For Those Who Were There

TABLE OF CONTENTS

OVERVIEW xiii
PREFACE xxxi
A NOTE ON PREPARATION OF THE TITLE V REPORT 1

Chapter I

THE INVASION OF KUWAIT 2
PRELUDE TO CRISIS 4
IRAQI MILITARY CAPABILITIES, 1990 9
    Republican Guard Forces Command 10
    Army 10
    Popular Army 11
Air Force 11
Air Defense Forces 12
Navy 13
Short Range Ballistic Missiles 13
Chemical Weapons 15
Biological Weapons 15
Nuclear Devices Program 15
Other Military Research and Development Programs 16
CONCLUSION 16

Chapter II

THE RESPONSE TO AGGRESSION 18
US RESPONSE — DRAWING A LINE 19
INITIAL WORLD RESPONSE 20
    International Organizations 21
    Western Reaction 21
    Asian Reaction 22
REGIONAL RESPONSE 23
Coalition Members in the Region 23
Other Regional Responses 24
Israeli Reaction 25
IRAQI FOLLOW-UP TO THE INVASION 26
Political Maneuvering 26
Iraqi Atrocities 27
Iraqi Hostage Taking 28

Chapter III

THE MILITARY OPTION — OPERATION DESERT SHIELD 30
MILITARY SITUATION, AUGUST 1990 31
MILITARY OBJECTIVES OF OPERATION DESERT SHIELD 32
CONCEPT OF OPERATIONS — OPERATION DESERT SHIELD 33
INITIAL DEPLOYMENT OF US MILITARY FORCES 34
WINDOW OF VULNERABILITY 37
EXPANDING THE DEFENSE 39
THE JOINT AND COMBINED COMMAND STRUCTURE 42
OBSERVATIONS 46

Chapter IV

MARITIME INTERCEPTION OPERATIONS .. 48
INTRODUCTION 49
STRATEGY AND OBJECTIVES 49
MULTINATIONAL RELATIONSHIPS OF THE MIF 50
OPERATIONAL PROCEDURES 53
SIGNIFICANT EVENTS DURING MARITIME INTERCEPTION OPERATIONS 57
EFFECTIVENESS 60
OBSERVATIONS 62

Chapter V

TRANSITION TO THE OFFENSIVE 64
INTRODUCTION 65
PLANNING FOR THE OFFENSIVE 65
   Evolution of the Offensive Plan 65
THE IRAQI THREAT IN OVERVIEW 70
Intelligence Estimates 71
Enemy Vulnerabilities 72
Iraqi Centers of Gravity 72
Prelude to Conflict 72
FINALIZING THE PLAN 73
National Policy Objectives and Military Objectives 73
THE PLAN IS ADOPTED 74
Air Campaign Plan in Overview 75
Ground Campaign Plan in Overview 75

Maritime Campaign Plan in Overview **76**
Deception Operations Plan in Overview **76**
THE DECISION TO REINFORCE, NOVEMBER 1990 .... **77**
REINFORCEMENT AND SUSTAINMENT **78**
DECISION TO BEGIN THE OFFENSIVE **80**
TRAINING FOR THE ATTACK **80**
EVE OF DESERT STORM **81**
   Status of Coalition Forces **81**
   Status of Iraqi Forces **82**
   Iraqi Defensive Concept of Operations **84**
   Military Balance **84**
OBSERVATIONS **87**

Chapter VI

THE AIR CAMPAIGN **88**
  INTRODUCTION **89**
    Decision to Begin the Offensive Ground
      Campaign **91**
  PLANNING THE OFFENSIVE AIR
    CAMPAIGN **91**
  The Early Concept Plan — Instant Thunder **91**
  Instant Thunder Evolves Into Operation Desert Storm Air Campaign **93**
THE OPERATION DESERT STORM AIR CAMPAIGN PLAN **95**
  JFACC Air Campaign Objectives **95**
  The Twelve Target Sets **95**
   Leadership Command Facilities **95**
   Electricity Production Facilities **96**
   Telecommunications And Command, Control, And Communication
     Nodes **96**
   Strategic Integrated Air Defense System **96**
   Air Forces And Airfields **96**
   Nuclear, Biological And Chemical Weapons Research, Production, And
     Storage Facilities **97**
   Scud Missiles, Launchers, And Production And Storage Facilities **97**
   Naval Forces And Port Facilities **97**
   Oil Refining And Distribution Facilities **97**
   Railroads And Bridges **98**
   Iraqi Army Units Including Republican Guard Forces In The KTO **98**
   Military Storage And Production Sites **98**
  Constraints on the Concept Plan **98**
   Avoid Collateral Damage And Casualties **98**
   Off Limits Targets **100**
  Phased Execution **100**

PREPARING TO EXECUTE THE PLAN 101
  The Joint Forces Air Component Commander 101
  The Master Attack Plan 102
  The Air Tasking Order 102
TRANSITION TO WARTIME PLANNING 103
  Deception 105
ON THE EVE OF THE AIR WAR 107
  Disposition of Air Forces 107
    CENTAF 107
    NAVCENT 107
    MARCENT 107
    Joint Task Force Proven Force 111
  Non-US Forces 112
EXECUTING THE AIR CAMPAIGN 112
  Evaluating the Results of the Air Campaign 113
  D-Day, The First Night 114
    First Night Reactions 120
    D-Day, Daytime Attacks 121
    D-Day, Second Night 122
    D-Day, Controlling Operations 123
    D-Day, Summary 123
  D+1 (18 January) 124
    D+1, Night 125
  D-Day through D+6: Summary of Week One (17-23 January) 125
  D+10 (27 January — CINCCENT Declares Air Supremacy) 127
    SEAD Operations 129
  D+7 through D+13: Summary of Week Two (24-30 January) 130
  D+12 through D+14 (29-31 January — The Battle of Al-Khafji) 130
  D+20 (6-7 February — Emphasis on Degrading the Iraqi Army
  and Navy) 133
    Cutting Off the Iraqi Army 134
    Degrading the Iraqi Army 135
    Kill Boxes 135
    Destroying the Iraqi Navy 136
  D+14 through D+20: Summary of Week Three (31 January-6 February) . . . 137
    Continuing to Disrupt Iraqi C^3 137
    Armored Vehicle Destruction 138
    Tanks Abandoned 139
    Psychological Operations Impact 140
  D+21 through D+27: Summary of Week Four (7-13 February) 141
  D+28 through D+34: Week Five (14-20 February) 141
  Summary of the Air Campaign, on the Eve of the Offensive
  Ground Campaign 142

D+38 (24 February — The Strategic Air Campaign Continues, and Air
    Operations Begin in Direct Support of the Offensive Ground Campaign) . . **144**
    Overview **144**
    Battlefield Air Operations **144**
    Air Interdiction **144**
    Close Air Support **146**
    Breaching Operations **146**
    Effect of Weather and Oil Well Fires **147**
D+35 through D+42: Week Six (21-28 February) **147**
RESULTS **148**
    Assessments By Target Set **149**
    Leadership Command Facilities **150**
    Electrical Production Facilities **150**
    Telecommunications and Command, Control, and Communication
        Nodes **151**
    Strategic Integrated Air Defense System **154**
    Air Forces and Airfields **154**
    Nuclear, Biological, and Chemical Weapons Research and Production
        Facilities **154**
    Scud Production and Storage Facilities **156**
    Naval Forces and Port Facilities **157**
    Oil Refining and Distribution Facilities, as Opposed to Long-term Oil
        Production Capability **157**
    Railroads and Bridges Connecting Iraqi Military Forces with Logistical
        Support Centers **158**
    Iraqi Military Units, Including Republican Guards in the KTO **158**
    Military Production and Storage **159**
  EPW Assessments **159**
  Safwan Revelations **160**
OPERATIONAL CONSIDERATIONS **161**
  Air Superiority and Air Supremacy **161**
  Suppression of Enemy Air Defenses **161**
  Aircraft Sorties **164**
  Technological Revolution **164**
  Tomahawk Land Attack Missile **164**
  GBU-28 . . . . **165**
  The Counter-Scud Effort **166**
  Patriot Defender Missile Defense System **169**
  Weather **169**
  Air Refueling **170**
  Reconnaissance and Surveillance **173**
  Forward Operating Locations (FOLs) Forward Area Rearming and
    Refueling Points (FARPs) **174**

HUMINT Assistance to Targeting Process **175**
Battle Damage Assessment **175**
Space Systems **176**
Civilian Casualties and Collateral Damage **177**
Aircraft Vulnerabilities to SAMs and AAA **178**
Coalition Fixed-Wing Aircraft Combat Losses **178**
OBSERVATIONS **179**

Chapter VII

THE MARITIME CAMPAIGN **182**
INTRODUCTION **183**
THE IMPORTANCE OF SEA CONTROL **184**
NAVCENT OPERATION DESERT STORM
   COMMAND ORGANIZATION **185**
THE MARITIME CAMPAIGN PLAN **187**
ANTISURFACE WARFARE (ASUW) **188**
The Iraqi Threat **190**
ASUW Command and Control **190**
Coalition ASUW Capabilities **191**
Destruction of the Iraqi Navy **193**
ANTIAIR WARFARE (AAW) **196**
The Iraqi Threat **197**
AAW Command and Control **197**
Coalition AAW Capabilities **198**
Significant Persian Gulf AAW Operations **199**
COUNTERMINE WARFARE **199**
The Iraqi Threat **200**
MCM Command and Control **202**
Coalition MCM Capabilities **203**
MCM Operations **206**
Impact of Iraq's Mine Warfare **207**
NAVAL GUNFIRE SUPPORT (NGFS) **208**
NGFS Missions **208**
NGFS Operations **210**
Use of UAVs **211**
NGFS Results **212**
AMPHIBIOUS WARFARE **212**
The Iraqi Threat **213**
Amphibious Warfare Planning **213**
Amphibious Operations **217**
Umm Al-Maradim Island **219**
Faylaka Island **219**

Ash Shuaybah Port Facility 220
Bubiyan Island 220
Landing of 5th MEB 220
Effectiveness of Amphibious Operations 221
SUBMARINE OPERATIONS 221
SUMMARY OF THE MARITIME CAMPAIGN 221
OBSERVATIONS 223

Chapter VIII

THE GROUND CAMPAIGN 226
INTRODUCTION 227
PLANNING THE GROUND OFFENSIVE 228
   Initial Planning Cell 228
   The Planning Process 229
   Operational Imperatives 229
Development of Courses of Action 230
Issues and Concerns Regarding the Plan 230
CINCCENT's Strategy and Concept 231
Secretary of Defense Reviews War Plans 231
Ground Campaign Phases 231
PREPARATION FOR THE OFFENSIVE 232
Ground Forces Buildup 232
Task Organization (US Ground Forces) 232
Task Organization (Non-US Ground Forces) 233
Command, Control, and Communications 234
Coalition Coordination, Communication, and Integration Center (C^3IC) 234
Liaison Teams 235
   Coordination and Control Measures 236
   Communications 236
Joint and Combined Operations 237
   Common Warfighting Doctrine 237
   AirLand Battle Doctrine 237
   Marine Air-Ground Task Force Doctrine 238
   Air Operations in Support of the Ground Offensive 238
   Naval Operations in Support of the Ground Offensive 239
   Roles of Non-US Coalition Forces 239
Tactical Intelligence 240
Logisitics 240
   Plan for Sustainment 241
   Establishment of Logisitics Bases 241
   Joint Logistics 242
   MARCENT Logistics 243

The Final Operational Plan **243**
Posturing for the Attack **245**
   Repositioning of I Marine Expeditionary Force **245**
   The Shift West of ARCENT Forces **245**
Preparing and Shaping the Battlefield **246**
   Deception Operations **247**
   Air Preparation of the Battlefield **248**
   Ground Preparation of the Battlefield **249**
   Reconnaissance and Counter-Reconnaissance **249**
   The Battle of Al-Khafji and Contact at Al-Wafrah **251**
The Threat as of 23 February — the Day Before the Ground Offensive **251**
   Iraqi Defensive Positions and Plan **251**
   Iraqi Combat Effectiveness **252**
   Iraqi Disposition and Strength in Theater Before the Ground Offensive . . . **254**
Weather **254**
Disposition of Coalition Forces on the Eve of the Ground Offensive **257**
   Army Component, Central Command **257**
   Joint Forces Command — North **258**
I Marine Expeditionary Force **258**
   Joint Forces Command — East **258**
CONDUCT OF THE GROUND OFFENSIVE **258**
  G-Day (24 February) — The Attack and the Breach **258**
   Enemy Actions and Dispositions **258**
   Army Component, Central Command **260**
     XVIII Airborne Corps **260**
     VII Corps **262**
   Joint Forces Command — North **264**
   I Marine Expeditionary Force **265**
   Joint Forces Command — East **267**
   Theater Reserve **267**
   Supporting Operations **268**
  G+1 (25 February) — Destruction of Enemy Tactical Forces **268**
   Enemy Actions and Disposition **268**
   Army Component, Central Command **270**
   Joint Forces Command — North **273**
   I Marine Expeditionary Force **273**
   Joint Forces Command — East **276**
   Supporting Operations **276**

G+2 (26 February) — Destruction of 2nd Echelon Operational Forces
and Sealing the Battlefield 276
   Enemy Actions And Disposition 276
   Army Component, Central Command 277
   Joint Forces Command-North 282
   I Marine Expeditionary Force 282
   Joint Forces Command — East 283
   Supporting Operations 283
G+3 (27 February) — Destruction of the Republican Guards 283
   Enemy Actions and Disposition 284
   Army Component, Central Command 285
   Joint Forces Command — North 288
   I Marine Expeditionary Force 289
   Joint Forces Command — East 289
   Supporting Operations 289
G+4 (28 February) — Offensive Operations Cease 290
   Army Component, Central Command 290
   Joint Forces Command — North 292
   I Marine Expeditionary Force 292
   Joint Forces Command — East 292
SUMMARY OF THE GROUND CAMPAIGN 292
CONCLUSIONS 294
OBSERVATIONS 297

Appendices

A 313   K 543
B 319   L 577
C 333   M 589
D 347   N 599
E 371   O 605
F 393   P 633
G 451   Q 639
H 471   R 647
I 487   S 651
J 523   T 657

G<small>LOSSARY</small> 811

OVERVIEW

THE CONDUCT OF THE PERSIAN GULF WAR

Saddam Hussein's invasion of Kuwait on August 2, 1990, unleashed an extraordinary series of events that culminated seven months later in the victory of American and Coalition forces over the Iraqi army and the liberation of Kuwait. Pursuant to Title V, Public Law 102-25, this report discusses the conduct of hostilities in the Persian Gulf theater of operations. It builds on the Department's Interim Report of July 1991. A proper understanding of the conduct of these military operations the extraordinary achievements and the needed improvements is an important and continuing task of the Department of Defense as we look to the future.

The Persian Gulf War was the first major conflict following the end of the Cold War. The victory was a triumph of Coalition strategy, of international cooperation, of technology, and of people. It reflected leadership, patience, and courage at the highest levels and in the field. Under adverse and hazardous conditions far from home, our airmen, soldiers, sailors, and marines once again played the leading role in reversing a dangerous threat to a critical region of the world and to our national interests. Their skill and sacrifice lie at the heart of this important triumph over aggression in the early post-Cold War era.

The Coalition victory was impressive militarily and important geopolitically; it will affect the American military and American security interests in the Middle East and beyond for years to come. Some of the lessons we should draw from the war are clear; others are more enigmatic. Some aspects of the war are unlikely to be repeated in future conflicts. But this experience also contains important indications of challenges to come and ways to surmount them.

America, the peaceful states of the Persian Gulf, and law-abiding nations everywhere are safer today because of the President's firm conviction that Iraq's aggression against Kuwait should not stand. Coming together, the nations of the Coalition defied aggression, defended much of the world's supply of oil, liberated Kuwait, stripped Saddam Hussein of his offensive military capability, set back his determined pursuit of nuclear weapons, and laid a foundation for peaceful progress elsewhere in the region that is still unfolding. The efforts and sacrifices of Operations Desert Shield and Desert Storm demand that we build on the lessons we have learned and the good that we have done.

THE MILITARY VICTORY OVER IRAQ

The Coalition victory was impressive militarily. Iraq possessed the fourth largest army in the world, an army hardened in long years of combat against Iran. During that war Iraq killed hundreds of thousands of Iranian soldiers in exactly the type of defensive combat it planned to fight in Kuwait. Saddam Hussein's forces possessed high-quality artillery, frontline T-72 tanks, modern MiG-29 and Mirage F-1 aircraft, ballistic missiles, biological agents and chemical weapons, and a large and sophisticated ground-based air defense system. His combat engineers, rated among the best in the world, had months to construct their defenses. Nonetheless, Iraqi forces were routed in six weeks by U.S. and other Coalition forces with extraordinarily low Coalition losses.

The Coalition dominated every area of warfare. The seas belonged to the Coalition from the start. Naval units were first on the scene and, along with early deploying air assets, contributed much of our military presence in the early days of the defense of Saudi Arabia. Coalition naval units also enforced United Nations economic sanctions against Iraq by inspecting ships and, when necessary, diverting them away from Iraq and Kuwait. This maritime interception effort was the start of the military cooperation among the Coalition members, and helped to deprive Iraq of outside resupply and revenues. The early arrival of the Marine Corps' Maritime Prepositioning Force provided an important addition to our deterrent on the ground. The Coalition controlled the skies virtually from the beginning of the air war, freeing our ground and naval units from air attack and preventing the Iraqis from using aerial reconnaissance to detect the movements of Coalition ground forces. Tactical aircraft were on the ground and the 82nd Airborne Division's Ready Brigade had been airlifted to the theater within hours of the order to deploy. Coalition planes destroyed 41 Iraqi aircraft and helicopters in air-to-air combat without suffering a confirmed loss to Iraqi aircraft. Coalition air power crippled Iraqi command and control and known unconventional weapons production, severely degraded the combat effectiveness of Iraqi forces, and paved the way for the final land assault that swept Iraqi forces from the field in only 100 hours. In the course of flying more than 100,000 sorties the Coalition lost only 38 fixed-wing aircraft. On the ground, Coalition armored forces traveled over 250 miles in 100 hours, one of the fastest movements of armored forces in the history of combat, to execute the now famous "left hook" that enveloped Iraq's elite, specially trained and equipped Republican Guards. Shortly after the end of the war, the U.S. Central Command (CENTCOM) estimated that Iraq lost roughly 3,800 tanks to Coalition air and ground attack; U.S. combat tank losses were fifteen.

The Coalition defeated not only Saddam Hussein's forces, but his strategy. Coalition strategy ensured that the war was fought under favorable conditions that took full advantage of Coalition strengths and Iraqi weaknesses. By contrast, Saddam's political and military strategy was soundly defeated. Despite his attempts to intimidate his neighbors, the Gulf states requested outside help; a coalition formed; the Arab "street" did not rise up on his behalf; and Israeli restraint in the face of Scud attacks undermined his plan to turn this into an Arab-Israeli war. Saddam's threats of massive casualties did not deter us; his taking of hostages did not paralyze us; his prepared defenses in Kuwait did not exact the high toll of Coalition casualties that he expected; and his army was decisively defeated. His attempts to take the offense his use of Scuds and the attack on the Saudi town of Al-Khafji at the end of January failed to achieve their strategic purpose. The overall result was a war in which Iraq was not only beaten, but failed to ever seize the initiative. Saddam consistently misjudged Coalition conviction and military capability.

GEOPOLITICAL CONSEQUENCES OF THE VICTORY

The victory against Iraq had several important and positive geopolitical consequences, both in the Persian Gulf and for the role the United States plays in the world. The geostrategic objectives set by the President on August 5, 1990, were achieved. Kuwait was liberated, and the security of Saudi Arabia and the Persian Gulf was enhanced. Saddam Hussein's plan to dominate the oil-rich Persian Gulf, an ambition on which he squandered his country's resources, was frustrated. The threat posed by Iraq's preponderance of military power in the region was swept away. Although underestimated before the war, Iraqi research and production facilities for ballistic missiles and nuclear, chemical and biological weapons were significantly damaged; furthermore, victory in the war was the prerequisite for the intrusive

United Nations inspection regime, which continues the work of dismantling those weapons programs. And even though Saddam Hussein remains in power, his political prestige has been crippled and his future prospects are uncertain. He is an international pariah whose hopes of leading an anti-Western coalition of Arab and Islamic peoples have been exposed as dangerous but ultimately empty boasts.

Although Saddam Hussein today has been reduced enormously in stature and power, we need to remember that the stakes in this conflict were large. Had the United States and the international community not responded to Saddam's invasion of Kuwait, the world would be much more dangerous today, much less friendly to American interests, and much more threatening to the peoples of the Middle East and beyond. The seizure of Kuwait placed significant additional financial resources and, hence, eventually military power in the hands of an aggressive and ambitious dictator. Saddam would have used Kuwait's wealth to accelerate the acquisition of nuclear, chemical and biological weapons and to expand and improve his inventory of ballistic missiles. Saddam had set a dangerous example of naked aggression that, unanswered, would ultimately have led to more aggression by him and perhaps by others as well. Having defied the United States and the United Nations, Saddam Hussein's prestige would have been high and his ability to secure new allies would have grown.

Saddam's seizure of Kuwait, left unanswered, threatened Saudi Arabia and its vast oil resources, in particular. He could have moved against Saudi Arabia; but even if he did not, the ominous presence of overwhelming force on the Kingdom's borders, coupled with the stark evidence of his ruthlessness toward his neighbors, constituted a threat to Saudi Arabia and vital U.S. interests. As Iraqi forces moved toward the border between Kuwait and Saudi Arabia, the world's largest concentration of oil reserves lay within reach. Iraqi forces could

have quickly moved down the Saudi coast to seize the oil-rich Eastern Province and threaten the Gulf sheikdoms. Iraqi control of Saudi Gulf ports also would have made military operations to recapture the seized territory extremely difficult and costly. But even without physically seizing eastern Saudi Arabia, Saddam threatened to dominate most of the world's oil reserves and much of current world production, giving him the ability to disrupt the world oil supply and hence the economies of the advanced industrial nations. He could have used this economic and political leverage, among other things, to increase his access to the high technology, materials, and tools needed for the further development of his nuclear, biological and chemical weapons and ballistic missile programs.

As the UN deadline for withdrawal approached in early January 1991, some wondered whether the use of force to free Kuwait should be postponed. The use of force will always remain for us a course of last resort, but there are times when it is necessary. By January of 1991, we had given Saddam every opportunity to withdraw from Kuwait peacefully and thereby avoid the risk of war and the cost of continued sanctions. By then he had made it clear that he considered it more important to hold on to Kuwait and had demonstrated his readiness to impose untold hardships on his people.

Further application of sanctions might have weakened the Iraqi military, especially the Iraqi Air Force; but delay would have imposed significant risks for Kuwait and the Coalition as well. Had we delayed longer there might have been little left of Kuwait to liberate. Moreover, the Coalition had reached a point of optimum strength. U.S. resolve was critical for holding together a potentially fragile coalition; our allies were reluctant only when they doubted America's commitment. Not only would it have been difficult to sustain our forces' fighting edge through a long period of stalemate, delay would have run the risk of successful Iraqi terrorist actions or a clash between Iraq and Israel or unfavorable political developments that might weaken the Coalition. Delay would also have given Iraq more time to thicken and extend the minefields and obstacles through which our ground forces had to move. It might have allowed the Iraqis to anticipate our plan and strengthen their defenses in the west. Worst of all, it would have given them more time to work on their chemical, biological, and even nuclear weapons. Since Saddam had made it clear that he would not leave Kuwait unless he was forced out, it was better to do so at a time of our choosing.

Unfortunately, Saddam Hussein's brutal treatment of his own people, which long preceded this war, has survived it. The world will be a better place when Saddam Hussein no longer misrules Iraq. However, his tyranny over Kuwait has ended. The tyranny he sought to extend over the Middle East has been turned back. The hold that he tried to secure over the world's oil supply has been removed. We have frustrated his plans to prepare to fight a nuclear war with Iran or Saudi Arabia or Israel or others who might oppose him. We will never know the full extent of the evils this war prevented. What we have learned since the war about his nuclear weapons program demonstrates with certainty that Saddam Hussein was preparing for aggression on a still larger scale and with more terrible weapons.

This war set an extraordinary example of international cooperation at the beginning of the post-Cold War era. By weakening the forces of violence and radicalism, it has created new openings for progress in the Arab-Israeli peace process, hopes that are symbolized by the process that began with the unprecedented conference in Madrid. This is part of a broader change in the dynamics of the region. It may not be a coincidence that after this war our hostages in Lebanon were freed. The objectives for which the United Nations Security Council authorized the use of force have been achieved. Potential aggressors will think twice, and small countries will feel more secure.

Victory in the Gulf has also resulted in much greater credibility for the United States on the world scene. America demonstrated that it would act decisively to redress a great wrong and to protect its national interests in the post-Cold War world. Combined with the dissolution of the Soviet Union, the victory in the Gulf has placed the United States in a strong position of leadership and influence.

THE LESSONS OF THE WAR FOR OUR MILITARY FORCES

The war was also important for what it tells us about our armed forces, and America's future defense needs. On August 2, 1990, the very day Saddam Hussein invaded Kuwait, President Bush was in Aspen, Colorado, presenting for the first time America's new defense strategy for the 1990s and beyond, a strategy that takes into account the vast changes in Eastern Europe and the former Soviet Union and envisions significant reductions in our forces and budgets. A distinguishing feature of this new strategy which was developed well before the Kuwait crisis is that it focuses more on regional threats, like the Gulf conflict, and less on global conventional confrontation.

The new strategy and the Gulf war continue to be linked, as we draw on the lessons of the war to inform our decisions for the future. As we reshape America's defenses, we need to look at Operations Desert Shield and Desert Storm for indications of what military capabilities we may need not just in the next few years, but 10, 20 or 30 years hence. We need to consider why we were successful, what worked and what did not, and what is important to protect and preserve in our military capability.

As we do so, we must remember that this war, like every other, was unique. We benefitted greatly from certain of its features such as the long interval to deploy and prepare our forces that we cannot count on in the future. We benefitted from our enemy's near-total international isolation and from our own strong Coalition. We received ample support from the nations that hosted our forces and relied on a well-developed coastal infrastructure that may not be available the next time. And we fought in a unique desert environment, challenging in many ways, but presenting advantages too. Enemy forces were fielded for the most part in terrain ideally suited to armor and air power and largely free of noncombatants.

We also benefitted from the timing of the war, which occurred at a unique moment when we still retained the forces that had been built up during the Cold War. We could afford to move the Army's VII Corps from Germany to Saudi Arabia, since the Soviet threat to Western Europe had greatly diminished. Our deployments and operations benefitted greatly from a world-wide system of bases that had been developed during, and largely because of, the Cold War. For example, a large percentage of the flights that airlifted cargo from the United States to the theater transited through the large and well-equipped air bases at Rhein-Main in Germany and Torrejon in Spain. Without these bases, the airlift would have been much more difficult to support. U.S. forces operating from Turkey used NATO-developed bases. In addition, bases in England and elsewhere were available to support B-52 operations that would otherwise have required greater flying distances or the establishment of support structures in the theater.

We should also remember that much of our military capability was not fully tested in Operations Desert Shield and Desert Storm. There was no submarine threat. Ships did not face significant anti-surface action. We had little fear that our forces sent from Europe or the U.S. would be attacked on their way to the region. There was no effective attack by aircraft on our troops or our port and support facilities. Though

there were concerns Iraq might employ chemical weapons or biological agents, they were never used. American amphibious capabilities, though used effectively for deception and small scale operations, were not tested on a large scale under fire. Our ground forces did not have to fight for long. Saddam Hussein's missiles were inaccurate. There was no interference to our space-based systems. As such, much of what was tested needs to be viewed in the context of this unique environment and the specific conflict.

Even more important to remember is that potential adversaries will study the lessons of this war no less diligently than will we. Future adversaries will seek to avoid Saddam Hussein's mistakes. Some potential aggressors may be deterred by the punishment Iraq's forces suffered. But others might wonder if the outcome would have been different if Iraq had acquired nuclear weapons first, or struck sooner at Saudi Arabia, or possessed a larger arsenal of more sophisticated ballistic missiles, or used chemical or biological weapons.

During the war, we learned a lot of specific lessons about systems that work and some that need work, about command relations, and about areas of warfare where we need improvement. We could have used more ships of particular types. We found we did not have enough Heavy Equipment Transporters or off-road mobility for logistics support vehicles. Sophisticated equipment was maintained only with extra care in the harsh desert environment. We were not nearly capable enough at clearing land and sea mines, especially shallow water mines. This might have imposed significant additional costs had large scale amphibious operations been required. We moved quickly to get more Global Positioning System receivers in the field and improvised to improve identification devices for our ground combat vehicles, but more navigation and identification capabilities are needed. The morale and intentions of Iraqi forces and leaders were obscure to us. Field commanders wanted more tactical reconnaissance and imagery. We had difficulty with battle damage assessment and with communications interoperability. Tactical ballistic missile defense worked, but imperfectly. Mobile missile targeting and destruction were difficult and costly; we need to do better. We were ill-prepared at the start for defense against biological warfare, even though Saddam had developed biological agents. And tragically, despite our best efforts there were here, as in any war, losses to fire from friendly forces. These and many other specific accomplishments, shortcomings and lessons are discussed in greater depth in the body of the report.

Among the many lessons we must study from this war, five general lessons noted in the Interim Report still stand out.

- Decisive Presidential leadership set clear goals, gave others confidence in America's sense of purpose, and rallied the domestic and international support necessary to reach those goals;
- A revolutionary new generation of high-technology weapons, combined with innovative and effective doctrine, gave our forces the edge;
- The high quality of our military, from its skilled commanders to the highly ready, well-trained, brave and disciplined men and women of the U.S. Armed Forces made an extraordinary victory possible;
- In a highly uncertain world, sound planning, forces in forward areas, and strategic air and sea lift are critical for developing the confidence, capabilities, international cooperation, and reach needed in times of trouble; and
- It takes a long time to build the high-quality forces and systems that gave us success.

These general lessons and related issues are discussed at length below.

Leadership

President Bush's early conviction built the domestic and international consensus that underlay the Coalition and its eventual victory. The President was resolute in his commitment both to expel the Iraqi forces from Kuwait and to use decisive military force to accomplish that objective. President Bush accepted enormous burdens in committing U.S. prestige and forces, which in turn helped the nation and the other members of the Coalition withstand the pressures of confrontation and war. Many counseled inaction. Many predicted military catastrophe or thousands of casualties. Some warned that even if we won, the Arabs would unite against us. But, having made his decision, the President never hesitated or wavered.

This crisis proved the wisdom of our Founding Fathers, who gave the office of the Presidency the authority needed to act decisively. When the time came, Congress gave the President the support he needed to carry his policies through, but those policies could never have been put in place without his personal strength and the institutional strength of his office.

Two critical moments of Presidential leadership bear particular mention. In the first few days following the invasion, the President determined that Saddam Hussein's invasion of Kuwait would not stand. At the time, we could not be sure that King Fahd of Saudi Arabia would invite our assistance to resist Iraq's aggression. Without Saudi cooperation, our task would have been much more difficult and costly. The Saudi decision to do so rested not only on their assessment of the gravity of the situation, but also on their confidence in the President. Without that confidence, the course of history might have been different. A second critical moment came in November, 1990, when the President directed that we double our forces in the Gulf to provide an overwhelming offensive capability. He sought to ensure that if U.S. forces were to go into battle, they would possess decisive force the U.S. would have enough military strength to be able to seize and maintain the initiative and to avoid getting bogged down in a long, inconclusive war. The President not only gave the military the tools to do the job, but he provided it with clear objectives and the support to carry out its assigned tasks. He allowed it to exercise its best judgment with respect to the detailed operational aspects of the war. These decisions enabled the military to perform to the best of its capabilities and saved American lives.

The President's personal diplomacy and his long standing and carefully-nurtured relationships with other world leaders played a major role in forming and cementing the political unity of the Coalition, which made possible the political and economic measures adopted by the United Nations and the Coalition's common military effort. Rarely has the world community come so close to speaking with a single voice in condemnation of an act of aggression.

While President Bush's leadership was the central element in the Coalition, its success depended as well on the strength and wisdom of leaders of the many countries that comprised it. Prime Minister Thatcher of Great Britain was a major voice for resisting the aggression from the very outset of the crisis. King Fahd of Saudi Arabia and the leaders of the other Gulf states Bahrain, Qatar, the United Arab Emirates and Oman defied Saddam Hussein in the face of imminent danger. President Mubarak of Egypt helped to rally the forces of the Arab League and committed a large number of troops to the ground war. President Ozal of Turkey cut off the oil pipeline from Iraq and permitted Coalition forces to strike Iraq from Turkey, despite the economic cost and the risk of Iraqi military action. Prime Minister Major of Great Britain continued his predecessor's strong support for the Coalition, providing important political leadership and committing substantial military forces. President Mitterrand of France also contributed sizable forces to the Coalition. Our

European allies opened their ports and airfields and yielded priorities on their railroads to speed our deployment. Countries from other regions, including Africa, East Asia, South Asia, the Pacific, North and South America, and a sign of new times Eastern Europe chose to make this their fight. Their commitment provided essential elements to the ultimate victory. Their unity underlay the widespread compliance with the UN-mandated sanctions regime, which sought to deprive Iraq of the revenues and imported materials it needed to pursue its military development programs and to put pressure on its leadership to withdraw from Kuwait. Once the war began, and the first Iraqi Scud missiles fell on Israeli cities, the Israeli leadership frustrated Saddam Hussein's plans to widen the war and disrupt the unity of the Coalition by making the painful, but ultimately vindicated decision to not take military action and attempt to preempt subsequent attacks.

The prospects for the Coalition were also increased by the vastly changed global context and the relationship that had been forged between President Bush and President Gorbachev of the former Soviet Union. During the Cold War, the invasion of Kuwait by Iraq a state that had close ties to the former Soviet Union might well have resulted in a major East-West confrontation. Instead, President Bush sought and won Soviet acceptance to deal with the problem not in the old context of an East-West showdown, but on its own terms. Without the Cold War motive of thwarting U.S. aims, the Soviet Union participated in an overwhelming United Nations Security Council majority that expressed an international consensus opposing the Iraqi aggression. No longer subordinated to East-West rivalry, the United Nations' action during the Persian Gulf crisis was arguably its greatest success to date: for the first time since the North Korean invasion of South Korea in June, 1950, the Security Council was able to authorize the use of force to repel an act of aggression.

Strong political leadership also underlay important international financial support to the war effort, including large financial contributions from Saudi Arabia, Kuwait, the United Arab Emirates, Japan, Germany, South Korea and others to help defray U.S. incremental costs. The total amount committed to defray the costs of the U.S. involvement in the war was almost $54 billion. This spread the financial burden of the war and helped to cushion the U.S. economy from its effects. In fact, the $54 billion that was raised, were it a national defense budget, would be the third largest in the world.

In sum, close examination of the successful international response to the invasion of Kuwait returns repeatedly to the theme of strong leadership. President Bush's early and firm opposition to the Iraqi invasion and the military force that stood behind it convinced Saudi Arabia and the other Gulf states that they could withstand Iraqi threats and led others to provide not only political support at the UN but also armed forces and money to a Coalition effort. This remarkable international effort coalesced because Coalition members could take confidence from the initial U.S. commitment, whose credibility derived from the U.S. willingness and military capability to do much of the job alone, if necessary. For at the military level, U.S. leadership was critical. No other nation was in a position to assume the military responsibility shouldered by the United States in liberating Kuwait.

A Revolutionary New Generation of High-Technology Weapons

A second general lesson of the war is that high-technology systems vastly increased the effectiveness of our forces. This war demonstrated dramatically the new possibilities of what has been called the "military-technological revolution in warfare." This technological revolution encompasses many areas, including stand-off precision weaponry,

sophisticated sensors, stealth for surprise and survivability, night vision capabilities and tactical ballistic missile defenses. In large part this revolution tracks the development of new technologies such as the microprocessing of information that has become familiar in our daily lives. The exploitation of these and still-emerging technologies promises to change the nature of warfare significantly, as did the earlier advent of tanks, airplanes, and aircraft carriers.

The war tested an entire generation of new weapons and systems at the forefront of this revolution. In many cases these weapons and systems were being used in large-scale combat for the first time. In other cases, where the weapons had been used previously, the war represented their first use in large numbers. For example, precision guided munitions are not entirely new they were used at the end of the Vietnam war in 1972 to destroy bridges in Hanoi that had withstood multiple air attacks earlier in the war but their use in large numbers represented a new stage in the history of warfare.

Technology greatly increased our battlefield effectiveness. Battlefield combat systems, like the M1A1 tank, AV-8B jet, and the Apache helicopter, and critical subsystems, like advanced fire control, the Global Positioning System, and thermal and night vision devices, gave the ground forces unprecedented maneuverability and reach. JSTARS offered a glimpse of new possibilities for battlefield intelligence. Our forces often found, targeted and destroyed the enemy's before the enemy could return fire effectively.

The Persian Gulf War saw the first use of a U.S. weapon system (the Patriot) in a tactical ballistic missile defense role. The war was not the first in which ballistic missiles were used, and there is no reason to think that it will be the last. Ballistic missiles offered Saddam Hussein some of his few, limited successes and were the only means by which he had a plausible opportunity (via the attacks on Israel) to achieve a strategic objective. While the Patriot helped to counter Saddam Hussein's use of conventionally-armed Scud missiles, we must anticipate that in the future more advanced types of ballistic missiles, some armed with nuclear, chemical or biological warheads, will likely exist in the inventories of a number of Third World nations. More advanced forms of ballistic missile defense, as well as more effective methods of locating and attacking mobile ballistic missile launchers, will be necessary to deal with that threat.

The importance of technology in the impressive results achieved by Coalition air operations will be given special prominence as strategists assess the lessons of Desert Storm. Precision and penetrating munitions, the ability to evade or suppress air defenses, and cruise missiles made effective, round-the-clock attacks possible on even heavily defended targets with minimal aircraft losses. Drawing in large part on new capabilities, air power destroyed or suppressed much of the Iraqi air defense network, neutralized the Iraqi Air Force, crippled much of Iraq's command and control system, knocked out bridges and storage sites and, as the war developed, methodically destroyed many Iraqi tanks and much of the artillery in forward areas capable of delivering chemical munitions.

Indeed, the decisive character of our victory in the Gulf War is attributable in large measure to the extraordinary effectiveness of air power. That effectiveness apparently came as a complete surprise to Iraqi leaders. This was illustrated by Saddam Hussein's pronouncement a few weeks after he invaded Kuwait that, "The United States relies on the air force, and the air force has never been the decisive factor in the history of war." Coalition land and sea-based air power was an enormous force multiplier, helping the overall force, and holding down Coalition casualties to exceptionally low levels. Air power, including attack helicopters and other organic aircraft employed by ground units, was a major element of the capability of the

ground forces to conduct so effectively a synchronized, high speed, combined arms attack. Moreover, it helped enable the Arab/Islamic and Marine Corps forces whose assigned missions were to mount supporting attacks against major Iraqi forces in place in southeastern Kuwait to reach Kuwait City in just three days.

Although the specific circumstances of the Coalition campaign were highly favorable to such an air offensive, the results portend advances in warfare made possible by technical advances enabling precision attacks and the rapid degradation of air defenses. That assessment acknowledges that the desert climate was well suited to precision air strikes, that the terrain exposed enemy vehicles to an unusual degree, that Saddam Hussein chose to establish a static defense, and that harsh desert conditions imposed constant logistical demands that made Iraqi forces more vulnerable to air interdiction. And, with Iraq isolated politically, the Coalition air campaign did not risk provoking intervention by a neighboring power a consideration which has constrained the U.S. in other regional wars. Nonetheless, while we should not assume that air power will invariably be so successful with such low casualties in future wars fought under less favorable conditions, it is certain that air power will continue to offer a special advantage, one that we must keep for ourselves and deny to our opponents.

On the other hand, air power alone could not have brought the war to so sharp and decisive a conclusion. Saddam not only underestimated the importance of the Coalition air forces, but he underestimated our will and ability to employ ground and maritime forces as well. The ground offensive option ensured that the Coalition would seize the initiative. A protracted air siege alone would not have had the impact that the combination of air, maritime and ground offensives was able to achieve. Without the credible threat of ground and amphibious attacks, the Iraqi defenders might have dispersed, dug in more deeply, concentrated in civilian areas, or otherwise adopted a strategy of outlasting the bombing from the air. For these purposes, even a much smaller Iraqi force would have sufficed. Such a strategy would have prolonged the conflict and might have strained the political cohesion of the Coalition. Given more time, Iraq might have achieved Scud attacks with chemical or other warheads capable of inflicting catastrophic casualties on Israeli or Saudi citizens or on Coalition troop concentrations. Even absent those contingencies, a failure to engage on the ground would have left Saddam Hussein able to claim that his army was still invincible. The defeat of that army on the ground destroyed his claims to leadership of the Arab world and doomed his hopes to reemerge as a near term threat.

As was recognized by senior decisionmakers from the earliest days of planning a possible offensive campaign, the combination of air, naval and ground power used together would greatly enhance the impact of each. The air campaign not only destroyed the combat effectiveness of important Iraqi units, but many that survived were deprived of tactical agility, a weakness that our own ground forces were able to exploit brilliantly. The threat of ground and amphibious attacks forced the Iraqis to concentrate before the ground attack and later to move, increasing the effect of air attacks. Similarly, while the air campaign was undoubtedly a major reason why more than 80,000 Iraqi soldiers surrendered, most of these surrendered only when advancing ground forces gave the Iraqis in forward positions the chance to escape the brutal discipline of their military commanders. The ground campaign also enabled the capture and destruction of vast quantities of Iraqi war materiel.

Evaluations of such complex operations inherently risk selective interpretation, which may miss the key point that the collective weight of air, maritime, amphibious, and ground attacks was necessary to achieve the exceptional combat superiority the Coalition forces achieved in the defeat of Iraq's large, very capable forces. In sum, while air power made a unique and significantly enlarged contribution to the decisive Coalition victory, the combined effects of the air, maritime and ground offensives with important contributions from many supporting forces were key.

The military technological revolution will continue to pose challenges to our forces both to keep up with competing technologies and to derive the greatest potential from the systems we have. For example, the extensive use of precision munitions created a requirement for much more detailed intelligence than had ever existed before. It is no longer enough for intelligence to report that a certain complex of buildings housed parts of the Iraqi nuclear program; targeteers now want to know precisely which function is conducted in which building, or even in which part of the building, since they have the capability to strike with great accuracy. In addition, the high speed of movement of the ground forces creates a requirement to know about the locations and movements of friendly and opposing formations to a greater depth than would have been the case in a more slowly moving battle. Such improvements can make our forces more effective and save lives that might otherwise be tragically lost to fire from friendly forces an area in which we still need to improve.

As we assess the impressive performance of our weaponry, we must realize that, under other circumstances, the results might have been somewhat less favorable. Conditions under which the Persian Gulf conflict was fought were ideal with respect to some of the more advanced types of weapons. Even though the weather during the war was characterized by an atypically large percentage of cloud cover for the region, the desert terrain and climate in general favored the use of airpower. The desert also allowed the U.S. armored forces to engage enemy forces at very long range before our forces could be targeted, an advantage that might have counted for less in a more mountainous or built-up environment.

In addition, future opponents may possess more advanced weapons systems and be more skilled in using them. In general, Iraqi equipment was not at the same technological level as that of the Coalition, and Iraq was even further behind when it came to the quality and training of its military personnel and their understanding of the military possibilities inherent in contemporary weaponry. A future adversary's strategy may be more adept than Saddam's. But, the U.S. must anticipate that some advanced weaponry will for a number of reasons become available to other potential aggressors. Relevant technologies continue to be developed for civilian use; the end of the Cold War is likely to bring a general relaxation in constraints on trade in high-technology items; and declining defense budgets in their own countries may lead some arms producers to pursue more vigorously foreign sales and their governments to be more willing to let them sell "top-of-the-line" equipment. Thus, much care is needed in applying the lessons of this war to a possible future one in which the sides might be more equal in terms of technology, doctrine, and the quality of personnel.

The war showed that we must work to maintain the tremendous advantages that accrue from being a generation ahead in weapons technology. Future adversaries may have ready access to advanced technologies and systems from the world arms market. A continued and substantial research and development effort, along with renewed efforts to prevent or at least constrain the spread of advanced technologies, will be required to maintain our advantage.

The High Quality of the U.S. Armed Forces

The third general lesson is the importance of high-quality troops and commanders. Warriors win wars, and smart weapons require smart people and sound doctrine to maximize their effectiveness. The highly trained, highly motivated all-volunteer force we fielded in Operations Desert Shield and Desert Storm is the highest quality fighting force the United States has ever fielded.

Many aspects of the war the complexity of the weapon systems used, the multinational coalition, the rapidity and intensity of the operations, the harsh physical environment in which it was fought, the unfamiliar cultural environment, the threat of chemical or biological attack tested the training, discipline and morale of the members of the Armed Forces. They passed the test with flying colors. From the very start, men and women in the theater, supported by thousands on bases and headquarters around the world, devoted themselves with extraordinary skill and vigor to this sudden task to mount a major military operation far from the United States and in conditions vastly different from the notional theaters for which our forces had primarily trained in the Cold War. Reflecting that American "can do" spirit, the campaign included some remarkable examples where plans were improvised, work arounds were found, and new ways of operating invented and rapidly put into practice. Over 98 percent of our all-volunteer force are high school graduates. They are well trained. When the fighting began, they proved not just their skills, but their bravery and dedication. To continue to attract such people we must continue to meet their expectations for top-notch facilities, equipment and training and to provide the quality of life they and their families deserve. In taking care of them, we protect the single most important strategic asset of our armed forces.

The units that we deployed to the Gulf contrast meaningfully with the same units a decade ago. Among our early deployments to Saudi Arabia following King Fahd's invitation were the F-15 air superiority fighters of the 1st Tactical Fighter Wing from Langley Air Force Base in Virginia.

Within 53 hours of the order to move, 45 aircraft were on the ground in Saudi Arabia. Ten years ago, that same wing failed its operational readiness exam; only 27 of 72 aircraft were combat ready the rest lacked spare parts.

The 1st Infantry Division out of Fort Riley, Kansas, did a tremendous job in the Gulf. When we called upon them to deploy last fall, they were ready to go. But, 10 years ago, they only had two-thirds of the equipment needed to equip the division, and half of that was not ready for combat.

Our forces' performance bore testimony to the high quality of the training they had received. Of particular note are the various training centers which use advanced simulation, computer techniques, and rigorous field operations to make the training as realistic as possible and to exploit the benefits of subsequent critique and review. For example, many of the soldiers who fought in Desert Storm had been to the armored warfare training at the National Training Center at Fort Irwin, California, which has been described as tougher than anything the troops ran into in Iraq. Similarly, the Air Force "Red Flag" exercise program, which employs joint and multinational air elements in a realistic and demanding training scenario, provided a forum for the rehearsal of tactics, techniques and procedures for the conduct of modern theater air warfare. The Navy's "Strike University" aided greatly in air and cruise missile operations, and the Marine Corps training at 29 Palms sharpened Marine desert war fighting skills. That is the way training is supposed to work.

The war highlighted as well the importance and capability of the reserves. The early Operation Desert Shield deployments would not have been possible without volunteers from the Reserves and National Guard. The call-up of additional reserves under the authority of Title 10, Section 673(b) the first time that authority has ever been used was critical to the success of our operations. Reserves served in combat, combat support and combat service support roles and they served well. However, the use of reserves was not without some problems. For example, the war exposed problems with including reserve combat brigades in our earliest-deploying divisions. Tested in combat, the Total Force concept remains an important element of our national defense. Nonetheless, as we reduce our active forces under the new strategy, we will need to reduce our reserve components as well.

Our success in the Gulf reflected outstanding military leadership, whether at the very top, like General Colin Powell, Chairman of the Joint Chiefs of Staff, and General Norman Schwarzkopf, Commander in Chief of the forces in U.S. Central Command; or at the Component level, like Lieutenant General Chuck Horner, who orchestrated the Coalition's massive and brilliant air campaign, or Vice Admiral Hank Mauz and Vice Admiral Stan Arthur, who led the largest deployment of naval power into combat since World War II, or Lieutenant General John Yeosock, who implemented the now-famous "left hook," or Lieutenant General Walt Boomer who led his Marines to the outskirts of Kuwait City, while continuing to divert Iraqi attention to a possible amphibious attack, or Lieutenant General Gus Pagonis who provisioned this enormous force that had deployed unexpectedly half-way around the world; or at the Corps or division commander, wing commander, or battle group commander level. The command arrangements and the skills of the military leadership were challenged by the deployment of such a large force in a relatively short period of time, the creation or substantial expansion of staffs at various levels of command and the establishment of working relationships among them, the melding of the forces of many different nations and of the different services into an integrated theater campaign, and the rapid pace of the war and the complexity of the operations. The result was a coordinated offensive operation of great speed, intensity and effectiveness.

This conflict represented the first test of the provisions of the Goldwater-Nichols Department of Defense Reorganization Act of 1986 in a major war. The act strengthened and clarified the authority of the Chairman of the Joint Chiefs of Staff. We were fortunate in this precedent setting time when joint arrangements were tested to have a Chairman with the unique qualities of General Colin Powell. General Powell's strategic insight and exceptional leadership helped the American people through trying times and ensured our forces fought smart. He drew upon all of our capabilities to bring the necessary military might to bear. We were also fortunate to have a superb Vice Chairman, Admiral Dave Jeremiah, and an outstanding group of Service Chiefs who provided excellent military advice on the proper employment of their forces. Working with their Service Secretaries, they fielded superbly trained and equipped forces, and saw that General Schwarzkopf got everything he required to prosecute the campaign successfully. The nation was well served by General Carl Vuono, Admiral Frank Kelso, General Merrill McPeak, and General Al Gray of the Joint Chiefs, as well as Admiral Bill Kime of the Coast Guard. To them and their associates, great credit must be given.

The act also clarified the roles of the Commanders in Chief of the Unified and Specified Commands and their relationships with the Services and the service components of their commands. Overall, the operations in the Gulf reflected an increased level of jointness among the services. Indeed, in the spirit of Goldwater-Nichols, General Schwarzkopf was well-supported by his fellow commanders. General H.T. Johnson at Transportation Command delivered the force. General Jack Galvin at European Command provided forces and support. General Donald Kutyna at Space Command watched the skies for Scuds. General

Ed Burba, commanding Army forces here in the continental U.S., provided the Army ground forces and served as rear support. Admiral Chuck Larson in the Pacific and Admiral Leon Edney in the Atlantic provided Navy and Marine Forces, while General Lee Butler at SAC provided bombers, refuelers, and reconnaissance. General Carl Stiner provided crack special operations forces. It was a magnificent team effort.

General Schwarzkopf and his counterparts from diverse Coalition nations faced the task of managing the complex relationships among their forces. This task, challenging enough under the best of circumstances, was particularly difficult given the great cultural differences and political sensitivities among the Coalition partners. The problem was solved by an innovative command arrangement involving parallel international commands, one, headed by General Schwarzkopf, incorporating the forces from the Western countries, and another, under the Saudi commander, Lieutenant General Khalid bin Sultan bin Abdul-Aziz, for the forces from the Arab and Islamic ones. In historical terms, the Coalition was noteworthy not only because of the large number of nations that participated and the speed with which it was assembled, but also because the forces of all these nations were participating in a single theater campaign, within close proximity to each other on the battlefield. The close coordination and integration of these diverse units into a cohesive fighting force was achieved in large part thanks to the deftness with which General Schwarzkopf managed the relations with the various forces of the nations of the Coalition and to his great skill as a commander.

The high quality of our forces was critical to the planning and execution of two very successful deception operations that surprised and confused the enemy. The first deception enabled the Coalition to achieve tactical surprise at the outset of the air war, even though the attack, given the passage of the United Nations deadline, was in a strategic sense totally expected and predictable. The deception required, for example, the careful planning of air operations during the Desert Shield period, to accustom the Iraqis to intense air activity of certain types, such as refueling operations, along the Saudi border. As a result, the heavy preparatory air activity over Saudi Arabia on the first night of Desert Storm does not appear to have alerted the Iraqis that the attack was imminent.

The second deception operation confused the Iraqis about the Coalition's plan for the ground offensive. Amphibious landing exercises as well as other activities that would be necessary to prepare for a landing (such as mine sweeping near potential landing areas) were conducted to convince the Iraqis that such an attack was part of the Coalition plan. At the same time, unobserved by the Iraqis who could not conduct aerial reconnaissance because of Coalition air supremacy, the VII Corps and XVIII Airborne Corps shifted hundreds of kilometers to the west from their initial concentration points south of Kuwait. Deceptive radio transmissions made it appear that the two Corps were still in their initial positions, while strict discipline restricted reconnaissance or scouting activity that might have betrayed an interest in the area west of Kuwait through which the actual attack was to be made. The success of this deception operation both pinned down several Iraqi divisions along the Kuwaiti coast and left the Iraqis completely unprepared to meet the Coalition's "left hook" as it swung around the troop concentrations in Kuwait and enveloped them.

Coalition strategy also benefitted immensely from psychological operations, the success of which is evidenced primarily by the large number of Iraqi soldiers who deserted Iraqi ranks or surrendered without putting up any resistance during the ground offensive. Our efforts built on, among other factors, the disheartening effect on Iraqi troops of the

unanswered and intensive Coalition aerial bombardment, the privations they suffered due to the degradation of the Iraqi logistics system, and the threat of the impending ground campaign. Radio transmissions and leaflets exploited this demoralization by explaining to the Iraqi troops how to surrender and assuring them of humane treatment if they did. More specific messages reduced Iraqi readiness by warning troops to stay away from their equipment (which was vulnerable to attack by precision munitions) and induced desertions by warning troops that their positions were about to be attacked by B-52s.

The skill and dedication of our forces were critical elements for the Coalition's efforts to design and carry out a campaign that would, within the legitimate bounds of war, minimize the risks of combat for nearby civilians and treat enemy soldiers humanely. Coalition pilots took additional risks and planners spared legitimate military targets to minimize civilian casualties. Coalition air strikes were designed to be as precise as possible. Tens of thousands of Iraqi prisoners of war were cared for and treated with dignity and compassion. The world will not soon forget pictures of Iraqi soldiers kissing their captors' hands.

In the course of Desert Shield and Desert Storm our troops spent long hours in harsh desert conditions, in duststorms and rainstorms, in heat and cold. The war saw tense periods of uncertainty and intense moments under enemy fire. It was not easy for any American personnel, including the quarter of a million reservists whose civilian lives were disrupted, or for the families separated from their loved ones. The fact that our pilots did not experience high losses going through Iraqi air defenses and our ground forces made it through the formidable Iraqi fortifications with light casualties does not diminish the extraordinary courage required from everyone who faced these dangers. It was especially hard for American prisoners of war, our wounded, and, above all, the Americans who gave their lives for their country and the families and friends who mourn them. Throughout these trials as America indeed, all the world watched them on television, American men and women portrayed the best in American values. We can be proud of the dignity, humanity and skill of the American soldier, sailor, airman and marine.

Sound Planning

The fourth general lesson of the Persian Gulf conflict is the importance in a highly uncertain world of sound planning, of having forces forward that build trust and experience in cooperative efforts, and of sufficient strategic lift.

Advance planning played an important role as the Persian Gulf conflict unfolded. It was important in the days immediately following Saddam Hussein's invasion of Kuwait to have a clear concept of how we would defend Saudi Arabia and of the forces we would need. This was important not just for our decisionmakers, but for King Fahd and other foreign leaders, who needed to judge our seriousness of purpose, and for our quick action should there be a decision to deploy. Our response in the crisis was greatly aided because we had planned for such a contingency.

In the fall of 1989, the Department shifted the focus of planning efforts in Southwest Asia to countering regional threats to the Arabian peninsula. The primary such threat was Iraq. As a result, CENTCOM prepared a Concept Outline Plan for addressing the Iraqi threat in the Spring of 1990. The outline plan contained both the overall forces and strategy for a successful defense of friendly Gulf states. This plan was developed into a draft operations plan by July 1990. In conjunction with the development of the plan, General Schwarzkopf had arranged to conduct an exercise, INTERNAL LOOK 90, which began in July. This exercise tested aspects of the plan for the

defense of the Arabian peninsula. When the decision was made to deploy forces in response to King Fahd's invitation, this plan was selected as the best option. It gave CENTCOM a head start.

However, while important aspects of the planning process for the contingency that actually occurred were quite well along, more detailed planning for the deployment of particular forces to the region had only just begun and was scheduled to take more than a year to complete. In the end, the actual deployments for Desert Shield and Desert Storm were accomplished in about half that time.

In the future we must continue to review and refine our planning methods to make sure that they enable us to adapt to unforeseen contingencies as quickly and as effectively as possible. General Eisenhower once remarked that while plans may not be important, planning is. The actual plans that are devised ahead of time may not fit precisely the circumstances that eventually arise, but the experience of preparing them is essential preparation for those who will have to act when the unforeseen actually occurs. If we are to take this maxim seriously, as our recent experience suggests we should, then several consequences seem to flow. Training must emphasize the speed with which these types of plans must be drawn up, as that is likely to be vital in an actual crisis. Management systems, such as those which support deployment and logistics, must be automated with this need for flexibility in mind. Overall, planning systems must increasingly adapt rapidly to changing situations, with forces tailored to meet unexpected contingencies.

Past U.S. investment and experience in the region were particularly critical to the success of our efforts. Saudi Arabia's airports and coastal infrastructure were well developed to receive a major military deployment. U.S. pilots had frequently worked with their Saudi counterparts. Each of these factors, in turn, reflected a legacy of past defense planning and strategic cooperation. U.S. steadfastness in escorting ships during the Iran-Iraq War, despite taking casualties, added an important element of credibility to our commitments. Without this legacy of past cooperation and experience in the region, our forces would not have been as ready, and the Gulf States might never have had the confidence in us needed for them to confront Iraq.

The success of Operations Desert Shield (including the maritime interception effort) and Desert Storm required the creation of an international coalition and multinational military cooperation, not just with the nations of the Arabian peninsula, but with the United Kingdom, France, Egypt, Turkey and a host of other nations. These efforts were greatly enhanced by past military cooperation in NATO, in combined exercises, in U.S. training of members of the allied forces, and in many other ways.

A key element of our strategy was to frustrate Saddam Hussein's efforts to draw Israel into the war and thereby change the political complexion of the conflict. We devoted much attention and resources to this problem, but we could not have succeeded without a history of trust and cooperation with the Israelis.

The Persian Gulf War teaches us that our current planning should pay explicit attention to the kinds of relationships which might support future coalition efforts. Building the basis for future cooperation should be an explicit goal of many of our international programs, including training, weapons sales, combined exercises and other contacts.

Long Lead Times

The forces that performed so well in Desert Storm took a long time to develop; decades of preparation were necessary for them to have been ready for use in 1991. The cruise missiles that people watched fly down the streets of Baghdad were first developed in the mid-'70s. The F-117 stealth fighter bomber, which flew many missions against heavily defended targets without ever being struck, was built in the early '80s. Development and production of major weapons systems today remain long processes. From the time we make a decision to start a new aircraft system until the time it is first fielded in the force takes on the average roughly 13 years.

What is true of weapons systems is also true of people. A general who is capable of commanding a division in combat is the product of more than 25 years' training. The same is true for other complex tasks of military leadership. To train a senior noncommissioned officer to the high level of performance that we expect today takes 10 to 15 years.

Units and command arrangements also take time to build and perfect. The units described earlier that were not ready for combat a decade ago took years to build to their current state. It takes much longer to build a quality force than to draw it down. Just five years after winning World War II, the United States was almost pushed off the Korean peninsula by the army of a third-rate country.

In the past, the appearance of new weapons has often preceded the strategic understanding of how they could be used. As a result, the side that had a better understanding of the implications of the new weapons often had a tremendous advantage over an opponent whose weapons might have been as good and as numerous, but whose concept of how to use them was not. German success in 1940, for example, was less the result of superior hardware than superior doctrine. Thus, appropriate doctrine and accumulated training will be critically important in the years ahead. Here, too, years of study and experiment are required to get the most from our forces. Study of Desert Storm will, itself, be of great importance.

Finally, as noted earlier, the war has reminded us of how important investments in infrastructure and practice in international cooperative efforts can be to build the trust and capabilities that will be needed to put together future coalitions and to enable them to operate successfully in future crises. It takes years of working together to build these kinds of ties.

IMPLICATIONS FOR THE FUTURE

The Persian Gulf conflict reminds us that we cannot be sure when or where the next conflict will arise. In early 1990, many said there were no threats left because of the Soviet withdrawal from Eastern Europe; very few expected that we would be at war within a year. We are constantly reminded of the unpredictability of world events. Few in early 1989 expected the dramatic developments that occurred in Eastern Europe that year. Fewer still would have predicted that within two years the Soviet Union itself would cease to exist. Looking back over the past century, enormous strategic changes often arose unexpectedly in the course of a few years or even less. This is not a lesson which we should have to keep learning anew.

Our ability to predict events 5, 10, or 15 years in the future is quite limited. But, whatever occurs, we will need high-quality forces to deter aggression or, if necessary, to defend our interests. No matter how hard we wish for a just peace, there will come a time when a future President will have to send young Americans into combat somewhere in the world.

As the Department of Defense reduces the armed forces over the next five years, two special challenges confront us, both of which were highlighted by Operation Desert Storm. The first is to retain our technological edge out into the future. The second is to be ready for the next Desert Storm-like contingency that comes along. Just as the high-technology systems we used in the Gulf war reflect conceptions and commitments of 15, 20, or 25 years ago, so the

decisions we make today will decide whether our forces 10 or 15 years from now have what they need to do the job with minimum losses. We want our forces of the year 2015 to have the same high quality our forces had in Desert Storm.

To provide a high-quality force for the future, we must be smart today. We must keep up our investment in R&D, personnel and crucial systems. But we must also cut unneeded production, reduce our active and reserve forces, and close unneeded bases so we can use our resources where they are most needed. M1A1 tanks, F-16s and F-14 aircraft are excellent systems, but we have enough of them; and some planned modernization can be safely deferred. We can better use the money saved by investing in the systems of the future. Reserve forces are valuable but, as we cut the active forces, we must cut the Reserves and National Guard units assigned the mission of supporting them. Our declining defense budgets must sustain the high level of training our remaining forces need. And, as we cut forces, we should cut base structure. Common sense dictates that a smaller force requires fewer bases.

To reach these goals, the Department has developed a new acquisition strategy, tailored to the post-Cold War world, that will enable us to get the most from our research and acquisition efforts at the lowest cost. We have proposed major cuts in new programs, shut down production lines, and sought significant cuts in active and reserve forces and domestic and overseas base structure. With the help of Congress and the American people, we can have a strong defense at greatly reduced cost.

As we reshape America's military and reduce its size, we must be careful that we do so in accordance with our new defense strategy and with a plan that will preserve the integrity of the military capability we have so carefully built. If we try to reduce the force too quickly, we can break it. If we fail to fund the training and high quality we have come to expect, we will end up with an organization that may still outwardly look like a military, but that simply will not function. It will take a long time, lost lives and many resources to rebuild; our nation's security will be hurt, not furthered by such precipitous defense cuts.

If we choose wisely today, we can do well something America has always done badly before we can draw down our military force at a responsible rate that will not end up endangering our security. We did not do this well after World War II, and we found ourselves unprepared for the Korean war barely five years later. We did not draw down intelligently after Vietnam, and we found ourselves with the hollow forces of the late '70s. We are determined to avoid repeating these costly errors.

Our future national security and the lives of young Americans of the next decade and beyond depend on our learning the proper lessons from the Persian Gulf war. It is a task the Department of Defense takes seriously. Those Americans lost in the Persian Gulf war and their families paid a heavy price for freedom. If we make the wrong choices now if we waste defense dollars on force structure we cannot support or on more weapons than we need or on bases we cannot afford then the next time young Americans go into combat we may not have the capabilities we need to win.

America can be proud of its role in the Persian Gulf war. There were lessons to be learned and problems to be sure. But overall there was an outstanding victory. We can be proud of our conviction and international leadership. We can be proud of one of the most remarkable deployments in history. We can be proud of our partnership in arms with many nations. We can be proud of our technology and the wisdom of our leaders at all levels. But most of all we can be proud of those dedicated young Americans soldiers, sailors, airmen and marines who showed their skill, their commitment to what we stand for, and their bravery in the way they fought this war.

Dick Cheney

PREFACE

The final report to Congress on the conduct of hostilities in the Persian Gulf (pursuant to the requirements of Title V of the Persian Gulf Supplemental and Personnel Benefits Act of 1991) is divided into two parts. The first part deals with the nature of Iraqi forces, Operation Desert Shield, the Maritime Interception Operations and Operation Desert Storm. The second part contains appendices dealing with specific issues.

Discussion in Chapters I through VIII focuses on how the threat in the Persian Gulf developed and how the United States and its Coalition partners responded to that threat at the strategic, operational, and tactical levels. The narrative is chronological to the extent possible. In this sense, it touches on issues such as logistics, intelligence, deployment, the law of armed conflict, and mobilization, among others, only as those issues have a bearing on the overall chronicle.

This is not to suggest that other issues are not important. In fact, examination of these issues is of great substantive value to future security plans and programs. To provide ready access to this information, discussions of specific issues have been structured into appendices. The intent is to provide as much detail as possible about a specific issue in one location. For all intents and purposes, the appendices are independent documents and with enough background to let the reader concerned with a particular area read the appropriate appendix and forego other parts of the report. Where cross-referencing or overlapping occurs, it is to achieve that objective.

The content of this report is the result of extensive research conducted through review of original source documents (such as orders, plans, estimates, and appraisals); information from the Office of the Secretary of Defense, Joint Staff, the United States Central Command, other unified and specified commands, component commands, and the military Services; and, in-depth interviews with many senior officers and policy makers involved in Operations Desert Shield and Desert Storm. Research to determine what lessons ought to be taken from the crisis began before the conflict ended. Throughout, officials at all levels willingly provided information. However, this conflict was exceptionally well documented compared with previous crises. Many data points remain in raw form and information on some aspects of the campaigns remains uncollated and unevaluated. The volume of available documents, perhaps in the millions of pages, will provide researchers with data for a number of years. Therefore, while the depictions, conclusions, and evaluations presented in this report are based on a thorough examination of the existing evidence, they are subject to modification as additional research makes more information available.

A NOTE ON PREPARATION OF THE TITLE V REPORT

Preparation of the interim and final versions of this report entailed an intensive twelve month effort involving hundreds of individuals. It was prepared under the auspices of Honorable Paul Wolfowitz, Under Secretary of Defense for Policy. The overall effort was directed by Honorable I. Lewis Libby, Deputy Under Secretary of Defense for Policy. Policy guidance was provided by Dr Zalmay Khalilzad, Assistant Deputy Under Secretary of Defense for Policy Planning.

The report was produced in consultation with the Chairman of the Joint Chiefs of Staff and the Commander-in-Chief, United States Central Command. Joint Staff efforts were directed by Rear Admiral David B. Robinson, USN, and Major General Alan V. Rogers, USAF, the Directors of Operational Plans and Interoperability (J-7). They were assisted by Colonel David L. Vesely, USAF; Colonel Douglas C. Lovelace Jr., USA; Lieutenant Colonel Daniel J. Pierre, USAF; Commander Stephen G. Gardner, USN; and Lieutenant Colonel Robert E. Nedergaard, USAF. Major General Burton R. Moore, USAF, Operations Directorate (J-3) directed contributions of the United States Central Command. He was assisted by Lieutenant Colonel Garry P. McNiesh, USA.

The Title V Report was researched, coordinated, and written by a joint team which was headed by Colonel George T. Raach, USA. Team members were: Colonel Phillip H. Bates, USAR; Colonel John R. Bioty Jr., USMC; Captain Paul W. Hanley, USN; Colonel Michael Peters, USA; Colonel Joe W. Robben, USMC; Captain Jerry Russell, USNR; Colonel Edward Soriano, USA; Captain A.H. White, USN; Lieutenant Colonel Edward A. Bondzeleske, USAF; Lieutenant Colonel Charles E. Byrd, USAF; Lieutenant Colonel Scott K. Gordon, USAF; Lieutenant Colonel Bernard E. Harvey, USAF; Lieutenant Colonel Daniel T. Kuehl, USAF; Lieutenant Colonel Gregory S. Laird, USA; Lieutenant Colonel Gerard J. Monaghan, USAR; Lieutenant Colonel John Peters, USA; Lieutenant Colonel Claudio J. Scialdo, USAR; Lieutenant Colonel Lloyd M. Scott, USA; Lieutenant Colonel Kenneth R. Straffer, USA, (ret); Major Richard C. Francona, USAF; Major Richard S. Moore, USMC; Major Alexander D. Perwich II, USA; Major David K. Swindell, USA; Captain Ralph A. Butler, USA; Lieutenant Gregory T. Maxwell, USN; and, Captain Kevin V. Wilkerson, USA; Lieutenant, Linda A. Petrone, USNR; Second Lieutenant Gail Curley, USA; and Cadet Patrick R. Brien, USAFA.

Lieutenant General Dale A. Vesser, USA, (ret), Assistant Deputy Under Secretary for Resources and Plans, and Captain Larry R. Seaquist, USN, Assistant to the Principal Deputy Under Secretary of Defense for Strategy and Resourses, also played a valuable role in the production of this report. Assisting Dr Khalilzad in his supervision of the report were Dr Wade P. Hinkle, his deputy, and Dr Abram N. Shulsky of the Policy Planning Staff, and Ms Carol Kuntz, Special Assistant to the Principal Deputy Under Secretary of Defense for Strategy and Resources.

Chapter I

Iraqi Armored Forces.

THE INVASION OF KUWAIT

At 0100 (Kuwait time), 2 August, three Iraqi Republican Guard Forces Command (RGFC) divisions attacked across the Kuwaiti frontier. A mechanized infantry division and an armored division conducted the main attack south into Kuwait along the Safwan-' Abdally axis, driving for the Al-Jahra pass. Another armored division conducted a supporting attack farther west. Almost simultaneously, at 0130, a special operations force conducted the first attack on Kuwait City — a heliborne assault against key government facilities. Meanwhile, commando teams made amphibious assaults against the Amir's palace and other key facilities. The Amir was able to escape into Saudi Arabia, but his brother was killed in the Iraqi assault on the Dasman Palace.

The three attacking armored and mechanized formations, supported by combat aircraft, linked up at Al-Jahra. The two divisions conducting the main attack continued east to Kuwait City, where they joined the special operations forces by 0530. By 1900, Iraqi forces had secured the city. Concurrently, the supporting armored division moved south from Al-Jahra to establish blocking positions on the main avenues of approach from the Saudi border. By the evening of 2 August, Iraqi tanks were moving south of the capital along the coast to occupy Kuwait's ports.

Kuwaiti armed forces were no match for the assembled Iraqi force. Although Kuwaiti armed forces had gone on full alert after Saddam Hussein's 17 July speech, they reduced alert

> *"Without warrant or warning, Iraq has struck brutally at a tiny Kuwait, a brazen challenge to world law. Iraq stands condemned by a unanimous UN Security Council...President Bush's taste for bluntness stands him in good stead: "Naked Aggression!" is the correct term for President Saddam Hussein's [1] grab at a vulnerable, oil-rich neighbor."*
>
> **New York Times**
> **3 August 1990**

levels a week later to 25 percent. This may have been done in an attempt to reduce the tension between Kuwait and Iraq. Kuwaiti military resistance was uncoordinated; despite individual acts of bravery, Kuwaiti forces were hopelessly outmatched. Army elements attempted to recapture the Amir's palace, and 35th Armored Brigade tanks tried to mount a defense against approaching Republican Guard armored formations. Kuwaiti casualties are estimated to have been light, but specific numbers are unknown. Some Kuwaiti forces successfully retreated across the Saudi border as defenses collapsed. Kuwait Air Force pilots flew limited sorties against attacking Iraqi units, but were forced to recover in Saudi Arabia or Bahrain, since the two Kuwaiti air bases had been overrun. By midday, 3 August, Iraqi forces had taken up positions near the Kuwaiti-Saudi border.

On 4 August, Iraqi tanks were establishing defensive positions. Hundreds of logistics vehicles were moving men and massive quantities of munitions and supplies south.

---

[1] Although the Arabic letters Hah (dammah)-Sin (fathah)-Yah-Nun are best renedered as HUSAYN, hereafter this document reflects the more commonly used HUSSEIN.

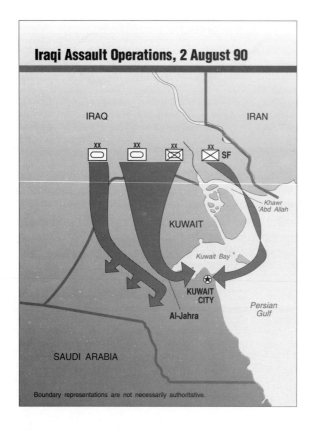

Iraqi Assault Operations, 2 August 90

Boundary representations are not necessarily authoritative.

replacement was ominous for, while it allowed a possible return of RGFC units to Iraq, it also freed these formations for a subsequent attack into Saudi Arabia, should Saddam order it.

By 6 August, the Iraqis had consolidated their gains and were resupplying their forces, another indication Iraq might continue its drive south. At this point, elements of at least 11 divisions were either in or entering Kuwait. This amounted to more than 200,000 soldiers, supported by more than 2,000 tanks. Two days later, Saddam announced the annexation of the country, describing Kuwait as the "19th Province — an eternal part of Iraq."

PRELUDE TO CRISIS

Emerging from the Iran-Iraq war at the helm of the dominant military power in the Gulf, Saddam saw himself as the premier leader in (and of) the Arab world. In April 1990, claiming an enlarged regional role, Saddam had

RGFC infantry divisions that had been deployed to the border area in late July moved into Kuwait, occupied Kuwait City, and secured the primary lines of communications to and from southern Iraq. By this time, more Iraqi divisions were moving south to Kuwait from garrisons in Iraq. These forces would replace the RGFC units in defensive positions in Kuwait. This

GEOGRAPHY OF KUWAIT

Kuwait, a country slightly smaller than New Jersey, consists of flat to slightly undulating desert plains. It has almost no defensible terrain. The only significant elevation in the country is the Al-Mutl'a Ridge, just north of the city of Al-Jahra. A pass in this ridge at Al-Jahra is the traditional defensive position against an approach from the north. British troops occupied the position in the 1961 defense of Kuwait when Iraq threatened to seize the newly independent country. In the Gulf War, Iraqi troops mined and fortified this pass as a defense against potential Coalition attacks north toward the Iraq-Kuwait frontier.

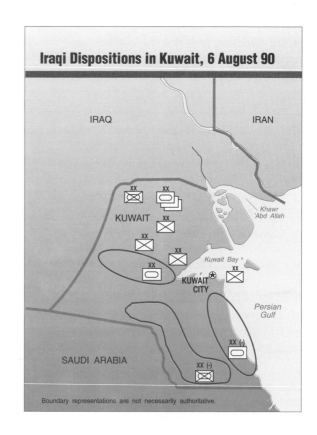

Iraqi Dispositions in Kuwait, 6 August 90

Boundary representations are not necessarily authoritative.

demanded withdrawal of US forces from the Gulf, claiming there no longer was any need for foreign presence in the region. On 1 July, Saddam declared Iraq now had binary chemical weapons (CW) — "a deterrent sufficient to confront the Israeli nuclear weapon." At the same time, the Iraqi leader made several threatening speeches, turning his attention to his Arab neighbors, claiming Iraq alone had defended the "Arab nation" against the age-old Persian threat.

On 17 July, Saddam accused Kuwait and the United Arab Emirates of complicity with the United States to cheat on oil production quotas. He blamed this overproduction for driving down the price of oil, causing losses of billions of dollars to Iraq. During this period, the Iraqi million-man armed forces and aggressive research and development programs (including Iraq's large nuclear development effort) were consuming enormous sums of money. Iraq's 1990 military budget was $12.9 billion, or approximately $700 per citizen in a country where the average annual income was $1,950. By mid 1990, Iraq had only enough cash reserves for three months of imports and an inflation rate of 40 percent.

Iraq largely had financed the military expenditures of the war with Iran through loans. By 1990, creditors were reluctant to extend new development loans until substantial parts of the old debt were paid. Many loans were in serious

IRAQ'S SADDAM: THE PRESIDENT-LEADER-MARSHAL

"He who launches an aggression against Iraq or the Arab nation will now find someone to repel him. If we can strike him with a stone, we will. With a missile, we will...and with all the missiles, bombs, and other means at our disposal."

18 April 1990

Saddam was born on 28 April 1937 near Tikrit and was raised in the home of his maternal uncle, after the breakup of his parents' marriage. After his bid to attend the Iraqi national military academy was rejected, an embittered Saddam turned to the Ba'ath Party. As a Party member, he took part in the aborted assassination attempt against the ruler of Iraq in 1959. Wounded in the attack, he escaped Iraq and made his way to Syria, and in 1961, to Egypt, where he reportedly attended college. He returned in 1963, after a successful Ba'ath coup in Baghdad. When the Ba'athis were ousted later that same year, Saddam was arrested and spent two years in prison. He escaped and spent two years underground, planning the successful 17 July 1968 coup. Saddam became vice chairman of the Revolutionary Command Council and de facto ruler of Iraq by eliminating any opposition. In July 1979, he convinced then-President Ahmad Hassan Al-Bakr to resign, and was named President of the Republic, Chairman of the Revolutionary Command Council, Supreme Commander of the Armed Forces, and Secretary General of the Ba'ath Party.

arrears, especially those made by other Arab states. Iraq's Arab neighbors were reluctant to write off more than $37 billion in loans made to Iraq. Baghdad did not believe it necessary to repay immediately what it considered "soft" loans from Gulf Cooperation Council members. (Saddam argued Iraq had gone to war with Iran to protect the Arabian Peninsula from the threat of Iranian expansionism. Thus, according to this argument, Gulf states ought not dun Iraq for expenses incurred on their behalf.) If not rescheduled, the required annual principal and interest payments on the non-Arab debt alone would have consumed more than half of Iraq's estimated $13 billion 1989 oil revenues. Debt

service in subsequent years would have had an equally deleterious effect.

Iraq's large expenditures on its military forces both aggravated its financial distress and provided the muscle with which to intimidate its rich, but weak, neighbor Kuwait. Saddam initially demanded money from Kuwait; this demand was rejected by the Kuwaiti Amir, who instead offered a small, long-term loan. Iraq again raised the long-standing question of ownership of the islands of Warbah and Bubiyan, which it claimed are important for secure access to its ports on the Khawr 'Abd Allah — the waterway leading to the Persian

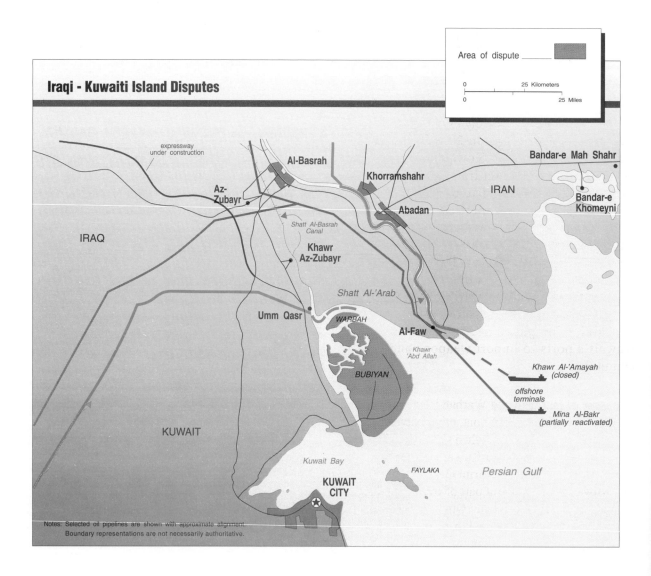

Iraqi - Kuwaiti Island Disputes

Area of dispute

0   25 Kilometers
0   25 Miles

expressway under construction

Al-Basrah

Khorramshahr

Bandar-e Mah Shahr

Az-Zubayr

IRAN

Bandar-e Khomeyni

Abadan

IRAQ

Shatt Al-Basrah Canal

Khawr Az-Zubayr

Shatt Al-'Arab

Umm Qasr

WARBAH

Al-Faw

Khawr 'Abd Allah

Khawr Al-'Amayah (closed)

BUBIYAN

offshore terminals

Mina Al-Bakr (partially reactivated)

KUWAIT

Kuwait Bay

FAYLAKA

Persian Gulf

KUWAIT CITY

Notes: Selected oil pipelines are shown with approximate alignment. Boundary representations are not necessarily authoritative.

Gulf that is the only alternative to the closed Shatt Al-'Arab, cluttered with debris from the Iran-Iraq war, sunken vessels, tons of unexploded ordnance (including nerve and blister agent rounds), and more than 10 years of silting. Iraq's limited access to the sea had forced the country to rely on its neighbors' ports since the Shatt was closed in 1980. (For example, Iraq's energy sector depended on the cooperation of Turkey and Saudi Arabia, whose ports handled 90 percent of Iraqi oil exports.) Efforts to clear the Shatt had been stymied by cost and difficulty. An Iraqi-built canal from Al-Basrah to Az-Zubayr could not handle large oil export vessels. In any case, vessels using this waterway must pass near the Kuwaiti islands of Warbah and Bubiyan. If held by a hostile government, the islands effectively could deny Iraqi access to the Persian Gulf. Kuwait, however, had taken no action to deny Iraq access to the Gulf.

Iraq had demanded repeatedly the two islands be transferred or leased to it. On 20 March 1973, Iraqi troops seized the Kuwaiti border post of As-Samitah and Iraq announced it was annexing a small strip of Kuwaiti territory near the Iraqi port city of Umm Qasr. Saudi Arabia immediately came to Kuwait's aid and, with the Arab League, secured Iraq's withdrawal. There was a minor border incident in this area in 1983, but this issue was temporarily shelved in 1984 because of the pressures of the war with Iran — Baghdad needed access to Kuwait's ports to import weapons and ammunition.

The issue of Bubiyan and Warbah islands was only part of the history of contention between Iraq and Kuwait. In 1961, when Great Britain ended its protectorate over Kuwait, then Iraqi Prime Minister 'Abd Al-Karim Qasim asserted that Kuwait is an "integral part of Iraq," because it had been part of the former Ottoman province of Al-Basrah. Iraq threatened to exert its sovereignty over Kuwait, but the resulting

deployment of British troops to Kuwait forced the Iraqis to back down. Although subsequent regimes have relinquished this claim by recognizing Kuwait's independence, Iraq never agreed formally to accept the existing boundary between the two countries. Iraq, in 1990, also claimed Kuwait was illegally extracting oil from the Iraqi-claimed Ar-Rumaylah oil field, which straddles the *de facto* boundary.

As the situation in July 1990 escalated from a war of words to deployment of a massive Iraqi force north of Kuwait, Arab leaders sought to resolve the crisis peacefully. Egyptian President Husni Mubarak and Saudi King Fahd offered their good offices. These leaders arranged a meeting between Kuwaiti and Iraqi officials in Jiddah, Saudi Arabia, on 1 August. But the Iraqi representative, Izzat Ibrahim Ad-Duri, walked out, complaining of Kuwaiti reluctance to discuss Iraqi claims to the islands or to forgive Iraq's debt to Kuwait. The Iraqi

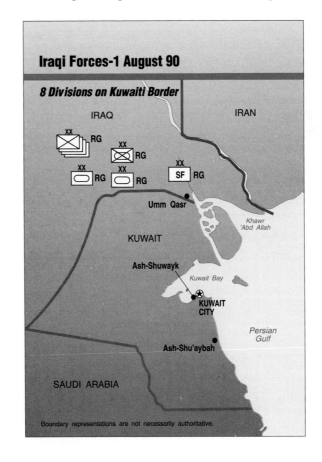

Deputy Prime Minister claimed "no agreement has been reached on anything because we did not feel from the Kuwaitis any seriousness in dealing with the severe damage inflicted on Iraq as a result of their recent behavior and stands against Iraq's basic interests."

Kuwait quite reasonably rejected Iraq's demands for money and territory. It had sought to ameliorate the crisis by concessions at the negotiation table. These concessions included guaranteed loans to the Iraqi government, and sharing of revenue derived from the Ar-Rumaylah oil field. By this time, however, Iraqi forces were on the move. Senior Iraqi military officers captured during Operation Desert Storm claimed the decision to invade had been made already in Baghdad.

In fact, Iraqi Republican Guard units had begun moving from garrisons around Baghdad as Saddam made his 17 July speech accusing Kuwait (among others) of cheating Iraq of oil revenue and of occupying territory belonging to Iraq. By 21 July, a RGFC armored division had deployed just north of Kuwait. There were reports that as many as 3,000 military vehicles were on the road leading south from Baghdad to the Kuwaiti border. In two weeks, the bulk of the combat power of Iraq's best military force — the Republican Guard — was moved hundreds of kilometers into positions that would permit an attack into Kuwait with almost no warning.

By 1 August, there were eight RGFC divisions (two armored, one mechanized, one special forces and four infantry) between Al-Basrah and the Kuwaiti border. The rapidity of this buildup indicated the quality and extent of Iraqi staff planning. Some units had moved as far as 700 kilometers from their home bases. The Iraqis had assembled almost 140,000 troops, supported by more than 1,500 tanks and infantry vehicles, plus the required artillery, and logistics. Iraqi air assets in the area increased as well. Attack, fighter, and fighter-bomber aircraft moved into

southern air bases, as did assault helicopters. Air defense systems were deployed to protect the assembling attack force.

In retrospect, it appears Iraq probably never intended to come to terms with Kuwait through

OVERVIEW OF THE IRAN-IRAQ WAR

After the fall of the Shah and the rise to power of the Ayatollah Ruhollah Khomeini, relations between Tehran and Baghdad deteriorated quickly. Khomeini called for the overthrow of Iraq's Ba'ath Party, actively supported anti-Ba'ath groups, and aided assassination attempts against senior Iraqi officials. Conversely, Iraq saw an opportunity to abrogate the 1975 Algiers Treaty, which had established joint Iraqi-Iranian control over the Shatt Al-'Arab by delineating the international border at the center of the navigable channel. Iraq believed its troops could defeat the Iranian armed forces, badly disintegrated by the Iranian revolution.

Iraq launched a two-corps attack into Iran in September 1980 and captured Iranian territory in the Arabic-speaking, oil-rich area of Khuzistan. Saddam expected the invasion to result in an Arab uprising against Khomeini's fundamentalist Islamic regime. This revolt did not materialize, however, and the Arab minority remained loyal to Tehran. After a month of advances, the Iraqi attack stalled; for a time, the situation was

characterized by small attacks and counterattacks, with neither side able to gain a distinct advantage. In 1982, when a major offensive failed, Saddam ordered a withdrawal to the international borders, believing Iran would agree to end the war. Iran did not accept this withdrawal as the end of the conflict, and continued the war into Iraq.

Believing it could win the war merely by holding the line and inflicting unacceptable losses on the attacking Iranians, Iraq initially adopted a static defensive strategy. This was successful in repelling successive Iranian offensives until 1986 and 1987, when the Al-Faw peninsula was lost and Iranian troops reached the gates of Al-Basrah. Embarrassed by the loss of the peninsula and concerned by the threat to his second largest city, Saddam ordered a change in strategy. From a defensive posture, in which the only offensive operations were counterattacks to relieve forces under pressure or to exploit failed Iranian assaults, the Iraqis adopted an offensive strategy. More decision-making authority was delegated to senior military commanders. The

negotiation. Rather, it may well have been that, in Iraq's view, the late-July political maneuverings and 1 August talks in Jiddah were only a pretext to provide time for final preparations and to give an air of legitimacy to the coming invasion.

success of this new strategy, plus the attendant change in doctrine and procedures, virtually eliminated Iranian military capabilities. The change also indicated a maturing of Iraqi military capabilities and an improvement in the armed forces' effectiveness.

Four major battles were fought from April to August 1988, in which the Iraqis routed or defeated the Iranians. In the first offensive, named Blessed Ramadhan, Iraqi Republican Guard and regular Army units recaptured the Al-Faw peninsula. The 36-hour battle was conducted in a militarily sophisticated manner with two main thrusts, supported by heliborne and amphibious landings, and low-level fixed-wing attack sorties. In this battle, the Iraqis effectively used chemical weapons (CW), using nerve and blister agents against Iranian command and control facilities, artillery positions, and logistics points.

Three subsequent operations followed much the same pattern, although they were somewhat less complex. After rehearsals, the Iraqis launched successful attacks on Iranian forces in the Fish Lake and Shalamjah areas near Al-Basrah and recaptured the oil-rich Majnun Islands. Farther to the north, in the last major engagement before the August 1988 cease-fire, Iraqi armored and mechanized forces penetrated deep into Iran, defeating Iranian forces and capturing huge amounts of armor and artillery. In the fall of 1988, the Iraqis displayed in Baghdad captured Iranian weapons amounting to more than three-quarters of the Iranian armor inventory and almost half of its artillery pieces and armored personnel carriers.

Iraq's victory was not without cost. The Iraqis suffered an estimated 375,000 casualties, the equivalent of 5.6 million for a population the size of the United States. Another 60,000 were taken prisoner by the Iranians. The Iraqi military machine — numbering more than a million men with an extensive arsenal of CW, extended range Scud missiles, a large air force and one of the world's larger armies — emerged as the premier armed force in the Persian Gulf region. In the Middle East, only the Israel Defense Force had superior capability.

IRAQI MILITARY CAPABILITIES, 1990

At the time of the invasion of Kuwait, the Iraqi armed forces were, by any measure, a formidable and battle-tested fighting force. Iraq began the crisis with one of the world's larger armies, equipped with great numbers of tanks, armored personnel carriers and artillery, some of which were state-of-the-art models. It had a sizable air force with many top-line fighters and fighter-bombers (F-1s, MiG-29s and Su-24s) and a modern air defense command and control (C^2) system. During the last six months of the Iran-Iraq war, the Iraqi army had demonstrated a capability to conduct multi-axis, multi-corps, combined-arms operations deep into hostile territory. The staff could conduct long-range planning; coordination of air and artillery preparations; timing of movements and operations; coordination of complicated logistics requirements; and movement of supplies, equipment, and troops to the right place at the designated time. They had developed excellent operational security and deception.

Iraqi armed forces were structured similarly to the British forces, but their operations were modeled more closely on Soviet armed forces. The senior military echelon in Iraq is the General Headquarters (GHQ), which integrates operations of the Republican Guard, Army, Navy, Air and Air Defense Forces, and Popular Army. It is dominated by ground force officers.

Iraqi ground forces were the largest in the Persian Gulf at the time of the invasion of Kuwait. They included the Republican Guard Forces Command, the regular Army, and the Popular Army. Iraqi ground forces had more than 5,000 main battle tanks, 5,000 armored infantry vehicles, and 3,000 artillery pieces larger than 100mm. These forces were supported by enough heavy equipment transporters to move a three-division heavy corps at one time. Iraqi troops were well practiced in conducting short-notice division moves across considerable distances, as well as other tactical operations.

The Iraqi military supply and transportation infrastructure was extensive and well-equipped, with ample supplies of ammunition, water, food and fuels. A modern transportation system had been built inside Iraq during the Iran-Iraq war to ease unit movement to and from combat areas and to keep them supplied. The logistic system was a hybrid of the Soviet system, in which materiel is delivered forward from higher echelons before it is needed, and the British system, in which lower echelons draw materiel as needed. In the Iraqi system, materiel was sent automatically from GHQ to the corps, based on estimated consumption requirements. Once at the corps depot, divisions and brigades drew replenishment supplies.

Republican Guard Forces Command

The RGFC was Iraq's most capable and loyal force, and had received the best training and equipment. It began as an elite organization tasked with regime protection. This organization served as the core around which to build an elite offensive force, which grew dramatically during the last two years of the war with Iran. Personnel recruited into the RGFC were given bonuses, new cars and subsidized housing. At the end of the war with Iran, the RGFC consisted of eight divisions. Combined with its independent infantry and artillery brigades, the RGFC comprised almost 20 percent of Iraqi ground forces. Most RGFC heavy divisions were equipped with Soviet T-72 main battle tanks, Soviet BMP armored personnel carriers, French GCT self-propelled howitzers and Austrian GHN-45 towed howitzers – all modern, state-of-the-art equipment. RGFC armored battalions had nine more tanks than Army tank battalions, giving them added firepower. Otherwise, the organization of combat arms units in the Guard and regular Army appeared identical.

The RGFC was subordinate to the State Special Security Apparatus, not the Defense Ministry; it was believed to be under GHQ operational control during combat. Although the Guard and regular Army were maintained as separate institutions, they had demonstrated the ability to fight effectively in the same offensive or defensive operation. The RGFC was the major assault force in each of the 1988 multi-corps offensive operations that reclaimed the Al-Faw peninsula, Fish Lake and the Majnun Islands from the Iranians. In these operations, regular forces fixed the enemy while the RGFC attacked. These offensive operations in 1988 were notable for their detailed preparation and planning.

The Guard's defensive mission was strategic reserve, withheld until it could influence the battle decisively with a counterattack, or shore up collapsing Army positions. To prevent the fall of Al-Basrah in 1987, 12 Guard brigades were committed to battle. Without the determined RGFC defense, the Iranians would have penetrated the Iraqi lines. In early 1988, RGFC elements again were sent hurriedly to shore up a weakness in the Al-Basrah defenses in anticipation of an expected Iranian offensive. GHQ usually reserved authority to commit the RGFC to battle. The RGFC also was an important political force supporting Saddam, used to counterbalance the regular Army in case of revolt or to deal with civil unrest.

Army

The regular Army in mid-1990 consisted of more than 50 divisions, additional special forces brigades, and specialized forces commands composed of maneuver and artillery units. Although most divisions were infantry, the Army had several armored and mechanized divisions. Some armored units had a small amount of modern Western and Soviet equipment, but most of the Army had 1960s-vintage Soviet and Chinese equipment. Training and equipment readiness of Army units varied greatly, ranging from good in the divisions that existed before the Iran-Iraq war, to poor in the largely conscript infantry formations.

The basic operational level formation was the corps, which consisted of several divisions and support units. Iraqi Army divisions were of three basic types: armored, mechanized and infantry. Divisions normally consisted of three brigades, division artillery, air defense, reconnaissance, combat support and combat service support units, although temporary assignment of other units was common. Armored and mechanized divisions were triangular in organization; armored divisions had two armored brigades and a mechanized brigade, while mechanized divisions had two mechanized brigades and an armored brigade. Infantry divisions were assigned three infantry brigades and a tank battalion. Iraqi divisions had at least four artillery battalions, but often were augmented by additional battalions. Armored and mechanized brigades normally consisted of four battalions. Armored brigades had three tank and one mechanized battalions, while a mechanized brigade had three mechanized and one tank battalion.

Popular Army

The Popular Army was created in 1970 as the Ba'ath Party militia. These units were poorly trained and equipped and, in August 1990, numbered approximately 250,000, down from 650,000 during the war with Iran. Originally restricted to party members, the Popular Army's mission was to secure the Ba'ath regime against internal opposition and provide a power base for the regime in case of a regular Army uprising. During the war with Iran, nonparty members were inducted into the ranks and as many as 100,000 Popular Army members were integrated into the regular Army and served for limited periods on the front lines. By 1990, however, membership once again was restricted to Ba'ath Party members and its mission restricted to rear area security.

Air Force

In terms of numbers of combat aircraft, the Iraqi Air Force was the largest in the Middle East in August 1990. The quality of the aircraft and aircrew, however, was very uneven. Its effectiveness was constrained by the conservative doctrine and aircraft systems limitations. While Iraqi pilots performed some impressive, relatively complex strikes with the F-1, air-to-air engagements were unimpressive. Lock on by Iranian fighters generally would cause Iraqi pilots conducting offensive counter air missions to abort their missions. Survival dominated their tactics, even when the odds were overwhelmingly in their favor. Aerial engagements were characterized by high-speed, maximum-range missile launches, and a lack of aggressive maneuvering. Saddam had proven reluctant to commit the air force to combat, preferring to keep it in reserve for a final defense of Baghdad and the regime. The Iraqi Air Force had been used most effectively in the war with Iran against economic targets such as oil facilities and tankers. During the war, tactics evolved from high-altitude level bombing to low-level attacks with precision guided munitions (PGMs). Iraq not only imported cluster bombs and fuel-air explosives, but also had acquired the technology to produce these weapons. Pilots had become adept at delivering both conventional and chemical-filled munitions during the final 1988 offensives.

Iraq had more than 700 combat aircraft in its inventory before the invasion of Kuwait. Fewer than half of these aircraft were either third generation (comparable to the US F-4) or fourth generation (comparable to US F-15 technology), and were flown by pilots of marginal quality, compared with US aviators. These aircraft included the Soviet MiG-29 and Su-24 (both fourth generation) as well as the MiG-23, MiG-25, and the French F-1 (third generation). The rest of the aircraft were 1950s and 1960s Soviet and Chinese technology, and were flown by poorly trained personnel. Nevertheless, under the proper conditions, even the older aircraft models were effective.

The 65 French-built F-1s and their pilots were the Iraqi Air Force elite. Iraq had acquired a wide range of weapons and electronic warfare gear for the F-1, including laser-guided air-to-surface missiles. French-trained pilots exhibited a high degree of skill and determination when attacking Iranian surface targets, and were more willing to engage in air-to-air combat than their colleagues flying Soviet-built aircraft. It was an Iraqi F-1 that fired two Exocet antiship missiles at the *USS Stark* (FFG 31) in 1987. During the Iraqi offensives of 1988, F-1s equipped with PGMs attacked Iranian armaments factories, oil refineries and facilities, bridges and causeways, as well as merchant shipping in the Gulf.

Iraqi aircraft were deployed at more than 24 primary and 30 dispersal airfields throughout the country. The main operating bases were well constructed, built to withstand conventional attack. The Iraqis could shelter almost all their aircraft in hardened shelters, some built by Yugoslav contractors to standards believed to be able to withstand the effects of air burst detonations of tactical nuclear weapons. Other air base facilities were placed in hardened shelters or took advantage of natural protection, such as caves.

Air Defense Forces

Iraqi air defenses were redesigned after the Israeli raid on the Osirak nuclear reactor in 1981. A network of radars, surface-to-air missiles (SAM) and antiaircraft artillery (AAA) was installed, primarily concentrated around strategic and industrial facilities in the Baghdad area. The national air defense operations center (ADOC) in downtown Baghdad controlled Iraq's air defenses. The ADOC maintained the overall air picture in

Iraq and established priorities for air defense engagements. Subordinate to this facility were sector operations centers (SOC), each controlling a specific geographic area. The SOC and the ADOC were connected by the French-built Kari command and control system. This modern, computerized system linked the diverse inventory of Soviet and Western radar and air defense weaponry. It provided a redundant C^2 capability.

Air defense weaponry included SA-2, SA-3, SA-6 and Roland SAM systems. Additional air defense was provided by Air Force interceptors and organic Army assets, including the SA-7/14, SA-8, SA-9/13, SA-16 missile systems, and the ZSU-23/4 self-propelled AAA system. In addition, the Iraqi air defense had more than 7,500 AAA pieces protecting all targets of value, some deployed on the roofs of numerous buildings in Baghdad housing government facilities. These weapons — 57-mm and 37-mm AAA pieces, ZSU-23/4 and ZSU-57/2 self-propelled AAA systems, and hundreds of 14.5-mm and 23-mm light antiaircraft weapons — formed the backbone of the integrated air defense network. In major high value target areas (such as Baghdad, airfields, chemical agent production complexes, and nuclear facilities) the combined arms air defense could prove lethal to aircraft operating below 10,000 feet.

The Iraqi air defense system was formidable, combining the best features of several systems. The multi-layered, redundant, computer-controlled air defense network around Baghdad was more dense than that surrounding most Eastern European cities during the Cold War, and several orders of magnitude greater than that which had defended Hanoi during the later stages of the Vietnam War. If permitted to function as designed, the air defense array was capable of effective protection of key targets in Iraq.

Navy

The navy consisted of a collection of Osa guided-missile patrol boats and numerous auxiliaries. Iraq's Soviet-built Osas were outfitted with the Styx missile with a maximum range of 46 or 95 kilometers, depending on the variant. While offensive capabilities were limited, the navy also had the 100-km range Silkworm surface-to-surface missile, whose half-ton warhead could sink a frigate or damage a battleship.

Another weapon in the Iraqi naval arsenal was a diverse inventory — numbering in the thousands — of moored contact and bottom influence mines. Iraqi mines were both imported and indigenously produced, reverse-engineered copies of at least five foreign models. Iraq's minelayers could lay extensive minefields in a nonhostile environment. Moored contact mines detonate when struck and normally are positioned at or below the water line, making detection possible but often difficult. Bottom influence mines, on the other hand, are extremely difficult to detect because they are laid on the ocean floor. They can be programmed to detonate in response to a variety of conditions, such as acoustic or magnetic stimuli, or after a designated number of ships have passed. The effect of a bottom influence mine is much more devastating than that of a contact mine.

Iraq realized the weakness of its navy; however, financial and political problems prevented timely correction. In 1980, Iraq signed a $1.8 billion contract with Italy for delivery of four Lupo class frigates, six Esmerelda class corvettes, one Stromboli class replenishment oiler, and one floating dry dock. These vessels had not been delivered by the time of the invasion of Kuwait. Further, Iran stated that any attempt to bring the vessels to the Gulf would provoke an Iranian effort to block their passage.

Short Range Ballistic Missiles

The Iraqis had launched almost 200 Al-Husayn missiles at targets in Iran in the February-April 1988 "War of the Cities." The Iranians responded with fewer than 50 standard Scuds. This was the first time Baghdad could strike Tehran with missiles. Because the circular error probable of the modified Scud missiles was approximately 3,000 meters, targets were Iranian cities rather than discrete military installations or facilities. Even with a small warhead, these attacks had great psychological impact on Tehran's population, causing almost one third of the residents to evacuate the city. It also gave the Iraqi population a psychological boost.

By the middle of 1990, the Iraqis had the basic Soviet-supplied Scud missile, plus two indigenous variants. The Al-Husayn missile could reach targets at 600 kilometers, and the Al-Hijarah could reach targets as far as 750 kilometers. (The Al-Husayn and Al-Hijarah were used to attack Israel and Saudi Arabia in 1991.) Iraq's modified Scud missiles could be fired from standard Scud transporter-erector-launchers or Iraqi-produced mobile erector-launchers. The Iraqi Scud family of

---

IRAQI MISSILE NAMES

Iraqi missiles were named for religious leaders or political causes. The first modified Scud produced by Iraq was named the Al-Husayn, for the grandson of the Prophet Muhammad and son of 'Ali. Both are revered in Shi'a Islam, whose adherents comprise the majority in Iraq. 'Ali was martyred in An-Najaf, and Husayn was killed in Karbala, both in Iraq and both now considered Shi'a holy places. Saddam is a Sunni; the name Al-Husayn may have been an attempt to appeal to the Shi'a population.

The Al-Hijarah, meaning "The Stones" was named for the Palestinian intifadhah, or uprising. The youth of the uprising are commonly known in the Arabic press as the "Children of the Stones." By naming the missile for the preferred weapon of the intifadhah, Saddam attempted to tie his weapons program (and anti-Israel stance) to the Palestinian problem.

Iraqi Missile Capabilities

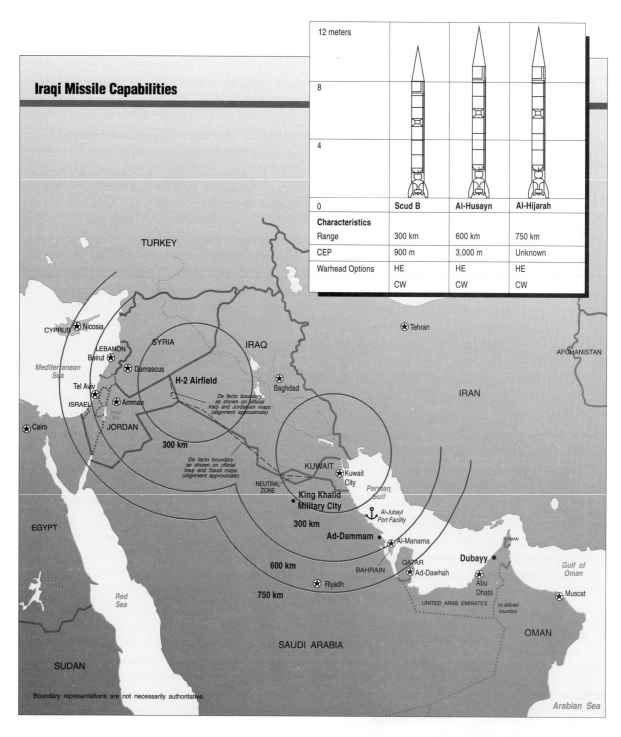

12 meters			
8			
4			
0	**Scud B**	**Al-Husayn**	**Al-Hijarah**
Characteristics			
Range	300 km	600 km	750 km
CEP	900 m	3,000 m	Unknown
Warhead Options	HE	HE	HE
	CW	CW	CW

Boundary representations are not necessarily authoritative.

missiles could carry conventional (high explosive) or unitary and binary nerve agent warheads.

In February 1990, US intelligence detected Iraqi construction of five Scud-type missile fixed launcher complexes in western Iraq. These complexes eventually contained 28 operational launchers. Assuming the standard 600-km flight trajectory of Iraqi-modified Scud missiles, missiles launched from the complexes could reach the Israeli cities of Tel Aviv, Haifa, and the nuclear facility at Dimona in the Negev desert. These sites also could strike targets in Syria and Turkey.

Chemical Weapons

By 1990, Iraq had the largest chemical agent production capability in the Third World, annually producing thousands of tons of blister agent mustard and nerve agents Sarin (GB) and GF. Sarin, a nonpersistent agent, is relatively easy to produce from readily available chemical precursors. GF, a semipersistent nerve agent similar to Soman (GD), was produced by the Iraqi research and development establishment when Western nations restricted the export of chemical precursors required for Soman. Iraqi delivery means, in addition to missile warheads, included aerial bombs, artillery shells, rockets, and aircraft-mounted spray tanks. During the war with Iran, Saddam exhibited the willingness to use CW against not only the Iranians, but also his own Kurdish population. In the spring of 1988, Iraqi troops used CW against Iraqi Kurdish insurgents in the town of Halabjah. Thousands of civilian men, women, and children died.

Four years earlier, Iraq had become the first nation in history to use nerve agents on the battlefield. While the agent was not used effectively in 1984, by the beginning of

1988, the Iraqis had developed an effective offensive doctrine for the use of nerve agents, which fully integrated CW into fire support plans. Both nerve and blister agents were used successfully in the final offensives that defeated the Iranians in 1988. These weapons were targeted specifically against command and control facilities, artillery positions and logistics areas.

Biological Weapons

By the time of the invasion of Kuwait, Iraq had developed biological weapons. Its advanced and aggressive biological warfare program was the most extensive in the Arab world. Although Baghdad stated in 1991 it was in compliance with the 1972 Biological and Toxin Weapons Convention, the program probably began in the late 1970s and concentrated on development of two agents — botulinum toxin and anthrax bacteria. (United Nations inspection teams were later to find evidence of these two toxins, as well as clostridium perfingens.) Large scale production of these agents began in 1989 at four facilities near Baghdad. Delivery means for biological agents ranged from simple aerial bombs and artillery rockets to surface-to-surface missiles.

Nuclear Devices Program

By 1990, Saddam had made the development of a nuclear device a high priority project. The Iraqi nuclear research program had reached the initial stages of producing enriched uranium. Iraqi scientists were involved in the design, engineering and nonnuclear testing required to ensure the viability of a nuclear device. The Iraqis had pursued at least five techniques for enriching uranium; their efforts using electromagnetic isotope separation had progressed the furthest. The program still required foreign technology and equipment; Iraq's covert procurement network had obtained much of it.

LETHALITY OF BIOLOGICAL WEAPONS

Experimental data indicate botulinum toxin is about 3 million times more potent than the nerve agent Sarin. A Scud missile warhead filled with botulinum could contaminate an area of 3,700 square kilometers (based on ideal weather conditions and an effective dispersal mechanism), or 16 times greater than the same warhead filled with Sarin. By the time symptoms occur, treatment has little chance of success. Rapid field detection methods for biological warfare agents do not exist. Although botulinum can debilitate in a few hours and kill in a little as 12, and anthrax takes two to four days to kill, anthrax is more persistent and can contaminate a much larger area using the same delivery means.

In March 1990, a joint US-British sting operation prevented the illegal export of US-built nuclear device-triggering components by Iraqi front companies and Iraqi Airways. In July 1990, the Defense Technology Security Administration discovered that US-built skull induction furnaces (needed for melting and casting of metals such as uranium, plutonium, and titanium) were destined for the Iraqi nuclear devices program. Further research revealed that similar British-made furnaces were also on order for the same research program. Both US and British shipments were halted.

Iraq did not have a nuclear device at the time of its invasion of Kuwait, although it may have been able to assemble one or two crude nuclear explosive devices within six months to one year, using the uranium in the French- and Soviet-supplied reactor fuel. Although information on Iraqi nuclear devices development was limited at the time of crisis, the conflict and resulting UN Special Commission inspections will provide greater details on the scope and progress of the program.

Other Military Research and Development Programs

On 5 December 1989, Iraq launched an indigenously designed prototype experimental space launch vehicle, the Al-'Abid. Although this vehicle was a crude attempt at space launch technology, it was an impressive achievement. In September 1988, the Israelis had placed a satellite in orbit; Saddam was eager to demonstrate his nation's technological achievements. The Al-'Abid appeared to have three stages; the first were engines in an indigenously built airframe. The second and third stages were inert, but needed for weight and aerodynamics. In wide-scale press and television coverage of the launch, Saddam claimed his engineers also had developed a 2,000-km range ballistic missile (the Tammuz, or July) using similar technology.

In March 1990, British Customs seized parts for a "Super Gun," called Project Babylon by the Iraqis. This 1,000-mm diameter bore weapon was designed to fire a gun-launched guided rocket with conventional, chemical or nuclear warheads hundreds of miles. Although the full-size weapon never was assembled (its components were destroyed after the war under UN auspices), a 350-mm research prototype had been fired at a site about 120 miles north of Baghdad.

CONCLUSION

It was this military machine that threatened the almost defenseless state of Kuwait on 1 August. Despite the numerous efforts of Arab and international diplomats and organizations, the Iraqi leader continued to rattle his saber against another Arab state. When the Kuwaiti Amir did not acquiesce to his demands, Saddam ordered his forces to attack. The resulting invasion shocked and outraged the world.

Chapter II

King Fahd and Secretary of Defense Cheney Confer in Early August 1990.

THE RESPONSE TO AGGRESSION

US RESPONSE — DRAWING A LINE

On 2 August, President Bush condemned the invasion, stating the seizure of Kuwait and potential Iraqi domination of Saudi Arabia through intimidation or invasion presented a real threat to US national interests, requiring a decisive response. The President immediately froze all Iraqi and Kuwaiti financial assets in the United States to prevent Iraq from gaining access to this wealth. On 5 August, after consultations with allies, President Bush characterized the invasion as "naked aggression" and stated "this shall not stand." The President decisively framed US national policy objectives:

- Immediate, complete, and unconditional withdrawal of all Iraqi forces from Kuwait;
- Restoration of Kuwait's legitimate government;
- Security and stability of Saudi Arabia and the Persian Gulf; and
- Safety and protection of the lives of American citizens abroad.

US military reaction to the invasion was immediate. Within one hour of the start of the 2 August attack, the Department of Defense (DOD) ordered the *USS Independence* (CV 62) battle group to move from near Diego Garcia in the Indian Ocean to the Gulf of Oman. The *USS Dwight D. Eisenhower* (CVN 69) battle group was ordered to sail to the eastern Mediterranean Sea in preparation for entering the Red Sea. Two Air Force KC-135 tanker aircraft in the United Arab Emirates (UAE) since 23 July were ordered to remain in the area. These aircraft were supporting UAE combat air patrols over its

> *"If history teaches us anything, it is that we must resist aggression or it will destroy our freedoms."*
>
> **President George Bush**
> **8 August 1990**

oil facilities in response to Saddam's accusations on 17 July.

On 5 August, three days after the invasion of Kuwait, the President dispatched the Secretary of Defense to consult with King Fahd of Saudi Arabia. The Secretary was accompanied by the Under Secretary of Defense for Policy, the Commander-in-Chief, US Central Command, and his Army and Air Force component commanders. Meeting with the King on 6 August, the Secretary reiterated President Bush's pledge of support for the Kingdom's security and stability and briefed the Saudi monarch on the US assessment of the situation. The world's premier oil-producing region — Saudi Arabia's Eastern Province — was within the easy reach of Saddam's army. Iraqi forces poised on the Saudi border had the ability, with little or no warning, to launch an armored thrust into the oil fields, move down the coast, and close Saudi Arabia's Gulf ports. Such a move would have threatened the Kingdom's survival, and would have allowed Saddam to control an additional 20 percent of the world's oil reserves, in addition to the 20 percent he controlled already in Iraq and Kuwait. Iraqi control of Saudi Arabia's Gulf ports also would have made any military operations to recapture the seized territory extremely difficult and costly. Whether Saddam actually planned to invade Saudi Arabia is unknown, but the ominous presence of overwhelming military force at the Kingdom's northern border, coupled with the fresh evidence of his willingness to attack his neighbors, constituted a threat to the vital interests of both Saudi Arabia and the United States. If Saddam's conquest of Kuwait were not reversed, he would have been in a position to intimidate all the countries of the Arabian Peninsula. Moreover, no effort to compel Iraq to withdraw from Kuwait could succeed if Saudi Arabia remained vulnerable to Iraqi attack.

The Secretary of Defense underscored the US willingness to provide the forces needed to defend Saudi Arabia, and emphasized US forces would leave the Kingdom when the job was done. In response, King Fahd invited the United States to send forces. President Bush immediately ordered DOD to begin deployments. (A detailed discussion of US force deployments is in Chapter III, with supporting information in Appendix E.)

INITIAL WORLD RESPONSE

The international coalition that opposed Saddam's wrongful invasion was put together almost as swiftly, largely through the President's decisive leadership that focused the international consensus against the aggression and galvanized the nations of the world to act promptly and forcefully. The United States played a leading role not only in opposing the invasion, but also in bringing together and maintaining this unprecedented effort.

From the outset of the Gulf crisis, it was clear that American leadership was needed. The United States was willing to assume the leading role both politically and militarily, but did not want to be alone. America's allies and friends understood that. They joined the United States in the United Nations. They joined American forces in the Gulf with soldiers, planes, ships, and equipment. They provided financial assistance to front-line states and helped with the United States' incremental

costs. What was accomplished in terms of responsibility sharing was unprecedented.

Nearly 50 countries made a contribution. Among those, 38 countries deployed air, sea, or ground forces. Together, they committed more than 200,000 troops, more than 60 warships, 750 aircraft, and 1,200 tanks. They came from all parts of the world, including Arab and Islamic countries. Their troops fought side by side with American forces. They faced danger and mourned casualties as did the United States. But they remained firmly committed to the Coalition.

Many countries contributed financially. They gave billions in cash to the United States, and provided valuable in-kind assistance, including construction equipment, computers, heavy equipment transporters, chemical detection vehicles, food, fuel, water, airlift, and sealift. They also gave billions in economic aid to countries most affected by the crisis.

Perhaps most remarkable was the amount of support provided by Coalition members to cover US incremental costs for the war. The contributions of US allies would rank, by a considerable margin, as the world's third largest defense budget, after that of the United States and the former Soviet Union. Few would have imagined this level of participation. US allies provided $54 billion against the estimated $61 billion of incremental costs. Roughly two-thirds of these commitments were from the Gulf states directly threatened by Iraq, with the other one-third largely coming from Japan and Germany.

Not only was unprecedented financial support forthcoming from friends and allies as the Coalition confronted Saddam's aggression, but the governments also worked effectively in common cause against the aggression. The diplomats coordinated positions together at the United Nations, the combat forces planned and fought effectively together, and the logisticians worked quickly and efficiently to transport needed items to the Gulf. This cooperation greatly contributed to the decisive victory over Iraqi aggression. It is not possible to detail here the responses of every nation that stood against Iraqi aggression; many are described throughout this report. As an introduction, this section briefly surveys some of these many cooperative acts. (Detailed information about financial contributions is in Appendix P, with amplifying information in Appendices F and I.)

International Organizations

The United Nations played an active and important role. The nearly unanimous manner in which the UN Security Council (UNSC) and the UN membership as a whole responded during this crisis was unprecedented. Operations Desert Shield and Desert Storm were conducted in accordance with UNSC resolutions and Iraq's refusal to abide by them. On 2 August, the UNSC passed Resolution 660, condemning the invasion as a violation of the UN Charter and demanding Iraqi withdrawal. The resolution passed 14-0, with Yemen abstaining. Four days later, the UNSC passed Resolution 661, imposing a trade and financial embargo on Iraq and establishing a special sanctions committee. This measure passed 13-0, with Cuba and Yemen abstaining. After these and nine subsequent resolutions failed to end the Iraqi occupation, on 29 November the UNSC authorized members to use "all means necessary" to enforce previous resolutions if Iraq did not leave Kuwait by 15 January. (All applicable UNSC Resolutions are in Appendix B.)

The Arab League convened an emergency summit in Cairo one week after the invasion. The summit passed a resolution calling for Iraq to withdraw from Kuwaiti territory. The membership voted 12 for (Egypt, Saudi Arabia, Kuwait, Morocco, Qatar, Bahrain, Somalia, Lebanon, Oman, UAE, Syria, and Djibouti); three against (Iraq, Libya, and Palestine); two abstaining (Yemen and Algeria); three

expressing reservations (Jordan, Sudan, and Mauritania); and one absence (Tunisia). The meeting was marked by heated rhetoric among the Iraqi, Saudi and Kuwaiti delegations.

Western Reaction

US allies in Western Europe responded immediately. In the United Kingdom (UK), the prime minister froze all Iraqi and Kuwaiti assets. On 6 August, two additional Royal Navy frigates were ordered to join the single British warship keeping station in the Persian Gulf. This flotilla's purpose was to show resolve and to help enforce sanctions. Two days later, after a request by King Fahd, the UK announced the start of what would be a major deployment of air and naval units as part of the multinational command forming against Iraq.

Also acting quickly, France sent an additional frigate on 6 August to augment two French warships already in the Gulf. Three days later, the French president announced he would commit ground units and advisers to Saudi Arabia although, in keeping with past policy decisions, they would not subordinate their forces formally to a multinational defense command. Initial French ground forces, code named *Force Daguet*, deployed to Hafr Al-Batin, near the convergence of the Saudi, Iraqi and Kuwaiti borders.

Italy, Spain and Germany declared that deploying American forces could use their air and naval bases. Greece later pledged this same support. This access was to become invaluable when the United States moved the VII Corps from Germany to Saudi Arabia late in 1990. Germany, whose constitution is interpreted to prohibit contribution of forces outside of the North Atlantic Treaty Organization, became a major logistic and financial supporter of the Coalition effort. On 10 August, the Canadian prime minister announced he would dispatch three ships — two destroyers and a supply ship — to the Persian Gulf.

Turkey played a crucial role in early opposition to the Iraqi invasion. Before the crisis, about half of Iraqi oil exports had passed through Turkey. Turkey's decision to shut down the Iraqi pipeline to the port of Ceyhan was vital in eliminating Iraq's ability to export oil and, combined with Saudi Arabia's closure of the Iraqi Pipeline Saudi Arabia, contributed substantially to Iraq's economic isolation.

Turkish military preparedness forced Iraq to maintain a sizable force on its northern border. Several squadrons of Turkish Air Force fighters and more than 50,000 troops were deployed to bases near the Iraqi border. On 12 August, the Turkish National Assembly gave the government power to declare war. This grant of authority was an indication of how seriously Turkey viewed the invasion. Ultimately, Turkey authorized the stationing of Coalition forces on its soil for operations against Iraq.

Although it was not a Coalition member, the Soviet Union's reaction was a key element in the success of the overall effort. Had the Soviet government chosen to oppose UN efforts, building a consensus would have been more difficult. Instead, on 2 August, the Soviets also demanded an immediate withdrawal of Iraqi troops from Kuwait. The Soviet government issued a statement that the Iraqi invasion of Kuwait "totally contradicts the interests of Arab states, creates new additional obstacles to the settlement of conflicts in the Middle East, and runs counter to the positive tendencies in improvement in international life."

In Eastern Europe, former Warsaw Pact members and Yugoslavia all supported the UN actions against Iraq — including the use of force — despite a substantial economic burden posed by compliance with UN sanctions. All of the Eastern European governments were Iraq's creditors and lost substantial amounts of money as a result of unpaid Iraqi debts and blocked exports. Poland, Czechoslovakia, Hungary, Romania, and Bulgaria responded to Iraq's

invasion of Kuwait with a willingness to commit noncombatant military units or humanitarian assistance to support the defense of Saudi Arabia. Many of these states granted overflight rights for aircraft carrying troops and materiel to the Gulf. Eventually, Czechoslovakia deployed a chemical defense unit to Saudi Arabia. Poland dispatched a medical ship, and an additional 100 medical personnel to Saudi military hospitals. Hungary provided a 37-man medical team that was attached to Saudi forces.

Asian Reaction

Japan, heavily dependent on Middle East oil — it imports 12 percent of its annual needs from Iraq and Kuwait — denounced the invasion as unlawful and a rejection of the UN Charter. Japan's constitution, written in the aftermath of World War II, allows maintenance of forces only to defend its own territory — interpreted as proscribing deployments abroad. As a compromise, the Japanese prime minister announced a six-point plan, which allowed Japan to make available civilian ships and airplanes, but restricted the cargo to food, medicine, and other noncombatant items. Japan also agreed to pay for chartering aircraft and ships from foreign countries. An initial grant of $1 billion was earmarked immediately for the multinational forces in Saudi Arabia. Financial assistance was pledged for refugee relief as well, and to nations suffering economically as a result of adhering to the sanctions, specifically Jordan, Turkey, and Egypt.

The Chinese premier stated his government's opposition to Iraq's invasion and annexation of Kuwait. He further stated that China opposed any military intervention by world powers, believing that Gulf and Arab affairs were best handled by Gulf and Arab nations, or by the United Nations. On 5 August, the Chinese announced they would end arms deliveries to Iraq. China supported all but one UNSC resolutions concerning the Iraqi invasion of Kuwait; it abstained on Resolution 678 authorizing use of all necessary means to enforce other UNSC resolutions. In addition, on grounds that the use of force was premature at that time, China insisted on deletion of the phrase "using the minimum degree of military force" from the text of UNSC Resolution 665, which called for the enforcement of sanctions against Iraq.

REGIONAL RESPONSE

Coalition Members in the Region

The Gulf Cooperation Council (GCC) — Saudi Arabia, Bahrain, Qatar, the UAE, Oman, and Kuwait — formed in 1981 as a reaction to the Iran-Iraq war, reacted strongly. Kuwait's ambassador to the United States requested US military assistance as Iraqi troops crossed the border on 2 August. As American and other forces began to deploy to Saudi Arabia, other GCC states committed forces, offered increased access to bases, and provided logistic assistance. These contributions of the GCC states, often attended by direct risks of Iraqi reprisals, proved important to the overall effort.

Egypt played a particularly important role. Egyptian denunciation of the Iraqi invasion of Kuwait was strong and immediate. When the invasion of Kuwait occurred, the Egyptian president had been trying to defuse the crisis. Reportedly, Saddam had assured him only a few days before 2 August that Iraq would not resort to military force to resolve differences with Kuwait. He regarded the action as a breach of faith between fellow Arab leaders and the Arab Cooperation Council members (Egypt, Iraq, Jordan, and Yemen). Egypt would become a major party in the Coalition's Arab/Islamic forces, sending more than two heavy divisions to Saudi Arabia. Also, Cairo became a center for Kuwaiti exiles; with Egyptian government support, Kuwaiti television, radio, and print media continued to report from Cairo on the crisis to its citizens throughout the Middle East and Europe.

Relations between Baghdad and Cairo had been tense for some time. As many as 800,000 Egyptians had been working in Iraq during the Iran-Iraq war. This number had been reduced forcibly to about 500,000 by the summer of

---

EGYPTIAN SUPPORT: PRESIDENTIAL LEADERSHIP

"We worked closely with the Egyptians and President Mubarak. President Mubarak and King Fahd were really the two very strong leaders in the Arab world that we worked with throughout this period.

"President Mubarak, on that very first weekend [after Iraq's invasion of Kuwait], was the first official I briefed after I talked with King Fahd and had gotten President Bush's approval to deploy the [US] force. I stopped, landed in Cairo, and then flew down to Alexandria in a small little twin engine prop plane that the US Army keeps at our

embassy over there, and landed right next to the Iraqi jet that was carrying the Iraqi Vice President who was making the rounds and trying to drum up support for the Iraqi position and justify their action of having invaded Kuwait. I had to wait to get in to see President Mubarak, as he was seeing the Iraqis first. We did not meet coming in. They kept me in a building across the street to avoid a diplomatic confrontation.

"But I went in to see President Mubarak and told him what we were doing. He, of course, had been talking with President Bush. One of the things that's characteristic throughout the

whole crisis is the President working the phones. Every place I went, he had greased the skids, so to speak, in front of me, which was enormously helpful, building on his personal relationships. I told President Mubarak we were going to deploy forces. He, at that point, had decided he wanted to convene the Arab League in Cairo, which was vital, which he did a few days later.

"I asked him for a number of things — overflight rights, because we had a lot of aircraft coming from the United States that would have to overfly Egypt to get to Saudi Arabia — which

he readily agreed to. I also asked permission to pass one of our aircraft carriers through the Suez Canal. The carrier was the *Eisenhower*, which was deployed in the Med, and we wanted to immediately move it down to the Red Sea just off the Saudi coast and provide air cover in case Saddam Hussein did make a move south. President Mubarak said when do you want to move the carrier? I said tonight. He said okay, and immediately signed up for it."

Secretary of Defense
Dick Cheney
December 1991

1990, and was a source of tension between Cairo and Baghdad. Remittances to Egypt in 1989 had totaled almost $550 million. On 2 August, these remittances ceased, as well as the remittances from the approximately 185,000 Egyptians working in Kuwait. The Egyptian government estimated the annualized loss at $400 million to $600 million.

Syria, a long-time rival of neighboring Iraq, condemned the invasion of another Arab state. Demonstrations erupted in Damascus, both in support of the Kuwaiti ruling family, and against Western intervention. The Syrians joined other regional states opposing Iraq and pledged deployment of a special forces regiment to Saudi Arabia. The first Syrian troops arrived in Saudi Arabia in mid-August, at the request of the Saudi government. Syria also moved two army divisions closer to its largely undefended border with Iraq. In October, Damascus began deployment of its 9th Armored Division to Saudi Arabia.

Morocco's King Hassan deployed troops to defend Saudi Arabia. Although other Arab Maghreb Union member states (Libya, Tunisia, Algeria and Mauritania are Morocco's partners) did not support the Iraqi invasion, they spoke out against foreign intervention and did not join the Coalition.

Other Regional Responses

Iran condemned the Iraqi invasion of Kuwait, but immediately declared its neutrality. For the last decade, Iran had demanded the withdrawal of foreign forces from the Gulf, especially US naval assets represented by ships of the Joint Task Force, Middle East. After the American commitment to deploy troops to the area, Iran labeled the move as "impudent" and called it a pretext to establish permanent military bases in the area. Nevertheless, it also called on the United Nations to respond to Saddam's aggression.

Nations in the multinational Coalition were very concerned about possible agreements between Tehran and Baghdad that would allow Iraq to import weapons through Iranian ports in violation of UN sanctions. Concern was heightened by Saddam's sudden reversal of his position regarding sovereignty of the Shatt Al-'Arab. In a surprise move, he accepted the *thalweg* (the center of the navigational channel) as the sovereign boundary between the two countries. He further withdrew all Iraqi forces from Iranian territory seized in the 1988 offensives. In essence, he gave up all he had won in eight years of war with Iran. Although there was smuggling of food, there is no evidence that Iran allowed weapons, munitions, or military materiel to cross the border.

During Operations Desert Shield and Desert Storm, most notably after December, Iranian smugglers were a major source of foodstuffs to Iraq, in violation of UN sanctions. The level of possible involvement of the Iranian government in these sanctions violations is not known. During Operation Desert Storm, Iraqi pilots flew more than 130 military and civilian aircraft to Iran where they remained impounded after the war.

The Hrawi government in Lebanon was the first Arab League member state to condemn Iraq's invasion of Kuwait. Apart from some pro-Iraqi demonstrations in Palestinian camps in the south, Lebanon played no direct role in the crisis.

Jordan's actions were the subject of intense international scrutiny throughout the crisis. Relations between Jordan and Iraq had been close since the beginning of the Iran-Iraq war. Because Iraq's sole outlet to the Persian Gulf was easily controlled by the Iranians in that conflict, Iraq had reached an agreement with Jordan for the use of the Red Sea port of Al-'Aqabah to import arms. The port and the associated land route into Iraq became one of the immediate focal points for maritime interception force scrutiny. An economically fragile Arab state, Jordan had received low-priced Iraqi oil, as well as increased business opportunities with Iraqi merchants, in return for Iraqi use of Al-'Aqabah .

The official level of Jordanian economic support for Iraq still is unclear. Some trade continued in violation of UN sanctions, although at a much lower level than before 2 August. The Jordanian government continued to accept Iraqi oil shipments, also technically in violation of the UN sanctions. Smuggling at an undetermined level almost certainly continued. Charitable and humanitarian groups were permitted to send food shipments through Jordan until 16 January and Jordan was the primary exit point for hundreds of thousands of refugees leaving Iraq and Kuwait.

Some Arabs were vocal in their support of Iraqi aggression. This was especially the case with the Palestine Liberation Organization (PLO). With the exception of the Damascus-based Popular Front for the Liberation of Palestine-General Command, all PLO member organizations supported Saddam.

Two other vocal supporters of Saddam were Yemen and the Sudan. In the Yemeni capital of Sana'a, demonstrations of support for Saddam took place outside the American, British, Saudi and Egyptian embassies on 11 August. Some

YEMENI AND SUDANESE VOLUNTEER TROOPS

Although Sana'a and Khartoum claimed thousands of their citizens volunteered to fight alongside Iraqi forces in the defense of Kuwait, only a few hundred probably went. Coalition forces captured some Yemenis and Sudanese during Operation Desert Storm. At the 3 March military talks at Safwan, Iraq, between senior Coalition and Iraqi officers, the Coalition provided the Iraqis an accounting of captured troops, including Yemeni and Sudanese volunteers. The senior Iraqi general disavowed any knowledge of these two groups, claiming all his forces in the KTO were Iraqis.

Yemenis volunteered to enlist in the Iraqi Popular Army, while students in Khartoum, Sudan, demonstrated in solidarity with Iraq. Support from these quarters for Saddam was more in the nature of a nuisance to the Coalition than an actual threat. However, because of long-standing border disputes between Saudi Arabia and Yemen, and between Oman and Yemen, that country's alignment with Iraq had to be treated as a potentially serious threat. A Yemeni invasion of southern Saudi Arabia or western Oman could not have succeeded; however, such a move would have diverted resources and attention away from the primary threat. Saudi Arabia remained concerned about potential threats to the kingdom's security from Sudan and Yemen throughout Operations Desert Shield and Desert Storm. Saudi concerns led to its expulsion of hundreds of thousands of Yemenis — a problem that continues in Saudi-Yemeni relations.

Israeli Reaction

On 6 August, Israel stated it was prepared to participate in any military attempt to prevent an Iraqi attack on Saudi Arabia, if asked by the United States. The Israeli prime minister warned Saddam an attack on Israel would "bring heavy disaster on himself." Coalition leaders were worried an Israeli-Iraqi confrontation would hinder creation of an international coalition and help Iraq shift attention away from its aggression against a fellow Arab country. Throughout the crisis, the United States worked closely with Israel to encourage a "low profile" posture.

The United States took unprecedented steps to persuade Israel not to respond to the Iraqi Scud attacks and committed a significant part of its own air assets to Scud suppression efforts. A special, secure communications link established between DOD and the Israeli Ministry of Defense enabled immediate and frequent contact between senior US and Israeli officials. Near-real-time warning of Iraqi Scud missile attacks on Israel gave the Israeli populace as much as five minutes to take shelter before missile impact. In the fall of 1990, the President authorized the transfer of two Patriot air defense missile batteries to Israel, and the training of Israeli crews for their operation. After the initial Scud attacks, Israel agreed to accept four additional Patriot batteries, to be manned by US troops. Finally, the Central Command devoted a substantial amount of its air power to combat the Scud threat. The President twice sent the Deputy Secretary of State and the Under Secretary of Defense for Policy to Israel to reaffirm the US commitment to Israel's security, to ensure US objectives were clearly understood, and to coordinate the common response to the crisis.

Israel's decision to restrain its own military response denied Saddam one of his key objectives, was crucial in keeping Jordan from becoming engulfed by the war, and contributed substantially to holding the Coalition together. The increased US cooperation with Israel was, in turn, crucial to its decision to exercise restraint in the face of extreme provocation. While there never was any doubt about Israel's will to defend itself or about the capability of its professional military, it is also clear that Israeli restraint was in its own best national interests; was its best policy option; and was overwhelmingly supported by the Israeli public, senior leadership, and strategic policy makers. Israel's extraordinary restraint, however, not only was in its best interests, but also in the best interests of the United States, the other Coalition members, and Jordan.

IRAQI FOLLOW-UP TO THE INVASION

Political Maneuvering

Immediately after the invasion of Kuwait, Iraq began campaigning for public support. This effort included defaming Kuwait's ruling family and portraying Iraq as the champion of anticolonialism, social justice, Arab unity, the Palestinian cause, and Islam. In an apparent move to defuse initial international condemnation of its invasion of Kuwait, Saddam announced Iraqi troops would begin pulling out of Kuwait on 6 August. In the first days following the invasion, he had justified the invasion with the fiction that Kuwaiti officers had engaged in a coup d'etat against the Amir. These officers had "invited" Iraq to send forces to assist them. Now, Saddam announced to the world the group that had conducted the coup was now in full control of Kuwait, and Iraqi troops would return to garrison.

There was a suitably staged "withdrawal" near the northern Kuwait border station at 'Abdally. This was recorded by the press and videotapes of a few tanks loaded aboard tank transporters were released for broadcast. At the same moment, however, at least four more heavy Iraqi Army divisions were deploying into Kuwait from Iraq. In addition to reinforcing Iraqi forces in Kuwait, Saddam took action on another front.

On 8 August, Iraqi media began broadcasting threats that regimes cooperating with the United States would be destabilized. The focus of these threats was Saudi Arabia and Egypt, which Saddam blamed for organizing Arab opposition to Iraq. Two days later, Iraq indicated it no longer recognized the legitimacy of the ruling family of Saudi Arabia. An extensive media disinformation campaign was begun to support this announcement. Two anti-Saudi radio stations named "Voice of Holy Mecca" and "Holy Madinah" began broadcasting programs condemning the Saudi royal family for allowing US "infidel" soldiers to defile the Islamic holy places with "alcohol, whores, and all kinds of heroin and narcotics." Public diplomacy and psychological warfare initiatives by Iraq would continue throughout the crisis.

On 12 August, Saddam stated he would not withdraw Iraqi forces from Kuwait unless all "issues of occupation" in the Middle East were resolved. He specifically called for Israel to first withdraw from the occupied West Bank and Gaza, and Syria to withdraw its military forces from Lebanon. The Iraqi leader also proposed defusing the current crisis by replacing US and Egyptian forces deployed to Saudi Arabia with UN troops.

Iraqi Atrocities

After Kuwait was firmly under Iraqi military control, Iraqi Popular Army "volunteers" began arriving in Kuwait. They were accompanied by members of the Iraqi Intelligence Service and the Directorate of Military Intelligence. The new arrivals' mission was to establish stringent control mechanisms in Kuwait City. They immediately went about their task with unbridled brutality. Kuwaiti resistance to Iraqi rule was systematically sought out and dealt with ruthlessly. The Kuwaiti Resistance fought the invaders for weeks after the Kuwaiti armed forces had been forced to evacuate the country. They continued to attack Iraqi soldiers, equipment, and facilities until the Iraqis inflicted brutal reprisals against whole neighborhoods. Even in the face of these horrible punishments, Kuwaitis continued to risk their lives to shelter innocent foreigners, including Americans.

Kuwaitis and foreigners fleeing Kuwait reported arrests and abuse on a grand scale. Influential Kuwaitis were rounded up and taken away, many to detention centers in Iraq. Iraqi intelligence and security officials combed the city, armed with lists of names of Kuwaitis who might prove troublesome to their rule. These lists were compiled by the extensive Iraqi intelligence network. As these persons were removed from the city, bus loads of Iraqi citizens began arriving to move into their homes, part of a campaign to resettle the "19th Province" with loyal Iraqi citizens.

Physical abuse and brutality were common. There are numerous reports of rapes of Kuwaiti and foreign women, often in the presence of family members. Anyone detained by Iraqi authorities was subject to torture, often resulting in death. Iraqi intelligence and security officials converted Kuwaiti schools and other public buildings to detention and interrogation centers. Summary executions were common. The Kuwaiti government estimates more than 1,000 civilians were murdered during the Iraqi occupation. Hundreds of people remain unaccounted for, and Kuwait claims more than 2,000 of its nationals still are being detained in Iraq.

All Kuwaiti citizens and residents were protected by the Geneva Conventions for the Protection of War Victims (12 August 1949). Kuwaiti armed forces members captured by Iraqi troops were entitled to treatment as prisoners of war. As an occupying power, Iraq had specific obligations to the civilian population of Kuwait. Kuwaiti resistance fighters captured by Iraqi forces were entitled to certain fundamental rights, such as protection from torture, and a regular trial for alleged offenses. All of these obligations frequently and systematically were breached throughout the seven-month Iraqi occupation. (See Appendix O for a discussion of the role of the law of war in the conflict.)

Soon after Iraqi gains in Kuwait had been consolidated, Baghdad began the organized, systematic plunder of the conquered country. In mid-August, flatbed trucks began loading shipping containers at the Ash-Shuwaykh port. Later, Iraqi ships were used to transport cargo to the Iraqi port of Umm Qasr. From there, the cargo was redistributed throughout Iraq by barge and truck. Large quantities of oil pipe sections and related materials also were shipped to Umm Qasr from Ash-Shuwaykh.

Iraqi troops broke into the Central Bank of Kuwait and removed the country's gold and currency reserves, which were transported by truck convoy to Baghdad. National museum holdings and government records also were transported to Baghdad or destroyed. Soldiers looted the gold and gem markets of the city and the homes of wealthy merchants, taking virtually anything of value. Almost all vehicles were taken by Iraqi soldiers; the more expensive vehicles were loaded onto heavy equipment transporters and taken to Iraq; many were stripped for parts to be sold on the black markets in Iraq.

After Saddam announced the annexation of Kuwait as Iraq's 19th province, Iraqi occupation officials began the relicensing of all vehicles remaining in Kuwait. The new license plates were standard Iraqi plates, with the word "Kuwait" appearing in the province identification block. Vehicle registration became a control mechanism for the occupation authorities. Foreigners — mostly Jordanians and Palestinians — allowed to leave Kuwait by vehicle through Iraq to Iran or Jordan, were required to display the new Kuwait province license plates before leaving Iraq.

Iraqi Hostage Taking

At the time of the Iraqi invasion of Kuwait, there were an estimated 3,000 Americans living in that country, in addition to thousands of other Westerners. Less than 10 days after the 8 August announcement that it had annexed Kuwait as its 19th province, Iraqi officials began the systematic rounding up of Western and Japanese nationals in Kuwait. They were detained in hotels in Kuwait City or transported to Baghdad. Those taken to Baghdad hotels were permitted contact with their diplomatic representations. The Iraqis appear to have respected the status and immunity of diplomatic personnel in Baghdad; however, this became an issue in Kuwait. Iraqi officials informed foreign ambassadors in Kuwait City that since Kuwait no longer was a sovereign state, embassies no longer were appropriate; all diplomatic functions were to be conducted in Baghdad. A deadline was set for the embassies to close, at which time the diplomatic status of the

representatives would expire. Iraqi occupation forces cut off water and electricity supplies to the embassies that refused to close and move their functions to Baghdad.

During the second week of August, the US Embassy in Baghdad received reports that Americans without diplomatic status in Iraq were to be taken to strategic installations as "human shields." There were about 500 Americans in Iraq at the time of the invasion. Many were seized during the next few days and detained at the Ar-Rashid Hotel. On 19 August, Saddam announced that as many as 10,000 Westerners would be sent to strategic sites to deter attacks. From the Ar-Rashid, these Americans and others were transported to power plants, oil production facilities and strategic military installations. On 20 August, President Bush labeled the detainees as hostages and demanded their immediate release.

Saddam's detention of Westerners for use as human shields was not limited to foreigners living in Kuwait and Iraq. More than 350 passengers on a British Airways 747 en route to India that had landed at Kuwait's international

---

"HUMAN SHIELDS"

Iraqi Foreign Minister Tariq 'Aziz claimed that Baghdad had detained foreign guests as a prudent peacemaking gesture, stating, "Our people and their representatives simply want to feel safe from a US attack on Iraq."

Information Minister Latif Nusayyif Jasim, in remarks directed at President Bush's claim that foreign detainees were being mistreated, said "Iraq's guests were being provided with all the means necessary for their comfort," in keeping with Arab and Islamic traditions of hospitality. He invited relatives of the "guests" to visit them for Christmas and New Year holidays.

Despite these claims, information from released detainees indicated that hostages — those sent to strategic sites as human shields — lived in appalling conditions, including poor to inedible food, unsanitary facilities, lack of medical care, and exposure to toxic waste.

airport for a one-hour refueling stop were detained. Many, including a 10-year-old American girl traveling alone, were taken to the Ar-Rashid and Al-Mansur Melia hotels in Baghdad. The girl later was turned over to the US Embassy. On 28 August, Saddam announced that all women and children being held hostage would be allowed to leave Iraq, although the departures did not begin until 6 September.

After limited hostage releases in late October, mostly as a result of appeals to the Iraqi leader by governments and private organizations, Saddam announced on 18 November that all hostages would be freed between 25 December and 25 March if peace continued in the region.

On 3 December, Iraq announced that 1,100 Soviet nationals would be allowed to return home, followed the next day by an announcement of the Iraqi Revolutionary Command Council that all 3,200 Soviets in Iraq were free to leave. Although never used as human shields, the Soviets, mostly civilian contractors, had been barred from leaving the country.

It was not until 6 December that Saddam announced that all hostages would be released at once. The first hostages to be freed as part of this release left Iraq on 9 December. Many others who had been in hiding in Kuwait were repatriated as well. All detainees and hostages who wished to leave did so in the next few days.

Chapter III

US Forces on Alert in the Saudi Arabian Desert.

THE MILITARY OPTION — OPERATION DESERT SHIELD

MILITARY SITUATION, AUGUST 1990

The Iraqi occupation of Kuwait was a difficult and urgent problem for US military planners. Iraqi forces, consolidating in Kuwait, appeared to be massing for possible further offensive operations into Saudi Arabia. By 6 August, the day before the first US force deployments, 11 Iraqi divisions were in or deploying to Kuwait. Far exceeding occupation requirements, Iraq had more than enough forces to launch an immediate invasion of Saudi Arabia's oil-rich Eastern Province. Intelligence reports indicated Iraqi units were being positioned along the Saudi border, while reinforcements continued to arrive in Kuwait.

If the Iraqis were contemplating an attack on Saudi Arabia, a course of action deemed possible by both the United States and Saudi Arabia in August, intelligence estimates identified three avenues of approach. First, the area along the Saudi coast road which runs through Al-Mish'ab, Al-Jubayl and Ad-Dammam seemed the most likely avenue, since it offered the most direct, high speed route to the port areas and coastal facilities. Although

---

> *"**I** view very seriously our determination to reverse this aggression. There are an awful lot of countries that are in total accord with what I've just said, and we will be working with them all for collective action. This will not stand. This will not stand, this aggression against Kuwait."*
>
> *President Bush*
> *5 August 1990*

---

somewhat restricted by marshy salt flats, called *sabkhas*, near Al-Mish'ab, the coastal road favored armor, mechanized forces and accompanying logistics vehicles. Captured Saudi desalinization plants also would provide advancing Iraqi columns essential water. The coastal area, however, was mostly flat or gently rolling terrain that offered defenders excellent observation and fields of fire. Advancing Iraqi forces would be exposed to long-range air and ground weapons. The most defensible terrain was about 40 miles northwest of Al-Jubayl, where several low hills dominate surrounding terrain and numerous Saudi rock and limestone quarries created obstacles.

The second avenue of approach ran from central Kuwait west of Al-Wafrah, across the Saudi border to the Trans-Arabian Pipeline (Tapline) road and then southeast to the coastal road. Although it only contained a few unimproved desert roads, Iraqi forces on this avenue could bypass the *sabkhas* that restricted off-road movement along the coast while still enabling them to seize the key coastal objectives of Al-Jubayl and possibly Ad-Dammam. Desert terrain was almost devoid of any vegetation and predominantly consisted of flat or rolling terrain, excellent for both armor maneuver and long-range defensive fires. Cover and

---

US NATIONAL POLICY OBJECTIVES

- **I**mmediate, complete, and unconditional withdrawal of all Iraqi forces from Kuwait;
- **R**estoration of Kuwait's legitimate government;
- **S**ecurity and stability of Saudi Arabia and the Persian Gulf; and
- **S**afety and protection of the lives of American citizens abroad.

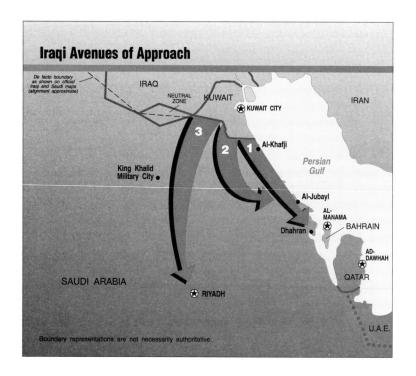

Iraqi Avenues of Approach

De facto boundary as shown on official Iraqi and Saudi maps (alignment approximate)

IRAQ

NEUTRAL ZONE

KUWAIT

KUWAIT CITY

IRAN

Al-Khafji

Persian Gulf

King Khalid Military City

Al-Jubayl

AL-MANAMA

Dhahran

BAHRAIN

AD-DAWHAH

QATAR

SAUDI ARABIA

RIYADH

U.A.E.

Boundary representations are not necessarily authoritative.

concealment was almost nonexistent, which would expose advancing forces to air attack. Other than a small oasis village near Al-Kibrit, the area contained no water sources between Kuwait and the town of An-Nu'ariyah along the Tapline Road, which would have constrained logistically any advance of large forces.

A third avenue, which Coalition planners assessed to be the least likely option, led from Kuwait straight for Riyadh on unimproved roads, soft sand, and mountainous desert. Although Riyadh's capture would have given the Iraqis a decisive political and military victory, the long desert distances, extremely rough terrain, and vulnerability to air attack while in the numerous narrow passes that channelized movement, made this option impractical. North of Riyadh, the desert turned to soft sand, which would have slowed advancing armor and, more important, the truck-mounted logistics tail. Absence of water, lack of roads to move the large quantities of fuel, water, and other supplies required by an army equipped with modern weapons, probably would have overtaxed the Iraqi logistics system.

Planners and intelligence analysts viewed the coastal area north of Ad-Dammam as crucial to both an attacking Iraqi force and the Coalition defense efforts. For the Coalition, loss of or serious damage to the port facilities at Al-Jubayl and Ad-Dammam would have made any force buildup in theater extremely difficult. For the Saudis, the loss of oil, port, water, and industrial facilities at Al-Khafji, Al-Mish'ab, Al-Manifah, Al-Jubayl, and Ras Tanurah would have been a serious economic and political blow. By seizing these areas, the Iraqis not only could have prevented a rapid Coalition military buildup, but also would have placed themselves in a politically strong position to negotiate a solution to the crisis on Baghdad's terms. They also could have achieved an important strategic victory, both in military and political terms. The mere threat of capture or destruction of these facilities by the large forces massing in Kuwait was seen as placing the Saudi government in a position that could have shifted the region's power balance substantially.

MILITARY OBJECTIVES OF OPERATION DESERT SHIELD

On the morning of 2 August, the Commander-in-Chief, Central Command (CINCCENT) briefed the Secretary of Defense, his key advisors, and the Chairman of the Joint Chiefs of Staff (CJCS) on two options for the use of military forces in response to the Iraqi invasion of Kuwait. One option involved retaliatory air strikes against targets in Iraq; the other involved deployment of air and ground forces in accordance with draft Operations Plans (OPLAN) 1002-90, Defense of the Arabian Peninsula. Two days later, at Camp David, the CJCS and CINCCENT briefed the President on available military options. CINCCENT discussed in detail the numbers and types of forces required to defend Saudi Arabia should that be necessary, estimating 17 weeks would be required to deploy all forces. The President, aware of the regional sensitivities of a large US military presence, made the decision that, if invited, the United States initially would deploy enough forces to deter further Iraqi attack, defend Saudi Arabia, and enforce UN resolutions, retaining the option to deploy more forces if needed to eject Iraq from Kuwait.

US military objectives during Operation Desert Shield were to:

■ Develop a defensive capability in the Gulf region to deter Saddam Hussein from further attacks;
■ Defend Saudi Arabia effectively if deterrence failed;
■ Build a militarily effective Coalition and integrate Coalition forces into operational plans; and, finally,
■ Enforce the economic sanctions prescribed by UNSC Resolutions 661 and 665.

These objectives provided planning staffs with the necessary direction to develop options and concepts.

CONCEPT OF OPERATIONS — OPERATION DESERT SHIELD

While Saudi forces established a thin defensive line along the Kuwait border, initial deployment of US ground forces secured key facilities to ensure uninterrupted follow-on deployments. This placed US units in positions from which they could support Coalition forces in any defensive battle. Ports and airfields along the Gulf coast, primarily Al-Jubayl and the Dhahran complex, were chosen since they offered the best unloading facilities and were near the primary avenue of approach for an Iraqi invasion. Thus, Saddam Hussein would be forced to fight US forces on the ground soon after attacking. Both land- and carrier-based air forces provided immediate combat power able, if necessary, to inflict severe casualties on advancing Iraqi mechanized columns. They also would be able to begin a limited strategic air campaign to reduce Iraqi military capabilities and isolate Saddam Hussein. Naval forces would seal off the region, enforcing the UN embargo against Iraq.

Based on these decisions, CINCCENT developed a concept of operations and began detailed planning. The initial deployment of air, naval, and light ground forces was intended to establish combat forces in theater quickly to deter an Iraqi ground attack and defend key

SHIFT IN SWA POLICY AND PLANS

In the fall of 1989, in the course of the Department of Defense's (DOD) regular planning process, the Under Secretary of Defense for Policy (USD(P)) recommended a shift in focus in the Persian Gulf. During most of the 1980s, security concerns in the Persian Gulf focused on the Soviet Union as the primary threat. Now, however, the USD(P) and the Commander-in-Chief, Central Command (CINCCENT) judged that this was no longer the primary threat. Instead, the disruption of the regional balance of power caused by Iraq's decisive defeat of Iran, the growing ambitions of Iraq, and the sharp disparity between its forces and those of the wealthy oil-producing nations of the Arabian Peniinsula pointed to the growing possibility of regional, vice Soviet, threats to US interests in this vital region. During planning deliberations, the Secretary of Defense emphasized the importance of the Persian Gulf. Accordingly, the Secretary directed DOD to sharpen its ability to counter regional conflicts on the Arabian Peninsula. In turn, the Chairman, Joint Chiefs of Staff directed CINCCENT to develop war plans consistent with this shift.

In the Spring of 1990, Central Command (CENTCOM) re-evaluated its operations plans for the Persian Gulf region in light of the new regional strategic and military situation. A new concept outline plan was completed in late spring. The outline plan included an estimate of the forces needed to respond to a regional threat. Based on the plan, the CENTCOM staff developed draft operations plan. In July 1990, the draft plan was tested during Exercise Internal Look 90. The exercise validated tactical concepts, logistics plans, and force requirements. The lessons learned served as a basis for subsequent deployments and operations during Operation Desert Shield.

ports and airfields along the Saudi northern Gulf coast. As heavier ground forces arrived in Saudi Arabia, defensive dispositions were to be expanded to block the two eastern avenues of approach. Continuing arrival of armored forces would let CINCCENT counterattack any attacking Iraqi forces with a strong mechanized reserve.

The area defense concept called for establishing initial defenses near Al-Jubayl and Dhahran, and using air power to reduce substantially the combat power of attacking Iraqi forces. The idea was to rely on an enclave strategy to hold key ports and airfields or, in essence, trade space for time while US combat forces deployed to Saudi Arabia. Coalition air power in conjunction with Saudi land forces in the forward area would bear the initial brunt of an Iraqi attack. During this initial phase, CINCCENT considered air power crucial to delaying an Iraqi attack. In early August, Central Command's (CENTCOM) Air Force planners had developed the "D-Day" air plan, with the objectives of maintaining air superiority over the Arabian Peninsula, establishing air superiority over Kuwait and southern Iraq, and attacking Iraqi forces. Behind the Saudi units, US ground forces were considered essential to defending arrival airfields and ports. Use of the ports and airfields at Al-Jubayl and Ad-Dammam placed US ground forces in blocking positions along the anticipated direct path of any advancing Iraqi forces.

The Saudis expressed some concern with the concept of operations. Understandably, the Saudis sought to defend all their territory and population centers. CINCCENT focused on defending key areas given the limited forces available. Desiring a forward defensive strategy that would place US forces along the Kuwait border and protect all Saudi territory and population, the Saudis suggested US forces enter through the northern ports of Ras Al-Khafji and Ras Al-Mish'ab rather than further south. US planners advocated a concept

of operations which would force the Iraqis to extend themselves and subject their forces to Coalition airpower and superiority in mobile warfare. These differing views did not affect the arrival and initial positioning of US forces. The discussions of alternatives continued until November when growing force levels had substantially eased the defensive problem. An interim combined operations order was published on 20 August. Intended to ensure US commanders understood Saudi defensive plans, it authorized liaison and coordination between US and Saudi units. This close liaison between commanders characterized much of the defensive planning and operations during Operation Desert Shield.

INITIAL DEPLOYMENT OF US MILITARY FORCES

After the decision to deploy US forces, the question facing CENTCOM and Saudi planners involved the order in which forces should be deployed and how those forces should be used. Pre-crisis planning had assumed 19 days of pre-hostility deployments and nine more days of deployments after hostilities began would be available before lead enemy elements reached defensive positions near Al-Jubayl. The emerging situation indicated these assumptions were too optimistic. A credible deterrence required the early presence of substantial numbers of combat units. The same sorts of forces would be required to defend Saudi Arabia if deterrence failed. However, available sealift meant the buildup of heavy ground forces would take several weeks, if not months. The overall intent of all deterrence and defense options was to confront Iraq with the prospects of unacceptable costs and a widened conflict with the United States if it launched further attacks.

A crucial CINCCENT decision was made early in the crisis. To ensure the greatest amount of ground combat power was available as soon as possible, CINCCENT accelerated deployment of combat forces and deferred deployment of theater logistics forces. He specifically requested Air Force (USAF) A-10 units and the Army 3rd Armored Cavalry Regiment (ACR) be moved up in the deployment schedule to get more antiarmor assets into Saudi Arabia as soon as possible. As a result, many ground combat units found themselves relying on organic supplies and equipment, initial combat sustainment, host nation support (HNS), and afloat prepositioned supplies. Although many units were largely self-sufficient initially, some combat units began to experience shortages. Both the 82nd Airborne Division and the 24th Infantry Division (Mechanized) relied for a short time on HNS and on Marine Corps (USMC) forces for resupply of food and water. The theater logistics structure did not mature until mid-November. Although placing arriving units in a somewhat precarious logistics position, the decision to deploy primarily combat forces in August and September let CINCCENT place a capable defensive and deterrent force in theater rapidly during the crucial weeks when the Iraqis greatly outnumbered the Coalition.

USMC and USAF units were not as severely affected as Army units by CINCCENT's decision to deploy ground combat forces before their logistics. Marine Expeditionary Brigades (MEB) are structured and deploy as integrated air-ground-logistics task forces. Able to draw on up to 30 days' supplies and equipment from Maritime Prepositioning Squadrons (MPS) ships, and with organic combat service support units, the MEBs proved largely self-sufficient. Arriving USAF squadrons deployed with organic aviation support packages designed to support 30 days of flight operations. Other support requirements were drawn from USAF prepositioned stocks or the host nation. Still, by C+60, both the USAF and USMC suffered from a lack of common item support normally provided by a theater logistics structure.

The initial order to deploy combat forces to the Gulf was issued on 6 August. CENTCOM

USS Dwight D. Eisenhower Moves Through the Suez Canal – August, 1990.

began to deploy its combat forces on 7 August, marking the beginning of Operation Desert Shield. Maritime Prepositioning Squadrons based at Diego Garcia and Guam sailed while USAF fighters and a brigade from the 82nd Airborne Division began deployment by air. (Consideration had been given to sailing MPS as early as 2 August to shorten response time and signal US intent; however, sailing orders were withheld until the President's decision to deploy air and ground forces to the region.)

Even before Operation Desert Shield began, the United States had combat forces in the region. Two carrier battle groups with more than 100 fighter and attack aircraft, and more than 10 surface combatant ships were directed to the Gulf region on 2 August. The carrier *USS Independence* (CV 62) and her battle group sailed from near Diego Garcia to the Arabian Sea, while the *USS Dwight D. Eisenhower* (CVN 69) battle group moved to the eastern Mediterranean Sea in preparation for entering the Red Sea. In the Persian Gulf, six Navy ships, on station as part of the permanent Joint Task

Force Middle East, were placed on alert and began active patrolling. Naval forces in the region soon began active operations as part of the UN embargo, beginning maritime intercept operations (MIO) in mid August, which would continue throughout the crisis. (See Chapter IV for a detailed discussion of MIO.) Two USAF KC-135s and a mobile operations center (MOC) also were operating in Abu Dhabi as part of a United Arab Emirates-requested deployment, Operation Ivory Justice. The MOC provided the only land-based secure satellite communications during the initial weeks of Operation Desert Shield. These naval and air units were, initially, the only substantial forces in theater.

Within a day of notification, USAF F-15C fighter aircraft of the 1st Tactical Fighter Wing (TFW) arrived in Saudi Arabia from Langley Air Force Base, VA. The aircraft flew non-stop for more than 14 hours, with seven aerial refuelings. By 9 August, these fighters were flying combat air patrols along the Iraq-Saudi border, supported by USAF RC-135 Rivet Joint reconnaissance platforms that had deployed from Europe and E-3 Airborne Warning and Control System aircraft just arrived from the United States. Also on 9 August, the first 82nd Airborne Division ready brigade troops from Fort Bragg, NC, arrived and established a defensive perimeter around the Saudi airport at

Dhahran. The entire brigade was in position by 13 August; a second brigade was in place eight days later. Rapid buildup of initial forces during these crucial days would have been impossible without strategic airlift. During the first two days of the deployment, Military Airlift Command aircraft flew 91 missions into theater and averaged more than 70 missions a day for the rest of August.

On 11 August, Strategic Air Command B-52G bombers with full weapons loads arrived within striking range and went on immediate alert under Air Force Component, Central Command (CENTAF) control. A USAF C-130 squadron arrived in Saudi Arabia to meet intra-theater airlift requirements. On 12 August, the 101st Airborne Division (Air Assault) began to deploy by air from Fort Campbell, KY. Two days later, the 7th Marine Expeditionary Brigade from southern California, a combined arms force with tanks, helicopters, and fixed-wing attack aircraft, began unloading its MPS at Al-Jubayl. In three weeks, CINCCENT had seven brigades, three carrier battle groups, 14 tactical fighter squadrons, four tactical airlift C-130 squadrons, a strategic bomber squadron, and a Patriot air defense missile umbrella 8,000 miles from the United States.

Other Army, Navy, USAF, and USMC forces had been alerted and were en route. To manage the massive flow of personnel and equipment to the theater, many logistics arrangements had to be made. On 10 August, the first 17 Ready Reserve Fleet ships were activated; the first fast sealift ship arrived at Savannah, GA, and began loading the 24th Infantry Division (Mechanized). The first agreement to charter a US-flagged ship was signed the same day. On 11 August, the first foreign-flagged ship was chartered. However, sufficient fast sealift, able to move heavy combat units, remained a problem throughout the crisis. To improve the speed of deployment to Saudi Arabia, Phase I of the Civil Reserve Air Fleet was activated on 18 August, adding 18

Us military capabilities to respond to crisis in the Gulf reflected the longstanding US commitment to the region. Since 1951, the US Military Training Mission had assisted Saudi Arabia in modernizing its military force. The Army Corps of Engineers entered into a continuous military construction program that included the Dhahran complex and King Khalid Military City. Naval forces had provided a continuous presence in the region for several decades. In the 1980s, US forces, under the newly activated Joint Task Force Middle East, protected Gulf shipping during Operation Earnest Will. Prepositioned equipment and supplies, both ashore and at sea, increased responsiveness. All these measures boosted regional confidence in the United States and eased the introduction of US forces during Operation Desert Shield.

passenger and 23 cargo aircraft of US commercial airlines to the effort.

On 22 August, the President signed Executive Order 12727 authorizing the Secretary of Defense, under Title 10, Section 673b of the US Code, to call to active duty selected Reserve units and individual Reservists. On 23 August, the Secretary of Defense delegated to the Service Secretaries the authority to order Selected Reserve members to active duty. Initial authorization provided for the recall of 25,000 Army, 14,500 USAF, 6,300 Navy, and 3,000 USMC Reservists. Simultaneously, the Secretary of Transportation authorized the Coast Guard to order to active duty as many as 1,250 Reservists. The first calls to active duty were announced on 24 August and, within the next few days, Army, Navy, and USAF Reservists had been notified to report.

While these mobilization and deployment actions were going on in the United States, Arab League member nations also deployed forces to Saudi Arabia. Egyptian and Syrian special forces were among the first Arab forces to arrive, augmenting Saudi and Gulf Cooperation Council (GCC) forces. It was around these initial deployments that the Coalition military force was built.

WINDOW OF VULNERABILITY

While US resolve had been demonstrated, offering a credible deterrent to an Iraqi invasion of Saudi Arabia and bolstering Coalition forces, the ability of Coalition forces to defeat a determined Iraqi attack into Saudi Arabia remained questionable. CINCCENT determined this would require deployment of heavy armored and mechanized forces. However, shortages of sufficient fast sealift with a roll-on/roll-off capability so crucial to loading and unloading armored equipment rapidly meant that heavy forces would deploy incrementally. The weeks that passed until adequate heavy forces arrived in theater became known as the

Armored Vehicles from the 24th Infantry Division (Mechanized) Wait to be Loaded Aboard Fast Sealift Ships at Savannah, GA – August, 1990.

"window of vulnerability". Primary defense continued to rely on air power and a thin line of Saudi units along the Kuwait border, and French and Egyptian forces staging in King Khalid Military City (KKMC). To the south of these forces, XVIII Airborne Corps, commanding all Army forces, and I Marine Expeditionary Force (I MEF), in command of 7th MEB and other USMC forces arriving in theater, dug into defensive positions north and west of Al-Jubayl and in the desert outside Dhahran. Capable of putting up a stiff fight, these ground units nonetheless lacked the combat power to defeat an Iraqi attack with forces estimated at three armored and two mechanized divisions in the initial assault, supported by additional armored, mechanized, and infantry divisions.

The deployment of heavy ground forces able to conduct mobile mechanized operations was possible only through rapid sealift which, unfortunately, did not exist in sufficient numbers. The 82nd Airborne Division, although deployable rapidly, is primarily a light infantry division, albeit one that has substantial antiarmor capabilities with its attack helicopters. I MEF, a mechanized air-ground task force deployed by airlift and MPS shipping, provided a strong mechanized capability, but not

Royal Saudi Air Force F-15 Taxis Past Arriving US troops – August, 1990.

reported by intelligence agencies in mid and late August, led to numerous alerts and often hasty defensive preparations. USMC and Army units arriving at Al-Jubayl and Dhahran were rushed to defensive positions to protect these crucial airfields and ports. Deploying combat units fully expected to fight shortly after arrival. Some units were issued ammunition before their deployment in case they landed at Saudi airfields under attack. Living under austere conditions and manning desert outposts, the troops who arrived in these early weeks performed missions under mentally and physically exhausting conditions. Aircrews who had ferried aircraft into Saudi air bases found themselves flying patrols or on strip alert within hours after arrival. Ports and airfields were furiously cleared of arriving supplies and equipment to minimize risks of major losses should Iraq choose to attack these concentrations with missiles or attack aircraft.

US ground forces continued to flow into the theater in September and October. The 4th MEB, able to conduct an amphibious assault into the flank of an Iraqi attack, arrived in the Northern Arabian Sea on 7 September. The final 1st MEB elements arrived on 12 September, integrated into I MEF, and its ground combat element filled out the 1st Marine Division (MARDIV). By mid-September, the 24th Infantry Division (Mechanized), with its mechanized brigades equipped with M-1 series tanks and M-2 series fighting vehicles had unloaded at Ad-Dammam. On 23 September, the final division elements arrived and moved into position alongside I MEF north and west of Al-Jubayl, establishing a line of mechanized US forces across the two most likely Iraqi avenues of approach. The 3d Armored Cavalry Regiment (ACR), just arrived from the United States, was assigned to the 24th Infantry Division. On 6 October, the rest of the 101st Airborne Division (Air Assault) arrived in Saudi Arabia, as did the European based 12th Aviation Brigade with AH-64 helicopters. Lead 1st Cavalry Division elements began arriving in

enough strength to defeat the Iraqis. USAF, Navy, Army and USMC attack aircraft could inflict serious damage to the Iraqis, but might not be decisive against a determined Iraqi ground attack.

During this period, commanders and troops acutely felt the uncertainty of their situation. Strong indicators of Iraqi attack preparation,

early October; the division's deployment was completed by 22 October.

Substantial air reinforcements also deployed to the theater, greatly increasing CENTCOM's combat power; total combat aircraft in the region numbered nearly 1,000 by early October. Elements of the Air Force's 4th, 37th, and 48th TFWs provided a long-range, precision strike capability. Iraqi air defenses could be suppressed or eliminated by the arriving electronic countermeasures capabilities of squadrons from the 366th and 35th TFWs. Finally, aircraft crucial for ground support arrived in the form of five squadrons of F-16Cs and four of A-10s. Additionally, the 3rd Marine Aircraft Wing had both fixed wing attack aircraft and AH-1W attack helicopters to support the ground forces, as well as fighters to help maintain air supremacy over the crucial coastal area. Carrier air wings aboard the *USS John F. Kennedy* (CV 67) and the *USS Saratoga* (CV 60), which had replaced the *USS Dwight D. Eisenhower* in the Red Sea and *USS Independence* in the Arabian Sea, respectively, added to the attack and fighter capabilities.

By early October, CINCCENT was satisfied the

USAF F-15C Flies Combat Air Patrol Over Saudi Arabia – September, 1990.

US Marines Conduct Chemical Defense Drill in Forward Positions Near Al-Jubayl – September, 1990.

"window of vulnerability" had narrowed and that he could conduct a successful defense of Saudi Arabia. The deployment of forces essential for the defensive mission, however, had taken nearly two months.

EXPANDING THE DEFENSE

Although Iraq may have been deterred from an early attack into Saudi Arabia, it remained a potent threat, still able to attack and inflict serious military and political damage to the Coalition. Intelligence sources estimated Iraqi forces in the Kuwait Theater of Operations (KTO) in mid-October represented most of the country's combat power. By that time, 27 Iraqi divisions were deployed, including all eight Republican Guard Forces Command (RGFC) divisions. Of these 27 divisions, nine were armored or mechanized, 17 were infantry, and one was special forces. These elements were organized into the II Corps, III Corps, IV Corps and VII Corps, as well as the RGFC, which operated as a corps. Iraqi manpower in the KTO numbered more than 435,000, supported by more than 3,600 tanks, almost 2,400 armored personnel carriers, and more than 2,400 artillery pieces.

On 13 September, CINCCENT met with Lieutenant General Khalid bin Sultan bin 'Abd Al-'Aziz, Commander, Royal Saudi Air Defense Forces and operational commander of Saudi forces committed to Operation Desert Shield, to discuss future strategy for defending Saudi Arabia. Lieutenant General Khalid re-emphasized the Saudi desire for defensive strongpoints and positions to retain territory and key population areas. CINCCENT urged that the strongpoint defenses be held to a minimum and used only as a last resort, preferring a more mobile defense. He also stressed that Saudi forces might be bypassed and destroyed by advancing Iraqi forces. Finally, CINCCENT

pointed out that I MEF defenses along the coast just south of the Saudi units might eliminate the need for strongpoints. As an alternative, the use of strongpoints was recommended as a temporary measure to wear down advancing Iraqi forces, with Saudi units withdrawn before they could be bypassed or overrun. CINCCENT recommended a deception plan to make the Iraqis think the Coalition's main defense was along the border. As the meeting ended, the two commanders agreed that defenses should focus on stopping the enemy north of Al-Jubayl to protect crucial facilities and cities to the south.

The agreed-upon concept of operations

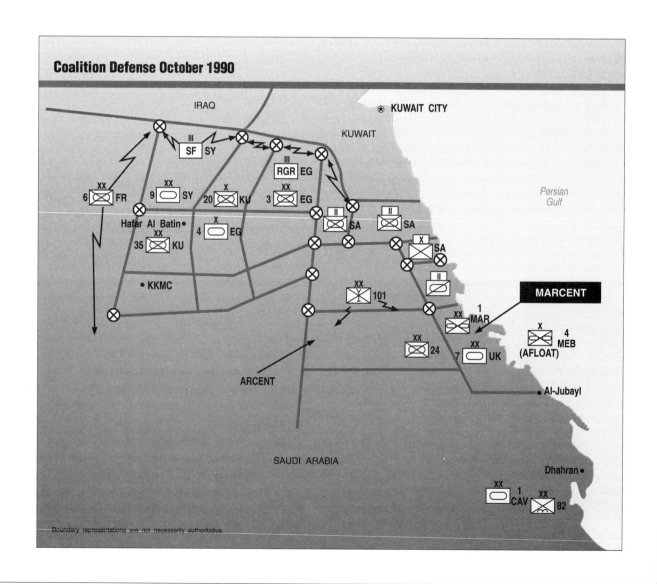

envisioned Coalition ground forces delaying an Iraqi attack as far forward as possible while inflicting increasing damage on the enemy, primarily through Coalition air power. In the Eastern Area Command (EAC), along the Gulf coast, defensive operations would concentrate on key cities, ports, and terrain starting at the Kuwaiti border. Behind the EAC, US forces would conduct a mobile defense designed to delay and then defeat the Iraqis before they reached Al-Jubayl. In the Northern Area Command (NAC), the defense hinged on screening the border area and strongpoints at KKMC, Hafr Al-Batin, Al-Qaysumah and Hail. If attacked, NAC was to defend in sector while evacuating population centers.

Arrival of additional Coalition forces in theater let CINCCENT and the Saudis establish defenses in accordance with this concept of operations. CINCCENT's defensive plan positioned I MEF's 1st MARDIV along the coastal road with forward positions 70 miles north of Al-Jubayl. The Marines would fall back on successive defensive positions, until reaching a final defensive line in the quarries and ridges 40 miles north of the port. On I MEF's left, XVIII Airborne Corps established a mobile defense in depth. The 101st Airborne Division (Air Assault) served as the Corps' covering force, forward and on the left of the 24th Infantry Division (Mechanized) which occupied the main battle area, ready to defend against an Iraqi attack along the Tapline Road and, more important, to act as a counterattack force into the flank of Iraqi forces advancing down the coast road against the Marines. To the rear, the 82nd Airborne Division assumed defensive positions in the oilfields near Abqaiq. Upon arrival, the 1st Cavalry Division, with its heavy armor, was placed in reserve, ready to counterattack Iraqi forces and drive them back into Kuwait. At sea, an amphibious task force threatened the potentially long Iraqi line of communications along the coast.

With his forces arrayed, CINCCENT intended

to fight a joint and combined battle to defeat an Iraqi attack. Defensive plans relied heavily on Coalition naval and air power and night-fighting capability to balance the numerical inferiority of Coalition ground forces. Intensive coordination between Coalition units was required to ensure plans could be executed smoothly. Saudi and other Coalition units were expected to withdraw through US forces, a complicated maneuver under the best of conditions. Withdrawal routes, link-up points, fire support coordination, and many other details demanded close cooperation. Special staffs and liaison teams were established to coordinate planning. On a less formal level, units and commanders conducted regular meetings, conferences, map exercises, and rehearsals. XVIII Airborne Corps and I MEF closely coordinated their actions. In late September, a joint conference ironed out fire support and air support issues among US air, naval, and ground forces. CINCCENT conducted a map exercise on 4 October for all commanders down to division level, ensuring each understood the defensive plan and his role; lingering questions were resolved. At lower levels, informal liaison solved the immediate problems of tactical commanders. As the last elements of the XVIII Airborne Corps arrived in theater, US forces were fully integrated into defensive plans.

Forward of US defenses, Coalition forces established a thin, but gradually strengthening, line along the Kuwait and southern Iraq border. These forces were to carry out the Saudi plan of defending key areas. Politically, they served notice to the Iraqis of Coalition resolve. In the NAC sector, elements of the 6th French Light Armored Division, the initial portion of Force Daguet, assumed positions west of Hafr Al-Batin, screening the Coalition forces' desert flank. North of Hafr Al-Batin, a Syrian Special Forces regiment patrolled the Iraqi and former Neutral Zone border area, backed by elements of the arriving 9th Syrian Armored Division. On their right, an Egyptian Ranger battalion screened the Kuwait border east of Wadi

Al-Batin in front of the 3rd Egyptian Mechanized Infantry Division. Saudi and other non-US units established additional strongpoints at Hafr Al-Batin and KKMC. In the EAC zone, Saudi forces, consisting of a thin screen of mechanized battalions, watched over the Kuwait border between the Egyptians and the Gulf.

At CINCCENT's recommendation, the three Saudi brigades positioned along the coast were shifted to defensive positions along the border, to provide better early warning of an attack and increase the impression that Coalition defenses were positioned well forward. As more Coalition forces arrived in November and December, they were integrated into the defensive line. These forces included a Qatari battalion, additional Egyptian and Syrian forces, the remainder of the 6th French Light Armored Division, numerous contingents from throughout the Coalition, and the growing strength of the Kuwait armed forces, which were being rebuilt at training camps near KKMC.

Throughout October, Coalition forces continued to refine defensive plans. Cross training between US and other Coalition units built mutual

Landing Craft from Amphibious Task Force Lands Marines During Exercise Imminent Thunder – November, 1990.

understanding. Coalition air forces conducted regular rehearsals of the actions they would take in an Iraqi attack. Amphibious exercises in Oman demonstrated the 4th MEB's capabilities. While the likelihood of an Iraqi attack had receded by the end of the month (CINCCENT believed it had become improbable), air, naval, and land forces continued to prepare defenses, rehearse, and, most importantly, ensure common joint and combined understanding. In late November, Exercise Imminent Thunder, a final defensive plan rehearsal, was conducted. This exercise integrated Coalition land, sea, and air forces.

The final combined defense plan for Operation Desert Shield was signed on 29 November and published in Arabic and English versions. Although supporting plans were not required from subordinate units and the OPLAN never was executed in its entirety, it confirmed actual plans and unit dispositions. While the plan also harmonized the views of both CINCCENT and Lieutenant General Khalid, it ensured common understanding and required detailed coordination at all levels. Although events already were overcoming the need to execute the plan, it can be viewed as a model of unity of effort and combined planning in coalition warfare.

THE JOINT AND COMBINED COMMAND STRUCTURE

Command arrangements were a matter of concern to all nations contributing forces to the Coalition. Several arrangements were considered and discussed, with unity of command the underlying consideration. It became clear an acceptable command structure must reflect the participating nations' national, ethnic, and religious pride. Political factors were of exceptional importance. Eventually, a dual chain of command, one under CINCCENT and the other under the control of a Saudi commander, was developed. This structure required maximum coordination and cooperation among commanders, but did achieve a high level of unity of effort.

CINCCENT relied on a clearly defined command structure that provided him with unambiguous command of all US forces in the theater. CINCCENT received his orders from the Secretary of Defense through the CJCS. CINCCENT submitted force requirements to the Secretary of Defense through the CJCS, who directed the military Services to identify and deploy those forces to the theater. As the supported commander-in-chief (CINC), he drew forces from the entire US military establishment. All forces in theater, except some specialized support units and strategic intelligence gathering assets, fell under subordinate component commanders who reported directly to CINCCENT. The Services thus provided forces to the components as directed by the Secretary of Defense through the CJCS, but held no command authority over those forces once they arrived in the theater.

Although structured along Service lines, these component commands reported directly to CINCCENT and assumed responsibility for administration, logistics, and operations of deployed forces. The Army Component, Central Command (ARCENT) commanded all Army forces in theater, other than those attached to other components. During Operation Desert Shield, these forces eventually consisted of XVIII Airborne Corps, VII Corps, and echelon above corps units providing logistics, intelligence, air defense, and other support.

The Marine Corps Component, Central Command (MARCENT) commanded all Marine forces ashore in Saudi Arabia. The tactical headquarters was I Marine Expeditionary Force, although the same person commanded both MARCENT and I MEF. Those Marines embarked aboard amphibious ships fell under Navy Component, Central Command, who

commanded all US naval forces in the Gulf region, less some naval special warfare units and those Navy units assigned directly to MARCENT, such as naval construction battalions.

CENTAF commanded all USAF units in theater and also was assigned the functions of airspace control authority and Joint Force Air Component Commander, responsible for planning, coordinating, allocating, and tasking theater-wide air operations in accordance with the CINC's apportionment decisions, to include air defense.

A subunified command, Special Operations Command, Central Command (SOCCENT), retained operational command of all special operations forces (SOF) in theater, but Service component commands provided administration and logistics. While the component commands were oriented primarily along Service lines (with the exception of SOCCENT), CINCCENT was free to, and did, cross attach units to meet changing situations.

CINCCENT exercised command by allowing component commanders maximum initiative within the scope of his guidance. He directed close coordination at those levels necessary to ensure operational effectiveness and resolve problems. Component commanders coordinated directly with each other and exchanged liaison detachments. Lower level commanders who found themselves relying on other component elements did the same. This command system allowed maximum flexibility and reduced friction. More importantly, the command structure let CINCCENT maximize each component's unique capabilities, while ensuring a joint approach to operations and planning at all levels.

The Coalition command structure enabled close coordination between US and other nations' military forces. Arriving United Kingdom (UK) forces were placed under CINCCENT's operational control (OPCON), while remaining under UK command. French forces operated independently under national command and control, but coordinated closely with the Saudis and CENTCOM. Islamic forces invited to participate in military operations did so with the understanding they would operate under Saudi control. Arab ground forces were under Saudi OPCON either in the Eastern Area Command, which held responsibility for the northern coastal region of Saudi Arabia, or the Northern Area Command, which included Hafr Al-Batin, KKMC and the area to the north and west. The EAC contained primarily Saudi and other GCC forces. The NAC commanded other GCC forces, as well as deployed Egyptian and Syrian units. Initially, all decisions for these forces were made by the Saudi Ministry of Defense and Aviation (MODA) Chief of Staff, a process that often proved time consuming. To streamline operational decision making, Lieutenant General Khalid was designated the Commander, Joint Forces and Theater of Operations in October, a position he held throughout the war.

To ensure close coordination between CENTCOM and forces under Saudi OPCON, an informal planning group was established in August that combined Saudi and CENTCOM military planners. The initial group included the CENTCOM Director of Plans and Policy, the MODA Director of Operations, several general officers from the Saudi armed forces, and a working group of US and Saudi field grade officers. The planning group conducted continuous coordination as forces were being rushed to the theater. It proved essential to resolving functional issues, preparing defensive plans, and arranging for ports and facilities for US forces. At lower levels, SOF teams were assigned to Islamic units down to the battalion level to assist with training and provide continuous liaison with US forces. These teams served with their Coalition counterparts throughout the crisis.

It quickly became clear that detailed coordination among Coalition ground forces would be necessary. In mid-August, the Coalition Coordination, Communication and Integration Center (C^{3}IC) was formed under the ARCENT's lead. The C^{3}IC became a clearinghouse for coordination of training areas, firing ranges, logistics, frequency management, and intelligence sharing. Manned by officers from all Coalition forces, the C^{3}IC served as the primary tool for coordination of the myriad details inherent in combined military operations. It soon expanded and was divided into ground, air, naval, logistics, special operations, and intelligence sections. The C^{3}IC became a vital tool in ensuring unity of effort among Coalition forces, remaining in operation throughout Operations Desert Shield and Desert Storm.

CENTCOM Command Structure

(Mid-October 1990)

A substantial difference in experience and expertise existed between US and Saudi military planners, understandable given the size, mission, and history of the two nations' armed forces. Continuous close coordination and daily meetings were required to ensure combined plans evolved. This process was made more difficult by language and cultural differences, which placed a premium on US Arab linguists with requisite operational experience and an understanding of the region. While senior Saudi officers meticulously reviewed Arabic translations of operations plans, the few available US linguists also reviewed plans to ensure accuracy.

Arrangements for Coalition C2 reflected the political concerns of the providing nations. Parallel chains of command that enabled commanders to refer to their governments on military questions placed a premium on cooperation and military leadership. That so few issues were elevated to the national level is a tribute to these commanders' professionalism. (For detailed discussion of Coalition C2, see Appendix I.)

OBSERVATIONS

Accomplishments

- Clearly defined and articulated political objectives ensured development of equally clear military objectives and decisively contributed to the success of Operation Desert Shield.

- Forward-deployed and rapidly deployable forces let the United States quickly establish a deterrent capability in theater.

- The US military command structure was unambiguous, letting CINCCENT exercise full command over all US forces in theater, maximizing the unique service capabilities of all forces, while ensuring unity of command.

- The Coalition command structure, while having no overall commander, was successful because of close coordination and the professionalism of the personnel assigned to the staffs and units at all levels.

Shortcomings

- Lack of fully developed defensive plans between the United States and Saudi Arabia hindered initial operational planning. CENTCOM continues to conduct planning and close coordination with Gulf region nations to ensure mutual understanding.

- Initial military options were limited by the time required to move large forces into the theater. Ground force deployment depended on sufficient, dedicated, fast sealift. Sealift shortages resulted in slow buildup of heavy forces during September and October.

Issues

- Successful buildup of forces depended on the availability of sealift, the Saudi port and airfield infrastructure, and host nation support. Shortages of fast, roll-on/ roll-off ships limited rapid deployment of heavy forces. The Department of Defense is addressing this issue.

- The complexities of joint military contingency planning are compounded by the requirement for rapid response, limitations on the availability of strategic lift, and operational differences among forces of a Coalition.

- Earlier MPS sailing could have provided additional military options, in terms of deterrence or rapid response, without committing US forces.

Chapter IV

A Navy Helicopter Queries a Liquid Natural Gas Carrier During Operation Desert Shield.

MARITIME INTERCEPTION OPERATIONS

INTRODUCTION

The Maritime Interception Force (MIF) was the primary instrument the Coalition used to enforce the United Nations Security Council (UNSC) economic sanctions against Iraq. Sanctions require a long and concerted effort. Although Maritime Interception Operations (MIO) continued after the cease fire, this report focuses on the period from 2 August to 28 February.

STRATEGY AND OBJECTIVES

One of the first steps the UNSC took to compel Iraq to relinquish its control of Kuwait was the imposition of economic sanctions. UNSC Resolution 661, which imposed these sanctions, was passed on 6 August. This resolution called on all States to prevent the import and export of all commodities and products to and from Iraq and Kuwait, except medical supplies and certain humanitarian shipments of foodstuffs. The resolution passed 13 to 0; Cuba and Yemen abstained. Within a few days of the Iraqi invasion, Coalition naval forces were gathering in the Red Sea and Persian Gulf. However, during the first two weeks of the crisis, the focus was on defending Saudi Arabia from a possible Iraqi invasion and building a coalition in support of Kuwait. Moreover, UNSC Resolution 661 had not authorized enforcement of the economic sanctions.

The initial Chairman, Joint Chiefs of Staff MIO alert order was dated 11 August and the Commander-in-Chief, Central Command's (CINCCENT) MIO operations order was drafted on 12 August. On 16 August,

> *"Calling upon those Member States cooperating with the Government of Kuwait which are deploying maritime forces to the area to use such measures commensurate to the specific circumstance as may be necessary under the authority of the Security Council to halt all inward and outward maritime shipping in order to inspect and verify their cargoes and destinations and to ensure strict implementation of the provisions related to such shipping laid down in Resolution 661 (1990)."*
>
> **United Nations Security Council Resolution 665**
> **25 August 1990**

CINCCENT was directed to execute MIO, effective 17 August, consistent with the scope of the United Nations (UN) Charter's article 51, and UNSC Resolution 661. At the same time, a notice to mariners was issued to alert merchant shipping of the operation and the potential for inspections.

A multinational MIF was developed to enforce the UNSC economic sanctions against Iraq by intercepting prohibited cargo on shipping headed for or leaving Iraqi and Kuwaiti ports, or Al-'Aqabah, Jordan. Because the United Nations did not have standardized operating procedures to enforce the sanctions, CINCCENT directed Naval Forces Component, Central Command (NAVCENT) to develop an operational plan for multinational MIO, with the understanding that multinational units participating in the MIF would operate under their national commands. Initially NAVCENT directed the Commander, Middle East Force (CMEF) to plan, coordinate, and execute US MIO. CMEF drafted an operational plan for the US MIF with two primary goals:

■ Effectively use available US naval forces to

monitor shipping channels used by Iraq throughout the region without compromising security objectives.

- Base MIO on the most universally accepted international legal principles to enforce the sanctions with minimal interference with legitimate maritime commerce.

The operational plan considered the danger that unnecessary use of force at the early stages of the crisis might undercut international support for the sanctions or even prompt an Iraqi military response at an inopportune time relative to Coalition building and Operation Desert Shield force deployment.

On 25 August, the UNSC authorized the use of force to enforce the sanctions and MIO began in earnest. While the use of force during MIO was justified under the UN Charter and authorized by UNSC Resolution 665, great efforts were taken to avoid not only the use of force during MIO, but also the appearance of taking any action that could be construed as the action of a belligerent during armed conflict. For example, the visit and search of suspect merchant vessels was announced to the merchant as an inspection, not a boarding. Although authorized by international law, seizure of vessels or cargoes that violated UNSC resolutions generally was

not done. Instead, vessels violating the sanctions were diverted to Coalition or non-aligned Middle East ports. Additionally, careful efforts were made to minimize interference with legitimate maritime commerce to avoid adverse effects on the economies of other nations.

Trade related to the Az-Zarqa free-trade zone in Jordan — much of it seaborne through Al-'Aqabah, some by air or truck — caused some confusion early in MIO. Free-trade zones are legal constructs Third World countries use to encourage industry to operate in the zone, by offering tax exemptions and other incentives. The Az-Zarqa free trade zone served as a transfer point for Iraqi-bound cargo. Initially, there was some uncertainty as to whether UNSC sanctions prohibited cargo destined for this free-trade zone. Ultimately, cargo consigned to this free trade zone was required to have an accurately documented final destination or the ships carrying it were diverted.

MULTINATIONAL RELATIONSHIPS OF THE MARITIME INTERCEPTION FORCE

The MIO's rapid development and smooth functioning was directly the product of extensive experience several of the key navies had accumulated. Importantly, during the "Tanker War" phase of the Iran-Iraq War, five European nations (members of both the Western European Union and the North Atlantic Treaty Organization (NATO)) and the United States conducted operations that protected reflagged merchant shipping in the Persian Gulf. Although

---

THE IRAQI MERCHANT FLEET AND PORT FACILITIES

At the time of Iraq's invasion, the total Iraqi merchant fleet consisted of about 140 vessels, but only some 42 ships were suitable for overseas cargo shipment. Of these 42 ships, there were 20 tankers, three roll-on/roll-off vessels, and 19 cargo vessels of various classes.

The major ports for seaborne cargo were Umm Qasr and Khawr Az-Zubayr in Iraq, and the Jordanian port of Al-'Aqabah, from which cargo for Iraq was shipped overland. Since oil pipelines through Saudi Arabia and Turkey were shut down shortly after the invasion, the Iraqi oil terminal at Mina Al-Bakr served as the only major facility with the potential to export substantial amounts of oil.

"Each naval force received Maritime Interception Force tasking . . . from its own national command authority. Even without a formal international command and control structure, MIF demonstrated superb international cooperation, enhanced through monthly MIF conferences. Conferences facilitated cooperation, ensured mutual protection, and reduced redundancy."

NAVCENT

these operations like Earnest Will (the name of the US effort) were separately mounted by each participating state, substantial collective experience in Persian Gulf naval operations was developed.

After UNSC Resolutions 661 and 665 were passed, nations continued to join the effort for several weeks. By 1 September, Australia, Canada, the United Kingdom (UK), the Netherlands, and France had dispatched 20

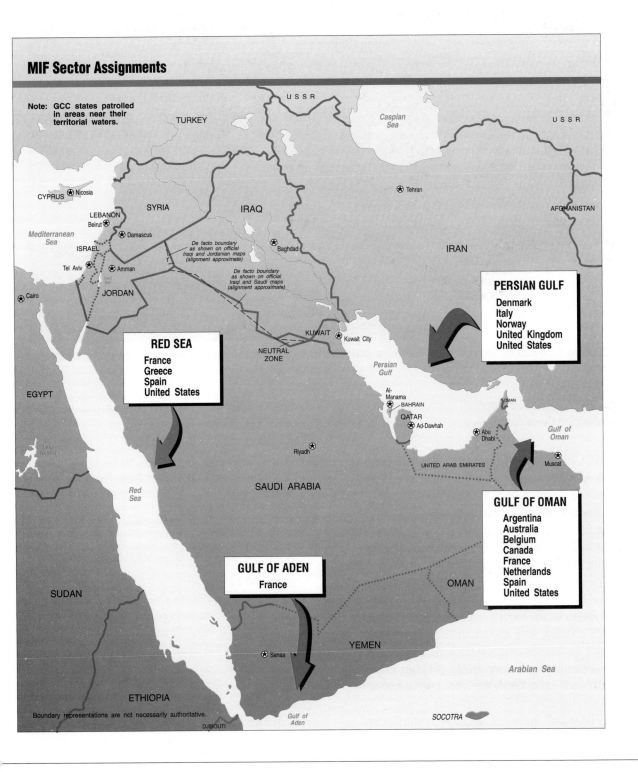

MIF Sector Assignments

Note: GCC states patrolled in areas near their territorial waters.

PERSIAN GULF
Denmark
Italy
Norway
United Kingdom
United States

RED SEA
France
Greece
Spain
United States

GULF OF OMAN
Argentina
Australia
Belgium
Canada
France
Netherlands
Spain
United States

GULF OF ADEN
France

Boundary representations are not necessarily authoritative.

A Boarding Team from the Spanish Frigate *Vencedora* (F36) Uses a Rigid-Hull Inflatable Boat to Conduct a Boarding in the Red Sea.

ships to Middle East waters, but had not yet committed these forces to the MIF.

CINCCENT assigned overall MIO coordination to NAVCENT, who initiated and chaired a series of monthly coordination meetings of representatives from each participating nation. The first conference was 9 September. After the first meeting, NAVCENT delineated operating sectors for the Coalition navies who committed ships to the MIF. Each sector generally included ships from more than one country, in addition to the forces of the local Gulf Cooperation Council (GCC) States, with the understanding that the senior naval officer in each sector would be the local sector coordinator. In the Red Sea and northern Persian Gulf, the local coordinators usually were the US carrier battle group (CVBG) and destroyer squadron commanders.

By 27 September, Australia, Belgium, Canada, Denmark, France, Greece, Italy, the Netherlands, Spain, and the UK had committed 42 ships to the MIF. The GCC states participated in MIO by preventing merchant vessels from using their coastal waters to avoid the MIF. In addition to the GCC states, 13 nations (Argentina, Australia, Belgium, Canada, Denmark, France, Greece, Italy, the Netherlands, Norway, Spain, the UK, and the United States) ultimately provided ships for the MIF. During Operations Desert Shield and Desert Storm, 22 nations participated in the MIF effort, providing support ranging from CVBGs to port logistics facilities.

The informal, multilateral MIF command structure achieved international cooperation and superb operational effectiveness. When implementing the sanctions under the UNSC resolutions, each country operated under its own national command directives. Although operational procedures varied, coordination among the Coalition naval forces resulted in an effective multinational effort. Information on operating procedures and tactics was routinely shared among the Coalition naval forces. For example, meetings, exchanges, and briefings among Greek, French, Spanish, and US MIF participants in the Red Sea served to increase mutual understanding and standardize operating procedures. Furthermore, uniform procedures and communications methods developed during years of NATO, Australia-New Zealand-United States (ANZUS), and various bilateral exercises greatly improved the Coalition's ability to work together effectively. Diplomatic support to prevent evasion of sanctions by merchant vessels in territorial waters also was crucial to the success of MIO.

OPERATIONAL PROCEDURES

MIO centered on surveillance of commercial shipping in the Persian Gulf, the Gulf of Oman, the Gulf of Aden, the Red Sea, and the eastern Mediterranean Sea, supported by worldwide monitoring of ships and cargoes potentially destined for Iraq, Kuwait, or Al-'Aqabah. When merchant vessels were intercepted, they were queried to identify the vessel and its shipping information (e.g., destination, origination, registration, and cargo). Suspect vessels were boarded for visual inspection, and, if prohibited cargo were found, the merchant ship was diverted. Rarely, and only when necessary, warning shots were fired to induce a vessel to allow boarding by the inspection team. As an additional step, takedowns — the insertion of armed teams from helicopters — were used to take temporary control of uncooperative, suspect merchant vessels that refused to stop for inspection.

The Naval Operational Intelligence Center (NOIC) provided detailed technical data on numerous merchant ships. The center also developed an inspection checklist for Coalition boarding teams. As an element of the overall US contribution to UNSC Sanctions Committee deliberations, which guided the UN effort, NOIC used its resources to develop watch lists of companies suspected of trading with, or on behalf of, Iraq.

Nearly 250,000 square miles of sea lanes were patrolled by Coalition naval forces. Maritime Patrol Aircraft (MPA) such as US Navy P-3 Orions, Royal Air Force Nimrods and French Navy Atlantiques ranged over the Persian Gulf and Red Sea. During Operation Desert Shield, the combined efforts of Coalition MPA resulted in the interception of more than 6,300 ships.

Queries requesting a vessel's identity, its point of origin, destination, and cargo were issued to merchant ships by radio from warships, MPA, helicopters, or tactical aircraft flying surveillance patrols. After vessels were queried, information from imagery, radar, intelligence, shipboard computer data bases, and public shipping records were used to corroborate the responses. Some warships, like *USS J. L. Hall* (FFG 32) (the first ship to challenge a merchant vessel), averaged 10 challenges daily.

To reduce the number of unnecessary boardings, intercepted shipping could be released without boarding if the vessel signaled its intention to proceed to a port other than one in Iraq, Kuwait, or Jordan. However, any ship that failed to

"The success of MIF operations was due in no small measure to experience and training provided by Coast Guard LEDETs."

NAVCENT

"The Coast Guard Law Enforcement Detachment hadn't been aboard but a few minutes when we realized that the Coast Guard had the corporate knowledge we needed badly."

Executive Officer, USS Goldsborough (DDG 20)

proceed as directed, or attempted to proceed to an Iraqi, Kuwaiti, or Jordanian port would be boarded. An exception to this policy applied to ferries and passenger liners, so long as there was no indication of subterfuge. Also, no boarding generally was required for any merchant visually confirmed to be riding high on the water (indicating the ship's holds were empty).

Two MIF warships normally conducted boarding operations. A team from one ship boarded the suspect vessel while the second ship remained nearby to provide assistance. To supplement the MIF assets, carrier-based

A Maritime Interception Force Team, Consisting of a US Coast Guard Law Enforcement Detachment and *USS W. V. Pratt* (DDG 44) Crew Members, Boards a Merchant Vessel in the Red Sea.

aircraft remained on alert, prepared to launch in support of an abnormal boarding (e.g., when only one Coalition ship was available to board a suspect Iraqi-flagged merchant). Helicopters also were tasked to inspect merchant vessels. If cargo holds were open, a helicopter visually confirmed whether the vessel was empty.

Reasons for diverting a merchant vessel to a port different from its intended destination included irregularities with the ship's manifest and blatant shipment of prohibited cargo destined for Iraq or Kuwait. Manifest irregularities included improper designation of consignees on the manifests and bookkeeping discrepancies. Prohibited cargo discovered and diverted by the MIF included such items as military equipment, food, cars stolen from Kuwait, chemicals, and spare parts.

Because of their experience and expertise, United States Coast Guard (USCG) Law Enforcement Detachments (LEDETs) proved to be invaluable to MIO. Previous drug interdiction operations in the Caribbean provided LEDETs an opportunity to become familiar with Navy shipboard operating procedures, capabilities, and support assets. These operations also provided the Navy and USCG experience in conducting at-sea inspections in potentially hostile environments. LEDETs provided Navy personnel with training in boarding procedures, handling of small arms, tactics used by smugglers, and the intricacies of shipping documentation and maritime law. A USCG officer normally led a 10-person boarding team composed of three USCG enlisted specialists, one Naval officer, and five Navy enlisted personnel.

Between 18 and 31 August, three Iraqi tankers refused to allow boarding inspections after being challenged by US naval forces. On 18 August, the first MIO warning shots were fired by *USS Reid* (FFG 30) after the Iraqi tanker *Khanaqin* refused to alter course in the Persian Gulf. Even after warning shots were fired, the Iraqi vessel

USS Mississippi's (CGN 40) Boarding Team Conducts a Cautious Search of a Merchant Vessel in the Red Sea.

was rescinded (see Significant MIO Events section). CINCENT's MIO operations order was revised on 1 September to require National Command Authorities approval for disabling fire. Disabling fire was authorized again on 14 September for *Al Fao*, but its master consented to boarding before disabling force was necessary. The last authorization was granted on 22 October against *Al Sahil Al Arabi*, which also consented to boarding before disabling fire actually was used.

Most merchant traffic the MIF queried was encountered inside the Persian Gulf (78 percent); however, most boardings occurred in the Red Sea (91 percent). Most takedowns took

refused to comply with the MIF's orders to halt and eventually was allowed to proceed to Aden, Yemen, where it anchored. Boarding operations were temporarily suspended while diplomatic efforts were made to obtain UNSC authorization to use force to obtain compliance with the sanctions. UNSC Resolution 665 was approved on 25 August and boarding operations resumed the same day.

On 27 August, US MIO procedures were changed to require NAVCENT's permission before warning shots could be fired at suspected vessels. From the beginning of MIO until 28 February, 11 interceptions required warning shots. At no time, however, was disabling gunfire used. The use of warning shots and disabling fire was tightly controlled to ensure all other means short of this display of force were used to induce compliance.

US warships were authorized to use disabling fire on Iraqi merchant ships three times during MIO. Permission for disabling fire was first granted on 18 August against *Khanaqin*, but

"Going through the boat was probably the most stressful part because you didn't know what was behind every door. We didn't know if it was going to be a regular boarding or if someone would be waiting for us."

Boarding Team Member, USS Brewton (FF 1086)

During a Training Exercise in the Red Sea, SEALs Fast Rope from a CH-46 onto the Deck of *USNS Humphreys* (TAO 188).

place against Iraqi ships in the Gulf of Oman and northern Arabian Sea. Because of concern for avoiding incidents involving infringement of territorial waters and oil spills, takedowns were purposely not conducted in the Persian Gulf. The UK was the first to conduct a takedown on 8 October, demonstrating the procedure's effectiveness.

Because of the risks involved and the potential for combat with hostile crews, takedowns were carried out by special forces using helicopter assets to insert the specially trained teams. Navy SEALS and special teams from the 4th Marine Expeditionary Brigade (MEB) and 13th Marine Expeditionary Unit (Special Operations Capable (MEU (SOC)) carried out most Coalition takedowns. (Marine Corps (USMC) teams were not always available to the MIF because of other tasking such as the Coalition's amphibious warfare preparations.)

Since any attempt to board a ship that had refused to stop could meet with a hostile reception, Coalition naval units typically sought to muster overwhelming force against such a ship. Usually three or four warships surrounded the challenged vessel while a helicopter gunship prepared to provide covering fire. Helicopters then hovered above the ship in question, and the takedown team "fast roped" (i.e., rappelled) onto the deck. The takedown team took control of the vessel and additional forces were brought aboard, often by small boats from the surrounding coalition warships, to secure and inspect the merchant ship.

Takedowns of uncooperative vessels evolved into an intermediate step between warning shots and disabling fire. Although successful, takedowns strained available shipboard helicopter resources. There were not enough helicopters capable of inserting a full 16-member takedown team onto a vessel. Though designed primarily for antisubmarine warfare, both the SH-3 and SH-60 were adapted to meet takedown requirements. The full

complement of a takedown squad usually required three SH-3s to conduct a successful insertion. The Navy's SH-60 helicopter was equipped with an M-60 machine gun and generally was used as the helicopter gunship during takedowns.

Iraq used many tactics in attempts to avoid the sanctions or frustrate the MIF. The families of Iraqi masters and crews were threatened with violence if any ship stopped for boarding. Iraqi crews often ignored verbal challenges, delayed responses to MIF interrogations, ignored warning shots, used water cannons against boarding parties, refused to cooperate after boarding, and refused to divert after verbally agreeing to do so. In most cases, the ship's master cooperated once he knew he could inform the Iraqi government he had been forced to comply. Iraqi masters sometimes labeled cargo as crew food or produced false manifests and documents. The Coalition countered these tactics by thorough searches of cargo and close scrutiny of documentation. To make it more difficult to produce fraudulent documentation, NAVCENT did not publish specific inspection criteria. In some cases, cargo was hidden in inaccessible areas of a merchant ship. Underway inspections in these situations were ineffective. With the government of Saudi Arabia's permission, suspect ships occasionally were diverted to the Saudi Red Sea port of Yanbu, where full inspections were conducted.

On 27 August, US naval forces participating in the MIF were authorized to offer safe haven to Iraqi masters and crews of vessels which refused to stop for inspection. Intercepting ships were authorized to communicate the following offer to the master of the ship: "If you fear persecution in Iraq for permitting boarding of your vessel in compliance with UN Security Council Resolutions, the United States will assist you in finding a safe haven outside Iraq." The term "safe haven" was developed to avoid confusion with existing policies concerning temporary refuge and asylum. Safe haven involved a pre-approved commitment by the State Department to protect an individual without guaranteeing asylum in the United States. No Iraqi ship master or crew requested safe haven.

SIGNIFICANT EVENTS DURING MARITIME INTERCEPTION OPERATIONS

More than 7,500 interceptions took place during Operations Desert Shield and Desert Storm, and it is not feasible to chronicle all those events in this chapter. The following descriptions, however, briefly highlight significant events that occurred.

On 18 August, the first boarding of a merchant vessel occurred when a team from *USS England* (CG 22) inspected the cargo and manifest of the Chinese freighter *Heng Chung Hai*. Later that day, the first diversion occurred when *USS Scott* (DDG 995) ordered the Cypriot merchant *Dongola* away from Al-'Aqabah after the vessel's master admitted carrying cargo bound for Iraq.

That same day, *USS Reid* intercepted the Iraqi tanker *Khanaqin* in the Persian Gulf. The Iraqi vessel refused to comply with boarding instructions or change course. *USS Reid* fired both 25-mm and 76-mm warning shots, which also failed to induce the ship's master to comply with the boarding instructions, but did cause some of *Khanaqin's* crew to don life jackets. *USS Reid* continued to follow the Iraqi vessel and later was relieved by *USS Goldsborough* (DDG 20). The Iraqi vessel was allowed to

"**O**ne cannot think about this activity without mentioning the Navy — the very quiet, very professional way they put the [Maritime Interception Operations] on . . . very, very effective — maybe one of the most important things we did."

General Merrill McPeak, Chief of Staff,
United States Air Force

proceed to Aden, Yemen, where it anchored. A similar incident occurred that same day between *USS R. G. Bradley* (FFG 49) and the Iraqi merchant vessel *Baba Gurgur*. The Iraqi vessel ignored three warning shots and was allowed to proceed to Aden, where it also anchored. In late November, both crews were transferred to the Iraqi roll-on/roll-off ship *Khawla Bint Al Azwar*, ferried to Al-'Aqabah, and then returned to Iraq.

On 31 August, *USS Biddle* (CG 34) boarded the first Iraqi merchant vessel, *Al Karamah*, en route to Al-'Aqabah. A thorough inspection revealed the vessel was empty and it was allowed to proceed.

In the early morning hours of 4 September, crew members of *USS Goldsborough* and a LEDET boarded the Iraqi vessel *Zanoobia*. The Iraqi merchant had enough tea to supply the entire population of Iraq for a month and was ordered to divert to a port outside the Persian Gulf. The Iraqi merchant's master refused to divert and *USS Goldsborough* was directed to take control of the Iraqi ship. More *USS Goldsborough* crewmen were brought aboard and took *Zanoobia* to the port of Muscat, Oman, where Iraqi diplomats advised the master to return to his port of origin in Sri Lanka.

In an attempt to break down the multinational Coalition and reduce the MIF's effectiveness, Iraq, on 11 September, offered free oil to Third World countries, if they would send ships to load it. No country responded.

On 14 September, US and Australian warships conducted the first multinational boarding of an Iraqi vessel. After 24 hours of radio negotiations, the Iraqi master of the merchant vessel, *Al Fao,* still refused to stop for inspection. The Australian Frigate *HMAS Darwin* (F 04) and *USS Brewton* (FF 1086) proceeded to the next step of the interception and fired warning shots ahead of the vessel, which caused the Iraqi vessel to slow down. The merchant vessel was boarded by a 13-member team consisting of Coast Guardsmen, *USS Brewton*, and *HMAS Darwin* crew members as *HMAS Darwin's* helicopter provided assistance. *Al Fao* was empty and allowed to proceed to the Iraqi port of Al-Basrah.

On 27 September, *USS Montgomery* (FF 1082), with the Spanish Frigate *SNS Cazadora* (F 35), intercepted the Iraqi merchant *Tadmur* outbound from Al-'Aqabah. The Iraqi vessel did not respond to several verbal warnings to stop. Eventually, the Iraqi master informed the Coalition ships his instructions were to proceed unless stopped by force. After *USS Montgomery* fired several .50-caliber warning shots, *Tadmur* agreed to stop and permit boarding. A US and Spanish team boarded the vessel as the Iraqi crew held up pictures of Saddam Hussein. Inspection revealed the vessel was empty. The purpose of the vessel's departure from Al-'Aqabah may have been to gather intelligence on MIO procedures and to test the Coalition's resolve.

On 2 October, the French frigate *Doudart de Lagree* (F 728), intercepted the North Korean vessel, *Sam Il Po*, which was carrying plywood panels. After the merchant vessel repeatedly failed to answer bridge-to-bridge radio calls, warning shots were fired across the vessel's bow. *Sam Il Po* then stopped and permitted the French ship to board. The North Korean master claimed he was not monitoring the bridge-to-bridge radio, and that stopping would have damaged his engines. The boarding team verified the cargo and ship's destination, and allowed the ship to proceed.

The Iraqi merchant *Alwasitti* was intercepted in the Gulf of Oman on 8 October by the British frigate *HMS Battleaxe* (F 89), *HMAS Adelaide* (F 01), and *USS Reasoner* (FF 1063). All three ships fired warning shots, but *Alwasitti* refused to stop or acknowledge any communications. *HMS Battleaxe* inserted four Royal Marines by helicopter and secured the vessel, executing the first takedown of the Gulf crisis.

Also on 8 October, the Iraqi vessel *Tadmur* was intercepted again by *HMS Brazen* (F 91), *USS Goldsborough*, and *HMAS Darwin*. The Iraqi vessel informed the Coalition ships that higher authority had instructed it not to allow boarding and it refused to stop. Royal Marines from *HMS Brazen* were inserted by helicopter and *USS Goldsborough* and *HMAS Darwin* crew members boarded by small boat. The boarding team instructed the Iraqi master to divert, but he refused and instead offered to jettison his cargo at sea. *HMS Brazen's* Commanding Officer, the local MIO coordinator, ordered the Iraqi merchant to divert to Muscat.

USS Brewton intercepted the Iraqi merchant *Almutanabbi* on 13 October, after it refused to heed verbal orders to stop. *HMAS Darwin* made a close, high speed crossing pass within 100 yards of *Almutanabbi's* bow. Two detachments of Marines from 13th MEU (SOC), aboard *USS Ogden* (LPD 5) were inserted and rapidly gained control of the ship. The Iraqi vessel was then boarded by additional teams from *USS Brewton, USS Ogden, HMAS Darwin,* and *HMS Jupiter* (F 60). This boarding was the first takedown by US Marines.

From 20 to 22 October, *USS O'Brien* (DD 975) intercepted and challenged the Iraqi vessel, *Al Sahil Al Arabi*, which was visually identified as a small cargo ship. The Iraqi master claimed the vessel was a fishing boat and, when boarded, it was confirmed to be a fishing refrigeration ship. However, the vessel was carrying lumber and piping, and was ordered either to divert to Bahrain or return to Iraq. The master, fearing he would be arrested if he went to Bahrain, initially agreed to return to Iraq. After the boarding party departed, the master apparently changed his mind about returning to Iraq and the crew started throwing wood over the side. When ordered to slow down, the Iraqi vessel increased speed and refused to stop.

The next day the Iraqi master again refused to turn back to Iraq, and *USS O'Brien* fired warning shots from .50-caliber, 25-mm, and 5-inch guns. Even after warning shots were fired, the vessel did not stop. On 22 October, *USS Reasoner* followed abeam of the Iraqi vessel while *HMAS Adelaide* made two close passes across the bow of *Al Sahil Al Arabi*. After the second pass, the Iraqi vessel stopped and allowed boarding. With US Marines standing by in *USS Ogden, HMAS Adelaide's* Commanding Officer, the local MIO coordinator, decided to insert *HMAS Adelaide's* takedown team. After the takedown, the Iraqi master cooperated fully with the team and complied with all MIF orders.

On 28 October, *USS Reasoner* intercepted the Iraqi merchant *Amuriyah*, which initially refused to answer bridge-to-bridge radio calls. *HMAS Darwin* made a close, high-speed crossing maneuver while towing a spar, which caused the Iraqi merchant to turn away and then resume its original course. In an effort to convince the vessel's master to submit to boarding, F-14s and F/A-18s from *USS Independence* (CV 62) made six low subsonic passes. The master remained extremely uncooperative and refused to accept a boarding party. *HMAS Darwin* and *USS Reasoner* fired warning shots, which only caused the Iraqi crew to don life-jackets. A 21-member USMC takedown team was inserted and initially reported no active resistance. The Iraqi master refused to muster his crew, and SEALs from *USS Ogden* were called in to help with the takedown. The crew of *Amuriyah* attempted to use a water cannon to prevent the SEALs from boarding. The crew then resisted passively as the vessel was secured; however, one crew member in the engineering spaces who tried to attack a Marine with an axe was disarmed and restrained. The ship's master also had to be restrained temporarily. Inspection revealed no prohibited cargo, so the vessel was not diverted. It appeared throughout the interception the Iraqi crew had received detailed guidance on how to avoid the sanctions and hamper Coalition boarding operations.

On 13 December, *USS Mississippi* (CGN 40) intercepted and boarded the Cypriot-flagged merchant vessel *Tilia,* outbound from Al-'Aqabah with motor vehicles and household goods. Careful inspection revealed most of the cars were stolen from Kuwait. The following day, *USS Sampson* (DDG 5) intercepted another ship with a similar load; both vessels were sent back to Al-'Aqabah.

In December, the Iraqi-flagged vessel *Ibn Khaldoon* attempted to carry food and approximately 60 peace activists to Iraq. On 26 December, *HMAS Sydney* intercepted the Iraqi ship after it refused to respond to challenges by bridge-to-bridge radio. A team of SEALs and 4th MEB Marines were inserted by USMC helicopters and met some resistance from women who formed a human chain across the vessel's midships to prevent access to the bridge. Some women also tried to grab the team's weapons and knocked one team member down. The team fired warning shots and used smoke grenades to restore order. After the takedown team gained control of the ship and slowed it down, a multinational team from *HMAS Sydney* (F 03), *USS Oldendorf* (DD 972), and *USS Fife* (DD 991) boarded the vessel. The vessel then was inspected and ordered to divert because it carried prohibited cargo (food), not authorized specifically by the UNSC as humanitarian assistance.

During the night of 27 December, a Swedish woman aboard *Ibn Khaldoon* became ill. A medical team was dispatched from *USS Trenton* (LPD 14) and the woman was treated for an apparent heart attack. The patient later was evacuated by helicopter to *USS Trenton* where she was stabilized and then transferred to a hospital in Muscat.

USS Mississippi and the Spanish frigate *SNS Infanta-Christina* (F 35) inspected the Russian merchant ship, *Dmitriy-Furmanov* on 4 January, while it was en route to Al-'Aqabah.

The vessel was carrying an unmanifested cargo of tank parts, detonators and rocket launchers. On 10 January, the vessel was reboarded by *USS Mississippi* and *SNS Diana* (F 32). Inspection revealed the cargo was still unmanifested and the vessel was allowed to depart the Red Sea via the Suez Canal.

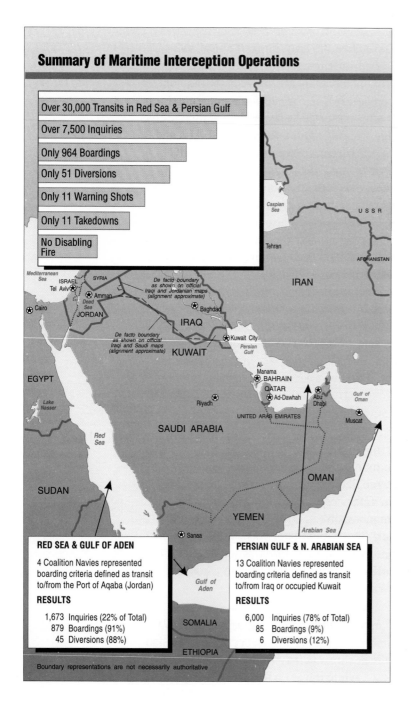

When Operation Desert Storm began, MIF boardings were stopped for one day, 17 January, to await Iraq's response to the initial attack and to allow US participants to fire Tomahawk missiles. Because of wartime conditions, NAVCENT modified his directions to the MIF to allow frequent travelers to the ports of Al-'Aqabah and Eilat to pass without boarding. Furthermore, all boardings were to be conducted in daylight, and all Iraqi ships were to be diverted automatically without boarding.

On 31 January, a Greek helicopter observed the St. Vincent-flagged cargo ship, *Superstar,* dropping what appeared to be mines in the northern Red Sea. A SEAL team from *USS John F. Kennedy* (CV 67) was inserted by helicopter and took control of the ship. Once the vessel was secured, a LEDET from *USS Biddle* boarded and inspected the vessel. The master was cooperative and provided logs and manifests. No evidence of minelaying was found.

EFFECTIVENESS

MIO appear to have been very effective. As a result of Coalition efforts during the seven months of the Persian Gulf crisis, more than 165 ships from 19 Coalition navies challenged more than 7,500 merchant vessels, boarded 964 ships to inspect manifests and cargo holds, and diverted 51 ships carrying more than one million tons of cargo in violation of UNSC sanctions. Commerce through Iraqi and Kuwaiti ports essentially was eliminated; ships were deterred from loading Iraqi oil while Turkey and Saudi Arabia prohibited use of Iraqi oil pipelines that crossed their territory. Virtually all Iraqi oil revenues were cut off; thus the source of much of Iraq's international credit was severed, along with 95 percent of the country's total pre-invasion revenues.

By severely restricting Iraqi seaborne trade, MIO played a major role in intercepting the

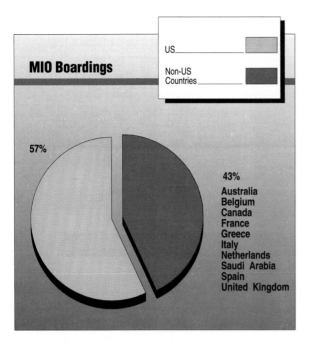

MIO Boardings

US

Non-US Countries

57%

43%
Australia
Belgium
Canada
France
Greece
Italy
Netherlands
Saudi Arabia
Spain
United Kingdom

import of materials required to sustain military operations and operate such equipment as surface-to-air-missile systems, command and control equipment, and early warning radar systems. Importantly, access to outside sources of tanks, aircraft, munitions, and other war material to replenish combat losses effectively was precluded. Iraq did obtain some imports by smuggling along its borders, and by air, but most high-volume bulk imports were completely cut off.

Between early October and 15 January, 18 tankers and cargo ships were identified in Kuwaiti and Iraqi ports. Most of these ships transported oil or food between Iraq and Kuwait. A Maltese cargo/bulk ship also transited between various Iraqi ports. Only eight of the ships attempted to leave the Persian Gulf and subsequently were boarded; however, two ships were unaccounted for and it was not determined if they had passed through the Strait of Hormuz. The low activity level of shipping observed in Iraqi and Kuwaiti ports, coupled with reports of immobile, fully loaded tankers, verified that the flow of shipping into and out of Iraq and Kuwait had been severely curtailed.

MIO could have been streamlined and made more effective if guidance detailing the sanctions and MIO procedures could have been provided to the international maritime community. Such guidance was slow to take form, primarily because of the volatile nature of the evolving crisis and the number of changes made to procedures as MIO progressed. Also, the commanders responsible for conducting the operations were concerned that, if more details concerning procedures were made public, more creative efforts to circumvent the sanctions could be developed. This concern was particularly applicable to shipping through Al-'Aqabah.

In retrospect, detailed information might have been promulgated earlier concerning the extent of at-sea inspections, the documentation requirements, and the need to ensure cargoes were accessible for inspection. Promulgation of guidance was hindered by the lack of international standards for cargo documentation and by the absence of a readily available medium by which such information could be transmitted effectively. Without prior notice of the procedures required to satisfy the UNSC sanctions, merchantmen often were ill-prepared for required inspections. Normal practices of peacetime documentation frequently were inadequate. There were countless instances of inaccessible cargo, improper manifests, and incorrect cargo labeling, which effectively precluded manifest verification. These vessels were diverted or their movement restricted until such problems could be remedied by rearranging cargo or by acquiring the correct documentation.

The UNSC sanctions against Iraq and the MIO that helped enforce them contributed significantly to the Coalition's victory. Although the Navy was involved in a majority of MIO, ranging from intelligence gathering and surveillance to boardings and takedowns, other Coalition navies participated in roughly half of all boardings. US ships conducted several combined boardings with Australian, British, Canadian, Greek, and Spanish warships. The MIF's multinational character built and sustained the Coalition's political and military effectiveness. Importantly, this multinational character promoted worldwide acceptance of MIO. The Coalition's procedures to enforce the UNSC sanctions were crafted in a manner least obtrusive to the rights of neutral nations and were accepted as legitimate by the majority of non-participating nations.

OBSERVATIONS

Accomplishments

■ MIO provided a foundation for Coalition building and were an example of multinational cooperation at its best. The legitimacy of their conduct and their basis in international law were internationally accepted, which contributed to the operational success.

■ International cooperation within the Coalition worked extremely well, even without formal command relationships. The uniform procedures and communications methods developed during years of NATO, ANZUS, and various bilateral exercises greatly improved the Coalition's ability to work effectively.

■ Diplomatic support to prevent evasion of sanctions by suspect ships transiting territorial waters was crucial to the success of MIO. Obtaining permission to use local ports for diversions and inspections also was important.

■ USCG expertise in boarding, small arms handling, maritime law, shipping documentation, and countersmuggling techniques proved to be invaluable.

■ Special forces successfully executed takedowns to board uncooperative merchant ships. Takedowns became the intermediary step in MIO enforcement escalation, occurring after warning shots, but before disabling fire. They were a substantial factor in the MIF's effectiveness and success. This innovation demonstrated resolve and allowed Coalition naval forces to prevent Iraqi merchant vessels from avoiding the sanctions without taking more extreme measures such as disabling fire.

Shortcomings

■ There were not enough helicopters able to insert a full takedown team onto a vessel. Three SH-3s normally were required to conduct a successful takedown. Takedowns also required a dedicated helicopter gunship to provide covering fire if the situation became hostile. The SH-60B usually was used as the helicopter gunship. These requirements strained the battle group's limited helicopter resources.

■ Small boats were vital for boardings. Rigid-Hull Inflatable Boats (RHIB) or Zodiac boats, available on only a few US warships, were more effective than the Navy's standard motor whaleboats because of the RHIB's better durability, speed, and sea-keeping abilities. Generally, the weather in the Red Sea and the Persian Gulf was good, but heavy seas sometimes precluded non-RHIB small boat operations. Many Coalition forces were equipped with RHIBs and Zodiacs and could board vessels when US boat crews could not.

■ Conducting MIO effectively required issuing detailed guidance to international merchantmen – guidance that often was slow to take form. Without prior notice of the procedures required to satisfy UNSC provisions, merchantmen often were ill-prepared for required inspections.

■ Normal practices of peacetime shipping documentation frequently were inadequate. There were countless instances of inaccessible cargo, improper manifests, and incorrect cargo labeling, which effectively precluded manifest verification.

Chapter V

Meeting in the Pentagon Gold Room – the usual meeting place of the Joint Chiefs of Staff, August 15, 1990, to discuss the U.S. military response to the Iraqi invasion of Kuwait, are: left to right: National Security Advisor Brent Scowcroft; General H. Norman Schwarzkopf, U. S. Army, Commander-in-Chief U.S. Central Command; Secretary of Defense Dick Cheney; The President of the United States George Bush; Chairman, Joint Chiefs of Staff, General Colin E. Powell, and Vice-Chairman, Joint Chiefs of Staff, Admiral Dave E. Jeremiah.

TRANSITION TO THE OFFENSIVE

INTRODUCTION

President Bush, speaking to the nation on 8 November, announced the United States would send more forces to the Gulf to give the Coalition a combined arms offensive capability. The President's statement marked a new phase in the crisis. Until that announcement, the United States and its allies had concentrated on deploying enough forces and materiel to deter Iraqi attack and defend Saudi Arabia from invasion. By early October, that goal had been achieved. Concurrently, the United States and several Coalition partners began discussing a wide range of military options in the event economic sanctions proved insufficient to convince Saddam Hussein to withdraw his army from Kuwait. While increasing the pressure on Saddam Hussein through further action at the United Nations and the application of sanctions, President Bush told his national security advisors in October he wanted them to develop a strong military option to force Iraq from Kuwait should that prove necessary. For the next three-and-a-half months, the Defense Department planned and prepared for offensive operations.

PLANNING FOR THE OFFENSIVE

Evolution of the Offensive Plan

Immediately after the Iraqi invasion of Kuwait, the Commander in Chief, Central Command (CINCCENT) developed several Deterrent Force Packages for consideration by the Chairman, Joint Chiefs of Staff (CJCS), Secretary of Defense, and the President. On 4 August, at a meeting in Camp David, MD,

> "*The first thing for a commander in chief to determine is what he is going to do, to see if he has the means to overcome the obstacles which the enemy can oppose to him, and, when he has decided, to do all he can to surmount them.*"
>
> **Napoleon**
> **Maxim LXXIX**

CINCCENT presented his initial ideas to the President. These Deterrent Force Packages included an array of forces which included carrier battle groups (CVBG), tactical fighter squadrons, tanker aircraft, Airborne Warning and Control System (AWACS), B-52s, Maritime Prepositioning Force Marine Expeditionary Brigades (MPF MEB), and an airborne division.

The Secretary of Defense instructed CJCS and CINCCENT to develop an offensive option that would be available to the President in case Saddam Hussein chose to engage in further aggression or other unacceptable behavior, such as killing Kuwaiti citizens or foreign nationals in Kuwait or Iraq. On 10 August, the Air Force (USAF) deputy director of plans for warfighting concepts briefed CINCCENT in Florida. The CJCS was briefed the following day and directed the Air Staff to expand the planning group to include Navy, Army, and Marine Corps members and to proceed with detailed planning under the authority of the Joint Staff's (JS) director of operations (J3). He reviewed the concept with the Secretary of Defense and received his approval. As the plan was developed further, it continued to be reviewed in detail by the Secretary of Defense and CJCS, culminating in an intensive two-day review of the plan in Saudi Arabia in December. If all went well, air attacks would paralyze Iraqi leadership, degrade their military capabilities, and neutralize their will to fight. (For more details of early air campaign planning, see Chapter VI)

After the Camp David meetings, planning continued at Central Command (CENTCOM) headquarters. On 25 August, CINCCENT briefed the Secretary of Defense and the CJCS on a four-phase offensive campaign, designed to provide a coordinated multi-axis air, naval and ground attack beginning with Phase I, "Strategic Air Campaign" against Iraq; Phase II, "Kuwait Air Campaign" against Iraqi air forces in Kuwait; Phase III, "Ground Combat Power Attrition" to neutralize the Republican Guard and isolate the Kuwait battlefield; and Phase IV, "Ground Attack" to eject Iraqi forces from

Kuwait. At this point, the plan for the ground campaign was in outline form, although no request was made for these forces at this time. CINCCENT concluded that assembling the necessary forces in theater for a ground offensive would take at least eight months. (The precise phase titles later were changed as the plan evolved.)

The development and refinement of the plans continued to be reviewed in detail by the Secretary of Defense and CJCS, culminating in an intensive two-day review of the plan in Saudi Arabia in December.

The initial concept of operations for the ground campaign included use of only a single corps and called for a night ground attack with the objective being an area of high ground north of the Mutla Pass and Ridge, near Al-Jahra and Kuwait City, on the main line of communication (LOC) northwest of Kuwait City. The plan involved an attack north by a single corps, fighting only selected enemy forces, conducting high tempo operations, and overwhelming enemy defenses with mass rather than finesse.

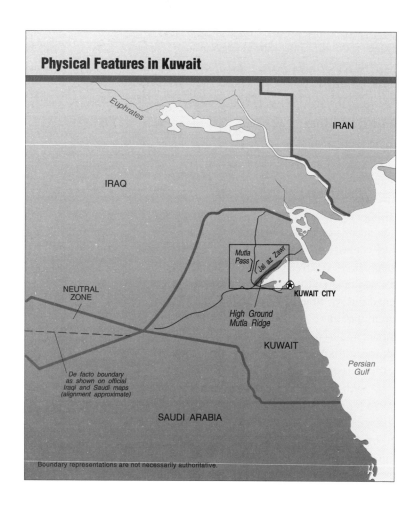

Physical Features in Kuwait

IRAN

IRAQ

Euphrates

NEUTRAL ZONE

Mutla Pass

Jal az Zawr

High Ground Mutla Ridge

KUWAIT CITY

De facto boundary as shown on official Iraqi and Saudi maps (alignment approximate)

KUWAIT

Persian Gulf

SAUDI ARABIA

Boundary representations are not necessarily authoritative.

On 11 October, this plan, with the single corps ground campaign, was briefed to the President, Secretary of Defense, and the CJCS, by the CENTCOM Chief of Staff who conveyed CINCCENT's assessment of the plan. Many risks were outlined, including the possibility of significant casualties; the difficulty of sustaining forces across an extended LOC; the lack of an armor force to serve as theater reserve; and the threat that Iraqi chemical attacks would slow the pace of operations. Further, success depended on several key accomplishments: the air campaign had to produce projected attrition of combat effectiveness to ensure success on the ground; the Coalition had to overcome interoperability obstacles; and the campaign had to end quickly with capitulation of Iraqi forces to avoid a protracted war of attrition. Planning for Phases I-III was sound. However, there were strong reservations concerning Phase IV. The draft plan called for advancing through the southern Kuwait border — 60 kilometers east of the Tri-border area. A frontal attack was to be directed at the enemy's obstacle belts and defensive fortifications and forces.

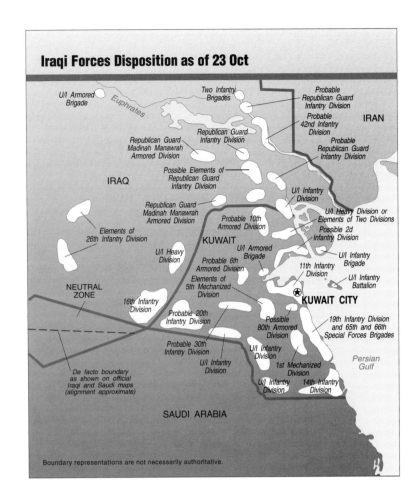

Iraqi Forces Disposition as of 23 Oct

Boundary representations are not necessarily authoritative.

The CENTCOM briefing produced two reactions. One was a concern because the plan called for an attack into the strength of the Iraqi positions. A second concern was that no matter what plan of attack was decided on, there was a need for more forces than were in the Kuwait Theater of Operations (KTO) at the time.

The day after the meeting with the President, the Secretary of Defense directed preparation of options for an attack on Iraqi forces through the western Iraqi desert in lieu of the riskier frontal attack. After consultation with the President, the Secretary of Defense directed CJCS to go to Saudi Arabia in order to find out from CINCCENT what he needed and to tell him that the President would be disposed to give him whatever forces he needed to do the job.

At a meeting of planners on 15 October, CINCCENT directed that the concept of the ground attack include a wider envelopment to the west. Although planning for a single corps attack would continue, CINCCENT directed consideration of a two-corps option as well. The concept of operations for the two-corps option assumed that attrition of crucial ground, air defense and command, control and communication (C^3) systems would be achieved by strategic and tactical air before Phase IV began, and that Iraqi forces would use chemical weapons during the ground attack. The intent was for the air campaign to establish favorable strategic conditions, and to set the stage for the ground offensive. On 21 October, CINCCENT was briefed on the revised offensive plan. He directed that the main effort would be to destroy the RGFC.

On 22 October, the CJCS was briefed in the CENTCOM headquarters on the ground offensive. The CJCS was briefed on both a single and a two-corps attack. The advantages and disadvantages of both options were assessed. Discussion ensued concerning the advisability of using a single corps attack. CINCCENT stated that a single corps frontal attack put the force at risk because Coalition strength was insufficient to attack a force the size of Iraq's. In terms of advantages, the concept for a two-corps attack would permit: massing of Coalition forces; high tempo of operations; fighting only selected Iraqi forces; bypassing of the obstacle belt; and surprise. The disadvantages were the risk to supply lines 180 km long and the risk to the flanks of the main attack which were exposed for about 100 km. The plan sacrificed simplicity and flexibility because of the relative complexity of multiple supporting attacks and the precise timing of the attacks. Discussion ensued concerning the advisability of employing a single corps attack. As a result of the meeting, the CJCS reiterated that CINCCENT should continue planning for a two-corps attack and agreed to seek approval from the Secretary of Defense and the President for additional forces consisting of the VII Corps, the 1st Infantry Division, a Marine division, additional CVBGs, an additional amphibious MEB, and tactical fighter wings.

On 27 October, CJCS asked CINCCENT to develop a plan to conduct an attack with ground forces against Scud fixed launcher complexes at H2 and H3 airfields in the extreme western part of Iraq (H2 and H3 are designations of pumping stations along the now-defunct Iraqi pipeline that terminated at Haifa). Although CENTCOM planners considered some options, this plan later was rejected because of the extended LOC to support the operation and the risk and the demands of planned corps operations.

With the rejection of the plan to attack H2/H3, CENTCOM focused on the corps envelopment options. Direction was issued to expand the area

CAMPAIGN PLANNING

A campaign plan is a plan for a series of related military operations designed to accomplish a common objective, normally within a given time and space. The "Combin-ed OPLAN for Offensive Operations to Eject Iraqi Forces from Kuwait" as finally adopted in January was a combined campaign plan jointly signed by CINCCENT and the Commander, Joint Force/Theater of Operations. It featured related air, land, sea, space and special operations. The common objectives of the plan were de-signed "to counter Iraqi aggression, secure Kuwait, and provide for the establishment of a legitimate government in Kuwait."

As a result of popular use of the word "campaign" when referring to air, land, and sea operations during Operation Desert Storm, confusion exists concerning how many campaigns actually were planned and conducted. Adding to the confusion are the titles used for campaign Phases I (Strategic Air Campaign) and IV (Ground Offensive Campaign) in the combined OPLAN. In fact, there was only one overall theater campaign, divided into four distinct phases: I — Strategic Air Campaign, II — Air Supremacy in the KTO, III — Battlefield Preparation, and IV — Ground Offensive Campaign. The campaign

of offensive operations farther to the west to a road the Iraqis had built from As Salman to the Saudi border. Guidance was given to investigate an area of operations from the vicinity of As-Samawh to the east along Highway 8 to select suitable terrain for a battle to destroy the RGFC in the KTO. Planning assumptions now were based on the availability of: two Army corps, one USMC corps, one corps consisting of two Egyptian divisions and one Syrian division, and Arab forces consisting of Saudi and Gulf Cooperation Council (GCC) forces.

Throughout, trafficability issues played a role in planning. There was concern as to whether wheeled vehicles could negotiate the terrain north of the Saudi-Iraqi border. A secondary concern was cross-country mobility for large trucks west of the Kuwait-Iraq border. A trafficability test was conducted by XVIII

Airborne Corps in the area east of Wadi Al-Batin and south of the Kuwait-Saudi border. The terrain in this location most closely resembled that west of the Wadi Al-Batin and north of the intended line of departure. Tracked and wheeled vehicles were driven cross-country to confirm the terrain could accommodate them.

CENTCOM planners met 1 November to discuss logistics requirements to support Operation Desert Storm. Sustainment in the desert for a second increment of deployments and for existing forces was a major concern. Initial force deployments in August had demonstrated it would be too difficult to receive, move, and sustain more forces in such an austere environment without first deploying additional combat service support (CSS) capabilities. (For a discussion of logistics considerations, see Appendix F). The planners decided to deploy more CSS before combat and combat support (CS) forces. The CSS forces were needed to provide support and transport forces. Contrary to the practice of marshaling units and their equipment at the ports of debarkation, the plan was to receive and push forces directly to assembly areas because the capacity of air and sea ports of debarkation would not support linkup and marshaling operations on the scale and in the time available for the second increment of forces.

On 14 November, CINCCENT conducted a commanders' conference at Dhahran to discuss offensive operations. CINCCENT explained his concept. XVIII Airborne Corps was to be used in the west in the vicinity of As Salman to As Samawah. The European-based VII Corps would be the main effort and destroy the RGFC. British forces would remain with the Marine Corps Component, Central Command (MARCENT) (a decision later reversed). A heavy division was to be assigned as the theater reserve. Supporting attacks would be conducted by the First Marine Expeditionary Force (I MEF), Joint Forces Command - North (consisting of Egyptian, Saudi, and Syrian forces) and Joint Forces Command - East (consisting of Saudi and GCC forces). Commanders were directed to have forces ready by mid-January.

Initially, the United States planned unilaterally for the offensive while simultaneously participating with the Coalition in the defense of Saudi Arabia. Coalition partners became fully involved in planning the overall offensive once the United Nations (UN) and Coalition members agreed to UN Security Council (UNSC) Resolution 678. (Discussion of Resolution 678 is in Appendix B). On 10 December, CINCCENT directed that combined planning begin on the offensive campaign. Each Coalition force had unique strengths and weaknesses which planners had to take into account to achieve the best overall results. Saudi Arabia and Egypt, as the designated planners for

Arab-Islamic forces, were then involved in the detailed planning. On 15 December, a combined warning order was issued to Coalition forces so they could begin their preparations for offensive operations.

On December 19 and 20, the plans were reviewed in detail by the Secretary of Defense and CJCS during the course of two full days of briefings at CINCCENT Headquarters in Riyadh. At the conclusion of that review, the Secretary of Defense gave his approval of the plan. On their return to Washington, he and the Chairman briefed the President, who also approved the plan. At that time, it was decided that if Saddam Hussein refused to withdraw from Kuwait and it became necessary to use force, the offensive would begin with the air campaign. While the ground campaign was approved, its start would be a separate and subsequent decision also requiring Presidential approval. Factors influencing the decision to begin the ground campaign are discussed in Chapter VIII, The Ground Offensive Campaign.

The operational imperatives outlined were:

- Achieve air superiority to allow Coalition freedom of movement and maneuver.
- Reduce to about half the combat effectiveness of Iraqi armor and mechanized forces with Coalition air assets . Of these, reduce selected brigades so the surviving unit was no larger than a battalion.
- Fight only selected Iraqi ground forces in close battle.
- Mass Coalition forces against selected Iraqi forces.
- Accept losses no greater than the equivalent of three companies per Coalition brigade.
- Achieve rapid theater tactical intelligence feedback on battlefield events.
- Use strategic deception to portray a defensive posture.
- Use operational deception to fix or divert Republican Guard and other heavy units

away from main effort.
- Use tactical deception to facilitate penetration of barriers.
- Friendly LOCs must support minimum daily supply requirements.

THE IRAQI THREAT IN OVERVIEW

A central element of military campaign planning is the estimation of enemy forces, including their strengths and weaknesses.

PRINCIPLES OF PLANNING

Decisive Force

In order to achieve assigned goals quickly and with minimum Coalition casualties, US defense planners applied the principle of decisive force. This contrasted with the incremental, attrition warfare which had characterized US operations in Vietnam. When US forces were committed to combat in Southwest Asia, planners were able to exploit every possible advantage in tactics, equipment, command and control, and the forces deployed to the theater at maximum speed. The Coalition used these advantages to conduct massive, simultaneous operations throughout the KTO and Iraq, rather than attacking centers of gravity and other crucial objectives piecemeal.

Strength Against Weakness

The overall offensive strategy was designed according to tested principles of applying strength against the enemy's weakness, while preventing him from doing the same to Coalition forces. Although the Coalition was operating in an environment seemingly more familiar to the opponent, uncertain about Saddam's Husayn's intent to use weapons of mass destruction, operating across an enormous area and with extended LOCs, and was, according to intelligence estimates, outnumbered, the Coalition nevertheless could exploit a number of distinct strengths. Among these were the high quality of Coalition air, ground, and naval forces, specifically:

- Superior personnel and training;
- Technological advantages in weaponry;
- The prospect of early and effective air superiority;
- A superior ability to acquire intelligence throughout the theater, including unimpeded access to space;
- Widespread international support; and,
- The high caliber of Coalition political and military leadership.

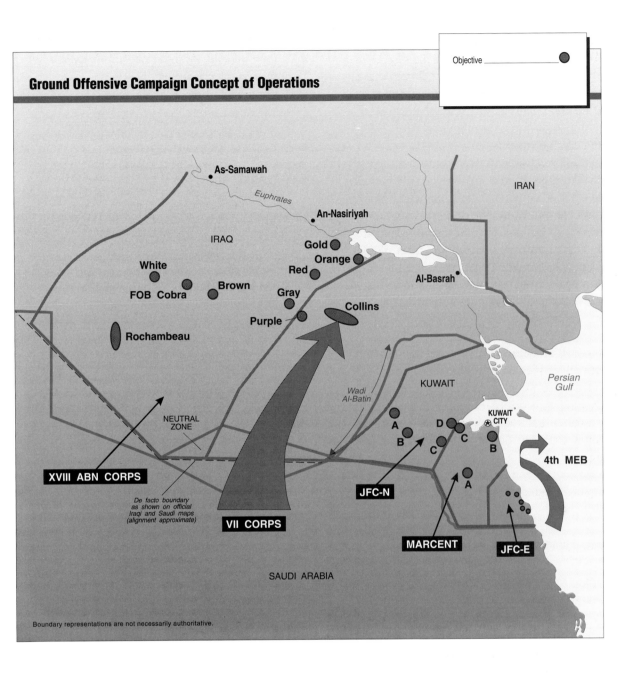

Ground Offensive Campaign Concept of Operations

Objective ———————— ●

As-Samawah

Euphrates

IRAN

An-Nasiriyah

IRAQ

Gold ●
Orange ●
Red ●

White ●

Brown ●

FOB Cobra

Gray ●

Al-Basrah

Collins

Purple ●

Rochambeau

Persian
Gulf

KUWAIT

Wadi
Al-Batin

KUWAIT
CITY

NEUTRAL
ZONE

A ●
B ●

D ●
C ●
C ●
C ●

B ●

4th MEB

XVIII ABN CORPS

A ●

De facto boundary
as shown on official
Iraqi and Saudi maps
(alignment approximate)

VII CORPS

JFC-N

MARCENT

JFC-E

SAUDI ARABIA

Boundary representations are not necessarily authoritative.

Intelligence Estimates

By mid-October, intelligence estimates indicated Saddam Hussein had more than 435,000 troops on the ground in Kuwait, dug in and arrayed in mutually supporting defenses in depth. These forces continued to grow, and were believed to have reached more than 500,000 by January. At least two defensive belts interspersed with formidable triangular fortifications had been established along the Saudi border with Kuwait. These defensive belts consisted of minefields and oil-filled fire trenches, covered by interlocking fields of fire from tanks, artillery, and machine gun positions. Strong, mobile, heavily armored counterattack forces, composed of the best elements of the Iraqi army, stood poised to strike at Coalition penetrations of the initial lines of defense. The Republican Guard units, augmented by army heavy divisions, served as the theater reserve and counterattack force. Equally strong positions were constructed along the sea coast, incorporating naval and land mines. Iraqi troops also fortified high rise apartment buildings fronting on the Gulf, turning them into multi-tiered fortresses.

Iraqi forces constructed an impressive system of roads, buried communications lines and supply depots. Command posts also were buried, often under 25 feet of desert soil. This infrastructure did much to multiply the combat power of an already powerful defensive force. It allowed reinforcements and supplies to move over multiple routes to any point on the battlefield. These roads, many of which were multi-lane, were so numerous that it was not feasible to destroy all of them. Buried telephone lines and fiber optic cables for command and control (C^2) purposes also were very difficult to attack. In early January, stocks of supplies in Kuwait and just north of the Iraq-Kuwait border were estimated to be sufficient to last through a month or more of sustained combat without replenishment, and many of these stocks had been dispersed to make detection and destruction more difficult.

Enemy Vulnerabilities

Despite Iraq's numerical strength and extensive military infrastructure, the Coalition knew the Iraqi forces had significant weaknesses:

■ A rigid, top-down C^2 system and the reluctance of Iraqi commanders to exercise initiative;

■ Ground forces and logistics especially vulnerable to air attack in desert conditions;

■ A generally defensive approach to battle and limited ability to conduct deep offensive operations;

■ An over-extended and cumbersome logistics system;

■ An uneven quality of military forces, built around a limited number of Republican

Guards divisions ;

■ Faulty understanding of Coalition forces' operational capabilities;

■ A limited ability to interfere with US space-based assets;

■ A limited air offensive capability; and,

■ Ineffective foreign intelligence.

Iraqi Centers of Gravity

In addition to these weaknesses, the Coalition had identified Iraq's centers of gravity. First was the command, control, and leadership of the Saddam Hussein regime. If rendered unable to direct its military forces, or to maintain a firm grip on its internal population control mechanisms, Iraq might be compelled to comply with Coalition demands. Second, degrading Iraq's weapons of mass destruction capability would reduce a major part of the threat to other regional states. This meant attacking the known Iraqi nuclear, chemical and biological (NBC) warfare production facilities along with various means of delivery — principally ballistic missiles and long-range aircraft. The third of Iraq's centers of gravity was the Republican Guard. Eliminating the Guard in the KTO as a combat force would reduce dramatically Iraq's ability to conduct a coordinated defense of Kuwait or to pose an offensive threat to the region later.

Prelude To Conflict

As the UN deadline approached, attempts to induce Saddam Hussein to withdraw from Kuwait and comply with UN resolutions continued. Late in December, the 12-member European Community (EC) called for a special session in Luxembourg in an effort to develop a solution to the crisis. On 3 January, President Bush, declaring his willingness to "go the extra mile for peace", offered to send the Secretary of State to meet with the Iraqi Foreign Minister. Such a meeting was conducted in Geneva on 9 January to no avail, as Iraq refused to accede to UN and Coalition demands. On 12 January, the

US Congress passed a Resolution supporting President Bush's decision to use force.

Saddam Hussein, despite repeated warnings and the demonstrated Coalition solidarity, remained defiant. He continued to reinforce his forces in the KTO, while attempting to divide the Coalition through propaganda and political maneuvering. The Iraqis repeatedly attempted to tie US and Western involvement in the crisis to Israel in an attempt to exploit Islamic sensitivities. In this, Saddam Hussein was aided to some extent by Iranian religious leaders who called for Islamic war against Western forces in the Gulf region. This attempt to create an Islamic-Western faultline sought to break up the Coalition by extracting Arab/Islamic states from it. Saddam Hussein repeatedly vowed to inflict massive casualties on US and Coalition forces should war occur — another gambit designed to disrupt the Coalition by eroding popular support. On 30 December, the ruling Ba'ath Party newspaper stated that a war with Iraq would not be confined to the Gulf, but would include a global terrorist campaign against the United States by Moslem guerrilla fighters. On 3 January, Iraq informed the foreign diplomatic corps in Baghdad the government would move all functions out of the capital in preparation for war. Inside Kuwait, harsh measures by Iraqi occupation forces reinforced Saddam Hussein's hard-line rhetoric. Indeed, reports of atrocities committed by Iraqi troops grimly attested to the cruelty of Iraqi occupation. Intelligence sources continued to report systematic looting in Kuwait City, as well as random killing and torture of Kuwait civilians. Saddam Hussein appeared committed to confronting the Coalition.

In the United States, and in many Coalition capitals, some debate continued about whether the economic sanctions and embargo should be given more time. More than $3 billion in Iraqi assets had been frozen worldwide, and Iraqi credit had been severed, along with almost 95 percent of its pre-crisis revenue. The air and naval embargo had sealed off Iraq from the rest of the world, reducing trade to overland smuggling, mostly of foodstuffs. The primary effect of the sanctions, however, was on the civilian rather than military side of the Iraqi economy. Food was rationed, but large-scale shortages had not occurred. Manufacturing of non-essential goods was curtailed. Oil refineries continued at reduced levels, and rationing provided adequate quantities of petroleum, oil and lubricants (POL) for military operations. Although spare parts and crucial components were in short supply, leading to some cannibalization and stripping of commercial vehicles in Kuwait, most units remained combat ready.

FINALIZING THE PLAN

National Policy Objectives and Military Objectives

Plans for possible offensive operations were completed while these events played out. The military objectives for the offensive operation were derived from the national policy objectives discussed in Chapter II. Operation Desert Storm departed from the "deter and defend" objectives of Operation Desert Shield and focused on forcing Iraq to withdraw from Kuwait.

CINCCENT

Mission Statement

CONDUCT OFFENSIVE OPERATIONS TO:
- Neutralize Iraqi National Command Authority
- Eject Iraqi Armed Forces from Kuwait
- Destroy the Republican Guard
- As Early As Possible, Destroy Iraq's Ballistic Missile, NBC Capability
- Assist in the Restoration of the Legitimate Government of Kuwait

In accordance with that mission statement, CINCCENT promulgated the key theater military objectives as stated in CENTCOM Operations Order 91-001, dated 17 January as follows:

- Attack Iraqi political-military leadership and C^2;
- Gain and maintain air superiority;
- Sever Iraqi supply lines;
- Destroy known nuclear, biological and chemical (NBC) production, storage, and delivery capabilities;
- Destroy Republican Guard forces in the KTO; and,
- Liberate Kuwait City.

THE PLAN IS ADOPTED

As a result of the extensive planning process described above with its attendant, frequent consultation among the political and military leaders of the Coalition, the final, four-phased concept of operations was developed and adopted.

As noted, the Coalition plan was crafted to emphasize Coalition strengths and to exploit Iraqi weaknesses. Years of experience in joint service, air-ground operations and similarly extensive experience in coalition operations in the North Atlantic Treaty Organization enabled CENTCOM to create the right mix of forces for the circumstances confronting the Coalition. Especially within US forces, the experience gained from many joint and combined exercises, the presence of first-rate equipment and weapons, and the advantage of well-trained, motivated personnel led by confident, competent leaders resulted in military forces that could not only execute their battle plans, but also could improvise and overcome the unexpected. (For a detailed discussion of US military preparedness see Appendix D.) Further, well-coordinated air, ground and naval operations were expected to produce a synergy that would overwhelm Saddam Hussein with minimum Coalition losses.

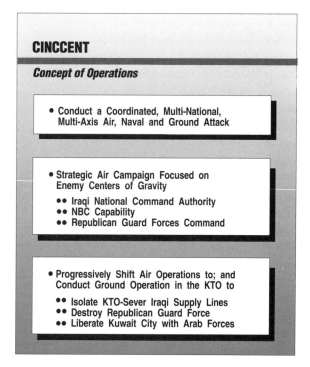

Just as the theater campaign plan contemplated Coalition strengths, it anticipated Saddam Hussein's weaknesses. The Coalition heavily targeted his rigid C^2 system, his strategy, doctrine, logistics infrastructure and air defense system vulnerabilities. Similarly, expecting the Iraqi army would be unable to see the battlefield in depth, the Coalition planned the long, sweeping ground force maneuvers through the desert against a blinded enemy.

Coalition political leaders and commanders planned to use air power and ground combat power to eject Iraq's forces from Kuwait. The Coalition also sought to destroy Iraqi ability to

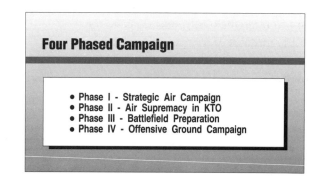

threaten regional peace and stability further. The Coalition would accomplish this by attacking carefully selected targets, but leave most of the basic economic infrastructure of the country intact. Collectively, these actions would weaken Saddam Hussein's regime and set the stage for a stable regional military balance.

Air Campaign Plan in Overview

The air campaign was developed to provide the President an offensive option in the early fall. It was a "strategic" plan designed to attack Saddam Hussein's vital centers of gravity. The concept was designed to paralyze the Iraqi leadership's ability to command and control (C^2) its forces, to destroy known Iraqi weapons of mass destruction, to render Iraqi forces in the KTO combat ineffective, to prepare the battlefield for ground force operations, and to minimize the loss of life for Coalition forces. The air campaign was designed to be executed in three phases and its success depended on overwhelming the Iraqi military command structure and air defenses, gaining accurate intelligence, exploiting technological advantages, and, ultimately, on the ability of the combat crews. Once the air attacks had brought the ratios of combat power to an acceptable level, and if the Iraqis had not yet complied with UN demands, multinational air and ground forces would conduct a coordinated combined arms attack to eject Iraqi forces occupying Kuwait and to destroy those forces remaining in the KTO. By January, there were enough air forces available that Coalition leaders decided to execute the three phases of the air campaign almost simultaneously, thus applying overwhelming pressure from the opening minutes of the war. (Chapter VI provides detailed discussion on the Air Campaign.)

The air campaign was intended to achieve the specific objectives listed below:

■ Gain and maintain air supremacy to permit

Theater Campaign Plan and Military Objectives

Theater Objectives	PHASE I Strategic Air Campaign	PHASE II Air Supremacy in the KTO	PHASE III Battlefield Prep	PHASE IV Ground Offensive Campaign
Leadership/C³	X			
Air Supremacy	X	X		
Cut Supply Lines	X	X	X	X
NBC Capability	X		X	
Destroy Republican Guards	X		X	X
Liberate Kuwait City				X

unhindered air and ground operations.
■ Isolate and incapacitate the Iraqi regime.
■ Destroy Iraq's known NBC warfare capability.
■ Eliminate Iraq's offensive military capability by destroying key military production, infrastructure, and power capabilities.
■ Render the Iraqi army and its mechanized equipment in Kuwait ineffective, causing its collapse.

Ground Campaign Plan in Overview

The ground campaign plan envisioned a main attack coming as a "left hook" by armor-heavy forces against Iraq's right flank, sweeping in from the west to avoid most fixed defenses and to attack one of Saddam Hussein's centers of gravity, the Republican Guard armored and mechanized divisions. Overwhelming combat power; rapid maneuver; deception; a sound, combined arms approach; a well-trained, highly motivated body of troops; and a skilled team of combat leaders in the field, were crucial factors in the plan for the success of the ground phase. The main attack would be supported by an elaborate deception operation, including an amphibious feint, and by supporting attacks along the Kuwaiti-Saudi border to fix Iraqi forces in Kuwait and to liberate Kuwait City. Throughout, the plan was intended to achieve the objectives decisively and with minimum casualties. (Chapter VIII provides detailed discussion on the Ground Campaign.)

Objectives for the ground attack were:

- To complete the envelopment with a US corps sized armored force positioned west of the Republican Guards Forces Command (RGFC) and a US corps armored force positioned south of the RGFC. A combined Egyptian, Syrian, Saudi, Nigerien, and Kuwaiti armored heavy force would be positioned on the north-south LOCs in Kuwait.
- Draw Iraq's reserve forces away from the main attack with deception, feints and two supporting attacks.
- The US supporting attack was to defend the right flank of the main attack from a counterattack by the tactical reserves, draw forces away from the main attack, and block LOCs.
- The main attack was to bypass forces and attack west of the Kuwait border, occupying a position to the west of the RGFC to prevent successful counterattack by Iraq's strategic reserve and attack the RGFC.
- Conduct psychological operations (PSYOP) to degrade Iraqi morale.
- Use Special Operations Forces (SOF) for deception, direct action, and surveillance.
- Use electronic warfare to disrupt Iraqi communications from corps to brigade after this first supporting attack began; from corps to General Headquarters before the western supporting attack began.

Maritime Campaign Plan in Overview

NAVCENT planned its major maritime tasks within the framework of CENTCOM's four-phased theater campaign plan. During phases I and II of the CENTCOM campaign plan, (strategic air strikes and air superiority over the KTO), the NAVCENT plan directed conduct of the air operation in accordance with the air tasking order; sea control and mine countermeasure operations in the northern Persian Gulf; and strikes at shore facilities threatening naval operations. During Phase III (battlefield preparation), Navy plans called for attacking Iraqi ground forces with naval air and gunfire and continuing phase I and II operations. The final tasks in the NAVCENT plan would take place during Phase IV (Offensive Ground Campaign). Naval and amphibious forces would conduct feints and demonstrations in the KTO; be prepared to conduct amphibious operations to link up with I MEF near Ash Shuaybah; and, continue execution of Phase I, II, and III tasks. (Chapter VII provides detailed discussion on the Maritime Campaign.)

Navy Component, Central Command (NAVCENT's) primary objectives were to:

- Provide naval operations in support of Coalition ground, air, and sea units.
- Support maritime interception operations.
- Provide naval tactical aircraft and Tomahawk land-attack missiles strikes against Iraqi forces.
- Maintain an expeditionary amphibious assault capability.
- Conduct offensive operations in the Northern Persian Gulf.
- Defend the coastlines of Saudi Arabia, United Arab Emirates, Qatar, Bahrain, Oman, and to patrol adjacent maritime areas.

Deception Operations Plan in Overview

Throughout the planning process, CINCCENT emphasized the need for a comprehensive plan to deceive Iraqi forces regarding Coalition intentions and to conceal the Coalition scheme of maneuver. The deception plan was intended to convince Iraq the Coalition main attack would be directly into Kuwait, supported by an amphibious assault. The plan also sought to divert Iraqi forces from the Coalition main attack and to fix Iraqi forces in eastern Kuwait and along the Kuwaiti coast.

All components contributed to the deception. Among the activities planned to support the deception were Navy feints and demonstrations in the northern Persian Gulf, Marine landing exercises along the Gulf and Omani coast, positioning of a large amphibious task force in the Gulf, and air refueling and training activity surges that desensitized the Iraqis to the real pre-attack buildup. The absence of air attacks on some western targets was also to contribute to the impression the Coalition main attack would come from the vicinity of the Saudi-Kuwaiti border and from the sea. This impression was to be reinforced by USMC and Joint Forces East (JFC-E) operations south of Kuwait to fix Iraqi divisions along Kuwait's southern border. Raids and some SOF activities were expected to contribute to Saddam Hussein's confusion as to the most likely location for the main attack.

In early November, intelligence projections indicated three more Iraqi infantry divisions could deploy to the KTO in the next two to three months. Buildup of Coalition forces south of Kuwait was attracting stronger Iraqi defensive deployments. Also, Coalition force buildup in the west caused the Iraqis to shift forces in the western KTO opposite Coalition forces. Because of Iraqi responses to Coalition deployments, a proposal to begin a near-term buildup of supplies at King Khalid Military City for the offensive was rejected. Such a buildup was certain to compromise the intended position for launching the main attack. For these same reasons, a proposed early buildup of combat forces in the west was prohibited. Instead, forces initially deployed to base camps in eastern Saudi

> "The President did things for us that were enormously helpful. When it was time to double the size of the force that we deployed, it would have been a relatively simple proposition to say let's see if we can't do it with smaller forces. He consistently said do whatever you have to to assemble the force and make certain that in the final analysis we can prevail at the lowest possible cost."
>
> *Dick Cheney*
> *Secretary of Defense*
> *21 March 1991*

Arabia and then moved forward to attack positions when their movements were covered by the air campaign.

None of the divisions would move until the air war had begun. Together, that and the planned ground, counter-reconnaissance battles would hinder Saddam Hussein's ability to detect and effectively react. The 1st Cavalry Division was to remain in the east, simulating the activities of the divisions which moved west, so Iraqi intelligence would not notice their absence. The 1st and 2nd Marine Divisions (MARDIV) conducted combined arms raids along the Kuwaiti border to confuse the Iraqis and focus their attention on the east. Finally, operations security practices supported deception.

THE DECISION TO REINFORCE, NOVEMBER 1990

As the weeks went by, Saddam Hussein showed no signs of abiding by the UNSC resolutions calling for his withdrawal from Kuwait. Operation Desert Shield appeared to have met its objective of deterring an Iraqi drive into Saudi Arabia; however, Kuwait was still under Iraqi occupation. CENTCOM had developed a viable offensive campaign plan which involved considerable risk.

Opposing the 27 Iraqi divisions in the KTO, US forces in October consisted of XVIII Airborne Corps with four Army divisions, I MEF, three CVBG, an amphibious task force (ATF), and more than five fighter and bomb wing equivalents.

On 8 November, the President announced the deployment of additional US forces into theater. Forces moved during this phase included more than 400 additional USAF aircraft; three additional CVBGs; the 1st Infantry Division (Mechanized) and an armored brigade from the United States; and the VII Corps from Germany, which included two armored divisions and an armored cavalry regiment. Additionally, the 2nd MARDIV, an ATF carrying the 5th MEB, and II MEF air and logistics elements were prepared for deployment. On 14 November, the Secretary of Defense increased reserve call-up authorization for the Army to 80,000 Selected Reserves; the Navy to 10,000; the USMC to 15,000; and the USAF to 20,000. On 1 December, the Secretary again increased the call-up authorization. The Service Secretaries now were authorized to call-up 188,000 Selected Reserve members. This authorization included as many as 115,000 from the Army; 30,000 Navy; 23,000 USMC and 20,000 USAF.

As these forces continued to deploy, so did those from other Coalition partners. The remainder of what would be the major combat elements of Joint Forces Command-North moved to positions north of Hafr Al-Batin. This included the rest of the 9th Syrian Armored Division and the 4th Egyptian Armored Division. The final elements of 1st UK Armoured Division, whose 7th UK Armoured Brigade had arrived earlier and was attached to I MEF, arrived in late December. Additional French reinforcements arrived during this period. By mid-January, all units that were to participate in the liberation of Kuwait had arrived in Saudi Arabia or were en route.

Iraq also increased its forces in the KTO. On 19 November, Saddam Hussein announced he was reinforcing with an additional 250,000 men. This was to be accomplished by mobilizing seven additional divisions and activating

150,000 reservists and draftees; these units began arriving immediately. By early January, the Iraqi KTO order of battle had reached the equivalent of 43 divisions organized into four corps and the RGFC. These included seven armored, four mechanized, 29 infantry, one special operations division, and several separate brigades. CENTCOM estimated the forces had more than 4,500 tanks, 2,800 armored personnel carriers, and 3,200 artillery pieces. Iraq could deploy no more meaningful combat power to the KTO. Nearly all of its armored and mechanized divisions were committed to the theater; more infantry would only add to the logistics burden and strip the rest of Iraq of internal security forces.

As additional US and Coalition air and ground combat forces arrived, offensive plans were adjusted to use the full array of available military power. Coalition strength increased steadily. By early February, with the deployment of 500 additional strike aircraft from the United States and Europe, the VII Corps from Germany, substantial Marine forces from II MEF, a MEB on amphibious ships and additional Naval reinforcement, as well as the arrival of substantial numbers of Arab/Islamic and allied troops and equipment, the Coalition had the forces necessary for ground offensive operations to liberate Kuwait with acceptable risk.

REINFORCEMENT AND SUSTAINMENT

As the combat forces grew in-country, the demand for support — CS and CSS — grew proportionately. The US theater force structure had to be tailored to meet the demand. Since most Army CS and CSS units as well as some essential combat units are in the Reserve Components (RC), the military services asked for and received additional authority to call more units and individuals to active duty. In late November, the Secretary of Defense determined the Presidential Call Up Authority announced 8 November was insufficient to meet the needs of the theater of operations. The JCS examined their requirements and prepared a decision briefing for the President. At that mid-December briefing, the Services explained their complete unit requirements. The President agreed to authorize the ceiling limits set forth in Section 673, Title 10, Partial Mobilization. A Presidential Order was drafted and enacted on 18 January. Even with the Partial Mobilization authority in place, additional latitude gained for the RC recall, stop-loss authority, and related measures, the military force structure still lacked certain types of CS and CSS units. Host Nation Support units and third nation donations covered the short-fall. (An in-depth discussion of non-US Coalition contributions is in Appendices I and P).

ARCENT's 22nd Support Command (SUPCOM) created the theater ground support plan, and provided and orchestrated most logistics support for US and some other Coalition forces. The ARCENT SUPCOM was the executive agent for food, water, bulk fuel, common ground munitions, port operations, inland cargo transportation, construction support, and grave registration for all US forces. The SUPCOM support plan included five phases. Phase Alpha involved repositioning support units and stocks to the north along main supply route (MSR) Dodge, while simultaneously receiving and moving VII Corps to its tactical assembly areas. SUPCOM also built large logistic bases during this phase along MSR Dodge to support ARCENT units. Phase Bravo involved moving simultaneously both the XVIII Airborne Corps and VII Corps to their attack positions. The 22nd SUPCOM helped by providing the heavy transportation assets needed to move the corps over the several hundred miles of desert. Two corps support commands established two new bases to support each corps when the offensive began. Phase Charlie entailed support and sustainment of the ground offensive into Iraq and Kuwait. The support plan called for transport of all classes of supply, especially fuel, water, and ammunition, and

construction of additional logistics bases deep in Iraq to sustain the offensive. During Phase Delta, SUPCOM and Civil Affairs units supported efforts to restore facilities and services inside liberated Kuwait. Phase Echo focused on preparations for the defense of Kuwait for the longer term.

SUPCOM benefited from extensive Saudi, European, and third-nation contributions in supporting Coalition combat forces. Saudi Arabia, for example, provided approximately 4,800 tents; 1.7 million gallons of packaged petroleum, oil and lubricants; more than 300 heavy equipment transporters (HETs); about 20 million meals; on average more than 20.5 million gallons of fuel a day; and bottled water for the entire theater. Even with this level of support, ARCENT still found it necessary to continue to hunt for such critical equipment as HETs to acquire enough rolling stock to move VII Corps to its attack positions.

The focus of combat service support for MARCENT was the 1st Force Service Support Group (FSSG). The 1st FSSG had the additional tasking to maintain the Al-Jubayl Port as a major logistical node for CENTCOM. The 1st FSSG used organic motor transport assets from the 7th and 8th Motor Transport Battalions, commercial vehicles driven by the Marines of 6th Motor Transport Battalion (USMCR), Army cargo trucks, CH-46 and CH-53 helicopters as well as USAF and USMC C-130s to move supplies from the ports to the forward combat service support areas. The 1st FSSG also provided mobile combat service support detachments to regimental-size maneuver elements.

As the US forces built up the in-theater logistics and sustainment base, they also undertook an ambitious modernization program. Units deploying from the Continental United States (CONUS) arrived with current equipment. Within about three months, these units had their equipment upgraded or replaced. The Army

Material Command managed some of the modernization effort through its control element in theater. Perhaps one of the more important new items issued was the global positioning system (GPS). The GPS enabled units to navigate accurately despite the absence of prominent terrain features to guide them. Other improvements included upgrades to the Bradley Fighting Vehicle, and new trucks to improve CSS capabilities.

DECISION TO BEGIN THE OFFENSIVE

The final decision to begin Operation Desert Storm was not made by the President until early January, allowing the diplomatic overtures to Saddam Hussein's government the opportunity to succeed. Senior commanders were given the tentative go ahead for the attack just four days before the 15 January deadline. These four days provided time to concentrate on last-minute details for the execution of the complex operational plan. Unit commanders worked throughout the last days refining their plans for when the "green light had been flashed," as one commander termed the time before launching the attack. Coordination between Airborne Warning and Control System, Joint Surveillance Target Attack Radar System, air refueling tankers and numerous Coalition air forces continued in exercises up until the day before the air attack.

TRAINING FOR THE ATTACK

Coalition forces conducted a wide variety of training once they arrived in the theater of operations, ranging from some common to all (e.g., desert survival, chemical and biological warfare protective measures, and local customs) to very mission-specific training once the war plans evolved in enough detail to allow units to rehearse. In addition, some units underwent extensive new equipment training to master M1A1 tanks and other major weapons systems issued in theater. (All of the Army divisions which deployed from the CONUS received the new tanks. This meant each division had to retrain about 325 tank crews, a major challenge for units about to go on the offensive.)

Air forces trained extensively after arrival in theater to become familiar with the desert flying environment. The deploying air forces faced the challenge of strange fields, bare base operating conditions, and long sortie durations because of the distances to targets in Iraq. The numbers and types of aircraft from all the Coalition members also meant that procedures had to be created for airspace management and common safety practices instituted. One example of this was the management of airspace and tankers to provide refueling for the thousands of aircraft that would fly daily in Operation Desert Storm. Because of the distances involved, most sorties required refueling. Although in-flight refueling is normally routine, the number of fighters and tankers operating near each other, often at night and sometimes in bad weather, added another layer of planning and difficulty to every mission. With a limited number of tankers available, procedures had to be established to get the maximum number of fighters serviced by each tanker in the shortest time possible.

The aircrews also trained to execute specific roles in the air operation. In some cases, this meant refining medium altitude tactics and practicing multiple weapons deliveries. The weather, threats, and targets in Kuwait and Iraq allowed medium altitude, multiple attacks instead of the low altitude, single pass attacks once the air environment had been shaped by air superiority and SEAD attacks. Advanced training programs such as Red Flag and Cope Thunder had laid an important foundation of skills upon which the aircrews of Operation Desert Storm built.

Ground forces generally practiced obstacle breaching techniques, attack of strongpoints, land navigation, night operations, and chemical defense. Commanders emphasized maneuver warfare in anticipation of the deep envelopment that was central to the scheme of maneuver. Most units also practiced combined arms training, integrating supporting arms, close-in fire support, air strikes, artillery fires, and use of attack helicopters with the scheme of maneuver. The 82nd Airborne Division built its own model of an Iraqi triangular defense work based on observer reports of the Iran-Iraq war. The 101st Airborne Division (Air Assault) used an abandoned village to practice fighting in an urban setting. I MEF conducted extensive live fire exercises to ensure all weapons were boresighted and zeroed. It also carried out extensive combined arms training, integrating supporting arms and close air support (CAS), to build mutual confidence between air and ground units. The MEF also constructed a mock-up of a typical Iraqi defensive strongpoint and rehearsed ways of attacking it.

Much training focused on the unique problems of desert warfare. Almost all of the Army's units benefited from training at the National Training Center (NTC), Fort Irwin, CA. Certain units like the 24th Infantry Division (Mechanized) and the USMC divisions stressed desert warfare in their training programs. Marines of the I MEF had extensive experience at the Marine Corps Air-Ground Combat Center (MCAGCC) at 29 Palms, CA. Prior training received at the NTC and MCAGCC major maneuver training areas proved to be of great value in the desert.

The USMC 2nd Tank Battalion and elements of the reserve 4th Tank Battalion had recently changed from the M60A1 to the M1 tank, and, when they arrived in theater, conducted extensive live fire training to hone their newly acquired skills.

Between late August and early January, the aircraft carriers *USS Saratoga* (CV 60), *USS Kennedy* (CV 67), and *USS Midway* (CV 41), together with their escorts, participated in exercises that were, in many ways, similar to the advanced training phase normally used by battle groups to prepare for overseas deployment. The training focus for the air wings included repulsing a potential Iraqi attack into Saudi Arabia, air and sea control, and airspace coordination in a dense air traffic environment.

In November, USMC, Navy, and USAF aircraft, and Navy Ships participated in Exercise Imminent Thunder. The final rehearsal of the Operation Desert Shield defensive plan included joint and combined air, ground, and naval portions, and an amphibious landing. The training was to prove invaluable in the offensive campaign.

Other local exercises dealt with the USAF and Naval Air Groups working on common tasks such as air interdiction, CAS, and combat search and rescue. These exercises were used to simplify peacetime rules and to coordinate procedures for implementation during the actual strike missions over Iraq or Kuwait. To increase the offensive posture and present a different air defense picture to the Iraqi defenders in Kuwait, the USAF began Operation Border Look on 17 December. The operation ran six days and allowed the Coalition to collect data on the Iraqi air defense radars and their ability to detect Coalition aircraft.

Exercises and training also were conducted across thousands of miles, between CENTCOM and Space Command (SPACECOM) forces, to develop and refine Scud warning procedures. SPACECOM cut the warning times for a Scud launch in half. CENTCOM developed ways to warn Patriot batteries and Coalition forces of Scud launches, letting Coalition units take cover and aiding Patriot units to intercept in-coming missiles.

EVE OF DESERT STORM

Status of Coalition Forces

As the UN deadline approached Coalition air forces conducted final preparations and ground forces continued to move into assembly areas.

Coalition aircraft were placed on ground alert and aircrews began mission planning as details of the air campaign were released. Along the Saudi coast south of the Kuwait border, JFC-E, composed of Saudi and CGG units, continued to train in preparation for attacking directly toward Kuwait City while manning defensive positions along the border. On their left, I MEF was displacing its logistics bases and moving the 1st and 2nd MARDIV into assembly areas for final attack rehearsals. Farther west, Arab-Islamic forces from JFC-N, consisting of Egyptian, Syrian, Kuwaiti, Nigerien, and Saudi units, continued to screen the border area north of Hafr Al-Batin. VII Corps, still arriving from Europe and including the 1st UK Armoured Division, continued to move its forces across the desert roads to assembly areas west of Wadi Al-Batin, while the XVIII Airborne Corps displaced even farther west, where it linked with the 6th French Light Armored Division. (Chapter VI — Air Campaign and Chapter VIII — Ground Campaign provide maps and graphics depicting disposition of Coalition Forces)

Coalition forces exhibited a readiness that, in many cases, exceeded peacetime expectations. For US forces, maintenance readiness of such major items as M1 tanks, M2/3 fighting vehicles, AH-64 attack helicopters, and AV-8B attack aircraft often exceeded 90 percent. Some units, such as the USMC 2nd Tank Battalion recently had received Abrams tanks. The 1st UK Armoured Division was equipped with the Challenger tank, considered one of the better main battle tanks built. Saudi, Qatari and Kuwaiti forces, accompanied by US and other advisors, trained constantly, displaying a confidence in their capabilities. Kuwait Army units had been rebuilt since the Iraqi invasion and were now equipped with modern Yugoslav M84 tanks and Soviet BMP-2 infantry fighting vehicles. Although long LOCs and harsh conditions strained the structure, equipment and supplies continued to flow into the theater in order to meet the stockage levels CENTCOM

established and supply points located at forward sites in the desert were stockpiling for combat.

Perhaps most important, the morale of Coalition troops, who felt confident they could defeat the Iraqis in battle, was high. Discipline problems were almost nonexistent. Cross-training between US and other Coalition forces, conducted throughout Operation Desert Shield, ensured mutual understanding. Among Coalition troops, high morale reinforced the advantages of superior equipment and training.

Status of Iraqi Forces

It was not clear until the offensive had begun that Saddam Hussein would choose to remain on the defensive. Iraqi preparations throughout the prior months had continued to raise the readiness of forces and it was estimated that they remained capable of launching an offensive (as they were later to attempt at Al-Khafji). The Iraqi Air Force stepped up training and defensive patrols from airfields in central and southern Iraq. Intelligence analysts estimated the Iraqi Air Force to be capable of surging up to 900 to 1,000 sorties daily, although the Iraqi capability to sustain such a sortie rate was questioned. Air C^2, logistics, and maintenance sites had been dispersed and hardened. Surface-to-surface missiles, most notably the Scud, had been on alert for several months and several test firings were conducted in the late Fall. The Scuds were capable of reaching targets in Saudi Arabia from southern Iraq. Some intelligence analysts predicted many launchers would be exceedingly difficult to locate because of their mobility and ability to hide. Iraq also emplaced Silkworm missiles at strategic coastal points and actively mined Persian Gulf waterways. Surface-to-air missiles (SAM) and antiaircraft artillery (AAA) remained concentrated around major population centers and strategic military targets. Many of Iraq's SAM launchers, even those with mobile capabilities, were tied to point defense of fixed targets. At least one battery of captured Kuwaiti

HAWK missiles was thought to have been positioned south of Baghdad. While the air defense system used by Iraq could provide centralized control of antiair assets, barrage fire was thought by Coalition intelligence analysts to be the most probable means of air defense engagements, particularly with AAA.

Iraqi weapons of mass destruction, particularly CW, posed a formidable threat. Although Iraqi nerve agents deteriorated after being placed in munitions, DIA assessed on 11 January that Iraq was probably in the final stages of an additional chemical production cycle and that munition fill activity was continuing, putting the chemical arsenal on a high level of readiness. Moreover, some Iraqi weapons, such as mustard agents, did not deteriorate and others remained dangerous even after deterioration. Most artillery in the Iraqi inventory was capable of firing chemical shells, and aircraft could be armed with chemical bombs or spray tanks. Iraqi training emphasized the use of CW. During the later stages of the Iran-Iraq war, tactical commanders displayed a keen understanding of the use of CW, often fully integrating them into their fire support plans. Although some units, particularly infantry and People's Army units, were short of chemical protective equipment, the stated willingness of Saddam Hussein to use CW combined with the Iraqi army's extensive prior use of CW made the threat of great concern to the Coalition.

Inside the KTO, at least 43 divisions were arrayed in depth with strong operational and tactical reserves. In Kuwait and stretching several miles into southern Iraq, Iraqi infantry had established two belts of minefields and obstacles, backed by trench lines and strongpoints. Thousands of mines had been sown in the sands, covered by extensive barbed wire obstacles, fire trenches, antitank ditches and berms. Dug-in infantry was reinforced by revetted tanks and artillery, all backed by armored reserves of brigade strength or larger.

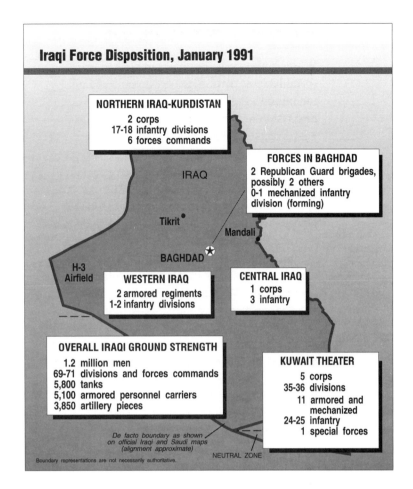

Iraqi Force Disposition, January 1991

NORTHERN IRAQ-KURDISTAN
2 corps
17-18 infantry divisions
6 forces commands

FORCES IN BAGHDAD
2 Republican Guard brigades, possibly 2 others
0-1 mechanized infantry division (forming)

IRAQ

Tikrit

Mandali

BAGHDAD

H-3 Airfield

WESTERN IRAQ
2 armored regiments
1-2 infantry divisions

CENTRAL IRAQ
1 corps
3 infantry

OVERALL IRAQI GROUND STRENGTH
1.2 million men
69-71 divisions and forces commands
5,800 tanks
5,100 armored personnel carriers
3,850 artillery pieces

KUWAIT THEATER
5 corps
35-36 divisions
11 armored and mechanized
24-25 infantry
1 special forces

De facto boundary as shown on official Iraqi and Saudi maps (alignment approximate)

Boundary representations are not necessarily authoritative.

NEUTRAL ZONE

Along the beaches, in testimony to Iraqi concern about an amphibious assault, no fewer than four infantry divisions and a mechanized division dug in behind minefields and obstacles, while strongly fortifying coastal sections of Kuwait City. In central Kuwait, roughly in the area between Ali As-Salim Air Base and the Kuwait International Airport, one armored and two mechanized divisions formed strong corps-level reserves. with additional forces to the northwest. Along the main north-south road from Kuwait City to Iraq stood an operational reserve of several regular Army armored and mechanized divisions. Positioned along the Iraq-Kuwait border, the theater reserve of at least six Republican Guards Divisions and other Army armored, mechanized, and infantry divisions formed the backbone of Iraqi forces in the KTO.

Iraqi Defensive Concept of Operations

While it was clear Iraq had established a formidable array of defenses in the KTO, its intentions were not clear at the time. The discussion in this section is drawn from post-war intelligence assessments.

The front line infantry divisions were to defend in sector from prepared positions. The commander of the 27th Infantry Division, VII Corps, stated his mission had been very clear, "to defend Wadi Al-Batin, period." Immediately behind the forward-deployed infantry divisions was a corps reserve. In addition to infantry divisions, the VII Corps, in the ARCENT main attack zone, deployed the 52nd Armored Division, and the IV Corps, just east of the Wadi and opposite the Multinational Force Corps, deployed the 6th Armored and 1st Mechanized divisions. The mission of the reserve forces was to counterattack any Coalition penetration within their respective sectors.

To the rear of the corps reserve was the operational reserve. In the western part of the KTO, the operational reserve was the Jihad Corps. It was composed of the 10th and 12th Armored divisions, its mission was to either counterattack, or to occupy blocking positions in the event of a Coalition penetration. In the eastern part of the KTO the operational reserve was the II Armored Corps comprised of the 51st Mechanized Infantry Division and the 17th Armored Division. Its missions were similar to the Jihad Corps, with the addition of countering expected airborne and amphibious assaults in Kuwait and Southern Iraq.

Behind the theater reserves, deployed in a crescent formation in Southern Iraq just north of the IV and VII Corps, was the RGFC as a theater reserve, composed of the Tawakalna Mechanized Infantry Division, the Medinah Armored Division, and the Hammurabi Armored Division. Once the main thrust of the Coalition was apparent and had been reduced by the forward divisions, the corps reserves, and the operational reserve, the RGFC would be committed as a corps to destroy the Coalition main attack.

Military Balance

By late December, CENTCOM had assessed the balance of ground forces using an assumption that the air campaign would succeed in destroying or neutralizing approximately half of the Iraqi forces in the KTO. The analysis was based on heavy brigades and was computed by axes of attack, for the main phases of the ground attack (i.e., before the breach, en route to final objectives, and before final objectives). The overall force correlations by attack axis were (Coalition forces/Iraqi forces): supporting attack 1.3/1; main attack 1.4/1; Egyptian/Syria attack 1.4/1; and MEF 0.75/1. The force correlations at the final objective (RGFC) for the supporting and main attacks were 2.7/1 and 2.2/1, respectively. These force ratios were believed to be sufficiently favorable to ensure success.

As noted earlier, Iraqi forces also exhibited several weaknesses, some of which were not appreciated until after action surveys were conducted. Although equipped with large numbers of fighter and attack aircraft, including modern French and Soviet fighters, the Air Force was built around a core of obsolescent planes. The Iraqis were almost totally reliant on tactical intelligence systems and human intelligence to discern Coalition dispositions; as the war proceeded, Iraqi forces became almost totally blind. Finally, the Iraqis had assumed a static defensive posture, conceding the initiative to the Coalition. Obstacles dug in September and October had been neglected in the following weeks. Some minefields had been exposed by wind and mines could be seen from the air or by approaching ground troops. Many alternate positions and trenches had filled with sand. Maintenance of equipment suffered from the embargo and extended logistics lines. In some cases, units resorted to cannibalization to meet maintenance needs. As the UN deadline approached, intelligence analysts detected some indications of morale and cohesion problems among some front line Iraqi troops in the KTO. Later information revealed that those problems had become increasingly severe in many units.

Despite its core of highly trained and motivated Republican Guards and a few elite regular Army units, the bulk of the Iraqi Army was composed of poorly trained conscripts. Most infantry divisions in Kuwait, charged with defending the extensive minefields, were made up of these second-class troops. As post-war information was to show, desertions, particularly in some front-line infantry units, became almost epidemic. Many soldiers simply went home. Iraqi propaganda and political maneuvering resulted in a backlash among Iraqi troops, particularly those in Kuwait. They began to realize they had been placed in the distasteful position of an occupying force in another Islamic country, faced with fighting their religious and cultural brothers. Increasing numbers of deserters expressed a growing antipathy towards Saddam Hussein, some claiming their comrades would not fight. Reports of Iraqi discipline squads, ordered to shoot deserters, began to filter into Coalition intelligence. Those Iraqi soldiers who remained suffered from food shortages. To induce them to stay, Saddam Hussein authorized special increases in pay; the troops were given worthless script which only served to make them more cynical.

Nevertheless, the Iraqi order of battle on the eve of war was formidable. DIA assessed Iraq to have 540,000 troops, more than 4,200 tanks, more than 2,800 armored personnel carriers, and approximately 3,100 artillery pieces fielded in the KTO. They could draw on up to 30 days of ammunition stockpiled in Kuwait and southern Iraq in the event of combat, with at least three days of ammunition being carried by each unit. An extensive air defense umbrella of AAA and SAM, to include several SA-2 and SA-3

launchers in Kuwait, provided some protection from air attack. These systems were highly mobile and capable of putting up a substantial challenge to Coalition aircraft, particularly those that attacked using low-level tactics. Although few aircraft were based inside the KTO, the Iraqi Air Force had demonstrated the capability to shift aircraft rapidly and conduct strikes and air defense operations throughout the KTO as well as into Saudi Arabia. The Iraqi Navy positioned missile-firing fast patrol boats and coastal defense surface-to-surface missiles along the Kuwaiti coast that could disrupt any attempts at amphibious landings. More importantly, Iraqi mine layers had begun sowing mines in the northern Gulf to help ward off any Coalition amphibious attack.

On the Coalition side, total numbers roughly equaled Iraqi totals, but ground forces were thought to be numerically inferior. Despite that apparent disadvantage, Coalition forces held several important tactical and operational advantages. These included high technology weapons, an extensive intelligence network, and a combined air-land-sea capability that sought to create strategic, operational, and tactical dilemmas with which the Iraqi command structure could not cope. While the state of training of the Coalition units varied, overall it was superior to that of the Iraqis, particularly those Iraqi forces occupying Kuwait.

In Saudi Arabia and the Gulf, seven Army divisions, two USMC Divisions, a British armored division, a French light armored division, and the equivalent of more than four Arab/Islamic divisions were moving into their assembly areas. There were 1,736 combat aircraft from 12 Coalition countries flying from bases and aircraft carriers throughout the theater and Turkey, and 60 B-52s waited at worldwide locations. In the Persian Gulf and Red Sea, naval forces including six aircraft carrier battle groups, two battleships, several submarines capable of launching cruise missiles, and the largest amphibious force mustered since the

Korean War, carrying nearly 17,000 Marines, were prepared to carry out their missions. A massive air and sea logistics effort continued to pour supplies into the theater. In all, more than 540,000 Coalition troops from 31 countries prepared to liberate Kuwait.

Of crucial importance, the Coalition would fight with a level of initiative and flexibility far superior to the Iraqis. Despite its disparate nature, the Coalition maintained unity of effort through a clear understanding of the mission, open coordination between elements, and a command structure that enabled each unit to carry out its mission unhindered by over-centralized control. US military warfighting doctrine emphasized the dislocation of enemy forces in a fluid battlefield. US and many Coalition commanders were capable of exercising a level of initiative of which the Iraqi commanders were totally incapable. C^2 systems enabled rapid shifting of forces, particularly aircraft, to crucial areas. In the ensuing fighting, this flexibility would become decisive. Superior training and organization enabled the US forces, and much of the Coalition as a whole, to outfight the centralized and cumbersome Iraqi armed forces.

With the likelihood of war looming, Saddam Hussein's warfighting strategy seems to have been based on several elements. First, he continued his efforts to divide the Coalition by appealing to radical Arab distrust of the West and Israel, while portraying Kuwait as a nation not worthy of Arab bloodshed. Continual references to the Israeli threat and attempts to tie negotiations to the Palestinian question played on the very real concerns of the Arab world. Subsequent attempts to draw the Israelis into the war reinforced these efforts. Second, he hoped to outlast the Coalition by prolonging the crisis and waiting for resolve to erode. This belief in his political ability to outlast the Coalition manifested itself in bellicose statements, occasionally conciliatory gestures, and continuous propaganda aimed at deterring a

Coalition attack with the threat of heavy casualties. Even after fighting started, Iraqi deserters and, later, enemy prisoners of war often expressed a belief that, somehow, Saddam Hussein would once again politically maneuver his way to a favorable resolution. Third, if these measures failed, Saddam threatened a costly war of attrition that, he hoped, would quickly turn public opinion against the war. This strategic objective was manifested in the Iraqi dispositions, reflecting the preconception that the Coalition would attack frontally through Kuwait into prepared defenses. Finally, Saddam Hussein may have calculated he would withdraw the bulk of his forces even after war began, if necessary.

Saddam Hussein suffered from several miscalculations, however. First, he underestimated the Coalition's resolve and strength. Believing he could sever the ties between the United States and Western nations and the Arab/Islamic states, he continually orchestrated propaganda and political overtures in an attempt to create internal strife, to no avail. When conflict seemed inevitable, he mistook democratic debate for weakness, threatening the Coalition with heavy casualties to shake its resolve. Next, the Iraqi defensive posture in the KTO, which seemed to ignore the exposed flank in the Iraqi desert, underscored the mistaken belief that the Coalition would not attack through Iraq to free Kuwait. Enhanced by the ongoing Coalition deception plan, this miscalculation positioned Iraqi forces facing south and east, intent on fighting a battle of attrition for which the Iraqi commanders were well trained, based on their combat experiences in Iran. Third, Saddam Hussein completely underestimated the efficacy of modern weapons and combat technology. Basing his calculations on his experiences in the Iran-Iraq War, he failed to comprehend the destructive potential of the air, land, and naval power that would be used against him. The battlefield advantages of precision-guided munitions, stealth technology, electronic warfare systems, a host of target acquisition and sighting systems, and highly mobile, lethal ground combat vehicles, used by highly trained personnel, were simply not understood by the Iraqis. First his air force and air defense forces, then his ground forces, and ultimately the Iraqi people suffered for Saddam Hussein's gross miscalculations.

Overall, the Coalition succeeded in what Sun Tzu calls the greatest achievement of a commander, defeating the enemy's strategy.

Saddam Hussein's strategy was to inflict casualties on the Coalition to break our will, to draw Israel into the war to break the Coalition and to inflict casualties on Israel to claim a victory among the Arabs. Expecting that the Coalition would blunder into these traps, Saddam found himself frustrated. Taking significant casualties himself, without inflicting any serious blows on his enemies, he launched the ground attack on Khafji. His disastrous defeat in that engagement foreshadowed his larger, ultimate defeat.

OBSERVATIONS

Accomplishments

- The Coalition developed and executed a coordinated, multi-national, multi-axis, combined arms theater campaign that succeeded in defeating Iraq.

- The Coalition built a multi-national armed force capable of offensive operations and the logistics to support and sustain it.

- Some Coalition forces modernized their units on the eve of battle, successfully undergoing new equipment training and improving the combat potential of their units.

- The services exploited the time available to reach the highest possible levels of unit proficiency.

- The United States demonstrated the ability to deploy and support large, complex forces far from home.

- The UNSC resolutions made US domestic support for offensive operations easier to garner, and contributed to US national political will. The UNSC resolutions made actions against Iraq legitimate in the eyes of much of the world, and made it easier for many nations to support Coalition actions with donations of money or supplies.

- Political will, excellent planning, prior training and exercises, and Coalition solidarity, were decisive determinants of success.

Shortcomings

- Availability of staging bases and a well-developed infrastructure, especially airfields and ports, were crucial to the Coalition's success. These facilities and resources may not be as readily available in future contingencies without considerable emphasis on HNS agreements.

- US strategic lift, the CS and CSS capabilities inherent in the active and RC units deployed, in-theater facilities, HNS, and the time to build the infrastructure in theater, facilitated transition to the offensive. The eventuality of short warning contingencies necessitates actions to improve strategic lift capabilities and enhance host nation support.

Issue

- The Coalition had sufficient time to plan and prepare for the offensive. This was a significant advantage that may not be the case in future crises.

Chapter VI

Shortly after 0230, 17 January, Iraqi Antiaircraft Artillery Illuminates the Baghdad Skyline in Response to the Air Campaign. *(Photo: Copyright Capital Cities/ABC, Inc. 1991).*

THE AIR CAMPAIGN

INTRODUCTION

In immediate response to the Iraqi invasion of Kuwait, the United States rapidly deployed substantial land- and sea-based air power to the Central Command (CENTCOM) area of responsibility (AOR) and increased the readiness level of forces outside Southwest Asia. Simultaneously, the Air Staff, in response to the Commander-in-Chief, Central Command's (CINCCENT) request, developed a concept plan, Instant Thunder, which formed the basis for CENTCOM's more comprehensive Operation Desert Storm air campaign. This, in turn, was devised to help achieve the President's four objectives: force unconditional Iraqi withdrawal from Kuwait, re-establish the legitimate Kuwait government, protect American lives, and ensure regional stability and security.

The air campaign was designed to exploit Coalition strengths (which included well-trained aircrews; advanced technology such as stealth, cruise missiles, precision-guided munitions (PGMs), superior command and control (C^2), and ability to operate effectively at night); and to take advantage of Iraqi weaknesses (including a rigid C^2 network and a defensive orientation). Coalition air planners intended to seize air superiority rapidly and paralyze the Iraqi leadership and command structure by striking simultaneously Iraq's most crucial centers of gravity: its National Command Authority (NCA); its nuclear, biological, and chemical (NBC) warfare capability; and the Republican Guard divisions.

The Strategic Air Campaign formed Phase I of the four phases of Operation Desert Storm.

"Gulf lesson one is the value of air power. . . . (it) was right on target from day one. The Gulf war taught us that we must retain combat superiority in the skies . . . . Our air strikes were the most effective, yet humane, in the history of warfare."

President George Bush
29 May 1991

Phase II focused on suppressing or eliminating Iraqi ground-based air defenses in the Kuwait Theater of Operations (KTO). Phase III emphasized direct air attacks on Iraqi ground forces in the KTO (including the Republican Guard Forces Command (RGFC) and the Iraqi Army in Kuwait). Phases I-III constituted the air campaign. Phase IV, the ground campaign to liberate Kuwait, used air attacks and sea bombardment in addition to ground attacks on concentrations of Iraqi forces remaining in the KTO. Concurrent with the Offensive Ground Campaign was an amphibious landing option, Operation Desert Saber, to be executed as required for the liberation of Kuwait City. The theater campaign plan recognized the phases were not necessarily discrete or sequential, but could overlap as resources became available or priorities shifted.

On 16 January, at 1535 (H — 11 hours, 25 minutes), B-52s took off from Louisiana carrying conventionally armed air-launched cruise missiles (ALCMs). They would launch their ALCMs approximately two hours after H-Hour. The first irretrievable hostile fire in Operation Desert Storm began at approximately 0130 (H-90 minutes), 17 January, when US warships launched Tomahawk land attack missiles (TLAMs) toward Baghdad. At 0238, while the TLAMs were still in flight, helicopters attacked early warning radar sites in southern Iraq. Stealth fighters already had passed over these sites enroute to attack targets in western Iraq and Baghdad. The helicopter, F-117A, cruise missile, F-15E Eagle fighter, and GR-1 Tornado fighter-bomber attacks helped create gaps in Iraqi radar coverage and the C^2 network for the non-stealth aircraft which followed. Powerful air strikes then continued throughout the country. Within hours, key parts of the Iraqi leadership, C^2 network, strategic air defense system, and NBC warfare capabilities were neutralized. By the conflict's first dawn, air attacks on Iraqi forces in the KTO had begun. These led to a steady reduction of their combat capability, and made it difficult for them to mass or move forces without coming under heavy Coalition air attack, according to the Defense Intelligence Agency (DIA) and CENTCOM. Hundreds of Coalition aircraft participated in these missions, marked by precision and impact, while suffering extremely low losses. Coalition air power continued to destroy strategic targets in Iraq and the KTO. Although hindered by bad weather, the air campaign, which extended throughout the 43 days of Operation Desert Storm, won air supremacy and met its key objectives, although suppression of Scud attacks proved far more difficult than anticipated and the destruction of Iraqi nuclear facilities was incomplete because of intelligence limitations.

Phase II of Operation Desert Storm sought the systematic neutralization or destruction of Iraqi surface-to-air missile (SAM) systems and large-caliber antiaircraft artillery (AAA) pieces that threatened Coalition aircraft in the KTO. The suppression of enemy air defenses (SEAD), which began in the air war's first minutes, not only attacked enemy air defense weapons, but also the C^2 centers that linked them. Many accompanying acquisition, fire control, and target tracking radars, according to DIA reports, also were put out of action or dissuaded from coming on line. In this way, Coalition air planners carved out a medium- and high-altitude

sanctuary, which allowed friendly aircraft to operate in the KTO with some degree of safety.

Coalition electronic warfare (EW) aircraft were invaluable during this phase. With active jamming, passive location systems, and antiradiation missile delivery ability, they either attacked enemy weapon systems or rendered them ineffective. Because of the number and mobility of enemy antiaircraft systems, SEAD continued throughout the war. It paved the way for strike aircraft to begin direct air attacks on enemy artillery, armor, and troops in the KTO.

Direct air attacks on Iraqi forces in the KTO continued until the cease-fire. In early February, the weight of Coalition air power shifted from strategic operations in Iraq to attacks on ground forces in the KTO, which could not resist the aerial attack effectively. By G-Day, interdiction of supply lines to the KTO reduced deliveries to a trickle. These and direct attacks on Iraqi supply points and in-theater logistical transportation, according to enemy prisoner of war (EPW) reports, resulted in major local shortages of food for fielded Iraqi forces in Kuwait. The RGFC and other high priority units, however, predominantly were located farther from Coalition forces, closer to rear-area supply depots, and tended to be better supplied than frontline forces.

Coalition aircrews developed innovative tactics to use PGMs against Iraqi armor. While estimates vary, by the start of the ground offensive, Army Component Central Command (ARCENT) estimated many of Iraq's tanks, other armored vehicles, and artillery in the KTO had been destroyed from the air. CINCCENT had stated he would not recommend starting the ground offensive until the combat effectiveness of the forces in the KTO had been degraded by half. The destruction of Iraqi operational command centers and communications links prevented effective military C^2 and helped prepare for the rapid, successful Offensive

Ground Campaign. When the Iraqis attempted their only substantial ground offensive operation, at the Saudi Arabian town of Al-Khafji, Coalition air power responded rapidly to help ground forces defeat the initial assault. At the same time, aircraft attacked and dispersed Iraq's two-division follow-on force before it could join the battle.

When ground forces encountered Iraqi resistance, Coalition airpower again was called on to attack the enemy and help minimize Coalition losses. This often required aircraft to fly lower into harm's way to identify and attack targets. Most Coalition air losses during the latter stages of the war were suffered in direct support of ground forces. During this final phase, the Coalition's speedy conclusion of the war, with minimal casualties, highlighted the synergy of powerful air and ground forces.

Decision to Begin the Offensive Ground Campaign

CINCCENT has said that several factors influenced his belief as to when the Offensive Ground Campaign should begin. These factors included force deployments and planning, logistics buildup, weather forecasts favorable for ground offensive operations, cohesion of the Coalition, and attack preparations, along with the air campaign. All were important in reducing risks and enhancing the probability of success with limited losses. While precise measurement of force ratios was not possible, senior commanders considered that Iraqi combat effectiveness needed to be reduced by about half before the ground offensive began. Combat effectiveness included both measures such as numbers of soldiers, tanks, armored personnel carriers (APC), and artillery (and degradation thereof), as well as less measurable factors such as morale. Once air operations began, Iraqi reactions could be analyzed to provide further evidence on their military capability. For example, the Iraqi failure at Khafji indicated an inability to orchestrate the sorts of complex

operations needed for a mobile defense. Further, the battle seemed to indicate a decline in the will of Iraqi soldiers while at the same time it provided a great boost in morale and confidence among Coalition Arab forces.

PLANNING THE OFFENSIVE AIR CAMPAIGN

The Early Concept Plan — Instant Thunder

During the initial days after the invasion of Kuwait, the CENTCOM and Service component staffs began planning for defensive and offensive operations from Saudi Arabia. The Air Force Component, Central Command (CENTAF) staff began planning an air campaign on 3 August; this provided the basic input for CINCCENT and CENTAF commander briefings to the Chairman of the Joint Chiefs of Staff (CJCS), the Secretary of Defense, and the President.

The Secretary of Defense instructed CJCS and CINCCENT to develop an offensive option that would be available to the President if Saddam Hussein chose to engage in further aggression or other unacceptable behavior, such as killing Kuwaiti citizens or foreign nationals in Kuwait or Iraq. This planning was the basis of CINCCENT's 8 August request to the Air Staff for a conceptual offensive air campaign plan directed exclusively against strategic targets in Iraq. He determined it would not be advisable to divert the deployed CENTAF staff from organizing the arrival and beddown of forces, while preparing a plan to defend Saudi Arabia from further Iraqi aggression. (See Chapter III for details of the D-Day plan). On 10 August, the Air Staff's deputy director of plans for warfighting concepts briefed CINCCENT in Florida on the Instant Thunder concept plan. The CJCS was briefed the following day and directed the Air Staff to expand the planning group to include Navy, Army, and Marine Corps (USMC) members and to proceed with detailed planning under the authority of the Joint Staff's director of operations. The CJCS reviewed the concept with the Secretary of Defense and received his approval.

When CINCCENT saw the expanded briefing again on 17 August, it bore the Joint Chiefs of Staff seal; by then both the Chief of Naval Operations and the Commandant of the Marine Corps also had accepted the concept plan. On 25 August, CINCCENT briefed the Secretary of Defense and the CJCS on a four-phase offensive campaign plan: Phase I, a Strategic Air Campaign against Iraq; Phase II, Kuwait Air Campaign against Iraqi air forces in the KTO; Phase III, Ground Combat Power Attrition to neutralize the Republican Guards and isolate the Kuwait battlefield; and Phase IV, Ground Attack, to eject Iraqi forces from Kuwait. The broad outlines of Operation Desert Storm had taken shape, but plans were further developed and refined for the next several months. As the plan was developed further, the Secretary of Defense and CJCS continued to review it in detail, culminating in an intensive two-day review in Saudi Arabia in December.

Non-US Coalition members became involved in planning during September. By the end of November, British Royal Air Force (RAF) and Royal Saudi Air Force (RSAF) planners were integrated fully.

The Air Staff concept plan had been called Instant Thunder to contrast it with Operation Rolling Thunder's prolonged, gradualistic approach to bombing North Vietnam during the 1960s. Instead of piecemeal attacks designed to send signals to enemy leaders, Instant Thunder was designed to destroy 84 strategic targets in Iraq in a single week. If all went well, air attacks would paralyze Iraqi leadership, degrade their military capabilities and neutralize their will to fight. There was, however, great concern on the part of CJCS and CINCCENT, particularly in August and the first part of September, that an aggressive Iraqi ground offensive in the absence of significant heavy Coalition ground forces

might succeed in seizing key airfields as well as ports, water facilities, and oil production sites.

As the air planners built Instant Thunder, they realized that in this war, the development of PGMs and active and passive antiradar technologies (stealth, jamming, antiradiation missiles) would allow attacks directly against the enemy leadership's ability to function. These attacks could neutralize the regime's ability to direct military operations by eroding communications, and depriving leaders of secure locations from which to plan and control operations. These leadership capabilities became key targets for Instant Thunder, and the main difference between it and more traditional strategic bombing campaigns.

In addition to attacks designed to influence the Iraqi leadership's ability to control their forces, the plan also envisaged attacks to reduce the effectiveness of forces in the KTO. Targets included NBC facilities, ballistic missile production and storage facilities, key bridges, railroads and ports that enabled Iraq to supply its forces in the KTO, and the Iraqi air defense system.

The Air Staff planning group (known as Checkmate), working under the Air Staff's deputy director of plans for warfighting concepts, categorized strategic targets as follows:

- Leadership — Saddam Hussein's command facilities and telecommunications
- Key production — electricity, oil refining, refined oil products, NBC, other military production, military storage
- Infrastructure — railroads, ports, and bridges (initial plans expected to attack only railroads; later, ports and bridges were added when the theater plan expanded to include attacks on the fielded forces in the KTO)
- Fielded forces — air defenses, naval forces, long-range combat aircraft and missiles, and airfields. (Although not included in the early drafts the Secretary of Defense

instructed CINCCENT to add the RGFC to the strategic target list because they were key to the Iraqi position in Kuwait and a serious offensive threat to Iraq's neighbors.)

Targets in each category were identified, imagery obtained, weapons and aiming points chosen, and an attack flow plan assembled using aircraft scheduled to deploy. Eventually, target identification became a joint-Service, multi-agency, and Coalition effort.

The Instant Thunder concept plan was designed to attack Iraq's centers of gravity. It envisioned a six-day (good weather and 700 attack sorties a day) attack on 84 strategic targets in Iraq. This initial plan, however, did not address some major target systems that became important in Operation Desert Storm.

Although suppressing Scud attacks later proved crucial to the strategic objective of frustrating Saddam Hussein's effort to draw Israel into the war, the missiles were not regarded initially as a threat to military forces — unless they were equipped with unconventional warheads — because of their inaccuracy. (In fact, however, a Scud strike on a barracks in February inflicted more US casualties than any single engagement. Moreover, Scud attacks elsewhere in the theater, for example on the ports of Ad-Dammam and Jubayl, in the early stages of the war when large concentrations of VII Corps troops were waiting for their equipment to arrive by sealift, potentially could have inflicted very large casualties.) In any case, trying to find and attack such mobile, easily hidden targets promised to absorb many sorties without likelihood of much success. The early plans, therefore, concentrated on attacking the fixed Scud launch facilities and production centers.

If Iraq attacked Saudi Arabia, the CENTAF commander, who also acted as the Joint Forces Air Component Commander (JFACC), planned to concentrate air attacks on the Iraqi ground forces which might move against the Saudi oil

fields and northern airfields. The Instant Thunder concept expected those targets to be attacked by RAF and Saudi Tornados, and US F-16s, AV-8Bs, A-10s, AH-64s, AH-1s, and F/A-18s.

Meanwhile, aircraft designed for long-range attacks would concentrate on strategic targets in Iraq. In time, this difference of focus lost much of its practical meaning, especially after the deployment of additional air and ground assets starting in November. An abundance of Coalition air and ground power gave assurance that an air campaign could be waged simultaneously against strategic targets in Iraq and Iraqi forces moving into Saudi Arabia, if necessary.

Instant Thunder Evolves Into Operation Desert Storm Air Campaign

During the fall, JFACC planners merged CENTAF's pre-deployment concept of operations with the Instant Thunder concept to form the foundation for the Operation Desert Storm air campaign plan.

Navy, USMC, and Army planners worked closely with Air Force (USAF) planners in August and September to draft the initial offensive air campaign plan. In Riyadh, Naval Component, Central Command (NAVCENT), Marine Corps Component, Central Command (MARCENT), and ARCENT were integral planning process members. RAF planners joined the JFACC staff on 19 September.

CENTCOM's offensive air campaign special planning group (SPG), in the RSAF Headquarters, was part of the JFACC staff and eventually became known as the Black Hole because of the extreme secrecy surrounding its activities. The Black Hole was led by a USAF brigadier general, reassigned from the *USS Lasalle* (AGF 3) where he had been serving as the deputy commander of Joint Task Force Middle East when Iraq invaded Kuwait. His small staff grew gradually to about 30 and included RAF, Army, Navy, USMC, and USAF personnel. Because of operational security (OPSEC) concerns, most of CENTAF headquarters was denied information on the plan until only a few hours before execution. By 15 September, the initial air planning stage was complete; the President was advised there were sufficient air forces to execute and sustain an offensive strategic air campaign against Iraq, should he order one.

During October, as planning began for a possible offensive ground operation to liberate Kuwait, air planners began to give more attention to Phase III, air attacks on Iraqi ground forces in the KTO. There was concern a ground assault against the well prepared KTO defenses might result in large and unnecessary loss of life. If Saddam Hussein did not comply with UN demands, air attacks would help the Offensive Ground Campaign meet its objectives rapidly and with minimal casualties. Computer modeling suggested to air planners it would take about a month of air attacks to destroy 75 to 80 percent of the armored vehicles, trucks, and artillery of the regular Iraqi army in Kuwait. Historical evidence shows attrition levels of 20 to 50 percent usually render a military force combat ineffective.

Another change from Instant Thunder was the decision to begin bombing the Republican Guards in southern Iraq at the start of Operation Desert Storm. The Secretary of Defense and CJCS identified the forces as the mainstay of the Iraqi defenses in the KTO, not only because they provided the bulk of Iraq's mobile reserves, but also because the regime counted on them to enforce the loyalty and discipline of the regular troops. In addition, weakening the Republican Guards would diminish Iraq's post-war threat to the region.

Given the SPG's small size, and the restrictions imposed by distance and limited communications, the director of campaign plans

needed help. Checkmate augmented the SPG as an information fusion and analysis center; it provided an educated pool of manpower with face-to-face access to the national Intelligence Community. Instant Thunder had identified only 84 targets, but by January, intelligence experts and operations planners identified more than 600 potential targets, of which more than 300 became part of the CENTCOM strategic target list.

The planners in theater also received help from the Strike Projection Evaluation and Antiair Research (SPEAR) team of the Navy Operational Intelligence Center. SPEAR helped complete the picture of the Iraqi integrated air defense system (IADS), which used a mix of Soviet and Western equipment and concepts tied together by a C^2 system largely designed by French technicians. Named Kari, this C^2 system coordinated Iraqi air defense forces which could inflict severe Coalition losses. As part of a joint analysis with USAF and national agency participation, SPEAR helped identify the extent and nature of the threat, the key IADS nodes, and the importance of destroying those nodes early in the campaign.

On the basis of the joint analysis, in-theater modeling using the Command, Control, Communications, and Intelligence simulation model (provided by the USAF Center for Studies and Analysis and Headquarters USAF Plans and Operations) predicted low-altitude attacks on key leadership, Command, Control, and Communications (C^3), and electrical targets in Baghdad would be extremely dangerous for both F-111F and A-6E aircraft. Consequently, these crucial targets were attacked from medium altitudes by F-117As and low altitudes by TLAMs. The SEAD effort to neutralize the Kari system proved vital to Coalition success; the initial blow, according to intelligence reports, was one from which Iraqi air defenses never recovered.

At first, planners could rely on fewer than 75

long-range aircraft with a laser self-designation capability: 18 F-117As and 55 A-6Es. The mid-August decision to deploy 32 F-111Fs was the first major expansion in the laser-guided bombing capability. After the November decision to deploy additional forces, the number of aircraft so equipped increased to more than 200 F-117As, F-15Es, F-111Fs, and A-6Es.

Instead of having to make the first attack, return to base to rearm, refuel, and then make a second attack, the larger number of aircraft would strike about as many targets with a single wave. This increased the number of targets attacked almost simultaneously, complicated Iraq's air defense task, and increased aircraft availability for later strikes.

THE OPERATION DESERT STORM AIR CAMPAIGN PLAN

The plan was based on achieving the five military objectives listed below. These objectives were derived from the President's objectives and a planning model developed by the Air Staff's deputy director of plans for warfighting concepts. Below each objective are listed the target sets that would be attacked to secure the objective. (Although degrading a target set commonly would help achieve more than one goal, target sets are listed only once.)

JFACC Air Campaign Objectives

■ Isolate and incapacitate the Iraqi regime:
  □ Leadership command facilities.
  □ Crucial aspects of electricity production facilities that power military and military-related industrial systems.
  □ Telecommunications and C^3 systems.
■ Gain and maintain air supremacy to permit unhindered air operations:
  □ Strategic IADS, including radar sites,

SAMs, and IADS control centers.
  □ Air forces and airfields.
■ Destroy NBC warfare capability:
  □ Known NBC research, production, and storage facilities.
■ Eliminate Iraq's offensive military capability by destroying major parts of key military production, infrastructure, and power projection capabilities:
  □ Military production and storage sites.
  □ Scud missiles and launchers, production and storage facilities.
  □ Oil refining and distribution facilities, as opposed to long-term production capabilities.
  □ Naval forces and port facilities.
■ Render the Iraqi army and its mechanized equipment in Kuwait ineffective, causing its collapse:
  □ Railroads and bridges connecting military forces to means of support.
  □ Army units to include RGFC in the KTO.

The Twelve Target Sets

The air campaign's 12 target sets are listed separately below. However, creating each day's attack plan was more complex than dealing with the target sets individually. The planners assessed progress toward the five military objectives, and how well they were accomplishing desired levels of damage and disruption, within each target set. The method for producing the daily attack plan involved synthesizing many inputs — battle damage assessment (BDA) from previous attacks, CINCCENT guidance, weather, target set priorities, new targets, intelligence, and the air campaign objectives. The target sets were interrelated and were not targeted individually. The available aircraft, special operations forces (SOF), and other assets then were assigned on the basis of ability and the most effective use of force.

Leadership Command Facilities
There were 45 targets in the Baghdad area, and

others throughout Iraq, in the leadership command facilities target set. The intent was to fragment and disrupt Iraqi political and military leadership by attacking its C^2 of Iraqi military forces, internal security elements, and key nodes within the government. The attacks should cause the leaders to hide or relocate, making it difficult for them to control or even keep pace with events. The target set's primary objective was incapacitating and isolating Iraq's senior decision-making authorities. Specifically targeted were facilities from which the Iraqi military leadership, including Saddam Hussein, would attempt to coordinate military actions. Targets included national-level political and military headquarters and command posts (CPs) in Baghdad and elsewhere in Iraq.

Electricity Production Facilities

Electricity is vital to the functioning of a modern military and industrial power such as Iraq, and disrupting the electrical supply can make destruction of other facilities unnecessary. Disrupting the electricity supply to key Iraqi facilities degraded a wide variety of crucial capabilities, from the radar sites that warned of Coalition air strikes, to the refrigeration used to preserve biological weapons (BW), to nuclear weapons production facilities.

To do this effectively required the disruption of virtually the entire Iraqi electric grid, to prevent the rerouting of power around damaged nodes. Although backup generators sometimes were available, they usually are slow to come on line, provide less power than main sources, and are not as reliable.

During switch over from main power to a backup generator, computers drop off line, temporary confusion ensues, and other residual problems can occur. Because of the fast pace of a modern, massed air attack, even milliseconds of enemy power disruption can mean the difference between life and death for aircrews.

Telecommunications And Command, Control, And Communication Nodes

The ability to issue orders to military and security forces, receive reports on the status of operations, and communicate with senior political and military leaders was crucial to Saddam Hussein's deployment and use of his forces. To challenge his C^3, the Coalition bombed microwave relay towers, telephone exchanges, switching rooms, fiber optic nodes, and bridges that carried coaxial communications cables. These national communications could be reestablished and so, required persistent restrikes. These either silenced them or forced the Iraqi leadership to use backup systems vulnerable to eavesdropping that produced valuable intelligence, according to DIA assessments, particularly in the period before the ground campaign.

More than half of Iraq's military landline communications passed through major switching facilities in Baghdad. Civil TV and radio facilities could be used easily for C^3 backup for military purposes. The Saddam Hussein regime also controlled TV and radio and used them as the principal media for Iraqi propaganda. Thus, these installations also were struck.

Strategic Integrated Air Defense System

The Iraqi strategic IADS was one of the more important immediate target sets; before Coalition air power could exercise its full aerial bombardment potential, the effectiveness of Iraqi air forces and ground-based air defenses had to be reduced to negligible proportions. Targets included the mid- and upper-level air defense control centers, SAM sites, radar sites, and the C^3 nodes that connected the system.

Air Forces And Airfields

The Iraqi Air Force posed both a defensive threat to Coalition air operations, and an offensive threat to Coalition forces in the region. In addition to a defensive capability, the Iraqi

Air Force had a chemical weapons (CW) delivery capability and had used PGMs.

Initial targeting of the Iraqi Air Force during Operation Desert Storm emphasized the suppression of air operations at airfields by cratering and mining runways, bombing aircraft, maintenance and storage facilities, and attacking C^3 facilities. Coalition planners anticipated the Iraqis initially would attempt to fly large numbers of defensive sorties, requiring an extensive counter-air effort. Air commanders also expected the Iraqis to house and protect aircraft in hardened shelters. An attempt to fly some aircraft to sanctuary in a neighboring country also was expected, although the safe haven was thought to be Jordan, rather than Iran.

Nuclear, Biological And Chemical Weapons Research, Production, And Storage Facilities

The extensive Iraqi NBC program was a serious threat to regional stability. Coalition planners intended to destroy weapons research and production capability and delivery vehicles. Because of the Iraqis' elaborate efforts to hide the extent of their programs, Coalition forces were uncertain of their exact scope.

Intelligence estimates varied, but the planning assumption was that Iraq could produce a rudimentary nuclear weapon by the end of 1992, if not sooner. Throughout the planning period, and during the conflict, finding and destroying NBC weapons facilities remained a top priority. International investigations continue to reveal the advanced character of Iraq's nuclear program, and to uncover additional facilities. The existence of the Al-Athir complex, 40 miles south of Baghdad, which was reported lightly damaged by bombing, was not confirmed until late in the war. It was the target of the last bomb dropped by an F-117A in the conflict.

Scud Missiles, Launchers, And Production And Storage Facilities

Iraq's Scud missile capability was considered a military and a psychological threat to Coalition forces, a threat to civilian populations in Israel, Saudi Arabia, and some other Gulf countries, and a threat to long-term regional stability. Along with targeting the fixed launch sites in western Iraq, Coalition planners targeted Iraq's ability to deploy existing missiles and build more.

Intelligence estimates at the time of the total numbers of mobile launchers and Scuds were sketchy and proved to be too low. As a working estimate, planners used 600 Scud missiles (and variants), 36 mobile launchers, and 28 fixed launchers in five complexes in western Iraq, plus some training launchers at At-Taji. Initial attacks concentrated on eliminating the fixed sites. Plans were developed for hunting and destroying mobile Scud launchers, but the missiles would prove to be elusive targets.

Naval Forces And Port Facilities

Although Iraq was not a major naval power, its naval forces posed a threat to Coalition naval and amphibious forces, and sealift assets. Iraqi forces had Silkworm and Exocet antiship missiles and mines; they could create a substantial political and military problem by destroying or seriously damaging a major surface ship. Coalition planners targeted Iraqi naval vessels, including captured Kuwaiti Exocet-equipped patrol boats, port facilities, and antiship missiles to prevent interference with Coalition operations and to reduce the threat to friendly ports and logistical systems in the Persian Gulf.

Oil Refining And Distribution Facilities

Fuel and lubricants are the lifeblood of a major industrial and military power. Iraq had a modern petroleum extraction, cracking, and distillation system, befitting its position as one of the world's major oil producing and refining nations. Coalition planners targeted Iraq's ability to produce refined oil products (such as gasoline) that had immediate military use, instead of its long-term crude oil production capability.

Railroads And Bridges

Most major railroad and highway bridges in Iraq served routes that ran between Baghdad and Al-Basrah. Iraqi forces in the KTO were almost totally dependent for their logistical support on the lines of communication (LOCs) that crossed these bridges, making them lucrative targets. Although Iraqi forces had built large stockpiles of supplies in southeast Iraq by January, DIA reported cutting the bridges prevented or reduced restocking, and prevented reinforcement of deployed forces once the air campaign began.

Iraqi Army Units Including Republican Guard Forces In The KTO

Iraq's means of projecting power into Kuwait and against the Coalition centered on its ground forces deployed in the KTO, especially its best

units, the Republican Guard. Although Iraqi forces were dug into strong positions built to defend against ground attack, they were vulnerable to air attack. Coalition planners hoped to reduce the combat effectiveness of these forces in the KTO by about 50 percent before the ground offensive.

Military Storage And Production Sites

The long-term combat effectiveness of Iraq's large military forces depended on military production facilities and continued support from its logistical base. Destruction of repair facilities, spare parts supplies, and storage depots would degrade Iraq's combat capability and long-term threat to the region. Planners knew there were too many targets to be eliminated entirely. For example, there were seven primary and 19 secondary ammunition storage facilities alone identified on target lists; each was composed of scores of individual storage bunkers. Consequently, they planned first to destroy the most threatening production facilities and stored materiel, then methodically to proceed with attacks on other storage and production facilities as time and assets allowed.

Constraints on the Concept Plan

Avoid Collateral Damage And Casualties

A key principle underlying Coalition strategy was the need to minimize casualties and damage, both to the Coalition and to Iraqi civilians. It was recognized at the beginning that this campaign would cause some unavoidable hardships for the Iraqi people. It was impossible, for example, to shut down the electrical power supply for Iraqi C^2 facilities or CW factories, yet leave untouched the electricity supply to the general populace. Coalition targeting policy and aircrews made every effort to minimize civilian casualties and collateral damage. Because of these restrictive policies, only PGMs were used to destroy key targets in downtown Baghdad in order to avoid damaging adjacent civilian buildings.

The Ancient Temple Depicted in This Drawing was not Targeted Despite the Placement of Iraqi Fighter Aircraft Nearby

Coalition Targeting Policy Was to Minimize Collateral Damage and Civilian Casualties. *Using Precision Weapons, Targets Such as the Iraqi Intelligence Service Headquarters in Baghdad were Struck Usually with Little or No Damage to Adjacent Buildings, According to Post-war Intelligence Assessments.*

Areas of Historical or Cultural Significance Were Not Targeted. *Mosques Were Among the Targets on the Off-limits List.*

Off Limits Targets

Planners were aware that each bomb carried a potential moral and political impact, and that Iraq has a rich cultural and religious heritage dating back several thousand years. Within its borders are sacred religious areas and literally thousands of archaeological sites that trace the evolution of modern civilization. Targeting policies, therefore, scrupulously avoided damage to mosques, religious shrines, and archaeological sites, as well as to civilian facilities and the civilian population. To help strike planners, CENTCOM target intelligence analysts, in close coordination with the national intelligence agencies and the State Department, produced a joint no-fire target list. This list was a compilation of historical, archaeological, economic, religious and politically sensitive installations in Iraq and Kuwait that could not be targeted. Additionally, target intelligence analysts were tasked to look in a six-mile area around each master attack list target for schools, hospitals, and mosques to identify targets where extreme care was required in planning. Further, using imagery, tourist maps, and human resource intelligence (HUMINT) reports, these same types of areas were identified for the entire city of Baghdad. When targeting officers calculated the probability of collateral damage as too high, the target was not attacked.

Only when a target satisfied the criteria was it placed on the target list, and eventually attacked based on its relative priority compared with other targets and on the availability of attack assets. The weapon system, munition, time of attack, direction of attack, desired impact point, and level of effort all were carefully planned. For example, attacks on known dual (i.e., military and civilian) use facilities normally were scheduled at night, because fewer people would be inside or on the streets outside.

Phased Execution

CINCCENT planners estimated that, with good

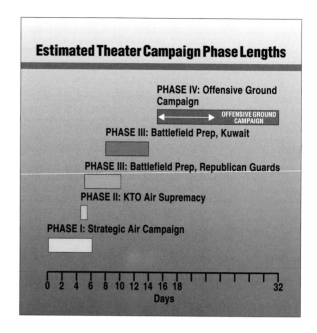

Estimated Theater Campaign Phase Lengths

weather and a specified level of effort, Phases I-III would last approximately 18 days. The main attacks of Phase I, the Strategic Air Campaign, would last about six days; a lower level of effort, against strategic targets, would continue throughout the remainder of the war to maintain pressure inside Iraq, to reattack targets not previously destroyed, and to attack newly discovered targets. The concentrated Phase II effort to establish air superiority over the KTO would last approximately one day; as was true for Phase I, a lower level of effort would continue to keep enemy air defense suppressed. Phase III, designed to reduce Iraqi combat effectiveness in the KTO by half, was to begin near the end of the Phase II SEAD effort and was expected to complete its objectives in about 10 to 12 days. Phase III attacks would continue until the President directed the start of the Offensive Ground Campaign. During Phase IV of Operation Desert Storm, air operations were designed to support the ground maneuver scheme by flying interdiction, battlefield air operations, and close air support (CAS) sorties. Interdiction would continue against enemy artillery, rockets, and reserve forces throughout the KTO. There was some planned overlap of the phases.

The original sequential air campaign execution was designed to reduce the threat to Coalition aircraft conducting Phase III, the systematic reduction of the Iraqi military forces in the KTO. With the increased amount of Coalition air power available in January, CINCCENT merged the execution of Phases I - III so Operation Desert Storm would begin with air attacks throughout the theater against the most crucial targets in each phase.

The predicted phase lengths were planning guidelines. CINCCENT built the Phase IV Offensive Ground Campaign plan on the assumption that air power alone would reduce Iraqi combat effectiveness in the KTO by about half. If all went as planned, Saddam Hussein and his forces in the Kuwait theater would be immobilized — unable to coordinate an effective defense, or to plan and execute large-scale counter offensives. Continued attacks and restrikes would maintain desired levels of disruption. If the Offensive Ground Campaign became necessary, it would be fought on Coalition terms. There would not be months of fighting and thousands of casualties as some had predicted, or as Saddam Hussein hoped. The ground offensive would last only days and Coalition casualties would be lighter. Together, the air and ground campaigns would ensure destruction of the Iraqi army's offensive capability, and the Coalition's success. Referring to the Iraqi Army in the KTO, the CJCS said in January, "First we're going to cut it off; then we're going to kill it."

PREPARING TO EXECUTE THE PLAN

The Joint Forces Air Component Commander

The historical problem of fragmented air operations command was solved when the CINCCENT operations order (OPORD) assigned the CENTAF Commander as the JFACC, responsible for planning the air campaign, and coordinating, allocating, and tasking apportioned Coalition air sorties to meet the theater objectives.

Although this concept had been used at least as early as World War II, Operation Desert Storm was the first regional conflict in which the JFACC was established formally. The concept proved its value; JFACC planned, coordinated, and, based on CINCCENT's apportionment decision, allocated, and tasked the efforts of more than 2,700 Coalition aircraft, representing 14 separate national or Service components. He integrated operations into a unified and focused 43-day air campaign using the master attack plan (MAP) and the air tasking order (ATO) process, which provided the necessary details to execute the attack.

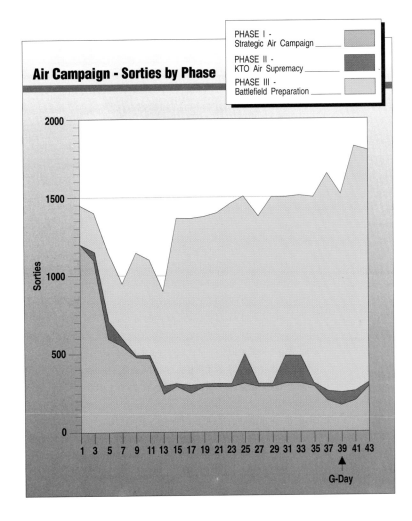

Chapter VI

101

The Master Attack Plan

The JFACC's intent for the air campaign was set forth in the MAP and the more detailed document derived from it, the ATO. The MAP was the key JFACC internal planning document which consolidated all inputs into a single, concise plan. CINCCENT had identified the crucial enemy elements or centers of gravity which had to be attacked effectively to achieve the President's stated objectives. From these centers of gravity, planners identified the Iraqi targets sets and, with the help of intelligence from a variety of agencies and institutions, set out to identify and locate the crucial nodes as well as those making up the bulk of the targets in each set. Using the concept of a strategic attack — striking directly at each target set's crucial nodes — the initial attack plan was developed. It focused on achieving desired effects appropriate to each target set rather than each target. As a subset of the CENTCOM joint target list, a JFACC master strategic target list was developed using a target reference number system based on the initial 12 target categories. However, the MAP did not merely service the target lists; it required timely analysis of BDA, and reflected changing target priorities, and other political and combat developments.

MAP preparation reflected a dynamic JFACC process in which strategic decision making was based on objectives, CINCCENT guidance, target priorities, the desired effect on each target, a synthesis of the latest multi-source intelligence and analysis, operational factors such as weather, the threat, and the availability and suitability of strike assets. In putting together the MAP, the best weapon system to achieve the desired effect was selected — regardless of Service or country of origin — and requested by the JFACC through CINCCENT if not already available in theater. Force packages were built to exploit enemy weakness and Coalition advantages (e.g., night operations, stealth, PGMs, cruise missiles,

drones, attack helicopters, SOF, and airborne refueling).

The result was a relatively compact document (the first day's MAP was only 21 pages) that integrated all attacking elements into force packages and provided strategic coherency and timing to the day's operations. It consisted of the sequence of attacks for a 24-hour period and included the time on target, target number, target description, number and type of weapon systems and supporting systems for each attack package. The MAP drove the process.

The Air Tasking Order

The ATO was the daily schedule that provided the details and guidance aircrews needed to execute the MAP. Through a laptop computer, it meshed the MAP with the air refueling plan. Weapon system experts from the JFACC staff and field units worked together with intelligence, logistics, and weather experts to add such details as mission numbers, target identification, and, sometimes, ordnance loads to the MAP. The weapon system experts included representatives from all of the Services, the RAF, the RSAF and, during the war, other Coalition air forces based on their degree of participation. Service and Coalition representatives served both as planners and as liaisons to their component or national staffs. Target assignments, route plans, altitudes, refueling tracks, fuel offloads, call signs, identification friend or foe codes, and other details were allocated for every Coalition sortie.

The ATO was a two-part document. The first focused on targeting and mission data and EW/SEAD support. The second contained the special instructions on topics such as communications frequencies, tanker and reconnaissance support, Airborne Warning and Control System (AWACS) coverage, combat search and rescue (CSAR) resources, routes into and out of enemy airspace, and many other details. If they did not adhere strictly to the ATO, Coalition air forces risked air-to-air and surface-to-air fratricide, inadequate fighter and SEAD support, or inadequate tanker support to reach the target and return safely. The ATO allowed C^2 elements to orchestrate combat and support operations. C^2 elements such as the land-based Tactical Air Control Center (TACC), EC-130 Airborne Battlefield Command and Control Center (ABCCC), AWACS and E-2Cs functioned more effectively and efficiently because the ATO provided a single attack script. While including Navy aircraft flights into Kuwait or Iraq, the ATO excluded Navy sorties over water. It tasked some aircraft originating outside the CENTCOM AOR, such as B-52s based in Spain, England, and the continental United States (CONUS).

Incorporating the closehold, offensive air campaign ATO into the normal planning process was challenging. During the planning phase for Operation Desert Storm, all the information was loaded into a laptop computer in the SPG, carried to the CENTAF ATO division in the middle of the night, and connected to heavy duty printers used for the daily training ATOs. When the hundred-page-plus ATOs were printed, they were carried back to the SPG where they were reviewed for accuracy, packaged, transmitted electronically by secure channels, flown around the theater, and delivered to units that were to participate in the air campaign. As the enemy situation changed, the MAP and the ATO were refined continuously.

The ATO was very effective and successful, particularly for the initial, preplanned stages of the Strategic Air Campaign. However, the ATO did not respond as rapidly when air operations progressed and emphasis shifted to more mobile targets. This was caused by a lengthy planning cycle, the size and perceived complexity of the ATO, and dissemination delays caused by some forces' not having compatible equipment. In addition, the ATO planning cycle was out of

phase with available BDA. Target selection and planning often were nearly complete before results of the previous missions were available. Plans were developed to use kill boxes, strip-alert aircraft, and uncommitted sorties in the ATO to ensure ATO execution flexibility and operational responsiveness.

TRANSITION TO WARTIME PLANNING

As the offensive approached, the JFACC merged his special-access planning program with the rest of his headquarters. The JFACC's director of air campaign plans (DCP) determined the SPG's compartmented nature was too cumbersome and that the planning process should be part of the daily ATO processing and execution cycle.

An early January SPG reorganization satisfied that need by consolidating several planning functions to establish the Guidance, Apportionment, and Targeting Division (GAT). The Black Hole became the Iraqi Strategic Planning Cell — primarily responsible for the Strategic Air Campaign. It functioned as before in creating the MAP, but no longer was responsible for the mechanics of ATO processing and distribution. The JFACC combat operations plans division became the KTO Planning Cell — primarily responsible for direct attack on Iraqi forces in the KTO. Planning cells for electronic combat, counter-Scud and NBC attack planning, ARCENT ground operations liaison, and an analysis cell, rounded out the GAT staff.

The DCP also was given responsibility for the ATO division, as well as the Airborne Command Element division, whose officers flew on board AWACS and helped control the air war. The DCP's responsibilities, therefore, encompassed planning, processing, and part of execution, with some people from every function participating in every other function. This organizational structure made it easier to carry the strategic focus of the air campaign from the MAP through the ATO to the AWACS mission director's console.

When the air offensive began, the DCP divisions began to operate on a 24-hour basis. The process began with CINCCENT guidance for adjustments to the air campaign plan passed through the JFACC 0700 staff meeting. Based on this guidance, the chief planners of the Iraqi/KTO planning cell created the MAP, which was approved by the DCP by 2000 that same day. Once approved, it was given to the intelligence division for aimpoint selection and verification for some specified targets. In other cases, planners and Navy, USMC, and RAF units selected aimpoints. Additional planning cell members transferred the MAP onto target planning worksheets (TPWs) and added details such as mission numbers required for processing the MAP into an ATO.

At 0430 the next day the TPWs were delivered to the ATO division, which worked out the details required to make the plan an executable ATO (e.g., airspace deconfliction, tanker routing, identification squawks, and special operating instructions). This information was then entered into the computer-aided force management system (CAFMS). Between 1700 and 1900, the final ATO was completed and sent to those units equipped to receive it electronically. The execution day the ATO covered began the next morning.

Three wars were going on each day — the execution war of today; the ATO building for tomorrow's war; and the MAP for the day-after-tomorrow's war. Weather, slow and limited BDA, the implications of Scud attacks and associated shifting of resources eventually compressed the three-day process into two. As a result, planners assumed more of the current operations tasks, improvised to work around BDA shortcomings, and developed a system to track the multitude of adjustments and changes to avoid unnecessary restrikes.

The ATO was much larger than the MAP, often more than 300 pages of text, and there were difficulties disseminating it. To transmit the ATO, the USAF deployed an existing electronic system, CAFMS, an interactive computer system for passing information that allows online discussion between the TACC combat operations section and combat units. CAFMS transmitted the ATO and real-time changes to most land-based units. However, CENTAF had problems using CAFMS to transmit the ATO to some B-52 units and aircraft carriers, in large part because of the complexity of the satellite relays to units outside the peninsula. Some problems were solved by extending CENTCOM's tactical super-high frequency satellite communications (SATCOM) network to include B-52 bases. After the MAP was written, planners rarely changed Navy sorties because of planning and communications concerns. Initially, this limited the flexible use of Navy air assets and resulted in USAF and USMC land-based air assigned to most short-notice changes.

The ATO reflects the USAF philosophy and practice for attack planning. The USAF focused on the potential for large-scale theater war and developed a system that allowed an orderly management of large numbers of aircraft. Because USAF doctrine separates intelligence, targeting, and flying functions, the ATO was designed to provide mission commanders with detailed direction about many aspects of the mission (including the target, weapon type, and strike composition, but not tactics).

Navy JFACC planning staff members provided targeting data before ATO dissemination through the Fleet satellite command net, and secure voice satellite telephone (INMARSAT). The Navy ultimately found the best way to distribute the final ATO and any strike support graphics and photos to the carriers was to use an S-3 aircraft or a courier. There were acknowledged difficulties with the mechanics of disseminating the ATO because of the lack of interoperability between the carriers' data systems and CAFMS. Nevertheless, it would have been impossible to achieve the air campaign's success and conduct combat operations as they were fought without the MAP and ATO.

Planners built flexibility and responsiveness into operations by delegating most detailed mission planning to the wing and unit level. Some aircraft were held in reserve or placed on ground alert to allow quick response to combat developments, Scud launches or missile transporter sightings, convoys or troop movements, and newly discovered targets. Many aircraft were assigned to generic or regional target locations, such as kill boxes in the KTO, where they might receive detailed attack instructions from air controllers. Most aircraft had alternate targets that allowed flexible response to changes in weather or other developments in the tactical situation.

At the beginning of Operation Desert Shield force deployment, there essentially was no existing US military command, control, communications, and computer (C^4) infrastructure in the region. By mid-January, the Coalition had established the largest tactical C^4 network ever assembled. This network provided for the C^2 of forces, dissemination of intelligence, establishment of an in-theater logistics capability and for myriad other combat service support activities such as personnel, finance, and EW. Despite this effort, the start of Operation Desert Storm made it clear the requirement for communications outstripped the capacity. This was especially true for the large amounts of imagery and intelligence data bases that needed to be transmitted throughout the theater. These products required large bandwidth capacity circuits for transmission. The available circuits simply were not able to handle the magnitude of data.

The Fleet pursued several initiatives to relieve some overloaded military circuits. One of the more effective innovations was use of INMARSAT to help with tactical communications. INMARSAT proved to be a vital link for coordinating the efforts of NAVCENT in the USS Blue Ridge (LCC 19) and staff elements in Riyadh, for communicating directly with CINCCENT, and for coordinating ATO inputs with the Persian Gulf battle force commander in USS Midway. (A discussion of C^3 is found in Appendix K.)

Deception

CENTCOM deception helped achieve the tactical surprise that set the stage for defeat of Iraq. A visible pattern of round-the-clock air activity was established as part of the overall deception plan. Placement of air refueling tracks and training areas emphasized support for a frontal assault against entrenched Iraqi defenses that helped CINCCENT play on Iraqi beliefs about Coalition intentions.

The Iraqis were conditioned to the presence of large numbers of AWACS and fighter combat air patrols (CAPs) on the borders with Saudi Arabia and the Persian Gulf. These aircraft flew defensive missions in the same orbits and numbers that would be used for the air offensive. A series of surges began to create a pattern of increased activity one night a week.

The final preparations for Operations Desert Storm were masked by placing many aircraft on ground alert. The published reason was as a precaution against a pre-emptive Iraqi attack before the 15 January UN deadline. The true reason was to permit mission planning, crew rest, and aircraft reconfigurations without revealing the Coalition's actual intentions. Ground alert weapons loads matched the loads listed in the ATO for the attack. However, F-15s flew daily operational CAP missions within EW coverage and could not stand down without leaving Saudi airspace unprotected and raising

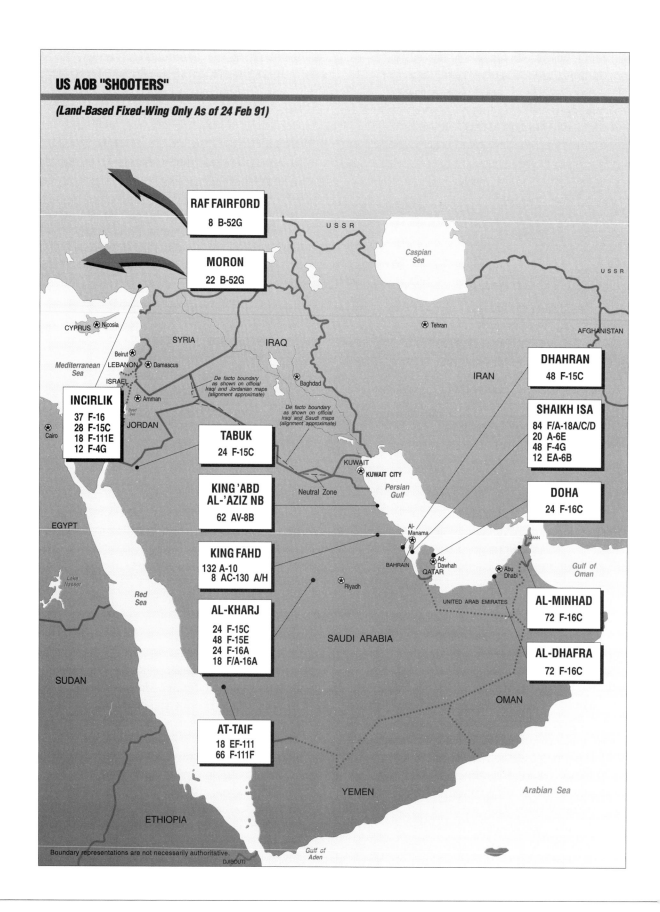

US AOB "SHOOTERS"

(Land-Based Fixed-Wing Only As of 24 Feb 91)

RAF FAIRFORD
8 B-52G

MORON
22 B-52G

DHAHRAN
48 F-15C

SHAIKH ISA
84 F/A-18A/C/D
20 A-6E
48 F-4G
12 EA-6B

INCIRLIK
37 F-16
28 F-15C
18 F-111E
12 F-4G

TABUK
24 F-15C

KING 'ABD AL-'AZIZ NB
62 AV-8B

DOHA
24 F-16C

KING FAHD
132 A-10
8 AC-130 A/H

AL-MINHAD
72 F-16C

AL-KHARJ
24 F-15C
48 F-15E
24 F-16A
18 F/A-16A

AL-DHAFRA
72 F-16C

AT-TAIF
18 EF-111
66 F-111F

Boundary representations are not necessarily authoritative.

Iraqi suspicions. To maintain the desired Iraqi perception of routine Coalition operations, but also allow F-15 units to make final preparations, F-16s not involved in the first attack were tasked to fill the defensive gaps. These and other Coalition deception efforts helped apply the principle of surprise in warfare.

ON THE EVE OF THE AIR WAR

Disposition of Air Forces

At the beginning of Operation Desert Storm, there were 2,430 fixed-wing aircraft in theater, just more than one quarter of which belonged to non-US Coalition partners. Thirty-eight days later, G-Day, that number had grown by more than 350. Approximately 60 percent of all aircraft were shooters, producing a relatively high tooth-to-tail ratio in the theater.

CENTAF

USAF aircraft were bedded down throughout Saudi Arabia and the other Gulf states, initially depending on where they could be received; relocations were based primarily on each aircraft's role in Operation Desert Storm. Some tanker assets, as well as unique reconnaissance platforms such as the TR-1s, and U-2s, and specialized combat aircraft such as the F-117As, EF-111s, and F-111Fs, were based at installations near Saudi Arabia's Red Sea coast. This increased security by keeping them well away from areas that could be reached by a sudden Iraqi pre-emptive strike. It also let them practice and refine most tactics outside of Iraqi radar range.

Air superiority fighters, such as the F-15C, and air-to-ground aircraft, such as the F-15E, were based relatively close to the Iraqi border, where they had the greatest reach and were near long-duration CAP stations over Iraq. Finally, battlefield attack assets such as the A-10s also were based close to the KTO, to allow rapid reaction to battlefield events and improve their

ability to generate a high number of sorties quickly. (The disposition of Air Force Special Operations Command, Central Command aircraft are in Appendix J.)

NAVCENT

The operating areas of the aircraft carrier battle forces at the beginning of Operation Desert Storm are shown on Map VI-4. The *USS John F. Kennedy* (CV 67), *USS Saratoga* (CV 60), and *USS America* (CV 66) battle groups operated in the Red Sea while the *USS Midway* (CV 41), *USS Ranger* (CV 61), and *USS Theodore Roosevelt* (CVN 71) battle groups operated in the Persian Gulf. *USS America* left the Red Sea on 7 February and arrived in the Gulf on 15 February to provide more air support for ground forces in the ground offensive. Typically, with three carriers present in the Red Sea early in the war, one carrier operated in a northern station and one in a southern station while the third replenished fuel and ammunition to the west.

In addition to the six carrier air wings, other Navy air assets in theater supported the Coalition effort. EP-3 and EA-3B aircraft conducted EW missions to support the strike offensive, while the P-3Cs conducted extensive reconnaissance, supporting maritime strike and Coalition maritime intercept operations.

MARCENT

In keeping with a Naval expeditionary posture, USMC aircraft were based both on amphibious ships in the Gulf and at bases ashore. The main operating bases ashore for 3rd Marine Aircraft Wing (MAW), the I Marine Expeditionary Force (MEF) aviation combat element, were at Shaikh Isa, Bahrain, and at Al-Jubayl Naval Air Facility and King 'Abd Al-'Aziz Naval Base, Saudi Arabia. Marine Aircraft Group (MAG) 11, based in Bahrain, was equipped with F/A-18A, C and D aircraft as well as A-6E, EA-6B and KC-130 aircraft. MAG 16 and MAG 26, the helicopter groups, initially were at Al-Jubayl with CH-46, CH-53, AH-1, and UH-1

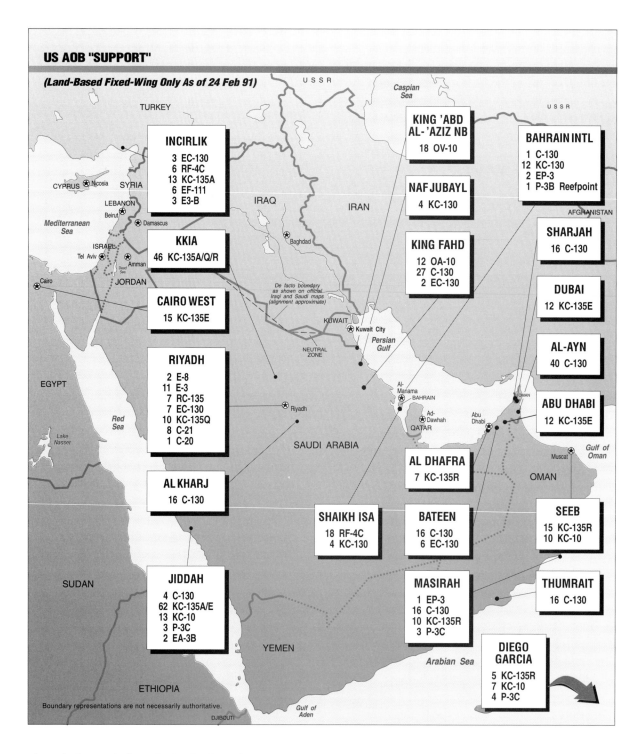

US AOB "SUPPORT"

(Land-Based Fixed-Wing Only As of 24 Feb 91)

INCIRLIK
3 EC-130
6 RF-4C
13 KC-135A
6 EF-111
3 E3-B

KKIA
46 KC-135A/Q/R

CAIRO WEST
15 KC-135E

RIYADH
2 E-8
11 E-3
7 RC-135
7 EC-130
10 KC-135Q
8 C-21
1 C-20

AL KHARJ
16 C-130

JIDDAH
4 C-130
62 KC-135A/E
13 KC-10
3 P-3C
2 EA-3B

KING 'ABD AL-'AZIZ NB
18 OV-10

NAF JUBAYL
4 KC-130

KING FAHD
12 OA-10
27 C-130
2 EC-130

AL DHAFRA
7 KC-135R

SHAIKH ISA
18 RF-4C
4 KC-130

BATEEN
16 C-130
6 EC-130

MASIRAH
1 EP-3
16 C-130
10 KC-135R
3 P-3C

BAHRAIN INTL
1 C-130
12 KC-130
2 EP-3
1 P-3B Reefpoint

SHARJAH
16 C-130

DUBAI
12 KC-135E

AL-AYN
40 C-130

ABU DHABI
12 KC-135E

SEEB
15 KC-135R
10 KC-10

THUMRAIT
16 C-130

DIEGO GARCIA
5 KC-135R
7 KC-10
4 P-3C

Boundary representations are not necessarily authoritative.

aircraft. Later, before the beginning of Operation Desert Storm, some helicopters were forward based at Al-Mishab to support the forward movement of I MEF. MAG 13 (Forward) was at King 'Abd Al-'Aziz Naval Base, with AV-8Bs and OV-10s. The AV-8Bs and OV-10s were the most forward land-based fixed-wing aircraft of any Service. Forward bases for both fixed- and rotary-wing aircraft also were established at various locations

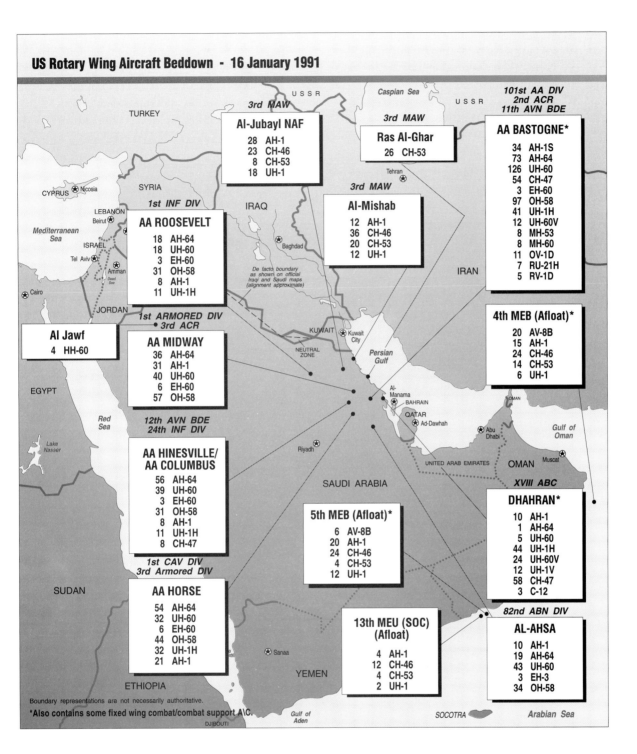

US Rotary Wing Aircraft Beddown - 16 January 1991

Al-Jubayl NAF
3rd MAW

28	AH-1
23	CH-46
8	CH-53
18	UH-1

Ras Al-Ghar
3rd MAW

26	CH-53

AA BASTOGNE*
101st AA DIV
2nd ACR
11th AVN BDE

34	AH-1S
73	AH-64
126	UH-60
54	CH-47
3	EH-60
97	OH-58
41	UH-1H
12	UH-60V
8	MH-53
8	MH-60
11	OV-1D
7	RU-21H
5	RV-1D

AA ROOSEVELT
1st INF DIV

18	AH-64
18	UH-60
3	EH-60
31	OH-58
8	AH-1
11	UH-1H

Al-Mishab
3rd MAW

12	AH-1
36	CH-46
20	CH-53
12	UH-1

Al Jawf

4	HH-60

AA MIDWAY
1th ARMORED DIV
3rd ACR

36	AH-64
31	AH-1
40	UH-60
6	EH-60
57	OH-58

4th MEB (Afloat)*

20	AV-8B
15	AH-1
24	CH-46
14	CH-53
6	UH-1

**AA HINESVILLE/
AA COLUMBUS**
12th AVN BDE
24th INF DIV

56	AH-64
39	UH-60
3	EH-60
31	OH-58
8	AH-1
11	UH-1H
8	CH-47

5th MEB (Afloat)*

6	AV-8B
20	AH-1
24	CH-46
4	CH-53
12	UH-1

DHAHRAN*
XVIII ABC

10	AH-1
1	AH-64
5	UH-60
44	UH-1H
24	UH-60V
12	UH-1V
58	CH-47
3	C-12

AA HORSE
1st CAV DIV
3rd Armored DIV

54	AH-64
32	UH-60
6	EH-60
44	OH-58
32	UH-1H
21	AH-1

**13th MEU (SOC)
(Afloat)**

4	AH-1
12	CH-46
4	CH-53
2	UH-1

AL-AHSA
82nd ABN DIV

10	AH-1
19	AH-64
43	UH-60
3	EH-3
34	OH-58

Boundary representations are not necessarily authoritative.

*****Also contains some fixed wing combat/combat support A\C.**

throughout the theater. Three locations were Tanajib, an ARAMCO facility 35 miles south of the Kuwait border, Al-Mishab, 28 miles south of the border, and Lonesome Dove, a logistics support base in the Saudi desert, also near the

border. Marine Air Control Group (MACG) 38 provided the Marine Tactical Air Command Center, an alternate Tactical Air Command Center, a ground-based Direct Air Support Center (DASC), a DASC Airborne (DASC-A) in a KC-130, a Tactical Air Operations Control Center, an associated early warning/control site, two I-HAWK missile battalions, and two Stinger antiaircraft battalions.

Marine aircraft also were positioned on amphibious ships in the Persian Gulf as part of the Amphibious Task Force (ATF) under NAVCENT. MAG 40, the 4th Marine Expeditionary Brigagde (MEB) aviation combat element, had arrived in the Gulf in September. Its aviation assets included fixed-wing and

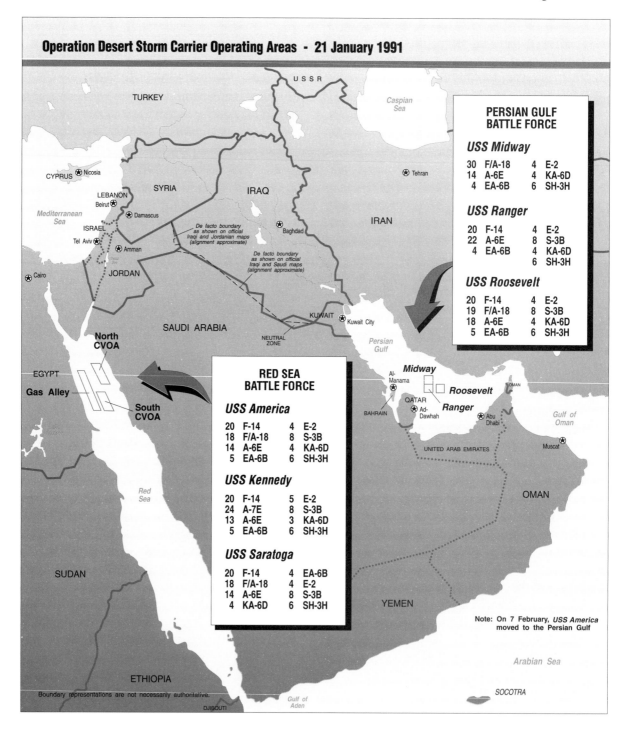

Operation Desert Storm Carrier Operating Areas - 21 January 1991

PERSIAN GULF BATTLE FORCE

USS Midway

30	F/A-18	4	E-2
14	A-6E	4	KA-6D
4	EA-6B	6	SH-3H

USS Ranger

20	F-14	4	E-2
22	A-6E	8	S-3B
4	EA-6B	4	KA-6D
		6	SH-3H

USS Roosevelt

20	F-14	4	E-2
19	F/A-18	8	S-3B
18	A-6E	4	KA-6D
5	EA-6B	6	SH-3H

RED SEA BATTLE FORCE

USS America

20	F-14	4	E-2
18	F/A-18	8	S-3B
14	A-6E	4	KA-6D
5	EA-6B	6	SH-3H

USS Kennedy

20	F-14	5	E-2
24	A-7E	8	S-3B
13	A-6E	3	KA-6D
5	EA-6B	6	SH-3H

USS Saratoga

20	F-14	4	EA-6B
18	F/A-18	4	E-2
14	A-6E	8	S-3B
4	KA-6D	6	SH-3H

Note: On 7 February, *USS America* moved to the Persian Gulf

De facto boundary as shown on official Iraqi and Jordanian maps (alignment approximate)

De facto boundary as shown on official Iraqi and Saudi maps (alignment approximate)

Boundary representations are not necessarily authoritative.

rotary-wing aircraft (20 AV-8Bs, 24 CH-46s, 14 CH-53s, 6 UH-1Ns, and 15 AH-1s). The 13th MEU (SOC), under the operational control of 4th MEB, had an additional 12 CH-46s, four CH-53s, four AH-1s, and two UH-1Ns. In January, the 5th MEB arrived in the Gulf, bringing an additional six AV-8Bs, 24 CH-46s, four CH-53s, 12 UH-1Ns, and 20 AH-1s to the ATF. The 5th MEB joined the 4th MEB, forming a major amphibious force that included 31 ships and more than 17,000 Marines and sailors in the landing force.

Joint Task Force Proven Force

During the first few weeks after the Iraqi invasion of Kuwait, Headquarters United States Air Forces Europe (USAFE) planners developed a concept to base EW support at Incirlik Air Base, Turkey. They envisioned complicating Iraqi defensive efforts by diverting attention electronically. The proposal eventually was endorsed by European Command (EUCOM) and the CJCS. The proposal was briefed to the Turks and discussions regarding authorization began.

Meanwhile, USAFE began to form the force package that eventually would coalesce at Incirlik as Joint Task Force (JTF) Proven Force, a composite wing (similar in concept to a Navy carrier air wing) of reconnaissance, fighter, bomber, tanker, EW, and C^3 aircraft. The Commander-in-Chief Europe (CINCEUR) and CINCCENT agreed that while EUCOM would retain operational control, CENTCOM would exercise tactical control and provide targeting requirements and tactical direction.

On 21 December, the CINCEUR Crisis Action Team telefaxed an advance copy of the preliminary JTF Proven Force OPORD to Headquarters USAFE. Two days later, on 23 December, CINCEUR sent Headquarters USAFE the formal OPORD message. The CINCEUR OPORD tasked USAFE to appoint a JTF commander in the rank of major general,

establish a staff to support the JTF commander, and coordinate air refueling, strike planning, and mission execution activities.

The first contingent of 39 JTF Proven Force headquarters personnel deployed from Ramstein Air Base, Germany, and arrived at Incirlik Air Base on 16 January. The next day, the Turkish Parliament empowered the Turkish government to use "those forces previously authorized (e.g. foreign military [forces] brought to Turkey since the Gulf Crisis) at the time and in the manner the government deems appropriate to carry out UN Security Council resolutions." The Turkish General Staff's rapid coordination and approval of airspace control, safe passage procedures, and air refueling tracks facilitated JTF Proven Force's entry into the air war.

JTF Proven Force was a powerful group of aircraft that included F-15s for air cover; F-16s for day strike; F-111Es for night strike; EF-111s, EC-130s and F-4Gs for EW and SEAD; KC-135s for aerial refueling; RF-4s for reconnaissance; and E-3Bs for airborne surveillance and C^3.

To reduce the amount of detailed communication required between Riyadh and Incirlik, JTF Proven Force missions were planned as part of the MAP, but their tasking was not as detailed, and in some cases was similar to mission type orders, which provide broad guidance on an expected outcome, such as, "Destroy CW production facilities at Mosul." JTF Proven Force planners were assigned targets on the master target list and then determined force size, mix, and desired weaponry — details normally included in ATO taskings for most other units. Their relative geographical isolation in northern Iraq allowed them to operate semi-autonomously, and the amount of coordination they required with mission packages from other Coalition air forces was limited. JTF Proven Force conducted most of its operations north of At-Taji. This was primarily because its location allowed aircraft to reach targets in northern Iraq more readily than could the forces based in Saudi Arabia.

Once Operation Desert Storm began, B-52s deployed to Moron Air Base, Spain, came under EUCOM control and sometimes flew missions coordinated with JTF Proven Force. Later, more B-52s deployed to RAF Fairford, United Kingdom. The decision to fly bombing missions from this location came after approval was granted to fly over French territory carrying conventional weapons. Once bombers based at Fairford began flying in support of JTF Proven Force, bombers at Moron switched to targets near the southern Iraq/Kuwait border under CENTCOM control.

Other EUCOM forces deployed to Turkey as well. On 12 January, the Secretary of Defense authorized the deployment of two EUCOM Patriot batteries from Dexheim, Germany, to Turkey to provide air defense for Incirlik Air Base. By 22 January, six of the eight launchers and 43 missiles were in place and operational.

Non-US Forces

A large contingent of the North Atlantic Treaty Organization's Allied Command, Europe, Mobile Forces (Air) deployed to Turkey to deter an Iraqi attack . Eighteen Luftwaffe Alpha Jets deployed with approximately 800 personnel. Three German reconnaissance aircraft also arrived with about 125 support personnel.

The non-US Coalition partners made a valuable contribution to the success of the air campaign through diplomatic, logistic, and operational support. Some partners who, for various reasons, did not send air forces, provided overflight or basing rights which made support of the effort in theater possible.

Others provided air forces which reinforced the Coalition's capabilities in numerous ways. The RAF provided tactical fighter squadrons

as well as helicopters, reconnaissance aircraft, tankers and transports. The Royal Canadian Air Forces (CAF) deployed air superiority and ground attack fighters available for defensive counter air missions, and support of ground forces. The French Air Force (FAF) provided tactical strike squadrons, air superiority fighters, tankers, transports, reconnaissance aircraft, maritime patrol aircraft (MPA), and helicopters. The Italian Air Force deployed attack fighters, transports, tankers, and reconnaissance aircraft, available to conduct and support air intercept and interdiction missions.

The Gulf Cooperation Council states provided logistic and operational support, as well as air superiority and ground attack fighter aircraft available to fly offensive counter air, defensive counter air, and interdiction sorties. Air forces also were available to conduct refueling, airborne command and control (C^2), reconnaissance, utility, and airlift missions.

EXECUTING THE AIR CAMPAIGN

In this section of Chapter VI, the air campaign is portrayed chronologically, primarily by week, to give an historical perspective of the effort — from the first hours of Operation Desert Storm through the application of air power in the KTO during the Offensive Ground Campaign. In some instances, a particular day (D-Day, D+1, D+2, D+20, and D+38) is highlighted to show the weight of effort applied. In other cases, particular subjects, such as armored vehicle destruction or attacks on hardened aircraft shelters, have received special attention because of their significance. In the last section of this chapter, the effects of the air campaign are recounted by target set, and some operational considerations (such as air supremacy, TLAMs, and the counter-Scud effort) are addressed. But before beginning the description of air operations, a brief discussion of the techniques used during the war to evaluate the effectiveness of the air campaign is necessary to place the campaign narrative in the proper context.

Evaluating the Results of the Air Campaign

Estimates of Iraqi losses were one of a number of tools CENTCOM used to manage combat operations. CENTCOM used loss estimates, among other things, to determine when combat capabilities of Iraqi ground forces had been reduced by half (which was one of the decision criteria for beginning the Offensive Ground Campaign). A methodology for assessing battle damage therefore was developed, and adjusted as circumstances warranted.

Estimating levels of destruction inflicted on the enemy always has been difficult. This was especially true during Operation Desert Storm, with its fast-moving, high-speed air, sea, and ground campaigns, which involved massive attacks throughout the theater of operations, using a wide variety of equipment and munitions. These difficulties were compounded by the fact that some new precision weapons allowed Coalition forces to place ordnance on targets in ways that made determination of actual damage difficult, and by the fact not all platforms had sensors and equipment to record the effects of their weapons. For example, PGMs gave pilots the unique ability to target precisely and strike sections of buildings or hardened shelters, significantly complicating bomb damage assessment. BDA was, therefore, by no means a precise science. It is quite possible that assessments of Iraqi losses during the course of the war, at various times, overestimated or underestimated actual results. Thus the estimates of Iraqi losses presented in this chapter and elsewhere in the report must be read in the proper context. The loss estimates shown in this report are accurate portrayals of the information provided to decision makers at the time. They were intended at the time to represent the best estimates of Iraq's losses then available. They were used at the time by

decision makers as one input into a decision making process that relied fundamentally on the exercise of professional military judgment. That, after all, is the primary purpose of military intelligence — to assist commanders in the field in making informed judgments.

It is possible the levels of damage never will be known with precision. That said, it is important to note that, even with these limitations, probably no set of American commanders has had more information available about the battlefield and enemy forces than the commanders of Operation Desert Storm. Tactical BDA was good enough to help CINCCENT make informed decisions. In retrospect, Operation Desert Storm's success strongly suggests the decisions were sound. In the end, it was professional military judgment — assisted by BDA and other information — that chose the right time to begin the ground offensive.

Two different BDA methodologies, based on fundamentally distinct purposes and guidance were used in the two principal periods of conflict during the Persian Gulf War. Before G-Day, 24 February, BDA estimates were designed to help CINCCENT determine when Iraqi forces in the KTO had been reduced to about half of their overall combat effectiveness — the point when he would be confident in starting the ground offensive. Consequently, ARCENT attempted to track carefully the number of tanks, APC, and artillery pieces destroyed, primarily by air attack, to produce an approximate measure of Iraqi unit degradation. This was one estimate available to CINCCENT for evaluating Iraqi combat effectiveness. He and his staff also used other information such as bridge destruction, communications degradation, estimates of supplies available, troop physical condition and morale, EPW debriefings, the results of the battle of Khafji, intelligence reports and assessments, and destruction of other vehicles.

After G-Day, the emphasis shifted to ground combat. Estimates of Iraqi losses were based on reports from advancing ground units as well as reports from air units. There was a fast-paced accounting of destroyed or captured tanks, APC, and artillery pieces with little attempt to determine if the equipment was destroyed by ground, air, or sea assets, or if the equipment were in working order or in use when destroyed. (For additional discussion of BDA during the Offensive Ground Campaign, see Chapter VIII.)

In connection with this report's preparation, there were extensive searches for any information available after cessation of hostilities that would improve the wartime estimates of Iraqi equipment losses. Postwar surveys were made of selected parts of the KTO, but none covered parts of the theater large enough to permit calculation of comprehensive estimates of overall losses. Many relevant areas were in Iraq itself, and thus inaccessible after the Coalition withdrew. Many parts of Kuwait also were difficult to study because of problems such as the lack of transportation infrastructure and danger from unexploded ordnance. The two analyses based on survey data that were completed after the war cover very small, and not necessarily representative areas. In the case of one study, many of the vehicles had been abandoned without substantial damage and less than half of the tanks destroyed appeared to have been destroyed from the air. However, the sample was small and may not have been representative. Efforts to analyze the available data further are continuing.

D-Day, The First Night

Early in the evening of 16 January, under the guise of routine AWACS station changes, the Coalition launched its first night crews to the standard Operation Desert Shield surveillance orbits.

At Coalition airfields and on board Coalition warships all across the Gulf region, the first hours after midnight 17 January were marked by activity with a new sense of urgency. At the air bases and on flight decks, crews prepared to launch the biggest air strike since World War II. On other warships, sailors were preparing TLAMs for their first combat launch. In cramped compartments, dozens of B-52 crew members, some of whom had left US bases hours earlier, prepared for combat. More than 160 aerial tankers orbited outside Iraqi early warning radar range and refueled hundreds of Coalition aircraft. Shifts of RC-135, U-2R, and TR-1 reconnaissance aircraft maintained normal 24-hour orbits to provide intelligence coverage of Iraq and Kuwait. E-3 AWACS and E-2Cs orbited over Saudi Arabia, powerful radars probed deep into Iraq and crews watched for Iraqi reactions. Meanwhile, the initial attack

Iraqi Air Threat

Aircraft
750 Shooters
200 Support

24 Main Operating Bases
30 Dispersal Bases

AAA AAA

AAA

BAGHDAD

Surface-To-Surface Missiles (SCUD) Chem-Bio Capability

AAA

AAA

AAA

AAA

AAA

Al-Basrah

Well Developed "State of the Art" Air Defenses
Radars
Missiles
AAA

AAA AAA

AAA

KUWAIT   Persian Gulf

De facto boundary as shown on official Iraqi and Saudi maps (alignment approximate)

NEUTRAL ZONE

Boundary representations are not necessarily authoritative.

packages marshaled south of the Iraqi and Jordanian early warning and ground control intercept (GCI) coverage. As H-Hour approached, the entire attack armada moved north, led by a fighter sweep of F-15s and F-14s. As the attack packages flew past, each AWACS moved forward to its wartime orbit. The huge air armada, comprising hundreds of aircraft from many different nations and Services, headed into the dark and threatening hostile airspace.

Even before the fighters struck Iraqi targets, three USAF MH-53J Pave Low special operations helicopters from the 1st Special Operations Wing (SOW) led nine Army AH-64 attack helicopters from the 101st Airborne Division (Air Assault) on a mission into southern Iraq. Shortly before H-Hour, the helicopters, organized as Task Force (TF) Normandy, completed the long, earth-hugging flight and sighted the assigned targets, two early warning radar sites inside Iraq. This mission was possible because of technological advances in night- and low-light vision devices, precise navigational capability resulting from space-based systems such as the Global Positioning System (GPS) satellites, and highly trained crews.

Commitment to hostilities occurred at approximately H-90 minutes when US warships launched TLAM cruise missiles toward targets in Baghdad. At approximately H-22 minutes, the AH-64s struck the opening blow of the conflict by destroying the radar sites with Hellfire missiles. Above and in front of TF Normandy, F-117 stealth fighters from the 37th Tactical Fighter Wing (TFW) already had passed the early warning sites and were well inside Iraqi radar coverage when the attacks occurred. The timing of the helicopter attacks was determined by the projected time when Iraqi air defense radar would detect the EF-111s scheduled to support air attacks on the Baghdad area. Its job complete, TF Normandy headed for home. Nine minutes before H-Hour, an F-117A dropped the

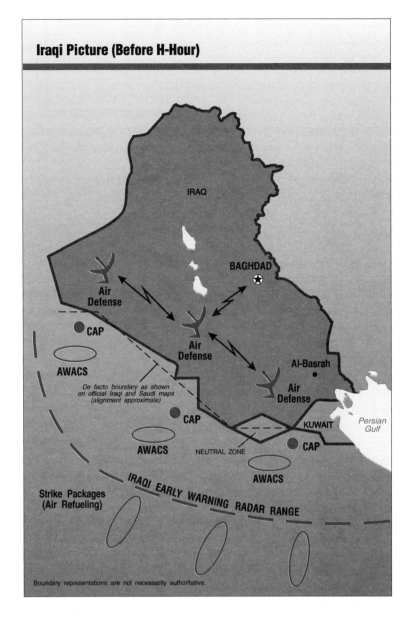

Iraqi Picture (Before H-Hour)

first bomb of the war, striking a hardened air defense intercept operations center (IOC) in southern Iraq, then continued on to drop a second bomb on a regional air defense sector operations center (SOC) in western Iraq. The helicopter and F-117A attacks created gaps in Iraqi radar coverage and in the C^2 network for the non-stealth aircraft which followed. Meanwhile, other F-117As were about to destroy several high-priority targets.

At H-Hour, 0300, two F-117As dropped the first

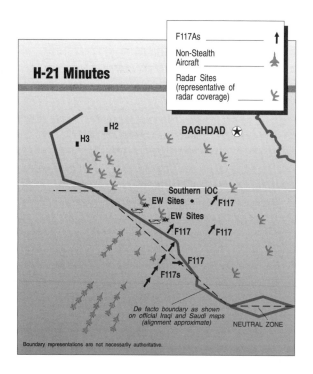

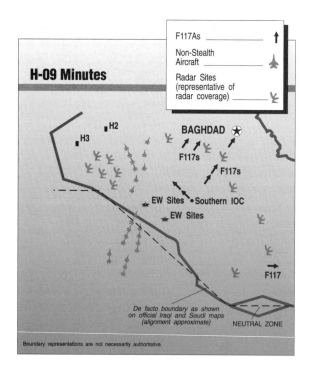

bombs on Baghdad. Shortly thereafter, TLAMs began to strike targets in the Baghdad area. Each F-117A carried two 2,000-lb hardened, penetrating laser-guided bombs (LGBs) and, within the offensive's first minutes, bombed

crucial installations in Baghdad and elsewhere. Each aircraft had an individual route through the Iraqi air defense system and a tailored target attack plan. The F-117A by virtue of its stealth characteristics allowed operations without the full range of support assets required by non-stealthy aircraft. Typically, F-117A sorties used no direct airborne support other than tankers.

An initial Coalition air task was to fragment and eventually destroy the Iraqi IADS. The initial fragmentation was accomplished by the early attacks by Apache helicopters, F-117As, cruise missiles, F-15Es, and GR-1s. Once the IADS was nullified, the enemy became increasingly vulnerable to attack and destruction from the air.

F-117As reached into the heart of downtown Baghdad to strike the Iraqi Air Force headquarters accurately. Ignoring flak, tracers, and SAMs, they systematically hit vital targets. One pilot high over Baghdad that night reported seeing Iraqi AAA wildly spraying fire over Baghdad, hitting the tops of buildings. AAA fire and expended SAMs probably caused some collateral damage inside the capital. Because of the density of the threat and the requirement to minimize collateral damage, F-117As, attacking at night, were the only manned aircraft to attack central Baghdad targets. The only weapon system used for daylight attacks on central Baghdad were TLAMs, which also struck at night. F-16s, B-52s, F/A-18s, A-6s, and A-7s attacked targets in the outskirts of the city. RF-4s, TR-1s, and U-2s flew over Baghdad later in the war, when the threat was reduced.

The first wave of attackers actually encompassed three separate groups that included 30 F-117s and 54 TLAMs. Within the first five minutes, nearly 20 air defense, C^3, electrical, and leadership nodes had been struck in Baghdad; within an hour, another 25 similar targets had been struck, as well as electric distribution and CW sites. By the end of the first

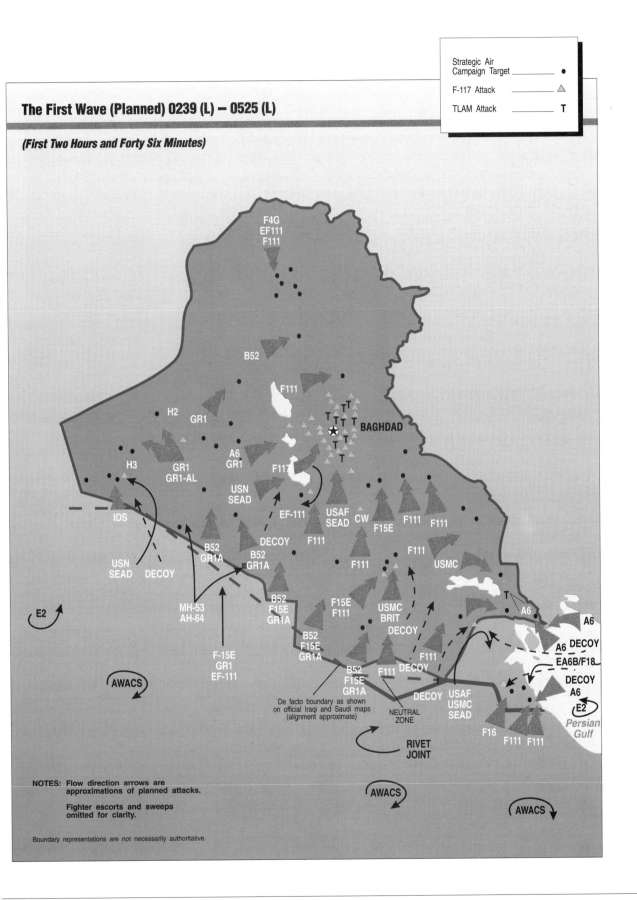

The First Wave (Planned) 0239 (L) — 0525 (L)

Strategic Air Campaign Target _____ ●

F-117 Attack _____ △

TLAM Attack _____ T

(First Two Hours and Forty Six Minutes)

F4G
EF111
F111

B52

H2 GR1

BAGHDAD

H3 GR1
GR1-AL

A6
GR1

F117

USN
SEAD

EF-111 USAF CW F111 F111
SEAD

F15E

IDS

F111 F111

USMC

USN DECOY B52 B52
SEAD GR1A GR1A

DECOY F111

E2

MH-53 B52 F15E USMC A6
AH-64 F15E F111 BRIT A6 DECOY
GR1A DECOY EA6B/F18

B52
F15E DECOY
GR1A A6

F-15E E2
GR1 B52 F111
EF-111 F15E DECOY Persian
GR1A DECOY USAF Gulf
USMC
AWACS De facto boundary as shown SEAD
on official Iraqi and Saudi maps NEUTRAL F16 F111 F111
(alignment approximate) ZONE

RIVET
JOINT

AWACS

AWACS

NOTES: Flow direction arrows are
approximations of planned attacks.

Fighter escorts and sweeps
omitted for clarity.

Boundary representations are not necessarily authoritative.

New Iraqi Air Force Headquarters, Baghdad, was a Vital Target. *The F-117A was the Only Aircraft to Attack Central Baghdad Targets.*

24 hours, nearly four dozen key targets in or near the enemy capital had been hit. These installations included more than a dozen leadership targets, a similar number of air defense and electric distribution facilities, 10 C^3 nodes, and installations in several other target sets. This was not a gradual rolling back of the Iraqi air defense system. The nearly simultaneous suppression of so many vital centers helped cripple Iraq's air defense system, and began seriously to disrupt the LOCs between Saddam Hussein and his forces in the KTO and southeastern Iraq. Nonetheless, the Iraqis always retained some ability to recover at least partially, given enough time and resources. Consequently, target categories required constant monitoring to measure residual capability and recovery attempts. Restrikes and attacks on new targets were used to maintain the pressure. As a result, according to DIA and

CENTCOM intelligence reports, it became increasingly difficult for the Iraqi political and military leadership to organize coherent, timely, and integrated responses to Coalition actions. In part, this was due to physical destruction of hardware and systems, such as C^3 links or CPs. It also was due to the psychological impact of the Coalition attacks. Leaders could not gather timely information on what was happening. When they did get information, they learned specific parts of the Iraqi government and military leadership had been destroyed, sometimes to the extent that individual offices had been bombed and eliminated.

First-day TLAM attacks, launched from cruisers, destroyers, and battleships in the Persian Gulf and the Red Sea, were coordinated with F-117A and other manned aircraft during the initial attacks as part of the carefully crafted

Strategic Air Campaign. The Aegis cruiser *USS San Jacinto* (CG 56) fired the first TLAM from the Red Sea. *USS Bunker Hill* (CG 52) followed moments later from the Persian Gulf. In the first 24 hours, 116 TLAMs from seven warships hit 16 heavily defended targets in Baghdad and its vicinity, damaging electrical power facilities and C^2 capabilities.

Conventional ALCMs also were used in the opening hours of the air campaign. B-52s that had taken from Barksdale AFB, LA, more than 11 hours before H-Hour launched 35 ALCMs to attack military communications sites and power generation and transmission facilities.

Nearly 700 combat aircraft, including fighters, bombers, and EW aircraft (jammers and high-speed antiradiation missile (HARM) shooters) entered Iraqi airspace that night. As they began their attacks, they benefited from encountering a foe who already was reeling and partly blinded from the opening strikes.

Strike packages were as small as a single F-117A or could contain more than 50 aircraft. The strike package against the Ahmad Al-Jabir Airfield complex, for example, consisted of 16 Low-Altitude Navigation Targeting Infrared for Night (LANTIRN)-equipped F-16s with MK-84 bombs, escorted by four F-4Gs configured with HARMs for SEAD, an EA-6B EW jammer, and four F/A-18s configured for the strike-fighter dual role. Supporting these strike packages were many tanker aircraft, including KC-135s, KC-10s, KA-6s, and KC-130s, which were airborne and waiting outside Iraqi airspace.

From the Red Sea and the Persian Gulf, and from bases along the Persian Gulf, Navy and Marine aircraft headed towards their targets near Baghdad and in southwestern and southeastern Iraq. Nineteen USAF F-15Es headed for Scud missile sites in western Iraq, passing through the

Each of the pilots of four F-15Cs from the 58th Tactical Fighter Squadron was flying his first combat mission on 17 January, sweeping for Iraqi fighters. Around Baghdad, "The whole ground was red with Triple-A fire as far as you could see," recalled one pilot. The four F-15s were inbound toward Mudaysis airfield when two Iraqi Mirage F-1 fighters took off and headed for them at low level. Using the look down, shoot down radar capability, one F-15 fired an AIM-7 radar-guided missile and saw the F-1 explode. The Iraqi wingman, evidently startled by this disaster, created an even greater one for himself when he turned right and dove straight into the desert floor.

58th TFS Unit History

gap the helicopters and F-117s had blown in the Iraqi defenses. From bases across Saudi Arabia and the Gulf states, other aircraft prepared to strike strategic centers of gravity throughout Iraq.

An overall depiction of the Coalition air armada at H-Hour would show a multipronged effort. Navy aircraft from the Red Sea carriers *USS John F. Kennedy* and *USS Saratoga,* together with USAF and RAF aircraft, were preparing to strike targets near Baghdad and at heavily defended airfields in western Iraq. Their targets included Scud missile sites, airfields, and air defenses. Navy aircraft also flew many SEAD and EW missions. In southeastern Iraq, between Baghdad and Kuwait, targets such as airfields, port facilities, and air defenses were attacked by Navy aircraft and other Coalition forces, including RAF, RSAF, and Kuwaiti Air Force aircraft, based in eastern Saudi Arabia. Coming up the middle were Coalition air forces striking fixed targets in southern and central Iraq.

Simultaneously, scores of USAF, Navy, USMC, Army, and other Coalition attack and support aircraft closed on strategic targets throughout Iraq and Kuwait, focusing on the IADS and Iraq's C^2 infrastructure, including communications and the electrical power distribution system, which supported Iraqi military operations. The Iraqi air defense

On the morning of 17 January, an EA-6B from Marine Tactical Electronic Warfare Squadron Two provided electronic warfare support for Marine, Navy, and Royal Air Force strike packages attacking strategic targets at the Al-'Amarah and Az-Zubayr command and control sites, as well as the Az-Zubayr railroad yards and the Al-Basrah bridges across the Tigris River. These targets were heavily defended by interlocking belts of surface-to-air missiles (SAM) and antiaircraft artillery (AAA). Iraqi fighters also were a potential threat. This was a dangerous mission — among the first daylight strikes of the war. Long before they approached the targets, the EA-6B crew started to work. The first enemy radar that came up was quickly jammed. Shortly after, however, additional radars were noted searching for the strike groups. Jamming of Iraqi long range early warning radars allowed the strikers to approach undetected. However, Iraqi ground control intercept radars as well as target tracking radars simultaneously began probing the Coalition strike package. The EA-6B crew quickly introduced intense electronic jamming into all modes of the Iraqi air defense system, which prevented the vectoring of enemy fighters. They also forced SAM and AAA systems into autonomous operation, uncoordinated by the command and control system which greatly reduced their ability to locate and track Coalition aircraft. To accomplish this, the EA-6B crew did not attempt evasive action but placed themselves into a predictable, wings-level orbit which highlighted their position amidst the beaconing and jamming strobes of the enemy radars. The severe degradation to radio transmissions caused by jamming interference limited the EA-6Bs ability to receive threat calls, making them vulnerable to enemy aircraft. Nonetheless, the crew remained on station, enabling all Coalition aircraft to strike the targets, accomplish the missions, and return home without loss or damage.

3rd Marine Aircraft Wing Award Citation

system was overwhelmed by the number of attacking aircraft. Nothing approaching the depth, breadth, magnitude, and simultaneity of this coordinated air attack ever had been achieved previously.

The first missions conducted to suppress enemy air defenses were difficult yet vital. At one time during that first hour, the lead F-4G flight countered more than 15 radar sites and several different type SAMs. More than 200 HARMs were fired against Iraqi radars, 100 by USMC F/A-18s alone. USAF EF-111s and F-4Gs, Navy and USMC EA-6Bs, A-6s, A-7s, and F/A-18s, determined threat locations then jammed enemy radar installations or attacked them with HARMs, while EC-130 Compass Call aircraft jammed enemy communications. These SEAD efforts helped keep Coalition losses low; in fact, most missions were possible only because of the SEAD aircraft.

One effective tactic to fool enemy air defenses involved Navy and Marine Corps (USMC) tactical air launched decoys (TALDs). The decoys caused Iraqi defenders to turn on their radars, revealing their locations and making them vulnerable to Coalition SEAD aircraft. The tactic confused the Iraqis and helped divert their defensive effort.

The joint SEAD effort also used 10 long-range Army tactical missile system (ATACMS) missiles to attack an Iraqi air defense site with good success. Overall, Coalition SEAD was highly successful and instrumental in limiting aircraft losses.

First Night Reactions

As these initial strikes took place, the pilots and ground crews back at base or aboard ship could only wait. No one knew how many losses the Coalition would suffer. Even more concerned were the commanders who sent the crews into combat. The commander of the F-111F wing at At-Taif airbase, for example, said, "losses were predicted to be at least 10 percent. I was figuring on ours being higher than that, because of the targets we had. I was personally convinced we were going to lose some airplanes that first night." No matter what the final cost, everyone anticipated the heaviest losses would be during

Baath Party Headquarters

Damaged Leadership
Facilities

Toppled Radio
Tower

10 March 1991

Coalition Air Strikes also Were Directed Against Iraqi Leadership Capabilities.

the first attacks, when the defenses were strongest and the air campaign had not had time to win air superiority.

Fortunately, all but one plane (an F/A-18 from the *USS Saratoga*) returned safely. But no one had any illusions that this would be quick or easy, that victory would be achieved without hard fighting and losses. Indeed, even as the air campaign's first wave of aircraft headed for home, the second wave was preparing to strike its targets.

D-Day, Daytime Attacks

The start of the second wave attacks roughly coincided with sunrise. This made available even more aircraft, as those best suited for daylight operations began flying missions. Throughout the day, USAF A-10s conducted more than 150 sorties against Iraqi ground forces in the KTO and radar sites in Iraq, while F-16s struck targets in the KTO, including airfields and many SAM sites. The initial USMC strikes during the dawn hours of the first day included attacks on enemy aircraft on runways or in revetments at the heavily defended Iraqi air bases of Tallil, Sh'aybah, Al-Qurnah, and Ar-Rumaylah. Thirty-one aircraft were assigned to hit Tallil Airfield alone. Thirty-six aircraft were tasked to strike

Tallil Airfield

7 March 1991

Aerial Attacks Against Iraqi Airfields Such as Tallil Airfield Further Denied the Iraqi Air Force Use of the Sky.

other targets in and around Al-Basrah, and more than a dozen aircraft struck the heavily defended airfield at Sh'aybah. Other attacks hit the airfield, bridges, and railroad yards at Al-'Amarah on the outskirts of Al-Basrah. AV-8Bs attacked armor and artillery targets in southern Kuwait.

Planners were unable to determine if F-15E strikes against fixed Scud launch sites had been successful. The Coalition did not know how many mobile Scud launchers Iraq had — in retrospect, some early estimates of the number were too low. A basic planning assumption always had been that Iraq would use its Scuds to attack Israel, intending to draw it into the war and fragment the Coalition. Scuds also would be targeted against Saudi Arabia and other regional states. This assumption proved correct, but the amount of effort and the length of time required to deal with the Scud threat was underestimated.

By nightfall on the first day of Operation Desert Storm, the Iraqis had suffered serious damage to the strategic C^3 network, the formerly robust strategic air defense system, and key leadership facilities. Part of the known NBC long-term threat already had been degraded, and Coalition air forces had defeated Iraqi Air Force attempts to offer a coordinated resistance.

D-Day, Second Night

The Coalition's ability to fight at night made it difficult for the Iraqis to use the cover of darkness to maintain and repair equipment, and replenish supplies. This was a key advantage helping to keep pressure on the Iraqis 24 hours a day. As night fell, a third wave of Coalition aircraft continued the attacks on key Iraqi strategic targets with emphasis on air defenses. The Iraqi Air Force coordination of defensive operations had been defeated up to this point; indeed they flew only about 50 air patrols during the first day. Shortly after nightfall on the second night of Operation Desert Storm, F-111Fs and A-6Es attacked Iraqi airfields. These aircraft made major contributions because their laser-designator systems let them identify and strike targets day or night without the need for a separate designator airplane. In addition, the F-111s' heavy bombload and relatively long range let them concentrate many precision bombs on target in a short period of time, deep in enemy territory, while exposing a limited number of aircraft to the threat. B-52s struck key Republican Guard elements, with several sorties targeted against the Tawakalna Mechanized Infantry Division.

On D-Day, JTF Proven Force concentrated on targets in northern Iraq in the Mosul, Kirkuk, Tikrit, Quayyarah, and Erbil areas. The EC-130, KC-135, and EF-111A aircraft, along with their F-15 protection, established orbits north of the border. The F-111Es turned south and arrived over their targets at 0410 on 18 January.

D-Day, Controlling Operations

Unity of effort in coordinating and tasking Coalition air power was crucial to ensuring that all Coalition aircraft operated in support of stated goals. The following air-to-air engagement was successful, in part, because airborne warning and control aircraft were part of a unified effort.

A strike package hit the oil facility at Habbaniyah and the airfield at At-Taqaddum with 32 F-16s; 16 F-15s provided air cover, while four EF-111s and eight F-4Gs provided jamming and SEAD support. Over Saudi Arabia and the Red Sea and Persian Gulf, the AWACS and E-2C surveillance planes watched the missions and identified who was friendly. During this particular F-16 mission, the AWACS controllers were able to alert the covering F-15s that two Iraqi MiG-29s were in the area and, in the ensuing action, the F-15s shot them both down. One victory went to a USMC exchange officer flying with the USAF's 58th Tactical Fighter Squadron.

D-Day, Summary

One key immediate objective was to seize air superiority so the full weight of Coalition air power could be brought to bear. The Iraqi Air Force's disorganized response was a positive and heartening sign that air superiority operations were succeeding. Air superiority was clearly important to the rest of Operation Desert Storm. Although the Iraqis would retain the ability throughout the war to react piecemeal to some Coalition strike packages, they would lose the ability to coordinate defensive actions, and each defensive sector would become increasingly isolated from the overall system.

Air superiority, or the dominance of a group of aircraft in a given time and space without prohibitive interference by the opposing force, was effectively gained in the first hours of the war. Coalition aircraft demonstrated they could control airspace of their choosing — the Iraqi Air Force could not coordinate an effective defense. Air supremacy (the degree of air superiority wherein the enemy is incapable of effective interference) would be announced on 27 January.

D+1 (18 January)

Day two operations continued the campaign against key strategic and tactical targets. Nuclear targets were again struck, as they were on D-Day. Between 0400 and 0530, the Coalition attacked air defense, BW and CW facilities, leadership targets, and airfields using more than 80 Coalition night-attack aircraft, including F-117s, F-15Es, F-111s, A-6s, and RAF and Italian Air Force GR-1s. Shortly after sunrise, F-16s and F/A-18s attacked Iraqi army units, including three Republican Guard division elements. Nearly 100 F-16 sorties struck the Tawakalna Division. Approximately 150 A-10 sorties were scheduled against Iraqi forces near, and west of the tri-border area, where the ground campaign's flanking maneuver would

pass through weeks later. F/A-18s and A-6s, supported by EA-6Bs, attacked Tallil Airfield. Large groups of USMC aircraft flew against the Republican Guard's Al-Madinah Division, just west of Al-Basrah. EA-6Bs provided composite active and passive electronic support for air strikes in and around Basrah.

JTF Proven Force aircrews flew their first combat missions shortly after midnight 18 January, when F-111Es raced into Iraq at low level to destroy four EW radar sites in northern Iraq and open an electronic gate. The sky was overcast at 3,000 feet with visibility at three miles with fog. Despite the poor weather, the F-111E crews found the targets and delivered their ordnance, encountering little Iraqi resistance. These, and subsequent missions forced Iraqi commanders to contend with attacks from all directions and to respond to a second air front as well as a potential second ground front. This pressured Iraq from the north, surrounded and forced them to retain forces in the northern region.

Early in Operation Desert Storm planning, CINCCENT had identified the RGFC as a key target; Phase III attacks on the RGFC and frontline armored forces in Kuwait began the first day. The RGFC began to feel real pressure starting the next day, when Coalition aircraft struck three divisions, the Tawakalna Mechanized Infantry Division, and the Hammurabi and Al-Madinah armored divisions, repeatedly throughout that day and the next.

During these two days, the three divisions were targeted for strikes by 214 F-16s, 36 F/A-18s, eight F-15Es, and 31 B-52s. Not included in these totals are missions not targeted directly against these divisions but which nonetheless affected their combat capability, such as air strikes against communications nodes outside the KTO.

The Navy attacked Iraqi naval installations near Umm Qasr, hit hangars and parking

ATO PLANNED ATTACK SORTIES AGAINST THE RGFC

	D+1	D+2
TAWAKALNA	90 F-16s, 8 F/A-18s, 3 B-52s	36 F-16s, 3 B-52s
HAMMURABI	16 F/A-18s, 3 B-52s	42 F-16s, 6 F/A-18s, 8 F-15Es, 12 B-52s
AL-MADINAH	24 F-16s, 3 B-52s	2 F-16s, 6 F/A-18s 7 B-52s

ramp areas at Sh'aybah and Ahmad Al-Jabir airfields during the late morning, and struck 17 oil, electric, and leadership targets with TLAMs.

D+1, Night

Darkness on D+1 did not mean the Iraqis would gain any respite. Coalition forward looking infrared (FLIR)- and radar-equipped aircraft attacked bridges behind the Republican Guards, to cut them off from their supply bases. Seven B-52 sorties took off from bases in the CONUS and bombed RGFC divisional elements in the KTO. An hour before midnight, a dozen F-117s bombed key C^3, leadership, and strategic air defense installations, including the ministries of Defense, Information, and Internal Security in downtown Baghdad.

By the end of the second day, Navy warships had fired 216 TLAMs, 64 percent of those fired during Operation Desert Storm, in support of the air campaign, while continuing to engage surface combatants, antiship missile bases and to track and destroy floating mines in the Persian Gulf. On 17 and 18 January, the Persian Gulf battle force flew more than half of its initial strikes against Iraqi naval facilities, coastal defense sites, and fortified oil platforms Iraq used in surveillance and small boat operations. Specific targets included the port facility, naval base, and Styx missile storage facility at Umm Qasr; the coastal defense sites at Al-Faw, Mina 'Abd Allah, Al-Qaruh Island and Umm Al-Maradim; the Mina Al-Bakr oil terminal and platform; and the Khawr Al-'Amayah oil platform. Naval aircraft flying from the Red Sea and Persian Gulf battle groups completed 1,100 sorties in support of the air campaign. USMC attack aircraft began shaping the battlefield during the first two days. F/A-18s, A-6s, and AV-8Bs attacked and destroyed armored vehicles, tanks, artillery, and Free Rocket Over Ground batteries throughout southern and central Kuwait. USMC F/A-18 and EA-6B aircraft struck Tallil airfield and bombed the Republican Guard's Al-Madinah Division as

well as a Republican Guard armored battalion. AV-8Bs nearly tripled their sorties from the first day, flying 55 missions against Iraqi front-line artillery battalions on the eastern side of Kuwait.

RAF GR-1s continued attacking Iraqi airfields, while A-6s attacked electricity-related and C^3 targets in the Al-Basrah, Az-Zubayr, and Al-Hadithah area. B-52s again bombed Republican Guard formations and began striking industrial targets, with eight sorties targeted against Iraqi oil installations in isolated areas where there was little probability of collateral damage. Finally, at 0300, the dividing line between D+1 and D+2, 10 F-117 sorties struck 17 C^3, air defense, and leadership targets around Baghdad and At-Taji.

D-Day through D+6: Summary of Week One (17-23 January)

At the end of Operation Desert Storm's first week, substantial results had been accomplished against several target categories, according to CENTCOM and intelligence reports. Many important targets had been destroyed by the first two days' operations, affecting several key Iraqi capabilities. The Coalition enjoyed air superiority, primarily because the Iraqi Air Force was not vigorously contesting the air campaign; still, the Iraqi Air Force remained a potential threat. Iraq's strategic air defenses and C^3 network had been fragmented, partly as a result of damage to the Iraqi national electric power grid. Iraq's known nuclear and BW programs, as well as its stocks of deployable CW were under daily attack. National political and military leadership was becoming increasingly cut off and isolated from preferred, secure means to direct operations. Iraqi ground and naval forces in the KTO were attacked from the beginning, to eliminate their ability to conduct substantial offensive operations and reduce their ability to oppose later military operations.

In combination with the naval embargo, the

Strategic Air Campaign's early effect on Iraqi war support infrastructure was substantial. Iraq's internal fuels refining and production capability was shut down, limiting its ability to produce fuel for its tanks, planes, and war-supporting infrastructure and resulting in government-imposed rationing of pre-attack inventory. Saddam Hussein's internal telecommunications capability was so badly damaged that, while he could broadcast televised propaganda to the world by portable satellite uplinks, he was limited in the use of telecommunications to influence the Iraqi populace.

During the first week, aircraft attacked Iraqi facilities throughout Iraq and Kuwait. USAF F-117As, F-16s, B-52s, A-10s, and F-4Gs, Navy and USMC A-6Es and F/A-18s, USMC AV-8Bs, and Navy A-7s attacked air defense radars, communications nodes, and military headquarters. During the first 24 hours alone, for example, 3rd MAW flew four major strategic strike packages. Another three waves hit such targets as the bridges in Al-Basrah and the RGFC Al-Madinah Division on days two and three. Aircraft such as RAF and RSAF GR-1 fighter-bombers attacked Iraqi airfields to destroy aircraft and bomb support facilities, and to suppress air defenses. USAF F-15s, Navy F-14s, and Navy and USMC F/A-18s provided

CAP and sweeps for attack packages and played an important role in establishing air supremacy quickly. USAF A-10s performed Scud-hunter and antitank missions.

The Iraqi Air Force had lost 39 aircraft, 14 of them in air-to-air combat. The Coalition's technology provided the ability to detect and destroy enemy fighters from beyond visual range. Coalition aircraft losses had been remarkably light, due in large measure to the successful initial attacks that quickly seized the initiative. Eleven US aircraft had been lost in combat, while other Coalition forces had lost six, most notably four RAF GR-1 Tornados lost on low-level airfield attack missions. With the possible exception of one F/A-18 loss still under investigation, all Coalition losses were inflicted by ground-based air defenses (antiaircraft fire or SAMs).

Perhaps the most significant tactical issue to arise in planning the air campaign concerned Coalition aircraft flying above the AAA and hand-held SAMs threat. Despite the strong peacetime emphasis on training for low-level delivery tactics, which exploit terrain to reduce aircraft detectability to radar and hence vulnerability to SAMs and to increase weapon delivery accuracy under the weather, the density of the Iraqi AAA and the dangers posed by unaimed barrage fire to low-flying aircraft drove some aircraft to higher altitude delivery tactics. After the initial attacks on Iraqi air defense nodes succeeded in largely neutralizing the SAMs able to engage at medium and high altitudes, a virtual sanctuary existed for Coalition aircraft above 10,000 feet, allowing medium-altitude delivery tactics.

Two factors slowed progress of the air campaign in its first week: bad weather and a greater-than-expected effort against Scuds. A weather front stalled over Iraq on the third day of the conflict, and disrupted operations for the next three days. Many sorties were canceled;

On 19 January, as more than 70 F-16s, along with F-15 escorts and EF-111 and F-4G support, headed toward Baghdad, the weather steadily worsened. Just after the package broke out of the weather north of the Iraqi border, antiaircraft artillery (AAA) fire disrupted the formation. About a fourth of the pilots could not find the rest of the formation and had to return home. The first group to strike were the F-16s from the 388th Tactical Fighter Wing, which hit the nuclear research facility near Baghdad. Unfortunately for the following F-16s, the Suppression of Enemy Air Defense package of F-4Gs had fired all its high-speed antiradiation missiles and left the area, as did the covering F-15s. That left the F-16s from the 614th Tactical Fighter Squadron with no air cover and no electronic support assets. The F-16s immediately came under heavy surface-to-air missile and AAA fire — two were shot down.

401 Tactical Fighter Wing Report

others were diverted to different and sometimes less important targets; some missions were less effective even when they got to their assigned targets, or flew into greater danger.

Because the effort to suppress Scud attacks proved more difficult than originally anticipated, greater emphasis against Iraqi Scuds began on the third day; this effort also took sorties away from other planned targets. Although the Army's Patriot air defense missile system experienced operational success against Scuds, the Coalition still faced an urgent requirement to prevent launches, and the Iraqi ability to hide before and after launch proved considerable.

D+10 (27 January — CINCCENT Declares Air Supremacy)

The air superiority gained in the first days of Operation Desert Storm, and the air supremacy declared on D+10, against some of the more heavily defended airspace in the history of warfare, granted Coalition aircraft a safety and freedom that permitted operations at high and medium altitudes over Iraq with virtual impunity. Air attacks continued on strategic targets in Iraq and to cut off and destroy the combat effectiveness of the Iraqi army in the KTO. For example, in Iraq, Coalition air forces continued to target Scud production and storage facilities, airfield facilities at H-2, Tallil, and Shaykhah Mazhar as well as the air defense headquarters, the Ministry of Industry and Military Industrialization and several secret police and intelligence headquarters buildings in Baghdad. In the KTO air forces targeted the Ar-Rumaylah ammunition storage area, the Al-Basrah radio relay and TV transmission facility, divisional logistics sites, and directed hundreds of sorties against Iraqi army artillery, armor, and support units.

The Iraqi Air Force was expected to react to Coalition attacks. However, Coalition fighter pilots were confident they would prevail.

Saddam Hussein Tried to Protect His Air Force in Hardened Aircraft Shelters. *Penetrating Bombs Denied This Sanctuary.*

Although the Coalition had air superiority at the end of D-Day, commanders wanted to guarantee the Iraqi Air Force would stay out of the fight; they wanted no surprises.

When Iraqi aircraft challenged the Coalition and suffered high losses, Iraq tried to shelter its aircraft. Iraqi doctrine envisioned keeping the Iraqi Air Force as a kind of strategic reserve, a role it had fulfilled during the war with Iran. Saddam Hussein thought his Air Force would be

The Power of the Weapons Used Against Airfield Shelters is Shown. *Concrete and Steel Blast Doors Weighing as Much as 60 Tons Sometimes Were Hurled up to 250 Feet Across the Tarmac.*

Exterior Shows Little Damage, but Interior and Contents Are Destroyed.

severely damaging a carrier. Any of these possibilities was highly undesirable in its own right, but, in addition, might galvanize western public opinion against the war, or split the Coalition. To preclude this possibility, the Coalition began attacking the hardened aircraft shelters.

This was a difficult task. The Iraqis had 594 shelters, some of which were believed to be hardened in a manner similar to missile silos, able to withstand the effects and blast over-pressures that would accompany nearby air-burst detonation of tactical nuclear weapons. Although Iraqi airfields had been attacked since the first hours of the war, the early emphasis was on denying the the use of the runways, not on destroying the shelters (except those suspected of hiding Scud missiles). On 23 January, however, the JFACC changed the tactic and started attacking directly the aircraft hidden in shelters, using 2,000-lb case-hardened penetrating LGBs. F-117As attacked Balad and other airfields. F-111s and RAF Tornados and Buccaneers attacked the shelters from medium-altitudes, which gave the crews a better, longer look at their targets than low-altitude attacks. Other Coalition aircraft provided SEAD support and fighter cover.

safe inside the extensive Iraqi aircraft shelter system.

For the first week of the war the Iraqi Air Force averaged only about 30 fighter sorties a day; it did not lose many airplanes that week because it did not fly much. Coalition planners considered the Iraqis might suddenly launch an aerial offensive, a last-gasp expenditure of the air force in an effort to engage Israel, attack Dhahran or Riyadh, cause significant Coalition ground casualties (perhaps through a CW attack), or strike a Fleet element in hopes of

The impact was dramatic. Post-strike target photos revealed the progressive destruction of the Iraqi Air Force. Each F-111 carried up to four bombs. In one attack, 20 F-111s made two passes each on an airfield, delivering PGMs directly on command bunkers and aircraft shelters, within seven minutes. This equates to a weapon impact about every five seconds. Most of these case hardened bombs penetrated many feet of reinforced concrete and detonated inside the shelters, causing catastrophic explosions that destroyed the shelters and their contents from the inside out. Concrete and steel blast doors weighing as much as 60 tons were hurled up to 250 feet. In some cases, the bombs penetrated the roof and the floor of the shelter before

Pinpoint Strikes Against Airfield Shelters and Personnel Bunkers.

detonation, crushing aircraft between the floor and ceiling.

Although the Iraqis had flown a few aircraft to Iran before Operation Desert Storm, most had been cargo or transport aircraft. On 26 January, however, the Iraqis suddenly began a mass exodus of their more capable combat aircraft to Iran. During the next three days, CENTCOM estimated nearly 80 combat aircraft fled across the border.

The Coalition responded by establishing barrier air patrols between Baghdad and the Iranian border with F-15s, and later with F-14s, which resulted in several MiG-23s being shot down. No Iraqi aircraft entered Iranian airspace for several days. However, when the patrols were reduced, the Iraqis resumed the flights. Between 6 and 10 February, more than 40 aircraft fled to Iran, where aircraft and pilots were interned by the Iranian government. The Coalition then increased the patrols and prevented most aircraft from leaving Iraq.

Meanwhile, in further attempts to prevent the air force's annihilation, the Iraqis also dispersed their aircraft around airfields, onto public roads, into civilian neighborhoods, and even in the shadows of ancient historical structures. Perhaps they guessed Coalition aircrews would not risk killing civilians or damaging historical monuments to destroy isolated aircraft. Although some dispersed aircraft were attacked during the remainder of the war, the Coalition considered them a low priority because they were difficult to service, launch, and maintain; they were effectively out of the fight. By 27 January, CINCCENT was able to announce the Iraqi Air Force was combat ineffective — air supremacy had been secured.

SEAD Operations

Establishment of air superiority in the KTO, planned as the second phase of the campaign, took place in conjunction with Phase I. The targets included Iraqi air defense weapons systems able to disrupt Coalition air strikes against Iraq and Kuwait. Particular emphasis was placed on enemy SAM systems, including mobile launchers, AAA, early warning and target tracking radars, and C^2 links that tied these systems together. Phase II was a combined operation involving the aircraft of several Coalition nations as well as Army, Navy, USMC and USAF assets. EW aircraft, dedicated to SEAD missions, were the heart and soul of Phase II operations.

In the early days of the air campaign, EA-6Bs, A-6Es, and F/A-18s escorted large strike packages into southern Iraq. The F/A-18s, A-6Es, A-7s, and S-3s successfully used TALDs to saturate, confuse, and deceive the air defense system. This tandem combination of soft and hard kill capability proved successful — no Coalition losses to radar-guided SAMs occurred during SEAD escort.

EA-6Bs and EF-111s also were highly effective in jamming Iraqi low-frequency early warning and higher frequency target-track and acquisition radars throughout the early air campaign, providing an umbrella for strikes. This jamming tactic was reduced as the war evolved because of the apparent success of HARMs and hard-kill weapons Coalition air forces delivered.

The carefully planned, large-scale SEAD operation, begun during the opening moments of the war, was successful. During the latter part of the war, many sites not destroyed by HARMs or bombs were wary about turning on radars for fear of being attacked. Although some target-acquisition and target-track radars were not destroyed, enemy radar activity decreased as the war progressed; consequently, the number of HARMs fired also declined. The captured commander of an Iraqi armored unit stated a fear of instant retaliation if his radars or radios were turned on. With this disruption of SAM and AAA radars, Coalition forces were able to operate at medium to high altitudes, staying out of the low altitude, highly lethal AAA and infrared (IR) SAM environment. SEAD helped degrade air defense capabilities and command links, stopping the effective flow of information throughout the Iraqi chain of command.

D+7 through D+13: Summary of Week Two (24 - 30 January)

As the bad weather that disrupted air operations during the first week of Operation Desert Storm cleared, the Coalition intensified its air attacks. The most notable aspects of week two operations were the interdiction of Iraqi LOCs in the KTO, the start of hardened aircraft shelter destruction, and the direct attacks on Iraqi forces in the KTO. Additional Coalition members began or increased their participation — the Qatari Emirates Air Force began flying combat missions and the FAF extended its combat operations into Iraq. Air attacks against strategic targets continued. The Iraqi strategic air defense system was so badly fragmented that only three of 16 IOC were fully operational. The anti-Scud effort continued unabated, although Iraq continued to launch Scuds at both Israel and Saudi Arabia. Coalition air losses were extremely light, with only three aircraft (an F-16, an AV-8B, and an RAF GR-1) lost to enemy action in seven days' operations. The Iraqi Air Force lost 11 aircraft in air-to-air combat.

On 25 January, Saddam Hussein began fouling the Gulf with millions of barrels of heavy, black crude oil. The damage inflicted through pumping crude oil directly into the Gulf was unprecedented. Iraq's intent may have been to block Coalition amphibious operations, or to threaten Saudi desalinization plants. Whatever the motive, the impact would have been even worse except for the Coalition's actions. Two F-111Fs used 2,000-lb GBU-15 bombs to destroy the pumping system and manifolds, cutting off the flow of oil into the Persian Gulf waters.

Air operations to cut Iraqi movements into the KTO began in earnest during week two. On 27 January, eight bridges were dropped or substantially damaged. These strikes not only caused traffic backups, which themselves became lucrative targets, but also further degraded Iraqi C^3 because some bridges carried communications cables. Once again, the ability of Coalition aircraft, especially F-111Fs, A-6s, F-15Es, F/A-18s, and RAF GR-1 (in cooperation with RAF Buccaneers), to deliver PGMs with extraordinary accuracy was a key factor in this effort.

Also on 27 January, Coalition air planners increased emphasis on the isolation and destruction of the Republican Guard and Iraqi Army in the KTO. The Republican Guard, Iraqi armor, artillery, C^3, and logistics throughout the KTO were marked for heavy attacks.

D+12 through D+14 (29 - 31 January — The Battle of Al-Khafji)

On 29 January, the Iraqis launched several small attacks into Saudi Arabia and captured the undefended, evacuated border town of Al-Khafji. Coalition air power played a key role in defeating these attacks, which ended with an important Coalition victory during the air campaign's third week. Other than Scud attacks on Saudi and Israeli cities, this was the only noteworthy Iraqi offensive action. Saddam Hussein's exact purpose is not known, although he might have sought to probe Coalition forces or provoke a large-scale ground battle. EPW reports show a major objective was to capture American troops. Although Iraqi forces occupied the nearly deserted town, their ultimate defeat said much about their combat capabilities 12 days into the air campaign (Coalition ground actions in Al-Khafji are discussed in more detail in Appendices I and J).

During the night of 29 and 30 January, Iraqi armored and mechanized infantry forces began several battalion-sized attacks against Coalition ground forces, including elements of the Saudi Arabian National Guard and USMC forces. The eastern most Iraqi force occupied the Saudi Arabian border town of Al-Khafji. Despite being outgunned by the heavier Iraqi forces, Coalition ground forces offered stiff resistance. Saudi M60 tanks destroyed Iraqi tanks and armored personnel carriers. Farther to the west at Al-Wafrah and across the southwestern corner of Kuwait , the USMC inflicted substantial losses on the Iraqis, using Light Armor Vehicles equipped with TOW anti-tank missiles.

The Iraqi forces were from the 5th Mechanized and the 3rd Armored divisions of the regular army, equipped with several hundred tanks and other armored vehicles, but they had no air support.

While Coalition ground forces were fighting the advancing Iraqis, Coalition air power had a major effect on the battle. While USMC helicopter gunships provided close-in fire support, a steady stream of Coalition fixed-wing aircraft struck the Iraqis. AV-8Bs, A-6s, and F/A-18s, working with OV-10 forward air controllers (FACs), delivered general

purpose and cluster bombs against Iraqi troops near Coalition ground forces. A-6s used radar beacons broadcasting from special forces on the ground to guide their bombing of Iraqi artillery positions, while A-10s using Maverick missiles and LANTIRN-equipped F-16s using CBU-87 combined effects munitions attacked armor and vehicles. Three AC-130 gunships from the 1st SOW delivered minigun and cannon fire against vehicles and armored personnel carriers; one AC-130 was shot down. The combination of dogged resistance by the ground forces and the constant pounding from Coalition air forces stopped the Iraqi advance.

During daylight on 30 January, Coalition ground and air forces continued to maul the Iraqis, demonstrating the degree to which Coalition military power was coordinated and integrated. That night, Saudi Arabian and Qatari armored elements launched a counter strike against the Iraqis holding Al-Khafji; by midday on 31 January, they had destroyed the remaining Iraqi forces in the town, taking several hundred EPWs.

This ended the ground engagements of the battle of Al-Khafji, but a lesser known aspect had taken place that night, 30-31 January, farther north, inside occupied Kuwait. During the daylight hours of 30 January, while Coalition aircraft conducted tactical strikes on Iraqi forces in contact with Coalition ground forces, manned and unmanned reconnaissance, and intelligence assets gathered a clearer picture of what was going on behind the leading Iraqi elements. New reconnaissance technologies such as the TR-1, Joint Surveillance Target Attack Radar System (JSTARS), and Navy and USMC unmanned aerial vehicles played an important role.

For eight hours, throughout the night, Coalition air power systematically attacked and decimated the two divisions; by daybreak the divisions were retreating in disarray. If they had been able to attack into Saudi Arabia in good order, they might have precipitated a large-scale ground

> **O**n 30 January, two Iraqi divisions were detected marshaling for a follow-on attack into Al-Khafji. This offered Coalition air power a lucrative target and, shortly after nightfall, Coalition aircraft took full advantage of their night combat capabilities. Heavy Coalition air attacks were directed onto the two Iraqi divisions. B-52s dropped armor-sensing mines, AV-8Bs, A-6s, and F/A-18s delivered cluster and precision munitions, A-10s and F-16s fired Maverick missiles, and F-15Es and F-16s dropped combined effects munitions. In some cases, when Iraqi vehicles were found in columns, the first aircraft took out the lead and trail vehicles, trapping the rest of the vehicles for follow-on attacks. In another case, the Tactical Air Control Center used Airborne Warning and Control System aircraft to redirect a three-ship B-52 formation to strike Iraqi armor north of Al-Khafji. The strike caught more than 80 Iraqi vehicles in column and broke it apart, making it easier for other aircraft to destroy the rest of the column.
>
> *CENTCOM Messages and Unit Reports*

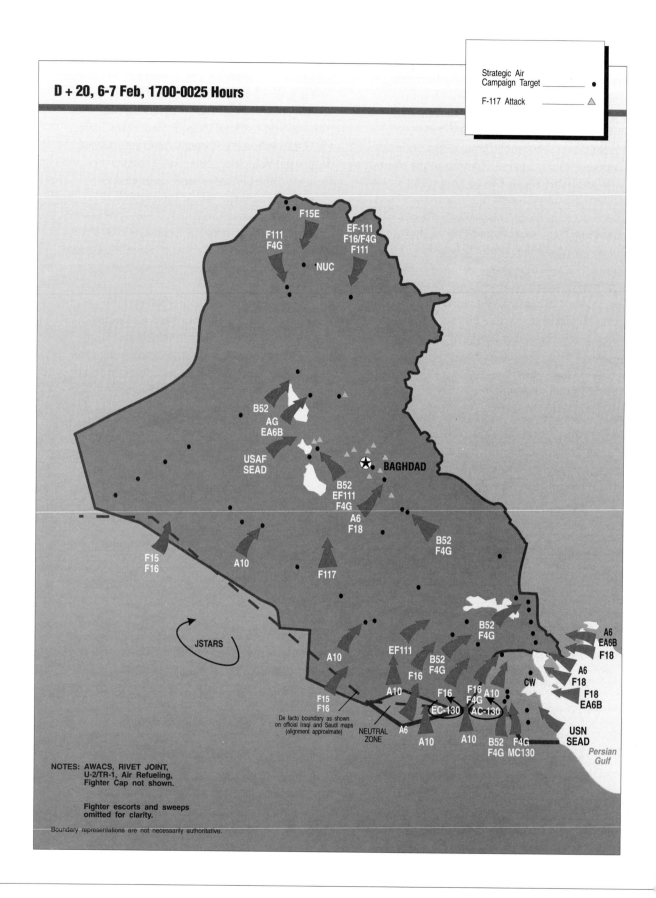

D + 20, 6-7 Feb, 1700-0025 Hours

Strategic Air
Campaign Target _____ ●

F-117 Attack _____ △

F15E

EF-111
F16/F4G
F111

F111
F4G

NUC

B52
AG
EA6B

USAF
SEAD

B52
EF111
F4G

★ BAGHDAD

A6
F18

B52
F4G

F15
F16

A10

F117

JSTARS

A10

EF111

B52
F4G

B52
F4G

F16

A10

F16
F4G

F16 A10
F4G

CW

A6
F18

A6
EA6B
F18

F18
EA6B

F15
F16

EC-130

AC-130

De facto boundary as shown
on official Iraqi and Saudi maps
(alignment approximate)

NEUTRAL
ZONE

A6

A10

A10

B52
F4G

F4G
MC130

USN
SEAD

*Persian
Gulf*

NOTES: AWACS, RIVET JOINT,
U-2/TR-1, Air Refueling,
Fighter Cap not shown.

**Fighter escorts and sweeps
omitted for clarity.**

Boundary representations are not necessarily authoritative.

engagement and caused significant Coalition casualties. Instead, they were repulsed. III Corps suffered numerous casualties and lost a substantial number of tanks and an undetermined number of other vehicles, according to combat unit and intelligence reports.

The Battle of Al-Khafji was important for the Coalition; the only ground offensive operation Saddam Hussein mounted had been defeated. The Pan-Arab forces had defeated the Iraqis in a pitched battle, launching a difficult night counterattack against enemy armor. The destruction inflicted on two Iraqi divisions by Coalition aircraft seemed to presage what awaited any Iraqi force that left dug-in defenses to conduct a mobile operation. The strategic significance: Any Iraqi unit that moved probably would be struck from the air. Any unit that remained in place eventually would be struck either from the air, or by the impending ground assault.

D+20 (6-7 February — Emphasis on Degrading the Iraqi Army and Navy)

During the air campaign's 21st day, attacks continued across the theater, although CINCCENT was shifting the emphasis from strategic targets in Iraq to direct attacks on Iraqi forces in the KTO. Map VI-10 depicts the D+20 planned sorties during 6 to 7 February, 1700 to 0025 hours. These attacks were roughly concentrated in four geographic regions — strategic targets in Baghdad; strategic targets in northern Iraq; Scud-related targets in the southwest and southeast of Iraq; direct attack on Iraqi forces in the KTO.

Attacks in northern Iraq were planned primarily against airfields and hardened aircraft shelters,

Precision Strikes Against Rail Lines Reduced Iraqi Resupply in the Kuwait Theater of Operations.

CW and nuclear weapons storage and production facilities. As examples, a dozen F-111s from At-Taif bombed the nuclear production and storage facilities at Mosul (Al-Mawsil); JTF Proven Force F-111s hit communications transmitters and a railroad station near Kirkuk.

Attacks in and near Baghdad concentrated on leadership, C^2, and airfields. F-117A sorties were planned against leadership command facilities and a Signals Intelligence facility in Baghdad. Other F-117As were scheduled to bomb leadership facilities and hardened aircraft shelters at Ar-Rashid and Balad Southeast airfields near Baghdad. B-52s were tasked to bomb the military production plant at Habbaniyah. More than a dozen A-6s and F/A-18s were scheduled to attack the SAM production and support facility at Al-Falliyah. Concurrently, Red Sea Battle Force aircraft were bombing targets north of Baghdad in the target complexes around Samarra.

During the same period, taking advantage of

night detection and targeting systems, dozens of F-15Es and LANTIRN-equipped F-16s were scheduled to respond to JSTARS and AWACS, which would direct attacks on Scud launchers and transporters, and other targets of opportunity such as convoys and Iraqi Army forces.

Meanwhile, waves of attacks were to take place in the KTO against Iraqi armored and mechanized units, personnel, artillery, headquarters facilities, C^2 facilities, supply vehicles and bridges, and storage areas. MC-130s were to drop 15,000-lb BLU-82 bombs against front line Iraqi positions in southern Kuwait. Silkworm missile sites and an infantry division at Al-Faw were scheduled for attacks by A-6s and B-52s. Scores of sorties by B-52s, AV-8Bs, F-16s, A-10s, F/A-18s, A-6s, A-7s, and an AC-130 were directed to attack Iraqi ground forces in kill boxes inside Kuwait.

Cutting Off the Iraqi Army

Air interdiction attacks were planned to reduce and slow resupply for the forces in the KTO, which were almost totally dependent on outside sources for supplies, including food and water. The Iraqis had extensive stockpiles in rear areas which were only moderately degraded by air

Resupply Movements from Baghdad to Al-Basrah

Solid Line Depicts Steady Reduction in Resupply Movement Capacity

- Required to Sustain Offensive Operations
- Required to Sustain Defensive Operations (30-42K MT/D)
- Required to Subsist in Place (Non Combat) (12-17K MT/D)

Metric Tons/Day — Days

(Curve Based Upon DIA Wartime Estimates)

The executive officer of Marine Attack Squadron 311, and his division went on standby alert for the first morning of the war. At 0740 an OV-10 reported Iraqi artillery was firing on the Saudi town of Al-Khafji. The Major led his four AV-8Bs, each loaded with four 1,000 pound bombs, Sidewinder missiles, and guns, north over the Persian Gulf. From their position 20,000 feet over the sea they could see smoke from burning oil tanks billowing 10,000 feet into the air. The OV-10 controller briefed the AV-8Bs, which then rolled in on six Iraqi artillery pieces. From out of the morning sun, the AV-8B pilots watched artillery tubes tossed high into the air from the impact of their bombs, then they headed back to base. The AV-8Bs' first combat mission was a success.

Marine Attack Group 13 (Forward)
Commanding Officer Report

attacks — but air attacks dramatically slowed resupply. The key interdiction targets were identified as about 40 of the 54 bridges across the Tigris and Euphrates rivers, along with railroad marshaling yards, fuel depots and supply concentration areas. Truck convoys also were hit.

Cutting the one rail line running south from Al-Basrah through Az-Zubayr to the KTO and the bridges over the Tigris and Euphrates rivers reduced the ability of the Iraqi army to resupply the theater. Once stockpiled supplies had been destroyed from the air or consumed, the Iraqi army would be unable to sustain itself.

Interdiction attacks reduced the flow of supplies from Baghdad to the KTO and made supply movements within the KTO extremely difficult and slow. By 4 February (D+18), intelligence estimated the amount of supplies reaching Iraqi forces in the KTO was below the level needed to sustain combat operations. One captured senior Iraqi infantry officer said that one week after the bombing began, there was no more resupply. Food shortages apparently caused desertion rates to escalate. Air interdiction attacks left most of the Iraqi army in the KTO weak and demoralized, although frontline forces in Kuwait bore the brunt of these privations. These and other air attacks, according to Military Intelligence reports, psychologically disarmed some Iraqi soldiers.

Degrading the Iraqi Army

Beginning on D-Day, Coalition air power, naval gunfire bombardment from the Gulf, and ground based artillery and rocket systems methodically struck Iraqi armor, artillery, and infantry forces. During the war, more than 35,000 attack sorties were flown against KTO targets, including 5,600 against Republican Guard forces. Artillery, CPs, C^2 facilities, armor, and logistics installations were hit daily. As the ground offensive approached, more sorties were allocated to

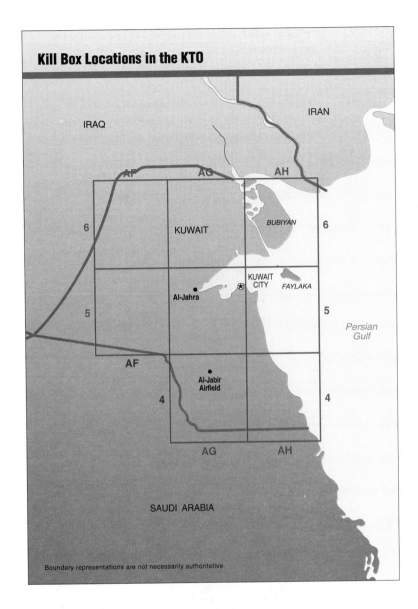

Kill Box Locations in the KTO

Boundary representations are not necessarily authoritative.

battlefield preparation and breaching operations. B-52s and USMC A-6s were used along enemy front lines in conjunction with MC-130s and other aircraft to deliver more than 21 million psychological warfare leaflets to warn Iraqi forces of what to expect if they did not leave Kuwait.

Kill Boxes

Locating and destroying the enemy in the tight confines of the KTO, while deconflicting Coalition air strikes, was a major concern. With the large number of Coalition aircraft operating over the KTO, especially in bad weather and the limited visibility caused by the smoke from burning oil fields, it was imperative to separate air strike elements, both to prevent the inefficiency of striking the same target and to prevent fratricide or mid-air collisions. Before Operation Desert Storm began, air planners devised a kill box system.

Kill boxes were assigned on the ATO and aircraft operating in them were allowed to locate and attack targets of opportunity. The boxes were 30 miles on a side (more than three times the size of New York City) and were subdivided into four quadrants to be assigned to a flight for a specified period of time. This system not only deconflicted the many Coalition aircraft operating in the region but also simplified the task of locating targets. When possible, airborne FACs and strike units were assigned repeatedly to a specific kill box increasing their familiarity with its features and terrain and making operations more effective. Within the I MEF area of operations, the kill boxes were further subdivided into maneuver boxes and fire support boxes, which simplified the task of coordinating and controlling air strikes at known locations.

Destroying the Iraqi Navy

The maritime campaign plan called for neutralization and destruction of Iraqi naval combatants and Iraqi mine layers. This effort was considered a prerequisite to moving Coalition naval forces into the northern Persian Gulf to support the anticipated ground offensive and a possible amphibious assault. (See Chapter VII, Maritime Campaign, for detailed description of naval operations.) To carry out these attacks, Navy commanders used, in

An Iraqi Tank Dug-in and Camouflaged to Avoid Detection and Increase Survivability. *The Effort Was Not Successful.*

addition to Coalition warships, carrier-based aircraft (A-6Es, F/A-18s, F-14s, and S-3A/Bs), MPA (P-3Cs and RAF Nimrods), helicopters (Navy SH-60Bs, RAF Lynxes, and Army OH-58Ds), and land-based Coalition aircraft (CAF CF-18s). These assets used such weapons as Mark 80 series 500- and 1,000-lb bombs, 1,000-lb LGBs, Skipper air-to-surface missiles, Zuni 5-inch rockets, and MK-20 Rockeye 500-lb cluster bombs. Sea Skua helicopters launched air-to-surface missiles, and used .50 caliber and 20-mm aircraft machine guns. By 2 February, the Iraqi navy was assessed as being incapable of offensive action.

D+14 through D+20: Summary of Week Three (31 January - 6 February)

Week three focused attacks on the Republican Guard and other Iraqi forces in the KTO, with the overall emphasis shifting from strategic attacks towards KTO objectives. JTF Proven Force kept up the pressure over northern and central Iraq. The Iraqi Navy was eliminated as a fighting force.

Convoys jammed up behind destroyed bridges and made large numbers of Iraqi supply vehicles vulnerable to destruction. Newly implemented FAC techniques, such as operating special scout FACs within designated geographic kill boxes, increased the efficiency and destructiveness of battlefield air operations. Psychological Operations (PSYOP) were mounted to weaken Iraqi morale and increase desertion. These included operations such as leaflet drops to warn Iraqi units of impending attacks (to spur desertion), and the use of BLU-82 bombs to send a threatening signal to Iraqi ground soldiers.

Coalition losses during this week were again quite low, with only three planes (an A-10, an AC-130, and A-6E) lost to enemy action.

Scattered Debris of an Iraqi Tank Destroyed by a LGB. *Some Aircrews Called this a "Plinked" Tank.*

Continuing to Disrupt Iraqi C³

Some bridges between Baghdad and the KTO were used not only to move supplies but also as conduits for Iraqi communications cables. Bombing these bridges would help cut the supply line, and a link in the Iraqi military communications network into the KTO. The fiber optic network Saddam Hussein used to communicate with his field commanders also included many switching stations (one of which was in the basement of the Ar-Rashid Hotel) and dozens of relay sites along the oil pipeline from Baghdad through Al-Basrah to the south of Iraq. However, hitting some of these targets was not desirable, despite their military significance, because of possible collateral damage.

By mid-February, according to CENTCOM and EPW reports, communications between corps and division headquarters and their subordinate units along the Kuwaiti-Saudi border had become sporadic. In many instances, Iraqi commanders had to use messengers to communicate with other units and with different command levels. Some captured Iraqi commanders indicated they had no communications at all with their headquarters for more than a week before G-Day.

Armored Vehicle Destruction

It was necessary to reduce Iraqi armored and mechanized forces because they were a threat to Coalition ground forces during the final phase of the war. Not only were they the underpinning of Iraq's position in Kuwait, but they also strengthened Iraq's ability to threaten its Gulf neighbors.

Locating and destroying this equipment was difficult. In many cases, tanks and artillery

An AGM-65 (Maverick), at Lower Left of Target, Just Before Impact.

pieces were spread out, dug in up to their turrets, sandbagged and surrounded by berms, trading mobility for supposed survivability.

Before the war, reconnaissance systems provided extremely accurate depictions of the Iraqi deployments, and planners realized there might be ways to exploit the Iraqis' visible and predictable deployment patterns. A F-16 pilot from the 614th TFS said "Flying in the area of the Republican Guard was a fighter pilot's dream come true. There were revetments full of tanks, armored personnel carriers, ammunition, AAA and artillery as far as the eye could see." In some areas, CENTCOM reported during the war that air power damaged or destroyed a large percentage of the Iraqi armored vehicles.

Aircrews learned that desert conditions created some unique opportunities for weapons that use thermal imaging or IR seekers. In early February, F-111 crews returning to base near sunset noted the presence of buried armor could be detected by FLIR equipment, because the metallic surfaces cooled slower than the surrounding sand. On 8 February, F-111Fs tried a new tactic, that informally became known as "tank plinking," in which an F-111, carrying four GBU-12, 500-lb LGBs, located and bombed individual Iraqi tanks.

The JFACC was satisfied with the results of these efforts. Soon, A-6Es and F-15Es joined the fray and achieved similar results. There were several instances, according to JFACC staff reports, when two F-15Es carrying 16 bombs were believed to have destroyed 16 tanks. These tactics demonstrate the creativity of American airmen and are a good example of excellent technology being improved on by outstanding personnel. The F-111 was designed to conduct long-range, strategic bombing runs, not to destroy tanks one by one. Yet when the need arose, crews responded and developed a tactic (permitted by air supremacy) that helped meet a vital objective. A-6Es and A-10s, on the other hand, do train for day and night attacks on armored vehicles.

The AGM-65 Maverick missiles (fired from A-10, F-16, AV-8, and F/A-18) had electro-optical, IR, or laser seekers, and were effective against tanks. The Coalition fired more than 5,100 AGM-65s; A-10s fired 4,801. In fact, more than 90 percent of the tank kills credited to the A-10 were achieved with IR Mavericks and not with its 30mm GAU-8 gun. (This was in part a factor of the Iraqi AAA threat, which forced the aircraft to operate at altitudes where the gun was less effective.) More importantly, the innovative and aggressive use of PGMs sped the destruction of Iraq's armored forces in the KTO. (For more details on AGM-65, see Appendix T.)

Tanks Abandoned

An Iraqi officer commented that during the war with Iran, the tank had been the soldier's friend, keeping him safe from enemy fire during cold desert nights. During the Operation Desert

Leaflet Samples

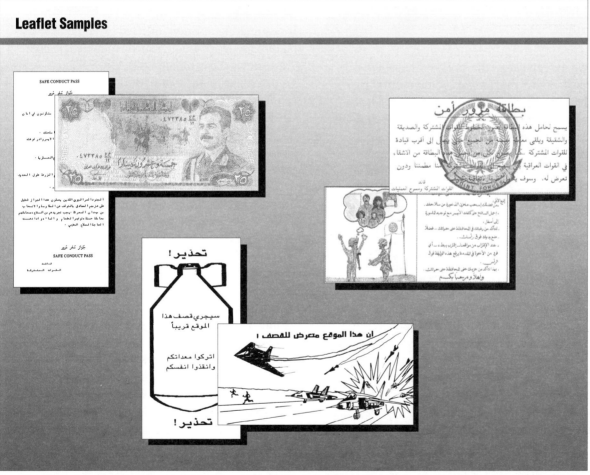

Samples of Psychological Operations Leaflets Dropped During Operation Desert Storm. *The Arabic Script on the Reverse of the 25 Dinar Note (With Saddam Hussein's Likeness) Reads, "If you want to escape the killing, be safe, and return to your families, do the following things: 1- Remove the magazines from your weapons; 2- Put your weapon over your left shoulder with the barrel pointed down; 3- Put your hands over your head; 4- Approach military positions slowly. Note: Beware of the minefields sown along the border. Now, use this safe conduct pass. The Iraqi soldiers who are carrying this pass have indicated their desire for friendship, to cease resistance, and to withdraw from the battlefield. You must take their weapons from their hands, afford them proper treatment, provide food and water, and render any needed medical treatment."*

Equipment Degradation in KTO Before G-Day

(Historical/Cumulative)

	TANKS	APCs	ARTILLERY
Original	4,280	2,880	3,100
22 Jan	14	0	77
27 Jan	65	50	281
01 Feb	476	243	356
06 Feb	728	552	535
11 Feb	862	692	771
16 Feb	1,439	879	1,271
21 Feb	1,563	887	1,428
23 Feb	1,688	929	1,452
24 Feb	1,772	948	1,474

Storm air campaign, the tank was his enemy because high flying aircraft could destroy it without warning, even at night. As a result, soldiers would leave their vehicles and live in trenches a hundred yards away. Some US ground forces commanders reported that many enemy tank crews had abandoned their tanks presumably in part because of Coalition air and artillery attacks. We do not know if this was a widespread phenomenon.

Psychological Operations Impact

Millions of PSYOP leaflets were dropped; they called on the Iraqis not only to surrender, but also warned them to stay away from their equipment because it was the target of Coalition air strikes. Most leaflets were dropped by MC-130s. F-16s and other aircraft flew several missions a day carrying the MK 129 leaflet container, showering the Iraqi troops with messages and warnings. USMC A-6s dropped another version of the leaflet in Kuwait. UH-1N used loudspeakers and Arab linguists to convince Iraqi soldiers to surrender along the Kuwait border. One leaflet depicted a mosque and a schoolyard, in which Saddam Hussein had liberally interspersed tanks, AAA guns, and other military equipment. The

message to the Iraqi soldier was that Saddam Hussein was deliberately endangering their religion and families.

The detonation of several 15,000-lb bombs, dropped from MC-130 special operations planes, also seemed to have a psychological effect on Iraqi troops. Senior Iraqi officer EPWs frequently commented their troops also were terrified of B-52s, and could clearly see and hear their strikes, even when miles away. (PSYOP are discussed in greater detail in Appendix J.)

CINCCENT assigned ARCENT responsibility for estimating attrition inflicted by aerial attack on three types of Iraqi ground equipment. Table VI-4 shows the estimates that ARCENT prepared during the war of attrition. These estimates were among several tools used by CINCCENT in making his decision on when to begin the Offensive Ground Campaign. The objective of the battlefield preparation phase of the air campaign was to reduce Iraqi capabilities in the KTO by about 50 percent in preparation for ground operations. Consequently, BDA methodology was focused on developing estimates of Iraqi equipment that contributed to those capabilities. In this methodology, the estimates began by using flying unit reports of equipment destruction. A-10, F-111, and F-15E reports accounted for most ARCENT counted claims, although other aircraft also were involved. Pilot reports had to be supported by either an aircraft generated video tape recording (VTR), or imagery produced by other sources. The unit's mission reports and imagery were reviewed by a Ground Liaison Officer (GLO). If the GLO confirmed the claim, ARCENT then adjusted the estimates to account for imprecision in the pilot reports and the imagery. For example, an A-10 mission report of a destroyed tank was counted as one third of a tank destroyed. An F-111 report would be counted as one half of the report's claim. These adjustment factors were changed several times during Operation Desert Storm. BDA methodology is addressed in more detail in this chapter in the section entitled, "Evaluating the Results of the Air Campaign."

D+21 through D+27: Summary of Week Four (7 - 13 February)

Week four maintained the emphasis on attacking Iraqi forces in the KTO. It was notable for the full implementation of tank plinking attacks on enemy armor forces, and for a strategic attack on an alternate military command bunker in which, regrettably, Iraqi civilians were killed.

Because of Coalition air superiority, the Iraqi Air Force was unable to gather intelligence about, or interfere with, the westward flanking movement Coalition ground forces were making as they prepared to execute the ground offensive. The air campaign had degraded the combat effectiveness of major parts of the Iraqi Army in the KTO.

The Strategic Air Campaign continued, although at a lower level of effort because of the focus on direct air attacks on deployed Iraqi forces. After four weeks of intense air attack, Iraq was strategically crippled. Its navy had been eliminated as an effective combat force, much of its air force either interned in neutral Iran or destroyed in Iraq, and its strategic air defenses neutralized. Iraq's forces and military capabilities were vulnerable to Coalition air power. The national electric grid had collapsed and refined oil products production halted. NBC facilities and systems had been struck, and Iraq's ability to produce CW munitions and agents badly damaged. Based on the reduced frequency of Scud launches after mobile Scud-hunting air operations began, the combined effects of the counter-Scud effort and the continued degradation of Iraqi military capabilities appeared to reduce Iraq's ability to launch missiles. Table VI-10 shows that during the first 10 days of Operation Desert Storm, Scud launches averaged five a day; during

February, the average was slightly more than one a day.

Careful targeting and use of PGMs minimized collateral damage and civilian casualties, reflecting US policy that Saddam Hussein and his military machine, not the Iraqi people, were the enemy. Regrettably, there were civilian casualties. One of the more publicized incidents was the destruction of the Al-Firdus district bomb shelter and alternate military CP in Baghdad on the night of 13-14 February. The Al Firdus bunker originally was constructed as a bomb shelter, but had been modified to serve as part of the national C^3 network providing C^2 of Iraqi forces.

When Coalition intelligence sources reported the bunker had been activated and its communications capabilities were being used by senior Iraqi military officials, Al Firdus was placed on the MAP. The attack was carried out by two F-117s, which each dropped one case-hardened penetrating 2,000-lb LGB, which set the bunker afire and destroyed it. Unfortunately, Iraqi authorities had permitted several hundred civilians into the facility, many of whom were killed or seriously injured. Intelligence had reported there were no civilians using the bomb shelter facilities. The resultant loss of civilian life led to a review of targeting policies, which were determined to be proper. (See Appendix O, The Role of Law of War, for further discussion.)

Coalition aircraft losses remained low during the week's operations. Two AV-8Bs and an RSAF F-5 were shot down. Iraqi air-to-air losses also were light (five aircraft shot down) because they continued to avoid combat.

D+28 through D+34: Week Five (14 - 20 February)

During Week Five, heavy attacks continued to focus on Iraqi forces in the KTO, while operations against strategic targets and the SEAD effort continued. Iraq's strategic air defenses remained quiescent, with only six of the more than 70 operations centers and reporting posts active. JTF Proven Force struck NBC and missile production facilities in Kirkuk and Mosul in northern Iraq. The counter-Scud effort continued with direct attacks on suspected Scud launch vehicles, mining and bombing of suspected launch and hide areas, and airborne alert sorties to search for targets of opportunity. These efforts appeared to make Scud movements more dangerous and probably narrowed the mobile launchers' operating areas.

Interdiction of LOCs leading into the KTO continued, as Coalition aircraft attacked pontoon bridges, which replaced previously destroyed fixed bridges. The Iraqis' heavy vehicle losses led to the use of civilian vehicles, even garbage trucks, to transport supplies to the KTO.

The emphasis was now shifting to attacks on front line Iraqi units and direct battlefield preparation for the impending ground offensive. While the antiarmor effort continued to damage or destroy a number of armored vehicles every night, other aircraft struck front line defenses and vehicles during the day. AV-8Bs dropped napalm on Iraqi fire trenches by day while, after dark, F-117s destroyed the pumps that supplied crude oil to the trenches. B-52 mine-breaching strikes continued, while MC-130s dropped the giant BLU-82.

The greatest threat to Coalition aircraft remained ground-based defenses; during the week, the Coalition lost five aircraft: An OA-10, two A-10s, an F-16 and an RAF GR-1. The loss of two A-10s on the same day while attacking the same Republican Guard target led to restrictions on the use of A-10s in the higher threat areas. Again, due to the Iraqi Air Force's almost total incapacitation in the face of Coalition air supremacy, the remaining fixed-wing force did not fly any combat sorties. Many Iraqi EPWs commented on the lack of air support they received during the war.

Summary of the Air Campaign, on the Eve of the Offensive Ground Campaign

The Operation Desert Storm air campaign helped isolate Iraq's leadership, seriously degraded the ability to conduct effective offensive and defensive operations, and reduced the threat to regional stability and security. Nearly 100,000 combat and support sorties were flown and 288 TLAMs and 35 ALCMs launched before G-Day. Of all sorties flown, 60 percent were combat missions. Damage to Iraqi forces was extensive, and Iraqi C^2 was disrupted radically. In some cases, corps, division and brigade commanders lost touch with their commands. Moderate amounts of equipment and supplies Iraq positioned to support the KTO were destroyed, and the road nets on which replenishment had to pass were degraded. Interdiction operations against fielded forces during Phase III sapped Iraqi forces' morale — according to intelligence reports in the week before the ground offensive, confirmed by subsequent reports from captured Iraqi officers, desertion rates were substantial. Phase III greatly reduced Saddam Hussein's ability to bring the strength of his army to bear against the Coalition forces. At the end of a month of bombardment, Iraqi forces remained in Kuwait; however, most were in poor condition with heavy desertions, low morale, and a severely degraded capability to coordinate an effective defense.

By G-Day, CENTCOM intelligence estimated Iraqi front line divisions had been reduced in effectiveness by approximately 50 percent due to desertion, supply degradation, and casualties the air campaign inflicted. Air attacks had been so effective that some Iraqi forces in the KTO were largely immobilized, cut off from effective C^2, increasingly isolated from their supply

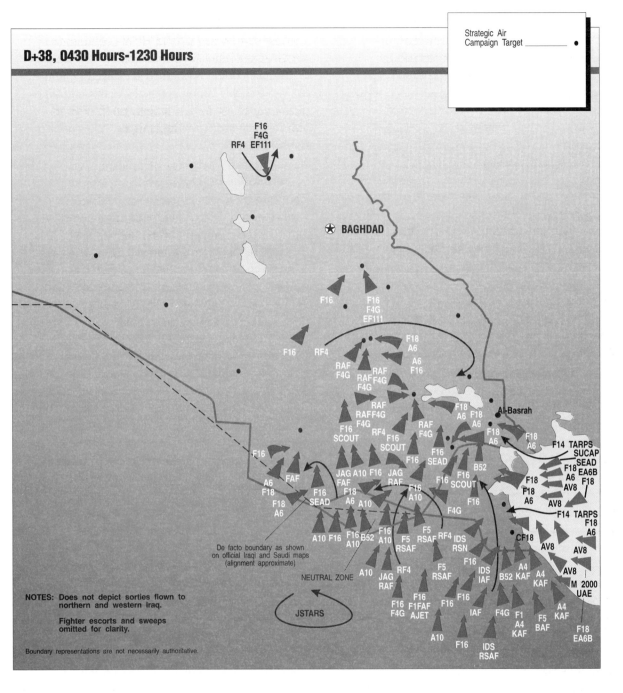

Strategic Air
Campaign Target _____ •

F16
F4G
RF4 EF111

⊛ **BAGHDAD**

F16
F16
F4G
EF111

F16   RF4

F18
A6
A6
F16

RAF
F4G   RAF
RAF F4G
F4G

RAF
RAFF4G
F4G   F18   Al-Basrah
A6 F18
A6   A6

F16   RF4   F16   RAF   F18
SCOUT   SCOUT   F4G   A6   F18
F16   A6   A6
F16

F16   F16   F18
SEAD   A6

F16   B52   F18
F16   SCOUT   A6   F18
AV8
F18
A6   AV8

F14 TARPS
SUCAP
SEAD
F18 EA6B
A6   F18

F16   F16
F16   JAG   A10   F16   JAG
FAF   RAF
A6   F15
A10

A6
F18   F16   F18
A6   SEAD   A6   A10
F16   F18   A6   A10

F4G
F16   F14 TARPS
F18
A6

A10 F16   F16   B52   F16   F5   RF4   IDS   CF18   AV8   AV8
A10   A10   F5 RSAF   RSN
RSAF

De facto boundary as shown
on official Iraqi and Saudi maps
(alignment approximate)

A10   RF4   F5   F16   IDS   A4   A4   M 2000
JAG   RSAF   IAF   B52 KAF   KAF   UAE
RAF
AV8

NEUTRAL ZONE

F16   F16
F16 F1FAF   F16   IAF   F4G   F1   F5   A4
F4G AJET   A4   BAF   KAF
KAF   F18
EA6B

A10   F16   IDS
RSAF

**NOTES: Does not depict sorties flown to
northern and western Iraq.**

**Fighter escorts and sweeps
omitted for clarity.**

Boundary representations are not necessarily authoritative.

JSTARS

sources, and demoralized. Not only were the front line forces unaware of the overall situation, but some Iraqi leadership and command elements also were unaware of the condition of their forces. CENTCOM estimated the combat effectiveness of Iraqi forces, before G-Day, was reduced by approximately 25 percent in the rear (which principally were the more potent Republican Guard forces), and by about half in the front echelon of regular army units. The Republican Guards were not attacked more heavily because of targeting priorities, as well as resource and BDA limitations. Nonetheless, when Coalition ground forces launched their offensive, they were met by an Iraqi army already demoralized and severely degraded in combat effectiveness. The CJCS subsequently said, "...air power took a terrible toll, not only by destroying equipment, but by breaking formations and breaking the will of the Iraqi armed forces."

D+38 (24 February — The Strategic Air Campaign Continues, and Air Operations Begin in Direct Support of the Offensive Ground Campaign)

Overview

During the Offensive Ground Campaign's four days, strategic air operations continued throughout Iraq and Kuwait. RAF GR-1s and Buccaneers, escorted by F-4Gs, bombed hardened aircraft shelters at Tallil and Jalibah airfields. A large package of F-16s and F-4Es escorted by F-15s, EF-111s, and F-4Gs attacked the Al Mawsil military research and production facility in northern Iraq. F-16s bombed the Shahiyat liquid fuel research and development facility. F-15Es sat ground alert and flew airborne alert ready for rapid response to Scud targeting by JSTARS and other surveillance systems. LANTIRN-equipped F-16s also flew in response to JSTARS target advisories during the night. B-52s bombed C^3 sites in southern Iraq.

Interdiction attacks also continued to disrupt the movement and resupply of Iraqi forces in the KTO. F-16s and A-10s, responding to JSTARS targeting, flew armed reconnaissance along Iraqi roads. Restrikes were conducted against bridges to curtail Iraqi reconstruction.

Battlefield air attack sorties increased to support ground forces. On G-Day, scores of ground attack aircraft assigned to kill boxes attacked artillery, armor, APC, supply vehicles, CPs, and troops. F/A-18s and A-6s with EA-6B SEAD, E-2 early warning and C^2, and KA-6 refueling support, attacked ZSU-23-4 AAA and SAM batteries in the KTO. Sections of AV-8Bs attacked Faylaka Island about every half hour throughout the day in preparation for the pending Coalition occupation. RSAF F-5s,

United Arab Emirates Air Force M2000s, and Kuwaiti Air Force (KAF) F-1s attacked artillery batteries and other Iraqi forces in the KTO. F-16s and Tornados bombed sites used to pump oil into trenches along planned Coalition ground attack corridors. Italian GR-1s and FAF F-1s and Jaguars struck artillery, armor, and troops in the KTO.

Battlefield Air Operations

Coalition air forces provided invaluable assistance to CINCCENT's ground scheme of maneuver. But the ground offensive's speed required innovative actions beyond what is considered to be the norm for combined arms operations. For example, determining the exact position of the forward edge of Coalition ground forces was difficult because they moved faster than anticipated. Ground liaison officers, air liaison officers, and airborne C^2 posts (such as FACs, AWACS, and ABCCC) worked to deconflict the movements and attacks in the KTO. In effect, each attack was deconflicted on a case-by-case basis.

Air attacks used in conjunction with ground forces will be discussed in three categories. These operations over and around the battlefield can be described as interdiction, close air support (CAS), and breaching operations support.

Air Interdiction

By the ground offensive's start, Coalition air interdiction of Iraqi LOCs had destroyed key logistical system elements. Interdiction of supply lines to the KTO reduced deliveries to a trickle. These and direct attacks on Iraqi supply points and transportation resulted in major supply shortages for fielded Iraqi forces in Kuwait, although the Republican Guards and other high priority units in Iraq appeared to suffer less. The effort to disrupt, delay, and destroy enemy forces and capabilities before they could be used against friendly forces continued, but the focus shifted to Iraqi systems nearer to Coalition forces. Air power engaged Iraqi supply elements that attempted to move food, fuel, and ammunition. Combat elements that attempted to shift position, retreat or advance, were identified by Coalition reconnaissance and surveillance systems such as U-2, TR-1, JSTARS, and RC-135s and were subjected to air attack. Iraqi forces thus were on the horns of a dilemma: if they remained in position, they would be struck either from the air or by advancing Coalition ground forces; if they tried to move, they made themselves extremely vulnerable to patrolling Coalition aircraft, including attack helicopters.

One of the more important targets for Coalition aircraft was Iraqi artillery, because of its long range and ability to fire chemical projectiles. Two days before ground operations started, air planners, in response to a request from the VII Corps commander, switched the F-111s from the Republican Guard to the Iraqi 47th Infantry Division artillery, because that unit had an abnormally large artillery component (204 instead of the normal complement of 72 pieces) and was in a position to fire on either the Egyptian forces or VII Corps. In less than a day, many artillery pieces were destroyed as a result of airstrikes and artillery raids. Thirty-six hours later, when the VII Corps began its breaching operation, Iraqi artillery near the breaching site was ineffectual, and the Corps completed breaching operations with minimal casualties. Large numbers of Iraqi soldiers began surrendering to advancing Coalition forces throughout G-Day. By day's end, more than 8,000 had been collected, and their condition said much about the effectiveness of Coalition efforts. Many were weak from hunger, sick, lice-infested, demoralized or in shock.

Another example of interdiction operations occurred on the night of G+2, when JSTARS detected large numbers of Iraqi vehicles moving from Kuwait towards Iraq. III Corps, trying to reach Al-Basrah and avoid destruction by I MEF

and the Arab Joint Forces Command-East (JFC-E) forces, became enmeshed with Iraqi occupation forces in Kuwait City. North and west of Kuwait City the roads and causeways formed a bottleneck and the mass of vehicles presented a lucrative target for Coalition airpower. Coalition commanders, aware that forces escaping with their combat equipment could regroup and pose a danger to Coalition ground forces, focused repeated air strikes in the area. Striking first at night, then into the daylight hours, Coalition aircraft destroyed a large number of vehicles, many abandoned by their crews who fled into the desert.

Military formations — particularly armored units in the open desert — exposed to constant attack from the air suffer losses and degradation of combat effectiveness. The many different Coalition air power elements served to magnify this effect on the Iraqis. One Iraqi officer stated he surrendered because of B-52 strikes. "But your position was never attacked by B-52s," his interrogator exclaimed. "That is true," the Iraqi officer stated, "but I saw one that had been attacked." After one BLU-82 bombing of an Iraqi minefield, leaflets were dropped on Iraqi troops that had witnessed the explosion, warning they would be next. Not knowing the bomb had been targeted on a minefield, mass defections resulted, including virtually the entire staff of one Iraqi battalion.

On 24 February, an Air Force captain leading a flight of four F-16s from the 10th Tactical Fighter Squadron was redirected to support a 16-member Special Forces (SF) team in trouble more than 135 miles from the flight's original target. The SF team was surrounded by a company-size Iraqi force. The lead pilot directed his flight to attack the approaching enemy troops. With disregard for intense enemy 23-mm and 37-mm anti-aircraft fire, his flight made multiple attacks, placing cluster bomb munitions on target — as close as 200 meters from friendly positions. On the last pass, while low on fuel, the captain put his bombs exactly on target, causing numerous enemy casualties and forcing the remaining enemy troops to retreat. Army helicopters extracted the SF team without a single Coalition casualty.

50th Tactical Fighter Wing Report

Close Air Support

The USAF, Navy, and USMC provided FACs and air naval gunfire liaison companies (ANGLICOs) to select and identify targets, and to guide strike aircraft to them; this procedure is the principal means for controlling CAS. The USAF and USMC used FACs with the ground forces, and in a liaison role with non-US Coalition ground forces; for example, a USAF officer accompanied the 4th Egyptian Armored Division. The USMC positioned tactical air control parties from 1st ANGLICO team with JFC-E.

During the months before Operation Desert Storm, Coalition aircraft flew simulated CAS sorties under the direction of the 1st ANGLICO FACs. This practice paid dividends at the battle of Al-Khafji. Airborne FACs also were used extensively; the USMC used the F/A-18D and the OV-10, while the USAF used OA-10s. The F-16s also performed FAC duties informally called Killer Scouts.

Locating and marking targets in this phase of the air war was crucial to effective CAS. FACs marked targets with a white phosphorus rocket or a laser designator so attack pilots could find and strike dug-in artillery, armor and troops. FACs sped and improved the effectiveness of attacks on ground forces in the KTO.

The basic CAS plan during the ground offensive involved multi-sortie surge operations, particularly by those aircraft designed for CAS operations and operating from forward operating locations (FOLs) near the battlefield, the A-10s and AV-8Bs. Since Iraqi artillery posed the greatest immediate threat to ground forces penetrating the minefield breaches and obstacle belt, it was a prime Coalition aircraft target. USMC aircraft began increased operations into Kuwait two days before the ground offensive. Operations were based on a system in which fixed-wing aircraft were launched according to schedule, instead of against specific targets, and flew to a series of stacks or holding points. AV-8Bs, for example, flew to a stack east of the battle zone and orbited for approximately 20 minutes while awaiting tasking. If no CAS were needed at that moment they were sent deeper into the KTO to receive targeting from a FAC in a kill box. During the daytime, a section of two USMC aircraft entered the stack every seven and a half minutes; at night, a section of A-6s or other USMC aircraft checked into the stack every 15 minutes. To the east and west, EA-6Bs orbited to provide jamming and EW support, effectively blocking Iraqi battlefield radars.

With the concurrence of the JFACC, I MEF used a high density air control zone (HIDACZ) to coordinate and control the large number of aircraft, artillery, and rockets within I MEF's AOR. Aircraft conducting interdiction or CAS missions within the HIDACZ worked with Marine Air Command and Control Systems for air traffic control and FAC handoffs. The HIDACZ size and shape was under continuous negotiation with the JFACC as other users requested the airspace. Despite some airspace dimensions restrictions, the HIDACZ effectively gave the Marine ground commander a flexible means of coordinating and controlling battlefield air attacks.

As G-Day approached, the JFACC modified the directions to Coalition pilots. Instead of remaining in the relative safety of the medium altitudes from which they bombed strategic and interdiction targets, they were to press home their attacks at lower altitudes. However, the effects of Coalition operations against Iraqi forces before G-Day, and the overall light resistance by Iraqi forces, limited the amount of CAS Coalition ground forces needed.

Breaching Operations

Coalition ground forces south of Kuwait faced a series of formidable defensive positions the Iraqis built during the five months before Operation Desert Storm. Coalition air power was used in several ways to help disrupt these defenses. B-52s bombed the minefields with 750-lb M-117 and 500-lb MK-82 bombs; MC-130s dropped 15,000-lb BLU-82 bombs to create over-pressure and detonate mines. A few days before G-Day, USMC AV-8Bs dropped napalm on the Iraqi fire trenches and attacked the pumping stations to ignite and burn off the oil, while fuel air explosives also were used against minefields. F-117As dropped 500-lb LGBs on oil pipes and distribution points in the fire trenches. Despite the extensive bombing to reduce the size of the Iraqi minefields and obstacles, these bombing efforts were not always effective. Most ground units used their organic countermine and counterobstacle equipment to breach enemy minefields and obstacles.

Effect of Weather and Oil Well Fires

Air attacks were affected by the weather, which turned bad on G-Day and stayed that way until hostilities ended. Conditions varied from solid cloud cover with severe icing from the surface up to 35,000 feet, to crystal blue sky above a thick carpet of ground fog that totally obscured targets. This forced pilots to make choices about the feasibility of some missions. To acquire targets visually, pilots had to go under the cloud layer, which made them vulnerable to Iraqi ground forces and to air defense weapons. On the first day of the ground offensive the Coalition lost four airplanes to Iraqi ground fire. Some A-10 pilots noted their green aircraft were quite visible to ground forces, because the dark paint made them stand out against the overcast skies. Fortunately, the effect of these problems was ameliorated by the speed of the ground advance, the rapid collapse of the Iraqis, and the ceasefire.

Just before and during the Offensive Ground Campaign, Iraqi forces detonated charges placed around Kuwaiti well heads, pipelines, and oil facilities. Thick, viscous pools of crude oil many acres wide formed from some ruptured pipes while more than 700 oil wells burned furiously,

sending great balls of flames and clouds of thick, greasy smoke into the air. The fumes and vapors were noxious and the clouds of smoke were a hazard to flying. Weapons also were affected. Sensitive optical devices such as seeker heads on missiles that earlier had been affected by gritty, windblown sand, also were affected by filmy drops of oil.

D+35 through D+42: Week Six (21 - 28 February)

During the four days before the ground offensive, the Coalition continued heavy emphasis on interdiction of the KTO and destruction of Iraqi forces in their defensive positions. Nearly 90 percent of all combat sorties were targeted into the KTO against armor, artillery, and other elements that threatened Coalition ground forces. According to CENTCOM rough estimates at the time, based only on pilot reports, air attacks on 23 February destroyed 178 tanks, 97 APCs, 202 vehicles, 201 artillery pieces or multiple rocket launchers, 66 revetments, buildings, and bunkers, and two AAA/SAM facilities.

Because of the Coalition ground forces' rapid advance, and the light resistance most ground elements met, relatively more air effort was expended on interdiction than on direct battlefield support. By G-Day, thousands of Iraqi soldiers had deserted, either returning home or crossing the border to surrender to Coalition forces.

Bad weather caused cancellation or diversion of many planned sorties, and forced many others to operate at lower altitudes and use

> "If there is one attitude more dangerous than to assume that a future war will be just like the last one, it is to imagine that it will be so utterly different that we can afford to ignore all the lessons of the last one."
>
> *Former RAF Marshal, Sir John Slessor*
> *Air Power and Armies, 1936*

attack profiles that increased their exposure to Iraqi air defenses. The combination of poor weather, the smoke and haze caused by Saddam Hussein's deliberate torching of hundreds of Kuwaiti oil wells, the fluid nature of the rapid ground advance, and the Coalition decision to operate and fight at night placed severe demands on Coalition forces and played a role in the few instances of fratricide that occurred.

Coalition air forces continued to strike strategic targets until the last moments of the war. Airfields were hit to prevent any Iraqi Air Force attempt to interfere with Coalition operations. Scuds remained a key target. Other attacks continued against NBC, missile production, and C^3 targets, including a mission just before the cease-fire that used a specially developed hard-target penetration bomb (the 4,700-lb GBU-28) to destroy a leadership C^3 bunker near At-Taji.

The Coalition lost eight aircraft during this final week of the war: Three AV-8Bs, one OV-10, one OA-10, one A-10, and two F-16s. Several US and UK troops were killed, wounded, or themselves captured in attempts to reach and rescue downed pilots. (CSAR Operations are discussed in Appendix J.)

RESULTS

Not all the Coalition advantages enjoyed during Operation Desert Storm will be present during the next conflict. However, all modern industrial and military powers share certain universal vulnerabilities. The technological advances that make them powerful also are their great vulnerabilities: these include computer dependent C^3 systems; networked air defense systems and airfields; and easily located sources of energy. When the key nodes are destroyed, such systems suffer cascading, and potentially catastrophic, failure.

Baghdad Ministry of Defense

Damaged Buildings

10 March 1991

Ministry of Defense, Baghdad (Post-Strike). *A Crucial Leadership Facility.*

The initial Operation Desert Storm air strikes attacked the entire target base nearly simultaneously to produce visible pressure and destructive effects against Iraqi centers of gravity. The highest initial priority was to establish air supremacy by degrading the Iraqi IADS, making enemy air forces ineffective, and preventing use of CW biological weapons. Achieving air supremacy allowed continuous air attacks with non-stealth aircraft against the complete range of targets. Stealth aircraft and cruise missiles allowed the Coalition to keep pressure on key leadership, as well as C^2 nodes, in the more heavily defended areas, around the clock.

CINCCENT neutralized the enemy with decisive air attacks. Iraq's sophisticated air defense system was defeated by stealth, large packages of EW aircraft, decoy drones, and attack aircraft using PGMs and gravity weapons, while key nodes in the electrical power system, air defenses, C^2 structure, and intelligence apparatus were attacked by stealth and conventional aircraft using PGMs and by cruise missiles. Scores of aircraft attacked Iraqi forces and facilities across the KTO and Iraq, using mostly gravity bombs and cluster bomb units, as well as PGMs (which constituted about 10 percent of the total munitions delivered). Saddam Hussein was unable to coordinate an effective response to the rest of Coalition military operations. What came after was not easy, and ground forces had to eject Saddam Hussein's forces from the KTO and secure the liberation of Kuwait, but air power set the stage and helped the Offensive Ground Campaign exploit a weakened enemy.

Assessments By Target Set

This section describes what air power, supported

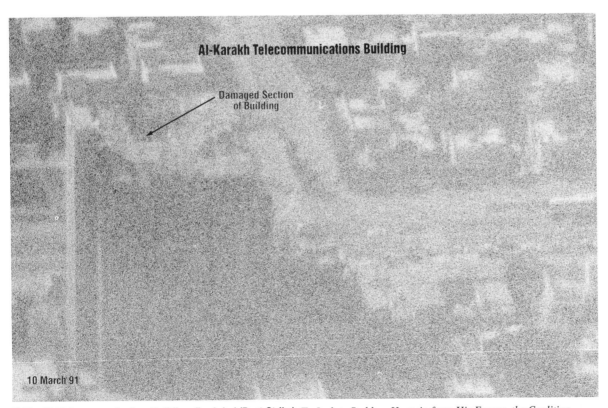

Al-Karakh TelecommunicationsBuilding, Baghdad (Post-Strike). *To Isolate Saddam Hussein from His Forces, the Coalition Conducted Strikes Against Key Communications Facilities.*

by some special operations and artillery attacks, accomplished by target set. These assessments cannot be definitive, because not all the data have been collected, analyzed, and examined in detail. For the most part, they must be both tentative and subjective because of the magnitude of Coalition air operations, difficulties with gathering records for each of some 60,000 attack sorties, and inaccessibility of enemy soldiers, equipment and facilities.

Leadership Command Facilities

A Strategic Air Campaign objective of overriding importance was the isolation and incapacitation of Saddam Hussein's regime. In Iraq's rigid, authoritarian society, where decision-making power is highly centralized in the hands of Saddam Hussein and a few others, destruction of the means of C^2 has a particularly crippling effect on forces in the field. Bombing several leadership facilities, (i.e., places from which Saddam Hussein controlled operations), caused him and other important leaders to avoid facilities that were best suited for C^3, and made them move often. This reduced the ability to communicate with their military forces, population, and the outside world. It also forced them to use less secure communications, thereby providing valuable intelligence.

Electrical Production Facilities

Attacks on Iraqi power facilities shut down their effective operation and eventually collapsed the national power grid. This had a cascading effect, reducing or eliminating the reliable supply of electricity needed to power NBC weapons production facilities, as well as other war-supporting industries; to refrigerate bio-toxins and some CW agents; to power the computer systems required to integrate the air defense network; to pump fuel and oil from storage facilities into trucks, tanks, and aircraft; to operate reinforced doors at aircraft storage and maintenance facilities; and to provide the lighting and power for maintenance, planning, repairs, and the loading of bombs and explosive agents. This increased Iraqi use of less-reliable backup power generators which, generally, are slow to come on line, and provide less power. Taken together, the synergistic effect of losing primary electrical power sources in the first days of the war helped reduce Iraq's ability to respond to Coalition attacks. The early disruption of electrical power undoubtedly helped keep Coalition casualties low.

Coalition planners in the theater directed that the switching system be targeted, rather than the generator halls. There were several deliberate exceptions made to this policy. For

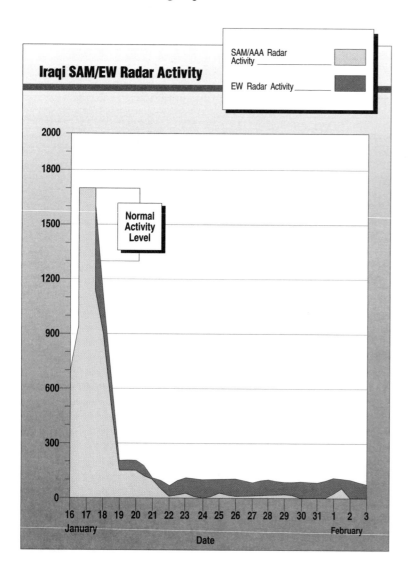

Iraqi SAM/EW Radar Activity

SAM/AAA Radar Activity

EW Radar Activity

Normal Activity Level

2000
1800
1500
1200
900
600
300
0

16 17 18 19 20 21 22 23 24 25 26 27 28 29 30 31 1 2 3
January   February

Date

the first three days, the ATO explicitly contained specific aimpoints for strikes against electrical production facilities. Subsequent to that, the specific aimpoints were only sporadically included. When wing-level planners lacked specific guidance on which aimpoints to hit at electrical power plants, they sometimes chose to target generator halls, which are among the aimpoints listed in standard targeting manuals.

Telecommunications and Command, Control, and Communication Nodes

Saddam Hussein's ability to transmit detailed, timely orders to his senior field commanders deteriorated rapidly. The physical destruction of the Iraqi C^3 capability began before H-Hour with attacks on key nodes of the air defense and C^3 systems. The destruction of the Iraqi Air Force headquarters, publicized by the CENTAF commander's press briefing in late January, was one of many attacks against

Iraq's ability to control combat operations effectively.

In Iraq, the civil telecommunications system was designed to serve the regime — it was an integral part of military communications. For example, approximately 60 percent of military landline communications passed through the civil telephone system. Degrading this system appears to have had an immediate effect on the ability to command military forces and secret police.

The bombing campaign seriously degraded Iraq's national communications network by destroying Saddam Hussein's preferred secure system for communicating with his fielded forces. However, this national-level capability could be repaired and thus needed to be attacked repeatedly. Also, redundancy was built into the national communications network; these other systems tended to be more vulnerable to

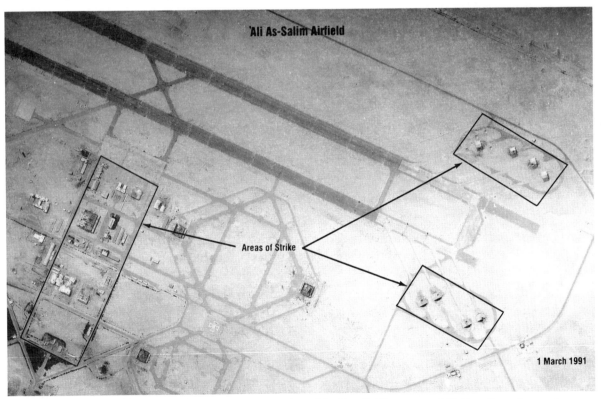

'Ali As-Salim Airfield, Kuwait (Pre-Strike). *Photograph Shows Part of the Parallel Runways and Air Base Operations and Support Facilities (Area Shown is Approximately 1.5 Miles Square).*

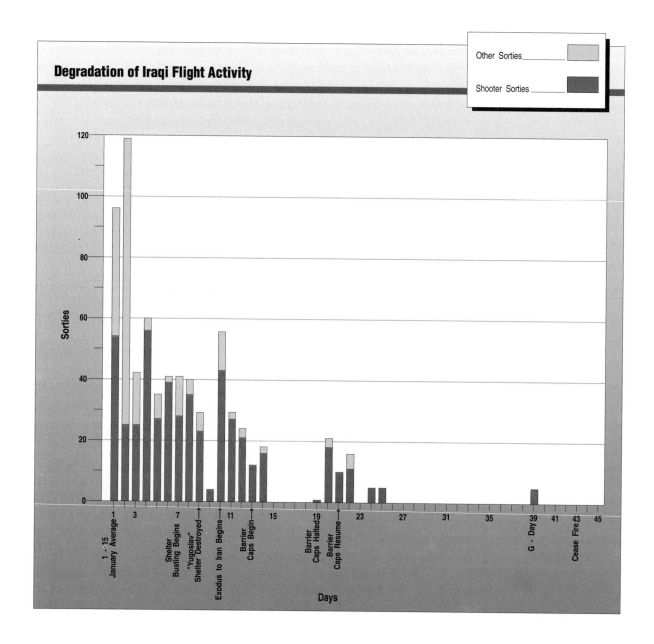

Degradation of Iraqi Flight Activity

Other Sorties

Shooter Sorties

Sorties

Days

1 - 15 January Average
Shelter Busting Begins
"Yugoslav" Shelter Destroyed
Exodus to Iran Begins
Barrier Caps Begin
Barrier Caps Halted
Barrier Caps Resume
G - Day
Cease Fire

eavesdropping but difficult to destroy because they included a dispersed network of CPs with radio transmission capability. These sites could be bombed if planners had precise targeting intelligence, but were difficult to destroy.

To deepen this isolation and incapacitation, telecommunications sites in Baghdad and elsewhere were attacked heavily during the first three days of the war. Internal radio and

television systems also were attacked. The Iraqis had a reduced capability to broadcast outside the country and could broadcast only sporadically inside the country.

By G-Day, regular means of electronic communication were reduced dramatically. During the Offensive Ground Campaign, communications continued to deteriorate. This also greatly improved intelligence collection against Iraqi communications.

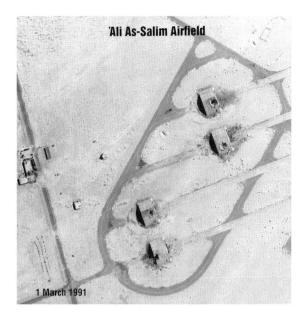

1 March 1991

1 March 1991

'Ali As-Salim Airfield, Kuwait (Post-Strike). *The Coalition Continued Its Pursuit of Air Superiority/Supremacy by Attacking Airfields and Their Facilities.*

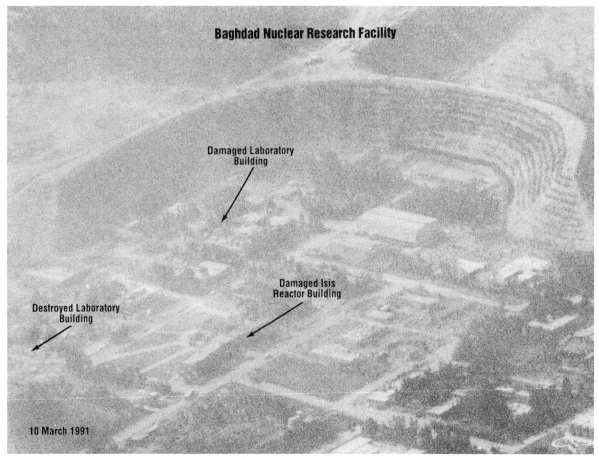

10 March 1991

The Tuwaythah Nuclear Research Facility, Baghdad (Post-Strike).

Strategic Integrated Air Defense System

On the eve of the air campaign, Iraq's strategic IADS was dense, overlapping, and dangerous. It used a mix of Soviet and Western equipment, including radars, interceptor aircraft, SAMs, and AAA, and was tied together by a French-built, computerized C^2 system, Kari. The AAA was either radar or optically guided; SAMs used either radar or IR guidance. The AAA was most dangerous below 12,000 to 15,000 feet, while Iraqi SAMs provided overlapping coverage from virtually ground level to above 40,000 feet. Coalition air operations neutralized most of the effectiveness of these systems through innovative tactics, technology, massive waves of aircraft, cruise missiles, SEAD, intelligence, and careful targeting.

Within hours of the start of combat operations, the IADS had been fragmented and individual air defense sectors forced into autonomous operations. Most hardened SOC and IOC were destroyed or neutralized within the first few days, markedly reducing the Iraqis' ability to coordinate and conduct air defense. The early warning radar net had been so badly damaged that the Iraqis were forced, in many cases, to rely on individual SAM battery radars to provide warning of attacks. After the first week, Coalition aircraft were able to operate at medium and high altitudes with virtual impunity; during the next three weeks, the Coalition lost only seven aircraft to Iraqi defenses. Not until the final few days of the war did air operations move down into the lower altitudes and higher threat posed by Iraqi battlefield defenses (handheld IR SAMs and small-caliber AAA, for example), and aircraft losses increased.

Air Forces and Airfields

The neutralization of the Iraqi Air Force occurred when Coalition air forces destroyed Iraqi aircraft in the air and on the ground. The destruction began with several air-to-air victories on the first night, and continued with

the shelter-busting effort during the air campaign's second week. This effort caused the Iraqi Air Force to disperse around airfields, into civilian neighborhoods, and to fly to Iran. By the war's end, 324 of the original 750-plus Iraqi fixed-wing combat aircraft, were reported destroyed, captured, or relocated outside Iraq. According to CENTAF estimates, 109 Iraqi combat fixed-wing aircraft flew to Iran; 151 were destroyed on the ground; 33 were shot down by Coalition fighter aircraft; and 31 were captured or destroyed by ground forces (the status of others was unknown). Fewer than 300 were believed to remain in Iraq and their combat readiness was doubtful because of the disintegrated air defense C^3 system, inadequate maintenance, and lack of other necessary support. Of the 594 Iraqi aircraft shelters, 375 were severely damaged or destroyed. Within six weeks, the world's sixth largest air force had been decimated.

Nuclear, Biological, and Chemical Weapons Research and Production Facilities

A key objective was degrading the threat from Iraqi NBC weapons of mass destruction and their delivery systems (one of Iraq's centers of gravity). Air power was one of the more effective ways to reach research and production facilities deep inside Iraq. Damage to the known nuclear weapons program was substantial. The Baghdad Nuclear Research Center was damaged, including both research reactors. However, UN inspection teams and US intelligence sources subsequently discovered Iraq's nuclear weapons program was more extensive than previously thought, and did not suffer as serious a setback as was desired.

During December, a team was formed in CONUS to determine the most effective way to attack Iraq's arsenal of CW/BW weapons. Several experiments were conducted which attempted to find a way to destroy these weapons without releasing BW agents or causing significant collateral damage. Finally, through timing of attacks and choice of munitions, planners were able to minimize the chance for toxins to spread. No chemical of biological agents were detected after the attacks and no CW/BW collateral damage was experienced.

During Operation Desert Storm, the BW program was damaged and its known key research and development facilities were destroyed. All known BW research and production capabilities were made unusable. Most of Iraq's refrigerated storage bunkers were destroyed.

Iraq's CW program was seriously damaged. At least 75 percent of Iraq's CW production capability was destroyed. At Samarra, Coalition forces destroyed or severely damaged most known primary CW production, processing, or production support buildings. All three buildings used to fill munitions at Samarra were

As-Samawah Petroleum Refinery (Post-Strike).

Coalition Air Strikes Inflicted Serious Damage to the Umm Qasr Port Facility.

destroyed, although the Iraqis may have moved the equipment from one building before Operation Desert Storm for safekeeping. All three precursor chemical facilities at Habbaniyah were seriously damaged. Although Iraq previously had produced and distributed many CW agents to storage sites throughout the country, the means for delivering the weapons was badly damaged. Coalition air supremacy made Iraqi Air Force delivery of these weapons unlikely; most artillery (Iraq's preferred method of delivering CW) was disabled.

Why Iraq did not use CW still is a matter of conjecture. Concerted efforts, both public and private, were made before the war to warn Saddam Hussein of severe consequences of CW use. The fact that almost no chemical munitions were distributed to Iraqi forces in the KTO suggests Saddam Hussein chose to retain tight control over this capability. UN inspections since the war have confirmed Iraq did have chemical warheads for its Scud missiles, which Iraq continued to fire until the end of the war. This suggests deterrence worked. However, Coalition attacks also disrupted the Iraqis' ability to move, load, and fire weapons, and eliminated many battlefield delivery systems. The rapid ground offensive against the already

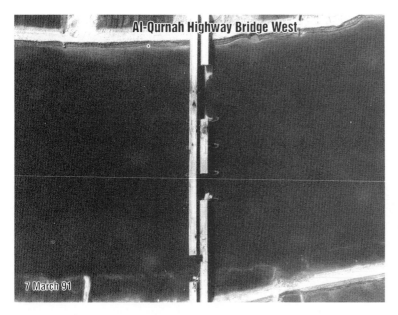

Al-Qurnah Highway Bridge West (Post-Strike). *Strikes Against the Iraqi Bridge System Helped Isolate Iraqi Forces in the Kuwait Theater of Operations.*

blinded and confused Iraqis made effective use of CW against the Coalition offensive almost impossible. At present, there is no conclusive answer.

Scud Production and Storage Facilities

Immediately after the war, estimates, based on imagery analysis of heavily damaged or destroyed complexes associated with Scud production, concluded Iraq's overall ability to modify or produce Scud missiles and support equipment was severely degraded and that Baghdad's overall potential to build liquid-propellant missiles had been reduced. More recently, UN inspection teams have determined most production equipment, components, and documents had been removed before the beginning of the air campaign. Recent intelligence estimates confirm that actual damage to Scud production and storage facilities is less than previously thought.

Attacks Against Bridges Cut into the Supply Effort as Evidenced by this Truck Convoy Stalled Before It had a Chance to Cross.

Naval Forces and Port Facilities

Coalition air strikes and naval gunfire effectively destroyed the Iraqi Navy in the first three weeks of Operation Desert Storm. While Iraq did not have major surface combatants, it did have dangerous antiship missile capabilities that could have inflicted politically significant damage to Coalition ships, giving Iraq a needed psychological victory. Approximately 87 percent (143 of 165) of Iraqi combatant naval vessels were destroyed or damaged. By 2 February, 11 of the 13 Iraqi missile-capable boats were destroyed, and the remaining Iraqi naval forces were assessed as incapable of offensive operations. The Umm Qasr Naval Base and Khawr Az-Zubayr port facility, the primary Iraqi naval operating areas, sustained substantial damage to storage facilities. Coalition air strikes also destroyed three of Iraq's seven shore-based Silkworm antiship missile launchers and an unknown number of missiles. Because of the destruction of the Iraqi naval threat, Coalition naval forces were able to move farther north in the Persian Gulf to increase the pressure on Iraqi forces, and to support better the Offensive Ground Campaign.

Oil Refining and Distribution Facilities, as Opposed to Long-term Oil Production Capability

Reducing Iraq's ability to refine and distribute finished oil products helped reduce Iraqi military forces' mobility. Aircraft carried out about 500 sorties against Iraqi oil facilities, dropping about 1,200 tons of bombs to shut down the national refining and distribution system. This offers another illustration of the effect modern PGMs and other advanced technologies have on the nature of war. For about half the bomb load dropped on one typical refinery in Germany during World War II, the

In Past Conflicts, it Might Have Taken Numerous Sorties to Achieve the Results Shown Here Against the Al-Basrah Highway Bridge. *Today's Technology Usually Requires Only a Few Missions.*

Coalition effectively stopped all Iraqi refined fuels production.

The air campaign damaged approximately 80 percent of Iraq's refining capacity, and the Iraqis closed the rest of the system to prevent its destruction. This left them with about 55 days of supply at prewar consumption rates. This figure may be misleading, however, because the synergistic effect of targeting oil refining and distribution, electricity, the road, rail and bridge infrastructure, and the national C^3 network, all combined to degrade amounts of oil and lubricants Iraqi commanders received. Saddam Hussein apparently was counting on a relatively protracted conflict in which conserving Iraqi fuel supplies could be important.

Railroads and Bridges Connecting Iraqi Military Forces with Logistical Support Centers

About three fourths of the bridges between central Iraq and the KTO were severely damaged or destroyed. Iraqi LOCs into the KTO were vulnerable because they crossed bridges over the Tigris and Euphrates rivers. The bridges were destroyed at the rate of seven to 10 a week, and the supply flow into the KTO dropped precipitously. While the supply routes into the KTO were being interdicted, Iraqi supply troops also were subjected to heavy air attacks. As bridges were destroyed, long convoys of military trucks waiting to cross were stranded and attacked. Air attacks also destroyed supplies stockpiled in the KTO and severely disrupted their distribution. In an environment where literally nothing was available locally, these efforts resulted in major shortages of food for fielded forces, particularly for those units farthest forward.

The effort to cut the rail and road LOCs from central Iraq into the KTO further demonstrated the effect of advanced technology. During the early years of the Vietnam War, hundreds of USAF and Navy aircraft bombed the Thanh Hoa bridge in North Vietnam. It was not seriously

damaged, and many aircraft were shot down. During Operation Linebacker I in 1972, the bridge was knocked down by just a few sorties using LGB and Walleye II, both PGMs. The Operation Desert Storm air campaign saw the use of improved PGMs, including LGB, Maverick, and Standoff Land-Attack Missiles (SLAM).

Video footage of Iraqi bridges falling to LGB became commonplace during briefings and on the television news. Not every PGM hit its intended target. But so many bridges were knocked down (41 major bridges and 31 pontoon bridges) and so many supply lines cut that the effect on the Iraqi forces in the KTO was severe.

In addition, the air campaign effectively interdicted LOCs within the KTO and destroyed thin-skinned tankers and other vehicles that supplied food and water. This was made possible in part by the lack of cover for moving vehicles in the desert and by US night vision capabilities that exploited this advantage even at night.

Iraqi Military Units, Including Republican Guards in the KTO

Iraqi forces in the KTO posed a serious threat to Saudi Arabia and the other Persian Gulf states; until they either evacuated Kuwait, were ejected, or destroyed, Kuwait could not be liberated. The air campaign worked towards all three possibilities. Saddam Hussein refused to withdraw his forces; however, the Coalition began direct air attacks to degrade the more important capabilities and assets (especially armor and artillery) and to prepare for Coalition ground forces to reoccupy Kuwait. The degree to which these objectives were accomplished was virtually unprecedented in warfare. In less than six weeks, a combat experienced army of several hundred thousand troops, with thousands of tanks, other armored vehicles, and artillery pieces, dug into well-sited and constructed defensive positions, was severely degraded and weakened from the air. The Iraqi forces' overall combat effectiveness was reduced dramatically.

CINCCENT's Operation Desert Storm OPORD identified the Republican Guard as an Iraqi center of gravity. Primary targets included armor and artillery, because these represented a major threat to Coalition forces; logistics installations such as fuel, ammunition and supply dumps; and C³ facilities such as CPs. Not every Republican Guard division was hit equally hard; those in the path of the planned Coalition ground forces received the brunt of the attacks. Other divisions, such as those south of Al-Basrah, received less damage. The Republican Guard was not as heavily targeted as were the front-line regular Army divisions the Coalition ground forces would encounter first, for a number of reasons — they were farther from Coalition bases and better equipped than front-line forces, which required longer flights with more airborne support, and risked higher aircraft attrition. More importantly, CINCCENT directed that comparatively greater damage be inflicted on the front-line forces to reduce Coalition ground forces' casualties.

Military Production and Storage

Military production and storage areas made up 15 percent of the total Strategic Air Campaign targets, attacked by about 2,750 sorties. By the end of the war, military production facilities had been severely damaged. At least 30 percent of Iraq's conventional weapons production capability, which made small arms, artillery, small- and large-caliber ammunition, electronic and optical systems, and repaired armored vehicles, was damaged or destroyed.

Supply depots were so numerous and large that they could not be eliminated; however, they were methodically attacked throughout the war, resulting in moderate reduction in stored materials. As an example, the massive military supply complex at At-Taji occupied more than

Strategic Targets Level of Effort

	Percent of Total Effort	Number of Sorties
		Total: 18,276
Electrical Power	01	215
Naval	02	247
National CMD Authority	02	429
Air Defense	02	436
Oil	03	518
C3	03	601
Railroad & Bridges	04	712
NBC	05	902
Military Support	15	2,756
SRBM	15	2,767
Airfields	17	3,047
REP Guard	31	5,646

10 square miles. Thousands of targets were within its confines, and it was struck repeatedly. On 29 January, as another example, B-52s hit the ammunition storage facility at Ar-Rumaylah, touching off a tremendous explosion — the equivalent of an erupting volcano.

EPW Assessments

One benefit of the rapid Coalition ground advance was the capture or surrender of many Iraqi senior officers and thousands of Iraqi troops. The officers provided Coalition intelligence debriefers with a unique perspective.

According to sources from four different Iraqi Army and Republican Guard armor, infantry, and antiaircraft units, for example, the air campaign's effect was telling. According to selected EPW reports, in some divisions, up to half the personnel who had deployed to the KTO deserted because of shortages of food and water, hardships caused by the bombing, or fear of being killed or wounded. Selected senior officer EPW also described very high (roughly 77 percent) attrition rates for tanks or wheeled vehicles in particular units. Not all units suffered attrition rates as high as this. For example, senior EPWs from other Iraqi units, such as the

50th Armored Brigade, 12th Armored Division, and the 8th Mechanized Brigade, 3rd Armored Division, reported lower attrition rates.

An indirect impact of Coalition air supremacy was reflected in the Iraqis' ignorance of Coalition dispositions and operations. This was important in preparing for and executing the ground campaign's left hook. In addition, although some units did relocate, one senior officer said that, after the start of Operation Desert Storm, he could no longer safely move his forces because of the threat of air attack. The Iraqis' problems were compounded by the inability to train their forces and maintain their equipment. The air interdiction effort and degradation of the supply system stressed the Iraqi forces to and, in some cases, beyond the breaking point. Experienced armor officers were visibly shaken when they described helplessly watching the progressive destruction of their forces from the air.

The EPWs agreed almost unanimously that PSYOP at the battlefield level had a substantial effect on front line forces' morale. Air strikes made it impossible for Iraqi commanders to stop the flow of soldiers deserting from some units.

Safwan Revelations

On 3 March, CINCCENT met with Iraqi senior military officers, including the III Corps commander, to finalize cease-fire terms. After the Iraqis informed CINCCENT about the status of Coalition Prisoners of War (POW) in Iraqi hands, the Iraqis asked for an accounting of the Iraqi EPWs the Coalition held. When CINCCENT replied the counting was still going on, but the number exceeded 58,000, the Iraqi vice chief of staff, according to eyewitness accounts, appeared stunned. When he asked the III Corps commander if this were possible, he replied that it was possible, but he did not know. The discussion then turned to establishing a no-contact line to separate Coalition and Iraqi forces. When CINCCENT presented his proposed line, the Iraqi vice chief of staff asked why it was drawn behind the Iraqi troops. CINCCENT said this was the forward line of the Coalition advance. The Iraqi officer, again looking stunned, turned to the III Corps commander, who again replied that it was possible, but he did not know. Thus, three days after hostilities ended, the Iraqi senior military leadership did not know how many men they had lost or where the Coalition forces were. While their ignorance may in part reflect the

Date	Unit	Shooter Aircraft	Type Downed	Weapon Used
17 Jan 91	33 TFW	F-15C	MIG-29	AIM 7
17 Jan 91	1 TFW	F-15C	F-1 Mirage	AIM 7
17 Jan 91	33 TFW	F-15C	2/F-1 Mirage	AIM 7 (Both)
17 Jan 91	33 TFW	F-15C	MIG-29	AIM 7
17 Jan 91	33 TFW	F-15C	MIG-29	AIM 7
17 Jan 91	VFA-81	F/A-18	MIG-21	AIM 9
17 Jan 91	VFA-81	F/A-18	MIG-21	AIM 7
19 Jan 91	33 TFW	F-15C	MIG-25	AIM 7
19 Jan 91	33 TFW	F-15C	MIG-25	AIM 7
19 Jan 91	33 TFW	F-15C	MIG-29	AIM 7
19 Jan 91	33 TFW	F-15C	MIG-29	AIM 7
19 Jan 91	33 TFW	F-15C	F-1 Mirage	AIM 7
19 Jan 91	33 TFW	F-15C	F-1 Mirage	AIM 7
24 Jan 91	RSAF	F-15C	2/F-1 Mirage	AIM 9 (Both)
26 Jan 91	33 TFW	F-15C	MIG-23	AIM 7
26 Jan 91	33 TFW	F-15C	MIG-23	AIM 7
26 Jan 91	33 TFW	F-15C	MIG-23	AIM 7
27 Jan 91	36 TFW	F-15C	2/MIG-23	AIM 9 (Both)
27 Jan 91	36 TFW	F-15C	MIG-23	AIM 7
27 Jan 91	36 TFW	F-15C	F-1 Mirage	AIM 7
28 Jan 91	32 TFG	F-15C	MIG-23	AIM 7
29 Jan 91	33 TFW	F-15C	MIG-23	AIM 7
2 Feb 91	36 TFW	F-15C	IL-76	AIM 7
6 Feb 91	36 TFW	F-15C	2/SU-25	AIM 9 (Both)
6 Feb 91	36 TFW	F-15C	2/MIG-21	AIM 9 (Both)
6 Feb 91	926 TFG	A-10	Helo	Gun
6 Feb 91	VF-1	F-14A	Helo	AIM 9
7 Feb 91	33 TFW	F-15C	2/SU-7/17	AIM 7 (Both)
7 Feb 91	33 TFW	F-15C	SU-7/17	AIM 7
7 Feb 91	36 TFW	F-15C	Helo	AIM 7
11 Feb 91	36 TFW	F-15C	Helo	AIM 7
15 Feb 91	10 TFW	A-10	MI-8 Helo	Gun

Operation Desert Storm Air-to-Air Victories by Coalition Air Forces, 17 January to 28 February. Source: Joint Staff/J3 (Joint Operations Division).

weaknesses of a totalitarian system in which bad news travels slowly, it undoubtedly also reflects the crippling of Iraqi intelligence and communications by the air campaign, the effectiveness of the deception actions at all levels, and the sweep, speed, and boldness of the ground campaign.

OPERATIONAL CONSIDERATIONS

Air Superiority and Air Supremacy

Throughout Operation Desert Shield, Coalition air forces were flying defensive counter air sorties to ensure the arrival and movement of forces into the AOR remained unimpeded by hostile attack. These missions typically lasted several hours, with fighters patrolling the border and refueling periodically to maintain an around the clock umbrella over Coalition forces.

Once Operation Desert Storm began, defensive counter air patrols continued; while additional offensive counter air fighter sweeps and strike package escorts into Iraq sought out and engaged Iraqi Air Force opposition. Assisted by AWACS and E-2Cs, these fighters achieved and maintained air superiority throughout the Persian Gulf War.

The air campaign's pre-eminent initial objective was the fragmentation and virtual destruction of the Iraqi IADS, which was paralyzed in Operation Desert Storm's early hours. It is difficult, if not virtually impossible, for a modern, mechanized army to operate effectively once control of the sky above it is lost. American ground forces have not had to fight without air superiority since World War II; the last time an American soldier was killed by enemy aircraft attack was during the Korean War. Dominance of the airspace is not, however, an end in itself, but something to allow other forces to operate more effectively. Air supremacy allowed Coalition land, sea and air forces to maneuver, deploy, resupply, stockpile

DEDICATED COALITION ELECTRONIC WARFARE AIRCRAFT IN THEATER ON 20 JANUARY

Location	Unit/Service	No. of Aircraft	Type of Aircraft
Shaikh Isa, Bahrain	USMC	12	EA-6B
Shaikh Isa, Bahrain	USAF	48	F-4G
At-Taif, Saudi Arabia	USAF	18	EF-111A
King Fahd, Saudi Arabia	USAF	2	EC-130H
Riyadh, Saudi Arabia	USAF	7	EC-130H
Bateen, UAE	USAF	6	EC-130H
USS Midway, USS Ranger, USS America, US Roosevelt, USS Kennedy, USS Saratoga	USN	27	EA-6B
Jiddah, Saudi Arabia	USN	2	EA-3B
Bahrain Intl, Bahrain	USN	2	EP-3E
Masirah, Oman	USN	1	EP-3E
Bahrain Intl, Bahrain	USN	1	P-3B (RP)
JTF Proven Force (Incirlik, Turkey)	USAF	6	EF-111A
	USAF	3	EC-130H
	USAF	12	F-4G
	USAF	13	F-16C
Total		160	

NOTE: Some of these aircraft (e.g., F-4Gs and F-16Cs) eventually were used for missions other than suppression of enemy air defenses.

and fight as they desired — a luxury the enemy did not have.

In future conflicts against a sophisticated military, the battle for air supremacy will be a key determinant. The fate of the Iraqi military machine will be remembered for decades. The Soviet Air Force Chief of Staff, General A. Malyukov, remarked after the war: "The war in the Persian Gulf provided a textbook example of what air supremacy means both for the country that gained it, and for the country ceding it."

Suppression of Enemy Air Defenses

Coalition aircraft conducting air defense suppression missions saturated Iraqi airspace with jammers, shooters, and bombers. Iraqi defenses that attempted to engage were disrupted, and risked being destroyed.

A Destroyed Surface-to-Air Missile Launcher.

Antiaircraft Artillery Pieces at an Iraqi Airfield Succumbed to the Coalition Air Onslaught.

EF-111As and EA-6Bs were used in stand-off and close-in orbits to jam early warning, acquisition, and GCI radars. EC-130H Compass Call aircraft jammed radio communications, data links, and navigation systems. F-4Gs, F-16s, EA-6Bs, A-6Es, A-7Es, and F/A-18s used HARMs to destroy acquisition, GCI, and target tracking radars. Various aircraft dropped bombs on air defense emplacements and control facilities. SEAD forces and bomb droppers caused confusion, hesitation, and loss of capability, which degraded Iraqi air defense capability.

Navy, Marine, and USAF aircraft used HARMs during Operations Desert Storm. USAF F-4Gs used most of the HARMs. For Navy and USMC HARM-shooters, initial tactics were based on the pre-emptive use of HARMs and Electronic Countermeasures (ECM). Typically, the use of HARMs in the preemptive mode was more common when supporting attacks on heavily defended strategic targets inside Iraq. The target-of-opportunity mode was more frequently used during operations against less well-defended targets and fielded forces in the KTO. More than half of all HARMs used were expended during the first week of the war, with another third expended from 6 to 13 February when the emphasis on attacking Iraqi forces in the KTO increased. Both of these periods also saw a significant concentration of strike efforts on heavily defended strategic targets. By the end of the conflict, reactive HARMs and ECM became common as a result of combat experience and the perceived need to husband HARMs.

Because of the extensive air defense threat, coordination among the Services to provide mutual support was essential to Operation Desert Storm's success. The JFACC tasked apportioned SEAD sorties, guaranteeing a

A Destroyed FAN SONG Radar, Once Part of the Iraqi Air Defense System.

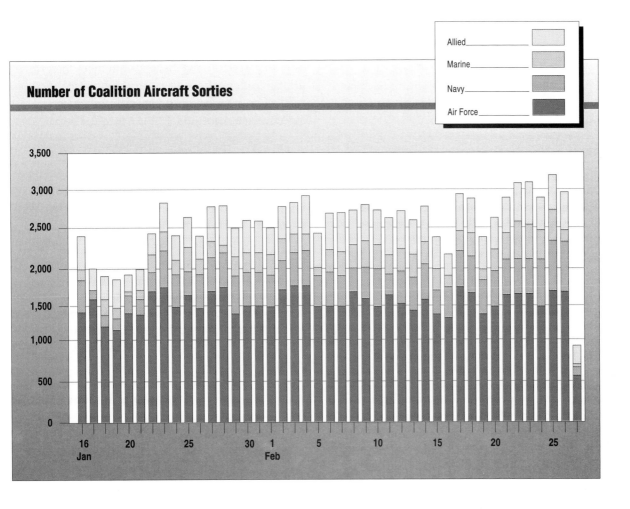

Number of Coalition Aircraft Sorties

Legend:
- Allied
- Marine
- Navy
- Air Force

coordinated, effective, and prioritized SEAD effort. Almost all Coalition aircraft contributed. In their first combat use, ATACMS demonstrated a rapid response capability. A Multiple Launch Rocket System launcher, armed with ATACMS, received a fire mission while moving in convoy, occupied a hasty firing position, computed firing data and launched a missile that neutralized an SA-2 site. On 20 February, an Army attack helicopter battalion conducted a deep strike in the Iraqi 45th Infantry Division rear area — EF-111As, F-4Gs, and EC-130Hs provided SEAD support on the way in, which helped the helicopters safely complete the mission.

SEAD tactics changed during the conflict, especially in the KTO. By using the APR-47

electromagnetic sensor system to see and attack threats as they came on the air, the F-4Gs conserved HARMs when threat activity diminished. The F-4Gs then were more available to support attack flights as they serviced kill boxes. For example, F-4Gs located and attacked mobile SA-6s deployed with the Republican Guards.

The attacks on the Iraqi electronic order of battle (EOB) affected every aspect of air supremacy operation. Using Tactical Electronic Reconnaissance Processing and Evaluation System, USMC EA-6Bs provided near-real-time (NRT) updates to the threat EOB.

The EC-130Hs also made major contributions,

flying from both Bateen, United Arab Emirates (UAE), and Incirlik, Turkey. Jamming enemy radio communications, data links, and enemy navigation systems, EC-130Hs disrupted air-to-air and air-to-ground Iraqi C^3 networks.

EF-111As flew from At-Taif, and from Incirlik. They were part of the initial surge of aircraft across the Iraqi border the first night of the war, and established orbits to escort strike packages into the H-3 and Baghdad areas. They jammed EW, height finder, GCI, and target-acquisition radars, and were effective in tricking the enemy into opening fire at false radar returns in areas where there were no Coalition aircraft.

The F-4G and the F-16 (in the SEAD role) flew from Shaikh Isa and from Incirlik, firing 1,061 HARMs. F-4Gs were among the first aircraft to cross the Iraqi border to protect strike flights in the Baghdad and H-2/H-3 areas. During the latter stages of the war, with the remaining Iraqi radars rarely emitting, F-4G aircrews used AGM-65D Maverick missiles against non-emitting radar targets.

Electronics intelligence data for the period 16 January to 10 February shows a high level of EOB activity initially, with a dramatic decrease 48 to 72 hours into the war. SAM operators frequently fired with limited or no radar guidance, reducing their overall effectiveness. This much reduced level continued for the remainder of the war.

Aircraft Sorties

The 43-day air campaign against Iraq and Iraqi forces in Kuwait involved more than 2,780 US fixed-wing aircraft, which flew more than 112,000 individual sorties. To support this enormous undertaking, the USAF committed more than 1,300 aircraft (about half of the Coalition total), the USMC about 240 aircraft (about nine percent of the total), and Coalition

partners more than 600 aircraft (about 25 percent of the total). The Navy deployed six aircraft carriers to the theater, with more than 400 aircraft, or about 16 percent of the Coalition total. (For more details on specific weapons systems, see Appendix T.)

Technological Revolution

Technological breakthroughs revolutionized air warfare. Because of its precision delivery capability and low-observable, or stealth technology, planners assigned F-117As to attack the most heavily defended, high-value, and hardened targets. Forty-two F-117As flew approximately two percent of Coalition fixed-wing attack sorties, and struck about 40 percent of the strategic targets. This advanced technological capability allowed aircrews to strike more targets using fewer aircraft.

The development and improvement of PGMs that use IR, electro-optical (EO), electromagnetic radiation, or laser guidance, improved the effectiveness and efficiency of air attacks. These technological breakthroughs, with improvements in such areas as electronic warfare and C^3I, combined to provide the Coalition an overwhelming air warfare capability.

Tomahawk Land Attack Missile

Unmanned TLAMs attacked high value targets day and night, helping deprive the Iraqi leadership of respite from attack, especially early in the air campaign. TLAMs were launched by surface warships and submarines at targets 450 to 700 miles away.

Two types of TLAM were used during Operation Desert Storm: The conventional missile with a unitary warhead (TLAM-C); and, a variant equipped with submunitions (TLAM-D). The TLAM-C delivered single, 1,000-lb warheads. The TLAM-D dispensed up to 166 armor-piercing, fragmentation, or

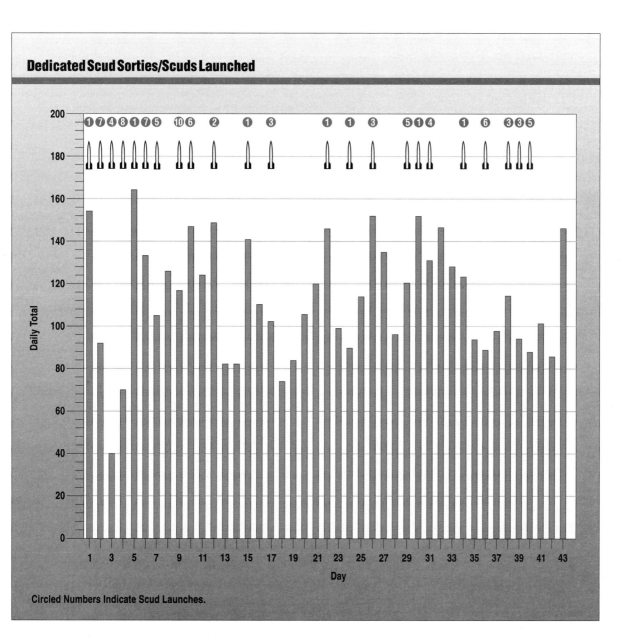

Dedicated Scud Sorties/Scuds Launched

Circled Numbers Indicate Scud Launches.

incendiary bomblets in 24 packages.

By the war's end, the Navy had fired 288 TLAMs from 16 surface ships and two submarines — an important part of the air campaign. TLAM missions required no airborne aircraft support.

GBU-28

The GBU-28, a 4,700-lb deep-penetrator LGB,

was not even in the early stages of research when Kuwait was invaded. The USAF did not ask industry for ideas until the week after combat operations started. Its rapid development and combat delivery were impressive.

The bomb was fabricated starting on 1 February, using surplus 8-inch artillery tubes. The official go-ahead for the project was issued on 14 February, and explosives for the initial units were hand-loaded by laboratory personnel into a bomb body that was partially buried upright in the ground outside the laboratory in New York.

The first two units were delivered to the USAF on 16 and 17 February, and the first flight to test the guidance software and fin configuration was conducted on 20 February. These tests were successful and the program proceeded, with a contract let on 22 February. A sled test on 26 February proved that the bomb could penetrate over 20 feet of concrete, while an earlier flight test had demonstrated the bomb's ability to penetrate more than 100 feet of earth. The first two operational bombs were delivered to the theater on 27 February — and were used in combat just before the cease-fire.

The Counter-Scud Effort

Long before the offensive, it was recognized that Saddam Hussein was likely to attack Israel with Scuds in the event of hostilities. Accordingly, considerable thought was given to how Israel could be protected from such attacks without Israel's own forces entering the war. Although there was never any doubt about the willingness of Israel's highly capable forces to take on this mission, the President realized this was precisely what Saddam Hussein hoped to achieve. At a minimum, this almost certainly would have led to a war between Israel and Jordan and allowed Saddam Hussein to change the complexion of the war from the liberation of Kuwait to another Arab-Israeli conflict. It might easily have brought down the government of Jordan and replaced it with a radical one. The Coalition's unity would be tested severely, with potentially major repercussions.

Accordingly, the President directed that unprecedented steps be taken to persuade Israel not to exercise its unquestioned right to respond to Iraqi attacks. A special, secure communications link established between the Department of Defense (DOD) and the Israeli Ministry of Defense (MOD) before the offensive began enabled immediate and frequent contact between senior US and Israeli officials. Early warning of Iraqi Scud missile attacks on this link gave the Israeli populace as much as five minutes to take shelter before missile impact. The President offered and Israel agreed to accept four US Patriot batteries manned with US troops which deployed from Europe in record time. Delivery of Israeli-manned Patriot batteries was accelerated.

One air campaign target was Iraq's strategic offensive capability, including Scud production, assembly and storage, and launch sites. The first counter-Scud missions were flown on D-Day against fixed launch complexes and Scud support depots. By the third day of air operations, attacks had begun on ballistic missile production and storage capability.

On the second day of Operation Desert Storm, Iraqi Scud missiles struck Tel Aviv and Haifa, Israel. Seven people were slightly injured by broken glass, but the political and emotional impact was tremendous. There was concern Saddam Hussein might use CW against Israel. In fact, 11 trucks were observed departing the Samarra CW storage facility in Iraq, heightening speculation about Iraqi CW preparations. Concern intensified that if the Scud threat were left unchecked, Israel might be forced to strike back.

When Iraq launched another Scud attack on Tel Aviv on 19 January, the pressure to respond was intense. A target intelligence officer assigned to the Black Hole identified what he believed to be a Scud launch site and recommended that F-15Es, loaded with CBU-89s and CBU-87s, strike the location. After this strike by the 4th TFW, which reported secondary explosions, there was a break of 85 hours before the Iraqis launched a single Scud against Israel, and more than five days before another mass launch.

The fourth day saw increased effort to locate, disrupt operations, and destroy mobile Scud missiles. Many sorties were diverted or replanned from their intended targets to hunt for and suppress the Scuds. Although the strategic target list included Scud missile capabilities only as one of several higher priority target sets, Scud suppression missions quickly took up an increasing share of air operations. Despite the poor weather conditions that caused the cancellation of nearly 300 sorties on 20 January, the JFACC kept planes on both air and ground alert for rapid response to Scud launches.

The Scud crews had several initial advantages. They fired from pre-surveyed launch positions. Mobile erector launchers are only about as large as a medium-sized truck and moved constantly. This enabled crews to set up relatively quickly, fire, and move before Coalition forces could respond. The area of western Iraq from which the missiles that struck Israel were launched is rugged, a good setting in which to conceal mobile launchers in ravines, beneath highway underpasses, or in culverts.

Scud launchers could be reconfigured and moving within a few minutes after a launch. Within 10 minutes after launch, a mobile Scud launcher could be anywhere within five miles of the launch site. If the Iraqi Scud crew were given five more minutes, it could be anywhere within nine miles of the launch point — 12 miles if it traveled on a road. Destruction of mobile Scud launchers depended on time — the faster strike aircraft could get to the target the better the chance of destroying the launcher. (See Appendix K and Appendix T for additional discussion of Scud launch detection.)

Of All the Scuds Fired by Iraq, Only One Proved Fatal to US Personnel. *Twenty-eight US Soldiers Were Killed When a Scud Hit Their Barracks.*

A considerable segment of the available intelligence-gathering capability was shifted to counter-Scud operations, including reconnaissance aircraft (U-2/TR-1s and RF-4Cs). Intelligence originally had estimated Iraq had 36 mobile Scud launchers, 33 of which were believed operational. Ad hoc groups were formed to develop options to the seemingly intractable problem of how to find and destroy Scuds. A special planning cell was set up in the US Embassy in Tel Aviv, headed by a Joint Staff flag officer, to give the Israelis a chance to analyze the available intelligence, and elicit their ideas. When one Scud hit a residential section in Tel Aviv on 22 January, killing three Israelis and injuring dozens more, the problem took on even greater urgency.

The next week saw an intense effort in western Iraq to eliminate the mobile Scud launchers. B-52s bombed suspected Scud hide sites and support facilities at H-2 and H-3 airfields in western Iraq during the day and at night. During the day, A-10s and F-16s patrolled the area; at night, LANTIRN-equipped F-16s and F-15Es, and FLIR-equipped A-6Es took up the task. Pilots often received target coordinates or patrol areas, based on the most up-to-date information, as they headed out to the planes. Using Defense Support Program (DSP) early warning information and other indications, CENTCOM directed aircraft to attack the launchers.

Satellite Weather Imagery Showing a Clear Day On 10 February.

JSTARS helped detect and report destruction of several possible mobile launchers north of the KTO on D+5. By D+10, the weather had cleared and A-10s joined in what came to be called the Great Scud Hunt.

The Scud-hunting effort in southeast Iraq was similar to that in the west. The search area was nearly as large, and the mobile Scud launchers were difficult to find. However, Coalition tactics made it dangerous for Scud transporters, and any other vehicles, to move; JSTARS and other surveillance assets alerted ground- and airborne-alert aircraft to vehicular movement, resulting in rapid attack in many cases. Following Scud launches, attack aircraft were concentrated in the launch area to search for and attack suspect vehicles.

By early February, the counter-Scud effort seemed to be having an effect, although no destruction of mobile launchers had been confirmed. The daily CENTCOM chronology for this period contains numerous entries such as, "one Scud launched towards Israel, no damage," and "Patriots destroyed the only Scud launched at Saudi Arabia." As more intelligence assets were brought to bear on the problem, specific Scud operating areas (Scud boxes) were more clearly defined; Coalition striking power was concentrated there. On 19 February, Coalition aircraft began dropping CBU-89 area denial mines into suspected operating areas, to hamper the launchers' mobility. A key element in this effort was small SOF groups on the ground who provided vital information about the Scuds.

On 25 February, a Scud struck a barracks in Dhahran, Saudi Arabia, killing 28 US soldiers and wounding almost 100 more. When the war ended, intelligence analysis showed the Iraqis had fired 88 modified Scuds, 42 towards Israel and 46 at Saudi Arabia and other Persian Gulf states.

Patriot Defender Missile Defense System

Scud ballistic missiles were the main weapon system with which Saddam Hussein took significant offensive action against Coalition forces, and the only one to offer him a possible opportunity, through the attacks on Israel, to achieve a strategic objective. Had they been more accurate or able to penetrate more successfully, they might have inflicted serious damage on military targets, including the large troop concentrations at Saudi ports at the start of the war. The Army's Patriot Defender missile defense system not only helped defeat the psychological threat of Iraq's Scuds, instilling a feeling of confidence in people in the targeted areas, but also almost certainly reduced civilian casualties. Scud attacks resulted in substantial property damage, including that caused by falling debris from the Patriots themselves. (For additional discussion of Patriot, see Appendix T.)

Weather

The worst weather in at least 14 years (the time the USAF has kept records of Iraqi weather patterns) was a factor during all phases of the war. Although no TLAM attack was canceled by poor weather, approximately 15 percent of scheduled aircraft attack sorties during the first 10 days were canceled because of poor visibility or low overcast sky conditions. Cloud ceilings of 5,000 to 7,000 feet were common, especially during the ground campaign's last few days. These conditions also had a negative effect on the ability to collect imagery and hindered the BDA process.

Before the air campaign began, forecasters warned the Baghdad region's weather would deteriorate the evening of 18 January as a frontal system moved into Iraq. A morning F-16 mission scheduled to strike the At-Taji Rocket Production Facility north of Baghdad, for example, was diverted to an alternate target, the Ar-Rumaylah airfield, because of a solid

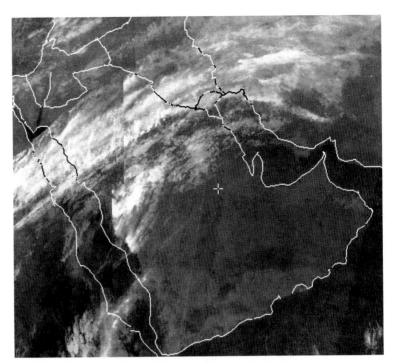

Satellite Photo Shows Clouds Covering the Area on 18 January.

undercast. However, mission results could not be assessed for several days because of cloud cover.

Weather and cloud cover also affected the delivery of LGB. Clouds could interfere with the laser beam used to illuminate targets, causing the LGB to lose guidance. Since JFACC directives required aircrews to avoid collateral damage, some aircraft returned to base with their weapons.

The Defense Meteorological Satellite Program (DMSP) helped the JFACC plan the most effective use of systems whose performance was affected by high humidity, fog, rain, and low clouds. DMSP was so important the JFACC kept a light table next to his desk to review the latest DMSP data, and the TACC waited for the latest DMSP images before finalizing the daily ATO.

An example on 24 January illustrates DMSP's value. Two DMSP images, only an hour and 40

A KC-10 Tanker Passes Fuel to an F-15.

Approximately 16 percent of USAF tanker missions supported Navy or USMC aircraft.

The mission's importance cannot be described by merely reciting the numbers of sorties, aircraft refueled, or gallons of fuel dispensed. The strike packages that hit Iraq on the first night of the war were able to reach their targets only because of repeated aerial refuelings going to and returning from their targets. The fighters that patrolled Iraqi airspace and kept the Iraqi Air Force on the ground needed several refuelings. By themselves, most attack aircraft are limited to a few hours' flight; with aerial refueling, their range and endurance is limited only by crew stamina. Missions by bombers and attack aircraft, AWACS, reconnaissance, EW, and special operations aircraft were either made possible or improved by aerial refueling.

Scheduling and coordinating refueling support for attack aircraft were major tasks. At JFACC headquarters, coordinating refueling was a separate event that took place after MAP strike sortie planning was completed. AWACS and E-2s played a key role in air refueling, but it was a major challenge. Initially, the air refueling plan was to have the tankers and receivers

minutes apart, showed cloudy skies over Baghdad clearing while sunny skies in Al-Basrah gave way to cloud cover. This type of timely, cloud cover assessment allowed the JFACC to make adjustments in the MAP, and Coalition aircrews to make tactical adjustments, in order to put more bombs on target.

Air Refueling

Aerial refueling was crucial throughout the crisis; the thousands of airlift missions to the Gulf, and the hundreds of combat aircraft deployments, could not have been accomplished without the KC-135s and KC-10s of the Strategic Air Command (SAC) tanker force.

Likewise, the air campaign could not have been conducted without the efforts of USAF KC-135s and KC-10s, USMC KC-130s, Navy KA-6s and tanker-configured S-3s, Saudi KE-3s, French KC-135s, and RAF Tristars and VC-10s. The single largest source of aerial refueling support came from SAC's tanker fleet; by the end of the war, SAC had committed 46 KC-10s and 262 KC-135s to Operation Desert Storm. Most combat sorties Coalition aircraft flew required one or more aerial refuelings. Navy, USMC, and other Coalition tankers flew more than 4,000 sorties, while USAF tankers flew more than

HC-130 Refuels Helicopters (HH-53, Left, HH-60, Right) While Training for Deep Reconnaissance Missions During Operation Desert Storm.

operate almost independently, with AWACS providing limited assistance, on request. However, this became unwieldy because of the large numbers of tankers and receivers. Eventually, an AWACS weapons director was assigned full time responsibility for tanker control. Also, the complexity of the air refueling task dictated that a tanker liaison be added to the AWACS airborne command element team on one of the five AWACS airborne at any given time.

One limiting factor for tanker operations was a lack of multipoint-equipped land-based tankers, although quick flow procedures for cycling aircraft off a single boom worked adequately in most cases. Airspace congestion also was a limiting factor. Strike package size sometimes was constrained by the number of tankers that could be scheduled into the heavily congested air refueling tracks. This was another Coalition air operation made more efficient through the unity of effort provided by the JFACC and the ATO. That there were no midair collisions between different packages was a tribute to the skill and professionalism of Coalition aircrews and the firm control of available airspace.

The Red Sea battle force was allocated about

On the afternoon of 17 January, two Air Force Reserve KC-135 tanker crews were orbiting near the Iraqi border, awaiting post-strike refueling requirements. An E-3A advised that a flight of four F-16s, some with battle damage and all low on fuel, were coming back from deep in central Iraq and needed immediate assistance. The two KC-135E tankers turned northwards into Iraq and towards the F-16s. Inside Iraqi airspace without fighter escort, and lacking good intelligence on the possible antiaircraft artillery and surface-to-air missile threat along the route, they located and joined up with the F-16s and provided enough fuel for the safe recovery of one battle-damaged and three fuel-starved aircraft.

CENTAF After Action Reports

twice as many tanker sorties as the Persian Gulf battle force, because of greater flight distances to assigned targets and because initial strike plans required two carriers to strike targets simultaneously from the Red Sea. Most tankers used for these sorties were either KC-135Es or KC-135Rs. To increase availability of refueling hoses, Navy KA-6 and specially equipped S-3s accompanied many KC-135 formations.

Processing large strike packages through the single-boom tankers was time consuming;

A KA-6 Tops Off a Flight of A-7 Aircraft.

A KC-130 Refuels Two CH-53Es.

aircraft over enemy territory to extend their range.

Strike packages from the Persian Gulf carriers evolved away from a reliance on ATO-scheduled tanking as the carriers moved north in the Gulf. The reduction in the range to targets and the consequent shift to normal carrier launch and recovery operations on 4 February substantially decreased the requirement for land-based refueling aircraft. After the fleet's arrival in the northernmost carrier operating areas on 14 February, Navy refueling aircraft provided virtually all refueling for Persian Gulf naval air strikes.

by the time the last aircraft had refueled, the first aircraft had burned up much of the fuel it had received. Tanking procedures evolved to include Navy organic tankers with the strike packages; the Navy tankers refueled from the USAF single-point and RAF multi-point tankers and helped refuel the rest of the strike package en route to the target.

Practice during Operation Desert Shield allowed other Services' pilots to become accustomed to refueling from the large USAF tankers. During Operation Desert Storm, this familiarity paid off, especially when tankers escorted attack

The USMC maintained 20 KC-130 refuelers in Bahrain and Saudi Arabia to support fighter, attack, and helicopter missions. Usually operating in a cell of three to five aircraft, the KC-130s refueled strike packages before and after missions in southern or central Iraq, flying 1,271 missions.

Aerial refueling operations normally are conducted in a no- or low-threat area, for obvious reasons. During Operation Desert Storm, however, Coalition tankers occasionally had to fly over hostile territory to enable strike forces to reach their targets, or to prevent the loss of fuel-starved Coalition aircraft. They flew over southern Iraq, for example, to refuel the fighters flying barrier patrols between Iraq and Iran. An SA-8 SAM exploded above a JTF Proven Force KC-135 tanker flying out of Incirlik.

USAF KC-135 Tanker with Navy F-14 Fighter.

Aerial refueling coordination with carrier-based aircraft was complicated by two requirements: JP-5 fuel which, because of its relatively high combustion temperature is used aboard ships for safety considerations, and basket adapters to fit KC-135 tankers for probe refueling. KC-10 tankers had the flexibility while airborne to refuel aircraft with either a basket or boom configuration, but the KC-135 had to be configured with a basket adapter before takeoff to refuel Navy, USMC, or most other Coalition aircraft.

Reconnaissance and Surveillance

Airborne reconnaissance and surveillance played a key role in Operations Desert Shield and Desert Storm. The Coalition's ability to monitor and control the battle area confirmed the Iraqis' ignorance of what Coalition forces were doing.

E-3B AWACS aircraft (among the first US assets to arrive in Saudi Arabia) maintained one to three 24-hour surveillance orbits during Operation Desert Shield. For Operation Desert Storm, this was expanded so the United States manned five orbits (four in Saudi Arabia and one in Turkey) and the RSAF manned one to three. With these orbits, AWACS provided comprehensive radar coverage 24 hours a day throughout the war. AWACS gave early warning of Iraqi air attack or other Iraqi Air Force movements, and helped control engagement of Iraqi aircraft. It also supported Coalition strike packages, and provided airborne surveillance and threat warning for other airborne assets such as SOF and CSAR missions.

U-2R and TR-1 aircraft provided valuable reconnaissance using a variety of sensors, and satisfied imagery collection requirements that could not be met by other collection sources. Initially, the aircraft remained over friendly territory but, when air supremacy was achieved, missions began to fly over Iraq.

RC-135 Rivet Joint aircraft was the first on-scene airborne reconnaissance system, flying the first operational sortie enroute from Hellenikon Air Base, Greece, to Riyadh on 9 August.

Naval electronic reconnaissance squadrons provided crucial support to Coalition forces beginning 7 August.

The 3rd MAW also flew the Senior Warrior package aboard a USMC Reserve KC-130T in support of MARCENT and the CENTCOM intelligence gathering effort.

Though still in development, CINCCENT requested E-8 JSTARS to be deployed in mid-December to give Coalition forces a tactical edge in combat. JSTARS provided theater commanders and other tactical users an NRT capability to locate and track moving ground targets across a wide area and quickly relay this information to air and ground commanders. The two JSTARS aircraft flew an 11-to-13 hour mission daily throughout Operation Desert Storm, with all sorties taking off in late afternoon or early evening. The aircraft usually flew in an eastern orbit just south of the KTO, where they were able to monitor ground activity. They also operated from a western orbit in northern Saudi Arabia near the Iraq/Jordan border to detect and track Scud launchers. An orbit in north central Saudi Arabia supported the Army's XVIII Airborne Corps before and during the Offensive Ground Campaign.

JSTARS tasking for the air campaign was to locate and target high-value armor, army forces, and resupply activity in the KTO (including the area encompassing the Republican Guard and secondary echelon forces). JSTARS also was tasked to find and target Scud locations, gather intelligence on the movement of forces within the KTO and eastern Iraq, and validate targets for other weapons systems. For the ground campaign, JSTARS was tasked to locate and target movement within the second echelon forces with emphasis on the Republican Guard, provide intelligence on the movement of forces within the KTO and eastern Iraq, and respond to immediate requests for support of engaged ground forces.

The information JSTARS provided during the ground offensive allowed CINCCENT to make key operational decisions at crucial moments. JSTARS found significant target groups, such as convoys. JSTARS detected the Republican Guard movement and massive retreats from Kuwait City during the ground offensive, which gave CINCCENT the opportunity to press the attack and destroy the Iraqi forces while they were moving.

Navy E-2C aircraft were the first US airborne early warning (AEW) and C^2 assets in theater. They provided continuous AEW, and were deployed to Bahrain during Operation Desert Shield to fill AWACS radar surveillance gaps. During Operation Desert Storm they primarily operated off aircraft carriers.

The E-2C was crucial for carrier-based naval aviation — it synthesized information, analyzed and corrected battlefield problems, and provided a more complete picture for strike leaders and warfare commanders. E-2Cs flew around the clock from carrier battle groups in the Red Sea and Persian Gulf, fusing tactical and strategic intelligence from AWACS, Aegis, and other assets to produce a comprehensive picture of the KTO. Airborne controllers provided tailored tactical control, intelligence filtering, and friendly forces deconfliction, and improved the situational awareness for Navy strike groups as well as other Coalition forces.

P-3 and S-3 aircraft made important contributions to maritime interception force operations, antisurface warfare, strike support, and the counter-Scud campaign. The Navy and USMC both used EA-6Bs to good effect.

Forward Operating Locations (FOLs) Forward Area Rearming and Refueling Points (FARPs)

Both the USMC and USAF attempted to base their primary attack assets at a home base, but also operated from FOLs to get closer to the target areas. The USAF based its A-10s at King Fahd International Airport in Saudi Arabia and operated from two FOLs, especially King Khalid Military City, while the USMC AV-8Bs operated from King 'Abd Al-'Aziz Naval Base as well as additional FOLs and forward area rearming and refueling points (FARP) near the Kuwaiti-Saudi border.

Before G-Day, the USMC established FARP for both fixed- and rotary-wing aircraft in northern Saudi Arabia. These locations allowed quicker aircraft response times. Fixed-wing sites were established at Al-Jubayl for F/A-18s and at Tanajib for AV-8Bs and OV-10s. The assets needed to refuel, rearm, and provide normal maintenance were at these sites; intelligence briefings and debriefings also were conducted. At Tanajib, an ARAMCO facility 35 miles south of the Kuwaiti border, AV-8B operations began on 18 February. AV-8Bs were able to rearm and refuel within 17 to 25 minutes and could reach the Kuwait border in five to seven minutes. The FARP allowed AV-8B aircraft to range farther north, without aerial refueling. These locations proved extremely valuable in attacking Iraqi troops in the I MEF area. FARP also allowed returning pilots an additional base for low fuel and other problems.

USMC rotary wing squadrons also deployed forward. AH-1s maintained a strip alert of four aircraft at Ras Al-Mish'ab, 27 miles south of the Kuwaiti border, beginning on D-Day. These aircraft responded to close-in fire support requests at Al-Khafji and during the ground offensive. Helicopter squadrons also deployed to Tanajib on 2 February, and on 16 February to a USMC expeditionary base in the desert, south of the "elbow," the bend in the

Kuwaiti border. This base, which included an AM-2 matting air strip, was named Lonesome Dove.

HUMINT Assistance to Targeting Process

Identifying military targets was difficult; however, information acquired by HUMINT operations improved targeting and destruction of significant military facilities in Baghdad, including the MOD and various communications nodes. In addition to blueprints and plans, HUMINT sources provided detailed memory sketches and were able to pinpoint on maps and photographs key locations, which subsequently were targeted.

Sources detailed the locations of bunkers underneath key facilities, including the Iraqi Air Force headquarters, which was composed of several main buildings and five underground bunkers, and the Iraqi practice of stringing coaxial communications cable under bridges rather than under the river beds in Baghdad and southern Iraq. This information was the deciding factor in the decision to target key bridges in Baghdad. Sources identified the communications center in Baghdad; less than 12 hours later, this facility was destroyed. Information obtained from EPWs also helped planners direct effective air attacks against troops and logistics targets.

Battle Damage Assessment

While the intelligence support to CENTCOM was considered an overall success, the BDA process was only a limited success. The following recounts some of the problems and successes with BDA support for the air campaign (see Appendix C).

The BDA process at the theater level suffered from a lack of adequate systems, procedures, and manpower and had difficulty trying to keep pace with the size, speed, and scope of the air campaign. Not since Vietnam had the DOD Intelligence Community been faced with such a large scale BDA challenge. With the beginning of Operation Desert Shield, DIA began extensive preparations to provide BDA to CENTCOM. These preparations included 13 DIA-led end-to-end exercises of imagery dissemination, and training for DIA personnel, as well as other participants. CENTCOM and its components took part in these preparations; however, not all aspects of the BDA architecture, especially within theater, were tested fully before Operation Desert Storm.

Further, the BDA process was not fully synchronized with the attack planning process. The air operations tempo and the massive number of targets outstripped the established system for collecting and reporting intelligence. This complicated the intelligence collection strategy and generally delayed BDA analysis and reporting. Additionally, BDA primarily relied on imagery and was severely hampered by bad weather. Even some of the better imagery analysts had difficulty assessing degrees of damage for targets not catastrophically destroyed.

Coupled with massive, fast-paced air attacks, it was difficult to provide aim point and damage criteria specifics in the MAP and ATO. Instead, planners at the air wing level often were forced to rely on cockpit video, pilot reports, and limited organic intelligence and planning capabilities to choose the best attack options and aimpoints. Doing that required access to recent target imagery and BDA information, which often were neither timely nor adequate. At times, this led to unnecessary restrikes.

At the tactical level, few assets were available to collect BDA after artillery or air strikes. Frustration at this level was increased by the competition at higher echelons for limited national intelligence collection assets. Further, communications down to the tactical level often were not adequate to pass reconnaissance results. Moreover, the disseminated BDA often was not useful to some tactical commanders. There was no system specifically designed to provide feedback from the tactical user to the national level producer.

Although BDA inputs from many different intelligence agencies were frequent and often timely, fusion of the BDA at the theater level posed problems. Throughout the war, damage assessment and intelligence information to support decisions to restrike particular targets were piecemeal affairs, requiring individual users, whether on a carrier or in Riyadh, to synthesize assessments independently.

The desire not to overstate operational accomplishments led to assessing damage based only on what could be proven using imagery. In some cases, this seems to have precluded making rapid judgments about what probably had been accomplished.

This practice did not serve well the needs of commanders operating under combat time pressures. They could not wait for in-depth analysis; decisions had to be made based on judgment. Consequently, planners were forced to make their own assessments of how attacks were succeeding, and whether restrikes were needed. In addition, some agencies doing BDA did not have some essential planning data, such as, the desired aimpoint, weapon destruction information, the target list priority, or the desired damage level.

Finally, neither training doctrine nor training standards existed; consequently, damage analysts were too few and not adequately trained to assess the effects of penetrating weapons or special weapons which typically reveal little visible damage beyond the entry hole.

The Defense Nuclear Agency (DNA) provided Checkmate with vulnerability analyses of Iraqi underground facilities. These analyses were submitted in a report format designed as a quick reference for attack planning. Requests for DNA assistance from Checkmate were handled on a rapid reaction basis; DNA's assessments usually were provided directly to the Checkmate staff within hours of the request. In addition, DNA received BDA data and provided munitions effectiveness assessments to Checkmate and DIA to help CENTCOM planning. (For additional assessment of BDA, see Appendix C.)

Ultimately CINCCENT relied upon a synergistic approach to determine BDA across the board and within individual target categories. He meshed BDA assessments from DIA and other national agencies and tactical reconnaissance (which tended to be conservative) with mission reports (which tended to be inflated) and gun camera imagery to provide a balanced assessment of the air campaign.

Space Systems

The war with Iraq was the first conflict in history to make comprehensive use of space systems support. All of the following helped the Coalition's air, ground, and naval forces: The DMSP weather satellites; US LANDSAT multi-spectral imagery satellites; the GPS; DSP early warning satellites; the tactical receive, equipment and related applications satellite broadcast; the Tactical Information Broadcast Service; as well as communications satellites. Space systems communications played a central role in the effective use of advanced weapon systems. (For more detailed discussion, see Appendices K and T.)

The largely featureless KTO terrain made precise electronic navigation crucial to many missions and functions. GPS was used by TLAM launch platforms to obtain accurate firing positions; by artillery for accurate targeting; by aircraft for more precise navigation; by SLAM for flight guidance; by minesweeping ships and helicopters to maintain accurate sweep lanes; by Navy CSAR and USMC medical evacuation helicopters to locate downed airmen or injured ground troops; and by many other units to provide grid locations for navigation aids and radars.

DSP was the primary Scud launch detection system during Operation Desert Storm. The DSP constellation and associated ground station processing provided crucial warning data of Scud launches. This data was disseminated by a variety of means. The national military command center used DSP data to provide military and civilian warning to Israel and the Gulf states.

Civilian Casualties and Collateral Damage

From the beginning, Coalition objectives made a clear distinction between the regime and the Iraqi populace — the regime and its military capabilities were the target; the Iraqi people were not.

Coalition planners followed stringent procedures to select and attack targets. Attack routes were planned to minimize the results of errant ordnance; the norm was to use PGMs, rather than less-accurate gravity weapons, in built-up or populated areas. Attack procedures specified that if the pilot could not positively identify his target or was not confident the weapon would guide properly (because of clouds, for example), he could not deliver that weapon. Several attack sorties were forced to return with their bombs for this reason.

Coalition planners recognized not all weapons would perform in every case as designed and, despite all efforts to prevent collateral damage, some would occur. Although the death or injury of any civilian is regrettable, the apparently low

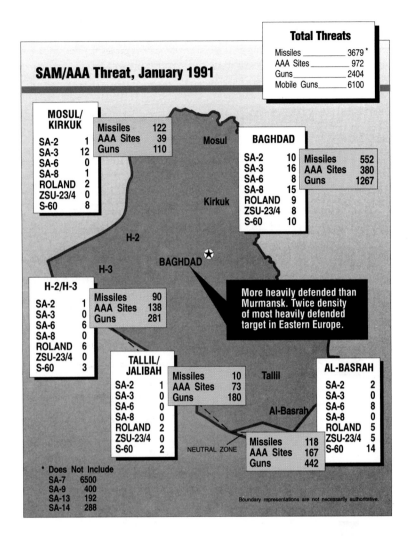

number clearly reflects Coalition efforts to minimize civilian casualties.

As discussed in Appendix O (The Role of Law of War), the problem of collateral civilian casualties was worsened by Saddam Hussein's failure to carry out routine air raid precautions to protect the civilian population and his conscious use of civilians to shield military objectives from attack.

There is also a probability that some casualties occurred when unexploded Iraqi SAMs or AAA fell back to earth. The often dense fire the Iraqis expended in attempts to shoot down Coalition aircraft and cruise missiles almost certainly caused some destruction on the ground from malfunctioning fuses or self-destruction features, as well as the simple impact of spent rounds.

Aircraft Vulnerabilities to SAMs and AAA

All aircraft are vulnerable to radar-guided weapons unless the radar tracking system can be denied crucial information such as altitude, heading, and speed. Coalition aircraft denied much of this information through stealth, jamming or chaff, and attacks on the radar systems (using bombs and missiles). Coalition aircraft also had to nullify the Iraqis' IR tracking systems; this was more difficult because jet exhausts produce heat. IR sensors cannot be jammed, but they can be defeated or fooled by flares the sensors detect.

The Coalition's aggressive SEAD defeated most Iraqi radar systems. This enabled Coalition aircraft to conduct operations in the middle

On the last day of the war, an A-10 pilot from the 511th Tactical Fighter Squadron was awaiting his next mission. Instead of an attack on the enemy, however, his last mission of the war offered a sobering reminder of the cost of freedom. It is best told in his own words: "As we're on our way out the door [to his plane], I overhear that there's a hog [A-10 Warthog] coming in with battle damage. He's been hit by an infrared surface-to-air missile in the tail, and he's flying [with] no hydraulics. Tower asks if we would mind flying a CAP over the airfield while he comes in, [so] we take off. We are overhead when he comes across the threshold [the end of the runway]. He is lined up and everything looks good. All of a sudden the aircraft hits the threshold very hard, all three gear collapse and shear out from under him. The aircraft bounces about 40 to 50 feet into the air. It then rolls into the wind, to the right. The flight lead starts yelling into the radio, and someone on the ground yells for him to punch out. It is too late, though, he is probably unconscious from the hard landing. The aircraft rolls and hits nose first. He didn't have a chance — the aircraft instantly goes up into a ball of flame . . . . We park our jets and go through debrief. Not more than two words are said. The next day the war is over, and we have won a big victory. Some have paid a higher price than others."

511 Tactical Fighter Squadron Unit History

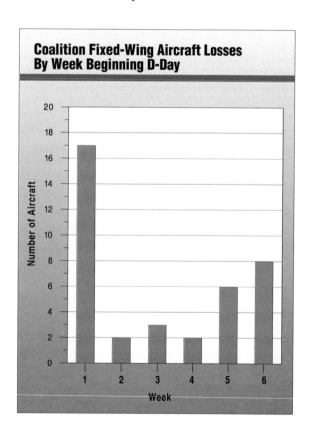

Coalition Fixed-Wing Aircraft Losses By Week Beginning D-Day

altitudes (about 15,000 feet) in relative safety because they were less vulnerable to IR-guided SAMs or unguided AAA. One of the greater dangers Coalition pilots faced was from IR- or EO-guided SAMs while they were flying at relatively low altitudes, supporting Coalition ground forces. Although sortie rates were relatively constant, approximately half of its fixed-wing combat losses occurred during either the first week of Operation Desert Storm (17 aircraft), before enemy defenses had been suppressed, or during the last week (eight aircraft), when aircraft were operating at lower altitudes in the IR SAM threat region.

Coalition Fixed-Wing Aircraft Combat Losses

Ten aircraft were lost during the final 10 days of the war (19 to 28 February), all in the KTO. During this period, Coalition aircraft often operated at lower altitudes, where the Iraqi defensive threat was still potent, to get below the prevalent bad weather and to support the ground forces better. This not only exposed the aircrews to battlefield defenses, such as hand-held IR SAMs that were not a threat at the middle altitudes, but also reduced aircrew reaction time and ability to evade SAMs.

OBSERVATIONS

Accomplishments

- Operation Desert Storm validated the concept of a campaign in which air power, applied precisely and nearly simultaneously against centers of gravity, significantly degraded enemy capabilities. Air power degraded much of the Iraqi command structure, markedly reduced military production, made the Iraqi Air Force ineffective, and significantly degraded the overall combat effectiveness of the Iraqi army in the KTO.

- The theater campaign strategy exploited wise investments, superior planning, people, training, doctrine, and technology to achieve surprise.

- Technology gave the Coalition a decisive edge. Stealth, PGMs, SEAD, C^3I, air refueling, reconnaissance and surveillance aircraft, space systems, night-fighting capabilities, tactical ballistic missile defense systems, logistics systems, airlift and sealift, cruise missiles, attack helicopters, remotely piloted vehicles, and flexible-basing aircraft made major contributions.

- The revolutionary combination of stealth aircraft and PGMs allowed nearly simultaneous attack against scores of targets across the theater. They enabled a relatively small number of offensive assets to attack effectively many more targets than would have been possible without stealth (which requires little airborne support) and PGMs (which require few munitions to achieve the desired effect). Without these capabilities, the attacks would have required many more sorties, and would have been much more costly. Many attacks would have been impractical (because they would have caused too much collateral damage or would have required too many assets) or impossible (because the desired level of damage against pinpoint or hardened targets could not have been achieved with conventional munitions).

- The TLAM played an important role in the air campaign as the only weapon system used to attack central Baghdad in daylight. The cruise missile concept — incorporating an unmanned, low-observable platform able to strike accurately at long distances — was validated as a significant new instrument for future conflicts.

- The JFACC concept was validated. JFACC planning, coordination, allocation, and tasking of apportioned sorties and capabilities secured unity of effort.

- Planning for air campaign levels of enemy force destruction, and crippling of enemy C^3 and logistics generally was accurate, despite the unusually bad weather. NBC destruction estimates suffered from incomplete target set information. Scud suppression, expected to be difficult, proved very much so.

- Mission capable maintenance rates were higher for most aircraft than peacetime rates, despite harsh desert conditions, high sortie rates, and flight under combat conditions.

- Despite difficulties with BDA, the NCA and Coalition commanders rated intelligence support to Operation Desert Storm as the best for any war. Improvements always are possible, but the intelligence and operations communities worked together, although sometimes in nonsystematic, innovative ways, to produce careful targeting and successful execution of massive air and ground campaigns.

(Continued)

OBSERVATIONS (Continued)

■ An ad hoc BDA system was developed using both objective (physical evidence) and subjective (military judgment) analysis, to determine damage inflicted by air power to strategic and operational targets.

■ Ad hoc cooperative efforts injected hardened target vulnerability expertise directly into the real-time targeting process. However, Operation Desert Storm experience demonstrated that such operations should be practiced to maximize effectiveness during future conflicts.

Shortcomings

■ The lack of PGM capability on many US aircraft required planners to select less-than-optimum attack options, such as delaying attacks or assigning multiple sorties with non-precision munitions. Operation Desert Storm results argue that a higher percentage of US attack aircraft should have PGM capability to increase the amount of target damage that can be inflicted by a finite number of aircraft.There was no published joint guidance on TLAM use. A joint TLAM strike-planning manual should be developed.

■ Operation Desert Storm highlighted the need for high resolution systems for capturing and rapidly exploiting mission results to allow accurate and timely BDA. Many aircraft that flew in the war had no system or a system that did not meet the BDA needs of a large-scale, rapid war, in which air attacks generated most BDA requirements.

■ In the Persian Gulf War, some target sets, such as electrical power production, were more heavily damaged than originally planned. As exceptions to the general targeting guidance to minimize long-term damage, some electricity-producing facilities purposely were severely damaged to ensure they remained unusable for the entire conflict. In some instances, wing-level planners were not briefed adequately on air campaign objectives. For example, JFACC planners had decided to target the switching systems at electrical power plants because they are easier to repair than other plant facilities. Unfortunately, this direction was not always passed to the units in the form of aimpoints in the ATO; this left some units to select their own aimpoints. As a result, many generator halls — which are easier to strike, but harder to repair — were damaged heavily. BDA limitations further complicated targeting. BDA sometimes was slow to reach air planners and did not assess fully the effects of modern munitions. Because disrupting electricity was time-crucial and considered vital to protect aircrew lives and ensure mission accomplishment, and BDA might never provide complete assessments of damage effects, commanders, based on the information available at the time, sometimes directed additional attacks. In some cases, this resulted in additional damage at facilities that apparently already were out of operation.

■ Although there were no ground-to-air or air-to-air losses caused by fire from friendly forces, some air-to-ground fire from friendly forces took place during the air campaign. (See Appendix M for discussion)

■ The lack of a tested, fully coordinated BDA system to support CENTCOM needs was a problem.

■ VTR imagery was very useful in Operation Desert Storm for providing BDA of PGM attacks. For the future, the resolution and overall capabilities of these sensors need to be improved to handle a variety of weapon delivery tactics at different flight levels. VTR for BDA should be provided to all attack aircraft. To obtain higher resolution, use of low-light-level, high-definition TV should be considered along with IR systems.

Issues

■ The theater Commander-in-Chief has the key role in theater-level targeting, but this role is not clearly defined in joint doctrine. This lack of definition caused confusion and duplication. Ground force commanders expressed discontent with the JFACC targeting process for not being responsive to pre-G-Day targeting nominations. On the other hand, the JFACC targeting process reacted to CINCCENT direction regarding priorities and maintenance of the overall deception plan. Difficulties were experienced in nominating and validating targets. CINCCENT has recommended, for future major military operations, the JFACC be staffed with personnel from all using as well as providing Services. This issue will be addressed in the DOD joint doctrinal development process.

■ Before Operation Desert Shield, the USAF had already begun developing an upgraded force management and planning system to replace CAFMS, which is relatively slow, and not fully interoperable with the other Services. The Services are working together on an interoperable follow-on system that will help shorten the ATO planning cycle.

■ Prudence dictates that national defense planning assume future adversaries will be more adept, better equipped, and more effective than Saddam Hussein.

■ Although the Coalition was able to take advantage of favorable environmental conditions in this war, in the future, elimination of an adversary's stockpile of chemical and biological weapons before deployment or use, with current conventional weapons inventories, is problematic.

■ Locating and destroying mobile missiles proved very difficult and required substantially more resources than planned. This could be a more serious problem in the future against an enemy with more accurate missiles or one who uses weapons of mass destruction.

■ More countries are expected to acquire ballistic missiles and will be prepared to use them in future conflicts. Tomorrow's forces must be defended against the more advanced missiles that soon will be found in some third world arsenals, perhaps armed with unconventional warheads. Continual expansion of the threat, as illustrated by Iraqi Scud attacks, indicates antiballistic missile defensive capabilities and counterforce location and targeting must be improved.

■ It appears at least 15 Coalition aircraft were lost to AAA or IR SAMs. When aircraft operated at lower altitudes to ensure target acquisition and destruction, they became more vulnerable to IR SAMs and AAA. SEAD can reduce, but not eradicate, these threats. All aircraft require improved protection. Possible improvements could come from automatic warning systems to indicate to the pilot his aircraft is being targeted by IR-, EO-, or radar-guided SAMs, and automatic defensive systems to react to the threat. Improved flares also may help.

■ There is a need to field an all-weather reconnaissance system to provide NRT battlefield intelligence and BDA at long range.

■ Future adversaries may be expected to invest in protective shelters and bunkers for aircraft and C^2 facilities. As other nations study the lessons of Operation Desert Storm, they may see the importance of a more balanced approach to passive air defenses. Shelters may be strengthened or facilities may be dispersed and made more mobile to avoid the increased likelihood that fixed targets will be vulnerable to attack. Further development of anti-hardened shelter weapons, methods for distinguishing decoys from targets, and methods to react quickly to mobile targets, all remain important issues.

Chapter VII

Part of the Red Sea Battle Force (from left): *USS Thomas S. Gates* (CG 51), *USS Saratoga* (CV 60), *USS San Jacinto* (CG 56), *USS John F. Kennedy* (CV 67), *USS Mississippi* (CGN 40), *USS America* (CV 66), *USS William V. Pratt* (DDG 44), *USS Normandy* (CG 60), *USS Philippine Sea* (CG 58) and *USS Preble* (DDG 46).

THE MARITIME CAMPAIGN

INTRODUCTION

The Navy benefited from years of operating experience in the harsh Middle East environment. Because there were no permanent US bases in the area, forward-deployed ships became increasingly important in the region. The Joint Task Force Middle East (JTFME) ships operated daily in the Persian Gulf before 2 August, conducting training exercises with Gulf Cooperation Council (GCC) nations, while their forward presence protected shipping routes.

In addition to the JTFME surface combatants, the United States routinely maintained an aircraft carrier battle group (CVBG) in the Indian Ocean. This battle group was tethered to the Persian Gulf region, requiring it to be in a position ready to respond to a crisis within a designated time period to support the National Command Authorities. As the Middle East political climate changed, this tether was shortened when tensions rose and lengthened during periods of stability.

The eight forward-deployed JTFME ships in the Persian Gulf, along with the *USS Independence* (CV 62) CVBG in the Indian Ocean and the *USS D. D. Eisenhower* (CVN 69) CVBG in the eastern Mediterranean Sea, were the only sustainable US combat forces nearby when Iraq invaded Kuwait. By 7 August, the Independence and Eisenhower battle groups (and embarked air wings) were operating under Commander-in-Chief, Central Command (CINCCENT) control. Eventually, the Persian Gulf conflict brought together the largest naval force assembled in a single theater since World War II.

"We continued heavy operations out in the sea because we wanted the Iraqis to believe that we were going to conduct a massive amphibious operation. The Iraqis thought that we were going to take them head on into their most heavily defended area. We launched amphibious feints and naval gunfire so they continued to think we were going to be attacking along the coast, and therefore fixed their forces there. Our hope was that by fixing the forces in this position and with a ground attack [from the south], we would basically keep the forces here [in southern Kuwait] and they wouldn't know what was going on out in this area [west of Kuwait]. We succeeded in that very well."

General H. Norman Schwarzkopf
Commander-in-Chief, Central Command

This chapter first discusses the importance of sea control in Operations Desert Shield and Desert Storm, and then reviews the planning and execution of Operation Desert Storm's maritime campaign, which was conducted to support the theater campaign. In this report, the maritime campaign is addressed by warfare area: antisurface warfare (ASUW), antiair warfare (AAW), countermine warfare, naval gunfire support (NGFS), and amphibious warfare. Each naval warfare area generally presents the specific Iraqi capabilities, followed by a discussion of Coalition capabilities in that area, and then a chronological description of significant operations. Also included is a discussion of the role US submarines played in support of Operations Desert Shield and Desert Storm. This chapter concludes with a maritime campaign summary followed by an observations section that lists significant accomplishments, shortcomings, and issues. (Chapter IV discusses Maritime Interception Operations (MIO) and Chapter VI discusses naval aviation's contributions to the air campaign.)

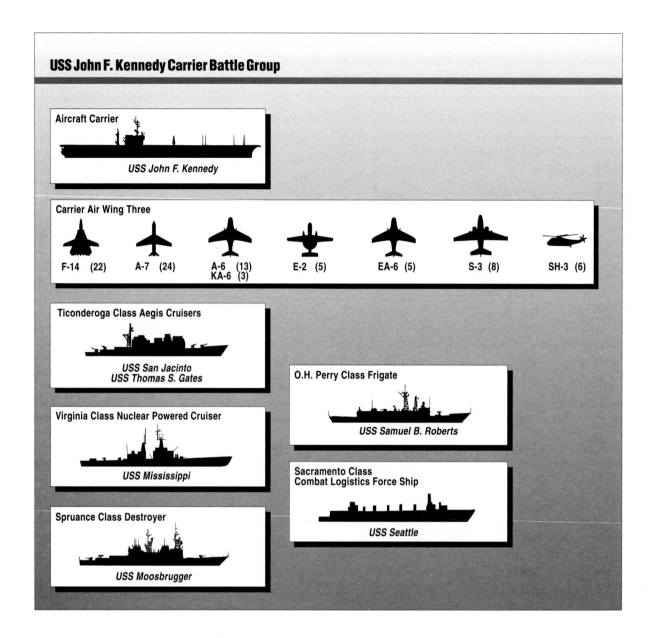

USS John F. Kennedy Carrier Battle Group

Aircraft Carrier
USS John F. Kennedy

Carrier Air Wing Three
F-14 (22)   A-7 (24)   A-6 (13)   E-2 (5)   EA-6 (5)   S-3 (8)   SH-3 (6)
                          KA-6 (3)

Ticonderoga Class Aegis Cruisers
USS San Jacinto
USS Thomas S. Gates

Virginia Class Nuclear Powered Cruiser
USS Mississippi

Spruance Class Destroyer
USS Moosbrugger

O.H. Perry Class Frigate
USS Samuel B. Roberts

Sacramento Class
Combat Logistics Force Ship
USS Seattle

THE IMPORTANCE OF SEA CONTROL

As the Coalition formed and plans were developed to restore the independence of Kuwait, the Navy set about classic naval missions — sea control and power projection. During the Persian Gulf conflict, the United States deployed more than 165 ships, including six carrier battle groups with embarked air wings, to the Persian Gulf, Arabian, Red, and eastern Mediterranean Seas. Other Coalition nations deployed more than 65 ships to Southwest Asia (SWA). As a result, the Coalition's control of the seas was never in question and naval forces made significant contributions to operations against Iraq.

Sea control allowed the Coalition to isolate Iraq from outside support. Maritime Interception Operations cut off Iraqi trade. In addition, sea control assured the free use of the sea lines of communication for the deployment of Coalition forces. Sealift carried 95 percent of the cargo required for Operations Desert Shield and Storm. As demonstrated during the Iran-Iraq War, mines, missile-firing patrol boats, antiship-missile-firing aircraft, and land-based antiship missile systems were capable of damaging and disrupting seaborne commerce. Without control of the sea and the airspace over it, that cargo would have been at risk, slowing the deployment of forces and support equipment, threatening US ability to charter foreign merchant vessels, and substantially increasing shipping costs. Because Coalition naval forces controlled the seas, this sealift effort was never challenged.

Control of the seas also permitted carrier battle groups to make maximum use of their mobility. Mobility is one of the carrier battle group's greater advantages. The America CVBG, initially used during the Strategic Air Campaign against targets in western Iraq, moved from the Red Sea to the Persian Gulf in early February. This redeployment reinforced the Persian Gulf battle force's participation in tactical operations against Iraqi forces in Kuwait. Similarly, repositioning the Persian Gulf battle force to operating areas farther north reduced the range to targets, thereby increasing the sortie rate of aircraft flying from those carriers. Mobility also made it possible to diversify attack axes against Iraq (from the Red Sea, GCC states, and the Persian Gulf), and provided the Coalition aircraft operating bases out of range of Iraq's short-range ballistic missile and chemical warfare threats.

Establishing control over the Persian Gulf also prevented Iraq from mounting small-scale surprise attacks against the coastlines of Saudi Arabia, the United Arab Emirates (UAE), Qatar, Bahrain, and Oman. During the Iran-Iraq War, both sides demonstrated the ability to attack both ships in the Persian Gulf and coastal facilities. Thus, Coalition naval forces were required to maintain constant vigilance against attacks from Iraq and Iran. At the same time, naval forces in the Persian Gulf added depth to the air defenses protecting Gulf states and the right flank of Coalition forces.

Finally, establishing sea control in the Gulf was an essential prerequisite to any amphibious operations against the Iraqi left flank in Kuwait. Although an amphibious assault never occurred, preparations for such an assault were part of the theater campaign's deception. The threat of amphibious attack induced the Iraqis to fortify the coast, diverting manpower and material from the area of the Coalition's actual assault.

The maritime campaign highlighted the crucial importance of the ability to:

- Take control of the sea and air, and to exploit that control to affect the course and outcome of maritime operations, even in the enemy's own territory;
- Operate in coastal waters such as the Persian Gulf; and
- Insert forces ashore, possibly against opposition, and sustain combat operations.

Furthermore, the Persian Gulf War demonstrated once again that sea control is fundamental to successful power projection, and revalidated the importance of maritime superiority to US global leadership.

NAVCENT OPERATION DESERT STORM COMMAND ORGANIZATION

As plans were developed for offensive operations, additional strike forces were deployed to the theater to augment forces already in place. This deployment of additional forces permitted Naval Forces Component, Central Command (NAVCENT) to restructure the command organization and form two carrier battle forces. Ultimately, six CVBGs were merged into these battle forces. Initially, the *USS Midway* (CV 41), *USS Ranger* (CV 61), and *USS Theodore R. Roosevelt* (CV 71) battle groups comprised the Persian Gulf Battle Force, with Commander, Carrier Group

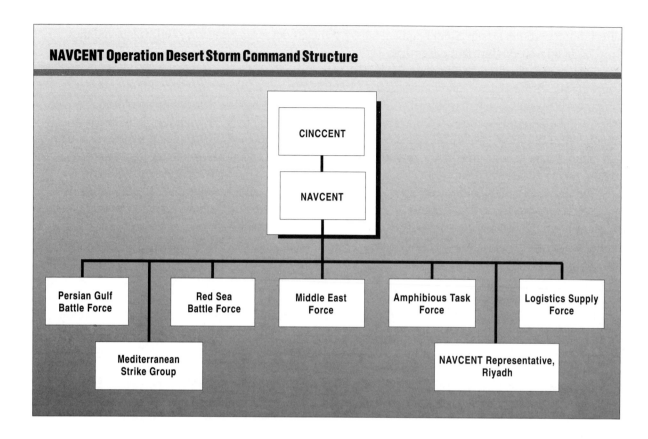

NAVCENT Operation Desert Storm Command Structure

CINCCENT

NAVCENT

Persian Gulf Battle Force

Red Sea Battle Force

Middle East Force

Amphibious Task Force

Logistics Supply Force

Mediterranean Strike Group

NAVCENT Representative, Riyadh

(COMCARGRU) 5 aboard *USS Midway* as battle force commander. The *USS John F. Kennedy* (CV 67), *USS Saratoga* (CV 60), and *USS America* battle groups formed the Red Sea Battle Force, with COMCARGRU 2 aboard *USS John F. Kennedy* as commander. In February, *USS America* joined the Persian Gulf battle force to provide more strike assets to support the anticipated ground offensive.

In addition to the Red Sea and Persian Gulf battle forces, NAVCENT controlled other task forces. The Commander, Middle East Force (CMEF) maintained operational control of the extensive US Maritime Interception Force, as well as the US mine countermeasure (MCM) forces and the Middle East Force surface combatant squadron in the Persian Gulf. The amphibious task force (ATF), which included the Marine Corps (USMC) landing force embarked in amphibious ships, also was under NAVCENT control. During some operations,

NAVCENT controlled the surface combatants and submarines in the Mediterranean Strike Group. NAVCENT also coordinated with the Navy's Atlantic, European, and Pacific fleets, which provided various forms of support (e.g., logistics, communications, intelligence, and maritime patrol aircraft (MPA) assets) to Operations Desert Shield and Desert Storm.

During Operation Desert Storm, NAVCENT exercised overall control of all warfare areas at sea, with Navy air strikes against occupied Kuwait conducted under the Joint Force Air Component Commander (JFACC) concept. NAVCENT assigned sea control and strike warfare tasks to his battle force commanders. Amphibious warfare tasks were assigned to the Commander, Amphibious Task Force (CATF) and the Commander, Landing Force (CLF) which comprised the ATF. NAVCENT's naval forces at sea implemented command and control (C^2), for the most part, through the Navy's

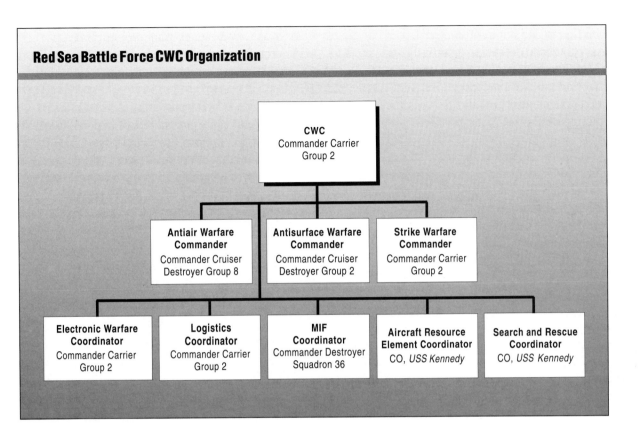

Red Sea Battle Force CWC Organization

```
                          CWC
                   Commander Carrier
                        Group 2

        ┌──────────────────┼──────────────────┐
  Antiair Warfare    Antisurface Warfare   Strike Warfare
   Commander            Commander           Commander
Commander Cruiser   Commander Cruiser    Commander Carrier
Destroyer Group 8   Destroyer Group 2        Group 2

┌──────────┬──────────┬──────────┬──────────┬──────────┐
Electronic    Logistics      MIF        Aircraft Resource   Search and Rescue
 Warfare     Coordinator  Coordinator   Element Coordinator    Coordinator
Coordinator
Commander    Commander    Commander     CO, USS Kennedy    CO, USS Kennedy
Carrier       Carrier      Destroyer
Group 2       Group 2     Squadron 36
```

standardized Composite Warfare Commander (CWC) concept. This concept embodies a basic organizational structure, which enables the CWCs (who were the battle force and task force commanders during Operation Desert Storm) to wage combat operations against air, surface, and subsurface threats to accomplish primary missions (such as sea control, strike warfare, or amphibious operations). During Operation Desert Storm, NAVCENT assigned missions to the battle force and task force CWCs, who planned and directed the execution of those missions.

To conduct combat operations, the CWC designates subordinate warfare commanders within his command organization, who are responsible to the CWC for conducting strike warfare, AAW, ASUW, and antisubmarine warfare (ASW). (ASW was not used in Operation Desert Storm). The warfare commanders are responsible for collecting, evaluating, and disseminating tactical information; executing assigned missions; and, at the CWC's discretion, are delegated authority to respond to threats. A wide range of options exist for the delegation of command authority to the warfare commanders. Regardless of the amount of authority delegated, the CWC always retains the option to overrule his subordinate commanders' decisions, if required.

THE MARITIME CAMPAIGN PLAN

The key pedestals of CINCCENT's theater campaign plan were the air campaign, the ground campaign, and an amphibious invasion, which evolved into part of the theater campaign's deception. In addition to supporting the air campaign, NAVCENT's other primary objective was developing and maintaining this amphibious invasion capability. Even though an amphibious invasion did not occur, the amphibious invasion threat had to be credible to induce Iraq to commit a substantial part of its military forces to defending against this threat. In addition to maintaining a well trained ATF, conducting amphibious operations first required extensive efforts in ASUW, mine countermeasures (MCM), and NGFS. Along with the amphibious invasion, NAVCENT was responsible for defending the coastlines of Saudi Arabia, the UAE, Qatar, Bahrain, Oman and the adjoining maritime areas. During the Iran-Iraq War, Iraq had demonstrated capabilities that could threaten Coalition ports, such as Ad-Dammam and Al-Jubayl, as well as Coalition naval forces operating in the Gulf.

To support CINCCENT's theater campaign plan, NAVCENT's major tasks during Operation Desert Storm phases I and II (Strategic Air Campaign and Establishment of Air Superiority over the Kuwait Theater of Operations (KTO)) were:

- Conduct the air campaign in accordance with the Air Tasking Order (ATO);
- Establish sea control and conduct MCM operations in the northern Persian Gulf; and
- Attack shore facilities that threaten naval operations.

During Phase III, battlefield preparations, NAVCENT was tasked to carry out phase I and II tasks as well as attack Iraqi ground forces with aircraft and naval gunfire. During Phase IV, the Offensive Ground Campaign, NAVCENT was to:

- Continue to carry out phase I, II, and III tasks;
- Conduct amphibious feints and demonstrations in the KTO; and
- Be prepared to conduct an amphibious assault to link up with Marine Corps Component, Central Command (MARCENT) near Ash Shuaybah.

To accomplish these tasks, NAVCENT assigned the following primary missions to his battle force commanders in the Persian Gulf and Red Sea:

- Conduct naval operations in defense of Coalition ground, air, and sea units;
- Support Maritime Interception Operations;
- Provide naval tactical aircraft and TLAM strikes against Iraqi forces and assets;
- Establish naval control of shipping in designated areas and provide air defense of the Coalition sealift effort; and
- Coordinate and provide Combat Search and Rescue in the Red Sea and Persian Gulf.

The Persian Gulf Battle Force also was directed to provide close air support and NGFS to the ATF and Coalition ground forces as required. The Red Sea Battle Force also was tasked to ensure the freedom of navigation of vital sea lines of communication such as the Bab Al-Mandab Strait. NAVCENT directed the ATF to plan, prepare for, and conduct amphibious operations.

ANTISURFACE WARFARE (ASUW)

ASUW played an important role in the liberation of Kuwait. While Coalition naval forces continued MIO, the Navy, with assistance from the British Royal Navy, the Kuwaiti Navy, and the Royal Saudi Naval Force (RSNF) destroyed the Iraqi Navy. By using an

Severely Damaged Iraqi Polnocy Class Amphibious Ship.

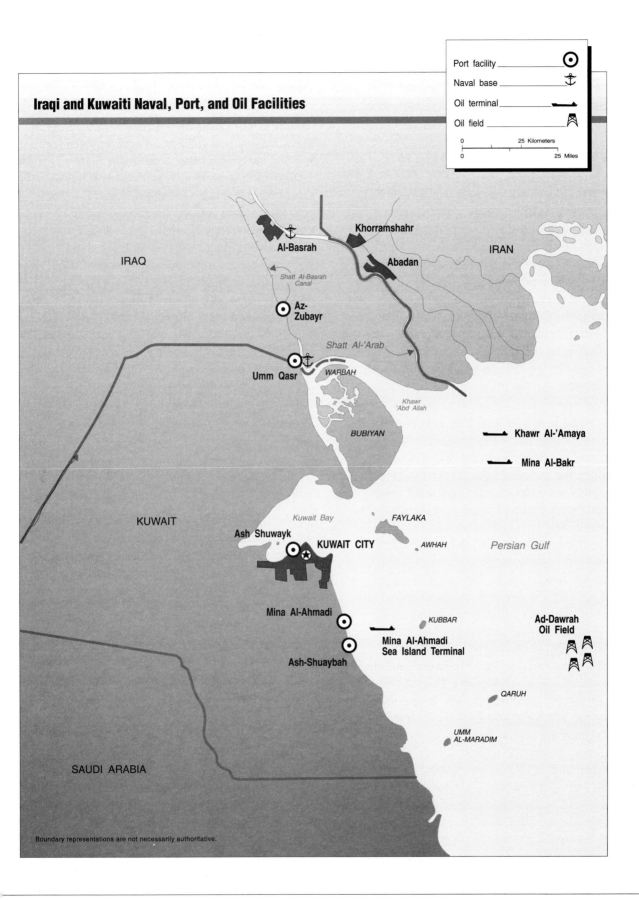

Iraqi and Kuwaiti Naval, Port, and Oil Facilities

Port facility	⊙
Naval base	⚓
Oil terminal	⌐⊷
Oil field	🛢

0 — 25 Kilometers
0 — 25 Miles

IRAQ

Al-Basrah

Khorramshahr

Abadan

IRAN

Shatt Al-Basrah Canal

Az-Zubayr

Shatt Al-'Arab

Umm Qasr

WARBAH

Khawr 'Abd Allah

BUBIYAN

⌐⊷ Khawr Al-'Amaya

⌐⊷ Mina Al-Bakr

KUWAIT

Kuwait Bay

FAYLAKA

Ash Shuwayk

KUWAIT CITY

AWHAH

Persian Gulf

Mina Al-Ahmadi

KUBBAR

Ad-Dawrah Oil Field

Mina Al-Ahmadi Sea Island Terminal

Ash-Shuaybah

QARUH

UMM AL-MARADIM

SAUDI ARABIA

Boundary representations are not necessarily authoritative.

aggressive and offensive ASUW concept during Operation Desert Storm, Coalition naval forces found and destroyed Iraqi naval vessels significantly beyond the range of enemy antiship missiles.

The Iraqi Threat

The Iraqi Navy and Air Force antiship capabilities posed a threat to Coalition naval forces in the Persian Gulf. The principal Iraqi port facilities and naval bases from which surface combatants could operate were concentrated near Al-Basrah, along the banks of the Shatt Al-'Arab, Iraq's only outlet to the Persian Gulf. Iraq also had the potential to use Kuwaiti ports and facilities, as well as several oil platforms in the northern Persian Gulf, as bases for small boat operations.

During the Iran-Iraq War, Iraqi F-1s conducted successful long range attacks against southern Persian Gulf shipping. In the Persian Gulf conflict, the principal Iraqi naval strength was its ability to conduct small scale, small boat operations, including missile attacks, mine warfare, and terrorist attacks against shipping in the northern Persian Gulf. The 13 Iraqi missile boats posed another lethal threat to Coalition naval forces and shipping. Iraq's missile boat inventory consisted of seven ex-Soviet Osa missile boats carrying Styx missiles (maximum range of 42 miles), five captured Kuwaiti TNC-45 and one FPB-57 missile boats carrying Exocet missiles (maximum range of 96 miles). This ASUW capability was used successfully during the Iran-Iraq War against at least one Iranian combatant and several merchant ships in the northern Persian Gulf. The rest of the approximately 165 Iraqi naval vessels were mostly small patrol boats, supplemented by minelaying boats and other specialized craft, such as hovercraft, Polnocny class amphibious tank landing ships, and auxiliary ships. The Iraqi Navy also operated one frigate, but this vessel historically had been used as a training ship and was not assessed as a serious threat.

To minimize casualties, destruction of the Iraqi surface threat was considered a prerequisite for moving the carrier battle force in the Gulf farther north to bring naval air power closer to targets and to prepare for amphibious operations. Iraqi surface threats also had to be eliminated to allow US and United Kingdom (UK) minesweepers and minehunting ships unimpeded access into enemy waters to clear lanes through the Iraqi minefields for amphibious operations or for NGFS. Other high-priority ASUW targets included land-based Silkworm antiship cruise missile batteries (using an active seeker with a 68-mile range), surface-to-air missiles (SAM), and aircraft capable of launching air-to-surface missiles. At the beginning of the conflict, Iraq had approximately 50 Silkworm missiles and seven launchers.

ASUW Command and Control

The battle force ASUW commander was tasked with neutralizing Iraqi naval forces in the northern Persian Gulf, as well as defending Coalition forces in the Persian Gulf and the GCC states' coastlines. Ensuring adequate surveillance for offensive ASUW, fleet defense, and coastal defense operations was a crucial concern of the Persian Gulf battle force ASUW commander. Continuous coverage of the surface vessel traffic in the entire Gulf was required and 24-mile exclusion zones for Iraqi combatants were established around each carrier and combat logistics force operating area.

At first, ASUW operations were directed by Commander, Destroyer Squadron (COMDESRON) 15 aboard *USS Midway*. In accordance with the maritime campaign plan, the ASUW commander set out the following objectives:

- Maintain accurate surface surveillance in the Persian Gulf;
- Establish sea control;
- Support MIO; and
- Conduct offensive ASUW operations.

The ASUW commander appointed several subordinate ASUW commanders to control specific operating areas and carry out these objectives. In the northern Persian Gulf, ASUW operations were directed by COMDESRON 35 embarked in USS Leftwich (DD 984), while the Commanding Officer of USS Wisconsin (BB 64) controlled the south/central Persian Gulf operating areas. A Canadian naval commander was assigned as the subordinate ASUW commander for the underway replenishment area and was responsible for protecting Coalition combat logistics ships.

After USS Ranger's arrival in the Persian Gulf on 15 January, responsibility for ASUW in the Persian Gulf shifted on 21 January to COMCARGRU 7, embarked in USS Ranger. COMCARGRU 7 adopted a more aggressive plan to eliminate the Iraqi naval threat as quickly as possible. To reflect this new offensive ASUW strategy, the ASUW objectives were changed to:

- Destroy all Iraqi surface combatants and minelayers;
- Deny Iraq the use of oil platforms for military purposes;
- Move back Iraqi surface forces in the northern Persian Gulf from south to north; and
- Prevent attacks or threats against Coalition forces and countries in the Gulf.

This plan called for using armed surface reconnaissance aircraft (ASR), helicopters and naval gunfire to achieve these goals.

COMCARGRU 7 continued to use local ASUW commanders, but modified the command structure and operating areas. COMDESRON 7, embarked in USS P. F. Foster (DD 964),

became the northern Persian Gulf local ASUW commander and was primarily responsible for conducting offensive operations against Iraqi naval forces. The Commanding Officer of USS Ranger was the south/central Persian Gulf local ASUW commander and was tasked to provide fleet defense of the Coalition naval forces. The Canadian naval force commander remained in control of the underway replenishment area.

Coalition ASUW Capabilities

Assets used in ASUW operations included carrier-based aircraft (A-6E, F/A-18, F-14, and S-3A/B), maritime patrol aircraft (P-3C and British Nimrod), ground-based Coalition combat air patrol (CAP) aircraft (e.g., Canadian CF-18), helicopters (Navy SH-60B, British Lynx, and Army OH-58D), and Coalition surface combatants. The following section briefly describes these ASUW assets. Some assets, such as MPA and helicopters, were under the ASUW commander's control. Other assets, such as strike, fighter, and E-2C airborne early warning (AEW) aircraft, also were used by other warfare commanders, who coordinated the use of these limited resources.

To increase the emphasis of offensive ASUW, the Persian Gulf battle force ASUW commander began ASR and armed scout missions on 21 January. Carrier-based A-6 and F/A-18 aircraft were used in ASR missions to search for and engage Iraqi surface vessels. However, since A-6s and F/A-18s also were the primary Navy strike aircraft used in the air campaign, ASR sorties were limited. S-3 aircraft conducted armed scout missions in the central Gulf and provided surveillance when maritime patrol aircraft were unable to support ASUW operations. S-3 aircraft actually engaged Iraqi naval forces twice during Operation Desert Storm and destroyed one enemy patrol boat. F-14 aircraft were not specifically launched for ASUW missions, but occasionally supported ASUW engagements when not engaged during CAP missions.

Surface surveillance in the northern Gulf was maintained by maritime patrol aircraft (MPA) — US P-3C from Masirah, and UK Nimrod aircraft from Seeb. These aircraft patrolled specified search areas near the aircraft carriers and surface ships. P-3C and Nimrod aircraft, which normally have a primary ASW mission, provided over-the-horizon (OTH) detection of targets. The aircraft then were able to prioritize surface contacts so Coalition aircraft could evaluate them efficiently. MPA also directed ASR aircraft to targets, and provided battle damage assessments (BDA). About 66 percent of all ASUW engagements were supported by MPA, primarily in the open Gulf south of Bubiyan Island. Engagements north of Bubiyan Island usually were initiated by ASR aircraft against targets of opportunity.

The ASUW commander also used ground-based Coalition aircraft, such as Canadian CF-18s, assigned to CAP duties over the Persian Gulf, to engage Iraqi naval vessels. Their use depended on AAW mission priorities, aircraft availability, and whether the CAP was within range of Iraqi surface combatants.

Helicopters were used extensively for ASUW operations. The battle force ASUW commander normally had two to five British Lynx, 10 to 23

SH-60Bs , and four OH-58Ds available for ASUW operations. The primary ASUW missions for the helicopters operating in the northern Persian Gulf were mine surveillance, surface surveillance and tracking, oil slick reconnaissance, and offensive ASUW engagements.

Mine surveillance was a primary helicopter mission until 23 January. Visual surveillance was conducted over Coalition ship operating areas. Between 24 January and 4 February, the primary mission of northern Gulf helicopters shifted to surface search, surveillance, and tracking of Iraqi naval combatants. The helicopters were instructed to find and interdict Iraqi patrol boats and minelayers, search oil platforms for evidence of Iraqi military activity, and conduct quick reaction engagements against Iraqi surface vessels.

Coalition helicopters operating in the northern Persian Gulf participated extensively in offensive ASUW engagements. These offensive operations most commonly used a tactic which took advantage of the SH-60B's superior electronic surveillance measures and radar capability and the British Lynx's radar-guided missile capability. The OH-58Ds were used primarily against armed oil platforms and land targets.

Oil slick reconnaissance (i.e., monitoring the spread of oil spills caused by Iraq's environmental terrorism) became the highest priority for northern Gulf helicopters beginning 5 February. Helicopters were required to record on videotape the affected oil terminals and the extent of sea contamination. This mission was conducted to help contain the spreading oil slick, to report on the oil flow situation, and to document Iraq's use of oil as an act of environmental terrorism.

In addition to the US and the GCC states' navies, surface combatants from Argentina, Australia, Canada, Denmark, France, Italy, the

Ad-Dawrah Oil Platforms.

Netherlands, Norway, Spain, and the United Kingdom (UK) participated in ASUW operations. Only US, UK, Kuwaiti, and Saudi surface combatants were involved in offensive ASUW operations against the Iraqi Navy. The GCC navies patrolled their coastal waters and defended Coalition facilities near shore against possible surprise attacks by Iraqi special forces operating from small boats. Other Coalition surface combatants provided fleet defense and protected the aircraft carriers and combat logistics forces. For example, France placed one frigate under US operational control on 15 February to carry out escort missions for the Coalition's combat logistics ships; however it was not authorized to engage in offensive operations.

Destruction of the Iraqi Navy

The first ASUW strike occurred on 18 January when strike aircraft from *USS Ranger* and *USS Midway* engaged and damaged two Iraqi gunboats, including an unconfirmed TNC-45 class missile boat, as well as a Sawahil class service craft supporting Iraqi forces operating from oil platforms.

Also on 18 January, several strike aircraft flying over the northern Gulf reported taking fire from Iraqi forces on oil platforms in the Ad-Dawrah offshore oil field, about 40 miles off of the Kuwaiti coast. The field's 11 oil rigs were along approach and departure routes used by Coalition aircraft to strike targets in Iraq. Nine platforms were believed to be occupied by Iraqi troops, who also were using them to spy on Coalition ship and aircraft movements. *USS Nicholas* (FFG 47) and embarked OH-58Ds, scouted the oil field and identified targets. That night, within range of Iraqi Silkworm missiles and near Iraqi combatant ships and aircraft armed with Exocet antiship missiles, *USS Nicholas* and the Kuwaiti fast attack craft Istiqlal (P5702) conducted the first surface engagement of the war. Masked by darkness and emitting no electronic transmissions, *USS Nicholas* approached the

platforms from the south. Over the horizon, the helicopter pilots, wearing night-vision devices, readied air-to-surface missiles. Flying low, the OH-58Ds, along with a Royal Navy Lynx helicopter and *USS Nicholas'* SH-60B, reached the targets — two platforms believed to be heavily armed and out of range of *USS Nicholas'* 76-mm gun. The OH-58D and Lynx helicopters attacked the platform with guided missiles. As an ammunition stockpile on the platform exploded, six Iraqi soldiers attempted to escape by using a Zodiac rubber boat. Istiqlal later captured them.

Soon after the helicopter attack, *USS Nicholas* and Istiqlal shelled nine of the 11 armed platforms to destroy remaining fortifications. The Coalition forces then picked up 23 Iraqis and landed a SEAL platoon on the platforms. Upon inspection, caches of shoulder-fired SAMs and a long range radio were discovered. The operation successfully removed a SAM threat to Coalition air forces, destroyed Iraqi surveillance posts, and captured the first enemy prisoners of war (EPWs) in Operation Desert Storm.

In an attempt to isolate Iraqi naval combatants in the northern Persian Gulf from the port facilities and naval bases at Al-Basrah, Az-Zubayr, and Umm Qasr (and to prevent more Iraqi vessels from leaving these bases), a mining operation was conducted 18 January at the mouth of the Khawr Az-Zubayr river. The entrance to this river is on the Iraqi-Kuwaiti border northwest of Bubiyan Island. Iraqi naval vessels which used this waterway were mostly fast patrol boats similar in size to a Soviet Osa class patrol boat. The mission involved 18 aircraft from USS Ranger, including four A-6s carrying Mark 36 Destructor mines. Forty-two of the 48 mines were successfully dropped on four separate locations. Six mines on one aircraft failed to release and the aircraft diverted to Shaikh Isa, Bahrain, to download the ordnance before returning to *USS Ranger*. One A-6 was shot down during the mission. Because no BDA was available, it was not possible to determine the effectiveness of the mining.

On the night of 22 January, a P-3C detected and tracked an Iraqi tanker carrying a hovercraft. The Iraqi merchant vessel had been conducting electronic warfare operations and was thought to be supporting small boats operating in the area. It also was suspected of carrying refined fuel, which could be used to ignite a crude oil spill. A-6s from *USS Midway* attacked the tanker as the hovercraft launched from the ship and took cover near the Mina Al-Bakr oil terminal. An A-6 then flushed the hovercraft away from the oil terminal and sank it with Rockeye cluster bombs.

After these initial actions in the northern Gulf and the capture of the Ad-Dawrah oil platforms, the pace of ASUW operations accelerated. On 24 January, A-6s from *USS Theodore R. Roosevelt* destroyed an Iraqi minelayer and another patrol boat. Also on 24 January, the Saudi Arabian patrol boat *Faisal* (517) launched a Harpoon surface-to-surface missile against a reported Iraqi utility craft with unknown results. Near Qaruh Island, a second enemy minelayer, attempting to evade an A-6E, sank after hitting one of its own mines.

Around noon on 24 January, OH-58Ds operating from *USS Curts* (FFG 38) attempted to rescue 22 Iraqis from the minelayer sunk near Qaruh Island. As the helicopters assisted the survivors, Iraqi forces on the island fired on the helicopters. The helicopters returned fire, and *USS Curts* maneuvered closer to the island and attacked the positions with 76-mm guns, beginning a six-hour operation to retake the first parcel of Kuwaiti territory. SEALs from Naval

USS Leftwich **Crew Members Survey Iraqi Weapons Captured by Coalition Forces on Qaruh Island.**

Special Warfare Group 1 landed on Qaruh aboard helicopters from *USS Leftwich*. With *USS Nicholas* and *USS Curts* covering the island, the SEALs reclaimed the island and raised the Kuwaiti flag. The Coalition forces captured 67 EPWs during the battle and obtained intelligence about Iraqi minefields in the area.

Although several Iraqi vessels were engaged before 24 January, the missile boats remained operational. As early as 27 January, the ASUW commander expressed concern that Iraqi naval forces might seek safe haven in Iran, just as the Iraqi air force had attempted. Surveillance regions for maritime patrol aircraft, helicopters, and ships were established to intercept fleeing ships. Coalition ships and aircraft were positioned along the northwest Persian Gulf

BATTLE OF BUBIYAN: IRAQI PATROL BOAT STRIKES

On the night of 29 January, a moonless night with restricted visibility caused by weather and oil fires, an A-6E on an armed surface reconnaissance mission located four suspicious vessels south of Al-Faw Peninsula. With their lights out, the vessels were headed toward Iranian coastal waters. The antisurface warfare commander assigned tactical control of the A-6 to an E-2C, which was in the area on an early warning mission. The vessels were identified as patrol boats, but their nationality could not be determined immediately. Several navies operated small boats in the northern Gulf so

suspected enemy vessels had to be identified positively before they could be engaged. Time was crucial to prevent Iraqi vessels from escaping to Iran, but fire from friendly forces, or an international incident involving Iran, had to be prevented.

Using available intelligence, the E-2C positively identified the vessels as hostile and authorized the A-6 to attack. The A-6 dropped a 500-lb laser-guided bomb (LGB) and guided it to a direct hit on the leading vessel. The other Iraqi boats scattered, but the A-6 continued to attack, dropping

another bomb on a second boat. The second direct hit destroyed the superstructure and caused the boat to go dead in the water. Meanwhile the E-2C located an F/A-18 to assist in the attack and directed it to the targets. The A-6E teamed with the F/A-18 to guide a 500-lb LGB dropped by the F/A-18 to a direct hit on the third boat. By this time both aircraft had expended their ordnance and the fourth Iraqi patrol boat continued its escape to Iran.

The E-2C contacted fighter control which released two Canadian CF-18 on CAP that had just completed refueling from a

tanker. The E-2C assumed tactical control of the Canadian aircraft and directed them to the last gunboat. Since the CF-18s were configured for a combat air patrol mission, they did not have any bombs, but attacked the Iraqi gunboat with strafing runs using 20-mm guns. Three Iraqi patrol boats were found capsized (a FPB-53, FPB-70, and a TNC-45). The fourth Iraqi vessel, an Osa patrol boat, later was located in an Iranian port with substantial strafing damage to its superstructure.

coast to detect Iraqi vessels leaving ports in Kuwait and Iraq. A barrier of ships and aircraft also was set up along the eastern coast of the Persian Gulf to intercept any Iraqi missile boats moving along the coastline under cover of merchant shipping.

On 29 January, Royal Air Force Jaguars detected 15 Iraqi fast patrol boats attempting to move from Ras Al-Qul'ayah to Mina Al-Saud as part of an apparent combined operation to attack the port of Ras Al-Khafji. Lynx helicopters from HMS Gloucester (D 96), Cardiff (D 108), and Brazen (F 91) located and engaged the Iraqi boats with Sea Skua missiles, leaving two sunk or damaged, and scattered the rest of the flotilla. Coalition aircraft then sank or severely damaged 10 more of the 15 small boats.

The next day, a large force of Iraqi combatants

based at Az-Zubayr and Umm Qasr attempted to flee to Iran, but was detected and engaged by Coalition forces near Bubiyan Island in what was later called "the Battle of Bubiyan." This battle lasted 13 hours and ended with the destruction of the Iraqi Navy. With P-3Cs providing target locations, helicopters, ASR aircraft on alert, and other aircraft diverted from strike and CAP missions conducted 21 engagements against Iraqi surface combatants. By the end of the Battle of Bubiyan, one FPB-57 missile boat and two TNC-45 missile boats were heavily damaged. An additional three Osa missile boats and possibly a third TNC-45 were damaged. Three Polnocny amphibious ships were damaged, two of them heavily, along with one T-43 minesweeper. Only two damaged ships, an Osa II missile boat and a Polnocny amphibious ship escaped to Iranian waters.

On 31 January, Coalition helicopters captured 20 EPWs on the Mina Al-Bakr oil platform after the Iraqis fled a sinking Iraqi Polnocny class amphibious ship, which had been laying mines when Coalition aircraft attacked. During that operation, a Lynx helicopter severely damaged

"With the burning Polnocny combatant only a mile away, the EPWs were searched and hoisted aboard the helos. Each helo picked up 10 EPWs with the mission completed well after dark."

Pilot, HS-12, CVW-5, USS Midway

> "We could identify the speed boat between Bubiyan Island and Iran. As the two Mk 82 500-lb bombs came off the aircraft, I quickly broke left and pumped out several flares in our defense. We realized that we had become the first Viking crew to sink a surface boat in combat."
>
> *Pilot, VS-24, CVW-8, USS Theodore Roosevelt*

an Iraqi TNC-45 combatant attempting to prevent the capture.

The Battle of Bubiyan and further air strikes against Iraqi port facilities essentially eliminated the Iraqi surface threat to Coalition shipping in the Gulf. By 2 February, all 13 Iraqi surface craft capable of delivering antiship missiles had been destroyed or disabled, and the Iraqi naval force was considered combat ineffective. NAVCENT declared Coalition sea control of the northern Persian Gulf on 8 February. Thereafter, the remaining Iraqi naval units conducted only minor, isolated operations at sea, and these vessels were engaged by Coalition aircraft. For example, after 8 February, five Iraqi vessels were engaged by Royal Navy Lynx helicopters.

Antisurface Warfare Results

- 143 Iraqi Naval Vessels Destroyed/Damaged

  11 Antiship Missile Boats Destroyed
  2 Antiship Missile Boats Disabled
  3 *Polnocny* Class Amphibious Ships Destroyed
  1 *Ibn Khaldun* Frigate Destroyed
  1 Bogomol PCF Patrol Boat Destroyed
  116 Small Patrol Boats and Auxilaries Destroyed/Damaged
  9 Minelayers Destroyed

- All Iraqi Naval Bases/Ports Significantly Damaged
- All Northern Persian Gulf Oil Platforms Searched and Secured
- No Attacks by Iraqi Surface Vessels Against Coalition Forces

On 16 February, an SH-60B helicopter from *USS P. F. Foster* located an Iraqi patrol boat operating with an Iraqi merchant ship and directed the Kuwaiti patrol boat Istiqlal to the target. Istiqlal fired an Exocet missile and its 76-mm gun against the patrol boat, causing an explosion and unknown damage.

ASUW forces also attacked land-based Silkworm antiship missile sites, which threatened Coalition naval forces. On 18 February, *USS Jarrett's* (FFG 33) SH-60B directed two OH-58Ds to a suspected Silkworm missile site on Faylaka Island. The OH-58Ds fired Hellfire missiles and reportedly destroyed a launcher.

On 20 February, the crew of a Navy S-3 aircraft from *USS T. R. Roosevelt*, but under the tactical control of *USS Valley Forge* (CG 50) engaged and destroyed an Iraqi gunboat with three 500-lb bombs, becoming the first S-3 crew to sink a hostile surface vessel in combat.

By using an offensive ASUW concept, Coalition naval forces found and destroyed Iraqi naval vessels well beyond the range of enemy antiship missiles. Carrier-based aircraft attacked and damaged many Iraqi ships while they were still alongside piers in Iraqi naval bases and port facilities. This ASUW strategy resulted in the destruction of, or damage to 143 Iraqi naval vessels. ASUW operations also extended beyond the destruction of naval vessels, attacking other threats to Coalition naval forces such as armed oil platforms and Silkworm antiship missile sites along the Kuwaiti and Iraqi coastlines.

ANTIAIR WARFARE (AAW)

The limited reaction times caused by the relatively short distances between Iraqi airfields and Coalition naval forces made it necessary to rely primarily on airborne, forward-positioned CAPs instead of deck-launched or ground-launched interceptors. Although both the

Red Sea battle force and Persian gulf battle force conducted AAW operations during Operation Desert Storm, this discussion focuses primarily on Persian Gulf operations. The relatively constrained Persian Gulf airspace resulted in using CAP aircraft in small, fixed operating areas. This geographical limit and the requirement for positive target identification before engagement prevented the use of standard fleet air defense tactics, including long-range indication and warning, layered air and SAM defenses, and beyond-visual-range engagements. Instead, fixed CAP stations were established in the central and northern Persian Gulf; these stations were manned 24 hours a day and were designed to respond quickly to an Iraqi air raid.

The Iraqi Threat

The Coalition's AAW operations in the Red Sea and Persian Gulf were influenced by the Iraqi antiship capabilities. During the Iran-Iraq War, Iraqi aircraft had used coordinated long-range antiship missile attacks with in-flight refueling. Furthermore, during Operation Desert Shield, Iraq practiced its antiship tactics in several large-scale exercises over Iraq and the northern Persian Gulf. Iraq had four types of airborne antiship-capable platforms. Each of the 32 strike-capable F-1 aircraft could fire two Exocet missiles. Iraq's four B-6D long-range bomber aircraft carried air-launched Silkworm missiles. However, these Chinese-made bombers were not deemed a significant threat because of their large size, slow speed, and ineffective navigation equipment. Iraq also had 25 Su-24s, capable of carrying the AS-7, 9, and 14 air-to-surface missiles, rockets, and laser-guided and general purpose bombs. The Su-24 also had the potential to use a sophisticated electronic countermeasure system. The French-built Super Frelon helicopter could launch two Exocet missiles and had been used by Iraq during the Iran-Iraq War in an antiship role before the F-1 was introduced.

The Navy's F-14 Fighter Was Used Extensively for Offensive and Defensive Counterair Missions during Operation Desert Storm.

AAW Command and Control

Since cruisers had trained and performed routinely in the role of Battle Force AAW commander, Aegis and New Threat Upgrade (NTU) cruisers were selected as AAW commanders in both the Red Sea and Persian Gulf. *USS Bunker Hill* (CG 52) and *USS Worden* (CG 18) alternated as AAW

The Aegis Cruiser *USS Bunker Hill* Was the AAW Commander in the Persian Gulf during Operation Desert Storm.

commander in the Persian Gulf. The AAW commander's primary mission was to establish and maintain air superiority over the Persian Gulf. To accomplish this mission, the following objectives were established:

■ Maintain an extended air space surveillance over the Persian Gulf, Gulf of Oman, and northern Arabian Sea;
■ Detect, identify, intercept, and engage or escort all hostile or unknown aircraft entering the Persian Gulf battle force AAW surveillance area;
■ Provide AAW protection for Coalition forces operating in the battle force surveillance areas; and
■ Establish air control and deconfliction procedures for Coalition air forces operating over the Persian Gulf.

Deconfliction involved distinguishing Coalition aircraft returning from missions over Iraq from hostile aircraft possibly attempting surprise attacks against Coalition forces or GCC states by trailing behind the returning Coalition aircraft.

Day-to-day AAW command and control were concerned mostly with the tasks of air control and deconfliction. Air controllers kept track of hundreds of aircraft entering the Red Sea and the northern Persian Gulf every day, including transiting Coalition strike aircraft, CAP, airborne early warning (AEW) aircraft, tankers, ASUW aircraft, maritime patrol aircraft, helicopters, and special mission aircraft. Coalition forces in the Persian Gulf shared AAW information over a high frequency radio data link. This Persian Gulf data link was interfaced with a larger, theater-wide data link, which included airborne warning and control system (AWACS) aircraft and ground-based Coalition air defense sites.

US naval forces took primary responsibility for deconfliction and target identification over the northern Persian Gulf, as well as the Red Sea. During the Persian Gulf Crisis, *USS Worden* used the NTU combat system successfully to deconflict more than 15,000 Coalition aircraft returning from missions, control 17 different types of US aircraft, and control the CAP of six Coalition nations. Designated return corridors and flight profiles proved the key methods to separate friendly aircraft from potentially hostile ones. These deconfliction methods required returning Coalition aircraft to fly within specific altitude bands and speeds along designated return corridors.

Coalition AAW Capabilities

AAW detection requirements in the Persian Gulf were particularly complex and demanding. Substantial numbers of ships were dedicated partially or totally to AAW responsibilities. For example, on 15 February, excluding the four aircraft carriers operating in the Gulf, 21 surface combatants, including six Aegis and three NTU cruisers and 12 US, UK, Australian, Spanish, and Italian destroyers and frigates, were under the AAW commander's control for AAW defense of Coalition naval forces. In addition to providing complete AAW surveillance, radar picket ships controlled hundreds of aircraft and helicopters in multiple warfare missions. For example, during the amphibious exercise Imminent Thunder, *USS Bunker Hill's* Aegis combat system, operated by well-trained shipboard air controllers, safely controlled more than 40 aircraft operating simultaneously in the amphibious objective area. AAW ships also controlled Coalition CAP aircraft over the Persian Gulf and Red Sea.

The E-2C, an all-weather, carrier-based AEW and command and control aircraft, provided

AEW coverage, some CAP control, and relayed communications for CVBGs in the northern and central Persian Gulf. At least one E-2C was kept airborne continuously during Operations Desert Shield and Desert Storm.

Of the approximately 18,120 sorties flown by carrier-based aircraft during Operation Desert Storm, about 21 percent were devoted to defensive counterair missions. Of these, 67 percent were flown by F-14s and 33 percent were flown by F/A-18s. Canadian CF-18 squadrons played an important role by manning one of the northern Persian Gulf CAP stations continuously from early October until the start of the war and then supplementing those stations through the end of hostilities.

Despite some degradation in performance because of weather and near-land operations, the complementary capabilities of the air search radars in NTU and Aegis cruisers, and the E-2 AEW aircraft provided complete coverage of air contacts in the Persian Gulf. (Since the E-2C was designed for open ocean operations, the aircraft's radar system experienced expected reductions in detection because of land clutter and weather effects. This limitation required the extensive use of surface platforms to ensure optimum airspace radar surveillance.)

Significant Persian Gulf AAW Operations

The only attempted airborne attack mounted by Iraqi aircraft against the Coalition occurred on 24 January. Two Iraqi F-1s, on a mission against the oil production facility and port in Ad-Dammam, Saudi Arabia, departed Iraqi airspace flying just to seaward of the Kuwaiti coastline, the boundary between the USAF AWACS and fleet air defense responsibilities. The AWACS aircraft directed four Saudi F-15s toward the incoming Iraqi F-1s and a Saudi pilot successfully shot down the two F-1s, thus thwarting the Iraqi attack before missiles were launched.

Only one actual antiair engagement against Iraqi missiles occurred during the hostilities. On 24 February, *USS Missouri* (BB 63), escorted by *USS Jarrett* and *HMS Gloucester*, approached within 10 miles of the Kuwaiti coast to provide naval gunfire support (NGFS) to advancing Coalition troops. As the battleship fired 16-inch guns in the early morning of 25 February, 10 USMC helicopters from *USS Okinawa* (LPH 3), along with the amphibious landing ship *USS Portland* (LSD 37), conducted a night heliborne amphibious feint near the Kuwaiti port of Ash Shuaybah.

Iraqis manning the Kuwait Silkworm missile sites reacted to the amphibious feint by firing two antiship missiles towards the *USS Missouri* and her escorts. The first missile landed between *USS Missouri* and *USS Jarrett*, possibly deceived by chaff fired by the two ships. The second missile was detected on radar by HMS Gloucester leaving the coastline 21 miles to the west and heading for *USS Missouri. HMS Gloucester's* crew identified the contact as a Silkworm missile, evaluated it as a direct threat to Coalition warships, and fired two Sea Dart surface-to-air missiles, which destroyed it.

The Silkworm activity then was reported to an E-2C, which assumed responsibility for coordinating an attack on the missile site. Using several intelligence assets, including an EP-3, the site was located and strike aircraft were directed to the target. An A-6E, evading heavy SAM and antiaircraft artillery activity near its target, dropped 12 Rockeye cluster bombs. Initial BDA reported heavy smoke from the target and all indications of Silkworm activity ceased. Later, reconnaissance confirmed the missile site's destruction.

COUNTERMINE WARFARE

The five months of Operation Desert Shield permitted Iraq to develop an extensive coastal defense system in Kuwait. The Iraqi mine threat affected almost all naval operations during the

US Ships Primarily Relied on Mine Watches Stationed on the Bow to Locate and Warn of Mines.

Russian contact mines. However, it also included high-technology magnetic and acoustic influence mines purchased from the Soviet Union and Italy. Specifically, Iraq had 11 types of mines including moored contact mines (e.g., the Myam, the Soviet M-08, and a similar Iraqi-produced LUGM-145) and bottom acoustic influence mines (e.g., the Italian Manta acoustic/magnetic mine, the Soviet KMD magnetic influence mine, the Soviet UDM acoustic influence mine, and the Iraqi-produced Sigeel acoustic influence mine). Before Operations Desert Shield and Desert Storm, Iraq was estimated to have 1,000 to 2,000 mines. After the cease fire, Iraq reported it had laid 1,167 mines during the conflict.

Iraq could deliver mines from surface and air platforms. Sea-based mine delivery platforms ranged from mine rail-equipped minesweepers to landing craft, auxiliaries, and even small boats. As Iran had demonstrated during the Iran-Iraq War, practically any surface vessel could become a minelayer. Iraq's Super Frelon helicopter was assessed as its principal airborne minelaying asset. Other possible air delivery platforms included Hip helicopters and B-6 bombers.

Iraq's minelaying strategy seemed to focus on protecting its seaward flank from an amphibious assault. Iraq apparently started laying mines in the northern Persian Gulf in late November. The Iraqis used two principal methods of offshore mining operations. They laid fields of moored and bottom mines and single mine lines to protect logistics sea lines of communication and the Kuwaiti coast from amphibious assault. In addition, it appears the Iraqis deliberately may have set some mines adrift in the Persian Gulf, perhaps so the mines would drift in the southern currents and damage Coalition ships, or at least disrupt Coalition naval operations. The first drifting mine was discovered by Royal Saudi MCM forces in the Zuluf oil field on 21 December. Although it is possible some floating mines accidentally broke free from their

Persian Gulf Conflict. After Operation Desert Storm began, the principal mission of Coalition MCM assets was to clear a path to the Kuwaiti coast for NGFS and a possible amphibious landing.

The Iraqi Threat

The bulk of Iraq's mine inventory consisted of Iraqi reproductions of pre-World War I designed

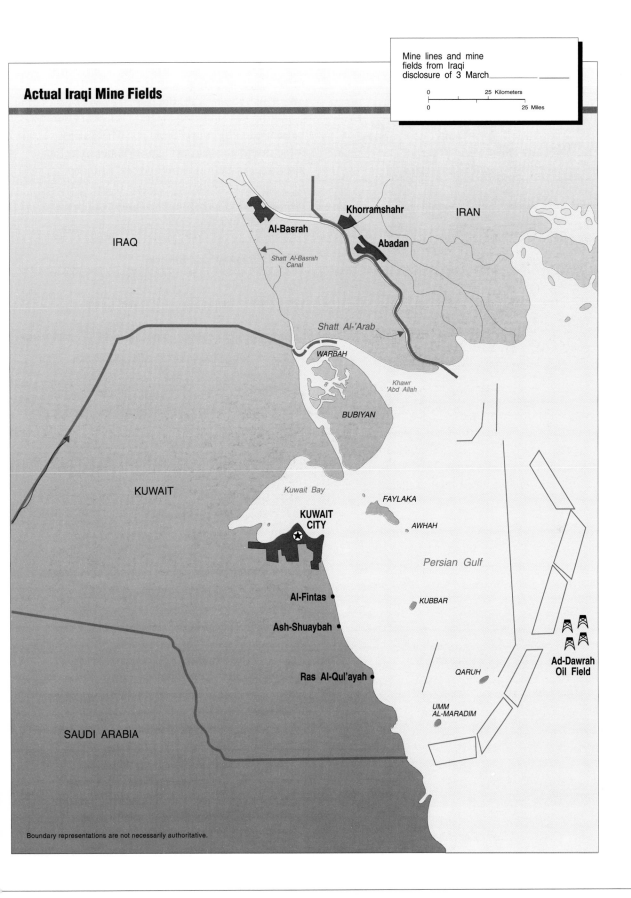

Actual Iraqi Mine Fields

Mine lines and mine fields from Iraqi disclosure of 3 March

0   25 Kilometers

0   25 Miles

IRAQ

Al-Basrah

Khorramshahr

Abadan

IRAN

Shatt Al-Basrah Canal

Shatt Al-'Arab

WARBAH

Khawr 'Abd Allah

BUBIYAN

KUWAIT

Kuwait Bay

KUWAIT CITY

FAYLAKA

AWHAH

Persian Gulf

Al-Fintas •

Ash-Shuaybah •

KUBBAR

Ras Al-Qul'ayah •

QARUH

Ad-Dawrah Oil Field

UMM AL-MARADIM

SAUDI ARABIA

Boundary representations are not necessarily authoritative.

USS Avenger and *USS Adroit* Are Offloaded from the Dutch Heavy Lift Ship Super Servant III (its Superstructure Can Be Seen in the Background) after Arriving in the Persian Gulf.

moorings, there is evidence (e.g., no mooring chains and little marine growth or corrosion) that approximately 20 percent of the floating mines recovered and destroyed by Coalition MCM forces were set adrift intentionally.

Intelligence reports during the war indicated the Iraqis used small rubber boats, each carrying a maximum of four mines, to deploy the drifting mines. These small boats operated from Ras

A Navy MH-53E AMCM Helicopter Conducts MCM Operations near a Royal Navy Hunt Class Mine Hunter in the Persian Gulf.

Al-Qul'ayah and probably set 20 mines adrift intentionally. After the Coalition's success in neutralizing the Iraqi Air Force, the drifting mines were viewed as the primary threat to Coalition naval vessels operating in the Gulf beyond antiship missile ranges. The drifting mine threat was a considerable concern to the aircraft carriers operating in the Gulf. The high-speed nature of the carrier flight operations reduced the effectiveness of mine watches and helicopter searches.

MCM Command and Control

NAVCENT established a US MCM Group (USMCMG) early in Operation Desert Shield to respond to the Iraqi mine threat. This group operated under Commander Middle East Force's (CMEF) control. The staff assigned to the USMCMG commander were both active-duty personnel from other naval commands and reservists. A British MCM force joined with the USMCMG to conduct most MCM operations during Operation Desert Storm. This British MCM group was under the operational control of the UK's Senior Naval Officer Middle East, but tactical control was given to the USMCMG commander.

MCM planning initially focused on supporting an amphibious assault north of Ash Shuaybah on the Kuwaiti coastline. CINCCENT made the final decision in early February to cancel this amphibious assault and directed NAVCENT to concentrate on an amphibious raid on Faylaka Island. MCM planning then shifted toward the new target. The mine clearance areas required for the Faylaka Island raid at first included a full set of fire support areas (FSA), a sea echelon area, and a cleared channel to the amphibious objective area. MCM objectives later were reduced to providing a safe path for *USS Missouri* to position herself off Faylaka Island to provide NGFS and present the Iraqis with credible indications of an amphibious landing.

Coalition MCM Capabilities

The US mine warfare concept was designed around a European war scenario which relied on North Atlantic Treaty Organization (NATO) allies to participate substantially in mine warfare operations, especially in MCM. The Navy's MCM capabilities in the Persian Gulf consisted of surface mine countermeasures (SMCM), aviation mine countermeasures (AMCM), and explosive ordnance disposal (EOD) teams. (Special Operations Forces also were used for MCM operations and are discussed in Appendix J.) SMCM capabilities included the newly commissioned *USS Avenger* (MCM 1) class MCM ship and three 30-year-old *USS Aggressive* and *USS Acme* (MSO 422 and 508) class minesweepers. The AMCM capability

An EOD Specialist Prepares a Moored Mine for Destruction.

Members of Helicopter Mine Countermeasures Squadron 14 (HM 14) Prepare a Mark 105 Hydrofoil Minesweeping Sled for MCM Operations.

A Drifting Mine near *USS Missouri* before Detonation by EOD Specialists.

deep waters. *USS Avenger* then used the AN/SLQ-48 mine neutralization system (MNS) to locate, examine, and destroy the detected mines. The MNS consists of a remotely piloted submersible vehicle equipped with sonar and two television cameras for locating mines, explosives for neutralizing mines, and cable cutters for cutting the mooring so the mine floats to the surface for destruction. The other US minesweepers used the AN/SQQ-14 MCM sonar to detect bottom and moored mines and mechanical minesweeping gear to cut mine cables.

AMCM helicopters towed a cable with a mechanical cutting device through the water, to cut a mine's mooring cable and release the mine to the surface. EOD teams or gunfire then detonated the mine. The helicopters also used acoustic and magnetic MCM sleds, which simulate a ship's propellers

Damage to *USS Tripoli* (LPH 10) Caused by an Iraqi Mine.

consisted of six MH-53E AMCM helicopters. More than 20 US EOD teams and a 23-man Australian team also were deployed to neutralize or destroy detected mines.

USS Avenger, the Navy's newest and most capable MCM ship, used the AN/SQQ-32 MCM sonar, a sophisticated mine-hunting sonar, to detect moored and bottom mines in shallow or

and magnetic signature to detonate influence mines.

The minesweepers *USS Impervious* (MSO 449), *USS Adroit* (MSO 509), *USS Leader* (MSO 490), and the MCM ship *USS Avenger* arrived in the theater 30 September on the Dutch heavy-lift ship Super Servant III. *USS Adroit* and *USS Impervious* were Naval Reserve Force minesweepers, which deployed to the Gulf augmented by Reserve crews. On 7 October, the six MH-53E AMCM helicopters arrived by USAF C-5A airlift. *USS Tripoli* (LPH 10), which had been part of the amphibious task force, was assigned to the USMCMG as a

support ship for the AMCM helicopters and as the USMCMG command ship. The USMC landing force disembarked and offloaded its equipment as the USMCMG staff embarked in *USS Tripoli* on 22 January. In addition, two UAE-flagged vessels, Vivi and Celina, were contracted as support ships for EOD teams that accompanied the USMCMG. These forces, along with the EOD teams, formed the USMCMG, based in Abu Dhabi, UAE.

In addition to the US MCM assets, two other NATO countries and Saudi Arabia provided SMCM ships during Operations Desert Shield and Desert Storm. The Royal Navy provided the

USS PRINCETON MINE INCIDENT

Commanding Officer, *USS Princeton* — "The ship was steaming slowly, barely maintaining steerageway in order to allow maximum reaction time if a mine was spotted. I had just told the crew that we had to be especially cautious and be on the lookout for mines because *Tripoli* had been hit just hours earlier. Just as I made that comment, the force of the mine explosion under the stern lifted up the ship and caused a whiplash. We on the bridge were moving up and down rapidly. We all grabbed on to something and tried to maintain our footing. . . My immediate reaction was that we had hit a mine. But the fact that the ship continued this violent motion for more than a second or two concerned me. I didn't expect the violent motion to continue as long as it did. At this point, both the Boatswain's Mate-of-the-Watch and I sounded General Quarters."

Two seconds after the mine exploded under the stern another mine exploded about 300 yards off the starboard bow. The combined effect of these two mines ripped the ship's

superstructure in two at the amidships quarterdeck.

"My first reaction was to notify someone else that we had struck a mine. We had to keep the ship from sinking. Another immediate reaction was that this was what we had been preparing for months. I had total confidence that my crew would do the right thing — that they would do what they had been trained to do."

"The first report that came in was about the injured people on the forecastle. Petty Officer . . . was already there giving first aid to Petty Officer . . ., who was the most seriously injured. Petty Officer . . . was standing right at the bullnose looking for mines when the blast went off under the stern. Petty Officer . . . was thrown 10 feet into the air."

Near the ship's stern, where the most serious damage occurred, the firemain ruptured and doused an electrical distribution switchboard, causing a major electrical fire hazard. The switchboard was remotely isolated after the rupture was reported to Damage Control Central. The mine blasts also

ruptured fuel tanks, forcing damage control parties to work in a mixture of fuel and water. Automatic sprinklers near the after 5-inch gun mount activated which aggravated the ship's flooding problem. The crew installed and activated dewatering systems within 10 minutes of the explosions and thus reduced the danger of both fire and flooding.

Loss of cooling water to electronic equipment, due to ruptured piping, disabled the ship's combat systems. Damage control teams quickly isolated the ruptures and immediately began emergency repairs to the cooling water systems.

"Within two hours the combat systems and combat information center teams had their equipment back on line with the forward gun and missile systems ready to shoot. *Princeton* reassumed duties as the local AAW commander and did not relinquish those duties until relieved by *USS Valley Forge*."

"As the day wore on I was concerned about drifting around

in the mine field. So I made the decision to have the salvage ship, *USS Beaufort*, take us in tow since our maneuverability was not good. Once under way, we moved slowly west with the minesweeper, *USS Adroit*, leading us, searching for mines. *USS Beaufort* continued to twist and turn, pulling us around the mines located by *USS Adroit* and marked by flares. Throughout the night, *USS Adroit* continued to lay flares. Near early morning, having run out of flares, she began marking the mines with chem-lights tied together. The teamwork of *USS Adroit* and *USS Beaufort* was superb."

"I felt the life of my ship and my men were in the hands of this small minesweeper's commanding officer and his crew. I directed *USS Adroit* to stay with us. I trusted him and I didn't want to let him go until I was clear of the danger area. All of us on *USS Princeton* owe a big debt to the officers and crew of *USS Beaufort* and *USS Adroit*. They were real pros."

most SMCM assets to the Coalition MCM effort. The UK initially deployed the Hunt Class mine hunters HMS Atherstone (M 38), HMS Cattistock (M31), and HMS Hurworth (M 39), along with the support ship HMS Herald (AGSH 138). Later, the mine hunters HMS Ledbury (M 30) and HMS Dulverton (M35) joined the MCM force. This UK MCM group operated closely with the USMCMG in clearing Iraqi mines in the northern Persian Gulf during Operation Desert Storm. Belgium contributed two Tripartite class mine hunters, Iris (M 920) and Myosotis (M 922), plus the support ship Zinnia (A 961). The Belgian MCM group operated mostly in the Gulf of Oman. Saudi Arabia's MCM ships included the minesweepers Addriyah (MSC 412), Al Quysumah (MSC 414), Al -Wadi'ah (MSC 416), and Safwa (MSC 418).

The SMCM and AMCM assets were responsible for clearing areas with water depths greater than 10 meters. The Coalition's MCM force provided the ability to survey the Persian Gulf open water areas, port approaches, harbors, potential amphibious objective areas, and sea lines of communication. The MCM force also had the ability to detect and counter all types of Iraqi bottom and moored mines.

MCM Operations

Before the start of Operation Desert Storm, the US ability to gather intelligence on Iraqi minefield locations, or observe and counter Iraqi minelaying activity in international waters (considered a hostile act under international law), was degraded by restrictions on naval and air operations in the northern Persian Gulf. To avoid any possibility of provoking Iraqi military action before Coalition defensive and later offensive preparations were complete, CINCCENT restricted naval surface forces in the Gulf to operating south of the 27-30'N parallel (approximately 72 miles south of the Kuwaiti-Saudi border) until early January. Similar restrictions kept the flight paths of

aircraft south of 27-45'N (approximately 55 miles south of the Kuwaiti-Saudi border) unless tactically required to exceed that limit. Those restrictions precluded gathering intelligence on Iraqi mining activity and also prevented NAVCENT from acting to deter or counter Iraqi forces from setting mines adrift in the Gulf.

After the RSNF discovered the first drifting mine in December, the USMCMG found and destroyed six drifting mines before Operation Desert Storm started. On 24 January, the USMCMG left Abu Dhabi and conducted training and maintenance while enroute to its designated MCM operating area in the northern Persian Gulf. On 14 February, the oceanographic survey vessel HMS Herald and five Royal Navy mine hunters joined the USMCMG. This task force started its MCM operations on 16 February, 60 miles east of the Kuwaiti coast, working initially to clear a 15-mile long, 1,000 yard wide path to a 10-mile by 3.5-mile FSA south of Faylaka Island.

While sweeping toward the shore of Faylaka Island on 17 February, the MCM force was targeted by Iraqi Silkworm antiship missile fire control radars in Kuwait. The ships moved out of the missile's range while Coalition forces located and attacked the radar site. With the Silkworm missile threat diminished, the MCM forces began to move back to the previous minesweeping areas at 0240 on 18 February. At 0435, after operating for 11 hours in an undetected Iraqi minefield, USS Tripoli hit a moored contact mine in 30 meters of water. The explosion ripped a 16 foot by 20 foot hole below the water line. As USS Avenger and USS Leader attempted to assist the damaged warship, USS Princeton (CG 59), while unknowingly heading along a line of Manta mines, continued to provide air defense for the MCM Group. At 0715, USS Princeton actuated a Manta mine in 16 meters of water. A sympathetic actuation of another mine about 350 yards from USS

Princeton occurred about three seconds later. These mine blasts caused substantial damage to *USS Princeton*, including a cracked superstructure, severe deck buckling, and a damaged propeller shaft and rudder. As damage control teams overcame fires and flooding aboard *USS Tripoli* and *USS Princeton*, the minesweepers *USS Impervious, USS Leader,* and *USS Avenger* searched for additional mines in the area. The minesweeper *USS Adroit* led the salvage ship *USS Beaufort* (ATS 2) toward *USS Princeton; USS Beaufort* then towed the damaged warship to safety.

USS Princeton restored her TLAM strike and Aegis AAW capabilities within two hours of the mine strike and reassumed duties as the local AAW commander, providing air defense for the Coalition MCM group for 30 additional hours until relieved. *USS Tripoli* was able to continue her mission for several days before being relieved by *USS Lasalle* (AGF 3) and *USS New Orleans* (LPH 11). The amphibious assault ship *USS New Orleans* detached from the ATF and provided the flight deck for AMCM helicopters while the USMCMG staff moved aboard *USS Lasalle* to continue coordinating the mine clearing operations. *USS Tripoli* then proceeded to Bahrain for repair.

Charts and intelligence captured from Iraqi forces showed the minefield where *USS Tripoli* and *USS Princeton* were hit was one of six in a 150-mile arc from Faylaka Island to the Saudi-Kuwaiti border. Within the arc, there were four additional mine lines, with more than 1,000 mines laid before Operation Desert Storm began.

The initial intelligence assessment, based on limited knowledge of Iraqi minelaying operations and on observations of the transit of an Iraqi merchant ship through the area, was that the Iraqis had placed their minefields closer to the coast. As a result, Coalition MCM forces initially passed through the outermost minefield and started MCM operations near a second

barrier of bottom mines. The *USS Tripoli* and *USS Princeton* incidents proved the initial assumption incorrect. The Coalition forces revised the MCM plan, extended the transit lanes 24 miles to the east, moved the MCM and NGFS task groups back out of the Iraqi minefield to unmined areas, and then resumed MCM operations.

On 27 February, *USS Avenger*, using the AN/SQQ-32 MCM sonar, detected, classified and marked a bottom influence mine similar to the type that had struck *USS Princeton* — the first bottom influence mine ever found intact during combat. Divers from EOD Mobile Unit 6 placed neutralizing charges and detonated the mine.

After the cease-fire, MCM assets from Belgium, France, Germany, Italy, Japan, and the Netherlands joined the MCM group. This MCM force swept paths to Kuwait's ports and completed Persian Gulf mine clearing operations by 10 September 1991.

Impact of Iraq's Mine Warfare

Although the Iraqi minefields were not placed to maximize their effectiveness and many mines were deployed improperly, mine warfare had a considerable effect on Coalition maritime operations in the Persian Gulf. Kuwait's relatively short coastline, combined with the large Iraqi mine inventory, caused the Coalition MCM forces to plan and conduct MCM operations in support of an amphibious landing through dense minefields while vulnerable to missile, artillery, and small boat attacks from fortified beaches. Considering hydrographic and operational characteristics, an amphibious landing probably could only occur between Kuwait City and Ras Al-Qul'ayah, along 30 miles of coastline.

Many deployed mines lacked sensors or batteries which prevented their proper operation. During MCM operations, 95 percent of the

UDM-type acoustic influence mines were evaluated as inoperable. Several moored contact mines were recovered on the bottom and apparently 13 percent of the moored mines broke away from their moorings. However, even the poorly planned and improperly deployed minefields caused damage to two combatants and were one of several reasons the amphibious invasion was not conducted. (Other factors, such as collateral damage to Kuwait's infrastructure, risks to the landing force, and lack of a MARCENT requirement for a coastal supply route, are discussed in this chapter's Amphibious Warfare section.)

NAVAL GUNFIRE SUPPORT (NGFS)

In addition to playing a major role in launching TLAM strikes against Iraq, the battleships *USS Wisconsin* and *USS Missouri* contributed the firepower of 16-inch guns in support of Coalition ground forces ashore. This NGFS marked the first time both battleships had fired in combat since the Korean War. The 16-inch NGFS in Operation Desert Storm also may have been an historical event — the final combat operations of the battleship.

NGFS Missions

To defend against an amphibious landing by Coalition forces, Iraq had positioned a large proportion of its troops and weapons along the Kuwaiti coastline. This positioning exposed Iraqi forces to offshore naval gunfire; however, the combination of local hydrographic features and the Iraqi mine threat precluded the effective

USS Missouri **Provides Night NGFS during Operation Desert Storm.**

use of the 5-inch gun against shore targets; therefore the battleship's 16-inch gun was used primarily for NGFS. (The limited water depths in the area held ships several miles off the coast, out of the 5-inch gun's effective range, while the Iraqi mine threat prevented free movement of ships up and down the coast).

NGFS missions were allocated to both amphibious forces and ground forces and were divided into four major target areas: the Kuwait-Saudi Arabia border area, the Ras Al-Qul'ayah area, the area north of Ash Shuaybah, and Faylaka Island. At the start of the theater campaign's battlefield preparation phase, neither battleship provided NGFS because of the mine threat and navigational hazards off the Kuwaiti coast. After the battle of Ras Al-Khafji, at least one battleship was stationed off the coast

> "The USMC OV-10 observation aircraft spotted an Iraqi artillery post in southern Kuwait that had been harassing Coalition troops in Saudi Arabia. The plane relayed the coordinates to USS Wisconsin which silenced the enemy emplacement with 16-inch shells. The emplacement was hit at an estimated range of 19 miles from USS Wisconsin. After the shelling the pilot of the OV-10 reported back, 'Artillery destroyed.'"
>
> *Intelligence Officer, USS Wisconsin*

of Ras Al-Khafji at FSA RK2 from 4 to 9 February. Until the start of the ground offensive, the battleships were on seven-hour alert to MARCENT requests for fire support. During the ground offensive, the theater campaign plan required at least one battleship to provide NGFS to the Commander, Joint Forces Command-East (JFC-E) and MARCENT.

During Operation Desert Storm, battleship

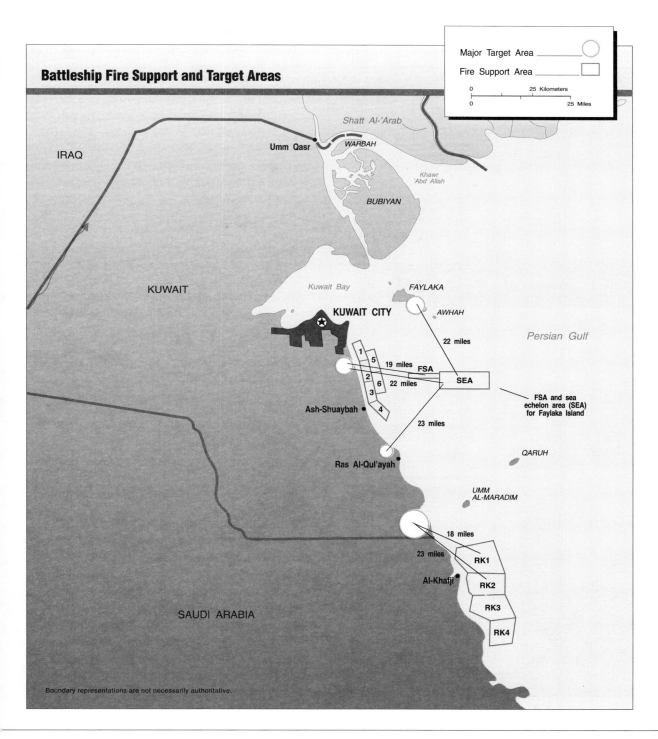

Battleship Fire Support and Target Areas

Major Target Area ⟶ ◯
Fire Support Area ⟶ ▢

0 ——— 25 Kilometers
0 ——— 25 Miles

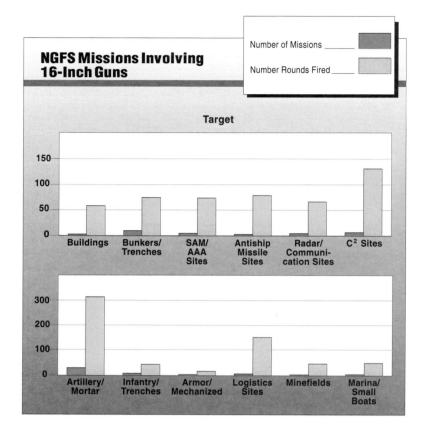

NGFS Missions Involving 16-Inch Guns

Number of Missions
Number Rounds Fired

Target

NGFS missions were generated in three ways: pre-arranged fires, self-determined targets of opportunity, and fires called for by ground forces. Before 15 February, NGFS missions focused more on command, control, and communications (C^3) facilities, radar sites, and electronic warfare sites. Once the ground offensive began, the focus shifted to artillery positions, mortar batteries, ammunition storage facilities, logistics sites, Silkworm antiship missile batteries, and troops on beaches. Only six percent of the missions were fired in a direct support role responding to calls from ground forces. This small percentage was due primarily to MARCENT's inland position beyond NGFS range before the ground offensive and the rapid Coalition advance during the ground offensive.

NGFS Operations

On 4 February, *USS Missouri*, escorted by *USS Curts* using an advanced mine avoidance sonar (a modified hull mounted SQS-56 sonar), threaded through a mine cleared channel and unlighted navigational hazards to a position close to the coast (FSA RK2). With Marines providing fire control direction, *USS Missouri's* 16-inch guns fired 2,700-pound shells onto Iraqi C^3 bunkers, artillery emplacements, radar sites, and other targets. Between 4 and 6 February, *USS Missouri* fired 112 16-inch shells, 12 five-inch shells, and successfully used an Unmanned Aerial Vehicle (UAV) in support of combat missions.

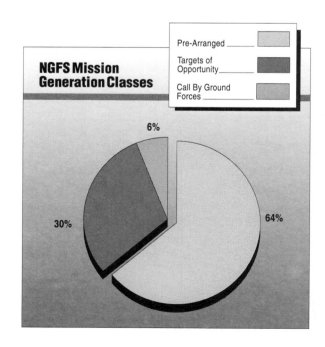

NGFS Mission Generation Classes

Pre-Arranged
Targets of Opportunity
Call By Ground Forces

6%
30%
64%

USS Wisconsin, escorted by *USS Nicholas*, relieved *USS Missouri* on 6 February. On her first mission, the most recently recommissioned battleship fired 11 shells 19 miles to destroy an Iraqi artillery battery in southern Kuwait. Using an UAV for spotting, *USS Wisconsin* attacked targets ashore, as well as small boats which were used during Iraqi raids along the Saudi coast. *USS Wisconsin's* guns opened fire again on 8 February, destroying Iraqi bunkers and artillery sites near Ras Al-Khafji.

USS Wisconsin's **UAV Heads for a Spotting Mission.**

Both battleships also used 16-inch guns to destroy enemy targets and soften defenses along the Kuwaiti coastline in preparation for a possible amphibious assault. On 21 February, the battleships moved north to

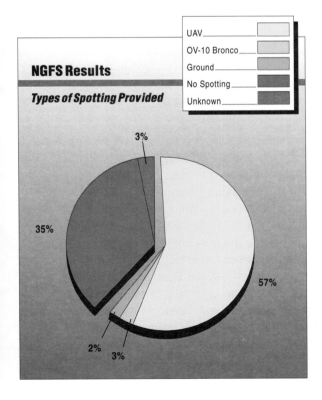

NGFS Results

Types of Spotting Provided

Legend	
UAV	
OV-10 Bronco	
Ground	
No Spotting	
Unknown	

3%
35%
57%
2%
3%

conduct battlefield preparation as the ground offensive neared. As *USS Wisconsin* and *USS Missouri* operated in the FSA south of Faylaka Island, which had been cleared recently of mines, the 16-inch guns continued to fire at Iraqi targets.

On 23 February, the night before the ground offensive started, *USS Missouri's* guns fired pyrotechnic shells onto Faylaka Island to convince Iraqi troops an amphibious invasion had begun. *USS Wisconsin*, accompanied by *USS McInerney* (FFG 8), moved in closer to the Kuwaiti coast to complement the deception. NGFS continued against Faylaka Island on 24 February to deceive the Iraqis that a large-scale amphibious assault was imminent.

As Coalition ground forces advanced around and through the Iraqi defenders in Kuwait , *USS Wisconsin* and *USS Missouri's* guns continued to support them. The battleships provided NGFS during the ground offensive to Joint Forces Command-East (JFC-E) on several occasions against dug-in Iraqi positions. On 26 February, the battleships provided support to the 1st Marine Division (MARDIV) when naval gunfire struck Iraqi tanks dug in at the Kuwait International Airport. *USS Wisconsin* fired the last NGFS of the war; together, both battleships passed the two million-pound mark in ordnance delivered on Iraqi targets by the cease-fire on 28 February.

Use of UAVs

The battleships used UAVs extensively in NGFS for target selection, spotting, and BDA. The UAV accounted for 52 percent of spotting and virtually all BDA support the battleships received. The battleships were able to generate NGFS missions using organic UAV for spotting. Targets of opportunity accounted for 30 percent of the total missions and about 40 percent of the shells fired. Using an UAV in this manner increased the battleship's flexibility to provide NGFS because it allowed each battleship to receive real-time target acquisition and BDA without relying on external spotting and intelligence assets.

In addition to direct support of NGFS missions, UAVs also were used to gather intelligence on Faylaka Island when national sensors were not available and weather prevented aircraft reconnaissance. Over Faylaka Island, *USS Wisconsin's* UAV recorded hundreds of Iraqi soldiers waving white flags — the first-ever surrender of enemy troops to an unmanned aircraft. After the cease-fire, UAVs monitored the coastline and outlying islands in reconnaissance support of occupying Coalition forces. Because UAVs were under direct tactical control of combat forces, they could respond quickly in dynamic situations. On one occasion, *USS Wisconsin's* UAV located two Iraqi patrol boats, which were sunk by aircraft directed to investigate.

NGFS Results

Sixty-five percent of all the fire support missions and 90 percent of all rounds fired received some degree of spotting support. When spotting was not available for a mission, only three or four rounds were fired, usually to harass Iraqi artillery or troop positions. The two battleships fired 1,102 rounds of 16-inch shells in 83 individual missions. Approximately 2,166,000 pounds of ordnance were delivered. The average range for the NGFS missions was approximately 22 miles, with all but 16 missions having ranges exceeding 18 miles.

BDA was obtained for 37 of the 52 missions where spotting was used. Damage was classified as light for 40 percent of these missions, while about 30 percent of the missions inflicted moderate to heavy damage or targets were evaluated as neutralized or destroyed. As expected, a higher percentage of point targets was destroyed, neutralized, or heavily damaged than area targets because area targets are made up of many, smaller individual targets. For point

target missions with BDA available, 28 percent were classified as heavily damaged, neutralized, or destroyed.

AMPHIBIOUS WARFARE

A major maritime campaign component centered on preparing for and executing amphibious operations during the ground offensive. For this purpose, the USMC deployed the 4th and 5th Marine Expeditionary Brigades (MEB) and 13th Marine Expeditionary Unit (Special Operation Capable) (MEU (SOC)) aboard amphibious ships to the Persian Gulf. Continuous planning for amphibious operations started when the lead elements of the 4th MEB and Amphibious Group 2 deployed to Southwest Asia (SWA) from the US East Coast in mid-August. Concurrently, the 13th MEU (SOC), aboard ships of Amphibious Squadron 5, which already were deployed to the Western Pacific, sailed for SWA. Upon its arrival, this amphibious force joined the East Coast amphibious force to form the amphibious task force (ATF). At the time of the these deployments, the distinct possibility existed that an amphibious assault would be required to defend against an Iraqi invasion of Saudi Arabia. In fact, during the initial deployment of Operation Desert Shield, the ATF provided CINCCENT's only forcible entry capability.

In the weeks leading up to the ground offensive, amphibious warfare planners afloat responded to tactical missions, which required them to develop plans ranging from large-scale amphibious assaults into Kuwait to raids and feints on islands and coastal areas. Additionally, as part of the theater campaign plan, the ATF conducted several well-publicized landings in Oman and the southern Persian Gulf. Finally, when the ground offensive began, the ATF conducted feints and raids, and was ready to conduct a large-scale amphibious assault if required. Although a major amphibious operation was not conducted, the ATF played a crucial part in the overall success of Operation

Desert Storm by fixing large numbers of Iraqi troops near the Kuwaiti coast and preventing their use in inland operations.

The Iraqi Threat

The unique geographic and military situation in the Persian Gulf meant an amphibious assault would be conducted against a heavily defended landing beach. The ATF was confronted with formidable coastal and beach defenses. One observer, who later examined Iraqi defenses along the Kuwait border, described them as more formidable than those encountered by Marines during many of the World War II Central Pacific battles. In the area close to shore, the Iraqis placed underwater obstacles, mines and barbed wire to ensnare and disable landing craft and vehicles. Between the low and high water marks, additional mines and barbed wire were positioned to stop infantry. Behind the beaches, the Iraqi defenders dug trench lines and bunkers, and, in the urban areas from Ash Shuaybah north, fortified buildings. Berms, minefields, antitank ditches, dug-in tanks and barbed wire blocked beach exits. To the rear, artillery, and mobile reserves stood ready to counterattack any Marines able to break through the beach defenses. At least three enemy infantry divisions were assigned to defend the Kuwaiti coast from Kuwait City south to the Saudi-Kuwaiti border. Additional Iraqi infantry divisions defended the coast north of Kuwait City. These forces were backed by the 5th Mechanized Division, in reserve near Al-Ahmadi. Similar defenses existed on Faylaka Island, defended by the Iraqi 440th Marine Brigade, and on Bubiyan Island.

Amphibious Warfare Planning

The ATF began preparations for offensive amphibious operations as soon as it reached the theater in mid-September. This force provided an important seaborne threat to the flank of Iraqi forces who, it was feared, might attack Saudi Arabia along the main coastal road from Ras

Iraqi Beach Defenses near Kuwait City.

Al-Khafji to Ad-Dammam. In late October, the ATF conducted amphibious exercises at Ras Al-Madrakah, Oman, providing the opportunity to rehearse generic landing plans. Meanwhile, the 13th MEU (SOC) participated in Maritime Interception Operations and then left SWA on 10 November to conduct exercises in the Philippines. In mid-November, the ATF conducted a highly publicized amphibious exercise along the eastern Saudi Arabian coast,

Marines Conduct an Amphibious Landing Exercise in Oman.

in conjunction with Exercise Imminent Thunder, a final rehearsal of CINCCENT's defensive plans. This exercise was the first in a continuous series of operations carefully designed to deceive the Iraqi command as to the direction of the Coalition's ground attack. A few weeks later, the ATF returned to Ras Al-Madrakah to conduct Exercise Sea Soldier III. By this time, the ATF had received preliminary guidance that its assault objective during the ground offensive would be along the Kuwaiti coast, precipitating staff rehearsals and planning to counter the extensive Iraqi coast defenses.

As Operation Desert Storm approached, amphibious planning intensified. On 30 and 31 December, an amphibious planning conference was conducted aboard USS Blue Ridge (LCC 19), during which the evolving ground offensive plan, and the ATF's role in it, was discussed. MARCENT continued to express concern, and VII Corps later concurred, that if the ground campaign became extended, then a secure port on the Kuwaiti coast would be needed to provide logistic support. I MEF had shifted more than 50 miles inland and MARCENT was concerned about the strain that position placed on logistics lines. Rather than trying to support the entire advance logistically from Saudi Arabia, MARCENT desired an amphibious landing to open a forward logistics base in Kuwait to take advantage of available sea-based logistics. The prospects for conducting an amphibious assault increased. Furthermore, the planning conference re-emphasized the ATF's requirement to plan for raids and feints along the Kuwaiti coast to fix Iraqi attention away from ground forces moving west.

On 6 January, NAVCENT issued a warning order directing the ATF to finalize plans for an amphibious assault on the Kuwaiti coast. The final plans for what had become known as Operation Desert Saber called for the ATF to conduct an amphibious assault north of Ash Shuaybah, establish the landing force ashore, and link up with MARCENT. The amphibious assault's objectives were to reduce the threat facing MARCENT by fixing enemy forces along the Kuwaiti coastline and destroying enemy forces in the beachhead area, and to seize the port facilities at Ash Shuaybah for sustained logistic support of MARCENT.

Based on the expected rate of advance of the ground offensive, the time needed to place amphibious forces into position after the ground campaign began, and the desire to fix as many Iraqi forces in coastal positions as possible, preliminary time lines scheduled the amphibious landing to take place four days after the ground offensive began. The plan envisioned the initial landing would be north of the Ash Shuaybah refinery. The landing force would then attack to the south to secure the port. A potentially serious obstacle to the attack was a liquid natural gas plant near the port complex; the plant's explosive potential posed a serious danger to the landing force. The damage the plant's destruction might cause to the surrounding Kuwaiti infrastructure caused CINCCENT to place it on the list of targets prohibited from attack by Coalition forces during the air campaign. In addition, a large number of high-rise apartment complexes and condominiums near the waterfront provided the Iraqis excellent defensive positions from which to oppose the landing. They, too, were not on CINCCENT's approved target list. These obstacles complicated the amphibious operations planning and decision making.

Available amphibious forces more than doubled in mid-January. Amphibious Squadron 5, with the 13th MEU (SOC) embarked, returned to the Persian Gulf on 12 January. Amphibious Group 3 with the 5th MEB embarked, which had left California in early December, also arrived in the theater on 12 January, and was integrated immediately into the ATF. Amphibious forces then consisted of 36 ships (31 amphibious assault ships and five Military Sealift Command ships) carrying the landing force (the assault echelon of the 4th and 5th MEBs, and the 13th

MEU (SOC). The landing force commander (CLF), preferring the flexibility the Marine Air-Ground Task Force (MAGTF) structure provided for multiple missions, opted to retain that structure for the subordinate units rather than attempt to combine them into one large MAGTF. The 13th MEU (SOC) was assigned the task of conducting advanced force operations and raids, while the 4th and 5th MEB remained capable of attacking separate objectives or, if necessary, joining as a single composite unit.

With the opening of the air campaign on 17 January, amphibious warfare planning and training accelerated. Along with 31 amphibious ships, the ATF also had one repair ship, 17 Landing Craft Air Cushion (LCAC) and 13 Landing Craft Utility (LCU). The landing force had approximately 17,000 Marines, built around two regimental landing teams, with five infantry battalions, plus supporting arms, including tanks, antitank vehicles, and light armored vehicles (LAV). In addition to the LCUs and LCACs available within the ATF, ship-to-shore movement also could be supported by 115 assault amphibian vehicles (AAV). The landing force's Air Combat Element included 19 AV-8Bs and 136 helicopters.

Exercises and planning surfaced several issues that needed resolution before the ATF could conduct an assault. Among them were problems of defining an amphibious objective area, given the expected close proximity of any landing to advancing Coalition ground forces; fire support and airspace coordination issues; and, link-up procedures in a rapidly moving ground offensive. Workaround procedures were developed, however. Foremost among the ATF's concerns was integrating its plans into the air campaign, and ensuring the JFACC targeting process considered the ATF's needs. To accomplish this, an ATF targeting cell was formed, composed of both Navy and USMC officers, who developed targets and submitted reports and requests directly to the JFACC in

Riyadh for incorporation into the ATO. To assist NAVCENT, and to provide closer liaison between NAVCENT, MARCENT, and CINCCENT, the USMC sent a planning staff to NAVCENT's flagship, *USS Blue Ridge*. This planning staff helped with the complex coordination between the ATF and forces ashore.

Because amphibious ships also were deployed to other regions to respond to potential crises, the number of amphibious ships deployed to the Persian Gulf, although sizable, was not enough to load the full assault echelons of two MEBs. Normal USMC practice involves loading amphibious ships so crucial pieces of equipment, particularly helicopters, are not concentrated on one or a few ships. The distribution of amphibious forces during the deployment to the Gulf resulted in the concentration of most or all of a particular aircraft type on a single ship. This practice had some administrative and maintenance advantages during the buildup and required fewer support personnel and equipment. However, it limited flexibility and exposed the landing force to serious degradation if ATF ships were damaged or, as later occurred, detached from the ATF to support MCM operations. Furthermore, because of the unavailability of amphibious lift in the theater, some of 5th MEB's assault echelon equipment was loaded aboard two MSC ships that were unsuitable for amphibious assault operations.

An additional concern centered on the composition of the Assault Follow-On Echelon (AFOE), which carried supplies and equipment for 4th MEB's sustainment of operations once ashore. Initially, the AFOE was loaded on five MSC ships. These ships, none of which had been specifically designed for amphibious assaults, had only a limited capability to conduct in-stream unloading, and virtually no capability for logistics-over-the-shore operations. In addition, two ships required pier cranes for unloading cargo because of inadequate onboard cranes. Moreover, Kuwaiti ports probably would not be available initially during an amphibious assault. These limitations severely reduced these ships' effectiveness in supporting an amphibious assault in such an austere operating environment. Because of the AFOE ships' operational shortfalls, they were unloaded in November and the equipment and supplies loaded onto two Maritime Prepositioning Squadron (MPS) roll-on/roll-off ships which had delivered their prepositioned equipment. These MPS ships were ideally configured for AFOE use because of their in-stream unloading capabilities.

Intelligence collection also became a concern during Operation Desert Storm. Because of competing theater requirements, the ATF was given lower priority for theater and national intelligence collection assets.

Near-shore and beach mines presented obstacles to the ATF. In an assault, AAVs emerging from the surf would be endangered, as would debarking infantrymen. The 4th and 5th MEB lacked the numbers and types of specialized engineer equipment available to the 1st and 2nd Marine Divisions. This shortage of mine clearing assets limited the size of planned initial surface assault waves, whose primary mission would be to clear the beaches. An amphibious assault would rely on heliborne waves that could secure the designated landing beaches from the rear. However, the primary USMC medium lift helicopter, the CH-46, had a limited range that would require the ATF ships to operate in areas suspected to be heavily mined.

An option considered for both a possible assault and a raid was an over-the-horizon (OTH) assault. The concept involves launching heliborne and surface assault waves at extended distances from the beach. OTH operations are practiced regularly as part of the MEU (SOC) training program and were demonstrated during Operation Eastern Exit in January when 4th

MEB, unexpectedly tasked by CINCCENT, landed Marines in Mogadishu, Somalia, to protect and evacuate US citizens. In this operation, the 4th MEB used CH-53E helicopters launched from *USS Trenton* (LPD 14) 466 miles off Somalia's coast. An OTH assault requires both long-range helicopters and assault craft capable of open ocean operations, both of which the ATF had, but in limited numbers. Enough CH-53E and CH-53D heavy lift helicopters, with the required range, were available to lift an infantry battalion. The ATF's 17 LCACs, capable of high-speed, open-ocean operations, could land the assault elements of a battalion landing team, reinforced by the necessary tanks and LAVs. With ATF ships remaining well offshore to avoid detection, engagement by Iraqi defenses, and the mine threat, a smaller, but still potent landing force of about two reinforced battalions could be put ashore. This concept also would use extensive air support to shape landing zones and destroy beach defenses. An OTH amphibious assault with the available assets had risks, but was considered feasible. Several smaller raid packages also were planned using this concept.

Amphibious planning continued to focus on several options as the ATF adjusted to continuous changes in the military situation and a host of possible missions. In late January, the enlarged ATF conducted Exercise Sea Soldier IV in Oman. The exercise was again highly publicized to ensure the Iraqi command understood the Coalition's amphibious capabilities.

On 2 February, CINCCENT and MARCENT met with NAVCENT aboard *USS Blue Ridge* to discuss the timing and feasibility of amphibious plans. Estimates assumed the main assault would need 10 days of MCM operations to clear a path through Iraqi minefields and three to five days of NGFS and air strikes to neutralize Iraqi beach defenses. Shore bombardment and air strikes also would be needed before the landing to allow MCM forces to clear mines from near-shore waters well inside the range of Iraqi land-based artillery. Without a concentrated MCM effort, offshore mines essentially kept the ATF off the coast by as much as 72 miles. NAVCENT also pointed out the possibility of collateral damage to Kuwaiti territory from the NGFS and air strikes against the highly fortified beach front during MCM operations and the amphibious landing. The wholesale destruction of the Kuwaiti infrastructure that could result from necessary pre-assault operations, and the evident risks to the assaulting landing force, were serious considerations. On the other hand, since the start of Operation Desert Storm, USMC service support units and Navy Seabees had worked diligently to improve the overland transportation routes in their area of responsibility. The deployment of substantial USMC reinforcements also improved I Marine Expeditionary Force's (I MEF) logistics capabilities. MARCENT now believed the ground attack could be supported logistically without the need to open a coastal supply route.

As a result of these and other considerations, CINCCENT decided to exclude the amphibious assault from the initial ground attack, but the ATF was directed to prepare for a possible amphibious assault on Ash Shuaybah if the ground offensive required it, and to continue active operations as part of the theater campaign plan. Such an assault would be timed to coincide with I MEF's advance, and thus would be executed on short notice. Although planning for Operation Desert Saber continued as a contingency in case an assault proved necessary, the planning focus shifted. In an 8 February message to NAVCENT, CINCCENT noted, "an amphibious assault into Kuwait, or the credible threat to execute one, is an integral part of the overall campaign plan for Operation Desert Storm." CINCCENT also ordered NAVCENT to establish an amphibious objective area and begin pre-assault operations, including MCM, NGFS, deception measures,

Iraqi Communication Facilities on Umm Al-Maradim Island.

air and sea control, and threat suppression.

Although a large scale, preplanned assault against the Kuwaiti coast had been decided against, the ATF identified several possible raid targets, ranging from the Kuwaiti border to the Al-Faw Peninsula and began detailed planning for an attack on Faylaka Island. A week later, CINCCENT approved continued planning for NAVCENT's proposed option for an attack, raid, or demonstration against Faylaka Island, where intelligence sources estimated a 2,500-man brigade was stationed. The advantages of such an operation were that it could accomplish the objective of distracting Iraqi attention, continue to fix enemy forces along the coast, minimize collateral damage in Kuwait, and also reduce the required MCM effort.

Amphibious Operations

In addition to exercises, the ATF conducted five amphibious operations during Operation Desert Storm. On 29 January, the 13th MEU (SOC) raided Umm Al-Maradim Island off the Kuwaiti coast. Amphibious operations supporting the ground offensive were

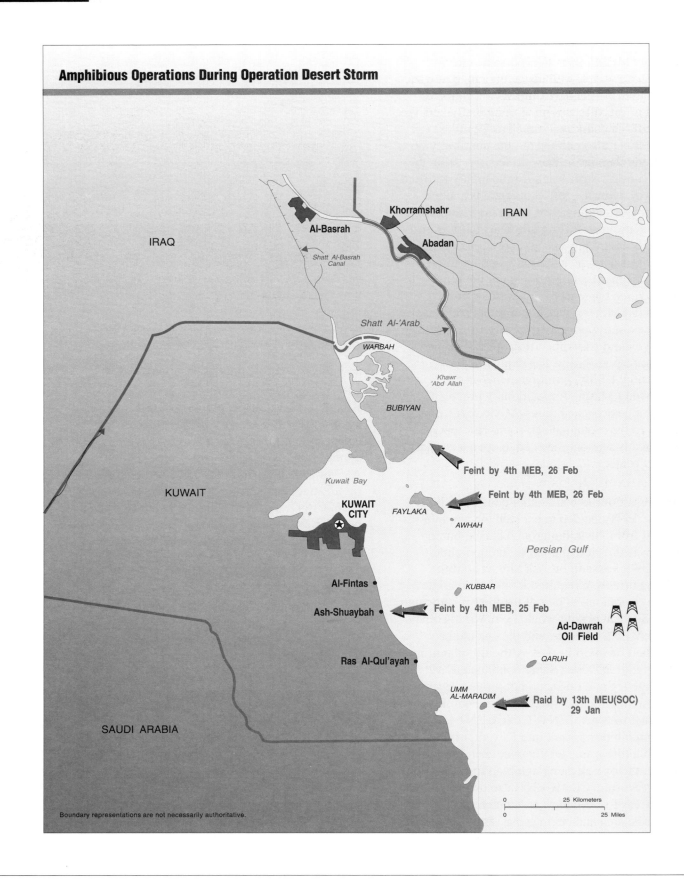

Amphibious Operations During Operation Desert Storm

IRAQ

Al-Basrah

Khorramshahr

Abadan

IRAN

Shatt Al-Basrah Canal

Shatt Al-'Arab

WARBAH

Khawr 'Abd Allah

BUBIYAN

Kuwait Bay

KUWAIT

KUWAIT CITY

FAYLAKA

AWHAH

Feint by 4th MEB, 26 Feb

Feint by 4th MEB, 26 Feb

Persian Gulf

Al-Fintas

KUBBAR

Ash-Shuaybah

Feint by 4th MEB, 25 Feb

Ad-Dawrah Oil Field

Ras Al-Qul'ayah

QARUH

UMM AL-MARADIM

Raid by 13th MEU(SOC) 29 Jan

SAUDI ARABIA

0   25 Kilometers

0   25 Miles

Boundary representations are not necessarily authoritative.

conducted from 20 to 26 February against Faylaka Island, the Ash Shuaybah port facility, and Bubiyan Island. The following section briefly describes these amphibious operations as well as the landing of the 5th MEB.

Umm Al-Maradim Island

Concurrently with Exercise Sea Soldier IV in mid-January, 13th MEU (SOC) moved into the Persian Gulf, having received a warning order to conduct a raid on Umm Al-Maradim Island off the Kuwaiti coast. To support this operation, Kuwaiti Marines were transferred to *USS Okinawa* to provide interpreter and EPW interrogation support as the MEU (SOC) moved toward the objective area. As an Iraqi radar and listening post, the island was thought to be occupied in company strength. Having rehearsed the raid during the preceding week, 13th MEU (SOC) assaulted the island on 29 January. For the Marines, however, the raid turned out to be anticlimactic. A Navy A-6, followed by Marine AH-1 helicopters overflew the island and reported it apparently abandoned. When riflemen from C Company, 1st Battalion, 4th Marines landed by helicopter a few hours later, they found no Iraqis. Quickly removing documents and equipment found there, they destroyed Iraqi heavy equipment that could not be removed and returned to the ATF ships. Many documents provided intelligence on the extent of Iraqi mining in the northern Persian Gulf. The raid demonstrated to the Iraqis the capabilities of the amphibious forces, reinforced the theater deception plan, and captured documents provided intelligence for amphibious operations planning.

Faylaka Island

NAVCENT issued a warning order on 6 February for a raid on Faylaka Island. The ATF was ordered to plan an OTH raid on the island as a diversionary attack before the ground offensive began. The warning order also specified the force was not to become embroiled

USMC AV-8Bs Prepare to Launch from *USS Nassau*.

in a fight with Iraqi defenders if that would make withdrawal difficult.

On 11 February, NAVCENT ordered preliminary operations for the raid to begin. On 12 February, the ATF commanders met aboard *USS Nassau* (LHA 4) to work out the plan's final details. The final concept of operations was issued on 13 February. The plan called for landing a reduced infantry battalion (two companies) supported by LAVs, tanks, and High Mobility Multi-purpose Wheeled Vehicles mounting TOW launchers and heavy machine guns. The raid's objectives were to destroy communications facilities, radar sites, and a command post that had been identified by intelligence sources, as well as to capture Iraqi troops.

A rehearsal was conducted 15 February as NAVCENT, CATF, and CLF briefed CINCCENT on the planned raid. After the meeting with CINCCENT, NAVCENT directed MCM operations to begin the next day. Approximately 48 hours later, on the morning of 18 February, *USS Tripoli* and *USS Princeton* struck mines.

Following these mine strikes, NAVCENT directed the ATF to examine the feasibility of conducting the raid from areas east of the Ad-Dawrah oil fields. MCM forces were staged from that area, and launching a raid from there would reduce the MCM requirements considerably. Although CLF judged the full scale raid was infeasible because of the extended ranges, a reduced raid was possible. Renewed planning centered on options requiring about half the original force and involving no more than one trip for each LCAC or helicopter. The final plan used heliborne forces from 13th MEU (SOC). On 20 February and continuing for the next two days, AV-8B attack aircraft from 4th MEB, operating from the *USS Nassau*, attacked Faylaka Island. The scope of the raid was scaled back on 22 February and was called off completely on 23 February. NGFS continued as planned on 23 and 24 February to deceive the Iraqis into believing a full-scale amphibious assault was imminent.

Ash Shuaybah Port Facility

Late on 24 February, NAVCENT ordered the ATF to conduct a demonstration or feint before dawn near Ash Shuaybah. Coalition ground forces were advancing faster than expected and it was important to hold Iraqi forces defending along the coast south of Kuwait City in position and prevent them from moving into blocking positions or from reinforcing other Iraqi forces further inland. At 0300, *USS Missouri* conducted four NGFS missions in the areas around the simulated landing beaches. Helicopters from 13th MEU (SOC), launched from *USS Okinawa* about 0400, proceeded toward Al-Fintas on a heliborne feint, turned away about three miles from the beach, and returned to the ship about 0450. In the early morning darkness on 25 February, 10 USMC helicopters, some carrying EW emitters, dashed towards Ash Shuaybah, turning away at the last moment within sight of beach defenders, while *USS Portland* maneuvered offshore. The Iraqi response to the feint was immediate — two Silkworm missiles were launched toward Coalition naval forces. As

described in detail earlier in this chapter, HMS Gloucester shot down one missile and the other missile landed in the water. At the same time, confused Iraqi antiaircraft batteries fired into the air.

Bubiyan Island

Shortly before noon on 25 February, NAVCENT ordered additional demonstrations, feints, or raids on Al-Faw and Faylaka Island because of indications that Iraqi forces were moving from the Bubiyan Island and Al-Faw regions. Again, the ATF's objective was to hold the Iraqis in their beach defenses. The next night, a combined Navy-USMC force of helicopters, EW aircraft, and A-6Es carried out a feint towards Bubiyan Island. When Iraqi defenses responded with flares and antiaircraft artillery, the A-6Es attacked. Concurrently with this feint, a smaller armed USMC helicopter force approached Faylaka Island, firing rockets and machine guns. Again, the Iraqi response was immediate, but confused.

Meanwhile, USMC AV-8Bs and AH-1W helicopter gunships from 4th and 5th MEB commenced operations in support of I MEF's attack into Kuwait. A detachment of six AV-8Bs from the *USS Tarawa* moved to a forward airfield at Tanajib to reduce response times for conducting deep and close air support missions, while the 4th MEB's AV-8Bs continued operating from *USS Nassau*. Both MEBs' helicopter gunships flew to forward sites near Al-Khanjar to support I MEF's advance.

Landing of 5th MEB

The largest direct contribution to the ground offensive by amphibious forces, came from the 5th MEB, which began landing through Al-Mish'ab and Al-Jubayl, Saudi Arabia on 24 February to assume the mission of I MEF reserve. Although experiencing little active combat, the MEB assisted in mopping up operations, EPW control, and security duties, while providing the MEF commander, whose two Marine divisions were fully committed, added tactical and operational flexibility.

Effectiveness of Amphibious Operations

Given the time required to conduct MCM operations, the potential for extensive collateral damage to the Kuwaiti infrastructure, and the risk to the landing force, coupled with the changing situation ashore, CINCCENT opted not to execute a large-scale amphibious assault. The ATF, trained and organized for amphibious landings, could have carried out such an assault, although offshore mines and beach defenses may have inflicted substantial casualties. Using the OTH concept, a smaller landing was planned, which could have been conducted on short notice, if required. Variations of this OTH assault plan were used to conduct the amphibious feints. Both assault options presented the Iraqis with a substantial threat to their seaward flank. In the end, the successes of the theater deception plan and the relatively short ground campaign made an amphibious assault unnecessary.

SUBMARINE OPERATIONS

Since Iraq had no submarines, there was no submarine threat to Coalition naval forces or merchant ships and ASW was not tested. However, Navy nuclear powered attack submarines (SSN) played a role in strike warfare and conducted a variety of missions in support of Operations Desert Shield and Desert Storm.

On 19 January, *USS Louisville* became the first submarine to launch a TLAM in combat when she fired five missiles at targets in Iraq in support of the Strategic Air Campaign. This action was the first combat for US submarines since World War II. *USS Louisville* launched three more TLAMs from the Red Sea before

being relieved by the *USS Chicago* (SSN 721) on 6 February.

SUMMARY OF THE MARITIME CAMPAIGN

Once Operation Desert Storm began, the Coalition's maritime campaign in the northern Persian Gulf, including the liberation of the first Kuwaiti territory, the capture of the first EPW, and the threat of an amphibious assault, focused Iraqi attention to the sea rather than to the desert to the west. Coalition naval forces in the Gulf also provided the Coalition with a solid flank to protect the forces and facilities on the Arabian Peninsula. The Coalition's naval presence also reassured the friendly nations of the Gulf and deterred any temptations Iran may have had to intervene directly or to allow Iraq to exploit Iranian territorial waters

A TLAM Flies Toward an Iraqi Target after Being Launched from *USS Pittsburgh* (view from periscope).

and airspace to strike at Coalition forces. This seagoing barrier was especially comforting in the early days of the Iraqi Air Force's exodus to Iran, when the implications of that action were uncertain.

Coalition naval forces essentially destroyed the Iraqi Navy in three weeks, secured control of the northern Gulf, and maintained the region's sea LOC with minimal Iraqi interference. The destruction of the Iraqi naval threat limited Iraq's ability to lay additional mines in the area and let Coalition naval forces establish operating areas farther north, increasing the number of aircraft strike sorties that could be launched against targets ashore and permitting amphibious operations.

The Persian Gulf conflict presented an unprecedented AAW deconfliction challenge. All air operations over the Persian Gulf were conducted safely and successfully. From Operation Desert Shield through Operation Desert Storm, there was no AAW fire from friendly forces. Restricted geography, unusual radar propagation conditions, the proximity of the threat from Iraq, the large number of commercial airfields and air routes in the vicinity, and the limited time available to establish positive identification of potential hostile air contacts before their entry into engagement envelopes combined to form a most complex, demanding AAW environment. The Aegis and NTU AAW systems performed as designed to provide battle force commanders complete coverage of all air contacts.

The five months of Operation Desert Shield permitted the Iraqis to develop an extensive coastal defense system in Kuwait. The Iraqi mine threat affected almost all naval operations during the Persian Gulf Conflict. The Coalition's ability to conduct amphibious operations and NGFS was constrained by the minefields in the northern Persian Gulf. The mine threat also affected naval air strike operations because it forced the carrier battle

groups in the Persian Gulf to operate at greater ranges from targets in Iraq. The presence of drifting mines in the southern Gulf or within a major port in the Gulf could have severely limited the rapid force build up in Operation Desert Shield. Similarly, the mines laid in Kuwaiti ports could have affected seriously the Coalition's ability to shift logistics support rapidly to those ports.

NGFS was a useful contribution to the Coalition's efforts during Operation Desert Storm. NGFS from *USS Wisconsin's* 16-inch guns supported JFC-E's attack up the Kuwaiti coast, especially when they breached Iraqi defenses. *USS Missouri's* NGFS contributed to maintaining the credibility of the amphibious assault option, particularly after a 16-inch bombardment of Ras Al-Qul'ayah induced the Iraqi defenders to abandon fortified positions. *USS Missouri* also supported Marines at the Kuwait International Airport. The UAV proved to be an excellent complement to the battleships, allowing them to attack enemy targets without the need of outside assistance, particularly aircraft, for spotting.

The ATF's contribution to the theater campaign cannot be quantified, yet it was significant to the Coalition's success. Beginning in late October, the ATF carried out amphibious exercises and operations that focused the Iraqi command's attention to the coast of Kuwait. In large measure, Iraq's preoccupation with the defense of Kuwait, and particularly against an amphibious assault, facilitated the ground offensive's now famous left hook maneuver. The amphibious invasion was not an idle threat; had the ATF been directed to do so, it could have conducted a successful assault, although possibly with substantial casualties. The decision not to conduct that assault is a tribute to the success of the theater deception efforts. Since the ATF's presence was sufficient, the ATF accomplished its mission without having to fight. The flexibility of amphibious forces was demonstrated by the

ATF's operations. Iraq's reactions, and refusal to evacuate coastal defenses even when ground forces were encircling the rear, testified to the effectiveness of these operations. In the same vein as the Coalition aircraft that bombed Iraqi forces, and the Coalition's ground forces that attacked through the desert, the ATF played a vital and integral role in Operation Desert Storm.

Although Iraq had no submarines and ASW was not tested, Navy nuclear powered attack submarines participated in the Strategic Air Campaign by launching TLAMs against many targets. Submarines also conducted such missions as intelligence and surveillance in support of Operations Desert Shield and Desert Storm.

OBSERVATIONS

Accomplishments

- The Persian Gulf conflict demonstrated that sea control is fundamental to successful power projection and revalidated the importance of maritime superiority to US global leadership.

- Coalition naval forces essentially destroyed the Iraqi Navy in about three weeks, which limited Iraq's ability to lay additional mines, allowed the carrier battle groups to move closer to Kuwait and increase the number of air strikes in the KTO, and permitted amphibious operations.

- All air operations over the Persian Gulf were conducted safely and successfully during the Persian Gulf conflict. There were no AAW engagements involving fire from friendly forces. Designated return corridors and flight profiles proved to be key methods to separate Coalition aircraft from potentially hostile ones.

- Battleship NGFS made a useful contribution to the Coalition's efforts during Operation Desert Storm. The 16-inch NGFS supported the JFC-E attack along the coast which secured the right flank of MARCENT's advance to Kuwait City and contributed to maintaining the continued credibility of the amphibious assault option.

- UAVs proved to be an excellent reconnaissance asset for the battleships, allowing them to attack enemy targets without the need of outside assistance, particularly aircraft, for spotting and intelligence support. Because the UAVs were under direct tactical control of the combat forces, they were able to respond quickly to changing situations and provide real-time information.

- The publicity associated with amphibious assault preparations, and the potential threat of an assault, forced the Iraqis to focus on their seaward flank, making it more difficult for them to reorient their defenses when the Coalition attacked their western flank. Although the assault never was carried out, the threat induced the Iraqis to fortify the coast and diverted manpower, materiel, and time from any westward extension of their fortified border positions.

Shortcomings

- Maintaining an accurate ASUW order of battle required the identification of Iraqi surface combatants and the accurate assessment of ASUW engagements. Lacking this information affected both the conduct of individual ASUW engagements and the strategy for future operations. Poor BDA resulted in unnecessary launches of additional ASUW aircraft to attack targets that were sinking or already sunk, or in missed opportunities to destroy targets that had been mistakenly reported as sunk by a previous strike.

(Continued)

OBSERVATIONS (Continued)

■ The Iraqi mine threat affected almost all Coalition naval operations during the Persian Gulf conflict. US MCM assets, developed in the Cold War context of a limited Soviet threat to US ports, performed as expected under a more strenuous scenario.

■ Using MSC ships which were unsuitable for amphibious operations to load some of 5th MEB's assault echelon equipment and the 4th MEB's AFOE equipment degraded the ATF's capability to accomplish its mission.

Issues

■ In addition to attacking underway Iraqi surface combatants, ASUW assets also struck other threats to the battle force, including actual and suspected Silkworm sites and high-value vessels detected in port. Considering such targets ASUW threats to the battle force allowed the ASUW commander to implement quick reaction strikes without any potential scheduling delays in the ATO targeting process. Allowing the ASUW commander to control strikes against battle force threats wherever they were located resulted in an operationally clearer division of offensive responsibilities between the ASUW commander and the strike warfare commander. The ASUW commander was responsible for protecting the battle force from antisurface threats and the strike warfare commander was responsible for conducting strike operations against theater targets.

■ The most effective ASUW tactic used by the Coalition was the British Lynx helicopter, working with a controlling SH-60B, firing the Sea Skua missile. Providing Navy shipboard helicopters with a similar weapon would make them more effective in ASUW and extend the range of the ASUW striking power of US combatants.

■ Amphibious assault remains one of the more difficult and dangerous military operations. However, amphibious forces provide a forcible entry capability and forward presence (independent of bases on foreign territory), which are of strategic and operational value.

Chapter VIII

M1A1 Abrams Tanks in Iraq.

THE GROUND CAMPAIGN

INTRODUCTION

Operation Desert Storm's final phase began early on 24 February, after more than 180 days of maritime interception operations and 38 days of aerial bombardment. The ground offensive's objectives were to eject Iraqi Armed Forces from Kuwait, destroy the Republican Guard in the KTO, and help restore the legitimate government of Kuwait. The plan envisioned a supporting attack along the Kuwait-Saudi Arabia border by the I Marine Expeditionary Force (I MEF) and Arab Coalition forces (JFC-E and JFC-N) to hold most forward Iraqi divisions in place. Simultaneously, two Army corps, augmented with French and United Kingdom (UK) divisions — more than 200,000 soldiers — would sweep west of the Iraqi defenses, strike deep into Iraq, cut Iraqi lines of communication (LOC) and destroy the Republican Guards forces in the KTO.

By the morning of 28 February, the Iraqi Army in the Kuwait Theater of Operations (KTO), including the Republican Guards, was routed and incapable of coordinated resistance. Iraqi forces were fleeing from Kuwait or surrendering to Coalition forces in large numbers. In 43 days, culminating in 100 hours of ground combat, the Coalition had shattered the fourth largest army in the world. The victory testified to the capabilities of the men and women who waged the ground operation and to the overall flexibility and effectiveness of the US military.

CINCCENT has said that several factors influenced his belief as to when the Offensive Ground Campaign should begin. These factors

"You may fly over a land forever; you may bomb it, atomize it, pulverize it and wipe it clean of life — but if you desire to defend it, protect it, and keep it for civilization, you must do this on the ground, the way the Roman legions did, by putting your young men into the mud."

T. R. Fehrenbach
This Kind of War

included force deployments and planning, logistics buildup, weather forecasts favorable for ground offensive operations, cohesion of the Coalition, and attack preparations, along with the air campaign. All were important in reducing risks and enhancing the probability of success with limited losses. While precise measurement of force ratios was not possible, senior commanders considered that Iraqi combat effectiveness needed to be reduced by about half before the ground offensive began. Combat effectiveness included both measures such as numbers of soldiers, tanks, armored personnel carriers, and artillery (and degradation thereof) as well as less measurable factors such as morale. Once air operations began, Iraqi reactions could be analyzed to provide further evidence on their military capability. For example, the Iraqi failure at Khafji indicated an inability to orchestrate the sorts of complex operations needed for a mobile defense. Further, the battle seemed to indicate a decline in the will of Iraqi soldiers while at the same time it provided a great boost in morale and confidence among Coalition Arab forces.

While Coalition air forces relentlessly pounded Iraqi defenses, Coalition ground forces completed combat preparations. They clandestinely repositioned from defensive sectors in eastern Saudi Arabia to forward assembly areas farther west. In positioning forces and supplies for the ground attack, logisticians and movement planners faced many challenges. The Coalition moved the equivalent of 17 divisions laterally hundreds of miles over a very limited road network. The trucks used for this movement were mobilized from US units, purchased and leased from US firms, donated or procured from foreign countries, and supplied by Saudi Arabia as host nation support (HNS). The move continued 24 hours a day for two weeks under the air campaign's cover. Forward logistics bases were established to support the ground offensive. This involved moving thousands of tons of supplies — food, water, fuel, ammunition, spare parts — on the same constrained road network used to move combat forces. This repositioning and logistical build up, completed on schedule and undetected by Iraqi forces, was vital to success.

At the same time, ground combat forces focused on battle preparation. Plans were refined, completed, issued, and rehearsed. The rehearsals were particularly important since much of the initial effort involved breaching extensive Iraqi minefields, obstacles, and fortifications — operations that required close coordination.

Meanwhile, ground forces conducted reconnaissance to prepare the battlefield for the ground attack and counter-reconnaissance to deny Iraq crucial information about Coalition ground forces' dispositions. Army and Marine forces conducted helicopter raids and armed aerial reconnaissance missions into Iraq and Kuwait. The Coalition used laser-guided artillery rounds, Hellfire missiles, and the Army Tactical Missile System (ATACMS) to strike headquarters, conduct counter-battery fire, and suppress air defense. Indirect fire units focused on destroying the command, control, communications, intelligence and fire support capabilities of the first-echelon Iraqi divisions. Artillery raids caused forward Iraqi artillery to fire counter battery missions, allowing US radar

to pinpoint the positions and then destroy them with multiple launch rocket systems, other artillery, and air attacks. Scout and attack helicopters, flying at night, identified Iraqi positions and engaged enemy observation posts.

This chapter discusses the planning and execution of Phase IV of the theater campaign — the Offensive Ground Campaign. It addresses the planning process, the operational considerations, and reasons for certain decisions. Next, it discusses the buildup of ground forces, battlefield preparations, logistics considerations, and intelligence requirements. An assessment of the enemy just before G-Day follows to set the stage for the ground offensive.

A detailed narrative describes the intensity of ground combat, the firepower and rapid maneuver of US ground forces, and the integration of joint and combined forces to attain the theater objectives. The chapter concludes with a summary of the accomplishments, shortcomings, and issues.

PLANNING THE GROUND OFFENSIVE

Initial Planning Cell

As early as 25 August, Commander-in-Chief, Central Command (CINCCENT) outlined a four-phased campaign ending with a ground offensive to drive Iraqi forces from Kuwait. At CINCCENT's request, in mid-September the Army assembled a group of officers to form the Central Command J5-Special Planning Group (CCJ5-SPG). CINCCENT chartered this group, graduates of the Army School of Advanced Military Studies (SAMS), Fort Leavenworth, KS, to develop courses of action for the ground offensive. A product of post-Vietnam military education improvements, SAMS provides a year of concentrated study of the theory and practice of warfare at the operational level (corps and above) and campaign planning. Because of this focus, CINCCENT requested SAMS graduates for his planning staff. The instruction at SAMS also is guided by the Army's AirLand Battle doctrine, which is compatible with other service doctrine, particularly Marine maneuver warfare. Therefore, the cell shared a common educational background and used the precepts of AirLand Battle as the basis for their planning.

The ground operations plan was developed from an integrated joint and combined campaign plan. CINCCENT chose to retain the function of land force commander over Army and Marine ground forces, although these component commanders had a major role in refining CINCCENT's concept of operations. The Central Command (CENTCOM) Plans and Policy Directorate and Combat Analysis Group, augmented by the SAMS graduates, had primary responsibility for developing and analyzing courses of action for the overall ground offensive plan. Meanwhile, ARCENT and the Marine Component, Central Command (MARCENT) had responsibility for developing and analyzing courses of action to implement the Theater Campaign Plan.

The ground forces' responsibilities (particularly Army Component, Central Command (ARCENT)), did not end with the cease-fire. Tasks such as post-war reconstruction, re-establishment of civil authority, and caring for refugees, displaced persons, enemy prisoners of war, and repatriated friendly prisoners of war remained. This planning and preparation had to be accomplished concurrent with the planning for combat operations and required substantial resources and effort.

The Planning Process

As previously discussed in Chapter 5, Transition to the Offensive, planning for the ground operation was evolutionary. Initially, planning for ground and air operations was unilateral and highly compartmented. This was due to political sensitivities and security concerns regarding an offensive campaign. After the President's November decision to deploy additional forces,

ARCENT was assigned the lead for planning the ground offensive. ARCENT commanded most US Army units in theater and exercised tactical control over selected non-US coalition forces. ARCENT focused primarily on the Army's joint and combined coordination role. At the same time, CINCCENT began to develop a combined Operation Desert Storm Operations Plan (OPLAN), integrating the Coalition's full combat capability. As the overall land component commander, CINCCENT provided a focal point for the combined planning of the Coalition. UK, Egyptian and French representatives augmented the existing US-Saudi combined planning team during this period.

CINCCENT initially instructed the planners to develop an Offensive Ground Campaign using the forces available in theater at the time: one corps of two heavy, one airborne, and one air assault division; an armored cavalry regiment (ACR), and a combat aviation brigade (CAB); a Marine Expeditionary Force (MEF) ashore along the coast and a Marine Expeditionary Brigade (MEB) afloat in the Gulf; and other Coalition forces.

Operational Imperatives

Planners had reached several significant conclusions that were designated as operational imperatives and would remain as central planning tenets throughout planning for the offensive. The planners concluded that for the ground campaign to be successful, the air campaign would have to reduce Iraqi combat effectiveness in the Kuwait Theater of Operations by about half. A second operational imperative was that Coalition ground forces should fight only those enemy units necessary to achieve Coalition objectives while bypassing other enemy forces. The third operational imperative was that battlefield tactical intelligence would be required in the hands of battlefield commanders so rapidly that fire power could be placed on target before the target could move sufficiently to require retargeting. It was felt that this tactical intelligence-targeting feedback loop would be critical to success on the battlefield.

Development of Courses of Action

The planning cell briefed their courses of action and recommendation to CINCCENT on 6 October. The preferred course of action called for a one corps frontal attack directly into Kuwait from Saudi Arabia. The objective for this attack was an area of high ground north of the Mutla Pass and Ridge. The risk with this plan was that the attack would encounter major portions of the enemy's strength and operations to breach Iraqi defenses might be extremely difficult. CINCCENT judged that while such an attack probably would succeed, casualties could be sizable, and the Republican Guards, one of Iraq's centers of gravity, might escape. To avoid the enemy's main defensive positions, a wider, deeper envelopment with additional forces was required.

On 11 October, the CENTCOM chief of staff briefed the Chairman of the Joint Chiefs of Staff (CJCS), the Secretary of Defense, and the President. The CENTCOM chief of staff stressed that, although the US ground forces could attack, success could not be guaranteed because of the existing balance of forces. Additional risks included extended supply lines, the lack of an armored force in theater reserve, and the threat of chemical warfare.

Based on guidance from the Secretary, CINCCENT subsequently directed his planning staff to consider an envelopment by two US Army corps west of the Wadi Al-Batin. The purpose of the envelopment was to get behind the main Iraqi forces while supporting attacks were conducted by other Coalition forces into Kuwait. The main attack's objective was the destruction of the Republican Guards forces.

The CJCS was briefed on this concept on 22

October. Following the briefing, his guidance to CINCCENT was straightforward. "Tell me what you need for assets. We will not do this halfway. The entire United States military is available to support this operation." The conclusion was that a second Army corps, initially two divisions and an ACR, should provide the necessary forces to carry out the maneuver to the west, around the Iraqi main defenses. The CJCS agreed to seek approval for deployment of the additional force . VII Corps, based in Germany, was a logical choice for deployment because of its proximity to the theater, high level of training, and modern equipment. VII Corps began its movement immediately after the President's 8 November announcement.

In addition to the European-based corps, other forces were required. At ARCENT's request a third division, the Army's 1st Infantry Division from Fort Riley, KS, was added to give VII Corps more capability. MARCENT saw the need for an additional division and reinforcement of the 3rd Marine Aircraft Wing (MAW) in order to conduct effective supporting attacks. These forces would let the Marines breach the Kuwait border defenses and defeat the 11 Iraqi divisions thought to be in eastern Kuwait. Planning also continued for an amphibious assault along the Kuwaiti coast to flank Iraqi defenders on the Kuwaiti border. Although the amphibious assault was not conducted, it became an integral part of the theater deception plan, which was intended to portray a Coalition main attack along Kuwait's southern border. To satisfy the requirement for additional forces, elements of II MEF, to include the 2nd Marine Division (MARDIV), a large part of the 2nd MAW, 2nd Force Service Support Group (FSSG), and the 5th MEB were deployed from the Continental US (CONUS).

Issues and Concerns Regarding the Plan

Several concerns were raised during the plan's final development. These included:

- What arrangements could be made for effective command and control (C^2) of Coalition forces?
- What was the trafficability for heavy vehicles in the area of operations?
- Was the concept of operations logistically supportable and feasible?
- Could the Coalition penetrate Iraq's defensive belts and formidable obstacles?

In addition, there was the crucial question of the overall size of the Iraqi force that would be deployed to defend the KTO.

CINCCENT's Strategy and Concept

On 14 November, CINCCENT briefed his concept for the operation to all his ground commanders down to division level. XVIII Airborne Corps was to be used in the west. VII Corps would be the main effort and would destroy the RGFC in the KTO. British forces would remain with MARCENT (a decision later reversed). A heavy division was to be assigned as theater reserve. Supporting attacks would be conducted by the I MEF, Joint Forces Command - North (consisting of Egyptian, Saudi, and Syrian forces) and Joint Forces Command - East (consisting of Saudi and GCC forces). Commanders were directed to have forces ready by mid-January.

Secretary of Defense Reviews War Plans

On 19 and 20 December, the Secretary of Defense and CJCS were provided an update on war plans in Riyadh. NCA objectives were reviewed and CENTCOM's mission was summarized. Ground offensive plans were summarized by phases of preparation and operations. The logistics buildup, which would be initiated when the air campaign started, would take two weeks and similarly, force repositioning to attack positions would consume two weeks. The actual ground offensive was estimated to take up to two weeks, followed by a period of consolidation that would last up to

Commander's Intent

Maximixe Friendly Strength Against Iraqi Weakness and Terminate Offensive Operations with the RGFC Destroyed and Major US Forces Controlling Critical LOC's in the Kuwaiti Theater of Operations.

four weeks. Subsequent logistics buildup and force repositioning would occur simultaneously. The commander's intentions were presented. Victory would be achieved through the destruction of the RGFC in the KTO, preservation of the offensive capability of the combined forces, and restoration of the sovereignty of Kuwait. Attacking ground forces were to penetrate and bypass static Iraqi defensive forces which included infantry and other forces that were not mobile and could not pose a threat to a fast moving Coalition armor forces. It was CINCCENT's intention to physically and psychologically isolate the Iraqi forces in Kuwait. Operations would fix and block Iraq's first operational echelon reserves, with the objective of securing Coalition flanks and LOCs. Ground operations would culminate in the destruction of RGFC divisions in the KTO.

The Secretary of Defense approved CINCCENT's plan. Upon his return to Washington, he and the CJCS briefed the President who also approved the plan. However, it was determined that the actual start of the ground campaign would require a subsequent Presidential decision, which was made in February.

Ground Campaign Phases

The planning process continued within CINCCENT's general parameters. When Operation Desert Storm OPLAN was issued, it directed the ground campaign part of the theater campaign be conducted in four phases:

- Phase I — Logistical buildup;
- Phase II — Force repositioning;
- Phase III — Ground attack; and
- Phase IV — Tactical consolidation.

PREPARATION FOR THE OFFENSIVE

Ground Forces Buildup

The first US ground forces, lead elements of the 82nd Airborne Division, arrived in theater on 9 August. Figure VIII-4 shows the buildup, by brigades, of US ground forces within the theater. By early December, approximately half of the US combat brigades had arrived. Within 40 days, most of the remaining forces had arrived. By the end of January, the ground forces in

A US Army Division, totalling approximately 17,500 soldiers, is organized from a common division base that consists of a division headquarters, three maneuver brigades, an aviation brigade, an artillery brigade, an air defense artillery battalion, an engineer battalion, a signal battalion, a military intelligence battalion, a military police company, a chemical company, and a support command. The heavy divisions that served in Operation Desert Storm each consisted of a mix of 10 armor and mechanized infantry battalions along with necessary combat support and combat service support units.

A US Marine Division is normally organized around three infantry regiments of three battalions, an artillery regiment, and separate tank, light armored vehicle, reconnaissance, assault amphibian vehicle, and combat engineer battalions, totalling approximately 20,000 Marines. During combat,

Ground Forces Command Structure on G-Day

Operational Command

Coalition Coordination, Communication, and Integration Center

Tactical Control

theater could conduct the type of offensive operations envisioned by CINCCENT. However, some VII Corps units literally moved directly from the ports into their tactical assembly areas (TAA) and forward attack positions the day before the ground offensive began.

Task Organization (US Ground Forces)

Coalition ground forces were task organized along corps lines to improve C^2 and in accordance with the ground operation mission. ARCENT provided C^2 to Army forces in the theater.

I MEF had two reinforced infantry divisions and the 3rd MAW with 222 fixed-wing aircraft and 183 helicopters. Its combat power greatly exceeded that normally found in a MEF. In addition, I MEF could call on 20 AV-8Bs and 141 helicopters afloat in the Gulf with 4th and 5th MEBs.

The 1st MARDIV, composed of units from all three active MEFs plus Reservists, deployed during the early stages of Operation Desert

Shield. To build esprit among the many units assigned to 1st MARDIV, it was divided into task forces, each organized and equipped for specific missions and bearing a unique title.

The 2nd MARDIV deployed in December, minus the 2nd Marine Regiment (Reinforced) afloat with 4th MEB; it also was augmented with Reserves. It retained its traditional regimental titles although it also was task organized. The 2nd MARDIV was given the 1st (Tiger) Brigade, 2nd Armored Division with M1A1 tanks and M2/M3 fighting vehicles, to serve as an exploitation or counterattack force.

Special Operations Forces (SOF) included Army Special Forces (SF) and Army Special Operations Aviation units; Navy SEALs and Special Boat Units; Air Force (USAF) Special Operations squadrons and Special Operations Combat Control Teams; and Psychological Operations (PSYOP) and Civil Affairs (CA) units. A Joint Special Operations Task Force controlled reconnaissance, special reconnaissance (SR), and direct action operations to support battlefield preparation.

SOF teams were attached to non-US Coalition units down to battalion level; their presence increased commanders' confidence. These teams assessed Coalition forces' readiness levels, provided training and communication capability, coordinated tactical operations, assisted with fire support coordination, and provided information CINCCENT needed to ensure effective operational coordination with Coalition forces. (SOF organizations and operations are further discussed in Appendix J.)

Task Organization (Non-US Ground Forces)

Arab-Islamic ground forces were organized in two corps, the Joint Forces Command-North (JFC-N) and Joint Forces Command-East (JFC-E). Ground forces in JFC-N and JFC-E represented 14 countries.

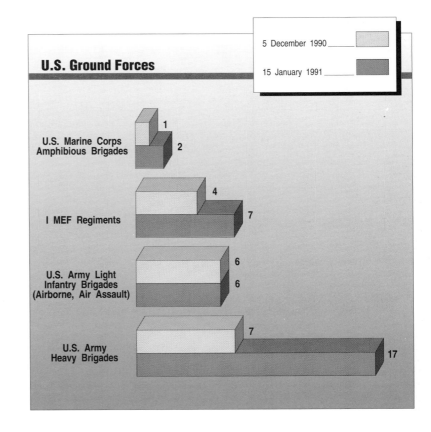

Task Organization

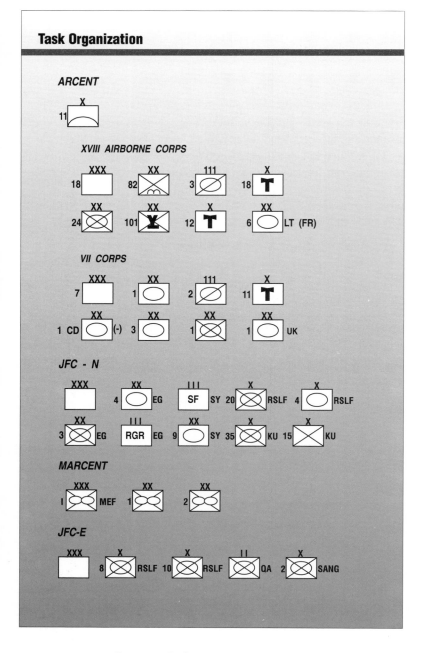

ARCENT

XVIII AIRBORNE CORPS

VII CORPS

JFC - N

MARCENT

JFC-E

Command, Control, and Communications

Coalition Coordination, Communication, and Integration Center (C ^{3}IC)

The Gulf War presented unique challenges in developing Coalition C^2 relationships and assigning missions. Faced with the diversity of forces from more than 23 nations, often with

unique doctrine, language, customs, religion, equipment, and capabilities, CINCCENT was aware of the operational contradictions that threatened the Coalition's vitality. Political considerations, national pride, and public perceptions could, in some instances, complicate military requirements.

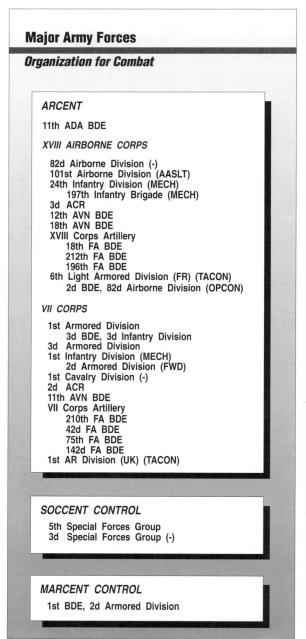

Major Army Forces

Organization for Combat

ARCENT

11th ADA BDE

XVIII AIRBORNE CORPS

82d Airborne Division (-)
101st Airborne Division (AASLT)
24th Infantry Division (MECH)
    197th Infantry Brigade (MECH)
3d ACR
12th AVN BDE
18th AVN BDE
XVIII Corps Artillery
    18th FA BDE
    212th FA BDE
    196th FA BDE
6th Light Armored Division (FR) (TACON)
    2d BDE, 82d Airborne Division (OPCON)

VII CORPS

1st Armored Division
    3d BDE, 3d Infantry Division
3d Armored Division
1st Infantry Division (MECH)
    2d Armored Division (FWD)
1st Cavalry Division (-)
2d ACR
11th AVN BDE
VII Corps Artillery
    210th FA BDE
    42d FA BDE
    75th FA BDE
    142d FA BDE
1st AR Division (UK) (TACON)

SOCCENT CONTROL

5th Special Forces Group
3d Special Forces Group (-)

MARCENT CONTROL

1st BDE, 2d Armored Division

To harmonize Coalition forces actions and achieve unity of effort (especially with respect to land forces), CINCCENT, ARCENT, and Saudi military leaders created the Coalition Coordination, Communication, and Integration Center (C³IC). ARCENT and the Saudi Arabian Armed Forces (SAAF), initially operated the C³IC. The C³IC gave ARCENT and the SAAF the ability to bring Coalition forces together to coordinate tasks and missions. In December, responsibility for the US operation of the center transferred to the CENTCOM staff. The C³IC did not command; it integrated the Coalition land forces into one solid effort, receiving reports, collecting data, improving the information flow, and harmonizing operational planning in areas such as host nation support, movement control, and training. The C³IC was the combined operations cornerstone, helping meld the Coalition into an effective combat force. The planning process, involving C³IC members, did much to help form and hold the Coalition together. In addition, the scope of the operation, movement of forces across great distances, and the forces' political and cultural complexion demanded innovative techniques and hard work at all levels to ensure battlefield success. Further information on the C³IC is in Appendix K.

Liaison Teams

Liaison teams from ARCENT, SOF, USAF Forward Air Controllers (FACs), Air Liaison Officers (ALO), and Air Naval Gunfire Liaison Company (ANGLICO) Marines also were key to coordination and control. Service warfighting doctrine requires liaison teams between flanking units, from higher to lower headquarters, among components and among Coalition forces. For example, ARCENT liaison teams with substantial communications capabilities were sent to the two Army corps and I MEF.

Liaison teams also were attached to other Coalition forces. ARCENT teams attached to JFC-N and JFC-E averaged 35 soldiers and became battle staff members, helping plan

I MEF Task Organization

I MEF Command Element

> 1st Surveillance, Reconnaissance, and Intelligence Group
> 3d Civil Affairs Group
> 3d Naval Construction Regiment (USN)
> 24th Marines (USMCR) (Rear Area Security)

1st Marine Division

> 1st Marines (TF Papa Bear)
> 3d Marines (TF Taro)
> 4th Marines (TF Grizzly)
> 7th Marines (TF Ripper)
> 11th Marines (TF King)
> 1st Light Armored Infantry Battalion (TF Shepherd)
> 1st Battalion, 25th Marines (USMCR) (TF Warden)
> TF Troy (Deception)
> (1st and 3d Tank Battalions, 1st Combat Engineer Battalion, 1st Reconnaissance Battalion, and other combat support units were attached to the task forces)

2d Marine Division

> 6th Marines
> 8th Marines
> Tiger Brigade, 2d Armored Division (USA)
> 10th Marines
> 2d Light Armored Infantry Battalion
> 2d Tank Battalion (M1A1)
> 8th Tank Battalion (USMCR) (M60A1)
> 2d Reconnaissance Battalion

3d Marine Aircraft Wing

> Marine Aircraft Group-11
> Marine Aircraft Group-13 (Forward)
> Marine Aircraft Group-16
> Marine Aircraft Group-26
> Marine Air Control Group-38
> Marine Wing Support Group-37

1st Force Service Support Group

> General Support Group-1
> General Support Group-2
> Direct Support Command
> > Direct Support Group-1
> > Direct Support Group-2

5th Marine Expeditionary Brigade

> 5th Marines
> Marine Aircraft Group 50 (Composite)
> Brigade Service Support Group-5

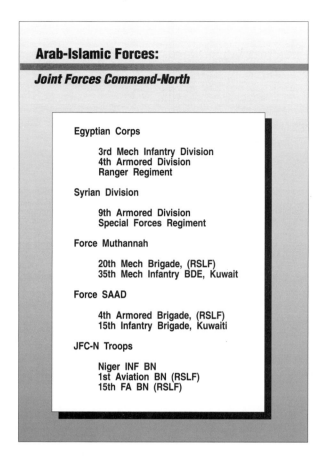

Arab-Islamic Forces:

Joint Forces Command-North

Egyptian Corps

    3rd Mech Infantry Division
    4th Armored Division
    Ranger Regiment

Syrian Division

    9th Armored Division
    Special Forces Regiment

Force Muthannah

    20th Mech Brigade, (RSLF)
    35th Mech Infantry BDE, Kuwait

Force SAAD

    4th Armored Brigade, (RSLF)
    15th Infantry Brigade, Kuwaiti

JFC-N Troops

    Niger INF BN
    1st Aviation BN (RSLF)
    15th FA BN (RSLF)

offensive operations and easing coordination with higher and adjacent units. These teams were equipped with satellite communications (SATCOM) packages that allowed them to communicate directly with ARCENT and CENTCOM headquarters. They became the eyes and ears of the ARCENT commander and CINCCENT, and provided an accurate battlefield picture in the non-US Coalition sectors as offensive operations progressed. These liaison teams were crucial to the synchronization, coordination and control of the combined battle.

Coordination and Control Measures

Coordination and control on a battlefield of this magnitude requires extensive measures, not only to permit joint and combined operations and synchronize the combat power of the multinational effort, but also to increase

Coalition forces' safety. Commanders were concerned about casualties from friendly fire from the beginning and took account of this danger in formulating their operational plans. It is almost impossible, however, to prevent casualties from friendly fires, given the speed of operations, lethality of weapons and the environmental conditions under which the war was fought. (Friendly fire incidents are discussed in Appendix M.)

Every level from company to theater used extensive coordination and control measures. Boundaries between units, phase lines to coordinate advances, fire support coordination lines (FSCL), and restricted fire lines were among the measures used. For the most part, these measures are found in doctrine or standard operating procedures. During the offensive, additional procedures were developed to meet specific needs for additional coordination.

Communications

To support Operation Desert Storm, CENTCOM created the largest theater communications system in history. It connected US sustaining bases, CENTCOM, Coalition forces, and subordinate elements. Because the system expanded rapidly, communications frequency management and asset availability became crucial. Providing reliable and continuous command, control and communications with a rapidly moving force across vast distances during the ground war raised a whole new set of challenges.

To meet the needs of field commanders, multichannel SATCOM was used. These systems required detailed frequency management and constant attention. There were 115 super high frequency (SHF) tactical satellite (TACSAT) ground terminal relocations during the Offensive Ground Campaign, with 33 multichannel satellite terminals in Iraq and Kuwait at the end of the operation. Planning and executing these satellite terminals' movement to support the ground offensive was a major challenge. Signal units frequently displaced nodes and terminals to maintain and sustain communications for advancing units.

Because of the distances between units, deploying units augmented their organic equipment with ultra high frequency (UHF) TACSAT ground terminals. UHF single channel TACSAT terminals were used for C^2, intelligence dissemination and logistics support. The need for this capability across long distances was identified early; the requirement increased steadily throughout the operation. (More detailed discussion of C^3I is in Appendix K.)

Joint and Combined Operations

Common Warfighting Doctrine

Evolving joint operations doctrine guided the planning and conduct of the ground offensive. The basic principles of initiative, depth, agility, synchronization and combined arms are understood and practiced by all Services. Forces

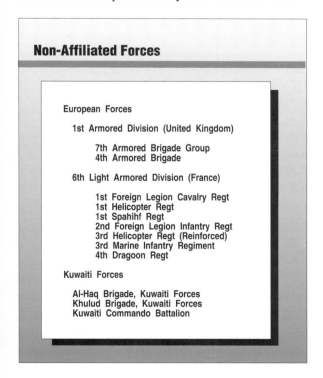

Non-Affiliated Forces

European Forces

1st Armored Division (United Kingdom)

7th Armored Brigade Group
4th Armored Brigade

6th Light Armored Division (France)

1st Foreign Legion Cavalry Regt
1st Helicopter Regt
1st Spahihf Regt
2nd Foreign Legion Infantry Regt
3rd Helicopter Regt (Reinforced)
3rd Marine Infantry Regiment
4th Dragoon Regt

Kuwaiti Forces

Al-Haq Brigade, Kuwaiti Forces
Khulud Brigade, Kuwaiti Forces
Kuwaiti Commando Battalion

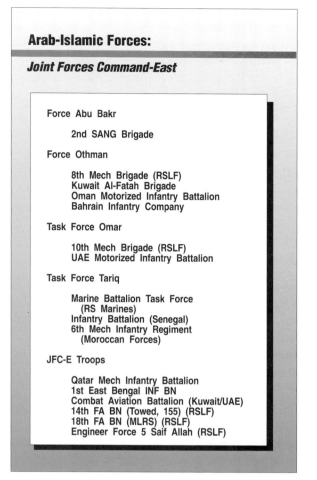

Arab-Islamic Forces:

Joint Forces Command-East

Force Abu Bakr

2nd SANG Brigade

Force Othman

8th Mech Brigade (RSLF)
Kuwait Al-Fatah Brigade
Oman Motorized Infantry Battalion
Bahrain Infantry Company

Task Force Omar

10th Mech Brigade (RSLF)
UAE Motorized Infantry Battalion

Task Force Tariq

Marine Battalion Task Force
(RS Marines)
Infantry Battalion (Senegal)
6th Mech Infantry Regiment
(Moroccan Forces)

JFC-E Troops

Qatar Mech Infantry Battalion
1st East Bengal INF BN
Combat Aviation Battalion (Kuwait/UAE)
14th FA BN (Towed, 155) (RSLF)
18th FA BN (MLRS) (RSLF)
Engineer Force 5 Saif Allah (RSLF)

are trained to fight using common principles and techniques to ensure battlefield interoperability. Each Service, however, has developed its own doctrinal concepts, operational principles, and internal organizational and tactical concepts to maximize capabilities. For example, USMC warfighting doctrine is based on many of the same principles as Army AirLand Battle doctrine, but it is adapted to the USMC organization and structure. Technical terminology and procedures are being standardized at the joint level. These include common maneuver and fire support control measures, air support procedures, and operational planning and reporting formats.

AirLand Battle Doctrine

The basis for ARCENT operations was AirLand

Battle doctrine. The essence of AirLand Battle is to defeat the enemy by conducting simultaneous offensive operations over the full breadth and depth of the battlefield. It is the intellectual road map for operations, conducted at corps and above, and tactics, conducted below corps. This doctrine places tremendous demands on combat leaders. Commanders must fight concurrently what are known as close, deep, and rear operations, all as interrelated parts of one battle. Commanders fight close — to destroy enemy forces where the battle is joined. They fight deep — to delay or attack enemy reserves. These operations are intended to disrupt the enemy's plan and create opportunities for success in close operations. They fight rear, behind forward units, to protect CSS assets and to retain freedom of action for friendly sustainment and movement of reserve forces.

AirLand Battle doctrine is centered on the combined arms team, fully integrating the capabilities of all land, sea and air combat systems, and envisions rapidly shifting and concentrating decisive combat power, both fire and maneuver, at the proper time and place on the battlefield.

Ultimately, success on the AirLand battlefield is predicated on four basic tenets:

- Initiative — to set or change the terms of battle by offensive action;
- Agility — the ability of friendly forces to act mentally and physically faster than the enemy;
- Depth — the extension of operations in space, time, and resources; and,
- Synchronization — the arrangement of battlefield activities in time, space, and purpose to produce maximum relative combat power at the decisive point.

Marine Air-Ground Task Force Doctrine

Marine Air-Ground Task Force (MAGTF) doctrine guided I MEF as it planned and executed its part of Operation Desert Storm. Seeking to unhinge the enemy's cohesion,

Marine forces exploited enemy vulnerabilities while maximizing their own strengths. Initiative, flexibility, and combined arms synchronization were keys to battlefield success, and to fully achieve these principles, the MAGTF concept was stressed. Task-organized for specific missions, the MAGTF is a balanced air-ground-logistics team composed of four elements — the command element, the ground combat element (GCE), the aviation combat element (ACE), and the CSS element. These elements fall under one commander, who can fight a three-dimensional battle at both the tactical and operational levels.

Central to MAGTF doctrine is the close integration of ground and air combat elements. Trained to work in close cooperation, this is more than a relationship in which aircraft provide close support to ground forces, although that is a key element. The GCE, task organized to accomplish its mission, can range from a light infantry force to a mechanized combined arms task force. Common warfighting doctrine and training lets units from different parent commands or geographic locations be meshed quickly into a fighting team (as occurred in the 1st MARDIV in Operation Desert Shield). The GCE, however, is only one MAGTF maneuver element. The ACE, with fighter, attack, and rotary wing aircraft, extends the battlefield and operates in the enemy's rear areas, seeking to inflict extensive damage and disruption before ground forces clash. During the ground battle, Marine aircraft ranged throughout the battle area, under the MAGTF commander's control, providing close air support (CAS) to ground forces and interdiction of enemy forces throughout the depth of the MAGTF AOR.

Air Operations in Support of the Ground Offensive

In CINCCENT's theater campaign plan, elimination of strategic targets and attrition of Iraqi combat effectiveness in the KTO were prerequisites for the Offensive Ground Campaign. However, many factors affected this plan and the realignment of air targeting priorities to support CINCCENT's objectives. These included: the air defense threat; the need to find and strike Scud missile launcher locations; the deception plan, which placed the weight of battlefield preparation initially in the MARCENT and JFC-N zone; ranges and capabilities of some airframes, which were not suited for certain types of missions; and an unusually long period of poor weather and low visibility.

Because the ground offensive's start was predicated on reduction of Iraqi forces in the KTO, the ground force commanders were directly involved in battle damage assessment and provided assessments to CENTCOM. CINCCENT's desired level of attrition was approximately half of the Iraqi combat effectiveness.Ground forces and supporting air assets closely coordinated the targeting effort to achieve the required attrition levels.

Army aviation operations during the ground offensive were an integral part of the ground commanders' scheme of maneuver. In addition to the traditional missions of attack, assault, armed reconnaissance, intelligence gathering, and C^2, non-traditional missions, such as counter-battery and counter-reconnaissance missions, were flown. Cooperative planning between fire support units and other air assets capitalized on the strengths of both systems.

I MEF relied on 3rd MAW assets. Trained to operate with Marine ground forces, 3rd MAW provided I MEF with an important combat multiplier, letting I MEF conduct an integrated air-ground operation that included not only the increased firepower of CAS, but also the ability to prepare the battlefield and to attack enemy forces throughout its zone. 3rd MAW, in effect, acted as an additional I MEF maneuver unit, operating in concert with the MEF attack plan, but able to strike the enemy and influence the battle well forward and to the flanks of the advancing ground forces.

Naval Operations in Support of the Ground Offensive

While Coalition naval forces continued to operate in the Red and Northern Arabian seas, primary support to the ground offensive was provided by forces in the Persian Gulf. This support included an amphibious task force, two battleships and two carrier battle forces, as well as escorts, smaller vessels and minesweepers from both the United States and several other Coalition nations. The primary focus of naval support for the ground offensive was an amphibious assault on the Kuwait coast.

Naval forces in the Gulf also conducted several other missions to support the ground offensive. The battleships *USS Missouri* (BB 63) and *USS Wisconsin* (BB 64) bombarded Iraqi coastal positions, and later provided naval gunfire support (NGFS) to advancing Coalition units. Naval aircraft destroyed Iraqi naval forces based in Kuwait and Al-Faw and conducted bombing attacks, which helped prepare the battlefield. Beginning in late January, SEALs conducted coastal reconnaissance. Finally, maritime forces ensured the continued flow of supplies and equipment to the Gulf coast ports, enabling the VII Corps and additional Marine forces to arrive. A detailed discussion of naval operations is in Chapter VII.

Roles of Non-US Coalition Forces

The various Coalition forces each had different abilities. The theater plans considered these differences and assigned roles and missions to achieve the best results. Final assignments of Arab-Islamic forces were coordinated between CINCCENT and Commander, Joint Forces/Theater of Operations. These missions considered the Arab-Islamic forces' relative capabilities, tactical mobility, and logistics supportability.

As the plan developed, CINCCENT redistributed missions. The 6th French Light Armored Division was placed under XVIII Airborne Corps tactical control (TACON); it was used to secure the theater's left flank. With the arrival of the remainder of the 1st UK Armoured Division from Germany, the 7th UK Armoured Brigade, attached to MARCENT, reverted to its parent unit. The 1st UK Armoured Division was placed under VII Corps TACON. To compensate for this loss in MARCENT's armor capability, the 1st (Tiger) Brigade, 2nd Armored Division was detached from the 1st Cavalry Division and attached to MARCENT.

Tactical Intelligence

Ground commanders at corps and below required as much information as possible about Iraqi forces and defensive positions, particularly along the Kuwait-Iraq border, where extensive minefields, complex obstacles, and interlocking defenses had to be breached. Deception and operations security (OPSEC) requirements precluded those same commanders from conducting intelligence collection operations to the depth of their respective areas of interest. As a result, the echelons above corps intelligence systems and organizations were tasked to provide detailed intelligence support to tactical commanders. At the same time, those sensors and organizations were expected to continue to provide intelligence support to other areas of vital US interests.

Competition for scarce and capable resources was intense and resulted in situations where requirements were not validated or were included in higher headquarters taskings. Sensors (particularly imagery) were unavailable or were incapable of being reoriented on short notice, and national-level analysts did not respond in the detail ground tactical commanders required.

Overall, intelligence organizations attempted to apply innovative solutions to difficult problems. Intelligence provided to ground tactical commanders from the theater and national levels was not always timely and often came in

unfamiliar formats. In confronting these difficulties, commanders often generated additional requests for information which, in turn, further taxed the over burdened theater and national intelligence systems. Consequently, ground tactical commanders were not confident with the tactical intelligence picture as G-Day approached.

Logistics

From the first day of Operation Desert Shield, the logistical effort was a major priority. Committed to a theater of operations without a broad, well-developed logistics infrastructure or transportation network, and lacking established alliance support relationships, US forces had to create these capabilities in the midst of a massive deployment, with the prospect of imminent combat.

Saudi air and sea ports are modern, sophisticated and complex, rivaling those of Europe and the Pacific in terms of capacity and capability. Major coastal roads and road systems around principal Saudi cities were also excellent. These provided a foundation which was critical to the overall effort. In contrast, the meager inland transportation system dictated a major road building effort and field logistics infrastructure development.

The ability to support and sustain the force was perhaps the most crucial operational consideration as CINCCENT planned the theater offensive. Massive logistics assets would have to be in place to support the ground offensive. Accordingly, two contingency plans were developed. The first was to shorten the LOC by building roads following the attacking corps. The second was a logistics over the shore operation, if a port in Kuwait could be made available. A base along the Kuwaiti coast, at Ash Shuaybah or farther north, would shorten logistics lines by hundreds of miles and enable supplies to be carried by sea from main bases in Al-Jubayl and Ad-Dammam.

Plan For Sustainment

The forces to be supported for the ground offensive were sizable. ARCENT, British, and French forces totaled 258,701 soldiers, 11,277 tracked vehicles, 47,449 wheeled vehicles, and 1,619 aircraft. In accordance with joint doctrine and agreements, ARCENT also retained responsibility for much of the theater logistics support of Air Force Component, Central Command (CENTAF) and MARCENT. In preparation for G-Day, 29.6 million meals, 36 million gallons of fuel, and 114.9 thousand tons of ammunition were moved from the port to forward positions west of Wadi Al-Batin. These supplies had to be moved in a very short period; however, to preserve security, logistics bases could not be set up west of the Wadi Al-Batin before air operations began.

The plan for logistical support and sustainment envisioned moving all classes of supplies, but especially fuel, ammunition, food, and water, forward to the ground forces as they pushed into Iraq. The corps support commands (COSCOM) in turn received and moved these supplies and equipment forward to the appropriate division support commands (DISCOM). The DISCOM then sent these supplies to the respective forward support battalions which supported the ground maneuver forces. The plan for theater logistics sustainment further called for support to be echeloned forward to temporary logistics bases, as the battle unfolded and tactical objectives were seized. Logistics planning and sustainment below the theater level were conducted according to established doctrine.

Establishment of Logistics Bases

The establishment of logistics bases was a key feature of the plan. CSS assets were required well forward and positioned to sustain the momentum of the attack once the ground offensive began. The bases had to be able to sustain the combat forces in their initial deployment areas and serve as intermediate storage areas for supplies to be moved to sites west of the Wadi Al-Batin. These sites

Forward Operating Logistics Base.

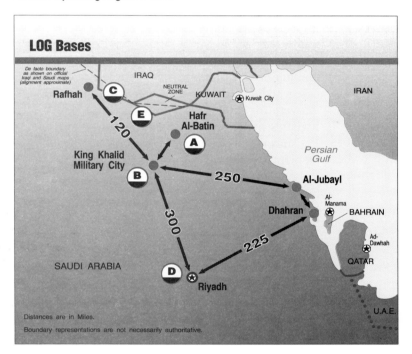

would, in turn, support operations into Iraq and Kuwait.

ARCENT established six sites to sustain the XVIII Airborne and VII Corps. In the I MEF area, four CSS areas were set up near the Kuwait border. All forward sites were stocked

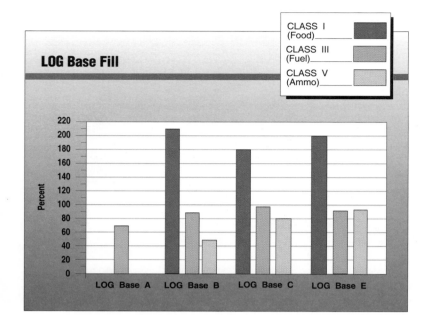

LOG Base Fill

Legend:
CLASS I (Food)
CLASS III (Fuel)
CLASS V (Ammo)

with bulk potable water, both bottled and from reverse osmosis water purification units, ammunition, equipment, food, petroleum, construction materials and spare parts for delivery forward as needed. At these forward logistics sites, the components organized logistics units to support and sustain forward elements according to their assigned missions.

ARCENT's 22d SUPCOM shifted vast quantities of supplies to these bases in the west. The supply bases contained enough materiel to support combat operations for up to 60 days. Some were moved several times, first to the west and then north once the operation began. Several lessons emerged from planning for this initial shift, including the fact that US forces lack sufficient heavy equipment transporters (HETs) and trucks with off-road capabilities. Just one of the five heavy divisions, the 24th Infantry Division (Mechanized), for example, needed 3,223 HET, 445 lowboys, and 509 flatbed loads to move its heavy equipment from forward assembly areas into attack positions. The problem was further complicated because units arrived at the ports at irregular intervals. While trucks could be surged to meet arriving

units, the limited road space upon which to move them remained constant. The necessary trucks were obtained with other Coalition countries' help. HNS, Coalition forces' support, and support from non-traditional allies, including the former Warsaw Pact nations, were substantial and essential. Although the Army sent considerable numbers of the most modern wheeled vehicles to the theater before Operation Desert Storm, off-road truck transport remained a problem throughout the ground offensive.

The extended maneuver of US ground combat units, characterized by rapid advance and continuous operations, was successfully sustained from the established logistics bases during the offensive. The greatest challenge for CSS operators at the logistics bases and supply operators with the maneuver units was trying to manage transportation assets effectively to ensure resupply across the rapidly expanding battlefield. Keeping the combat vehicles supplied with fuel was the greatest challenge. The Heavy Expanded Mobility Tactical Truck was one of the few vehicles that could keep going when rain turned roads into a quagmire. (Appendix F includes a further discussion of heavy equipment transporters.)

Joint Logistics

In addition to supporting Army elements, ARCENT supported the other CENTCOM components. ARCENT was responsible for food, water, bulk fuel, ground munitions, port operations, inland cargo transportation, construction support for all US forces and for graves registration after a Service exceeded its own organic capability.

Support for the Tiger Brigade attached to MARCENT for the ground offensive was an excellent example of how joint logistics was managed. The USMC system is not structured to support and maintain an Army brigade equipped with M1A1 tanks and M2/M3 fighting vehicles. To meet this requirement, back-up direct support and general support was provided through a provisional forward area support company tailored from elements of the ARCENT 593rd Area Support Group and the 176th Maintenance Battalion. These elements augmented the brigade's direct support battalion and operated with the USMC 1st FSSG. The relationship between the Army forward area support operations and the USMC logistics structure provided the necessary support to the brigade.

MARCENT Logistics

CSS in the MARCENT sector was equally challenging. Organized and equipped to conduct operations relatively close to the shore, the 1st FSSG operated more than 50 miles inland and 100 miles from its main supply base at Al-Jubayl. As an innovative partial solution, Marine Reservists, primarily from the 6th Motor Transport Battalion, formed "Saudi Motors", a collection of several hundred drivers with commercial trucks provided by the Saudis to link Al-Jubayl with the forward logistics sites. Marine assault support helicopters shuttled back and forth between the rear and forward logistics sites, carrying cargo and delivering high priority items. I MEF requested and received some direct support line haul, transportation and theater level fuel support in the form of HETs, fuel tankers and other motor transport assets from 22nd SUPCOM.

To support the tactical units, 1st FSSG divided itself into general support and direct support groups, with mobile service support detachments providing support to each assault regiment or task force. This decentralized structure let 1st FSSG distribute supplies from Al-Jubayl directly to front-line units without a cumbersome intervening support organization. Each level operated to help the next element forward. Although not a part of USMC doctrine, this innovative organization of the service support structure may have been one of the more successful aspects of the ground campaign. I MEF supported its combat forces at distances far exceeding those anticipated in

peacetime, and given the volumes of supplies and speed of advance, Marine logistics abilities were stretched to the limits.

The Final Operational Plan

The final CINCCENT ground offensive plan involved several interrelated operations. ARCENT would lead the main effort. XVIII Airborne Corps would attack in the west and deep into Iraq to control the east-west LOC along Highway 8 and cut off Iraqi forces in the KTO. VII Corps would conduct the main Coalition effort, attacking east of XVIII Airborne Corps and west of Wadi Al-Batin, driving to the north and then east to destroy Republican Guard forces. VII Corps adjusted its plan by calling an "audible" during a CPX conducted 6-8 January 1991, to move two armored divisions and a cavalry regiment to the west to take advantage of a gap in the Iraqi defenses. This was made possible when the 1st Cavalry Division was made OPCON to VII Corps to prevent a Khafji-type attack by Iraqi forces into Hafir Al Batin. VII Corps moved the 1st Cavalry Division to prevent an Iraqi attack and to fix Iraqi forces in place to allow the envelopment to take place.

On the right flank, JFC-N, MARCENT, and JFC-E, would hold the enemy's tactical and operational forces in place by breaching Iraqi defenses in Kuwait and encircling Iraqi forces in the heel of Kuwait and Kuwait City. JFC-N would block Iraqi LOC north of Kuwait City. MARCENT would destroy enemy forces and seize key objectives southeast of Al-Jahra. MARCENT also would protect JFC-N's right flank. Navy and Marine forces in the Gulf would create a deception through amphibious exercises and feints before and during the ground offensive. JFC-E would protect MARCENT's right flank by destroying Iraqi forces and securing key objectives along the coast. Once Kuwait City was encircled and Iraqi forces were ejected or defeated, Arab-Islamic forces from both JFC-E and JFC-N, would

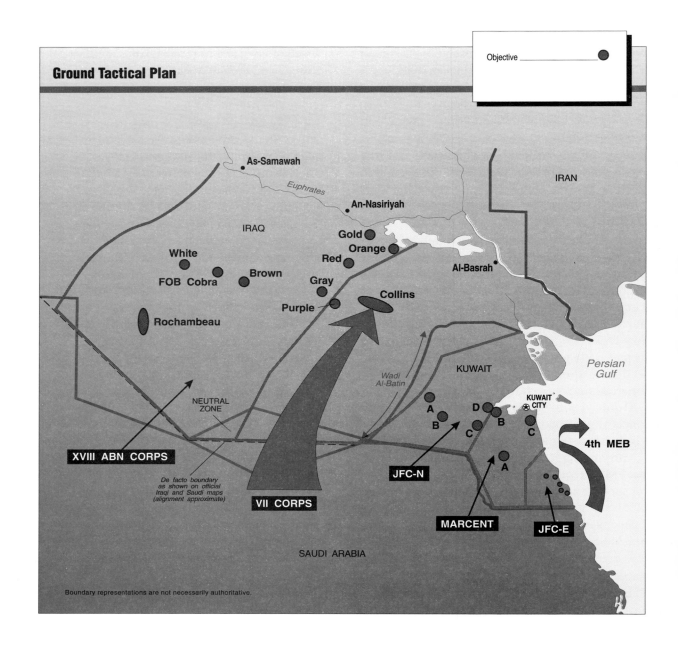

Ground Tactical Plan

Objective ●

As-Samawah

Euphrates

An-Nasiriyah

IRAQ

Gold
Orange

White
Red

FOB Cobra
Brown
Gray

Al-Basrah

Purple
Collins

IRAN

Rochambeau

Persian Gulf

KUWAIT

Wadi Al-Batin

KUWAIT CITY

NEUTRAL ZONE

A
B
D
C
B
C

4th MEB

XVIII ABN CORPS

De facto boundary as shown on official Iraqi and Saudi maps (alignment approximate)

JFC-N

A

VII CORPS

MARCENT

JFC-E

SAUDI ARABIA

Boundary representations are not necessarily authoritative.

liberate Kuwait City. CINCCENT initially designated the 1st Cavalry Division from Fort Hood, TX, as the theater reserve.

To further confuse the Iraqis and perhaps draw off tactical and operational reserves, the ground offensive was to be sequenced. The XVIII Airborne Corps' 6th French Light Armor Division, 82nd Airborne Division, and the 101st Airborne Division (Air Assault) would attack at 0400 on G-Day, in the general direction of Baghdad and the lower Euphrates River to secure the left flank of the main attack. The Marines would attack at the same time, followed by the JFC-E on the coast. The I MEF's specific mission was to attack into Kuwait west of Al-Wafrah to hold and destroy Iraqi forces to their front, hold Iraqi tactical and operational reserves to prevent reinforcement of Iraqi forces in the West, block Iraqi forces' retreat from southeast Kuwait and Kuwait City and help Arab forces enter Kuwait City. The theater main effort, the VII Corps, was not intended to begin until G+1, followed an hour later by an attack from JFC-N forces.

The main attack was designed to avoid most fixed defenses, drive deep into Iraq, envelop Iraqi forces from the west and attack and destroy Saddam Hussein's strategic reserve — Republican Guard armored and mechanized infantry divisions augmented by several other Iraqi Army heavy divisions. This wide left sweep, sometimes referred to as the "Hail Mary" plan, emphasized the key tenets of AirLand Battle doctrine. Accurate intelligence, air supremacy, the reduction of combat power by air operations and technological advantages, such as the Small Lightweight Global Positioning System Receivers (SLGRs) sent to the theater during the six-month buildup prior to the offensive, made it possible to cross the desert undetected and effectively apply overwhelming ground combat power from a direction and in a way the Iraqis did not expect.

During the operation, some adjustments were made to the original ground offensive plan. The most significant alteration was the acceleration of the time for the main attack. The high rate of advance by I MEF, JFC-E, and the XVIII Airborne Corps let CINCCENT accelerate the time table for the operation. As a result, VII Corps crossed the line of departure 15 hours ahead of schedule. In addition, after it was apparent the attack by JFC-N was proceeding satisfactorily, the 1st Cavalry Division was released from theater reserve and attached to the VII Corps on Tuesday morning, 26 February. The 1st Cavalry Division moved rapidly around the VII Corps left flank and was in position to conduct the northern assault of the planned corps double envelopment.

Posturing for the Attack

Repositioning of I Marine Expeditionary Force

Because I MEF's area of responsibility had shifted away from the coast, its assault would be conducted through the defenses covering Ahmad Al-Jabir Airfield west of Al-Wafrah. To support this move, supply points at Al-Mish'ab and along the coast had to be moved to newly constructed bases at Al-Kibrit and Al-Khanjar. Two expeditionary airfields and a helicopter complex were built at Al-Khanjar while the existing dirt strip at Al-Kibrit was improved to handle C-130s to support the ground attack. The two divisions leapfrogged past each other, placing the 1st MARDIV on the right and 2nd MARDIV on the left. This simultaneous movement of nearly 60,000 Marines and all their equipment was accomplished using a single dirt road that stretched across 100 miles of desert. Difficult to execute under the best peacetime conditions, the shift was carried out while I MEF elements remained in direct contact with enemy forces.

Once in assembly areas, assault units honed their skills by conducting extensive training and rehearsals. Full scale mock-ups of breach areas were constructed. New engineer equipment arrived, to include armored combat earthmovers and mine-clearing plows loaned by the Army.

The Shift West of ARCENT Forces

Throughout December, the 22nd SUPCOM shifted supplies from the ports to bases near King Khalid Military City. From 17 January to 24 February, while the Coalition air forces waged the air operation, VII Corps, XVIII Airborne Corps, and other coalition elements moved more than 270,000 troops and supplies into position for the attack. XVIII Airborne Corps displaced approximately 260 miles and VII Corps maneuvered west over 150 miles in the same tactical formations that it would use to attack from south to north. This was done

Convoy During the Shift of Forces.

with the near continuous flow of fighters to targets in Iraq. The C-130s averaged a takeoff and landing out of King Fahd International Airport every seven minutes, 24 hours a day, for the first 13 days of the move.

Once forces were at Rafha, the C-130s helped build up the supplies, combat replacements, and the logistics bases. At log base Charlie, the combat engineers blocked a one mile strip of the Trans Arabian Pipeline (Tapline) Road to serve as an airstrip. Only nine miles from the Iraqi border, it was essential to get in and out quickly. Perhaps the most important cargo delivered was fuel. Aircraft equipped with special bladders brought in more than 5,000 gallons of fuel on each lift and pumped it into waiting fuel trucks.

Preparing and Shaping the Battlefield

Preparation and shaping of the battlefield is intended to seize the initiative from the enemy, forcing him to fight in accordance with your plan rather than his, thus allowing the attacker to exploit the enemy's weaknesses and to maneuver more freely on the battlefield. The concept of preparation and shaping entails two aspects — physical degradation of the enemy's capabilities and psychological operations to

without HETs and was a corps level rehearsal for the actual attack. This movement, which continued 24 hours a day for more than three weeks before the start of the ground war, was one of the largest and longest movements of combat forces in history. The total number of personnel and amount of equipment exceeded that moved by General George S. Patton during his attack into the German flank at the Battle of the Bulge. Whole divisions and extensive support structures moved hundreds of miles, undetected by the Iraqis. The move was conducted on largely unimproved roads. The road network not only made repositioning physically difficult, but also complicated movement management. To avoid massive traffic jams, movement schedules were worked out to the last detail. In the dense traffic, vehicles were moving at 15 second intervals.

The tactical airlift fleet also supported the westward shift. C-130s established air tactical routings to Rafha, the XVIII Airborne Corps' destination, from airfields near the Corps rear staging areas. These routings were established at low altitudes to ensure the movement would not be detected by the Iraqis and to deconflict them

Combined Arms Forces Move Forward During Combat Operations.

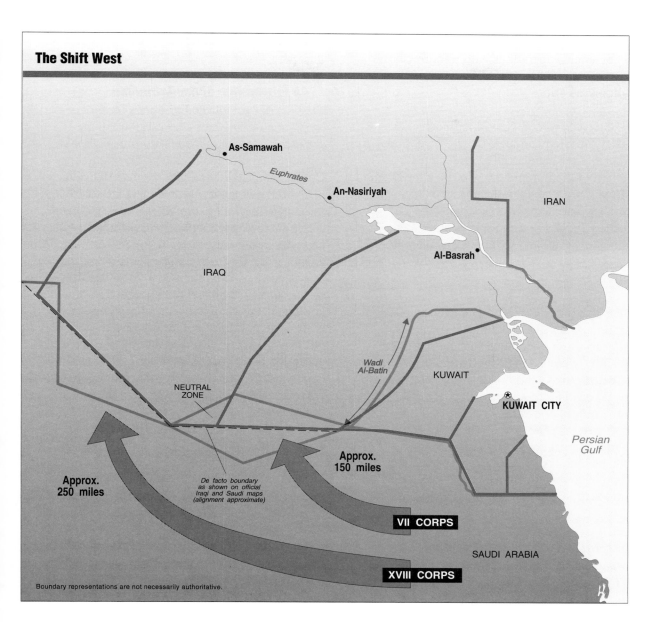

The Shift West

As-Samawah

Euphrates

An-Nasiriyah

IRAN

Al-Basrah

IRAQ

Wadi Al-Batin

KUWAIT

NEUTRAL ZONE

⊛ KUWAIT CITY

Persian Gulf

Approx. 250 miles

De facto boundary as shown on official Iraqi and Saudi maps (alignment approximate)

Approx. 150 miles

VII CORPS

SAUDI ARABIA

XVIII CORPS

Boundary representations are not necessarily authoritative.

deceive and demoralize the enemy. Both are carried out throughout the depth of the battlefield. Physical degradation requires extensive use of supporting arms and raids, both ground and air, to attack and destroy enemy abilities to conduct operations. PSYOPS attack the enemy's will to fight and deceive him, thereby forcing him to react to, rather than anticipate the actions of the attacker. Coalition air and ground forces extensively prepared and shaped the battlefield.

Deception Operations

CINCCENT placed a high priority on deception operations which were intended to convince Iraq that the main attack would be directly into Kuwait, supported by an amphibious assault. All components contributed to the deception operation. Aggressive ground force patrolling, artillery raids, amphibious feints and ship movements, and air operations all were part of CINCCENT's orchestrated deception operation. Throughout, ground force units engaged in reconnaissance and counter-reconnaissance operations with Iraqi forces to deny the Iraqis information about actual Coalition intentions.

For 30 days before the ground offensive, the 1st Cavalry Division conducted aggressive feints, demonstrations, and artillery raids in the direction of the Iraqi defenses nearest the Wadi Al-Batin. These activities reinforced the deception that the main attack would be launched directly north into Western Kuwait. It also held five infantry divisions and an armored division in place, well away from the actual VII Corps zone of attack.

I MEF also implemented a detailed deception operation. A series of combined arms raids, similar to those conducted in January, drew Iraqi fire, while PSYOP loud speakers broadcast across the border. For 10 days, Task Force (TF) Troy, consisting of infantry, armor, reconnaissance, engineers, Seabees and Army PSYOPS created the impression of a much larger force, engaging enemy elements in the Al-Wafrah area, conducting deceptive communications, and building dummy positions.

These operations complemented the deception effort carried out by amphibious forces off Kuwait's coast. The amphibious task force (ATF), assigned the mission of deceiving the Iraqis into expecting an assault against Kuwait, and conducting that assault should it become necessary, began posturing in the Gulf in mid-January. A well publicized amphibious rehearsal in Oman attracted media attention in the end of January while, simultaneously, Marines from the 13th Marine Expeditionary Unit (Special Operations Capable) conducted a raid on tiny Umm Al-Maradim Island off the Kuwait coast. As the ground offensive approached, the ATF moved into the northern Gulf, conspicuously preparing for a possible assault. Overall, the deception operation was key to achieving both tactical and operational surprise and, ultimately, the ground offensive's success.

Air Preparation of the Battlefield

CINCCENT established priorities for air preparation of the battlefield. Although the ground commanders made recommendations regarding targets and timing of the operation, CINCCENT aligned it with the overall theater plan. Ground tactical commanders found this discomforting, since they were most concerned about the forces immediately to their front and had only limited information on how CINCCENT was using air power to shape the entire theater. Additionally, by CINCCENT direction, air operations did not initially emphasize destruction of front line Iraqi forces in the KTO until just before the ground offensive. This was done in part to enhance the deception plan. This also concerned the ground commanders, who naturally wanted air power to degrade the Iraqi units immediately in their line of advance.

Coalition air forces flew more than 35,000 sorties against KTO targets, including more than 5,600 against the Republican Guards Forces Command (RGFC). The Service components nominated targets, but CINCCENT apportioned sorties, and the Joint Force Air Component Commander tasked them. Artillery, CPs, C^2 facilities, armor, and logistics installations were hit repeatedly. As the ground war approached, the percentage of sorties allocated to the destruction of Iraqi forces in the KTO increased.

In preparation for ground attacks in the eastern portion of the KTO, 3rd MAW used primarily AV-8Bs and F/A-18s to attack targets inside Kuwait. Priority was given to locating and destroying enemy artillery, armor and troops in the central and southern parts of Kuwait. Marine aviation intensified its attacks in Kuwait as the date for the ground offensive approached. By mid-February, 3rd MAW was used almost totally to prepare the battlefield. Aircraft were kept on continuous alert to provide immediate

CAS, and to respond to enemy sightings, artillery attacks and Iraqi cross-border incursions.

Ground Preparation of the Battlefield

Iraqi artillery was a primary objective in the battlefield preparation. Iraqi artillery, modern by any standard, often out-ranged Coalition guns, and had been effective in the Iran-Iraq war. While the Coalition could hold Iraqi maneuver forces in position; left unchecked, Iraqi artillery alone might disrupt the Coalition ground assault. Properly used, enemy artillery could have delayed breaching operations long enough for some Iraqi units to counterattack. Additionally, there was a real concern that Iraqi commanders might use artillery-delivered chemical weapons. Accordingly, Iraqi artillery, particularly their most modern systems, were high priority targets during Phase III of the theater campaign. Air, attack helicopters, and Multiple-Launch Rocket Systems (MLRS) were used to destroy enemy artillery. 3rd MAW AV-8Bs and F/A-18s, assisted by Marine unmanned aerial vehicles (UAVs) and airborne FACs, searched out batteries for destruction. The Army and Marines also conducted many artillery raids to destroy Iraqi artillery.

Reconnaissance and Counter-Reconnaissance

During the air campaign, ground forces conducted extensive reconnaissance to determine the extent and locations of Iraqi obstacles and defensive positions and counter-reconnaissance operations to deceive the enemy regarding Coalition forces disposition. Ground forces conducted raids, patrols, feints and long-range reconnaissance.

Both air and ground maneuver benefited from Army aviation reconnaissance in depth. Attack, scout, and special operations aircraft performed repetitive armed reconnaissance missions in each division zone for days before the ground offensive. Even with the array of deep acquisition platforms, one of the most

> **D**uring night operations, 30 January, the 24th Infantry Division's Apache attack helicopter battalion, conducting reconnaissance, found an electronic warfare site with their long-range optics. Early in the morning of 31 January, the Battalion Commander ordered Apache A Company across the border to attack it. "It was a great start for the Apaches and a successful raid," the battalion commander said.
>
> *The US Army Aviation Center*

reliable and timely sources of battlefield information for tactical commanders was human source intelligence (HUMINT) provided by aviation.

Another innovative approach was the extensive use of helicopters to locate Iraqi observation posts and CPs. Flying at night, Army and Marine observation and attack helicopters found and destroyed these positions using Hellfire and other laser-designated munitions such as Copperhead. The same tactics proved effective for air defense sites, and contributed to joint suppression of enemy air defense activities.

On the left flank, in the days immediately before the ground offensive XVIII Airborne Corps conducted aerial and mounted raids deep into Iraqi territory to hit armor, artillery, bunkers, and observation posts. The XVIII Airborne Corps reported, that in one armed aerial reconnaissance operation on 20 February, the 101st Airborne Division (Air Assault) aviation brigade destroyed 15 bunkers with air and TOW missile fire and induced 476 Iraqis to surrender. The division, with attack helicopter support, sent CH-47 Chinook helicopters and troops forward to gather the EPWs. By 22 February, 82nd Airborne Division helicopters were penetrating deep into Iraqi territory in daylight.

In the VII Corps area, in preparation for the attack, the 2nd ACR pushed 15 kilometers into Iraq to cover engineers cutting openings in the border berm. Just before the ground offensive, VII Corps reports show that the 1st Infantry

Division (Mechanized) engaged 20 Iraqi tanks and killed several enemy soldiers patrolling the border.

SOF operated deep in enemy territory and along the coast, reporting enemy disposition and activities. Early in the crisis, the 5th Special Forces Group (SFG), (Airborne) in cooperation with Saudi paratroopers, had manned observation posts and conducted patrols along the Kuwaiti border to provide early warning of an Iraqi attack. 3rd SFG (A) carried out valuable long-range patrols north of the border. One team used low-light cameras and probing equipment to determine if the terrain north of the border would support armored vehicles. Others, including the British Special Air Service (SAS), watched suspected Iraqi reinforcement routes and searched for Scud launchers. SEALS conducted reconnaissance operations along the coast to determine enemy dispositions and to clear mines.

In mid-January, I MEF established observation and signal intelligence collection posts along the Kuwait border to try to locate enemy defenses and concentrations. Reconnaissance teams and light armored vehicles kept a watchful eye on the border while screening the forward movement of the 1st and 2nd MARDIVs. The Iraqis reacted quickly; on 17 January, forward elements of 1st Surveillance Reconnaissance and Intelligence Group at Al-Khafji received artillery fire. Marine AV-8Bs on strip alert at King 'Abd Al-'Aziz Expeditionary Airfield in northern Saudi Arabia were launched to silence the Iraqi artillery. On 19 January, several Iraqi soldiers crossed the border and surrendered to Marines, the first prisoners the MEF took.

Beginning 20 January, and continuing for the next 10 days, I MEF conducted combined arms raids along the Kuwaiti border. These raids were designed to deceive the enemy as to the location and disposition of Coalition forces, focus attention toward Kuwait, keep the Iraqis

AH-64 Apache Helicopters Returning From a Combat Mission. *Note: Aircraft on right has Hellfire missiles, aircraft on left has expended its ordnance.*

off-balance, and test their response. Marines manning outposts along the border continued to call on AV-8Bs to conduct counterbattery attacks, while UAVs flying from Al-Mish'ab located targets. Although air operations over Iraq absorbed much of the world's attention, the Kuwaiti border had become a scene of active fighting.

As the ground offensive approached, I MEF increased reconnaissance and surveillance, both to deny enemy intelligence collection and to gain a more accurate picture of his dispositions. Reconnaissance teams from both 1st and 2nd MARDIV crossed the border and moved into Kuwait a week before the attack. Elements of two regimental sized task forces from 1st MARDIV began infiltrating on the night of 21 February and during the next two nights, remaining hidden and largely undetected during the day. These elements eliminated Iraqi forward observers, cleared minefield lanes, and positioned themselves to support the mechanized task forces when they attacked on the morning of 24 February.

In the 2nd MARDIV sector, conditions differed markedly. Only a few kilometers separated its attack positions from the Iraqi defenses. The two defensive lines were only two to three kilometers apart and intertwined within the Umm Qudayr oilfields. Obstacles included forward outposts, berms, and fire trenches in addition to the minefields and trenchlines. Before G-Day, the 2nd MARDIV's 2nd Light Armored Infantry (LAI) Battalion crossed into Kuwait on a three-day operation to clear Iraqi outposts and defenses forward of the first obstacle belt.

The Battle of Al-Khafji and Contact at Al-Wafrah

On 29 January, attention abruptly shifted from air operations to the JFC-E and Marine areas. Iraqi armored forces launched cross-border attacks, the most newsworthy at Al-Khafji. However, a second attack, directed at the area south and west of Al-Wafrah, engaged I MEF's TF Shepherd. A young Marine corporal in the 2nd LAI Battalion scored a TOW antitank missile kill in the dark from more than 3,000 meters as a T-55 tank emerged through the border berm, blocking the exit and halting further Iraqi advance. The next day, the 6th Marine Regiment rushed northward and dug in south of Al-Wafrah, ending any Iraqi threat in that sector, although sporadic artillery fire continued for several days.

At Al-Khafji, Arab forces, supported by Marine forward observers, who called and adjusted artillery and CAS, pushed invading Iraqi columns back into Kuwait. At the height of the fighting, a Marine reconnaissance team, cut off in the town and cornered on the roof of a building, continued to report enemy movements and call in air and artillery fires. These battles proved costly to the Iraqis while instilling new confidence in the Coalition and providing

Marines combat experience. (See Chapter 6 for details on air operations at Al-Khafji.)

The Threat as of 23 February — the Day Before the Ground Offensive

Iraqi Defensive Positions and Plan

As discussed earlier, the Iraqi Army was prepared to defend the KTO. Operational and tactical level plans existed, preparations for contingencies were made and executed, and, while some units in the forward areas were composed of second class troops, many Iraqi regular and heavy units put up a fight. The Iraqi defensive strategy, however, was not prepared for the Coalition's offensive strategy. The Iraqi assumption that the tactics used in the Iran-Iraq War would be applicable against the Coalition proved faulty, as did their assumption that the attack would be terrain-oriented in support of the Coalition's political goal of liberating Kuwait. Further, once the air war began, Iraqi tactical intelligence became virtually blind. Most importantly, Iraqi defensive planning was rendered ineffective due to the speed, maneuver, firepower, and technological advantages of the Coalition offensive, which surprised and overwhelmed the Iraqis.

The Iraqis prepared for the expected assault into Kuwait in a manner that reflected the successes of their defensive strategy during the Iranian War. They constructed two major defensive belts in addition to extensive fortifications and obstacles along the coast. The first belt paralleled the border roughly five to 15 kilometers inside Kuwait and was composed of continuous minefields varying in width from 100 to 200 meters, with barbed wire, antitank ditches, berms, and oil filled trenches intended to cover key avenues of approach. Covering the first belt were Iraqi platoon and company-size strongpoints designed to provide early warning and delay any attacker attempting to cut through.

The second obstacle belt, up to 20 kilometers

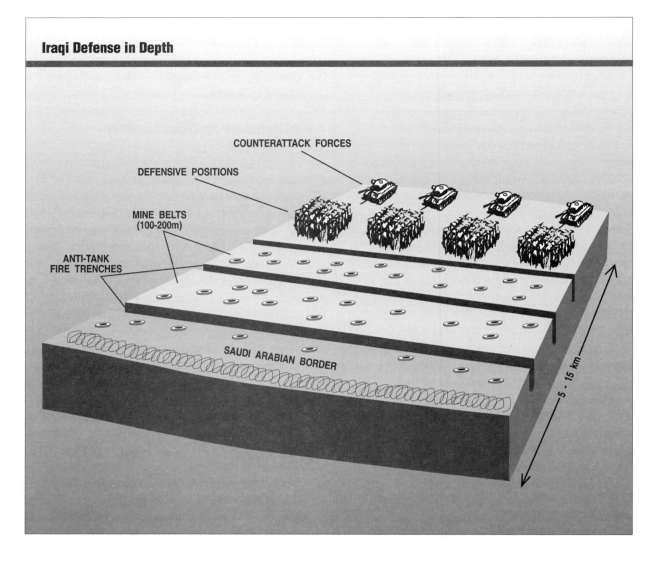

Iraqi Defense in Depth

COUNTERATTACK FORCES

DEFENSIVE POSITIONS

MINE BELTS
(100-200m)

ANTI-TANK
FIRE TRENCHES

SAUDI ARABIAN BORDER

5 - 15 km

behind the first, began north of Al-Khafji and proceeded northwest of the Al-Wafrah oilfields until it joined with the first near Al-Manaqish. This second obstacle belt actually constituted the main Iraqi defensive line in Kuwait. Obstacles and minefields mirrored those of the first belt. They were covered by an almost unbroken line of mutually supporting brigade-sized defensive positions composed of company trench lines and strongpoints. The minefields contained both antitank and antipersonnel mines.

The Iraqi tactical plan was designed to slow the attacker at the first belt, to trap him in

prearranged kill zones between the two belts, and to destroy him before he could break through the second belt. Any attacking forces able to breach the second belt would be counterattacked immediately behind the strongpoints by division and corps level armor reserves.

Iraqi Combat Effectiveness

One objective of the initial phases of the theater campaign was to shift the balance of forces more in favor of the Coalition; this goal was achieved. In all, almost 100,000 total combat and support sorties were flown and

288 Tomahawk land-attack missiles launched during the first three phases of the campaign. Of the total sorties flown, 60 percent were combat missions. Damage to Iraqi forces was extensive, and Iraqi C2 was severely degraded. Saddam Hussein's ability to direct his fielded forces was impeded and in many cases, forward corps, division and brigade commanders lost touch with their subordinate commands. Large amounts of equipment were damaged or destroyed. Vast stockpiles of Iraqi supplies, positioned to support the KTO, were destroyed and the road nets on which replenishment had to pass were degraded. Air operations against fielded forces, in conjunction with PSYOPS, helped sap Iraqi morale. Phase III of the campaign greatly reduced Saddam Hussein's ability to bring the

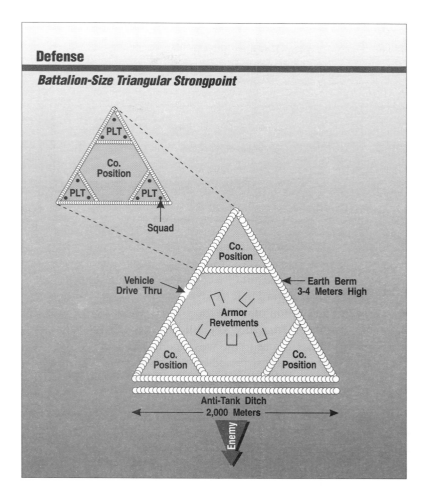

Defense

Battalion-Size Triangular Strongpoint

Oil Ditch that Iraqis Planned to Ignite as an Obstacle.

strength of his army to bear against the Coalition ground forces.

At the end of more than a month of bombardment, Iraqi forces remained in Kuwait; many, particularly in the front line units, were in poor condition, with their ability to coordinate an effective defense along the border severely reduced. When the ground war started, CINCCENT assessed that, largely through the results of the Coalition air operation, the overall combat effectiveness of the opposing Iraqi forces had been reduced by about half.

It should be noted that while the forward infantry divisions suffered high attrition, a substantial portion of the more capable units, such as the Republican Guards, and Iraqi

Iraqi Buildup in KTO

As of 15 January 1991:

- Over 545,000 Iraqi Troops in Kuwait Theater
- Approximately 43 Divisions
- Estimate: 4,280 Tanks
              3,100 Artillery
              2,800 APCS

armored and infantry divisions to the west and north, still were combat effective. This was, in part, the result of a conscious decision to target the forward defensive positions as a part of the deception plan. As the ground offensive unfolded, many Republican Guards units and other forces to the west and north, even though they were surprised by the advancing Coalition formations, retained much of their combat capability and put up a fight.

Iraqi Disposition and Strength in Theater Before the Ground Offensive

The build-up of Iraqi forces in the KTO as estimated by DIA on 15 January 1991, just before Operation Desert Storm began, had reached more than 540,000 troops.

DIA intelligence assessments of enemy attrition and disposition before the ground offensive began indicated the combat effectiveness of all first-line defensive divisions were reduced to less than half. The 45th Mechanized Division south of As-Salman was estimated to be at 50 to 75 percent strength as were the 12th, 52nd, 17th and 10th Armored divisions, the tactical reserves. The two most western Republican Guards divisions, the Tawakalna Mechanized and Al-Madinah Armored divisions, were estimated to be at 50 to 75 percent effectiveness. The general assessment was that the tactical echelon and artillery were severely degraded, the operational echelon's sustainment capability had been

eliminated, and the Republican Guard somewhat degraded.

Iraqi ground forces in the KTO included elements of up to 43 divisions, 25 of which were assessed as committed, 10 the operational reserve, and eight the strategic reserve. Some independent brigades were operating under corps control. The RGFC and Iraqi Army heavy divisions remained deployed in defensive positions behind the tactical and operational forces. On the eve of the ground offensive, the Iraqi forces were arrayed on the ground.

Despite these assessments, the Iraqi military's weaknesses were not so apparent to the ground commanders. They saw an Iraqi force of up to 43 divisions in the theater, arrayed in depth and with strong operational and tactical reserves. Dug-in infantry was reinforced by revetted tanks and artillery, all backed by armored reserves of brigade strength or larger. In central Kuwait, roughly in the area between 'Ali As-Salim airfield and the Kuwait International Airport, one armored and two mechanized divisions formed strong corps-level reserves, with additional armored forces to the northwest of Al-Jahra. Along the beaches, in testimony to the Iraqi fear of an amphibious assault, no fewer than four infantry divisions and a mechanized division occupied positions behind minefields and obstacles. Finally, along the Iraq-Kuwait border, at least six Republican Guards divisions and other armored, mechanized, and infantry divisions were poised to counterattack. On the eve of the ground offensive, Coalition planners thought nearly 450,000 Iraqi troops remained in the KTO.

Weather

Weather was a factor during the entire campaign. Approximately 15 percent of all scheduled attack sorties during the first 10 days of air operations were canceled because of poor visibility or low overcast in the KTO. Ceilings of 5,000 to 7,000 feet were not

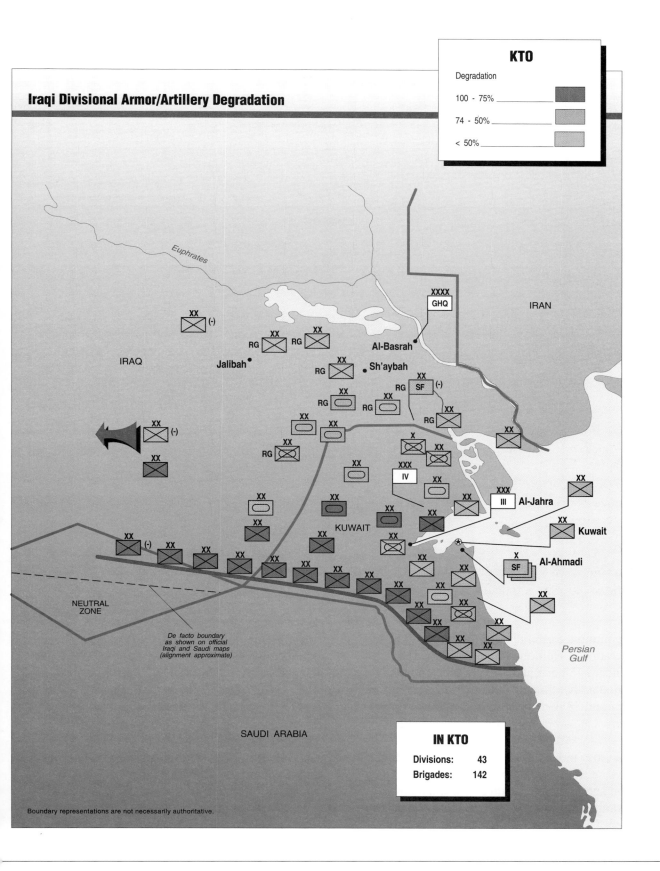

Iraqi Divisional Armor/Artillery Degradation

KTO

Degradation

100 - 75% _____

74 - 50% _____

< 50% _____

IRAN

Euphrates

XXXX
GHQ

XX (-)

RG XX RG XX

IRAQ

Jalibah

Al-Basrah

RG XX Sh'aybah

XX
RG SF (-)

XX
RG

XX
RG

RG XX

XX
RG

XX (-)

XX

RG XX

XX

X

XXX
IV

X

III Al-Jahra

XX

KUWAIT

XX Kuwait

XXX

X
SF Al-Ahmadi

XX (-) XX XX XX XX

XX

NEUTRAL
ZONE

De facto boundary
as shown on official
Iraqi and Saudi maps
(alignment approximate)

Persian
Gulf

SAUDI ARABIA

IN KTO

Divisions: 43
Brigades: 142

Boundary representations are not necessarily authoritative.

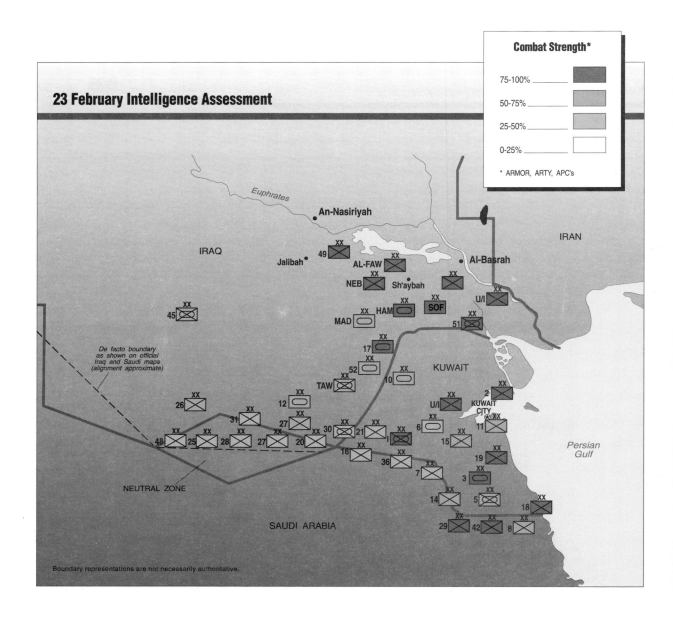

23 February Intelligence Assessment

Combat Strength*

75-100% _____

50-75% _____

25-50% _____

0-25% _____

* ARMOR, ARTY, APC's

uncommon, especially during the ground operation. Coalition planners assumed the standard 13 percent cloud cover, typical for the region at that time of year. In fact, cloud cover persisted 39 percent of the time, the worst in 14 years.

The early morning of G-Day was marked by adverse weather throughout the area. Blowing sand and rain, along with dense smoke from burning oil wells, made visibility extremely poor. These conditions early in the ground

operation improved the US technical advantage in electro-optics. At the same time, it inhibited CAS and proved the value of the Joint Surveillance Target Attack Radar System (JSTARS) as both an operational indicator of enemy movement and a deep targeting system. The bad weather at the beginning of the attack also threatened sustainability by making cross-country mobility difficult for wheeled logistics vehicles. Fortunately, the skies cleared and the cease-fire was declared before serious sustainment problems developed.

Disposition of Coalition Forces on the Eve of the Ground Offensive

When the ground offensive began, Coalition forces were poised along a line from the Persian Gulf 300 miles west into the desert, in four major formations.

Army Component, Central Command

ARCENT, which consisted of the XVIII Airborne Corps and VII Corps, was on the western flank of the theater. Positioned on ARCENT's left flank was the XVIII Airborne Corps; VII Corps was to the right. These two corps covered about two thirds of the line occupied by the multi-national force.

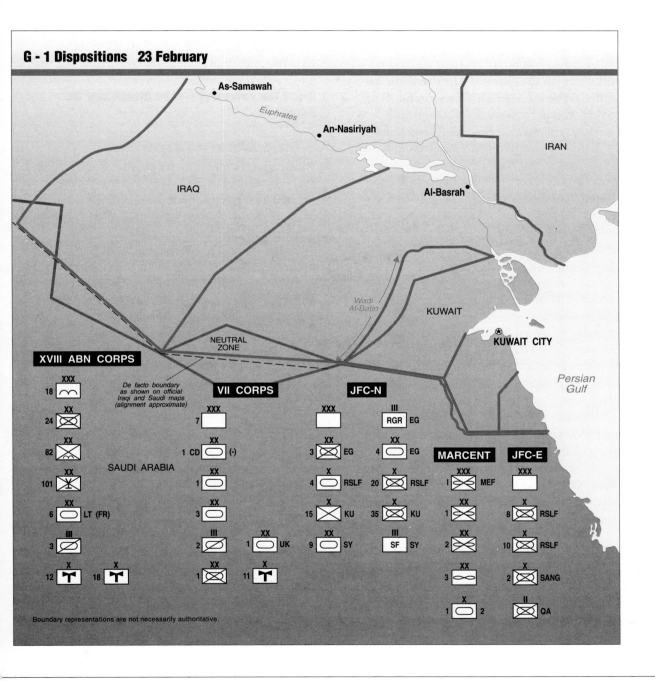

G - 1 Dispositions 23 February

Joint Forces Command — North

JFC-N, in the center, consisted of the 3rd Egyptian Mechanized Division, the 4th Egyptian Armored Division, the 9th Syrian Division, the Egyptian Ranger Regiment, the Syrian Special Forces Regiment, the 20th Mechanized Brigade, Royal Saudi Land Forces (RSLF), the Kuwaiti Ash-Shahid and Al-Tahrir Brigades, and the 4th Armored Brigade (RSLF).

I Marine Expeditionary Force

I MEF, on the right of JFC-N, had the 2nd MARDIV, with the attached Tiger Brigade on the left and the 1st MARDIV on the right. The 5th MEB, coming ashore at Al-Jubayl and Al-Mish'ab and staging near Al-Khanjar, acted as the MEF reserve. 3rd MAW flew from bases in Saudi Arabia and Bahrain, basing AV-8Bs and attack helicopters forward at Tanajib and Al-Khanjar, respectively.

Joint Forces Command — East

On the right flank, along the coast, JFC-E anchored the Coalition line. Like JFC-N, JFC-E was under the command of Saudi Lieutenant General Khalid bin Sultan. JFC-E consisted of units from all six Gulf Cooperation Council (GCC) member states. There were three task forces — TF Omar, consisting of the 10th Infantry Brigade (RSLF) and an United Arab Emirates (UAE) Motorized Infantry Battalion; TF Othman, consisting of the 8th Mechanized Infantry Brigade (RSLF) an Omani Motorized Infantry Battalion, Bahrain Infantry Company, and the Kuwaiti Al-Fatah Brigade; TF Abu Bakr with the 2nd Saudi Arabian National Guard (SANG) Motorized Infantry Brigade and a Qatar Mechanized Battalion.

CONDUCT OF THE GROUND OFFENSIVE

At 0400 24 February, the ground assault to liberate Kuwait began. CENTCOM unleashed combined arms attacks against Iraqi forces at three points. In the far west, the French 6th Light Armored Division, (with the 2nd Brigade, 82nd Airborne Division under its operational control) , and 101st Airborne Division (Air Assault) conducted a massive air and ground envelopment to secure the Coalition western flank and establish forward support bases deep in Iraq. In the center of the Coalition line, along the Wadi Al-Batin, the dry ravine that separates Kuwait from Iraq, the 1st Cavalry Division, the theater reserve, feinted an attack north toward a heavy Iraqi concentration. In the east, I MEF and JFC-E, attacked north into Kuwait.

G-Day (24 February) — The Attack and the Breach

Enemy Actions and Dispositions

When the ground offensive started, Iraqi ground forces remained in defensive positions in the KTO. There were no indications of any Iraqi troop withdrawal. Iraqi front line units, including the 7th, 14th and 29th Infantry divisions in the I MEF zone and the 19th Infantry Division in the JFC-E zone, offered sporadic, but sometimes stiff, resistance. These forces were bypassed, withdrew or surrendered. Despite these initial setbacks, the Iraqi III Corps, opposite I MEF and JFC-E and the Iraqi IV Corps, generally opposite JFC-N, still could counterattack with units from the 3rd Armored Division south of Kuwait International Airport. However, the large number of III Corps soldiers surrendering suggested many had lost the will to fight. For the Iraqis to stop the Coalition ground offensive, mobile forces would have to leave their revetted positions, making them vulnerable to Coalition air attack.

Iraqi artillery fired at Coalition forces during the ground offensive was persistent but inaccurate. The Iraqis appeared to fire on known points, but did not shift or follow targets. The infantry fought initially, but surrendered when Coalition forces approached their positions. Coalition forces found ammunition stored throughout the trenches. The front line infantry forces'

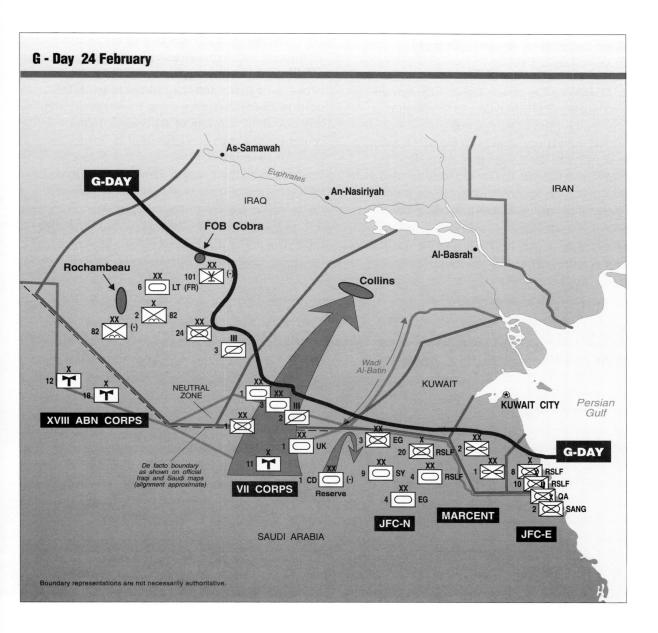

G - Day 24 February

G-DAY

As-Samawah

Euphrates

IRAQ

An-Nasiriyah

IRAN

FOB Cobra

Rochambeau

Al-Basrah

Collins

101 (-) LT (FR)

6

2 82

82 (-)

24

3

12

18

Wadi Al-Batin

KUWAIT

NEUTRAL ZONE

XVIII ABN CORPS

1

3 III

2

1 UK

KUWAIT CITY

Persian Gulf

KUWAIT CITY

De facto boundary as shown on official Iraqi and Saudi maps (alignment approximate)

11

1 CD (-)
Reserve

3 EG

20 RSLF

2

9 SY

4 RSLF

1

8 RSLF

10 RSLF

QA

2 SANG

G-DAY

VII CORPS

4 EG

JFC-N

MARCENT

JFC-E

SAUDI ARABIA

Boundary representations are not necessarily authoritative.

performance demonstrated serious shortcomings, particularly in coordinated indirect fire, air defense, and morale. Perhaps Iraqi commanders anticipated difficulties since intelligence sources indicated some RGFC artillery units were assigned to regular army divisions in southeastern Kuwait.

Enemy prisoners of war (EPWs) and deserters who crossed the Saudi border before the ground offensive began, complained of the lack of food and water and poor sanitation. A former battalion commander reported morale was poor, and he had not communicated with his brigade since the end of January. Expressing surprise that Americans were in front of his forces, he lacked specific Coalition force dispositions: this illustrates Iraq's weak battlefield intelligence capabilities, the breakdown of communications with higher headquarters, and the success of the Coalition in achieving surprise.

Army Component, Central Command

XVIII Airborne Corps

XVIII Airborne Corps was tasked to penetrate approximately 260 kilometers to the Euphrates River, cut the Iraqi LOC along Highway 8 to Baghdad, isolate Iraqi forces in the KTO, and help destroy the theater reserve — the RGFC. The 6th French Light Armored Division with a brigade from the 82nd Airborne Division under operational control (OPCON) and the 82nd Airborne Division (with two brigades) were along the western Corps boundary and began the theater ground attack. The 101st Airborne

Division (Air Assault) was east of the French. Its mission was to penetrate rapidly by air assault to the Euphrates River, cut the LOC between Baghdad and Iraqi forces in the KTO, destroy all enemy forces along those routes, and turn east to block north of Al-Basrah. In the center of the Corps zone, the 24th Infantry Division (Mechanized) was to attack through Iraqi forces in their zone to the Euphrates River, then turn east to destroy RGFC forces trapped in the KTO. On the Corps eastern boundary, the 3rd ACR was to secure the Corps right flank and maintain contact and coordination with VII Corps.

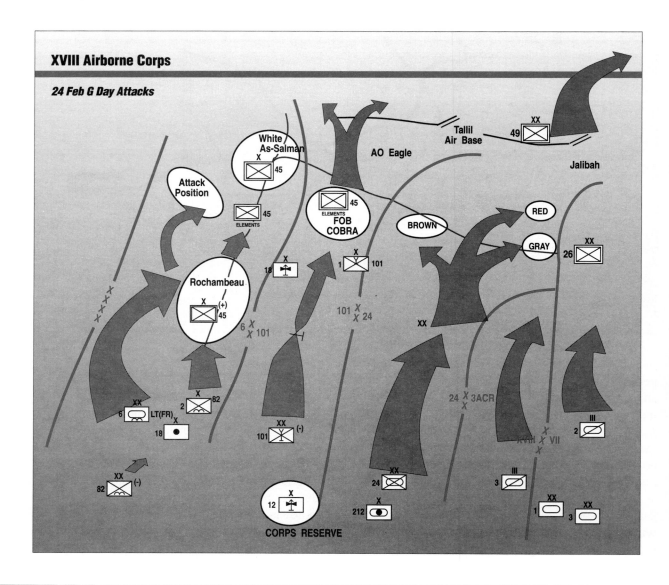

At 0400, 6th French Light Armored Division scouts advanced into Iraq. Three hours later, the French main body attacked through a light rain. Its objective was As-Salman, a small airfield about 90 miles inside Iraq. Reinforced by the 2nd Brigade, 82nd Airborne Division, the French crossed the border unopposed and attacked north. Short of their objective, the French ran into outposts of the 45th Iraqi Mechanized Infantry Division. After a brief battle, using missile-armed Gazelle attack helicopters against dug-in enemy tanks and bunkers, the French captured 2,500 prisoners and controlled the objective. The French moved on through Objective Rochambeau and onto As-Salman, known as Objective White in the plan, without opposition. Less than seven hours into the operation, the French 6th Light Armored Division, supported by the 82nd Airborne Division, secured its objectives and continued the attack north. The left flank was secured.

The remaining two brigades of the 82nd Airborne Division, following the French advance, were tasked to clear and secure a two-lane highway into southern Iraq. This road, Main Supply Route (MSR) Texas, would be used to move troops, equipment and supplies supporting the corps' advance north. The 101st Airborne Division (Air Assault) was scheduled to attack at 0500, but fog over the initial objective forced a delay. While the weather posed problems for aviation, indirect fire support missions continued. Corps artillery and rocket launchers fired on objectives and approach routes. Two hours later, the 101st Airborne Division (Air Assault) began its attack with its AH-64s, AH-1s, 60 UH-60s and 40 CH-47s augmented by the XVIII Airborne Corps' 18th Aviation Brigade and began lifting the 1st Brigade into what became Forward Operating Base (FOB) Cobra, 93 miles into Iraq and halfway to the Euphrates River. Over three hundred helicopter sorties ferried the troops and equipment into the objective area in the largest heliborne operation in military history.

At approximately 0700 hours, 60 UH-60 Blackhawks and 30 CH47D Chinooks carrying 1st Brigade's first air assault element climbed from the brigade's pickup zone in TAA Campbell. In just over an hour, the aircraft had safely deposited some 500 soldiers 93 miles deep into Iraq. The 1st Battalion, 82nd Brigade of Iraq's 49th Infantry Division had entrenched themselves just north of MSR Virginia. The 1/327th Infantry discovered the Iraqi battalion while clearing FOB Cobra in zone. A sharp firefight ensued. The Iraqi battalion commander surrendered once the 1/327th attacked his position. Upon his capture, the Iraqi commander was persuaded to use a bullhorn to convince his 300-plus soldiers to lay down their arms.

Situation Report from the 101st Airborne Division (Air Assault)

The Iraqis were scattered and disorganized. By mid-afternoon, the number of EPWs increased. Chinook helicopters lifted artillery, ammunition, refueling equipment, and building materials into FOB Cobra to create a major logistics base and refueling point. By the end of G+2 the 101st Airborne Division (Air Assault) had 380,000 gallons of fuel at FOB Cobra. This logistics base allowed the XVIII Airborne Corps to move infantry and attack helicopters north quickly to block Highway 8 and served as a springboard to move eight attack helicopter battalions and

UH-60 Blackhawks and AH-64 Apaches Lift Off for Air Assault.

M2 Bradley Fighting Vehicles During Offensive.

cavalry squadrons 200 km to the east to interdict forces fleeing on the Al Hammar causeway toward Al-Basrah on G+3.

As the air assault began, the 101st Airborne Division (Air Assault) CSS assets started a 700-vehicle convoy north along MSR New Market, carved in the desert by the 101st Division Engineers, to link up with the CH-47s at FOB Cobra. As soon as the Division secured Cobra and refueled the helicopters, it continued its assault north. By the evening of 24 February, the Division had moved approximately 170 miles into Iraq and cut Highway 8. The first of several roads connecting Iraqi forces in Kuwait with Baghdad was closed.

Because the initial attacks by the 6th French Light Armored Division and the 101st Airborne Division (Air Assault) were so successful, the 24th Infantry Division (Mechanized) crossed the line of departure about five hours ahead of schedule. The division attacked with three brigades abreast. The division cavalry squadron conducted reconnaissance and protection operations to the front. The 24th Infantry Division (Mechanized) advanced rapidly, maintaining a speed of 25 to 30 miles an hour, and pushed about 50 miles into Iraq against light

opposition. Their attack continued into the night. The division kept on its course with the aid of long range electronic navigation, image enhancement scopes and goggles, infrared (IR) and thermal imaging systems (TIS), and GPS. By midnight, the Division was 75 miles into Iraqi, poised to continue the attack.

VII Corps

VII Corps conducted the theater main attack with the mission of destroying the armor-heavy RGFC. The VII Corps plan of advance paralleled that of the XVIII Airborne Corps — a thrust north into Iraq, and a massive right turn toward the east. Once the turn was completed, both corps were to coordinate their attacks to trap the Republican Guards divisions. They were then to press until the RGFC was eliminated. The original plan was for VII Corps to attack on 25 February, but initial success attained by I MEF, JFC-E, and the XVIII Airborne Corps enabled the theater commander to accelerate the schedule by 15 hours.

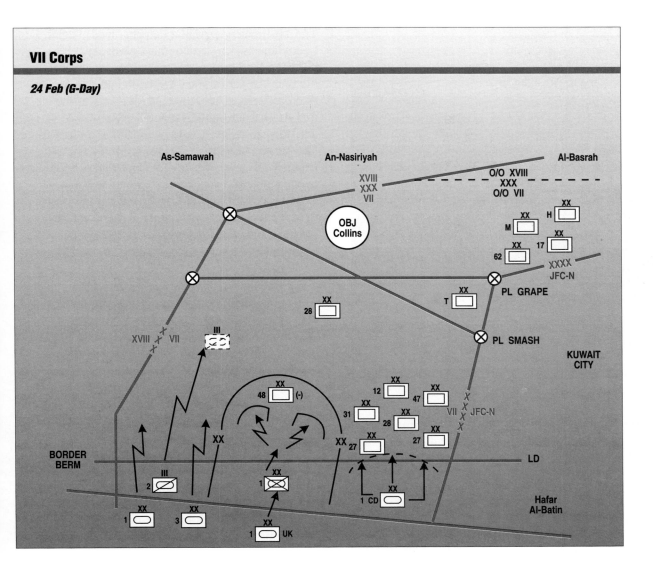

VII Corps

24 Feb (G-Day)

The VII Corps' plan was a feint and envelopment, much like the overall theater strategy. The 1st Cavalry Division, still the theater reserve at this point, would make a strong, but limited attack and feint along the Wadi Al-Batin, causing the Iraqi forces to believe the main attack would come from that direction. While Iraq's attention was focused on the 1st Cavalry Division, the VII Corps commander would send two divisions through the berms and mines along the corps' east flank and the ACR, followed by two more divisions, around the Iraqi defenses on the corps' west flank. 1st UK Armoured Division was assigned the mission to pass through the breach created by the 1st Infantry Division and to attack the Iraqi armored division in its zone to prevent it from moving into the flank of advancing VII Corps. VII Corps planned to move considerable fuel and ammunition through the breach to a logistics site in the 1st Infantry Division (Mechanized) zone. Clearing the breach of enemy infantry and artillery was a priority so as not to interrupt either the passage of 1st UK Armoured Division or the Corps CSS assets.

M-109 Self-propelled Howitzer Provides Fire In Support of Attack.

Before the start of the VII Corps main attack, 2nd ACR swept to the west of the Iraqi obstacles and crossed into Iraq. AH-64 attack helicopters and artillery raids intensified across the VII Corps front. With the 2nd ACR leading on the corps west flank, 1st and 3rd Armored divisions crossed the line of departure and attacked north.

Engineer Equipment Typical of that Used in 1st Infantry Division Breaching Operations.

The 1st Infantry Division (Mechanized) began to cut lanes through a complex obstacle belt of wire and land mines against little resistance. By the time the 1st Infantry Division had crossed the line of departure, the lead elements of the 2nd ACR, leading the 1st and 3rd Armored divisions along the Corps' west flank, already had pushed more than 30 km into Iraq. The 1st Infantry Division was given a warning order to leave a battalion task force in the breach and, after passage of the 1st UK Armoured Division, to move forward to make the third division of the three division force against the RGFC. 1st Cavalry Division was still under CENTCOM control.

Breaching the mine fields posed more problems than enemy fire. By nightfall, the 1st Infantry Division had successfully breached about 50 percent of the enemy's obstacle belt and forward defenses, and captured several hundred EPW. During the night of 24 February, the 1st Infantry Division consolidated, repositioned artillery, and coordinated for the 1st UK Armoured Division's passage of lines through the 1st Infantry Division positions. Since the 1st UK Armored Division would not be able to clear the breach that evening, VII Corps halted the advance of the 1st and 3rd Armored divisions for the night. Across the VII Corps front, in-depth artillery fire against the enemy continued throughout the night.

On line from west to east, 1st Armored and 3rd Armored divisions followed the axis cleared by the 2nd ACR. In the center, 1st Infantry Division continued its deliberate breach of the Iraqi defenses by plowing through the berms. On the Corps eastern flank, the 1st UK Armoured Division prepared to pass through the 1st Infantry Division to attack the Iraqi tactical reserves.

Joint Forces Command — North
At 1600 hours 24 February, the 3rd Egyptian Mechanized Division, TF Khalid and TF

Muthannah began to attack Iraqi positions in Kuwait. They encountered Iraqi fire trenches, minefields, barriers, and harassing fires as they crossed the border in their zone. Saudi and Kuwaiti forces began the offensive shortly after the Egyptians. The Egyptians, concerned about an Iraqi armored counterattack, halted their advance short of their initial objectives and established blocking positions in sector for the night. They resumed offensive operations at daybreak the following day. Meanwhile, the 4th Egyptian Armored Division prepared to follow the 3rd Egyptian Mechanized Division. The 9th Syrian Armored Division followed the Egyptian Divisions as the JFC-N reserve and conducted screening operations with one reconnaissance battalion on the right flank to tie in with MARCENT.

I Marine Expeditionary Force

I MEF began the assault at 0400, aimed directly at its ultimate objective, Al-Mutl'a Pass and the roads leading from Kuwait City, 35 to 50 miles to the northeast. I MEF faced the strongest concentration of enemy defenses in theater. The 1st MARDIV led the attack from a position just west of the "elbow" of the southern Kuwait border. The 2nd MARDIV attacked 90 minutes later. Against sometimes stiff resistance, I MEF succeeded in breaching two defended defensive belts, opened 14 lanes in the east and six lanes in the west, and established a solid foothold inside Kuwait. These breaching operations were successful because of detailed preparation, including reconnaissance and mapping of obstacles, followed by extensive training and rehearsals.

Most importantly, I MEF diverted the attention of the Iraqi high command, which remained focused on Kuwait, largely oblivious to the enveloping threat to the west. At the end of the day, I MEF had captured more than 8,000 EPW and attacked 20 miles into Kuwait.

On the right, 1st MARDIV, led by TF Ripper and covered by the two TFs that had infiltrated

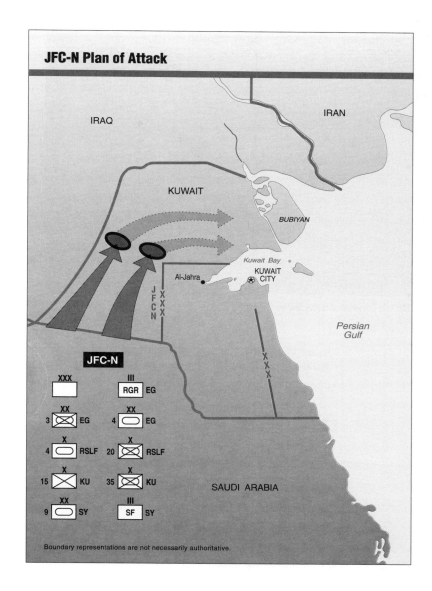

earlier, completed its breach of the two defensive belts. The division's after action report indicated they destroyed the older Iraqi T-55 and T-62 tanks with M60A1 tanks, TOW-equipped High Mobility Multi-Wheeled Vehicles (HMMWVs), and heavy artillery. The 3rd MAW provided both CAS and interdiction. There were several individual acts of heroism during this intense fighting.

Advancing north, the division bypassed Ahmad Al-Jabir airfield, opting to clear its buildings and bunkers later with infantry. Light Armored

1st Marine Division Advances as Oil Wells Burn in the Background.

Infantry (LAI) screened the right flank of the division while Marines continued to clear the enemy in zone.

To the west, 2nd MARDIV, with the reinforced 6th Marines in the lead, blasted its way through the obstacle belts against moderate resistance. The leading regiment advanced in three battalion columns through mortar and artillery fire. The initial opposition came from Iraqi defenders dug in behind the first minefields. The Iraqis were silenced quickly by Marine infantrymen and tanks supporting the combat engineers. Here too, there were examples of heroism. A young Marine reserve combat engineer twice raced into the minefields to reprime a failed line charge while under small arms and artillery fire.

After clearing the first obstacle, the 6th Marines turned left and attacked the more heavily defended obstacles. Marine engineers used M-154 Mine Clearing line charges and M60A1 tanks with forked mine plows and rakes to clear six lanes in the division sector. Temporarily delayed on the right, the regiment pushed its battalions through the center and left breach lanes, turned and eliminated resistance on the right. Once through, the regiment advanced to its objectives, overrunning elements of the Iraqi 7th and 14th Infantry divisions. The 2nd MARDIV noted in its after action report that the regiment captured more than 4,000 EPW including the Iraqi 9th Tank Battalion with 35 operational tanks.

Iraqi Tank Takes a Fatal Hit.

Having secured its objectives by 1400, the 6th Marines spread out and prepared for an Iraqi counterattack, while the remainder of the 2nd MARDIV passed through the breach lanes and assumed positions to its right and left. By nightfall, the bulk of the 2nd MARDIV had passed through the breach.

Iraqi troops had displayed dogged fighting qualities when attacked frontally, only to quickly surrender when flanked or attacked from the rear. By day's end, I MEF had overrun the Iraqi defensive line and eliminated the better part of three infantry divisions. As the Marines consolidated, CH-46s and CH-53s shuttled into landing zones, replenishing ammunition and picking up EPWs.

The initial Marine air focus was on support to the ground forces and second to targets deeper inside Iraq. The 3rd MAW provided support to JFC-E as well as to MARCENT during this period. To provide 24-hour support to ground forces, the 3rd MAW developed the concept of push flow, which entailed a section of attack aircraft checking in with the ground units through the Direct Air Support Center every seven minutes. Prebriefed on the scheme of maneuver, the pilots would then be "pushed" to a requesting unit or, if not needed, "pushed" to an airborne FAC for direction to targets behind enemy lines. Airborne or ground FACs exercised positive control throughout the mission.

A key factor in the day's success was 3rd MAW CAS. AV-8Bs and F/A-18s orbited overhead, waiting for requests to support ground elements. AH-1s waited at holding areas behind advancing Marines, quickly popping up and eliminating Iraqi armored vehicles and strongpoints. Particularly effective at eliminating enemy tanks were the laser-guided Hellfire missiles carried by AH-1Ws, with target designation provided by spotters with front-line infantry.

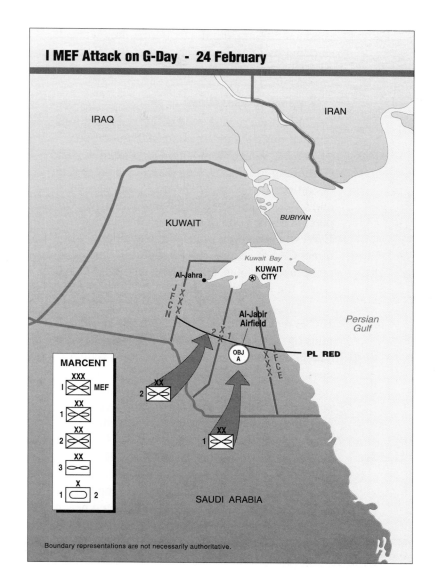

I MEF Attack on G-Day - 24 February

Boundary representations are not necessarily authoritative.

Joint Forces Command — East

In the east, JFC-E began moving at 0800 and cut six lanes through the first obstacle belt. The 8th and 10th Saudi Mechanized Brigades secured their respective objectives during the initial attacks. JFC-E secured all its initial objectives by the end of the first day, capturing large numbers of Iraqis. The 2nd SANG Brigade continued a reconnaissance in force along the coastal highway.

Theater Reserve

The 1st Cavalry Division, as theater reserve,

conducted feints into the tri-border area while standing by to assist JFC-N east of the Wadi Al-Batin.

Supporting Operations

On 24 February, as ground offensive operations began, integrated air, sea and SOF operations continued. While maintaining air supremacy and continuing to attack selected strategic targets, air operations increasingly shifted to interdiction and CAS, which represented more than 78 percent of the combat sorties on 24 February. Even when weather reduced the availability of direct CAS missions, interdiction missions continued to isolate Iraqi forces in the KTO and attack the Republican Guards.

JFC-E received fire support from the 16-inch guns of the *USS Missouri* and *USS Wisconsin*. The Navy continued strike operations, fighter cover, Gulf Combat Air Patrol (CAP), armed reconnaissance, countermine operations and surface surveillance missions in support of ground forces and the theater campaign.

Before dawn on 25 February, 4th MEB helicopters conducted an amphibious feint off Ash Shuaybah to hold Iraqi forces along the coast. Simultaneously, SEALs conducted beach reconnaissance and detonated charges to the

British Forces Pause Momentarily During the Advance North.

south. Other Naval Special Warfare (NSW) units entered Kuwait City with returning Kuwaiti resistance fighters. These elements were to prepare to link up with Coalition ground forces entering Kuwait City later in the operation.

G+1 (25 February) — Destruction of Enemy Tactical Forces

Enemy Actions and Disposition

As the ground offensive progressed, Iraqi units' ineffectiveness became more clear. The Iraqi III Corps units had suffered severe damage. CENTCOM assessed the Corps' 7th, 8th, 14th, 18th, and 29th Infantry divisions, in the I MEF and JFC-E zones, as combat ineffective and the Iraqi 5th Mechanized Infantry and the 3rd Armored divisions of III Corps as badly mauled.

On the western side of III Corps, the 14th and 7th Infantry divisions in front of I MEF were combat ineffective. The 36th Infantry, 1st Mechanized Infantry, and the 56th Armored Brigade established hasty defensive positions south/southwest of Al-Jahra, northwest of Kuwait City. The Iraqi 3rd Armored Division was trying to hold blocking positions between Kuwait International Airfield and Al-Jahra.

On the eastern side of III Corps, the 18th and 8th Infantry divisions, in front of JFC-E, were assessed as combat ineffective, although they offered stiff resistance against JFC-E forces near Mina As-Sa'ud. The 29th Infantry Division, withdrawing to the east, also was combat ineffective.

The Iraqi 19th, 11th, and 15th Infantry divisions and three SF brigades in Kuwait City were assessed at full strength. These divisions continued to focus on an amphibious assault and prepare for military operations in Kuwait City.

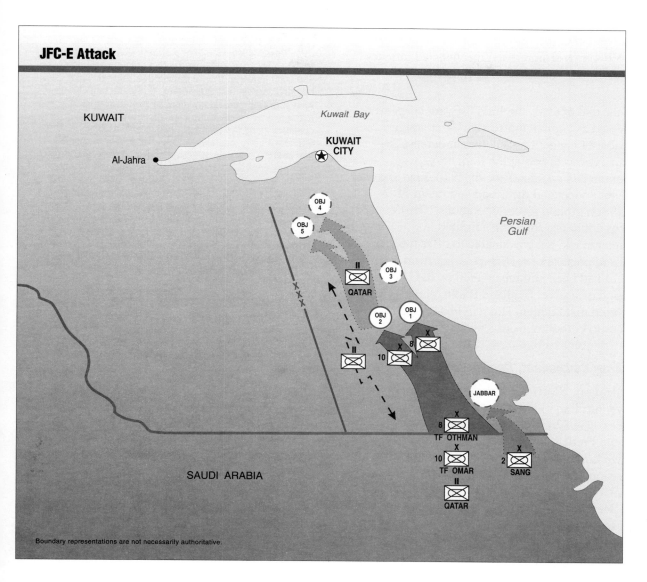

JFC-E Attack

KUWAIT

Kuwait Bay

KUWAIT CITY

Al-Jahra

Persian Gulf

OBJ 4

OBJ 5

OBJ 3

QATAR

OBJ 2

OBJ 1

8

10

JABBAR

8

TF OTHMAN

10

TF OMAR

2

SANG

QATAR

SAUDI ARABIA

Boundary representations are not necessarily authoritative.

The deep penetration of Coalition forces in the western side of the III Corps prompted several Iraqi battalion-size counterattacks from divisions along the flanks of the penetration. These units took heavy losses.

In the IV Corps area of western Kuwait, in front of JFC-N, the Iraqi 20th and 30th Infantry divisions were assessed as combat ineffective by the end of the first day of the ground offensive. The 21st and 16th Infantry divisions appeared to be falling back to a defensive line south and west of 'Ali As-Salim Airfield. The 6th

Armored Division, west of 'Ali As-Salim Airfield, was heavily reduced.

By the end of G+1, five VII Corps infantry divisions, one in US VII Corps zone in the tri-border area, were in jeopardy of being isolated on the front lines. The 12th Armored Division, in front of the 1st UK Armoured Division, was engaged with Coalition armored forces as it attempted to maintain a LOC for the 47th, 27th, and 28th Infantry divisions along the US VII Corps eastern flank. From west to east in front of the VII Corps, the 48th, 25th, 26th,

31st, and 45th Infantry divisions were engaged by VII Corps armored and mechanized infantry divisions and rendered combat ineffective.

By the end of G+1, the Iraqi forward corps were assessed as combat ineffective — no longer capable of conducting a coherent defense in sector. It was apparent the Iraqi corps commanders could not see the battlefield and did not understand the scope and intent of Coalition ground forces operations. The IV Corps could use forces in a limited counterattack, but was unable to offer more than isolated pockets of resistance. Iraqi front line forces had been outmaneuvered by the Coalition ground offensive. Baghdad Radio, at this point, reported that Saddam Hussein had ordered his forces to withdraw from Kuwait.

Army Component, Central Command

In the west, XVIII Airborne Corps continued to drive into Iraq to interdict LOC and isolate Iraqi forces. The 82nd Airborne Division followed the 6th French Light Armored Division along Phase Line Smash. As the 82nd Airborne Division entered FOB Cobra, the 101st Airborne Division (Air Assault) sent its 3rd Brigade on the deepest air assault in military history. The 3rd Brigade air assaulted north from its TAA along the Saudi-Iraqi border 175 miles to occupy observation and blocking positions on the south bank of the Euphrates River, just west

"**A**s troopers from the 82nd Airborne Division advanced to the valley, they were faced with a unique challenge. The commander of the 1st Battalion (Airborne), 505th Infantry, relates: 'The 3rd Brigade's mission largely was to secure Tallil Airfield and destroy enemy aircraft. A major concern in securing the airfield was the local civilians, many of whom were engaged in battling Saddam's army themselves. Our charter was to capture and destroy weapons. We had to be careful we didn't have any confrontations with the local peasants or with the resistance fighters. After a couple of days, you got to know who was who on the resistance fighters – who you could trust and who you couldn't. Soon, the area became a major treatment center for Iraqi refugees.' 'We treated well over 1,000 civilians who were fighting with the resistance,' said a 3rd Brigade medical NCO. 'They were pretty messed up. I've seen every kind of combat wound that you could imagine – everything, it was there.' "

Army Times, 21 October 1991

of the town of An-Nasiriyah and a few miles north of the Iraqi air base at Tallil.

In the early morning the same day, the 24th Infantry Division (Mechanized) moved toward its first major objective. At 0300 hours the 197th Infantry Brigade attacked Objective Brown, in the western part of the division sector. The brigade found hungry prisoners, dazed by the heavy artillery preparation. By 0700, the 197th secured its objective and established blocking positions to the east and west along MSR Virginia. Shortly thereafter, the 2nd Brigade, 24th Infantry Division (Mechanized) attacked

M1 Abrams Tanks Move Forward While Vulcan (SP) Provides Air Cover.

Typical Result of Tank Hit on Iraqi Armor. (Iraqi turret in foreground.)

Chapter VIII

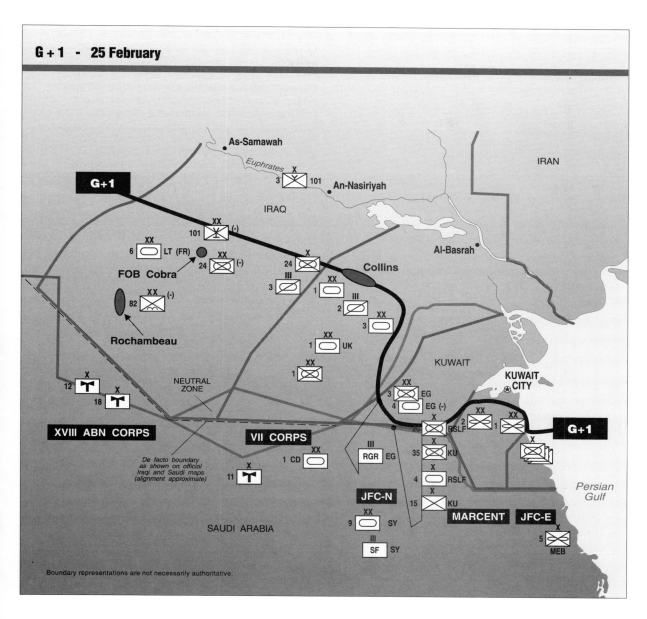

Objective Grey, encountering no enemy fire and capturing 300 prisoners; it also established blocking positions to the east. 1st Brigade, 24th Infantry Division (Mechanized) continued northwest in the center of the division sector and attacked and secured Objective Red.

The 24th Infantry Division (Mechanized) had taken three major objectives and hundreds of prisoners against weak resistance from the Iraqi 26th and 35th Infantry divisions. By the

end of the day, XVIII Airborne Corps had advanced in all division sectors, established an FOB, placed brigade-size blocking positions in

> "A sergeant of D Company, 1st Battalion, 35th Armor, commented: 'At 2,800 meters, the tankers engaged tanks. I watched Iraqi tank turrets flip 40 feet into the air, and was dumbfounded. I was amazed by how much firepower we had, how much destruction we could do. It was a sobering thought.' "
>
> *Army Times, 16 September 1991*

Apache Helicopter Prepares for a Mission.

the Euphrates River Valley, and taken thousands of prisoners.

On the VII Corps left flank, the 1st Armored Division resumed its attack shortly after daybreak and made contact first with units of the Iraqi 26th Infantry Division. While the division was about 35 to 40 miles from its objective, CAS strikes began, followed by attack helicopter strikes. As it approached the objective, artillery, rocket launchers, and tactical missile batteries delivered preparatory fires. When Division lead elements came into visual range, PSYOP teams broadcast surrender

M1 Abrams Tanks Move Forward in the Attack.

appeals. However, the Iraqis attempted to mount an attack, and a brigade of the 1st Armored Division reported destroying 40 to 50 tanks and armored personnel carriers of the Iraqi 26th Infantry Division in 10 minutes at a range of 2,000 meters.

Approaching Al-Busayyah in early afternoon, the 1st Armored Division directed CAS and attack helicopter sorties to the Iraqi brigade position, destroying artillery pieces, and several vehicles, and taking almost 300 prisoners.

The 3rd Armored Division continued its attack north, and by the night of 25 February both the 2nd ACR and the 3rd Armored Division had turned east, and were encountering isolated enemy units as high winds and heavy rains began.

Later in the night of 25 February, the 2nd ACR encountered elements of the Tawakalna Division and the 50th Brigade of the 12th Armored Division. It destroyed the 50th Brigade then assumed a hasty defense and prepared to continue the attack against the Tawakalna at first light on 26 February.

In the 1st Infantry Division sector, the 1st UK Armoured Division passed through the breach lanes the 1st Infantry Division had opened. While the 1st Infantry Division expanded the breach by defeating enemy brigades to the front,

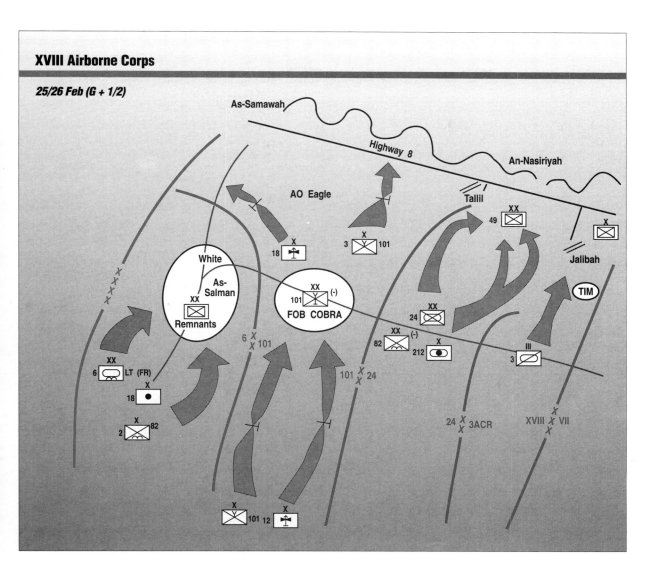

XVIII Airborne Corps

25/26 Feb (G + 1/2)

the British turned right to hit the Iraqi 52nd Armored Division. That easterly attack by the British marked the start of nearly continuous combat for the "Desert Rats" during the next two days.

Joint Forces Command — North

JFC-N, in the center, continued to advance. At approximately 0400 hours the Egyptian forces continued their breaching operations and advanced towards their initial objectives. The Egyptian Corps had secured a 16-square kilometer bridgehead, but their objective had not been secured by the early hours of 26 February.

TF Khalid continued breaching obstacles and advanced toward its objectives early on 25 February. By the end of the day, the Saudis and Kuwaitis on the right flank had seized their objective and consolidated positions. Other units, including the 9th Syrian Armored Division followed and supported. The Syrian reconnaissance battalion continued to screen along the border between JFC-N and MARCENT.

I Marine Expeditionary Force

On G+1, I MEF advanced against the fiercest resistance it encountered during the ground

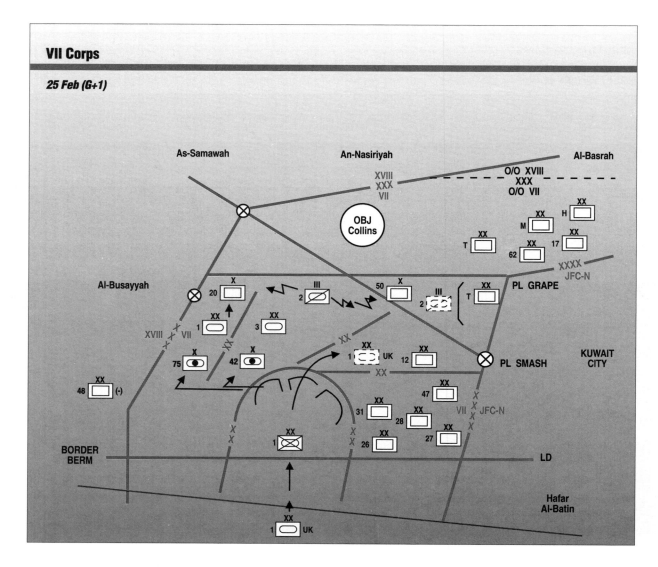

VII Corps

25 Feb (G+1)

As-Samawah An-Nasiriyah Al-Basrah

XVIII
XXX
VII

O/O XVIII
XXX
O/O VII

OBJ
Collins

Al-Busayyah

PL GRAPE

XXXX
JFC-N

KUWAIT
CITY

PL SMASH

VII JFC-N

BORDER
BERM

LD

Hafar
Al-Batin

offensive. In the 2nd MARDIV sector, an Iraqi armored counterattack was repulsed by the 6th Marine Regiment using a combination of CAS, artillery, tanks, and TOW missiles. Attacked by aircraft as they formed for the attack south of Kuwait City, the Iraqis were reduced to less than brigade strength by the time they actually attacked the regiment. Attacking on schedule, the 2nd MARDIV, with the Tiger Brigade on the left, 6th Marines in the center, and 8th Marines on the right, advanced against elements of the Iraqi 3rd Armored Division and 1st Mechanized Division that had assumed defensive positions on the high ground to the

north and northwest and in an area of buildings and fences known as the "ice-cube tray". Weather combined with intense smog from burning oil wells reduced visibility to a few

---

Silver Star citation of a Marine Corporal: "The next morning [G+1], the enemy counterattacked . . . with tanks and infantry. Acting immediately and with no regard for his personal safety, the Corporal grabbed an AT-4 and moved forward through thick smoke and automatic weapons fire. Sighting a tank, he worked himself close to its right flank, fired, and singlehandedly destroyed the tank."

I MEF Award Citation

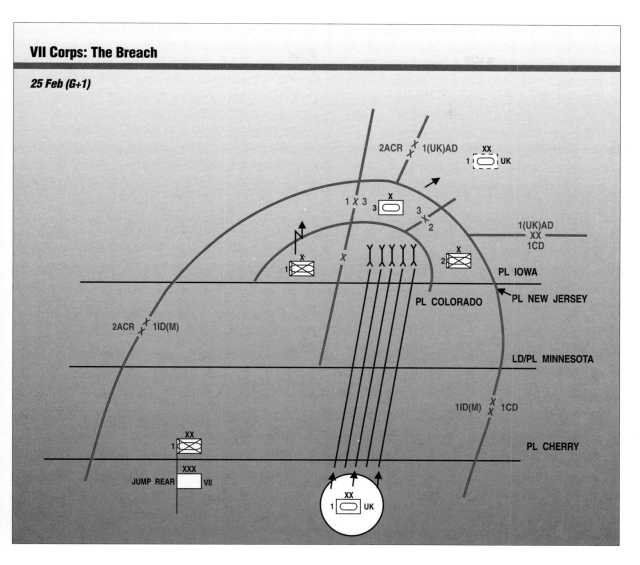

yards. Fighting in near darkness, Marine M1s of the 2nd Tank Battalion (supporting the 8th Marines) and the Tiger Brigade, equipped with the M1A1 and enhanced optics, proved particularly successful at engaging armor at long ranges. Other Marine tank crews, in M60A1 tanks, relied on crew skill to outfight the enemy. In the "ice-cube tray", tanks and infantry cleared buildings and trenches at close ranges in the darkness, finally securing the area after 2200 against stiff resistance.

On the right of the I MEF sector, the 1st MARDIV encountered a strong counterattack near the Al-Burqan Oil field which, at one point, was fought within 300 meters of the division CP. It lasted several hours, and involved close combat.

AH-1W and AV-8B maneuvered in conjunction with tanks and LAV to overwhelm the enemy thrust. One FAC found himself controlling the simultaneous attacks of eight different aircraft. At times the fighting became so confused that Marine and Iraqi units intermingled. One Iraqi tank commander drove his tank up to the TF Papa Bear Command Post and surrendered. In the end, the attacking formations were destroyed. In this type of fighting, GPS and thermal imaging systems proved their worth, as did training and discipline. The final tally of the battle (according to 1st MARDIV) included more than 100 Iraqi armored vehicles destroyed and at least 1,500 EPWs. The 1st MARDIV completed consolidation of Ahmad Al-Jabir airfield and pushed to within 10 miles of Kuwait City.

Joint Forces Command — East

JFC-E secured its objectives against light resistance and with very few casualties; however, progress was slowed by the large number of Iraqis who surrendered. TF Omar and Othman continued their advance toward their objectives. The 2nd SANG Brigade continued its advance along the coastal highway and assigned one battalion to escort EPW to the rear. Qatari units followed TF Omar as the JFC-E reserve.

Supporting Operations

With the Coalition ground advance well under way, a Navy amphibious force made its final effort to convince the Iraqi command that CENTCOM would launch a major over-the-beach assault into Kuwait. Beginning late on 24 February and continuing during the following two days, the Navy landed the 5th MEB, a 7,500-man force at Al-Mish'ab which was attached to MARCENT as the I MEF reserve. An ATF also conducted strike missions against Faylaka and Bubiyan islands, along with simulated Marine helicopter assaults and artillery raids along the Kuwaiti coast. Feints and demonstrations by Navy and US amphibious forces off the coast tied down up to 10 divisions. Both the *USS Missouri* and *USS Wisconsin* continued to provide NGFS for I MEF and JFC-E. The 4th MEB remained afloat, ready for commitment. 4th MEB also conducted air strikes against Faylaka Island and continued to carry out amphibious feints along the coast at Bubiyan Island.

Coalition air forces flew a record number of sorties — 3,159, of which 1,997 were direct combat missions. Priority missions remained counter air, CAS, and interdiction. USMC air priority went to ground forces with second priority to targets further inside Iraq. In the early morning hours, Iraqi 3rd Armored Division elements, massing west of Kuwait International Airport, were caught in the open. Air strikes destroyed the force's counterattack potential, eliminating an obstacle to the rapidly advancing ground forces.

SOF conducted SR patrols that reported enemy dispositions. SOF liaison teams remained with Coalition units and continued to advise and support these forces in battle.

G+2 (26 February) — Destruction of 2nd Echelon Operational Forces and Sealing the Battlefield

Enemy Actions And Disposition

During this period, the massive exodus of Iraqi forces from the eastern part of the theater began. Elements of the Iraqi III Corps were pushed back into Kuwait City by I MEF and JFC-E. They were joined by Iraqi occupation troops from Kuwait City. Iraqi units became intermingled and disordered. During the early morning of 26 February, military and commandeered civilian vehicles of every description, loaded with Iraqi soldiers and goods looted from Kuwait, clogged the main four-lane highway north from Kuwait City. To deny Iraqi commanders the opportunity to reorganize their forces and establish a cohesive defense, these forces were struck repeatedly by air attacks.

Although many Iraqis surrendered, some did not. There were several intense engagements, particularly with the Republican Guards. But by sunset on G+2, Coalition forces had pushed hundreds of miles into Iraq; DIA assessments reflected that they captured more than 30,000 EPW; destroyed or rendered combat ineffective 26 of 43 Iraqi divisions; overwhelmed the Iraqi decision making process and rendered its C^2

ineffective; and forced the Iraqi Army into full retreat.

Army Component, Central Command

XVIII Airborne Corps turned its attack northeast and advanced into the Euphrates River Valley. With the 6th French Light Armored Division, the 101st Airborne Division (Air Assault) and 82nd Airborne Divisions protecting the western and northern flanks, the 24th Infantry Division (Mechanized) led the Corps attack into the valley. Weather became a factor at this point in the offensive; a dust storm in the objective area kicked up thick clouds of swirling dust. The 24th Infantry Division (Mechanized) moved out at 1400, with three brigades heading toward the Iraqi airfields at Jalibah and Tallil. During these attacks, the 3rd ACR screened the division's southern and eastern flanks and the 24th Infantry Division (Mechanized) encountered its heaviest resistance of the war.

The Iraqi 47th and 49th Infantry divisions, the Republican Guard Nebuchadnezzar Infantry Division, and the 26th Commando Brigade stood and fought. The terrain gave them a clear advantage. Iraqi artillery and automatic weapons were dug into rocky escarpments. For four hours, the 1st Brigade of the 24th Infantry Division (Mechanized) received intense tank and artillery fire. The division reported that American artillery crews located enemy batteries with Firefinder radars and returned three to six rounds for every round of incoming, destroying six Iraqi artillery battalions.

In the dust storm and darkness, American technology gave the US forces a clear advantage. Tank, infantry fighting vehicle, and attack helicopter crews worked so well together that they could spot and hit Iraqi tanks at ranges over 3500 meters long before the Iraqis saw them. Precise tank gunnery, M-19 automatic grenade launcher fire from the fighting vehicles and armored personnel carriers, overwhelming artillery, rocket, and AH-64 support took the 24th Infantry Division (Mechanized) through

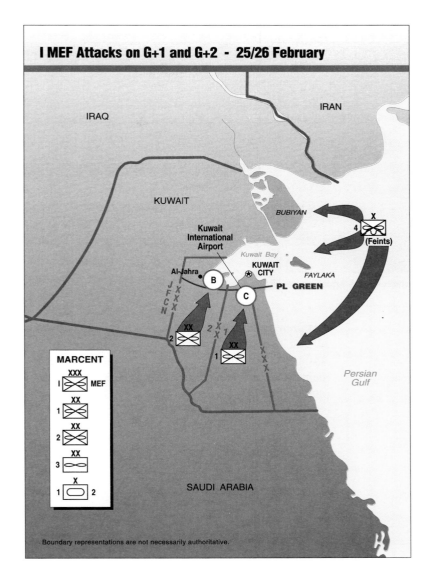

the enemy armor and artillery units. This combination of superior weaponry and technique forced Iraqi troops out of their bunkers and vehicles. They surrendered in droves.

After a day and night of hard fighting, all three brigades of the 24th Infantry Division (Mechanized) were poised just south of the airfields. The 6th French Light Armored Division secured and cleared all of its objectives and moved to protect the theater left flank. The 82nd Airborne Division continued to perform

Coalition Forces Attack on Iraqi Positions.

crossed Corps Phase Line Smash just after daylight, and attacked objective Collins, east of Al-Busayyah. With the capture of those objectives, VII Corps turned its advance to assault directly east into Republican Guards' strongholds.

rear area security, especially protection of the MSRs. The 101st Airborne Division (Air Assault)'s 3rd Brigade continued to interdict the main LOC between Baghdad and the KTO and planning began to move its 2nd Brigade to the east to secure FOB Viper and attack the North Al-Basrah road.

The XVIII Airborne Corps had achieved all its objectives; interdicting the LOC in the Euphrates River Valley, blocking reinforcement of Iraqi forces in the KTO, and completing the envelopment of Saddam Hussein's forces in southern Iraq and Kuwait.

VII Corps continued its deep envelopment into Iraq before turning right and attacking reserve units and continuing the attack to destroy the Republican Guards. CINCCENT directed VII Corps to accelerate the pace of its attack. The 11th Aviation Brigade's AH-64 Apaches made two attacks deep into Iraqi territory, one at 2100 hours, and the next at 0300 hours. These attacks destroyed significant numbers of Iraqi armored vehicles and, including air interdiction, extended VII Corps battle in depth to over 100 kilometers.

In the 3rd Armored Division zone, the division

"**A**s the 1st Armored Division moved into the Euphrates River Valley and approached Al-Busayyah, the scene is described by members of the 6th Battalion, 6th Infantry: 'At 1500 meters, a T-55 with its turret swinging toward the advancing, US forces was spotted and destroyed, as were three others in rapid succession. We killed the tanks so quickly they didn't get a round off. A fifth tank trying to flee was taken out by an M1A1 main round. The turret flew through the air like a Frisbee. We moved up to the town expecting them to wave white handkerchiefs, and they started shooting at us.' "

" 'The word was they were going to have the white flags up.' a C Co, 6/6 Inf Bradley vehicle commander said. 'We stopped about 200 meters out, started scanning for white flags, didn't see any.' He spotted a machine-gun position in a building on the left flank, and the Bradley fired 60 rounds into it, turning the building into rubble and taking out the gun."

"The commander of the battalion's C Company, reported some Iraqi soldiers coming to the edge of the town with their hands up. 'My instructions to him were have them come out to you, do not take yourself into RPG range. Immediately after they waved their hands and some shirts, they dropped back behind fortifications and started shooting at us again, so we knew we were going to have to go in and get him.' "

"The battalion commander pulled his forces back and ordered the 2nd Battalion, 1st Artillery Regiment to fire a 10-minute artillery prep on the town. He then sent three companies to the east side of town, a tank-heavy security element to the north end of town to catch escaping Iraqi, and a small assault team consisting of a platoon of Bradleys, two Armored Combat Earthmovers and a combat engineer vehicle to the south side of town.

"Once the forces were in position, the three companies opened up. Fire was lifted to allow the assault team to enter from the south. They were hit by small-arms fire and the engineer vehicle opened up. Its huge 165-mm demolition gun fired 21 rounds with devastating impact. 'That totally destroyed all the resistance in the town.' "

Army Times, 16 September 1991

As the attack east began, VII Corps presented in the northern part of its sector a front of three divisions and one regiment: 1st Armored Division on the left (north), 3rd Armored Division in the center, 2nd ACR and the 1st Infantry Division on the right (south). Farther south, the 1st UK Armored Division advanced on a separate axis into Objective Waterloo, and on to the junction of Phase Line Smash and the Corps boundary. The 3rd Armored Division pressed on, turning northeast, and hitting the Republican Guard Tawakalna Division. Late that night, the 1st Armored Division mounted a night assault on the elite enemy unit, and in fighting that continued into the next day, destroyed a substantial number of tanks and other vehicles.

Soldiers from the 101st Airborne Division (Air Assault) Operating a 105mm Howitzer.

In the early afternoon, the 2nd ACR advanced east through a sandstorm to Objective Collins. The regiment was screening in front of the 1st Infantry Division, which had just arrived after clearing the mine belt along the Saudi border. The Iraqis had long expected the American attack to come from the south and east, and were now frantically turning hundreds of tanks, towed artillery pieces and other vehicles to meet the onslaught from the west. On the Iraqi side, unit locations were changing almost by the minute. As the 2nd ACR neared Phase Line Tangerine, 20 miles east of Objective Collins, it received fire from a building on the "69 Easting," a north-south line on military maps. The regiment returned fire and continued east. They were met with more enemy fire for the next two hours. About 1600, the regiment found T-72 tanks in prepared defensive positions at "73 Easting." Using its thermal imagery equipment, the regiment destroyed every tank that appeared.

This was a different kind of battle from what Americans had fought so far. The destruction of the first tanks did not signal the surrender of hundreds of Iraqi soldiers. The regiment had found two Iraqi divisions willing to put up a hard fight, the 12th Armored and the Republican

Guard Tawakalna divisions. The regiment found a seam between the two divisions, and for a time became the only American unit obviously outnumbered and outgunned during the campaign. But here again, thermal imaging equipment cut through the dust storm to give gunners a long-range view of enemy vehicles and grant the first-shot advantage. For four hours, the 2nd ACR destroyed tanks and armored personnel carriers while attack helicopters knocked out artillery batteries.

Scouts of I Troop, 3rd Squadron, 2nd Armored Cavalry Regiment Move Forward Through the Battle Zone Inside Iraq.
(Photo courtesy of Soldier Magazine, May 1991).

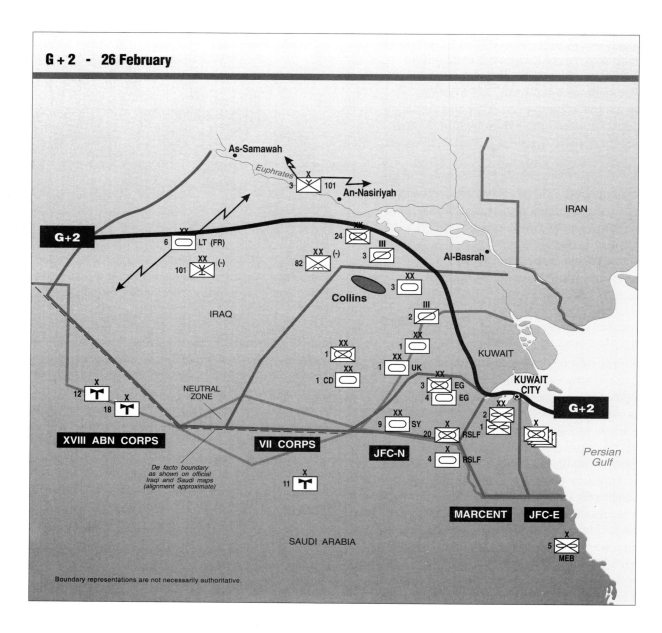

G + 2 - 26 February

As-Samawah

Euphrates

3 | 101

An-Nasiriyah

IRAN

G+2

6 | LT (FR)

24

101 (-)

82 (-)

3

3

Collins

IRAQ

3

2

Al-Basrah

KUWAIT

1

1 | UK

1

1 CD

12

18

NEUTRAL ZONE

XVIII ABN CORPS

3 | EG

4 | EG

9 | SY

KUWAIT CITY

G+2

2

1

20 | RSLF

VII CORPS

JFC-N

4 | RSLF

Persian Gulf

De facto boundary as shown on official Iraqi and Saudi maps (alignment approximate)

11

MARCENT **JFC-E**

SAUDI ARABIA

5

MEB

Boundary representations are not necessarily authoritative.

When this "Battle of 73 Easting" ended early in the evening of 26 February, the 2nd ACR reported they had destroyed at least 29 tanks and 24 armored personnel carriers, and had taken 1,300 prisoners. That night, the 1st Infantry Division (Mechanized) passed through the regiment and continued the attack east.

The evening of 26 February, the 3rd Armored Division attacked due east through an enemy reconnaissance screen and into the Republican

"**T**he Iraqi vehicles were dug into defensive revetments that limited their fields of fire to the south and southeast. 'You could just see the top of the turret over the berm,' said a tanker. 'So I started shooting two or three feet down from the top. We were shooting sabot rounds right through the berms. You'd hit it and see sparks fly, metal fly, equipment fly.' 'We were told before the battle that you've got to hit 'em in a certain place. But, anything you shot 'em with, they blew up. Using sabot, we blew one turret out of the hole about 20 feet. It landed upside down,' said an Abrams tank commander."

Soldier Magazine, June 1991

1st UK Armoured Division.

Guards' Tawakalna Division. This attack, under extremely adverse weather conditions, was typical of the heavy fighting encountered by the VII Corps as it engaged Republican Guard Forces. These forces were heavily armored and occupied well constructed defensive emplacements. They had also prepared alternate positions which enabled them to reorient to the west to face the VII Corps attack. Even after extensive bombardment, most elements of the Tawakalna Division remained combat effective. Weather conditions continued to deteriorate and winds gusted from 25-42 knots. Heavy rain and blowing sand often reduced visibility to less than 100 meters. The ceiling was generally very low, and in the words of one senior armor commander, "neither Army aviation nor air forces could fly."

Under these conditions, the 1st and 2nd Brigades of the 3rd Armored Division simultaneously conducted a hasty attack against the 29th and 9th Brigades of the Tawakalna Division. Spearheaded by the division cavalry squadron and a tank heavy task force, supported by five battalions of cannon artillery and 27 MLRS launchers, the 3rd Armored Division succeeded in destroying numerous Iraqi armored vehicles and tanks in intense fighting. This action effectively destroyed the Tawakalna Division as a coherent fighting force. US

artillery proved extremely effective in the counterfire role during this battle. Although Iraqi artillery was able to fire initially, it was quickly targeted and rapidly suppressed or destroyed.

Later in the engagement, visibility improved enough to employ the division's Apache-equipped attack battalion. In the northern portion of the division zone where the 2nd Brigade operated, the timely arrival of the Apaches (guided by intelligence from JSTARS) caught an enemy mechanized infantry task force as it moved diagonally across the brigade's sector but outside of direct fire range. Their unit was evidently attempting to reinforce other elements of the Tawakalna Division. According to unit after action reports, this engagement resulted in the destruction of eight tanks and nineteen armored vehicles.

Farther south, the 1st UK Armoured Division fought a series of sharp fights with enemy units trying to withdraw. In the largest engagement, the "Desert Rats" destroyed 40 tanks and captured an Iraqi division commander.

Released from its theater reserve mission and attached to the VII Corps, 1st Cavalry Division (Mechanized) raced to the northern limit of the VII Corps to help attack the Republican Guards.

Joint Forces Command-North

The JFC-N continued to attack, seizing its intermediate and final objectives before the evening of 26 February. Egyptian forces secured their objective near Al-Abraq and turned east, pushing 60 kilometers toward their next objective, 'Ali As-Salim airfield. The plan was to pass through the US Marine forces and liberate Kuwait City. TF Khalid secured its objectives and also turned east towards Kuwait City. The 9th Syrian Armored Division screened the Saudi border east of TF Khalid and secured JFC-N supply routes with two brigades. The 3rd Syrian brigade followed TF Khalid toward Kuwait City.

I Marine Expeditionary Force

After refueling and replenishing during the night and early morning hours, I MEF continued to attack north on 26 February. Its objectives were Kuwait International Airport and the Al-Mutl'a Pass. The I MEF advanced with the 2nd MARDIV attacking to the northwest towards Al Jahra and the 1st MARDIV turning towards Kuwait International Airport. The Tiger Brigade headed toward Al-Mutl'a Ridge, terrain that dominated the roads leading from Kuwait City and key to cutting off the Iraqi retreat. Occupation of these dominant terrain features would close the main road, the 6th Ring Road, from coastal Kuwait.

The Iraqi command, belatedly realizing its forces in Kuwait faced entrapment, had issued orders to begin withdrawing. It was too late. The 2nd MARDIV began the attack at 1200. In a classic example of joint operations, the Tiger Brigade, with 3rd Battalion, 67th Armor in the lead supported by USAF and USMC aircraft, smashed its way to the high ground northwest of Al-Jahra, destroyed the remaining Iraqi resistance and cutting off further Iraqi retreat. Approaching Al-Mutl'a Ridge, the brigade found a minefield and waited for the plows to cut a safety lane. Once through the minefield, the brigade began to find enemy bunker complexes and dug-in armor units. They destroyed the enemy tanks and bunkers. Moving up and over Al-Mutl'a Ridge, the brigade destroyed many antiaircraft artillery (AAA) positions and began to consolidate its position.

The Tiger Brigade now controlled the highest point for hundreds of miles in any direction. The roads were choked with Iraqi vehicles and armor. The previous night, aircraft had begun destroying enemy military and commandeered vehicles retreating from Kuwait on these highways. The Tiger Brigade added its firepower to the continuous air strikes. Up and down the multi-lane highways were hundreds of burning and exploding vehicles of all types. The result brought the road the name "Highway of Death." Soldiers escaped from their vehicles and fled into the desert to join the growing army of prisoners.

The rest of the 2nd MARDIV reached Al-Jahra, overcoming the Iraqi rear guard dug in south of the city in quarries and dumps. The 6th Marines advanced into the quarry area, encountering stiff resistance from elements of the Iraqi 3rd Armored and 5th Mechanized divisions, some equipped with T-72 tanks. Elaborate bunkers were uncovered that housed brigade CPs, complete with kitchens and classrooms. 1st Battalion, 6th Marines advanced to the outskirts of Al-Jahra, the first Marine unit to reach Kuwait City. Relatively few prisoners were taken since the Iraqi rearguard chose to fight rather than surrender. Hundreds of civilians were encountered for the first time in the operation.

The 1st MARDIV ran into a desperate Iraqi armored defense centered on Kuwait International Airport. With TF Papa Bear in the center leading the attack, TF Ripper on the left, and TF Shepherd on the right, the division fought into the night of 26 February, assisted by 16-inch naval gunfire from the *USS Wisconsin* and Marine CAS. Darkness and intense smoke restricted visibility to only a few yards. TF Shepard was ordered to clear the airport while the other units held up, to ease coordination. The 1st MARDIV finally seized Kuwait International Airport at 0330, 27 February. I MEF After Action Reports reflect more than 250 destroyed tanks and 70 armored vehicles were counted in or near the airport, a testament to the final Iraqi stand. By early morning on 27 February, I MEF had secured all its assigned objectives. I MEF now awaited the arrival of JFC-E and JFC-N, which would liberate Kuwait City.

Joint Forces Command — East
Coalition forces continued operations well ahead of schedule, meeting generally light resistance. TF Omar continued its attack in the western sector reaching its objectives. The Qatari battalion pressed forward and also secured its objectives south of Kuwait City, as did TF Othman. The UAE motorized infantry battalion screened the 10th RSLF Mechanized Brigade's left flank. JFC-E was so successful that its western boundary was changed twice, and it was given four additional objectives. By day's end, preparations were made for a Pan-Islamic force to enter Kuwait City on 27 February.

Supporting Operations
Air Force Special Operations Command (AFSOC) and Army helicopters from 160th Special Operations Aircraft Regiment (SOAR) recovered SF teams from western Iraq. AFSOC PSYOP EC-130's flew numerous missions dropping leaflets and broadcasting prerecorded messages for Iraqi forces to surrender or be destroyed.

Despite the adverse weather, Coalition air crews continued the destruction of vehicles, artillery pieces and fortifications. Support of ground operations took on increased importance in an effort to destroy the Iraqi forces in the KTO.

As I MEF advanced, 3rd MAW fixed- and rotary wing aircraft continued to push forward. A large percentage flew interdiction missions as the MEF attempted to eliminate resistance before it could disrupt advancing ground units. Directed by airborne FACs, attack aircraft, some of whom flew from amphibious ships offshore, blocked the bottleneck formed by the Al-Mutl'a Pass. This action was instrumental in the destruction of major elements of the retreating enemy force.

G+3 (27 February) — Destruction of the Republican Guards

Coalition forces pressed the attack on the night of 26 February and pursued the Iraqi forces throughout 27 February against disintegrating resistance.

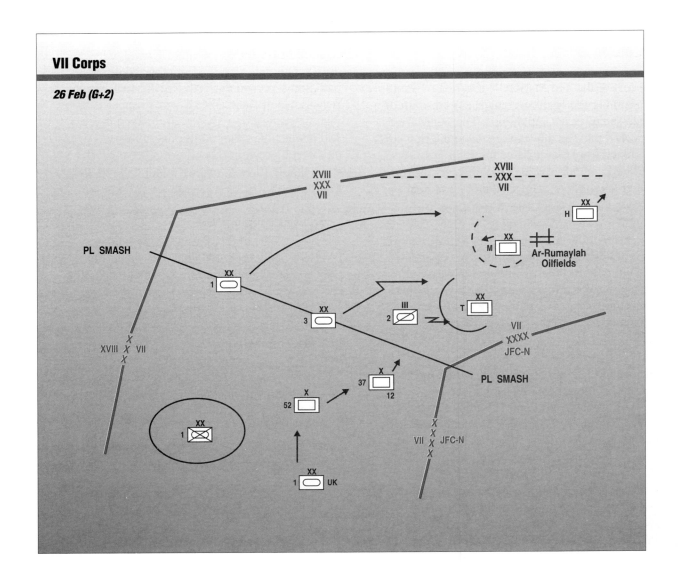

VII Corps

26 Feb (G+2)

Enemy Actions and Disposition

By the end of G+3, 33 Iraqi divisions were assessed by DIA as combat ineffective. Only isolated pockets of Iraqi forces remained in Kuwait. Most Iraqi Army units had surrendered, been destroyed, or were retreating. Many retreating units abandoned their equipment as they fled toward Al-Basrah. Coalition forces were involved in several brisk engagements with the RGFC; however, these remaining RGFC elements were operating independently and could no longer conduct cohesive operations.

West and south of Al-Basrah, remnants of Iraqi operational and theater reserve forces attempted to defend against heavy pressure from the Coalition. Remaining elements of the 10th Armored Division linked up with the remains of the RGFC Al-Madinah Division just north of the Iraq-Kuwait border and attempted, unsuccessfully, to defend against advancing US forces. To the west of the city, elements of the RGFC Hammurabi Armored Division with scattered elements of RGFC infantry divisions continued to defend under heavy pressure from advancing Coalition forces. Some parts of these

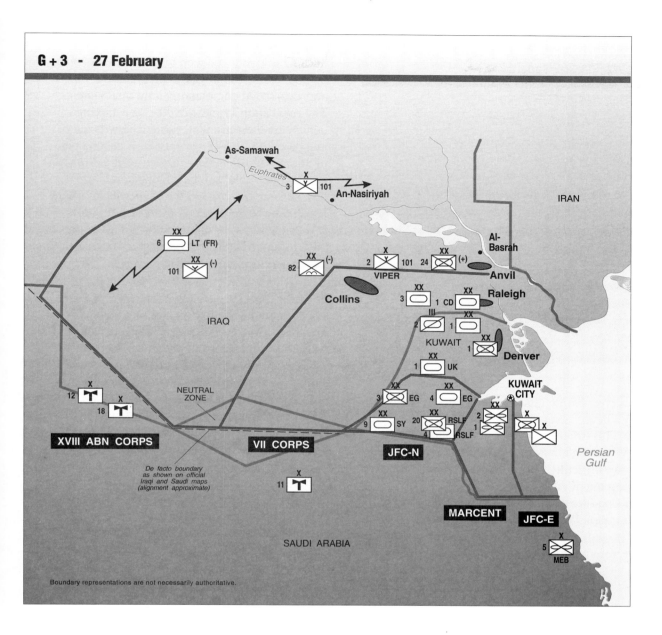

units succeeded in escaping across the Euphrates River. DIA estimates that upwards of 70,000 to 80,000 troops from defeated divisions in Kuwait may have fled into the city of Al-Basrah.

Army Component, Central Command

On the morning of 27 February, XVIII Airborne Corps was prepared to continue its advance east toward Al-Basrah. But before the assault could be resumed, the 24th Infantry Division (Mechanized) had to secure the Euphrates River Valley by taking two airfields still in Iraqi hands. Tallil airfield was about 20 miles south of the of An-Nasiriyah and Jalibah airfield lay farther east, near the lake at Hawr Al-Milh. The mission of taking these two airfields went to the units which had ended the previous day in positions closest to them. 1st Brigade would support the 2nd Brigade's attack on Jalibah airfield. The 197th Infantry Brigade, moving north, would take Tallil.

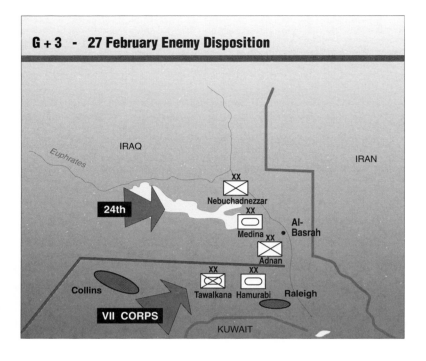

G + 3 - 27 February Enemy Disposition

IRAQ

IRAN

Euphrates

24th

XX
Nebuchadnezzar

XX
Medina

XX
Adnan

Al-Basrah

Collins

XX
Tawalkana

XX
Hamurabi

Raleigh

VII CORPS

KUWAIT

However, before attacks against the airfields could begin, a supply problem had to be solved. The 24th Infantry Division (Mechanized) had moved so fast in two days that fuel tankers were having difficulty keeping up. After halting during the night of the 26 February, the lead tanks had less than 100 gallons of fuel in their 500-gallon tanks. Replenishment fuel was with the brigade trains, but lead elements were not sure where to rendezvous in the desert. Through the initiative of a number of junior officers, the leaders managed to refuel the 24th Infantry Division (Mechanized) vehicles by midnight on 26 February. At 0600 27 February, 1st Brigade moved east; by 1000, Jalibah airfield was secured.

At 1200, the first XVIII Airborne Corps and 101st Airborne Division (Air Assault) attack helicopter battalions closed on a new FOB Viper, 200 km east of FOB Cobra which had been secured by the 2nd Brigade, 101st Airborne Division (Air Assault) assaulting at 1000. Two attack helicopter battalions from the 101st Airborne Division (Air Assault) were first

to the Al-Basrah causeway. Smoke from the burning oil wells reduced visibility to less than 1,000 meters, and it was so dark that the aircrews relied completely on thermal sights. The two battalions destroyed every moving vehicle on the causeway, scattering wreckage and blocking further movement. A second pair of attack battalions flew further north across the Al Hammar Lake and began engaging targets that had already crossed the causeway. With the last escape route now cut, most of Iraqi units were caught between advancing forces of the 24th Infantry Division (Mechanized), the VII Corps and the Euphrates River.

With the 24th Infantry Division (Mechanized) now oriented east after its northern advance, new phase lines were drawn between Tallil airfield and the Ar-Rumaylah oilfields west of Al-Basrah. From the line of departure east of Jalibah airfield, the 24th Infantry Division (Mechanized) advanced east, centering on Highway 8, and tying in with VII Corps to the south. Through the afternoon and night of 27 February, tankers, fighting vehicle gunners, helicopter crews and artillerymen destroyed hundreds of vehicles trying to redeploy to meet the new American attack or simply escape north across the Euphrates River.

In the VII Corps sector, the attack rolled east. VII Corps conducted a coordinated main attack against the three mechanized Republican Guard Divisions — the Tawakalna, the Al-Madinah, and the Hammurabi. As this operation began, the 1st Infantry Division, in the south of the Corps zone, conducted a night passage through the 2nd ACR, and immediately engaged the Iraqi forces. To the north, the 1st and 3rd Armored divisions attacked to the east and the 1st Cavalry Division attacked on the northern flank to prevent an Iraqi breakout in that direction. These attacks were closely synchronized combined arms and joint operations. CAS was first shifted deeper to attack the next expected targets. Waves of artillery and AH-64 battalions then were called in to fix the Iraqis and prevent them from maneuvering effectively against the approaching Americans. With the Iraqis set up, the massed maneuver elements of VII Corps struck one decisive blow after another. In other sectors, Iraqi elements broke and ran. Here, they stood and fought.

The battles begun the previous afternoon continued through the morning of 27 February as VII Corps divisions bore into Republican Guard units trying to escape or reposition. As the assault gained momentum, the VII Corps, for the first time, deployed its full combat power. The 1st Cavalry Division headed north to join the VII Corps assault. By 2100, the 1st Cavalry Division was in position on the extreme left of the corps sector, tying in with the 24th Infantry Division (Mechanized) across the corps boundary. Now the VII Corps could send five divisions and an ACR against the Republican Guard. From left (north) to right, VII Corps deployed the 1st Cavalry Division, 1st Armored Division, 3rd Armored Division, 1st Infantry Division (Mechanized), 2nd ACR, and the 1st UK Armoured Division. GPS receivers helped keep unit flanks aligned with one another and helped avoid friendly engagements.

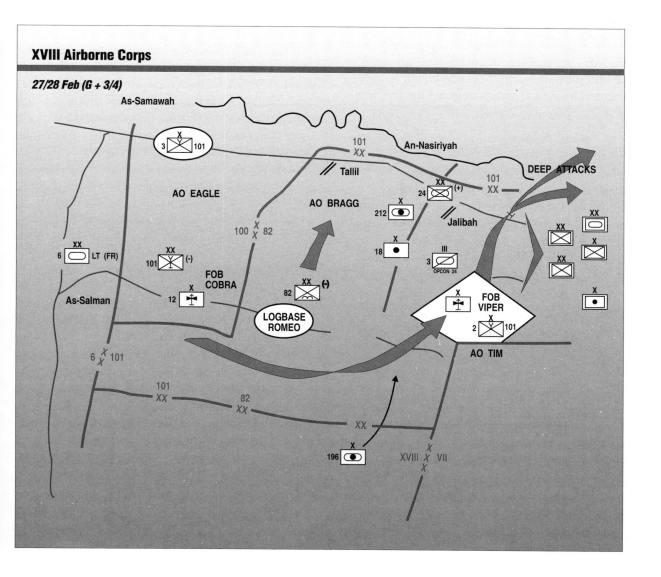

Early on 27 February, after a night of intense fighting, the 3rd Armored Division's 3rd Brigade moved through the 2nd Brigade, conducting a passage of lines while in contact with the enemy. This demanding maneuver required extensive coordination in order to preclude inflicting casualties on friendly forces. The level of training and the high quality soldiers and leaders were crucial to the success of this maneuver. Under a supporting artillery barrage, the 3rd Brigade then attacked the Iraqi 12th Armored Division. After a sharp fight, the 3rd Brigade broke through the enemy's defensive positions and drove into Kuwait.

Late in the evening on 27 February, the 3rd Armored Division again employed Apaches under adverse weather conditions and struck deep into the rear area of the enemy 10th Armored Division. These attacks behind the Iraqi lines broke the continuity of their defense

Coalition Forces Move North.

and forced them to abandon both their positions and much of their equipment. Together with attacks by the 1st Infantry Division , heavy frontal pressure from the 1st and 3rd Brigades of the 3rd Armored Division, supported by MLRS fires, forced front line enemy units to retreat directly into the disorganized rear elements. This combined arms operation prevented reorganization and completed the rout of the Iraqi 10th Armored Division.

The 1st Armored Division also fought remnants of the Tawakalna, Al-Madinah and Adnan Republican Guards Divisions. The 2nd Brigade, 1st Armored Division, destroyed 61 tanks and 34 armored personnel carriers of the Al-Madinah Division in less than one hour. The 1st Infantry Division (Mechanized) overran the 12th Armored Division and scattered the 10th Armored Division into retreat. On the south flank, the 1st UK Armoured Division destroyed the 52nd Armored Division, then overran three infantry divisions. To finish the RGFC destruction, VII Corps conducted a double envelopment involving the 1st Cavalry Division on the left and 1st Infantry Division (Mechanized) on the right. The trap closed on disorganized bands of Iraqis streaming north in full retreat.

The VII Corps pressed its attack farther east. The 1st Infantry Division (Mechanized) established blocking positions on the north-south highway connecting Al-Basrah to Kuwait City. In the early morning hours of 28 February, corps artillery units fired an enormous preparation involving all long-range weapons: 155-mm and 8-inch self-propelled artillery pieces, rocket launchers, and tactical missiles. Attack helicopters followed to strike suspected enemy positions. The advance east continued until offensive operations were halted at 0800, with VII Corps' armored divisions just inside western Kuwait.

Joint Forces Command — North

Egyptian forces closed on 'Ali As-Salim

airfield. The Kuwaiti Ash-Shahid Brigade and 4th Armored Brigade (RSLF) secured Objective Hotel. Syrian units continued to handle EPWs for JFC-N. One Syrian Brigade continued to secure the JFC-N LOC. Another Syrian Brigade, screening the Saudi border moved northeast to join the rest of the division. A brigade size force entered Kuwait City and prepared to occupy the western part.

I Marine Expeditionary Force

In the I MEF sector on 27 February, the 2nd MARDIV began the fourth day of the ground war by holding positions and maintaining close liaison with JFC-N units on the left flank. At 0500 27 February, Tiger Brigade troops made contact with Egyptian units, and four hours later JFC-N columns passed through the 2nd Marine Division. The Division remained on Al-Mutl'a Ridge and Phase Line Bear until offensive operations ended at 0800 28 February. To the east, 1st MARDIV consolidated its area, clearing the last pockets of resistance from near Kuwait International Airport and linking up with JFC-E units advancing along the coast.

Two small, but symbolic, incidents occurred on this final day of combat. Twelve Marines from the 2nd Force Reconnaissance Company infiltrated into Kuwait City in the early morning darkness of 27 February, to be greeted by jubilant Kuwaitis and American flags waving from buildings, despite sporadic fire from Iraqi stragglers. In Al-Jahra, a Marine officer slipped into the city on the afternoon of 27 February to contact the Kuwaiti Resistance, which was battling Iraqi rear-guard forces and stragglers. After conducting a reconnaissance patrol of key facilities in the city in the company of six well-armed Kuwaiti resistance fighters, he found himself the guest of honor at a dinner celebrating the liberation of Kuwait.

Joint Forces Command — East

JFC-E's offensive actions secured final objectives south of Kuwait City. Forward elements continued into Kuwait City and linked up with JFC-N forces which were entering Kuwait City from the west. JFC-E forces began to occupy the eastern part of Kuwait City.

Supporting Operations

Coalition air forces continued to provide air interdiction (AI) and CAS in adverse weather. A-10s and F-16s flew from bases in Saudi Arabia during the day while F-15Es and LANTIRN-equipped F-16s attacked during the night. Carriers in the Gulf provided A-6s, A-7s and F/A-18s to strike targets beyond the fire support coordination line (FSCL). F/A-18s and A-6s from Bahrain and forward-based AV-8Bs attacked targets and responded to requests for CAS in Kuwait. AH-64s and AH-1W s provided close-in fire support for ground forces. Some aircraft flying combat missions were damaged and lost to AAA and IR missiles as deteriorating weather conditions forced aircraft to fly at lower, more vulnerable altitudes.

The 3rd MAW, still pushing AH-1W attack helicopters and attack aircraft to Marine ground units, shifted its main effort to the north, along the main highway from Kuwait City to Iraq. Joining in the effort were AV-8Bs flying from the *USS Nassau* (LHA 4) in the Gulf, the first time in Naval history that attack aircraft had conducted missions from an amphibious ship. Behind I MEF's lines, heavy lift CH-53s and medium lift CH-46Es shuttled back and forth between ground combat units and logistics bases, carrying supplies forward and returning loaded with enemy prisoners, who were shuttled to Coalition EPW compounds.

SOF recaptured the American embassy in Kuwait City as other coalition forces liberated the city and linked up with Kuwaiti Resistance forces and helped clear key government buildings. Naval Special Warfare units took the former Kuwaiti Police Headquarters and captured numerous documents depicting C^2 of the Iraqi-supported terrorist campaign.

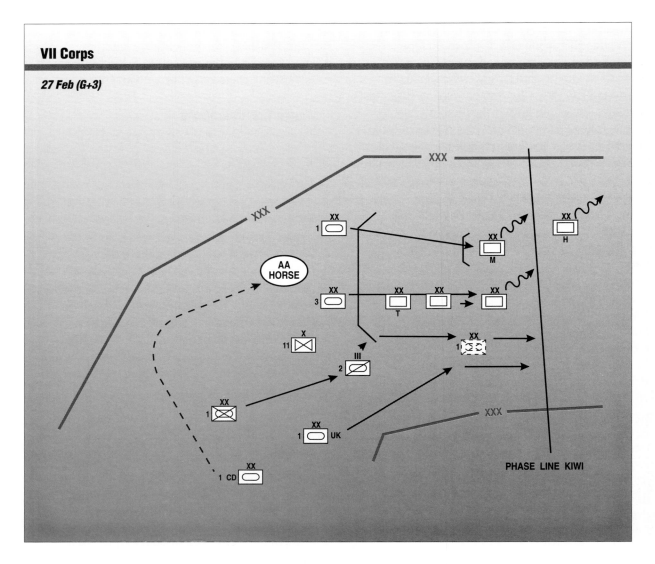

AA HORSE

PHASE LINE KIWI

G+4 (28 February) — Offensive Operations Cease

Army Component, Central Command

By the time offensive operations were halted, XVIII Airborne Corps had completed its advance into Iraq, cutting off Iraqi retreat and helping with the RGFC's final destruction. The 24th Infantry Division with the 3rd ACR continued its attack to the east to block enemy withdrawal and completed the elimination of the RGFC. The 82nd Airborne Division continued to clear objectives Red, Gold, and Orange. The 101st Airborne Division (Air Assault) continued

operations along Highway 8 while securing FOBs Cobra and Viper and interdicting the North Al-Basrah road.

When offensive operations ended at 0800 28 February, the 24th Infantry Division (Mechanized) lead elements stood along a phase line only 30 miles west of Al-Basrah. The division established a hasty defense along the appropriately named phase line "Victory," and there the XVIII Airborne Corps advance ended.

In the VII Corps sector, VII Corps continued to attack early on 28 February to destroy elements of remaining Iraqi divisions west of Al-Basrah. 1st Armored Division attacked and secured Objective Bonn. 3rd Armored Division cleared Objective Dorset after meeting stiff resistance and destroying more than 250 enemy vehicles, then pursued remaining enemy elements towards Objective Minden. The 1st UK Armoured Division attacked to the east to clear Objective Varsity, encountering limited resistance. After attacking across the zone and destroying RGFC remnants, the VII Corps established blocking positions with the 1st Infantry Division and 1st Armored Division along the Al-Jahra/Al-Basrah MSR. 1st Cavalry Division, 1st Armored Division, 3rd Armored Division, and the 2nd ACR secured their objectives and cleared positions short of the Corps limit of advance, which was the MSR between Al-Jahra and Al-Basrah.

In 90 hours of continuous movement and combat, VII Corps achieved devastating results

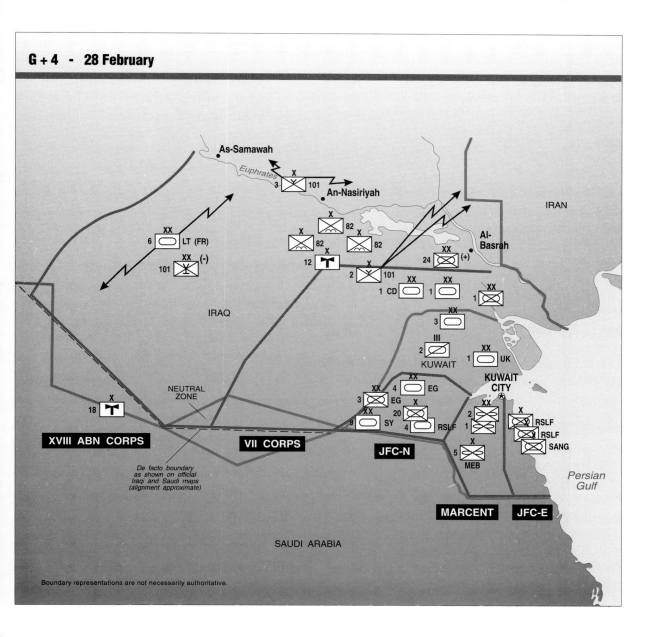

G + 4 - 28 February

against the best units of the Iraqi army. VII Corps reported destroying more than a dozen Iraqi divisions; an estimated 1,300 tanks, 1,200 fighting vehicles and APCs; 285 artillery pieces and 100 air defense systems;and captured nearly 22,000 enemy soldiers. At the same time, the corps had extremely light casualties and combat vehicles losses.

After defeating the enemy, VII Corps focused attention on humanitarian operations as did other US units. US forces ensured that Iraqi citizens, including Iraqi military personnel, were treated compassionately and with dignity. To do this essential services were restored as quickly as possible. For example, VII Corps humanitarian support included treating almost 30,000 Iraqi civilians in military health care facilities, supplying over a million meals, and reopening the health clinic and school in Safwan. In addition, VII Corps protected 12,000 Iraqi refugees in Safwan and at a camp near Rafhah, built a camp north of Rafhah that would hold 30,000 refugees, and provided transportation for refugees who chose to leave Iraq.

Joint Forces Command — North

JFC-N ceased offensive operations, secured enemy locations in their area, and consolidated positions. Elements of the Egyptian Ranger Regiment secured the Egyptian Embassy and the 6th Brigade, 4th Egyptian Armored Division began clearing the western part of Kuwait City. The 3rd Egyptian Mechanized Division screened north from its position at Al-Abraq.

I Marine Expeditionary Force

The final day of the ground offensive found I MEF in defensive position outside of Kuwait City. In the 2nd MARDIV sector, the 6th and 8th Marines had spent the previous night planning to attack into Al-Jahra to seize the key Kuwait military bases in the area and secure the northern road. Liaison had been established with the Kuwaiti resistance, now in control of most

of the city, to ensure that Marines and resistance fighters would not fire on one another. However, when offensive operations ended, the Marines remained outside the city as planned. 1st MARDIV consolidated its positions. I MEF assisted the passage of Arab-Islamic forces into Kuwait City. The 3rd MAW, ordered to stand down, provided helicopter support, moving supplies and logistics to forward units, and flew CAP over the MEF sector. During the ground offensive, 3rd MAW had flown 9,569 sorties in support of Marine and Coalition forces, 8,910 of which were fixed-wing sorties in support of the advancing ground troops.

Joint Forces Command — East

JFC-E ceased offensive operations and consolidated south of the Seventh Ring Road in Kuwait City. TF Victory of the Saudi SF secured the Saudi Embassy. One battalion-size task force entered Kuwait City and remained near the Sixth Ring Road. Royal Saudi Marines occupied Mina As-Sa'ud. Other JFC-E forces continued to clear enemy in their area.

SUMMARY OF THE GROUND CAMPAIGN

When offensive operations ended, the Coalition faced the beaten remnants of a once-formidable foe. Coalition ground forces, with tremendous support from air and naval forces, had defeated the Iraqi Army. Coalition armies stood on the banks of the Euphrates River, stretched across the Iraqi and Kuwaiti deserts and patrolled a liberated Kuwait City.

The ground campaign's results were impressive. The ground offensive lasted 100 hours and achieved all of CINCCENT's objectives. US and Coalition forces:

- Controlled critical Lines Of Communications in the KTO;
- Ejected Iraqi forces from Kuwait;
- Secured Kuwait International Airport and

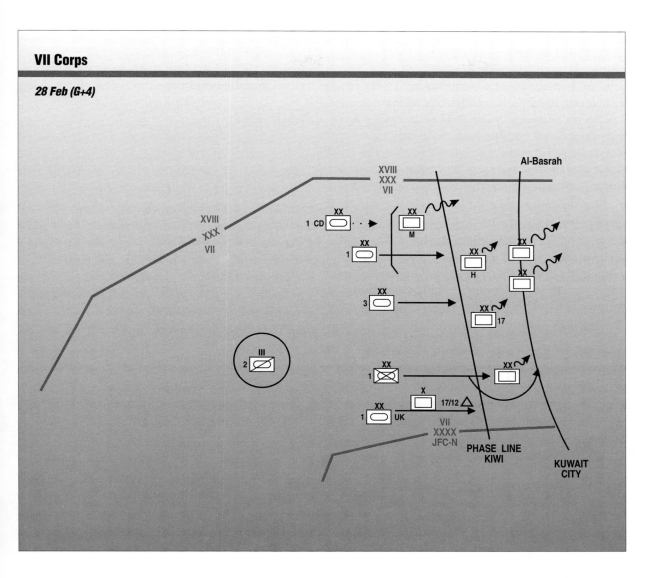

VII Corps

28 Feb (G+4)

Al-Basrah

XVIII
XXX
VII

PHASE LINE KIWI

KUWAIT CITY

crossroads west of Kuwait City;

■ Flanked, cut off, and destroyed Republican Guards Forces; and,

■ Liberated Kuwait City.

When the ground offensive started, the rapid rate of advance coupled with the violence with which enemy forces were encountered and suppressed or destroyed precluded an accurate assessment and count of battle damaged or destroyed enemy equipment. Ground commanders remained focused on reaching their final objectives with the thought that an

accurate battle damage assessment would be conducted after completion of combat operations.

After cessation of hostilities, most ground unit intelligence sections sent teams of soldiers to walk the battlefields and more accurately assess the number of enemy armored vehicles damaged, or captured. Information from these teams was sent to CENTCOM. The CENTCOM Joint Intelligence Center analyzed the numbers reported from the field and in many cases validated them with imagery or other sources of intelligence. Analysis and correlation of data was completed by 18 March 1991. The final numbers of enemy vehicles estimated by CENTCOM as destroyed or captured by Coalition forces during the entire Operation Desert Storm campaign were 3847 tanks, 1450 armored personnel carriers, and 2917 artillery pieces. It is important to note that these numbers are estimates only. (Chapter VI contains additional information on BDA evaluations.)

Final CENTCOM estimates were that only five to seven of their 43 combat divisions remained capable of offensive operations and an estimated 86,000 prisoners had been captured (64,000 by US forces). The combined Coalition forces — ground, air, naval, special, and supporting forces — had won one of the fastest and most complete victories in military history.

CONCLUSIONS

The ground campaign was clearly a success and the final, crucial element in a decisive Coalition victory. The Coalition forged an effective fighting force, destroyed much of the Iraqi army, and liberated Kuwait while sustaining light casualties. This overall victory was achieved through detailed planning and bold, aggressive execution. Coalition air forces

Summary of the Offensive Ground Campaign

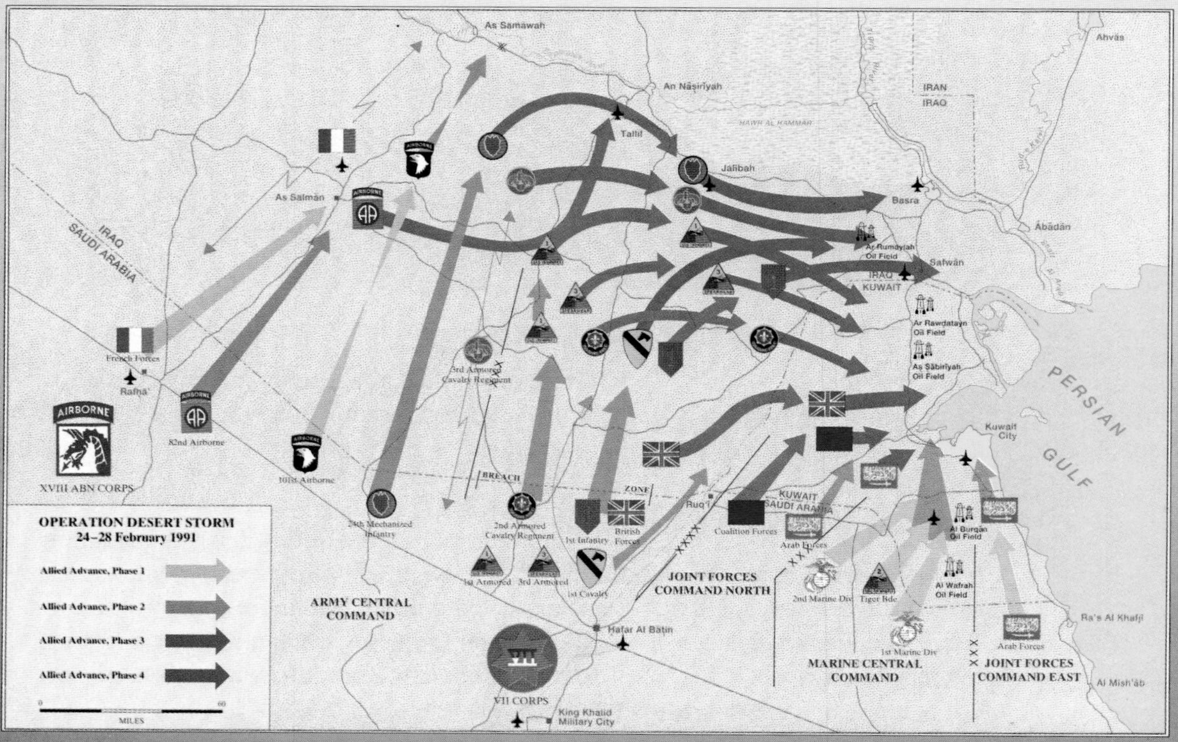

OPERATION DESERT STORM
24–28 February 1991

Allied Advance, Phase 1
Allied Advance, Phase 2
Allied Advance, Phase 3
Allied Advance, Phase 4

rapidly achieved air superiority in the KTO and set the stage for the Coalition ground forces' dramatic envelopment, destruction of the combat effectiveness of the Republican Guards and defeat of Saddam Hussein's forces in detail. This is not to say Coalition forces executed flawlessly, or always operated strictly according to the dictates of established doctrine; but they showed great professionalism and often improvised brilliantly. Finally, the enemy's limitations and aspects of the weather and terrain each contributed at times to ultimate Coalition victory.

However, no examination of the ground campaign would be complete if it dealt solely with assembly of forces and support structure in the theater of operations and the execution of the battle plans. The foundation of Operation Desert Storm was laid in the immediate aftermath of Vietnam. Developments within the US military were set in the context of the US-Soviet conflict and focused on combat operations in central Europe against a massive, armor-heavy threat. Programs begun in the mid-1970s reorganized the armed services on a volunteer basis, began to revise doctrine based on maneuver warfare, revitalized the noncommissioned officer and officer education programs, and formulated a long-range modernization effort. These and other steps combined to create the most capable land force in US history. It was this force that defeated one of the largest armies in the world — with more than 43 committed divisions and 10,000 items of combat equipment.

One hundred hours of ground combat was

too short a period to form comprehensive judgments about specific strengths or shortcomings. Much evidence remains anecdotal. In addition, the theater, the enemy and the global political situation were unique. Nonetheless, the Operation Desert Storm victory was unquestionably enabled by many years of thought, realistic planning, new doctrinal concepts, new unit designs and structures, an investment strategy for equipment modernization, and a training strategy for all components. The following observations reflect the essential elements of the land force's success.

Quality people are the single most important requirement for US forces. Without capable, motivated young men and women, technology alone will not be decisive. Good leadership and training are essential to readiness. Well-trained forces are confident in themselves, their leaders, and their equipment. The leaders of Operation Desert Storm were developed through a combination of practical experience and formal instruction. US combat units were led by seasoned professionals at every level — platoon sergeants with 10 years' troop duty; company commanders, developed through progressive assignments for six years to prepare them for command; and battalion commanders with 17 years' service behind them, much of it in tactical assignments. Operation Desert Storm was rapid, successful, and cost relatively few American casualties because US forces maintained high levels of combat readiness in peacetime.

The systematic evolution of doctrine before Operation Desert Storm served the land forces well. Service doctrines that stressed maneuver warfare fundamentals, coupled with joint doctrine for air, land, and maritime operations under a unified commander were a significant advantage. Operation Desert Storm was a clear demonstration of the overwhelming effectiveness of joint and combined operations synchronized by sound doctrine and experienced leaders.

The proper balance of land forces — light, airborne, air assault, armored, special operations and amphibious, along with appropriate combat support (CS) and combat service support (CSS) Active and Reserve, gave the Coalition the range of capabilities necessary to defeat Saddam Hussein.

Modern weapons systems and technology, in the hands of well-trained and well-led forces, provide the critical edge in modern combat. US ground forces had equipment that enabled them to decisively defeat the Iraqi forces. Moreover, US forces were trained to maximize this equipment's effectiveness. Tough training, technological superiority, and continued modernization are crucial to ensuring the lethality of the smaller forces of the future.

The weather and terrain conditions, on balance, favored Coalition victory. As demanding as the climate was, Coalition forces were well-equipped and supported. Iraqi forces, often isolated in static defenses for long periods, were steadily demoralized by air and psychological operations along with the harsh conditions. Accordingly, many Iraqis lost the will to resist by the time the ground operation began. The combination of austere terrain and desert weather coupled with extended periods of reduced visibility let US forces exploit the advantages of long-range weapons and all-weather, day-night sight systems. In many instances, this provided the crucial edge for success and contributed to the low casualty rate.

Joint and combined exercises, security assistance, and military-to-military contacts produced valuable relationships and infrastructure within the region that contributed to the creation of a militarily effective Coalition. Many US military leaders were accustomed to operating with Arab and other Islamic forces, and thus were adept at modifying US operational practices to accommodate other nations' requirements. The US doctrine, strategy, and tactics, developed originally in response to the Soviet threat to Western Europe, stressed maneuver warfare based on continuous operations, flexibility, agility, initiative and synchronization, attributes that served Coalition commanders well as they planned and executed the ground operation against Saddam Hussein. Years of cooperation and combined operations within the North Atlantic Treaty Organization (NATO) smoothed integration of European allies into the operation. In the end, the Coalition executed an integrated campaign that combined the combat power of each Coalition partner. Although CINCCENT did not exercise total control over all Coalition forces, unity of effort was achieved through careful and systematic coordination.

OBSERVATIONS

Accomplishments

- An overwhelming, rapid, continuous, joint and multi-national ground offensive enveloped Iraqi forces, destroyed the combat effectiveness of Iraqi units in the KTO and liberated Kuwait.

- Service doctrine for land warfare worked. Army AirLand Battle and USMC maneuver warfare doctrine were compatible and set the example for Coalition ground operations.

- Deception played a crucial role in ground operations and was integrated in all phases of the plan. Coupled with strict OPSEC, it helped fix Iraqi forces until it was too late for them to react to Coalition ground attacks. Deception was especially important during ground operations due to the need for surprise, and the vulnerability of large numbers of massed combat and support troops just before G-Day.

- Despite the difficult terrain and weather, Coalition maneuver forces moved rapidly over great distances. In 100 hours of combat, XVIII Airborne Corps maneuvered its lead elements approximately 260 miles. Armor-heavy VII Corps maneuvered over 150 miles as it enveloped Iraqi forces. I MEF also demonstrated tremendous agility as it breached two minefields and obstacle belts, fought off several armored counterattacks, and destroyed or trapped numerous Iraqi divisions.

- US Soldiers, Marines, British and French forces, and the forces of JFC-N and JFC-E outfought their Iraqi foes. Courage, determination, training and leadership at all levels were decisive in hundreds of individual fire fights and contributed directly to Coalition victory.

Shortcomings

- Intelligence support to tactical commanders was sufficient, but suffered from a lack of available assets and difficulties in disseminating national and theater intelligence. Tactical intelligence dissemination was constrained by a lack of sophisticated and secure communications below division level.

- Logistics units were hard-pressed to keep up with the rapid pace of maneuver units. Both logistics structure and doctrine were found wanting in the high tempo offensive operation. HET and off-road truck mobility were limited, and MSRs into Iraq few and constricted. Had the operation lasted longer, maneuver forces would have outrun their fuel and other support.

Issues

- The US had time to prepare its ground offensive while coalition-building, political and diplomatic efforts, and commercial sanctions ran their courses. The ability to rapidly move robust fighting forces will be a key challenge.

- The ground campaign was conducted by heavy, airborne, and air assault forces, all of which depend on large, bulky equipment for much of their combat power. Ways to improve strategic lift and tactical mobility continue to be a major priority.

- Measures to improve US chemical and biological defense readiness contributed to the ability of the Coalition to pursue the campaign in the face of a significant Iraqi chemical/biological warfare threat. The effectiveness of US chemical and biological defensive equipment and procedures was not challenged during the conflict.

- Breaching minefields under enemy fire proved demanding. Requirements for countermine and engineer equipment should be reviewed carefully.

Appendices Table Of Contents

A   **List Of US Fatalities And Prisoners Of War During Operations Desert Shield And Desert Storm** 313
LIST OF FATALITIES PROVIDED BY THE SERVICES 313
PRISONERS OF WAR DURING OPERATIONS DESERT SHIELD
   AND DESERT STORM 317

B   **United Nations Resolutions On Iraq** 319
SUMMARY OF UN SECURITY COUNCIL RESOLUTIONS
   ON IRAQ 319
   Resolution 660 of 2 August, 1990 319
   Resolution 661 of 6 August, 1990 319
   Resolution 662 of 9 August, 1990 319
   Resolution 664 of 18 August, 1990 319
   Resolution 665 of 25 August, 1990 319
   Resolution 666 of 13 September, 1990 319
   Resolution 667 of 16 September, 1990 319
   Resolution 669 of 24 September, 1990 319
   Resolution 670 of 25 September, 1990 319
   Resolution 674 of 29 October, 1990 319
   Resolution 677 of 28 November, 1990 319
   Resolution 678 of 29 November, 1990 319
   Resolution 686 of 2 March, 1991 320
DETAILS OF UNITED NATIONS RESOLUTIONS ON IRAQ 320
   Resolution 660 (2 August, 1990) 320
     The Security Council 320
   Resolution 661 (6 August, 1990) 320
     The Security Council 320
   Resolution 662 (9 August, 1990) 321
     The Security Council 321
   Resolution 664 (18 August, 1990) 322
     The Security Council 322
   Resolution 665 (25 August, 1990) 322
     The Security Council 322
   Resolution 666 (13 September, 1990) 323
     The Security Council 323

Resolution 667 (16 September, 1990) **324**
   The Security Council **324**
Resolution 669 (24 September,1990) **325**
   The Security Council **325**
Resolution 670 (25 September, 1990) **325**
   The Security Council **325**
Resolution 674 (29 October, 1990) **327**
   The Security Council **327**
Resolution 677 (28 November, 1990) **329**
   The Security Council **329**
Resolution 678 (29 November, 1990) **329**
   The Security Council **329**
Resolution 686 (2 March 1991) **330**
   The Security Council **330**

C   INTELLIGENCE **333**
PROLOGUE **333**
NATIONAL INTELLIGENCE **334**
THEATER INTELLIGENCE **337**
  Central Command **337**
  CENTCOM Components/Subunified Command **339**
  Coalition Intelligence **339**
  Operation Proven Force **340**
TACTICAL INTELLIGENCE **340**
  I MEF **340**
  ARCENT Corps **340**
  CENTAF Units **341**
  NAVCENT Units **341**
  Intelligence Collection and Dissemination **341**
BATTLE DAMAGE ASSESSMENT **343**
COUNTERINTELLIGENCE **345**
CONCLUSION **345**
OBSERVATIONS **346**

D   PREPAREDNESS OF UNITED STATES FORCES **347**
INTRODUCTION **347**
INTERESTS AND PRIOR COMMITMENTS **347**
  Military Involvement **347**
PLANNING **349**
  Changes in the Strategic Environment **349**
  New Policy Assessments **349**
  New Operations Plan **350**

Deployment Planning **351**
Planning and Preparations for Joint Operations **352**
Planning and Preparations for Combined Operations **353**
TRAINING **353**
Realistic Combat Training **353**
Combined and Joint Exercises **356**
Training In-Theater **357**
DEPLOYMENT PREPAREDNESS **358**
Strategic Lift **358**
Prepositioned Equipment **359**
FORCE MODERNIZATION **359**
Army Modernization **360**
Air Force Modernization **362**
Navy Modernization **362**
Marine Corps Modernization **363**
Other Modernization Issues **364**
PUBLIC AND FAMILY SUPPORT **365**
SUMMARY **365**
OBSERVATIONS **365**
Table 1, History of Defense Planning and Program
   Development for Persian Gulf/Southwest Asia Presence
   & Crisis Response **367**

E   **DEPLOYMENT** .... **.371**
INTRODUCTION **371**
DEPLOYMENT PLANNING **372**
EARLY DEPLOYMENT ISSUES, DECISIONS,
   AND PRIORITIES **374**
STRATEGIC LIFT CAPABILITIES **375**
Airlift **375**
   Civil Reserve Air Fleet (CRAF) **376**
Sealift **377**
   Ready Reserve Force (RRF) **378**
   Fast Sealift Ships (FSS) **378**
   Sealift Readiness Program (SRP) **379**
   Prepositioned Equipment **379**
   Afloat Prepositioning Ships (APS) **379**
   Air Force Prepositioning **380**
   Maritime Prepositioning **380**
DEPLOYMENT OVERVIEW AND EXECUTION **381**
Phase I **381**
   Army Component, Central Command (ARCENT)
      Deployments **382**

Marine Component, Central Command (MARCENT)
Deployments **384**
Air Force Component, Central Command (CENTAF)
Deployments **384**
Navy Component, Central Command (NAVCENT)
Deployments **386**
Other Force Deployments **387**
Phase II **387**
SUMMARY **389**
OBSERVATIONS **390**

F   LOGISTICS BUILDUP AND SUSTAINMENT 393

LOGISTICS PLANNING, PREPARATION, AND STRUCTURE ... 394
Army 394
Air Force 397
Navy 399
Marine Corps 400
REGIONAL NATIONS' SUPPORT 401
Infrastructure 402
Aerial Ports of Debarkation (APODs) 402
Sea Ports of Debarkation (SPODs) 403
Storage Facilities 403
Surface Transportation Network 403
Supply Support 404
SUSTAINMENT 405
Nature of the Sustainment Base 405
Expanding Logistic Requirements 406
EUCOM Support 409
Proven Force 410
TRANSPORTATION 411
Strategic Lift 412
Airlift 412
Civil Reserve Air Fleet (CRAF) 413
Air Refueling — The Force Multiplier 413
Desert Express 415
Sealift 416
Afloat Prepositioning Force 418
Fast Sealift Ships (FSS) 418
Ready Reserve Force (RRF) 419
Chartered Ships 419
Sealift Express 419
Importance of Forward Deployed Assets 419
The Importance of Lift to Sustainment 420

INTRATHEATER TRANSPORTATION 421
   Intratheater Airlift 422
   Building the Land Transportation Network 423
MATERIEL DISTRIBUTION SYSTEM 427
   Item Visibility 427
   Use of Containers 428
   Priority System 428
CONSUMABLES STORAGE 429
INDUSTRIAL BASE 432
WAR RESERVE STOCKS 435
EQUIPMENT MAINTENANCE STRATEGY 437
   Army 437
   Air Force 438
   Navy 440
   USMC 441
ENGINEERING SERVICES 442
OTHER ALLIED SUPPORT 444
   Foreign Military Sales 445
SUMMARY 446
OBSERVATIONS 448

G   **MEDICAL SUPPORT** 451
INTRODUCTION 451
   Overview of Health Service Support Concept 451
   Patient Care and Movement 452
   Army Health Services Operations 452
   Patient Movement 454
   Navy Health Service Operations 454
   Air Force Health Service Operations 455
   Veterinary Services 456
OPERATIONS DESERT SHIELD AND DESERT STORM 456
CONUS OPERATIONS 458
DEPLOYMENT 459
   Personnel 460
HEALTH CARE PLANNING AND SUPPORT IN CENTCOM 460
   Patient Evacuation 463
   Logistics 464
   Blood 465
   Systems Support 465
   C^3 467
   Chemical and Biological Defense 467

Medical Force Structure 468
OBSERVATIONS 469

H   **RESERVE COMPONENT FORCES** 471
INTRODUCTION 471
TOTAL FORCE POLICY, THE RESERVE COMPONENTS,
     AND PERSIAN GULF CONFLICT 471
RESERVE FORCES PREPAREDNESS — LEGACY
     OF THE '80s 471
INITIAL VOLUNTEERS 472
DECISION TO ACTIVATE, MOBILIZE, AND DEPLOY
     RESERVES 474
     Initial Involuntary Call-Up 474
     Second Involuntary Call-Up 475
     Third Activation 476
ACTIVATION, MOBILIZATION, AND DEPLOYMENT
     PROCESS 478
POST MOBILIZATION TRAINING 479
     Army National Guard Combat Brigades 480
     Air, Naval, and Marine Elements 481
INTEGRATION OF RESERVE COMPONENT FORCES 481
USE AND PERFORMANCE OF RESERVE COMPONENT
     FORCES IN THE THEATER 483
USE AND PERFORMANCE OF RESERVE COMPONENT
     FORCES OUTSIDE THE THEATER 484
ASSESSMENT 484
OBSERVATIONS 486

I   **COALITION DEVELOPMENT, COORDINATION,
     AND WARFARE** 487
HISTORICAL PERSPECTIVE 487
FOUNDATIONS FOR MILITARY COALITION 488
     Political Consensus 488
     International Environment 488
     Access and Resources 488
       Within the Gulf Region 488
       Outside the Gulf Region 489
BUILDING THE MILITARY COALITION 489
     Cultural Sensitivity 489
DEFENSIVE PHASE — OPERATION DESERT SHIELD 490
     Planning 490
     Forces 492

Command Arrangements 493
Summary 497
Offensive Phase — Operation Desert Storm 497
    Planning 497
    Forces 500
    Command Arrangements 500
    Summary 501
COALITION OPERATIONS 501
  Sanctions 501
    Within the Gulf Region 501
    Outside the Gulf Region 504
  Defensive Phase 504
    Within the Gulf Region 504
    Kuwaiti Resistance to Iraqi Occupation 506
    Outside the Gulf Region 506
    Host Nation Support by NCPs 506
    NATO Activities 507
    Eastern European Countries 507
    Pacific and Indian Ocean Area 508
    Supporting US CINCs 508
  Summary 509
  Offensive Phase 509
  Within the Gulf Region 509
    Coalition Air Operations 509
    The Battle of Khafji 510
    The Ground Offensive 512
  The Liberation of Kuwait City 516
  Outside the Gulf Region 516
  Host Nation Support By NCPs 517
  NATO Activities 518
  Eastern European Countries 518
  Pacific and Indian Ocean Area 518
  Supporting US CINCs 519
  Summary 519
  Arrangements for Enemy Prisoners of War 520
OBSERVATIONS 521

J   SPECIAL OPERATIONS FORCES 523
INTRODUCTION 523
COMMAND AND CONTROL RELATIONSHIPS 523
SOF MISSIONS 526

SOF OPERATIONS DURING OPERATIONS DESERT SHIELD
  AND DESERT STORM **527**
    Reconstitution of Kuwaiti Military **527**
    Coalition Warfare Support **528**
    Special Reconnaissance (SR) **529**
    Direct Action (DA) Missions **531**
    Electronic Warfare **533**
    Combat Search and Rescue (CSAR) **533**
LOGISTICS.................................... **534**
COMBATTING TERRORISM (CT) **535**
PSYCHOLOGICAL OPERATIONS (PSYOP) **536**
    Command Relationships for the Psychological
    Operation Group **537**
CIVIL AFFAIRS **538**
    Planning **538**
    Operations **539**
CONCLUSION **540**
OBSERVATIONS **541**

K   COMMAND, CONTROL, COMMUNICATIONS (C³)
  AND SPACE **543**
INTRODUCTION **543**
    Historical Perspective of CENTCOM Involvement in SWA ... **543**
COMMAND AND CONTROL STRUCTURE **545**
COMMAND AND CONTROL STRUCTURE OF COMPONENT
  COMMANDS **549**
    Army Command Relationships **549**
    Air Force Command Relationships **551**
    Navy Command Relationships **552**
    Marine Corps Command Relationships **553**
    Special Forces Command Relationships **554**
COALITION FORCES RELATIONSHIPS **555**
    Coalition Coordination, Communication, and Integration
    Center **558**
COMMUNICATIONS **559**
    Joint Command,Control,and Communications (C³)
    Structure **559**
    Combined Command and Control Communications **562**
SATELLITE COMMUNICATIONS SYSTEMS **563**
    Multichannel Satellite Communications **563**
    UHF Satellite Communication **564**
    Leased Commercial Satellite Communications **565**

TACTICAL COMMUNICATIONS SYSTEMS 566
   EUCOM Communications Support 567
INTELLIGENCE AND RECONNAISSANCE COMMUNICATIONS
   SUPPORT 568
   Weather Systems 568
   Multi-Spectral Imagery 569
NAVIGATION SYSTEMS 569
   NAVSTAR Global Positioning System (GPS) 569
   Position Location Reporting System (PLRS) 570
CONTROL OF COMMUNICATIONS RESOURCES,
   PROCEDURES, AND POLICY 570
   Frequency Management 571
COMMUNICATIONS INTEROPERABILITY 571
SUMMARY 572
OBSERVATIONS 573

L   **ENEMY PRISONER OF WAR OPERATIONS** 577
INTRODUCTION 577
AGREEMENTS 578
FORCE STRUCTURE 579
CAMP CONSTRUCTION 580
SAUDI RESPONSIBILITIES FOR EPWS 583
UNITED KINGDOM AND FRENCH FACILITIES 584
EPW HANDLING AND PROCESSING 584
INTELLIGENCE OPERATIONS 585
REPATRIATION 586
OBSERVATIONS 588

M   **FIRE FROM FRIENDLY FORCES** 589
INTRODUCTION 589
HISTORICAL PERSPECTIVE 589
MODERN WARFARE AND FIRE FROM FRIENDLY FORCES 590
FIRE FROM FRIENDLY FORCES INVOLVING UNITED
   STATES UNITS 591
ACTIONS TAKEN TO PREVENT FIRE FROM FRIENDLY
   FORCES DURING THE CONFLICT 592
   Technological Initiatives 592
   Training 592
   Control Measures 593
ONGOING EFFORTS 594
   Technology Initiatives 595
   Training 595

SUMMARY 596
OBSERVATIONS 597

N   **CIVILIAN SUPPORT** 599
INTRODUCTION 599
ARMY CIVILIAN PERSONNEL 600
AIR FORCE CIVILIAN PERSONNEL 600
NAVY AND MARINE CIVILIAN PERSONNEL 601
DEFENSE AGENCIES' CIVILIAN PERSONNEL 601
PLANNING AND OPERATIONS 602
AMERICAN RED CROSS PERSONNEL 604
OBSERVATIONS 604

O   **THE ROLE OF THE LAW OF WAR** 605
BACKGROUND 605
ROLE OF LEGAL ADVISERS 607
TAKING OF HOSTAGES 607
TREATMENT OF CIVILIANS IN OCCUPIED TERRITORY 608
TARGETING, COLLATERAL DAMAGE, AND CIVILIAN
    CASUALTIES 611
ENEMY PRISONER OF WAR PROGRAM 617
TREATMENT OF PRISONERS OF WAR 619
REPATRIATION OF PRISONERS OF WAR 620
USE OF RUSES AND ACTS OF PERFIDY 620
WAR CRIMES 621
ENVIRONMENTAL TERRORISM 624
CONDUCT OF NEUTRAL NATIONS 626
CONCEPT OF "SURRENDER" IN THE CONDUCT OF
    COMBAT OPERATIONS 629
OBSERVATIONS 632

P   **RESPONSIBILITY SHARING** 633
INTRODUCTION 633
RESPONSIBILITY SHARING TO OFFSET US INCREMENTAL
    DEFENSE COSTS 633
RESPONSIBILITY SHARING FOR CALENDAR YEAR 1990 –
    DESERT SHIELD COSTS 634
RESPONSIBILITY SHARING FOR CALENDAR YEAR 1991
    DESERT SHIELD AND DESERT STORM INCREMENTAL
    COSTS 636
IN-KIND CONTRIBUTIONS OTHER THAN HOST NATION
    SUPPORT 636

EQUIPMENT, MATERIAL, AND SUPPLIES 637
IN-KIND AIRLIFT AND SEALIFT 637
OBSERVATIONS 638

Q　**CHEMICAL AND BIOLOGICAL WARFARE DEFENSE** 639
INTRODUCTION 639
THE IRAQI THREAT 640
COALITION CW/BW DEFENSIVE MEASURES 640
　CW/BW Defense Force Structure 640
　CW/BW Defense Training 641
CW/BW DEFENSE EQUIPMENT 641
　Detection, Identification and Warning Systems 641
　Individual Protective Clothing and Equipment 643
　Collective Protective Systems (Vehicles and Shelters) 644
　Decontamination Equipment 644
LOGISTICS ASPECTS OF CW/BW DEFENSE 645
SUMMARY 645
OBSERVATIONS 646

R　**ROLE OF WOMEN IN THE THEATER OF OPERATIONS** 647
INTRODUCTION 647
JOB FUNCTIONS OF WOMEN DURING DESERT SHIELD/
　STORM 647
DEPLOYMENT OF WOMEN TO COMBAT ZONES 647
OBSERVATIONS 649

S　**MEDIA POLICY** 651
INTRODUCTION 651
PUBLIC AFFAIRS OPERATIONS 652
　National Media Pool 652
　Joint Information Bureau 652
　Media Concerns 652
　Media On the Battlefield 652
　Media Briefings 654
OBSERVATIONS 655

T　**PERFORMANCE OF SELECTED WEAPON SYSTEMS** 657
CAVEATS 657
　Scope 657
　System Performance and Mission Accomplishment 657
　Data Limitations and Biases 658

Aircraft Systems

A-6E INTRUDER ATTACK AIRCRAFT 661
A-10 THUNDERBOLT II ATTACK AIRCRAFT 664
AH-1 COBRA ATTACK HELICOPTER 666
AH-64 APACHE ATTACK HELICOPTER 669
AV-8B HARRIER STOVL AIRCRAFT 671
B-52 STRATOFORTRESS BOMBER 674
CH-46 SEA KNIGHT TRANSPORT HELICOPTER 677
CH-47D CHINOOK TRANSPORT HELICOPTER 679
E-2C HAWKEYE AEW AIRCRAFT 681
E-3 AWACS AIRCRAFT 684
EA-6B PROWLER ECM AIRCRAFT 686
F-4G WILD WEASEL ECM AIRCRAFT 688
F-14 TOMCAT FIGHTER 690
F-15C EAGLE FIGHTER 692
F-15E EAGLE FIGHTER 694
F-16 FIGHTING FALCON MULTI-ROLE AIRCRAFT 696
F-111 AARDVARK STRIKE AIRCRAFT 699
F-117A NIGHTHAWK STEALTH FIGHTER 702
F/A-18A/C HORNET STRIKE FIGHTER 704
F/A-18D HORNET STRIKE FIGHTER 707
JOINT SURVEILLANCE AND TARGET ATTACK RADAR
    SYSTEM (JSTARS) 709
KC-135 STRATOTANKER REFUELING AIRCRAFT 712
LIGHT AIRBORNE MULTIPURPOSE SYSTEM (LAMPS)
    HELICOPTER 715
MH-53E SEA STALLION MINE COUNTERMEASURES
    HELICOPTER 717
OH-58D SCOUT HELICOPTER 719
PIONEER UNMANNED AERIAL VEHICLE (UAV) 722
S-3B VIKING MULTI-MISSION AIRCRAFT 725
SH-3H SEA KING MULTI-MISSION HELICOPTER 727
UH-60 BLACK HAWK UTILITY HELICOPTER 729

Ground Systems

ASSAULT AMPHIBIAN VEHICLE (AAV) 735
BRADLEY FIGHTING VEHICLE 738
LAND MINE COUNTERMEASURE AND OBSTACLE
    BREACHING SYSTEMS 741
LIGHT ARMORED VEHICLE (LAV) 746
M1A1 ABRAMS TANK 749
MULTIPLE LAUNCH ROCKET SYSTEM (MLRS) AND
    ARMY TACTICAL MISSILE SYSTEM (ATACMS) 752
PATRIOT AIR DEFENSE SYSTEM 755

TACTICAL WHEELED VEHICLES (HEAVY FLEET) 757
TACTICAL WHEELED VEHICLES (MEDIUM FLEET) 762
TACTICAL WHEELED VEHICLES (LIGHT FLEET) 764
TRAILBLAZER RADIO INTERCEPT AND DIRECTION
    FINDING SYSTEM 766
TROJAN SPIRIT SATELLITE COMMUNICATIONS SYSTEM 768

Munitions

AIR-LAUNCHED CRUISE MISSILE 773
LASER GUIDED BOMBS (LGB) 775
MAVERICK AIR-TO-GROUND MISSILE 777
SIDEWINDER AIR-TO-AIR MISSILE 779
SPARROW AIR-TO-AIR MISSILE 780
STANDOFF LAND ATTACK MISSILE (SLAM) 782
TACTICAL AIR-LAUNCHED DECOY 784
TOMAHAWK MISSILE 786

Naval Systems

AIRCRAFT CARRIER (CV/CVN) 791
MINE COUNTERMEASURES SHIP 794
NAVAL GUNFIRE SUPPORT (NGFS) 796

Space Systems

DEFENSE METEOROLOGICAL SATELLITE
    PROGRAM (DMSP) 801
DEFENSE SATELLITE COMMUNICATIONS SYSTEM (DSCS) ... 803
GLOBAL POSITIONING SYSTEM (GPS) NAVSTAR-GPS 806
MULTI-SPECTRAL IMAGERY: LANDSAT 808

Appendix A

List Of US Fatalities And Prisoners Of War During Operations Desert Shield And Desert Storm

LIST OF FATALITIES PROVIDED BY THE SERVICES

UNITED STATES FATALITIES AND PRISONERS OF WAR ATTRIBUTED DIRECTLY TO OPERATIONS DESERT SHIELD AND DESERT STORM FROM 3 AUGUST 1990 TO 15 DECEMBER 1991

List of Fatalities Provided by the Uniformed Services . . . 313

List of Prisoners of War 317

Adams, Thomas R., Jr., Lance Corporal, USMC

Alaniz, Andy, Specialist, USA

Allen, Frank C., Lance Corporal, USMC

Allen, Michael R., Staff Sergeant, USA

Ames, David R., Staff Sergeant, USA

Anderson, Michael F., Chief Warrant Officer Three, USA

Applegate, Tony R., Staff Sergeant, USA

Arteaga, Jorge I., Captain, USAF

Atherton, Steven E., Corporal, USA

Auger, Allen R., Corporal, USMC

Avey, Hans C. R., Private First Class, USA

Awalt, Russell F., Staff Sergeant, USA

Bartusiak, Stanley W., Specialist, USA

Bates, Donald R., Staff Sergeant, USA

Bates, Tommie W., Captain, USA

Beaudoin, Cindy M., Specialist, USA

Belas, Lee A., Sergeant, USA

Belliveau, Michael L., Aviation Electrician's Mate Third Class, USN

Benningfield, Alan H., Boiler Technician Second Class, USN

Bentzlin, Stephen E., Corporal, USMC

Benz, Kurt A., Corporal, USMC

Betz, Dennis W., Sergeant, USMC

Bianco, Scott F., Corporal, USMC

Bland, Thomas C., Jr., Captain, USAF

Blessinger, John P., Staff Sergeant, USAF

Blowe, James, Mr., Army/Contractor

Blue, Tommy A., Sergeant, USA

Bnosky, Jeffrey J., Captain, USA

Boliver, John A Jr., Specialist, USA

Bongiorni, Joseph P., III, Sergeant, USA

Bowers, Tyrone, Private First Class, USA

Bowman, Charles L., Jr., Specialist, USA

Boxler, John T., Sergeant, USA

Brace, William C., Specialist, USA

Bradt, Douglas L., Captain, USAF

Bridges, Cindy D. J., Private First Class, USA

Brilinski, Roger P., Jr., Sergeant, USA

Brogdon, Tracy D., Sergeant, USA

Brooks, Tyrone M., Boiler Technician Fireman, USN

Brown, Christopher B., Airman Apprentice, USN

Brown, Darrell K., Airman Apprentice, USN

Brown, James R., Specialist, USA

Budzian, Steven A., Airman Apprentice, USN

Buege, Paul G., Senior Master Sergeant, USAF

Bunch, Ricky L., Staff Sergeant, USA

Burt, Paul L., Sergeant, USA

Butch, Michael R., Aviation Structural Mechanic Second Class, USN

Butler, Tommy D., Specialist, USA

Butts, William T., Sergeant First Class, USA

Caldwell, Thomas R., Captain, USAF

Calloway, Kevin L., Private First Class, USA

Campisi, John F., Staff Sergeant, USAF

Carr, Jason C., Sergeant, USA

Carranza, Hector, Jr., Lieutenant Colonel, USA

Carrington, Monray C., Seaman, USN

Cash, Clarence A., Specialist, USA

Chapman, Christopher J., Sergeant, USA

Chinburg, Michael L., Captain, USAF

Clark, Barry M., Sergeant, USAF

Clark, Beverly S., Specialist, USA

Clark, Larry M., Airman, USN

Clark, Otto F., Master Sergeant, USA

Clark, Steven D., Specialist, USA
Clemente, Samuel J., Mr,Army/Contractor
Codispodo, Edward M., Lance Corporal, USMC
Cohen, Gerald A., Private First Class, USA
Collins, Melford R., Private First Class, USA
Connelly, Mark A., Major, USA
Conner, Michael R., Sr., Staff Sergeant, USMC
Connor, Patrick K., Lieutenant, USN
Cooke, Barry T., Lieutenant Commander, USN
Cooke, Michael D., Corporal, USMC
Cooper, Ardon B., Private First Class, USA
Cooper, Charles W., Captain, USA
Cormier, Dale T., Captain, USAF
Costen, William T., Lieutenant, USN
Cotto, Ismael, Corporal, USMC
Crask, Gary W., Specialist, USA
Craver, Alan B., Sergeant, USA
Crockford, James F., Aviation Structural Mechanic
    Third Class, USN
Cronin, William D., Jr., Captain, USMC
Cronquist, Mark R., Specialist, USA
Cross, Shirley M., Aerographer's Mate First Class,
    USN
Crumby, David R., Jr., Sergeant, USA
Cruz, George, Mr., Navy/Contractor
Cunningham, James B., Lance Corporal, USMC
Curtin, John J., Chief Warrant Officer Three, USA
Dailey, Michael C., Jr., Private First Class, USA
Damian, Roy T., Jr., Specialist, USA
Daniel, Candace M., Private First Class, USA
Daniels, Michael D., Specialist, USA
Danielson, Donald C., Sergeant, USA
Daugherty, Robert L., Jr., Private First Class, USA
Davila, Manuel M., Specialist, USA
Davis, Marty R., Private First Class, USA
Dees, Tatiana, Staff Sergeant, USA
Delagneau, Rolando A., Specialist, USA
Delgado, Delwin, Signalman Third Class, USN
Delgado, Luis R., Sergeant, USA
Dierking, Ross A., Sergeant, USA
Diffenbaugh, Thomas M., Warrant Officer One,
    USMC
Dillon, Gary S., Captain, USMC
Dillon, Young M., Sergeant, USA
Dolvin, Kevin R., Captain, USMC
Donaldson, Patrick A., Chief Warrant Officer Two,
    USA
Dougherty, Joseph D., III, Lance Corporal, USMC
Douthit, David A., Lieutenant Colonel, USA
Douthit, David Q., Staff Sergeant, USA
Durrell, Robert L., Sergeant, USA

Dwyer, Robert J., Lieutenant, USN
Edwards, Jonathan R., Captain, USMC
Eichenlaub, Paul R., II, Captain, USAF
Fails, Dorothy L., Private, USA
Fajardo, Mario, Captain, USA
Farnen, Steven P., Specialist, USA
Felix, Eliseo C., Lance Corporal, USMC
Fielder, Douglas L., Sergeant, USA
Finneral, George S., Aviation Machinist's Mate
    Third Class, USN
Fitz, Michael L., Private First Class, USA
Fleming, Anthony J., Aviation Ordnanceman Third
    Class, USN
Fleming, Joshua J., Private (E-2), USA
Fontaine, Gilbert A., Aviation Storekeeper Airman,
    USN
Foreman, Ira L., Sergeant, USA
Fowler, John C., Specialist, USA
Galvan, Arthur, Captain, USAF
Garrett, Mike A., Staff Sergeant, USA
Garvey, Philip H., Chief Warrant Officer Four, USA
Garza, Arthur O., Lance Corporal, USMC
Gay, Pamela Y., Private First Class, USA
Gentry, Kenneth B., Staff Sergeant, USA
Gillespie, John H., Major, USA
Gilliland, David A., Boiler Technician Third Class,
    USN
Godfrey, Robert G., Chief Warrant Officer Three,
    USA
Gologram, Mark J., Sergeant, USA
Graybeal, Daniel E., Captain, USA
Gregory, Troy L., Lance Corporal, USMC
Grimm, Walter D., Captain, USAF
Guerrero, Jorge L., Airman, USN
Haddad, Albert G., Jr., Corporal, USMC
Haggerty, Thomas J., First Lieutenant, USA
Hailey, Garland V., Staff Sergeant, USA
Hampton, Tracy, Sergeant, USA
Hancock, Joe H., Jr., Lieutenant Colonel, USA
Hansen, Steven M., Staff Sergeant, USA
Harris, Michael A., Jr., Staff Sergeant, USA
Harrison, Timothy R., Staff Sergeant, USAF
Hart, Adrian J., Specialist, USA
Hatcher, Raymond E., Jr., Staff Sergeant, USA
Haws, Jimmy D., Staff Sergeant, USA
Hawthorne, James D., Sergeant, USMC
Hector, Wade E., Specialist, USA
Hedeen, Eric D., First Lieutenant, USAF
Hein, Kerry P., Chief Warrant Officer Two, USA
Hein, Leroy E., Jr., Sergeant, USAF
Henderson, Barry K., Major, USAF

Henry-Garay, Luis A., Specialist, USA
Herr, David R., Jr., Captain, USMC
Heyden, James P., Specialist, USA
Heyman, David L., Specialist, USA
Hill, Timothy E., Specialist, USA
Hills, Kevin J., Aviation Electrician's Mate Airman, USN
Hoage, Adam T., Lance Corporal, USMC
Hodges, Robert K., Technical Sergeant, USAF
Hogan, Larry G., Sergeant, USMC
Holland, Donnie R., Lieutenant Colonel, USAF
Hollen, Duane W., Jr., Specialist, USA
Hollenbeck, David C., Specialist, USA
Holt, William A., Aviation Electronics Technician Third Class, USN
Holyfield, Ron R, Damage Controlman Third Class, USN
Hook, Peter S., Major, USAF
Hopson, Trezzvant, Jr., Mr., Navy/Contractor
Horwath, Raymond L., Jr., Corporal, USMC
Howard, Aaron W., Private First Class, USA
Hughes, Robert J., Chief Warrant Officer Three, USA
Hurley, Patrick R., Sergeant Major, USA
Hurley, William J., Captain, USMC
Hutchison, Mark E., Boiler Technician Second Class, USN
Hutto, John W., Private First Class, USA
Huyghue, Wilton L., Fireman, USN
Jackson, Arthur, , Staff Sergeant, USA
Jackson, Kenneth J., Private First Class, USA
Jackson, Mark D., Lieutenant, USN
Jackson, Timothy J., Fire Control Technician Third Class, USN
James, Jimmy W., Specialist, USA
Jarrell, Thomas R., Specialist, USA
Jenkins, Thomas A., Lance Corporal, USMC
Jock, Dale W., Machinist's Mate Fireman, USN
Joel, Daniel D., Corporal, USMC
Jones, Alexander, Airman Apprentice, USN
Jones, Daniel M., Electrician's Mate Third Class, USN
Jones, Glen D., Specialist, USA
Jones, Phillip J., Corporal, USMC
Kamm, Jonathan H., Staff Sergeant, USA
Kanuha, Damon V., Staff Sergeant, USAF
Keller, Kenneth T., Jr., Sergeant, USMC
Kelly, Shannon P., Second Lieutenant, USA
Kemp, Nathaniel H., Mess Management Specialist Seaman App., USN
Keough, Frank S., Specialist, USA

Kidd, Anthony W., Specialist, USA
Kilkus, John R., Staff Sergeant, USMC
Kimbrell, Allen, Mr., Army/Corps of Engineers
Kime, Joseph G., III, Captain, USA
King, Jerry L., Private First Class, USA
Kirk, Reuben G., III, Private First Class, USA
Koritz, Thomas F., Major, USAF
Kramer, David W., Private First Class, USA
Kutz, Edwin B., Sergeant, USA
LaMoureux, Dustin C., Private First Class, USA
Lake, Victor T., Jr., Corporal, USMC
Lane, Brianz L., Lance Corporal, USMC
Lang, James M., Lance Corporal, USMC
Larson, Thomas S., Lieutenant, USN
Lawton, Lorraine K., Second Lieutenant, USA
Lee, Richard R., Chief Warrant Officer Three, USA
Linderman, Michael E., Jr., Lance Corporal, USMC
Lindsey, J. Scott, , Sergeant, USA
Long, William E., Major, USA
Lumpkins, James H., Lance Corporal, USMC   .
Lupatsky, Daniel, Electrician's Mate Second Class, USN
Madison, Anthony E., Specialist, USA
Mahan, Gary W., Specialist, USA
Maks, Joseph D., First Lieutenant, USA
Malak, George N., Warrant Officer, USA
Manns, Michael N., Jr., Fireman, USN
Martin, Christopher A., Warrant Officer, USA
Mason, Steven G., Specialist, USA
Matthews, Kelly, L., Sergeant, USA
May, James B., II, Senior Master Sergeant, USAF
Mayes, Christine L., Specialist, USA
McCarthy, Eugene T., Major, USMC
McCoy, James R., Sergeant, USA
McCreight, Brent A., Airman, USN
McDougle, Melvin D., Sergeant, USA
McKinsey, Daniel C., Boiler Technician Fireman Apprentice, USN
McKnight, Bobby L., Specialist, USA
Middleton, Jeffrey T., Sergeant, USA
Miller, James R., Jr., Specialist, USA
Miller, Mark A., Private First Class, USA
Mills, Michael W., Specialist, USA
Mills, Randall C., Sergeant, USA
Mitchell, Adrienne L., Private, USA
Mitchem, Earnest F., Jr., Sergeant First Class, USA
Mobley, Phillip D., Specialist, USA
Moller, Nels A., Sergeant, USA
Mongrella, Garett A., Sergeant, USMC
Monroe, Michael N., First Lieutenant, USMC
Monsen, Lance M., Staff Sergeant, USMC

Montalvo, Candelario, Jr., Sergeant, USMC
Moran, Thomas J., Staff Sergeant, USMC
Morgan, Donald W., Staff Sergeant, USA
Morgan, John K., Warrant Officer, USA
Mullin, Jeffrey E., Staff Sergeant, USA
Murphy, Donald T., Sergeant First Class, USA
Murphy, Joe, First Sergeant, USA
Murray, James C., Jr., Specialist, USA
Myers, Donald R., Specialist, USA
Neberman, James F., Mr., Army/Material Command
Neel, Randy L., Airman Apprentice, USN
Nelson, Rocky J., Airman First Class, USAF
Noble, Shawnacee L., Private First Class, USA
Noline, Michael A., Private First Class, USMC
Noonan, Robert A., Specialist, USA
O'Brien, Cheryl L., Sergeant, USA
Oelschlager, John L., Technical Sergeant, USAF
Oliver, Arthur D., Lance Corporal, USMC
Olson, Jeffery J., Captain, USAF
Olson, Patrick B., Captain, USAF
Ortiz, Patbouvier E., Staff Sergeant, USA
Pack, Aaron A., Sergeant, USMC
Paddock, John M., Chief Warrant Officer Four, USN
Palmer, William F., Specialist, USA
Parker, Fred R., Jr., Boiler Technician Second Class, USN
Patterson, Anthony T., Private, USA
Paulson, Dale L., Specialist, USA
Perry, Kenneth J., Specialist, USA
Phillips, Kelly D., Specialist, USA
Phillis, Stephen R., Captain, USAF
Plasch, David G., Warrant Officer, USA
Plummer, Marvin J., Aviation Boatswain's Mate Second Class, USN
Plunk, Terry L., First Lieutenant, USA
Poole, Ramono L., Senior Airman, USAF
Poremba, Kip A., Lance Corporal, USMC
Porter, Christian J., Lance Corporal, USMC
Poulet, James B., Captain, USAF
Powell, Dodge R., Sergeant, USA
Rainwater, Norman R., Jr., Private First Class, USA
Randazzo, Ronald M., Sergeant, USA
Reel, Jeffrey D., Private First Class, USA
Reichle, Hal H., Chief Warrant Officer Two, USA
Reid, Fredrick A., Captain, USAF
Rennison, Ronald D., Specialist, USA
Ritch, Todd C., Private First Class, USA
Rivera, Manuel, Jr., Captain, USMC
Rivers, Ernest, , Sergeant, USMC
Robinette, Stephen R., Sergeant, USA
Robson, Michael R., Staff Sergeant, USA

Rodriguez, Eloy A., Jr., Master Sergeant, USA
Rollins, Jeffrey A., Sergeant, USA
Romei, Timothy W., Corporal, USMC
Rossi, Marie T., Major, USA
Rush, Scott A., Private First Class, USA
Russ, Leonard A., Sergeant, USA
San Juan, Archimedes P., Lance Corporal, USMC
Sanders, Henry J., Jr., First Sergeant, USA
Sapien, Manuel B., Jr., Specialist, USA
Satchell, Baldwin L., Sergeant, USA
Schiedler, Matthew J., Data Systems Technician Third Class, USN
Schmauss, Mark J., Staff Sergeant, USAF
Schmidt, Paul L., Mr., Navy/Contractor
Scholand, Thomas J., Lance Corporal, USMC
Schramm, Stephen G., Lieutenant Colonel, USAF
Schroeder, Scott A., Lance Corporal, USMC
Scott, Brian P., Sergeant, USA
Seay, Timothy B., Disbursing Clerk Third Class, USN
Settimi, Jeffrey A., Mess Management Specialist Seaman App., USN
Shaw, David A., Staff Sergeant, USMC
Shaw, Timothy A., Private First Class, USA
Sherry, Kathleen M., Second Lieutenant, USA
Shukers, Jeffrey W., Fire Control Technician Chief, USN
Siko, Stephen J., Specialist, USA
Simpson, Brian K., Specialist, USA
Smith, James A., Jr., Machinist's Mate Third Class, USN
Smith, James M., Jr., Staff Sergeant, USA
Smith, Michael S., Sergeant, USA
Smith, Russell G., Jr., Sergeant First Class, USA
Snyder, David T., Lance Corporal, USMC
Snyder, John M., Lieutenant, USN
Speicher, Jeffrey W., Private First Class, USA
Speicher, Michael S., Lieutenant Commander, USN
Spellacy, David M., Captain, USMC
Squires, Otha B., Jr., Specialist, USA
Stephens, Christopher H., Staff Sergeant, USA
Stephens, John B., Specialist, USA
Stephenson, Dion J., Lance Corporal, USMC
Stewart, Anthony D., Lance Corporal, USMC
Stewart, Roderick T., Radioman Seaman, USN
Stokes, Adrian L., Private First Class, USA
Stone, Thomas G., Specialist, USA
Streeter, Gary E., Sergeant First Class, USA
Strehlow, William A., Sergeant, USA
Stribling, Earl K., Major, USA
Sumerall, Roy J., Staff Sergeant, USA

Swano, Peter L., Jr., Specialist, USA

Swartzendruber, George R., Chief Warrant Officer Two, USA

Sylvia, James H., Jr., Corporal, USMC

Talley, Robert D., Private, USA

Tapley, David L., Sergeant First Class, USA

Tatum, James D., Specialist, USA

Thomas, Phillip J., Aviation Structural Mechanic Second Class, USN

Thorp, James K., Captain, USMC

Tillar, Donaldson P., III, First Lieutenant, USA

Tormanen, Thomas R., Lance Corporal, USMC

Trautman, Steven R., Specialist, USA

Turner, Charles J., Lieutenant, USN

Underwood, Reginald C., Captain, USMC

Valentine, Craig E., Lieutenant (junior grade), USN

Valentine, Roger E., Private First Class, USA

Vega Velazquez, Mario, Sergeant, USA

Vigrass, Scott N., Private, USA

Viquez, Carlos A., Lieutenant Colonel, USA

Volden, Robert L., Boiler Technician First Class, USN

Wade, Robert C., Private First Class, USA

Waldron, James E., Lance Corporal, USMC

Walker, Charles S., Private First Class, USA

Walker, Daniel B., Lance Corporal, USMC

Wallington, Michael C., Lieutenant Colonel, USA

Walls, Frank J., Specialist, USA

Walrath, Thomas E., Specialist, USA

Walters, Dixon L., Jr., Captain, USAF

Wanke, Patrick A., Private First Class, USA

Ware, Bobby, M., Specialist, USA

Weaver, Brian P., Aviation Electrican Second Class, USN

Weaver, Paul J., Major, USAF

Wedgwood, Troy, M., Specialist, USA

Welch, Lawrence N., Sergeant, USA

West, John D., Aviation Structural Mechanic Airman, USN

Whittenburg, Scotty L., Sergeant, USA

Wieczorek, David M., Private First Class, USA

Wilbourn, James N., III, Captain, USMC

Wilcher, James, , Sergeant, USA

Wilkinson, Philip L., Mess Management Specialist Second Class, USN

Williams, Jonathan M., Corporal, USA

Winkle, Corey L., Private First Class, USA

Winkley, Bernard S., Chief Warrant Officer Two, USMC

Witzke, Harold P., III, Sergeant First Class, USA

Wolverton, Richard V., Specialist, USA

Worthy, James E., Specialist, USA

Wright, Kevin E., Specialist, USA

Zabel, Carl W., Specialist, USA

Zeugner, Thomas C. M., Major, USA

PRISONERS OF WAR DURING OPERATIONS DESERT SHIELD AND DESERT STORM

Acree, Clifford M., Lieutenant Colonel, USMC

Andrews, William F., Captain, USAF

Berryman, Michael C., Captain, USMC

Coleman, Melissa A., Specialist, USA

Cornum, Rhonda L., Major, USA

Dunlap, Troy A., Specialist, USA

Eberly, David W., Colonel, USAF

Fox, Jeffrey D., Lieutenant Colonel, USAF

Griffith, Thomas E. Jr., Major, USAF

Hunter, Guy L. Jr., Chief Warrant Officer Four, USMC

Lockett, David, Specialist, USA

Roberts, Harry M., Captain, USAF

Sanborn, Russell A. C., Captain, USMC

Slade, Lawrence R., Lieutenant, USN

Small, Joseph J. III, Major, USMC

Stamaris, Daniel J. Jr., Staff Sergeant, USA

Storr, Richard D., Captain, USAF

Sweet, Robert J., First Lieutenant, USAF

Tice, Jeffrey S., Major, USAF

Wetzel, Robert, Lieutenant, USN

Zaun, Jeffrey N., Lieutenant, USN

Appendix B

UNITED NATIONS RESOLUTIONS ON IRAQ

SUMMARY OF UN SECURITY COUNCIL RESOLUTIONS ON IRAQ

Resolution 660 of 2 August, 1990

Condemned invasion. Demanded withdrawal. Adopted 14-0-1, Yemen abstaining.

Resolution 661 of 6 August, 1990

Imposed a trade and financial embargo. Established special sanctions committee. Called on UN members to protect Kuwaiti assets. Adopted 13-0-2, Cuba and Yemen abstaining.

Resolution 662 of 9 August, 1990

Declared Iraq's annexation of Kuwait null and void. Adopted unanimously.

Resolution 664 of 18 August, 1990

Demanded immediate release of foreigners from Kuwait and Iraq. Insisted Iraq rescind its order closing missions in Kuwait. Adopted unanimously.

Resolution 665 of 25 August, 1990

Called on UN members cooperating with Kuwait to enforce sanctions by inspecting and verifying cargoes and destinations. Adopted 13-0-2, Cuba and Yemen abstaining.

Resolution 666 of 13 September, 1990

Affirmed Iraq was responsible for safety of foreign nationals. Specified guidelines for delivery of food and medical supplies. Adopted 13-2, Cuba and Yemen against.

Resolution 667 of 16 September, 1990

Condemned Iraqi aggression against diplomats. Demanded immediate release of foreign nationals. Adopted unanimously.

Resolution 669 of 24 September, 1990

Emphasized only special sanctions committee could authorize food and aid shipments to Iraq or Kuwait. Adopted unanimously.

Resolution 670 of 25 September, 1990

Expanded embargo to include air traffic. Called on UN members to detain Iraqi ships used to break the embargo. Adopted 14-1, Cuba against.

Resolution 674 of 29 October, 1990

Demanded Iraq stop mistreating Kuwaitis and foreign nationals. Reminded Iraq it is liable for damages. Adopted 13-0-2, Cuba and Yemen abstaining.

Resolution 677 of 28 November, 1990

Condemned Iraq's attempts to change Kuwait's demographic composition and Iraq's destruction of Kuwaiti civil records. Adopted unanimously.

Resolution 678 of 29 November, 1990

Authorized UN members to use "all means necessary" to enforce previous resolutions, if Iraq does not leave Kuwait by 15 January 1991.

Adopted 12-2-1, Cuba and Yemen against, China abstaining.

Resolution 686 of 2 March, 1991

Demanded Iraq cease hostile action, return all POWs and detainees, rescind annexation, accept liability, return Kuwaiti property, and disclose mine locations. Adopted 11-1-3, Cuba against, Yemen, China, and India abstaining

DETAILS OF UNITED NATIONS RESOLUTIONS ON IRAQ

Resolution 660 (2 August, 1990)

The Security Council,

Alarmed by the invasion of Kuwait on 2 August 1990 by the military forces of Iraq,

Determining that there exists a breach of international peace and security as regards the Iraqi invasion of Kuwait,

Acting under Articles 39 and 40 of the Charter of the United Nations,

1. Condemns the Iraqi invasion of Kuwait;

2. Demands that Iraq withdraw immediately and unconditionally all its forces to the positions in which they were located on 1 August 1990;

3. Calls upon Iraq and Kuwait to begin immediately intensive negotiations for the resolution of their differences and supports all efforts in this regard, and especially those of the League of Arab States;

4. Decides to meet again as necessary to consider further steps to ensure compliance with the present resolution.

VOTE: 14 for, 0 against, 1 abstention (Yemen)

Resolution 661 (6 August, 1990)

The Security Council,

Reaffirming its resolution 660 (1990) of 2 August 1990,

Deeply concerned that resolution has not been implemented and that the invasion by Iraq of Kuwait continues with further loss of human life and material destruction,

Determined to bring the invasion and occupation of Kuwait by Iraq to an end and to restore the sovereignty, independence and territorial integrity of Kuwait,

Noting that the legitimate Government of Kuwait has expressed its readiness to comply with resolution 660 (1990),

Mindful of its responsibilities under the Charter of the United Nations for the maintenance of international peace and security,

Affirming the inherent right of individual or collective self-defence, in response to the armed attack by Iraq against Kuwait, in accordance with Article 51 of the Charter

Acting under Chapter VII of the Charter of the United Nations,

1. Determines that Iraq so far has failed to comply with paragraph 2 of resolution 660 (1990) and has usurped the authority of the legitimate Government of Kuwait;

2. Decides, as a consequence, to take the following measures to secure compliance of Iraq with paragraph 2 of resolution 660 (1990) and to restore the authority of the legitimate Government of Kuwait;

3. Decides that all States shall prevent:

(a) The import into their territories of all commodities and products originating in Iraq or Kuwait exported therefrom after the date of the present resolution;

(b) Any activities by their nationals or in their territories which would promote or are calculated to promote the export or trans-shipment of any commodities or products from Iraq or Kuwait; and any dealings by their nationals or their flag vessels or in their territories in any commodities or products originating in Iraq or Kuwait and exported there from after the date of the present resolution, including in particular any transfer of funds to Iraq or Kuwait for the purposes of such activities or dealings;

(c) The sale or supply by their nationals or from their territories or using their flag vessels of any commodities or products, including weapons or any other military equipment, whether or not originating in their territories but not including supplies intended strictly for medical purposes, and, in humanitarian circumstances, foodstuffs, to any person or body in Iraq or Kuwait or to any person or body for the purposes of any business carried on in or operated from Iraq or Kuwait, and any activities by their nationals or in their territories which promote or are calculated to promote such sale or supply of such commodities or products;

4. Decides that all States shall not make available to the Government of Iraq or to any commercial, industrial or public utility undertaking in Iraq or Kuwait, any funds or any other financial or economic resources and shall prevent their nationals and any persons within their territories from removing from their territories or otherwise making available to that Government or to any such undertaking any such funds or resources and from remitting any other funds to persons or bodies within Iraq or Kuwait, except payments exclusively for strictly medical or humanitarian purposes and, in humanitarian circumstances, foodstuffs;

5. Calls upon all States, including States non-members of the United Nations, to act strictly in accordance with the provisions of the present resolution notwithstanding any contract entered into or license granted before the date of the present resolution;

6. Decides to establish, in accordance with rule 28 of the provisional rules of procedure of the Security Council, a Committee of the Security Council consisting of all the members of the Council, to undertake the following tasks and to report on its work to the Council with its observations and recommendations:

(a) To examine the reports on the progress of the implementation of the present resolution which will be submitted by the Secretary-General;

(b) To seek from all States further information regarding the action taken by them concerning the effective implementation of the provisions laid down in the present resolution;

7. Calls upon all States to co-operate fully with the Committee in the fulfillment of its task, including supplying such information as may be sought by the Committee in pursuance of the present resolution;

8. Requests the Secretary-General to provide all necessary assistance to the Committee and to make the necessary arrangements in the Secretariat for the purpose;

9. Decides that, notwithstanding paragraphs 4 through 8 above, nothing in the present resolution shall prohibit assistance to the legitimate Government of Kuwait, and calls upon all States:

(a) To take appropriate measures to protect assets of the legitimate Government of Kuwait and its agencies;

(b) Not to recognize any regime set up by the occupying Power;

10. Requests the Secretary-General to report to the Council on the progress of the implementation of the present resolution, the first report to be submitted within thirty days;

11. Decides to keep this item on its agenda and to continue itsefforts to put an early end to the invasion by Iraq.

VOTE: 13 for, 0 against, 2 abstentions (Cuba and Yemen)

Resolution 662 (9 August, 1990)

The Security Council,
Recalling its resolutions 660 (1990) and 661 (1990),

Gravely alarmed by the declaration by Iraq of a comprehensive and eternal merger with Kuwait,

Demanding, once again, that Iraq withdraw

immediately and unconditionally all its forces to the positions in which they were located on 1 August 1990,

Determined to bring the occupation of Kuwait by Iraq to an end and to restore the sovereignty, independence and territorial integrity of Kuwait,

Determined also to restore the authority of the legitimate Government of Kuwait,

1. Decides that annexation of Kuwait by Iraq under any form and whatever pretext has no legal validity, and is considered null and void;

2. Calls upon all States, international organizations and specialized agencies not to recognize that annexation, and to refrain from any action or dealing that might be interpreted as an indirect recognition of the annexation;

3. Further demands that Iraq rescind its actions purporting to annex Kuwait;

4. Decides to keep this item on its agenda and to continue its efforts to put an early end to the occupation.

VOTE: Unanimous (15-0)

Resolution 664 (18 August, 1990)

The Security Council,
Recalling the Iraqi invasion and purported annexation of Kuwait and resolutions 660, 661 and 662,

Deeply concerned for the safety and well being of third-state nationals in Iraq and Kuwait,

Recalling the obligations of Iraq in this regard under international law,

Welcoming the efforts of the Secretary-General to pursue urgent consultations with the Government of Iraq following the concern and anxiety expressed by the members of the Council on 17 August 1990,

Acting under Chapter VII of the United Nations Charter:

1. Demands that Iraq permit and facilitate the immediate departure from Kuwait and Iraq of the nationals of third countries and grant immediate and continuing access of consular officials to such nationals;

2. Further demands that Iraq take no action to jeopardize the safety, security or health of such nationals;

3. Reaffirms its decision in resolution 662 (1990) that annexation of Kuwait by Iraq is null and void, and therefore, demands that the Government of Iraq rescind its orders for the closure of diplomatic and consular missions in Kuwait and the withdrawal of the immunity of their personnel, and refrain from any such actions in the future;

4. Requests the Secretary-General to report to the Council on compliance with this resolution at the earliest possible time.

VOTE: Unanimous (15-0)

Resolution 665 (25 August, 1990)

The Security Council,
Recalling its resolutions 660 (1990), 661 (1990), 662 (1990) and 664 (1990) and demanding their full and immediate implementation,

Having decided in resolution 661 (1990) to impose economic sanctions under Chapter VII of the Charter of the United Nations,

Determined to bring an end to the occupation of Kuwait by Iraq which imperils the existence of a Member State and to restore the legitimate authority, the sovereignty, independence and territorial integrity of Kuwait which requires the speedy implementation of the above resolutions,

Deploring the loss of innocent life stemming from the Iraqi invasion of Kuwait and determined to prevent further such losses,

Gravely alarmed that Iraq continues to refuse to comply with resolutions 660 (1990), 661 (1990), and 664 (1990) and in particular at the conduct of the Government of Iraq in using Iraqi flag vessels to export oil,

1. Calling upon those Member States cooperating with the Government of Kuwait which are deploying maritime forces to the area to use such measures commensurate to the specific circumstance as may be necessary under the authority of the Security Council to halt all inward and outward maritime shipping in order to inspect and verify their cargoes and destinations and to ensure strict implementation of the provisions related to such shipping laid down in resolution 661 (1990);

2. Invites Member States accordingly to co-operate as may be necessary to ensure compliance with the provisions of resolution 661 (1990) with maximum use of political and diplomatic measures, in accordance with paragraph 1 above;

3. Requests all States to provide in accordance with the Charter such assistance as may be required by the States referred to in paragraph 1 of this resolution;

4. Further requests the States concerned to co-ordinate their actions in pursuit of the above paragraphs of this resolution using as appropriate mechanisms of the Military Staff Committee and after consultation with the Secretary-General to submit reports to the Security Council and its Committee established under resolution 661 (1990) to facilitate the monitoring of the implementation of this resolution;

5. Decides to remain actively seized of the matter.

VOTE: 13 for, 0 against, 2 abstentions (Cuba and Yemen)

Resolution 666 (13 September, 1990)

The Security Council,

Recalling its resolution 661 (1990), paragraphs 3 (c) and 4 of which apply, except in humanitarian circumstances, to foodstuffs,

Recognizing that circumstances may arise in which it will be necessary for foodstuffs to be supplied to the civilian population in Iraq or Kuwait in order to relieve human suffering,

Noting that in this respect the Committee established under paragraph 6 of that resolution has received communications from several Member States,

Emphasizing that it is for the Security Council, alone or acting through the Committee, to determine whether humanitarian circumstances have arisen,

Deeply concerned that Iraq has failed to comply with its obligations under Security Council resolution 664 (1990) in respect of the safety and well-being of third State nationals, and reaffirming that Iraq retains full responsibility in this regard under international humanitarian law including, where applicable, the Fourth Geneva Convention,

Acting under Chapter VII of the Charter of the United Nations,

1. Decides that in order to make the necessary determination whether or not for the purposes of paragraph 3 (c) and paragraph 4 of resolution 661 (1990) humanitarian circumstances have arisen, the Committee shall keep the situation regarding foodstuffs in Iraq and Kuwait under constant review;

2. Expects Iraq to comply with its obligations under Security Council resolution 664 (1990) in respect of third State nationals and reaffirms that Iraq remains fully responsible for their safety and well-being in accordance with international humanitarian law including, where applicable, the Fourth Geneva Convention;

3. Requests, for the purposes of paragraphs 1 and 2 of this resolution, that the Secretary-General seek urgently, and on a continuing basis, information from relevant United Nations and other appropriate humanitarian agencies and all other sources on the availability of food in Iraq and Kuwait, such information to be communicated by the

Secretary-General to the Committee regularly;

4. Requests further that in seeking and supplying such information particular attention will be paid to such categories of persons who might suffer specially, such as children under 15 years of age, expectant mothers, maternity cases, the sick and the elderly;

5. Decides that if the Committee, after receiving the reports from the Secretary-General, determines that circumstances have arisen in which there is an urgent humanitarian need to supply foodstuffs to Iraq or Kuwait in order to relieve human suffering, it will report promptly to the Council its decision as to how such need should be met;

6. Directs the Committee that in formulating its decisions it should bear in mind that foodstuffs should be provided through the United Nations in co-operation with the International Committee of the Red Cross or other appropriate humanitarian agencies and distributed by them or under their supervision in order to ensure that they reach the intended beneficiaries;

7. Requests the Secretary-General to use his good offices to facilitate the delivery and distribution of foodstuffs to Kuwait and Iraq in accordance with the provisions of this and other relevant resolutions;

8. Recalls that resolution 661 (1990) does not apply to supplies intended strictly for medical purposes, but in this connection recommends that medical supplies should be exported under the strict supervision of the Government of the exporting State or by appropriate humanitarian agencies.

VOTE: 13 for, 0 against, 2 abstentions (Cuba and Yemen)

Resolution 667 (16 September, 1990)

The Security Council,

Reaffirming its resolutions 660 (1990), 661 (1990), 662 (1990), 664 (1990), 665 (1990) and 666 (1990),

Recalling the Vienna Conventions of 18 April 1961 on diplomatic relations and of 24 April 1963 on consular relations, to both of which Iraq is a party,

Considering that the decision of Iraq to order the closure of diplomatic and consular missions in Kuwait and to withdraw the immunity and privileges of these missions and their personnel is contrary to the decisions of the Security Council, the international Conventions mentioned above and international law,

Deeply concerned that Iraq, notwithstanding the decisions of the Security Council and the provisions of the Conventions mentioned above, has committed acts of violence against diplomatic missions and their personnel in Kuwait,

Outraged at recent violations by Iraq of diplomatic premises in Kuwait and at the abduction of personnel enjoying diplomatic immunity and foreign nationals who were present in these premises,

Considering that the above actions by Iraq constitute aggressive acts and a flagrant violation of its international obligations which strike at the root of the conduct of international relations in accordance with the Charter of the United Nations,

Recalling that Iraq is fully responsible for any use of violence against foreign nationals or against any diplomatic or consular mission in Kuwait or its personnel,

Determined to ensure respect for its decisions and for Article 25 of the Charter of the United Nations,

Further considering that the grave nature of Iraq's actions, which constitute a new escalation of its violations of international law, obliges the Council not only to express its immediate reaction but also to consult urgently to take further concrete measures to ensure Iraq's compliance with the Council's resolutions,

Acting under Chapter VII of the Charter of the United Nations,

1. Strongly condemns aggressive acts perpetrated by Iraq against diplomatic premises and personnel in Kuwait, including the abduction of foreign nationals who were present in those premises;

2. Demands the immediate release of those foreign nationals as well as all nationals mentioned in resolution 664 (1990);

3. Further demands that Iraq immediately and fully comply with its international obligations under resolutions 660 (1990), 662 (1990) and 664 (1990) of the Security Council, the Vienna Conventions on diplomatic and consular relations and international law;

4. Further demands that Iraq immediately protect the safety and well-being of diplomatic and consular personnel and premises in Kuwait and in Iraq and take no action to hinder the diplomatic and consular missions in the performance of their functions, including access to their nationals and the protection of their person and interests;

5. Reminds all States that they are obliged to observe strictly resolutions 661 (1990), 662 (1990), 664 (1990), 665 (1990) and 666 (1990);

6. Decides to consult urgently to take further concrete measures as soon as possible, under Chapter VII of the Charter, in response to Iraq's continued violation of the Charter, of resolutions of the Council and of international law.

VOTE: Unanimous (15-0)

Resolution 669 (24 September, 1990)

The Security Council,
Recalling its resolution 661 (1990) of 6 August 1990,

Recalling also Article 50 of the Charter of the United Nations,

Conscious of the fact that an increasing number of requests for assistance have been received under the provisions of Article 50 of the Charter of the United Nations,

Entrusts the Committee established under resolution 661 (1990) concerning the situation between Iraq and Kuwait with the task of examining requests for assistance under the provisions of Article 50 of the Charter of the United Nations and making recommendations to the President of the Security Council for appropriate action.

VOTE: Unanimous (15-0)

Resolution 670 (25 September, 1990)

The Security Council,
Reaffirming its resolutions 660 (1990), 661 (1990), 662 (1990), 664 (1990), 665 (1990), 666 (1990), and 667 (1990);

Condemning Iraq's continued occupation of Kuwait, its failure to rescind its actions and end its purported annexation and its holding of third State nationals against their will, in flagrant violation of resolutions 660 (1990), 662 (1990), 664 (1990) and 667 (1990) and of international humanitarian law;

Condemning further the treatment by Iraqi forces of Kuwaiti nationals, including measures to force them to leave their own country and mistreatment of persons and property in Kuwait in violation of international law;

Noting with grave concern the persistent attempts to evade the measures laid down in resolution 661 (1990);

Further noting that a number of States have limited the number of Iraqi diplomatic and consular officials in their countries and that others are planning to do so;

Determined to ensure by all necessary means the

strict and complete application of the measures laid down in resolution 661 (1990);

Determined to ensure respect for its decisions and the provisions of Articles 25 and 48 of the Charter of the United Nations;

Affirming that any acts of the Government of Iraq which are contrary to the above-mentioned resolutions or to Articles 25 or 48 of the Charter of the United Nations, such as Decree No. 377 of the Revolution Command Council of Iraq of 16 September 1990, are null and void;

Reaffirming its determination to ensure compliance with Security Council resolutions by maximum use of political and diplomatic means;

Welcoming the Secretary-General's use of his good offices to advance a peaceful solution based on the relevant Security Council resolutions and noting with appreciation his continuing efforts to this end;

Underlining to the Government of Iraq that its continued failure to comply with the terms of resolutions 660 (1990), 661 (1990), 662 (1990), 664 (1990), 666 (1990) and 667 (1990) could lead to further serious action by the Council under the Charter of the United Nations, including under Chapter VII;

Recalling the provisions of Article 103 of the Charter of the United Nations;

Acting under Chapter VII of the Charter of the United Nations:

1. Calls upon all States to carry out their obligations to ensure strict and complete compliance with resolution 661 (1990) and in particular paragraphs 3, 4 and 5 thereof;

2. Confirms that resolution 661 (1990) applies to all means of transport, including aircraft;

3. Decides that all States, notwithstanding the existence of any rights or obligations conferred or imposed by any international agreement or any contract entered into or any license or permit granted before the date of the present resolution, shall deny permission to any aircraft to take off from their territory if the aircraft would carry any cargo to or from Iraq or Kuwait other than food in humanitarian circumstances, subject to authorization by the Council or the Committee established by resolution 661 (1990) and in accordance with resolution 666 (1990), or supplies intended strictly for medical purposes or solely for UNIIMOG;

4. Decides further that all States shall deny permission to any aircraft destined to land in Iraq or Kuwait, whatever its State of registration, to overfly its territory unless:

(a) The aircraft lands at an airfield designated by that State outside Iraq or Kuwait in order to permit its inspection to ensure that there is no cargo on board in violation of resolution 661 (1990) or the present resolution, and for this purpose the aircraft may be detained for as long as necessary; or

(b) The particular flight has been approved by the Committee established by resolution 661 (1990); or

(c) The flight is certified by the United Nations as solely for the purposes of UNIIMOG;

5. Decides that each State shall take all necessary measures to ensure that any aircraft registered in its territory or operated by an operator who has his principal place of business or permanent residence in its territory complies with the provisions of resolution 661 (1990) and the present resolution;

6. Decides further that all States shall notify in a timely fashion the Committee established by resolution 661 (1990) of any flight between its territory and Iraq or Kuwait to which the requirement to land in paragraph 4 above does not apply, and the purpose for such a flight;

7. Calls upon all States to co-operate in taking such measures as may be necessary, consistent with international law, including the Chicago Convention, to ensure the effective implementation of the provisions of resolution 661 (1990) or the present resolution;

8. Calls upon all States to detain any ships of

Iraqi registry which enter their ports and which are being or have been used in violation of resolution 661 (1990), or to deny such ships entrance to their ports except in circumstances recognized under international law as necessary to safeguard human life;

9. Reminds all States of their obligations under resolution 661 (1990) with regard to the freezing of Iraqi assets, and the protection of the assets of the legitimate Government of Kuwait and its agencies, located within their territory and to report to the Committee established under resolution 661 (1990) regarding those assets;

10. Calls upon all States to provide to the Committee established by resolution 661 (1990) information regarding the action taken by them to implement the provisions laid down in the present resolution;

11. Affirms that the United Nations Organization, the specialized agencies and other international organizations in the United Nations system are required to take such measures as may be necessary to give effect to the terms of resolution 661 (1990) and this resolution;

12. Decides to consider, in the event of evasion of the provisions of resolution 661 (1990) or of the present resolution by a State or its nationals or through its territory, measures directed at the State in question to prevent such evasion;

13. Reaffirms that the Fourth Geneva Convention applies to Kuwait and that as a High Contracting Party to the Convention Iraq is bound to comply fully with all its terms and in particular is liable under the Convention in respect of the grave breaches committed by it, as are individuals who commit or order the commission of grave breaches.

VOTE: 14 for, 1 against (Cuba)

Resolution 674 (29 October, 1990)

The Security Council,
Recalling its resolutions 660 (1990), 661 (1990), 662 (1990), 664 (1990), 665 (1990), 666 (1990), 667 (1990) and 670 (1990),

Stressing the urgent need for the immediate and unconditional withdrawal of all Iraqi forces from Kuwait, for the restoration of Kuwait's sovereignty, independence and territorial integrity, and of the authority of its legitimate government,

Condemning the actions by the Iraqi authorities and occupying forces to take third State nationals hostage and to mistreat and oppress Kuwaiti and third State nationals, and the other actions reported to the Council such as the destruction of Kuwaiti demographic records, forced departure of Kuwaitis, and relocation of population in Kuwait and the unlawful destruction and seizure of public and private property in Kuwait including hospital supplies and equipment, in violation of the decisions of this Council, the Charter of the United Nations, the Fourth Geneva Convention, the Vienna Conventions on Diplomatic and Consular Relations and international law,

Expressing grave alarm over the situation of nationals of third States in Kuwait and Iraq, including the personnel of the diplomatic and consular missions of such States,

Reaffirming that the Fourth Geneva Convention applies to Kuwait and that as a High Contracting Party to the Convention Iraq is bound to comply fully with all its terms and in particular is liable under the Convention in respect of the grave breaches committed by it, as are individuals who commit or order the commission of grave breaches,

Recalling the efforts of the Secretary-General concerning the safety and well-being of third State nationals in Iraq and Kuwait,

Deeply concerned at the economic cost, and at the loss and suffering caused to individuals in Kuwait and Iraq as a result of the invasion and occupation of Kuwait by Iraq,

Acting under Chapter VII of the United Nations Charter,

Reaffirming the goal of the international community of maintaining international peace and security by seeking to resolve international disputes and conflicts through peaceful means,

Recalling also the important role that the United Nations and its Secretary-General have played in the peaceful solution of disputes and conflicts in conformity with the provisions of the United Nations Charter,

Alarmed by the dangers of the present crisis caused by the Iraqi invasion and occupation of Kuwait, directly threatening international peace and security, and seeking to avoid any further worsening of the situation,

Calling upon Iraq to comply with the relevant resolutions of the Security Council, in particular resolutions 660 (1990), 662 (1990) and 664 (1990),

Reaffirming its determination to ensure compliance by Iraq with the Security Council resolutions by maximum use of political and diplomatic means.

A

1. Demands that the Iraqi authorities and occupying forces immediately cease and desist from taking third State nationals hostage, and mistreating and oppressing Kuwaiti and third State nationals, and from any other actions such as those reported to the Council and described above, violating the decisions of this Council, the Charter of the United Nations, the Fourth Geneva Convention, the Vienna Conventions on Diplomatic and Consular Relations and international law;

2. Invites States to collate substantiated information in their possession or submitted to them on the grave breaches by Iraq as per paragraph 1 above and to make this information available to the Council;

3. Reaffirms its demand that Iraq immediately fulfill its obligations to third State nationals in Kuwait and Iraq, including the personnel of diplomatic and consular missions, under the Charter, the Fourth Geneva Convention, the Vienna Conventions on Diplomatic and Consular relations, general principles of international law and the relevant resolutions of the Council;

4. Reaffirms further its demand that Iraq permit and facilitate the immediate departure from Kuwait and Iraq of those third State nationals, including diplomatic and consular personnel, who wish to leave;

5. Demands that Iraq ensure the immediate access to food, water and basic services necessary to the protection and well-being of Kuwaiti nationals and of nationals of third States in Kuwait and Iraq, including the personnel of diplomatic and consular missions in Kuwait;

6. Reaffirms its demand that Iraq immediately protect the safety and well-being of diplomatic and consular personnel and premises in Kuwait and in Iraq, take no action to hinder these diplomatic and consular missions in the performance of their functions, including access to their nationals and the protection of their person and interests and rescind its orders for the closure of diplomatic and consular missions in Kuwait and the withdrawal of the immunity of their personnel;

7. Requests the Secretary-General, in the context of the continued exercise of his good offices concerning the safety and well-being of third State nationals in Iraq and Kuwait, to seek to achieve theobjectives of paragraphs 4, 5 and 6 and in particular the provision of food, water and basic services to Kuwaiti nationals and to the diplomatic and consular missions in Kuwait and the evacuation of third State nationals;

8. Reminds Iraq that under international law it is liable for any loss, damage or injury arising in regard to Kuwait and third States, and their nationals and corporations, as a result of the

invasion and illegal occupation of Kuwait by Iraq;

9. Invites States to collect relevant information regarding their claims, and those of their nationals and corporations, for restitution or financial compensation by Iraq with a view to such arrangements as may be established in accordance with international law;

10. Requires that Iraq comply with the provisions of the present resolution and its previous resolutions, failing which the Council will need to take further measures under the Charter;

11. Decides to remain actively and permanently seized of the matter until Kuwait has regained its independence and peace has been restored in conformity with the relevant resolutions of the Security Council.

B

12. Reposes its trust in the Secretary-General to make available his good offices and, as he considers appropriate, to pursue them and undertake diplomatic efforts in order to reach a peaceful solution to the crisis caused by the Iraqi invasion and occupation of Kuwait on the basis of Security Council resolutions 660 (1990), 662 (1990) and 664 (1990), and calls on all States, both those in the region and others, to pursue on this basis their efforts to this end, in conformity with the Charter, in order to improve the situation and restore peace, security and stability;

13. Requests the Secretary-General to report to the Security Council on the results of his good offices and diplomatic efforts.

VOTE: 13 for, 0 against, 2 abstentions (Cuba and Yemen)

Resolution 677 (28 November, 1990)

The Security Council,

Recalling its resolutions 660 (1990) of 2 August 1990, 662 (1990) of 9 August 1990 and 674 (1990) of 29 October 1990,

Reiterating its concern for the suffering caused to individuals in Kuwait as a result of the invasion and occupation of Kuwait by Iraq,

Gravely concerned at the ongoing attempt by Iraq to alter the demographic composition of the population of Kuwait and to destroy the civil records maintained by the legitimate Government of Kuwait;

Acting under Chapter VII of the Charter of the United Nations,

1. Condemns the attempts by Iraq to alter the demographic composition of the population of Kuwait and to destroy the civil records maintained by the legitimate Government of Kuwait;

2. Mandates the Secretary-General to take custody of a copy of the population register of Kuwait, the authenticity of which has been certified by the legitimate Government of Kuwait and which covers the registration of population up to 1 August 1990;

3. Requests the Secretary-General to establish, in co-operation with the legitimate Government of Kuwait, an Order of Rules and Regulations governing access to and use of the said copy of the population register.

VOTE: Unanimous (15-0)

Resolution 678 (29 November, 1990)

The Security Council,

Recalling and reaffirming its resolutions 660 (1990), 661 (1990), 662 (1990), 664 (1990), 665 (1990), 666 (1990), 667 (1990), 669 (1990), 670 (1990) and 674 (1990),

Noting that, despite all efforts by the United Nations, Iraq refuses to comply with its obligation to implement resolution 660 (1990) and the above subsequent relevant resolutions, in flagrant contempt of the Council,

Mindful of its duties and responsibilities under the Charter of the United Nations for the maintenance and preservation of international peace and security,

Determined to secure full compliance with its decisions,

Acting under Chapter VII of the Charter of the United Nations,

1. Demands that Iraq comply fully with resolution 660 (1990) and all subsequent relevant resolutions and decides, while maintaining all its decisions, to allow Iraq one final opportunity, as a pause of goodwill, to do so;

2. Authorizes Member States co-operating with the Government of Kuwait, unless Iraq on or before 15 January 1991 fully implements, as set forth in paragraph 1 above, the foregoing resolutions, to use all necessary means to uphold and implement Security Council resolution 660 (1990) and all subsequent relevant resolutions and to restore international peace and security in the area;

3. Requests all States to provide appropriate support for the actions undertaken in pursuance of paragraph 2 of this resolution;

4. Requests the States concerned to keep the Council regularly informed on the progress of actions undertaken pursuant to paragraphs 2 and 3 of this resolution;

5. Decides to remain seized of the matter.

VOTE: 12 for, 2 against (Cuba and Yemen); 1 abstention (China)

Resolution 686 (2 March, 1991)

The Security Council,
Recalling and reaffirming its resolutions 660 (1990), 661 (1990), 662 (1990), 664 (1990), 665 (1990), 666 (1990), 667 (1990), 669 (1990), 670 (1990), 674 (1990), 677 (1990), and 678 (1990),

Recalling the obligations of Member States under Article 25 of the Charter,

Recalling paragraph 9 of resolution 661 (1990)

regarding assistance to the Government of Kuwait and paragraph 3(c) of that resolution regarding supplies strictly for medical purposes and, in humanitarian circumstances, foodstuffs,

Taking note of the letters of the Foreign Minister of Iraq confirming Iraq's agreement to comply fully with all of the resolutions noted above (S/22275), and stating it's intention to release prisoners of war immediately (S/22273),

Taking note of the suspension of offensive combat operations by the forces of Kuwait and the Member States cooperating with Kuwait pursuant to resolution 678 (1990),

Bearing in mind the need to be assured of Iraq's peaceful intentions, and the objective in resolution 678 (1990) of restoring international peace and security in the region,

Underlining the importance of Iraq taking the necessary measures which would permit a definitive end to the hostilities,

Affirming the commitment of all Member States to the independence, sovereignty and territorial integrity of Iraq and Kuwait, and noting the intention expressed by the Member States cooperating under paragraph 2 of Security Council resolution 678 (1990) to bring their military presence in Iraq to an end as soon as possible consistent with achieving the objectives of the resolution,

Acting under Chapter VII of the Charter,

1. Affirms that all twelve resolutions noted above continue to have full force and effect;

2. Demands that Iraq implement its acceptance of all twelve resolutions noted above and in particular that Iraq:

(a) Rescind immediately its actions purporting to annex Kuwait;

(b) Accept in principle its liability under international law for any loss, damage, or injury arising in regard to Kuwait and third States, and their nationals and corporations, as a result of the invasion and illegal occupation of Kuwait by Iraq;

(c) Immediately release under the auspices of the International Committee of the Red Cross, Red Cross Societies, or Red Crescent Societies, all Kuwaiti and third country nationals detained by Iraq and return the remains of any deceased Kuwaiti and third country nationals so detained; and

(d) Immediately begin to return all Kuwaiti property seized by Iraq, to be completed in the shortest possible period;

3. Further demands that Iraq:

(a) Cease hostile or provocative actions by its forces against all Member States, including missile attacks and flights of combat aircraft;

(b) Designate military commanders to meet with counterparts from the forces of Kuwait and the Member States cooperating with Kuwait pursuant to resolution 678 (1990) to arrange for the military aspects of a cessation of hostilities at the earliest possible time;

(c) Arrange for immediate access to and release of all prisoners of war under the auspices of the International Committee of the Red Cross, Red Cross Societies, or Red Crescent Societies, and return the remains of any deceased personnel of the forces of Kuwait and the Member States cooperating with Kuwait pursuant to resolution 678 (1990); and

(d) Provide all information and assistance in identifying Iraqi mines, booby traps and other explosives as well as any chemical and

biological weapons and material in Kuwait, in areas of Iraq where forces of Member States cooperating with Kuwait pursuant to resolution 678 (1990) are present temporarily, and in the adjacent waters;

4. Recognizes that during the period required for Iraq to comply with paragraphs 2 and 3 above, the provisions of paragraph 2 of resolution 678 (1990) remain valid.

5. Welcomes the decision of Kuwait and the Member States cooperating with Kuwait pursuant to resolution 678 (1990) to provide access and to commence immediately the release of Iraqi prisoners of war as required by the terms of the Third Geneva Convention of 1949, under the auspices of the International Committee of the Red Cross;

6. Requests all Member States, as well as the United Nations, the specialized agencies and other international organizations in the United Nations system, to take all appropriate action to cooperate with the Government and people of Kuwait in the reconstruction of their country;

7. Decides that Iraq shall notify the Secretary-General and the Security Council when it has taken the actions set out above;

8. Decides that in order to secure the rapid establishment of a definitive end to the hostilities, the Security Council remains actively seized of the matter.

VOTE: 11 for, 1 against (Cuba), 3 abstentions (China, India, Yemen).

Appendix C

INTELLIGENCE

The contributions and problems of intelligence support to Operations Desert Shield and Desert Storm have received widespread attention in reports, studies, testimonies and hearings. Assessing the successes and failures is difficult because of the magnitude of the effort; the diversity of intelligence requirements, functions, and systems; the size of the area of operations; and unique aspects of the Gulf crisis. Intelligence support, overall, was better than in past conflicts, as evidenced by the conduct and outcome of the war. Although some details of intelligence operations in the Gulf war are presented here, much of the information, of necessity, remains classified.

PROLOGUE

The Intelligence Community had been concerned about Iraq for years before the Gulf conflict. However, Iraqi regimes under the Ba'ath Party have been aggressive in security and counterintelligence operations, complicating the intelligence collection environment. Iraqi citizens are barred from contact with foreigners, even to the extent that the use of international mail and telephone circuits require permission from the Interior Ministry. Iraqi security services are pervasive in their surveillance and scrutiny of Iraqi citizens and foreigners alike. The difficult collection environment resulted in shortfalls in US knowledge of the extent and exact disposition of Iraqi nuclear research and chemical and biological weapons facilities. Although US intelligence agencies were aware of Iraqi military capabilities, they lacked access

"No combat commander has ever had as full and complete a view of his adversary as did our field commander. Intelligence support to Operations Desert Shield and Desert Storm was a success story."

General Colin Powell, USA
Chairman
Joint Chiefs of Staff

"The great military victory we achieved in Desert Storm and the minimal losses sustained by US and Coalition forces can be directly attributed to the excellent intelligence picture we had on the Iraqis."

General H. Norman Schwarzkopf, USA
Commander-in-Chief
Central Command

"At the strategic level, [intelligence] was fine. But we did not get enough tactical intelligence — front-line battle intelligence."

Lieutenant General William M. Keys, USMC
Commanding General
2nd Marine Division during Operation Desert Storm[1]

to information on the Iraqi leadership's intentions.

In late 1989, Central Command (CENTCOM) began reassessing its operational plans in the context of a declining Soviet threat and concerns about increased regional proliferation of weapons of mass destruction and advanced delivery systems. (Iraqi military programs and capabilities are detailed in Chapter I.) Battlefields during the Iran-Iraq war had witnessed use of chemical weapons and ballistic missiles, large-scale armor engagements, and substantial loss of life. As Iraqi demands for US withdrawal from the Gulf grew more strident

---

[1]   Reprinted from Proceedings with permission, copyright 1991, US Naval Institute.

and details of Saddam Hussein's[2] aggressive military research and development programs became better known, CENTCOM's Directorate of Intelligence (J-2) focused on Iraq as a potential threat to US interests in its area of responsibility.

Although relations between Iraq and Kuwait had, in the past, been affected by the unresolved border issue and the question of ownership of Warbah and Bubiyan islands, Kuwaiti leaders nevertheless were surprised at the antagonism of Saddam's 17 July speech commemorating the 22nd anniversary of the 1968 Iraqi revolution. (See Chapter I for details of the Kuwaiti-Iraqi disputes.) In his speech, Saddam accused Kuwait and the United Arab Emirates of complicity with the United States and Israel in a plot to cheat Iraq out of billions of dollars of oil revenue. The ferocity of the speech caused concern among the Intelligence Community, as did detection of movements of Republican Guard Forces Command (RGFC) units from the Baghdad area towards the Kuwaiti border.

CENTCOM, the Defense Intelligence Agency (DIA), the Central Intelligence Agency (CIA), and the National Intelligence Officer for Warning all were monitoring events closely and reporting on their significance. On 23 July, DIA began twice-daily production of Defense Special Assessments on the developing situation. All US intelligence agencies provided detailed reporting on the continuing Iraqi military buildup, and issued warnings of possible Iraqi military action against Kuwait. By 1 August, Iraqi forces between Al-Basrah and the Kuwaiti border included eight Republican Guard (RGFC) divisions supported by at least 10 artillery battalions. This force consisted of almost 150,000 troops, with by more than 1,000 tanks, and required support forces. That same day, CIA, DIA, and CENTCOM issued warnings that

an Iraqi invasion of Kuwait was likely, if not imminent.

On 2 August, at 0100 (Kuwait time), the three heavy divisions and a special operations division of the Iraqi RGFC launched a coordinated, multi-axis assault on Kuwait. (See Chapter I for a discussion of the invasion.) CENTCOM and DIA analysts evaluated the Iraqi force in or near Kuwait as more than sufficient to conduct a successful follow-on attack into Saudi Arabia's oil-rich Eastern Province.

On 4 August, the DIA Deputy Director for Joint Chiefs of Staff (JCS) Support accompanied the Secretary of Defense, the Chairman of the Joint Chiefs of Staff, and the Commander-in-Chief, Central Command (CINCCENT) to Camp David, MD, to brief President Bush on the situation in Kuwait and the potential threat to Saudi Arabia. On 5 August, the President sent the Secretary of Defense to Saudi Arabia to brief King Fahd on US perceptions and to offer American forces to help defend the Kingdom. The next day, King Fahd invited US forces to Saudi Arabia, marking the start of Operation Desert Shield.

Thus began one of the larger efforts in the history of the US Intelligence Community. The subsequent effort reflected the investment of billions of dollars in technology and training, and the contributions of thousands of intelligence professionals, both military and civilian, from a variety of agencies and staffs. These quality people were often the key. When systems or procedures proved inadequate or too cumbersome, the problems were remedied by innovative solutions and hard work.

NATIONAL INTELLIGENCE

Coinciding with the release of DIA, CIA, and

---

[2] Although the Arabic letters Hah (dammah)-Sin (Fathah)-Yah-Nun are best rendered as HU SAYN, this document reflects the more commonly used HUSSEIN.

CENTCOM warnings of possible Iraqi military action against Kuwait, DIA activated an Intelligence Task Force (ITF) in the National Military Intelligence Center (NMIC) at the Pentagon, and augmented the Operational Intelligence Crisis Center (OICC) at the Defense Intelligence Analysis Center on Bolling Air Force Base, DC. The ITF mission was to provide direct support to the JCS operations and planning staffs, and to serve as a clearinghouse for the flood of requests for information (RFI) pouring into the NMIC from commands worldwide. The OICC was augmented to coordinate and manage all DIA research and analytical efforts to provide responses to RFI, and to produce specialized targeting packages.

Concurrent with CENTCOM's initial force deployments on 7 August, DIA deployed a National Military Intelligence Support Team (NMIST) to Riyadh. NMIST have self-contained satellite communications equipment providing direct connectivity to DIA for the submission of RFI and the direct dissemination of intelligence information and imagery to the theater. Eleven NMIST eventually were deployed to support forces involved in Operations Desert Shield and Desert Storm. The NMIST network was to prove crucial to the CENTCOM J-2 since it eventually would be the sole dedicated intelligence communications capability between the CENTCOM J-2, the component and subunified command intelligence staffs, and the national intelligence community. These teams were vital sources of timely information, to include imagery, especially when the existing communications circuits between the United States and the theater became saturated with operational message traffic.

The National Security Agency (NSA) increased operations to support deployed military forces as well as national-level decision makers. CIA established 24-hour task forces in its Operations and Intelligence directorates. All national and Service intelligence organizations eventually deployed intelligence operations specialists, area specialists, and analysts to the theater to provide direct support, or to augment CENTCOM or component intelligence staffs.

The Intelligence Community initially was not prepared to cope with the volume of intelligence requirements to support the large scale of Operations Desert Shield and Desert Storm. During the initial period of Operation Desert Shield, various agencies and staffs produced a very high level of duplicative, even contradictory, intelligence to support deploying and deployed forces. Both JCS and CENTCOM recognized a need for some order in the Department of Defense (DOD) intelligence community, consisting of more than 30 producers. DIA assumed a new wartime role of production guidance — addressing order of battle, targeting, imagery exploitation, estimates, and battle damage assessment (BDA).

Under DIA guidance, Service intelligence staffs and organizations refocused ongoing production to complement the national agencies' efforts. The Army Intelligence and Threat Analysis Center (ITAC) produced detailed analyses on Iraqi doctrine and tactics, drawing on the lessons of the Iran-Iraq war. ITAC, in cooperation with DIA, produced thousands of copies of an unclassified "How They Fight" booklet for distribution to deploying US forces. This booklet contained Iraqi equipment descriptions, Iraqi tactics, and drawings of typical Iraqi defensive positions. ITAC also produced map overlays of actual defensive positions of Iraqi divisions in the Kuwait Theater of Operations (KTO). These templates were valuable tools for unit-level intelligence officers during the ground campaign. Often, these products were of greater detail and accuracy than captured Iraqi overlays of the same positions. Templates were distributed to all Coalition forces involved in the ground campaign.

The Navy Operational Intelligence Center (NOIC) supported the maritime campaign by providing merchant shipping analyses directly to maritime interdiction forces. This was supported by a major Intelligence Community, including CIA, effort to provide information about ship movements to assist in the maritime interdiction operations. NOIC's Crisis Action Team, working with the Marine Corps Intelligence Center, developed special support projects for amphibious warfare planning in the I Marine Expeditionary Force (MEF) area. The Navy Technical Intelligence Center produced two versions of a "Persian Gulf Fact Book" on the characteristics of Iraqi and Iranian naval systems, and provided quick reaction exploitation of Iraqi mines encountered in the Persian Gulf.

The Air Force Assistant Chief of Staff for Intelligence produced an "Iraqi Threat Reference Guide", and the Air Force Foreign Technology Division provided in-depth studies on the characteristics, capabilities and weaknesses of top line Iraqi fighter aircraft, such as the MiG-29 and F-1. The Air Force Intelligence Agency and Air Staff intelligence specialists directly supported the Air Staff's Checkmate operational planning group. (See Chapter VI for details on Checkmate.)

The Military Intelligence Board (MIB) — an advisory and decision-making body chaired by the Director, DIA, and made up of Service intelligence chiefs and the Director, NSA — supported the CENTCOM intelligence mission. (For support to Operations Desert Shield and Desert Storm, the MIB also included nonvoting representatives of the Joint Staff Directorate of Command, Control and Communications; and the Defense Support Program Office.) The MIB addressed theater shortfalls as identified by the CENTCOM Directorate of Intelligence (J-2) and coordinated the deployment of needed personnel, equipment, and systems to support operations in the Gulf.

In Washington, the DOD Joint Intelligence Center (DOD-JIC) was established in the NMIC

on 2 September to provide a single, integrated DOD intelligence position to national decision makers and the theater commander. The DOD-JIC was a landmark effort; for the first time, analysts from DIA, NSA, and all Service intelligence commands were organized in one location in one chain-of-command and focused on one DOD, all-source intelligence position. CIA provided some staffing to the DOD-JIC.

During the early months of Operation Desert Shield and throughout Operation Desert Storm, CENTCOM and DIA collection managers, working in close coordination with other Intelligence Community elements, optimized US national collection systems against CENTCOM intelligence requirements. The State Department Bureau of Intelligence and Research adjusted its coverage from other issues to become the primary agency for compilation of UN economic sanctions violations.

Mapping, charting, and geodesy (MC&G) products were key to the targeting, planning, and operations efforts of Operations Desert Shield and Desert Storm. Imagery also was acquired from US, foreign, and commercial sources to support MC&G requirements. Initially, the airlift priority for MC&G items was too low to support deploying forces adequately . CENTCOM resolved the problem by raising MC&G to the same priority as medical supplies. Ninety million maps were transported to theater.

During Operations Desert Shield and Desert Storm, the national intelligence agencies produced numerous reports and special national intelligence estimates. Field commanders have criticized some of these products as being overly caveated and footnoted, too broad, and non-predictive. The national-level intelligence structure, including the National Intelligence Council, DIA, and CIA, adhered to the peacetime concept of competing analysis, which gives intelligence consumers the benefit of alternative views and predictions. This is appropriate for high-level policymakers; however, to a combat commander, this reporting method often presents too broad a picture and too wide a range of options to affect combat force posturing or employment.

THEATER INTELLIGENCE

Central Command

The primary focus of intelligence operations, particularly during Operation Desert Shield, was to provide the theater and component commanders with an accurate picture of Iraqi capabilities and intentions. To do so, the theater-level intelligence structure made extensive use of national capabilities as well as a wide array of deployed Service and component capabilities. In some cases, collection platforms and systems organic to tactical units were tasked for missions that did not directly support their parent organizations. Although some shortfalls surfaced, theater-level intelligence efforts met the requirements of CINCCENT and his component commanders.

Before Operation Desert Shield, the CENTCOM intelligence staff did not have the resources, equipment, or organizational structure needed to deploy and support operations of the level and scope of Operation Desert Storm. Nor did it have the types or numbers of trained personnel needed to execute the wartime mission, and had to be augmented with personnel with the required specialized skills. The CENTCOM J-2 identified these shortfalls and conveyed them to DIA and the MIB. The J-2 directed the drafting of an architecture plan to augment the organization with the numbers and types of personnel the mission required. In response to a CENTCOM Director of Intelligence request, the MIB deployed a joint-service team to theater in November to help develop a wartime intelligence staff. The MIB was instrumental in identifying and/or providing qualified Service personnel to fill the manpower gaps.

The CENTCOM Joint Intelligence Center (JIC) was created and operated as the senior intelligence organization in theater, maintaining contact with the Directors of Intelligence at the components and subunified command headquarters. Analytic tasks were shared, with each component providing analysis of its geographic area of operations and in its functional area of expertise. The JIC acted as the clearinghouse for intelligence requirements and as the collection manager for theater assets. Theater and component collection managers met daily at CENTCOM. RFI that could not be answered using theater assets were validated, prioritized, and referred to the DOD-JIC. The CENTCOM JIC used scarce theater assets effectively by eliminating duplicative efforts, and ensured component and subunified command intelligence requirements were addressed by national elements.

Wartime intelligence organizations and functions, nonexistent or seldom used and exercised in peacetime, were created within the CENTCOM JIC. The Combat Assessment Center included the Combat Assessment Cell, which provided an assessment of enemy intentions 24 to 96 hours into the future — an effort not only previously nonexistent at CENTCOM, but also nonexistent at the national level throughout Operations Desert Shield and Desert Storm — and the BDA cell, created to evaluate achievement of mission objectives and provide targeting recommendations.

Reconnaissance and airborne intelligence collection efforts in theater were managed by the Joint Reconnaissance Center (JRC), a standard function in most unified and specified commands. The notable difference is that the CENTCOM JRC was an integral part of the CENTCOM JIC rather than part of the Directorate of Operations (J-3) staff. This allowed direct and effective contact between the reconnaissance and intelligence platform managers, collection managers, and the theater-level intelligence analysts who needed timely information to respond to CINCCENT's requirements. The JRC also controlled some corps-level reconnaissance and intelligence collection assets, effectively harmonizing their capabilities and areas of coverage in response to overall theater intelligence requirements. The placement of the JRC within the intelligence domain ensured the timely acquisition and dissemination of needed information. To coordinate and deconflict airborne intelligence collection and surveillance operations between CENTCOM components and other Coalition nations, CENTCOM conducted a Daily Aerial Reconnaissance and Surveillance (DARS) conference. Representatives of the United States, United Kingdom, France and Saudi Arabia were standing members of the DARS committee.

Many national and tactical systems were operated at the theater level throughout Operations Desert Shield and Desert Storm. The distinction between their strategic and tactical roles blurred during preparation for combat and during combat operations. The Air Force-Army Joint Surveillance Target Attack Radar System (JSTARS), still in project development and testing, provided all-weather, near-real-time targeting information in coordination with other tactical and theater systems, such as the Army OV-1D. (A detailed description of JSTARS is in Appendix T.) The OV-1D normally is a corps asset, but its operations were routinely tasked by the CENTCOM JRC during Operation Desert Storm.

Although CENTCOM JRC tasking of corps-level assets may have been frustrating to the corps commanders, CINCCENT needed these platforms' capabilities to meet theater-unique requirements. The mobile Scud threat was a case in point. The CINCCENT requirement to suppress Iraq's ability to launch Scuds at Israel — a threat to the cohesiveness of the Coalition — required use of the JSTARS in a Scud-hunting role (particularly in western Iraq, from where the missiles were launched at

---

JSTARS

The Joint Surveillance Target Attack Radar System (JSTARS) provided useful information concerning Iraqi forces during the 29 January Iraqi attack on Al-Khafji. Iraqi follow-on forces were tracked by JSTARS and destroyed by Coalition air power — north of the Saudi border. Information such as this was provided to ground and air commanders in near-real-time via the Army's JSTARS Interim Ground Station Modules (IGSMs). IGSMs were deployed with Army Component, Central Command (ARCENT) headquarters, ARCENT Forward Command Post, ARCENT Main Command Post, I Marine Expeditionary Force headquarters, VII Corps, XVIII Airborne Corps, and the Air Force Component, Central Command Tactical Air Control Center.

Just before the Offensive Ground Campaign began, JSTARS confirmed that Iraqi forces remained in their defensive positions against which the attack had been planned. During the attack itself, JSTARS detected the positioning of Iraqi operational reserve heavy divisions into blocking positions in response to the VII Corps advance.

Israel) and use of the OV-1D to fill resulting gaps in coverage. This need superseded the corps' requirements for use of the OV-1D.

Imagery was vital to Coalition operations, especially to support targeting development for precision guided munitions and Tomahawk Land Attack Missile attacks, and for BDA. Operations Desert Shield and Desert Storm placed great demands on national, theater and tactical imagery reconnaissance systems. The insatiable appetite for imagery and imagery-derived products could not be met.

The SR-71, phased out in 1989, was evaluated for possible reactivation to alleviate the imagery shortfall. The SR-71 could have been useful during Operation Desert Shield if overflight of Iraq had been permitted. In that case, the system would have provided broad area coverage of a large number of Iraqi units. However, since overflight of Iraq was not allowed, it would have provided no more coverage than available

platforms. During Operation Desert Storm air operations, the SR-71 would have been of value for BDA and determining Iraqi force dispositions. During Operation Desert Storm ground operations, the SR-71 would not have made greater contributions than other platforms, given the speed of the advance. Unique aircraft requirements also would have limited potential SR-71 operating locations.

Although national and theater imagery reconnaissance platforms could collect substantial amounts of imagery, getting it to the tactical commander proved difficult. Components deployed with numerous incompatible secondary imagery dissemination systems (SIDS) — each bringing the systems procured by its parent Service. While national imagery was available at CENTCOM and the components, dissemination below that level required workarounds, often at the expense of precious communications circuits. At times, couriers had to be used to ensure delivery.

Through an ad hoc communications architecture involving both national and theater intelligence systems, Army Patriot batteries deployed to Saudi Arabia, Israel, and Turkey were able to receive warnings of Iraqi-modified Scud missile launches, which proved key to early target detection and acquisition.

From the beginning of the crisis through the end of Operation Desert Storm, there was a theater-wide shortage of trained, proficient Arabic linguists. This shortage, coupled with a lack of linguists familiar with the Iraqi dialect, reduced the ability to collect and produce intelligence, as well as operate effectively within a Coalition that included nine Arabic-speaking countries. This situation was alleviated somewhat by an Army initiative to recruit, train, and deploy some 600 Kuwaiti volunteers as interpreters and interrogators in Army and Marine Corps units.

CENTCOM Components/Subunified Command

CENTCOM's components and subunified command were supported by organic and/or augmented intelligence organizations. The Army Component, Central Command (ARCENT) was supported by the 513th Military Intelligence (MI) Brigade, which conducted all-source intelligence operations in support of ARCENT echelons above corps. The brigade was headquartered in Riyadh, with elements operating with ARCENT Forward at Hafr Al-Batin and other locations throughout the theater. The Air Force Component, Central Command (CENTAF) was supported by the 9th Tactical Intelligence Squadron, the 6975th Electronic Security Squadron, and a detachment of the Air Force Special Activities Center, all in Riyadh. The Navy Component, Central Command (NAVCENT) was supported by the intelligence staff resident on the Seventh Fleet flagship, the USS Blue Ridge (LCC 19). The Marine Corps Component, Central Command (MARCENT) was supported by the 1st Surveillance, Reconnaissance, and Intelligence Group (SRIG), a task-organized intelligence command that also supported I MEF and its subordinate units. The Special Operations Commmand, Central Command was supported by a heavily augmented intelligence staff. Intelligence personnel from all four components formed the Joint Air Intelligence Cell in Riyadh to support the CENTAF Commander in his role as Joint Force Air Component Commander (JFACC).

Coalition Intelligence

Coalition intelligence efforts worked well during the crisis. Intelligence officers from the United Kingdom, Canada and Australia were integrated fully into the CENTCOM JIC. The Royal Air Force operated its GR-1 photoreconnaissance variant aircraft to collect against theater requirements. Saudi aerial reconnaissance capability was made available to CENTCOM intelligence collection managers. Royal Saudi Air Force (RSAF) RF-5C photoreconnaissance aircraft conducted border surveillance missions along Saudi Arabia's border with Kuwait and Iraq, as well as over Iraqi territory during Operation Desert Storm. Marine Corps and RSAF intelligence personnel in Riyadh interpreted RF-5C photography. Other Coalition nations provided intelligence collected by their fielded systems.

Arabic-speaking US intelligence officers were on duty 24 hours a day in the Coalition Coordination, Communication, and Integration Center to provide intelligence support to Coalition forces, and receive intelligence information. Coalition commanders acknowledged the United States provided most of their intelligence. The liberal provision of American intelligence during Operations Desert Shield and Desert Storm likely will cause pressure for continued access to sensitive information, possibly straining the ability to protect sources and methods.

Operation Proven Force

European Command (EUCOM) and its component commands produced intelligence to support US combat operations from Turkey. EUCOM assumed intelligence responsibilities for northern Iraq to support US forces operating from bases in Turkey as part of Joint Task Force Proven Force.

TACTICAL INTELLIGENCE

Perhaps in no other conflict in American history have tactical commanders — corps-level and below — been able to call on as capable an intelligence system as in the Gulf War. Yet, despite the impressive capabilities of collection systems at the national, theater, and tactical levels, many division, brigade, and wing commanders expressed frustration and dissatisfaction with the intelligence support they received. The detail desired in some cases, was,

and will continue to be, beyond the capabilities of the intelligence system. Additionally, many of the more capable tactical intelligence collection systems were restricted in their use because of operational security considerations before Operation Desert Storm. Others were controlled or tasked at the theater (CENTCOM or component) level. Wing, division and brigade commanders' intelligence needs that could not be met with organic assets had to be validated and prioritized at higher echelons; many times their requirements, although validated, fell too low on the list to be satisfied by heavily tasked theater and national resources.

I MEF

I MEF deployed to the theater, having recently reorganized its tactical intelligence structure. Marines ashore depended on the recently created 1st SRIG, a regimental sized unit that meshed all ground intelligence collection assets, covering all intelligence disciplines. Additionally, each Marine division had a ground reconnaissance battalion of Marines specially trained in patrolling, and a light armored infantry battalion, capable of mechanized cavalry and reconnaissance operations using light armored vehicles. Many of these assets were attached to assault units to provide direct support during the ground attack.

A serious shortfall the Marines faced was the absence of a tactical aerial reconnaissance platform able to provide imagery responsive to ground commanders' requirements. The RF-4B, recently taken out of service, had not yet been replaced by the reconnaissance pods programmed for the F/A-18D.

ARCENT Corps

The tactical intelligence capability initially deployed with Army units was midway through a modernization effort, resulting in mobility, targeting, communications, and processing problems. Consequently, the Army had to custom design a battlefield intelligence system. An MI brigade supported each of the two corps, and each division had a full MI battalion organic to it. Communications paths to disseminate intelligence, targeting data, and imagery from producers to corps and division commanders in near-real-time did not exist, or had insufficient capacity. Many collection systems, such as JSTARS and the Pioneer unmanned aerial vehicle (UAV) were prototypes. Through urgent fielding of such prototypes and off-the-shelf systems, the Army fielded an all-discipline battlefield intelligence capability that met the most immediate needs of commanders and provided them with necessary targeting and intelligence data.

CENTAF Units

The unique nature of Operation Desert Storm air operations tended to blur the distinction between tactical and theater level intelligence. Air tasking and targeting was centralized at the JFACC level, with intelligence requirements originating at the theater level and results pushed downward, in contrast to the decentralized nature of ground-combat intelligence. Because of this, many theater systems provided direct support to air planners. Squadrons, groups, and wings have limited organic intelligence sources other than aircrew debriefings and assigned collection platforms. However, the Airborne Warning and Control System , Airborne Battlefield Command and Control Center , Tactical Information Broadcast System , and Tactical Receive Equipment and Related Applications gave aircrews timely intelligence-derived warning of pending threats.

NAVCENT Units

Naval operations also tend to blur the distinction between theater and tactical assets. At sea, P-3C patrol aircraft and E-2 airborne early warning aircraft were able to meet the requirement for immediate threat identification. Navy battle

groups and amphibious groups were manned with complete intelligence staffs and capabilities to support their operations.

Intelligence Collection and Dissemination

VII Corps, I MEF, and NAVCENT ships operated the Pioneer UAV to provide real-time imagery intelligence and targeting data. Pioneer was deployed in late August as part of the 7th Marine Expeditionary Brigade. I MEF incorporated UAV missions into its battlefield preparation, often using them to locate targets and adjust artillery fire and close air support. Navy battleships used Pioneer to refine naval gunfire support accuracy during operations off Kuwait in late January and February. The VII Corps' system became operational on 1 February. Pioneer proved excellent at providing an immediately responsive intelligence collection capability. VII Corps flew 43 UAV missions during February, providing situation development and targeting support. During one mission, a Pioneer located three Iraqi artillery battalions, three free-rocket-over-ground launch sites, and an antitank battalion. Since the system still was in the test and evaluation stage of development, it had inadequate communications and down-link capabilities to be completely effective and widely available. (See Appendix T for a description of the Pioneer system.)

One additional UAV system, Pointer, was used by the 82nd Airborne Division and the 2nd Marine Division. An experimental, hand-launched, very short-range UAV designed for direct support of small units, Pointer was operated from the front lines, but was of limited use in the open desert because of its fragility and range.

A variety of tactical signals intelligence systems was deployed to the theater to support tactical commanders. Although hindered somewhat by the shortage of Arabic linguists, operators were able to provide timely and useful intelligence throughout Operations Desert Shield and Desert Storm.

Human source intelligence proved its value to tactical commanders during Operation Desert Storm. For units at the brigade and lower levels, it often was the primary source of intelligence on enemy capabilities and intentions. ARCENT, NAVCENT, MARCENT and CENTAF attached interrogators to front-line units to extract perishable information of immediate tactical significance, some of which was used immediately to target enemy forces. Once the ground offensive began and American units began capturing large numbers of Iraqi enemy prisoners of war, US interrogators had access to a variety of Iraqi military personnel. Iraqi officers and soldiers proved quite willing to divulge details of tactical dispositions and plans. The large numbers of prisoners quickly overburdened intelligence unit interrogators.

As in past conflicts, combat operations in the Persian Gulf again demonstrated the value of the individual soldier, sailor, airman, and Marine in conducting reconnaissance and surveillance. Aircrew debriefings provided valuable data on Iraq air defense tactics and weapons capabilities, as well as continually updating BDA and data on the ground situation. Through Operation Desert Shield and in the weeks leading to the ground offensive, Special Operations Forces and Marine Corps units established observation posts along the Kuwait border. Later, as Army units closed on southern Iraq, XVIII Airborne Corps and VII Corps established similar posts in their areas of operations. During the final days before the ground attack, Marine Corps reconnaissance patrols crossed the Kuwaiti border to determine exact locations and composition of enemy obstacles and minefields. Army scouts performed similar missions to the west, some penetrating several miles into Iraq. All these ground reconnaissance units, along with operational reports from units in contact with the enemy, provided tactical

commanders with valuable information on enemy capabilities.

Because much of the intelligence gathered originated at corps and higher levels, tactical commanders found intelligence provided to them was too broad. Frequently, tactical units were sent finished estimates and summaries produced for senior commanders rather than the detailed, tailored intelligence needed to plan tactical operations, with the notable exception of targeting templates. Tactical units, restricted in the use of their own intelligence and surveillance assets and reliant on a tenuous dissemination process, often found themselves trying to piece together an intelligence picture of the enemy in their sectors using the limited information they could draw from intelligence being produced at higher levels.

Operation Desert Storm validated again the requirement for timely dissemination of intelligence to the tactical level. However, system capabilities, coupled with the lack of communications capacity or systems, did not meet tactical commanders' expectations — either in quality or quantity. Component commanders generally lacked the organic imagery collection assets to satisfy their own requirements, let alone those of their subordinate units.

Tactical imagery dissemination also was slowed by the geographic separation of collection platforms from the intelligence production facilities in theater. Film from the U-2R had to be flown from the aircraft operating base at At-Taif to Riyadh for exploitation. Likewise, RF-4C imagery had to be flown to Riyadh from the operating base at Shaikh Isa, Bahrain.

Overall, intelligence support for tactical commanders was good, better than that commanders had experienced in the past. Because of the unique situation faced in the Gulf, particularly for ground commanders before the ground offensive, many deployed tactical intelligence systems could not be exploited fully. National and theater systems often were used in an attempt to fill the gap, with mixed success. Tactical commanders remained frustrated, because their demands exceeded their organic intelligence systems' capabilities, and because they were forced to rely on higher echelons to provide them intelligence. Particular areas requiring improvement include tactical imagery reconnaissance, intelligence dissemination, and intelligence analysis responsive to the tactical commanders' needs. DIA and the Services are examining these issues.

BATTLE DAMAGE ASSESSMENT

BDA is a wartime function necessary to determine if desired effects are being achieved by the application of force. BDA serves decision makers and commanders at all levels. At the national level, BDA is used to determine which national or theater options are to be pursued. At the operational level (the component command in this instance), BDA is necessary to determine if the required level of damage has been done to a target or target set, or if objectives have been sufficiently achieved to permit progression to the next phase of attack. At the tactical level — aircrews, ground combat units, and naval combatants — BDA is used to validate tactics and weapons performance. However, BDA is not a precise science.

BDA in the Gulf War, as a whole, has been criticized as too slow and inadequate. It is quite possible that assessments of Iraqi losses at various times overestimated or underestimated actual results. These criticisms, however, are not entirely accurate, given the nature of the war and the unprecedented BDA requirements it generated. In terms of traditional analysis, assessments were timely and accurate. Strike evaluators were able to ascertain the effectiveness of missions directed against targets such as bridges, building complexes, and storage sites. Damage to these facilities was readily

apparent, and analysis posed few problems. In essence, analysts applied the same techniques used during past wars, although most data was provided by state-of-the-art imagery reconnaissance systems.

However, the revolutionary changes in the way American forces conducted combat operations during Operation Desert Storm outstripped the abilities of the BDA system. Analysts were unable to meet the requirements for timely data on a variety of new types of targets or targets struck in new ways. For example, the precise targeting and striking of sections of buildings or hardened shelters complicated the assessment process. In many cases, all that was visible to imagery analysts was a relatively small entry hole on the surface of a structure with no indication as to the extent of internal damage. Another example involves damage to individual tanks or vehicles, such as mobile missile launchers. Unless the destruction was catastrophic, a destroyed tank might still appear operational. Even if secondary explosions accompanied the destruction of a suspected missile launcher, it was not possible to conclude with a high degree of certainty that a Scud had been destroyed.

In short, the BDA system was called upon to produce results it had not been asked for in the past. Even though there was enough general information to enable CINCCENT to prosecute the war, some targets that had been destroyed may have been struck again and some that had not been destroyed may have been neglected. Targeting at the theater and tactical levels was less effective in the absence of more precise damage assessment. While there will never be enough information to satisfy all levels of command, improvements are clearly needed to ensure that BDA capability keeps up with the ability to strike targets with precision and penetrating weapons. DOD will continue to examine this requirement.

CENTCOM J-2 developed a BDA methodology

for Operation Desert Storm to incorporate all available sources. CENTCOM BDA coupled information from national systems, mission reports, deserter reports, and gun camera film with subjective analysis and sound military judgment to determine to what degree an objective had been achieved. While CENTCOM BDA support to CINCCENT was relatively successful, there still is no DOD-wide, formalized BDA training or needed organizational structure, doctrine, methodology, or procedures. Lastly, there is no existing automated data processing software available to handle the massive volume of information which must be collated by BDA analysts. While the BDA process evolved to the point where it provided sound military assessments at the strategic and operational levels, institutionalization of an effective process remains to be done.

As part of the CENTCOM BDA methodology, the component intelligence staffs provided BDA analysis to the theater BDA cell, based on their individual areas of expertise. The CENTAF Director of Intelligence provided his analysis of all BDA on targets struck by air during the air campaign. NAVCENT did BDA of naval facilities and vessels. Likewise, assessment of combat effectiveness of Iraqi ground forces in the KTO with the exception of MARCENT's

area was an ARCENT responsibility. MARCENT was responsible for BDA in its area of responsibility.

CENTCOM J-2 analysts displayed each target set with an indicator of actual observable damage and an assessment of the degree to which CINCCENT's objectives had been met. On a single map, Iraqi Army divisions were color coded to portray current estimated combat effectiveness. This map was used by CINCCENT for force posturing and employment. Major CINCCENT operational decisions depended on BDA. These included determining: the effectiveness of air operations; when to shift from the Strategic Air Campaign to preparation of the battlefield; emphasis during preparation of the battlefield; when to initiate the Offensive Ground Campaign; and when and where to maneuver combat forces.

CENTCOM, by fusing intelligence information derived from both national and theater systems as well as inputs from its component commanders, met BDA requirements of both national decision makers and the theater commander. However, BDA for tactical commanders, who wanted more specific detail, was more difficult. At the tactical level, it often was impossible to get the information to commanders fast enough to affect decision making. Additionally, CIA and DIA BDA estimates using information available solely from national intelligence sources conflicted greatly with those produced in theater. Independent CIA reporting of this conflicting BDA to the White House sometimes caused confusion between national decision makers and the theater commander. Because of the availability of additional data in theater, CENTCOM-produced BDA was more accurate and useful to CINCCENT.

Other factors were crucial in addressing BDA issues. The combat tempo of the war was greater than the ability to collect BDA data.

Poor weather early in the campaign severely hampered verification of target destruction. BDA will continue to be a problem for the foreseeable future. However, many difficulties encountered in Operations Desert Shield and Desert Storm can be minimized or eliminated by developing standard BDA doctrine and procedures that meet the needs of operational and intelligence communities. The intelligence and operations communities must collaborate in this effort. BDA must also become an integral part of joint training and periodic exercises. (Additional discussion of BDA is included in Chapters VI and VIII.)

COUNTERINTELLIGENCE

Operations Desert Shield and Desert Storm provided the first opportunity to conduct theater-level counterintelligence according to doctrine developed since the Vietnam conflict, both in the United States and in theater. This allowed CINCCENT to exercise operational control of these assets through the components.

DOD counterintelligence agencies successfully detected and interdicted US military members attempting to sell classified defense information to foreign intelligence services.

Arab/Islamic countries' services also are good at internal security and counterintelligence. To coordinate operations between US and other Coalition services, Joint Counterintelligence Liaison Offices were established in Saudi Arabia.

CONCLUSION

The Coalition forces' overwhelming military victory against Iraqi armed forces was due in large part to accurate intelligence provided to decision makers, particularly at the national and theater level. The shortfalls in the intelligence support to American forces, which have been detailed in this report, are being addressed.

OBSERVATIONS

Accomplishments

- Intelligence support to national and theater decision makers was excellent.

- DOD-JIC, manned by DIA, NSA and Service intelligence staffs, provided agreed DOD intelligence positions to the theater and helped eliminate duplicative efforts.

- CENTCOM JIC provided effective intelligence and BDA to theater commander. Placement of JRC within the JIC allowed effective tasking of theater assets against theater and tactical requirements.

- JSTARS provided useful targeting and situational data on enemy ground forces throughout the war.

- The UAV demonstrated its tactical intelligence collection value.

Shortcomings

- Support to tactical commanders was sufficient, but suffered from a lack of available assets and difficulties in disseminating national and theater intelligence. This was aggravated by numerous incompatible secondary imagery dissemination systems in theater.

- There was a lack of information on the scope and exact disposition of chemical, biological, and nuclear weapons programs, and poor understanding of Iraqi intentions.

- Community-wide shortage of Arabic linguists affected intelligence, counterintelligence, and liaison efforts.

- The BDA process was difficult, especially for restrike decisions. BDA doctrine and organization must be determined. DIA, the Services, and the unified and specified commands have begun to institutionalize a BDA structure that will satisfy combat commanders' requirements.

Issues

- Tactical commanders considered intelligence support at the division, wing and lower levels insufficient, because of overreliance on national and theater systems, lack of adequate tactical imagery systems, and limited imagery production. Although better dissemination of national and theater intelligence can meet some intelligence requirements, commanders need more and better organic assets.

- Combat commanders were concerned that national intelligence often was caveated and proved of limited value. The cornerstone of the national intelligence process is competitive analysis. When this process produces differing judgments within the Intelligence Community, the nature and supporting rationale for these different opinions must be made clear to senior leaders. Intelligence judgments must convey all the options open to an adversary, as well as the ambiguities surrounding his intent and likely future actions. At the same time, the type of intelligence product that is appropriate for senior national leaders may not be useful for a combat commander. Therefore, there is a need to examine how national estimates dealing with military contingencies are developed. An interagency task force is reviewing this process.

- Joint intelligence doctrine must be developed that addresses unified command requirements on a fast-moving battlefield. Joint Publication 2-0, Doctrine for Intelligence Support to Joint Operations, has been published in the test phase. Development has begun on a more detailed Joint Tactics, Techniques, and Procedures document for intelligence support to joint operations. A JIC concept of operations also is under development. JICs must be adequately manned, organized, and equipped to support the command mission fully.

Appendix D

PREPAREDNESS OF UNITED STATES FORCES

INTRODUCTION

Military preparedness is the ability to introduce properly equipped and trained forces quickly into a crisis situation. This ability normally cannot be generated in a short period of time. Preparation for Operations Desert Shield and Desert Storm did not begin when Iraq invaded Kuwait on 2 August. That date was preceded by years of preparation; a change in the global environment; a shift in strategy; previous defense planning; investments in people, equipment, and training; and forward presence in Europe and the Middle East, which placed US forces in a particularly favorable position to accomplish the mission. (The table at the end of this appendix highlights some of the activity that preceded this crisis.)

Few elements of preparedness can be reduced to mathematically quantifiable terms. The following sections discuss several factors that improved US armed forces' ability to react rapidly to a major crisis in Southwest Asia (SWA) only months after the Revolution of 1989 in the Soviet Union and Eastern Europe had capped a strategic shift away from four decades of deterring a global war centered in Europe. These factors include national interests, previous commitments and security agreements, planning for regional crises, training, deployment, and force modernization.

INTERESTS AND PRIOR COMMITMENTS

Military Involvement

The United States has had an enduring interest in the security and stability of the Middle East

> *"In just 24 months the Cold War was ended, Panama was freed, and Iraqi aggression reversed. America's military played a vital role in each of these national triumphs. These accomplishments were not achieved by accident. They are the product of 20 years of dedication, planning, training and just plain hard work. The warfighting edge of our military is the result of quality people, trained to razor sharpness, outfitted with modern equipment, led by tough competent leaders, structured into an effective mix of forces, and employed according to up-to-date doctrine."*
>
> **General Gordon R. Sullivan**
> **Chief of Staff, US Army**

and SWA, particularly since the 1940s. In support of its objectives, the United States has maintained a presence in the region and developed programs to improve responsiveness to contingencies there.

The earliest post-World War II permanent presence in the region began in 1949 when the Commander Middle East Force (CMEF), took up station in the Persian Gulf. In 1988, CMEF became a dual-hatted position with Joint Task Force Middle East (JTFME), under Central Command (CENTCOM). Although normally less than a half dozen vessels, this task force has been a symbol of US interest in regional stability for 40 years. It has served as the base for larger US operations in the Gulf on several occasions, and it played a crucial role in the early days of this crisis. The value of this presence cannot be overstated. JTFME provided the operational expertise needed to establish patrol areas, rendezvous points, and contingency plans for responses to attacks on merchant shipping. It also made possible the rapid construction of a viable maritime interception program. The task force includes planners and staff officers from all Services and its presence is welcomed by friendly regional states.

US policy makers always have valued Saudi Arabian support for regional stability and have used several initiatives to cultivate that support. Weapons sales and infrastructure development encouraged through US Government security assistance programs were part of this strategy. For example, a large part of the Saudi infrastructure was built under Foreign Military Sales (FMS) construction programs, managed by the US Army Corps of Engineers and paid for by the government of Saudi Arabia.

After the revolution in Iran, several Presidential policies, including the Carter Doctrine, defined vital US national security interests in the region. Like their predecessors, the Reagan and Bush administrations reconfirmed the region's importance. In order to protect US interests in the Gulf, they decided to sustain a forward military presence, develop a credible capability to help regional states respond to military threats, protect freedom of navigation, and ensure the unimpeded flow of oil to global markets.

Major elements of US forward presence were JTFME and security assistance. Under US security assistance programs, training, weapons, supplies and construction assistance to develop roads and ports were provided to most countries, with the notable exception of Iraq.

An important part of the security assistance provided to regional states since World War II included training of military forces. The US provided schooling in the United States and in the region for officers and enlisted personnel through the FMS system and the grant-aid International Military Education and Training (IMET) program. Through these diverse educational opportunities, many nations developed a familiarity with US military equipment and doctrine. Many personnel had

been trained to operate equipment to the same standards expected of US service members. Many regional air forces had received some United States Air Force (USAF) training, and Saudi ground forces had been given extensive training by American military personnel. For example, the US military maintains a multi-service training mission, headed by a major general, in Saudi Arabia. Of notable importance, these training programs have fostered a mutual understanding, improved rapport, and sharpened language skills on all sides. The United Kingdom (UK) and France, both Coalition members, had provided training to regional militaries as well, as part of a long association with several regional states. Relationships which began as the by-products of training were strengthened by several US forces operations at the request of regional states.

In the aftermath of the fall of the Shah of Iran in 1979, the Department of Defense (DOD) had to reassess its ability to respond to contingencies in the region, shifting from relying on regional allies to building up our own power projection capabilities to respond to a conflict. The region had also become of greater concern because of the oil price shocks of the 1970s. A DOD study, Capabilities for Limited Contingencies in the Persian Gulf, was completed in 1979 in response to an earlier National Security Council directive requiring such a study. It and subsequent DOD reviews in 1979 resulted in program initiatives such as maritime prepositioning and improvement of facilities for enroute refueling, as well as preliminary consideration of more extensive initiatives to improve power projection. In the aftermath of the Soviet invasion of Afghanistan in December 1979, the threat of a Soviet invasion of Iran became the principal concern in the region. A host of mobility programs were initiated (Maritime Prepositioning as it now exists, procurement of SL-7s, and many others), base access was pursued with regional allies, regional exercises begun, and importantly, a new dedicated command was created — the Rapid

Deployment Force (RDF) which was given responsibility for developing operational capabilities for SWA. The Reagan administration expanded and refined the RDF initiative, transforming it into the United States Central Command (CENTCOM).

In 1980, at the request of the Kingdom of Saudi Arabia, the US deployed four Airborne Warning and Control System (AWACS) aircraft and supporting air refueling tankers to Riyadh. These aircraft provided 24-hour-a-day surveillance of the northeastern Arabian Peninsula. In addition, USAF personnel manned the Eastern Sector Command Center, working alongside Saudi counterparts. In 1988, in response to Kuwaiti requests, several Western states deployed naval forces to the region to protect shipping during the latter stages of the Iran-Iraq war. (A brief discussion of this war is contained in Chapter I.) The United States played a major role in escorting ships in the region as part of Operation Earnest Will.

Operation Earnest Will was a watershed event entailing substantial commitment of US forces under combat conditions at the request of a Gulf state. In addition to JTFME assets, the United States deployed Navy warships, a contingency Marine Air-Ground Task Force (MAGTF) embarked on amphibious ships, Army helicopters, and Air Force aircraft to guarantee the passage of Kuwaiti ships registered under the American flag. Upon successful completion of Operation Earnest Will, the US withdrew the additional assets promptly. The trust and confidence created during this experience made it easier for friendly regional states to accept readily the US presence during Operations Desert Shield and Desert Storm. Because Operation Earnest Will was a multinational effort involving several North Atlantic Treaty Organization (NATO) partners, it set the precedent for future cooperative efforts in the region. Similarly, close collaboration of US diplomats and military officials also greatly eased the coordination of effort between US embassies in the region and DOD during the Gulf crisis.

PLANNING

Changes in the Strategic Environment

The changes in the global security environment which resulted from the Revolution of 1989 in Eastern Europe and the ongoing change in the Soviet Union caused national security planners to begin to redefine US security strategy.

During the early summer of 1990, as the dramatic events reshaped Eastern Europe and the Soviet Union, DOD had begun to incorporate the tenets of the new defense strategy President Bush announced on 2 August. Intense studies and planning had identified the chief threats to US strategic interests in the Gulf as regional rather than global. (Earlier plans for contingencies in the region were predicated on the threat of a Soviet attack through Iran. These plans envisioned such an incursion in the context of a much larger Soviet aggression that included Western Europe, in essence leading to global war.)

The new strategic framework the President articulated in August made it clear that threats from regional actors would likely be the principal challenges to peace in the rapidly changing geostrategic climate. It was understood from the beginning that such threats had to be countered decisively, and that they now could be countered without necessarily incurring the risks of a confrontation with the Soviet Union.

New Policy Assessments

In the fall of 1989, during DOD's regular planning process, the Under Secretary of Defense for Policy (USD(P)) recommended and the Secretary approved a shift in the principal US focus in the Persian Gulf. While during the 1980s DOD had focused principally on developing the power projection capabilities to counter a Soviet invasion into Iran, the USD(P) and the Commander-in-Chief, Central Command (CINCCENT) now judged that — while still a concern worth planning against — it no longer was the most likely or worrisome challenge in the region, given the increasing turmoil and political changes in the Soviet Union and the fact that it was perceived as unlikely that Iran would ask for US assistance in a timely manner to counter such an invasion. Instead, the growing military capability and ambitions of Iraq — with its forces toughened by its war with Iran — and the sharp disparity between its forces and those of the wealthy oil-producing nations of the Arabian Peninsula pointed to the growing possibility of conflict between these regional powers. During deliberations for the planning process, the Secretary emphasized the continuing importance of the Persian Gulf and approved this shift in emphasis. Accordingly, the Secretary directed DOD to sharpen its ability to counter such a regional conflict on the Arabian Peninsula. In turn, the Chairman of the Joint Chiefs of Staff (CJCS) directed CINCCENT to develop war plans consistent with this shift in emphasis.

New Operations Plan

CENTCOM had long maintained a plan for the defense of the Saudi Arabian Peninsula. This plan was undergoing routine revision consistent with guidance provided by the JCS in the Joint Strategic Capabilities Plan (JSCP). The revision process was on schedule according to the agreement between the Joint Staff (JS) and CENTCOM.

In accordance with the Secretary's direction, planning for the defense of the Arabian Peninsula was elevated to the highest priority and it was accelerated with the objective of completing a comprehensive plan by July 1990 for use in a scheduled command post exercise. Significant manpower and

computer resources were allocated to speed the plan.

In response to CJCS guidance and a complete mission analysis of likely contingencies, CINCCENT prepared a Concept Outline Plan (COP) early in 1990 for the defense of the Arabian Peninsula. The COP was an expansion of CINCCENT's concept of operations and was unique to CINCCENT; it is not a standard Joint Strategic Planning System (JSPS) document. The COP, based on a threat scenario developed by Defense Intelligence Agency and the CENTCOM Directorate for Intelligence (J-2), included an estimate of forces needed to respond to a regional threat. The COP, which the CJCS approved in April, provided the basis for the operations plan (OPLAN) developed in response to the Iraqi invasion of Kuwait.

CENTCOM developed courses of action for defending against an attack by Iraq. These courses of action were refined continually by planners and included war gaming against computer simulations of a conflict between US forces and the forces of Iraq that intelligence estimated would participate in an an attack on Kuwait and Saudi Arabia. War gaming simulations permitted planners to study different courses of action in terms of equipment and personnel casualties projected for both sides and measured by an estimate of the territory that could be defended, lost, or recovered. The simulation included the contribution of air power to the ground campaign.

After an initial review of courses of action, CINCCENT approved the basic planning concept for the defense of the Arabian Peninsula which involved trading space for time as US forces reduced attacking Iraqi forces. This approach would permit US forces to continue their deployment into Saudi Arabia and complete their subsequent movement to defensive positions. US ground forces would fight a delay and avoid decisive engagement while tactical air and indirect fire by other forces continued to reduce attacking Iraqi forces. When US forces had sufficient combat power, they would conduct a counter offensive to regain lost territory.

CENTCOM draft OPLAN 1002-90 (Defense of the Arabian Peninsula) was prepared based upon the COP. OPLANs are detailed documents that require meticulous preparation, take considerable time to develop, and must be carefully coordinated. OPLAN 1002-90 had the highest CENTCOM planning priority in the Spring of 1990. The second draft of OPLAN 1002-90 was published in July 1990 with a third draft scheduled to be published in October 1990 in preparation for a Phase I Time Phased Force Deployment Data (TPFDD) conference in October/November 1990.

CENTCOM scheduled Exercise Internal Look 90 in late July 1990 to test the validity of operational and logistic support concepts in OPLAN 1002-90. Focused on an Iraqi incursion on the Arabian peninsula, the exercise revealed the need for a revised troop list, and an armor heavy and highly mobile force to fight a high-speed tank battle in the expanses of the Arabian desert. Furthermore, Exercise Internal Look 90 reviewed the current order of battle of potential combatants and provided the impetus to include Patriot as an antitactical missile capability and for protection and defense during the initial troop deployments.

Exercise Internal Look 90 also validated the concept of air defense for Saudi Arabia and provided insights on where to best position air defense aircraft. It exercised the joint air tasking order used for coordinating air operations. Boundary issues between component land commanders were given full visibility. The need to deploy additional mine countermeasures to counter the Iraqi mine threat was highlighted. All these results and lessons were subsequently applied during the formulation of the final plan.

The exercise identified the need to restructure

NAVCENT command and control relationships and organization. As a result, early in Operation Desert Shield, the Commander, Seventh Fleet, (COMSEVENTHFLT) was assigned as Commander, Naval Component, Central Command, (NAVCENT) , the principal naval commander for the significantly enlarged naval force deployed to the Middle East. JTFME was disbanded, and its functions were retained by the Commander, Middle East Force, reporting to NAVCENT. The exercise also indicated the distance from carriers outside the Gulf to the battlefield and targets in Iraq reduced the number of Navy sorties available to attack important targets and required substantial support of land based refueling. The Navy began a review of the feasibility of operating carriers in more restrictive waters and as a result, the decision was made to operate carriers in the Gulf. This increased significantly the number of carrier-based aircraft available for employment against targets in Kuwait and Iraq and reduced land-based refueling requirements.

Exercise Internal Look 90 was instrumental in refining concepts and plans by CINCCENT, his staff, and the component commanders used. With these insights, the basic concepts for Operations Desert Shield and Desert Storm were established before a single Iraqi soldier entered Kuwait.

Deployment Planning

CENTCOM OPLAN 1002-90 was undergoing final review in August 1990. Detailed deployment requirements depend on approved plan requirements. The JSCP apportions the major combat forces to support OPLAN and contingency plan CONPLAN taskings. The Services then select and identify the forces for each commander-in-chief (CINC). The CINC, through his concept of operations, then selects the forces to be used and identifies the flow of forces into the theater. Support requirements (supplies and support units) are then identified in the various TPFDD conferences.

TPFDD conferences, which involve representatives from all service elements, were scheduled for November 1990 and February 1991. A final deployment plan was due to be published in April 1991 and supporting plans in August 1991. The Iraqi invasion of Kuwait disrupted this timetable. Computerized systems can provide valuable help in constructing deployment schedules, assuming disruptions are minimal. However, as described in Appendix E, Deployment, the lack of a final TPFDD and the need to deploy rapidly certain types of units to the theater necessitated manual entry of the initial deployment data into the computer instead of using an existing data base.

Although OPLAN 1002-90 was not complete and specific deployment data was lacking, it provided a sound foundation. As with all plans, some modifications were made to account for circumstances unique to the crisis. Nevertheless, much of the OPLAN was not modified. Modification of other parts was done with relative ease compared with the requirements of starting operations without a base document.

Planning and Preparations for Joint Operations

The ability to conduct effective joint operations has been a primary DOD concern for years. The Goldwater-Nichols DOD Reorganization Act of 1986 (GNA) strengthened the system which provided for the formulation, promulgation, and periodic review of joint operations plans. GNA required the Secretary of Defense to issue contingency planning guidance that links national military strategies with the JSCP, streamlining the planning process. GNA also gave the USD(P) a role in reviewing contingency plans. GNA also strengthened and clarified the authority of the CINCs of unified commands such as CENTCOM. It also clearly defined the relationship between supported and supporting unified commands and clarified the relationship among these commands, the National Command Authorities and the military Services.

Progress made in joint doctrine development contributed to the preparation of the theater campaign plan. Joint Test Publication, Doctrine for Unified and Joint Operations, drafted by the Army as the JS agent and released for evaluation in 1990, served as a guide for development of the Operation Desert Storm theater campaign plan. However, problems remained. There are differences in interpreting joint doctrine, such as the concept of operations for the Joint Force Air Component Commander (JFACC) and the limits of JFACC authority over aircraft belonging to other component commanders. Not all intelligence systems were interoperable. Finally, much combined combat power achieved by the integrated theater campaign was the result of innovative procedures adopted on the scene. These innovations bridged the gaps between Service planning procedures in intelligence, operational and logistics systems; but some procedures require refinement to achieve maximum joint efficiency.

The US military was relatively well prepared to conduct joint operations when Iraq invaded Kuwait. Operations Desert Shield and Desert Storm demonstrated a quantum advance in joint interaction among Army, USAF, Marine (USMC), and Navy forces. Preparation for joint operations before the crisis meant a broad range of interdependent relationships between the Services could be tapped with little or no delay because of procedural matters. Many procedures and numerous points of doctrine had been agreed upon and, as discussed in the section on military preparedness in this Appendix, were implemented and validated by numerous joint exercises. Where agreements did not exist, previous experience with joint operations made expeditious innovation possible. Problem areas with logistics, intelligence, and operational interoperability have been identified and remedies are under consideration. Additional discussion of these points is contained in the appropriate sections of this report.

Planning and Preparations for Combined Operations

Combined operations involving armed forces of more than one nation, were a crucial part of Operations Desert Shield and Desert Storm and owe much success to advanced planning and experience. The United States conducted Combined Operations Bright Star with Egypt, as well as numerous exercises with those coalition partners belonging to NATO. This NATO experience was especially valuable for maritime interception operations in support of the UN imposed embargo on Iraq and for air and ground operations against Iraq.

NATO experiences provided a number of procedural agreements that made the interaction of these forces more efficient. NATO doctrine and exercises had provided for the sophisticated interoperability of land, air, and maritime forces. The NATO experience also eased logistics support as critical supplies such as ammunition were shifted among NATO allies. There is little doubt that basing and overflight rights were expedited as a result of alliance relationships.

There was less experience in operating with Islamic Coalition members. As described later in this appendix, some combined exercises had occurred with some Islamic members. Because the United States had developed some Arabic linguists, and because some Arab officers and noncommissioned officers had been educated in US Service schools, it was possible to establish effective communication among partners. Interactions between US and Arab land forces were managed by US liaison teams, whose linguistic and regional expertise allowed them to serve as bridges between very disparate national military forces. These skilled linguists also improved the effectiveness of the Command, Control, Coordination and Integration Center. A more detailed explanation of the interaction between Coalition members is in the appendices concerning Special Operations Forces (SOF), Coalition Development, Coordination, and

Warfare, and Command, Control, Communications and Intelligence . (Appendices I, J, and K.)

TRAINING

Realistic Combat Training

High quality training was one of the more important contributors to the preparedness of US forces and subsequent success in the Gulf operations. Service and joint training centers provided realistic operational experiences, including live fire, against realistic threats, in a simulated wartime environment. The value and importance of modern tactical maneuver warfare centers, such as the Army National Training Center (NTC), the USAF Tactical Fighter Weapons Center, the Navy Strike Warfare Center (NSWC), and the Marine Corps Air-Ground Combat Center (MCAGCC) were demonstrated during Operations Desert Shield and Desert Storm.

The Combat Training Center (CTC) Program is central to the Army's strategy of maintaining a force able to deploy rapidly for ground conflict. Their program has made a greater contribution to improving and sustaining the professionalism and war fighting capability of the Total Army than any other single program. The CTCs encompass the NTC at Fort Irwin, CA; the Joint Readiness Training Center (JRTC) at Fort Chaffee and Little Rock Air Force Base (AFB),AR; the Combat Maneuver Training Center (CMTC) at Hohenfels, Germany; and the Battle Command Training Program (BCTP) at Fort Leavenworth, KS. These centers provided advanced unit training and training in joint operations for the full range of Active and Reserve Component (RC) units under realistic conditions, with immediate feedback to commanders. The exercises include live-fire scenarios involving the integration of artillery, armor, and infantry weapons as well as close air support. Nearly all US and European-based units and commanders that deployed to

Operations Desert Shield and Desert Storm had trained at a CTC during the year before the war.

NTC scenarios concentrate on armored and integrated armored and light unit operations under mid to high -intensity conflict conditions. The NTC conducts 12 brigade level rotations a year. The NTC proved to be invaluable as the training ground for active and RC units preparing for deployment to the Persian Gulf. The JRTC, based on the NTC model, focuses on low- to mid-intensity contingency operations. This center trained airborne, air assault, light infantry, and other rapid deployment units, including SOF. The CMTC provides CTC training to Army forces deployed in Europe. Armored and mechanized units in the VII Corps trained there before Operation Desert Storm.

Substantial USAF participation in the Army CTCs further improves joint operations. For example, USAF units frequently have participated in exercises supporting the JRTC at Fort Chaffee. In addition to providing Army elements with close air support (CAS) and tactical resupply, USAF provides tactical training for Air Force elements. Military Airlift Command (MAC) and Tactical Air Command participate by providing the necessary airlift and CAS. Army units work with USAF elements to plan and execute deployment of personnel and equipment. CAS planning and execution is tested at all CTCs. The USAF typically provides 120 sorties for a JRTC exercise, using a variety of aircraft.

It is difficult to train an entire division or corps, because there are no training areas large enough to deploy such complex organizations. Thus, to simulate the battlefield and train higher level commanders and staffs properly, BCTP was developed to extend CTC training to division and corps commanders and their staffs. It is a two-phased program, consisting of a war-fighting seminar, followed by a computer-assisted battle simulation command post

exercise (CPX), usually conducted at the corps or division home station. A BCTP team deployed to Saudi Arabia and, using OPLANs developed in theater, war gamed the various courses of actions in computer assisted battle simulation exercises, with corps and division commanders participating. This served to train division and corps commanders and staffs in theater and prepare them for offensive operations.

The USAF conducts numerous exercises at various training centers. One is Green Flag, an electronic combat exercise conducted several times each year on the Tonopah Electronic Combat Range, NV. The exercise's objectives are to improve electronic combat proficiency, train battle staffs, conduct suppression of enemy air defense (SEAD) operations, and evaluate current electronic combat systems.

Red Flag is another large scale tactical training exercise. Its purpose is to expose combat air crews to a realistic combat environment while they use their aircraft against simulated threat systems. Conducted at Nellis AFB, NV , the exercise focuses on the integration of various types of combat aircraft, with supporting aircraft such as air refueling tankers and electronic jammers, while opposing systems provide a credible air threat. Red Flag exposes air crews to the complexity and dangers associated with the first missions of any war. The exercise is conducted four to six times a year, and involves up to 100 aircraft, which fly up to 3,500 sorties in two weeks. Scenarios vary; however, the integration of attack aircraft and air-to-air fighters and the execution of the orchestrated attack plan on Nellis ranges provide a close replication of the air campaign conducted during Operation Desert Storm. The Nellis ranges are instrumented to provide real-time force attrition and accurate debriefing visualizations to enhance air crew learning and awareness in large scale operations. The exercises include elements from all Services; other nations often are represented. (The UK,

Germany, Italy, France, Egypt, and Canada, among other nations, have participated in Red Flag exercises.)

Established in the mid-1980s at Naval Air Station, Fallon, NV, the NSWC is the Navy's foremost authority on strike warfare, the offensive air, land, and sea operations to destroy enemy military facilities and forces. As the single site for Navy strike warfare training, NSWC provides selected air crews and key staff personnel an intensive ground and flight training program. Prospective strike planners and strike leaders undergo a two-week Strike Leader Attack Training course. Air crews and staff also deploy to Fallon as an integrated air wing for a three-week course which includes exposure to realistic combat scenarios. Air crews plan, brief and fly simulated combat missions against an integrated air defense system using surface-to-air and air-to-air threats. Hundreds of missions are flown over the highly instrumented range complex, using the latest integrated air wing tactics. Crews return to an extensive debriefing including high-technology wide-screen displays to show the entire mission and to highlight the key lessons. The training provides the most realistic combat training available and prepared air crews well for Operation Desert Storm.

The Navy also has established Fleet Combat Tactical training centers (FCTC) and a Battle Group Tactical Training Continuum (BGTT) to support the carrier battle group's (CVBG) preparation for deployment. Before deploying to SWA, nearly every CVBG had the opportunity to train both in port and at sea. The FCTCs and the BGTT's Tactical Training Groups (TACTRAGRU) are in both Dam Neck, VA, and San Diego, CA. FCTCs provide realistic tactical training to individual units and CVBGs while in port. The TACTRAGRUs provide training in coordinated tactical warfare against multiple threats in a battle force environment, and have been stressing joint training in recent years. Integral to the BGTT is the Enhanced

Naval Warfare Gaming System (ENWGS). ENWGS assists fleet and CVBG staffs in examining organizational and command and control (C^2) concepts, and testing staff management and tactical proficiency in Fleet training scenarios. ENWGS supports training in all naval warfare areas (e.g., antiair, antisurface, antisubmarine, and amphibious warfare). During preparations for Operation Desert Storm, CVBG commanders used ENWGS extensively to develop warfighting capabilities for the unique SWA situation.

The MCAGCC at 29 Palms, CA, is the USMC's premier CTC. The MCAGCC combined arms exercises provide the only opportunity in which the full range of combat capabilities can be tested. Air-ground task forces regularly conduct live-fire maneuver exercises that integrate ground and air weapons in an environment that closely simulates combat. Ten battalion or regimental sized task force rotations, involving both regular and Reserve Component (RC) forces, are conducted each year; each rotation lasts three weeks. Task forces consist of ground, aviation and combat service support (CSS) elements formed and deployed in accordance with MAGTF doctrine. These components participate in a live-fire training program that emphasizes Command, Control, Communications and Intelligence (C^3I) in fire support coordination in combined arms operations, with priority placed on air-ground integration in mechanized warfare and rapid movement across hundreds of kilometers of desert terrain.

There were two specific instances in which training at 29 Palms proved invaluable in preparation for Operation Desert Storm. First, the 2nd Tank Battalion, and two companies from the Reserve 4th Tank Battalion deployed to MCAGCC during November to train on newly acquired M1A1 tanks. These Marines conducted gunnery, maneuver, and combined arms training to qualify with these tanks. Crews of the 4th Tank Battalion played an important role in exploiting the Marine breach into Kuwait during the ground offensive.

The second, and perhaps the most important, MCAGCC contribution during the crisis, was the development and testing of engineering equipment and techniques for minefield and obstacle breaching. The Reserve 6th Combat Engineer Battalion constructed extensive models of Iraqi obstacles and conducted breaching exercises to evaluate newly fielded equipment and test tactical concepts. These were crucial to the success of the combat engineer teams that were to cut gaps in Iraqi defenses.

Through its exercises before the Gulf crisis and its training in the months before Operation Desert Storm, the MCAGCC had prepared the Marines extensively for the combat challenges they faced in SWA.

Combined and Joint Exercises

Large scale exercises provide an opportunity to synchronize maneuver and support forces in realistic, stressful situations. Short of combat, exercises are the best method to determine training and readiness strengths and weaknesses. Often, exercises involve operations at the centers discussed in the section on training or in environments similar to the ones in which forces are expected to fight. In recent years, several training initiatives, including exercises and deployments, were designed to present challenges similar to those involved in moving troops and materiel enormous distances. Many involved major multinational training commitments which, as mentioned previously, helped develop the procedures that facilitated combined operations during the crisis. A discussion of some of these exercises will underscore this point.

One of the more important training exercises during the 1980s was the Gallant Eagle series. These war games involved large scale air, land, and sea maneuvers in California and Nevada.

They were designed to simulate the rapid intervention of US forces to help an allied nation repel an invasion force.

US forces also have participated in combined and joint exercises in the Gulf region for several years. The major exercise in the region was Bright Star, conducted in Fiscal Years 83, 85, 87, and 90. Bright Star is a large scale deployment exercise with US forces deployed to Egypt, Oman, Jordan, Somalia, and Kenya. Major participants include Army Component, Central Command and Air Force Component, Central Command. USMC participation has included all levels of MAGTFs: Marine Expeditionary Units conducting amphibious landings; Maritime Prepositioning Force brigades unloading equipment and supplies; a Marine Expeditionary Force command element participating in CPX as well as deployment exercises (e.g. Bright Star). All units were combined and a full range of training was conducted. CVBGs also participated at sea and with strikes ashore. For example, the USS Saratoga (CV 60) Battle Group participated in Bright Star 87. Several small scale SOF deployment exercises to SWA also have been conducted during the past several years. In addition, CENTCOM periodically has conducted training exercises in the continental United States using a SWA scenario. An example of this sort of exercise was Exercise Internal Look 90 discussed earlier.

One of the more important joint and combined exercises instrumental in preparing US forces is the annual Return of Forces to Germany (REFORGER) exercise. Although focused on a completely different part of the world, REFORGER exercises provided an opportunity to test doctrinal and tactical concepts. Many RC elements were mobilized and deployed as they would be under actual crisis conditions. Of equal importance, forces gained experience deploying under tight time schedules, in shipping equipment by air and sea, and in operating with prepositioned equipment.

Strategic lift systems were used as were deployment management systems. In all, REFORGER provided large scale training for the requirements of Operations Desert Shield and Desert Storm.

Other important exercises included multi-CVBG training exercises including FleetEx, Northern Wedding, and PacEx. While these were conducted outside of the CENTCOM area of operations, they played an important role in developing multi-carrier battle group operations, tactics, and skills.

Training In-Theater

The availability of time to train in theater, ranging from a few days to several months, proved invaluable. Initially, the broad spectrum of mission-essential requirements was reviewed to determine the deployed and deploying forces' live-fire and maneuver area needs. By the end of September, live-fire and live bombing practice ranges were established in the Saudi desert for training. Training to that point included cultural and regional orientation as well as multi-echeloned training such as decontamination exercises, squad and platoon maneuver live fire exercises, CPXs at all levels, and indirect fire integration exercises that included joint and combined forces.

By mid-October, training had evolved to company- and battalion-level exercises, artillery live firing, Joint Air Attack exercises with the USAF, and combined fire coordination exercises with Saudi and other coalition forces.

Forces conducted repeated rehearsals of virtually every aspect of defensive and offensive operations. Rehearsals and backbriefs of combat plans and maneuvers were conducted regularly as a result of numerous training exercises including battle drills, battle staff training, gunnery, and mass casualty exercises. Among these in-theater rehearsals were the widely publicized USMC amphibious operations. Less

visible than the landing rehearsals, but equally crucial, were countless ground force obstacle-breaching rehearsals.

The threat of chemical or biological attack forced allied units to train and operate frequently in a Mission-Oriented Protective Posture (MOPP). All units deployed to SWA with standard chemical and biological defense equipment; these were used extensively both in training exercises during the buildup phase and during the offensive operations. Extensive training, in the form of battle drills and rehearsals in full MOPP, acclimatized forces so the additional stress of this protective equipment would not slow unduly the pace of operations. Based on this extensive training, commanders and troops expressed confidence in their ability to survive chemical/biological warfare (CW/BW) attacks and continue to fight. (Additional discussion on CW/BW is in Appendix Q.)

Aviation units with CAS missions practiced with ground units. Navy, USMC, and USAF strike forces and Army aviation attack helicopters thoroughly rehearsed their missions. Individuals and units endlessly repeated CW/BW defensive drills. Naval units en route to and in the theater conducted Rules of Engagement exercises. These regularly scheduled and coordinated exercises were designed to ensure US forces understood their obligations under international law.

The ability of units to adapt quickly to the particulars of the Saudi environment is a product of the Service's training doctrine. Training conducted in-theater was essentially the same as that done as a rule throughout the Services. Tough, realistic training at home stations and in-theater served the US military well in the preparation for and the conduct of the war. The result of this training was to raise US forces to an exceptional peak of combat readiness and to maintain that peak throughout the crisis.

DEPLOYMENT PREPAREDNESS

Strategic Lift

Military preparedness includes the ability to project forces into a crisis area. Determination of preparedness levels must include an assessment of the quantity and readiness of deployment forces, capabilities, and prepositioned assets. Other sections of this report focus specifically on deployment and more detailed information is contained in those discussions. (See Appendices E and F.) However, the following overview will improve the overall discussion of preparedness in this appendix.

Airlift readiness was a key factor in US preparedness to project power rapidly. MAC has a peacetime mission serving a worldwide network of military and other governmental customers. The strategic airlift fleet — active duty USAF, Air Force Reserve, and Air National Guard — on the eve of Operation Desert Shield consisted of a total inventory of 265 C-141s and 126 C-5s. The Civil Reserve Air Fleet (CRAF) represents investments in preparedness extending back to the 1950s and was available to help in deployment and sustainment operations. Tactical airlift with C-130 aircraft maintained a rotational squadron flying airlift missions throughout Europe and SWA, supplementing the C-130s based at Rhein-Main Air Base, Germany. Because of these requirements, airlift was available almost immediately to begin moving personnel and equipment to and within the region. In a sense, the investment in aircraft to help in peacetime operations provided a dividend in the form of ready availability during crisis.

Military Traffic Management Command (MTMC) readiness was shown in the early loading in the Continental United States (CONUS) of the 24th Infantry Division (Mechanized) through Savannah, GA, the 101st Airborne Division (Air Assault) through Jacksonville, FL, and the XVIII Airborne Corps through Wilmington, NC. MTMC also demonstrated expertise by rapidly loading VII Corps through European ports on short notice and during severe weather. MTMC's Reservists, including 200 volunteers in August, were crucial to efficient operations and performed very well. These volunteers supervised the loading of early deployers until other Reservists were available.

Approximately $7 billion was invested to improve sealift during the 1980s. That investment provided the Military Sealift Command (MSC) a force structure with specific programs designed to improve mobilization and deployment of US armed forces. These programs included the Afloat Prepositioning Force, Fast Sealift Ships, and the Ready Reserve Fleet (RRF). Ships could have been added to the MSC fleet from the Sealift Readiness Program (SRP) or through requisitioning, although the ready availability of other sources of sealift made this unnecessary. Prepositioning ships were available and arrived in the region relatively quickly. However, sealift was degraded by previous decreases in maintenance and exercise funds. Given the resources available, sealift was relatively well prepared.

One key to the effectiveness of strategic lift is the availability of aerial and sea port facilities, overflight rights and en route bases to support deployment. The availability of these assets, both in the US and overseas is an example of sound defense planning. Air and sea ports in the United States that could accommodate the deployment of large numbers of service members and their equipment had been identified. In the case of military terminals, many needed facilities were constructed years before the crisis. Facilities to load heavy equipment onto rail cars and ships also were available.

Bases to provide refueling and other support to air and sea transport were available in Portugal, Spain, Germany, Italy, UK, France, Greece,

Egypt, and Turkey. Many of these facilities, such as Rota, Spain, were made available on very short notice — sometimes only a few hours. While availability of such bases became routine as the crisis lengthened, it is worth noting that availability in the crucial first days required rapid decisions by all governments involved. Many governments had not yet publicly declared their support for US initiatives and were unsure of the temper of their constituents with respect to the crisis. Nevertheless, rights were made available when the deployment began, in part owed to previous US security relations with these states, including security assistance programs, and the quick actions of State Department officials.

Ports of embarkation and support en route are crucial to deployment; however, equally as crucial are ports of debarkation within the crisis area. Largely because of previous programs, Saudi Arabia had a sophisticated air and sea port infrastructure. State of the art debarkation sites were available in harbors and at airfields. Although not all desired facilities were made available, substantial assets were designated for deployment and sustainment support.

Decisions to release ramp space at Saudi airfields required time. Some ramps were dedicated to reception of Saudi national aircraft or the aircraft of other nations. In other cases, dormant ramp space had to be brought on line. There also were concerns about the adequacy of airfield refueling facilities and, initially, there were concerns about the reliability of third country refueling crews. Although some delays were experienced initially, most problems were overcome quickly.

Seaports in Saudi Arabia were among the more advanced in the world, with a substantial number of berths and modern materiel handling equipment. However, the ability to move goods through the ports quickly was constrained by an inadequate road system away from the coastal region. This caused a backlog of supplies and equipment to develop at the ports. The problem was compounded by a lack of suitable warehouse space at the ports to accommodate this backlog.

Prepositioned Equipment

Prepositioning equipment and sustainment supplies is an important strategic lift multiplier that reduces the initial strain of air and sealift and provides deploying commands with substantially increased flexibility. Whether ashore or afloat, prepositioned materiel is available readily and can be brought to bear on a crisis virtually as soon as units can be airlifted to it.

In depth discussions of prepositioning and its implications are in Appendices E and F. From the standpoint of preparedness, DOD had invested substantially in stocks and in the establishment of storage facilities on ships and at selected sites within the Persian Gulf region. These investments were complemented by plans to deploy forces to the appropriate locations quickly. As described in the discussion of deployment, lessons were learned from Operations Desert Shield and Desert Storm to improve prepositioning. However, on the whole, current prepositioning programs improved US preparedness markedly.

FORCE MODERNIZATION

Another aspect of military preparedness is the level and state of force modernization. Modernization is a continuous process by which the Services develop and field warfighting capabilities designed to take advantage of technology and to counter potential threats. There are several aspects of force modernization. While the focus in this discussion is equipment modernization, equally important are the development and implementation of modern doctrine, organizations, leader development, and training programs to capitalize on the capabilities of this equipment and, in some cases, determine what additional types of equipment should be procured. Force modernization ensures the United States maintains its superiority in research and development (R&D) and fielded high technology systems.

Force modernization before and during Operations Desert Shield and Desert Storm improved combat capabilities and force preparedness and readiness. Investments in R&D, and testing and evaluation (T&E) during the past several decades produced systems used during the war. The armed forces deployed for operations in the Persian Gulf benefited from the leadership of previous Presidents, government, congressional, and DOD leaders.

The forces in Operations Desert Shield and Desert Storm deployed both old and new equipment. Some systems had been used in combat before the Gulf War, but most were not yet combat proven. Some equipment still was in the developmental stage when the war began and was used before completion of normal research and development and test and evaluation programs. Acquisition of a number of these systems was accelerated and sent directly to the theater for use by US forces.

The fact the United States has such a menu of defense hardware in research or in development with options to deploy contributed to the ability to respond on 2 August in at least two ways. First, there was a highly modernized force of aircraft, ships and ground forces with appropriate C^3I deployed in significant numbers. In addition, there were numerous systems in various stages of R&D, some of which were accelerated to the field. There also was an industrial base and an acquisition process able to take several needed items from concept through R&D and deployment to the field during the conflict. These systems and technologies were in either in research (early in development), in full scale engineering

development, or in early stages of development before deployment.

Perhaps the salient example of a system in an early stage of research was the Joint Surveillance Target Attack Radar System (JSTARS). This prototype system provided both wide area coverage and more focused views of moving or fixed equipment of interest. Other examples of R&D systems that were accelerated and fielded included the Constant Source intelligence fusion system, the Standoff Land-Attack Missile (SLAM), the Advanced Medium Range Air-to-Air Missile, the Army Tactical Missile System (ATACMS), JSTARS Ground Support Module (GSM), and the Light Applique System Technique ceramic armor for the USMC Light Armored Vehicles (LAV).

Examples of systems in low rate, early production that were accelerated by the acquisition system included the Low-Altitude Navigation and Targeting Infrared System for Night (LANTIRN) for the F-15E and F-16, and the associated targeting pod for the F-15E. Perhaps most remarkable were a few systems that were taken from concept to fielding in the time allowed, such as the Guided Bomb Unit (GBU-28) laser-guided 5,000-lb bomb, and an initial, but limited number of identify-friend- or-foe (IFF) beacons for US armored vehicles.

Army Modernization

The modernization effort so successful in Operations Desert Shield and Desert Storm is the result of a modernization program begun in the 1970s. Army forces benefited from a coherent, integrated and dynamic modernization strategy with the goal of increasing warfighting capability and ability to survive in combat by taking advantage of technological strengths. Driven by this goal and in accordance with established modernization principles ("first to fight" units have priority; field deployable, sustainable systems that are lethal and improve survivability; field advanced warfighting capabilities before potential opponents; design equipment for future modernization; and, modernize by force package according to unit missions and potential for use), ground force modernization resulted from normal planned programs as well as Operations Desert Shield and Desert Storm unique initiatives.

Before notification for deployment, many units already had been equipped with modernized weapons, equipment and munitions developed during the past several decades. The M1A1 Abrams tank, M2 and M3 Bradley fighting vehicles, Patriot missile, M9 Armored Combat Earthmover, Multiple Launch Rocket System (MLRS), High Mobility Multi-Purpose Wheeled Vehicle (HMMWV), the AH-64 Apache helicopter, and OH-58D Kiowa helicopter were established in units prior to August.

Once deployment began, a major effort was undertaken to provide Army forces with the most modern and lethal weapons and support systems in the Army inventory. Modernization initiatives included equipping three divisions and an armored cavalry regiment (ACR) with M1A1 Abrams tanks (with 120-mm gun); one division and two ACR with improved, high survivability M2A2/M3A3 Bradley fighting vehicles; and numerous units with M9 Armored Combat Earthmovers; optical laser protection for all improved TOW vehicles and HMMWV TOW systems. Also fielded during the crisis were two M270 deep attack MLRS launchers capable of firing the Army Tactical Missile System (ATACMS); approximately 1,000 Heavy Expanded Mobility Tactical Truck (HEMTT) for divisions and ACRs; six divisions, one brigade and two ACRs worth of HMMWV light tactical vehicles; and three battalions of AH-1F helicopters. Some new equipment - notably the Small Lightweight Global Positioning System Receiver (SLGR) - was procured commercially specifically to meet SWA requirements. A few developmental

systems, such as JSTARS, communication, command, and control projects also were fielded quickly and played crucial roles.

Several systems were upgraded or modified to address concerns associated with the theater. For example, the M1A1 tanks were given heat shields, armor plates, and an optical improvement program which increased fire prevention, survivability, and lethality. Helicopters were modified with the engine advanced particle separator and blade taping, both of which addressed the maintenance problems encountered as a result of the desert environment. Upgrades to the Patriot PAC-2 missile software improved lethality, range and capability. More than a dozen modifications were applied to systems in SWA.

Completing Army modernization initiatives, ammunition and missile deliveries were accelerated and assets diverted from units not scheduled for deployment. Similar support was provided to other services, most notably providing the USMC with M1A1 tanks, mine/countermine devices, and engineer systems.

The Army's success on the battlefield, was due, in large part, to the technological advantages afforded by modernized systems. Most systems met or exceeded performance requirements. Their contributions during the theater campaign were substantial. The M1A1 Abrams tank and the M2 and M3 Bradley fighting vehicles were effective. The AH-64 Apache helicopter was proven against armor and hard targets. the M9 increased mobility on the battlefield . Army deep attack artillery (ATACMS MLRS) provided a crucial asset for SEAD. The Patriot was key in keeping Israel out of the war and provided the only fielded anti-Scud capability. The SLGR proved invaluable in allowing Coalition forces to bypass enemy kill zones, navigate unmarked terrain, use artillery rapidly, improve C^2, and reduce fratricide. The

HEMTTs delivered fuel and cargo when no other vehicles could move in the desert.

Indeed, before the ground offensive campaign began, all essential CINCCENT requested Army modernization objectives were achieved. The modernization underscores a profound lesson for the future - modern warfighting capabilities are essential for US forces to be successful on the modern battlefield.

Air Force Modernization

USAF modernization efforts since the late 1970s also paid dividends during Operation Desert Storm. Revolutionary aircraft such as the F-117, evolutionary aircraft such as the F-15E, and the solid designs of the F-16, F-15C, and A-10 contributed to the success of the strategic air campaign and air operations. The performance of these aircraft, as well as that of others, was improved through the addition of several new systems and recent modifications.

The Pave Tack infrared navigation and targeting pod allowed the F-111 to use precision guided munitions with lethal accuracy. The LANTIRN pod carried on the F-15E and some F-16Cs, and the F-15E's LANTIRN targeting pod (which was still under development at the start of the conflict) allowed aircraft to fly and fight more effectively at night.

The combination of new aircraft systems and improved air-delivered weapons developed during the last decade has been effective. For example, the improved 2,000-lb bomb mated to a laser guidance kit became the GBU-27. Delivered by the F-117, the GBU-27 could penetrate all but the hardest and deepest Iraqi targets. To be able to destroy targets impervious to the GBU-27, the USAF developed and tested the GBU-28 bomb (5,000 pounds) in less than six weeks. The GBU-15, another precision guided weapon, allowed the destruction of point targets from moderate standoff ranges.

Improved antiarmor munitions like the AGM-65D imaging-infrared Maverick, CBU-87 Combined Effects Munition, and CBU-89 Gator mines were very effective against Iraqi armor and artillery. Additionally, 500-lb GBU-12 laser-guided bombs proved to be a very cost effective munition for use against Iraqi dug-in armor. GPS greatly increased target acquisition and blind bombing of area targets. High-speed antiradiation missiles (HARM), with precision targeting information from F-4Gs equipped with APR-47 electronic receivers, destroyed many mobile Iraqi threat radars. Newer versions of the proven air-to-air missiles, the AIM-7 Sparrow and AIM-9 Sidewinder, accounted for the majority of kills of Iraqi aircraft in air-to-air combat, performing with nearly the exact success rate predicted by pre-war training and testing.

Modernization of support aircraft and systems also contributed significantly. KC-10 and KC-135R tankers were able to refuel more aircraft per mission than the older KC-135A models, thus playing a key role in maintaining the tempo of the war. The C-141B stretch/aerial refueling modifications and the C-5A wing replacement program greatly increased strategic lift capability. Improvements of C^2 aircraft systems kept commanders aware of what was going on in their sectors of responsibilities. Two JSTARS still in developmental testing and evaluation when they deployed to Saudi Arabia provided unique advantages. Tracking most ground force movements, the system was one of the key elements of the Scud-hunting effort. Working with Coalition attack aircraft, it effectively denied the enemy a night sanctuary and kept continual pressure on Iraqi forces in the theater.

Navy Modernization

Navy modernization included both ships and aircraft, which received new or upgraded weapons systems to improve their warfighting capabilities and keep pace with global threats.

Navy Tomahawk Land Attack Missiles (TLAM) were used in combat for the first time in Operation Desert Storm. The weapon's success confirmed the results of operational testing in the 1980s and demonstrated the value of distributed firepower since TLAMs were launched from both surface combatants and submarines. The TLAMs uses a wide array of advanced technology. Launched with a solid rocket booster and propelled by a turbofan engine, the missile follows complex guidance commands from its on-board computer. Skimming the desert floor at 100 to 300 feet, it literally reads the terrain to avoid enemy radars and other defenses as it navigates to the target. TLAMs were effectively used against a wide array of targets, including CW and nuclear weapons facilities, surface-to-air missile sites, and C^2 centers.

An upgraded A-6 aircraft was the principal long-range Navy strike aircraft in Operation Desert Storm. It performed well in an environment of established air superiority, using a wide variety of precision weapons including laser-guided bombs, HARMs, and the first successful use of the new SLAM in combat.

The F/A-18's performance confirmed the validity of the multi-mission strike/fighter concept. The EA-6B and other defense suppression aircraft were instrumental in the air operation's success. The F-14 was the primary fighter for the Navy during Operation Desert Storm and will remain the principal Navy fighter for the foreseeable future.

USS Avenger (MCM 1), the Navy's newest and most capable mine countermeasures ship, used the AN/SQQ-32, a sophisticated mine hunting sonar, to detect moored and bottom mines in shallow and deep waters. Using this sonar, USS Avenger successfully detected, classified and marked a bottom influence mine similar to the type that struck USS Princeton (CG59). USS Avenger also used the AN/SLQ-48 mine neutralization system (MNS) to locate, examine and destroy mines. The MNS consists of a remotely piloted submersible vehicle equipped with sonar and two television cameras for locating mines, explosives for neutralizing mines, and cable cutters for cutting a mine's mooring so it floats to the surface for destruction.

Marine Corps Modernization

USMC modernization before the Persian Gulf crisis involved wide-ranging overhaul of both ground and air elements during the preceding decade. During the late 1980s, the LAV family of vehicles, consisting of scout and reconnaissance, antitank, mortar, command, and logistics variants, entered service in each division, adding substantial mechanized capability. Equipment modernization programs completed in the late 1980s included the M198, 155-mm howitzer, which replaced the aging and shorter range M101 105-mm and M114 155-mm. howitzers; the HMMWV; Kevlar body armor; the TOW-2 antitank missile system; and a new, longer range 81-mm mortar; and new small arms and infantry weapons ranging from the M16A2 rifle to the MK19 40-mm grenade launcher. Logistics capabilities were improved by the introduction of the Logistics Vehicle System (LVS) and the M900 series of trucks. Not only was Marine units' equipment modernized, but older equipment aboard maritime prepositioning ships also was replaced during scheduled maintenance cycles.

Marine armored capability remained dependent on the venerable M60A1 battle tank, with its 105-mm main gun. These tanks, scheduled to be replaced by the M1A1 beginning in 1991, still formed the core of Marine tank units during the war. Delivery of initial M1 tanks was advanced to October, when the Army provided 108 tanks to the USMC. These were issued to the 2nd Tank Battalion of the 2nd Marine Division and attached elements of the reserve 4th Tank Battalion when deployed to SWA.

Perhaps the most innovative new item was the Pioneer Unmanned Aerial Vehicle (UAV). This system allowed real time reconnaissance and provided a capability to adjust supporting arms fires in hostile enemy airspace virtually undetected.

USMC aviation modernization programs provided up-to-date multi-purpose equipment. Beginning in December 1982, the first F/A-18 entered service, replacing F-4 fighters. By 1991, transition to this new aircraft, with its dual fighter and attack capability had been completed. New fighters also were placed in Reserve squadrons. Included in this modernization was the introduction of the F/A-18D, a two-seat attack aircraft that carried forward looking infrared radar (FLIR). During the crisis, this aircraft was used extensively for airborne forward air control of close and deep air support missions, markedly improving attack accuracy and reducing the chances of fire from friendly forces.

The AV-8B, introduced in 1983, improved the ability of USMC aviation to support Marines on the ground by enabling aircraft to be based near ground commanders, greatly reducing response times. The OV-10 observation aircraft was in the midst of a Service Life Extension Program, which upgraded the largely visual capabilities of the OV-10A to the day-night capabilities of the OV-10D with improved avionics and FLIR. Both types of aircraft were deployed.

CH-53E heavy lift helicopters were introduced during the 1980s. This helicopter nearly doubled lift capability from the older CH-53D. The CH-53E was able to lift up to 32,000 pounds of cargo and was equipped for aerial refueling. The AH-1W attack helicopter, with Hellfire antitank missiles and improved night vision systems, had begun to replace the older AH-1T in the late 1980s. Although the change had not been completed in August, those helicopters that were available improved USMC

antitank capabilities. While Marine helicopter aviation generally had been modernized during the 1980s, a shortfall continued to exist in terms of medium lift. The aging CH-46, in service since the mid-1960s, is rapidly nearing obsolescence. Its short range and relatively slow speed limited its tactical use, particularly for long-range amphibious assaults.

Other Modernization Issues

The ever increasing demand for real-time information exchange and command, control and communications (C^3), was stretched to the limit during the war. Tactical satellites (TACSAT) is an area that should be exploited further for combat use, including space-based TACSAT systems for weather and tactical ground systems. A need to continue development and procurement of such items as a GPS, other space-based systems and anti-fratricide systems were identified.

Development and procurement of items such as the global positioning system and its user components must continue. Solutions to the difficult problems of detecting and targeting mobile relocatable targets and sorting out friend from foe on the fast paced modern battlefield must be found. There is a recognized need to improve the capability to deliver precision-guided munitions in all weather conditions, and to rapidly compile and disseminate accurate battle damage assessments. Finally, and equally important, problems in the orchestration of air war emphasize the need to develop interoperable systems for passing air tasking and intelligence data quickly to tactical units in all Services. (A discussion of some of these systems is in Appendix K)

Modernization of strategic deployment capabilities by land, air, and sea must continue to ensure future national security objectives can be met.

PUBLIC AND FAMILY SUPPORT

An aspect of US preparedness that was fundamental to success was the tremendous support US forces received from the American people and family support programs within the respective Services. Public support was instrumental in the high morale and outstanding performance of US forces. US forces knew the American people were behind them. The Services' support for families of deployed forces played a crucial role in the ability of US forces to respond quickly and for a sustained period of time. Family support plans, support groups, and assistance programs were developed to take care of deployed forces families. Deployed soldiers, sailors, airmen, and Marines took great comfort knowing this. These programs contributed to the overall preparedness of US forces in future operations.

SUMMARY

The high level of US preparedness clearly contributed to the tremendous success in Operations Desert Shield and Desert Storm. This preparedness was a product of years of involvement and forward presence in the region; longstanding security assistance programs; previous detailed crisis planning by the Office of the Secretary of Defense (OSD), the JS and CENTCOM; investments in quality people; tough, demanding, and realistic training; and, force modernization programs that provided US forces with the best equipment possible. Most importantly, US forces had the American people behind them and they knew, as they deployed, their families were being cared for. In these respects, US forces were trained and ready to go to war.

OBSERVATIONS

Accomplishments

■ US forces were well prepared for Operations Desert Shield and Desert Storm.

■ Previous commitments to the region, a US forward presence, exercises, basing and access arrangements in and enroute to the region — supported in large part by longstanding, security assistance arrangements — improved preparedness.

■ Planning for crises in the region began long before Iraq's invasion of Kuwait. These plans were based on Secretary of Defense and CJCS guidance and detailed analyses of the region. CINCCENT had developed a plan for the defense of the Arabian peninsula and had tested that plan immediately before the crisis. Lessons learned from that exercise provided much valuable information with which to modify the plan to fit the situation.

■ Joint doctrine and exercises prepared US forces for operations with each other and with the forces of Coalition states.

■ Training at sophisticated CTCs whose scenarios closely approximate actual combat prepared service members for Operations Desert Shield and Desert Storm. Large scale exercises provided interoperability and deployment experience.

■ R&D choices, together with procurement decisions, made state-of-the-art equipment available to all Services.

■ Family support programs were organized to provide support, information, and assistance to families of deployed soldiers, sailors, airmen, Coast Guardsmen, and Marines.

(Continued)

OBSERVATIONS (Continued)

Shortcomings

- Deployment data was not fully developed in August. Initial deployments were done manually rather than automated. In this sense, US forces were not as well prepared as they might have been; however, innovation on the part of deployment managers in all organizations made the system work despite problems. Deployment data depends on approved plans and there is always the risk that plans will not be fully mature or that developments will require changes. The solution is to continue to develop automated systems that can respond rapidly to emerging requirements.

- Initial deployments were slowed because not all debarkation facilities were available. Lack of information on availability of support equipment and facilities delayed decisions and impeded the flow of in-bound personnel and equipment. One solution to problems of this nature is to conclude host nation support agreements long before projected need. This procedure for prior agreements has been used in Europe for years; it has relevance for regional contingencies as well.

- When road and rail infrastructure is inadequate, tactical airlift can improve intratheater transportation if enough airports are available.

- Insufficient numbers of large, roll-on/roll-off (RO/RO) ships, and the RRF slow response precluded CINCCENT from building combat power as rapidly as the situation required. Strategic sealift could not meet the requirements for rapid lift.

Issues

- Preparedness for future conflicts begins long before the crisis. In many respects, the forces that go to war are the forces inherited as a result of earlier decisions.

- As forces are drawn down and the defense budget becomes smaller, it is important to continue to improve those things that contributed to the preparation of forces for Operations Desert Shield and Desert Storm. These include: forward presence and military-to-military contacts to facilitate regional operations; security assistance to improve regional stability through the transfer of equipment and the provision of services and training; sound analysis and planning guidance that improves operational plans; joint and combined training and exercises under realistic conditions; and, continued investments in deployment infrastructure, mobility capabilities, and R&D.

- Maintaining a technological edge is one of the more important aspects of preparedness. As regional threats become more sophisticated, technology becomes more important to deter crises and to protect US interests. However, technology is only one part of an overall structure, and the edge in high quality service members who can use advanced equipment in innovative ways also is crucial.

TABLE 1, Appendix D

HISTORY OF DEFENSE PLANNING AND PROGRAM DEVELOPMENT FOR PERSIAN GULF/SOUTHWEST ASIA PRESENCE AND CRISIS RESPONSE

The following highlight the key decisions and major events in the policy and programmatic actions to develop and improve US defense capabilities in the region:

1951

The Army Corps of Engineers (COE) involvement in Saudi Arabia began with the rebuilding of the airfield at Dhahran. COE completed the construction of the Dhahran Civil Air Terminal in 1961.

15 November 1951

United States Military Assistance and Advisory Group (MAAG) to Saudi Arabia established to complement COE efforts in the Kingdom.

2 April 1957

United States MAAG to Saudi Arabia expands to become US Military Training Mission (USMTM), now the largest US security assistance organization in Asia.

May 1965

The US Ambassador to Saudi Arabia and the Saudi Minister of Foreign Affairs signed the Engineer Assistance Agreement in which the US agreed to provide advice and assistance for construction of certain military facilities for the Saudi Ministry of Defense and Aviation (MODA).

1972-88

COE directed five major construction projects funded entirely by the Kingdom of Saudi Arabia at a total cost of $14 billion. King Khalid Military City was completed in 1988 as part of this program.

1976 Saudi Naval Expansion Program

The US began sales, training, and logistics support in the expansion and modernization of the Saudi Navy.

1977 Presidential Review of US Regional Security Commitments and Capabilities

Conducted primarily within the Office of the Secretary of Defense, the effort resulted in a series of Presidential Review Memorandums (PRMs), including PRM 10 that stipulated the need for:

- A limited number of relatively light combat forces (such as USMC divisions and some light Army divisions).
- Naval and tactical air forces.
- Strategic mobility forces with the range and payload to minimize dependence on staging and logistical support bases.

July 1977

The US and Bahrain concluded an agreement for continued leasing of docking and shore facilities by the US Middle East Force (which had been stationed at Manama since 1949).

July 1978

Presidential Directive 18 identified a strike force of about 100,000 troops to respond to regional contingencies. Department of Defense identified two Army divisions, one heavy and one light, and a USMC amphibious force. The Pentagon also was instructed to increase its strategic airlift and sealift capability so it could quickly transport these forces to potential combat zones. The strike force was to be backed up by two to four aircraft carrier task forces and by up to three USAF tactical air wings totaling about 200 airplanes.

25 January, 1979

In his second annual report to the Congress, Secretary of Defense Harold Brown spoke of rapid deployment forces, saying that "we must have sufficient capabilities to permit the rapid movement of substantial forces to threatened theaters."

June 1979

As a result of the Iranian Revolution and increasing tension, the Secretary of Defense increased naval task force deployments to the Indian Ocean from two every other year to four a year and gradually expanded the duration of the deployments.

August 1979

In Department of Defense (DOD) Amended Program Decision Memorandum, maritime prepositioning was announced. It encompassed a combination of airlift and sealift, to include 13 Maritime Prepositioning Ships (MPS). These would carry the equipment and supplies for three USMC Amphibious brigades for a rapid global response capability.

1 October, 1979

In an address to the Nation, President Carter announced that "rapid deployment forces" would be used to meet contingencies anywhere in the world. This publicly announced the new US emphasis on the importance of an intervention capability to be used in Third World contingencies.

5 December, 1979

At a press conference, Major General P.X. Kelley, Deputy Chief of Staff for Requirements and Programs at Headquarters USMC revealed the Secretary of Defense had ordered the USMC to organize a 50,000 man spearhead for the Rapid Deployment Force (RDF). He also discussed the MPS program and underscored the glaring deficiency "in strategic mobility assets, particularly airlift" to respond to contingencies.

13 December, 1979

Secretary Brown described before the Senate Armed Services Committee the initial programs for improving rapid deployment capabilities. Previewing the FY81 budget and the FYDP, the Secretary said: "We are undertaking two major initiatives to help the US cope with crises outside Europe. The first will be Maritime Prepositioning Ships that will carry in dehumidified storage the heavy equipment and supplies for three Marine brigades. These ships would be stationed in peacetime in remote areas where US forces might be needed. The Marines would be airlifted to marry up with their gear and be ready for battle on short notice. The other initiative will be the development and production of a new fleet of large cargo aircraft able to carry Army equipment, including tanks, over intercontinental distances. These aircraft would be used initially to deliver the outsize equipment of the advance forces necessary to secure air bases or the ports or the beaches needed by the MPS to deliver their heavy gear."

December 1979

DOD began negotiating with Oman, Somalia, Djibouti and Kenya to permit the increased use of ports in those countries by US forces.

23 January, 1980

In the aftermath of the Soviet invasion of Afghanistan in December 1979, President Carter enunciated the "Carter Doctrine," which designated the Persian Gulf as an area of vital interest to the United States. Specifically, the doctrine stated, "Any attempt by any outside force to gain control of the Persian Gulf region will be regarded as an assault on the vital interests of the USA and will be repelled by any means necessary, including military force."

29 January, 1980

In his third annual report, Secretary Brown further described the RDF. In addition to the hardware programs, the Secretary reported the creation of an RDF based in the Continental United States (CONUS) under a USMC lieutenant general.

1 March, 1980

The Rapid Deployment Joint Task Force (RDJTF) was established to protect US national interests, including assured access to oil, stable and secure regimes in SWA,

and prevention of the influence or takeover of the region whose interests are inimical to those of the US and the region.

5 March, 1980

DOD announced the Pentagon would deploy to the Indian Ocean seven existing cargo ships with enough equipment and supplies for early arriving forces of the RDF. This formalized the Near-Term Prepositioning Ships (NTPS) program.

Other Events

The RDJTF began planning for contingency operations and exercises throughout SWA under a variety of scenarios and potential threats to US security interests.

The RDJTF began exercises outside CONUS (Bright Star) with Egypt, Oman, Sudan, and Somalia and emphasized desert warfare training for component forces.

The RDJTF began to examine areas for desert training support. The Army National Training Center (NTC) and the Marine Corps Air Ground Combat Center (MCAGCC) were ultimately established, in part, to support realistic terrain and environmental training for Southwest Asia (SWA).

The NTPS was expanded to include six additional ships to support RDJTF contingency responses in the region and development of Fast Sealift Ship (FSS).

The United States expanded security assistance programs and defense cooperative efforts with friendly states throughout the region:

- Sales of modern US military equipment to Jordan, Egypt, Saudi Arabia and the rest of the Gulf Cooperation Council (GCC) states.
- Facilities support arrangements with Kenya, Somalia, Egypt, Saudi Arabia, Sudan, Oman, the United Arab Emirates, and Bahrain. Specifically concluded the only formal access agreement with a Gulf nation with Oman for aircraft landing rights.
- Programs were initiated (throughout the 1980s) to improve support for US military capabilities in the region including land-based prepositioning, brigade staging areas, water production, logistics-over-the-shore, RRF expansion and hospital ships.
- Increased deployments of naval combatants and Amphibious Ready Groups (ARGs) to the North Arabian Sea and Indian Ocean.

1981

Military construction and improvements to existing facilities in Oman, Kenya, Somalia, Egypt, and Diego Garcia to support an increased capability for US forces in the region were approved.

The Royal Saudi Air Force bought US Airborne Warning and Control System aircraft.

President Reagan requested $81 million to begin development of a new transport plane, the CX, which could carry US military equipment several thousand miles non-stop in support of Persian Gulf security.

1 October, 1981

In a national press conference, President Reagan declared that "...there's no way the US could stand by and see that (Persian Gulf oil) taken over by anyone that would shut off that oil."

Congressionally Mandated Mobility Study (CMMS) completed. This analysis identified significant airlift requirements shortfalls in virtually every scenario investigated. The programmed buy for airlift through the present has been predicated on a fiscally constrained goal of 66 million ton-miles per day (MTM/D) which has never been realized. Airlift requirements in CMMS exceeded 100 MTM/D in some scenarios and exceeded 66 MTM/D in every scenario. Currently, airlift capability rests near 48 MTM/D.

1 January, 1983

The RDJTF took on unified command status and became the US Central Command (CENTCOM).

20 October, 1983

After Iran's threat to close the Persian Gulf and the Strait of Hormuz, President Reagan declared during a news conference that the Strait of Hormuz would not be allowed to be closed for oil traffic.

Prepositioning of USAF equipment in Oman in support of CENTCOM missions began.

6 April, 1984

At the National Leadership Forum of the Center for International and Strategic Studies at Georgetown University, President Reagan stated, "...given the importance of the region (the Middle East), we must also be ready to act when the presence of American power and that of our friends can help stop the spread of violence. I have said, for example, that we'll keep open the Strait of Hormuz, the vital lifeline through which much oil flows to the US and other industrial democracies."

May 1984

CENTCOM spearheaded Operation Intense Look (Red Sea mine clearing operations) after a Libyan Roll-On/Roll-Off ship probably dropped mines during its transit of the Red Sea/Suez Canal.

June 1984

CENTCOM commenced Shadow Hawk special operations exercises with Jordan.

1987-89

CENTCOM created the JTFME to spearhead efforts of the US reflagging of 11 Kuwaiti oil tankers (Operation Earnest Will) during the Iran-Iraq war. The US effort included a military structure of 22 naval combatants/support ships, Four US Airborne Warning and Control System (AWACS) aircraft and eight KC-135/KC-10 aircraft, two mobile sea bases used for operations against the Iranian Revolutionary Guard Corps Navy, five P-3 surface surveillance aircraft, 10 patrol boats, eight attack helicopters, eight mine clearing helicopters, and a Contingency Marine Air Ground Task Force (MAGTF) of approximately 400 Marines, and approximately 800 USAF aircrew and support personnel. US efforts in asserting the principle of freedom of navigation, providing distress assistance to neutral shipping, clearing mines from shipping lanes, and repelling Iranian gunboat and missile attacks clearly improved US economic, military, and political ties to friendly Arab states while reaffirming the resolve to protect US interests in the Middle East.

17 January, 1989

In his FY 1990 Annual Report to the Congress, Secretary of Defense Frank Carlucci defined maintaining access to regional oil supplies and promoting the security and stability of friendly states to be US regional goals in SWA. The report cited the continuing need for US rapid force deployment and resupply, access to local facilities, and assistance from local military forces to respond adequately to regional threats.

May 1989

CENTCOM conducted the CINCCENT War Game to review and examine newly revised Operations Plan OPLAN 1002 for SWA.

1988-89

CENTCOM revised its OPLAN 1002, originally to plan operations to counter an intra-regional conflict, without Soviet involvement, to specifically address the US capability to counter an Iraqi attack on Kuwait and Saudi Arabia.

October 1989

President Bush stated that "access to Persian Gulf oil and the security of key friendly states in the area are vital to US national security. Accordingly, the US remains committed to defend its vital interests in the region, if necessary and appropriate through the use of US military force." He further stated that the US is also committed to "support the individual and collective self-defense of friendly countries in the area to enable them to play a more active role in their own defense and thereby reduce the necessity for unilateral US military intervention."

January 1990

The Secretary of Defense's guidance made the US central objective for SWA the prevention of a hostile power from gaining control over a share of oil supplies or shipment routes sufficient to provide it with leverage over the US and its allies.

DOD was directed to reassess the appropriate response capability to the range of threats in the region. Accordingly, the Under Secretary of Defense for Policy directed a review to re-examine US policy, strategy, and programs for defense of US interests in Southwest Asia. The study also examined present threats in the region, specifically Iraqi military capabilities and Saddam Hussein's ability to threaten Kuwait and the GCC.

8 August, 1990

In an address to the nation, President Bush noted that his administration, as has been the case with every president from Roosevelt to Reagan, remained committed to the security and stability of the Persian Gulf.

Appendix E

DEPLOYMENT

INTRODUCTION

On 7 August , President Bush directed deployment of US forces in response to a request for assistance from the government of Saudi Arabia. Operation Desert Shield had begun. The first US soldier, a member of the 82nd Airborne Division, was on the ground in Saudi Arabia within 31 hours of the initial alert order. What followed during the subsequent months was the fastest build up and movement of combat power across greater distances in less time than at any other point in history.

"Operation Desert Shield was the fastest build up and movement of combat power across greater distances in less time than at any other time in history. "It was an absolutely gigantic accomplishment, and I can't give credit enough to the logisticians and transporters who were able to pull this off."

General H. Norman Schwarzkopf
Commander-in-Chief,
CENTCOM

Although deployment of US forces in the operation ultimately was successful, it identified several weaknesses in US rapid deployment capabilities. As the US moves to implement a

24th Infantry Division (Mechanized) Tanks and Fighting Vehicles Staged for Loading Aboard the Cargo Ship *USNS Bellatrix* in Savannah, Georgia.

national military strategy based on the projection of power from the United States and forward bases, these deficiencies must be addressed. Deployment planning systems must be reviewed in light of changing priorities in response to regional contingencies; the need for structured, but flexible deployment schedules; and the requirement for transportation feasibility studies to ensure assets are sufficient and able to accommodate unit requirements. Equally important is the continued emphasis on improving worldwide mobility — airlift, sealift, land movement, and prepositioning — necessary to ensure that the United States can deploy and project power credibly.

The following discussion focuses on the deployment of US forces, supplies, and equipment to the theater of operations. Deployment planning, priorities, and execution will be reviewed in detail. Mobility will be addressed by examining current capabilities and how these assets were used in support of Operations Desert Shield and Desert Storm. An assessment of these capabilities is included so that future improvements may be developed. A summary of observations, to include accomplishments, shortcomings, and issues, is provided at the end of this appendix. (Discussion of deployment often overlaps with discussion of logistics. A report on logistics is contained in Appendix F.)

DEPLOYMENT PLANNING

Operation Desert Shield deployment planning required close coordination and interaction between Central Command (CENTCOM), the Services, the Joint Staff (JS), and Transportation Command (TRANSCOM). This planning was conducted within established joint systems; however, it became readily apparent during early deployments that modifications and adjustments had to be made to developed deployment plans, based on deployment priorities and orders.

Department of Defense (DOD) planning for deployment operations is conducted within the framework of the Joint Strategic Planning System (JSPS); Joint Operations, Planning and Execution System (JOPES), and the accompanying Time Phased Force Deployment Data (TPFDD). These systems, which the Services use to plan and execute deployment actions, provide forces to meet military Commander-in-Chief (CINC) requirements. Procedures and systems have been tested in numerous exercises and have worked well; however, Operation Desert Shield surfaced some areas where refinements are required.

The JSPS translates national security policy into strategic guidance, force structure requirements, and provides long and short term operational planning guidance to the CINCs and Services. The JOPES establishes polices and procedures and provides automated systems for the development of Concept Plans (CONPLANs) and Operation Plans (OPLANs) required by JSPS. JOPES, a developmental system, has shown its utility in the past as an effective planning tool.

However, in the initial Operation Desert Shield deployment phases, three factors prevented full use of the JOPES. First, information necessary for deployment was not loaded into the TPFDD. Second, operational considerations in the area of responsibility (AOR) required CENTCOM to repeatedly change the priority and the scheduling of unit movements in midstream. Given its current level of development, JOPES cannot react quickly enough to changes of such frequency and magnitude. Third, the infrequent use of JOPES in peacetime resulted in a shortage of JOPES-capable operators during the early days of Operation Desert Shield.

Essentially, the initial phases of the deployment were done manually while the Services, CENTCOM, and TRANSCOM constructed a TPFDD. This document, initially established in the third week of August, provided discipline to the system, improved deployment procedures, enabled JOPES to begin functioning as designed, and gave TRANSCOM the necessary perspective on total deployment requirements.

Planning for the deployments of US forces is based on operations plans (OPLANs) and the accompanying TPFDD; actual deployments are predicated on operations orders (OPORDs) and Time Phased Force Development Lists (TPFDL). The TPFDD contains deployment data, including ports of embarkation and debarkation; the amount of cargo and personnel deploying; and the type lift required to deploy them. Because there were no approved plans in August, CENTCOM planners had to improvise a solution quickly. Deployment data had not been reviewed to determine transportation feasibility, or revised to reflect actual capability. Accordingly, early movements of units to Saudi Arabia were accomplished with a draft TPFDD, which was built as it was executed.

This meant that early deployments were orchestrated through staff-level conversations between CENTCOM, JS, TRANSCOM, and the Service components. As the need for particular units arose, the CENTCOM staff notified the Joint Staff Crisis Action Team, which, in turn, began producing a deployment order. At approximately the same time, CENTCOM discussed transportation requirements with TRANSCOM. Simultaneously, the Services, CENTCOM, and TRANSCOM began work on the construction of a deployment list. (An in-depth discussion of the planning prior to Operation Shield deployment is contained in Appendix D).

Based on CINCCENT's requirements, TRANSCOM directed strategic lift assets to permit the timely flow of forces and material. TRANSCOM is the unified command responsible for strategic mobility planning; direction, coordination, and management of air and sealift assets for the movement of forces

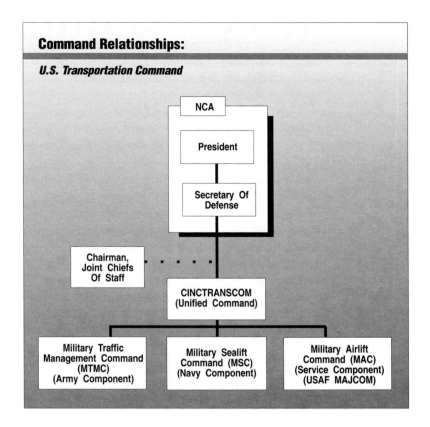

Command Relationships:

U.S. Transportation Command

- NCA
- President
- Secretary Of Defense
- Chairman, Joint Chiefs Of Staff
- CINCTRANSCOM (Unified Command)
- Military Traffic Management Command (MTMC) (Army Component)
- Military Sealift Command (MSC) (Navy Component)
- Military Airlift Command (MAC) (Service Component) (USAF MAJCOM)

and materiel in crisis and war; maintaining JOPES; and wartime traffic management. Its mission is to provide global air, land, and sea transportation to meet national security needs. The command has three components: Military Airlift Command (MAC), Military Sealift Command (MSC), and, Military Traffic Management Command (MTMC).

TRANSCOM exercised command over assigned common user- transportation resources of each of its components. During Operations Desert Shield and Desert Storm, TRANSCOM was responsible for common-user airlift and sealift, Continental United States (CONUS) land transportation, port loading operations, and management of chartered or donated commercial lift.

MAC common-user transportation resources include active, Air Force Reserve (AFR), and Air National Guard (ANG) C-141 and C-5 strategic airlift and support units. MAC also manages the DOD Civilian Reserve Air Fleet (CRAF) program — a systematic activation of commercial passenger and cargo aircraft to support crisis airlift situations — providing additional airlift capability and flexibility to the strategic air flow.

MSC common-user assets available during crisis include Fast Sealift Ships (FSS) and Ready Reserve Force Ships (RRF). FSS consists of eight ships capable of 33 knots at full power, usually dedicated to rapidly deploy Army mechanized units, but available for use by any Service as the supported CINC desires. These ships are maintained in a reduced operating and manning status in peacetime, but are kept ready to sail in 96 hours or less. RRF ships are also maintained in reduced operating conditions, and consist primarily of break-bulk ships, roll-on/roll-off (RO/RO) ships, barge carriers, and tankers. These ships are older vessels and are activated according to a multi-tiered schedule.

Afloat Prepositioning Ships (APS) and Maritime Prepositioning Ships (MPS) can be made available to TRANSCOM for common-user transportation after they have discharged their initial cargo and are released by the supported CINC. APS consists of 11 ships carrying ordnance, supplies, and fuel for the Army and Air Force (USAF) and Navy fleet hospital ships. MPS consists of 13 ships, divided into three squadrons: two squadrons with four ships and one squadron with five ships. Each squadron carries a full complement of equipment and 30 days of supplies for a Marine Expeditionary Brigade (MEB).

MTMC is the DOD single manager for military traffic management, CONUS land transportation, common-user worldwide water terminals, and intermodal movement. MTMC relies upon its active and Reserve Component (RC) personnel to support deployments by air and sea. During Operations Desert Shield and Desert Storm, MTMC was responsible for loading 560 ships, carrying 945,000 vehicles and other cargo, and for arranging the transport of 37,000 containers.

EARLY DEPLOYMENT ISSUES, DECISIONS, AND PRIORITIES

During the first few weeks, several complex issues developed which complicated TRANSCOM's contribution. In addition to the lack of a structured schedule and the absence of transportation feasibility studies, CENTCOM made an early decision to deploy as many combat elements as possible. Although this meant that logistics and administrative units (needed to ensure expeditious reception of units and supplies) were late in arriving, this decision seemed prudent given the fact that Iraq might have attacked Saudi Arabia. The decision to change deployment priorities also necessitated corrections in the flow of units already enroute to ports of embarkation. The immediate impact that such changes had on transportation assets were significant. Each time a short notice change was made, crews and transportation assets had to be repositioned.

CINCCENT was aware of the difficulties imposed by changes in deployment priorities. However, he clearly required immediate combat power to deter Iraqi aggression, and the decision was easier to implement because of the availability of host nation logistics support and port infrastructure. The ability to use Saudi resources to support arriving forces was providential. The assets available were considerable, and, although there were some initial problems in rapidly concluding formal agreements, dependence on host nation support (HNS) — in Saudi Arabia and other Persian Gulf states — worked relatively well. However, Persian Gulf states have infrastructures that are unusual among countries where the United States may deploy forces to resolve regional crises. A more detailed discussion of HNS provided by Saudi Arabia and other GCC states is contained in Appendix F.

Another issue which arose early involved transportation feasibility. Transportation feasibility studies examine the assets needed to move personnel and equipment. Rapid response units, such as the 82nd Airborne Division, the 1st and 7th MEBs, and the USAF tactical fighter squadrons, were the only ones for which current transportation feasibility data was available. The feasibility of moving other units was determined while deployment decisions were being made.

Manual intervention and management to meet short notice deployments and changes in the theater tactical situation cannot be totally eliminated. In fact, some degree of personal intervention will always be required to account for unforeseen circumstances and to provide flexibility. However, as JOPES continues to mature and more sophisticated software becomes available, planning and execution of deployments will become more efficient. The tasks of balancing the deployment ledger and matching units to available transportation assets will be performed more or less automatically. At that time, changes in priorities or the deployment of forces without fully developed deployment data will be easier to accommodate.

A discussion of the deployment of forces must focus on two aspects: the assets available to transport personnel and equipment and the actual deployment. The former governs to a great extent the options for the latter. The following discussion focuses on the assets that were available to successfully deploy US forces and equipment and also identifies some of the difficulties encountered as the deployments occurred.

STRATEGIC LIFT CAPABILITIES

The US ability to project and sustain combat power from CONUS or forward bases is crucial to attaining US national security objectives.

Operations Desert Shield and Desert Storm clearly demonstrated the capability to deploy and project combat power. The United States projected forces, equipment, and sustainment farther, faster and in greater quantities than ever before. Airlift and sealift formed the core of the US strategic lift capabilities. These assets, coupled with land movement and prepositioned equipment and supplies, formed the mobility capabilities so crucial to success in the Gulf War.

Land movements and port operations — in CONUS, Europe, SWA, and elsewhere — include the movement of materiel and loading of aircraft and ships to meet rapid deployment schedules. MTMC arranged all commercial rail and truck moves in CONUS.

This conflict also served to identify deployment capability shortcomings. Requirements substantially stressed capabilities. A credible power projection strategy cannot be executed without adequate worldwide capability and deployability. This requires reviewing capabilities and exploring improvements in worldwide mobility — land movement, airlift, sealift, and prepositioning.

Airlift

A very quick and flexible part of US mobility capability is airlift. TRANSCOM directed, and MAC executed, strategic airlift for rapid force projection during Operations Desert Shield and Desert Storm. Key to US airlift capability is the augmentation provided by the AFR and ANG; their aircraft and crews augmented the active component by providing a total USAF airlift force of 118 out of a total 126 C-5 airlift force and 195 of 265 C-141 cargo planes used during Operations Desert Shield and Desert Storm. These assets were further augmented by Navy C-9s in January, February, and March 1991. USAF KC-10s were employed as cargo carriers when not involved in refueling missions. Airlift system flexibility was also demonstrated by meeting unexpected requirements, such as airlifting Patriot missiles to Israel, rapidly moving particular munitions which were used at higher rates than expected, and deploying additional vehicles to the theater to meet land transportation requirements.

Civil Reserve Air Fleet (CRAF)

CRAF is a program in which commercial airlines agree to make aircraft available for DOD deployments in exchange for peacetime military business. The CRAF is organized into three stages which can be activated incrementally to support DOD airlift requirements of increasing intensity. Thirty-four airlines took part in CRAF operations during this period. US civil air carriers also voluntarily provided passenger and cargo aircraft to support deployments.

CRAF Stage I was activated on 17 August to supplement MAC's organic aircraft during Phase I deployment. This provided 18 long-range international (LRI) passenger aircraft and crews and 21 LRI cargo aircraft and crews. Additional cargo requirements during Phase II of Operation Desert Shield deployments required implementing CRAF II on 17 January. This provided access to another 59 LRI passenger aircraft and 17 more LRI cargo aircraft, some of which already had been committed voluntarily. Throughout the deployment, air carriers volunteered more aircraft than required by the CRAF activations. Commercial assets delivered 27 percent of the air cargo and 64 percent of the air passengers. (Commercial assets included aircraft which were not part of the CRAF).

While CRAF aircraft are very effective in transporting large volumes of passengers, CRAF is less flexible for cargo than MAC organic assets. For example, some kinds of military cargo cannot be carried on civil aircraft because of its size or hazardous nature. Large communications vans, Patriot missile components and helicopters are characteristic of the cargo that can only be moved on organic

military transports. Also, some crews were unfamiliar with military cargo and had difficulty determining what they could or could not carry without first consulting airline officials.

Some CRAF members volunteered aircraft and crews before formal activation; volunteer lift in excess of activated CRAF aircraft continued throughout deployment operations. However, some air carriers were reluctant to volunteer additional passenger aircraft for MAC use during the December holiday travel period — a time when Phase II deployments were under way. Throughout Operations Desert Shield and Desert Storm, DOD also received donated airlift support from government carriers in South Korea, Japan, Luxembourg, and Italy.

Strategic airlift depended on enroute bases in Germany, Italy, Portugal, and Spain. Key facilities such as Torrejon Air Base, Spain; Rhein-Main Airport, and Ramstein Air Base, Germany; the bases at Sigonella, Italy; and Diego Garcia in the Indian Ocean, were well established, integral part of the airlift infrastructure and proved invaluable during deployment. Eighty-four percent of all aircraft missions flowed through Torrejon and Rhein-Main, emphasizing the importance of well-established bases with the capacity necessary for deployment.

Saudi Arabian infrastructure — especially airfields and ports — was well developed. The Saudis were forthcoming in providing access to their facilities — even though there were initial delays that were ultimately remedied. Ramp space at these airfields was also limited, as were ground refueling facilities. In some cases, this meant that aircraft were refueled in the air prior to, or just after, departure. These constraints highlight several key points. First, it is important to have pre-existing host nation support arrangements to ensure access to arrival facilities whenever possible. A second factor illustrated by air deployment is that there were difficulties in servicing aircraft, even though Saudi Arabia has some of the most up-to-date facilities in the world. These difficulties would certainly be exacerbated were there a requirement to deploy a similar sized force to less developed airfields.

Several additional observations emerge from reviewing the airlift. First, airlift delivered more than 544,000 tons of cargo (about 5 percent of the total cargo) and more than 500,000 passengers (about 99 percent of the total passengers moved). During the early deployment period, more than 25 percent of the cargo delivered by air was outsized (larger in size than commercial standard pallets), deliverable today only on C-5s. Another 60 percent was oversize (too large for commercial carrier), most of which could be more efficiently delivered by military aircraft. Secondly, Air Reserve Component (ARC) volunteers augmented the MAC effort for varying periods of time from the outset. The airlift system relies on the call-up of these ARC members to sustain airlift capability. Had they not been available, the airlift system would have run out of crews to sustain the aircraft. Eventually, more than 18,000 ARC volunteers augmented MAC. Reserve units called to duty consisted of seven C-5 squadrons, 11 C-141 squadrons, and 10 C-130 squadrons, comprising more than 80 percent of USAF lift assets.

It also should be noted that the US provided substantial strategic airlift, primarily C-5s, to other Coalition members during Operations Desert Shield and Desert Storm. This included support to NATO allies and several East European and Arab-Islamic countries. For example, MAC lifted equipment and personnel from France and the UK to Saudi Arabia, and German Roland and Dutch Patriot air defense units to Turkey. The US also transported Czech and Romanian chemical defense units to the theater and airlifted equipment for both Saudi Arabia and Kuwait directly from CONUS to SWA. US aircraft were even used to fly crucial

Troops Board CRAF Aircraft.

spare parts from Argentina.

The Navy also provided organic airlift support to supplement the heavily stressed TRANSCOM system. Four of the 11 Navy Reserve Transportation squadrons flying C-9 aircraft were recalled and, together with additional support from the other squadrons, flew more than 9,000 hours, carrying passengers and cargo between Europe and the Middle East.

Sealift

Strategic sealift was crucial both for deploying forces to Saudi Arabia and for their sustainment. Although personnel usually were flown to the Gulf, most equipment and supplies were sent by sea. Because of the huge amounts of heavy equipment requiring transport, and the limited strategic assets available to lift this equipment within the time CENTCOM specified, TRANSCOM had to manage sealift assets carefully and put sealift elements in motion immediately. Close coordination among the entire transportation network was necessary to ensure that airlifted personnel reached the theater near the date their equipment was scheduled to arrive. Arrival of personnel before their equipment would increase the burden on the Saudi infrastructure. It also would expose troop concentrations in the port areas to possible enemy attack by ballistic missiles, aircraft and terrorists.

Ready Reserve Force (RRF)

The RRF was activated for the first time, providing additional RO/RO ships, break-bulk cargo ships, and barge carriers. In the late 1970's, the Navy began purchasing militarily useful ships to bolster the aging mothballed fleet of World War II-era cargo ships. During the next 10 years, the RRF grew and was maintained at various sites by the Maritime Administration in an unmanned status.

The RRF program was designed to provide militarily useful ships in five, 10, or 20 days depending on each ship's current readiness status. There are 17 RO/RO ships in the RRF, and these were the first ships activated. Upon activation, RRF ships moved to a shipyard or dock and were prepared for deployment. They were manned by civilian merchant mariners. Initially, there were problems which led to slow RRF activations. Only 12 of the initial 44 RRF ships were activated within the specified time and only six of 27 additional RRF ships required for deployment of follow-on forces were activated within their established times. Ships scheduled for five-day breakout took, on the average, 11 days to prepare. It took an average of 16 days to prepare 10-day ships. Delays were directly related to prior year funding cuts for RRF maintenance and activation exercises. Once activated and brought to operating condition, however, RRF ships performed well. They maintained a respectable 93 percent reliability rate and delivered 22 percent of the unit cargo for US forces. Figure 4 below depicts RRF activation distribution and reflects the amount of time it took to breakout the RRF fleet.

The advantages of RO/RO and container vessels were clear in this deployment. Most of the RRF consists of break-bulk ships which generally have a smaller cargo capacity and take two to three days longer than RO/ROs to load and unload.

The use of containerized cargo shipments was not as widespread as it might have been during deployment. Increased containerization could have substantially increased the throughput capability of ports. Had events moved more quickly, the two or three days of delay caused by the lack of containerized cargo shipments might have been crucial. However, despite its advantages, containerization presents its own set of problems. For example, there is currently no West coast port equipped to handle containerized ammunition. (Appendix F contains further information on this subject).

Fast Sealift Ships (FSS)

The MSC's FSS had a good performance record. FSSs have both RO/RO and limited container capabilities and are a rapid and versatile transportation means for unit equipment. They have a larger capacity than break-bulk ships and require less time to load and unload. However, there are only eight FSS ships, thus availability was limited. Unfortunately, one FSS, *USNS Antares*, failed off the East coast of the United States with a considerable amount of the 24th Infantry Division (Mechanized) equipment aboard. The ship was towed to Spain. Some of the cargo was airlifted to Saudi Arabia but most had to be unloaded and reloaded aboard another FSS returning from her initial voyage. This cargo arrived about three weeks later than planned. (Before the war, *USNS Antares* had been scheduled for major overhaul, but this was delayed. Thus a degree of risk was accepted in the decision to use *USNS Antares* to speed the deployment.)

The FSS size and speed allowed the remaining seven ships to deliver more than 13 percent of the total cargo of the unit equipment. FSS carried the 90,000 short tons of equipment for the 24th Infantry Division (Mechanized) at average speeds of 27 knots. Although normally on 96-hour standby, the first FSS was ready to deploy in 48 hours. The typical FSS load included more than 700 Army vehicles such as M-1 tanks, M-2 fighting vehicles, and fuel trucks. By comparison, 116 World War II Liberty Ships would have been required to move the same tonnage in the same period.

In conjunction with the FSS and RRF, chartered commercial ships played a vital role in the deployment. There were a total of 213 ships chartered by the US when redeployment began on 10 March. US charters carried 14 percent of all dry cargo and foreign flag charters carried 20 percent. In addition, MSC contracted with US shipping companies to transport containers aboard regularly scheduled United States-Middle East liner service. Through this contracting arrangement, the Special Middle East Shipping Agreement, MSC delivered almost one million short tons of containerized cargo, capitalizing on the strength of US maritime industry.

Sealift Readiness Program (SRP)

Another program that can be called upon when necessary is the SRP. The SRP, a contractual program, requires that shipping companies that bid on MSC contracts commit 50 percent of their cargo capacity to the program. Additionally, those ships built with construction subsidies or receiving operating subsidies are committed to the SRP. The SRP, as currently structured, was not used during the crisis because the US maritime industry responded voluntarily with an adequate number of vessels available for charter.

Several other points in regard to sealift need to be emphasized. First, sealift delivered 95 percent of all cargo, including 85 percent of the dry cargo and 99 percent of the petroleum products. Additionally, once ships became available, overall shipping performance was

Heavy Equipment Being Loaded onto a Fast Sealift Ship.

sound. During Phase I, only six out of 110 ships that entered the sealift system had reliability problems that delayed them in accomplishing their missions. On the other hand, because there are so few fast cargo ships, delivery times were relatively slow.

Prepositioned Equipment

DOD had been preparing for a major expeditionary operation in the Gulf since the 1970s and had made improvements in its expeditionary prepositioning capabilities as part of these preparations. The value of prepositioning — both afloat and ashore — was proven during Operations Desert Shield and Desert Storm. Prepositioning allowed for a more rapid response by combat forces to the theater, providing essential supplies and equipment to early deploying forces.

Afloat Prepositioning Ships (APS)

During the 1980's, the Army established afloat prepositioning of equipment in support of Southwest Asia. These ships are referred to as APS and, when the war started, consisted of 12 ships (eight dry cargo and four tanker).Two tankers were already being used in a fleet support role. These vessels were located at Diego Garcia and one ship was in the Mediterranean. This program involved storage of cargo on four Army APS which would be strategically positioned and could be moved to support CENTCOM contingencies carrying equipment, fuel, and supplies for the Army.

During Operations Desert Shield and Desert Storm, these ships sailed from forward bases in Diego Garcia to the Middle East, and the first APS arrived in Saudi Arabia on 17 August. The war reserve cargo on board these ships included: subsistence, general supplies and equipment, packaged fuel, construction and barrier material, ammunition, and medical supplies. One semi-submersible heavy lift vessel carried port operating equipment (e.g. tugboats, floating cranes, utility landing craft, rough terrain forklifts, containers, and support parts). These ships proved to be indispensable during the operation's first days providing a readily available source of supplies.

Air Force Prepositioning

The USAF prepositioned $1 billion worth of fuel, ammunition, and equipment on the Arabian Peninsula, complementing materiel stored on its three prepositioned ships. Prepositioned assets stored in Oman and Bahrain (as well as on APS) included rations, munitions, medical supplies, aircraft fuel tanks, vehicles, and basic support items consisting of shelters, materiel handling equipment, power generation and distribution equipment, kitchens, water purification and production equipment, and airfield support items. These bare base support items were designed to support 1,200 personnel at each of 14 aircraft bed-down locations but eventually supported 21 locations. HNS initially provided some feeding and facilities support, reducing the need for all available prepositioned assets. (Saudi Arabia had built many airfields that could be used for deployed forces. Those airfields often were bare bases which required improvements, but were available to receive Coalition forces in August).

Maritime Prepositioning

The Navy-USMC maritime prepositioning program was begun in the late 1970s as a result of a DOD strategic mobility enhancement initiative to improve response times for SWA contingencies. Until the full MPF capability (specially built or converted ships) was achieved in the mid 1980s, an interim measure known as Near Term Prepositioning Ships was created in 1980 to provide an initial response capability. The NTPS ships were on station at Diego Garcia by July 1980 and contained the equipment and 30 days of supplies for a USMC Brigade. By early 1985, the first combination RO/RO and break-bulk ships specifically built or converted for the Navy had been commissioned and were loaded with prepositioned vehicles, equipment, and supplies. By 1987, 13 ships organized in three squadrons had been commissioned, crewed with civilian mariners, loaded, and deployed.

The ships were more than just floating warehouses. Each of the three MPS carried equipment for a MEB, along with enough supply sustainment for at least 30 days. The squadrons were associated with a specific MEB to ensure effective planning and training. MPS-1, associated with the 6th MEB, stationed at Camp Lejeune, NC, was deployed in the western Atlantic; MPS-3, associated with the Hawaii-based 1st MEB, was home ported at Guam/Saipan; MPS-2, associated with the 7th MEB in California, was anchored at Diego Garcia. Together, each squadron and its associated MEB become an MPF.

The MPF concept performed largely as expected during the crisis, due to an aggressive training, exercise, and maintenance program carried out during the 1980s. Exercises had established planning goals of about 250 strategic airlift sorties to deploy a MEB; this figure was confirmed by the 7th MEB which deployed to Saudi Arabia using 259 sorties. (The additional nine sorties reflected the addition of an infantry battalion and more helicopter antitank assets to the MEB.) The expected time of 10 days to unload ships and marry equipment with arriving units was met by all three MPFs . In fact, 7th MEB combat elements occupied defensive positions near Al-Jubayl in August within four days of their arrival. The only problem encountered during initial deployment of the 7th MEB centered on refueling support to Marine fixed wing aircraft flying from CONUS, which competed for scarce assets with other service aircraft. Elements of 1st MEB and II MEF, although deployed using MPF concepts, did not do so as complete units. Instead, their air, ground, and logistics elements were deployed and integrated into I MEF as they arrived, drawing their equipment from their associated MPS ships.

DEPLOYMENT OVERVIEW AND EXECUTION

Force deployments were initially based on a Concept Outline Plan (COP) and draft OPLAN developed as part of the DOD deliberate planning process in the spring and summer of 1990. These were put into immediate use as the best available plans at the time of the Iraqis' invasion of Kuwait. The OPLAN was translated into an Operations Order (OPORD) which provided deployment instructions, and priorities to CENTCOM's component Services and provided tasking direction to supporting unified and specified commands. The order also requested intergovernmental support from the departments of State, Transportation, and Justice. The OPORD directed that Operation Desert Shield deployments occur in two phases.

Phase I

Phase I began on 7 August which was designated as C-Day, the day on which deployments began, and lasted until mid-November. This phase was designed to deploy enough forces to deter further Iraqi aggression; prepare for defensive operations; and conduct combined exercises and training with multinational forces in theater. Although the US build-up of forces was larger and occurred faster than any in history, during this phase of the deployment, the ground forces,

major ports and airfields in Saudi Arabia remained vulnerable to Iraqi attack. (Combat forces from other Coalition nations, particularly Egypt, Syria, France, and the United Kingdom joined the US and Saudi forces during this period as well.)

In the first 10 days, a significant joint force of Army, USAF, Navy, and Marine (USMC) units deployed to the theater. Modern airfield and port facilities contributed substantially to the initial deployment's success. These facilities and years of experience with the Saudis gave the United States a head start. Ultimately, during Phase I deployments, the United States deployed about 1,000 aircraft, 60 Navy ships, an amphibious task force, and 240,000 military personnel.

Phase I deployments involved a number of simultaneous movements by elements of all Services. Because a number of events occurred at once, it is easier to consider force deployments in terms of individual Service movements rather than by laying out all of the deployments that occurred on a particular date. The following discussion deals with each Service, and how together they contributed to the accomplishment of the CINC's objectives.

USMC MPS Ship Being Off-Loaded At Al-Jubayl.

Army Component, Central Command (ARCENT) Deployments

Because the US did not have substantial ground forces or prepositioned equipment in Saudi Arabia, a major deployment of these assets was required. To ensure a more efficient deployment, the MTMC Contingency Response Program was activated on 8 August. This organization ensured that DOD requirements for commercial transportation within CONUS were appropriately coordinated and met. Civil aircraft, under MAC contract, began arriving in Saudi Arabia on 9 August with troops from Pope Air Force Base. As early as 8 August, Defense Fuel Supply Center and its Middle East regional office were arranging rapid expansion of contract fuel support at MAC reception points. Elements proceeded rapidly after initial preparations were made.

During Phase I, US strategic lift moved substantial forces into the region. However, much was required before all of these elements were available in theater. Early-arriving troops established defenses around the airfield at Dhahran to provide security. The Army's XVIII Airborne Corps' assault command post and lead elements of the 82d Airborne Division's ready brigade departed Pope Air Force Base, NC, on 8 August. The following day, the 101st Airborne Division (Air Assault) stationed at Fort Campbell, KY, began to deploy by air.

Armored and mechanized infantry forces from the 24th Infantry Division (Mechanized) (augmented by the 197th Separate Infantry Brigade in place of a round-out brigade), 1st Cavalry Division, 1st Tiger Brigade, 2nd Armored Division and the 3rd Armored Cavalry Regiment (ACR) were selected as the initial follow-on forces for the deployment order issued on 10 August.

On 10 August, orders for the activation of the first 17 RRF ships were issued. On the same day the first FSS ship arrived at Savannah, GA, and began loading the tanks, infantry fighting vehicles, and self-propelled artillery of the 24th Infantry Division (Mechanized) under MTMC supervision. The first contract to charter a US ship also was signed on 10 August.

The rapid deployment of the 82nd Airborne Division continued. By the afternoon of 13 August, most of the 82nd's first ready brigade had arrived in Saudi Arabia. As the only significant ground combat force in theater during the first days of the crisis, the brigade provided security for critical sites, ports, and airbases, including the port of Al-Jubayl which was vital to the arrival of MPS, APS, and unit equipment.

Eighteen M-551 armored assault vehicles (Sheridans) and 15 AH-64s of the 82nd Airborne Division arrived on 14 August. Combined with the arrival of air Force elements and the mechanized air-ground capability of the 7th MEB, the three airborne battalions and Army aviation task force that comprised the ready brigade gave CENTCOM a mechanized force with supporting air early in the operation.

By 17 August, the first of four Army APS arrived in Saudi Arabia with enough supplies, equipment, and fuel to support the 82nd Airborne Division and other deployed or deploying forces. (As requirements increased, they surpassed the capability provided by MAC and volunteer civil aircraft. As a result, Stage 1 of the CRAF was activated on 17 August.) The first element of the 101st Airborne Division (Air Assault) arrived in Saudi Arabia two days later. The capabilities of the Army Component, Central Command (ARCENT) forces in theater during this early stage were further increased during the next several days with the arrival of the lead elements of the Army's 24th Infantry Division (Mechanized) with its M1 tanks, M2/M3 infantry fighting

Unit Deployment Flow

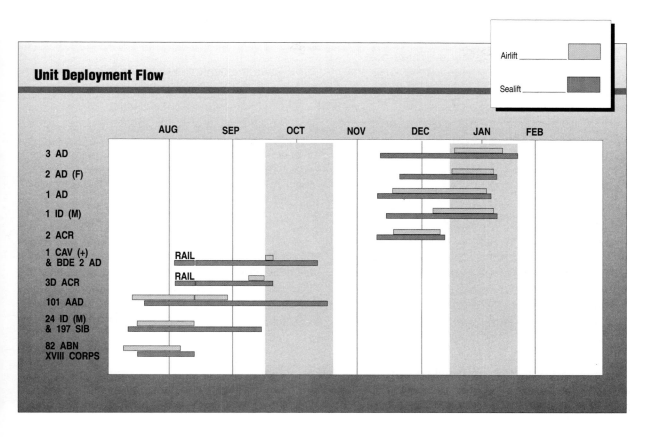

vehicles, and self-propelled howitzers on 27 August.

The first elements of a Patriot missile battery of the 11th Air Defense Artillery Brigade also deployed in August. Eventually, twenty-nine Patriot batteries were deployed in support of Operation Desert Shield and Desert Storm: 21 in Saudi Arabia, six in Israel (four-US/two- Israeli Defense Forces), and two in Turkey.

The 3rd ACR movement began on 22 August with equipment unloading finished in Saudi Arabia by 17 October. The 1st Cavalry Division began loading 6 September and was in defensive positions during the first week of November.

The 12th Combat Aviation Brigade, assigned to V Corps in Germany, was the first major combat unit to deploy from Europe to the Middle East. The brigade began arriving by 27 September and was in its assembly area by early October. Army divisions had their own logistics organizations, capable of supporting operations for limited periods.

During the Phase I deployments, the Army deployed an airborne division, an air assault division, a mechanized infantry division, an armored division, and an ACR along with logistical and administrative units to support not only Army forces, but those of US forces and other nations as well. This effort ultimately involved the deployment of more than 115,000 soldiers by the end of October and more than 700 tanks, 1,000 armored personnel carriers, 145 AH-64 Apache helicopters, 294 155mm self-propelled howitzers, and hundreds of other major items of equipment and thousands of ancillary pieces.

Marine Component, Central Command (MARCENT) Deployments

On 7 August, 7th MEB received its deployment order; simultaneously, ships from MPS-2 were ordered to sail. The first three ships deployed from their homeport of Diego Garcia and arrived in Saudi Arabia on 15 August, marking the first use of the MPS in a crisis. The airlift arrival of the 7th MEB began on 14 August. CONUS-based fixed wing attack aircraft from 7th MEB, from CONUS, began arriving on 20 August. This Marine Air-Ground Task Force (MAGTF), consisted of a mechanized ground combat element with more than 50 M60A1 tanks, self-propelled artillery, and a supporting aircraft group with attack helicopters and fixed-wing aircraft. Within four days of their arrival in the port of Al-Jubayl, Navy cargo handlers and Marines unloaded the three 755-foot MPS ships containing the MEBs equipment and 30 days of combat supplies. The 17,000 Marines of the 7th MEB linked with their MPS equipment and supplies and were ready for combat on 26 August. This provided the first mechanized ground combat capability for CINCCENT.

On 25 August, the 1st MEB initial units deployed by strategic airlift to Al-Jubayl to link with MPS-3. By 11 September, the final elements arrived and were integrated into the I MEF major subordinate commands.

The I MEF command element which arrived in Saudi Arabia on 4 September, assumed command of all Marine forces ashore. These included ground, air, and logistics elements organized into the 1st Marine Division (MARDIV), 3rd Marine Aircraft Wing, and 1st Force Service Support Group (FSSG), respectively. Continued deployments of reinforcements brought these units to full strength by early October. (The 7th and 1st MEBs, having carried out their deployment mission, were dis-established and their assets were distributed among other I MEF units.) Reinforcements continued to arrive during the next three months to bring the I MEF command to full strength.

USMC aviation deployed to the theater in three increments: fly-in echelon; elements brought in on MPS; and, aviation logistic support ships (TAVB). The aircraft, initial spares and supplies, and support personnel constituted the fly-in echelon. Ordnance, support equipment, aviation fuel, and other items arrived aboard MPS. Aviation logistics support ships provide the maintenance and repair capabilities essential to sustaining aircraft readiness. Competing requirements for aerial refueling tankers caused several days' delay in deploying USMC aircraft. This delay concerned the 7th MEB commander, who relied on these aircraft for much of his combat power. Despite these difficulties, the actual arrival date corresponded fairly closely to arrival of the first MPS squadron and associated USMC ground units.

By the end of August, the USMC had deployed 48 FA-18A/Cs, 40 AV-8Bs, 10 A-6Es, 12 EA-6Bs, and six KC-130s, as well as 90 helicopters, which included 40 AH-1Ws. These numbers increased during the next several weeks as additional attack aircraft, OV-10s and helicopters arrived in theater, to include 20 AV-8Bs embarked aboard amphibious ships.

Air Force Component, Central Command (CENTAF) Deployments

Before Iraq's invasion of Kuwait, the USAF had a small operations support detachment in Dhahran that provided ground handling service for regularly scheduled airlift missions. At the time of the invasion, KC-135 air refueling tankers were operating in the United Arab Emirates as part of exercise Ivory Justice. Also, USAF pilots and support personnel were stationed as instructors at key Royal Saudi Air Force F-15C and F-5 fighter bases throughout Saudi Arabia, as part of the US Military Training Mission — Saudi Arabia.

Additional USAF assets were sent immediately after the invasion. MAC began moving airlift control elements (ALCEs) to key air facilities around the world in anticipation of deployment requirements. The MAC crisis action team had prepared plans and began the notification process to use enroute staging bases in Europe to support a possible large-scale deployment to Saudi Arabia.

The first USAF combat aircraft from the 1st Tactical Fighter Wing (TFW), supported by five AWACS from Tinker AFB, OK, arrived in Riyadh on 8 August. Twenty-four F-15Cs from the 71st Tactical Fighter Squadron, Langley AFB, VA, arrived in Dhahran 34 hours after receiving the deployment order, and were on combat air patrol alert four hours later. Enroute to Dhahran, the F-15Cs were refueled by KC-10 tankers from Zaragoza Air Base, Spain, Royal Air Force Base (RAF) Mildenhall, UK, and Sigonella, Italy. The first RC-135 Rivet Joint aircraft began providing support on 9 August. By 19 August, four RC-135s were operating from Saudi Arabia.

On 8 August, strategic airlift began its movements in earnest. The first aircraft supporting the 1st TFW from Langley began to arrive in Saudi Arabia on 8 August. On 9 August, a MAC mission carrying the first CENTCOM command elements landed in the Saudi capital. In the early days of deployment, on average, one airlifter left from both Langley and Pope AFB every hour.

By 10 August, 45 air superiority F-15Cs, 19 deep strike interdiction F-15Es and 24 multi-role F-16s were in the AOR, fully armed and either on airborne patrols or on ready alert. A day later, the first squadron of C-130 transports arrived in Saudi Arabia. The same day, MAC deployed a theater ALCE to Riyadh; it was fully operational on 11 August. Twenty additional F-16s and seven B-52s arrived on 12 August. The same day, USAF C-130s arrived at Thumrait and Masirah, Oman, where they began

Marine Corps Deployment of Forces

Unit	Combat Ready	Deployment Option
7th MEB	25 Aug	MPS
13th MEU(SOC)	7 Sep	Amphibious (FWD deployed to WESTPAC)
1st MEB	10 Sep	MPS
1MEF* (1st MARDIV, 3d MAW, 1st FSSG)	3 Sep	MPS, Airlift, Sealift
4th MEB	16 Sep	Amphibious
2d Marine Division	8 Jan	MPS, Airlift, Sealift
5th MEB	14 Jan	Amphibious
II MEF (Air, CSS Elements)	15 Jan	Airlift, Sealift

*NOTE: I MEF assumed command of all marine forces ashore, compositing the ground, air, and service support elements of 7th MEB and 1st MEB (along with follow-on forces) into 1st marine division, 3d marine aircraft wing, and 1st force service support group, respectively.

immediate distribution of equipment, armament and supplies.

By 14 August, more than 200 USAF combat aircraft had deployed to the theater. By 24 August, the USAF force structure in SWA included three squadrons of air-to-air superiority fighters, eight squadrons of air-to-ground fighters, and U-2/TR-1 aircraft to provide imagery intelligence (IMINT) coverage of Iraq and Kuwait.

Deployment continued through September and October. By 8 November, the Coalition air forces had increased significantly. The USAF had more than 1,030 aircraft. These forces included the deployment of more than 590 combat aircraft from CONUS and European

Command (EUCOM) since 14 August. More than 90 US fighter aircraft were dedicated to air superiority missions; more than 260 were dedicated to air-to-ground operations; and, more than 240 dual role aircraft to air-to-air and air-to-ground missions.

Navy Component, Central Command (NAVCENT) Deployments

Additional forces soon were deployed to reinforce the Naval presence in the theater of operations. Ultimately, the total naval forces deployed consisted of six CVBGs, two battleships, the command ship *USS Blue Ridge,* (LCC 19), several support ships, four mine warfare ships, maritime patrol aircraft, several submarines, an amphibious task force that numbered 31 ships, and Naval Special Warfare (NSW) Units.

Two carrier battle groups with more than

100 fighter and attack aircraft and more than 10 surface combatant ships were directed to sail to the Gulf region on 2 August. The carrier *USS Independence* (CV 62) battle group sailed from near Diego Garcia to the North Arabian Sea, while the *USS Dwight D. Eisenhower* (CVN 69) battle group moved to the eastern Mediterranean in preparation for entering the Red Sea. MPS 2 and 3, based in Diego Garcia and Guam, were ordered to sail on 7 August.

Amphibious deployments were supported by both Atlantic and Pacific Fleet forces. The Amphibious Ready Group (ARG) in the Mediterranean Sea, the closest amphibious force, was not diverted to Operation Desert Shield because of its involvement in the Liberian evacuation and the need to maintain some expeditionary capability in the Mediterranean. In the Atlantic, the 4th

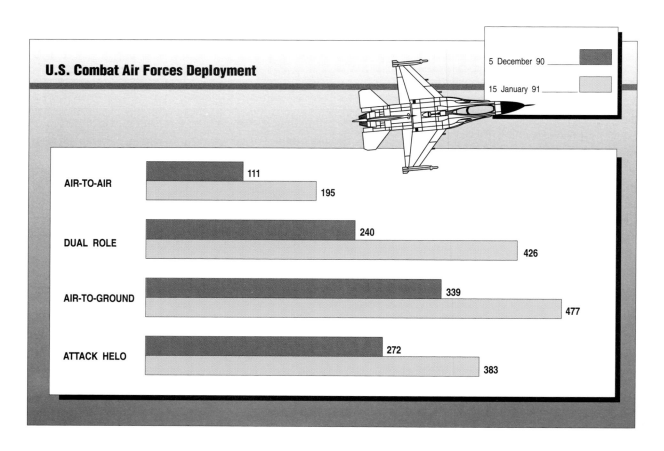

U.S. Combat Air Forces Deployment

5 December 90

15 January 91

	5 December 90	15 January 91
AIR-TO-AIR	111	195
DUAL ROLE	240	426
AIR-TO-GROUND	339	477
ATTACK HELO	272	383

MEB had been scheduled to participate in North Atlantic Treaty Organization (NATO) exercises in September. When the order was received, 4th MEB deployed on 13 amphibious ships and one RO/RO ship with 8,340 Marines. Arriving in the North Arabian Sea between 11 and 16 September, the 4th MEB began a series of amphibious exercises in Oman and the Gulf.

Pacific Fleet amphibious forces sailed from several locations. The 13th Marine Expeditionary Unit (Special Operations Capable) (MEU (SOC)), consisting of five amphibious ships and 2300 Marines, arrived from the Philippines on 7 September and was integrated into the 4th MEB, which arrived in the Gulf of Oman on 11 September. This force was supplemented by a Battalion Landing Team (BLT) that had been deployed with III MEF in Okinawa, and amphibious ships home-ported in the western Pacific. The combined force contained eight ships and 4,600 Marines. The landing team disembarked at Al-Jubayl and reinforced the 1st MARDIV in mid-September. Three ships of the Pacific ARG remained in the Gulf for several weeks to provide additional amphibious capability before returning to the Pacific fleet.

Other Force Deployments

While US forces were deploying, several Arab League member nations announced they would send forces to Saudi Arabia also. Egyptian and Syrian special operations forces were among the first Arab forces to deploy. They arrived in August to augment Saudi Arabia and Gulf Cooperation Council forces. Other forces followed throughout the fall.

By 1 September, the Coalition had deployed a small, but militarily well-balanced and highly capable force. The rapid projection of combat power to an area 8,000 miles from the United States demonstrated tremendous capability to project power and served to deter further Iraqi aggression.

Phase II

At the end of October, the NCA decided it would be prudent to increase the forces available in theater to provide an offensive option to eject Iraqi forces from Kuwait with minimal casualties. Phase II deployment began with the President's announcement on 8 November that the US presence in the theater would be reinforced by approximately 200,000 additional personnel.

Decisions were made to move forward-deployed elements of the Army VII Corp from Europe as well as additional forces from CONUS. Additional RC personnel were mobilized and deployed to assist the deployment of forces from Europe and the United States.

Forces moved during this phase included the 1st Infantry Division (Mechanized), a heavy division from Fort Riley, KS; the European based VII Corps (consisting of the 1st and 3rd Armored divisions, the 2nd ACR, a headquarters, and the VII Corps, associated combat and support elements); three additional CVBGs, one battleship and Amphibious Group 3 with the 5th MEB; substantial air and service support elements of the II MEF including MPS -1 and the 2nd MARDIV. Four hundred and ten additional USAF aircraft were also deployed, (including 24 F-15C, 18 F-117, 24 F-15E, 32 F-111F, 42 F-16, 12 RF-4C, 12 F-4G, eight B-52, 32 C-130, aerial refueling tankers, and other supporting aircraft). By 15 January, the number of US forces in the theater effectively doubled and the strength of the other Coalition forces also increased.

The deployment of the VII Corps was considered essential to the theater campaign's success. Because it was forward based in Europe, it could be moved into the SWA theater of operations and declared combat ready somewhat more rapidly than the forces from the US. Additionally, VII Corps' degree of modernization and preponderance of active

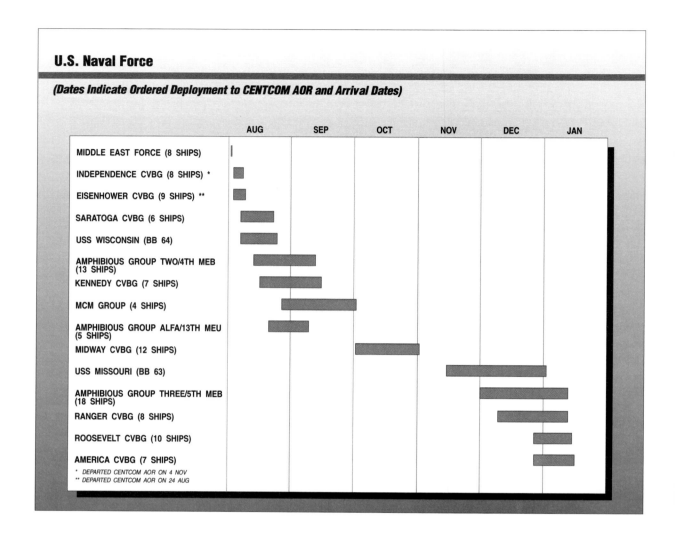

U.S. Naval Force

(Dates Indicate Ordered Deployment to CENTCOM AOR and Arrival Dates)

	AUG	SEP	OCT	NOV	DEC	JAN
MIDDLE EAST FORCE (8 SHIPS)						
INDEPENDENCE CVBG (8 SHIPS) *						
EISENHOWER CVBG (9 SHIPS) **						
SARATOGA CVBG (6 SHIPS)						
USS WISCONSIN (BB 64)						
AMPHIBIOUS GROUP TWO/4TH MEB (13 SHIPS)						
KENNEDY CVBG (7 SHIPS)						
MCM GROUP (4 SHIPS)						
AMPHIBIOUS GROUP ALFA/13TH MEU (5 SHIPS)						
MIDWAY CVBG (12 SHIPS)						
USS MISSOURI (BB 63)						
AMPHIBIOUS GROUP THREE/5TH MEB (18 SHIPS)						
RANGER CVBG (8 SHIPS)						
ROOSEVELT CVBG (10 SHIPS)						
AMERICA CVBG (7 SHIPS)						

* DEPARTED CENTCOM AOR ON 4 NOV
** DEPARTED CENTCOM AOR ON 24 AUG

component units were key factors in the decision to deploy them to SWA. Finally, the military threat was significantly lower in Europe and would safely permit the removal of one Corps. Although significant cross-leveling was required to support VII Corps and prepare it for deployment, the value of forward basing US combat power in geostrategic areas from which they can then be redeployed was demonstrated in this instance. However, as discussed later in this Appendix, there were some difficulties in meeting deployment requirements.

Substantial numbers of Army Reserve and Army National Guard personnel and units

began deployment during Phase II. Although there were some combat units, these units were primarily CS and CSS units intended to augment support units already deployed in theater and to replace VII Corps units deployed from Europe.

Additional USMC forces deployed in December, eventually raising the total of Marines ashore to more than 70,000. II MEF forces deployed by sea, air, and MPS. MPS-1, located in the Atlantic, arrived in theater on 12 December and began unloading equipment and supplies. The 2nd MARDIV arrived by 8 January. In early December, the 5th MEB, onboard Amphibious Group-3 ships, deployed from California. They arrived in theater on 12 January and joined afloat forces already in the Gulf. The amphibious task force now numbered 31 amphibious ships and 17,000 Marines. USMC air and ground forces were in theater by 19 January. This was the largest amphibious force assembled in nearly 40 years.

Simultaneously, and at CENTCOM's request, support from the Departments of State, Transportation, and Justice was being requested. The State Department initiated diplomatic actions to establish Status of Forces Agreements, basing, staging, enroute refueling locations, and overflight rights. It also requested embassies in the AOR to help DOD elements arrange for HNS, especially, water, fuel, transportation, air and sealift facilities service. The Transportation Department was asked to activate additional RRF vessels for transfer to the DOD. The Justice Department, through the Federal Bureau of Investigation, was asked to provide pertinent counterintelligence and security information.

During this phase, US Army, Europe (USAREUR) deployed Patriots to provide air defense capabilities in Turkey and Israel. On 12 January, the Secretary of Defense authorized the deployment of two USAREUR Patriot batteries from Dexheim, Germany, to Turkey to provide air defense for Incirlik Air Base. By 22 January, six of the eight launchers were in place and operational, with 43 missiles on hand. The United States and Israeli political authorities also agreed to deploy Patriot units to counter Scud threats to Israel. Shortly after the war began, Iraq attacked Tel Aviv and Haifa, Israel, with an extended range variant of the Scud B missile. A direct Israeli military response to these attacks might have weakened the commitment of Coalition Arab members to Operation Desert Storm. Task Force Patriot Defender, created from 32nd Air Defense Command (USAREUR), deployed to Israel to provide antitactical ballistic missile defense of priority Israeli assets and to provide training and maintenance support for the two newly formed IDF Patriot batteries. Patriot units from the 32nd Air Defense Command were ordered to deploy on 18 January, and within 29 hours from verbal notification to deploy, the task force was operational and ready to conduct fire missions. A second deployment of two more batteries to Israel began on 23 January and was completed and operational by 26 January.

SUMMARY

Iraq's failure to move into Saudi Arabia allowed sufficient time to deploy substantial countervailing forces. The success of the deployment was dependent on the availability of aircraft, ships, and crews; timely decisions to augment active force lift assets with the Selected Reserve, CRAF, RRF; ability to load effectively; forward staging bases for international flights; forward deployed forces; superb Saudi ports facilities; cooperation of European allies; and TRANSCOM's effectiveness. The focus for the future must be on further strengthening both military and civil transportation capability, completing HNS agreements with allies in areas of potential crisis, and integrating those logistical requirements that may have to be met by organic resources. To project military power, sustain it, and decisively win future conflicts, the United States must be able to execute deployment plans in a timely manner, gain access to local ports and airfields, and possess adequate airlift and sealift to accomplish the mission.

Time is one factor over which DOD may not have much control in future crises. Although US forces arrived quickly, there was a lengthy period of vulnerability during which Coalition forces could not have repulsed an Iraqi invasion into Saudi Arabia. DOD can improve its ability to respond to crises by taking several actions in advance. First, sea and land based prepositioning and forward deployed forces can provide ready forces and initial sustainment early, easing lift requirements. Comprehensive

HNS agreements with those nations where there are vital US interests will be essential for deployment, sustainment, and employment of most foreign US military operations.

A comprehensive Joint Chiefs of Staff exercise program, which includes movement of Army heavy divisions, is essential. As the US moves toward a strategy that bases a larger proportion of forces in CONUS, the ability to respond to regional contingencies must be convincing and expeditious. In that regard, strategic lift capabilities, particularly sealift, must be able to meet surge requirements to deploy forces and associated sustainment into a theater. While sealift resources are available, the number of specific types of vessels to accommodate requirements, the readiness posture of these vessels, and the amount of time it takes to activate and make operational these assets should be reviewed.

Unit operational and logistics readiness of CONUS-based forces and strategic lift also will play a crucial role in sharpening the US ability to respond quickly. The Mobility Requirements Study (MRS) and further analysis of deployments in Operations Desert Shield and Desert Storm will help assess those needs.

OBSERVATIONS

Accomplishments

- Policy and contingency planning aided deployment

- Airlift, sealift, and landlift moved enormous quantities of personnel and equipment.

- Airlift transported about 5 percent of all cargo and 99 percent of all passengers in support of Operations Desert Shield and Desert Storm. CRAF, volunteer civil carriers, and donated foreign lift delivered 27 percent of the air cargo and 64 percent of the air passengers. Organic MAC aircraft delivered the rest.

- Reservists who augmented MAC, MSC, and MTMC early were crucial to expeditious deployment.

- Sealift delivered 95 percent of all cargo.

- Prepositioned ships and MPS worked well and added flexibility to strategic lift.

- Staging bases in Europe were crucial to efficient strategic airlift. Forward basing in Europe of combat and service support elements also increased the speed of deployment. These units should be routinely trained in deployments.

- Investments in sealift (the RRF, APF, MPF, FSS, hospital ships, and aviation support ships) have proven their value.

Shortcomings

- If the Coalition had lacked the extended period of time to deploy, the tactical situation might have been precarious. DOD needs the ability to bring forces to bear more quickly, effectively, and decisively, with minimum risk to human life.

- Maintenance and repair, logistics and spare parts, and test activations of RRF vessels have been underfunded.

- CRAF is intended to augment organic aircraft, but is less capable of handling effectively more demanding loads of equipment that must be deployed. CRAF does not have the degree of flexibility expected from military aircraft, especially in terms of handling military cargo and equipment. This limitation, although long recognized, requires careful oversight for scheduling CRAF missions involving unit equipment and cargo.

(Continued)

OBSERVATIONS (Continued)

- Most RRF ships were not activated on schedule. Ships with breakout schedules of five and 10 days took, on the average, 11 and 16 days to break out. RRF crew availability (quantity and quality) affects activation and timeliness.

- Some delays were created because there were insufficient RO/RO assets in the RRF and because of the longer times required to load and unload break-bulk ships compared with RO/ROs and container vessels. The mix of RRF ship types may require adjustment.

Issues

- Efficient strategic airlift for long distance deployment depends on enroute staging bases. More than 80 percent of all airlift missions flowed through two bases scheduled to close: Torrejon and Rhein-Main. If enroute staging bases are not available, reliance on air refueling increases and overall payloads decrease. Forward based forces can both provide staging bases for aircraft that originate in the US and shorten the distances to hasten deployments.

- To address the problems encountered in activating the RRF, the Deputy Secretary of Transportation and Deputy Assistant Secretary of Defense (Logistics), agreed to form a joint DOD and Transportation Department Ready Reserve Force Working Group (RRFWG) to study and make recommendations regarding RRF management based on lessons learned from Operations Desert Shield and Desert Storm. The RRFWG submitted its report, "The Ready Reserve Force, Enhancing a National Asset," on October 23, 1991. The report addresses the ability of the RRF to augment DOD organic sealift assets and the nation's commercial merchant marine fleet in time of national emergency. It also documents DOD and Transportation Department agreements on an integrated plan for the RRF based upon experience during the recent activation of RRF ships. The RRFWG will continue to meet and monitor the implementation of its recommendations.

- There were early problems in airlift systems management. Coupled with the absence of a TPFDD and the uncertain situation confronting CINCCENT, the airlift system did not operate initially at full capacity.

- There are reports that more lift than programmed was required to transport deploying forces. What appears to have happened is that units which had previously deployed only for exercises took much more equipment and supplies when they deployed for actual combat missions.

- There was difficulty in using the developmental JOPES system. An automated airlift scheduling capability, linked between JOPES and an airlift scheduling function is required. OPLANs must also be updated to identify changes or additional requirements for existing systems.

- While the overall utility of the MPS was proved out, the lack of an early decision to sail MPS — which is designed to be unilaterally deployed in international waters in ambiguous situations — reduced the options available to CINCCENT in the early days of the crisis.

- TRANSCOM was not the fully operational common-user manager needed. TRANSCOM's peacetime activities should be organized the same as its wartime activities. Action is under way to identify CINCTRANS as the single manager for common-user transportation and assign all transportation component commands and all common-user transportation forces to CINCTRANS.

- Some prepositioned assets, nominally deployed for other contingencies, were in areas not convenient to the KTO. Nevertheless, they were closer to the KTO than if they had been stored in CONUS. Requirements for prepositioning and for continued US cooperative presence in the Persian Gulf region will remain crucial to US ability to exercise a stabilizing influence there.

Appendix F
Logistics Buildup And Sustainment

The logistician's trade is an essential element of the art of war. From 2 August until hostilities ended 28 February, a common thread that linked Coalition forces' success was the logistics effort to transport, sustain, and maintain a force in the often hostile Arabian peninsula environment as well as a large number of forces, from all Services, outside the theater. A force is only as combat capable as the effectiveness of the logistics support it receives. Logistics is the science of planning and carrying out the movement and maintenance of forces. In its most comprehensive sense, logistics encompasses those aspects of military operations that deal with: design and development, acquisition, storage, movement, distribution, maintenance, removal, and disposition of materiel; movement, evacuation, and hospitalization of personnel; acquisition or construction, maintenance, operation, and disposition of facilities; and acquisition or provision of services.

Although each nation was responsible for its own logistics, in addition to the support Coalition members provided to US forces there were occasions when the United States had to give assistance to other Coalition partners. Also, when deployed for major operations, the Services become more interdependent. Strategic land, sea and airlift are examples of this. Often, commanders-in-chief (CINCs), in their operations plans (OPLAN), designate a Service to provide a common logistics function for the entire theater beginning, for example, 60 days after deployment. For Operation Desert Shield, in some cases, common item support responsibilities exceeded the providing Service's capabilities. After the first 60 days, for

> *"The overall logistics effort to mobilize and support Desert Shield/Storm was herculean, especially in the weeks prior to initiating hostilities. The superb performance of the logistics community deserves high praise."*
>
> **General H. Norman Schwarzkopf**
> **Commander-in-Chief, Central Command**

example, the other Services and host nation support (HNS) helped the Army provide supply class I (subsistence), and class III (petroleum, oil and lubricants (POL)). In fact, Saudi HNS provided a large share of subsistence, averaging 250,000 meals a day and an estimated two million gallons of potable water a day.

Because of the size of the Coalition response to the Saudi request for assistance, theater support could not simply be integrated into the existing infrastructure. Distribution systems were developed, storage depots and repair facilities built, and supply communications established. Logisticians ensured that complex support systems worked efficiently in a remote theater's very demanding environmental conditions, where the well-developed coastal infrastructure becomes a rudimentary road system inland. Operations Desert Shield and Desert Storm logisticians succeeded despite the lack of complete information resulting from rapidly changing and often uncertain situations. Finally, very complex force structures magnified logistics challenges.

Though not without its problems, the logistics efforts of the United States and its allies were among the more successful in history. Moving a combat force halfway around the world, linking supply lines that spanned the entire globe, and maintaining unprecedented readiness rates, are a tribute to the people who make the logistics system work. Logisticians from all Services supported more than half a million US Service members with supplies, services, facilities, equipment, maintenance, and transportation. A survey of logisticians' accomplishments shows, among other things, that they:

- Maintained many major weapons systems at or above normal peacetime standards
- Moved more than 1.3 billion ton-miles of cargo from ports to combat units
- Shipped and received more than 112,500 tracked and wheeled vehicles
- Armed weapons systems with more than $2.5 billion worth of munitions
- Constructed more than $615 million worth of support facilities, and,
- At the peak of operations, issued up to 19 million gallons of fuel a day.

These feats were made possible by and are a tribute to the foresight of military logistics planners and investments made in modernization, reliability, and maintainability over the past two decades. Conceptually, the logistician draws the line beyond which the tactician cannot go.

LOGISTICS PLANNING, PREPARATION, AND STRUCTURE

The Army deployed a much larger proportion of combat service support (CSS) than combat units. Army truck transportation is a case in point. Despite the deployment of 72 percent of its truck companies in support of 25 percent of its combat divisions, the Army still relied on HNS trucks to meet requirements. Also, the Navy deployed most of its Combat Logistics Force (CLF) ships to the Central Command (CENTCOM) area of operations (AOR). Within the Army, many support units which eased the logistics mission came from the Reserve Component (RC). Although this was anticipated

in force structure planning, the availability and mix of Active Component and RC must be monitored as the Total Force draws down.

Another fundamental influence on the ability to sustain the forces in the theater was the lack of a theater-wide contingency plan before August for supporting the forces that became part of the effort. The discussions in Chapter V and Appendix D highlight the fact there was no approved plan for dealing with the crisis when it occurred. The concept plan had been war gamed extensively during Exercise Internal Look 90, and senior commanders and planners were aware of factors to be considered. However, because logistics support plans are based upon OPLANS and the tactical commander's concept of operations, there was no existing logistical support plan for the scope of support required. The seemingly ad hoc creation of the required support organization and structure was carried out quickly and effectively and was based on Service doctrine and experience. Preparation by the Services, their organization, and structures for dealing with the logistics effort should be explained so the context of the effort is better understood. A brief description of some Service-unique arrangements follows.

Army

Army divisions and regiments have Combat Service Support (CSS) units organic to their structures. These units are fixed organizations and generally are the same for comparable types of divisions and regiments. They provide immediate support to the combat elements of those organizations. However, their capabilities for sustaining combat forces are limited, and they depend on organizations at higher echelons to provide a more complete and longer lasting sustainment base.

Absolutely crucial to the successful sustainment of deployed forces is the correct determination and timely introduction of the logistics force structure into the theater. Above the division level, that is at Corps and Theater Army, the composition of logistics units is tailored to the specific force being supported. Size and type of units deployed dictate CSS unit requirements. In addition, the level of enemy activity, expected duration of deployment, geographic location, and theater infrastructure all influence decisions on the scope of support requirement and the type and quantity of CSS units to deploy. Typically, support detachments, companies, battalions, and groups are formed and distributed to support brigades and support groups, which are further organized into support commands (SUPCOMs). The Theater Army Area Command analyzes the commander's logistics requirements, then prepares the plans to satisfy them. These plans are executed by SUPCOM subordinate elements. The theater support command headquarters determines, in large measure, whether support will be provided quickly.

When Operation Desert Shield began, there was a brief period when an adequate command and control (C^2) structure for Army logistics units was not available in the theater. Deployment of these headquarters units was delayed while combat units with higher priority missions were moved into the theater. Earlier in Chapter III, the discussion of deployment priorities explained that Commander-in-Chief, Central Command (CINCCENT) determined his primary need was combat forces. This assessment resulted in lowering the priority for support unit deployment and thus detracted from the support available to early-deployed combat units.

Since the deployment's length was unknown, and the authority to activate RC forces initially was limited, Army Component, Central Command (ARCENT) elected to establish an ad hoc logistics headquarters to oversee this part of the force. This provisional support command became a satisfactory solution during the first phases of the deployment. When the size of the force increased in November, ARCENT did not request mobilization of a theater-level logistics

C^2 element because this would have disrupted an already functioning system.

This ad hoc logistics command element quickly discovered early in the deployment it alone could not effectively handle the massive deployment of combat troops. The soldiers who began arriving in Saudi Arabia on 9 August needed food, shelter, equipment, supplies, sanitation facilities, and transportation. Anticipating this problem, Forces Command sent a general officer to the theater to serve as ARCENT deputy commander for logistics. He and a small handpicked staff were the nucleus of logistics support in the theater. They had experience in deployment and sustainment of large forces as a result of their involvement in annual Return of Forces to Germany exercises and that experience served as the model for creating the Operation Desert Shield logistics support plan.

This small staff was charged with coordinating logistics for the Army. The initial concept had three major tasks:

- Reception of arriving forces;
- Onward movement of those forces; and,
- Sustainment of all soldiers, equipment, and supplies arriving in theater.

These tasks occurred almost simultaneously, and required complex arrangements to ensure coordination throughout the logistics effort.

The decision to deploy combat forces versus CSS units first, while tactically prudent, was a principal reason for the initial burden on the logistics system. The placement of CSS units later in the deployment flow meant deployed units' support was delayed. Initial delays led to support backlogs that grew geometrically and required time and intense management to correct.

Another problem force planners and logisticians faced early was identification of specific units required to support deploying combat forces. Most of these units were not large, but were crucial to sustainment. They included water purification, storage, and distribution detachments; petroleum operating units; supply and service companies; and truck companies. Many of these units are in the RC; rapid mobilization of RC units that could provide vital services became an imperative. Until these units were deployed, Saudi HNS was the logistics mainstay. The ARCENT logistics cell in Riyadh established special contracting teams to expedite service support agreements for housing, storage facilities, water, food, transport, and more. Another expedient theater logisticians used was to use the logistics elements organic to deploying units to assist with support efforts. Commanders of units arriving in theater frequently provided manpower, drivers and vehicles for the common good of all forces.

The support for the first deployed units was augmented by prepositioned stocks from Army and Air Force (USAF) Afloat Prepositioning Ships (APS) and Marine Corps Maritime Prepositioning Squadron (MPS) vessels, air deployable packages of war reserve materiel (WRM), and agreements with local suppliers for essential items. In early September, Saudi Arabia agreed to provide all food, fuel, water, facilities, and local transportation at no cost for all US forces in Saudi Arabia and surrounding waters. As a result, CINCCENT asked the Department of Defense (DOD) to send a team to negotiate HNS agreements with the Saudis. Because of the lack of any formal HNS agreement with Saudi Arabia, a DOD team of experts, led by a general officer, went to Saudi Arabia on 17 October to work out detailed arrangements. The DOD team eventually concluded an agreement with the Saudis by mid November called "Implementation Plan for Logistics Support of the United States Forces in Defense of the Kingdom of Saudi Arabia."

The plan was retroactive to the beginning of the deployment, and the Saudis subsequently provided $760 million in cash to the US Defense Cooperation Account as reimbursement for US expenses incurred from August to October for items covered by the implementation plan. This effort bore fruit and the Saudis provided a large amount of logistics support. The initial process was difficult as a result of the administrative difficulty of coordinating such a massive transfer of in-kind assistance. Equally important was the HNS for US forces deployed in other nations of the region, which also included free fuel, water, food, and housing provided by the respective host. To facilitate CINCCENT's ability to support his force and to develop a theater infrastructure, advance agreements to enable more expeditious support should be concluded whenever possible.

By 17 August, four Army APS had arrived in theater and provided rations, cots, tents, blankets, and medical supplies, as well as refrigerated trailers, reverse osmosis water purification units (ROWPU), forklifts, packaged fuel, construction and barrier material, ammunition and medical supplies. One semi-submersible Heavy Lift Preposition Ship (HLPS) carried port operating equipment such as tugboats, floating cranes, landing craft, rough terrain forklifts, and repair parts. This satisfied the immediate needs of the new arrivals and eased the most immediate crises in supplying and sustaining them.

Two days after the APS arrived, the ad hoc logistics staff became the ARCENT SUPCOM (Provisional). As requirements grew, so too did the SUPCOM staff. Eventually, the staff consisted of more than 750 personnel, of which more than 60 percent were RC soldiers; the mature logistical structure responsible for planning and providing CSS in Saudi Arabia consisted of a theater support command and the two Corps Support Commands (COSCOM).

In addition to meeting its own requirements, CINCCENT appointed ARCENT as executive agent for support of certain common items for all US forces in the theater. Common-item support, provided directly (or arranged through contracting or HNS), consisted of inland surface transportation, port operations, food, backup water support, bulk fuel distribution, common munitions, medical, veterinary services, and graves registration. For various reasons, including lack of items and lack of CSS units, the Army could not meet its common-item support obligations for some items by the specified time. As a result, the other Services relied on organic supply systems much longer than planned. (A diagram of the Army theater organization is in the discussion of C², in Appendix K.)

The effectiveness of logistics automation during Operations Desert Shield and Desert Storm was substantially degraded by the lack of tactical communications support below corps level. Because of this, CSS units became dependent on commercial telecommunication to augment C² tactical communications. In Southwest Asia (SWA), the host nation telecommunications infrastructure in the remote regions of the country was limited to nonexistent.

Army supply transactions were consolidated each day and carried to the next higher level support activity for processing. Supply requests often had to be couriered more than 100 kilometers by tactical vehicle or helicopter. The terrain and long distances between units resulted in delays of eight to 15 days to pass requisitions from company level to the US wholesale system. During the peak of supply activity, requisitions reached as many as 10,700 per day. The effect on the supply system included the loss of manpower to courier transactions, longer order-ship times, and a larger number of parts in the supply pipeline. Processing delays resulted in a loss of confidence in the supply system; the abuse of priority requisitions, with 64.9 percent of all requisitions submitted as high priority; and, in the submission of multiple requisitions and status requests, thus worsening run time, backlog and system saturation problems. Both

the Corporate Information Management and Total Asset Visibility initiatives will help to correct these practices and restore confidence in the system.

Air Force

The concept of operations for deployed USAF combat units centers on the unit's ability to deploy with its own organic supply, spares and maintenance personnel to be self sustaining for 30 days, if combined with munitions, fuels and rations. A key aspect of this concept is the War Readiness Spares Kit (WRSK) maintained by deployable aircraft units, and prepackaged for rapid movement. These kits are stocked with spare parts, common use items and hardware according to predicted and known failure rates and contain necessary parts and supplies to repair the unit's aircraft. Within an established theater of operations, USAF units link to an established supply system, usually at the component command level (such as Air Force Component, Central Command (CENTAF) in SWA). The concept then provides for 30 days to get the lines of communication (LOC) in place to support the longer term requisition system for crucial replacement parts and supplies.

To orchestrate the deployment, beddown, and sustainment of CENTAF units as they arrived in the AOR a CENTAF logistics staff was created and a CENTAF Logistics Readiness Center established. More than 100 personnel coordinated the movement into and within the theater of necessary items such as prepositioned stocks and those supplies required to sustain follow on forces.

Initial USAF logistics support in SWA hinged on effective investments made during the past several years in support systems for bases with little or no improved facilities, called bare bases, investments in WRSK, and prepositioned munitions. The WRM for use in a contingency to convert a bare base into a functional airfield was procured and maintained through a series of

Harvest Programs. For example, in addition to the Harvest Eagle housekeeping sets, each capable of supporting more than 1,100 people, and a 4,400-person Harvest Bare package capable of supporting 72 aircraft, a WRM package known as Harvest Falcon was being procured and maintained at the time of the SWA contingency. Harvest Falcon is a bare base contingency package to support 55,000 people and 750 aircraft at 14 separate locations. It includes hardwall shelters, temper tents, vehicles, materiel handling equipment, power generation and distribution equipment, kitchens, water purification and production equipment, and airfield support equipment. At the start of Operation Desert Shield, this package was about 82 percent complete. Even though much equipment had to be maintained in the continental United States (CONUS), having approximately 35 percent of it available in the region made beddown at 21 principal airfields more rapid and much easier than otherwise might have been possible. The equipment and prepositioned munitions worked well despite years in storage.

Units deployed from various commands to Operations Desert Shield and Desert Storm. As mentioned earlier, USAF contingency plans for providing supply support to deployed squadrons called for the units to deploy with their combat supply system to maintain accountability and inventory control of resupply to the WRSK, with kit replenishment provided by a computer support base mainframe computer. The WRSK replenishment was dependent on getting the combat supply system transaction files back to the unit's computer support base. Original plans called for the deployment of a mainframe computer with tactical shelter systems (TSS). The TSSs, however, were not deployed. Because computer-to-computer links were not available, combat supply system transactions were updated at the unit computer support base by mailing, hand carrying floppy diskettes, or modem transmission by phone. This was cumbersome and less than satisfactory. Also, as

the US presence in the AOR was extended, a longer term approach to provide sustainment supply support had to be developed. As a result, the CENTAF Supply Support Activity, which regionalized computer support for the 21 individual supply accounts and integrated these efforts under a single CENTAF chief of supply, was created. This system was installed and fully operational on 5 January.

The Activity was established at Langley AFB, VA, with a central data base to which all supply, equipment, and fuels transactions were funneled by satellite. Base supply systems specialists orchestrated the transfer of supply records from home station to Langley. This eased online processing of supply transactions and improved weapon system support. The Activity was manned by 109 personnel from all USAF major commands, who maintained constant liaison with deployed chiefs of supply and remote processing stations. This online standard base supply system capability represented a truly revolutionary way of doing business for deployed units and, while indicative of the lack of adequate organization to provide for unique USAF unit needs, it improved logistics support.

In keeping with operational plans, USAF units deployed with WRSK for initial support of their aviation packages. Each kit was as robust as possible, designed to support the unit for the contingency's first 30 days. For example, when the 317th Tactical Airlift Wing (TAW) arrived in theater, it operated solely out of its WRSK during the initial stages of the deployment. After 60 days of operation, the 317th TAW had maintained a 94 percent mission capable rate, validating the WRSK concept as an essential element of the core wartime materiel requirement.

A contributing factor to this success was funding to support the purchase of aircraft WRSK through FY87, which provided an excellent baseline for most systems in Operations Desert Shield and Desert Storm.

From FY 84 through FY 87, WRSK funding averaged 92 percent of the required fill of parts and supply. This funding baseline was instrumental to the mission capability (more than 92 percent) of the deployed tactical aircraft. However, WRSK funding in FY 88 and 89 was cut to less than 35 percent, which caught new systems (such as the F-15E with no established parts supply line) in a funding gap. This caused a significant amount of cannibalization from non-deploying F-15E units to support F-15E requirements for robust WRSK before to deployment. Cannibalization also was required to support other systems with short lead time parts no longer available from earlier funding. Where there were parts shortcomings, the shortcomings were overcome by the surge of logistics centers, discussed in greater detail under Industrial Base, later in this appendix.

Before the air campaign began, USAF units simultaneously sustained ambitious training while maintaining high alert states. Units deployed to SWA maintained average in-commission rates some 10 percent higher than normal peacetime rates, and were able to effectively surge before the air campaign. The overall mission capable (MC) rate of combat aircraft in the AOR on the day prior to Operation Desert Storm was 94.6 percent.

Another contribution to USAF logistics performance during Operation Desert Shield was in the area of reliability and maintainability (R&M). R&M improvements in the 1980s meant less spare parts money was needed for newer generation aircraft (e.g. F-16s require only one sixth the dollar value in spare parts of the F-111, and less than half that required for the F-15C). This has produced higher peacetime readiness rates and an improved wartime sortie capacity at lower operating costs and manpower levels. Improved components reduced maintenance loads, which increased the maintenance crews' ability to keep weapon systems at a high state of readiness.

Dedicated and innovative personnel performance also played a role in the mission readiness levels sustained during Operations Desert Shield and Desert Storm. Despite the harsh environment, USAF logisticians developed effective work arounds. For instance, in 120-degree plus temperatures, some air-cooled engines, such as those on ground-support equipment for aircraft maintenance, tend to shut down as designed after prolonged, uninterrupted use. Effective work arounds included equipment rotation pools, scheduled cool down periods, and the more frequent changing of air filters to catch the fine sand prevalent in certain parts of the region. On-the-spot modifications enabled the relocation of voltage regulators, power supplies, and other temperature sensitive components away from engine hot spots to cooler locations.

Finally, the contributions to readiness achieved through effective analysis were crucial. The recently modernized logistics management systems allowed immediate distribution of depot products to the requester. The weapons system management information system allowed deployed wing commanders to do hypothetical requirements analysis of their assets while it simultaneously determined repair priorities for the depots.

Navy

CLF ships supported the Navy's battle groups in the Persian Gulf and Red Sea much as the Navy performs peacetime battle group resupply. These CLF ships were, in turn, supplied from forward expeditionary logistics sites. CLF ships, along with various Military Sealift Command (MSC) and Ready Reserve Force (RRF) ships, were responsible for the logistics support of more than 115 combatants. In general, CLF operations successfully supported the fleet both in the Red Sea and the Persian Gulf. Most Navy CLF ships were deployed to the CENTCOM AOR, however, this heavy commitment left a minimal mobile logistics support capability in

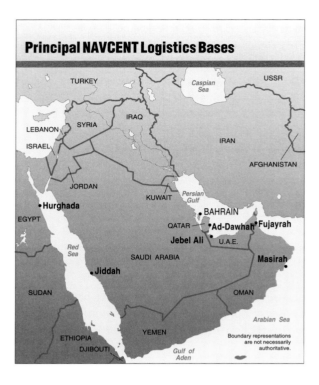

Principal NAVCENT Logistics Bases

other theaters. By the time Operation Desert Storm began, the increased operations tempo (OPTEMPO) had increased resupply requirement substantially.

Forward logistic sites in Jiddah, Al-Fujayrah, Djibouti, Hurghada, Masirah, Ad-Dawhah (Doha) and Bahrain for both airhead and port operations, and an additional surface resupply port established at Jebel Ali to resupply CLF ships in the Persian Gulf and north Arabian Sea, proved crucial to the fleet logistic operations. They were used as transshipment points for commercial shipping that brought material from the United States.

By the end of Operation Desert Storm, the forward logistic support sites in Bahrain, Al-Fujayrah, and Jabal 'Ali supplied more than 100 Coalition ships in the Persian Gulf. The combat logistics stores facility in Jiddah provided the CLF ships assigned to the Red Sea the ability to restock, repair, and rearm without depending on the Suez Canal as the logistics link. Airfields in Saudi Arabia and Bahrain also were used as bases for 25 helicopters and fixed-wing aircraft dedicated to logistics support.

The Navy also was responsible for coordinating port security and harbor defense (PSHD) for the three major ports in the Gulf region. Three PSHD groups, consisting of a Mobile Inshore Undersea Warfare Unit (providing radar and sonar surveillance), a Coast Guard small boat security team, and a Navy explosive ordnance disposal diving team, protected the key ports of Al-Jubayl and Ad-Dammam, Saudi Arabia, and Bahrain.

Marine Corps

Marine Corps (USMC) logistics forces are structured to be expeditionary and integral to a Marine Air-Ground Task Force (MAGTF). Task-organized CSS elements assigned to MAGTFs are tailored for the specific force they support; they deploy with the MAGTF to provide immediate support to air and ground combat units. In the early stages of Operation Desert Shield, this structure proved itself, as the 7th and 1st Marine Expeditionary Brigades (MEB), both linked to MPS ships, deployed to Saudi Arabia and were able to establish logistics support facilities immediately. USMC CSS units assumed control of Al-Jubayl port operations, and established logistics sites near the city. In early September, the two deployed MEB service support groups were combined and reinforced to form the 1st Force Service Support Group (FSSG), a logistics command able to meet I Marine Expeditionary Force (MEF) logistics requirements. The 1st FSSG subsequently expanded to meet all additional USMC needs from USMC and Army common-user stocks. Before the crisis, USMC planners had anticipated these actions .

USMC doctrine states that a MEF deploy with 60 days' sustainment, a MEB with 30 days and a Marine Expeditionary Unit with 15 days. MPS ships carry the unit equipment and 30 days' sustainment for a mechanized MEB of 16,500

Marines and sailors. Once a MEB is committed, additional sustainment is shipped based upon the assigned mission. Equipment and supplies from MPS-2 and MPS-3 contributed to the rapid I MEF buildup. The nine MPS ships provided the equipment and 30 days' sustainment for food, fuel, ammunition, medical supplies, two days of supply (DOS) of potable water, and repair parts for two-thirds of the USMC forces ashore.

While expeditionary in nature, USMC logistics forces are not structured for sustained operations ashore, at great distances from the coast. To conduct such operations, Marines rely on joint doctrine and service agreements for such support as intratheater transportation, common-item support, and establishment of extensive base areas and theater-level logistics structures. Joint doctrine and service agreements call for much of this support to be assumed by the Army and USAF after 60 days. The late deployment of Army logistics forces strained USMC logistics capabilities, and the Marines found themselves not only providing support beyond the 60-day sustainment, but also providing support, particularly rations and water, to Army combat forces from MPS stores. Later, when I MEF moved inland before the ground offensive, the USMC relied on extensive HNS and the other Services for heavy ground transportation.

To ensure aviation maintenance and supply support, Aviation Logistics Support Ships (TAVB), activated from reduced operating status, were loaded at the beginning of the crisis with adequate supplies and facilities to provide intermediate maintenance support for both fixed-wing and helicopter aircraft. TAVB operation is described in greater detail under equipment maintenance strategy.

Each Service had unique logistics capabilities, matched to the unique strength it brought to the conflict. But just as important to the logistics preparation was the infrastructure within which they had to sustain combat operations.

CENTCOM's ability to bring together a complex array of forces was eased by the regional Coalition partners' cooperation. While some aspects of the region's infrastructure were among the more modern in the world, the vastness of the area, the variable topography, the recent decade's industrial boom from oil revenues, and limited

societal need for complex road and rail networks each affected the success of the sustainment operation. Before describing that operation, it is useful to understand the support provided by the region's nations.

REGIONAL NATIONS' SUPPORT

US forces rapidly deployed a large, heavy force with no prior Saudi Arabia/US HNS planning or acquisition procedures in effect. US military organic support capabilities in August and September were austere and inadequate to support the mission. Large, crucial support shortfalls surfaced immediately. Saudi Arabia reacted well to meet US requirements and considerable HNS was provided immediately for support needs at airports, seaports, and initial base camps. By 15 August, US logisticians laid out the initial HNS requirements into these 20 functional areas.

- Accommodations
- Airports
- Construction
- Communications
- Facilities
- Fuel
- Hygiene
- Medical
- Maintenance
- Materiel
- Seaports
- Security
- Services
- Specialized equipment
- Storage
- Subsistence
- Supplies
- Transportation
- Utilities
- Water (includes ice)

As HNS requirements grew, it became readily apparent that a formal Saudi/US HNS organization was needed to request, acquire, and integrate HNS assets into organic US support systems. An assistant chief of staff for host nation activities was established to deal with all Saudi Arabian and allied support for US forces to include contingency contracting policy and civil-military operations.

In November, Saudi Arabia signed the Saudi Arabia HNS Implementation Plan agreeing to support US forces. This plan rolled the original 20 HNS functional area requirements into five areas: fuel, food, water, transportation, and accommodations/facilities. The HNS Implementation Plan did three things. It provided US forces with government controlled/owned assets, contracted to obtain assets to be provided US forces, or reimbursed the United States for contracts the US let to provide for US forces' needs. As of 1 August 1991, Saudi Arabia had provided US forces with HNS amounting to $13.4 billion.

Infrastructure

While the region's major seaports and airports were modern, there still were many limits on the region's ability to support the rapid influx of a large force. Away from the immediate arrival facilities, the support infrastructure was less robust. The major transportation arteries were primarily between the major population centers. The secondary road network also had limited fresh food and developed housing. The national infrastructure's strengths caused by the build up of the oil industry in the 1970s and 1980s also highlight the limitations it presented to such a large fighting force. The industry had developed an infrastructure that principally supported those avenues of access required for that industry's particular operations. This left the vastness of the country relatively less developed, complicating military transportation requirements and delaying resupply that would accommodate the sudden influx of more than half a million people.

US development of the theater infrastructure also was constrained. Because spending was limited to minor construction, it was difficult to

improve the infrastructure to receive and sustain a large force. Most required construction exceeded the $200,000 limit in Section 2805, Title 10, USC, for new construction using US operations and maintenance (O&M) funds. While this limit adequately constrained peacetime spending, it curtailed the Service component's ability to provide timely facilities support, using US funds, to their forces during a contingency. Even when raised to $300,000, as recommended in the President's FY92 budget submission, the limit constrains crucial construction support requirements during contingencies. Emergency construction authority under Section 2808, Title 10, USC, allowing use of unobligated military construction funds, was obtained by Executive Order on 14 November. However, because of this late approval, and the availability of host nation construction support and assistance-in-kind from the Government of Japan, the unobligated funds authorization was used for only two projects. Since future contingencies may not enjoy this extensive host nation and third party support, procedures should be implemented to trigger access to higher O&M limits and early activation of Section 2808, Title 10, USC, to ensure responsiveness of construction funding support to the combatant commander.

Aerial Ports of Debarkation (APODs)

The two initial primary aerial ports of debarkation (APODs), Dhahran and Riyadh, had long, modern runways, associated airport environment structures such as navigation aids, modern facilities, communication capabilities, and more ramp space than most commercial airports. The ability to handle large numbers of aircraft, however, was limited. And, because of the large numbers of rapidly arriving aircraft, there was limited available ramp space for parking aircraft. Despite this, primary APODs were better than most in the region. Eventually, the United States expanded the airlift operation to other airports, principally King Fahd, King

Khalid, and others. Also of importance were the airport facilities provided by Oman at the preposition bases of Thumrait and Masirah. Each offered long, well-established runways.

Sea Ports of Debarkation (SPODs)

The Coalition was fortunate that Saudi Arabia has an excellent port infrastructure, with seven major ports capable of handling large quantities of material daily. Four of the major ports are on the Persian Gulf coast; three are on the Red Sea coast. The two principal theater seaports, Ad-Dammam and Al-Jubayl, had heavy lift equipment, warehouses, outdoor hardstand storage and staging areas, and good road networks around the port facilities. The warehouses generally were full, though, and there was not enough storage capacity at these port facilities to handle the large amount of equipment and supplies that arrived in such a short period. Saudi Arabia cooperated fully in making the port facilities available, and allocated more than 70 percent of the throughput capability in the theater to support Coalition forces. Other in-theater port operations, used to move prepositioned stocks and provide storage, were conducted in Bahrain, Oman, and the United Arab Emirates (UAE).

Storage Facilities

While some large storage facilities existed at the main ports, there was a significant shortage of storage capacity at virtually every location. At the sea port of debarkation SPOD, the Army Engineers and Navy Seabees constructed storage space to protect arriving shipments until they could be moved from the ports. The lack of good road networks inland and the overall shortage of trucks worsened the problem at the ports. The same was generally true at the APOD as well, where Army and USAF engineers also constructed temporary storage space. Warehouses and staging yards also were leased from local owners, using a combination of US funds and HNS.

Surface Transportation Network

The transportation network in theater consists of a mix of six-lane, four-lane and two-lane asphalt roads. Hard surface roads connect Saudi Arabia to Kuwait, Iraq, Jordan, Qatar, the UAE, Bahrain, and Yemen. Secondary roads connect the major cities and towns to minor towns and villages and into the outlying region. Paralleling the Trans-Arabian Pipeline is the Tapline Road, a crucial east-west roadway. The other significant roadway is the 500-km/300-mile-long coastal highway from the Kuwaiti border south to the Qatari border. In terms of rail network, there is only one active rail line in the country, a standard-gauge single track from the port of Ad-Dammam to Riyadh.

Distances from the ports of debarkation to the final combat positions were great. From Dhahran to the theater logistical base at King Khalid Military City (KKMC) is 334 miles along the northern main supply route and 528 miles through Riyadh. The XVIII Airborne Corps forward tactical assembly area was more than 500 miles from Ad-Dammam by the northern route and 696 miles by the southern road. The highways became high-speed avenues for combat units and supplies moving to their destinations. Because large stretches were multi-lane roads, they allowed heavy volumes of traffic to move fast, both as individual vehicles and as convoys. Even those roads that were not multi-lane were paved and generally in good condition. Unfortunately, the established road network, while good where it existed, was limited to major arteries between major cities. US engineers and host nation contractors solved the limited road network problem by constructing or maintaining more than 2,150 miles of roads used to support the deployed forces.

To increase the road network's efficiency, ARCENT established convoy support centers. These truck stops operated 24 hours a day and had fuel, latrines, food, sleeping tents, and limited repair facilities. They added to the comfort, safety, and morale of the forces traveling in the theater. Because of the long distances, these rest areas quickly became favorite landmarks to those who drove the main supply routes (MSR).

Supply Support

Another factor that multiplied the logistics effort effectiveness was the supply support other nations provided. In fact, this support was crucial to the rapid deployment of forces to the theater and allowed the flexibility of deploying substantial amounts of combat power early in the sequence when risks were greatest. Had HNS or assistance in-kind not been provided by the Coalition partners and other responsible allies and friends, some combat units would have been displaced by support units when that did not seem prudent. This sort of support was crucial to US efforts throughout the operation. Food supplements, fuel, and services provided by the Gulf Cooperation Council states were invaluable.

Early in the deployment, the newly established ARCENT SUPCOM began to formalize requests for Saudi Government assistance. As early as 18 August, the logistics operations center developed a list of the command's basic HNS needs for 45 days. Discussed in greater detail in the assistance-in-kind section in this report, the Saudis agreed to provide tents, food, transportation, real estate, and civilian labor support.

However, HNS within the context of Operations Desert Shield and Desert Storm was much broader than the substantial Saudi Arabian support. The preposition storage facilities at Thumrait, Masirah, and Seeb, Oman, were significant to the CENTAF operation. Oman also provided construction materials, food preparation facilities, local worker labor support, and helped correct the transportation problems the initial units encountered. The

UAE, another aircraft beddown location, provided port facilities for the Coalition ships as well as lodging, food, fuel and security. Bahrain hosted a large segment of the fighter and tanker force, and provided important port facilities to maintain Coalition shipping. It also provided lodging, food, and facilities support for the forces based there. All countries in the region increased output of refined petroleum products and made them available to Coalition forces, in certain cases putting themselves in the position of having to import a particular type of fuel for domestic use.

Host nation contributions were a major factor in the fuels operation's success. All ground fuels, and most jet fuel, except for JP-5 and jet fuel, thermally stable (JPTS), were provided from in the theater. Commercial airport contractors provided refueling support, host military provided aircraft refueling at military bases, and host nation trucks and drivers provided most inland distribution to move fuel from refineries and depots to the bases. This removed a major burden from ARCENT, which was responsible for bulk fuel inland distribution and had committed most of its truck companies to moving fuel for ground forces. By the time the offensive started, US fuels personnel and mobility equipment, such as portable hydrants, bladders, pumps and fuel transfer systems, combined with host nation personnel and fuels facilities, were available at each deployed location to provide refueling support to sustain the operation. Additionally, fuel distribution and storage equipment from the Southwest Asia Petroleum Distribution Operational Project (SWAPDOP) was deployed from CONUS to the AOR. It consists of pipeline, tactical petroleum terminals, and pump stations used to distribute large quantities of fuel across great distances. During Operations Desert Shield and Desert Storm, more than 127 miles of tactical pipeline were laid to provide a quick response to urgent operational support requirements, enabling the movement and storage of greater quantities of fuel farther forward.

Most sustainment fuel was acquired in the AOR from the host nations. The inland fuel delivery to air bases and component units behind the Corps area was done by host nation transport and organic line-haul tank truck, freeing tactical military vehicles to deliver fuel forward of the Corps rear boundary to divisions and brigades. Requirements for specialty fuels, however, posed a special challenge.

JPTS was required for some aircraft deployed to the Theater. Initially, no JPTS supply was available in the AOR; the closest sources were in southern Europe. The JPTS at one location consisted of 3,000 55-gallon drums which were airlifted to the Theater using organic KC-10 and Transportation Command (TRANSCOM) C-141 airlift. The JPTS at another consisted of approximately 700,000 gallons which was stored in bulk fuel tanks. Approximately 100,000 gallons were airlifted from this location to the AOR by Aerial Bulk Fuel Delivery Systems, mounted in C-141s. Additional needs were moved in drums by truck from the refinery in Texas to Barksdale AFB, LA, where it was airlifted to the AOR. Once 60 DOS was established in theater, resupply was established using sealift and line-haul tank trucks. This requirement was the exception to the single fuel used by most forces in the AOR.

The single fuel concept, which involves the ability of land-based air and ground forces to operate with a single, common fuel, was successfully used by several USAF, USMC, and Army units. JET A-1 was used as the common fuel for aircraft and ground vehicles, weapons systems, and equipment within these units. The use of a single, common fuel increased tactical flexibility, simplified battlefield logistics, and maximized available fuel transport equipment. Some Army units chose to use diesel fuel since it was readily available in theater and produces a better smoke screen when used in the M1A1 engine exhaust smoke system. USAF aircraft operating from host nation air bases used the same type fuel as the host nation forces except

USAF injected anti-ice, antistatic, and anti-corrosion additives.

The availability of facilities, supplies, and manpower at the host nation locations established the baseline for the initial sustainment requirement. The requirement, however, was a complex iteration of needs that encompassed all aspects of receiving, storing, expenditure planning, and consumption prediction. To accommodate this intricate planning and sustaining process, a sustainment base was established that lashed together the forces' needs and capabilities.

SUSTAINMENT

Nature of the Sustainment Base

Within the theater, a complex logistics sustainment effort was required to maintain and improve combat capability. Deploying forces depended on extensive lateral support from other theaters, requiring the movement of stocks between theaters for some items, known as cross leveling. Most notable was the heavy use of equipment and stocks from the European Command (EUCOM), explained in greater detail throughout this section. Extensive use of depot resupply before deployment to overcome normal peacetime deficits also was required. Post-deployment support and sustainment of forces in theater was significantly improved by the surge of organic depot production, Defense Logistics Agency (DLA) efforts, the availability of lateral support from EUCOM, industrial base responsiveness, and the availability of airlift to bring high priority items into the theater quickly and sealift to move efficiently the large volume of sustainment cargo.

Sustainment includes providing and maintaining the force and equipment a combatant CINC requires to accomplish the national objectives. Establishment of a sustainment base involves determining what is required to let a force achieve those objectives within a specific period of time. As a general rule, the theater commander estimates the length of time the operation will require. This estimate is passed to the logistician in the form of a stockage objective. Logisticians then calculate, and combat force commanders approve, the amount of supplies and services required based on time, environment, type of operation, type of force, and the number of troops in theater.

The computations involved are relatively complex and the data must be tempered by judgment. Supply calculations resulting from this process are expressed in terms of days of supply (DOS). Although the calculations themselves are more sophisticated, involving failure rates, order times and demand analysis, DOS are shorthand expressions of tonnages or gallons. For example, rather than give the number of tons of a particular commodity available in the theater — a relatively meaningless figure in itself — logisticians speak of the number of days those tonnages will support the force at the present or anticipated consumption rates. Thus, to report there are 10 DOS of a particular commodity on hand indicates that, if there is no change in plans, the stocks available are sufficient to sustain the force for 10 days.

The DOS also tell logisticians how close the sustainment base is to satisfying the commander's stockage objective and whether expenditure controls should be imposed. If, for example, the commander has estimated the operation will require 10 DOS of ammunition and there are seven DOS on hand, action must be taken to increase stock levels or limit expenditures by establishing priorities.

Supply calculations for the size of the sustainment base also are used as part of the formula to compute transportation requirements and the need for units to receive, store, and issue supplies. Both requirements are predicated on the quantities of materiel at the base and the need to distribute it to using units.

Although it is not difficult to understand the November decision to increase the size of the force in terms of personnel, the fact this decision had significant meaning for the sustainment base is not always as clear. Essentially, as initial deployments were made, sustainment stocks were introduced into the theater, first through the use of prepositioned ships, and later from CONUS or stocks in forward bases. As the deployment flow slowed, more lift became available to increase sustainment base shipments. As these shipments arrived in theater, they were distributed to units that required them or to theater storage areas. When the decision to deploy additional forces was made, the demands for these stocks increased, and increased the requirement for the transportation system to bring additional amounts into the region.

Expanding Logistic Requirements

The logistics requirements visualized in August were far less than those projected just a few months later. In August, the concept of operations was primarily defensive, with logistics sustainment requirements developed accordingly. However, the decision to move into offensive posture required increases in: forces deployed; operations tempo (OPTEMPO), with its corresponding expansion in the geographic AOR; expected consumption of munitions, fuel, spare parts, storage requirements; maintenance; and demands for intratheater transportation. The change in sustainment requirements also had other effects. It necessitated establishing additional forward logistics support bases to reduce the distance between fighting forces and the support base and making the transportation system more efficient. In addition, CINCCENT directed the stockage levels in theater for food and ammunition be increased from 30 to 60 DOS. The increase in the number of forces, the requirements for new bases and the increase in stockage levels caused a major increase in logistics workload. A discussion of the effect of these factors on petroleum and munitions provides insights to the logistics challenges to the theater.

The CENTCOM Joint Petroleum Office developed petroleum requirements and passed them to the Defense Fuel Region/ Middle East (DFR/ME), a subordinate element of the DLA Defense Fuel Supply Center (DFSC) at Cameron Station, Alexandria, VA. In turn, DFR/ME identified sources of supply and, in coordination with MSC, scheduled the tanker ships to carry the bulk petroleum to the AOR. Although fuel was shipped to the AOR from both CONUS and other regions, the primary fuel source throughout the operation was Saudi Arabia and, to a lesser degree, other Coalition nations; the remaining fuel required to attain the desired stockage levels was shipped from other sources.

Fuel already had been prepositioned both in and near the AOR before the Iraqi invasion. Defense Fuels Supply Points (DFSP) had also been established. Support also was provided from DFSPs in Spain, Italy, Greece, Turkey, Singapore and Hawaii. Three Afloat Prepositioning Force (APF) ships with POL also had been stationed at Diego Garcia. The DFSP, along with the APF ship cargoes, represented approximately 32 DOS of prepositioned stocks for the early plans. In addition to the prepositioned WRM stocks ashore and afloat, on-base stocks of USAF-owned fuel in theater added another two DOS. And, each MPS squadron had enough fuel on board its ships to sustain its deployed Marines for 30 days.

But when the force levels were increased, in-theater requirements increased proportionately. Even though the 30 DOS theater stockage policy did not change with the increase in force levels, the ability to stock the larger quantities required by the increased number of users became more of a challenge. A more complete discussion of storage follows in the consumable storage section of this appendix.

The increase in force levels and the commensurate optempo increase anticipated by the change from defense to offense called for a substantial increase in the amount of fuel required to sustain the force. Increasing the share of output from Saudi refineries for jet fuel, bringing tanker ships to safe haven berths as floating storage capacity, and the laying of tactical pipelines to ease movement to forward storage bladders are but a few of the methods used to increase the available usable fuel for the forces. Munitions, however, posed an even more challenging task for the logistician.

The increase in the force structure, and the increased stockage objective from 30 to 60 DOS had perhaps the greatest impact on munitions supply functions. This was because stocks of munitions generally require significant amounts of material handling equipment (MHE) (e.g., forklifts and roller conveyors), special handling and shipping precautions, and must be sent to storage sites reasonably near the user. Because of the weight and handling characteristics associated with munitions, early identification of requirements is crucial to planning the most efficient shipment and delivery. Airlift is an extremely inefficient means of movement because munitions tend to be too heavy to carry in efficient loads when that aircraft could be carrying greater quantities of other high-value goods. Sealift is the most efficient for moving munitions, but requires time for the transfer from land transportation to sea ports, sea transit time, and then movement to the point of intended use. Transport is limited by the number of trucks available to move the ammunition within the theater and the nature of the road network. The effect of some factors is reduced if ammunition is containerized. However, there is a need for the necessary infrastructure — in terms of containers, container ships, port handling equipment, line haul equipment, and MHE for unloading containers at their destinations. Therefore, careful planning and positioning of munitions is crucial.

Before Operation Desert Shield, munitions of all Services aboard the MPS and the APS were being upgraded in both quantity and quality. The Committee for Ammunition Logistics Support had made reallocation decisions concerning the worldwide stockage levels of munitions and the types allocated to each theater. As a result of these decisions, part of the worldwide munitions assets were reallocated to CINCCENT. This action began the process of identifying preferred munitions, or those that would most likely be used against the types of anticipated targets within the planned threat scenario, and the requirements for modernization. This gave the CENTCOM logisticians a better understanding of the shortfalls and requirements for munitions in the theater.

As the initial 30 DOS requirement was established, munitions requirements, though not fully satisfied, were met initially by APS, USAF preposition stocks in theater, and APF and MPS munitions ships. Except for the MPS ships which unloaded at Al-Jubayl, these ships started to arrive at Ad-Dammam, a principal SPOD, on 17 August, and continued to arrive through 31 August. Unloading these vessels was delayed by port congestion. This was, in part, a result of an inadequate CSS structure, which included a shortage of trucks and drivers to move the cargo out of the ports and into the storage sites. Inadequate CSS structure also delayed development of ammunition storage sites in the Corps and Theater areas, which also contributed to port congestion.

The arrival of the *USS Cleveland* on 21 September continued the flow of sustainment munitions to the theater. The requirements for munitions varied with the many types of weapons the forces had in the theater. The services focused on stockpiling munitions such as Hellfire, 120-mm tank ammunition, Maverick air-to-ground missiles, 30-mm rounds, laser-guided bombs (LGB) and anti-tank cluster bombs, all of which are effective antitank munitions. These types of ammunition were

crucial to effective defensive as well as offensive operations.

The decision to deploy an armor force composed mainly of M1A1s required an exchange of 105-mm tank rounds for 120-mm tank rounds. During the sustainment buildup, nearly 220,000 120-mm tank rounds were supplied. However, because of the short duration of the war and fewer active engagements than anticipated during the ground campaign, expenditures were only about 3,600.

Requirements calculations improved as the planning for conflict got closer to actual execution. Requirements determination by the Service components reflected frequent changes in planning assumptions and optempo reassessments. Coupled with malpositioning, these changes in requirements were reflected in perceived shortages of some types of munitions. For example, Marine Component, Central Command (MARCENT) did not achieve a satisfactory stockage level in air munitions until early February. This was due to delays in determining aviation munitions requirements because of the changes in plans, the length of the sustainment pipeline, and dependence on obtaining common aviation ordnance items from Navy and USMC stocks.

Also, CENTAF munitions requirements were adjusted during planning for the air campaign, but while the initial stockage levels were within the planned expenditure rate at the beginning of hostilities, once the air campaign began, expenditure rates increased well beyond the anticipated resupply levels for certain preferred munitions, such as the 500-lb LGB. This affected sustainment by changing the requirement for the 500-lb LGB. Another early emphasis was on movement of Maverick antitank missiles and high-speed antiradiation missiles, and this emphasis was validated by the expenditure rates experienced during the air campaign. Also, though the high expenditure rate of precision-guided munitions (PGM) was anticipated, full stockages were not received until after the air campaign began. The short notice approval for introduction of B-52 operations in Theater caused special airlift requirements for M-117 (750-lb bomb) from alternate storage locations.

The successful effort to provide the material required to sustain a force of a half million people was not without its difficulties. However, robust support infrastructure near the theater was invaluable to the success of the sustainment effort of Operations Desert Shield and Desert Storm. That robust support infrastructure was in Europe, under EUCOM, which played an important role in establishing an adequate sustainment base from which CENTCOM could operate.

EUCOM Support

Because of its location so near the CENTCOM area of responsibility, EUCOM provided en route support; munitions, maintenance, materiel and equipment; major combat forces; and Joint Task Force (JTF) operations in support of Operations Desert Shield and Desert Storm. As a major command charged with the defense of Europe, EUCOM is home to major US fighting forces. As such, units and assets not readily available from other areas added their strength to the Coalition forces.

As the SWA situation developed, EUCOM geared up to support the operation. Forward-deployed forces helped maintain strategic agility. The value of existing facilities and prepositioned stocks and equipment reaffirmed the concept of forward basing. Individual relationships and personal trust developed during years of close work with the North Atlantic Treaty Organization (NATO) paid great dividends. Bases within EUCOM received cargo and personnel en route to the conflict and set up intermediate maintenance facilities. These facilities were established to support increased repair requirements dictated by increased use of weapon systems and the harsh SWA desert environment.

As a transit and staging base, 84 percent of all US strategic airlift, combat aircraft, and naval vessels passed through the EUCOM AOR. Bases in England, Germany, Spain, Italy, Greece, and Turkey provided support, personnel, and supplies to help sustain the forces of Operations Desert Shield and Desert Storm.

EUCOM supply support to the CENTCOM area of operations was substantial. To help feed and protect deployed troops, more than 2.1 million meals, ready to eat (MREs), more than one million T- and B-rations, and more than one million chemical garments were provided from EUCOM stockpiles. Considerable amounts of munitions, including preferred munitions and Patriot missiles, also were shipped. Support extended beyond expendables; major end items also were contributed. More than $2 billion of the Prepositioned Organization Materiel Configured in Unit Sets (POMCUS), totaling 1,300 tanks and armored combat vehicles, were sent to the AOR. EUCOM's largest contribution to sustainment of the deployed forces in SWA for the long term was its European-based maintenance complex.

EUCOM sites were used as a readily available base for the repair of equipment that required facilities or test equipment beyond that available in theater. US air bases in Europe repaired avionics components not only for assets deployed from US Air Forces in Europe (USAFE), but for units deployed from CONUS as well. Jet engines also required extensive facilities to provide maintenance and overhaul necessary to maintain high readiness rates. European bases provided these engine repair shops. Bitburg and Hahn provided F-15 and F-16 support and the Rhein Main Air Base C-130 engine shop was expanded to provide support for all C-130 aircraft within the CENTCOM AOR. More than 4,500 avionics and 500 engine repairs were performed.

The desert environment and amount of complex repair and test equipment needed also made existing US bases in Europe the choice for some repairs. For example, C-130 propeller repairs require large amounts of heavy, low-technology equipment and fixtures as well as a clean room for assembling hub gear boxes. Instead of moving all this to the desert, it was decided to expand the existing shop at Rhein Main Air Base and perform the repairs there. Completed propellers then were shipped to the AOR for final assembly of hubs and blades.

Army Materiel Command (AMC), Europe, also provided a ready military industrial base to repair ARCENT engines, transmissions, transfer cases, and other end items. AMC shops completed more than 7,500 repairs, which were set aside for CENTCOM use. These repairs included 1,800 engines, 832 transmissions, and 852 transfer cases.

Naval Forces, Europe (NAVEUR), provided similar support for deployed naval forces both in and around the theater of operations. NAVEUR repaired more than 200 jet engines for MARCENT aircraft. These efforts kept both end items and components from being sent to CONUS for maintenance and repair.

In addition to support for forces deployed to the SWA AOR, EUCOM also supported combat operations from within its own theater. JTF Proven Force, based in Turkey, a country for which EUCOM has responsibility, conducted military operations into the AOR in direct support of CENTCOM. EUCOM provided continuing support to forces including fighter and tanker aircraft, naval forces, Army special operations forces and Patriot batteries. The support EUCOM provided allowed CENTCOM logisticians to concentrate on the problems associated with beddown of the forces within the AOR, and relieved many aspects of the long supply lines to SWA.

Proven Force

EUCOM support to Operation Proven Force included all aspects of logistics. From an initial plan to support a small force designed to divert enemy equipment and resources, the concept quickly grew to support deployed Army units and 1.2 fighter wing equivalents.

Deployed aircraft assets quickly took on the aspects of a composite wing, made up of small numbers of aircraft from many units. This created a challenge for maintenance personnel since EUCOM had not tested true, composite support organizations previously. Fighter units were consolidated under a single support organization umbrella using a two-level maintenance concept, while Strategic Air Command (SAC), MAC and the Airborne Warning and Control System (AWACS) detachment maintenance support was provided by their own deployed personnel. The two-level concept relied heavily on each unit's home station to provide intermediate level repair support. The timely repair of parts by home station, coupled with a responsive transportation flow, was very effective as demonstrated by a low total not mission capable supply rate of 9.5 percent for the fighter aircraft fleet. A drawback to this support concept was that it placed an added burden on an already-taxed transportation system.

After initial delays with Turkish customs concerning the inspection and release of large quantities of equipment and supplies arriving in the AOR, airlift became the life blood of deployed operations. Transportation personnel prepared, packaged, loaded, moved and unloaded tens of thousands of items in direct support of JTF Proven Force. Ninety-eight C-5, 102 C-141, 82 C-130, and 35 other support aircraft moved more than 8,000 short tons of cargo and more than 4,000 passengers into the AOR. In addition, more than 3,300 short tons of cargo were moved by surface. This large quantity of items destined for several different deployed units posed not only a tremendous workload for transportation personnel but also a special challenge for the supply system in Turkey.

USAFE opted to establish a separate supply account for each deployed aircraft unit to provide better support. This necessitated establishment of five new supply accounts at Ramstein Air Base, since the Incirlik supply computer already was saturated. With a framework in place, supply operations began in earnest. Units processed up to 45 Mission Impaired Capability Awaiting Parts (MICAP) requests daily. Most MICAP parts were located in hours in the European theater, using the MICAP Asset Sourcing System. The problem was to get the parts to the user quickly. To solve this transportation problem, two pallet spaces were dedicated on daily C-130 missions to Turkey. Project code Fox pallet space was used only for MICAPs, WRSK replenishment, and other high priority assets. Fuel support, however, proved to be as much of a challenge for supply as parts support.

The fuels infrastructure in Turkey was saturated. USAFE, EUCOM/J-4, the DFSC, and the Defense Fuels Region/ Europe negotiated with the Turkish government to ensure adequate fuel supplies were available. This effort added almost eight million gallons of fuel storage and pipeline time to existing capabilities. Contacts also were let for daily tank truck deliveries of more than 600,000 gallons of aviation fuel to Incirlik Air Base.

In addition to fuel, USAFE provided operational contract support in several areas. Besides providing support to units deployed to Incirlik Air Base, contracting support also was required for a forward base for the Joint Special Operations Task Force. In all, contracting officers obligated $5.7 million on more than 1,100 actions.

TRANSPORTATION

The detailed discussion on strategic lift in the section on mobilization and deployment in Appendix E emphasizes the accomplishments and limitations of US mobility capabilities within the context of deploying forces. But the importance of lift to the sustainment of the Coalition forces cannot be overlooked. While the scale of the deployment is impressive, equally impressive is the sustained operation to supply the forces even while the deployment was occurring. To place the sustainment lift effort in context, the fact that in little more than seven months more than 544,000 tons of equipment and supplies were airlifted, more than 3.4 million tons of dry cargo and more than 6.1 million barrels of petroleum products were moved by sea reflects the intensity of the sustainment effort. By comparison, cargo delivered during the Persian Gulf Conflict was greater than the cargo moved across the English Channel to Normandy in support of the D-Day invasion during a comparable seven-month period, and significantly exceeded the more than 2.3 million tons of coal, food, and medical supplies that had been moved to West Berlin during the Berlin airlift. The transportation of the sustainment cargo for Operations Desert Shield and Desert Storm involved all aspects of available lift — including land, sea and airlift, water terminal operations, Civil Reserve Air Fleet (CRAF) elements, foreign-flagged air and sea carriers either donated or leased, and tactical air and ground transportation assets, organic, donated or leased from foreign sources.

MHE to load and unload unit equipment and supplies is a crucial factor in deploying and sustaining forces. A large amount of MHE was deployed, including 204 40,000-pound capacity cargo loaders to support military cargo aircraft and specialized equipment to support wide-body cargo aircraft, which was sent to the AOR. A shortage of equipment to support wide-body contract cargo aircraft slowed commercial operations and resulted in some extended ground times in the AOR in August. (The 40,000-pound loaders are not compatible with the wide-body cargo aircraft and rapidly are completing their useful life. Additionally, the weight capacity of current equipment limits some operations.)

The first major phase of the transportation effort was the initial deployment of combat forces, covered in the appendix on deployment. Of equal magnitude was the task of receiving and moving troops and their equipment to operating areas once they arrived in theater. The arriving forces began the task of developing high combat readiness levels while concurrently preparing for sustained combat. As the arrival of forces, support material, and supplies began to stabilize, ARCENT SUPCOM began work on a comprehensive plan to support the arrival of additional forces, sustain operational requirements during offensive operations, and provide for redeployment after hostilities.

The SUPCOM faced severe limitations from the beginning. While the region's infrastructure, such as the sea and air ports, was large and modern by any standard, the requirements to house, feed, and move troops to their combat locations overwhelmed available facilities. Also, when the decision was made to deploy combat units first, the long supply lines, limited host nation transportation infrastructure, and limited initial HNS increased the difficulty. Innovative command and personal involvement at all levels made the logistics support work. But the requirements levied on the logistics system changed as the decision to increase the number of forces in the theater changed, and the lift, sustainment, intratheater transportation, storage and maintenance requirements became all the more taxing on an already stressed logistics system.

Strategic Lift

The sustainment of combat forces and equipment would not have been possible without the combined assets of MAC, MSC, and Military Traffic Management Command (MTMC); supporting civil assets; and the material prepositioned in or available to be moved to the theater. These three elements comprise the nation's strategic lift capability. During Operations Desert Shield and Desert Storm, airlift delivered more than 544,000 tons of cargo — five percent of the total cargo or 15 percent of all cargo when bulk petroleum is excluded — while simultaneously delivering more than 500,000 passengers during the deployment and sustainment phases. Sealift was the work horse of the deployment and sustainment operations and, for Operations Desert Shield and Desert Storm, delivered 95 percent of all cargo. The role of the prepositioned equipment and supplies was crucial to the early combat capability and the sustainment of the forces, and reduced the number of airlift and sealift missions required into the theater.

Airlift

After the initial surge to deploy forces, strategic airlift objectives shifted to sustaining the force. There normally were 50 to 65 Operation Desert Shield C-5 and C-141 missions into the theater each day during the August surge, simultaneously deploying troops and sustainment cargo for the units already in the theater. C-5 and C-141 Operation Desert Shield activity tapered to an average of 44 missions a day when the sustainment supply effort was beginning to meet the required delivery rates into the theater by mid September. The sustainment requirements will be discussed in detail in the sustainment section of this appendix. By the end of September, the average number of airlift missions flown daily (including commercial aircraft, KC-10 tankers and C-130s in addition to the C-141s and C-5s) increased to approximately 100 a day. MAC missions supporting non-Operation Desert Storm areas averaged 25 a day, providing resupply to other service supply points such as the Navy's Cubi

Point, Philippines, and repositioning equipment and supplies in other theaters in anticipation of their use in SWA. From early October through Thanksgiving, C-5 and C-141 Operation Desert Shield sustainment activity leveled off at 36 missions a day to the Arabian peninsula.

By the time Operation Desert Storm began on 16 January, after 165 days of airlift activity, MAC organic aircraft and contracted commercial carriers had completed more than 10,500 missions to move more than 355,000 short tons of cargo from CONUS, Europe, and elsewhere to APODs in the Persian Gulf region. The level of effort by the airlift forces is illustrated by the fact that all but a few of MAC's active C-5 and C-141s were committed to flying Operation Desert Shield missions in August 1990. Two weeks after C-day, on 21 August, 94 percent of the USAF C-5s (118 of 126) and 73 percent (195 of 265) C-141s were supporting Operation Desert Shield.

SAC KC-10 and KC-135 aircraft also played a vital role in cargo and passenger movement. These tankers moved more than 4,800 tons of cargo and more than 14,200 passengers to support SAC operations alone. Part of this effort was conducted by shuttles established on a scheduled basis to improve resupply efforts to the Pacific, European, and SWA theaters. Additionally, KC-10s transported more than 1,600 tons of cargo and more than 2,500 passengers in a dual-role capacity for USAF and USMC fighter unit moves, providing refueling support and airlift for the units on the same sorties. Up to 20 KC-10s also were assigned to MAC for pure airlift sorties, moving more than 3,800 tons of cargo and more than 4,900 passengers in this capacity.

Civil Reserve Air Fleet (CRAF)

From the moment Operation Desert Shield began, MAC depended on the civilian airline industry to help fulfill its enormous airlift requirements. The CRAF program, through

C-141 and C-5 Aircraft.

which participating US civil air carriers voluntarily commit their aircraft and other resources to support US national interests, was a crucial asset. Daily commercial air carrier operations peaked at approximately 25 missions a day in support of Operation Desert Shield, with additional aircraft supporting other airlift requirements.

The airlift system effectively meshed active airlifters, Air Reserve Component (ARC) members, and the CRAF to provide the flexibility and short response time needed to meet time-sensitive requirements. When TRANSCOM implemented Stage I CRAF on 18 August, an additional 18 passenger and 21 cargo aircraft were added to the fleet, the cargo aircraft dedicated primarily to sustainment operations. When Stage II CRAF was implemented on 17 January, an additional 59 passenger and 17 cargo aircraft were available for service, increasing the available sustainment lift considerably.

Air Refueling — The Force Multiplier

The tremendous productivity of the airlifters would not have been as impressive were it not for the synergistic interaction of tankers and

A CRAF Plane Unloads at Riyadh.

transports. Modification in the 1970s added air refueling capability to transport aircraft. This had substantial effect on readiness, rapid deployment, and the sustainment of forces to the theater. In the first few weeks of the deployment, as many as 16 percent of the airlift missions were aerial refueled for non-stop flights. Sometimes the C-5s and C-141s were aerial refueled by tankers just before landing or shortly after taking off to help reduce refueling congestion at the APOD in the theater. This action also helped ease the shortage of refueling points and parking space at the airfields.

Air refueling was important to the logistical support of Operations Desert Shield and Desert Storm, and went far beyond the initial airlift support. SAC used 262 KC-135s and 46 KC-10s during Operation Desert Storm; they flew more than 17,000 sorties, to include more than 11,500 air refueling sorties and nearly 75,000 hours; refueled more than 33,000 receivers, including 5,500 Navy and USMC aircraft; with nearly 70 million gallons of fuel, in six months. Tankers surpassed this effort during the six weeks of Operation Desert Storm when they flew almost 17,000 sorties (more than 15,000 of these air refueling sorties) logged more than 66,000 hours, and refueled almost 52,000 aircraft with more than 125 million gallons of fuel. Approximately 12 percent of the fuel and 17 percent of the sorties supported the Navy and USMC. Nearly every air refueling

capable aircraft used USAF tankers at some point.

The USAF was responsible for providing much of the aerial refueling for the Navy during Operations Desert Shield and Desert Storm. To support the requirement, JP-5 storage sites were established in the Theater. Resupply from DFSC stocks in theater and afloat storage tankers in the Red Sea was established. USAF tankers operated from Seeb and Jiddah to provide JP-5 aerial refueling for the Navy, in addition to the other locations throughout the AOR where the tankers operated with the standard JP-8. Although JP-5 is the preferred Navy aviation fuel, it was not practical to designate part of the tanker force to carry JP-5 only to support the Navy, because of the lead time required to refuel tankers, the vast numbers of refueling requirements, and the need for mission tasking flexibility. JET A-1, the primary jet fuel available in the theater, provided by Saudi Arabia, was dispensed to the Navy most of the time. JET A-1 is the same

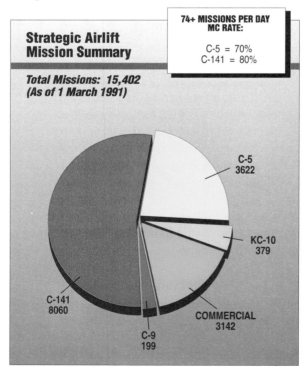

74+ MISSIONS PER DAY
MC RATE:

C-5 = 70%
C-141 = 80%

Strategic Airlift Mission Summary

Total Missions: 15,402 (As of 1 March 1991)

C-5
3622

KC-10
379

COMMERCIAL
3142

C-9
199

C-141
8060

basic fuel as the military fuel JP-8. The difference is that additives for anti-ice, antistatic, and corrosion have been added to JET A-1 to make JP-8. The flash point for JP-8 is 100 degrees Fahrenheit; the Navy requires a 140 degree F flash point for carrier safety and JP-5 meets that requirement. The reason JP-5 is not the US forces standard fuel is its availability and cost; only two percent of a barrel of crude oil can be refined into JP-5.

The success of the USAF's air refueling contribution was not without its trade offs, however. The additional air refueling requirements, including the Navy, USMC and Coalition, prevented wider use of the KC-10 in an airlift only role and affected the ability to plan for KC-10 apportionment in this role. Also, the demand for tanker support was so great that the USAF allocated a larger part of the total world wide tanker fleet to the effort. Fully 81 percent of the USAF's KC-10 fleet and 44 percent of the KC-135 fleet was committed to the Gulf crisis. While these may be comparably high percentages, the strategic deterrence posture of SAC was not adversely affected.

The sustained airlift operation would not have been possible were it not for dedicated crews, including those who flew the aircraft and those who loaded and maintained them. Long missions from CONUS to the theater stretched aircrew resources to the limit. Until the ARC call up on 22 August, all C-5 and C-141 missions to the Arabian peninsula were performed by active duty air crews and ARC volunteers. In addition to the time spent flying between designated locations, each crew day included the time an aircrew spent waiting for its aircraft to be loaded, unloaded, and refueled. As a result of long in-flight times and unpredictable ground times, MAC extended the maximum consecutive duty hours between rest periods for a basic air crew from 16 (the peacetime limit) to 20 hours. Backlogs of cargo at many stateside terminals and delays in

A USAF Tanker refuels Fighter Aircraft.

refueling en route compounded an already demanding situation for the crews. Actions such as staging crews at forward locations such as Rhein Main Air Base, Germany, and Torrejon Air Base, Spain, through which more than 80 percent of the airlift staged, helped ease demands on aircrews.

Desert Express

Hundreds of aircraft, tanks, and other equipment in the theater of operations created the need for extraordinary logistics pipeline support. In late October, with 200,000 American forces in theater, MAC, at TRANSCOM's direction, began a special airlift called Desert Express. This operation, flown daily from CONUS to the theater, provided overnight delivery of spare parts considered absolutely crucial to accomplish the mission and ensure maximum wartime readiness. While the idea of aerial resupply of crucial items is not new, the concept of a regularly scheduled, dedicated aircraft operation was innovative. The Desert Express system included a dedicated C-141 aircraft flying each day from Charleston AFB, SC, to deliver high priority logistics items to the AOR. TRANSCOM designated Charleston as the collection point for logistics parts the Army,

Loading and Ramp Operations at Rhein Main AB, Germany.

USAF, Navy and USMC needed to provide a link with commercial air express services. Functioning like the commercial overnight express delivery systems, Desert Express departed daily at 1230. Cargo destined for SWA had to arrive at Charleston by 1030 to be on that day's Express. The 1030 cutoff time dovetailed with CONUS overnight mail and air express parcel delivery schedules and the flight schedules of LOGAIR, (a private cargo airline under contract to the Air Force Logistics Command (AFLC) and AMC) and QUICKTRANS (under contract to the Navy). Desert Express reduced the response time for high priority shipments from as long as two weeks to as little as 72 hours.

Deployment of additional forces to the Arabian peninsula in November increased the requirement for overnight delivery of high-priority spare parts. To provide a link with the logistics and maintenance support facilities in Europe, a similar dedicated, special airlift operation was started from Europe and dubbed European Desert Express. The mission aircraft

departed Ramstein and picked up cargo at Rhein Main Air Base, Germany, once daily, seven days a week. The C-141 left Ramstein at midnight and arrived at Rhein Main 45 minutes later. After loading cargo and fueling, the aircraft departed for Saudi Arabia with a scheduled arrival time at Dhahran of 0530. Unloaded and refueled, the C-141 returned to Ramstein.

When crucial parts arrived in Saudi Arabia, they were taken to their final destinations within the theater by surface transportation or by MAC's theater based C-130s. These were part of the Camels and STARS airlift system, explained later in this appendix in intratheater airlift. As of the end of February, the cumulative Desert and European Desert Express airlift had moved nearly 2,500 tons of cargo to the AOR.

SAC tankers also flew regular missions from Castle AFB, CA, to support operations at Andersen AFB, Guam and Diego Garcia during Operations Desert Shield and Desert Storm. These Desert Express type missions were important in providing mission capability support and high-priority surge and sustainment cargo to these locations. In addition to these efforts, SAC began Mighty Express in mid January primarily to sustain deployed B-52 operations. Six KC-135 aircraft airlifted 680 personnel and 198.8 tons of cargo in four months.

Sealift

Key to the buildup and sustainment of forces was the workhorse of the strategic mobility triad, sealift. Sealift in Operations Desert Shield and Desert Storm was composed of ships under MSC operational control, and domestic and foreign ships under charter to MSC. The size and swiftness of the buildup required the United States to use almost every element of its sealift capability. Almost all Navy sealift elements were involved in the operation, and they were

Desert Express/European Desert Express

(Cargo in Short Tons)

| | Desert Express[1] | | | | | European Desert Express[2] | | |
	Army	AF	Navy	MC	Total	Army	AF	Total
Aug 90	-	-	-	-	-	-	-	-
Sep 90	-	-	-	-	-	-	-	-
Oct 90	2.17	0.27	-	-	2.44	-	-	-
Nov 90	171.45	52.53	1.49	9.31	234.78	-	-	-
Dec 90	229.31	124.62	26.32	17.07	397.32	19.58	61.55	81.13
Jan 91	266.25	251.42	36.01	22.59	576.27	110.42	184.72	295.14
Feb 91	274.58	273.74	39.49	40.88	628.69	91.17	168.76	259.93
Total	943.76	702.58	103.31	89.85	1839.50	221.17	415.03	636.20

[1]Start Date: 30 October 1990; Discontinued: 19 May 1991
[2]Start Date: 8 December 1990; Discontinued: 9 March 1991

supplemented by large numbers of chartered domestic and foreign ships. During the entire operation, 385 ships delivered unit equipment, related support, and petroleum products.

The sealift logistics deployment and sustainment effort of Operations Desert Shield and Desert Storm took place in two phases. The first sealift phase extended from August to November, and was designed to deploy and sustain forces to deter further Iraqi aggression. During that period, sealift moved the equipment of more than four Army divisions along with sustainment for the initial defensive support requirements. By September, more than 100 of TRANSCOM's MSC-controlled ships had delivered the equipment and sustainment for the 100,000 US military personnel who had deployed to the theater. When the first sealift

phase ended, more than 180 ships were assigned or under charter to MSC and nearly 3.5 million tons of fuel and 1.2 million tons of cargo had been delivered.

By 15 January, the total number of US forces deployed in the theater had more than doubled. From the beginning, while deploying a unit, ships also would be loaded with sustainment supplies required by the forces in theater. By March, an average of 4,200 tons of cargo arrived in theater daily. The average one-way voyage for the Operations Desert Shield and Desert Storm sealift covered nearly 8,700 miles.

Strategic sealift made a vital contribution to logistics sustainment in Operations Desert Shield and Desert Storm. RRF ships with

Break Down of Sealift Ships Utilized

Ship Classification	Total Number of Ships
Afloat Prepositioning Ships	
MPS (Marine Equipment)	13
PREPO (Army & Air Force Cargo)	8
PREPO Tankers	3
Fast Sealift Ships (FSS)	8
Ready Reserve Force (RRF)	71
Chartered Ships	
US Flagged or Controlled Cargo	25
Foreign Flagged Cargo	187
US Flagged or Controlled Tankers	47
Foreign Flagged Tankers	23
Total Sealift Ships Utilized (Entire Operation)	**385**

breakout schedules of five and 10 days took, on the average, 11 and 16 days to break out. However, they performed well once activated, carrying the largest percentage of dry cargo of all the sealift assets. RRF ships began arriving in theater on 8 September and the first chartered ship, which had been under contract when Operation Desert Shield began, arrived the next day. The first ship chartered after the beginning of Operation Desert Shield arrived in the AOR on 9 September. In addition to shipments to the theater on US government owned or controlled and chartered ships, many US-flagged container ships delivered cargo in support of Operations Desert Shield and Desert Storm as part of their regularly scheduled service to the region. These ships delivered cargo under the Special Middle East Sealift Agreement (SMESA). Fuel deliveries required MSC to increase the number of tankers in its fleet from 22 in August to 48 in early February.

Afloat Prepositioning Force

The APF consisting of the MPS and APS fleets worked well and added flexibility to strategic lift. All ships delivered their initial loads, and 11 ships made subsequent deliveries after reverting to a common-user status when CINCCENT had no further requirements for them in theater. Three MPS were out of position on 7 August because of regularly scheduled maintenance and training exercises. Because the other MPS and APS were so well positioned relative to the crisis scene, their response was excellent.

Fast Sealift Ships (FSS)

The Fast Sealift Ships (FSS) performed well in their part of the overall logistics effort, doing more relative to their numbers than any other type of sealift asset. This performance was due to their large size, the special configuration to accommodate the equipment, and speed. There are eight FSS and, although they only represent four percent of the total sealift ships, they delivered 13 percent of unit cargo. One FSS, Antares, broke down on its initial trip. Before the crisis, Antares had an electrical fire in an automatic combustion control system. She had been scheduled to begin regular maintenance on one boiler in mid-August, which would have delayed her activation by about 90 days. The decision was made to defer the maintenance and take the calculated risk of a breakdown to speed delivery of the equipment. After a series of boiler breakdowns during her initial Atlantic crossing, Antares put into Rota, Spain, for repairs; the FSS Altair subsequently picked up Antares' cargo after delivering her own initial load. Antares break down delayed the complete delivery of the first wave of FSS-delivered material and reduced the FSS fleet delivery capacity by about 12 percent, for the duration of the conflict. The remaining FSS fleet responded as planned, although speeds on the initial trips, about 27 knots, were lower than their rated capability. After the initial crossings, FSS averaged 24 knots for the entire operation.

Ready Reserve Force (RRF)

RRF activation orders started 10 August with 18 ships (including 17 roll-on/roll-off (RO/RO) ships). During Phase I of the sealift, 44 ships were activated. In Phase II, 27 more ships were activated. In general, activation requirements were not met; only 18 of the 71 activations were ready on time. Of the 32 ships that were late or failed to activate in Phase I, mechanical failures were a contributing factor in at least 24 cases. Six ships incurred short delays because of a lack of available shipyard workers or crew members. Once activated, RRF ships performed as expected.

Chartered Ships

During Operation Desert Shield, MSC made extensive use of chartered ships to move military cargo. There were two basic reasons why chartered ships were used in addition to RRF. First, RO/RO ships were preferred because of larger size and better loading efficiency, but there are only 17 RRF RO/RO ships. Second, relative to the cost of activating, operating, and then deactivating RRF ships, charters were much less expensive. Even though MSC afforded preference to US ships, most chartered ships were foreign flagged because the types of cargo ships required by MSC were more available in foreign fleets.

MSC negotiated the SMESA with US flag commercial container carriers to ship 40-foot containers, the preferred means to move sustainment cargo to the AOR. The vessel capacity of US flag carriers participating in SMESA was 3,400 containers a week. The estimated DOD requirement was 1,200 containers per week but the system successfully surged to more than 2,000 per week in February 1991.

Sealift Express

Much like the requirement for air delivery of

high value parts and supplies, there was a need to move containerized cargo to the theater as rapidly as possible. Normal over-ocean shipping time to SWA is 30 to 35 days for containers. Sealift Express was established to improve on those times for priority containerized surface cargo. At TRANSCOM's direction, MTMC and MSC, in coordination with the ocean shipping lines, established and managed Desert Storm Sealift Express. Using commercial shipping procedures, containers were not shipped directly to Saudi Arabia, but were interlined (transshipped) to smaller feeder vessels in the Mediterranean Sea and then shuttled to SWA. Sealift Express had a 23-day goal for shipment from the last CONUS port of embarkation to the SWA port of debarkation. Actual Sealift Express shipping times averaged 25 to 27 days, reducing over-ocean time by approximately one week. The initial six sealift express sailings departed intermittently during a 35-day interval, before weekly sailings were established to support sustainment requirements. Sealift Express proved a valuable transportation tool for moving priority cargo.

Importance of Forward Deployed Assets

Prepositioned stocks played a crucial role in sustaining of the forces deployed to SWA. The MPS that brought USMC equipment ashore provided the initial sustainment effort for the bulk of the first arriving ground forces, the 7th MEB and the 82nd Airborne Division. The ship's stockage stabilized the most immediate requirements for the initial wave of forces. In the 1980s, DOD established a Near-Term Prepositioning Force in support of SWA. This program began the storing of cargo on four ships which were be strategically positioned and moved to support CENTCOM contingencies. These ships proved to be indispensable during the first days of Operations Desert Shield and Desert Storm by providing a readily available source of crucial supplies to the AOR.

The war reserve cargo on these ships included

rations, general supplies and equipment, packaged fuel, construction and barrier equipment, munitions, and medical supplies. One semi-submersible HLPS carried port operating equipment including tugboats, floating cranes, forklifts, and utility landing craft. Those ships allowed CENTCOM to give priority to combat units in the deployment sequence. Together, the MPS, the Army and USAF's APS, and the USAF Harvest Falcon and Harvest Bare equipment that was maintained in theater, were crucial to the initial sustainment effort.

The Importance of Lift to Sustainment

In theory, deployment operations and sustainment occur sequentially and are distinguishable. During Desert Shield and Desert Storm, however, they occurred simultaneously. Units deployed with some limited organic sustainment, such as munitions, food, and fuel. But the scope of the effort demanded initial emphasis on deployment of forces and the sustainment of those forces already in or about to be in theater. Several features of the operation, such as the lack of ongoing hostilities impeding the flow of materiel, and the robustness of the receiving port facilities, allowed shifting emphasis between deployment and sustainment. During the early movement period, more than 25 percent of the cargo delivered by air was outsized, deliverable today only on C-5s. Another 60 percent was

MPS Unloads USMC Equipment in Saudi Arabia.

oversize, and, while not requiring a C-5, had to be delivered by C-141 or C-130 aircraft because it could not fit into civilian aircraft.

Additional cargo requirements during Phase II of Operation Desert Shield deployments required implementing CRAF II on 17 January, providing access to another 59 long range international (LRI) passenger aircraft and 17 more LRI cargo aircraft. Because of the number of volunteer aircraft, only nine additional cargo aircraft became available when Stage II activated. With the activation of CRAF Stage II, commercial aircraft operations grew to an average of 25 missions a day and represented substantial capability to meet deployment and sustainment needs. However, CRAF aircraft are less able to handle effectively the more demanding unit equipment that must be deployed and specialized loading equipment may be necessary for the most useful CRAF aircraft (wide-body cargo aircraft). Additionally, many civil air carriers frequently do not handle many of the large items or hazardous materials common to military deployments and special escorts or procedures are required to minimize the effect of this situation. Overall, airlift transported about 15 percent of all dry cargo and nearly 544,000 passengers in support of Operations Desert Shield and Desert Storm. Of this airlift total, CRAF and chartered volunteer civil carriers delivered 27 percent of the air cargo and 64 percent of the air passengers. Organic MAC aircraft delivered the remainder.

As was discussed previously, European staging bases were crucial to efficient strategic airlift. The forward basing in Europe of combat and CSS elements also speeded deployment. Despite the substantial Saudi infrastructure, another factor initially limiting airlift effectiveness was the lack of adequate ground equipment at some Saudi airfields. At the beginning of the deployment, Saudi sensitivities limited MAC to two main deployment bases. These limitations illustrate the importance of maintaining adequate overseas support bases as part of a forward basing structure. They also serve to highlight the need to give priority to pre-crisis agreements on the development and use of host nation infrastructure assets.

Throughout the logistics sustainment effort, early and accurate identification of lift requirements was difficult and logistics requirements were very dynamic. Close coordination by TRANSCOM, MAC, MSC, and the MTMC kept cargo moving. Overall, the APF response to the crisis was excellent, partly because the ships were so well positioned. The RRF responsiveness was slower than planned, but its reliability after activation exceeded 93 percent. The FSSs' large size and high speed allowed them to lift more cargo relative to their numbers than any other type of sealift. Problems encountered during some RRF ships' activation reflected shortfalls in maintenance and exercise funding in previous years. Improved maintenance and more frequent activations would improve RRF readiness. Because of the absence of a maritime threat, foreign-flagged ship owners were not reluctant to charter their ships to MSC to support Operations Desert Shield and Desert Storm. This reduced the need to activate the Sealift Readiness Program or to resort to ship requisitioning, which would have adversely affected the US maritime industry in the world shipping market. Finally, the extraordinary speed and efficiency of the entire strategic lift operation was aided considerably by the modern condition and large size of the Saudi Arabian ports, airfields, and contingency bases, discussed previously under HNS.

A discussion of the value of sealift in Operations Desert Shield and Desert Storm is incomplete without a comment on the status of the US Merchant Marine. Past traditional US focus on NATO has brought a feeling of comfort relative to sealift capability. NATO agreements make some 400 NATO merchant vessels available in support of a NATO contingency. However, in a non-NATO environment, the United States

found itself depending on the merchant fleet (which had dwindled from 578 ships in 1978 to 367 in 1990), Coalition shipping, and the world market. Foreign-flagged shipping provided more than 20 percent of the dry cargo lifted.

The FSS concept to improve force movement was validated during Operations Desert Shield and Desert Storm, and this validation makes clear the need to review Government-controlled strategic sealift composition. The focus of US strategy on rapid response to crises mandates rapid movement of heavy forces and sustainment supplies by sea. In turn, this requirement for speed requires reduction in time allocated for every aspect of movement including: movement to sea ports of embarkation (SPOE); loading merchant vessels; steaming time; unloading times; and movement to depots and forward assembly areas. Because of ease in loading and unloading, RO/RO ships provide a means to reduce transit times. The fleet is heavily oriented toward the break-bulk type ships. In this context, it may be advisable to change the composition of the RRF by increasing the number of RO/RO ships. Similarly, planners need to explore positioning RRF vessels at ports most advantageous to rapid deployment of key forces.

INTRATHEATER TRANSPORTATION

The intratheater transportation requirements that existed from the beginning of Operation Desert Shield were extraordinary, and with the initial deployment of combat forces, seemed overwhelming. The combination of an austere highway system beyond the main routes, and a requirement for massive amounts of inland cargo line haul, presented one of the operation's major logistical challenges, compounded by several factors. The first was the decision to delay the flow of CSS into theater until after combat forces arrived. The adverse conditions in the extensive geographic AOR was a second factor, while the change in mission in November was a third.

The flow of troops, aircraft, and equipment into the theater increased steadily. As each increment arrived, the demands on the intratheater transportation system increased disproportionally. More than 600 shiploads were discharged at the SPODs and more than 10,500 aircraft loads were received at APODs during Operation Desert Shield. Movement of these forces, their supplies and equipment from the APODs and SPODs to their positions in the field was instrumental in achieving combat capability. As distances from the port facilities increased, however, existing supporting infrastructure rapidly dissolved. This complicated an already difficult transportation problem. Essentially, two modes of transportation — airlift and overland — were available to move personnel, equipment and sustainment supplies and were not adequate to meet all requirements. Some commodities, such as mail, were delayed due to higher priority requirements for food, water, and ammunition.

Intratheater Airlift

Simultaneously with the deployment of troops from Fort Bragg, N C, C-130 transport aircraft of the 317th TAW from neighboring Pope AFB, deployed to the Arabian peninsula. This unit established the first intratheater transportation network in SWA on 11 August. Initially deployed to the prepositioned equipment bases in the AOR, the C-130s began immediate flight operations. They transported crucial equipment, ammunition, tents, supplies and construction materials from prepositioned stocks to the beddown locations, or initial operating bases, of the arriving forces. Within a few days, four additional squadrons of C-130s began arriving in theater to fly support missions. By the end of December, the 96 C-130s deployed before November had flown more than 8,000 sorties, amounting to more than 19,400 flying hours, transferring cargo and passengers throughout the theater.

It is important to note the limitations to the rapid

movement of personnel and supplies through the aerial ports. Throughput capacity — the rate at which personnel and cargo could be received and processed — depended on several factors. First, personnel, MHE, and the supporting structure had to be in place to cope with the massive quantity of arriving material and passengers. This task was accomplished by mission support teams from aerial port units deployed to the theater with the first airlifters. These units served the dual function of acting as the advance party in many areas, as well as providing service to arriving strategic airlift and the turnaround of intratheater airlift.

Another important factor for throughput efficiency was reduction of ground time for the transports. Ramp space was extremely limited, which severely reduced efficiency in terms of aircraft turn around times. Sometimes C-130s were forced to unload without shutting down engines, or to park off the ramp. It was crucial that cargo and passengers be moved away from the APOD as rapidly as possible to free the facilities for new arrivals. To get the forces away from the APODs, many host nation buses and trucks were contracted to supplement the available but overtaxed organic land transportation assets. (Details of the land transportation problems are covered below in the section on building the land transportation network.)

In the theater of operations, C-130s flew two generic types of CENTCOM support missions known as STAR and Camel. STAR (Scheduled Theater Airlift Route), a joint intratheater airlift operation, had the primary mission of moving people and mail among the operating bases on the Arabian peninsula. The Camel missions, in contrast to STAR, provided a daily cargo transport service throughout the theater of operations. C-130s committed to Camel airlifted cargo to destinations throughout the peninsula, according to regular airlift schedules similar to those MAC uses for its worldwide peacetime strategic airlift missions. Passengers were transported on a space-available basis. Camel schedules were planned to align the movement of cargo in theater with the arrival of airlift Express missions at the principal APODs, Dhahran and Riyadh. At the height of the buildup, 147 USAF C-130s were in theater. Of these, as many as 25 were used daily for Camel and STAR support at the peak of offensive operations.

The Navy operated its own Navy-unique Fleet-essential airlift. With five C-130s, seven C-2s, two US-3s, five C-12s, and CH-53 and H-46 helicopters, these airlift assets were used primarily for Service-unique support missions within the theater. In conjunction with four Naval Reserve C-9 squadrons (a total of 12 aircraft) mobilized in December and based at Bitburg and Sembach Air Bases, Germany, and Naples, Italy, these aircraft linked with the scheduled MAC supply APODs, the Camel and STAR delivery routes, and the carrier on-board delivery and vertical on-board delivery pick up points. Pick up points were in Bahrain, Jiddah, Saudi Arabia, and Hurghada, Egypt, to serve the Persian Gulf and Red Sea Fleet activities for shipboard delivery. Navy airlift assets also provided some service to support virtually all major logistics sites along the coast.

The 20 USMC active and Reserve C-130s also linked the principal MAC supply APODs and the USMC units. Based at Bahrain International and at Al-Jubayl, Saudi Arabia, these aircraft flew between theater logistics bases and the forward logistics bases in northeastern Saudi Arabia. CH-46s and CH-53s were links to the theater logistics bases, forward logistics bases, and the USMC forces deployed forward serving as the internal USMC distribution.

An episode that illustrates the importance of the intratheater airlift role throughout the operation is the forward resupply and movement of forces within the theater. USAF C-130s ran shuttle missions between staging areas and the logistics base along Tapline Road; aircraft used part of

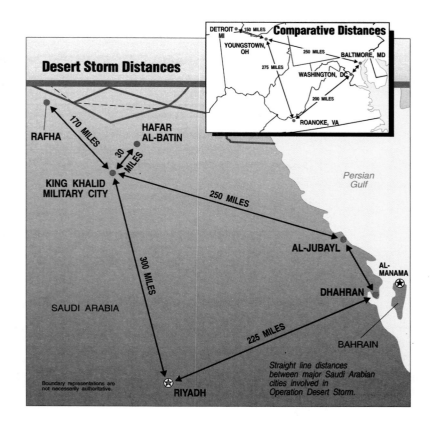

this narrow road as an airstrip. During the movement of the XVIII Airborne Corps after the air campaign began, C-130s at one point were averaging a takeoff and landing every seven minutes, 24 hours a day, for the first 13 days of the move from one of the rear staging areas near King Fahd airport delivering troops, fuel, and ammunition to the forward logistics base.

Building the Land Transportation Network

The movement of massive amounts of military equipment and supplies across the long distances was accomplished by coordinated land and airlift transportation assets. Throughout the operation, however, vehicle requirements far exceeded capabilities. The initial ground transport assets were provided from preposition sites in theater and the preposition ship, Advantage. In addition to vehicles deployed with the units, nearly 2,600 vehicles were distributed from prepositioned supply to support

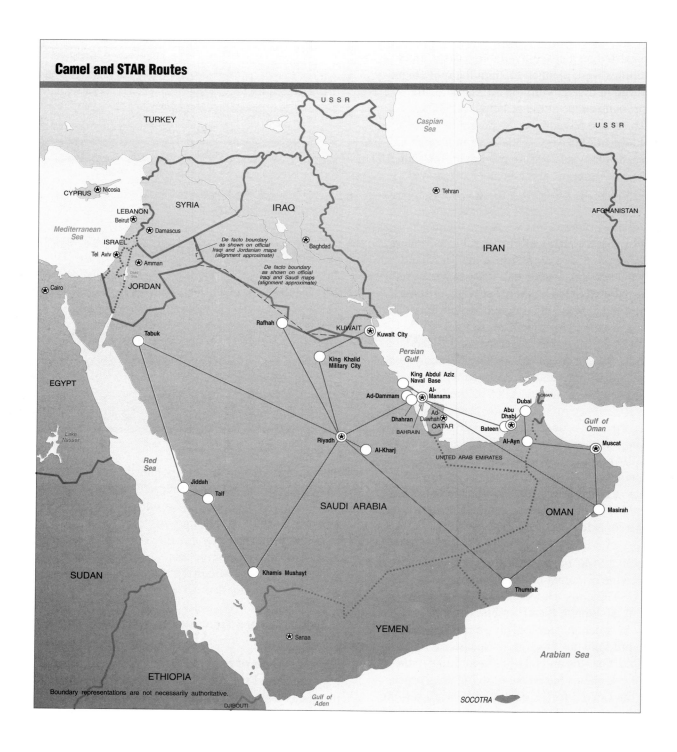

Camel and STAR Routes

the first phase of arriving forces. But the realization the available assets were being overwhelmed called for innovation by the small logistics staff. The oil industry uses large vehicles to transport heavy equipment to various well sites, and many heavy equipment transporters (HETs) and tractor trailer cargo trucks were available in Saudi Arabia. Many passenger buses also were available because of increased urban population and an expanding pool of expatriate workers. Efforts to increase quickly the ability to move troops and equipment from the port facilities involved on-the-spot contracting of buses and trucks. These contracting efforts helped fill the void experienced by the fledgling movement infrastructure.

The arrival of the Army's 7th Transportation Group to the theater provided some relief. Quickly folded into the provisional SUPCOM, some personnel were assigned SUPCOM staff duties while the remainder ran airport and seaport operations. The more robust staff was able to satisfy the immediate requirement of buses and trucks to get the equipment moved out of the port areas.

Good off-road mobility is required to move large forces and to keep them supplied over great distances with limited road networks common to many third world countries. To meet this challenge, Army combat units and their support elements were pure-fleeted (all vehicles from the same series) with the latest and highest mobility tactical wheeled vehicles. High mobility multi-purpose wheeled vehicles (HMMWVs), which could negotiate the desert terrain easily, replaced the older commercial utility cargo vehicle (CUCV). The older medium tactical 5-ton trucks were replaced with the newer M939A2 series truck with a central tire inflation system. Heavy expanded mobility tactical trucks (HEMTTs), with excellent off-road mobility, also were shipped to supplement 5-ton truck/trailer combinations. The HEMTTs were critical to the resupply of combat units with fuel, ammunition, rations and other critical supplies. The most efficient means to move armored vehicles over long distances is either by rail or by HETs. This reduces the number of mechanical breakdowns and ensures that crews arrive rested and prepared to conduct tactical operations. More than 1,200 HETs were required to support US operations during Operations Desert Shield and Desert Storm. In addition to Army assets, HETs came from

View of Tapline Road Landing Strip From a C-130 on Final Approach.

sources ranging from former Warsaw Pact members to leases from the US trucking industry. More than 4,000 trucks including HETs, flatbeds, lowboys, water and POL tankers, refrigeration trucks, and trailers were provided by other countries to Coalition forces in Saudi Arabia. These vehicles equated to saving the equivalent of 67 Army truck companies.

The magnitude of the transportation mission can be seen in statistics from COSCOMs on the movement of material by truck during the 21 days before the ground campaign began. More than 3,500 truck convoys — involving 1,400 Army and 2,100 Saudi vehicles — traveled

HET Contributions to Operation DS/DS

US Deploying	497
Commercial	48
US Trucking Industry	51
HNS - Commercial	333
Egypt	100
Italy - Military	60
Germany	181
Czechoslovakia	40
Total	1,310

more than 2,700 miles of MSR. These convoys logged more than 35 million miles and included more than 1,700 moves by HET; 5,800 moves by other equipment transporters (sometimes referred to as low boys); and 10,100 trips by flatbed trucks hauling bulk cargo. The figures convey only a partial idea of the nature of the transportation requirements. The fact most moves occurred on relatively unimproved dirt roads underscores further the nature of the Operation Desert Storm logistics challenges.

The newly introduced HEMTT and the USMC Logistics Vehicle System performed well in this mission, but there were not enough of them. Other trucks, especially those originally designed for long-haul, improved-surface use and without a true off-road capability, such as HETs and petroleum tankers, did not fare as well. Once the ground offensive began, many types of trucks struggled to keep up with the speed of the maneuver forces. While they were able to keep pace with the requirements — largely through the efforts of drivers and mechanics — the experience clearly demonstrated the need for more vehicles with off road capabilities.

In addition to the thousands of civilian heavy trucks, more than 2,000 civilian drivers were employed. The civilian drivers and commercial vehicles were organized into battalions with cadres of American soldiers. Concern about the reliability of civilian drivers when the war started prompted the SUPCOM to acquire from other US units within the AOR more than 3,000 US soldiers as backup drivers.

A similar problem the USMC encountered involved the large numbers of civilian trucks and HETs Saudi Arabia provided. As the USMC deployed close to the Kuwaiti border, civilian drivers became reluctant. The Marines assumed control of the vehicles, provided drivers, performed maintenance (learning as they went along), and developed a system in which repair parts were obtained directly from the Saudi government. Necessity and innovation enabled the Marines to keep this civilian truck fleet operational throughout Operation Desert Storm.

In transportation planning for conflict in other parts of the world, rail and inland waterways are crucial because of the large tonnage of materiel they can move. Ideally, railroad movement would play a major role in the movement of equipment and supplies. But because the only railroad was a single track between Riyadh and Ad-Dammam, rail transportation played a relatively minor role initially. Later during the operation, the rail line was used to move ammunition and containers from the ports to inland ammunition storage sites. Army water craft used coastal waterways to transport cargo from the primary seaports to other ports on the Persian Gulf coast of Saudi Arabia, moving prepositioned munitions and equipment or repositioning cargo for storage.

Because the deployment flow emphasized the early arrival of combat forces, ARCENT could not meet the demands for common-user land transportation. In particular, delay in munitions movements caused an excessive backlog at the ports. As previously mentioned, contracting and HNS solved much of the transportation problem. Eventually, more than half of the heavy transportation assets were either contracted commercial trucks or trucks provided by other nations. Japan contributed almost 2,000 4x4s, water trucks, refrigerator vans, and fuel vehicles. The commercial vehicles added crucial mobility assets to US vehicles and increased the flexibility and C^2 of many units. A large part of the initial HET shortage was nearly satisfied by HETs obtained from many sources mentioned earlier. These were crucial to moving forces from Saudi ports to desert tactical assembly areas, many of which were more than 300 miles away. Without these assets, it would have been very difficult to move forces quickly across the vast distances.

CENTAF also created a land transportation network to satisfy its requirements for support, dubbed the Blueball Express. In the early deployment stages, common-user land transportation shortfalls required CENTAF to let its own commercial long-haul contracts to support its operating locations. During this operation, CENTAF established an organic long-haul capability consisting of 200 USAF drivers and 100 leased tractor trailers and tankers. This system moved cargo, such as jet aircraft engines and aerospace ground support equipment, and repositioned some munitions and fuel resupply.

Naval Component, Central Command's) inland transportation needs were satisfied using established air and land transportation networks, and leased host nation trucks with Navy personnel escorting local national drivers.

Theater transportation was a success story. Though difficulties highlighted shortfalls in organic transportation for a deployment of this magnitude, the contracting efforts of the logisticians in the theater, the contributions of Saudi Arabian government and the contributions of many allies helped to create success. But while transportation was successful, the material distribution system did have some problems.

MATERIEL DISTRIBUTION SYSTEM

The materiel distribution system in support of Operations Desert Shield and Desert Storm, in general, performed satisfactorily. The systematic distribution of material involves a close connection between supply and transportation systems. However, as noted elsewhere in this report, the adequacy of material distribution performance was attributable largely to extended deployment time and large amounts of HNS that may not necessarily be available in other contingency operations. It also relied heavily on innovation of all Services' logisticians.

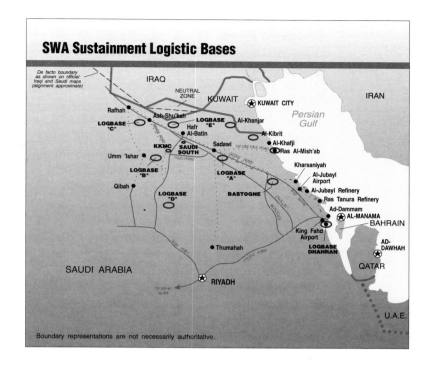

This section identifies some problems which, while manageable in Operation Desert Shield, could have been more serious under other circumstances. Among these problems were the lack of item visibility, ineffective use of containers, abuse of prioritization, and less-than-desirable effectiveness of providing some common support functions.

Item Visibility

Asset visibility means knowing the status of requested materiel at every stage of the process from requisition to delivery. It includes informing the requesting authority when the requisition has been received, the disposition of the request (e.g., filled or back ordered), and shipment status (e.g., date and mode of transportation).

During Operations Desert Shield and Desert Storm, asset visibility in the US wholesale system generally was adequate. However, visibility of assets while in-transit and in-theater was poor. This lack of visibility resulted in considerable confusion and reordering (sometimes multiple reordering),of the same itemsby field units concerned about existing or projected shortages of crucial items.

The problem can appear at any point in the distribution system. In the United States, vendor shipments — especially containerized and palletized cargo — made directly to the port of embarkation quite often were inadequately marked or documented. Shipments arrived at ports of debarkation with the destination classified or marked as Operation Desert Shield. Even if adequately documented, frequently pallets that contained material for several units were broken down on arrival in theater and reconsolidated into shipments by destination unit. This almost always destroyed any visibility that may have existed, pertaining to the pallet's contents. As a result, in-transit visibility was virtually nonexistent for some munitions, chemical warfare defense equipment, repair parts, and food shipments once they arrived in SWA. There were several reasons for this problem.

First, the materiel distribution system involved thousands of people around the globe in many different organizations,inventory control points, depots, vendors, and transportation agencies. This diverse system fed through air and sea ports of debarkation to the enormously complex and rapidly changing in-theater distribution system. The distribution system was confronted with units spread across great distances, constantly changing unit locations, often marginal communications, and early saturation of the ground transportation system.

Second, there was a lack of discipline in the use of the military's standard supply and transportation system. This resulted in a lack of status information, either through supply activity error, or a lack of necessary communications and automation capability. In the case of Operation Desert Shield, there were inadequate

communications and automation capabilities in theater to receive and process status and transportation manifest information.

Another reason contributing to the asset visibility problem was that manifest data received at water terminals was not shared quickly with materiel management centers because of the backlog that accumulated. Thus, there was a lack of visibility of materiel scheduled to arrive in theater.

Finally, RC port units and their MHE, including heavy fork lifts, were not among the early-deploying elements for reasons discussed elsewhere. This led to large materiel accumulations at the ports, adding to the visibility problem and delaying delivery to already anxious users.

Use of Containers

The improved efficiency available through the use of containerized shipments rather than break-bulk shipments is well documented. In Operations Desert Shield and Desert Storm, most ammunition was moved by break-bulk shipping because of limited availability of containers to carry ammunition, lack of containerized ammunition capability at the West Coast ammunition port, delayed deployment of ammunition units, lack of container handling equipment at the units in the field and ports of debarkation, and availability of RC CSS units to unload. Also there was inadequate container handling and unloading capability at some ports along the transshipment route. Inability to use containers delayed ammunition delivery to theater users because of extended loading and unloading times at the ports. It also resulted in increased use of inadequate land transportation assets.

Priority System

Abuse of the supply prioritization system (the system designed to give priority to crucial supplies, spares and equipment) was a problem. The Uniform Material Movement and Issue Priority System provided guidance on the shipping priority of parts as that priority applied to customer requests. The system was excellent in treating individual items but not quite as good in discriminating among large amounts of material. Further, the priority system requires review because it did not adequately recognize the need to return critical unserviceable items to the depot or intermediate repair facilities for repair. Ad hoc procedures were established to ensure high priority items were moved first. The return of reparable spares became important because support procedures depend on the repair and return of recoverable assets. Retrograde of these items moved well from the AOR to consolidation ports. However, bottlenecks occurred at Rhein Main Air Base, Germany; Dover AFB, DE; and, Charleston AFB, SC as pallets had to be broken down to move property to end destinations. The Pacer Return program was developed to alert transportation personnel of priority retrograde items. Pallets with cargo containing this project code were broken down ahead of other pallets. The end effect of the prioritization system used in Operations Desert Shield and Desert Storm was the abuse of high-priority requests, inability to discriminate among these requests, and subsequent movements of mis-prioritized items.

The current distribution system was designed to work under normal conditions using an established infrastructure such as that in NATO. The need to respond quickly to crises requires a distribution system responsive to requirements and fits well into regional crises' infrastructure; provides visibility of high-demand, crucial supply items; and allows for the expeditious movement to satisfy these needs.

CONSUMABLES STORAGE

The storage of consumable items posed another challenge for logisticians. The initial requirement was to provide storage for the large amounts of consumables entering the theater. The storage problem became particularly acute as the CENTCOM mission changed, the force and stockage objectives increased, and the ground distances expanded, requiring additional storage sites.

When the ground offensive began, 300,000 soldiers, 12,400 tracked vehicles, 114,000 wheeled vehicles and more than 1,800 helicopters required support. The development of the theater logistics support plan was integral to sustaining of these forces. A key feature of this support plan and its execution were provisions to ensure CSS assets were maintained well forward and positioned to sustain the attack's momentum. Chief among these provisions were the establishment of logistics bases. The logistics bases had to be able both to sustain the forces in their initial deployment areas and serve as intermediate storage areas for supplies destined to be forwarded to additional logistics sites, which were to be constructed as the ground offensive progressed.

In October, ARCENT SUPCOM established two forward logistics bases as supply depots and sites for crucial items including medical materiel, maintenance activities, fuel, and ammunition. These support bases were large by any standard, with perimeters as much as 80 miles long. The bases, Bastogne and Pulaski, provided storage sites for arriving materiel and allowed terminal service units to clear ports for incoming shipments. In December, ARCENT SUPCOM established additional logistics bases near KKMC. These bases were designated Alpha, Bravo, and Delta, and were to contain all classes of supply to support the XVIII Airborne Corps, VII Corps, and echelons above corps. Upon movement of both Corps from tactical assembly areas to attack positions, the COSCOMs and ARCENT SUPCOM established two new logistics bases, Echo and Charlie, to provide support during the ground campaign.

The plan for logistics support and sustainment envisioned forward movement of all classes of supply, but especially fuel, ammunition, food, and water. In preparation for G-Day, more than 29 million meals, 36 million gallons of fuel, and almost 115 thousand short tons of ammunition were transported forward to be in place 14 days after the air campaign started.

Initial XVIII Airborne Corps support was based at logistics base Charlie. As the tactical objectives were seized, support was echeloned forward to temporary logistics bases. Once the tactical operation allowed, logistics base Mars was established to support the remainder of the offensive, with the temporary logistics bases, now to the rear, allowed to dry up.

Initial VII Corps support was from logistics base Echo. Logistics base Nellingen also supported VII Corps through the end of the offensive. The maneuver of US ground combat units was successfully sustained from the preestablished logistics bases during the ground offensive.

The USMC placed a combat service support area (CSSA) at Al-Kibrit, close enough to the southern border of Kuwait to support an attack at any point along that border. The CSSA was fully stocked by 4 February with several day's worth of all classes of supply. The decision to move the USMC attack to the west required the movement of the USMC and its supplies approximately 80 miles to the northwest from Al-Kibrit. Within two weeks, a CSSA was created at Al-Khanjar. Al-Khanjar covered 11,000 acres with 24 miles of berms, and included almost 800 acres of munitions storage, five million gallons of fuel, one million gallons of water, a hospital with 14 operating rooms, and two C-130 capable airfields.

These logistics bases stored everything needed to supply the fighting force, from food, fuel, and water to bombs, bullets, and spare parts. The vastness of the area across which such a large

force was deployed required large amounts of consumables to be stored at Army and USMC logistics bases throughout the theater, as well as aboard MPS off the coast. Millions of gallons of fuel were stored in anticipation of the ground offensive. The forward logistics bases stored tons of ammunition, and acted as forward ammunition supply points with numerous clusters of several dozen ammunition boxes dispersed across many thousands of square yards. Also tons of munitions were stored at air bases throughout the theater. Munitions supply ships also were used as floating ammunition dumps.

The logistics bases also contained another commodity crucial to the sustainment of forces — food. The increase of the sustainment requirement to 60 DOS and the influx of additional forces after November placed a tremendous strain on the ability to feed the troops. SUPCOM's plan for feeding personnel involved a mix of two MREs and one T-ration, or one MRE and two T-rations, each day. The rapid increase in the number of personnel severely strained the the system's ability to supply MREs and T-rations. Troops never missed a meal. Sufficient supplies were in theater, including perishable foods for special Thanksgiving and Christmas meals.

At one time, however, inventory records showed supplies down to less than one DOS. Although adequate meals were on hand, there was no system that could maintain accurate inventory control or accurate visibility of available meals on hand. Innovative host nation arrangements to include contract kitchen support ensured enough meals were available. Other measures included contract meals in theater, and substitutes of off-the-shelf meals. DLA provided large amounts of provisions, peaking at approximately 20 million meals a month. These included bulk and unitized B-rations. DLA also arranged for substitutes of a commercial, shelf-stable meal called the meal, ordered-ready-to-eat (MORE). To further ensure sufficient meals were available, DLA depots assembled more than 48,000 pallets of tray packs. The tray pack consists of 12 to 36 serving meal modules of breakfast and lunch or dinner entrees, including accessory packets. As supplies increased, there was a 60-DOS of food in-theater by the time Operation Desert Storm began, including 29 DOS of MRE.

Fuel was another concern for logisticians. The overall stockage objective was 30 DOS. During Phase I of the deployment, the 30-DOS objective included five DOS stored by the Services at forward locations. An additional 10 DOS were held in reserve in each country at various depots, bases and refineries, and 15 DOS were maintained by the DFSC at DFSPs in Bahrain, UAE, Oman, Djibouti, Somalia, and aboard tankers under way in the Arabian Sea and Red Sea. However, additional requirements were generated by the increase of forces and the anticipated OPTEMPO increase as CENTCOM prepared for offensive operations. Against these additional requirements, the fuel storage capacity was inadequate. Therefore, several additional actions were taken to satisfy the 30 DOS objective.

To store the increased quantities of fuel, additional portable fuel storage bladders were deployed to ensure that Services could continue to store five DOS in forward locations. DFSC increased its number of afloat storage tankers in the AOR to increase capacity to the 15-DOS level. US negotiations with the Saudis resulted in an agreement for the Saudis to increase their reserves. Because all onshore facilities were filled to capacity, this agreement required the Saudis to position an additional one DOS aboard tankers afloat in the AOR.

Before the ground campaign began, DFSC stocks rose to 17 DOS. As a result, combined with the other stored fuel in theater, the 30-DOS stockage objective was exceeded. This provided a cushion and would have done much to sustain operations had storage or reception sites been

CREATION OF THE "WOLF BURGER." An Army chief warrant officer, handpicked as theater food service advisor, improvised from the beginning. The feeding plans involved contracting for Saudi operated mess halls with American-trained cooks in large troop concentrations. While adequate, the meals were not quite American; the chicken was cut differently, the seasonings were strange, and the general method of preparation was different. A short-order grill was created to serve hamburgers and hotdogs; to increase availability, barbecue grills were made from cut-up 55-gallon oil drums. Another ambitious solution was using a mobile food truck. The Saudis helped by providing a mobile kitchen on a recreational vehicle chassis — it was an instant success. The troops began calling it the Wolfmobile (named for the warrant officer), and the burgers became Wolfburgers. Both names stuck; soon more than 20 Wolfmobiles, some self contained and some towed, were institutions in the theater.

subject to attack. This level was maintained throughout the war. For the most part, fuel was distributed to DFSP, air bases, and logistics bases by host nation commercial assets. Army, USMC, and USAF vehicles distributed fuel from the logistics bases to units in the forward areas. C-130 and CH-47 aircraft also were used to move more than 300,000 gallons of fuel to sites as far north as Kuwait in support of allied forces.

Although the review of the fuel distribution and storage system provides an understanding of the complexity of the logistics sustainment base for the theater, other commodities such as potable water also posed unique sustainment challenges. Requirements for potable water were filled either through procurement of commercial bottled water or by the use of municipal potable water systems in various Saudi cities and military installations. These sources were to be supplemented by the arrival of ROWPUs. (Army ROWPUs were drawn from stocks on prepositioned ships, while the USMC used ROWPUs from MPS assets and follow-on shipping. Also, the afloat MEBs had additional ROWPUs that could have been placed in service, if needed.)

Upon arrival of the prepositioning ships in the AOR, both Services began to produce and to distribute bulk potable water. However, when the Army's prepositioned ships arrived, some reverse osmosis elements were unserviceable. This fact and the delayed arrival of CSS water production personnel caused an Army (and later an USAF) decision to continue to use the abundant supply of bottled water and keep the ROWPUs in reserve. As the ground campaign progressed and the forward displacement of Army forces continued, ROWPUs provided potable water in forward locations using water from inland wells.

The Army was tasked to provide six million gallons of potable water a day. As Executive Agent to provide backup water support to the USAF, Navy, and the USMC ashore, the Army used a combination of host nation water sources, prepositioned water equipment, barge-mounted ROWPUs, unit equipment, foreign donated equipment, and prototype 3,000 gallon-an-hour ROWPUs. To make the water palatable, the Army provided water chillers which, when attached to water trailers, could cool 800 gallons of water a day to 60 degrees F. The USAF also began to use ROWPU-produced water at bases that had no capability to provide potable water.

Operations Desert Shield and Desert Storm also posed some unique munitions problems. Storage requirements were extensive and facilities were almost nonexistent in Saudi Arabia. Although studies during the previous decade had identified the need for covered munitions storage, such sites were not available during Operations Desert Shield and Desert Storm. Therefore, field expedients were developed. In many instances, large caches of munitions were kept in their containers and covered with sand to provide protection. In some larger munitions storage areas, containers were dispersed and protected with berms. As the quantities of munitions continued to arrive during the later phases of Operation Desert Storm, large

quantities of munitions were kept aboard ships anchored in relatively safe ports.

Throughout the operation, consumables storage was a challenge. The quantities required to sustain a fighting force and the austere infrastructure for storage and distribution created unique problems. Limitations on refinery facilities for fuel storage required a great amount of HNS. Innovative procedures for both fuel and munitions ensured enough was available at forward locations in the theater. Contributions from the industrial base were significant to this buildup of the sustainment effort.

INDUSTRIAL BASE

Forces deployed to the theater relied on the ability of industry and DOD depot facilities to respond to new and increased demands. AMC let more than 23,000 contracts involving more than 1,500 contractors for nearly $4 billion dollars to accelerate production of crucial items and services to include munitions, water systems, repair parts, chemical and environmental protection systems, generators, maintenance and support services. Additionally, DLA placed more than 94,000 contracts valued at nearly $5 billion with more than 1,000 prime contractors to accelerate production and delivery of such crucial items as desert battle dress uniforms, chemical defense clothing, desert boots, MREs, T-rations, repair parts, equipment, weapons, and fuel. The Services also let millions of dollars worth of contracts to support forces deployed to SWA. Items procured included containers, batteries, medical supplies, repair parts, refabrication kits, nuclear/biological/ chemical (NBC) suits and electronic equipment.

Literally thousands of items were accelerated to meet increased CENTCOM requirements. From weapons systems to individual supply items, a tremendous demand was placed on part of the nation's industrial base. Items such as chemical protective clothing were surged from 33,000 a month to 200,000 a month, desert combat boots went from zero to 157,000 pair a month, and desert camouflage uniforms went from zero to 376,000 a month in six months. Many contractors were still ramping toward maximum capability at the end of February. In some cases, the production rate increase was the direct result of government action to accelerate an individual contractor's performance on an existing contract; in other cases, sources were identified and new contracts executed.

The phased buildup of support and short duration of the war meant few items were unavailable. Nevertheless, there were instances where some items were not available in the desired quantities. Demands for some things increased 20 to 30 times the peacetime rate. The industrial base generally performed well for emergency and accelerated procurements, but there were instances where industry was strained to the limits to meet minimum production needs. Not withstanding the remarkable production increases achieved during Operation Desert Storm, substantial time was required to achieve maximum production rates, even for some common, relatively inexpensive items. Table F-5 shows that six to nine months was required to achieve maximum production capacity for a variety of items. The time required to increase production rates of major items is greater still. For example, it would take 19 months to increase the AH-64 production rate from six to eight a month.

One example of industry's surge limitations is T-rations. The Army's field feeding plan relied on ample supplies of T-rations, which require only heating before serving. Although T-rations are the preferred ration, they were not in war reserve stocks in large numbers due to shelf-life limitations and low peacetime demand. Industry was unable to gear up production quickly enough to meet the Army's increased requirements. War reserve stocks of MRE and additional procurement

of B-rations filled the gap until industry could increase production. Substitutes such as the MORE-CT also were used to conserve MREs and T-rations. Although contractors invested in additional production equipment to expand capacity further, requirements still exceeded this expanded capacity. DLA acted to expand MRE and T-ration capacity even further through government investment in production equipment.

Industry's response to increased demand for desert camouflage clothing and boots also was delayed because the cloth had to be produced before the uniforms could be made. There was no specific requirement for these items until September, and no purchases had been made of desert pattern uniforms since 1986. Thus, a substantial part of the force deployed with woodland pattern uniforms. Within 30 days, more than three million desert camouflage uniforms were on contract.

Certain preferred munitions could not be provided in desired quantities because the industrial base was not able to respond quickly enough. This was the result of many factors, some of which include: the size of the industrial base for defense manufacturing; inability to reprogram emergency funds for munitions; and the difficulty of changing industrial priorities.

Among the more remarkable surge performances were those of the DOD organic depot facilities in accelerating the overhaul and repair of major items and components such as critical spare parts. These organic depots also installed major modifications to fielded equipment. USAF Air Logistics Center (ALC) at San Antonio, TX, accelerated 12 C-5 aircraft through its depot repair facility. This figure represented nearly 10 percent of the entire C-5 fleet. The ALC at Warner-Robins AFB, GA, accelerated depot level repair on 41 C-141 aircraft. Thirty-five of these were repaired in the ALC facility and six were repaired by contractor. By the end of the war, 70 aircraft had been accelerated through the depot repair facilities, providing the operating commands the equivalent of nearly 1,000 additional flying days.

In addition to complete aircraft, the ALC also increased repair of aircraft engines and engine components. The ALCs at San Antonio and Oklahoma City, OK, accelerated repair on more than 260 complete engines and more than 550 major engine sections. These overhauls involved procurement of more than half a million individual parts, in addition to the normal workload. To meet crucial wartime requirements, these engines were rebuilt 20 to 60 days faster than in peacetime by working longer shifts and accelerating parts deliveries.

Perhaps even more important than aircraft and engines, in terms of the effect on mission was the repair of spare parts and assemblies. To complete WRSK and provide resupply of crucial parts, the AFLC expedited maintenance on thousands of parts throughout Operations Desert Shield and Desert Storm, supporting the

combat aircraft, ensuring no shortages would occur for combat systems. AFLC also continued to support the routine requirement of an average of more than 60,000 parts a month.

The Army Depot System Command (DESCOM) dispatched more than 430 employees as members of materiel fielding teams to help inspect, repair, and issue equipment to deploying military personnel. Support was provided to units at Fort Hood, TX; Fort Benning, GA; Fort Drum, NY; Fort Sill, OK; Fort Campbell, KY; Fort Knox, KY; and many other sites. DESCOM personnel were at all deployment sites to help units achieve the highest possible combat readiness before deployment.

DESCOM's maintenance depots accelerated to meet expanded requirements and to ensure there were few shortages for deploying combat forces. One thousand temporary employees were hired and overtime was increased from seven percent to 20 percent. A few examples of this surge effort include the manufacture of 59 mine rakes for M1 tanks, in anticipation of the need to breach Iraqi defenses. Also, 800 replacement tracks for M1A1 tanks were assembled within two weeks; this required connecting 67,000 individual track shoes. Another major task was the retrofit of 70 M551A1 airborne assault reconnaissance vehicles with thermal imaging systems to give the vehicles advanced night vision capabilities and the fabrication of more than 200 M60 machine gun mounting kits.

Depot level overhaul of other items also was improved by increased overtime. For example, overhaul of AH-1F expanded from five to 30 a month. Also, the depots increased overhaul of VRC-12 radios. The normal program of 350 radios a month was expanded to 1,350. And finally, the depots increased overhaul of Patriot power generation units from 40 to 60.

DESCOM's supply operations also expanded substantially to meet Operations Desert Shield

Selected Production Surge Capabilities

Item	Pre-ODS production (per month)	Maximum capacity (per month)	Time (months) to reach maximum capacity
Desert BDU Coat	0	446K	9
Desert Boot	0	157K	8
Chemical Protective Suit	33K	200K	9
Nerve Agent Injectors	60K	717K	8
Sandbags	84K	326K	6
Tray-pack Rations	1.3M(meals)	4.7M(meals)	9

and Desert Storm requirements. Total ammunition shipments from August through March were 523,000 short tons, 3.5 times the amount of ammunition shipped during a normal eight-month peacetime period. Shipments of other supplies also were expedited. To accomplish this increased supply workload, DESCOM hired approximately 900 temporary personnel and rehired 800 previously released through a reduction in force.

Ship depot maintenance facilities also accelerated activities to support Fleet operations during the crisis. The facilities conducted pre-voyage repairs to ships to allow the vessels to arrive in theater in a high state of readiness. Contractor-operated depot facilities were called on for rapid work on deploying ships. On the East Coast, the Norfolk area was the most active, conducting unscheduled repairs to three battle groups, consisting of 25 ships, including three aircraft carriers; providing technical, material and on-site support for *USS Biddle* (CG 34) rudder replacement in Toulon, France; and normal support for two additional carrier battle groups in August.

The USMC depot maintenance activities at Marine Corps Logistics Bases (MCLBs) Albany, GA, and Barstow, CA, significantly increased their supply and maintenance activities to meet the needs of the forces deployed to SWA. More than 33,000 items were processed to support the USMC and other Services. These included the design, fabrication and shipment of armor protection kits for the D7G dozer and its operator, applique armor kits for M60A1 tanks, and bracket assemblies and cables to attach night sight equipment to the Light Armored Vehicle. The depots dispatched teams of Marines and civilians to SWA to support retrofit modifications to TOW-2A missile guidance systems and install tank applique armor. Also, the traffic management office, Barstow, CA, maintained an airlift challenge program that resulted in a cost avoidance of about $8 million.

The availability of sufficient war reserve stocks of principal items such as tanks meant there was no requirement to increase planned production of them during the crisis. Relatively low loss rates and the planned reductions in the size of the armed forces indicate there will be no post-crisis requirement for increased production to replace battle damaged or lost items.

Another indication of the innovative use of contractor and industrial base assets is the Joint Surveillance Target Attack Radar System (JSTARS) aircraft. Designed to support the AirLand Battle in central Europe, JSTARS was contractor controlled and had been used as a test bed in Europe during Exercise Deep Strike in the fall of 1989. Based on that performance, the decision was made to deploy JSTARS to Operations Desert Shield and Desert Storm even though the system had not completed developmental test and evaluation. The two available aircraft (a Boeing 707 airframe, designated an E-8A) flew 54 combat sorties with a system availability exceeding 80 percent. JSTARS detected and tracked everything that moved and some things that did not, including Iraqi concertina wire erected as a barrier across highways. The systems located, identified, and targeted assembly areas, POL storage sites, Scud assembly areas and missiles, convoys, trucks, tanks, and even surface to air missile sites and artillery. Linked with AWACS aircraft by the Joint Tactical Information Distribution System, and teamed with the F-15Es, F-16s, and F-111s, JSTARS denied the enemy its night sanctuary. JSTARS is scheduled to complete development and be fully operational in 1997.

WAR RESERVE STOCKS

War reserves are those stocks of materiel amassed in peacetime to meet wartime increases in military requirements until industrial production can meet demand. War reserves provide interim support to sustain operations until resupply began; stockage objectives are a function of, among other things, the threat and industrial base dynamics. WRM actually procured is a function of funding priorities. These materials are geographically located as strategically as possible, and at the beginning of Operation Desert Shield could be found in CONUS, Europe, the Pacific, and SWA, both ashore and afloat.

Use of WRM began when deployment started. APS with WRM were shifted to the Gulf area, and deploying USAF squadrons carried 30-day WRSK. Navy battle groups routinely carry enough material to sustain operations for 60 days (90 days for aviation spares). For USAFE and SAC units that would normally fight from their home base, WRSK support was not planned or procured.

Another impact of low WRM in the form of WRSK was the initial response by logistics depots. In cases where deploying squadrons lacked crucial components to fill out WRSK, parts were removed from another non-deploying squadron's WRSK. This was most apparent with the initial deployment of the F-15Es from Seymour Johnson AFB, NC Twenty-four aircraft made the journey and all were ready for combat only hours after arriving in theater. Some F-15E components even were removed from new, unfinished aircraft on the McDonnell-Douglas production lines. This early shortfall occurred because the aircraft was new and a complete stock of spare parts did not yet exist. However, the additional 24 F-15Es from Seymour deployed on schedule 60 days later, fully ready for combat missions.

A noteworthy accomplishment by industry for the war effort was the design, testing, and employment of the GBU-28 deep penetrating bomb which was accomplished jointly by the Air Force and industry. From the initial proposal for the bomb to the air campaign planners on 30 January, the bomb was designed, produced, tested, deployed and dropped on 27 February. Four GBU-28s were used during the war, two during testing and two against hardened underground Iraqi bunkers.

Eventually, all classes of WRM were provided from other theater (Pacific Command, Atlantic Command, and EUCOM) and CONUS stocks. Issues of POMCUS stocks from six division sets in Germany began in August with the shipment of 10 laundry trailers. Further issues remained limited until a decision was made as to whether these sets also would support unit rotations then under consideration. When the decision was made to leave deployed units in theater for the duration of the operation and to modernize them in the field, more extensive POMCUS issues began. For example, all 865 M1A1 Abrams tanks were shipped complete with machine guns and radios. Residual equipment was used to establish theater reserves. More than 1,000 HMMWVs were shipped, as well as HET and MHE not required in Europe to move the VII Corps and additional supplies to port. The air campaign was especially dependent on war reserve munitions stocks, particularly PGMs.

During Operations Desert Shield and Desert Storm the Army received stocks from 22 (43 percent) of its 52 operational storage sites, from every major command except Southern Command. These supplies included life support materiel, hot weather clothing and equipment, water support equipment, POL pipeline systems, desert clothing, rations, aluminum airfield matting, bridging equipment, aerial delivery equipment, and special operations equipment.

Operations Desert Shield and Desert Storm demonstrated the need for modernized theater reserves. The Army used six of its 14 prepositioned theater reserve stockpiles outside of CONUS and two of its three CONUS theater reserve stockpiles to provide Coalition forces with preferred warfighting equipment and munitions, such as tanks, trucks, chemical protective clothing, 155-mm munitions, TOW missiles, Multiple Launch Rocker Systems and Stingers. More than $469 million worth of clothing, packaged fuel products and repair parts was issued from US reserves. A major part of the T-Rations, MRE, and B-rations were drawn from theater reserve stocks.

The USMC withdrew approximately $345 million in prepositioned war reserve stocks from logistics bases at Albany, GA, and Barstow, CA, to support Marines in SWA. Responding in as little as two days, the logistics bases filled requirements for vehicles, armor, spare parts, clothing and more. Fill rates were greater than 90 percent for preplanned requirements and more than 75 percent for new requests.

Other types of war reserve material proved equally effective and necessary. These included the USAF Harvest programs (Harvest Eagle, Harvest Bare, and Harvest Falcon) for converting unimproved air bases into functional operating air bases; a Navy program that provides a capability for developing an austere forward logistics support base; and air and sea transportable Army, USAF, and Navy hospitals (in addition to the two MSC-operated, Navy-staffed hospital ships that also were deployed from war reserves). All of these systems make heavy demands on the transportation system and on engineering services for construction and support. (Engineering functions to establish bases are performed by Army Engineers, USAF RED HORSE, and Navy Seabees.) Often overlooked, but of crucial importance, were map and chart products to support deployed forces during Operations Desert Shield and Desert Storm. Operational requirements confirmed the need to review and update stocks of mapping, charting, and geodesy products. In addition to type and quantity, the usefulness of any WRM material is based upon its location.

The redistribution of WRM stocks during the crisis was a carefully managed process. High-level attention was necessary because the ability to respond to other possible regional contingencies was affected by the redistribution

of WRM. Since the end of hostilities, much attention has also been accorded the redeployment and reconstitution of these war reserve assets. US ability to respond effectively to future regional contingencies rests in part on maintaining adequate levels of war reserve stocks.

EQUIPMENT MAINTENANCE STRATEGY

Equipment maintenance was especially important in Operations Desert Shield and Desert Storm because of the duration and intensity of the operations and the adverse environmental conditions. The diverse weapon systems which were deployed, the degree to which the Services depend on the RC and civil sector for maintenance skills, and the Services' varied missions and respective maintenance strategies, required considerable diversity in how maintenance was performed. Crucial to the success of the maintenance effort in SWA was the support provided by EUCOM for both the Army and USAF.

Army

Recognizing the necessity to reduce repair and maintenance times, the Army created two maintenance activities in theater: one for ground elements and one for aviation components. The Army's maintenance strategy in SWA was in line with the doctrine of forward support maintenance, the goal of which is to maximize combat system availability by shortening the distance between the failure and repair points. This was accomplished by performing required maintenance at all levels according to unit capabilities. The current philosophy for ground units is to perform maintenance at four levels of increasing complexity: unit, direct support, general support, and depot. This structure was adhered to for ground assets in the AOR. Aviation maintenance, however, is performed at three levels: unit; a combination of unit and direct support; and intermediate, a combination of the remaining direct support and limited general support maintenance, and depot. Each division had unit and intermediate level maintenance capability, while each COSCOM had an intermediate capability to support corps and divisional aviation units. Intermediate-level maintenance also was provided at echelons above corps for aviation assets in or passing through the area. The Aviation Support Command established a Theater Aircraft Maintenance Program (TAMP) for all aviation units in the AOR.

The TAMP in SWA consisted of 47 military, 62 DOD civilians and 655 aviation contractors. It provided wholesale level maintenance and supply for unit level maintenance activities, contract maintenance, and backup aviation intermediate maintenance support. Contract field service representatives and AMC logistics assistance representatives were assigned to help units down to the aviation unit level. These representatives were in the field with the troops and provided invaluable technical expertise.

To augment established intermediate- and depot-level repair facilities, and to support crucial systems such as aviation, communications, intelligence, electronic warfare (EW), tracked and wheeled vehicles, missile, and tactical Army CSS systems, AMC deployed and operated several specialized repair activities. These organizations employed more than 850 AMC depot government civilians and more than 1,000 civilians representing 60 contractors. Specialized repair activities performed equipment modernization upgrades increasing the unit's mobility, survivability, lethality, and supportability.

AMC established the US Army Support Group (USASG) to provide a wholesale-level maintenance and supply system within the theater and to manage contract maintenance support. The USASG was tailored to provide selected general support and depot level repair. In terms of supply, the USASG managed high-dollar, high-tech, low-density items such as

avionics; reduced the amount of materiel in the supply pipeline; and, provided retrograde management. The USASG began operations 17 November, with the objective to repair 70 percent of the major assemblies in theater, to expedite return of repaired items to the supply system, and minimize the evacuation of crucial materiel from the theater. During its operation, the USASG repaired more than 34,000 components.

Air Force

USAF maintenance strategy is a modified three-level system. Most organizations perform organizational (unit)-level maintenance and selected intermediate-level maintenance based on ease of repair, or mean time between failure at the base level. Above the unit, depot-level maintenance (those repairs beyond unit level capability or economically unfeasible) is performed.

The maintenance strategy for units deployed to the AOR was based on this model. Units deployed with an organizational maintenance capability and a WRSK designed to sustain the unit for 30 days. Some intermediate maintenance capability was deployed to a few bases in the AOR earlier than planned. Though not available at all bases, all units had access to the capability through arrangements with a similarly equipped unit at another base. For instance, if an F-16 unit required intermediate repair service, parts needing repair were sent to a more robust F-16 maintenance unit elsewhere in the theater. Also, links to European maintenance facilities through European Desert Express enabled less robust maintenance units to acquire needed capabilities. For this reason, together with an initial lower-than-planned sortie rate and rapid resupply of parts, WRSK assets of many deployed fighter units were not used as much as anticipated.

Following the initial flurry to get combat aircraft, personnel, and basic material into the

AOR, the USAF began assembling the assets and dispatching supplies to sustain prolonged training and combat operations. Complex aircraft require equally complex test equipment to remain operational. Accordingly, dozens of aircraft test equipment sets were sent to the region. To augment deployed units, depots sent specialized teams to support units and bases with enhanced repair capabilities.

Depot combat logistics support squadrons (CLSSs) provided aircraft battle damage repair (ABDR) capability. Forty-two ABDR teams (39 active and three Reserve) were deployed to the theater to provide combat maintenance before the war and battle damage repair services after hostilities began. These CLSS personnel performed battle damage repair on 30 aircraft including an F-15, F-16s, and A-10s.

Also, to avoid sending sophisticated electronic aircraft components back to CONUS for periodic calibration, the Aerospace Guidance and Metrology Center deployed a mobile calibration laboratory (the recently acquired field assistance support team for calibration (FASTCAL) unit) to Saudi Arabia in September. FASTCAL measured the accuracy of repairs performed on the guidance systems used by almost every type aircraft in theater as well as many precision guided weapons, including the Army's Patriot missile.

Each Service used European maintenance facilities, and each augmented those facilities with uniformed maintenance personnel from CONUS. For example, the USAF designated certain USAFE bases as principal intermediate-level maintenance sites for particular types of aircraft. The largest of these was the intermediate repair facility at Rhein Main Air Base, Germany. At this facility, all major repair work for the C-130 engines was done. For SAC, a Contingency Intermediate Level Maintenance Center (CILMC) operation was established at Moron Air Base, Spain. The

CILMC provided full avionics and intermediate-level maintenance capabilities. The Army relied on EUCOM to provide intermediate and depot-level maintenance on many crucial parts and systems. USMC participation was limited to the temporary assignment of aviation maintenance personnel to augment the engine repair capability of the Naval Aviation Maintenance Facility at Naval Air Station, Sigonella, Italy. The USMC was able to draw on the pool of available engines to support fixed wing and helicopter assets in SWA.

Sand and dust affected operations, but did not stop them. Jet engine manufacturers helped define inspection points to detect calcium-based buildup in the engines' hot section. Experience showed this to be a very gradual process; however, it was not necessary to remove a single fighter engine for this problem. Nevertheless, due principally to sand induced erosion, the T-64 engines powering the MH-53 Pave Low helicopters had to be removed at the 100-to-200 hour point as opposed to the normal 700-to-1,200-hour point. Together with the Army and Navy facilities that repair these engines for the USAF, an interim solution was developed to ensure serviceable spares were available ahead of time. Increased activity at Navy North Island, San Diego, CA, the Army's establishment of an in-theater T700 engine depot; and MAC's dedicated transportation arrangements, kept on-hand spares ahead of needs.

Each deployed tactical fighter squadron also had a US Government civilian technician. This individual was assigned to a billet and served as an on-site technical expert, as well as performing liaison functions between the deployed squadron and the AFLC depot system.

Computer-dependent aircraft systems also required constant software updates to adjust to changing threats. Initially, updating aircraft software required the shuttling of magnetic tape and punched computer tapes between CONUS and the theater. However, 162 early production units of the Digital Computer System were rushed to the field. When linked to terminals in CONUS by a secure communications network, CONUS computer programmers could update software in theater through computer link. During Operations Desert Shield and Desert Storm, software changes were engineered, tested, and transmitted to tailor EW system information against the Iraqi threat environment. With this system, EW reprogramming elements in the United States could perform the reprogramming and incorporate changed mission data shortly after the receipt of new information for the USAF and Navy aircraft operating in the Gulf.

Navy

Operations Desert Shield and Desert Storm validated the Navy's ship maintenance policy and practice. Ships on scene initially and those that arrived later were ready for combat immediately. The maintenance system sustained this readiness while deployed and repaired two battle damaged vessels. Navy ship maintenance policy and execution supports its expeditionary mission to conduct sustained combat operations at sea. The Navy's mission is realistically and routinely practiced through local operations and deployments and self-sufficiency is a principle which threads its way through all ships' maintenance plans.

Maintenance actions are planned and accomplished within the broad Navy mission. These actions are conducted by a three-tiered hierarchy: first, each ship at the unit or organizational level; second, afloat and ashore intermediate maintenance activities; and third, shipyards for depot level. All three levels accomplish planned and corrective maintenance. Maintenance requirements are progressively assigned from each level as determined by ability and capacity.

The units and respective chains-of-command participate in all three levels of maintenance. Operations Desert Shield and Desert Storm required use of all three levels. Ships and submarines perform their own organizational level actions. Since operators of ships and submarines also perform the unit level actions, a fixed unit level maintenance capability is inherent in every class of ship. On larger ships such as aircraft carriers and amphibious assault ships, the capabilities to perform maintenance is considerably larger than the smaller ships. These assets contributed measurably to the Navy's ability to carry out the operation continuously.

Intermediate level is tailored for the size and length of deployment. Tenders and repair ships formed the backbone for ship maintenance during Operations Desert Shield and Desert Storm, as they do for more routine deployments. They moored near or moved with the warships to minimize the transit times to assist with or perform maintenance. The crews are military; they carried out the everyday tasks of repairs beyond the capability or capacity of individual ships, both on-board the tenders and on-board the ships. The tenders performed tasks such as rebuilding electric motors and pumps, and troubleshooting and repairing printed circuit boards.

These ships were manned and equipped to perform ship battle damage repair, but fortunately were not required to use it. Tenders also performed corrective maintenance on-board individual ships, which provided greater convenience for the operational commander. This was done by means of fly-away teams, or by traveling to the ship in need. These teams performed maintenance on a variety of systems from ice-making machines to guided missile fire control radars. One tender, *USS Yellowstone* (AD 41), based in the Red Sea for most of her deployment, completed more than 10,000 maintenance actions on 30 Coalition ships. These tenders were augmented by a unit ashore in Bahrain that consisted of a group of civil servants who were specialists in unique weapons and weapons support (hull structure, communication, electric and propulsion power) systems. These people moved to the individual ships to help and train sailors maintain these unique systems; people in this group rotated from CONUS; this ship support group averaged 30 people.

Planned depot maintenance cycles depend on the type of ship. Maintenance is scheduled at intervals that average 18 to 24 months. Depot work estimated to require less than six months is accomplished in or near the ship's homeport, if possible. Deviations from schedules are kept to a minimum to maintain program integrity and avoid workload disruption and associated additional costs. Only unplanned depot maintenance associated with the dry docking and repair of the two mine damaged ships was accomplished in the theater. These repairs were accomplished by Master Ship Repair Agreement contractors (private shipyards) in theater. In addition other, less complex voyage repair maintenance was accomplished by these contractors when the ships' crews or tenders were not immediately available.

In addition, Naval Aircraft Depots, shipyards, and Systems Command Field Activities sent teams, composed of US government civilian employees tasked for aircraft and ship repair. Those repair teams, with agreements to support other Services, also were available to provide aircraft engineering, inspection, and repair services to Army and USAF units. On average, the Navy had 500 to 600 US government civilian employees ashore or afloat in Operations Desert Shield and Desert Storm.

Naval aircraft maintenance varied little from peacetime procedures. Aircraft deployed with carrier battle groups underwent normal maintenance schedules and activities. Depot maintenance requirements were deferred, as long as deferred requirements did not prevent mission completion.

Aircraft Damage Repair (ADR) teams were formed and sent to SWA. There were 23 civilian engineers from the Navy depots and 108 contract workers at various locations both in country and aboard carriers to conduct routine depot-level maintenance and to repair battle damaged aircraft. Additionally, one ADR training team with equipment was sent to Bahrain to augment fleet ADR personnel. Each carrier/wing/squadron had a cadre of ADR-trained Fleet personnel to support repair requirements when needed. USMC aviation, however, requires both shipboard and ashore maintenance capability.

USMC

USMC aviation maintenance is conducted using Navy procedures, since USMC and Navy aircraft are intended to be interchangeable. Shipboard maintenance for aircraft aboard amphibious ships, such as helicopters and AV-8Bs, is accomplished with an intermediate maintenance block aboard amphibious assault ships. Some elements are a permanent part of the ship, while other elements are brought on board ship by Marines. USMC aircraft operating from Navy carriers are incorporated into existing Navy facilities.

USMC aircraft maintenance procedures functioned as designed during Operations Desert Shield and Desert Storm. Primary intermediate maintenance facilities were established at Jubayl and in Bahrain. Two TAVBs were deployed and arrived in theater in September. The origin of the TAVB concept was an innovation technique developed during the early MPS implementation planning as a means to deploy USMC aviation maintenance capability without placing a heavy demand on strategic airlift. Fixed wing intermediate maintenance facilities subsequently were unloaded to provide ashore capabilities. Rotary wing maintenance facilities were retained aboard the ships, which operated as intermediate maintenance activities while pierside at Al-Jubayl. To improve aircraft maintenance, the USMC also used an experimental Defense Advanced Research Projects Agency small communications satellite known as the Multiple Access Communications Satellite (MACSAT). Spare parts requirements and other administrative information were relayed by MACSAT to the 2nd Marine Air Wing (MAW) at Cherry Point, NC.

USMC ground maintenance is organized with five echelons of repair. First- and second-echelon maintenance is conducted at the unit level. Third- and some fourth-echelon maintenance is conducted at the force service support group level. Fifth-echelon depot maintenance is conducted at MCLB Barstow, CA, or Albany, GA.

Parts needed for maintenance are obtained from the USMC Intermediate Supply Activity (ISA) which links with an automated services center to order parts not on hand. During Operations Desert Shield and Desert Storm, the ISA was established at Al-Jubayl. As units deployed farther from Al-Jubayl, repair of essential combat equipment slowed due to ground transportation limitations. Rations, water, fuel and ammunition were the first priority for ground transportation. According to existing USMC doctrine, mobile combat service support detachments were sent forward to support regimental-sized maneuver elements. The parts delivery problem eased only when CH-53s began making several parts deliveries a day to support the ground equipment maintenance effort. Though the system was unresponsive at times, work arounds and innovation kept equipment running.

Each Service used maintenance capabilities appropriate to support its mission. The high operational readiness rates indicate long-term DOD investments in training, reliability and maintainability, war reserve stocks of repair parts and components, and deployable maintenance facilities were prudent. Equally important is the fact that high levels of combat readiness and effectiveness could not have been achieved without the experience and teamwork and contribution of the Active, Reserve, and Government civilians, and support from civilian defense contractors.

ENGINEERING SERVICES

The CENTCOM decision to adopt austere construction standards, the minimum required to sustain the forces in the field and support the operation, limited construction requirements and minimized the effect on host nation construction capabilities. As mentioned previously, construction support capability also was constrained by lack of adequate authority for quick accomplishment with O&M and military construction appropriations. Further, military troop construction capability was late developing in theater. Engineers were delayed in arriving since combat units received the lift priority. Facility requirements generally were satisfied through the use of existing host nation or leased facilities as first priority before turning to host nation contractor, or troop unit construction. Fortunately, the governments of Japan and Saudi Arabia were willing to provide contract construction support to US forces on an in-kind or HNS basis. Each Service provided crucial organic engineering capability that became the foundation for the ability to receive and process forces rapidly into theater.

The Air Force's Prime BEEF (Base Emergency Engineering Force) teams, RED HORSE (Rapid Engineer Deployable, Heavy Operations Repair Squadrons, Engineer), and Prime RIBS (Readiness in Base Services) teams were the key elements of base support that bedded down more than 1,200 aircraft and 55,000 USAF personnel at 21 airfields and a total of more than 25 locations. These locations ranged from bare bases to fully operational host nation bases. Approximately 3,700 engineers and 1,450 service personnel erected air conditioned tents, dining facilities, showers, and latrines;

established water and electrical systems; constructed air traffic flow control units and aircraft shelters in addition to extending runways, ramps, and aprons; and provided feeding, billeting, laundry, and mortuary services. During Operations Desert Shield and Desert Storm, the Air Force's Prime BEEF, RED HORSE, and Prime RIBS teams erected more than 5,000 tents; paved more than two million square feet to expand aircraft parking areas; constructed 39 facilities with to 192,000 square feet for munitions storage, maintenance, and warehouse space; paved roads; built more than 200 aircraft revetments; erected fencing; and built berms to protect high value assets that included Patriot missile batteries. This effort was equivalent to building a complex the size of Moody AFB, GA, complete with buildings, runways, parking aprons and all necessary facilities to support a wing of aircraft and associated personnel. Their most notable success story was the construction of Al-Kharj, the largest bare base ever built by USAF combat engineers. Working around the clock, forces built a fully operational combat base from the ground up in less than 40 days; it housed more than 5,000 personnel and five fighter squadrons.

Since some Saudi airfields were little more than runways in the sand, major construction had to be done to prepare them to receive modern combat aircraft. LANDSAT (a civilian multi-spectral imagery satellite) imagery of the area around a runway was converted into engineering drawings of the airfield sites. These drawings then were used to plan and build some of the larger air bases in the world.

Navy Seabees played a major role in expanding the infrastructure to support US force deployment. These units expanded airfields, set up berthing facilities, built ammunition storage bunkers, roads and defensive barriers. The Seabees also were responsible for building a 500-bed Fleet hospital and a 400-bed Army field hospital. More than 5,000 Seabees, including

1,000 from the RC, participated in Operations Desert Shield and Desert Storm. In all, the Naval construction force built 14 mess facilities capable of feeding 75,000 people; an Enemy Prisoner of War (EPW) camp capable of housing up to 40,000 personnel; six million square feet of aircraft parking aprons; four ammunition supply centers; and 4,750 other buildings. They also improved and maintained 200 miles of unpaved desert four-lane highways which were used as MSRs. These roads played a vital role in the Coalition's flanking movement.

MARCENT used two FSSG Engineer Support Battalions. Their most notable accomplishments were at Al-Khanjar and Al-Kibrit. At Al-Khanjar, engineers built 24 miles of berms in seven days; built the largest ammunition supply point in USMC history (768 acres containing 150 cells); built a fuel farm with a 4.8 million gallon capacity in 10 days; completed 26 miles of LOC to the Kuwait border; and built an EPW camp with a capacity of 4,000. At Al Kibrit, they built more than 2,000 bunkers and fighting positions; transformed a one-lane desert track into an eight lane MSR and upgraded an abandoned airstrip to handle C-130 aircraft.

Army engineers, both military and civilian, established and expanded the facilities to receive, lodge, and sustain US forces. One early deploying unit, the Middle East/Africa Projects office, Army Corps of Engineers, acted as the DOD construction agent. The organization provided in-country engineering planning, facilities design, construction contract administration, and real estate services for the theater. The unit included Army officers and civilian engineers, real estate specialists, contract administrators and construction inspectors. It leased facilities, designed and awarded construction contracts, and contracted for engineering services and supplies.

Leases totaling approximately $110 million provided: sleeping accommodations for more than 45,000 troops; maintenance facilities;

supply warehouses; cold storage buildings; and, medical facilities. Contracts were let for construction and for services and supplies including field latrines, field showers, helicopter facility sunshades, solid and human waste disposal, and construction equipment rental. Between the mid-October arrival of the first heavy engineer construction battalion and the beginning of the ground offensive, 11,000 military engineers worked in Saudi Arabia. In large part commanded and controlled by the 416th Engineer Command, Army Reserve (USAR), this force of active, USAR, and Army National Guard units built, upgraded and maintained more than 2,000 miles of roads; installed approximately 200 miles of coupled pipeline to move bulk petroleum; developed seven major logistical support bases in the desert; provided large scale electrical power to critical facilities; and, within 30 days, constructed four camps together capable of housing as many as 100,000 EPW.

As mentioned previously, development of theater infrastructure was constrained. Available host nation construction and assistance-in-kind from Japan helped relieve construction limitations US law imposed; however, it remained difficult to improve the infrastructure needed to receive and sustain a large force. This inadequacy emphasizes the need for procedures to trigger access to higher O&M limits and early activation of Section 2808, Title 10 USC, to ensure responsiveness of construction funding support to the combatant commander.

Construction management also required innovation. CENTCOM chose not to use the traditional construction management process and executed a new concept for regional contingencies. The result of discussions the weeks before the Iraqi invasion, the process, called Regional Contingency Construction Management (RCCM), provided a joint team of engineers with representatives from each component to help CENTCOM set theater-wide construction policy, priorities, standards, and

allocate crucial construction support. The RCCM concept worked well during Operations Desert Shield and Desert Storm, and is one model for construction management in future contingencies.

US forces' success in engineering services, supply, transportation, and maintenance, can be attributed to planning and flexibility. While existing logistics concepts were followed where practical, they were modified when needed to provide the most capable, complete, and responsive support for combat forces in the theater. Combat engineers built bases in some of the more demanding terrain on earth. Transporters moved many thousands of tons of supplies across great distances to ensure Coalition forces had what they needed, where they needed it, when they needed it. Maintenance kept the forces on the move, ensuring the pressure on Iraq never faltered even though the environment conspired to clog filters, contaminate fuel, and erode crucial parts on an around-the-clock basis. These accomplishments alone do not tell the whole story. Had it not been for the additional support Coalition partners provided, US forces would not have been as logistically well prepared to prosecute the offensive.

OTHER ALLIED SUPPORT

Another factor that multiplied the effectiveness of the logistics effort was the support provided by other nations. In fact this support was absolutely crucial to the rapid deployment of forces to the theater and it allowed the flexibility of deploying substantial amounts of combat power early in the sequence when risks were greatest. Had support in the form of host nation or assistance in-kind not been provided by Coalition partners and other responsible allies and friends, some combat units would have had to have been displaced by support units when that did not seem prudent. This sort of support was essential to US efforts throughout the operation. Food supplements, fuel and services provided by the Gulf Cooperation Council states were invaluable. Assistance in-kind provided by other nations was similarly important. An example is the 60 Fuchs NBC reconnaissance vehicles, provided by Germany, which filled an equipment shortfall that might have been crucial had things gone differently. Another example of support from other nations as well as an indication of NATO interoperability was the provision of 120-mm tank gun ammunition to US forces by Germany.

Other operations, such as those by KC-135 tanker squadrons, were supported from United Kingdom (UK), Italy, France, Greece, Egypt, and Spain. Fuel consumption in Spain increased 300 percent from peacetime rates. This resulted in a demand on the Spanish-owned pipeline system, which provides resupply to US bases and the Spanish private sector, that could not be met. USAFE officials negotiated with Spanish authorities and augmented fuel deliveries with tank trucks. At one time, as many as 60 tank trucks were delivering jet fuel, some of which came from refineries several hundred miles away. Additional mission requirements prompted a request by US officials for more fuel. Based on this request more Spanish pipeline time was made available for fuel deliveries at the expense of civil requirements.

Overall, however, the support received by the Coalition within the theater from out-of-theater countries presented a two-edged situation. No other nation had enough lift to deploy its forces or material rapidly, and only the United States had outsize airlift capability. This prompted numerous requests from Coalition partners for rapid deployment using US airlift. An example of this was the movement of the Dutch Patriot Batteries to Incirlik, Turkey, by US C-5s. However, adjustments to the airlift flow to support allied requests generally had a one-for-one impact on the delivery of US units or sustainment cargo. Although ammunition expenditures were low during the ground war, air munition expenditures were higher than most

participating allies had anticipated, resulting in shipments of US munitions' to UK air forces. But even without the large ammunition requirements during the ground war, high mobility still incurred great POL and maintenance resource requirements unanticipated by some Egyptian, Syrian and French units. The US-established supply networks to provide replenishment for these as well.

Foreign Military Sales

The need for US supplies and equipment highlighted another aspect of allied and Coalition support. This was the first time the US was involved in a conflict that required both the US and Foreign Military Sales (FMS) customers to be supported through the US supply system. While host nations and Coalition partners were helped and greatly influenced US ability to sustain forces throughout the area, their participation also placed additional demands on the US military supply system.

Participation by Coalition forces resulted in a tremendous increase in provisioning requirements which, for the most part, the US was prepared to meet. Since many Coalition partners had peacetime security assistance relationships with the United States, the United States had a military and political commitment to continue to help these countries. Peacetime US security assistance arrangements with Coalition partners, particularly Saudi Arabia, and with other non-coalition countries in the region, formed the basis to move military assets and helped build Coalition members' preparedness. In response, US military departments, in conjunction with the Defense Security Assistance Agency, activated a contingency team for expediting FMS cases. Working within the guidelines of the Arms Export Control Act, the security assistance community processed more than 350 FMS cases worth more than $12 billion for Coalition partners.

After Iraq's invasion of Kuwait, the Saudis' requested and received an emergency FMS package that included F-15 aircraft, M-60 tanks, and Stinger missiles, and was valued at more than $950 million. US ability to respond to these requests added credibility to the pledge of support to the region. Existing open-ended FMS supply cases were used to provide non-sensitive defense articles on a priority basis to numerous Coalition, NATO and other allied countries. The Special Defense Acquisition Fund (established to buy defense items in anticipation of FMS and to avoid diversion from US military inventories) provided approximately $130 million for defense equipment to Coalition partners. Under FMS terms, US stockpiles were drawn down to provide priority shipments of chemical protective gear for Coalition forces. Dutch-owned Patriot fire units purchased through FMS were deployed to Turkey and Israel to address Iraqi Scud threats. The Germans offered Patriot batteries to the Israelis. The German offer was never consummated because Patriot units ultimately were provided by the United States to Israel under emergency authority. However, the willingness of US allies to divert their FMS orders to the Persian Gulf Coalition was not unique to the Netherlands, Germany, and other NATO allies. In one case, Colombia contributed an FMS purchase of aviation parts, diverted to US military inventory, to be replaced after the war.

These relationships were supported by using security assistance and maintaining international cooperation agreements. Under the Foreign Assistance Act, Section 506 emergency authority, crucial Patriot units were provided to Israel and AIM-9M missiles and miscellaneous ammunition were provided to Turkey. Under Section 61 of the Arms Export Control Act, M548 cargo carriers, howitzers and Pave Spike targeting pods were leased to the UK for Operation Desert Storm support activities. Finally, reobligation-deobligation authority relating to foreign military credit financing was exercised to provide an additional $50 million of

credit funds to Turkey. With this increase, Turkey purchased TOW 2/2A and Stinger missiles.

The security assistance program and the FMS process worked well in providing essential support to Coalition, NATO and allied members. Peacetime cooperation through the US FMS system formed the basis for crucial military infrastructure development in Saudi Arabia and ensured most Coalition partners were equipped and trained on US-origin equipment, bringing a high level of interoperability to Coalition forces.

SUMMARY

Success does not preclude lessons to be learned, and the difficulties which beset the logistics support of the Gulf War should not be allowed to diminish the magnitude of the achievement — perhaps the most impressive short-term buildup of people and materiel in the history of warfare. It was an ambitious undertaking, and its complexity assured that, however well done, it could have been done better. The most important criticisms of the effort stem from the fact that more time was required to overcome the emergent difficulties than may be available in future crises. The most significant successes are attributable to the foresight of policymakers and planners, and the creativity and flexibility of logisticians on scene.

Most of the major aspects of Gulf War logistics included both strengths and shortcomings. Saudi infrastructure was invaluable as far as it had been developed, but was limited to a few major sites; highways were excellent where they had been built, but over two thousand miles of road construction was required where they had not. The tactical advantage of first deploying combat versus support forces, as well as the decision to stock 60 rather than 30 days of supply, had a price: they created backlogs which strained the supply system and contributed to the breakdown of user confidence. As a result, new procedures have been developed which will improve item visibility in the future and obviate the inflation of requester priorities.

The large number of participants complicated the operation, but the assistance of host nations and supporting CINCs was invaluable. The extraordinary distances involved in transportation and supply tested the Coalition's resources, but the foresight of forward deployed assets and innovations in the approach to strategic lift got the job done.

Thanks in large part to the prudence of previous years, there were sufficient supplies on hand to fight the war, and the US industrial base responded with imagination and alacrity to meet accelerated delivery dates for numerous specific requirements. On the whole, however, there was no requirement for a major industrial surge, and there were some indications that industry's ability to respond to a more protracted crisis might not match its enthusiasm to assist.

In short, the victorious participants in Operations Desert Shield and Desert Storm should congratulate themselves on the unqualified success of the outcome. They should also redouble their efforts to support the logistics of a longer war fought at shorter notice.

OBSERVATIONS

Accomplishments

■ The Coalition's logistics effort was unprecedented. Operations Desert Shield and Desert Storm used virtually every facet of the US military and civilian transportation system. The first-ever CRAF and RRF activation worked well; and the activation of elements of sealift, though not without problems, carried the sustainment effort due to its bulk delivery ability. And the wisdom of the previous decade to fund and develop a prepositioning program for the region proved to be a valuable means to improve combat capability half a world away.

■ To acknowledge the strengths and weaknesses of the logistics effort, one must first comprehend the scope of that effort. Despite organizational and systemic flaws, the innovative and dedicated people, both civilian and military, were the key ingredients that made the operation a success. The Services' logistics forces met all essential requirements without experiencing any shortfalls that turned into war stoppers. In those cases where established procedures and systems proved inadequate, logisticians developed effective solutions. This was accomplished for a combat force exceeding half a million people in the harsh, vast, distant environment of the Arabian peninsula.

■ Logisticians provided continuous support, despite the challenges of a distant theater half a world away; an expansive operational area with limited roads; demanding environmental and operational conditions; and a very complex force structure characterized by Coalition, Joint Service, Active, and RC forces.

Shortcomings

■ This operation highlighted some significant limitations. The decision to sequence the deployment of the service support units later in the deployment flow severely affected the ability of the Army to provide the common-user requirements for the other services. In some cases, even those logistics forces that did arrive were unable to meet all requirements, and CENTCOM had to rely on HNS to make up the shortages. There were not sufficient heavy equipment and petroleum transport, water supply units, graves registration, and theater material management units, even though virtually all in the Total Force were deployed to the theater. For example, 73 out of 108 (68 percent) of the medium truck companies in the Army's Total Force was in the theater; also, 28 out of 31 (90 percent) petroleum truck companies, and 17 out of 17 (100 percent) heavy truck companies (operating the HET) were deployed. Of more than 1,200 HETs in theater, only 497 were US government owned; the balance came from host nations and other countries. As force reductions are undertaken, the balance between support units and combat units must be closely monitored and controlled to ensure the national security strategy is supportable.

■ Operations Desert Shield and Desert Storm clearly demonstrated the Army had not yet fielded adequate numbers of high mobility tactical wheeled vehicles to support its armored and mechanized divisions. The new Heavy Equipment Transporter System, the Palletized Load System and the family of medium tactical vehicles had not yet entered production. The M939A2 5-ton trucks were in production, but did not arrive in sufficient numbers before the end of the war. The pure-fleeting initiative to replace CUCVs with HMMWVs in divisions, armored cavalry regiments and units operating in the division area had not been fully implemented at the start of the war. Current procurement programs will do much to correct this problem.

■ Wartime HNS was essential for rapid force sustainment and was a force multiplier. However, very few support agreements had been negotiated with governments in the region before 2 August. A concentrated effort resulted in completion of the necessary agreements. Early support of the troops would have been improved if effective HNS programs had been in place before the conflict. HNS may become even more crucial as US forward-deployed forces decrease worldwide.

■ Arriving personnel found a wide spectrum of facilities, from exceptionally well developed to extremely austere. It is widely recognized how the key APODs and SPODs facilitated the operation. While the ports were important to the flow of personnel and materiel, the limited initial ability to move troops and equipment away from the ports to their preliminary combat positions became a weak link in the logistics chain. Inadequate numbers of US organic trucks, especially those with good off-road capability, and a limited MSR network became severe challenges that had to be overcome.

■ Assistance in-kind made up for crucial shortfalls of equipment, especially HETs provided by other nations. There also were other items provided to US forces during deployment and Operations Desert Shield and Desert Storm that were essential to success, such as fuel from some regional Coalition partners.

■ The effectiveness of Army logistics automation during Operations Desert Shield and Desert Storm was substantially degraded by the lack of tactical communications support below corps level. Due to the limited availability of tactical communications support, CSS units have become dependent on commercial telecommunications to augment C^2 tactical communications.

■ The Gulf War did not (with some exceptions) provide a strenuous test of production surge capabilities. A general mobilization was not necessary, in large measure due to the existence of some war reserves for most items. There were some valuable insights, however, from surging in the production of those items which were (or potentially were) in short supply. The greatest demand for increased production was for secondary items such as engines, transmissions, spare parts, and troop support items, rather than major end items (e.g., tanks, aircraft, etc.). The need was for quick surge capability to overcome deficiencies in war reserves of those secondary items. The response by industry was overwhelmingly supportive and enthusiastic. However, in some cases, industry's ability to meet surge demands was marginal and could have had serious consequences had the offensive begun sooner, lasted longer, or been more demanding. For many items, the time required for industry to surge to maximum production capacity was six to nine months, even for relatively inexpensive, low-technology items, such as clothing, sandbags, and barbed wire.

■ In the context of the new national military strategy which emphasizes the ability to respond quickly to regional crises, coupled with an anticipated decline in defense procurement, even warm production lines are limited in the ability to respond to a short warning or short duration contingency. Response to short warning scenarios must be made with war reserves, plus what can be quickly produced by warm production lines. This suggests a need for balancing procurement of war reserve stocks with industrial surge capability, and making investments in industrial preparedness that would enable a quick production surge.

■ The present makeup of government-controlled shipping is not conducive to early force movement. The relative high number of break-bulk ships in the RRF, the rapidly diminishing number of merchant marine vessels and the merchant mariners available for manning the RRF, and the focus on rapid response to crisis situations require certain actions be taken. These actions include: evaluate the need for additional RO/ROs in the RRF and FSS; enhancement of the readiness of RRF vessels; increase containerizable materiel and equipment in Army heavy divisions; increase the overall ability of the force to move sustainment tonnage (particularly munitions) in containers; increase the availability of mariner crews; and finally, achieve the capability to provide visibility of what is in each vessel or container.

Issues

■ It is necessary to ensure that sustainment stocks meet requirements. An assumption should not be made that in future contingencies shortfalls in one AOR can, or should be, alleviated by redistributing assets from another theater.

■ Operations Desert Shield and Desert Storm acquisition and procurement experience indicates a requirement for additional study on the appropriate balance between war reserve programs and industrial base capability, and on the need to identify and fund surge capabilities, especially for crucial secondary items. Again, draw down of the force will have a significant negative effect on the responsiveness of the defense industrial base.

■ Prepositioned equipment proved itself invaluable. But improvement in the types of equipment and consumables stored, as well as increasing the quantities, would improve forces capabilities significantly.

Appendix G

MEDICAL SUPPORT

INTRODUCTION

Operations Desert Shield and Desert Storm were supported by medical organizations in Central Command (CENTCOM), European Command (EUCOM), Pacific Command and the Continental United States (CONUS). The medical support structure was tailored to meet the command's needs based on the number of troops in the theater and the Commander-in-Chief, Central Command's (CINCCENT) casualty estimates for various types of combat operations.

Medical units from all Services began deployment to Southwest Asia (SWA) on 8 August. As the deployed force's mission evolved from deterrence to offensive operations, medical support requirements expanded. Beds also were provided by EUCOM and through host nation support (HNS) agreements with Saudi Arabia, Bahrain, United Arab Emirates (UAE), Qatar, and Oman. Additionally, requirements for extensive health services in the United States emerged with the decision to retain full medical care for military members and their dependents worldwide.

Immediately after Operation Desert Shield began, Forces Command was directed to develop a concept of operations to execute the Integrated CONUS Medical Mobilization Plan (ICMMP), which would ensure the Services were prepared to care for casualties evacuated from the Theater to the CONUS. Had it been necessary, the Department of Veterans Affairs (VA) and Department of Defense (DOD) Health Resources Sharing and Emergency Operations Act could have been implemented. DOD also

"It was the fastest mobilization of medical assets in history — we did in three months what took us three years in Korea."

Lieutenant General Frank F. Ledford, Jr.
Army Surgeon General

was prepared to request activation of the National Disaster Medical System (NDMS) to augment DOD and VA capacity.

Although the actual operational situation ultimately required the use of only a small part of the available assets, a detailed description of how the medical system was organized to meet the medical needs of the forces is, nevertheless, instructive. This appendix discusses the doctrine for and the application of health care in support of Operations Desert Shield and Desert Storm.

Overview of Health Service Support Concept

The joint health service support (HSS) mission is to minimize the effects of disease, injuries, and wounds on unit readiness, effectiveness, and morale. The HSS system used in Operations Desert Shield and Desert Storm was an outgrowth of existing Service and joint operations procedures. While the SWA environment and operational requirements were unique, medical care nonetheless was planned, arranged, and delivered through optimum use and integration of component command HSS resources, along the lines established by each Service for health service support. This mission was accomplished using a phased health-care system that begins with those measures taken near where initial disability occurs and extends through evacuation from the theater for treatment at a CONUS hospital. The system's effectiveness is measured by its ability to return patients to duty quickly and as far forward in the theater as possible, while minimizing morbidity and mortality. Through application of HSS principles and use of the levels of care, requirements for replacement personnel, patient evacuation, and logistics support were minimized.

Patient Care and Movement

Progression through the health care system is determined by the nature of the disability. For example, patients with minor wounds may not be evacuated through all levels of health care and are returned to duty after treatment at the lowest level that meets the patient's needs. The patient's condition, threat, time, distance, and terrain are considered when the evacuation mode is selected. Centralized evacuation management procedures match the patient's condition and urgency of movement with the transport method. In the forward area, treatment facilities are not bypassed unless the patient has been treated at a medical treatment facility (MTF) and stabilized for flight or ground transportation. These facilities also provide the opportunity to refine further and designate the transportation mode for evacuation to the rear.

Movement of casualties from one level of care to the next in the forward area usually is done within hours. Distances and times vary with the tactical situation, but casualties quickly travel between the battlefront and hospitals. Modern concepts of increased mobility, as well as the vulnerability of rear areas to aerial or missile attacks, require all medical units, wherever located, be prepared to receive and treat casualties.

The health care operations described below for the Army outline the Joint doctrinal health service concept all Services use. While the concept highlights the Army's theater health

service operations, it also provides a description of the levels, or echelons, of care each Service used. In their inception, care levels and HSS principles did not specifically address joint or combined operations as experienced during Operations Desert Shield and Desert Storm. Their implementation, however, is common among the Services and applies to HSS planning and execution by joint force commanders. Joint operation HSS is continuous planning, coordination, and training by the Services to achieve unified health care. While each Service brings unique capabilities and requirements to a theater, the single joint doctrine provides for more effective HSS application. The Army operations section below describes the joint HSS care levels and principles; it is typical of the entire theater HSS concept. Each Service's unique HSS aspects are described separately.

Army Health Services Operations

HSS within a theater is organized into levels which extend throughout the theater. Each level is designed to meet the needs of the operational environment and play a specific part in the progressive, phased treatment, hospitalization, and evacuation of casualties. Each succeeding support level has the same treatment capabilities as those levels more forward, and adds a new level, or increment, of treatment which sets it apart from the previous level. (Echelon of care can be used interchangeably with the term level of care.) Medical resources are tailored to provide the greatest benefit to the largest number of persons within the theater.

Joint Services health care is provided in five levels. This system treats and evacuates patients from forward theater areas to hospitals that match patient treatment needs. Level I medical support is provided by individual soldiers; by specifically trained individuals; or by elements organic to combat, combat support (CS), and designated medical units. Emphasis is placed on emergency lifesaving measures to stabilize and allow evacuation of the patient to the next level of care. Level I medical support also includes medical evacuation from supported units to a higher level of medical treatment.

Level II care is given at division or Corps clearing stations. Level II functions are performed typically by company-sized medical units at brigades, in divisions, and by similar units in the corps and theater rear area. These Level II units are located in the Brigade Support Area (BSA), Division Support Area (DSA), Corps Support Area, and the Theater rear area. An initial surgical capability is organic to these units in airborne and air assault divisions. Other types of divisions are augmented with surgical capability as the combat situation requires. At this level, the casualty is more closely examined. Wounds and general status are evaluated to determine priority for further care or evacuation. Emergency care, including basic resuscitation and stabilization, is continued. If necessary, additional emergency measures are instituted; however, these measures generally do not go beyond immediate treatment.

In Level III care, the casualty is treated in a MTF staffed and equipped to provide resuscitation, initial wound surgery, and postoperative treatment. Casualties whose wounds are life-threatening receive surgical care in a hospital close to the clearing station. Those whose injuries permit additional transportation without detriment receive surgical care in a hospital farther to the rear. Hospitalization at this level is provided by the Mobile Army Surgical Hospital (MASH), the Combat Support Hospital (CSH), and the Evacuation (EVAC) Hospital. The MASH provides intensive care for up to 60 patients. The CSH provides intensive, intermediate, and minimal care for up to 200 patients (40 intensive care, 80 intermediate care, and 80 minimal care). The EVAC hospital provides intensive, intermediate, and minimal care for up to 400 patients (40 intensive care, 160 intermediate care, and 200 minimal care).

In Level IV medical care, the casualty is treated

An Army Deployable Medical Systems Hospital.

in a MTF staffed and equipped for general, specialty, and surgical care and reconditioning rehabilitation for return to duty. Hospitalization at this level is provided by the field hospital (which also may be part of Level III treatment facilities if the situation warrants), the station hospital, and the general hospital. To provide flexibility, the field hospital can be divided into three hospital units, which can operate at separate locations for a limited time. The field hospital can accommodate up to 400 patients, or each hospital unit up to 100 at a time. Station and general hospitals have no fixed size.

In Level V, further HSS is found in CONUS, and available for this crisis, EUCOM hospitals. Normally, mobilization requires the expansion of peacetime military hospital capacities, but does not include the peacetime level of care for all eligible, non-active duty beneficiaries. It also includes VA and civilian hospital beds to meet the increased specialized requirements (e.g., burns and spinal injury) of patients evacuated from the theater. This level is usually associated with long term reconstructive, rehabilitative, or more definitive care.

Some medical care facilities have the ability to relocate, should this be necessary. These units can move relatively rapidly to sustain the force. In some cases, small HSS units operate independently. In other cases, HSS units shift to react to the flow of the battle or to meet requirements for unit reconstitution.

Forward combat unit reconstitution is accomplished in part through the return to duty rate of casualties. Should medical units require reconstitution, resources normally come from the next higher HSS level. Each level is designed to reconstitute, within limits, the next lower level. Cross-leveling of medical assets, or the supplementing of one unit that is short personnel or equipment with that of another unit, also may permit reconstitution and reinforcement. Cross-leveling actions are done with every expectation that the units will be replenished as soon as additional personnel or equipment is made available.

Patient Movement

To speed the movement of casualties to the more comprehensive medical care available back from the forward line of troops, ground ambulance capability is supplemented by aeromedical evacuation assets. The Air Ambulance Company has 15 helicopters, each able to evacuate litter and ambulatory patients and is a Corps medical asset. Its main role is to provide aeromedical evacuation support within the Corps area and in direct support of divisions. Aeromedical evacuation elements locate with medical companies in the BSA and DSA to evacuate patients to Corps hospitals. These aircraft operate as far forward as the tactical situation permits. (Individual aircraft may operate beyond friendly lines in support of special operations or unique mission requirements.) The Air Ambulance Detachment, another aeromedical evacuation unit, is a small, flexible aeromedical organization with six helicopters, each able to evacuate litter and ambulatory patients. It can be used in the Corps area in a role similar to the Air Ambulance

Company, or in the theater rear area to transfer patients between hospitals or to Air Force Aeromedical Staging Facilities.

Navy Health Service Operations

While subscribing to joint concepts, the Navy maintains the capability to provide medical care on board each ship. HSS operations during hostilities are much the same as peacetime procedures. As a combat theater is established, the Navy component commander determines additional requirements for health care based on the theater commander-in-chief's (CINC's) operational plan and the population at risk. Factors which are considered include the requirement for higher levels of care to support combat operations, size of the Marine Corps (USMC) forces deployed in theater, size of the fleet, and operating tempo. The CINC staff then designates the Primary Casualty Receiving and Treatment Ships (PCRTS), deployable fleet hospitals, hospital ships, and coordinates the manning and transportation of the medical and dental treatment units. The Navy also augments USMC Level I and II medical units as required. All Navy PCRTSs are Level II medical support capable and their beds are considered flow-through beds. Simultaneously, the Navy staff coordinates the movement of the required equipment sets, such as Fleet Hospitals, with the supporting Navy component command for deployment to the theater.

Navy medical platforms and units deployed to SWA with a full complement of capabilities. The hospital ships USNS Comfort and USNS Mercy are dedicated afloat MTFs, providing Level III care. The hospital ships each have 1,000 beds; of these, 500 are acute care and 500 are minimal care. The acute care beds consist of 80 intensive care units, 20 recovery, 280 intermediate, and 120 light-care beds. The minimal care beds generally are for post-treatment wound care, follow-up diagnostic procedures, and minimal nursing care. The shore-based Fleet hospitals are transportable medical facilities designed for rapid deployment and assembly in the field. They each have 500 beds; of these 80 are intensive care and 420 are acute care. The amphibious assault ships have a secondary role to the Fleet as Casualty Receiving and Treatment Ships. During an amphibious assault, these ships perform the PCRTS role for the combat troops.

In the USMC, as in each of the Services, Level I care is provided by individual hospital corpsmen and medical elements organic to combat and combat support units, such as battalion-level aid stations. Level II care is provided by units of the Medical Battalion of the Force Service Support Group. Within each medical battalion are surgical support companies and collection and clearing companies. The mission of the surgical support company is to provide general medical support to the Marine Expeditionary Force (MEF). Each company has five operating rooms and 150 flow-through beds. The mission of the collecting and clearing company is to provide direct medical support to the MEF and has two operating rooms and 60 flow-through beds. The USMC is dependent on the Navy for medical care above Echelon II.

Air Force Health Service Operations

The Air Force (USAF) concept of operations for deployed medical support also conforms with joint doctrine and closely parallels the methodology used for peacetime health care. Initial medical support (Level I and II treatment) at deployment locations is provided by air transportable clinics (ATC) and preexisting medical facilities. Each ATC contains first aid and emergency medical supplies and is staffed by a squadron medical element consisting of a flight surgeon and three technicians. An ATC is assigned to and supports each combat flying squadron and is an integral part of the deployment package. Level III and higher care for combat or prolonged deployment in an underdeveloped region requires the more

USNS Mercy and *USNS Comfort* Hospital Ships were deployed to Southwest Asia.

sophisticated medical services of an air transportable hospital (ATH), or large contingency hospital.

A complete ATH is capable of delivering surgical, X-ray, and laboratory services; blood storage; medical and dental outpatient services; and beds for 50 patients. Each hospital is designed to meet the medical needs of a deployed fighter wing with more than 4,000 people. Most ATHs are attached to CONUS-based fighter wings for rapid deployment where needed. Expansion packages are available to increase the ATH's surgical capability. Patient decontamination teams often deploy with ATHs to manage chemical casualties.

Preestablished medical facilities in theater (active or warm bases) also can be expanded and staffed by host nation support (HNS) or manpower packages from CONUS to provide increased medical capability. Contingency hospitals, ranging from 250 to 1,500 beds, are prepositioned primarily in the European and Pacific theaters and are prepared for rapid activation. They offer a wide range of sophisticated medical services and represent the final provider of medical care before evacuation to CONUS.

This 50-bed Air Transportable Hospital was Assembled and Fully Operational Within 24 hours of Arrival in Saudi Arabia.

The Military Airlift Command, assisted by USAF aeromedical evacuation and staging teams, and medical evacuation units from the Army and Navy, establishes a coordinated, multi-theater aeromedical evacuation system for casualties. Medically configured C-130 aircraft normally are used for dedicated evacuation flights within the theater, while both dedicated and other available C-141s evacuate patients to facilities outside the theater and to CONUS. (The theater evacuation policy, established in planning guidance, determines whether patients are retained for treatment in theater or evacuated to CONUS.)

In CONUS, active duty and Air Reserve Component units and personnel provide support to deploying medical units and expand CONUS hospitals identified for casualty reception. According to current planning concepts, medical care at most CONUS facilities normally would be scaled back to serve principally active duty personnel. VA and NDMS facilities also are available on call to treat patients returning from theater.

Veterinary Services

Another important part of HSS is the veterinary service. It provides for control of zoonotic diseases, care and control of local and DOD-owned animals (e.g. working dogs), veterinary laboratory support, and inspection and laboratory examination of subsistence items for wholesomeness and quality. A key contribution of veterinary services for fielded combat forces is inspecting facilities that supply, store, and issue subsistence items. This, in conjunction with the responsibility for inspection of all subsistence items after exposure to chemical or biological warfare (CW/BW), is a crucial role in a theater of operations.

OPERATIONS DESERT SHIELD AND DESERT STORM

During the early phases of Operation Desert Shield, the CENTCOM Surgeon established a requirement for 7,350 hospital beds in theater with an additional 5,500 beds in EUCOM, a requirement that remained constant until offensive operations planning began. CENTCOM also identified a requirement for 17,000-to-22,000 beds in CONUS.

When the decision was made to augment the forces in theater to provide an offensive capability, medical requirements were adjusted accordingly. In-theater bed requirements increased to 18,530, of which 4,600 were to be provided by host nations with staffing or augmentation provided by US military personnel. When the air campaign began on 17 January, 7,680 fully staffed beds were in the CENTCOM AOR and 6,160 were operational. (Fully staffed beds means all required personnel are in place, but not all equipment is set up; operational means all personnel are in place and facilities fully set up.) The full complement of beds was available in EUCOM, but they awaited augmentation of selected medical providers to become fully operational. When the land campaign began on 24 February, all assets to support the 18,530-bed requirement were in-theater and 15,430 beds were operational. To retain an appropriate degree of flexibility,

Bed Capacity of Medical Assets in CENTCOM by Month[1]

	Aug 15	Sep 15	Oct 15	Nov 15	Dec 15	Jan 15	Feb 15
USAF	100	300	450	450	450	750	950
USN	0	1,500	1,500	1,500	1,500	1,500	3,500
USA	0	600	660	1,460	1,860	4,460	9,480[2]
HNS	350	350	350	500	500	500	4,600[3]
Total	450	2,750	2,960	3,910	4,310	7,210	18,530

Notes: [1] These figures represent fully staffed and equipped beds in theater, but are not necessarily total operational beds.

[2] Containerized equivalent of more than 3,100 beds were loaded on trucks to deploy to casualty concentrations as required. On 26 February, Day 3 of the ground war, several hospitals still were enroute to their objectives when the cease fire was issued. At that time, there were enough hospital beds operational in theater to support the workload. 1,933 beds remained uploaded to support contingency operations.

[3] After extensive negotiations, 4,100 were HNS beds staffed by Army personnel and 500 were provided by host nations with staffing augmentation provided by the Navy.

however, the remaining beds were kept loaded in containers on trucks to follow the combat forces forward.

EUCOM's 5,500 bed requirement was provided by both the USAF and Army. EUCOM identified the personnel from the United States that would be required to augment their staff, and those required to activate EUCOM's prepositioned contingency hospitals in order to support CENTCOM requirements. CINCCENT decided to delay until January the full manning of facilities in EUCOM for CENTCOM support.

In addition to mobilization to support CENTCOM, medical personnel were mobilized to support CONUS facilities. Some of these personnel were used to expand capacity to treat casualties returned to the United States. Primary receiving hospitals were designated and received priority for augmentation. Other

medical personnel were used to maintain peacetime levels of health care for non-deployed personnel and military dependents (including those of activated reservists). The latter requirement was unanticipated. Before the crisis, DOD planning guidance for contingencies assumed that civilians and CHAMPUS would provide care when mobilization occurred. When the crisis began, however, the Department decided to maintain full peacetime levels of service at military medical facilities for service members and their families (including families of activated reservists) as one means of providing the maximum degree of support possible for their efforts; but not all RC beneficiaries are near military facilities and many did not understand CHAMPUS. Both factors hindered the rapid filing and settlement of claims.

In some instances, units were tailored so only

direct care personnel (i.e. physicians, nurses, dentists) were called up for this purpose, while the augmentation units for hospitals as a whole were not always activated. Generally, units were not aware their personnel would be recalled incrementally and the procedure led to some morale problems. (A discussion of the mobilization of Reservists is contained in Appendices E and H.)

CONUS OPERATIONS

Acting for the National Command Authorities, the Chairman of the Joint Chiefs of Staff directed the Commander-in-Chief, Forces Command (CINCFOR) to prepare for possible implementation of the ICMMP. This plan integrates the existing Service medical mobilization plans, which govern use of CONUS medical resources to care for returning casualties. Difficulties in the planning process resulted in some confusion and demonstrated the need for closer coordination between CINCFOR and the Services.

To avoid premature activation of the NDMS, arrangements were made for small numbers of patients requiring specialized medical care primarily available in the civil sector (e.g. burn and spinal cord injury beds) to be sent to a military medical facility, which would then obtain care at nearby civilian hospitals, using established procedures. Current agreements with the VA and the military's ability to place active duty patients in civilian hospitals using the supplemental care program provide access to specialty care not normally provided in DOD facilities.

The USAF used approximately 6,600 Reserve Component (RC) personnel to backfill CONUS medical facilities to meet the overall demand for CONUS support. The requirement was met through the use of volunteers, reserve units on active duty for annual training, manning assistance by temporary duty assigned personnel, gains resulting from the Stop Loss program, and activation of RC units and personnel. The individual mobilization augmentation program afforded valuable support with flexibility to match specific provider requirements in RC units and CONUS casualty receiving hospitals.

The Army called up more than 4,200 RC personnel to replace deployed active duty medical personnel. In many cases, the active duty personnel went with the units deployed to the area of operations (AOR), while RC replacements maintained the peacetime medical support and expanded the CONUS based hospital capacity to continue health care delivery at near normal peacetime capability. Primary receiving hospitals, such as

Bed Capacity of Medical Assets in EUCOM by Month

	Aug 15	Sep 15	Oct 15	Nov 15	Dec 15	Jan 15	Feb 15
USAF	490	490	490	490	490	490	3,740
USA	622	622	622	622	622	622	1,760
Total	1,112	1,112	1,112	1,112	1,112	1,112	5,500

Walter Reed Army Medical Center in Washington, DC, were given priority. In some instances, derivative units were created so only specific direct care personnel (e.g. thoracic surgeons, cardiologists) were called up, not entire RC organizations. Eventually, 199 Army medical units were called to serve in SWA, or to support medical operations in Europe or in CONUS.

The Navy activated more than 10,500 medical and non-medical support RC personnel to support Operations Desert Shield and Desert Storm, and for CONUS backfill requirements. There were plans to call-up 6,000 more RC personnel when the war ended. Included in the call-up were reserve medical personnel required to augment two hospital ships, to meet mission requirements for the Fleet Marine Force, two reserve Fleet hospitals, and additional theater driven requirements. The need to expand CONUS medical facilities rapidly to receive potentially large numbers of casualties from SWA required an increase of medical RC augmentation. Maintaining the peacetime level of health care to beneficiaries in CONUS also required RC call-up and a Stop Loss Initiative for active duty personnel.

DEPLOYMENT

Deployment of medical assets occurred according to a CENTCOM established schedule. This schedule was consistent with CINCCENT's prioritization of movement for combat, CS, and combat service support (CSS) units. Preparation for deployment of medical units and personnel provided challenges, however. For example, current law requires an equivalent of 12 weeks military training for personnel before deployment. Army RC medical officers who did not meet the criteria were awarded constructive credit for their professional training and were taught field skills in a special two-week orientation course. About 2,000 RC officers were trained in this program. This requirement not only taxed the training

This Aircraft Hangar Doubled as a Ward in a Contingency Hospital.

base, but also identified a training shortfall. Alternatives will be examined to eliminate this shortfall and ensure RC personnel are ready for operational deployment.

The Army used existing regional medical training sites, and deployed mobile training teams in the theater to conduct new equipment training for active and RC units being modernized with Deployable Medical Systems (DEPMEDS) equipment. Selected RC units also received refresher training at the regional sites before deployment.

Another example of an expanding training requirement occurred upon activation of the two Fleet Hospitals to be staffed with RC personnel. Some additional training for staffs was necessary to ensure peak efficiency with field equipment. This training was conducted at Fort Dix, NJ, to provide a single training center that also permitted development of unit cohesiveness.

The USAF deployed ATHs and ATCs which travel with their flying squadrons and wings. USAF equipment identified for deployment was complete. However, because the FY91 Revolving Funds were not fully funded for War

Reserve Material, many dated and limited shelf-life items had expired and had to be replaced using peacetime operations and maintenance funds and supplies. The USAF also accelerated deployable medical unit training for selected active and RC units to improve proficiency with equipment employed in SWA. In response to a CINCCENT theater requirement, the USAF increased active and RC unit participation in the Tri-Service Field Medical Management of Chemical Casualties Course before deployment.

Personnel

Although programs were in place to compensate RC health care providers, many endured severe financial hardships because of Operations Desert Shield and Desert Storm. Legislation was enacted to provide special pay for activated health care practitioners. Also, an amendment to the Soldiers' and Sailors' Civil Relief Act provided important relief in professional liability protection for health care providers. Even with these positive actions, many reserve physicians called to active duty suffered financially.

Many RC practitioners sustain their skills by actively practicing the medical profession. However, others whose interests may have been redirected into teaching or administrative roles may not be as proficient as they once were. Existing policies must be enforced to ensure practitioners' abilities are current for their wartime position and the personnel classification systems accurately reflect the current area of expertise. This is particularly true of physicians whose specialty allows them to be placed in a substitutable position, and medical enlisted service members.

The quantity of dental care assets deployed to the theater was less than doctrine would have required. However, dental problems were minimal. This was due in part to the efforts of both active and RC dental personnel to prepare personnel for deployment. Clinics worked to

ensure that personnel did not deploy with conditions likely to produce dental emergencies. As an example, by the outset of Desert Storm, DOD had sent to the Gulf approximately 150,000 RC personnel. Nearly 22 percent reported with dental conditions likely to produce an emergency problem, but only eight personnel were not deployed due to dental disease.

HEALTH CARE PLANNING AND SUPPORT IN CENTCOM

Medical plans were refined continually as the mission in the theater evolved from defense and deterrence to an offensive role. Contingency plans developed in support of Operation Desert Storm and for reaction to other events proved to be adequate. As with any plan, fine tuning was required as exemplified by the periodic relocation of medical assets to provide better support to the forces. There also was a reallocation of aeromedical lift to link the tactical and strategic airflow better as the theater matured.

Planned medical staffing of the CENTCOM and EUCOM Surgeons' offices was adequate for the initial defense phase, but as the mission changed to an offensive role, the operational population of units and personnel more than doubled, and additional staff was required. Areas requiring augmentation included operations, logistics, administration, the Joint Medical Regulating Office (JMRO), the Joint Blood Program Office, special consultants for nuclear, biological and chemical warfare, and aeromedical evacuation.

CENTCOM identified requirements for medical support as missions evolved. The Services provided the assets CINCCENT requested, and they were combined to form a comprehensive health care delivery system within the theater. Ultimately, this system consisted of 65 hospitals (two Navy hospital ships, three Navy Fleet hospitals, 44 Army hospitals, and 16 USAF hospitals), and organic medical assets supporting the USMC.

Early-arriving USAF ATHs were the primary source of medical care for forward deployed USAF units and nearby units from the other services until the arrival of more comprehensive medical resources.

The Navy provided immediate staffing for 350 host nation beds in Bahrain and later increased the HNS number to 500 beds with the addition of 150 beds in Qatar. Additional staffing for host nation hospitals was provided by nine Army RC hospital units. These units deployed without unit equipment and staffed 4,100 beds in nine permanent hospitals in Saudi Arabia, Oman and UAE. These hospitals were assigned to echelons above corps and represented the highest level of fixed medical treatment capability available in the AOR.

The five early-deploying Active Army units were equipped with Medical Unit Self-Contained Transportable or conventional hospital sets. Following DOD guidance, these units had not been modernized with DEPMEDS equipment because the Service fielding policy gave priority to unequipped units (primarily the RC) to expand the the Army's total bed capability. When it became apparent that early deploying units could not provide satisfactory care because of equipment failures from environmental causes, the Army quickly developed and executed a modernization program to equip these units with DEPMEDS equipment.

This program was completed before the air campaign began. In addition, all follow-on deploying hospitals were provided DEPMEDS equipment from storage, such as from prepositioned stocks in Europe, or Primary Mobilization Stocks stored in Ogden UT. All of the stored hospital sets had known shortages, including potency items and dated material that was not available when the set originally was fielded. These shortages were documented before the crisis by the specific set and module to which the shortage applied. An automated system, called Ship Short, built unit - specific packages of supplies and equipment, and became operational during the early phase of Operation Desert Shield. As a result, each hospital was provided a tailored package to fill critical shortages before the ground offensive began.

Medical intelligence and forward laboratory support from the Navy, assisted by Army personnel, aided in identification and verification of biological and chemical agents in the theater. In addition, the environment presented a number of endemic diseases for which there was no proven treatment. An ad hoc tri-Service working group worked with the Office of the Assistant Secretary of Defense for Health Affairs and the Food and Drug Administration (FDA) to field a number of investigational drugs. The use of these drugs afforded the best available protection quickly and provided the only possible treatment for certain specific endemic diseases.

Disease, non-battle injury (DNBI) rates were markedly lower than expected. This is attributable to several factors: strong command emphasis on preventive medicine, especially regarding environmental threats to health such as prevention of heat injuries; well-trained preventive medicine, environmental health, and bio-environmental engineering officers and specially trained enlisted personnel; a very strong veterinary presence for food inspection; an adequate supply of potable water; a lower than predicted threat from infectious diseases; and, minimal contact with indigenous personnel. The Gulf War marks the first time a comprehensive DNBI program was used throughout a combat theater to monitor health. It provided commanders and medical personnel with a weekly summary of those injuries and illnesses that affected deployed units. However, not all Services participated equally in this program. During future deployments, DNBI surveillance programs will receive continued emphasis and include the entire force structure.

Inpatient Care in CENTCOM by Month (Cumulative Inpatient Days)

	Sep 15	Oct 15	Nov 15	Dec 15	Jan 15	Feb 15	Mar 15
USA	474	2,930	8,376	7,775	11,934	10,766	11,279
USN	197	961	1,448	1,430	1,492	1,507	1,189
USMC	438	2,247	3,005	2,410	3,241	2,032	1,688
USAF	364	901	1,211	1,280	1,572	1,693	1,111
EPW	0	0	0	0	0	295	9,942
USC	9	17	14	52	47	55	92
OC	0	6	35	21	40	8,693	15,622
Other	25	41	166	113	92	3,317	4,156
Total	1,507	7,103	14,255	13,081	18,418	28,358	45,079

Outpatient Care in CENTCOM by Month (30 Day Increments)

	Sep 15	Oct 15	Nov 15	Dec 15	Jan 15	Feb 15	Mar 15
USA	5,038	13,713	30,331	35,198	34,318	20,495	23,985
USN	690	2,974	4,025	4,103	4,979	7,125	7,595
USMC	1,983	4,021	5,152	4,635	5,052	4,381	3,775
USAF	6,986	16,869	15,600	15,917	18,530	23,503	15,233
EPW	0	0	0	0	0	94	373
USC	60	215	201	176	227	446	346
OC	2	42	117	81	121	1,188	1,272
Other	61	238	761	695	753	2,883	4,904
Total	14,820	38,072	56,187	60,805	63,980	60,115	57,483

The number of combat casualties experienced during Operation Desert Storm did not test the capabilities of the medical units supporting forces in the theater. However, the speed and distances covered by maneuvering combat elements tested the ability of forward support medical units to keep up with advancing units. MASHs and CSHs were loaded on trucks, ready to deploy to casualty concentration sites in a rapidly changing tactical situation and in anticipation of a ground transportation shortfall. Surface transportation was a problem because of the competing demands for heavy trucks and transportation assets. This problem, coupled with the size of the container requirement to move a MASH or CSH, left some medical assets with limited mobility. (The transportation shortfall is discussed in greater detail in Appendix F, Logistics.)

Patient Evacuation

The elements of the health care system in CENTCOM, EUCOM and CONUS were linked by the patient evacuation system. The CENTCOM AOR offered unique challenges for patient evacuation, which required innovative solutions. Some tactical evacuation legs were too long for Army medical evacuation (MEDEVAC) helicopters. USAF C-130s were prepared to fly into the Corps areas (including Iraq) to satisfy this requirement. In addition, 12 Army MEDEVAC helicopters were used to transport patients to and from the Navy hospital ships in the Persian Gulf.

The rapid movement of ground forces to the west stretched the medical evacuation lines considerably. During Operation Desert Storm, CENTCOM used more than 220 dedicated medical helicopters and more than 1,000 ground ambulances (including 60 German ambulances and 100 medical evacuation buses). During the ground campaign, more than 30 C-130 missions a day were committed to aeromedical evacuation support, if needed, and an additional 74 C-130 missions a day were available. USAF

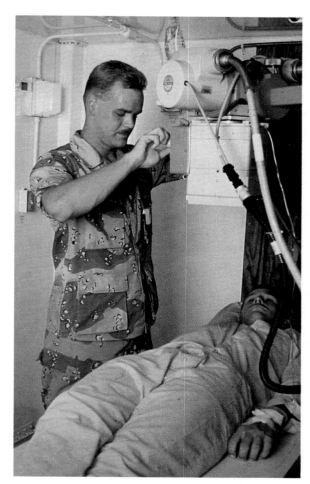

A Medical Technician Operates the X-Ray Unit of a Deployable Hospital.

Aeromedical Evacuation assets in the CENTCOM AOR, EUCOM, and CONUS included 18 aeromedical staging facilities, 13 mobile aeromedical staging facilities, 31 aeromedical evacuation liaison teams, 18 aeromedical evacuation control elements, and three theater aeromedical evacuation control centers.

The aeromedical evacuation system performance can be illustrated by the missions flown in support of CENTCOM. During Operation Desert Shield, 242 C-130 aeromedical evacuation missions were flown, transporting 2,136 patients. During Operation Desert Storm, 173 C-130 missions were flown which transported 2,375 patients, including Coalition and Iraqi casualties.

In order to provide strategic patient evacuation between SWA, EUCOM and CONUS, Transportation Command (TRANSCOM) considered using aircraft in the dedicated aeromedical segment in Stage III of the Civil Reserve Air Fleet (CRAF) to reduce competition for C-141s. At TRANSCOM's request, the USAF contractor prepared to speed production of 10 sets designed to convert CRAF III Boeing 767 interiors for aeromedical use. Delivery was scheduled for April 1991; however, with the end of hostilities, accelerated production was no longer necessary.

While the MEDEVAC system was not taxed in this operation, operational considerations may affect future requirements for all Services. The JMRO would have been significantly busier had casualties been higher, and JMRO joint staffing was too austere to manage a heavier workload effectively. Future deployments should increase JMRO staffing. In addition, tracking patients in the entire health care delivery system, including the aeromedical evacuation system, was ineffective. Substantial efforts are in progress to remedy this.

Logistics

While initial medical resupply support was provided by each respective Service, by the end of November, Army Component, Central Command, was designated as the single integrated medical logistics manager for the theater and assumed the total medical supply support mission. Though having experience in this role in Europe and Korea in normal peacetime operations, this was the first time the Army (or any Service Component) served in this role during a contingency. There were some difficulties, including obtaining access to host nation warehousing and insufficient joint logistical staffing for the deployed Medical Supply and Optical Maintenance (MEDSOM) Units.

The Army Medical Materiel Center Saudi Arabia (USAMMCSA) was established by colocating two Army MEDSOMs. The center served as the primary medical resupply source for all DEPMEDS equipped units in the CENTCOM AOR. Though some supply shortages occurred in some hospitals, supplies were eventually provided by the Services. At full theater maturity, USAMMCSA, with an additional three deployed MEDSOMs, provided medical resupply support to 65 hospitals, nine equivalent Army Divisions, and one MEF. USAMMCSA was able to provide only approximately 40 percent of the medical material requirements to the Navy hospital ships. This was due in part to the non-DEPMEDS material and platform specific

UH-60 MEDEVAC Helicopter.

requirements not handled by Army MEDSOMs. As a result, the hospital ships used both Army and Navy supply channels. In addition to the five Army MEDSOMs in SWA, a backfill MEDSOM was sent to Europe to replace the EUCOM MEDSOM deployed to SWA. The MEDSOM sent to EUCOM assisted the Army Medical Materiel Center Europe, which served as the primary resupply source for the USAMMCSA. The Defense Logistics Agency also provided key resupply support to both Europe and SWA. The designation of a single integrated medical logistics manager for a theater of operations was useful, and should be used in the future.

Because of short shelf life, certain drugs, to include chemical and biological defense drugs, were available only in limited quantities. DOD is investigating options for insuring future availability of these drugs in the future while at the same time minimizing the recurring costs of maintaining them in inventory.

Blood

Sufficient quantities of freshly collected liquid blood and frozen blood components were moved to and maintained in the CENTCOM and EUCOM AORs to satisfy expected requirements. The Armed Services Blood Program Office activated the US tri-Service contingency military blood resupply system. Contingency contracts with the American Red Cross and the American Association of Blood Banks were used to supplement the Armed Services Blood Program. The Persian Gulf War provided the impetus to quickly complete the CENTCOM frozen blood depot in the region. This depot can store up to 2,000 units of frozen red blood cells for more than 20 years.

The Persian Gulf crisis underscored the value of current blood programs. In addition, for frozen blood to meet its potential as a prepositioned contingency asset, increased emphasis must be put on training those who will

Operation Desert Shield/Storm Aeromedical Evacuation Workload

(12 August 1990 - 31 March 1991)

	Litter	Ambulatory	Total	Missions
Intratheather	1,816	2,695	4,511	415
Intertheater	3,283	4,838	8,121	256
Total	5,099	7,533	12,632	671

deglycerolize the product. There also must be increased use in peacetime medical treatment facilities of frozen blood components, and education of military physicians concerning the benefits and characteristics of using frozen blood.

Systems Support

Automated systems and established reporting procedures were used extensively throughout Operations Desert Shield and Desert Storm to determine requirements, execute the plan, and provide information to decision makers at all levels. For example, the Medical Planning Module within the Joint Operation Planning and

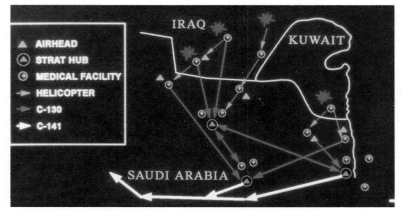

Operation Desert Storm Aeromedical Evacuation Routes.

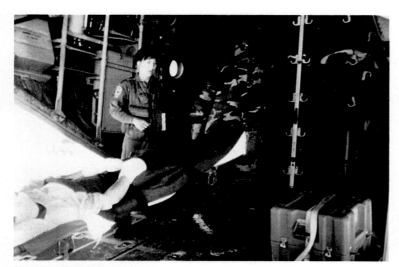
C-130 MEDEVAC with patients.

joint medical information management, if it can be modified to meet specific Navy, USMC and USAF requirements. These modifications are under way, and TAMMIS is the baseline for the Theater Medical Information System, being developed under the auspices of the Corporate Information Management Program.

The Defense Medical Regulating Information System (DMRIS) was used to match specialty medical care requirements and capabilities at medical treatment facilities in CENTCOM, EUCOM and CONUS. Some operational difficulties were experienced and resolved. An interface was developed to link DMRIS and TAMMIS; however, hostilities ended before it could be fielded.

Preestablished interoperable message text formats designed for the automated system were used to pass medical information in Situation Reports. The inability of hospitals to communicate across long distances and the inability of TAMMIS to interface with DMRIS required the use of contingency regulating procedures which compounded problems with casualty reporting and tracking. Although this system worked well in isolated regions within the theater, improved theater communications are required to afford a unified patient tracking and reporting system that provides workload

Execution System (JOPES) was used to develop gross bed requirements. JOPES was used to communicate requirements, determine which units could best satisfy these requirements, to schedule strategic movement, as well as to provide information to decision makers, and to monitor the flow of medical assets.

Parts of the Theater Army Medical Management and Information System (TAMMIS) were sent to the theater two years ahead of the scheduled fielding date and used to varying degrees of success by the Service components and medical units. TAMMIS has the potential to improve

Blood in CENTCOM by Month

	Sep 15	Oct 15	Nov 15	Dec 15	Jan 15	Feb 15
Liquid	2,387	3,025	2,457	2,988	12,752	28,944
Frozen	3,966	5,988	6,378	6,372	7,627	7,552
Total	6,353	9,013	8,835	9,360	20,379	36,496

Blood in EUCOM by Month

	Sep 15	Oct 15	Nov 15	Dec 15	Jan 15	Feb 15
Liquid	1,411	1,902	1,366	748	1,168	6,543
Frozen	255	298	599	924	1,363	4,439
Total	1,666	2,200	1,965	1,672	2,531	10,982

data to decision makers at all levels. These message text formats will be modified to include the most current functional information requirements of the joint medical community, and these requirements will be included in the Medical Planning and Execution System developed within JOPES.

C³

Clear command relationships were established and medical support concepts of operations documents were prepared. Although joint command, control and communications, together with joint use of medical resources, has advanced significantly during the past decade, there were communications problems. Communications among medical elements of the various services need to be upgraded and made more interoperable. Some emerging medical technologies, such as teleradiography, may exceed the limit of current communications systems. New communications systems, such as portable satellite communications terminals, would improve the ability to support technological advances and reduce the possibility of communications confusion. These systems must meet the tactical and the non-tactical requirements for voice and data networks. Many other problems experienced with planning and deploying of communication

systems can be corrected through better JOPES planning and education of the several theater medical staffs.

Chemical and Biological Defense

Years of research and training, coupled with medical-related intelligence, enabled the Services to prepare for treatment of chemical casualties and provide the force with solutions to avoid significant loss of life had the threat materialized. There were some problems; however, the medical community was able to attain a level of medical defense unavailable before this conflict. (CW and BW defense are more fully covered in Appendix Q.)

Principles of managing chemical casualties are well described in a tri-Service publication and taught to military medical practitioners. Special training classes were provided to medical personnel to improve a chemical casualty's chance of survival. Exportable packages and teams were provided to all medical elements, hospitals, and the other Services by the Army, which is the DOD Executive Agent for CW/BW training. Training focused on patient management, decontamination, and treatment of chemical casualties. In addition, both the Army and the USAF organized special teams to support chemical decontamination at hospitals.

Protocols were developed for use at casualty collection points and at medical treatment facilities. The Services are evaluating how to expand this training to health care providers during peacetime.

Dealing with the threat posed by BW was more problematic. For example, there were limited stockpiles of drugs and vaccines for biological defense before and during Operations Desert Shield and Desert Storm. The industrial base could not supply all the items needed. Long production lead times, and the legal and medical problems related to the use of these drugs delayed their fielding. Continued close coordination with the FDA is expected to resolve some major issues.

Medical management of casualties caused by biological agents received little emphasis before Operation Desert Shield began. The Army, as the DOD Executive Agent for Biological Defense, prepared a manual which addressed potential threats. The manual was distributed to theater medical personnel in November, and in January the CENTCOM Surgeon's office provided two other booklets, one classified and one unclassified, to Coalition forces.

Collective protection for medical facilities was virtually nonexistent. All serviceable M51 Collective Protective Shelters (CPS) were shipped from depots to Saudi Arabia for division Battalion Aid Stations and Medical Company use. The vehicle-mounted Chemical Biological Protection Shelter replacement for the M51 was approved for rapid production. The XM28 CPS for hospitals also was approved for rapid production. This was beneficial during the crisis, although both systems are now back on a normal development and procurement schedule with limited funding.

The USAF, Navy and USMC currently have no CW/BW protected facilities; however, there is a project under way to develop and field a medical facility which will afford protection to the medical staff and patients from airborne chemical and biological agents. During Operation Desert Shield, the USAF deployed a team of 19 medical personnel trained in chemical decontamination procedures with each ATH at risk in anticipation of the chemical threat.

Medical Force Structure

Several force structure deficiencies were identified during the crisis. An example is highlighted by the need to confirm the use of biological or chemical agents by Iraq. As mentioned previously, the Navy and the Army pieced together a theater laboratory. While the concept was sound, control of operations was difficult. Another deficiency was a potential shortfall in MEDEVAC support to Navy hospital ships. There also were shortfalls in staffing levels for theater medical management. There seems to be a need to provide joint staffing for all Theater Medical Materiel Management Centers at more robust levels.

RC policies requiring activation of entire RC units instead of selectively mobilizing individuals or tailoring manpower packages caused some problems with use of these forces to satisfy medical requirements. Examination of these policies to engender greater flexibility appear warranted.

Actions were taken to involuntarily cross-level Army RC soldiers from units not selected for activation to those identified for call-up to achieve properly staffed Army units (This expedient, which was used in combat, CS, and CSS as well as medical units, had a less than desirable effect on morale and cohesiveness.) This policy may have long-term detrimental effects on retention. An alternative to involuntary cross-leveling must be developed for future contingencies. Options might include manning Reserve units to full wartime strength levels, developing a more flexible reserve force structure or making earlier use of the Individual

Ready Reserve, which exists to fill unit vacancies and to provide casualty replacements.

(This issue is discussed in greater detail in Appendix H.)

OBSERVATIONS

Accomplishments

■ The largest medical force since World War II was deployed to one of the harshest environments in the world. Establishing health care facilities with more than 18,500 beds in the immediate theater of operations, 5,500 beds in EUCOM (with provisions for more in host nation hospitals), up to 22,000 beds in CONUS, and an aeromedical evacuation capacity to move stabilized casualties, demonstrated an impressive combat medical capability.

■ DOD provided medical care not only for a combat force of more than half a million, but maintained simultaneously its care commitments worldwide, despite the fact that no force structure provisions had been made for such an expansive requirement.

■ Investments in prepositioned equipment, rapidly transportable ATHs, and the availability of *USNS Comfort* and *USNS Mercy* contributed to the readiness of health care forces deployed to the theater.

■ The modernization and conversion of the Army hospitals during Operations Desert Shield and Desert Storm was successful. The Army employed the new DEPMEDS system ahead of schedule and the system proved flexible, rugged, and capable of satisfying most field medical treatment requirements.

Shortcomings

■ Training of some Active and RC medical personnel may not have been optimum for rapid deployment of forward medical facilities. Current law requires 12 weeks (or its equivalent) of military training for military personnel before deployment on land overseas. Army RC medical officers who did not meet the criteria were provided a special two-week orientation course and granted 10 weeks of credit for professional education and experience. About 2,000 RC officers were trained in this program before deployment. This requirement taxed the training base. Options to eliminate this shortfall and ensure RC personnel are ready for operational deployment are under consideration.

■ Ground transportation of medical facilities was a problem because of a lack of heavy trucks. Many medical assets for the support of front line units had limited mobility.

■ At the beginning of the deployment, the Services were not adequately prepared to deal with the full range of CW/BW. There were limitations with respect to drug availability, protection, detection, decontamination, prophylaxis, and therapy. Only the Army had an initial protective shelter system for decontamination and treatment of chemical casualties, although this capability was available to the other Services before hostilities began. Training was also an issue initially. By the time hostilities began, however, almost all physicians and health care providers had received chemical casualty training.

Issues

■ Certain short-lived drug stocks (i.e. some drugs, including antibiotics, CW and BW vaccines) were available only in extremely limited test quantities.

■ The optimum mobility of MASH and CSH assets in a rapidly changing environment may require further analysis.

(Continued)

OBSERVATIONS (Continued)

- The theater offered unique tactical challenges, which required innovative solutions. While some tactical evacuation legs were too long for Army MEDEVAC helicopters, USAF C-130s were used to satisfy this requirement. In addition, Army MEDEVAC helicopters were used to transport patients to and from hospital ships. These operational considerations may affect overall requirements for the Services.

- The call up of RC personnel caused an overall increase in health care costs since family members of RC service members became service medical beneficiaries.

- Prolonged activation places a substantial financial burden on reserve medical personnel, particularly physicians.

- Further training is required in the area of crisis action system communications. Medical communications planning guidance recently has been inIn August 1991, the Deputy Secretary of Defense assigned executive agency responsibilities to the Secretary of the Army for BW Defense. The Services have embarked on a long term project for an integrated DOD response to biological threats, to include protection and stockpiling necessary vaccines and antitoxins, the deployment and fielding of appropriate detection systems, and the development and fielding of appropriate protective and decontamination systems.cluded in the appropriate JOPES documents, and action is under way to establish a Joint Medical Planners' course.

- In August 1991, the Deputy Secretary of Defense assigned executive agency responsibilities to the Secretary of the Army for BW Defense. The Services have embarked on a long term project for an integrated DOD response to biological threats, to include protection and stockpiling necessary vaccines and antitoxins, the deployment and fielding of appropriate detection systems, and the development and fielding of appropriate protective and decontamination systems.

Appendix H
RESERVE COMPONENT FORCES

INTRODUCTION

Operations Desert Shield and Desert Storm required the largest mobilization and deployment of Reserve Component (RC) forces since the Korean Conflict and represented the first major test of the Reserve's role under the Total Force Policy that emerged after Vietnam. Two hundred forty-five thousand Reservists from all Services were ordered to active duty in support of the crisis; approximately 106,000 served in Southwest Asia (SWA). Reserve forces played a vital role, participating in all phases of the Persian Gulf crisis from the initial response through the redeployment of forces. What the Department of Defense (DOD) accomplished in resolving the Persian Gulf crisis simply could not have been done without the full integration of the capabilities of the thousands of Reservists and National Guard personnel who served in combat, combat support (CS), and combat service support (CSS) roles in the theater and elsewhere. Most importantly, the mobilization and use of Reserve Forces validated the key concepts of the Nation's Total Force Policy.

TOTAL FORCE POLICY, THE RESERVE COMPONENTS, AND PERSIAN GULF CONFLICT

The Reserve force that deployed to SWA and the Reserve force that supported that deployment, like the Active force, was created in the aftermath of Vietnam. The "Total Force" concept was conceived in 1970; the RC were equipped, manned, and trained in consonance with the 1973 decision to adopt the Total Force

> *"The success of the Guard and Reserve participation in Desert Shield cannot be overemphasized. Their participation has been a significant factor in affording us flexibility and balance, and reinforces the policies and decisions made over the last 10 years to strengthen the Total Force concept."*
>
> **General Colin Powell, USA**
> **Chairman, Joint Chiefs of Staff**
> **3 December 1990**

Policy as a cornerstone of the nation's national defense strategy. As initially developed and subsequently implemented, that policy has had two principal tenets. First, planners were to consider Reserve forces as the primary augmentation for the Active force. Second, military response would involve the integrated use of all forces available, including Active, Reserve, civilian and allied. As the 1990 DOD Report to Congress on the Total Force Policy stated, those functions that require high levels of activity in wartime but comparatively low levels in peacetime are well-suited for Reservists. Missions that require extended peacetime deployments, on the other hand, are generally more appropriate for Active Components (AC). The objective of the Total Force policy has been to integrate the AC and RC force capabilities and strengths in the most cost-effective manner. As a result of these efforts, on 2 August, the Services, individually and collectively, had one integrated structure — the Total Force.

RESERVE FORCES PREPAREDNESS — LEGACY OF THE '80s

During the 1980s, major improvements were made in Reserve force readiness to perform wartime missions. By the fall of 1990, modernization efforts had given the RC the ability to field approximately 84 percent (in dollar value) of the equipment they required for war. The DOD policy of "First to fight, first to equip" required resourcing both AC and RC units in the sequence in which they were required to perform their wartime missions. Successful recruiting efforts, the assignment to the RC of important peacetime and wartime responsibilities, and substantially improved training opportunities, also contributed significantly to improved Reserve force readiness.

The increase in RC readiness levels in the 1980s occurred concurrently with the largest ever expansion of the RC peacetime structure. From 1980 to the end of the decade, the number of Selected Reservists increased by 35 percent, growing from approximately 850,000 to more than 1,150,000. This growth did not come at the expense of personnel readiness. On the contrary, throughout the decade, the Services devoted considerable resources to ensure individual proficiency of Selected Reserve members. During this same period, more emphasis was placed on the Individual Ready Reserve (IRR), the pool of pre-trained individuals.

INITIAL VOLUNTEERS

Individual RC volunteers were integrated into the Active force from the start of the Persian Gulf crisis, even before the involuntary Reserve call-up. By 22 August, more than 10,500 volunteer RC members already were serving on active duty. Their contributions were essential to provide capabilities required from the first days of the crisis — particularly strategic airlift — and to perform missions almost exclusively assigned to Reserve units including, for example, water purification and port security.

Thousands of Air Reserve Component (ARC) personnel volunteered within hours of the initial US response to support the time-sensitive movement of US personnel and materiel to the Persian Gulf. ARC volunteers flew 42 percent of all strategic airlift missions and 33 percent of the aerial refueling missions. They also provided Continental United States (CONUS) base maintenance, medical, civil engineering, aerial port, and security police support to deploying Air Force (USAF) units and airlift missions. By 22 August, Air Force Reserve volunteers had moved seven million tons of cargo and 8,150 passengers to the theater. As of 25 August, Air Force Reserve volunteers began operating Westover AFB, MA as a major eastbound staging operation on a 24-hour basis. Westover continued to operate on a volunteer basis for four months until these same volunteers were mobilized on 3 December.

US Naval Reserve (USNR) volunteers contributed medical, logistics, and cargo-handling skills to CONUS base support operations. While approximately 50 percent of all USNR volunteers were involved in health care, Naval Reservists also were deployed outside the United States for other tasks. For example, a detachment of Active Seabees at Subic Bay, Philippines, was deployed to SWA in August with their parent battalion. When a strike by 3,000 civilians of the public works center was imminent, 150 volunteers from a Reserve public works center augmented units deployed to Subic Bay and helped keep essential services in operation. As a result, the base suffered no interruption in operations, and response time to trouble calls noticeably improved. Some volunteers subsequently were deployed to Bahrain to augment the Navy Logistics Support Force's public works force.

Approximately 1,100 US Marine Corps Reserve (USMCR) volunteers supported the preparation for deployment of Marine Corps (USMC) forces to SWA. They not only provided maintenance and logistical support for deploying Active USMC units but also transport services, to include KC-130T crews who flew transatlantic refueling missions. In addition, they were assigned liaison and linguist duties with deploying Active units.

US Coast Guard (USCG) Reserve volunteers provided port security and supervised the loading of explosives and hazardous cargo at US east and Gulf Coast ports. The USCG activated Port Security Harbor Defense Units (PSHD) from its Ninth District (Cleveland) to work with US mobile inshore underwater warfare units in SWA. This marked the first extended use of USCG volunteers for this mission.

More than 5,580 Army RC personnel volunteered for temporary tours of active duty. For example, during Operation Desert Shield, Army Reserve (USAR) terminal transportation unit members volunteered to work with the Military Traffic Management Command to manage the flow of combat forces from US east

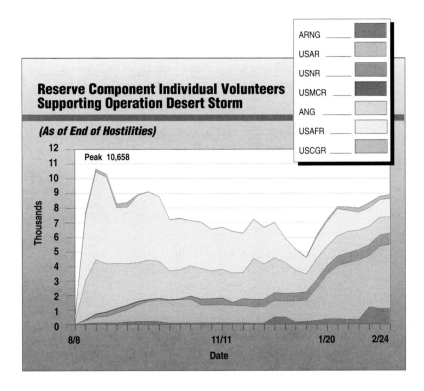

and Gulf Coast ports. Other USAR and National Guard (ARNG) volunteers provided maintenance and logistics support, chemical defense training, and aviation operations assistance for AC forces. RC medical personnel also backfilled active Health Service Command professionals, who deployed during the first days of the crisis. Some volunteers deployed directly to theater. South Carolina ARNG members deployed with Third US Army to help establish strategic communications for the headquarters.

The large number of RC members who volunteered during the conflict's early stages vividly demonstrates their commitment and dedication. Individual volunteers also provided essential manpower before the decision to involuntarily activate the Reserves had been made. This provided excellent support during a difficult time. However, a problem was created by the absence of those who had volunteered from their units when the units were later activated. Subsequent investigation indicates the problem was corrected by cross-leveling and other personnel actions. The general success with RC volunteers demonstrates the value of using them early in future crises before a decision is made to activate Selected Reserve units.

DECISION TO ACTIVATE, MOBILIZE, AND DEPLOY RESERVES

By 9 August, as RC volunteers were supporting the initial phases of Operation Desert Shield, the Defense Department began planning for a possible RC call-up to support the evolving strategy. It quickly became apparent that Reserve forces would be needed for deployment to the Persian Gulf to meet Commander-in-Chief, Central Command (CINCCENT) requirements; to backfill positions in the US and other theaters vacated by AC personnel deployed to Saudi Arabia; and for essential CONUS-based missions.

The Office of the Secretary of Defense (OSD), the Joint Staff, the Services, Department of Transportation, and the USCG worked together in coordination with Central Command (CENTCOM) to ensure various policy and operational issues during the mobilization process were dealt with as quickly and efficiently as possible.

Initial Involuntary Call-Up

For the first time since it became law in 1976, the President exercised his authority under Title 10, Section 673b of the US Code, by which he may direct the involuntary activation of up to 200,000 Selected Reservists for 90 days, plus a 90-day extension in the interests of national security, to augment Active forces for any "operational mission." He signed Executive Order 12727 on 22 August. The recall began expeditiously; prior planning by OSD and the Military Departments, and JS directed mobilization exercises proved to have been extremely useful to ready DOD for efficient activation.

After the President's announcement, the Secretary of Defense delegated authority to the Service Secretaries to order Selected Reserve members to active duty. Initial authorization provided for the recall of 25,000 Army Selected Reservists (combat support and combat service support forces only); 14,500 USAF; 6,300 Navy; and 3,000 USMC reservists. Simultaneously, the Secretary of Transportation authorized the USCG to order to active duty as many as 1,250 USCG Reservists.

The first calls to active duty were announced on 24 August and, by the end of September, 26,653 Army, Navy, and USAF Reservists had reported for duty under the authority of 673b. Consistent with USMC doctrine, selected Marine Corps Reserve units were not activated until 11 October.

Early in the crisis, US Forces Command (FORSCOM) planned for the activation of Army Reserve forces in two parts. The first envisioned a call-up of RC units to support the deployment — to flesh out the mobilization base and support Active combat unit deployment. The second called for the activation of additional Reserve forces by the end of September that would deploy mainly to SWA to logistically support forces in theater — to provide in-country food, petroleum, oil and lubricants (POL), water, and ammunition support to the theater. RC support to meet CINCCENT's requirements, as envisioned in the FORSCOM plan, was consistent with Total Force Policy.

By the end of October, the Army had activated 235 RC units, consisting of nearly 24,000 soldiers from 44 states and Puerto Rico. Approximately 5,000 Naval Reservists and 355 units from 39 states, Puerto Rico and the District of Columbia had been ordered to active duty, as were 32 Selected Reserve units and more than 5,000 ARC personnel. The USMC activated its first unit of 157 personnel to backfill an active force deployed from Hawaii.

Initial Reserve Force Package

Service	SWA Theater Requirements	CONUS Base Requirements
USA	35 Combat Support Units 166 Combat Service Support Units	Port Operations Medical Installation Support
USN	2 Minesweeper Crews Port Security Military/Sealift Shipping Control Cargo HDLC/Logistics Support	Medical (CONUS Backfill) MSC/Shipping Control Cargo Handling/Logistics Support Intelligence
USAF	CENTCOM Staff Augmentation	Strategic Airlift 12 AFRES Squadrons 3 ANG Squadrons LOG/Maintenance
USMC	CENTCOM Staff Augmentation 5th MEB Augmentation	Headquarters Staff Augmentation Air Station Augmentation
USCG	3 Port Security Units	CONUS Port Operations

Second Involuntary Call-Up

On 8 November, the President announced his intention to deploy 200,000 additional troops to SWA to provide offensive options to resolve the Persian Gulf crisis. On 14 November, the Secretary of Defense authorized the Military Departments to activate a total of 115,000 Selected Reservists. In accordance with Section 673b(i) of Title 10 US Code, the duration of service for all activated Reservists was extended to 180 days. On 1 December, the Secretary of Defense authorized the Military Departments to call to active duty as many as 188,000 Selected Reservists. The additional RC forces were needed to complete the work of building a mature theater logistics base in SWA before to the start of an offensive, to sustain the CONUS logistics pipeline to the Middle East, and to ensure the readiness of US forces in Europe and the Pacific.

By mid-December, the Military Departments had ordered to active duty nearly 120,000 Selected Reserve members, including substantial RC combat elements. The Defense Appropriations Act for Fiscal Year 1991, which became law in November, included new authority permitting the President to retain RC combat units on active duty for as many as 360 days, but it did not become necessary for the President to exercise the new authority. When the President extended the period of activation for Selected Reservists for an additional 90 days, the Army and USMC began activating Reserve combat units. In November and early December, the Army activated three ARNG "round-out" brigades and two field artillery brigades. The USMC called key elements of its 4th (Reserve) Marine Division (MARDIV) to active duty.

Throughout December and January, many

Title 10 US Code 673B Allocations to Military Departments and US Coast Guard during Desert Shield (1990)

Service	August 24	November 14[1]	December 1
Army	25,000[2]	80,000	115,000
Navy	6,300	10,000	30,000
Air Force	14,500	20,000	20,000
Marine Corps	3,000	15,000	23,000
Coast Guard	1,250	1,250	1,250
Total	51,050	116,250	189,250

[1] Provision of 10 USC 673B (i) executed (Selected Reservists extended on active duty to 180 days).

[2] Combat Support and Combat Service Support only.

Selected Reserve units deployed to SWA. The Army deployed the two field artillery brigades — the 142nd Field Artillery (FA) Brigade from Arkansas and Oklahoma, and the 196th FA Brigade from Tennessee, West Virginia, and Kentucky. The USMC sent a substantial part of the 4th MARDIV, the 4th Marine Aircraft Wing, and the 4th Force Service Support Group, including four infantry battalions, elements of two tank battalions, several artillery batteries, and composite attack and transport helicopter squadrons. The ARC deployed three tactical fighter squadrons, one special operations group, two special operations squadrons, and a tactical reconnaissance squadron. The Navy sent two minesweepers, two combat search and rescue detachments, one Seabee battalion, four logistics squadrons, and several mobile inshore undersea warfare detachments. The USCG continued to operate the three PSHD, which had deployed to the theater in October.

From 9 December through 15 May 1991, 19,433 Army personnel were deployed through three CONUS Replacement Centers (CRC) established by Army Training and Doctrine Command. Although most personnel deployed through the CRCs were IRR members, the number also includes active soldiers, Selected Reservists, and civilians (DOD, Red Cross and contractor personnel).

By mid-January, the size of the US force in the Persian Gulf had reached more than 400,000 personnel, including 63,998 RC members or 16 percent of the US forces in the theater. The total number activated had reached approximately 150,000 personnel.

Third Activation

On 18 January, pursuant to Section 673 of Title 10, the President authorized the departments of Defense and Transportation to order Ready Reserve members to active duty, including members of both the Selected Reserve and the IRR. This action authorized the retention of all RC personnel on active duty for as long as one year and permitted the departments to call additional RC personnel to active duty. On 19 January, the Secretary of Defense authorized the Military departments to call as many as 360,000 to active duty, including 220,000 members of the Army Ready Reserve, 44,000 members of the Naval Ready Reserve, 44,000 members of the USMC Ready Reserve, and 52,000 members of the USAF Ready Reserve. The USCG was authorized to call as many as 5,000 Ready Reservists to active duty.

The availability of members of the IRR was particularly important. During Operation Desert Shield, Reserve units earmarked for call-up experienced several difficulties. In some cases, particularly in Army CS and CSS forces, Reserve units had been organized at less than wartime strength requirements. In others, they were manned at less than peacetime approved operating levels. In addition, and like some

Service Employment of Activated Reserve Component Personnel in Desert Shield as of December 16, 1990

Army

CONUS (Augmentation/Training)	66,180
Transportation	5,837
Military Police	1,997
Supply & Service	6,979
Maintenance	2,866
Command & Control	411
Engineer	929
Intelligence	266
Medical	1,040
Total	**86,505**

Navy

Medical	3,591
Mobile Inshore Undersea Warfare	185
Mine Sweepers	47
Military Sealift Command (MSC)	303
Naval Control Of Shipping	78
Intelligence	250
Logistics Support	576
Other/Misc.	217
Combat SAR (HCS)	28
Cargo Handling Battalions/Staff	192
Seabees	1,731
Ship Augment	0
Total	**7,198**

Air Force

CONUS (Augmentation/Training)	1,817
Strategic Airlift	4,172
Tactical Airlift	1,298
Medical	346
Combat Communications	84
Reconnaissance	130
Security Police	349
Supply & Service	45
Refueling	6
Total	**8,247**

Marine Corps

CONUS (Base Augmentation)	387
OCONUS (Augmentation)	2,325
I MEF (Augmenting/Reinforcing)	11,852
Individual Mobilization Augmentees	120
Intelligence	26
Total	**14,710**

Coast Guard

CONUS (Augmentation/Training)	57
Port Security (USA)	422
Port Security (Middle East)	282
Total	**761**

Active units, most Selected Reserve units contained some personnel who were non-deployable because of medical disqualifications or established policies (e.g., because they had not completed basic training). Since individual Reserve filler personnel were not immediately available to Selected Reserve units activated under Section 673b, Reserve personnel were cross-leveled or cross-assigned, on both a voluntary and involuntary basis, from units not scheduled for activation. (Despite these efforts, in some cases after activation, additional personnel had to be assigned to RC units to bring them up to wartime fill standards.) Cross-leveling in this fashion, while effective in

the short term, reduced the readiness of non-activated or later deploying units. Thus access to the IRR at this juncture provided needed fillers to meet personnel shortages in both Active and Reserve units.

Equipment cross-leveling also occurred and involved two types of equipment transfers: those made within the RC to prepare a unit for call-up, and those made from an RC to an AC unit to correct an equipment shortfall. The cross-leveling of equipment within the RC was practical, especially for equipment unique to the RC where no other source of supply was immediately available. Under the provisions of DOD Directive 1225.6, the Army requested and received DOD authority to withdraw specified equipment (e.g., helicopters and heavy equipment transports) from the RC to the AC for the duration of the conflict. The Army was the only Service to request this delegation of authority. As a result of these procedures, both Active and RC forces were assured of equipment to meet mission requirements.

When ground combat operations began in the Kuwait Theater of Operations (KTO) on 24 February 1991, 202,337 Selected Reservists and 20,277 IRR had been called to active duty. At the peak of the mobilization of Reserve forces (10 March 1991), a total of 231,000 Ready Reservists were serving on active duty in support of CONUS base, Operation Desert Storm, and other worldwide commitments.

ACTIVATION, MOBILIZATION, AND DEPLOYMENT PROCESS

Requests for increased authority to activate RC units throughout the mobilization process were based on both CINCCENT and Service requirements validated by CENTCOM component commands and by other Unified Commands to the Chairman, Joint Chiefs of Staff. The Military Departments, in conjunction with the JS, made the decision as to which units to deploy. For example, the Army Component Central Command (ARCENT) passed requirements to FORSCOM, which then recommended specific ARNG and USAR units to Department of the Army for approval and subsequent activation.

Army Readiness Groups (ARG) were extremely valuable during the mobilization process. They knew the units and their shortcomings. They helped unit commanders plan and conduct training. The Readiness groups did much to ensure that soldier support was provided so unit leaders could concentrate on training their soldiers. Army Mobile Training Teams (MTT)

drawn from 2nd US Army, Readiness Groups, and FORSCOM (supplemented by training cadre at the National Training Center [NTC] and other training areas) helped units attain proficiency in the shortest time possible. Army Readiness Groups (ARG) verified the current state of readiness of the tentatively selected RC units. Readiness Group officials also sought to verify unit training status.

Reserve units were called initially to provide strategic and tactical airlift, water purification and distribution, maintenance, transportation, terminal operations, movement control, law enforcement, port security, chemical defense, medical and legal. When Reserve units with these skills began to arrive at the mobilization stations, their actual status often differed considerably from their readiness reports. The readiness reports were resource status reports often completed months before the call-up, and the personnel and equipment status of units often had changed substantially in the interim. Moreover, as specific Operation Desert Shield requirements became known, even fully resourced RC units sometimes did not meet these requirements.

As an example of RC personnel and force structure mismatches, some Reserve medical units contained a number of doctors who were not qualified for their assigned position, (e.g., a psychiatrist filling a surgeon's position). Cross-leveling within the Army provided mobilized units with doctors of appropriate specialties. Rather than call up an entire unit, derivative units were created to allow the call-up of only those personnel who were actually needed. In some medical units, only doctors in certain specialties were needed. Only those doctors were called while other members of the unit remained behind. This practice ensured that operational requirements were filled without exceeding mobilization quotas, but often at an inconvenience to those soldiers activated. Personnel in derivation units appear to have taken longer to integrate into the Active force and were, in general, less satisfied with terms of their service.

Some Army and USMC RC units spent several weeks at mobilization stations before deployment (as long as five or six weeks in a few cases). Because of strategic lift constraints, theater infrastructure limits, and operational security concerns, a decision was made to hold units in the United States beyond the planned training period until shortly before their equipment was scheduled to arrive in Saudi Arabia. During the pre-deployment period, units finished processing and received further training. All units received chemical and biological training that included requalification in basic skills (this training was emphasized in theater by all Services as well). As a general rule, ground combat maneuver units needed more training than CS and CSS units. In some cases, mobile training teams (MTTs) from Army service schools taught courses at mobilization stations. For example, water purification equipment operators and mechanics were trained to repair the Army's newest purification equipment, since it had not previously been issued to RC units.

One of the problems that impeded the mobilization process was the incompatibility of some AC and RC automated data processing systems. It was sometimes impossible to transfer pay and personnel data directly between systems, causing delays in pay and a variety of reporting problems. Personnel accountability surfaced as one of the major problems. The current automation infrastructure cannot capture, process, and transmit data to all echelons for management of personnel during mobilization. With the exception of the Marine Corps, automation cannot support deployment, redeployment, location, and status of mobilized personnel and units.

The activation and deployment of RC forces and their full integration into the Active structure were accomplished with no significant

Reserve Component Selected Reserve Personnel Activated as of January 13, 1991

Service	Activated	FY 90 Authorized End Strength	% of Total
Army	102,828	779,700	13.2
Navy	11,390	153,400	7.4
Air Force	14,806	201,100	7.4
Marine Corps	16,558	44,000	37.6
Coast Guard	641	15,000	4.3

problems. In part, this was caused by ensuring the welfare of Reserve members, thereby allowing them to concentrate on mission assignments. Prompt action by OSD in seeking Congressional support for changes in the Soldiers' and Sailors' Civil Relief Act and the Veterans Re-employment Rights Act was necessary to ensure equal treatment of Reservists called up under Title 10 US Code 673b. Ultimate amendment of those statutes ensured the welfare of Reservists and their families. While the Services took steps to mitigate the trauma Reservists felt from family separation through a variety of family support activities, employers of activated Reserve members were generally supportive of US goals in the Persian Gulf crisis and their Reserve employees' absence from the workplace. Finally, the activation of Reservists from all walks of life and every state in the union, as well as their full integration into the plans to enforce the United Nations resolutions against Iraq, helped the American public to understand the seriousness of the Persian Gulf crisis and to ensure their support for the operation.

POST MOBILIZATION TRAINING

The nature and the amount of post-mobilization

training that was required of Reserve component units depended upon several factors. The primary factors were the type of mission assigned to particular units, the training readiness condition of the units, and the levels of organization in the units that had been maintained in peacetime. The civilian job skills of individual National Guardsmen and Reservists and other factors were important to certain units depending upon the nature of the wartime mission assigned to the units. There were also instances where post-mobilization development of certain individual skills was necessary because of the use of new equipment or the unique requirements of theater-specific missions. Most units of the Reserve components were ready to be deployed on schedule and the timing and sequence of their deployment was determined by the needs of the theater commanders and similar factors, rather than by post mobilization training requirements. However, there were some notable instances where post mobilization training was a constraint.

Army National Guard Combat Brigades

On 8 November, the Secretary of Defense announced that three ARNG ground combat brigades would be ordered to active duty, including the 155th Armored Brigade from Mississippi, the 48th Infantry Brigade (Mechanized) from Georgia, and the 256th infantry Brigade (Mechanized) from Louisiana. The brigades constituted less than seven percent of the total number of Reservists called to active duty, but they were the subject of much controversy.

Some attention resulted from the fact that when the Army's 24th Infantry Division (Mechanized) was deployed to Saudi Arabia, it was not yet clear it would be necessary to order any RC forces to active duty. The division thus deployed without the 48th Infantry Brigade (Mechanized), its round-out brigade. Instead, the Army sent an available

Active duty brigade from Georgia. When the President authorized the RC activation on 22 August, Section 673b of Title 10, US Code restricted activations of Reservists to an initial period of 90 days and one 90 day extension. That restriction made a call-up of such large combat units impractical. The time required to complete the post call-up training that had long been planned and to ship their equipment by sea to the war zone, meant that such reserve combat units could not have been retained in the theater as long as necessary.

When the decision to activate the three brigades was made, they received extensive training at various locations and, when the cease-fire took place on 28 February, they either had been certified or were about to be certified by the Army as ready for combat, if needed. The Secretary of Defense had made it clear from the beginning of the conflict that no military unit would be sent into combat until it was ready. Any other policy would have been irresponsible and completely disloyal to those whose lives would have otherwise been at greater risk.

The state of training and readiness of the roundout brigades and the plans for their use have often been misunderstood. Brigades are large, complex organizations. Their wartime missions require extensive synchronization, integration and coordination of high speed, continuous fire, maneuver and support operations. The complex, collective combat skills required by the commanders, staffs, and soldiers of armor and mechanized infantry brigades are difficult to achieve by RC soldiers who receive limited training each year. The challenge for the roundout brigades was made greater by the absence of extensive experience among the brigade's leadership. In one of the brigades, less than 10 percent of the officers had extended active duty experience. Such challenges were difficult to overcome, even by the high motivation and exceptional quality of the RC personnel who serve in the brigades.

Premobilization training is focused on specific, critical small unit tasks, and on improving the ability of RC commanders and staffs to plan and conduct ground combat operations. Post-mobilization training was required to bring the units to required levels of combined arms proficiency before deployment.

The 1990 DOD Total Force Policy study noted that readiness of reserve units was a function not only of resource and training levels, but also of various intangible factors, such as motivation and experience. The training experience of the three ARNG combat brigades corroborate these observations. The remarkable enthusiasm of the RC round-out brigade personnel made a significant contribution to their successful performance in strenuous combat training.

Air, Naval, and Marine Elements

USMC Reservists arrived at their stations of initial assignment (SIAs) well trained. They received additional training, however, to meet unique SWA challenges, including the Iraqi order of battle, and operations under chemical warfare conditions, obstacle breaching techniques, desert warfare, and customs and cultures of the Arabian Peninsula. USMC MTTs deployed to SWA and provided this training to both Active and RC units. Perhaps the best example of the effectiveness of this training is the performance in the Gulf War of Company C of the 4th Tank Battalion, 4th MARDIV. This unit had been equipped with M60A1 tanks, much different from the more modern M1 and M1A1. Following activation, it completed a 23-day M1 training program in 18 days. The unit arrived in Saudi Arabia 19 February and went into battle 24 February. During the next three days, it engaged and destroyed numerous enemy armored vehicles and tanks.

In most cases, some theater-unique training was necessary to familiarize deploying personnel with the Persian Gulf environment. For example, Naval Reservists, who augmented active commands, generally were well trained in basic skills but received training for specific mission requirements. Reservists assigned to Fleet Hospitals were trained in desert survival, combat trauma care, and medical management of chemical casualties. Those assigned to cargo handling battalions received training in hazardous material handling and storage, small arms, and chemical decontamination.

Air Force Reserve units, aircrews, maintenance crews and support personnel required little-to-no post-mobilization training before performing their respective missions. All mobilized Air Force Reserve flying units mobilized in 24 hours or less, and were prepared to deploy or did deploy in less than 72 hours. For example, the 926th Tactical Fighter Group (TFG), an A-10 unit, was recalled on 29 December, deployed on 1 January, and flew proficiency sorties until the unit began combat operations with the launch of the Air Campaign. Air Reserve Component (ARC) met USAF qualification standards but also received training in chemical and biological defense.

Continuous training was carried out by all units throughout the operation. Exercises, drills and rehearsals were conducted regularly by forces in SWA to keep skill levels high and increase force proficiency. This training helped the forces — AC and RC — to hold their edge in the long buildup period before the offensive.

INTEGRATION OF RESERVE COMPONENT FORCES

During the 1980s, the military Services made considerable progress integrating AC and RC forces into an effective Total Force. Many RC units, particularly those assigned missions requiring early deployment, had been modernized to the same level as the AC units with whom they were aligned. RC training plans were extracted from published Service doctrine and training material. For a several years, Reserve forces had been integrated into JCS-directed and Service training exercises, such as REFORGER, Team Spirit, Cobra Gold, Certain Sage, and many US-based joint exercises.

Therefore, integration of RC units in the Operations Desert Shield and Desert Storm force structures was very effective overall. RC units and individuals filled crucial manpower and capabilities shortfalls. The Air Force established provisional wings that consisted of both AC and RC units. For example, 86 percent of the strategic and tactical airlift assets were activated RC forces, which amounted to seven C-5, 11 C-141, and 10 C-130 units. Seventeen of 20 RC air refueling squadrons (16 KC-135E units and one KC-10 unit) were also mobilized. Army RC units also were effectively integrated with AC units. For example, the 20th Special Forces Group (SFG) (Airborne) was rapidly integrated into the Army Special Forces Command to support other worldwide operations.

Naval Reservists augmented in-theater combat search and rescue capability, working very closely with USAF AC elements, and contributed substantively to this important task. Two USNR Ocean Mine Sweeper vessels, the USS Adroit (MSO 509) and the USS Impervious, (MSO 449) were activated and deployed to the Gulf with Reserve crews. Reserve USCG law enforcement detachments were integrated into Naval units, where their expertise in boarding operations was invaluable during maritime interception operations. The Reserve 3rd Naval Construction Regiment was called to operate as the command and control headquarters for the three active and one Reserve Seabee battalions supporting I Marine Expeditionary Force (MEF) in SWA. In addition, Reserve Cargo Handling Battalions (RCHB) 3 and 13 were called to active duty to provide cargo movement support throughout the Persian Gulf area.

The USAR's 416th Engineer Command served as the theater Army engineer command, performing tasks crucial to the sustainment of forces and the success of the operation. In this command, Active and RC units served side-by-side. Two Army National Guard (ARNG) Field Artillery (FA) brigades provided fire support to both VII Corps and XVIII Airborne Corps during Operation Desert Storm. Furthermore, the 142nd FA Brigade was assigned to support the 1st British Armoured Division. In that role, it was integrated rapidly. USAR and ARNG combat support (CS) and combat service support (CSS) units were integrated with both VII Corps and XVIII Airborne Corps, often with RC commands structured to include both Active and Reserve components. The ARNG and USAR provided considerable engineering, logistics, and military police support not only to the Army but also to other Services and allied forces.

USMC Reservists increased combat power by providing armor, artillery, infantry, aviation, engineer and combat service support forces to

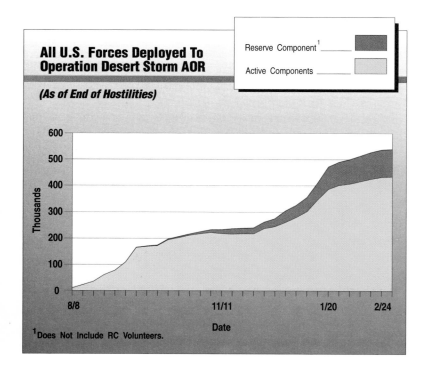

All U.S. Forces Deployed To Operation Desert Storm AOR

(As of End of Hostilities)

Reserve Component[1]

Active Components

[1]Does Not Include RC Volunteers.

complement active USMC units. For the most part, USMCR personnel and units fought as integral components of active units. The 8th Tank Battalion, for example, fought with the 6th Marine Regiment throughout the ground offensive. In many cases, USMC artillery and armor battalions, although part of the AC, contained RC detachments and units. Artillery batteries from the 14th Marines, a Reserve regiment, were assigned to the active 10th and 11th Marines in the ground offensive.

USE AND PERFORMANCE OF RESERVE COMPONENT FORCES IN THE THEATER

RC forces performed to expected standards during Operations Desert Shield and Storm. Individual mobilization augmentees were ordered to active duty and filled key wartime positions including duty at DOD, Service, JS, Defense agency, and unified and specified command headquarters. They multiplied the existing capabilities of the force and in several cases, performed unique missions, which proved crucial to the overall success of the operation. RC air crews flew air reconnaissance, close air support, and special operations missions in support of the air and ground campaigns. The first A-10 air-to-air kill was recorded by a pilot of the 926th Tactical Fighter Group (AFR) who shot down an Iraqi helicopter. During Operations Desert Shield and Desert Storm, KC-10s flown by Reserve Associate crews and ARC KC-135s refueled more than 22,000 aircraft. ARC air crews helped move more than 525,000 tons of equipment and supplies and nearly 330,000 personnel. More than 400 Naval Intelligence and more than 70 Security Group cryptology reservists served in more than 30 commands and frequently were cited by commanders for their performance.

The 142nd FA Brigade, ARNG, providing fire support to the 4th British Armoured Brigade, moved 350 kilometers in the ground campaign's four days and fired 422 tons of ordnance. This was one of the larger amounts of ammunition expended by any Coalition FA brigade during the operation. The Navy depended upon Reserve forces for medical care, construction of beddown facilities, ammunition storage, harbor and port security, the Naval air logistics effort, countermine efforts, and the Military Sealift Command. The Marine Corps Reserve combat units success has been well publicized. B Company, 4th Tank Battalion was credited with destroying over 30 Iraqi armored vehicles during the attack into Kuwait. In addition, USMCR infantrymen, artillerymen, tank crewmen, and air crewmen acquitted themselves well.

When the cease fire was ordered on 28 February more than 105,000 RC personnel were serving in the theater of operations, including; 37,692 ARNG; 35,158 USAR; 6,625 USNR; 13,066 USMCR; 10,800 ARC; and 281 USCGR.

After the cease-fire, RC forces performed

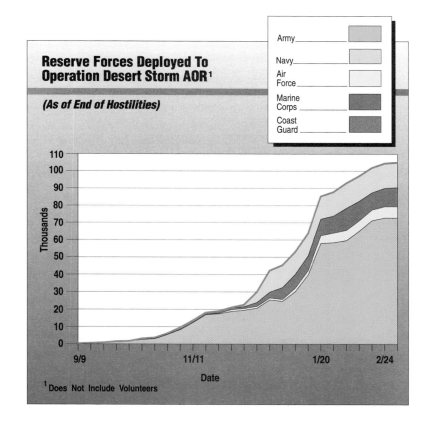

Reserve Forces Deployed To Operation Desert Storm AOR[1]

(As of End of Hostilities)

[1] Does Not Include Volunteers

missions in support of consolidation and redeployment. Reserve Civil Affairs, engineer, Military Police, water purification, and medical assets were engaged in humanitarian missions and restoration of crucial services in Southern Iraq and Kuwait. Reserve CS and CSS units remained in theater. Much of the recovery, backhaul, preparation for shipment, and loading of the tremendous amounts of US materiel and supplies that had accumulated in the Persian Gulf were entrusted to RC combat service support forces. By the end of August 1991, 1,022 Reservists, involuntarily activated, remained in the Persian Gulf. Another 4,463 Reserve volunteers were also in the theater to help in the redeployment.

USE AND PERFORMANCE OF RESERVE COMPONENT FORCES OUTSIDE THE THEATER

RC units and personnel also fulfilled important roles by backfilling units and personnel that deployed to SWA from both the US and overseas locations. USMCR stood in for Active USMC units in both II and III MEF, enabling the USMC to continue to fulfill its global commitments. Infantry battalions, artillery batteries, helicopter squadrons, and a fixed-wing squadron replaced deployed units on Okinawa and Iwakuni, thus maintaining US forward-deployed presence in the Western Pacific. The USMCR 2nd Marine Expeditionary Brigade (MEB) was activated and participated in Exercise Battle Griffin in Norway, in place of the deployed 4th MEB.

Army RC members were used to provided crucial support functions in the United States and Europe. These included terminal operations, force protection, installation support, and sustainment of the AC medical care system. The Army also activated an USAR infantry battalion for duty in Europe and an ARNG Special Forces Group to respond to worldwide contingencies.

Naval Reservists deployed outside of the

theater also provided support. For example, when the Fast Support Ship USNS Antares was disabled at sea, RCHB 4 mobilized and deployed to Rota, Spain, to unload the cargo within 72 hours. RCHBs 5 and 11 managed the greatly increased volume of Navy cargo at Guam and in the Philippines. Seabee battalions were recalled to replace active battalions which had deployed to SWA from Guam, Okinawa, and Puerto Rico.

ARC members provided crucial support services such as aerial refueling, aerial port and air base operations, aeromedical evacuation, and rear echelon medical support. They also provided medical support for units remaining in the United States and the dependents of deployed personnel.

Use of the RC to replace AC units deployed to the theater of operations gave the DOD considerable flexibility. It allowed US forces to deploy more rapidly and to get into place needed combat elements and their supporting activities, while maintaining commitments throughout the world.

ASSESSMENT

During Operations Desert Shield and Desert Storm, the Total Force Policy and the nation's reliance on Reserve forces were tested in ways unprecedented since the adoption of the policy. The call to active duty and the performance of the RC members who served in connection with the Gulf conflict were marked by extraordinary success. In his 6 March, 1991, address to the Congress, the President declared that the magnificent victory in the war "belongs...to the regulars, to the reserves, to the National Guard. This victory belongs to the finest fighting force this nation has ever known in its history."

It should be recognized, however, that Operations Desert Shield and Desert Storm took place as the nation was adopting a new military

Reserve Components Ready Reserve Activated as of February 24, 1991

	Selected Reserve (Unit Members and IMAs)			Individual Ready Reserve		
	Activated	FY 90 Authorized End Strength	% of Total	Activated	Strength as of 30 Sep 1990	% of Total
ARNG	60,427	458,000	13	0	0	0
USAR	65,277	321,700	20	13,841	284,221	5
USNR	17,980	153,400	12	15	87,439	<1
USMCR	23,271	44,000	53	5,268	37,433	14
ANG	10,456	116,200	9	0	0	0
AFR	21,024	84,900	25	767	68,714	1
USCGR	877	15,000	6	0	5,109	0
Total	199,312	1,193,200	17	19,891	482,916	4

strategy, a new force structure, and a new AC/RC force mix to meet the requirements of rapidly changing geopolitical circumstances. The success of the Total Force Policy in Operations Desert Shield and Desert Storm will provide a solid foundation for the planning currently under way to ensure the future Total Force remains effective.

OBSERVATIONS

Accomplishments

- Operations Desert Shield and Desert Storm required the largest mobilization and deployment of RC forces since the Korean Conflict.

- Operations Desert Shield and Desert Storm validated the key concepts underlying the DOD Total Force Policy.

- RC contributions were essential to success in the KTO and were instrumental in meeting challenges in other overseas theaters and in CONUS.

- RC volunteers were effectively used to support the early phases of the Persian Gulf contingency. Many volunteers augmented each Service. They accomplished many missions until the involuntary activation of RC units.

- The first large scale involuntary call-up of RC units and individuals was implemented in a systematic fashion in accordance with the provisions of Title 10 of the US Code, Sections 673b, 673c, and 673.

- For the most part, when RC forces were activated, their readiness levels were sufficiently high to ensure mission accomplishment with a minimum of post-mobilization training.

- The integration of AC and RC units generally was good. Reserves performed a wide range of missions including combat, combat support, and combat service support.

- Rapid DOD action in requesting Congressional assistance in updating and increasing Reserve Component entitlements was significant in providing for the welfare of Reserve personnel and their families.

- The activation of Reserve forces from thousands of communities across the nation and the full integration of their capabilities into CINCCENT's campaign plan helped to ensure the American public's support for the operation.

- Employers of activate Reservists were generally supportive of their Reserve employees, and the Services took steps to mitigate the trauma of Reservists' separation from their families.

Shortcomings

- Absence from units of those RC personnel who had volunteered earlier caused some initial difficulties which were overcome through cross-leveling and other personnel actions.

- Some RC forces, particularly large ground combat maneuver units, need some post-mobilization training, often in CONUS, to prepare them for operational missions. During Operations Desert Shield and Desert Storm, a misperception existed that the three Army RC brigades could be made ready for deployment with little or no post-mobilization training. This was never the intent.

- Incompatibility of automation systems between AC and RC, particularly in the Army, complicated the transition of RC personnel to active duty, created pay and personnel tracking problems, and hindered post mobilization training. Personnel automation support was a shortcoming in mobilization operations. Current infrastructure cannot satisfy the demands placed on it during mobilization. Current systems are not designed to meet wartime needs.

- Operations Desert Shield and Storm demonstrated the importance of premobilization family preparedness and of family support in the National Guard and Reserve. Overall, the family programs worked well and provided cross-service support to all military families. Nevertheless, DOD is reviewing the peacetime structure and is studying ways to strengthen family support as the force structure and organization changes. This review includes a survey of RC members and their spouses and field visits to National Guard and Reserve units to assess the effectiveness of family support programs.

Issue

- Operations Desert Shield and Desert Storm demonstrated the importance of timely access to the RC — both individuals and units. OSD is studying ways to improve access based upon the experience gained in the Gulf crisis.

Appendix I

COALITION DEVELOPMENT, COORDINATION, AND WARFARE

HISTORICAL PERSPECTIVE

One of the more important and interesting aspects of the Gulf War was the remarkable coalition of nations that joined ranks to turn back Saddam Hussein. It is useful to examine the conditions that facilitated the creation of this coalition, and to trace its evolution from the initial response to Saddam Hussein's invasion of Kuwait through the one-sided victory which Coalition efforts achieved seven months later.

Coalitions are different from alliances inasmuch as they tend to be more loosely structured and often focus on a single objective. Alliances more often are agreements to promote the allies' security in whatever situations arise for an extended period. Operations Desert Shield and Desert Storm underscored the advantages of common strategy, doctrine, tactics, and procedures developed by decades of training with North Atlantic Treaty Organization (NATO) allies. By the same token, exercises with friends in the Gulf region, where the United States has maintained a continuous military presence for more than 40 years, paid similar dividends. Still, the Gulf War underscored the need for further improvement in the ability of Coalition forces to conduct combined operations. Overall, the overwhelming success of this operation, combined with its lessons, comprises a possible model for international cooperation in future crises.

Since the 1950s, US foreign policy has included a long-term commitment to security assistance,

> *"We learned — and relearned — a lot of lessons from this partnership. The first was that life is a lot easier when you're not alone."*
>
> **Senior US Desert Storm Participant**

which helped develop strong relationships with NATO and Coalition partners. Security assistance and defense sales provide compatibility of equipment; the training that comes with US hardware often leads recipients to adopt US doctrine and tactics, resulting in operational compatibility as well. The US Foreign Military Sales (FMS) system provided Saudi military infrastructure, US-origin equipment and training for most of the partners, and the foundation of peacetime cooperation and interoperability on which the Coalition was built.

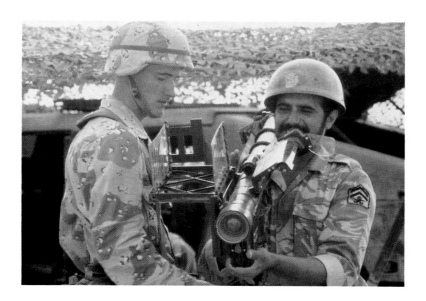

FOUNDATIONS FOR MILITARY COALITION

Political Consensus

Most nations perceived Iraq's invasion of Kuwait as entirely without justification. Furthermore, Iraq's posture after the invasion would have had unacceptable political consequences in the Gulf. Many feared the brutal attack would introduce an era in which Gulf states would be intimidated by Iraq's overwhelming military superiority. There also was the possibility that Iraq would continue its aggression and attack Saudi Arabia if the conquest of Kuwait were unopposed. Leading world powers soon formed a consensus to deny Iraq the possibility of further aggression. This widely shared view, that Iraq's aggression had created a threat to stability in an important part of the world, was the basis for formation of the Coalition to defend Saudi Arabia and eventually eject Iraq from Kuwait.

Saudi Arabia's request for military assistance to defend against the possibility of attack was a prerequisite for effective collective action against Iraq. Saudi Arabia's geographic position, wealth, and political prominence on the Arabian Peninsula meant its decision to grant access to friendly foreign military forces was indispensable to building the Coalition. Following Saudi Arabia's decision, the other Gulf states granted access to friendly military forces for their defense.

While Saudi Arabia made bilateral arrangements for assistance by friendly foreign nations, the United Nations condemned Iraq and initiated economic sanctions, isolating Iraq politically and economically.

International Environment

Internal difficulties distracted the Soviet Union from greater attention to Southwest Asia (SWA), and improved East-West relations removed many obstacles to international consensus. This central feature of the international environment made cooperation among nations easier. Unfettered by the antagonisms of the Cold War, the United Nations closed ranks, opposed Saddam Hussein's illegal occupation, and, ultimately, authorized measures necessary to expel Iraq from Kuwait.

Access and Resources

Within the Gulf Region

King Fahd's request for US help in defending the Kingdom was essential to the Coalition's success. Conscious of the need for decisive action, on 5 August President Bush sent the Secretary of Defense, the Under Secretary of Defense for Policy, the Commander-in-Chief, Central Command (CINCCENT) and the commanders of the Army and Air Force Components of Central Command (ARCENT and CENTAF) to Riyadh to see the King. The next day, the delegation and the US Ambassador to Saudi Arabia were given a royal audience, and they showed the King intelligence indicating Iraq had brought far more forces into Kuwait than were necessary to occupy it. The implication was that Saddam Hussein might commit further acts of aggression, and the obvious target was the oil fields in the Saudi Eastern Province and the other Gulf Cooperation Council (GCC) countries.

Saudi Arabia's request for assistance authorized friendly foreign nations to deploy, station, and operate large military forces on Saudi territory and in its airspace. This included authority to use telecommunications, roads, airfields, ports, bases, and buildings. Saudi Arabia also provided water, food, shelter, and fuel for friendly forces. Other Gulf states authorized similar access for friendly foreign forces.

A unique and crucial advantage to the Coalition was Saudi Arabia's creation, during the past 20 years, of an extensive and highly capable infrastructure of air and sea ports, including some roads, power generation and distribution systems, and water and petroleum production facilities. Saudi foresight in building this infrastructure greatly eased the task of receiving and supporting the deployment of large military forces. Much of the military construction in Saudi Arabia was accomplished under the US FMS program. This process is discussed in greater detail in Appendix F.

Saudi Arabia and other Gulf states also acquired military equipment from western suppliers and through the US FMS programs. They have adopted western military doctrine and tactics, modified to meet their specific needs. Some GCC nations' military officers have attended western military schools. Before the Gulf War, western military forces had participated with the GCC in limited exercises involving mainly naval and air forces. Peacetime cooperation through the FMS program, training, education, and these limited exercises formed a basis for more intensive wartime collaboration.

Security assistance emerged as a central pillar of coalition warfare, and when Operation Desert Shield began, FMS requests surged. Countries in the region found their stocks insufficient, as did distant Coalition members who had either forces participating in theater or defensive commitments to countries bordering Iraq. As both the US and its Coalition partners scrambled to meet these sudden shortfalls, stockage and production capability lagged demand, and the Diversion Decision Consideration process, developed to resolve FMS needs for scarce supplies, became necessary for more than 240 FMS crucial requests.

Outside the Gulf Region

Outside the Gulf region, Operations Desert Shield and Desert Storm deployments required a massive transportation effort made possible only by extensive international cooperation. Of particular importance, many nations granted access for overflight and landing rights,

overland transportation, and use of port facilities. In addition, as discussed in Appendix P, several nations provided cash and in-kind material and lift support to offset the costs of the US deployments.

Key to arranging for the movement of US forces to the theater was the role outside the Gulf region of those Unified and Specified commanders supporting the Central Command (CENTCOM). This support consisted of two principal elements, one the military assets and resources provided to CENTCOM, and the other the orchestration of the support. This orchestration was essential to deployments into the theater during Operation Desert Shield and to preparation for the conduct of combat during Operations Desert Shield and Desert Storm. In effect, there was within the larger Coalition a network of US activities overseas — the unified Commanders-in-Chief (CINCs), their subordinate commanders, embassies, attaches, and security assistance offices — which arranged overflight, access, transit, staging rights, and other support, such as hospital facilities and security services for the deploying forces. The European Command (EUCOM) and Pacific Command (PACOM) organizations were particularly instrumental in coordinating this support.

BUILDING THE MILITARY COALITION

Cultural Sensitivity

Deployment of large numbers of US forces to Saudi Arabia meant harmonizing western culture with the the birthplace of Islam. A rigorous indoctrination program was undertaken to orient US personnel on the region's unique history, customs, religion, law, and mores.Since Islam eschews alcohol, CINCCENT issued a general order prohibiting consumption of alcohol in the CENTCOM area of operations (with waivers granted on a country-by-country basis). In recognition of Islamic sensitivities regarding attire, CINCCENT established a civilian dress code designed to reduce the likelihood of inadvertent offense.

Saudi Arabian standards of propriety in public media are considerably more conservative than those of the United States, so programming transmitted by the Armed Forces Radio and Television Service was monitored to avoid material that would be offensive, and service members were asked to comply with standards concerning material sent in the mail. United Service Organization entertainers were given area orientation briefings and performers cooperated by ensuring their tours were in consonance with Saudi sensibilities.

Saudi practice of Islam includes specific rules governing most aspects of female conduct. US women were provided thorough briefings concerning these rules and effectively adapted to the situation. Saudi Arabia also made some accommodations of cultural difference — for example, the prohibition against women driving was lifted if that was part of their official duty.

To provide some access to recreation of a Western flavor, as well as some relief for service men and women from the harsh environment and arduous duty of Operation Desert Shield, the US government chartered the cruise ship Cunard Princess which docked in Bahrain and began its first cycle of rest and recuperation (R&R) operations on 24 December. With a berthing capacity of 900 in 398 cabins, the Cunard Princess made available a four-day, three-night R&R package for more than 50,000 service men and women of all branches and ranks (the vast majority junior) in its first six months of operation. Lodging, dining, sports, recreation activities, and local tour packages were paid for by the government; discretionary costs, such as snack foods, beverages, retail and concessionaire purchases were borne by the service members. At the request of the US Ambassador to Bahrain, the ship had the additional mission of evacuating US citizens in an emergency. Armed Forces

> "It was hot. The daytime temperatures in the summer were often over 115 degrees, and sometimes 120. And drier than Phoenix — you could get dehydrated just from taking a nap. Then in the winter it would freeze at night, down into the twenties or even the teens. There were scorpions all over — in your bed, in your shoes, in your pack — but they weren't as bad as the flies. Those flies were huge, and swarmed so thick you had to learn to eat with one hand and swat with the other. And sand. Fine, powdery sand that got everywhere — in your clothes and in your equipment, no matter what you did to try and screen it. When the wind blew, you didn't have to brush your teeth — just smile and they'd get sand-blasted clean."
>
> *Desert Storm Airman*

Reserve Center — Bahrain, as it was officially called, ceased operations on 23 September 1991, and the Cunard Princess was released from contract.

It is a tribute to American service men and women that, under conditions of considerable stress and hardship, they demonstrated impeccable respect for a culture much different from their own. They recognized the importance to their mission of the overall relationship between Saudi Arabia and the United States. Their superb conduct will have a long-lasting, positive effect; the reputation they established will make it easier to build future coalitions with Middle Eastern and other partners.

DEFENSIVE PHASE — OPERATION DESERT SHIELD

Planning

On 8 August , after King Fahd had requested assistance and granted access for deployment of US forces, senior CENTCOM and Saudi planners agreed to establish a combined group to plan the defense of Saudi Arabia, with the additional responsibility of proposing command arrangements for their respective commanders. The combined planning group concentrated on the ground campaign since the bulk of Arab forces were ground forces. Later they produced the Combined Operations Plan (OPLAN) for offensive operations to eject Iraqi forces from Kuwait (Operation Desert Storm) and numerous other contingency plans.

By mid-August, the combined planning group was briefed on the US unilateral plan (OPLAN 1002-90) to defend Saudi Arabia. This initial combined planning group was composed of the CENTCOM J5, the Ministry of Defense and Aviation (MODA) J3, general officers from the various Saudi armed forces, and a working group of US and Saudi field grade officers. The Saudi officers were the operations deputies for their respective services, and the press of requirements to prepare for an imminent attack by Iraq made it impossible for them to devote sufficient time to the combined planning group. As a result, the CENTCOM J5 and MODA J3 agreed to share responsibility for developing a combined OPLAN for the defense of Saudi Arabia.

There is an aphorism that plans are worthless, but planning is indispensable. Although four major combined OPLANs eventually were developed, the most valuable aspect of the combined planning process was that it required that the Saudis plan for the reception, sustainment, and integration of Coalition forces and it provided the only forum to identify and resolve combined issues across all functional areas. Moreover, it provided a mechanism for rapid access to US and Saudi decision makers and institutionalized the plan development process for the Saudis.

Initial planning for the defense of Saudi Arabia (Operation Desert Shield) evolved from the concept developed earlier by the US for the defense of the Arabian Peninsula, modified to include a larger force. The concept of operations was to establish initial defenses with US forces in the vicinity of Al Jubayl and reduce enemy forces with tactical airpower as they attacked across the 100 miles from the Kuwait border to US defensive positions. Concurrently, US forces would continue to deploy into Saudi Arabia through Ad Dammam, Dhahran and Al-Jubayl.

On 20 August, CINCCENT published Operation Order (OPORD) 003 as an interim combined defense plan. The purpose of OPORD 003 was to ensure US commanders understood the capabilities, intentions, and tasks of Saudi forces and to authorize the liaison and coordination necessary to establish a fully integrated Coalition defense. Although OPORD 003 was disseminated to only US forces, it was developed by the US/Saudi combined planning group and represented the first combined planning product of the crisis.

On 13 September, the combined planning team briefed a combined concept of operations for defense of Saudi Arabia to CINCCENT and Lieutenant General Khalid Bin Sultan Bin 'Abd Al-'Aziz. The commanders approved continued development of a combined defense plan and provided specific planning guidance. In October, Lieutenant General Khalid was designated Commander, Joint Force/Theater of Operations (later, Joint Forces Command (JFC)) and the MODA J3 was also the JF/Theater of Operations J5. The net result of this reorganization was that minor planning decisions no longer required approval of the MODA Chief of Staff. Lieutenant General Khalid's new position increased his decision-making authority and improved US access to top Saudi officials. These changes substantially improved the combined planning process.

As additional countries continued to provide forces for the defense of Saudi Arabia and the Coalition's combat capability increased, the concept for defending Saudi Arabia with a US-only force, or a US/Saudi force as reflected in OPORD 003, became obsolete. The initial combined defense concept relied on an economy of force in the Northern Area Command (NAC) and in the sector between NAC and the Eastern

Area Command (EAC). As other nations offered additional combat units, the opportunity arose to establish substantially stronger defenses and reduce the risk to Coalition forces. By 15 October, Syria agreed to provide one combat division and the Egyptians already were defending north of Hafr Al-Batin with one mechanized division and offering to provide another division if requested by Saudi Arabia.

War game analyses confirmed the inadequacy of available forces to defend the NAC, encompassing a large area surrounding Hafr Al-Batin and King Khalid Military City (KKMC). These analyses showed that with the addition of an Egyptian division and a Syrian division, a successful defense of the NAC was possible. Saudi Arabia accepted the Egyptian offer.

The final combined defense plan for Operation Desert Shield (Combined OPLAN for the Defense of Saudi Arabia) was signed on 29 November and published in Arabic and English versions, and Coalition forces generally were used accordingly. CINCCENT's intent was to wait until all forces arrived in theater and issue an execute order. As it transpired, there was no major Iraqi attack beyond Kuwait; and the need for supporting plans from subordinate commands and a CINCCENT execute order was obviated by the decision to deploy additional forces and begin repositioning Coalition units in preparation for offensive operations.

Forces

Forces from outside the Gulf region began deployment to Saudi Arabia soon after Iraq's invasion of Kuwait. Egyptian and Syrian special forces were among the first Arab forces to arrive, augmenting Saudi and GCC forces already present. US naval combatants were present in the Gulf of Oman and Persian Gulf when the Iraqi forces attacked. US forces began deploying on 7 August, and elements of the

82nd Airborne Division arrived the next day. US Air Force (USAF) air superiority fighters, airborne warning and control system (AWACS) aircraft, and air refueling tankers arrived in Saudi Arabia on 8 August; bomber aircraft began deploying on 11 August and, four days later, 20 were in place. On 8 August, Maritime Prepositioning Ships sailed from Diego Garcia and US Marines prepared to join them at Al-Jubayl. United Kingdom (UK) Jaguar air-to-ground fighters and Tornado strike fighters were in the region by the end of August. The arrival of substantial numbers of ground attack aircraft from the United States during August combined with the carrier-based air already in the Gulf of Oman to produce a formidable force. In addition, many nations contributed light forces that could be deployed quickly. These early commitments signalled global resolve and served as a deterrent to further Iraqi aggression.

Heavier forces began arriving by September. The 3rd Egyptian Mechanized Division began deployment on 21 September and had completed deployment on 6 October. In CINCCENT's assessment, by early October there were enough ground forces available to defend against further invasion. The 7th UK Armoured Brigade began deploying 15 October and completed deployment by 20 November, augmenting the Marines deployed near Al-Jubayl (although they ultimately moved to and fought with VII Corps). Deployment of the 9th Syrian Armored Division began on 1 November and was completed on 18 December. The 4th Egyptian Armored Division deployed initially on 19 December and completed deploying by 7 January.

The deployment of air-delivered munitions built up steadily to support land-based air forces. CINCCENT reported that by mid-September, there was enough capability to conduct an offensive air campaign as well as defensive air operations against the full range of Iraqi targets, had there been an invasion.

Naval forces that participated in the maritime operations of Desert Shield and Desert Storm included those of Argentina, Australia, Bahrain, Belgium, Canada, Denmark, France, Germany, Greece, Italy, Netherlands, Norway, Oman, Poland, Portugal, Qatar, Saudi Arabia, Spain, Turkey, the United Arab Emirates (UAE), UK, and United States. Further discussion of maritime operations is in the ensuing section on sanctions in this appendix.

Command Arrangements

Command arrangements for Operation Desert Shield evolved as Saudi Arabia made agreements with friendly nations for deployment of their forces. Foreign Islamic forces were invited with the understanding they would operate under Saudi operational command. US forces would be commanded by the US National Command Authority (NCA) with CINCCENT exercising command in theater. The initial agreement allowing the entry of US forces into Saudi Arabia provided for "strategic direction" of US forces by the Saudi Military Command, consistent with the constraints of the US Constitution. "Strategic direction" was never defined. After researching precedents, CENTCOM assumed the phrase to mean general guidance at a strategic level with no actual command authority, since the Constitution contains no provision for foreign command of US troops. The net effect of the wording was to accommodate both Saudi and US sensitivities, by allowing the Saudis to claim authority over the foreign forces on their soil, while at the same time respecting US requirements to adhere to the provisions of the Constitution.

The UK arranged with Saudi Arabia for British forces to be under tactical control (TACON) of CINCCENT while the UK NCA maintained command. France arranged for an independent chain of command for French forces reporting to the French NCA while agreeing to coordinate operations in theater with Saudi Arabia's military command. Later, the Coalition shifted to an offensive plan and the French ground forces were placed TACON to ARCENT around mid-December, ultimately to serve on the westernmost flank of XVIII Airborne Corps. Thus the NCAs retained command of their forces while selected Western and all Islamic nations authorized the US or Saudi Arabia to exercise operational control of their forces.

Arab forces in the Kuwaiti Theater of Operations (KTO) were under EAC or NAC operational control depending on their location. The EAC tactical sector for Operation Desert Shield lay from Kuwait south to the northernmost limit of the US sector and from the east coast west to a line extending roughly south from the westernmost part of the Kuwait panhandle. The main forces assigned to EAC were Saudi and GCC forces. The NAC encompassed the area south of Kuwait and Iraq excluding the EAC sector. The NAC included Hafr Al-Batin, KKMC and the terrain feature Wadi Al-Batin, a dry river bed that runs along the Kuwait-Iraq border south-southwest into Saudi Arabia. Most major Arab forces that eventually deployed to Saudi Arabia were in NAC, including two Egyptian divisions and a Syrian division. While EAC and NAC exercised operational control (OPCON) during Operation Desert Shield, OPCON during Operation Desert Storm was exercised by forward tactical headquarters with different commanders and staffs. These new commands were called Joint Forces Command East and North (JFC-E and JFC-N). EAC and NAC functioned as rear area commands during offensive operations.

Arrangements for command and operational control of military forces reflected the sense of national, ethnic, and religious pride which were of great importance to every nation participating in the Coalition. Parallel chains of command satisfied these political considerations and placed a premium on cooperation among the leadership of major Coalition forces. It is a tribute to the commanders involved that they were able to establish an effective and cooperative relationship.

The combined group described earlier did the planning for the Coalition. Operational coordination was facilitated by establishing the Coalition, Coordination, Communications, and Integration Center (C^3IC) in the MODA building that served as the headquarters for both CINCCENT and Commander Joint Forces/Theater of Operations, the Saudi commander of Islamic forces. C^3IC was the center for intelligence and operational information exchange and assessment. A metaphor for the cooperative spirit of the Coalition, it ensured coordination of operations among the Coalition forces from the theater command level, as well as providing resolved informally and collegially among staff officers.

The C^3IC grew out of the requirement, recognized in the first days of Operation Desert Shield, to establish some kind of combined command center which was not a section of an existing US or Saudi headquarters. It began in mid-August with a small, lean, multi-service team built from the staffs of component commands by a US and a Saudi major general. After an initial period in which the members strove to establish their role, the C^3IC emerged as a bridge between CENTCOM and the Saudi-created EAC and NAC. Mid-grade officers established personal relationships with the staffs of their respective national commands which permitted them to bring information into the C^3IC. Saudi and US counterparts then worked closely together to produce briefings which could be delivered by both Saudi and US officers. The congenial atmosphere at the action level reflected the amity of the most senior leaders; but a key to the effectiveness of the arrangement was the formality of the meeting and briefing structure. The resulting predictability helped prevent surprises and embarrassment, and the presence of very senior

officers on both sides underlined the importance of the work produced.

As early as August, with the prospect of more and more Coalition forces being committed to support Operation Desert Shield using different equipment and command and control (C^2) procedures, CINCCENT had recognized two important requirements: to assess their capabilities and limitations, and to ensure they were integrated at the operational and tactical level. In the case of front-line, combat units, the Coalition Warfare Support mission was tasked to US Special Operations Forces (SOF) because of their unique capabilities — language and cultural orientation skills, wide range of tactical and technical expertise, and high levels of training. A fuller discussion of their activities is in Appendix J. Other US forces provided liaison teams to non-US Coalition partner (NCP) support units. The United States assigned these teams to NCP commanders down to battalion level. Using US communications systems, they coordinated with appropriate US and NCP commands in their area of responsibility (AOR). The liaison officers who helped train Arab units in combined tactics and procedures during Operation Desert Shield worked with the same units during hostilities to smooth battlefield coordination. Among the most important tasks of US liaison teams was indirect fire support coordination for the NCP units to which they were assigned. Most Coalition nations also exchanged liaison personnel with nearby ground and air units. Coordination of ground operations was improved by the assignment of AORs designed to minimize mutual interference between forces speaking different languages. The network of US liaison officers provided the best (and sometimes the only) comprehensive command, control, and communications (C^3) system among the diverse Coalition forces, insuring that commanders of all units remained well informed of emerging developments.

As a complementary program, Kuwait also provided interpreters for liaison with US forces

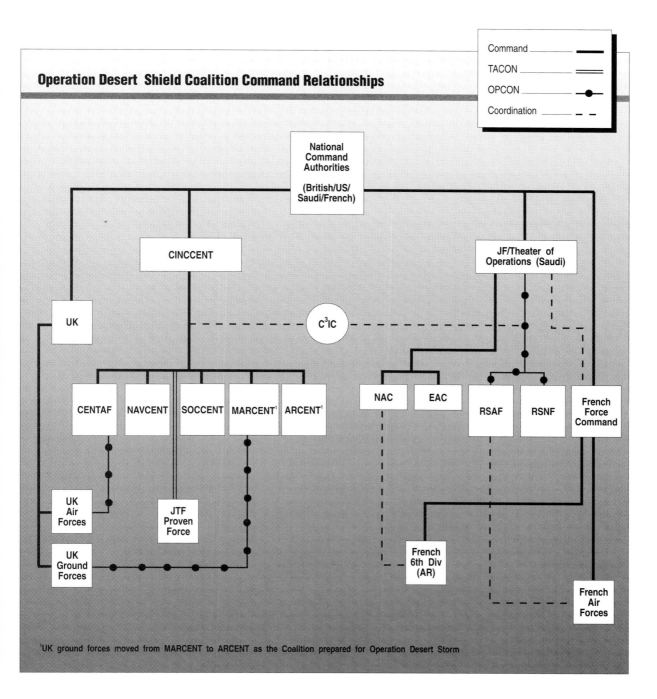

Operation Desert Shield Coalition Command Relationships

Command ——————
TACON ——————
OPCON ——————
Coordination —— ——

National Command Authorities

(British/US/Saudi/French)

CINCCENT

JF/Theater of Operations (Saudi)

UK

C³IC

CENTAF NAVCENT SOCCENT MARCENT¹ ARCENT¹

NAC EAC

RSAF RSNF French Force Command

UK Air Forces

JTF Proven Force

UK Ground Forces

French 6th Div (AR)

French Air Forces

¹UK ground forces moved from MARCENT to ARCENT as the Coalition prepared for Operation Desert Storm

assisting in the liberation of their country. Soldiers, teachers, students — all manner of people fluent in English who had escaped the invasion — measurably improved Coalition cooperation by donating their linguistic skills.

The presence of large numbers of aircraft from many nations and services presented a significant challenge to C² of air operations. Aircraft operations were concentrated in the Persian Gulf region and northeastern Saudi Arabia. During the defensive phase, air operations typically included strategic and theater airlift, air defense, surveillance and reconnaissance, intense training, and commercial airlift flights. Planning and exercising for the defense of Saudi Arabia envisioned a massive air attack that included close air support (CAS), battlefield interdiction, air defense, and sustained bombing against strategic targets in Iraq.

While Saudi Arabia had a substantial civil and military aviation capability and infrastructure, the magnitude of Coalition air forces and the scope of their operations required extraordinary resources and adherence to procedures to coordinate operations safely and effectively. CENTAF prepared a daily air tasking order

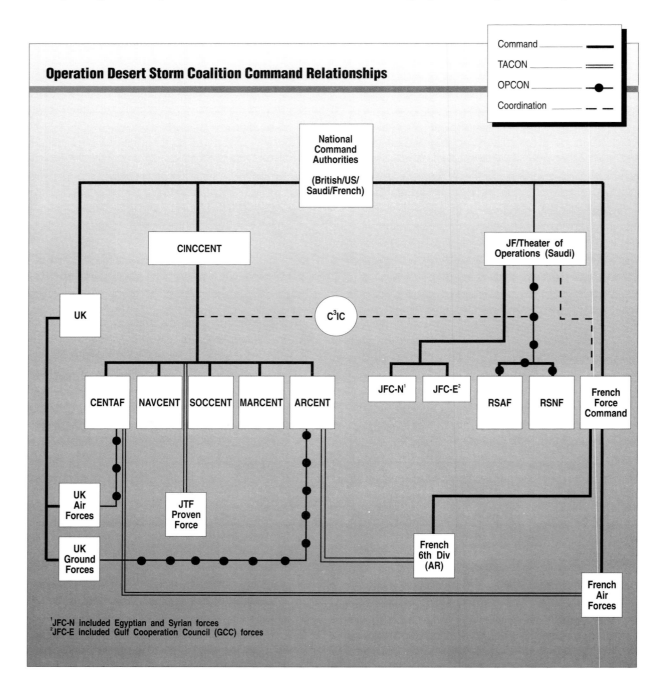

Operation Desert Storm Coalition Command Relationships

Command ————
TACON ————
OPCON ——●—
Coordination — — —

National Command Authorities (British/US/Saudi/French)

CINCCENT

JF/Theater of Operations (Saudi)

UK

C³IC

CENTAF   NAVCENT   SOCCENT   MARCENT   ARCENT

JFC-N¹   JFC-E²   RSAF   RSNF   French Force Command

UK Air Forces

JTF Proven Force

French 6th Div (AR)

UK Ground Forces

French Air Forces

¹JFC-N included Egyptian and Syrian forces
²JFC-E included Gulf Cooperation Council (GCC) forces

(ATO) in coordination with the Royal Saudi Air Force (RSAF) with inputs from Coalition air elements. This procedure maintained readiness of Coalition air forces and ensured flight safety. Despite the fact that during Operations Desert Shield and Desert Storm more than 2,700 aircraft from 10 countries flew some 112,000 missions, cooperation among Coalition air forces resulted in a perfect record of no friendly air-to-air engagements and no mid-air collisions. Considering the tempo of air operations and the diversity of the Coalition, this was a monumental achievement.

Coalition nations' NCAs maintained command of naval forces with a high level of multinational cooperation orchestrated by the United States. Individual national naval commanders in theater exercised OPCON of Coalition naval forces, with units of one nation occasionally operating under the tactical control of another. The benefits of an effective peacetime exercise program and cooperation among the commanders and units of Coalition navies made for well coordinated maritime intercept operations (MIO).

Summary

Operation Desert Shield was a political and military success because there was time to create a broadly based coalition which isolated Iraq, deterred it from further invasion, implemented sanctions, reassured Gulf states of the world's resolve to defend them against aggression, maintained access to Gulf oil, and empowered the United Nations to act effectively against aggression. Coalition military forces cooperated in the defense of Saudi Arabia and arranged for C^2 of defensive operations.

Deployment would have been impossible without the contribution of strategic airlift and sealift from around the world, but the emplacement of a force adequate to defend Saudi Arabia took several weeks. Prepositioning more equipment and supplies in the region could

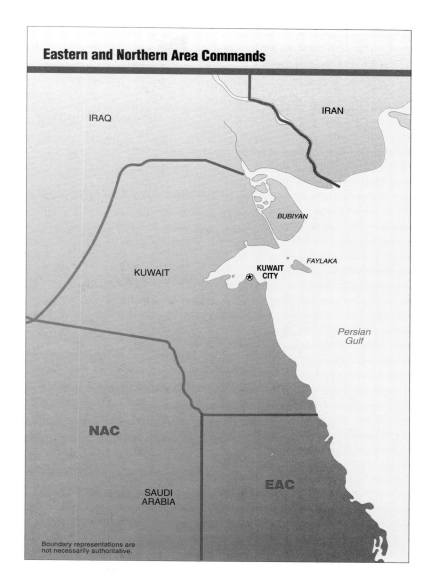

Eastern and Northern Area Commands

IRAQ

IRAN

BUBIYAN

KUWAIT

FAYLAKA

KUWAIT CITY

Persian Gulf

NAC

SAUDI ARABIA

EAC

Boundary representations are not necessarily authoritative.

accelerate the process in another emergency, when there may be less time to deploy.

Offensive Phase — Operation Desert Storm

Planning

Anticipating the possible requirement to eject Iraq from Kuwait, CINCCENT began unilateral contingency planning for offensive operations in August, while at the same time planning with the NCPs for the defense of Saudi Arabia. Although the UK took part in the preliminary planning for offensive operations from late

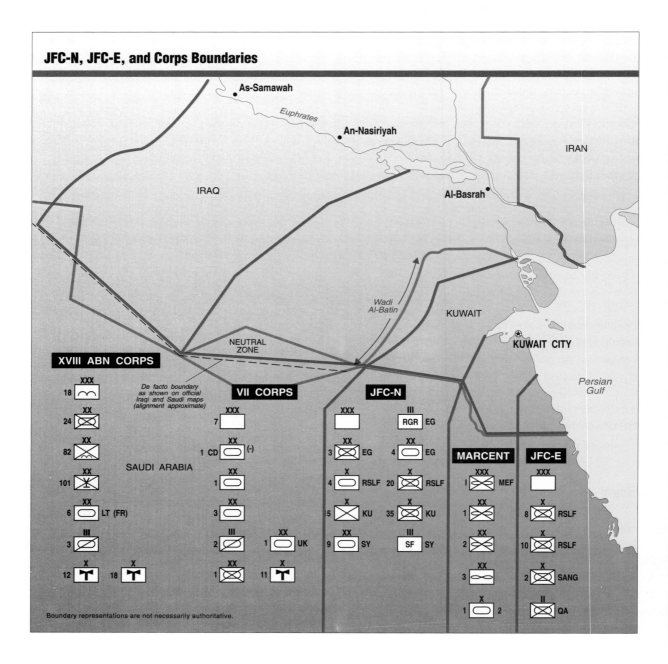

JFC-N, JFC-E, and Corps Boundaries

As-Samawah

Euphrates

An-Nasiriyah

IRAQ

IRAN

Al-Basrah

Wadi Al-Batin

KUWAIT

NEUTRAL ZONE

KUWAIT CITY

Persian Gulf

XVIII ABN CORPS

De facto boundary as shown on official Iraqi and Saudi maps (alignment approximate)

VII CORPS

JFC-N

MARCENT

JFC-E

SAUDI ARABIA

Boundary representations are not necessarily authoritative.

October, other NCPs were not formally involved until the United Nations and Coalition partners agreed to the operations in December.

Preliminary planning for offensive operations involved two major mutually supporting efforts. First, CENTAF planned for an air campaign that involved strikes against strategic targets deep in Iraq as well as targets in the KTO. Second, the

CENTCOM staff began planning for a ground campaign in conjunction with ARCENT.

During Exercise Internal Look in the weeks before the invasion, CINCCENT had formed the opinion that to eject Iraq from Kuwait with acceptable levels of risk and losses would require more forces than were on hand for Operation Desert Shield — that is, a single US

Army corps and a Marine division (MARDIV) augmented by an Egyptian corps, a Syrian division, Saudi and other GCC forces, a UK brigade and French forces. Nevertheless, initial ground campaign planning assessed all courses of action using this mix of forces. The process confirmed CINCCENT's conviction: at those force levels, the attack would have to drive straight into the teeth of Iraq's strongest defenses. It might well succeed, but the risk of failure was too great and the potential cost in casualties too high. More forces, on the other hand, would permit the now famous maneuver around the enemy's right flank to surprise and destroy his elite Republican Guard in strategic reserve. This would allow not only the liberation of Kuwait but also the reduction of Iraqi potential for future aggression, and it would do so without risk of inordinate casualties. The President, the Secretary of Defense, and the Chairman of the Joint Chiefs of Staff (CJCS) agreed. In November, the President announced the deployment of an additional Army corps, another MARDIV and amphibious brigade, increased combat service support, and double the existing Operation Desert Shield air and naval forces to ensure a short conflict with minimum casualties. An expanded account of the evolution of this thinking is in Chapters III and V.

On 29 November, the UN Security Council (UNSC) approved Resolution 678 to use all means necessary to enforce previous resolutions. By mid-December virtually all members were committed, and the same combined team that had planned the defense of Saudi Arabia began Coalition planning for offensive operations.

US planners briefed their NCP counterparts on preliminary proposals, including attacks by the Joint Forces/Theater of Operations (Arab forces) into Kuwait with Egyptian forces attacking in the west to secure Al Abraq and thence eastward to block approaches to Kuwait City. Saudi and GCC forces would attack along the coast east of

the Marine attack as well as in the west on the right flank of the Egyptian attack. It was proposed that Arab forces would liberate Kuwait City.

The combined operations plan was designed to achieve national goals of the Coalition partners and specified the following campaign objectives:

- Destroy Iraq's military capability to wage war
- Gain and maintain air supremacy
- Cut Iraqi supply lines
- Destroy Iraq's chemical, biological, and nuclear (NBC) capability
- Destroy Republican Guard forces
- Liberate Kuwait City with Arab forces

The plan called for battlefield preparation through early deception operations, air operations, and counter-reconnaissance operations which would fix Republican Guard forces in the KTO and cause Iraq to focus efforts in the eastern areas of Iraq and Kuwait.

The concept of operations also directed forces to continue to defend Saudi Arabia while preparing for offensive operations. The air attack was to focus on Iraqi centers of gravity: C^2, NBC capabilities, and the Republican Guard. The air campaign would move progressively into the KTO to isolate it and reduce the Iraqi defenses' effectiveness. A multi-axis ground, naval, and air attack would create the perception of a main attack in the east; however, the main effort would be in the west.

The combined operations plan directed JFC-E to conduct a supporting attack to penetrate Iraqi defenses and protect the Marine Component, Central Command (MARCENT) right flank. When directed, JFC-E forces were to secure Kuwait City.

JFC-N was directed to conduct a supporting

attack to penetrate Iraqi defenses and protect the right flank of VII Corps as far north as Al Abraq. When these objectives were achieved, JFC-N forces would continue the attack to block Iraqi lines of communication (LOC) north of Kuwait City and then help secure and clear it.

All commands were directed to secure crucial rear area facilities and LOCs. A separate Combined Theater Rear Operations Plan was promulgated as an annex to the Desert Storm OPLAN.

While it took almost four months to complete the combined plan for the defense of Saudi Arabia, it required only four weeks to plan the combined ground offensive campaign. Lessons learned from defensive planning accelerated the greater challenge of offensive planning. Translation of plan revisions from English to Arabic was the most time consuming task in plan preparation. It required Arab officers with considerable operational experience and English proficiency to translate important instructions to reflect the commander's intentions accurately. To streamline this process, the two theater commanders eliminated all but the most essential guidance from the offensive plan.

By keeping plan documents brief, the combined planning group was able to produce several contingency plans concurrently with the offensive plan: to respond to an Iraqi unilateral withdrawal from Kuwait; to clear and secure Kuwait City, assuming Iraq defended it; and to defend Saudi Arabia and Kuwait after offensive operations. The planning process was one of the Coalition's strengths.

Forces

NCPs contributed important forces to Operation Desert Storm. Egypt contributed the 4th Armored Division, 3rd Mechanized Division, and 20th Special Forces Regiment, all of which

played a key role in the attack into Kuwait. The UK contributed the 1st Armoured Division that participated in the main attack with VII Corps. The 6th French Light Armored Division participated with XVIII Airborne Corps in the westernmost attack into Iraq, protecting the left flank of the entire Coalition. Saudi Arabia's forces included five independent brigades and smaller units. Syria's 9th Armored Division and special forces regiment participated as the reserve for JFC-N. Saudi Arabia, Bahrain, Kuwait, Oman, and Qatar also contributed forces to the JFC-E Force. Kuwait forces included three independent brigades and smaller units. Overall, the contribution of the 160,000 non-US Coalition forces was essential to the success of the ground operation. This includes the forces of several smaller nations, which made a significant contribution to the success of Operation Desert Storm and, in some cases, made sacrifices disproportionate to their size.

In addition to ground forces, the UK contributed five tactical fighter squadrons, France provided three tactical fighter squadrons, Italy and Canada one fighter squadron each, Saudi Arabia five fighter wings, and Kuwait two tactical fighter squadrons.

Command Arrangements

Command arrangements during Operation Desert Storm evolved from arrangements in effect for Operation Desert Shield. US, Saudi, UK and French forces remained under the command of their respective national authorities. French forces retained their coordinating relationship with the Commander, Joint Forces/Theater of Operations, while the 6th French Armored Division was placed under ARCENT's TACON for Operation Desert Storm where it operated as a unit of XVIII Airborne Corps. British air and ground forces were under CENTAF and ARCENT TACON, respectively. With their forces split between two separate reporting chains, neither of which was British, UK commanders needed unusual flexibility and imagination. The smooth battlefield coordination is a tribute to their effectiveness. CINCCENT was the land component commander for ground forces assigned to ARCENT and MARCENT. Participating forces from Islamic nations were under the command of the Saudi Arabian Joint Forces/Theater of Operations Commander.

There were parallel command structures, for the forces controlled respectively by US and Saudi commanders. They agreed any military action or operation would be subject to mutual discussion and approval.

The plan established liaison teams to coordinate both operations between ground units and CAS to ground forces. While all Coalition partners provided liaison personnel, US liaison teams were assigned to Coalition units at every command level down to the battalion. US teams assigned to the NCP corps level had significant operational planning expertise as well as robust communication capabilities. They exchanged timely operational, planning, intelligence and logistics information between US and NCP commands during preparation for and conduct of the offensive.

Tying the Coalition ground forces into the C^{3}IC at the headquarters used by CINCCENT and Commander Joint Forces/Theater of Operations ensured that theater level commanders had a clear picture and issued coordinated guidance to forces participating in the ground campaign. The C^{3}IC and US liaison teams with their capable communications were important to effective C^2 during the ground war.

Summary

The achievement of broad-based support for offensive operations to eject Iraq from Kuwait required delicate diplomacy at the highest levels, which took place in consonance with the doubling of US forces in theater. Their resolve bolstered by UN Resolutions, the Coalition partners proved adept at planning, having learned the value of keeping combined planning

documents brief. The multi-corps ground forces were organized and employed in a manner which accommodated the individual sensitivities and political requirements of each nation, while matching missions with capabilities. The liaison teams of several nationalities and the C^{3}IC exerted a strong cohesive influence on the Coalition by streamlining communication and coordination.

COALITION OPERATIONS

Sanctions

Within the Gulf Region

Initial Coalition operations during Operation Desert Shield consisted mainly of the steady introduction of major ground forces by Coalition partners, and MIO to cut off resupply of Iraq's commerce and war materiel. On 16 August, CJCS directed CINCCENT to execute the MIO, effective 17 August, consistent with the scope of the UN Charter, article 51, and UNSC Resolution 661. At the same time, a notice to mariners was issued to alert merchant shipping of the operations and the potential for boardings. Coalition naval forces encountered merchant shipping bound for Iraqi ports with prohibited cargo during the earliest stages of Operation Desert Shield.

The Navy's extensive operating experience with foreign navies paid handsome dividends during the Maritime Intercept Force (MIF) operations. In fact, the Operation Desert Shield MIF was not the first multinational response to a crisis in the Persian Gulf. During the 1987-1988 Earnest Will operation, five nations, who were members of both the Western European Union (WEU) and NATO, participated with the United States in protecting reflagged shipping in the Persian Gulf. The broad-based cooperation during Operation Earnest Will improved working relationships among the participating nations, particularly between the US and France, and deepened trust and cooperation between the US and the GCC states. This experience helped pave the way for the successful Coalition effort during Operations Desert Shield and Desert Storm.

On 25 August, UNSC Resolution 665 approved the use of force in imposing trade sanctions against Iraq, and a growing number of nations began to assist in the MIO. To organize this increasingly complex operation, CINCCENT assigned overall MIF coordination to Naval Component, Central Command (NAVCENT). Accordingly, he sponsored the first monthly international Naval Planning Conference in Bahrain on 9 and 10 September, attended by 20 countries. Several approaches to MIO coordination were proposed, including use of WEU auspices; but the delegates decided on a loosely organized arrangement in which NAVCENT would take the lead. After the meeting, NAVCENT organized MIF operating sectors for the 17 Coalition navies who provided ships to the MIF — the six GCC states (Bahrain, Kuwait, Oman, Qatar, Saudi Arabia, and UAE), plus Australia, Belgium, Canada, Denmark, France, Greece, Italy, the Netherlands, Spain, UK, and United States. Of the remaining conferees, Argentina and Norway soon also provided ships, and Egypt made ports available for diverted shipping (as did Oman, Saudi Arabia, and UAE), as well as helping with surveillance. Each sector generally included ships from more than one country, in addition to the forces of the local GCC states, with the understanding that the senior naval officer in each sector was to act as the local sector coordinator. In the Red Sea and Northern Persian Gulf, the local coordinators usually were the US aircraft carrier battle group (CVBG) and destroyer squadron commanders. The GCC states played a vital role in the MIO by preventing merchant vessels from using their littoral waters to avoid the MIF.

Each participating naval force received its tasking, reporting requirements, interception, boarding, search and seizure guidance, and rules of engagement from its own NCA. Coalition navies coordinated their operations by ultra high frequency (UHF) and teletypewriter radio circuits. Ships equipped to do so used tactical data link. NAVCENT's monthly coordination meeting settled operating areas, ship availability, and procedures.

Disabling fire was authorized with NAVCENT approval, but was never used, although warning shots were fired on several occasions, hundreds of ships were boarded, and many were diverted for carrying prohibited cargo. Two MIF

Non-US Coalition Partners in Maritime Intercept Operations*

Country	Location
27 September 1990: 10 Countries, 42 Ships	
Australia	Gulf of Oman
Belgium	Gulf of Oman
Canada	Gulf of Oman
Denmark	Gulf of Oman
France	Djibouti
	Persian Gulf
	Red Sea
Greece	Red Sea
Italy	Arabian Sea
	Persian Gulf
Netherlands	Gulf of Oman
	Persian Gulf
Spain	Gulf of Oman
	Red Sea
	Strait of Hormuz
United Kingdom	Gulf of Oman
	Persian Gulf
15 December 1990: 12 Countries, 50 Ships	
Argentina	Gulf of Oman
	Persian Gulf
Australia	Gulf of Oman
Belgium	Gulf of Aden
	Gulf of Oman
Canada	Gulf of Oman
Denmark	Gulf of Oman
France	Djibouti
	Gulf of Oman
	Red Sea
Greece	Red Sea
Italy	Persian Gulf

* GCC ships patrolled in areas near their nation's territorial waters.

combatants normally conducted boarding operations. Efforts were made continually to maximize the participation of NCP navies in MIO to enhance multinational coordination and demonstrate international resolve. Boarding teams from one ship boarded the suspect vessel while the second ship remained nearby to render assistance.

Although the US Navy was involved in most of the MIO, ranging from intelligence gathering and surveillance to boardings and take downs,

Country	Location
Netherlands	Gulf of Oman
	Persian Gulf
Norway	Persian Gulf
Spain	Gulf of Oman
	Red Sea
	Strait of Hormuz
United Kingdom	Persian Gulf
15 February 1990: 12 Countries, 66 Ships	
Argentina	Gulf of Oman
	Persian Gulf
Australia	Gulf of Oman
Belgium	Gulf of Oman
	Port Said
Canada	Gulf of Oman
	Persian Gulf
Denmark	Persian Gulf
France	Djibouti
	Gulf of Oman
	Persian Gulf
	Port Said
	Red Sea
	Yanbu, Saudi Arabia
Greece	Red Sea
Italy	Persian Gulf
Netherlands	Gulf of Oman
	Persian Gulf
Norway	Persian Gulf
Spain	Gulf of Oman
	Red Sea
	Strait of Hormuz
United Kingdom	Persian Gulf

NCP navies performed almost half of all boardings. French, Greek, and Spanish ships participated in more than 85 percent of all boarding operations that did not involve the United States. US ships conducted several joint MIF boardings with Australian, Canadian, Greek, Spanish, and UK warships. The MIF's multinational character proved essential to the integration of the Coalition's political will and military power.

For example, among the first intercepts conducted by an NCP, the Saudi patrol boat *Hitteen* stopped, boarded, and searched a vessel carrying prohibited cargo on 1 September. Hitteen escorted the vessel to a UAE port for further inspection.

Another example of a multinational intercept occurred on 8 October, when *HMS Battleaxe* (F 89), *HMAS Adelaide* (F 01), and *USS Reasoner* (FF 1063) intercepted the Iraqi *MV Al Wasitti*. Al Wasitti refused to stop despite warning shots fired across the bow. Al Wasitti was then boarded by UK Marines inserted by helicopters, who forced the ship to stop. A law enforcement detachment from Reasoner boarded the ship, found it empty of cargo, and allowed it to proceed in accordance with procedures.

Also on 8 October, the Iraqi merchant ship Tadmur was boarded by *HMS Brazen* (F 91), *HMAS Darwin* (F 04), and *USS Goldsborough* (DDG 20) in the North Arabian Sea while the Tadmur was enroute from Aqaba to Iraq. Tadmur was carrying foodstuffs and was diverted to Muscat, Oman, where it was searched by British and Omani officials.

These examples of multinational participation in intercept operations emphasize the smooth tactical coordination of wartime operations, the necessity of having divert ports nearby, and the cooperation of the GCC nations in searching and administering ships diverted to their ports.

The Coalition naval embargo authorized by UNSC Resolution 665 and air embargo authorized by UNSC Resolution 670 were very effective in applying economic sanctions. The air embargo was never challenged; and as a result of Coalition efforts during the seven months of the Persian Gulf crisis, more than 165 ships from Coalition nations challenged more than 7,500 merchant vessels, boarded nearly a thousand ships to inspect manifests and cargo holds, and diverted 51 ships carrying more than one million tons of cargo in violation of UN sanctions. Commerce through Iraqi and Kuwaiti ports essentially was eliminated; ships were deterred from loading Iraqi oil while Turkey and Saudi Arabia prohibited use of Iraqi oil pipelines which crossed their territory. Virtually all Iraqi oil revenues were cut off, and the source of much of Iraq's international credit was severed, along with 95 per cent of the country's total pre-invasion revenue.

Outside the Gulf Region

While the principal military actions to enforce the UN sanctions occurred within the Gulf Region, there were supporting activities outside that area. In Europe and elsewhere, NCPs prepared naval ships for deployment and sailed them to SWA to support the MIO. Some nations, unable for various reasons to support Gulf operations directly, assisted by assuming patrol and presence duties which freed other Coalition naval forces for Gulf deployment. EUCOM developed defensive operations for the key LOCs running through the Mediterranean Sea. Control of these operations later were transferred to NATO and monitored by Allied Forces Southern Europe command structure.

Another action occurred in Italy which was of significance to the Persian Gulf naval operations. Iraq had ordered four frigates and six corvettes, all modern types and well armed, as new construction from Italian shipyards. Essentially ready and, in several cases, with Iraqi crews in place, the ships had not been delivered because contractual agreements were incomplete. When Operation Desert Shield began and the UN sanctions were implemented, Italy determined the ships would not be delivered to Iraq and began marketing them elsewhere.

Defensive Phase

Within the Gulf Region

While MIO were being conducted, initial Coalition ground operations during Operation Desert Shield involved deployment, debarkation, marshalling equipment and troops, movement to tactical assembly areas, training, and defensive employment. The largest NCP deployments were made by Egypt, Syria, France, and UK. Early arrival of Egyptian and Syrian heavy forces was delayed, in part, because Saudi Arabia was unable to receive them and provide support such as food, water, shelter, fuel, and transportation from ports of debarkation to tactical assembly areas (TAAs). The reason for the difficulty was that Saudi Arabia was already fully extended in providing these resources for the large US deployment. A key contribution in this process was 100 heavy equipment transporters (HETs) made available by Egypt. HET shortages plagued the Coalition on many occasions, and Egypt's timely assistance made a significant difference in the Coalition's ability to disperse heavy equipment from ports of entry and, later, to get it to the battle.

After most of the Phase I US deployments were completed, the most vulnerable area was the NAC where the force to space ratio was too thin. Deployment of Egyptian and Syrian heavy divisions in the NAC considerably improved the defenses and increased confidence in a successful Coalition defense against an Iraqi attack.

Egypt, Syria, and France transported their forces and equipment in ships to Red Sea ports where they were moved across Saudi Arabia to assembly areas in the NAC. In part, this path for deployments was made necessary by congestion in the east ports and LOCs as US forces deployed. Early deploying units remained near developed areas for water and other vital support during the hot season. Arrival in ports of debarkation involved consolidating troops with their equipment. This was facilitated by staging areas adjacent to piers where large numbers of personnel and quantities of equipment could be assembled and prepared for further movement. While expedient, this dense concentration of large numbers of troops inevitably presented a lucrative target.

After arrival in TAAs, units began a process of familiarization, organization, maintenance of equipment, and initial training. Familiarization and organization involved arranging for logistical support from the Saudis and exchanging orientation visits with previously deployed units or local troops in the area. Preparations included fortifying positions, providing screens, and establishing communications.

From the start, CENTCOM and ARCENT had placed a high priority on training Coalition forces although, at first, not all Coalition members were equally convinced of the value and necessity of combined training. The achievement of a consensus on this matter was important, because of the value of combined training in building trust and coordinating doctrine and tactics of Coalition forces. Although the Army had worked with Egyptians and Jordanians in past exercises, it never had trained with the Saudis or most of the other Arabs in the Coalition. The US Army Training and Doctrine Command deployed about 130 Mobile Training Teams and New Equipment Training Teams consisting of some 800 personnel to train soldiers in Europe and the Middle East. In addition to basic training for UAE females, they provided an abbreviated basic training course for more than 500 Kuwaiti linguists assigned to US Army units. Elements

of the 5th Special Forces Group had deployed with the first American troops to arrive in Saudi Arabia, and by 1 December, they already had instructed 13,000 NCP troops in 43 different subjects. Since the Coalition troops would have to rely on a largely American air force, communications and CAS received especially heavy emphasis, but the Green Berets also stressed weapons training and instruction in basic small unit tactics, chemical countermeasures, and land navigation.

Late in the defensive phase, training was increasingly oriented towards preparation for the offensive. US forces trained Coalition forces for breaching operations and constructed a full-scale replica of an Iraqi defensive position including mine fields, fortifications, trenches, and strong points. XVIII Airborne Corps also trained its counterparts, instituting a partnership program which paired each of its units with a corresponding Saudi formation from the EAC. The 3rd Armored Cavalry Regiment, for example, conducted live fire exercises with the 8th Saudi Armored Brigade, and American engineers instructed their Saudi counterparts in breaching techniques. Marines in the EAC also trained with Saudis and GCC forces, usually at the small unit level. Since many Arabs spoke English and some Americans Arabic, language did not prove a major barrier, but cultural sensitivities still made combined training a challenge for both sides from time to time.

Air operations during the defensive phase were designed for air defense of friendly air space, to prepare to conduct an offensive air campaign, to train, to rehearse operational procedures for the first three days of the air attack, and to condition Iraqi air defenses to regard as routine the same maneuvers eventually used to launch the air attack. Air operations were intensive and the large number of Coalition aircraft deployed required the closest control for effective training and safety of flight. In addition to US, Kuwaiti, and Saudi Arabian air forces, Coalition combat air forces were contributed by the GCC, UK,

France, Italy, and Canada. NCP air forces participated with US air forces in air defense operations and training. Training included strike, strike support, counter-air, air defense, CAS, antishipping, and reconnaissance missions.

Coalition partners contributed ships that participated in the MIO and provided mine countermeasures (MCM) capabilities. Participation in MIO and MCM attracted several nations unable to contribute ground or air forces in theater.

Kuwaiti Resistance to Iraqi Occupation

The crushing weight of Iraqi military superiority did not deter thousands of brave men and women who chose to resist the invaders and fight on from inside Kuwait. Despite acts of vicious retribution by the occupying forces — often including the abuse or murder of Kuwaitis in the presence of their family members — the Resistance tied down an estimated two divisions of Iraqi occupation troops in Kuwait City to maintain order and suppress acts of sabotage and harassment. Besides engaging targets of opportunity such as Iraqi personnel and command C^2 facilities, the Resistance hid, sheltered, and smuggled out of Kuwait many Western and third-country nationals. Understandably, these resistance forces were eager to cooperate with the Coalition.

The experience with the Kuwaiti Resistance underscores the usefulness of SOF to help train, equip, and organize such forces to considerable military advantage. Apart from the occupying forces Iraq had to dedicate to the maintenance of order, the Resistance operatives were a valuable touchstone for the state of Iraqi troop morale and organizational characteristics. They also exerted a sizeable negative influence themselves on Iraqi morale, while encouraging their compatriots. Indeed, observers of Kuwaiti society have pointed out the galvanizing influence of the occupation on the structure and values of Kuwaiti neighborhoods. Clearly, coalition building must take account of the potential of Resistance movements as an important force multiplier.

Outside the Gulf Region

Immediately after the decision to send US forces to SWA, and before the maturation of the coalition concept, US Allies and friendly nations became involved in support of actions to counter Iraq's aggression. Particularly in Europe but also in the Pacific and Indian Ocean areas, the granting of transit and overflight rights, and access to bases, dramatically assisted the strategic deployment of US forces by air and sea, which continued throughout the defensive phase of Operation Desert Shield. Additional allied support was provided as forward positioned US stocks and selected tactical units were deployed to SWA, although the bulk of this support occurred after the decision to build an offensive capability. Security became a concern for the air and sea LOCs for strategic movement, particularly as they passed through the restrictive and potentially vulnerable Mediterranean region, and NATO acted in September to provide security forces there. Finally, within the various Allied national capitals, deliberations regarding the extent of commitment to be provided the Coalition were conducted in a compressed schedule at the urging of the United States and the United Nations. It is worth noting that August is traditionally a holiday period in Europe, normally characterized by greatly reduced government staffing and an inability to react rapidly; against this background the speed with which the Coalition took shape was impressive.

Host Nation Support by NCPs

One event that required significant international cooperation was the deployment of the 12th Combat Aviation Brigade from Wiesbaden, Germany, through France to Pisa and Livorno, Italy, to SWA. As a hint of things to come after transition to the offensive buildup, the hiring of trains and provision of border crossing clearances involved the commercial transportation facilities of Germany, France, and

Italy. The governmental customs and interior ministries provided rail clearances as well as overflight rights for the unit's organic helicopters. The Italian government additionally became involved in loading and clearing the unit from Livorno and Pisa; strikes by Italian workers about pay issues were potential interruptions but, not entirely coincidentally, occurred only when there was no need for their support.

As mentioned earlier, the extensive deployment of forces from the continental United States (CONUS) to SWA was facilitated by prompt granting of overflight rights by all the European countries, and landing rights at 90 European airfields, with Torrejon, Spain and Rhein Main, Germany as the principal support locations. The host nations provided excellent coordination of airlift movement, an impressive feat in light of the potential for interference between the heavy strategic flow to support the Coalition and the normal commercial operations, particularly at Frankfurt am Main and Madrid International.

PACOM coordinated similar staging support, including overflight and landing rights, in the Pacific and Indian Ocean area.

NATO Activities
NATO established significant security arrangements for forces moving through the Mediterranean Sea to SWA. The threat of international terrorism was real and great throughout Operation Desert Shield and Desert Storm, whether initiated by Saddam Hussein, by Libya, by others supporting Iraq, or by those anxious to harm the Coalition forces (particularly the West and the United States) at any opportunity. Accordingly, NATO arranged for the following actions during August and September:

- Established NATO Airborne Early Warning (NAEW) orbits with E-3As in Mediterranean region

- Activated the On Call Naval Force Mediterranean (NAVOCFORMED)
- Activated a Mediterranean MCM Force
- Deployed the Standing Naval Force Channel (STANAVFORCHAN) to the Mediterranean.

These operations committed a total of 45 ships and 29 surveillance aircraft from eleven nations (Belgium, France, Germany, Greece, Italy, the Netherlands, Norway, Spain, Turkey, the UK, and the United States), plus 10 NATO AWACS aircraft.

Another NATO action during this same period was the initial declaration of measures from the NATO alert system. These measures were for preparatory steps to review procedures, staff headquarters, and increase security and reporting. It is noteworthy that the NATO allies did not mobilize or enact the emergency national crisis legislation required before the provision of formal Wartime host nation support (HNS) under existing bilateral agreements. Nevertheless, allied support provided to the US was, in many cases, nearly identical to that agreed to during a NATO war, although often using commercial contracts rather than processes planned for wartime. For example, military personnel and resources often were substituted for civilian assets, which were not mobilized.

Eastern European Countries
During the defensive phase, Poland, Czechoslovakia, Hungary, Romania, and Bulgaria also provided support, reflecting the historic changes that were taking place in Eastern Europe at that time. They offered many items of potential use to the Coalition in SWA. With a view to future requirements, EUCOM initiated a diplomatic effort to develop overflight rights for US aircraft supporting Operation Desert Shield. This initiative was crucial to the development of mutual understanding and was the forerunner for many substantive contributions during the buildup of the offensive capability, including Hungary's

deployment of medical teams and Czechoslovakia's deployment of a chemical detection and analysis team.

Pacific and Indian Ocean Area

Friends and allies in the Pacific region were a great help, too. Japan and Korea contributed significant funds to the Coalition, as well as sealift and airlift to assist US deployments. Japan also donated computers, vehicles, construction equipment, and other valuable in-kind material. The Philippines, Australia, New Zealand, and South Korea pledged various assistance from warships to medical personnel.

Supporting US CINCs

Coalitions must be mutually supportive. During the defensive phase, there were several requests for US support from NATO allies and from other NCPs. The US provided a wide range of assistance such as intelligence support, air refueling, ammunition, specialized equipment, communications equipment, and even aircraft (25 F-15s to Saudi Arabia as part of FMS). A real challenge was to establish appropriate procedures and channels of communication to process the requests rapidly, and to maintain the paperwork necessary for an audit trail to allow final accounting.

The efforts of the unified and specified commands supporting CENTCOM were crucial from the outset of Operation Desert Shield. Earlier it was noted that the orchestration of HNS and of access rights was a substantial contribution of the overseas CINCs. There were additional contributions. During the defensive phase in Europe, the Coalition provided whatever support was required for the defensive buildup. The deployments to SWA of the assigned CVBG, tactical USAF units, and a CAB were among the key forces that arrived in minimum time. In addition, the Commander-in-Chief, Europe approved the reduction of theater precision-guided munitions below minimum supply to support CINCCENT. Deployments of special equipment such as

communications gear, intelligence, and medical material were primarily supported by US forces in theater. Army modernization equipment such as the latest version of the main battle tank was shipped from theater reserve stocks. Sustainment stocks including ammunition and spare parts also were sent forward.

An interesting innovation was EUCOM's establishment of a rear area support base for CENTCOM called EUCOMM-Z. This support base provided maintenance for Army tank engines, Navy and USAF aircraft engines, and all service avionics in Europe. EUCOMM-Z was expanded to include other functions such as intelligence, communications, and medical support to be conducted within the European area to support CENTCOM. A network of airlift channel flights was established to move equipment requiring repair from Saudi Arabia to Europe and return. The EUCOMM-Z concept relieved CENTCOM of having to establish similar support capabilities in SWA.

During this phase other commanders participated in a similar fashion: Forces Command (FORSCOM) and Tactical Air Command (TAC) provided the CONUS-based Army and USAF reinforcing units; Atlantic Command (LANTCOM) and PACOM deployed naval forces such as CVBGs, Marine Corps (USMC) units, and the key prepositioning ships which delivered essential equipment to SWA early in the crisis. Transportation Command (TRANSCOM) was a particularly significant supporting command, scheduling the air and sea lift, deploying elements of its sealift, airlift, and sea terminal component commands to overseas locations both in and outside SWA to speed transportation and movements, and dispatching small planning cells to other CINCs' headquarters, particularly CENTCOM and EUCOM, to assist deployment planning. Strategic Air Command (SAC) made an indispensable contribution with massive tanker support across the Atlantic and Mediterranean.

Summary

Coalition operations during the defensive phase of Operation Desert Shield were wide-ranging, and crucial to the establishment of a defensive, deterrent posture to counter Saddam Hussein in SWA. The infusion of ground and air forces steadily improved the security posture of the Coalition, but it required a system of command arrangements tailored to accommodate the various sensitivities of the partners. Coalition naval operations began early to enforce the UN sanctions against Iraqi trade, incorporating a loosely defined but effective system of cooperation under on-scene commanders. Outside the theater, the most noteworthy activities were the granting of basing, transit and overflight rights for the heavy strategic lift, and tightening security in the Mediterranean region. Additional support, both to the United States, and by the United States to NCPs, in many cases served to activate a process that would be more heavily stressed in Phase II.

Offensive Phase

The full narrative of the offensive operations can be found in Chapters 5 (Transition to the Offensive), 6 (Air Campaign), 7 (Maritime Campaign), and 8 (Ground Campaign). Since the British fought as an integral part of VII Corps and the French of XVIII Airborne Corps, the story of their ground forces is in those chapters also. Discussed below are the principal operations of the other NCPs.

Within the Gulf Region

Coalition Air Operations

Besides the air forces of the GCC (Bahrain, Kuwait, Oman, Qatar, Saudi Arabia, and UAE), the chief participants in the air operations were the British, Canadians, French, and Italians. Notably, there were a number of exchange pilots scattered among the partners — in fact, two Royal Air Force officers on exchange duty in separate Groups of the 3rd Marine Air Wing received US Air Medals for their actions in the Iraq and Kuwait theater. Some participants provided a few aircraft, and some provided hundreds — in all, there were more than 3,000. The magnitude of these forces prompted all partners to participate in the ATO. Not only was this the policy of the Coalition leadership; it offered the only means of ensuring flight safety in theater. In this way communication and cooperation were built into the system, and all the capabilities of the Coalition could be orchestrated efficiently. For example, most members took part in the preliminary deception procedures which conditioned the enemy to disregard patterns of behavior which, on D-Day, were the prelude to attack.

In addition to the tactical aircraft, NCPs made a crucial contribution to the logistic effort by making civilian aircraft available as a kind of non-US supplement to the Civil Reserve Air Fleet (CRAF) under TRANSCOM. The national airlines of Italy, Kuwait, Luxembourg, the Netherlands, and South Korea significantly reduced the airlift problem, especially by the movement of people. Some nations, for divers reasons unable to offer combat units, furnished transport aircraft for use in theater, a precious commodity considering the short haul airlift requirements of the XVIII Airborne and VII Corps' long LOCs.

The start of Operation Desert Storm brought all the Coalition air forces into action. It is a tribute to the effectiveness of the ATO that there were no friendly aircraft shoot-downs. This is not to say there were no difficulties. As in the case of units in the ground campaign, a substantial issue was that of discriminating between friendly and enemy aircraft, or Identification Friend or Foe (IFF). Some Coalition members had been among the main suppliers of Iraqi military hardware for some years before the conflict, so the Iraqis had a wide range of equipment closely resembling, and in some cases identical to, the Coalition's. This, combined with the unprecedented density of sorties, made for a constant challenge.

On the other hand, Coalition coordination and cooperation achieved numerous successes. The orchestration of all theater air operations ensured that each partner made the maximum use of its arsenal. The most sophisticated weapon systems were used against the best defended targets, while those aircraft whose performance was more limited also were used fully against targets within their capabilities. AWACS aircraft manned by Coalition crews of different nationalities helped coordinate the air battle for all partners. One outstanding example of multinational cooperation came when an RSAF pilot, directed by a USAF AWACS aircraft, shot down a pair of Iraqi fighters.

The Battle of Khafji

The JFC-E, with three reinforced brigades consisting of Saudis and GCC forces, was preparing for offensive operations on the right flank of the Coalition when, on the night of 29 January, Iraq attacked Ras Al Khafji, achieving some tactical surprise.

In all, there were five separate Iraqi attacks during the night and the following day. First, an Iraqi armored brigade attacked across the Saudi border 17 miles west of Al Wafrah, where they were engaged by a Marine Light Armored Infantry (LAI) battalion supported by USMC AV-8s, F/A-18s, A-6s, and AH-1Ws, and USAF A-10s and AC-130s. The Iraqis returned across the border, having lost 10 tanks and four enemy prisoners of war (EPWs). The Marines lost eleven killed and two wounded when two Light Armored Vehicles were destroyed by fire from friendly forces. At about the same time, an Iraqi tank column attempted to cross the Saudi border south of Wafrah, but withdrew with the loss of one tank when its lead tanks came under long-range fire from the USMC 2nd LAI

"THE BANDITS ARE DESTROYED...."

A Royal Saudi Air Force (RSAF) captain (referred to hereafter as "Captain S") was flying combat air patrol on 24 January in command of a formation of four RSAF F-15 aircraft, when he was given a bearing and range to a possible target by Airborne Warning and Control System (AWACS). Turning his formation toward the threat, Captain S detected a radar contact and headed towards it. Rules of Engagement required the RSAF to visually identify all targets as hostile, and receive authenticated clearance from AWACS, before engaging. This made the RSAF's job more difficult but helped to ensure against fratricide. Captain S continued to approach the target and locked his fire control radar onto it at a distance of approximately 85 miles. The target was 5,000 feet above ground level, flying southeast at 660 knots, almost directly toward Capt S's oncoming fighters.

The four Saudis held course until, at approximately 35 miles, they separated into two flights of two planes each so as to be able to follow the target if it suddenly turned left or right. During the Saudis' approach, the target was descending to an altitude of 250 to 500 feet, so the Saudis began to descend too. Captain S and his wingman had good radar contacts throughout the intercept, and at a range of about 30 miles were able to distinguish two separate target aircraft flying in formation about half a mile apart. A sudden turn by the targets at 15 miles placed the other two Saudis too far away to be able to participate in the engagement, but left Captain S's flight on the targets' tail. Having taken his final radar lock at about 15 miles, he continued to close on the targets using full afterburner and his remaining advantage in altitude.

He chased the targets for two to three minutes at altitudes of 250 to 1,000 feet and airspeeds of 720 to 780 miles per hour. Due to haze, Capt S had to close to within 3,500 feet to be certain of the targets' identity: they were Iraqi F-1 Mirage fighters. At first, because of the range from AWACS, he had trouble receiving permission to fire, but as soon as he was given clearance, he fired two AIM-9L air-to-air missiles without effect. Captain S's third missile struck one Iraqi, and he maneuvered to reposition for a shot at the other. The second F-1 began a hard turn, but Capt S downed it with an AIM-9L from approximately 6,000 feet. Both Iraqis jettisoned external fuel tanks as the first missile was fired, and Capt S does not believe they knew he was intercepting them until then. After the encounter, he transmitted the message, "The bandits are destroyed," and the Saudi formation returned to base unscathed.

Battalion. Iraqi forces staged through the Wafrah area, occasionally patrolling south of the Saudi border and directing artillery fire at Marine and Saudi positions. The Wafrah cultivated area became an assembly point for enemy forces fighting in Khafji.

Two hours later, an Iraqi mechanized infantry battalion crossed the border north of Khafji , where it met a screening force of the 2nd Saudi Arabian National Guard (SANG) and tactical air support. The outnumbered screening force broke contact and withdrew to the south, whereupon elements of the Iraqi battalion occupied Ras Al Khafji. The Coalition destroyed 13 Iraqi vehicles in this engagement with no friendly losses. The 1st and 2nd MARDIV then moved regiment-sized forces to block any further Iraqi advances and to reinforce JFC-E. The Iraqis were unaware that, by coincidence, a small reconnaissance team of Marines had entered Khafji unobserved before the attack began, were trapped when the town was captured, and had concealed themselves.

Not long after midnight on 30 January, shortly after they had occupied Khafji, the Iraqis sent mechanized infantry and tanks across the Saudi border 20 miles northwest of the town. A Marine LAI battalion supported by USMC, Navy, and USAF tactical air drove them back north of the border. After sunrise, another force of 40 Iraqi tanks crossed the border west of Al Wafrah: it also was engaged and thrown back by a Marine LAI battalion supported by additional tactical air. The Marines destroyed 15 enemy tanks and captured nine EPWs without friendly losses.

In the early afternoon, another Iraqi mechanized infantry battalion was reported at the Saudi border north of Khafji. The Iraqis withdrew north of the border after being attacked by Coalition ground forces and USMC AV-8s, F/A-18s, A-6s, and AH-1Ws, and USAF A-10s.

By the afternoon of 30 January, both sides could claim a measure of success. Whereas the Iraqis had had much the worse of their five engagements with the Coalition on the ground, only one incident had pitted Iraqi forces against Coalition Arabs, and the result was the tactical withdrawal of the Coalition forces and the Iraqi occupation of Khafji. The question was, would the Coalition now attempt to retake the town, risking heavy losses or perhaps failure; or would they concede the geographically insignificant Iraqi gains but thereby leave unresolved the fate of the hidden Marines and offer Iraq a much-needed psychological victory?

The Iraqis learned the Coalition Arabs' decision at 0230 on 31 January, when the counterattack began. With Qatari forces blocking to the north and the 8th Royal Saudi Land Forces (RSLF) Brigade blocking to the south, the 2nd SANG Task Force (TF) engaged the Iraqis, supported by USMC artillery and CAS and naval gunfire. Initially thwarted by the ferocity of the defense, the Coalition Arabs nevertheless redoubled the attack and, after several hours of intense fighting, cleared the town. An hour after Khafji was declared liberated, the 2nd SANG TF engaged the remaining enemy tank forces seven miles to the north, taking 160 EPWs. They proceeded to eliminate the remaining pockets of resistance around Khafji, and, as the afternoon of 31 January ended, the last Iraqi forces withdrew across the Kuwaiti border. The JFC-E repulsed an Iraqi company-size armor attack on 2 February in the vicinity of Khafji, ending the episode.

Saddam Hussein's purpose in attacking Khafji is not known for certain. He may have sought to probe Coalition forces or provoke the ground battle he had repeatedly said he wanted. Although Iraqi forces were able to mount the probing attack, their effort had three major consequences, all beneficial to the Coalition. First, it exposed the limitations of the Iraqi ground forces and confirmed their vulnerability to Coalition tactics. Second, it catapulted the morale and self-confidence of the Arab forces, who had heard much about the invincibility of the war-hardened Iraqis. Finally, the incident erased any misperception there may have been on the part of the other Coalition members as to the quality of the Arab troops. In the words of a young USMC officer eyewitness, "Because we train differently and because our methods are not the same, many Marines initially questioned the effectiveness of the Saudi and Qatari soldiers. At Khafji, without any but the most rudimentary plan, Arab soldiers conducted a night counter-attack against enemy armor with just this guidance: 'Attack Khafji.' And they did — without question or hesitation. Some 19 were killed and 36 wounded, some terribly. Khafji put to rest any doubt about the courage, decisiveness, aggressiveness or willingness to obey their orders and earned them the respect reserved for the best amongst us."

The Ground Offensive

Besides the defense and recapture of Khafji, the highlights of the Coalition ground operations were the Arab assault on Iraqi concentrations in Kuwait culminating in the liberation of Kuwait City, the 1st UK Armoured Division's participation in the main attack, and the 6th French Light Armor Division's seizure of objectives in Iraq. These Coalition ground forces, in conjunction with the US, produced the necessary combat power for an attack across a wide front that achieved all objectives swiftly with minimum casualties. The UK and French forces operated as part of VII Corps and XVIII Airborne Corps respectively, and the account of their operations is covered in Volume II, Chapter VIII.

Final preparation for offensive operations began on D-Day when the Coalition was confident that Iraq would be unable to observe forces moving to attack positions or to determine the location of the main attack. To clear their area for movement of the VII Corps, JFC-N forces

moved to their attack positions, and were in place by 21 January.

Coalition forces for the ground offensive were arrayed from left to right (west to east) in five major formations. On the left flank was the XVIII Airborne Corps including the 6th French Armored Division. To the right of XVIII Airborne Corps was the VII Corps which included the 1st UK Armoured Division. In the center was JFC-N which consisted of the 3rd Egyptian Mechanized Division, 4th Egyptian Armoured Division, an Egyptian Ranger Regiment, 9th Syrian Armored Division, a composite Syrian Commando Regiment, and a consolidated unit under Saudi command called Task Force Khalid made up of the 20th Mechanized Brigade (RSLF), the Kuwaiti Shaheed and Al-Tahrir Brigades, and 4th Saudi Armored Brigade. Also under JFC-N was Forward Forces Command 'Ar'Ar, a blocking force west of Rahfa comprising three Saudi battalions and the 7th Pakistani Armored Brigade. On the right of JFC-N was the I Marine Expeditionary Force (MEF). On the extreme right flank was JFC-E made up of three task forces. TF Omar was composed of the 10th Infantry Brigade (RSLF), UAE Motorized Infantry Battalion, and an Omani Motorized Infantry Battalion. The second task force, TF Othman, consisted of the 8th Mechanized Infantry Brigade (RSLF), Bahrain Infantry Company, and Kuwaiti Al-Fatah Brigade. The final task force, Abu Bakr, comprised the 2nd SANG Motorized Infantry Brigade and a Mechanized Battalion from Qatar.

At 0400, 24 February (G-Day), the ground offensive to eject Iraq from Kuwait began. In the east, JFC-E cut six lanes through the first obstacle and began moving at 0800. It secured its initial objectives and continued north, capturing large numbers of Iraqis as it went. The high rate of advance of JFC-E and US units enabled the theater commanders to accelerate the time table for initiating the attack by the remainder of the force. When this had been done, the Egyptians in JFC-N also attacked on 24 February, about 1500. The Egyptian preparatory attack caused the Iraqis to light their fire trenches and give away their artillery positions, and destroyed the Iraqi security force. On the morning of 25 February, the 3rd Egyptian Mechanized Division launched a successful main attack through fire trenches, minefields, and harassing fire. The Egyptians, concerned about an Iraqi armored counterattack, established blocking positions in sector.

On G+1 (25 February), Coalition forces continued to press the attack. The JFC-E secured its objectives against light resistance and with very few casualties; however, by this point, progress was slowed by the large number of Iraqis who had surrendered. In the center, JFC-N continued to attack together with VII Corps. The 3rd Egyptian Mechanized Division continued its attack to the north and captured 1,500 EPWs and two tanks. Other units, including the 9th

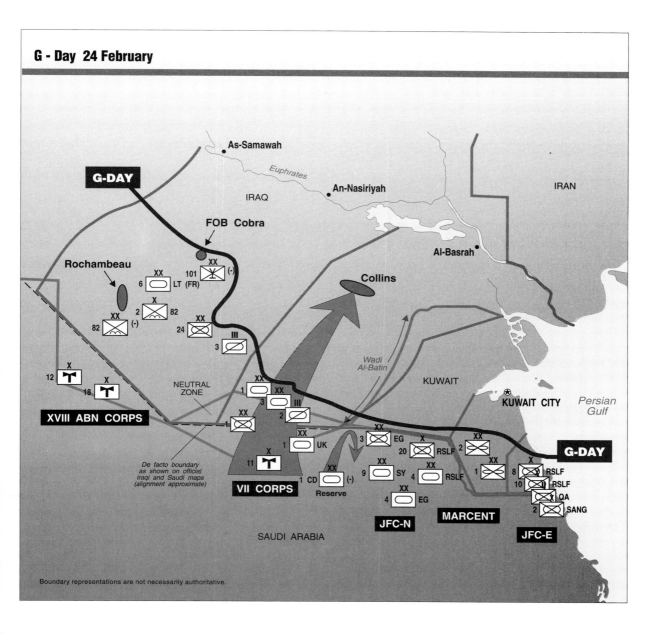

G - Day 24 February

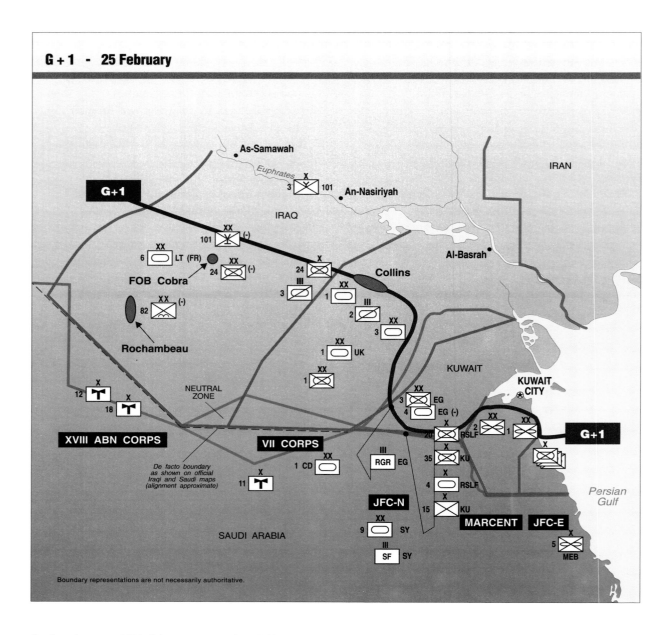

G + 1 - 25 February

During this period, the massive exodus of Iraqi forces from the eastern part of the theater began. Elements of the Iraqi III Corps, commanded by one of the best Iraqi field commanders, were pushed back in Kuwait City by JFC-E and I MEF. Iraqi units became intermingled and disorder ensued. These forces were joined by Iraqi occupation troops based in Kuwait City. During the early morning hours of 26 February,

Syrian Armored Division, prepared to follow.

military and civilian vehicles of every description, loaded with Iraqi soldiers and goods looted from Kuwait, clogged the main four-lane highway north from Kuwait City. To deny Iraqi commanders the opportunity to reorganize their forces and establish a cohesive defensive line, the Coalition struck these forces repeatedly from the air.

Coalition forces continued operations well ahead of schedule on G+2 (26 February), meeting generally light resistance, although there were several sharp engagements. The JFC-E was so successful that its boundary was changed twice, and it was given four additional objectives. By day's end, units of the JFC-E, which was composed of forces from each GCC nation, were positioned to lead a drive into Kuwait City.

Meanwhile in the center of the front, the JFC-N continued to attack, seizing intermediate and final objectives before evening. The Egyptian Corps secured its objective in the vicinity of Al Abraq, and then turned east and maneuvered 60 kilometers to seize 'Ali Al-Salim airfield.

Exploitation and pursuit continued through G+3 (27 February) against rapidly disintegrating resistance. The JFC-E consolidated its position in southern Kuwait City and coordinated a link-up with JFC-N forces which were preparing to enter Kuwait City from the west.

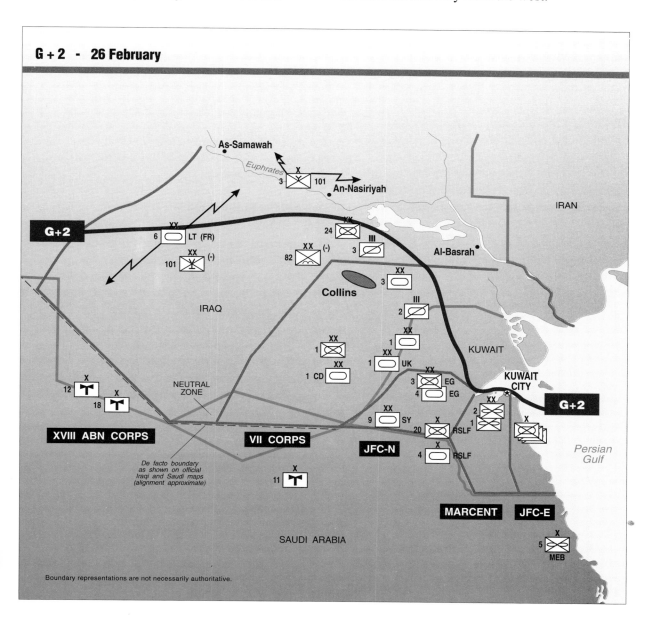

The Liberation of Kuwait City

The Coalition leadership desired that Kuwait forces alone should clear and secure Kuwait City. To accommodate this preference and to provide for the worst case, planning for this operation provided for two contingencies. The first was that Iraq would defend Kuwait City as a means of prolonging the war and inflicting heavy casualties. In this case, Coalition forces would conduct a siege of the city for an unspecified time followed by an operation conducted by Arab forces to secure and clear the Iraqis from the built-up areas. Planners envisioned the length of the siege would be influenced by the condition of the population, the level of Iraqi resistance, and the length of time required to deploy Arab forces to their siege positions around the city after they had secured and cleared their zones outside the populated areas. It was assumed that clearing and securing of the zones outside the city would be required to neutralize Iraqi forces bypassed during the initial armor attack and advance.

The Kuwait Army Commander felt the Iraqis would not stand and fight in the populated areas. Accordingly, a second variation of the plan provided for relief of the city by Kuwaiti forces with provision for reinforcement by other Arab forces if the Kuwaitis ran into heavier resistance than they had expected.

A brigade-size force from JFC-N approached from the west and prepared to occupy the western part of Kuwait City. Forward elements of JFC-E, approaching from the south, linked up with JFC-N and prepared to occupy the eastern part of the city.

As events unfolded on the battlefield, the Kuwaiti Commander's prediction proved correct, the Iraqis fled the populated areas, and the Kuwaitis were able to secure and clear Kuwait City with minimal assistance from other Arab forces. They completed this operation with a degree of pride and emotion to

be expected from an army of liberation freeing its people from the grip of a long and brutal occupation.

As a footnote to this story, 45 Marines served with JFC-E forces, providing liaison with I MEF; and 1st and 2nd Air/Naval Gunfire Liaison Companies coordinated air, artillery, and naval gunfire. Also, at the request of Kuwait's Army commander, Special Forces had been operating with the Kuwaitis extensively, as they had with other NCP forces, since August. SOF assisted with C^2 and performed foreign internal defense with Kuwait's forces. Foreign internal defense involves training friendly security forces in basic skills and small unit tactics. Appendix J gives more details of SOF operations.

On G+4 (28 February), Coalition offensive operations were suspended, Iraq having been ejected from Kuwait.

Outside the Gulf Region

Host nations met extensive specific US support requests, just as the US met host nation and NATO requests. This interactive support of the NCPs in Europe resulted in large part from the cooperative planning done for many years within NATO. Long time relationships with host nation personnel and organizations were invaluable in obtaining support. Officials in various military branches knew their counterparts personally, as well as their

> "**A** last important lesson is that what we have seen this week is not an Arab defeat. On the contrary — it is a resounding Arab victory. The Arab League roundly condemned the invasion of Kuwait. Troops from nine Arab countries, representing more than half the world's Arab population, participated in coalition operations. Arab armies and air forces performed superbly in this conflict and played a leading role in the liberation of Kuwait."
>
> *Paul Wolfowitz*
> *Under Secretary of Defense for Policy*

administrative organizations, and their regulations. Although its charter prevented NATO from participating directly in Operations Desert Shield and Desert Storm, the familiarity of US forces with the European NCPs and vice versa measurably increased support for Coalition operations in SWA.

Host Nation Support By NCPs

During the offensive phase of Operation Desert Shield and Desert Storm, the Germans supported 73 road convoys of 25 to 30 vehicles each on the autobahns with road march authorizations and rest and overnight facilities. Although there had been similar road and rail support during exercises in the past, never had such an extensive demand been levied at such short notice, with such unusual conditions (e.g., vehicles loaded with ammunition on trains), and in such a concentrated period of time. The German rail system (Deutsches Bundesbahn) already was severely taxed by seasonal requirements but, despite the considerable hardships incurred by many Germans during the Christmas holidays, VII Corps was given adequate priority and all of its equipment was at the sea port of embarkation (SPOE) 42 days after the Phase II deployment order was issued.

Another example of a movement requirement met in an unprecedented manner by several NCPs (Germany, the Netherlands, the UK, and Italy) was the loading of nearly 300,000 short tons of ammunition through seven SPOEs; several of the ports used had been excluded from supporting any ammunition movements in the past and net explosive weight limits frequently were raised or waived to expedite the movements. Nearly as much ammunition to sustain SWA operations came through European ports as from CONUS.

A unique capability of the German forces which the US required on a priority basis was the Fuchs NBC reconnaissance vehicle. This is a six-wheeled, amphibious, armored vehicle equipped with sensors that detect and identify all known chemical warfare agents and measure radioactive contamination. Germany responded by providing 60 Fuchs vehicles: 50 supported the Army and 10 the USMC. In the important area of HETs, the Coalition acquired 181 from the Germans which had formerly been used by East Germany.

Additionally, the NCPs in Europe supported the Coalition with significant amounts of money; especially noteworthy was Germany. NATO also augmented theater tactical airlift. Nine countries provided more than 800 aircraft sorties within Europe to help the US move high priority cargo and personnel, which would have remained backlogged while waiting for US aircraft. The six C-160 transports Germany made available flew nearly 3,400 hours carrying US requirements within EUCOM.

Most importantly, the host nations provided security. The terrorist threat, which was extremely high throughout Europe and even higher in Turkey, lasted longer than ever before. The host nations provided security at facilities and installations, to deploying units both at ports and while enroute within their country, and to the otherwise unguarded family housing areas where dependents of deploying soldiers remained. A new HNS agreement strictly for security was executed with German authorities. There were no terrorist incidents and the large number of demonstrations were mostly peaceful. The extent to which the host nations' security efforts were responsible for that welcome situation cannot be determined, but the cooperation and support were unstinting.

Especially within Germany, where the dependents of deployed US soldiers remained in place rather than relocate to CONUS, host nation communities, organizations, and individuals supported US families generously. Some assistance was specifically requested by the United States; however, much was volunteered at the hosts' initiative, including free transportation, tours, food, facility access, and in many cases gifts of money.

Overflight and landing rights and other access continued to be an invaluable contribution to US deployments, originating in both CONUS and Europe. Sixteen countries in Europe provided enroute staging support at 90 airfields as the buildup accelerated. (As a matter of interest, Greece made bases available for the US to operate aircraft bound for Turkey.) More than 95 percent of the flights to SWA staged through Europe, and consisted of about 2,200 tactical, and 15,402 strategic airlift (including 3,142 CRAF) sorties. Additionally, tanker aircraft operated from 10 airbases in seven countries (France, Greece, Italy, Portugal, Spain, Turkey, and the UK).

B-52s conducted combat operations from Britain and Saudi Arabia to strike targets in Iraq; and similar B-52 operations were conducted from Moron, Spain, which was without precedent. Turkey provided bases for the US Joint Task Force Proven Force to conduct tactical air combat into Iraq, as well as the deployment of the Allied Command Europe Mobile Force (Air). Although not all European NCPs deployed forces into SWA, in other ways each supported the overall Coalition mission.

NATO Activities

NATO expanded its support during Phase II. The Defense Planning Committee and the Military Committee maintained NATO at an increased alert status, with a total of 43 measures ultimately activated to respond to threats from Saddam Hussein — by far the most extensive use of the NATO alert system since its inception.

Within the Mediterranean area, a NATO Communications Information System Network linked the surface ships, NAEW, and controlling commands using satellite communications to exchange radar and other C^2 and threat information. The Allied Command Europe Mobile Force (Air) of 60 aircraft (Alpha Jets, Mirage, RF-104, F-15, E-3A) and air defense units (Patriot, I-Hawk, and Roland) from Belgium, Germany, Italy, the Netherlands, Turkey, and the United States, and NATO AWACS operated at five Turkish bases as a deterrent, flying more than 1,600 air sorties in all. Finally, Supreme Headquarters Allied Powers Europe (SHAPE) headquarters became actively involved in the theater airlift process by activating an airlift cell which matched requirements of the various nations in Europe with assets made available by Belgium, Germany, and others.

Eastern European Countries

The support initiated during the defensive phase increased in the offensive phase. The Eastern European countries approved overflight rights and made available specific equipment urgently needed in SWA. In addition, Czechoslovakia sold 40 HETs to the US, which reflected the significant changes then taking place in Eastern Europe's relations with the West. These HETs proved invaluable not only in moving heavy equipment from ports of entry to staging areas, but in the long offensive drive into Iraq as well. Czechoslovakia also provided chemical detection and analysis equipment along with trained operators. Hungary, Romania, and Poland sent medical teams to Saudi Arabia.

Pacific and Indian Ocean Area

Throughout this period PACOM continued to coordinate support across a wide spectrum, ranging from military units such as Canadian and Australian Navy ships, to funding like that pledged by Korea and Japan, to the overflight rights granted by numerous Coalition friends. South Korea deployed C-130 airlift assets and a medical team to SWA, while Australia, New Zealand, the Philippines, and Singapore provided additional medical support.

Supporting US CINCs

The unified and specified commands expanded their support to CENTCOM during both the second phase of Operations Desert Shield and Desert Storm. For example, major force units were deployed forward from EUCOM. As a measure of that effort, some 40 percent of Army personnel stationed in Europe, 16 percent of USAF personnel (but 54 percent of the aircraft), and 38 percent of naval personnel deployed from Europe to SWA, along with approximately 292,000 short tons of ammunition of all Services. Training facilities in Europe were used to receive nearly 5,000 Army Individual Ready Reserves, train them on combat vehicles, and deploy them to SWA as replacement crews. Other EUCOM support in this period included the establishment of Operation Proven Force in Turkey, consisting of 6,000 US personnel and more than 120 aircraft of 13 types deployed to Incirlik Air Base. Approximately 4,400 sorties were flown, striking 120 targets in Iraq and downing five Iraqi aircraft.

In a similar fashion, the other CINCs, and the individual Services and Defense Agencies as well, continued their support with the result that the US force in theater was essentially doubled from Phase I. In addition to the earlier and continuing deployment and sustainment activities of EUCOM, PACOM, LANTCOM, TRANSCOM, and FORSCOM was the support by SAC. The SAC tanker services for the deploying strategic and tactical aircraft were essential to maintain the flow to SWA, and, once the war started, SAC provided CINCCENT with B-52 bombers to expand his conventional bombing capability. Finally, Commander-in-Chief, US Space Command supported CENTCOM. US Space Command (SPACECOM) crews called Scud warnings directly into CENTCOM Headquarters, and SPACECOM personnel operated the Global Positioning System and weather satellites to enhance coverage over the KTO in direct support of air, ground, and naval operations.

Direct US support to the European NCPs increased significantly in Phase II and fell into three principal areas: airlift (C-5 sorties, for example, to lift Dutch Patriots into Turkey); C^3 capabilities to help establish key networks linked with UHF satellites and to provide secure communication facilities at the most senior national levels as well as at operational locations; and intelligence support for the national leadership. US support to deploying UK forces included 3,000 Multiple Launch Tocket System (MLRS) pods, 20,000 M82 primers, and 150 M548A1 tracked ammunition carriers as well as miscellaneous C^3 equipment and transportation support. France received C^3 equipment and intelligence support. Turkey received 200 AIM-9M missiles and significant C^3 equipment. Italy received air refueling services. NATO (SHAPE, Allied Forces Southern Europe, and 6th Allied Tactical Air Force, for example) received extensive C^3 equipment (primarily for secure communications), other equipment such as night vision goggles, and extensive intelligence support.

In addition to its support for members of the Coalition, the TF Patriot Defender deployment into Israel was conducted at very short notice (less than 29 hours from alert in Germany to initial operational capability in Israel) and resulted in 13 known Scuds destroyed.

Summary

The stunning success of the Coalition forces on the ground and in the air during the offensive phase of Operation Desert Shield and Desert Storm owed a great deal to the combined planning process, the willingness of the partners to incorporate one another's political requirements into military arrangements, the deconflicting influence of the ATO in the air and the liaison teams on the ground, the opportunity to prepare for the assault, and of course the courage and determination of the individual service members of all nationalities who adapted to each other so harmoniously and fought together so bravely.

As the Coalition changed its mission from defense to offense, the mutual support provided outside the Gulf Region increased significantly. Demands were heavy, and support was provided willingly and often before it was requested.

Arrangements for Enemy Prisoners of War

Coalition commanders anticipated the capture, confinement, and support of up to 100,000 Iraqi EPWs, and began discussions early with Saudi Arabia to arrange for HNS, detention, and repatriation assistance.

US policy requires that a formal international agreement be concluded as a prerequisite to transferring EPWs to a coalition partner for custody. Intensive US and Saudi effort through December bore fruit when an agreement was signed in early January. Arrangements made with Saudi Arabia provided that custody of EPWs would be transferred by the United States to the Saudis after registration of EPWs by US forces.

The effort to construct, staff, and organize the EPW system was another logistical feat achieved through the combined efforts of the United States and Saudi Arabia. Both partners worked to ensure their respective camps, which were inspected by the International Committee of the Red Cross, met international standards. The Saudis intended to establish model EPW camps where, as hosts, they desired that Iraqis would be treated as guests in the Arab custom. It was a Coalition objective that Iraqis would have much better conditions as EPWs than as soldiers in the Iraqi army, a theme conveyed to the Iraqi soldiers as psychological warfare prior to the ground war. Efforts to prepare for a large number of EPWs were rewarded when more than 85,000 arrived.

Expeditious repatriation of EPWs became a high Coalition priority when offensive operations were suspended. Coalition officials initiated talks on EPW exchanges with Iraq's representatives. Iraq said it was anxious to turn over Coalition prisoners of war but was unwilling to accept large numbers of Iraqi EPWs in return. While most Iraqis accepted repatriation, some exercised their right not to return to Iraq and they still are being cared for by the Saudis.

OBSERVATIONS

Accomplishments

- Coalition was perhaps the most successful in history.

- Coalition reduced length of conflict and friendly casualties.

- United States emerged as the logical leader of future coalitions in Gulf and probably elsewhere.

- NATO experience was invaluable for coordinating warfighting, C^3I, and logistics.

- Out of area operations with NATO members are enhanced by NATO experience.

- Forty years of Gulf presence and, in particular, US performance in Operation Earnest Will paid off in willingness of GCC to trust the United States.

- US military personnel demonstrated outstanding professionalism in adapting to the Islamic culture.

- The US FMS system provided Saudi military infrastructure, US origin equipment and training for most of our regional partners, and contributed importantly to the foundation of peacetime cooperation and interoperability on which the Coalition was built.

Shortcomings

- Present strategic airlift and sealift assets are inadequate to move enough coalition people and materiel far and fast enough to cover some possible contingencies.

- Combined forces C^3 is still rudimentary, IFF is inadequate.

Issues

- US needs to cultivate global network of regional partnerships as basis for forming coalitions during crises.

- Next time, there might not be such a long period to develop a coalition.

- Need for right mix of forces and equipment early implies rapid mobility and prepositioning.

- Organization of coalitions must reflect political as well as military requirements.

- Security assistance programs have excellent potential for inexpensive coalition building in advance (e.g. international military education and training, service school exchanges, English language training, mobile training teams, etc.).

- Acquisition of US equipment by coalition states promotes interoperability.

- Combined exercises are invaluable to effective coalition operations.

Appendix J

SPECIAL OPERATIONS FORCES

INTRODUCTION

Four days after President Bush's announcement that US forces would deploy to the Persian Gulf, Special Operations Forces (SOF) were on the ground in Saudi Arabia. Constituting only a small percentage of the total forces deployed into Southwest Asia (SWA), SOF played a unique and important role in Operations Desert Shield and Desert Storm. This was the largest SOF deployment and the largest integrated use in history of Special Operations units in one geographical region.

Virtually every aspect of the wide range of specialized SOF capabilities and skills was tested. Many missions were directed at high value and often perishable targets at great distances from established support bases. These required sophisticated communications and rapid long range transports. Other invaluable accomplishments included training and assistance for Coalition forces, special reconnaissance (SR), and personnel recovery operations. Throughout, SOF did not operate independently, but were fully integrated in every stage of planning and executing the theater campaign. They operated with conventional forces as part of the combined arms team.

This appendix focuses on the SOF organization and capabilities deployed to the Gulf and details many of the operations they carried out during Operations Desert Shield and Desert Storm.

COMMAND AND CONTROL RELATIONSHIPS

During Operation Desert Shield, SOF operated

"The Special Forces made an invaluable contribution. I have my own special operations command, SOCCENT, Special Operations Command, CENTCOM. They were the very first ... to be deployed. As you know, the overall SOCOM responsibility is to raise, train, and equip the Special Operations Forces, and then the employment of the Special Operations Forces falls to the theater commander through his component commander."

General H. Norman Schwarzkopf
Commander-in-Chief
Central Command

under a command relationship begun with the passage of the Cohen-Nunn Amendment to the Goldwater-Nichols Defense Reorganization Act of 1986 (GNA). This amendment created the Special Operations Command (SOCOM). Before SOCOM's creation, SOF was the responsibility of the US Readiness Command (REDCOM), the Services, and the Joint Staff (JS). The establishment of SOCOM as a unified command was designed to improve operational capability and give joint focus to Special Operations.

As prescribed in Title 10, USC Section 167, all SOF based in the Continental United States (CONUS), to include Army and Air Force Psychological Operations (PSYOP) and Army Civil Affairs (CA), are assigned to CINCSOC, who exercises Combatant Command (COCOM) of these forces. Before deployment of SOF assets, CINCSOC exercises operational control (OPCON) through subordinate joint functional commands or Service components. CINCSOC usually provides SOF to other regional commanders-in-chief who, in turn, assume COCOM of these committed forces. During Operations Desert Shield and Desert Storm,

SOF were reassigned to Central Command (CENTCOM), which assumed COCOM. CENTCOM and a sub-unified command, US Special Operations Command, Central (SOCCENT), then assumed OPCON of SOF forces (less PSYOP and CA and Naval Special Warfare (NSW) forces afloat.)

SOCCENT was a joint command with

subordinate Army Special Operations Forces Task Force (ARSOTF), the Naval Special Warfare Task Group (NSWTG), and Air Force Special Operations Command Central (AFSOCCENT) and a separate Special Forces Group (SFG). The Service components retained responsibility for administrative and logistical support of their SOF elements. Although SOCCENT was a sub-unified command, it

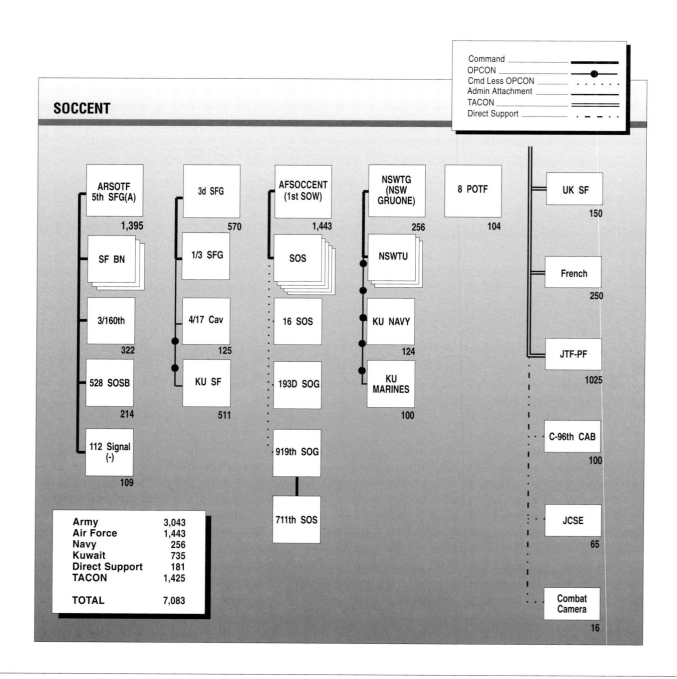

worked with other CENTCOM elements to plan missions and to select areas of operations and targets for SOF missions in Kuwait and Iraq.

SOCCENT deployed to SWA in early August. The command was based temporarily in Riyadh before establishing permanent headquarters at King Fahd International Airport in mid-August. In order to improve operations with forward deployed Coalition forces, SOCCENT later established a forward command center, located with the forward headquarters of 5th SFG, in King Khalid Military City (KKMC). During Operation Desert Storm, SOCCENT also established a forward tactical operations and communications center for combat search and rescue (CSAR) in Al Jouf near the Iraqi-Saudi border. This location improved coordination and communications with SOF aviation assets flying missions into Kuwait and Iraq.

Service SOF elements were integrated into the SOCCENT structure primarily through the command relationship of Operational Control or OPCON. This is the authority delegated to a commander to direct assigned forces to accomplish specific missions or tasks. The relationship relieves the commander of the requirement to provide logistic and administrative support to those elements. This simplifies both the gaining commander's responsibilities and helps to ensure adequate support for operating forces in the most efficient manner possible.

Army forces which were OPCON to SOCCENT included the 3rd Special Forces Group and the Army Special Forces Task Force (ARSOTF) which was comprised primarily of the 5th Special Forces Group and other Army SOF elements.

Although Civil Affairs (CA) and Psychological Operations (PSYOPs) units are part of the CINCSOC force structure, they were not placed OPCON to SOCCENT. Instead, the 352nd Civil Affairs Command and other civil affairs assets were attached to Army Component Central Command (ARCENT). Psychological Operations units including those in or centered on the 4th Psychological Operations Group, were also attached to ARCENT. The intent was to place these units under the operational control of the units they would support during actual hostilities. Nevertheless, much of the planning for the use of Psyops units was done at CENTCOM.

SOCCENT exercised OPCON of all Naval Special Warfare (NSW) assets except for

---

US FORCES OPCON TO SOCCENT

ARMY

5th Special Forces Group (Abn)
3rd Special Forces Group (Abn)(-)
A Company,10th Special Forces Group (Abn)
TF 3-160 Special Ops Aviation Regiment
4th Squadron, 17th Air Cavalry
528th Special Ops Support Bn
112th Special Ops Signal Bn (-)

AIR FORCE

8th Special Operations Squad (MC-130E)
9th Special Operations Squad (HC-130)
20th Special Operations Squad (MH-53J)

55th Special Operations Squad (MH-60G)
71st Special Operations Squad (HH-3)

NAVY

Naval Special Warfare Group One
SEAL Team One (2 Platoons)
SEAL Team Five (2 Platoons)
Swimmer Delivery Vehicles Team One (1 Platoon)
Special Boat Unit 12 (high Speed Boat Det and Rigid
    Inflatable Boat Det)
Mobile Communication Team
Naval Special Warfare Development
Group (High Speed Boat Det)

SEALs assigned to Fleet units. Fleet SEALs were under OPCON of Naval Component, Central Command (NAVCENT) and conducted operations in support of Maritime Interception Operations (MIO) (A discussion of this support is contained in Chapter IV.). SEALs assigned to SOCCENT were made available to NAVCENT for combat search and rescue (CSAR). NSW, under the operational control of SOCCENT, provided support to NAVCENT, Marine Corps Component, Central Command (MARCENT), as well as SOCCENT.

As an exception to the lines of control described previously, the Air Force Component, Central Command (CENTAF), exercised OPCON of AC-130 gunships from the 16th Special Operations Squadron (SOS), 919th SOS, and EC-130 Volant Solos from the 193rd Special Operation Group (SOG) Pennsylvania Air National Guard. These two squadrons directly supported MARCENT and ARCENT forces during the ground operations.

Considerable numbers of SOF forces deployed directly from CONUS, although some NSW elements were afloat with carrier battle groups and Amphibious Ready Groups (ARG) in the Red Sea, Mediterranean Sea, and Persian Gulf. Other SOF deployed to SWA from Europe.

Each Special Operations component assigned to SOCCENT had an intermediate level headquarters in theater to coordinate logistics support for assigned forces with ARCENT. As the theater logistics provider, ARCENT initially was responsible for providing assigned SOF with logistics support for supply, petroleum, oil, and lubricants (POL), ammunition, rations, maintenance, and required base operations functions to the Army. Later this support responsibility was extended to all on-shore SOF.

SOF MISSIONS

CENTCOM's Operation Order (OPORD) 003-90, developed between August and November, stated the following general SOF mission: "USCENTCOM Special Operations Forces will conduct special operations in Kuwait, Iraq, and Northern Saudi Arabia in support of all phases of the USCINCCENT campaign plan." The order was published in December and allowed SOCCENT latitude and flexibility in executing its missions. This general mission statement was applicable throughout Operations Desert Shield and Desert Storm.

From the CENTCOM general mission statement, SOCCENT derived the following tasks:

- Position Special Operations teams and liaison officers (LNO) with forward deployed coalition units in the Eastern Area Command (EAC) and Northern Area Command (NAC) and conduct Foreign Internal Defense (FID) training as required;
- Conduct special reconnaissance (SR) of Iraqi forces from Combined Special Operations Areas (CSOA);
- Coordinate CSOA forces passage through friendly lines with appropriate ground force commanders; and,
- Be prepared to conduct CSAR in Iraq and Kuwait.

Special Operations Forces were Capable of Conducting a Variety of Missions.

> "The variety of missions that the Special Operations Forces provided over there was across the entire spectrum of what they are expected to do. First of all, foreign internal defense; they were absolutely magnificent, number one, in training the Coalition forces — the Arab forces. But number two, probably more importantly, they were right with them during the entire conduct of the war, to act as advisors to control air support, to coordinate gunfire, and that sort of thing. They also did strategic reconnaissance missions. They were very, very effective in their strategic reconnaissance missions."
>
> *General H. Norman Schwarzkopf*
> *Commander-in-Chief*
> *Central Command*

When the Operation Desert Shield OPORD was published, the SOCCENT J-3 planning staff began to prepare the next order to support offensive operations. SOCCENT's taskings from CINCCENT for Operation Desert Storm were changed to:

- Conduct CSAR operations in Iraq and Kuwait; and,
- Continue to provide Special Operations LNOs to ensure coordination of coalition warfare activities.

These operational taskings taxed the SOF resources of all Services assigned to SOCCENT. As a result, SOCCENT requested and received one additional battalion from the 3rd SFG and an additional company from the 10th SFG.

Although not specifically included in the tasking, there also was a requirement for direct reconnaissance support to the tactical corps. This mission was implied, however, by the requirement to provide SR missions in Kuwait and Iraq.

SOF OPERATIONS DURING OPERATIONS DESERT SHIELD AND DESERT STORM

The tasks listed above represent all facets of

SOF doctrinal missions, for which SOF units are trained, equipped, and manned to perform. The following discussion describes how these tasks, categorized by mission areas, were accomplished.

Reconstitution of Kuwaiti Military

A key SF mission was to reconstitute Kuwaiti military capabilities. The intent was to train, advise, and help the Kuwaiti forces and to increase their interoperability for future operations. The reconstitution mission was developed in meetings between COMSOCCENT and the Kuwaiti Armed Forces Chief of Staff. The plan was to train a SF battalion and a commando brigade, organized from former Kuwaiti military personnel at KKMC. The mission was given to the 5th SFG on 11 September; in mid-September, 60 Kuwaitis began a training program conducted by six Special Forces Operational Detachments (SFOD). The program was in four-phases: individual, squad, platoon, and company level. Each phase lasted two weeks. The mission's initial phase was completed by the end of September, with 57 of the initial 60 Kuwaitis successfully meeting training requirements. (The instruction later was modified and 20 students added.)

The mission to reconstitute Kuwaiti military capabilities was expanded to encompass four new Kuwaiti infantry brigades organized at KKMC. Training for these units extended from 26 December 90 to 22 February 91, when the units joined Coalition formations for the ground offensive phase of Operation Desert Storm. A total of 6,357 personnel from the Kuwaiti SF battalion, commando brigade (later redesignated as the Al-Tahrir Brigade), and the Al-Khulud, Al-Haq, Fatah, and Badr Infantry Brigades were trained. Subjects included weapons training, tactics, staff procedures, law of land warfare, close air support (CAS), forward observer procedures, antiarmor operations, and nuclear, chemical and biological (NBC) defense.

The primary constraint on the training program was the lack of training ammunition and equipment for remnants of the Kuwaiti regular army. Training was suspended from 7 November to 10 December, pending receipt of necessary equipment and supplies. Training continued once additional ammunition and equipment were received.

The reconstitution of the Kuwait Navy began in mid-September. Continuing until commencement of hostilities on 17 January, Naval Special Warfare Task Group Central (NSWTG-CENT) played a key role in preparing the ships Sawahil, Istiqlal, and Sambovk for combat operations. From October through December, NSWTG-CENT SEALs and Special Boat Unit (SBU) personnel trained and equipped the crews of the three ships. Additionally, they helped with maintenance and repair actions, as well as helping establish standard operating procedures on the ships. These ships were later used to support CSAR and other NSW operations.

Coalition Warfare Support

SOF's capabilities, particularly in language

SOF Teams Trained Coalition Forces.

skills, cultural orientation, broad tactical and technical expertise, and level of training, allowed them to perform a wide range of missions supporting Coalition forces. Coalition warfare support missions were assigned to SOCCENT who, in turn, tasked Army Special Forces (SF) and SEALs.

Shortly after arriving in country, NSWTG-CENT was directed to train Royal Saudi forces in the EAC. For three weeks, a 20-man SEAL element worked with the Saudis and taught not only CAS, but also small-unit tactics and weapons. The SEALs were relieved by the 5th SFG on 7 September. These combined teams provided surveillance and early warning along borders out to the neutral zone, providing security as VII Corps and XVIII Airborne Corps forces deployed west. A SEAL platoon with units from the Royal Saudi Naval Forces (RSNF) conducted border surveillance in the coastal area near the Al-Khalij border station north of Ras Al-Khafji from 14 October 90 to 29 January 91. They withdrew only after Iraqi armored forces attacked through their positions enroute to Ras Al-Khafji.

SOCCENT also provided specifically tailored SF Coordination and Training Teams to work with Coalition partners. Initially, the mission was limited to support of the Royal Saudi Land Forces (RSLF) and the Saudi Arabian National Guard (SANG). However, as forces from Egypt, Syria, Oman, Morocco, Bahrain, the United Arab Emirates (UAE), and Qatar arrived in Saudi Arabia, they also sought US training and support assistance. Eventually, 109 SF Coordination and Training Teams (CTT) were created. SF CTT also were later sent to French forces.

Included in the Coalition training was an exercise that had a significant impact not only on current readiness, but on future training programs as well. A Combined Arms Live Fire Exercise (CALFEX) was conducted by elements of the RSLF and ARCENT. SOF teams trained with elements of the RSLF and acted as facilitators for the exercise.

The integration of the non-US Coalition members with US forces was improved by the use of Army SF teams, which linked the CENTCOM maneuver planning staff and the Arab-Islamic units. Regularly scheduled situation reports were passed by SOF liaison teams through the US chain of command to CENTCOM. Islamic forces provided activity reports to the Saudis, occasionally a time-consuming process; Army SF liaison teams provided the theater commander a more expeditious means of acquiring information about forces locations, status, and capabilities. These teams also provided coordination between adjacent Coalition forces, which helped in command and control, and did much to prevent casualties from the fire of friendly forces. Additionally, they passed support requests when needed.

Another Army Special Forces team task was to help conduct realistic training. The teams built replicas of objectives and worked with commanders to rehearse attack plans. Rehearsals developed confidence among soldiers. Some examples of training include instructing the Royal Saudi Land Forces (RSLF) general purpose forces in CAS, naval gunfire support (NGFS) and fire support coordination. The 1st Battalion, 5th SFG and a SEAL platoon also trained Royal Saudi Naval Forces (RSNF) and Marines in small unit tactics, diving operations, air operations, demolitions, weapons, mission planning, and high-speed boat operations.

Overall Coalition warfare support was a success and attests to SOF's ability to integrate those Coalition units into the overall theater plan. Arab forces were effectively integrated into the command and control, communications and intelligence structure of the joint forces. However, two shortcomings warrant mention and subsequent review. First, overall language

proficiency skills and the number of language-trained SOF personnel was insufficient to meet Coalition warfare support requirements. Secondly, because SOF operations normally emphasize smaller unit skills and unconventional warfare, some liaison teams had limited experience and training in larger unit (battalion level and higher) operations. Consequently, advice and assistance in mobile armored warfare and employment was limited. Battalion and brigade level combined arms operations and doctrine should be a part of SOF training programs and professional development.

Special Reconnaissance (SR)

SOF conducted SR missions throughout Operations Desert Shield and Desert Storm. SR operations are reconnaissance and surveillance actions to obtain or verify, by visual observation or other collection methods, information about enemy capabilities, intentions, and activities, or to gather data about the meteorological, hydrographic, or geographic characteristics of a particular area. SR missions complemented national and theater intelligence collection assets through border reconnaissance and deep penetration missions to obtain specific,

SOF Elements Conducted Special Reconnaissance Operations Along the Kuwaiti Coast.

SOF Helicopters Conducted Aerial Reconnaissance of Key Areas.

time-sensitive information of strategic and tactical significance.

NSW units conducted security missions along the Kuwaiti coast from 23 August to 12 September. Navy SEALs and Navy SBU detachments conducted nightly patrols off Al-Jubayl Harbor while Marine Corps (USMC) maritime pre-positioned ships (MPS) unloaded. Beginning in October, SEAL platoons maintained a continual presence north of Ras Al-Khafji. These platoons provided real-time intelligence and coordinated close air support. For example, in late January, SEALs photographed the Iraqi minelayer, T-43, while it was actively laying mines in Kuwaiti territorial waters. Additionally, four hours after Coalition air strikes began on 17 January, SEALs called in CAS and destroyed the Iraqi border station, 400 yards north of the Saudi-Kuwait border.

When the offensive began, NSW units conducted 11 SR missions onto the Kuwaiti beaches and north of Al-Khafji. A SEAL platoon, north of Ras Al-Khafji, was directly involved in the battle for Al-Khafji. As Iraqi forces prepared to move south, the SEALs called in CAS. The unit remained in position on the border, providing real-time intelligence on Iraqi troop and vehicular movement until they were forced out by enemy fire.

SR operations were not limited to the Kuwait-Saudi-Iraq border and along the coast of Kuwait; missions also were conducted farther north and deep into Kuwait and Iraq during the offensive. Extensive planning for these missions began in early January. SOCCENT forces conducted 12 SR missions during Operation Desert Storm; in these deep reconnaissance missions, some Army SF operated for lengthy periods behind enemy lines — one team had spent 60 hours behind enemy lines by the time the cease fire was declared.

NSW units continued to patrol the coastal areas as the offensive began, providing valuable intelligence on enemy coastal defenses while increasing Iraqi concerns about amphibious landings.

During the same period, Army SF performed SR missions to support XVIII Airborne Corps and VII Corps. Army SF teams provided essential information to ground tactical commanders during the final ground offensive preparations. This information included analyzing soil conditions to determine whether it would permit passage of heavy armored vehicles.

Additionally, SOF aircraft also conducted aerial reconnaissance and photographic missions of the Mina Al-Ahmadi oil terminal after Iraq released oil into the Persian Gulf. Using both USAF and Army MH-60 aircraft, NSWTG SEALs and photographers from the combat camera detachment conducted aerial reconnaissance. These missions documented the

Air Force Special Operations AC 130 Supported Operations Over Kuwait.

extent of contamination from the oil spill and verified the success of Coalition airstrikes in stopping the oil flow.

Direct Action (DA) Missions

DA missions include raids, ambushes, or other assault tactics. These missions may involve placement of munitions and other devices and conduct of standoff attacks by coordinating fire from air, ground, or maritime fire support platforms. SOF forces planned for, but did not conduct any DA missions during Operation Desert Shield; however, several DA missions were conducted during Operation Desert Storm.

In the planning for Operation Desert Storm, SOCCENT was given the mission of destroying two key Iraqi early warning radar sites near the Saudi-Iraqi border. Destruction of these sites facilitated Coalition air strikes at the start of the air campaign deep into Iraqi territory. SOCCENT developed a plan which coupled the firepower of the AH-64 Apache with the long range navigational capability of the MH-53 Pave Low helicopter. The MH-53s led the AH-64s to a point approximately 10 kilometers from the radar sites 22 minutes prior to H-Hour. The AH-64s then destroyed the radar sites with Hellfire missiles and 30 mm cannon fire.

In addition to the opening attack on the Iraqi radar sites, SOF aircraft were also involved in other DA missions. The MC-130E Combat Talon, was selected to support operations to breach Iraqi minefields and reduce obstacles facing the Coalition forces. BLU-82s, powerful 15,000-pound bombs supported counter-obstacle operations, PSYOP operations, and targeted enemy command and control (C^2) headquarters during the early phase of Operation Desert Storm. Five of these missions dropped 11 BLU-82s on nine different Iraqi positions, including Faylaka Island. Although there were mixed reports of the effectiveness of the bombs against minefields, a collateral result was psychological intimidation and degradation of morale in the targeted units. Numerous Iraqi EPWs cited these bombs as significant factors in their decision to surrender.

On 24 January, SOCCENT NSW forces conducted a daylight raid on enemy forces on Qaruh Island and recaptured the area — the first Kuwaiti territory Coalition forces recaptured. These forces successfully captured Iraqi soldiers, along with substantial amounts of weapons and ammunition without sustaining any casualties. Once secured, the island was used as a staging area for other NSW reconnaissance and DA missions, including those conducted against offshore oil platforms.

NSW operations were extensive during the ground phase of Operation Desert Storm, particularly counter-mine operations. Mine-hunting missions were conducted off the coast of Kuwait.

SEALs participated in aerial mine hunting with USN helicopters. The patrols searched for floating mines, and when found, SEALs dropped from hovering helicopters, swam to the mine, and attached a pre-timed demolition charge; 25 floating mines were destroyed in this manner. Additionally more than 145 floating mines were destroyed by USN Explosive

Soldiers Witness the Symbolic Raising of the Colors at the Embassy in Kuwait.

Ordnance Disposal divers and Coalition mine clearance divers.

As Operation Desert Storm began, direct action missions were conducted to seize enemy-held off-shore oil platforms. Reconnaissance patrols determined the platforms had antiaircraft weapons on them and served as observation posts, monitoring Coalition ship and air movements in the approaches to Kuwait City. The offshore platforms also could provide launch platforms for missiles directed against the Coalition. The elimination of these platforms became an essential part of the preparations for an amphibious landing near Kuwait City. On 19 January, Navy SEALs aboard Rigid Inflatable

Boats, and supported by the *USS Nicholas* and the Kuwaiti patrol craft Istiqlal, boarded and recaptured the Ad-Dawrah oil field platforms.

In late January, Special Operations AC-130 Spectre gunships began DA and fire support missions in southern Iraq, northwest Kuwait, and near Kuwait City. The aircraft armed with 20mm, 40mm, and 105-mm cannons, provided support for Coalition forces. AC-130 Spectre gunships were able to operate over friendly positions providing effective fire on enemy positions for several hours at a time. They were particularly effective in attacking Iraqi ground forces in the KTO and in support of Joint Forces Command-East (JFC-E) units during the battle of Al-Khafji.

The Iraqi forces apparently believed an amphibious assault would be a key component of the Coalition maneuver scheme and retained several divisions in the Kuwait City area to repulse the invasion. A significant mission in support of the CENTCOM deception plan involved simulating beach preparations for an amphibious landing to convince the Iraqis that such a landing was imminent. As the ground operations were about to begin, SEALs entered the water and swam ashore to plant delayed charges and set up lane markers to deceive the Iraqi forces as to the Coalition forces' intent.

On 26 and 27 February, SOCCENT planned and coordinated use of assets in the liberation of portions of Kuwait City. The 3rd SFG with attached SEALs secured and cleared the US Embassy simultaneously with actions taken by UK and French units to occupy their embassies. Using a heliborne assault, SOF teams touched down inside the abandoned US Embassy compound and sealed the area and recaptured the buildings. The next day, SOF turned the compound over to the State Department. SOCCENT elements working with Kuwaiti resistance groups, helped seize and clear the

Kuwaiti Police Headquarters and other key government buildings.

Electronic Warfare

Using both ground and air assets, SOCCENT conducted signal monitoring and radio direction finding operations against Iraq shortly after arriving in SWA. Special Forces Electronic Warfare Teams established joint and combined electronic listening posts to detect and monitor Iraqi signals. These operations added to the surveillance reports along the border and fixed the locations of Iraqi headquarters and artillery observers. Once additional forces had arrived and the SOF command infrastructure was established, SOCCENT moved ground listening and monitoring stations into CSOAs Shannon and Cochise. The data was sent back to SOCCENT, where analysts processed the information and coordinated with targeting teams.

Combat Search and Rescue (CSAR)

CINCCENT designated CENTAF as the theater CSAR coordinator. CENTAF established and operated the Joint Rescue Coordination Center (JRCC) to coordinate these missions. Because SOF aircraft were best suited to conduct long-range personnel recovery missions, the SOCCENT commander was designated as commander of combat rescue forces. SOF provided 24-hour, on-call CSAR for Coalition aircrews. Army SOF helicopters (MH-60), upgraded with mini-guns, and Naval Reserve HH-60H helicopters, and MH-47 helicopters were available for these missions in addition to Air Force Special Operations Command, Central (AFSOCCENT) assets.

SOF aircraft supporting the CSAR mission were located in Saudi Arabia. SOCEUR aircraft covered the northern area of Iraq. In addition to Iraq and Kuwait, SOCCENT's CSAR area extended 12 miles in the Arabian Gulf. The Navy was responsible for CSAR beyond 12 miles in the Gulf and in the Red Sea.

CSAR procedures required a reasonable confirmation of a survivor's situation and location before a mission could be launched. This required the downed crews to call-in using hand-held survival radios.

Radios like the PRC-112, have optional preset frequencies and codes, in addition to the international channels. Unfortunately, there was only a limited number of PRC-112s available to units in SWA, with more than half of the radios in SOF units. Sufficient numbers of these radios did not exist for all Coalition aircrews. An immediate attempt was made to procure additional PRC-112 radios and associated power sources from US, Asian, and European sources.

There were 38 downed Coalition aircraft and many downed crew members. Several downed crew members ejected over or near heavily fortified Iraqi positions, deep inside Iraq, making rescue attempts impossible due to distances involved and the enemy situation. Seven CSAR missions were launched. There were three successful recoveries; all rescued

Successful CSAR Missions Were Conducted During the War.

crew members were Americans. Kuwaiti partisan forces also recovered a downed Kuwaiti pilot. Three of the successful CSAR missions are described below.

The first rescue of a downed air crewmember was a daylight recovery of a Navy pilot deep inside Iraq on 21 January. AWACS controlled the flights of air cover from two A-10s and a pair of AFSOC Pave Low helicopters which flew more than 160 miles into Iraq for the recovery. As the Pave Lows were on final approach for the pick-up, an Iraqi radio intercept truck headed straight for the pilot. The A-10s on station immediately responded by attacking and destroying the van. The aircraft continued to fly overhead, covering the helicopters as they landed. After a successful pickup, the helicopters returned to base, nearly eight hours after the Navy aircraft was shot down.

Another recovery occurred on 23 January. The frigate USS Nicholas, (FFG 47) was on station off the Kuwaiti coast. Using the ship's SH-60 helicopter, SEALs aboard the ship recovered a pilot from within two miles of the Kuwaiti coast who had ejected from his stricken aircraft. The CSAR mission took only 35 minutes to complete. The third rescue occurred on 17 February and involved the night rescue of a USAF pilot 60 miles behind enemy lines. Army SOF responded with two MH-60s, and while in the process of recovering the crewman, the pilots, who were wearing night vision goggles, evaded an Iraqi surface-to-air missile.

There was a strong demand for SOF aircraft during Operation Desert Storm. Special Operations aircraft provide capabilities not normally found in similar types of aircraft. As a result of these sophisticated capabilities, the aircraft were requested to perform innovative missions outside the traditional Special Operations role. As a consequence, SOF aircraft had one of the higher utilization

rates in theater. In the case of CSAR missions, SOF aircraft were preferred because of their radar evasion, communications, and weapons system countermeasures capabilities that were considered important for aircraft survivability. However, the combination of CSAR requirements and the other demands for these assets left little room for contingency missions.

LOGISTICS

Special Operations logistics support, in the past, has depended upon the Service's logistics support structures to meet the bulk of SOF sustainment requirements. During Operations Desert Shield and Desert Storm, SOF requirements exceeded theater support capabilities. These problems were caused, in many cases, by the early deployment of SOF tactical units, the limited initial logistics infrastructure in the AOR, and the slow buildup of the theater logistics system. Support to the SOF logistics base was neither adequately prioritized nor organized.

The 5th Special Operations Support Command (Theater Army) (TASOSC), was designed to plan and coordinate the support and sustainment for Army SOF. However, 5th TASOSC was not organized until after most SOF were in theater. During peacetime conditions, 5th TASOSC, is a planning cell and not manned at the required operational level. Deployment required personnel augmentation. In addition, the 5th TASOSC was not sufficiently integrated into the theater logistics network. USAF and Navy SOF did not have similar organizations at theater level, and were dependent on logistics support from their own component organizations.

Most SOF-specific items had to be procured from non-military sources, transported to Saudi Arabia, and transshipped to the requesting unit in theater. SOCCENT received support from SOCOM, who coordinated acquisition of most

SOF-specific items and forwarded them to the theater.

For Army SOF, direct support was provided by the 528th Special Operations Support Battalion (SOSB). The 528th SOSB was under the operational control of the ARSOTF, and not a subordinate element of 5th TASOSC. The support battalion provided rations, fuels, repair parts, transportation and maintenance. This small battalion also operated an arrival and departure airfield control group (A/DACG) at KKMC. The tasks for the 528th SOSB expanded when SOCCENT directed it to provide maintenance and repair support to NSW units. The 528th was not structured properly to accomplish all these missions.

The 528th SOSB deployed to Saudi Arabia without enough repair parts because they did not yet have a fully established Authorized Stockage List (ASL). Pending receipt of repair parts, the 528th received support from the 1st Corps Support Command (COSCOM), and eventually from the 101st Airborne Division (Air Assault) Support Command (DISCOM). Most major assemblies replaced by the 528th SOSB during the first two months were obtained from these sources. The 528th SOSB had only light maintenance capability and sent night vision devices and laser range finders to the 101st Airborne Division (Air Assault) for repair. Due to the additional taskings, the 528th performed as a general support maintenance and supply unit, although neither structured nor resourced to do so.

USAF SOF were supported by maintenance squadrons that deployed with them to the theater. The accelerated air movement of materiel caused a backlog in reception and onward movement of supplies because forward logistics support bases were inadequately manned and equipped. Specifically, the lack of ground transportation specialists and materiel handling equipment slowed the receipt of repair parts shipments and delayed the retrograde of repairable aviation components. This resulted in longer supply procurement times and delayed the receipt of repair parts at the unit level. The slow movement of retrograde parts severely hampered repairs of aircraft, affecting the mission-ready rate. Specific examples include rotor blades, T-700 MH-60G engines, C-130 propellers, and HC-130 in-flight tanker refueling system components.

NSW forces deployed with a 30-day support package. Resupply for afloat NSW forces was handled through established Service support channels. For those NSW forces based ashore, ad hoc arrangements were made through Army supply channels to provide support including vehicles, climate-controlled tentage, messing facilities, and consumables. Examination of the NSW support requirements and structure is recommended for future operations.

Due to operational tempo requirements, environmental conditions, and the slow buildup of the maintenance support base, high failure rates were experienced with certain types of communications equipment. A mobile communication team provided repair for this equipment. Replacements radios were available in CENTCOM for issue, and this helped to maintain a high level of readiness of communications equipment.

Aerial refueling support was provided by the 9th SOS in two geographic operating areas. The bulk of the 9th SOS' missions were flown in the eastern area of operations throughout Operation Desert Storm. As the war evolved, the 9th SOS also provided tanker support to the western area of operations. In total, the 9th SOS flew 103 sorties and 316 hours, including 89 combat sorties and six combat support sorties, that involved 47 refueling missions with the transfer of 412,000 pounds of fuel.

COMBATTING TERRORISM (CT)

From the beginning of Operation Desert Shield,

the United States was concerned about possible terrorist attack. Consultations and exchanges of information among Coalition partners and other members of the UN led to the expulsion of over 200 Iraqi diplomatic personnel, embassy staff, and intelligence personnel from their posts throughout the world. This undoubtedly had a disruptive effort on Iraqi terrorist operations.

Within the US Government, the National Security Council took the lead in producing a well-founded, coordinated policy. Throughout the conflict OSD met frequently in the interagency arena to consult and formulate policy options, including employment of SOF. These policy determinations involved both components of CT: antiterrorism, which involves defensive measures to reduce vulnerability or individuals and property to terrorist acts; and counterterrorism, which involves offensive measures taken to prevent, deter, and respond to terrorism.

The OSD Combatting Terrorism Program served as a pivotal basis for antiterrorism actions on a global basis. The principal mechanism to facilitate inter-Service coordination and support of US Government antiterrorism activities was the DOD Antiterrorism Coordinating Committee (ATCC). Its membership includes representatives from the intelligence, law enforcement, and security communities. Ongoing antiterrorism actions reported by the membership at that time included a wide variety of activities. Concerns that the draw-down and deployment of CONUS-based military security and law enforcement personnel could have made DOD installations more vulnerable to terrorist attacks were passed to the Federal Bureau of Investigation (FBI). In turn, the FBI instructed its field offices to establish liaison with military installations to explain its role in terrorist situations and to alert local and state law enforcement agencies to

report any indications of terrorist activity.

A cross section of other DOD antiterrorism activities included the Commander-in-Chief, Forces Command's accelerated identification and security planning for key DOD assets. These are industrial and infrastructure facilities (owned by private sector or by government agencies) that are essential to mobilize, deploy, or sustain the armed forces. EUCOM commanders, working with military security police and with local officials, established protective measure to be taken by their troops or in their communities. CENTCOM provided antiterrorism awareness training to its military personnel. This training raised individual and collective awareness of the general terrorist threat and the measures that could be taken to reduce personnel vulnerability. Vulnerability surveys were also made of command and billeting facilities, both in CONUS and in the Persian Gulf AOR.

As part of the Combatting Terrorism Program, SOCOM developed and prepared counterterrorism contingency plans and was prepared to respond to terrorist acts and possible hostage situations. OSD was prepared to address policy aspects of multiple CT contingency operations, however, terrorism never materialized.

PSYCHOLOGICAL OPERATIONS (PSYOP)

PSYOP focused on destroying Iraqi morale and encouraging mass surrender and desertion. After the cease fire, an Iraqi division commander stated that next to the Coalition bombing operations, PSYOP was the greatest threat to his troops' morale. PSYOP leaflets and radio broadcasts undermined unit morale, provided instructions on how to surrender, instilled confidence that prisoners would be treated humanely, and provided advanced warning of impending air attacks, thus encouraging desertion. PSYOP objectives were:

Command Relationship for Psychological Operations

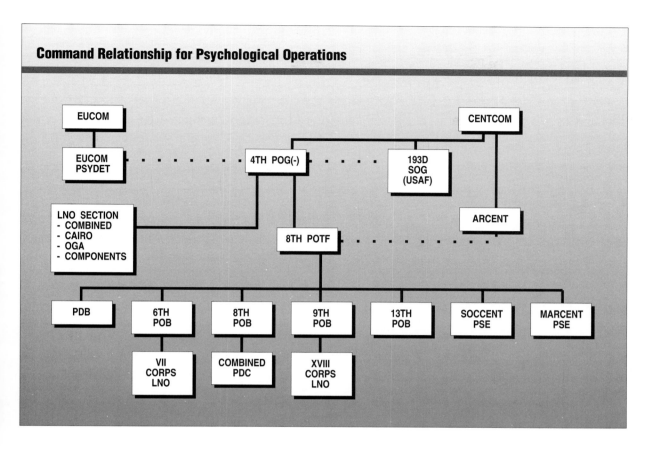

- Gain acceptance and support for US operations;
- Encourage Iraqi disaffection, alienation, defection and loss of confidence;
- Create doubt in Iraqi leadership;
- Encourage non-cooperation and resistance;
- Strengthen confidence and determination of friendly states to resist aggression; and,
- Improve deterrent value of US forces.

Command Relationships for the Psychological Operation Group

Planning for psychological operations began immediately after the invasion of Kuwait. A PSYOP planning group consisting of military and civilian personnel from CENTCOM, SOCOM, and the 4th Psychological Operations Group (POG) was formed at CENTCOM Headquarters, MacDill Air Force Base, FL. in early August. This group

became the nucleus of the PSYOP command and control element that deployed to Saudi Arabia in late August.

Leaflet, radio and loudspeaker operations were combined and this combination was key to the success of PSYOP. Leaflets were the most commonly used method of conveying PSYOP messages. Twenty-nine million leaflets consisting of 33 different messages were disseminated in the Kuwait theater of operations. Delivery means consisted of MC-130, HC -130, A-6, F-16, B-52, and artillery. A building block approach for leaflet operations was used with the first leaflet themes being ones of peace and brotherhood. Increasing the intensity of the PSYOP message as events evolved, leaflet themes transitioned to emphasizing the United Nations imposed 15 January deadline. After the UN deadline passed and Operation Desert Storm began, themes

PSYOP Leaflet

أه ياولــــدي متى تـــرد

OH, MY DEAR SON, WHEN WILL YOU RETURN?

emphasizing abandonment of equipment and desertion were used. Exploiting the effects of specific munitions, leaflets were also used to inform Iraqi units that they were going to be bombed. Feedback from interviews with enemy prisoners of war validated the success of leaflet operations.

"Voice of the Gulf" was the Coalition's radio network that began broadcasting on 19 January from ground based and airborne transmitters, 18 hours per day for 40 days. The radio script was prepared daily and provided news, countered Iraqi propaganda and disinformation, and encouraged Iraqi defection and surrender.

Loudspeaker teams were used effectively throughout the theater. Each tactical maneuver brigade had loudspeaker PSYOP teams attached. Many of the 66 teams came from the Army Reserve Components (RC). Loudspeaker teams accompanied units into Iraq and Kuwait, broadcasting tapes of prepared surrender messages. Messages were transmitted in Arabic and were developed by

cross cultural teams. These messages were similar to those on the leaflets being dropped. Iraqi soldiers were encouraged to surrender, were warned of impending bombing attacks, and told they would be treated humanely and fairly. Many Enemy Prisoners of War (EPW) mentioned hearing the loudspeaker broadcasts in their area and surrendered to the Coalition forces because they feared more bombing.

PSYOP proved very successful during the war; however, there are some areas that require further review. As noted earlier, there was a significant delay in the approval processes. PSYOP capabilities are best used when they are employed early in an operation to promote deterrence and/or decrease an opponent's will to resist. Thus, the machinery to do so must be in place as soon as possible. Also, a concerted effort to recruit, train, and maintain linguists is needed.

Additionally, PSYOP unit structuring, both in the active and Reserve Components, must be reviewed, as well as the wartime command relationships among these units. Active and RC force mix should be evaluated to ensure sufficient PSYOP assets are available to provide support should more than one contingency occur.

CIVIL AFFAIRS

Planning

One of the functions of civil affairs is to assist in integrating US forces smoothly with the population and forces of the host nation. Deployment of large numbers of US forces to Saudi Arabia meant harmonizing our western culture with the culture of our host. The challenge facing US personnel was to adapt to the customs of Saudi Arabia so conduct created an impression of respect for the Saudis and their culture. A rigorous indoctrination program was undertaken to orient US personnel on the region's uniqueness and its history, customs, religion, law, and mores.

Civil Affairs planners were active in identifying, planning, coordinating, and integrating host nation support (HNS) which was crucial to effective military operations. They identified sources of contract labor, services, materials, and supplies. Civil affairs planners assisted the Saudi in civil defense emergency planning. They kept the status of the Saudis civil defense preparedness including dispersal locations, warning systems, shelters, and NBC defense resources for civilians. Prior to offensive operations and at the request of the US embassy, civil affairs officers met with US civilian nationals living and working in Saudi Arabia to assure them of Coalition military capabilities so as to relieve some of their anxiety about being in a war zone.

Operations

Units from the US Army, US Army Reserve, and the USMC Reserve provided the Civil Affairs support for pre-combat, combat, and emergency reconstruction missions during Operations Desert Shield and Desert Storm in the Kuwait Theater of Operations (KTO). Units involved included the Army's 96th CA Battalion, the only active Army unit, 16 USAR units, and two USMC(Reserve) CA groups. Missions included coordinating and facilitating host nation support (HNS); emergency services and support to the civil sector; support to combat operations by minimizing civilian interference and casualties; providing for movement and control of civilians; emergency water, food, shelter, and medical care for displaced civilians and enemy prisoners of war (EPWs); and providing emergency services and reconstruction assistance to the Government of Kuwait in rebuilding its infrastructure following the cessation of hostilities.

In October, the Government of Kuwait requested US government help to plan the

Civil Affairs Operations in Kuwait.

Kuwait Emergency and Recovery Program and the State Department turned to DOD for assistance. In early December, the Kuwait CA Task Force was formed, largely around personnel of the 352nd CA Command, a USAR unit from Riverdale, MD. The task force helped marshal resources, from both the private and public sector, which Kuwait needed to restore emergency services once the country was liberated. The task force objectives included mobilizing the Kuwaiti government-in-exile to plan for the necessary services, supplies and equipment. Initially, the task force worked with ministerial representatives of the Kuwaiti government in exile to plan and contract for the necessary services, supplies and equipment needed in the post-combat phase of the operation. The organization deployed to Saudi Arabia in January to complete final civil affairs planning and preparation to execute the plan.

CA forces contributed to the procurement of host nation support (HNS) by locating and arranging for supplies and services from US allies in the region. Initially, the 96th CA Battalion, and later USAR CA units, particularly the 304th CA Group, worked in direct support of ARCENT's 22nd Support Command on HNS matters. Their efforts helped sustain the force buildup in the KTO.

CA forces assigned to combat units performed the essential function of controlling and providing humanitarian assistance to displaced civilians, refugees, and EPWs encountered on the battlefield. In doing so, they minimized the effect these persons had on military operations and safeguarded them from combat operations. In the rear areas, CA forces organized and managed the displaced civilians and refugee collection points and camps and assisted the transition of responsibility for these groups from military to international relief organizations.

Deployment of CA forces competed in the early stages of Operation Desert Shield with the urgent requirements for combat capability, including combat forces, and the necessary logistical support units, equipment and supplies needed to sustain combat operations. As the force structure to meet tactical requirements were met, CENTCOM began to increase priority to post-hostility considerations, including deployment and employment of CA units. Most of the CA units were deployed between mid-January and mid-February.

Despite notable CA successes discussed in this report, the civil implications of military operations did not receive as much early planning attention as would have been preferred. In some instances, combat forces had already moved forward to their pre-assault

> "**W**hen used properly and when synchronized with other battlefield assets, SOF is a combat multiplier that offers commanders a capability that will extend their vision of the battlefield, increase their flexibility, and enhance their initiative."
>
> *General Carl W. Stiner, USA*
> *Commander-In-Chief*
> *Special Operations Command*

positions by the time their supporting CA units arrived in-country. The planning assistance to the Kuwait government, although requested in October, did not commence until December and it was done in isolation from the war plans prepared by CENTCOM.

CONCLUSION

SOF played a valuable role in Operations Desert Shield and Desert Storm, conducting a wide range of missions. Through these successful missions, SOCCENT forces achieved total integration with the conventional forces and proved the applicability of SOF in a medium-high intensity conflict.

Use of Special Operations capabilities requires tradeoffs between the political risk that often accompanies the conduct of special operations and the military advantage provided. Cross-border operations provided both real-time tactical and operational level advantages to the force commanders; however, inadvertent compromise of these operations can signal strategic objectives, incurring both military and political repercussions.

OBSERVATIONS

Accomplishments

- Operations Desert Shield and Desert Storm were the largest deployment of SOF units and personnel in modern history. They operated in all environments, on land, water, and in the air. SOF teams remained hidden behind enemy lines, conducting SR for CINCCENT and tactical commanders alike, and conducted DA missions to include the first offensive attack to begin the air campaign. SOF contributions also were particularly valuable in support of Coalition Warfare, reconstructing the Kuwaiti military, supporting CINCCENT's deception plan, and CSAR.

- SOF actions with the Coalition forces were important to the success of the operation.

- PSYOP contributed significantly to the collapse and defeat of the Iraqi army.

- CA forces were instrumental in acquiring HNS, handling dislocated persons, and the reconstruction of Kuwait.

- SOF RC augmented the Active component forces and performed well.

Shortcomings

- There was a strong demand for SOF aircraft during Operation Desert Storm. The combination of CSAR requirements and other demands left little room for contingency missions.

- There were insufficient numbers of the newer PRC-112 hand-held survival radios available for all Coalition aircrews. The newer PRC-112 radio has additional optional preset frequencies and codes to provide confirmation of a downed aircrew's situation and location.

- The PSYOPs process requires review and should be streamlined for timely implementation and execution.

- SOF theater language requirements and the number of available linguists were short of the required level. There is a continuing need to identify requirements in all Service Components and to ensure resources are available to train and maintain linguists.

- SOF were assigned to train and go into battle with Coalition partners. The preponderance of Coalition units were general purpose forces. SOF teams with Coalition units were required to have a working knowledge of combined arms maneuver doctrine. Some SOF members did not have detailed knowledge of the combined arms tactical considerations for large mechanized forces.

- NSWTG required conventional services and support when operating from the fleet. Future combat scenarios may require that they be able to operate and sustain themselves as a member of a joint force. NSW forces deployed in SWA relied on many ad hoc support agreements to accomplish the mission, instead of from a structured, in-place organization. The types of agreements, while successful in this case, are short lived and may not be available for other contingency deployments.

- Civil Affairs implications in military operations did not receive appropriate attention early in the theater planning process and was done in isolation from the theater plans. Future planning should include CA considerations earlier in the process.

Issues

- In Operations Desert Shield and Desert Storm, SOF operated where contingency planning was not fully developed. Service SOF operated out of their traditional environments and relied heavily on theater level conventional support services. In doing so, several areas where joint procedures need to be established were identified. To validate current requirements, test draft joint procedures, and help plan for future deployments, regularly scheduled joint SOF and general purpose support forces mobilization and deployment exercises should be conducted.

- SOCOM role in TPFDD determination should be established and cyclical planning for force call up and deployments reviewed and defined.

- PSYOP and CA assets were able to support CINCCENT requirements, however, support for a second contingency would have been difficult. Active and RC force mix should be evaluated to ensure sufficient PSYOP and CA assets are available should more than one contingency occur.

Appendix K

COMMAND, CONTROL, COMMUNICATIONS (C³), AND SPACE

INTRODUCTION

Historical Perspective of CENTCOM Involvement in SWA

"Our superiority in precision munitions, stealth, mobility, and command, control, communications and computers proved to be decisive force multipliers"

General H. Norman Schwarzkopf
Commander-in-Chief, Central Command

Beginning in the early 1960s, a succession of commands was given the responsibility for planning Middle East operations. The first was the US Strike Command (STRICOM). Established at MacDill Air Force Base, FL, in 1962, STRICOM had responsibility for joint planning of operations in the Middle East, South Asia and sub-Saharan Africa. Although a

The Lines of Authority and Lines of Responsibility Were Clear from the President and Secretary of Defense, Through the Chairman, Joint Chiefs of Staff, to the Commander-in-Chief, Central Command, Which Meant a Much More Effective Fighting Force in the Gulf.

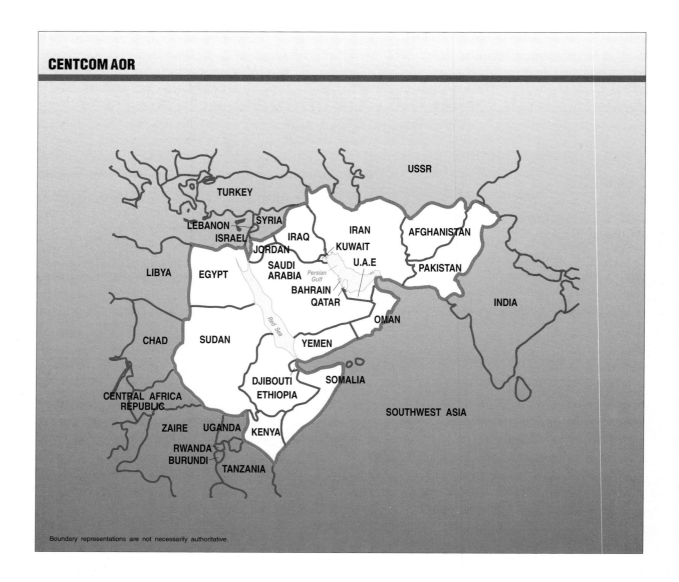

CENTCOM AOR

Boundary representations are not necessarily authoritative.

unified command, it controlled no Navy or Marine Corps (USMC) units. During STRICOM's existence, the Fast Deployment Logistics concept was formulated. Although never implemented, it became the forerunner of today's prepositioning ships.

In late 1971, the Joint Chiefs of Staff (JCS) implemented a new Unified Command Plan. This plan replaced STRICOM with the US Readiness Command (REDCOM), and split STRICOM's responsibilities among existing unified commands. Three organizations gained

operational responsibility for various parts of the Middle East/Southwest Asia (SWA): European Command (EUCOM), Pacific Command, and Atlantic Command. Although REDCOM was a unified command, it had no geographic area of responsibility (AOR). In essence, it became a training command, charged only with providing forces to other unified commands, and with the land defense of the continental United States (CONUS).

Another step in the development of a rapid deployment force came in 1980 with establishment of the Rapid Deployment Joint Task Force (RDJTF), under REDCOM's administrative control. Its initial worldwide mission soon was narrowed to SWA. In October 1981, the RDJTF was made a separate joint task force (JTF), reporting to the National Command Authorities (NCA) through the JCS. A final metamorphosis took place on 1 January 1983, when Central Command (CENTCOM), a unified command, replaced the RDJTF. Its AOR consisted of portions of SWA.

CENTCOM was organized with Service component commands, each responsible for all aspects of its respective Service's functions. In peacetime, except for the Navy Component, Central Command (NAVCENT), component commands have no forces assigned. Other CENTCOM forces are designated for planning purposes only for wartime requirements and assigned elsewhere in peacetime. For example, units designated for Army Component, Central Command (ARCENT) are subordinate to Forces Command (FORSCOM) in peacetime; Marine Component, Central Command (MARCENT) is an additional command responsibility assigned to I Marine Expeditionary Force (I MEF). Additional forces, if needed, would be made available from other commands within each Service. In peacetime, Commander-in-Chief, Central Command (CINCCENT) headquarters is at Tampa, FL. Except for Special Operations Component, Central Command (SOCCENT), each CENTCOM component commander is stationed elsewhere.

CENTCOM produced a draft operations plan (OPLAN), including annexes, for the wargame exercise Internal Look 90 in July 1990. CENTCOM and its Service components validated the OPLAN during Internal Look 90 and, as a result, this draft became the genesis for Operation Desert Shield.

COMMAND AND CONTROL STRUCTURE

The Secretary of Defense, the Under Secretary of Defense for Policy, CINCCENT, ARCENT,

GOLDWATER-NICHOLS ACT

The Goldwater-Nichols Department of Defense Reorganization Act of 1986 (GNA) sought to strengthen civilian control and oversight of military operations; improve the military advice provided to civilian authority; establish the Chairman, Joint Chiefs of Staff (CJCS) as the principal military advisor to the National Command Authorities; and place clear responsibility on combatant commanders while ensuring the Commanders-in-Chief's (CINC) authority was commensurate with their responsibilities. GNA gives the Under Secretary of Defense for Policy authority to review contingency plans. Operations Desert Shield and Desert Storm provided the first major occasion to assess the effect of the GNA in a joint environment. There were several areas in which GNA affected the Commander-in-Chief, Central Command's (CINCCENT) combatant command authority. GNA clarified the chain of command and the lines of communication, from the President and Secretary of Defense, through the CJCS, to CINCCENT. The CJCS role was strengthened, increasing his ability to provide timely military advice; roles of Services, Defense agencies, and supporting CINCs were clarified, which improved providing timely assistance to CINCCENT. GNA's creation of the position of the Vice Chairman, Joint Chiefs of Staff (VCJCS) allowed the CJCS to devote his full attention to Operations Desert Shield and Desert Storm while the VCJCS conducted day-to-day business, with no loss of continuity.

and Air Force Component, Central Command (CENTAF) commanders and key staff officers arrived on 6 August in Saudi Arabia with an offer to deploy US forces to defend Saudi Arabia. After acceptance from the Saudi King in Jiddah, the Secretary, Under Secretary, and CINCCENT returned to the United States, leaving the officers who had accompanied them in Riyadh to begin Operation Desert Shield. The CENTAF commander was designated Commander, CENTCOM Forward, and remained in Saudi Arabia with the other general officers to coordinate with the Saudis and monitor the reception of US forces. The component commanders also served as CINCCENT's agents until he and his staff arrived and assumed the duties involved in building a combined coalition force.

CINCCENT returned to Tampa where he could best influence the prioritization and deployment of forces and organize the command and control (C^2) structure. CENTCOM had begun only recently to identify detailed needs in support of the operations plan for the defense of the Arabian Peninsula. The lack of an approved plan was especially crucial in the fluid situation in August. (In peacetime, once a unified campaign plan is approved, it provides the Services with the force requirements to execute the plan.) In support of Operation Desert Shield, it took time to identify all requirements and then match requirements with specific units. The problem was not serious in dealing with large units such as corps and divisions, but became acute in identifying the many smaller separate units needed to support the larger force.

After the deployment of forces was under way, CINCCENT deployed his headquarters from MacDill Air Force Base (AFB) to Riyadh. In addition to deploying, supporting, and training the combat forces necessary to halt and reverse Iraqi aggression, it also was

> "**G**oldwater-Nichols established very, very clear lines of command authority and responsibilities over subordinate commanders, and that meant a much more effective fighting force in the Gulf. The lines of authority were clear, the lines of responsibility were clear, and we just did not have any problem in that area — none whatsoever."
>
> *General H. Norman Schwarzkopf*

crucial that CENTCOM establish the theater command, control, and communications (C^3) structure. This process included organizing, testing, and modifying lines of communications and developing an efficient scheme to control forces.

CINCCENT's command structure and relationships had been evolving for several years. For example, in 1980, military relationships were established during joint US/Saudi use of the Airborne Warning and Control System (AWACS). These were refined while conducting escort missions of reflagged oil tankers in the Persian Gulf during the 1987-1990 Operation Earnest Will.

In establishing the Operation Desert Shield command structure, joint procedures and doctrine provided a basis for integration of US forces. While each service provided forces to CENTCOM, CINCCENT commanded and decided how to organize them. He organized US forces using both Service components (similar to the peacetime organizational structure) and a Joint Force Air Component Commander (JFACC) to integrate and coordinate combat power. This structure maintained continuity, ensured component commanders were responsible for Service missions in theater, and smoothed the transition to a wartime organization. SOCCENT remained a sub-unified command, allowing centralized operational control of special operations forces (SOF) from the military Services under a single commander. While there were no changes in the US command organization during the transition to Operation Desert Storm, non-US Coalition forces moved either under CINCCENT's operational control (OPCON) or tactical control (TACON).

The Chairman, Joint Chiefs of Staff (CJCS) established these command relationships:

- CINCCENT was the supported combatant commander and responsible for all military operations within his AOR.
- Commanders-in-Chief, Europe, Atlantic, Pacific, Special Operations, Space, Transportation, South, Forces, and Strategic Air Commands (CINCEUR, CINCLANT, CINCPAC, CINCSOC, CINCSPACE, CINCTRANS, CINCSO, CINCFOR, CINCSAC) were supporting commanders and Commander, Tactical Air Command (TAC), a supporting resource manager.
- Army, Marine Corps (USMC), SOF forces ashore in the AOR, Air Force (USAF) TAC forces in the AOR, and Naval forces assigned to Commander, Middle East Force (CMEF) were assigned Combatant Command (COCOM) to CINCCENT.
- Transportation Command (TRANSCOM) air/sea lift control units in the AOR, and Strategic Air Command (SAC) B-52s were OPCON to CINCCENT.
- SAC tanker forces and the other Commanders-in-Chief (CINCs) forces (e.g.

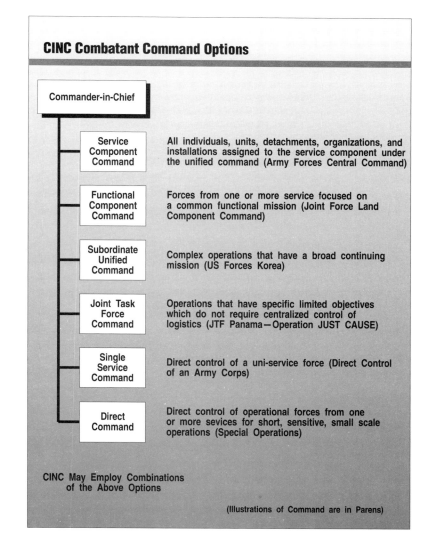

CINC Combatant Command Options

Commander-in-Chief

Service Component Command	All individuals, units, detachments, organizations, and installations assigned to the service component under the unified command (Army Forces Central Command)
Functional Component Command	Forces from one or more service focused on a common functional mission (Joint Force Land Component Command)
Subordinate Unified Command	Complex operations that have a broad continuing mission (US Forces Korea)
Joint Task Force Command	Operations that have specific limited objectives which do not require centralized control of logistics (JTF Panama—Operation JUST CAUSE)
Single Service Command	Direct control of a uni-service force (Direct Control of an Army Corps)
Direct Command	Direct control of operational forces from one or more sevices for short, sensitive, small scale operations (Special Operations)

CINC May Employ Combinations of the Above Options

(Illustrations of Command are in Parens)

The types or levels of command authority are well defined by Joint Pub 0-2, Unified Action Armed Forces (UNAAF) and Joint Pub 1, DOD Dictionary of Military and Associated Terms. The only recent addition occurred with the 1986 revision to the UNAAF, which expanded operational command (OPCOM) and operational control (OPCON) into combatant command, OPCON, tactical control and support, to better define GNA authorities. Support and coordination remained essentially unchanged. OPCOM still applies to allied command relationships in the North Atlantic Treaty Organization.

TRANSCOM lift assets and EUCOM's aircraft operating from EUCOM's AOR), while operating in CENTCOM's AOR, were assigned TACON to CINCCENT.
- Other supporting CINCs' forces supporting CINCCENT were assigned to CINCCENT's TACON while operating in the AOR.
- CINCSAC, as both a supporting and supported commander, retained OPCON of all strategic reconnaissance forces in the AOR.

In addition, CINCCENT chose to retain the Joint Force Land Component Commander

EXPLANATION OF COMMAND RELATIONSHIP TERMINOLOGY

- **C**ombatant command (COCOM): COCOM equates to owning forces. All Army forces in the AOR are under COCOM of CINCCENT — allows broadest command relationship.

- **O**perational control (OPCON): OPCON equates to leasing forces. B-52s remain COCOM under CINCSAC but are OPCON to CINCCENT — allows maximum control without burden of support.

- **T**actical control (TACON): TACON equates to renting (short term) forces. CINCEUR F-111s operating from CINCEUR were TACON to CINCCENT while operating in CENTCOM's AOR — allows use and control of another CINC's assets.

- **C**omponent: NAVCENT, for example, is the Navy component for CINCCENT and is responsible for coordinating all Navy functions.

- **S**upport is providing a service: CINCTRANS C-141s and C-5s provide airlift and transportation support to CINCCENT.

function rather than delegate the Land Component Command responsibility. CENTCOM's broad, complex mission required unity of effort and the integration of vastly different US and allied forces. CINCCENT directed the ground service components — ARCENT and MARCENT — and maintained coordination with the Saudi ground force command at his level. However, ARCENT and MARCENT had primary responsibility for developing and analyzing courses of action for their respective ground offensives.

On 9 August, all Gulf Cooperation Council states except Qatar, agreed to permit access to US forces, and the first increment of the CENTCOM Forward Headquarters Element (FHE) arrived in Saudi Arabia. (Qatar agreed to permit access a week later.) By mid-August, the FHE was established in the National Defense Operations Center bunker,

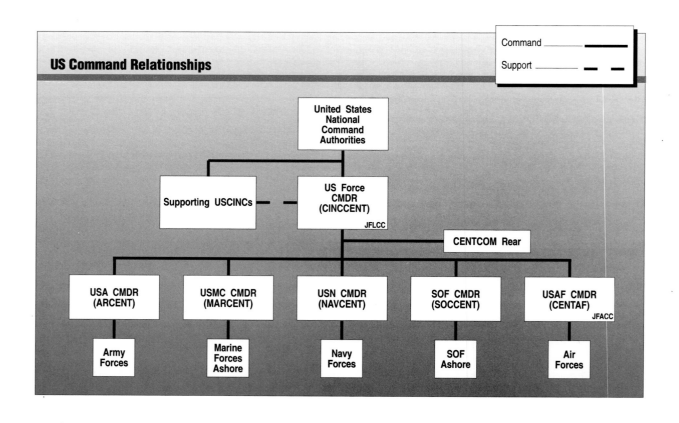

US Command Relationships

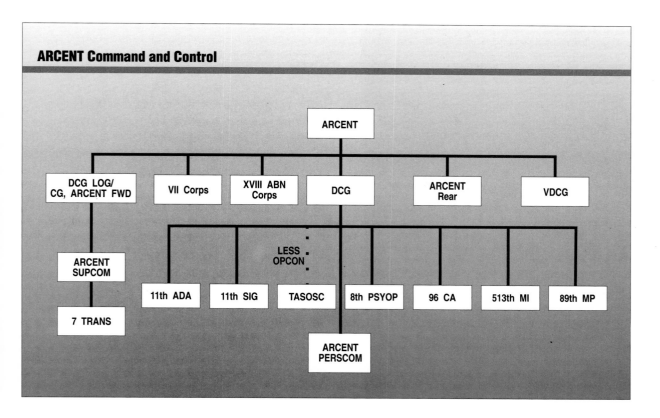

ARCENT Command and Control

ARCENT
- DCG LOG/ CG, ARCENT FWD
  - ARCENT SUPCOM
    - 7 TRANS
- VII Corps
- XVIII ABN Corps
- DCG
  - 11th ADA
  - 11th SIG
  - TASOSC (LESS OPCON)
  - 8th PSYOP
  - 96 CA
  - 513th MI
  - 89th MP
  - ARCENT PERSCOM
- ARCENT Rear
- VDCG

under the Saudi Arabia Ministry of Defense and Aviation (MODA) building in Riyadh. Initial requirements were to provide communications between components and CENTCOM Rear; monitor and coordinate maritime intercept operations; track deployment of US and friendly forces; and help coordinate aircraft beddowns. Other immediate tasks included defining command relationships, initiating combined planning, and integrating third-country participation into Operation Desert Shield.

COMMAND AND CONTROL STRUCTURE OF COMPONENT COMMANDS

Army Command Relationships

The 3rd US Army commander also served as the ARCENT commander. He developed a wartime command structure in Saudi Arabia to control deploying Army units. This structure practically doubled in size on 8 August with the arrival of the ARCENT Advance Command and Control Element. (The ARCENT headquarters main body arrived next, in two echelons, bringing the headquarters to an effective strength of 266 on 23 August.) ARCENT (Main) was established in Riyadh on 16 August to oversee the arrival, sustainment, and combat planning for deploying Army units. Until CINCCENT arrived in theater, the ARCENT commander was responsible for preparing for the joint force's arrival. CINCFOR assumed the additional duty of ARCENT (Rear) headquarters. (FORSCOM is a specified major Army command whose responsibilities include providing forces to meet worldwide contingencies and defending CONUS.)

Third Army had three different structures to meet its responsibilities for joint and combined coordination, theater support operations, and operational direction. As the Army component, ARCENT was responsible for all aspects of Army operations, rear operations and certain

ARCENT Receives an Update on the Ground War while Inside the Army Command Operations and Intelligence Center.

Given the size of the theater and the scope of responsibilities, a C^2 system was needed to provide timely assessments and to permit rapid reallocation of resources. ARCENT increased its C^2 capability by creating seven liaison teams, a mobile alternate command post (CP) positioned forward, and a more robust, integrated operations and intelligence center in Riyadh, using the 513th MI Brigade's capabilities.

Liaison teams were assigned to major ground forces (XVIII Airborne Corps, VII Corps, Joint Forces Command-North (JFC-N), Joint Forces Command-East (JFC-E), the Egyptian Corps, I MEF, and 1st Cavalry Division). Liaison personnel were detailed from units deployed around the world, while equipment (e.g., communications) was taken directly from production lines, stocks and units in CONUS and Europe. The teams were a vital link for CINCCENT and the ARCENT commander, playing a crucial role in coordinating operations between Coalition units, and for disseminating standardized procedures among all ground forces within the theater. CINCCENT used the liaison teams as a link with other Coalition forces, while the ARCENT commander used them as a network among subordinate and adjacent units. They also let the commander communicate his intent quickly in fast moving operations. The mobile CP, a scaled down version of the main CP, could displace to forward locations, improving ARCENT's control of battle operations. It also served as an alternate CP and had the communications and staff to support the commander, as necessary. More importantly, it provided an additional capability for the commander to gather information, adding to his ability to quickly reallocate resources to solve short-term problems.

Integration of the three nodes provided effective C^2 of Army forces: the Main CP maintained operational continuity and and monitored the balance of the army units; the liaison teams kept

types of multi-service logistics support throughout the CENTCOM AOR. As a Theater Army, it established the extensive logistics systems and infrastructure needed to receive and sustain deploying forces and directed the emplacement of the Patriot antitactical ballistic missile system. Later in the crisis, as a numbered Field Army, it exercised C^2 of the movement of army forces into attack positions, combat operations in Iraq, and reconstruction efforts in Kuwait.

Army deployments continued from August through March and ultimately exceeded 330,000 active and Reserve Component soldiers. The XVIII Airborne Corps deployed from US bases from August through November; the Europe-based VII Corps deployed from November through January; and echelons above corps units deployed from August 1990 through March 1991. (The latter units make up the support structure that performs specific functions to increase or support corps capabilities. These units include artillery, engineer, signal, Military Intelligence (MI), Military Police, transportation, medical, and Civil Affairs (CA) organizations, among others.)

the commander informed of immediate developments; and the Mobile CP provided another means to focus on potential problems.

Air Force Command Relationships

The Commander, 9th Air Force, served as the CENTAF commander. He was designated CENTCOM Forward Commander from 6 to 26 August while CINCCENT organized the command and directed the deployment of forces to support Operation Desert Shield from his MacDill AFB headquarters. Since CENTAF was acting as the CENTCOM Forward, the vice commander, CENTAF, arrived to serve temporarily as CENTAF commander in Saudi Arabia. A large part of the 9th Air Force staff also moved to help plan and deploy the forces. Rather than transfer personnel to 9th Air Force Headquarters at Shaw AFB, SC, to augment the CENTAF Rear staff, Headquarters TAC at Langley AFB, VA, assumed the responsibilities of CENTAF Rear on 12 August.

Managing the planned force required modification of the CENTAF organizational structure. USAF units ultimately were organized into provisional wings during Operation Desert Shield, with each initially reporting through the CENTAF staff to the CENTAF commander. An Air Division concept was created in December to form clearer command relationships between the wings and CENTAF. Control of USAF assets was divided into four provisional divisions, set up in accordance with mission specialities. The 14th Air Division (P) consisted of all fighter aircraft; the 15th Air Division (P) consisted of electronic warfare and C^2 aircraft; the 17th Air Division (P) consisted of SAC aircraft; and the 1610th Air Lift Division (P) consisted of all Military Airlift Command aircraft. The Commander, 14th Air Division (P), also was Director of the Campaign Plans Division, which developed and planned the Strategic Air Campaign.

CINCCENT also designated CENTAF as the

The JFACC Was Implemented to Provide for Aviation Unity of Effort. *This Was the First Time It Was Used in a Major Regional Conflict.*

JFACC, with responsibility for coordinating all Coalition air forces to ensure focus of effort in the air campaign. The JFACC planned, coordinated, allocated, and tasked apportioned air sorties in coordination with other Service component commanders. The JFACC integrated area air defenses as the Area Air Defense Commander. The Commander, CENTAF, also designated as the Airspace Control Authority, managed theater airspace requirements.

The JFACC, in Riyadh, used a daily Master Attack Plan and Air Tasking Order (ATO) to carry out his responsibilities. This same

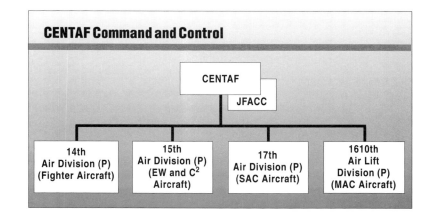

mechanism served as the basis for JFACC's pre-offensive air campaign planning. Normally transmitted at Immediate precedence, the daily ATO still required hours to arrive at the hundreds of addressees. As a result, couriers often were used to deliver the ATO on diskettes. Real-time control of aircraft missions was managed through the ground-based Tactical Air Control Center and the Airborne Command Element, operating from USAF AWACS aircraft orbiting inside Saudi airspace. While the JFACC concept had been discussed for several years, this was the first time it was used in a major regional conflict. The JFACC is discussed in greater detail in Chapter VI.

Navy Command Relationships

In early August, the commander of the US Seventh Fleet (SEVENTHFLT) was designated the NAVCENT commander. CMEF normally commands NAVCENT; however, the Navy wanted a more senior commander for Operation Desert Shield. These changing relationships required a steep learning curve with new people and command arrangements under the urgent pressures of planning and training for large-scale combat, which seemed imminent. Commander, SEVENTHFLT, deployed by air on 15 August to the AOR with key members of his staff. Taking up residence on board the *USS LaSalle* (AGF 3), the Commander, Joint Task

USS Blue Ridge, Seventh Fleet Flagship, Became the NAVCENT Command Ship Upon Arrival in the Gulf.

Force Middle East (JTFME) flagship, he remained there until the SEVENTHFLT flagship, *USS Blue Ridge* (LCC 19), arrived 1 September. NAVCENT also assumed the command of the Fleet at sea, which included Navy and USMC elements and was designated as Task Force 150. At the same time, CMEF took over JTFME functions, and reported directly to NAVCENT. (CMEF maintained operational control of the extensive US Maritime Interception Force (MIF), as well as the US mine countermeasure forces and the Middle East Force surface combatant squadron.) The Persian Gulf and Red Sea carrier battle groups (CVBG) also were assigned to NAVCENT. Before Operation Desert Shield started, the JTFME, established in 1987, had served as the primary on-scene CENTCOM military commander in the Persian Gulf region.

NAVCENT brought a Fleet Coordinating Group (FLTCORGRU) with him from Japan and immediately installed it in Riyadh to work with the JFACC on all aspects of air operations. FLTCORGRU, whose purpose was to coordinate land and sea-based joint air operations, had worked extensively with the USAF in Western Pacific exercises. NAVCENT also provided a mobile satellite communications (SATCOM) capability to FLTCORGRU to improve communications between Riyadh and the Fleet.

Since NAVCENT operated from onboard ship, he established NAVCENT-Riyadh as a staff organization to provide continuous Navy representation at CENTCOM headquarters. This mission was assigned initially to Commander, Carrier Group Three (COMCARGRU 3). During succeeding months, the NAVCENT-Riyadh staff was augmented substantially but remained small, relative to the ARCENT and CENTAF staffs. In November, the NAVCENT-Riyadh command was transferred from COMCARGRU 3 to Commander, Cruiser Destroyer Group 5. This change resulted in the Navy flag officer at

NAVCENT-Riyadh's remaining relatively junior to other Service representatives, particularly CENTAF. This imbalance in size and seniority between the Navy and other staffs, coupled with the geographic separation with NAVCENT headquarters, made it difficult for NAVCENT-Riyadh to represent the interests of the Navy in the overall coordination and planning efforts.

Marine Corps Command Relationships

The commanding general of I MEF is also the MARCENT commander, responsible for both component and tactical command of Marine forces ashore. To carry out his component command duties, MARCENT assigned a deputy commander to Riyadh, designated MARCENT (Rear), to represent MARCENT. While MARCENT provided liaison officers (LNO) and staff officers to CINCCENT to coordinate tactical matters, the MEF commander did not feel the need to establish separate tactical and component command elements; instead, he retained responsibility for both functions. Later, the MARCENT commander reported he was in constant communication with CINCCENT and believed tactical and component issues could be resolved. CINCCENT's style of leadership gave considerable leeway to subordinate commanders.

To coordinate fully with other component commanders, MARCENT provided LNO and communications to ARCENT and the JFACC, as well as adjacent Coalition units. Although there was only one commander, two staffs evolved to handle the different challenges of a component and a tactical command. An additional requirement surfaced with the arrival of amphibious forces in theater, particularly during the planning for an amphibious assault on the Kuwaiti shoreline. USMC forces ashore came under MARCENT command, while USMC forces afloat were under NAVCENT. Although plans envisioned that I MEF would command all Marines ashore, coordination of amphibious forces with USMC land operations

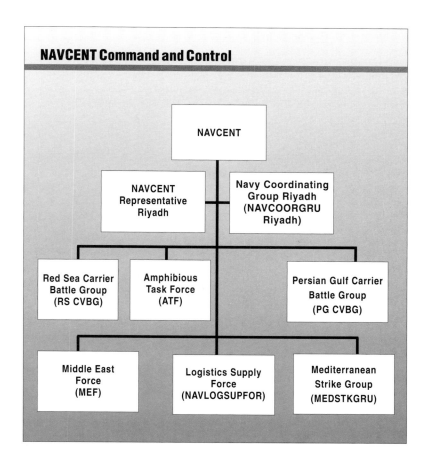

before and during the initial stages of an amphibious assault presented unforeseen problems. Details of landing sites, airspace coordination, fire support coordination, tactical boundaries and control measures, as well as

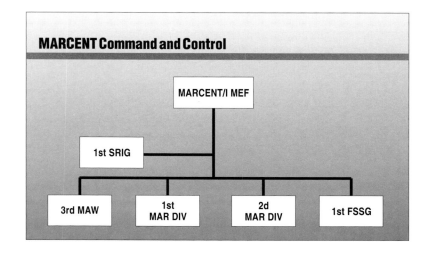

The 3rd Marine Air Wing Tactical Air Operations Center, Located North of Al-Jubayl, Controlled Aircraft Operating in the I MEF AOR.

tasking for future operational planning had to be routed officially through a command chain that included CENTCOM and NAVCENT, a process sometimes complicated by the distances between the commanders and staffs. To resolve this difficulty, MARCENT located a forward headquarters (MARCENT (FWD)) with NAVCENT aboard the USS Blue Ridge in mid-January 1991. This small staff conducted detailed coordination with NAVCENT and ensured ground and amphibious plans were fully coordinated.

Internally, I MEF exercised both tactical and administrative command of all Marine forces ashore. These forces consisted of the 1st and 2nd Marine Divisions (MARDIV), the 3rd Marine Aircraft Wing, the 1st Force Service Support Group and the 1st Surveillance Reconnaissance and Intelligence Group. Faced with a significantly expanded Marine force, and the requirement to provide LNO and staff officers to adjacent and higher headquarters, the I MEF command element was augmented by personnel and equipment from organizations throughout the USMC. The Army and USAF provided communications

equipment to I MEF to ensure interoperability. Structured for expeditionary and amphibious operations, the MEF found itself controlling the operations of a corps-sized force operating across extended inland distances. While this taxed the pre-war command structure, the MEF command element adjusted rapidly . The need for a separate USMC component commander, as well as the structure of the USMC component command headquarters and the MEF command element, are being re-examined in light of these lessons.

Special Forces Command Relationships

SOCCENT was established to direct SOF elements from each military Service assigned to support CENTCOM. All SOF based in CONUS, including Army and USAF Psychological Operations (PSYOP) and CA elements, are assigned to SOCOM, a unified command established in 1986 to improve the operational capability and give joint focus to Special Operations. CINCSOC exercises OPCON of SOF, and as a supporting commander, provides SOF to combatant commanders who, in turn, exercise command authority over those forces. Throughout the crisis, SOCOM identified the forces required to support Operations Desert Shield and Desert Storm and assigned them OPCON to SOCCENT, less PSYOP and CA. As CA and PSYOP units arrived in Theater, they were detached from SOCOM and assigned to ARCENT. Reporting directly to SOCCENT were the Army Special Operations Task Force, the Naval Special Warfare Task Group , and Air Force Special Operations Command, Central Command.

SOCCENT began deploying to the theater in early August. The command was based briefly in Riyadh; it moved to King Fahd International Airport in mid-August. As the force structure built up, and to improve operations with the multinational force arrayed across the northern Saudi border, a forward command center was established 300 miles north at the Army's 5th Special Forces Group (Airborne) headquarters, in King Khalid Military City. As Operation Desert Shield evolved into Operation Desert Storm, SOCCENT established a forward tactical operations and communications center for Combat Search and Rescue (CSAR) activities in 'Ar'ar, near the Iraqi-Saudi border. This location provided better coordination and communications with SOF assets flying CSAR missions in Kuwait and Iraq.

Although SOCCENT was a sub-unified command, it did not work alone. ARCENT and SOCCENT planners worked closely to select areas of operation and targets for SOF missions in Kuwait and Iraq. Likewise, SOCCENT and CENTAF also worked closely in planning missions and selecting special operations targets for offensive operations.

While SOCCENT exercised OPCON of SOF, the components retained responsibility for administrative and logistical support of their respective Service SOF. Navy SEALs assigned to Fleet units were under NAVCENT OPCON; those assigned to SOCCENT were made available to NAVCENT for CSAR. The AC-130 gunships from the 16th Special Operations Squadron and EC-130 Volant Solos from the 193rd Special Operations Group directly

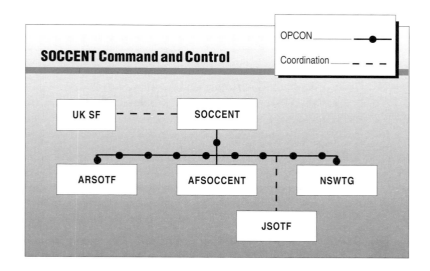

HQ, 5th Special Forces Group (Airborne) Command Post.

supported MARCENT and ARCENT forces during the ground campaign.

Other SOF deployed from Europe. Upon their arrival, OPCON was passed from Special Operations Command, Europe (SOCEUR), the EUCOM special operations sub-unified command, to SOCCENT.

Also located with SOCCENT headquarters was a coordinating element for the British Special Forces. British SOF remained under their own national command organization and were not OPCON to CINCCENT. Nonetheless, they were fully integrated into the SOCCENT and CENTCOM plans and operations. (A detailed discussion of SOF operations is in Appendix J.)

COALITION FORCES RELATIONSHIPS

Forming working relationships with Coalition partners was a crucial aspect of US operations in Operation Desert Shield and a basis for subsequent operations in Operation Desert Storm. The political and military dimensions of building an effective coalition against Iraq were basic concerns to ensure successful multinational operations during Operation Desert Shield. It was important to have a force with as many nations as possible, particularly

Arab states; however, Coalition force management stressed C³ and decision-making.

After the invasion of Kuwait, Saudi Arabia was preoccupied with marshaling enough forces from friendly nations against a potential Iraqi invasion. It soon was overwhelmed by the number and size of arriving forces. However, Iraq's failure to take advantage of the situation allowed the Saudis and their allies the time to develop a credible defense and modify command structures to use available forces more effectively. Establishing and implementing Coalition command relationships was difficult and a matter of great concern for all nations

contributing forces to the Coalition. National, ethnic, and religious pride, along with politics and public perception, played as large a role in determining these relationships as did military requirements.

As additional Coalition forces arrived in Saudi Arabia, command relationships continued to evolve and defense concepts changed constantly. Over time, Coalition forces C² was established with separate, but parallel, chains of command under the United States and Saudi Arabia. All forces ultimately remained under their respective national authority. The US-led western force had CINCCENT in COCOM of

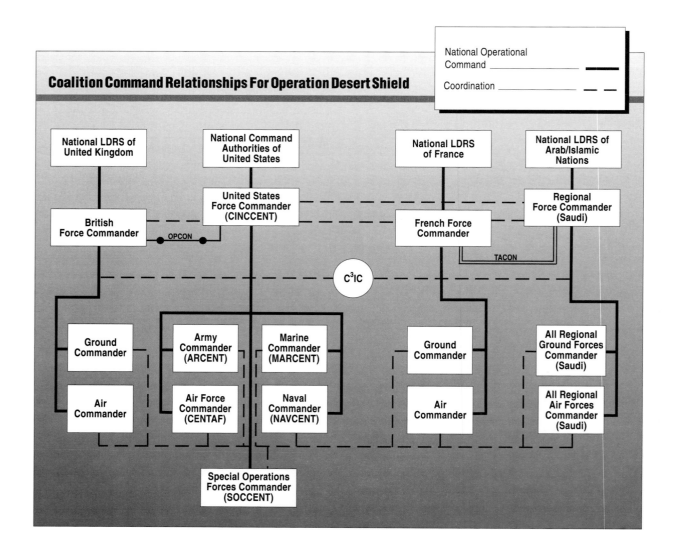

Coalition Command Relationships For Operation Desert Shield

National Operational Command _____
Coordination _____

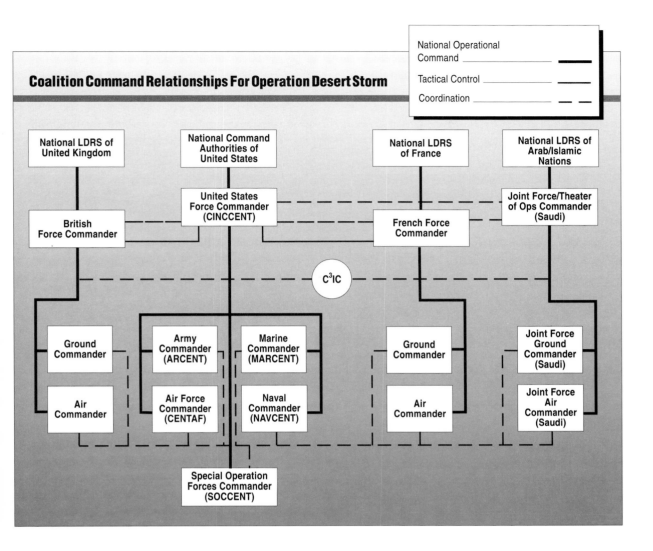

Coalition Command Relationships For Operation Desert Storm

National Operational Command _____ ——

Tactical Control _____ ——

Coordination _____ — —

National LDRS of United Kingdom

National Command Authorities of United States

National LDRS of France

National LDRS of Arab/Islamic Nations

United States Force Commander (CINCCENT)

Joint Force/Theater of Ops Commander (Saudi)

British Force Commander

French Force Commander

C³IC

Ground Commander

Army Commander (ARCENT)

Marine Commander (MARCENT)

Ground Commander

Joint Force Ground Commander (Saudi)

Air Commander

Air Force Commander (CENTAF)

Naval Commander (NAVCENT)

Air Commander

Joint Force Air Commander (Saudi)

Special Operation Forces Commander (SOCCENT)

---

forces from the United States, OPCON of forces from the UK, and other western nations and TACON of French forces. (The French forces, initially TACON to the Saudis, were placed TACON to ARCENT about mid-December 1990 in preparation for offensive operations.) The Saudi-led combined regional force component was called the Joint Force/Theater of Operations (later, Joint Forces Command (JFC)) and had OPCON of all Arab/Islamic forces. Through this structure, the National Command Authorities of western nations retained command of their forces, while Islamic nations authorized Saudi Arabia to exercise command of theirs.

Arab forces in the field were OPCON to either the Eastern or Northern Area Commands (EAC/NAC), depending on their location. By February, the Arab Coalition force commander exercised his authority through three operational theater commanders: JFC-E, JFC-N, and Forward Forces Command - 'Ar'ar (FFC-A), although the latter technically remained under JFC-N. Before establishment of this organization, there was only minimal coordination among Saudi forces. Establishing the JFC was necessary to provide more effective means for C^2 of Arab/Islamic regional forces. This also simplified matters for CINCCENT, because now he only had to coordinate with the

Saudis for all regional forces. The EAC and NAC functioned as rear area commands and continued to provide logistic and administrative support.

All ground operations were coordinated in the Coalition Coordination, Communication, and

General Schwarzkopf and Lieutenant General Khalid Discuss Operations in CENTCOM War Room.

Integration Center (C^3IC) and through periodic commanders' conferences. The ground component commanders were CINCCENT and Commander, JFC. UK ground forces were OPCON to VII Corps and French ground forces were under the TACON to XVIII Airborne Corps. Coalition air forces were integrated into the theater air campaign as detailed in the ATO.

Coalition Coordination, Communication, and Integration Center

Another vitally important challenge for the United States and Saudi Arabia was to forge a unified effort among Coalition ground forces without the benefits of a unified command. Unlike the North Atlantic Treaty Organization (NATO), there was no single commander or alliance to coordinate multinational activities. To facilitate the combined planning process and improve day-to-day integration of coalition operations, a combined operations center was needed. The ARCENT Commander, with extensive experience working with the Saudi Arabia National Guard (SANG), assumed responsibility in this task and quickly established the C^3IC.

The C^3IC was established on 13 August in Riyadh, in the National Defense Operations Center of the MODA headquarters building, the same complex that housed CENTCOM

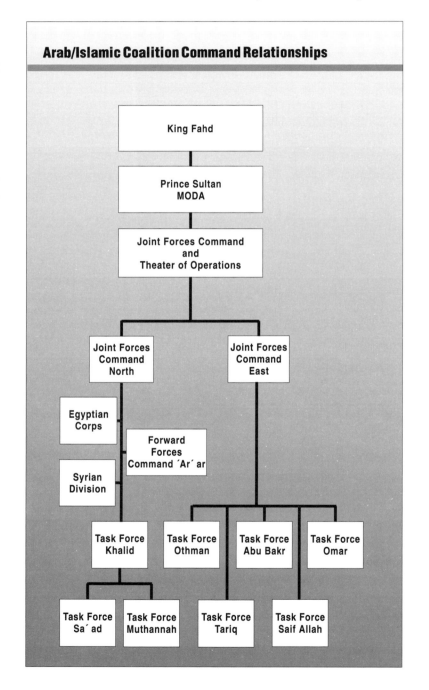

Arab/Islamic Coalition Command Relationships

- King Fahd
- Prince Sultan MODA
- Joint Forces Command and Theater of Operations
  - Joint Forces Command North
    - Egyptian Corps
    - Syrian Division
    - Forward Forces Command 'Ar' ar
      - Task Force Khalid
        - Task Force Sa' ad
        - Task Force Muthannah
      - Task Force Othman
  - Joint Forces Command East
    - Task Force Abu Bakr
      - Task Force Tariq
    - Task Force Omar
      - Task Force Saif Allah

headquarters. It was directly adjacent to the CINCCENT war room, the CENTCOM Joint Operations Center, and the CENTCOM Joint Intelligence Center. It was operated by ARCENT and the Saudi Arabian Armed Forces. The initial C³IC task was to coordinate the activities of the Coalition ground forces assembling in Saudi Arabia. In December, as Operation Desert Shield matured and the Coalition grew, responsibility for the US operation of the center was transferred to the CENTCOM staff, and its mission was primarily to prepare for operations to liberate Kuwait.

The C³IC served the link between the two major command structures that developed during Operation Desert Shield — the American, British and French (as well as air units from Italy and Canada) on one hand, and the Arab/Islamic (the JFC) forces on the other. The 24-hour center exercised no command authority, but was the conduit for all coordination between the Western and Arab/Islamic forces. It proved crucial to the success of Operation Desert Storm. During Operation Desert Shield, the C³IC became the clearinghouse for the coordination of training areas, firing ranges, logistic arrangements, frequency management, and planning activities. During Operation Desert Storm, the center coordinated the operations of the US/UK/French forces with those of the JFC-N, JFC-E, and FFC-A. This included coordination of boundary changes and movement of the fire support coordination line. Throughout the crisis, the C³IC also served as the focal point for the exchange of intelligence between the Saudis and US forces at the national, theater, and tactical levels. This included requests for both strategic and tactical reconnaissance to and from each command structure.

The Vice Deputy Commanding General, ARCENT and the Saudi JFC, each representing his command structure, directed the C³IC. The center was organized into Ground, Air Forces, Naval, Air Defense, Special Operations,

Logistics, and Intelligence sections, each jointly manned by Saudi and American officers. These officers were the points of contact between their CENTCOM and Saudi General Staff functional elements. The French Force Daguet, the SANG, and the VII Corps each provided an LNO to the C³IC.

The C³IC provided briefings and updates daily on the Iraqi and allied situation to senior officers from all Coalition countries. Presiding officers at these briefings normally were CINCCENT or his deputy, and the JFC commander. Briefing responsibilities alternated between US and Saudi officers. This helped to involve all parties in the preparation process and, in so doing, improved understanding throughout the crisis.

COMMUNICATIONS

Joint Command, Control, and Communications (C³) Structure

The communications network established to support Operations Desert Shield and Desert Storm was the largest in history. A flexible and responsive C³ system was installed in record time — and it maintained a phenomenal 98 percent readiness rate. The final architecture provided connectivity with the NCA, US sustaining bases, CENTCOM, other Coalition forces, and subordinate component elements. This was not an easy task.

In addition to equipment differences among various Coalition members, there were differences among US forces. Ultimately,

> "The services put more electronics communications connectivity into the Gulf in 90 days than we put in Europe in 40 years"
>
> *Lieutenant General James S. Cassity*
> *J-6, Joint Staff*

A Sophisticated Network of Multimedia Communications Capability Had to be Built from the Ground Up to Tie the Coalition Forces Together so That Timely Command and Control Could Become a Reality.

several generations of equipment and many different command and staff elements were melded. At the height of the operation, this hybrid system supported more than 700,000 telephone calls and 152,000 messages a day. Additionally, more than 35,000 frequencies were managed and monitored daily to ensure radio communication nets were free of interference from other users.

On 8 August, in support of the rapid deployment of US forces, CENTCOM deployed the first contingent of communications equipment and personnel to provide crucial links between the in-theater forces and CINCCENT at MacDill AFB. Included in the initial communications package was a super high frequency (SHF) multichannel satellite terminal, several ultra high frequency (UHF) single-channel tactical satellite (TACSAT) terminals, and associated

terminal equipment, to provide secure voice, facsimile and Defense Switched Network (DSN), Automatic Digital Network (AUTODIN), and Worldwide Military Command and Control System connectivity to the initial deployed headquarters elements. The Joint Communications Support Element (JCSE) was among the first of these deployments. (The

Originally formed in 1962 under US Strike Command, the Joint Communications Support Element has evolved into its current organization under the Chairman, Joint Chiefs of Staff (CJCS) with the purpose of providing crucial tactical command, control, and communications support for contingency operations and joint exercises for all unified and specified commands at CJCS's direction. To meet its global, rapid deployment mission, a contingency support package can be deployed within 24 hours and the entire unit within 72 hours.

JCSE is responsible to the CJCS for providing tactical communications to JTF headquarters and SOCOM.) At the same time, communications equipment from the XVIII Airborne Corps, I MEF, and the 9th Air Force began arriving and links were established quickly.

The rapidly deployable JCSE provided the primary communications support to CENTCOM and SOCCENT during the initial deployment. JCSE resources included UHF and SHF SATCOM radios, line-of-sight radios, High Frequency (HF) radios, and circuit and message switches. Throughout Operations Desert Shield and Desert Storm, JCSE communications provided continuous transmission and switching support for CENTCOM headquarters, linking the command with its components and the NCA. The final JCSE resources were deployed in mid-January in response to a requirement to support the CENTCOM Alternate CP, and to provide Ground Mobile Force/Defense Satellite Communications System (GMF/DSCS) satellite support to UK forces.

The Saudi national telephone service augmented early deploying communications packages. There were very limited in-place Defense Communications System (DCS) facilities anywhere in SWA and, although the Saudi telecommunications system is modern and reliable, it has neither the capacity nor the geographical dispersion to support a large military force. Available international telephone access also was only a small part of the total requirement.

Parallel to the rapid buildup of combat forces in SWA was the deployment of organic tactical communications systems from Army, USMC and USAF units to tie components and subordinate commands into a joint voice and message switching network. Because of the high demand for limited airlift resources, initial forces arrived with minimum essential

communications capabilities, usually single channel UHF SATCOM and sporadic access to the local commercial telephone system using secure telephone units (STU-III). This level of communications support would have been insufficient to conduct operations had hostilities begun immediately. The network continued to expand, however, as air and surface transports brought more communications equipment into the theater. The arrival of heavy tropospheric scatter and line-of-sight radio equipment (which provided the bulk of the intra-theater connectivity) improved multiple path routing, adding robustness to the joint network.

By November, there was more strategic connectivity (circuits, telephone trunks and radio links) in the AOR than in Europe. By the time Operation Desert Storm began, networks that included satellite and terrestrial communications links provided 324 DSN voice trunks into US and European DSN switches, along with 30 AUTODIN circuits to CONUS and European AUTODIN switches, supporting 286 communications centers. The Defense Data Network (DDN) was extended to the tactical level, providing high-speed packet switched data communications. At its peak, the joint

JCSE Element Deployed Provided Communications Support for CENTCOM Headquarters, Linking the Command With Its Components and the NCA.

DOD COMMUNICATIONS SYSTEMS

- **Automatic Digital Network (AUTODIN):** The principal long-haul network for transmitting record or message traffic. Serves two major communities of users: general purpose and special intelligence.
- **Defense Communications Systems (DCS):** The backbone long-haul communications systems in support of the Department of Defense.
- **Defense Data Network (DDN):** Provides worldwide digital packet switching networks designed to meet DOD data communications requirements. A composite of four separate data networks that operate at different security levels.
- **Defense Satellite Communications System (DSCS):** Military wideband, multichannel super high frequency (SHF) satellite communications system . Backbone of defense satellite communications. Provides secure, long-haul, worldwide communications service in support of unique and vital DOD and non-DOD users.
- **Defense Switched Network (DSN):** Provides a switched network for end-to-end, long distance, common-user and dedicated telephone, data, and video service on a worldwide basis. Replaces the Automatic Voice Network (AUTOVON).
- **Joint Tactical Communications Program (includes TRI-TAC):** Joint Service program to develop and field tactical multichannel and switched communications equipment.
- **Ultra High Frequency Satellite Communications (UHF SATCOM):** Military UHF satellite communications systems provide the requisite single channel connectivity for tactical users.
- **Worldwide Military Command and Control System (WWMCCS):** Provides the National Command Authorities, the Chairman, Joint Chiefs of Staff, and commanders of unified and specified commands with the means for planning, directing, and controlling US military forces worldwide.

communications network included 118 GMF satellite terminals, 12 commercial satellite terminals, 61 TRI-TAC voice and 20 TRI-TAC message switches. (This was the first major operational employment of the jointly developed TRI-TAC equipment.)

Combined Command and Control Communications

US forces worked extensively with Saudi communications managers to plan and implement a communications infrastructure for C^2 of Saudi and Islamic forces. Beginning in August, CENTCOM communications staffs helped the Saudis purchase more than 100 secure HF radios. These radios were an effective communication system from the Eastern and Northern province commands to the front line. In addition, the US provided other encryption systems to secure existing nonsecure radios and telephones. Interoperability was further improved when ARCENT liaison teams augmented the Saudi

communications capability with US communications assets immediately before the ground war began. The US-augmented systems were the most reliable C^2 systems for Saudi forces.

Coalition C^3 was improved by the use of STU-IIIs, personal computers, and fax machines, as well as the sharing of national and commercial satellite resources, and the exchange of liaison teams to overcome language and technical problems. Exceptions to policy were required to allow use of some items by foreign Coalition members. The variety of equipment in use meant that the communications architecture had to be improvised as additional requirements became known. For example, an interoperable Coalition secure voice system was needed. A system that satisfied this requirement was constructed; however, while it was possible to build the structure around existing equipment, many innovative modifications and upgrades were required.

SATELLITE COMMUNICATIONS SYSTEMS (SATCOM)

For the first time in history, satellite communications for both inter- and intra-theater played a major role in the combat forces' deployment, support and C^2. Even precision weapon systems depended on reliable, high speed data systems for success. Military satellite communications (MILSATCOM) formed the C^2 backbone and highlighted the growing dependence on MILSATCOM to provide operational flexibility tailored to prioritized C^2 needs. Central management of all MILSATCOM systems resulted in effective allocation of scarce resources and expedient solutions to crucial C^2 needs, consistent with Coalition force operations. Examples of this include moving two satellites to the AOR to support intra-theater communications for VII Corps and I MEF; using UK satellite capacity for US tactical satellite terminals in support of dispersed UK and US forces; exchanging Service MILSATCOM assets among the Army, USAF, and Navy.

Multichannel Satellite Communications

The rapid deployment, and need to conserve airlift for combat forces, coupled with a lack of an indigenous communications infrastructure, resulted in a heavy reliance on GMF satellite terminals using the DSCS. The GMF system was the primary in-theater long-haul, multichannel communications capability available for deployed CENTCOM forces. DSCS is the military wideband SHF satellite communications system that was the principal multichannel transmission means for CENTCOM forces for both strategic and tactical operations. To meet the additional communications needs of augmentation forces that began deploying to the theater in November, a third satellite joined the DSCS constellation in December. This reserve DSCS II was repositioned from its Pacific orbit, augmenting the primary Indian Ocean DSCS II and the East Atlantic DSCS III satellite.

It also was clear that providing reliable and continuous communications presented a unique set of challenges — how to maintain communications with a rapidly moving force across vast distances. One solution was to use the DSCS multichannel satellite terminal with a mobile eight-foot antenna dish. At the beginning of the offensive, DSCS provided 75 percent of all inter-theater connectivity and was used extensively to support intra-theater requirements across long distances, not supportable by terrestrial systems. The DSCS capacity, however, was limited by available power and bandwidth. To make maximum use of GMF with DSCS, larger, less mobile 20-foot satellite antennas were used, especially at the fixed

A Multichannel Satellite Communications Terminal and Dish Were Used in SWA.

SHF Satellite Communications

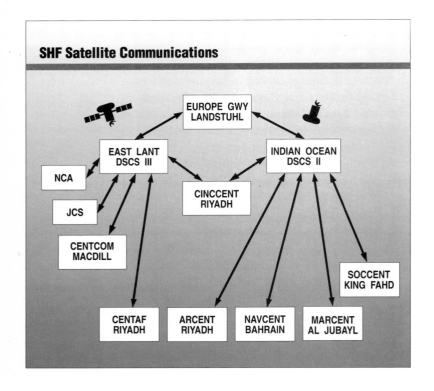

SHF GMF Terminal With the 8-foot Mobile Antenna Operating Over DSCS Carried Voice and Data Circuits That Linked Bases Within Theater and Extended Connectivity to the Defense Network.

headquarters and main logistics areas. Additionally, to meet surge demands, DSCS managers took steps to improve satellite performance. These measures included

reallocating user priorities, refocusing the primary DSCS II narrow beam antenna over Saudi Arabia, and reconfiguring DSCS III antenna feeds and patterns to improve coverage of the AOR. In anticipation of increased requirements for DSCS when the offensive began, supplemental satellite communications support was arranged through commercial leases and capacity on SKYNET, the British military communications satellite, in accordance with a pre-existing US/UK satellite communications memorandum of understanding.

UHF Satellite Communication

Military UHF SATCOMs provided requisite single channel connectivity for C^2, intelligence dissemination and logistics support throughout the operation. The need to have UHF TACSAT capability to support combat forces across long distances was established early and the requirement grew steadily. UHF TACSAT was used as a combat radio net where conventional FM radios did not provide the necessary range. During the deployment, initial UHF SATCOM usage grew until the 160-channel UHF constellation was nearly saturated with traffic. CENTCOM forces on ships, submarines, aircraft, and ground sites used hundreds of UHF MILSATCOM terminals. Deploying units augmented organic equipment with borrowed UHF TACSAT terminals.

The Navy, in particular, places heavy reliance on UHF communications. Approximately 95 percent of the Navy's message traffic went over UHF satellite communications. These satellite systems were oversubscribed and fragile, despite having the demand assigned multiple access multiplexing system, which permits one satellite channel to be shared by multiple users simultaneously. UHF communications were used so extensively that on 28 November, Naval Space Command stated there was no additional UHF coverage available. This was because the fleet satellite used to support CENTCOM and other users in the AOR had been completely

UHF TACSAT Terminal Can Be Transported and Set Up Quickly to Provide Single Channel Secure Voice and Data.

saturated. Additional users could not be supported without taking other users off. This limitation was eased somewhat in mid-December when a Lincoln Laboratories satellite, which used a different portion of the UHF spectrum, was made available to support US forces.

Rapid growth in requirements throughout the operation required continuous effort by the Joint Staff and CENTCOM staff to find space segment capacity to support the enormous demand for access.

All satellite communications, both military and commercial, were vulnerable to jamming had the enemy chosen to do so. Single-channel UHF communications systems, in particular, are extremely vulnerable due to the relative ease of jamming a transponder in any of the UHF satellites.

Leased Commercial Satellite Communications

Confronted with a substantial demand for multichannel capability, the JS, Defense Communications Agency (DCA) (renamed Defense Information Systems Agency in June 1991) and CENTCOM communicators used commercial satellites to supplement military requirements. At the CENTCOM J-6's

direction, with JS support and assistance and in cooperation with DCA and the National Communications System (NCS), actions were taken to lease turnkey (ready to use) SATCOM communications services. Especially noteworthy were the commercial C-band and Ku-band earth terminals deployed to the AOR. These terminals provided leased circuits that interfaced with the joint and component tactical switched networks in the theater.

The NCS provided more than 350 circuits in support of Operations Desert Shield and Desert Storm. They were used for emergency and essential services; carried AUTODIN, DSN, DDN; and had dedicated voice and data circuits. Users included the Secretary of Defense, the Secretary of State, the White House Communications Agency, CENTCOM, the Service component commands, DCA, and SAC. More than a dozen commercial local and long-distance carriers participated. Additionally, commercial vendors offered a wide array of services, including voice and facsimile, at no charge or at reduced cost.

The initial complement of commercial satellite circuits established in August and September linked CENTCOM Forward and Rear, and Fort Bragg, NC, and Dhahran in support of the XVIII Airborne Corps. There was significant expansion in the following months, including leased terminals deployed to Saudi Arabia to provide service through INTELSAT. (This system also supported VII Corps communications to Europe.)

The joint Command, Control, Communications, and Intelligence (C^3I) community examined other commercial satellite alternatives in anticipation of additional communications demands. However, initiatives were dismissed after it was determined that additional commercial communications were no longer needed or that their footprint did not adequately cover the area of interest.

Seeking improved data communications to relieve some of the overloaded military circuits to NAVCENT, the Navy arranged for commercial satellite communications capability to be installed on selected ships operating in the AOR. This capability proved to be a vital link for coordinating the efforts of NAVCENT on the command ship USS Blue Ridge and NAVCENT-Riyadh, and for communicating directly with CINCCENT. Additionally, it played an important part in the real-time coordination of ATO inputs between Riyadh and the Persian Gulf battle force commander on board the USS Midway (CV 41).

Commercial SATCOM proved a valuable resource to satisfy the requirements for satellite communications and to accommodate as many non-warfighting requirements as possible to relieve the overburdened MILSATCOM system.

TACTICAL COMMUNICATIONS SYSTEMS

An extensive network of tactical voice and message switches was installed in the AOR to provide communications across extended distances. Using three generations of equipment during the buildup of forces in SWA, and achieving a coherent, fully interoperable network, was a unique challenge. It required numerous interfaces,

> "The performance of the MSE system in the 1st Cav during Desert Shield has been superb. The dependability of the system is good and [it] has been operating 24 hrs/day in a harsh environment".
>
> *Commanding General, 1st Cavalry Division*
>
> "MSE is far superior to IATACS, especially in a highly mobile and intense conflict. During Operation Desert Storm, the division signaleers truly earned their combat pay."
>
> *Commanding General, 3rd Armored Division*

intensive management, and substantial, innovative workarounds in both equipment and software.

Deployed systems consisted of the Army's all digital Mobile Subscriber Equipment (MSE), used at echelons corps and below, and the TRI-TAC switches used by the JCSE, USMC, USAF and Army at echelons above corps, with both a digital and analog capability. The Army and USMC also deployed the Improved Army Tactical Communications System (IATACS) and AN/GRC-201 Troposcatter Multichannel Radio System, respectively, which are older generation analog systems.

MSE performed well, adding robustness to corps and division C^3. It interfaced with tactical satellite and tropospheric scatter communications systems, enabling commanders to extend their span of control across great distances. Through established DSN gateways, an MSE-equipped unit moving through the desert could be reached by direct dialing from the United States. Ease of operation and rapid installation added flexibility and mobility. Twenty node switches (major centers) and more than 100 extension switches with associated radio and secure radio telephones from five signal battalions were deployed. The MSE contractor deployed a Regional Support Center which provided technical and logistics support throughout. Contractor representatives worked on-site with Army personnel at the unit level. Division signal units reported high reliability, low maintenance and the ability of MSE to keep pace with maneuver units while providing telephone and data service on-the-move. The requirement for a system to do this was of great concern before the ground offensive. MSE successfully interoperated with the TTC-42 voice switch, an element of the USMC Unit Level Circuit Switch (ULCS); with TRI-TAC equipment; and with NATO equipment, including the French RITA communications systems.

The new electronic counter-countermeasures capable Single Channel Ground and Airborne Radio System (SINCGARS) worked well. However, only a few Army and USMC units were equipped with this radio. Approximately 700 were deployed with the Army and 350 with the Marines. They displayed an astounding 7,000 hours mean time between failure rate as well as a 30 percent range increase from older radios. SINCGARS is a tremendous improvement from the old VRC-12 family of radios in terms of reliability, maintainability, usable and dependable range, secure operations, and the ability to operate in extreme weather conditions. Other advantages are its resistance to

MSE, Deployed for First Time in a Hostile, Desert Environment, Provides Essential Telecommunications Links for Military Units Moving Through the Battle Area.

jamming and the ability to transmit data as well as voice. SOF used SINCGARS throughout the war and were exceptionally pleased by the seven-pound weight savings compared with the older backpack radio.

EUCOM Communications Support

EUCOM involvement in the Gulf began in July, before the invasion of Kuwait. UHF TACSAT systems and operators were deployed to Doha, Qatar, to support SAC tanker operations during Operation Ivory Justice, a SAC exercise. Shortly thereafter, during the early stages of Operation Desert Shield, EUCOM deployed many individual items of communications equipment and personnel to augment in-place communications units. Principal assets included SHF multichannel and UHF single channel tactical satellite systems, tropospheric scatter and tropo/satellite support radios, TRI-TAC voice and message switches, and secure FM radios. This rapid deployment not only underscored CINCEUR's commitment to support CENTCOM fully, but also reflected the changing political climate in Europe. Although unit readiness was, in some cases,

Microwave Communications Relay Site Providing Communications Link Between XVIII Abn Corps and Rear Area.

severely downgraded by the transfer of crucial, mission-essential systems, the rapidly fading threat from the Warsaw Pact allowed this transfer without degrading the security of Central Europe. US Army, Europe further minimized the effect by taking much of the equipment being sent to SWA from prepositioned stocks.

Also, during this time, significant initiatives were undertaken with European allies to make them interoperable with the Coalition forces. Throughout the buildup in Operation Desert Shield (and all through Operation Desert Storm), many requests for assistance were supported. These included secure voice/data connectivity and GMF terminals and TACSAT antennas.

With the deployment of the VII Corps in December, a considerable number of support units also had to be deployed to meet the increase in communications requirements. These units included three of the four European-based Echelons-Above-Corps signal battalions, the USAF Operations Center, elements of a Combat Communications Group and Tactical Control Wing, and a Communications Security Logistic Support Unit.

In January, EUCOM installed a UHF TACSAT system in Israel, which provided connectivity to a network supporting the Secretary of Defense. The network proved so reliable that, during Operation Desert Storm, it also was used to relay Scud missile warnings.

Providing essential C^3 support for Operation Proven Force proved a challenge. (Operation Proven Force was a EUCOM established JTF in Turkey to assist the Coalition forces in the liberation of Kuwait. It supported Operation Desert Storm by conducting offensive combat operations against targets in northern Iraq. Communications into the Turkish AOR had to be expanded substantially. Every satellite asset assigned to EUCOM was used to full capacity; prioritization of channels and terminals had to be carefully managed. A major communications effort involved expanding the capacity of the existing DCS transmission system in Turkey, as well as increasing the number of DSN voice trunks. Planned commercial upgrades were accelerated through coordination with the Turkish Post, Telephone and Telegraph System to provide additional capacity. Overall, the communications capacity available to the US military in Turkey increased by 200 percent within weeks.

INTELLIGENCE AND RECONNAISSANCE COMMUNICATIONS SUPPORT

CINCCENT recognized intelligence communications as crucial to meet vital collection, analysis, processing, and dissemination functions. Intelligence functions expanded in scope and efficiency as the communications infrastructure grew from a few voice circuits to a broad variety of voice, data, and message links connecting the United States, the AOR and points within the AOR. The Defense Intelligence Agency, National Security Agency (NSA), Central Intelligence Agency, the Service headquarters intelligence staffs and other unified and specified commands made significant contributions to the growth of intelligence information exchange capabilities to support CINCCENT. Telecommunications paths were required to connect the computers and workstations at all intelligence processing echelons.

Weather Systems

Weather satellites played a key role during the war. US and Coalition forces used data from the Defense Meteorological Satellite Program (DMSP) spacecraft and civil weather satellites to predict rapidly changing weather patterns. Meteorological satellites were the most reliable source of information on weather in Iraq. The information they provided was used extensively to plan and execute attack missions, to determine wind direction and potential spread of chemical agents, and to alert US forces of sandstorms or other phenomena. This access to current weather data allowed US forces to capitalize further on night vision and infrared targeting capabilities. Navy weather personnel on board the aircraft carrier USS Roosevelt (CVN-71) made extensive use of INMARSAT to supplement existing environmental data links, greatly improving the quality of weather forecasting for carrier air operations. (DMSP is discussed in detail in Appendix T.)

Multi-Spectral Imagery

When US forces deployed to the Gulf, many maps of Kuwait, Iraq, and Saudi Arabia were old and inaccurate. To correct this deficiency, multi-spectral imagery (MSI) satellite systems were used to map the AOR, resulting in up-to-date, very precise maps of the area. There also were requirements to plan amphibious and airborne operations, to track the movement of Iraqi forces, and to prepare for or practice strike operations — MSI helped meet these needs.

MSI satellites (e.g., the US LANDSAT) view specific areas of the earth and transmit images to ground stations. These images are more than black and white pictures; they show features of the earth beyond human visual detection capability. By using these MSI images, it is possible to identify shallow areas near coastlines or where equipment has traveled over the earth. MSI shows much that is hidden from normal view; everytime the ground is disturbed, which is almost unavoidable for a modern army, a spectral change occurs. This data is emphasized by comparing MSI computer images and instructing the computer to display changes. This type of information provided insights into Iraqi operations and was used to help plan the ground war.

NAVIGATION SYSTEMS

NAVSTAR Global Positioning System (GPS)

Use of space-based navigation and positioning was an unqualified success. The NAVSTAR Global Positioning System (GPS) played an important role in the success of the overall operation. Navigation and positioning data was provided to all Coalition forces. GPS proved an assured method of navigating in a featureless desert — one of the more difficult tasks the forces faced. GPS equipment was used to support a wide variety of missions, including:

- To provide mid-course guidance for the Stand-off Land Attack Missile, which allowed more efficient terminal sensor target acquisition.
- To improve navigation accuracy for F-16/B-52s.
- To improve emitter source location for RC-135s.
- To enhance deep penetration of enemy territory to rescue downed aircrews and other personnel.
- To make land navigation for ground forces

The Crisis Marked the First Combat Use of the Small, Lightweight GPS Receiver Commonly called "Slugger" by Soldiers.

easier and more precise.

- To reduce Patriot missile system radar emplacement times.
- To provide more precise methods for mapping and marking minefields, and to permit aerial mine-clearing under instrument flight rules.
- To provide precise navigational data for Tomahawk Land-Attack Missiles.

The Services purchased thousands of commercial GPS receivers to provide GPS access. Initially deployed ground forces were without this navigation means. GPS receivers remained in short supply until an emergency procurement action enabled the Services to acquire commercial receivers. Almost 90 percent of the GPS receivers US forces used were commercial, non-crypto capable receivers. This heavy reliance on commercial receivers forced the US to keep the GPS Selective Availability (SA) feature turned off. SA is a GPS function that preserves highly precise GPS data for authorized users, and is accomplished by degrading the unencrypted navigation data to make it less accurate. In future conflicts, the US may face adversaries capable of exploiting GPS or using weapons systems with GPS. The CINCs and the Services agree that the current DOD policy on GPS-SA should remain unchanged — SA should remain on. A mix of military GPS receivers and commercial receivers, to meet diverse DOD requirements, is being considered to control cost while maintaining needed operational performance. (GPS is discussed in detail in Appendix T.)

Position Location Reporting System (PLRS)

The Position Location Reporting System is an automated navigational aid that provides accurate and reliable near-real-time position and navigation information in display form. It consists of a master station and basic user units (BUU) and is used for fire support planning, C^2, and coordination. The USMC used this system extensively throughout SWA. Each Marine

As stated by the Assistant Signal Officer, 11th Air Defense Brigade when asked about GPS receivers: " If you mean those green position locators, they are lifesavers. Whenever we sent someone to another unit for coordination, we entered that unit's 10 digit coordinates and the SLGR (small lightweight GPS receiver) directs them to the command post. Before, we had people getting lost in the desert, but since we got the three GPS receivers, nobody has got lost."

Division maintained a master station that could monitor up to 370 BUUs used at all echelons, including the forward air controllers and reconnaissance teams. In addition to providing commanders with accurate and timely information about forces, the system contributed to fire support coordination, maneuver lane and corridor identification, convoy control, and the passing of short, free-text messages between users.

CONTROL OF COMMUNICATIONS RESOURCES, PROCEDURES, AND POLICY

Early in the operation, CENTCOM assumed control of the validation process for all long-haul strategic communications. Without this control, early deploying forces would have consumed most available resources. Centralized management of long-haul strategic communications, satellite capacity, and frequency spectrum allocations was vital to subsequent force deployments. Allocation of communications circuits on established networks also was centrally managed, resulting in substantial equipment savings. At the height of the operation, more than 2,500 joint circuits were sharing the transmission and switching capacity of two or more Services. Centralized control of procedures and policy (i.e., switch network routing tables and precedence assignments) also were used.

During the initial stages of the operation, it became apparent that a Joint Communications-Electronics Operating

Instructions (JCEOI) were essential to manage the theater-wide use of tens of thousands of tactical combat net radios. CENTCOM and NSA compiled this document and distributed it in September. The rapid force structure growth, coupled with the rigid design of the JCEOI, made it difficult to publish the changes required as the force structure increased. Eventually, the JCEOI provided information to operate more than 12,000 different radio nets. Although there were some delays in the process during Operation Desert Shield, a JS working group has examined this issue and developed a JCEOI concept that will improve the system substantially for future crises.

Frequency Management

Frequency management challenges were enormous. There was no single controlling agency in Saudi Arabia for radio frequency allocation or control. Consequently, CENTCOM frequency managers had to coordinate with a wide variety of Saudi government and military agencies, none of which had a complete picture of frequency use in Saudi Arabia. Progress in frequency allocation and deconfliction was slow until the publication of the combined operations order for the defense of Saudi Arabia in early November. This OPORD designated the CENTCOM Frequency Management Office (FMO) as the single point of contact for all joint and combined forces. This resulted in improved cooperation among Coalition force frequency managers.

This FMO, augmented by numerous frequency managers operating in Washington, coordinated and assigned more than 35,000 frequencies for Coalition forces, to provide for nearly interference-free use of the electromagnetic spectrum. Included in these assignments were more than 7,500 HF nets, 1,200 Very High Frequency (VHF-AM) nets, and 7,000 UHF-AM nets. To manage the VHF-FM frequency spectrum, which is the primary combat net radio band for Army and USMC

ground forces, CENTCOM (in close coordination with the components, JS, and the NSA) developed a theater-unique JCEOI which assigned daily changing frequencies and call signs.

COMMUNICATIONS INTEROPERABILITY

Operations Desert Shield and Desert Storm provided a fertile environment to validate and further develop joint communications doctrine and procedures, as well as to solve many technical problems. These efforts rapidly built upon work done by various C^3 groups, established to meet the challenges of creating a joint interoperable communications environment. Equipment not designed or intended to interoperate when procured originally was in use to support missions that became increasingly integrated as the theater developed. In many cases, as interoperation requirements emerged, the Services and agencies developed innovative modifications or upgrades to make interfaces possible. One example of such a success was the software modification that enabled the USMC ULCS to interoperate fully with TRI-TAC circuit switches (AN/TTC-39A). However, in some cases, interoperability was lacking, and these problems were documented in numerous after-action reports. The Joint Tactical Command, Control, and Communications Agency's Joint Interoperability Test Center now has in place a test bed of different equipment which will be used to test for and resolve such interoperability problems.

Interoperability between Coalition forces was accomplished in several different ways. The use of STU-II (NATO) and STU-IIIA (interoperable with STU-II) was one solution. Other techniques included sharing of national and commercial satellite resources and exchange of liaison teams. Of major importance was the loan of five tactical satellite terminals (from USAF and JCSE assets) to the UK, which resolved critical strategic C^2 shortfalls between the UK

Command headquarters and its dispersed ground forces. The integration of the French RITA communications system to interoperate with the robust MSE network also was a success.

At the beginning of Operation Desert Shield, CINCCENT announced a requirement for secure voice interoperability within the Coalition Forces. The solution was found in assembling a combination of equipment for use by US forces with different parties. STU-IIIAs were used to interface with NATO allies equipped with STU-ll equipment. Doctrinal exceptions were required to allow the use of STU-llls by selected foreign nationals. To communicate with the the non-NATO Coalition force members, NSA provided a commercial secure phone with enhanced security. Connectivity was provided by lending STU-ll equipment to embassies and STU-lllAs to US users.

SUMMARY

The best personnel, equipment, and plans are of little value without positive C^3. Building a communications infrastructure virtually from scratch was one of the more significant challenges of the operations in SWA. Never has the demand for real-time information been so great or the challenge met so effectively. The C^3 system was largely brought over with the forces and grew in capability as the forces arrived. A mix of long-haul military, tactical military, and commercial communications was used to support deployment and warfighting operations. Satellites, leased land lines and tactical equipment had to be woven into a sophisticated network to meet the communications needs of a dynamic and rapidly changing combat situation. The demand for, and subsequent use of, secure communications placed a heavy load on the system. Innovative use of STUs, personal computers, and fax machines allowed for timely, secure information transfer and fortified C^3 capability. The ability to quickly disseminate information was testimony to the successful efforts of those who provided the logistical and technical base.

DSCS, the principal multichannel transmission means for CENTCOM forces, was the mainstay of the operation. The need for MILSATCOM to support national requirements was clearly demonstrated. Commercial systems, though essential, cannot provide the operational flexibility and security required to support the large volume of tactical C^2 needs, nor accommodate the sensitivities associated with worldwide signal intelligence collection and dissemination. Because of the significant demand for communications connectivity, commercial satellites (e.g., INTELSAT) and allied satellites (UK SKYNET and NATO) added a surge capability to MILSATCOM systems. Heavy reliance was placed on single channel UHF systems for C^2, intelligence dissemination and logistics support. All satellite communications were vulnerable to jamming, intercept, monitoring, and spoofing. Deployment of MILSTAR satellites beginning in 1992 will significantly alleviate these shortfalls.

NAVSTAR GPS played a key role and has many applications in all functional war-fighting areas. Land navigation was the biggest beneficiary, giving Coalition forces a major advantage over the Iraqis.

Given technical interfaces and innovative workarounds, tactical communications systems proved interoperable and were robust enough to provide top-to-bottom connectivity throughout the Coalition. Three generations of tactical communications systems were deployed — MSE, TRI-TAC and IATACS. Of particular interest was the debut of the Army's MSE which performed well and added significant mobility and flexibility. SINCGARS demonstrated its effectiveness under harsh conditions in a combat environment, and is a significant improvement from the earlier version of the combat net radio.

Communications were part of the most successful and technologically sophisticated health, morale, and welfare service ever assembled in support of deployed US armed forces. Commercial satellite terminals provided almost 3,000 telephones for morale calls. More than 90 Military Affiliated Radio Stations (MARS) established in the AOR handled more than 3,000 phone patches and 8,000 MARS-grams a week. Desert Fax connectivity provided free facsimile service from CONUS and Europe to the AOR, handling more than 6,000 messages a day at the height of the war.

OBSERVATIONS

Accomplishments

- Organization of US forces and C^{3}I in Operations Desert Shield and Desert Storm was successful and may provide a model for future regional conflicts.

- Joint doctrine and procedures provided a basis for integration of US forces.

- The US command organization was simpler and had more unity of command than some of those that preceded it. GNA greatly clarified CINC authority and the CINC's relationship with the Services and the NCA.

- US command relationship doctrine of COCOM, OPCON, TACON, and Support was validated. The command relationships established reinforced Title 10, US Code, requirements for strengthening the role of the CINC.

- The JFACC concept was implemented as a method to provide for planning, allocating, coordinating, and tasking air activity. The ATO was used for coordination and allocation of sorties. All components and other Coalition nations with air forces participated in the ATO process.

- The United States provided liaison teams to all major Coalition forces. These were a source of accurate, timely information. They also were deployed to improve interoperability and reduce the potential for fratricide. LNOs well-versed in fire support procedures, communications, and US military doctrine, are vital.

- The technical competence and innovativeness of US forces allowed them to find solutions to many technical challenges to establish a workable C^3 system.

- Space systems played a crucial role for warning, surveillance, communications, navigation, weather, and multi-spectral imagery.

- Tactical systems such as MSE, TRI-TAC and SINCGARS, along with telephones, fax, and personal computers provided flexible connectivity and compatibility. The modernization efforts that resulted in these new systems allowed commanders to visualize, plan, and then execute the wide turning movements while maintaining unit alignment across vast distances.

- The JCSE's unique communications capability demonstrated that the design and concept of a joint communications support organization is sound and necessary.

- The DSCS was the principal multichannel transmission system for intra- and inter-theater communications during the early deployment. Initially, DSCS provided 75 percent of all inter-theater connectivity and was used extensively to support intra-theater requirements.

- Secure voice systems (STU-II/III, KY-57, KY-68, and SVX-2400) and commercial telephone and fax systems were reliable and effective.

- US surveillance and C^3 systems provided tactical warning and communications crucial in suppressing the Iraqi Scud threat.

(Continued)

OBSERVATIONS (Continued)

- Commercial satellites such as INTELSAT provided the necessary flexibility and backup to MILSATCOM.

- Civilian maintenance and repair worked well.

- The commercial telecommunications industry provided superb support.

Shortcomings

- A comprehensive C^3 interoperability plan between Services and other defense agencies had to be constructed with many workarounds.

- GPS is susceptible to exploitation, although the Iraqis did not do so. There is a need to continue to press for the production, distribution, and integration of GPS receivers incorporating SA decryption.

- Throughout the operation, DSCS connectivity remained fragile due to the age and condition of the satellites and some ground stations. Older DSCS satellites and DSCS ground terminals will require modernization. It may be advisable to increase the number of military satellites providing worldwide C^2 coverage, also. Consideration should be given to procuring terminals capable of using the worldwide coverage provided by commercial satellites. Emphasis also is needed to build smaller, more mobile terminals transportable by a single C-130. (The XVIII Airborne Corps used a prototype GMF terminal with a lightweight, eight-foot antenna. The antenna requires less space than the current mobile eight-foot antenna.)

- The United States does not have a reactive space-launch capability; this prevents replacement or augmentation of critical satellites when failures occur or crises arise.

- The ATO transmission process was slow and cumbersome because of inadequate interoperability. This was particularly true in the Navy, due to the lack of SHF communications on their aircraft carriers to permit on-line integration with the USAF computer-aided force management system. UHF and HF communications paths were used, but were not satisfactory because of the large data flow required. As a result, couriers often were used to deliver the ATO diskettes. The Services are working to streamline the ATO process. The Navy has a long range plan to equip all carriers with SHF by FY 95.

- DSP provided Patriot batteries with sufficient warning but, in the future, an improved sensor will be needed.

- Most SATCOM was vulnerable to jamming, intercept, monitoring, and spoofing, had the enemy been able or chosen to do so. Single-channel UHF systems have limited capacity and are extremely vulnerable, due to the relative ease of jamming a transponder in any UHF satellite. Future corrective actions to counter jamming include use of the extremely high frequency MILSTAR satellite system when it is fielded and the installation of an antijam modem for SHF fixed-base satellite terminals and tactical ground mobile terminals.

- Services should continue support of JCS actions intended to expand the effective UHF tactical satellite communications capacity. Concepts such as embedded COMSEC should be pursued, also.

- There is a continuing need to field lightweight, easily deployable communications equipment that can provide multichannel voice and data service for early deploying units. The MSE light forces contingency communications package, consisting of downsized, digital MSE, is being fielded to selected light divisions, such as the 101st Airborne Division (Air Assault), 82nd Airborne Division, and 7th Infantry Division (Light), in the first quarter of FY 93.

- Operations Desert Shield and Desert Storm demonstrated the need to field a digital radio such as SINCGARS quickly, to replace the VRC-12 series radios which experienced extensive alignment, reliability, and availability problems. The Army and USAF will field an airborne SINCGARS version; the Navy will field multi-functional radios capable of full interoperability with SINCGARS.

- The GPS was a success for US and Coalition land, sea, and air forces.

- Tactical Special Intelligence (SI) support to Naval forces afloat was improved through use of the UHF Tactical Intelligence communications system. The rapid reconfiguration of the system provided a medium for the delivery of SI information.

Issues

- Deploying component headquarters should not be burdened with the details of deploying forces when their primary task is to prepare arriving forces for combat. While recognizing there are some deployment functions best accomplished in theater, overall deployment management effort should reside in a headquarters not preoccupied with the preparation for combat. Force deployment responsibilities need to be revalidated.

- Some component headquarters were dual-tasked. NAVCENT doubled as the Fleet Headquarters and MARCENT as the MEF Headquarters. Although this arrangement provided direct communication between CINCCENT and the tactical commander, the geographic separation of these headquarters from CENTCOM headquarters prevented planning and conferring with all component commanders on a regular basis and made coordination among components more difficult. Component command structures are being re-examined. NAVCENT (Rear) has relocated from Pearl Harbor to MacDill AFB.

- The CINC must exercise with component commanders with whom he will fight. Upon execution of Operation Desert Shield, the JTFME initially was designated NAVCENT. SEVENTHFLT subsequently was designated NAVCENT and, while it overcame many obstacles during transition and performed its mission well, the changing relationships created a steep learning curve with new people and command arrangements, including a new Navy Support Command. War fighting component commanders must be the same as peacetime.

- Establishing and implementing coalition command relationships was difficult. The United States must remain innovative and flexible in establishing command relationships.

- For future operations, planners must consider the challenges of operating within another nation's C^3 infrastructure. Combatant commanders must have deployable C^3 systems that work well with all US and allied forces.

- The ARCENT headquarters (in peacetime) was a planning headquarters and manned to meet the peacetime and initial wartime requirements. Staff elements deployed in increments and manning slots were filled and augmented as necessary. The peacetime manning levels and concepts for deployment are under review.

- Intelligence requirements grew to unprecedented levels, exceeding the communications capacity allocated to the intelligence agencies and functions. Deployment of service-unique systems for intelligence dissemination exacerbated this problem due to a lack of interoperability.

- There is a need for a comprehensive joint architecture from which supporting communications architecture can be built and interoperability issues resolved.

- Warning capabilities must be improved or warning support could be limited in future conflicts by the type of tactical missile used or by solar, weather, or geographical limitations.

- The only US MSI capability is the aging LANDSAT system under Commerce Department control. DOD is analyzing improved collection capabilities of greater use to military users. A mission needs statement for remote earth sensing has been validated.

- The use of space-based support by operational and tactical commanders should be institutionalized into military doctrine and training, and routinely incorporated into operational plans.

Appendix L

ENEMY PRISONER OF WAR OPERATIONS

INTRODUCTION

The success of the enemy prisoner of war (EPW) operations during Operations Desert Shield and Desert Storm can be attributed, in part, to the lessons learned in the Vietnam War. During that conflict, US Armed Forces dealt with the international transfer of US and Allied EPWs to an ally; conducted military liaison with the EPW camp authorities of that ally; coordinated with the International Committee of the Red Cross (ICRC), determined training requirements for EPW units; and, established the need for an enemy prisoner of war information system, centralized management, and accurate accountability. It is also due in great measure to adherence to the various agreements and conventions dealing with enemy prisoners of war, displaced persons and refugees.

The most important requirements of international law pertaining to persons captured or detained during an armed conflict are detailed in the four Geneva Conventions for the Protection of War Victims. Specific requirements for the humane treatment and full accountability of prisoners of war are found in the 1949 Geneva Convention Relative to the Treatment of Prisoners of War (GPW). The 1949 Geneva Convention Relative to the Protection of Civilian Persons in Time of War (GC), governs similar treatment and accountability of civilians.

Treatment and accountability of EPWs generated international interest and concern. In addition to other concerns, religious and cultural sensitivities were a factor. All EPWs and

> "*The treatment of Iraqi prisoners of war by US forces was the best compliance with the Geneva Convention by any nation in any conflict in history.*"
>
> **International Committee of the Red Cross, Riyadh, Saudi Arabia, April 1991**

displaced civilians captured by Coalition forces during Operations Desert Shield and Desert Storm were eventually turned over to Saudi control to insure that Arab prisoners were treated in accordance with Arab culture and Islamic religious practice.

During Operation Desert Storm, Coalition forces captured 86,743 EPWs. Approximately 69,822 EPWs and displaced civilians were processed through US operated facilities between January, when the first EPW was captured, and May 1991. (By agreement, the United States also accepted EPWs and displaced

Iraqi Prisoners of War Are Taken to a Holding Area.

civilians from UK and France and transferred them to Saudi Arabian installations.) US forces provided food, shelter, and medical care to both EPWs and more than 1,400 civilian displaced persons or refugees during this period. Eight EPW died in US custody; all as a result of injuries or sickness contracted prior to capture. Five died from combat injuries, one from malnutrition/dehydration, and two from unknown causes. Three US transferred prisoners died in Saudi camps due to wounds received while interned in the Saudi controlled camps. These deaths were investigated and reported through command channels to the ICRC, as required by Articles 120, 122, and 123, GPW.

Interrogations of some detainees initially identified as EPWs determined that several were civilians who had not taken part in hostile actions against the Coalition forces. In some cases, they had surrendered to the Coalition to receive food and lodging. Under Article 5 of the GPW, tribunals were conducted to determine whether civilians were entitled to be granted EPW status. For those detainees whose status was questionable, tribunals were conducted to verify status, based upon the individual's relationship to the military and participation in the war. A total of 1,196 tribunal hearings were conducted. As a result, 310 persons were granted EPW status; the others were determined to be displaced civilians and were treated as refugees. No civilian was found to have acted as an unlawful combatant. (US Forces released 12 displaced civilians to Safwan, a US operated refugee camp, and 874 civilians to Raffa, a Saudi refugee camp.)

Centralized EPW management began during Operation Desert Shield and continued throughout Operation Desert Storm. The US National Prisoner of War Information Center (NPWIC) was fully operational before the ground offensive began, and a new automated program for compiling information on and accounting for captured personnel (as required by the GPW) was fielded in Operation Desert

CUMULATIVE EPW AND DISPLACED CIVILIANS CAPTURED/SURRENDERED	
United States Forces	63,948*
Arab Forces	16,921
British Forces	5,005
French Forces	869
Total All Forces:	86,743

* Displaced Civilians (1,492) are included in the US forces numbers.

Shield. Trained Reserve Component (RC) EPW units were activated, and camp advisory teams were sent to Saudi Arabia to establish liaison with Saudi units to provide technical assistance, and to maintain accountability for EPWs and displaced civilians transferred to the Saudis. (In accordance with Article 12, GPW, the United States retained residual responsibility for EPWs transferred to the Saudi Arabian government.)

AGREEMENTS

Agreements were concluded in theater to formalize EPW procedures between separate Services and Coalition partners. Early interservice agreements between the Army, Navy, and Marine Corps Component Commanders formalized procedures and apportioned responsibilities for EPWs and displaced persons.

US policy requires approval of a formal international agreement by the Assistant Secretary of Defense for International Security Affairs (ASD/ISA) and the State Department as a prerequisite to transferring EPWs to a Coalition partner. A government-to-government agreement was negotiated between Saudi Arabia and the United States authorizing the transfer of EPWs to Saudi custody. This document was signed formally on 15 January. Separate military-to-military agreements, authorized by the ASD/ISA and the State Department, were also negotiated. These negotiations resulted in the US/UK EPW transfer agreement of 31 January and US/French transfer agreement of 24 February. The agreements outlined the actions to be taken by capturing forces in processing EPWs and displaced civilians through US theater camps, and medical channels to Saudi facilities.

The agreement between the United States and Saudi governments provided the United States would transfer custody of EPW to Saudi control after EPW registration by US forces. This agreement also was applicable to EPW captured by the French and British and processed by the US. The Saudis established camps where Iraqi prisoners were treated well and in accordance with Arab customs. This procedure, while somewhat burdensome to the Saudis, eliminated the potential of intra-Coalition friction over the issue of treatment of captured personnel.

The United States and Saudi Arabia also worked closely to ensure that all EPW facilities met international standards. As part of the agreement on the treatment of EPWs, the United States agreed to provide liaison teams to work with the Saudis. These teams were organized to provide management, logistics, and administrative assistance. Also, they were to maintain accountability of EPWs transferred to the Saudis by the United States.

The number of prisoners captured and the size of the area of operations frequently complicated the handling of EPWs. The size of the Saudi EPW camps, distance between Coalition camps and transportation availability often limited the number of EPWs the United States could transfer. This meant that EPW remained at US camps longer than planned. However, extensive coordination among Coalition forces minimized these difficulties.

FORCE STRUCTURE

Headquarters, Department of the Army (HQDA) serves as the Department of Defense

EPW Liaison Teams Worked Well.

(DOD) executive agent for the EPW program. HQDA develops plans, polices, procedures, and force structure compatible with Geneva Conventions criteria to meet DOD requirements . HQDA also operates the NPWIC, the central agency for all information pertaining to prisoners of war.

Article 122, GPW, and Article 136, GC, require captors to establish a national information bureau as quickly as possible after the start of hostilities. The NPWIC, manned by Army Reserve (USAR) individual mobilization augmentees, volunteer Reservists, and retired personnel, served as a central repository for information related to EPW and displaced civilians captured or transferred to US forces. It also coordinated information with the ICRC pertaining to EPW held by Coalition forces and provided information pertaining to Americans (POW) in Iraqi hands. Additionally, the NPWIC consolidated information from the theater for dissemination to appropriate government agencies, Congress, and the ICRC.

Information provided to the ICRC on each EPW included:

■ Surname,first name, rank;

- Date of birth, place of birth;
- First name of father, maiden name of mother;
- Name and address of the person to be informed;
- Address for correspondence; and
- Army, regimental, or personal serial number, or equivalent.

In the KTO, ARCENT served as the Central Command (CENTCOM) executive agent for EPW operations, although staff responsibilities for EPW actions rested with the CENTCOM Provost Marshal . The 800th MP Brigade (PW), a USAR unit assigned to ARCENT, conducted the theater EPW mission. Planners estimated that there would be approximately 4,000 captured EPW within the first six months after hostilities began. During Operation Desert Shield, intelligence reports caused planners to question this estimate and figures were revised upwards until it was thought that as many as 100,000 EPWs could be captured within the first

week of the ground war. As a result, ARCENT increased force structure and support requirements for EPWs. Substantial resources were required to confine and support that many EPWs.

Programmed forces were increased to a brigade-size element consisting of 61 subordinate units and a theater prisoner of war information center (PWIC). An advance element of the EPW structure, consisting of personnel from the Headquarters, 800th MP Brigade, the 401st and the 403rd EPW Camps, the 400th MP Battalion, five MP escort /guard companies, and the 313th PWIC deployed to the theater early in December to conduct extensive planning. Later in December and January, the remaining EPW structure deployed.

The full structure of the 800th MP Brigade was comprised of more than 7,300 personnel to include: five EPW camps, six EPW battalion headquarters, five processing units, 40 escort guard and guard companies, seven camp advisory teams, and the PWIC. Because of a lack of EPW capable units in the force structure, an Adjutant General company was converted to serve as an MP processing company and 22 MP combat support companies were converted to perform duties as either MP guard or escort guard units. Additionally, the 313th Military Intelligence (MI) Detachment, components of the 6th and 13th Psychological Operations (PSYOPS) Detachments, and the 300th Field Hospital were attached to the brigade.

CAMP CONSTRUCTION

Early discussions with Saudi Arabia were initiated to arrange host nation support (HNS) for supplies,transportation, and medical and facility support. An implementation plan was developed and coordinated with the Saudis and appropriate engineer and logistic assets to construct four 24,000 EPW camps. (The original concept was for the United States to build six sites; however, the Saudis wanted the US to

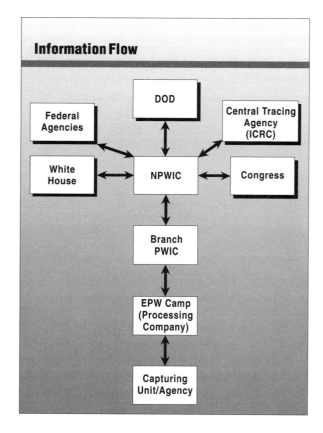

Information Flow

construct less since they planned to build four camps of their own.) Two camps were in the eastern part of the AOR southwest of Al-Mish'ab). These were called "Bronx". The other two farther west, north of King Khalid Military City were named "Brooklyn". Together, these camps could house up to 100,000 EPWs.

Bronx was designated to support the USMC holding areas. Brooklyn supported the VII Corps and the XVII Airborne Corps and each accepted EPW from French and UK forces. The camps were required to escort, process, and intern EPWs in a safe and secure environment. As previously described, US camps were required to transfer EPW to Saudi Arabia for detention until repatriation. (In addition to the theater camps, several holding facilities were established. For example, the Navy Seabees constructed a holding facility near Al-Kibrit which was capable of temporarily housing up to 40,000 EPWs. VII Corps, XVII Airborne Corps, the French and the British also established these types of facilities.)

Because initial construction of the camps was dependent upon the marshaling of resources that were in short supply and subject to competing demands, most camps were not complete when the first Iraqis were captured. The 22nd SUPCOM diverted resources to the EPW camp effort. Construction details were able to install approximately one mile of wire, eight guard towers, and two guard shacks each day. Intensive efforts ensured that camps were completed rapidly and in time to receive massive numbers of prisoners.

Construction of these camps, each of which encompassed approximately four square kilometers, was completed by the joint efforts of the 416th Engineer Command, the 800th MP Brigade, and the Saudi Arabian Government. The term "camp" should not be interpreted to mean one large enclosure. In some cases, camps consisted of several enclosures and each

Military Police and Engineers Construct EPW Camps.

enclosure had separate compounds. Logistics support was provided by the 22nd Support Command (SUPCOM) and HNS. At the outset, lack of understanding of the scope and magnitude of the operation caused slow growth of the camps initially. As priorities shifted and host nation support became more effective, the camps were inundated with supplies and materials. Construction and facilities support required 450 miles of chain link fencing; 35,000 rolls of concertina wire; 10,000 tents; 296 guard towers; 5,000 wash basins; 1,500 latrines; eight 210-kw generators; eight 50,000-gallon and 35 3,000-gallon water bladders; two tactical water

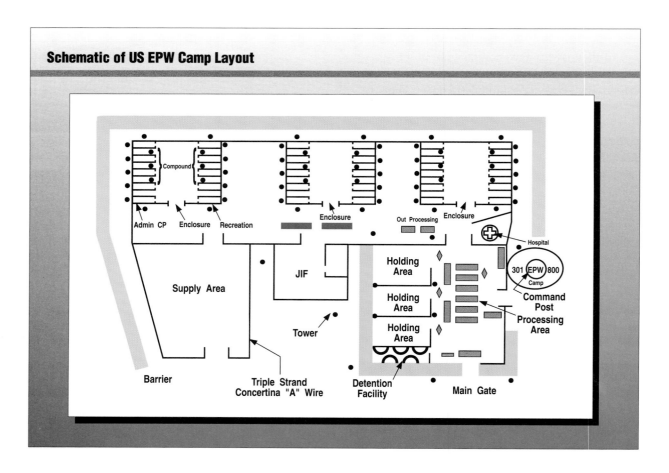

distribution systems; 200,000 sets of clothing and bedding; 100,000 towels; footwear, and nuclear, biological and chemical protective masks; 140,000 sundry packs, 300,000 meals a day and 1.5 million gallons of water a day; and, five tons of lindan powder for delousing operations.

The effort to build, staff, and organize the EPW system was a major achievement possible only through the combined efforts of the United States and Saudi Arabia. The Geneva Conventions require EPWs be given the same or equivalent quarters, food and treatment as soldiers of the capturing forces. US and Saudi officials worked diligently to ensure that this requirement was fulfilled. As a result of their efforts, many Iraqi EPWs had better living conditions in the internment sites than they had had in the Iraqi Army.

Joint interrogation facilities (JIF), a PSYOPS detachment, and a field medical hospital also were established at each site. This was the first time this type of support had been dedicated to EPW operations. Linguist support for interrogation was provided initially by Military Intelligence personnel; however, when internment facilities competed with demands for intelligence collection, linguists were returned to intelligence collection efforts. Thus, site administrators sometimes were hard pressed to communicate with internees.

Solutions to this problem required innovation. In addition to using EPWs who could speak English, actions were taken through Civil Affairs channels to employ Kuwaiti volunteers trained in the United States. Two hundred volunteers were identified for use in the EPW camps before their departure from the United

States. They were given training on the GPW, MP operations, and EPW handling techniques. Once these personnel arrived in theater, 137 were assigned EPW support duties. However, when hostilities ended, many Kuwaiti volunteers were anxious to return to Kuwait, and many did so. Actions were then taken to obtain linguistic support from the Saudis and other Coalition members. The attached PSYOPS detachment assisted in maintaining order by producing Arabic signs and audio tapes to provide instruction for inprocessing.

The requirements for medical personnel to process and care for EPWs grew as the EPW numbers increased. Additional medical assets were assigned to assist with EPW camp medical support.

SAUDI RESPONSIBILITIES FOR EPWS

The Saudi Arabia National Guard (SANG) was given the mission to administer the Saudi camp facilities. Four Saudi camps were

Soldiers Set Up an EPW Camp compound.

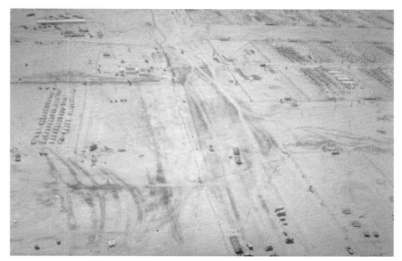

Aerial Views of US EPW Camps Portray their Size.

planned: SA Camp #1 at Hafr Al-Batin; SA#2 near An-Nu'ariyah; SA#3 near Al-Artawiyah; and SA#4 near Tabuk. Camps 1 through 3 were designed to accommodate a population of 12,000 enlisted EPW each, Camp 4 was built to house 5,000 officer EPW. Construction required extensive logistical support; however, lessons learned from initial construction of US camps and the use of advisory teams assisted the Saudis.

SANG infantry forces lacked the training and experience of the specialized US EPW units. Thus, US forces provided training on processing procedures and internment of EPWs. Courses of instruction were developed

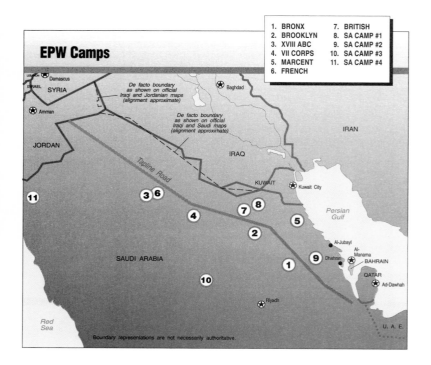

EPW Camps

1. BRONX	7. BRITISH
2. BROOKLYN	8. SA CAMP #1
3. XVIII ABC	9. SA CAMP #2
4. VII CORPS	10. SA CAMP #3
5. MARCENT	11. SA CAMP #4
6. FRENCH	

EPW HANDLING AND PROCESSING

Coalition forces treated EPWs and displaced civilians in accordance with respectively, the GPW and the GC. The GPW mandates humane treatment and full accountability for all EPWs from the moment of capture until repatriation, release, or death. The GC requires humane treatment for displaced civilians. The International Committee of the Red Cross (ICRC) was provided access to Coalition EPW and displaced civilian facilities, confirmed Coalition compliance with the 1949 Geneva Convention, and reviewed findings in periodic meetings in Riyadh. Coalition forces cooperated fully with the ICRC on matters pertaining to EPWs. (Unfortunately, neither the ICRC nor any other humanitarian organization was successful in gaining Iraqi compliance with the Geneva Conventions, especially those pertaining to humane treatment and full accountability.)

Evacuation flow from the forward divisional combat areas to a theater EPW camp was conducted as shown in the EPW flow diagram. Evacuation of EPW from the combat zone was done immediately after capture. In the combat zone, not only may EPWs become casualties, but the fluidity of battlefield movement, the wide dispersion of units, and the austerity of facilities requires rapid evacuation. Non-walking wounded and sick EPW were evacuated via medical channels but remained physically segregated from Coalition patients.

During the ground operations, ground forces were faced with enormous numbers of surrendering Iraqi soldiers. Coupled with the speed of the offensive, this created some problems. Normally, capturing forces conduct initial field processing which includes searching, segregation, safeguarding, providing immediate medical care, classifying, interrogating, and evacuating to rear camps. However, the sheer volume of surrendering Iraqis and the rapid pace of operations presented enormous challenges to

with the assistance of the US Project Manager for the SANG. Language problems were solved through the use of a mix of military and volunteer civilian linguists. After training and establishing the camp structure, some US teams stayed on to assist in camp administration and the transfer of EPWs to the repatriation point.

UNITED KINGDOM AND FRENCH FACILITIES

Maryhill, the British camp, was near Al-Qaysumah and Clemence ,the French EPW camp was near Raffa. Maryhill was constructed to house 5,000 EPWs; Clemence was able to hold 500. Both the UK and the French established close working relationships with the VII Corps and XVII Airborne Corps MP brigades. They transferred EPWs to Corps temporary holding facilities to be processed and transported to the theater camps. The UK assigned Royal Military Police representatives to the 800th MP Brigade's headquarters to ease processing and movement of British-captured EPWs.

initial EPW processing. Despite expedient processing measures, there were no reported or known incidents of maltreatment or misconduct on the part of coalition captors.

Divisional MP units accepted custody of EPWs brought into Division collection points. Corps MP units went to these points and transferred EPWs to the Corps holding facilities, pending movement by 800th MP brigade elements to the theater camps. Other EPWs began to flow from the forward division areas, through the Corps holding facilities to the Theater camps. Camp Bronx became the first operational US facility with the first EPWs arriving 23 January, within an hour after completing the first compound. Because logistics support was limited, US soldiers initially provided EPWs their own food, water, and blankets. EPWs initially were apprehensive about their captors, but this display of humanity allayed their fears. Accounts spread to EPWs brought in later, which may have helped ensure EPW cooperation.

While initial groups of EPWs were fairly small, eventually they arrived in groups of up to 2,000. Upon arrival, they were unloaded from their transports, directed to holding area compounds where they were cared for and systematically processed for transfer to holding compounds within the camp enclosures. EPWs were transferred to holding compounds in small groups of about 50. They were given physical examinations, medically assessed, segregated by rank, and briefed on rules and expectations. Once processed into the camp, the EPWs were required to conform to a structured daily schedule consisting of work details, meals, and accountability procedures to maintain camp order and sanitation.

Rations for EPW were nourishing. The usual menu consisted of: Four slices of bread w/jam, cheese,1/4 liter milk or juice for breakfast; 1 US meal ready to eat, North Atlantic Treaty Organization, or Saudi rations for lunch; and,

beans, tomatoes, rice, meat (lamb or chicken), and tea for supper. Items prohibited by local and regional religious beliefs were not served to EPWs. US personnel removed these items from ration packets and replaced them with acceptable substitutes.

The NPWIC and the theater EPW units used the Prisoner of War Information System (PWIS -2), an automated system designed to expedite processing and provide an information database on captured personnel. Fielding of the newly developed PWIS-2 system was accelerated during Operation Desert Shield. The system arrived in November with the first EPW processing unit deployed to SWA. Under the old manual system, an average of 190 EPW could be fully processed per day, per camp. With PWIS-2 automated processing procedures, Army EPW units eventually were processing more than 1,500 EPW a day, per camp. Processing accuracy was sustained at an unprecedented 99 percent level, although training, system connectivity and maintenance requirements initially limited capabilities. PWIS-2 information was transmitted from camps to the 800th MP brigade headquarters and entered into PWIC theater data files. This information was electronically sent to the NPWIC for accountability and was presented to the ICRC.

INTELLIGENCE OPERATIONS

Interrogation of EPWs provided valuable information. The 513th MI Brigade, augmented by Air Force, Marine, and some Arab

> "On more than one occasion, the EPWs were so eager to reach the EPW camps that they volunteered to drive. Thus many EPW cooperated in the backhaul transportation mission. Also, two Iraqi soldiers gave themselves up after traveling by a commandeered Toyota truck behind a US convoy into the US sector near Hafr Al Batin."
>
> *Report from 800th Military Police Brigade*

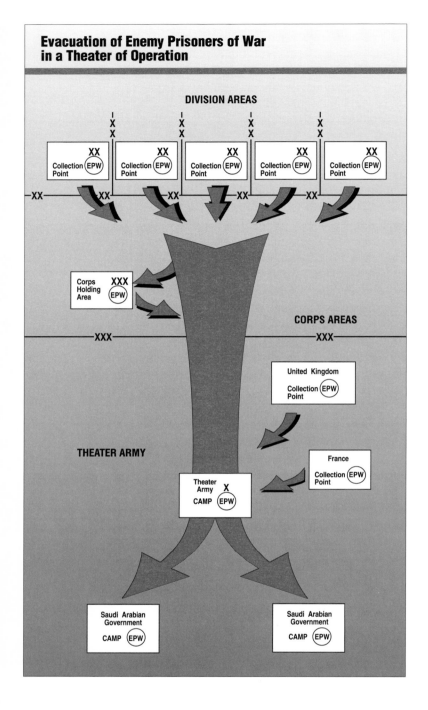

Evacuation of Enemy Prisoners of War in a Theater of Operation

DIVISION AREAS

Collection Point (EPW) | Collection Point (EPW) | Collection Point (EPW) | Collection Point (EPW) | Collection Point (EPW)

Corps Holding Area (EPW)

CORPS AREAS

United Kingdom Collection Point (EPW)

THEATER ARMY

France Collection Point (EPW)

Theater Army CAMP (EPW)

Saudi Arabian Government CAMP (EPW)

Saudi Arabian Government CAMP (EPW)

confirmation of growing morale problems and waning of the will to fight. Information was also obtained about bomb damage assessment, targeting, and artillery plans and procedures.

Interrogations of Iraqi general officers resulted in several instructive assessments. As an example, they indicated the air campaign was very effective in hitting Iraqi supply vehicles and revealed that the B-52 bombing had great psychological effect.

Interrogations were limited by a lack of capable interrogators fluent in Arabic. There were not enough of these specialists to support all committed brigades and simultaneously operate division interrogation facilities. The lack of interrogators in the front line brigades deprived the units closest to the fight of useful information.

REPATRIATION

After the cease fire, expeditious repatriation of EPWs was a high priority and Coalition officials promptly began talks with Iraqi representatives on EPW exchanges. Iraq said it was anxious to return Coalition POWs, but was unwilling to accept large numbers of EPWs in return, saying it was not prepared to receive them.

In March, Coalition forces and Iraq signed a memorandum of understanding detailing administrative procedures for the repatriation of the remaining EPW, under ICRC auspices. On 4 March, Iraq released the first group of 10 Coalition POWs, six of whom were American. On 6 March, the US reciprocated by releasing 294 EPWs to the ICRC for repatriation to Iraq.

> "Iraqi prisoners of war are so surprised by good conditions in allied EPW camps and our knowledge and honor of the Muslim religion, that many want to stay and become workers in the camps."
>
> *Commander, 22nd SUPCOM*

interrogators, set up two Joint Intelligence Facilities (JIFs) and one Joint Debriefing Center for extensive EPW exploitation. These facilities screened more than 48,000 EPWs, and interrogated 526, including 13 Iraqi general officers. Interrogations provided the first

Prisoner of War Information System Operations.

This was the only repatriation the United States sponsored. All future repatriations were accomplished by the Saudi Arabian government. Follow-on repatriation procedures, coordinated with all parties, provided for repatriation of EPWs and displaced civilians to Iraq at a planned rate of approximately 5,000 a day. Repatriation of EPW not in medical channels occurred at Judaydat ''Ar'ar, near the Jordan border. Those EPW in medical channels were flown directly to Iraq. By international convention, no EPW was forcibly repatriated. Coalition forces identified to the ICRC Iraqi EPW not desiring repatriation. When an Iraqi reached the exchange site, the ICRC reconfirmed willingness to be repatriated. Those who indicated they no longer desired to return to Iraq were returned to the custody of Saudi Arabia.

On 2 May 1991, the last EPW in US custody was transferred to the Saudi Arabian government. The Coalition repatriation began on 6 March and ended on 22 August. A total of 13,418 EPWs refused repatriation (13,227 remain at Camp Al-Artawiyah and 191 officer EPWs remain at Camp Tabuk). On 23 August, the ICRC announced the Iraqi EPW repatriation had been completed and that all Iraqi EPWs still refusing repatriation and remaining interned in Saudi Arabia should be treated as civilians protected under the Fourth Geneva convention. The Coalition governments have taken the position the Iraqi EPWs remaining in Saudi Arabia should be reclassified as refugees.

At the end of US custody of Iraqi EPW, ICRC officials advised the 800th MP Brigade the treatment of Iraqi EPW by US forces was the best compliance with the GPW in any conflict in history — a fitting tribute. Coalition measures to comply with the GPW had no significant adverse effect on planning and executing military operations; indeed by encouraging the surrender of Iraqi military personnel, they may have speeded and eased the operations.

OBSERVATIONS

Accomplishments

- The Coalition successfully built complex EPW camps, and processed and managed over 86,000 EPWs.

- Coalition members responsible for EPWs developed and maintained an effective working relationship with the ICRC.

- The NPWIC was activated before the offensive began, serving as the central manager for the Operations Desert Shield and Desert Storm EPW program, and the central US agency for information pertaining to POWs.

- The introduction of the automated PWIS allowed for accurate EPW accountability.

Shortcomings

- US EPW force structure should be deployed as soon as practical to develop HNS, contact with the ICRC, and to establish fully functional camp operations before the start of a conflict.

- Capture rate study data did not accurately forecast the situation in SWA.

- Planned use of US ground backhaul transportation assets could not support the large numbers of captured EPW.

Issues

- PWIS-2 system was limited by speed, equipment capacity and software, lack of training time before fielding in SWA, and inadequate power generation equipment and long-haul data-communication capabilities.

- Translator support for EPW MP and interrogation operations is a consideration for future operations. A shortage of Arabic translators early in the conflict caused processing, screening and camp management problems. This was corrected partially by the use of HNS, civilian volunteers, and English-speaking EPWs.

- Logistical support was hindered by the volume of EPWs, the competition for resources, procedural problems in ordering EPW logistical support, and an overburdened transportation system.

Appendix M
FIRE FROM FRIENDLY FORCES

INTRODUCTION

Of the total of 613 US military battle casualties in Operation Desert Storm, 146 service personnel were killed in action, including 35 killed by fire from friendly forces, and 467 were wounded, including 72 by fire from friendly forces. Incidents also occurred involving US forces with non-US Coalition forces, as well as fire among non-US Coalition forces. Casualties from friendly fire are never acceptable and warrant relentless corrective action to preclude further occurrences. The Department of Defense has launched concerted efforts to reduce the chances of future casualties from fire from friendly forces — although, given the confusion inherent in warfare, it will prove virtually impossible to entirely eliminate.

HISTORICAL PERSPECTIVE

Casualties from fire from friendly forces are not unique to Operation Desert Storm. For example, the number of incidents among air forces caused by aircraft and antiaircraft artillery in previous wars were serious enough to justify dedicated identification friend or foe (IFF) systems for these forces. An Army Training and Doctrine Command (TRADOC) study on ground fratricide published in the early 1980s sought to determine the approximate number of casualties from friendly fire and to determine the causes. In analyzing the causes in the previous major US conflicts, the TRADOC study reported about 26 percent were caused by target misidentifications, 45 percent by coordination problems, 19 percent by inexperienced troops and discipline problems, and 10 percent by unknown causes.

> *"It was round the clock battle, a blow deep in the heart of enemy territory. It was fought at a furious pace, in rainstorms and sandstorms, with killing systems of ferocious ability. It left many soldiers of VII Corps, some of the Army's most accomplished practitioners of armored warfare, looking for help when picking out the good guys from the bad guys . . . ."*
>
> **Army Times, 19 August 91**

In contrast, during Operation Desert Storm, approximately 39 percent of the incidents (11 out of 28) appeared to be as a result of target misidentification. Misidentification was a result of several factors — weather and battlefield conditions being the most predominant reasons. Coordination problems also accounted for approximately 29 percent (8 out of 28) of friendly fire incidents. Of the remaining nine incidents that occurred, six were due to technical and/or ordnance malfunctions; three incidents had insufficient or inconclusive findings to determine cause.

Three factors help explain the higher proportion of casualties from friendly fire in Operation Desert Storm as opposed to previous conflicts. First, a more thorough investigation of these incidents was possible in Operation Desert Storm. The war was short, the number of incidents few, and more sophisticated investigations were conducted. Second, fire from friendly forces may loom large principally because the total number of casualties was so small. A third factor is the duration of the conflict. Some incidents occurred because of the lack of battle experience among frontline troops. One could expect this type incident to decrease markedly as experience grew.

This problem requires both a technical and a training solution. Enhanced optics and more sophisticated identification devices and thermal sights to match longer weapons killing range is one answer. Training that includes a focus on fire from friendly forces incidents is another. However, all solutions must be sensitive to the nature of the modern battlefield.

MODERN WARFARE AND FIRE FROM FRIENDLY FORCES

During Operation Desert Storm, the risk of mistakenly firing on friendly forces was increased by several factors more common to this war than to others. These included faster paced maneuvers across vast distances, often at night or in reduced visibility. The nature of the tactics used in this type of warfare is that they change the shape of the battlefield from the relatively orderly line-vs.-line arrangement of most previous wars to a nonlinear configuration. Where one line opposed another across contested ground, it was less complicated to prevent friendly forces from firing on one another, although such incidents did occur. On a battlefield that is nonlinear — that is fluid — forces are less certain of the positions of adjacent friendly elements and the enemy. The strip of contested ground that was relatively free of forces in the past now is likely to be wider and contain intermingled elements of both sides. While increasing the danger of fire from friendly forces, these tactics, are more effective and much less costly than attacks into modern defensive strongpoints.

Another difference between this war and previous ones was the great number of long-range engagements and engagements in limited visibility. Fire control systems — sights and computers — are far more capable than in the past. Weapons and ammunition are able to achieve high probabilities of hits and kills at greater ranges. The nature of the desert permitted engagement of targets at ranges exceeding two and one half kilometers on a regular basis and in almost all weather conditions. Effective long-range fires do much to win battles with fewer casualties, but these engagements also place a premium on positive target identification.

In addition to increased ranges, desert warfare is characterized by periods of limited visibility. Weather conditions, such as the sand and rain storms that occurred during Operation Desert Storm, the dust and smoke of battle, and darkness often aid attacking forces by shielding them from enemy observation. It is reasonable to assume these conditions were, to some extent, responsible for relatively low Coalition casualties. However, these conditions also degrade somewhat the sighting systems air and ground forces use. In such conditions, state-of-the-art sights provide sufficient resolution to identify general targets, but often lack the resolution to provide clear identification of vehicle type. Long-range, limited-visibility engagements are part of the art of modern warfare.

Another factor is the requirement for rapid engagement decisions. Tank crews are routinely held to a standard of less than 10 seconds from the time a target is first detected until it is destroyed. Well trained crews complete the task in about six seconds. Combat targets are not passive and the history of tank-to-tank combat demonstrates that, where opponents have equally sophisticated fire control and equally lethal munitions, success usually belongs to the crew that fires first.

A final factor on the modern battlefield is the presence of Coalition forces equipped with different equipment. Coalition forces in the future may have equipment similar to that of the enemy. Likewise, potential future enemies could have military equipment purchased from long-term allies. There will be doubts as to the ownership of such equipment on the battlefield. Coalition warfare interjects a new difficulty into the challenges surrounding prevention of fire from friendly forces.

A more rapid paced, less structured battlefield with a mix of increasingly lethal equipment appears to be typical of modern conflict. New concepts and devices are necessary to operate successfully in these conditions. The risks of casualties from friendly fire has increased. However, by the same token, sophisticated weapons systems — whether air or ground — and innovative approaches to their use were key factors in the Coalition success.

FIRE FROM FRIENDLY FORCES INVOLVING UNITED STATES UNITS

Investigations have identified 28 incidents during Operation Desert Storm in which US forces inadvertently engaged other American forces, resulting in the deaths of 35 servicemen and the wounding of 72 others. Of the 28 US incidents, 16 were in ground-to-ground engagements, with 24 killed and 57 wounded, while nine were in air-to-ground engagements that resulted in 11 killed and 15 wounded. Other incidents included one ship-to-ship, one shore-to-ship, and one ground-to-air engagement. However, no casualties resulted from these incidents.

Before the ground offensive began on 24 February, 15 servicemen were killed and 18 were wounded in nine fire from friendly forces incidents. The remaining 74 casualties occurred during the ground offensive, in which 20 servicemen were killed and 54 were wounded in 11 separate incidents.

Most casualties involved crews of armored vehicles struck by high-velocity, non-explosive tank rounds that rely on the force of impact to destroy the target. The number of deaths and injuries from these incidents would have been higher had it not been for the built-in safety and survivability features of the M1A1 tank and the M2/M3 fighting vehicle, such as fire suppression systems, blow out panels, hardened armor, and protective liners.

Of the 21 Army soldiers killed, one was an M1A1 tank crewman; 15 were Bradley Fighting Vehicle (BFV) crewmen; one was a crewman of a modified M113 armored personnel carrier; and four were soldiers on the ground. Of the 65 Army soldiers wounded, 49 were BFV crewmen, seven were tank crewmen, and nine were on the ground. Of the 14 Marines killed, 11 were Light Armored Vehicle (LAV) crewmen and three were on the ground. Of the six Marines wounded, two were LAV crewmen and four were on the ground or in trucks. One sailor was wounded while serving with a Marine Corps (USMC) reconnaissance unit. Of the nine air-to-ground incidents, one was from an Army AH-64, four were from Air Force (USAF) aircraft, one from USMC aircraft, and three from high speed antiradiation missiles from undetermined sources.

A complete discussion of these incidents was released by the Office of Assistant Secretary of Defense for Public Affairs on 13 August 1991. These incidents represented all known and completed investigations of incidents involving fire from friendly forces as of that date.

Thorough investigations were conducted in each case to determine how the incidents happened, to prevent future incidents, and whether negligence was involved. Investigations included examination of damaged or destroyed equipment to determine angle of attack and the type of weapon involved. Projectiles sometimes leave distinctive signatures and, in those cases, determination was less difficult. However, in other instances, the damage caused by the projectile's impact was such that more time-consuming efforts were required. Equipment suspected to have fired on US forces was examined to determine mechanical problems. In several cases, investigators visited the battle sites to determine relative positions of vehicles and the nature of the terrain. Crews and other witnesses were interviewed. In effect, each incident was recreated and meticulously analyzed.

ACTIONS TAKEN TO PREVENT FIRE FROM FRIENDLY FORCES DURING THE CONFLICT

Technological Initiatives

After the first incident of losses on the ground due to fire from friendly aircraft, the Director of the Joint Staff required a review of current technology to develop a "quick fix" to the problem of firing on friendly forces. On 6 February, at the request of the Director of the Joint Staff, the Defense Advanced Research Projects Agency (DARPA) began work on a solution for Army and USMC ground combat vehicles. The Army, USMC, and USAF coordinated efforts, using off-the-shelf technology to achieve quick solutions for application during Operation Desert Storm. More than 60 proposals examining both air-to-ground and ground-to-ground problems were reviewed. These proposals represented 41 different technical approaches across five technology categories: thermal imagery, infrared imagery, laser, radio frequency, and visual techniques. Tests on various proposals were conducted between 15 and 22 February at Yuma Proving Ground and adjacent ranges.

GPS Was Crucial to Command, Control, and Coordination.

An intense government-industry effort produced the anti-fratricide identification device (AFID), also called the DARPA light. The AFID was available in Saudi Arabia in very limited numbers on 26 February, 20 days after receipt of the initial joint staff request. The AFID is a battery-powered beacon that uses two high-powered infrared diodes to generate a signal, visible through standard third-generation night vision goggles from a distance of approximately five miles under normal night-viewing conditions. The light can be attached to vehicles with high-technology velcro. Because the Coalition forces had air supremacy, there was little concern that Iraqi aircraft could use the emitters to target Coalition vehicles. The AFID had a protective collar to keep the device from disclosing the vehicle's position to hostile ground forces.

Although not specifically designed to prevent fire from friendly forces, high technology navigational systems, such as the Global Positioning System (GPS), helped reduce the risks of inadvertently firing on friendly ground forces. The small, lightweight GPS receiver provided units with exact coordinates and locations on the ground. This information, together with knowledge of the coordinates and locations of adjacent units, helped control maneuver forces. In addition, GPS was instrumental in navigating across long distances and helped ensure that units advanced and maneuvered to designated checkpoints on time, and successfully converged on objectives without mingling with other maneuver forces. Although 4,490 commercial and 842 military GPS receivers were fielded to Southwest Asia; wider distribution would have aided greatly the command, control, coordination, and safety of ground units. A discussion of the GPS is in Appendices K and T of this report.

Training

Extensive training was conducted in the theater before Operation Desert Storm to prevent fire from friendly forces. Commanders and leaders at all levels emphasized procedures and standards to preclude these incidents. The causes and prevention of the incidents were discussed in detail by the Services as they prepared for offensive actions. Command and control (C^2) measures, fire support coordination lines (FSCL), adjacent unit coordination, liaison teams, day/night operations, limited visibility considerations, rules of engagements (ROE), after action reviews (AAR), and commander's briefings were key topics.

Extensive and repeated rehearsals before the offensive campaign did much to reduce incidents. Large-and small-scale sand table

Rehearsing Battle Drills Enhanced Troop Confidence.

Walk-Through Rehearsals and Commander's Backbriefs Were Essential In Reducing Fire From Friendly Forces Incidents.

exercises were conducted at every level, allowing leaders to walk through operations orders and plans to ensure there was proper coordination, and that units and commanders clearly understood the scheme of maneuver and where units would be during the ground offensive. The extensive live fire exercises conducted in-theater emphasized troop safety and continuous fire coordination.

Control Measures

Identifying friendly forces requires extensive coordination. All standard control measures and some innovative ones were used; however, the speed of advance on a featureless desert posed new challenges. Nevertheless, control measures generally were successful in preventing friendly fire incidents. Results of investigations did not indicate lack of control measures as the most significant cause for these incidents, although it was a contributing cause in some cases.

The Services used widely recognized control measures such as Fire Support Coordination Line (FSCL), coordinated fire lines, boundaries, air-ground joint and combined procedures, and air defense engagement rules. Each measure has specific rules associated with it. Adherence to these rules does much to ensure that friendly forces do not fire on one another. Face-to-face contact enhances the effectiveness of these measures, and various liaison teams were exchanged between units. The fact there were no known ground-to-air incidents which resulted in casualties attests to the degree of coordination between air and ground units, and the fire discipline and adherence to air defense engagement rules demonstrated by air defense units on the ground.

Key to the effort to reduce the risk of firing on friendly forces was the liaison role of Forward Air Controllers (FACs), Special Operations Forces and Air Naval Gunfire Liaison Company teams. These liaison parties, together with the exchange of liaison teams between ground units from battalion to Corps levels, were instrumental in preventing massive friendly fire incidents. They identified friendly units to the headquarters they represented and provided information on the locations of their units to the headquarters to which they were accredited. The importance of these teams on the modern battlefield cannot be overstated.

Airspace coordination and control was a top priority, implemented by using US Central Command's Airspace Coordination Center, under the Joint Force Air Component Commander (JFACC) acting as Airspace Control Authority. All Coalition forces were briefed on airspace coordination procedures. Air crew orientation and increased situational awareness were emphasized during these briefings. Airspace control sectors were coordinated with Saudi Arabia and other Coalition air forces. Airborne command and control systems, E-2C airborne early warning planes, and ground sector control centers provided coordination for ground and air forces. Additional control measures were established for deconfliction of air within the USMC area of responsibility. An example of these control measures was the High Density Airspace Control Zones which defined airspace used by a large number of aircraft. Kill boxes were

another example; these were defined ground areas under the control of the Airborne Battlefield Command and Control Center.

Air-to-air rules of engagement were governed by the JFACC in his role as the Area Air Defense Commander. Procedures were distributed on a daily basis in the air tasking order (ATO). The ATO delineated the factors for determining whether a target was friendly or hostile. While the ATO was the central means for airspace deconfliction, it also specified aircraft IFF codes. Aircraft with IFF capabilities were required to operate these systems during flight operations. IFF codes were prescribed for a given time of day and geographic area. Where aircraft had no IFF transponder, or when an inoperable transponder was suspected, airspace corridors and altitude bands were established for safe passage and more stringent operational constraints were applied.

To improve ground-to-ground and air-to-ground identification and control, the inverted "V" and the VS-17 panel (a fluorescent orange cloth panel) were designated as standard vehicle markings for all Coalition forces. Ground vehicles were marked with VS-17 panels on the top and inverted "V" symbols on the sides. Inverted "V" symbols were made using fluorescent placards, white luminous paint, black paint, and thermal tape. However, the procedures and materiel Coalition forces used were only marginally effective.

ONGOING EFFORTS

Efforts to develop both short-and long-term solutions continue. The Army's Advanced Systems Concept Office at Fort Meade, MD, has delivered approximately 10,000 AFID units since the end of hostilities. These will be used by ground units for further evaluation in reduction of losses to fire from friendly forces, C^2 improvement, and future contingencies. Results of these

Inverted "V" Markings Helped Identify Friendly Vehicles.

evaluations and further technological improvements will continue to receive DOD attention.

Technology Initiatives

Efforts to develop both short and long term solutions continue. A TRADOC and Army Material Command Positive Combat Identification Task Force has been formed for extraordinary management of the combat identification issue. The effort is overseen by a general officer steering committee that includes representatives from each military Service.

Department of the Army has proposed a major R&D program for ground combat identification centered at the Army's Laboratory Command. This program is designed to examine a wide range of solutions to the problem.

Training

The risks of misidentification leading to fire from friendly forces can be reduced to some extent by training programs. This is an integral part of fratricide prevention efforts, such training is emphasized at each Service warfare training center. Lessons learned from the Gulf War have been incorporated into the exercises and in-depth AARs recognize and highlight incidents of friendly fire so incidents can be prevented.

At all three of the Army's Combat Training Centers (CTC), emphasis is placed on adjacent unit coordination, liaison teams, vehicle marking systems, troop leading procedures, risk assessments, rehearsals, vehicle recognition, fire control measures and fire support coordination. Observers/Controllers (personnel assigned to assess, evaluate, and control units being tested) have been trained to recognize specific events and incidents of fire from friendly forces and have been trained to coach units to prevent such incidents. AARs conducted after every training event highlight these incidents. Emerging data trends are identified, analyzed, and disseminated. An evaluation of quick-fix combat identification devices is scheduled at the National Training Center (NTC). This will be the first time the AFIDs will be used at a CTC. Analysis of the data will determine the effectiveness of these devices.

Several other initiatives in Army training to prevent fire from friendly forces also have been undertaken. At the NTC, "fratricide targets" have been introduced into both live-fire and force-on-force training. The live-fire target is a robotic M1A1. In maneuver training, an M1A1 moves from an out-of-sector area into an area where it is not expected to test force reactions. If a unit engages a target vehicle, the unit conducts an informal investigation to determine the cause. Results are discussed during AARs so lessons learned are understood and disseminated.

At the USMC Air-Ground Combat Center, the Combined Arms Exercise (CAX) program also includes fratricide-prevention training, particularly during live-fire exercises. Because all training is conducted with live ordnance during the CAX, fire support coordination procedures are clearly understood and friendly forces safety is of utmost importance. These exercises include both fixed and rotary-wing aircraft that conduct close air support and close-in fire support. Close coordination and understanding between air and ground units are emphasized to preclude fire from friendly forces.

USAF sponsored Red Flag Exercises and Naval Strike Warfare Center exercises routinely include fratricide prevention. Methods of prevention practiced by units during these exercises include deconfliction of aircraft by timing (ensuring that no more than one aircraft is at the same location at the same time when weapons and ordnance are being released), deconfliction of aircraft by routing around designated target areas, use of IFF codes and other electronic means which, when used by friendly aircraft, allow friendly recognition by electronic means.

In air-to-ground scenarios where USAF units participate in exercises with Army ground forces at the CTCs, use of FSCLs established by ground commanders and FAC parties are used. Positive control and coordination among the FAC, ground forces, and aircraft are stressed. Future initiatives may include more night, low-visibility training; more high-and medium-altitude training; and, more practice of higher altitude ordnance releases.

SUMMARY

The mistaken firing on friendly forces is not a new problem in warfare. Commanders and leaders at every level made extensive efforts to prevent it. While fire from friendly forces occurred, it should not detract from the bravery and performance of the superb soldiers, Marines, and sailors who were victims.

The characteristics of modern warfare demand a solution to the friendly fire problem. Solving the problem will be challenging. The more than 60 proposals examined during Operation Desert Storm for quick fix solutions to the fratricide problem indicate many ideas are available. No one single approach is likely to provide sufficiently reliable capability for all situations. An overall capability is needed, which consists of several techniques or approaches that can be integrated or can complement one another to improve the confidence of correct identification decisions in a variety of situations.

Ultimately, the optimum solution must be an approach that addresses the contributions of doctrine and procedures, organization, training, advanced technology and hardware.

OBSERVATIONS

Accomplishments

■ Coalition forces took several actions to reduce the risk among Coalition forces of mistakenly firing on friendly forces both before the conflict began and afterward. Efforts to minimize these incidents included aggressive leadership, training, and techniques such as vehicle markings.

■ Extraordinary government and industry efforts produced procedures and material in record time that would have made a positive contribution to reducing the risk of these incidents had the hostilities continued past 28 February.

Shortcomings

■ Despite Coalition efforts, there were casualties and damage due to fire from friendly forces.

Issues

■ A need exists for an identification system that identifies friendly vehicles from the air, as well as a ground-to-ground identification system, at extended ranges in reduced visibility and darkness without betraying these locations to hostile forces.

■ More GPS receivers are needed for units and vehicles to ensure better control of maneuver forces,thereby minimizing the risk of firing on friendly forces.

■ Continued efforts must be made to improve optics and thermal sights to match the extended killing range of weapons systems.

Appendix N

Civilian Support

INTRODUCTION

In Operations Desert Shield and Desert Storm, the United States employed civilians both as career civil service employees and indirectly as contractor employees. Civilians performed as part of the transportation system, at the forward depot level repair and intermediate level maintenance activities and as weapon systems technical representatives. Civilians worked aboard Navy ships, at Air Force (USAF) bases, and with virtually every Army unit. Only the Marine Corps (USMC) did not employ significant numbers of civilians in theater. This civilian expertise was invaluable and contributed directly to the success achieved.

By late February, US government civilians in Southwest Asia (SWA) numbered about 4,500, of which some 500 were merchant mariners employed by the Military Sealift Command (MSC). A large number of US civilians were employed by US contractors. A number of local nationals and third-country employees were hired by US and foreign contractors.

The civilian contribution to the Coalition success in Operations Desert Shield and Desert Storm must be viewed in a Total Force context, a force which includes civilians as well as military components. While the discussion which follows addresses and emphasizes the roles and performance of the civilian component serving in SWA, such emphasis must not be construed as denigrating or overlooking the contributions of the Continental US (CONUS) and Europe-based civilian Total Force component. The civilians in SWA accounted for about one percent of the

> *"Civilian employees, despite seemingly insurmountable logistical problems, unrelenting pressure, and severe time constraints, successfully accomplished what this nation asked of them in a manner consistent with the highest standards of excellence and professionalism."*
>
> **Senate Concurrent Resolution 36**

entire force and were part of a much larger civilian support structure.

Department of Defense (DOD) employees served in communications, intelligence, commercial contracting, depot and intermediate level maintenance, weapon system modernization, graves registration and mortuary services. Additionally, they performed environmental impact assessments; morale, welfare, and recreation programs; and in liaison

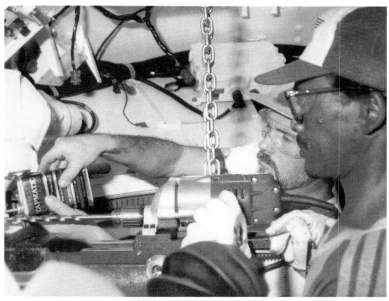

Civilians Overhaul a Turret of an Armored Vehicle in Saudi Arabia during Desert Operation Shield.

functions between forward deployed units and CONUS organizations. The contractors served mostly in the aviation trades and in weapon and automation systems and communications support. The ability to bring experts, government employee and contractor alike, quickly to the scene of a problem was a distinct advantage.

While the recitation of civilian roles and duties in this report is not exhaustive, it is illustrative of the degree to which the military has come to depend on the civilian employees and contractors. Many roles have been transferred to the civilian sector from the military because of force reductions, realignments and civilianization efforts. Civilians employed in direct support of Operations Desert Shield and Desert Storm were there because the capability they represented was not sufficiently available in the uniformed military or because the capability had been consciously assigned to the civilian component to conserve military manpower. It seems clear that future contingencies also will require the presence and involvement of civilians in active theaters of operations.

Although Central Command (CENTCOM) and DOD monitored the civilian personnel situation closely and provided policy guidance when necessary, civilian personnel requirements, management and administration were viewed as a Service component responsibility. Each Service and activity providing civilians to the Kuwait Theater of Operations (KTO) developed procedures which best suited its particular needs. The comprehensiveness of pre-Operation Desert Shield planning for the use of civilians in an active theater of operations varied widely among the organizations and activities. While generalizations are difficult in an operation of relatively short duration, those organizations best prepared were those that had more experience in posting civilians to overseas assignments. Several civilian personnel issues were identified; these will be discussed later.

ARMY CIVILIAN PERSONNEL

The Army, which had the greatest need for civilians in theater, had the most formal approach to preparing them for KTO duty: a five-day indoctrination and training program conducted initially at Aberdeen Proving Ground, MD, and later at Fort Jackson, SC. (The Army Corps of Engineers (COE) used facilities at Winchester, VA, to train its civilians). This period provided an opportunity for area indoctrination briefings, self-defense training, equipment training, issuance and inspection of individual equipment.

The Army Materiel Command (AMC) was the principal source of Army in-theater civilian support. Some 1,500 government and 3,000 contractor civilians were involved in new equipment issue as part of force modernization, and in maintenance of complex technical systems. AMC subordinate commands deploying civilians to the KTO did not provide adequate in-theater assistance for civilians arriving in country to ensure that reception, orientation, assignment assistance and personnel advisory services were provided. Eventually AMC established a civilian personnel advisor in Dhahran to assist civilians with problems.

The COE, with extensive and recent involvement in the Persian Gulf region, recognized the special requirements for special training, area familiarization, and family support programs. COE developed several initiatives to satisfy those needs. At the end of the operation, the COE had some 1,600 volunteers waiting to fill spaces in Saudi Arabia.

AIR FORCE CIVILIAN PERSONNEL

The USAF employed few civilians in theater. When Operation Desert Shield began, approximately 80 of the Air Force Logistics Command (AFLC) employees already were assigned to an on-going logistics support project in Saudi Arabia. After Operations Desert Shield and Desert Storm deployments, the cumulative total of USAF civilians in SWA had grown to about 200. This number included 44 engineering and technical services personnel regularly assigned to the Tactical Air Force operating squadrons. The remaining civilian personnel were associated with aircraft repair, contracting, mortuary affairs, and fuel quality control. In addition to the 200 in SWA, civilian personnel from various AFLC and Tactical Air Command (TAC) activities were detailed to aircraft overhaul and maintenance activities in Europe in support of Operation Desert Storm.

USAF civilian employees were deployed directly from home stations. Civilian deployment processing, such as issuing individual equipment, personal protection training, and indoctrination were accomplished by the employee's unit. Although different from the Army's centralized approach, it was consistent with USAF policy of decentralized deployment processing of military members.

NAVY AND MARINE CIVILIAN PERSONNEL

On average, the Navy had 500 to 600 civilian employees serving in theater with a similar number of MSC civilian mariners afloat. Those ashore were drawn mostly from the Navy Aircraft Depots, naval shipyards, and Navy field activities, and were engaged primarily in aircraft and ship repair. They performed duties ashore, but occasionally worked aboard ship when circumstances warranted. Twenty-five civilians supported USMC units on a temporary duty basis. Their specialties ranged from welding and heavy equipment operations to supply and quality assurance. Additionally, technical representatives from aircraft contracting firms accompanied 3rd Marine Aircraft Wing elements.

DEFENSE AGENCIES' CIVILIAN PERSONNEL

The Defense agencies (e.g., Communications,

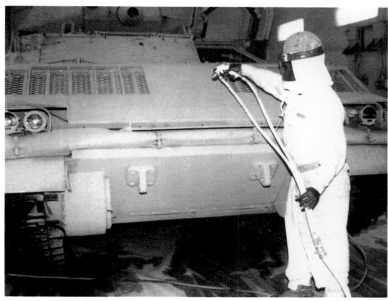

Federal Civilian Paints Equipment.

Intelligence, Logistics, Mapping, etc.) provided civilian support to in-theater forces. The Defense Logistics Agency (DLA) had the largest numbers of personnel in theater. Most performed fuel support functions, as they had before the crisis. In addition, DLA had some quality control specialists to assist in supply distribution and property disposal. Many of these specialities came from activities supporting Army forces in the European Command (EUCOM).

Civilian Longshoremen Load an Armored Vehicle onto a Transport Vehicle in Saudi Arabia.

PLANNING AND OPERATIONS

Peacetime and mobilization planning guidance concerning the use of civilians in an active theater of operations has been published. For example, DOD Directive 1404.10 defines "Emergency Essential" civilian positions and provides DOD policy to ensure continued performance of these duties during crisis situations. This policy directive, first issued in 1985 and up-dated in April 1990, focuses on both DOD civilians stationed overseas, with or in support of military organizations, and DOD civilians expected to deploy with US forces. It also provides guidance for issuing of Geneva Conventions Identity Cards. The Services were implementing DOD Directive 1404.10 when Operation Desert Shield began.

At the beginning, relatively few civilians sent to support Operations Desert Shield and Desert Storm were serving in pre-designated Emergency Essential billets. While many DOD civilians sent to Saudi Arabia had previous experience in deploying on temporary duty, few had experience supporting operations in a wartime environment. Most civilians who deployed to the KTO did so on very short

Civilian Merchant Marine Ship Delivers Supplies To an Aircraft Carrier.

notice. Identifying emergency essential positions in peacetime lets the employing activity manage more effectively the necessary pre-deployment administrative requirements such as next-of-kin identification, issuance of Geneva Convention Identification Cards, taking and storing panographic dental X-Rays, and maintenance of current immunization and passport documentation.

It is not surprising there were very few disciplinary actions or serious breaches of conduct among the civilians supporting Operations Desert Shield and Desert Storm. Nearly all were volunteers and enjoyed professional status.

There is, however, some anecdotal evidence to suggest the need for improvements. For example, support and training for civilians, appropriate danger and other pays, medical care and family support should be reviewed. Civilian employees would play a substantial role in future contingencies, and commanders-in chief must have the authority to manage, control, discipline, and protect them.

Some problems may have been caused by a failure to recognize the role of civilians in the Total Force. The fact not all civilians were deployed as organized units also contributed to some perceived inequities. Selected examples of areas that require additional emphasis or review include the following.

Civilians traveling to SWA via military aircraft were accorded a movement priority after military personnel. In future operations, transportation authorities should consider the relative importance of ability to the overall mission and assign movement priorities accordingly. Another area involves free mail privileges. Free mail privileges accorded military personnel in SWA were denied to the civilians. Free mail privileges for civilians should be provided via legislative change.

Civilian personnel accountability was another concern that requires review. Military and civilian personnel accounting systems are separate with no simple way to incorporate civilians into the automated personnel management systems the deployed forces used. The result is that headquarters do not have timely and accurate information concerning the identification, location, and numbers of civilian personnel. Such information, when integrated with emergency essential planning, provides a basis for civilian personnel support planning.

Civilian pay and compensation procedures also require additional review. Civilian personnel pay directives do not differentiate between peacetime procedures and combat zone procedures, nor do they provide a simple means for coding the changed status of Reserve Component (RC) members recalled to active duty. Civilians in theater had to send weekly time sheets to parent commands by facsimile. This added to the heavy communications load discussed in Appendix K. There was no uniform approach for overtime accounting and compensation in the theater.

The absence of a standard civilian ID card resulted in different identification systems. This practice caused occasional problems at security checkpoints when the security guard, often a local national with limited ability to speak English, failed to recognize the validity of a particular card.

Danger or hazardous duty compensation was a particularly complicated and contentious issue. Beginning on 19 September, the uniformed military received hazardous duty compensation of $125/month prorated from the day of arrival in theater. Civilians exposed to the same hazards, did not receive danger pay until January. In this case danger pay of 25 percent was authorized, however, it may vary from 5 percent to 25 percent depending on the level of danger. Foreign post differential allowance (five

percent to 25 percent of base pay, depending on the locale) is authorized for civilians serving outside CONUS to compensate for hardship conditions. Eligibility for employees on TDY began 42 days after arrival in theater. Eventually payment was made retroactive. Merchant mariners initially received $130 imminent danger pay a month; this subsequently was increased to 100 percent of base pay, but was received only when the ship was in the combat zone. Additionally, exclusion, for income tax purposes, of part of the military member's pay while serving in theater was not accorded civilians serving in theater.

The disparity between military and civilian award systems also became an issue during the war. The military commander has a wide range of awards at his disposal, and a great deal of flexibility for awarding them quickly. He does not have similar flexibility for recognizing superior performance for the civilians supporting the operation. Civilian awards may have a monetary dimension and they require greater administrative procedures which often impose significant delays. The prestige attached to government service would have been enhanced substantially had the on scene commander had the authority to present the lower level military awards (e.g., Commendation Medal or Meritorious Service Medal) or a civilian equivalent to civilian government employees. This subject is currently under study.

The guidance for treating civilian war zone casualties lacks the specificity provided by the Services for handling military fatalities. For example, military fatalities are returned with a military escort. Perhaps civilian casualties should be similarly treated.

DOD published policy discussing family support opportunities, but this was not implemented consistently. Family assistance organizations, activities, and services for military members were not consistently available to family members of deployed civilians.

AMERICAN RED CROSS PERSONNEL

The American Red Cross (ARC) supported Operations Desert Shield and Desert Storm as it has in every war since its inception. Field workers in the United States, Europe, and SWA played a vital role in helping commanders with personnel emergency matters and managing messages concerning family members. The first Red Cross staff person arrived in Saudi Arabia on 12 August. The number of Red Cross personnel serving in theater eventually reached 158; those in theater and in CONUS processed more than 200,000 messages. Red Cross chapters played an important role in providing access to military resources for families of RC troops as well as support groups for all military families. DOD needs to assure that Red Cross personnel receive the same support as DOD civilian personnel.

OBSERVATIONS

Accomplishments

■ Civilians, contractors, and other non-military personnel performed crucial combat support and combat service support functions. This participation contributed directly to the high degree of success of Operations Desert Shield and Desert Storm.

■ Civilian employees and contractor personnel brought many special skills necessary to support Operations Desert Shield and Desert Storm.

Shortcomings

■ Civilian mobilization planning was sometimes not adequate. Current full-time mobilization planners do not always consider the need and requirements of civilians deployed in support of contingency operations. This hampers the efforts to train, equip, and manage civilians designated to support contingency operations.

■ Preparedness exercises did not always challenge the civilian personnel and support system to identify and prepare for support of contingency operations.

■ Family assistance organizations, activities, and services for military members were not consistently available to family members of deployed civilians.

■ CENTCOM assigned no overall employee coordinator to monitor issues common to all components such as theater entrance requirements, ID cards, pay, benefits, training, equipping, and processing within the theater.

■ The absence of a standard civilian ID card resulted in some components' using pre-existing ID cards, creation of ID cards, and some elements not having any form of standard identification. This practice caused occasional problems at security check-points.

Issue

■ Although DOD and the Services assumed some responsibility, the issue of the extent of responsibility, rights, adequate guidelines for deployment, and administration of contractor personnel needs clarification for future deployments.

Appendix O

THE ROLE OF THE LAW OF WAR

BACKGROUND

The United States, its Coalition partners, and Iraq are parties to numerous law of war treaties intended to minimize unnecessary suffering by combatants and noncombatants during war. The US military's law of war program is one of the more comprehensive in the world. As indicated in this appendix, it is US policy that its forces will conduct military operations in a manner consistent with US law of war obligations. This appendix discusses the principal law of war issues that arose during Operation Desert Storm.

As defined in Joint Publication 1-02, Department of Defense (DOD) Dictionary of Military and Associated Terms (1 December 1989), the law of war is "That part of international law that regulates the conduct of armed hostilities. It is often termed the law of armed conflict." While the terms are synonymous, this appendix will use "law of war" for consistency. Both concepts of jus ad bellum and jus in bello are covered in this appendix.

In addition to the United Nations Charter, with its prohibition against the threat or use of force against the territorial integrity or political independence of any state, treaties applicable to the Persian Gulf War include:

- Hague Convention IV and its Annex Respecting the Laws and Customs of War on Land of 18 October 1907 ("Hague IV").
- Hague Convention V Respecting the Rights and Duties of Neutral Powers and Persons in

> "*Decisions were impacted by legal considerations at every level, [the law of war] proved invaluable in the decision-making process.*"
>
> *General Colin Powell,*
> *Chairman, Joint Chiefs of Staff*

Case of War on Land of 18 October 1907 ("Hague V").

- Hague Convention VIII Relative to the Laying of Automatic Submarine Contact Mines of 18 October 1907 ("Hague VIII").
- Hague Convention IX Concerning Bombardment by Naval Forces in Time of War of 18 October 1907 ("Hague IX").
- Geneva Protocol for the Prohibition of the Use of Asphyxiating, Poisonous or Other Gases, and of Bacteriological Methods of Warfare of 17 June 1925 ("1925 Geneva Protocol").
- Convention on the Prevention and Punishment of the Crime of Genocide of 9 December 1948 ("the Genocide Convention").
- The four Geneva Conventions for the Protection of War Victims of August 12, 1949:
- Geneva Convention for the Amelioration of the Condition of Wounded and Sick in Armed Forces in the Field ("GWS").
- Geneva Convention for the Amelioration of the Wounded, Sick and Shipwrecked Members of Armed Forces at Sea (hereinafter "GWS" [Sea]).
- Geneva Convention Relative to the Treatment of Prisoners of War ("GPW").
- Geneva Convention Relative to the Protection of Civilian Persons in Time of War ("GC").
- Hague Convention for the Protection of

Cultural Property in the Event of Armed Conflict of 14 May 1954 ("1954 Hague"). Since Iraq, Kuwait, France, Egypt, Saudi Arabia, and other Coalition members are parties to this treaty, the treaty was binding between Iraq and Kuwait, and between Iraq and those Coalition members in the Persian Gulf War. Canada, Great Britain, and the United States are not parties to this treaty. However, the armed forces of each receive training on its provisions, and the treaty was followed by all Coalition forces in the Persian Gulf War.

The United States is a party to all of these treaties, except the 1954 Hague Cultural Property Convention. While Iraq is not a party to Hague IV, the International Military Tribunal (Nuremberg, 1946) stated with regard to it that:

The rules of land warfare expressed in . . . [Hague IV] undoubtedly represented an advance over existing International Law at the time of their adoption . . . but by 1939 these rules . . . were recognized by all civilized nations and were regarded as being declaratory of the laws and customs of war.

As customary international law, its obligations are binding upon all nations. Neither is Iraq a party to Hague V, Hague VIII, or Hague IX. However, the provisions of each cited herein are regarded as a reflection of the customary practice of nations, and therefore binding upon all nations.

The United States, other Coalition members, and Iraq are parties to the 1925 Geneva Protocol which prohibits the use of chemical (CW) or bacteriological (biological) weapons (BW) in time of war. Both Iraq and the United States filed a reservation to this treaty at the time of their respective ratifications. Iraq's reservation accepted the 1925 Geneva Protocol as prohibiting first use of CW or BW weapons; the United States, having unilaterally renounced the

use of BW in 1969, accepted without reservation the prohibition on BW and first use of CW. (The United States also is a party to the Convention on the Prohibition of Development, Production and Stockpiling of Bacteriological [Biological] and Toxin Weapons and on Their Destruction of 10 April 1972; Iraq is not.) All nations party to the Persian Gulf conflict, including Iraq, are parties to the four 1949 Geneva Conventions for the protection of war victims. The precise applicability of these treaties will be addressed in the discussion of each topic in this appendix.

Three other law of war treaties were not legally applicable in the Persian Gulf War, but nonetheless bear mention. They are:

■ 1977 Convention on the Prohibition of Military or Any Other Hostile Use of Environmental Modification Techniques ("ENMOD Convention"). While the United States and many of its Coalition partners are parties to this treaty, Iraq has signed but not ratified the ENMOD Convention; therefore it was not legally applicable to Iraqi actions during the Persian Gulf War.

■ 1977 Protocol I Additional to the Geneva Conventions of 12 August 1949 ("Protocol I"). From 1974 to 1977 the United States and more than 100 other nations participated in a Diplomatic Conference intended to supplement the 1949 Geneva Conventions and modernize the law of war. That conference produced two new law of war treaties: Protocol I deals with the law of war in international armed conflicts, while Protocol II addresses the law of war applicable to internal armed conflicts. Iraq and several Coalition members, including the United States, Great Britain, and France, are not parties to Protocol I; therefore it was not applicable during the Persian Gulf War. For humanitarian, military, and political reasons, the United States in 1987 declined to become a party to Protocol I; France reached a similar decision in 1984.

- 1980 Convention on Prohibitions or Restrictions on the Use of Certain Conventional Weapons. Iraq and most of the Coalition partners, including the United States, are not parties to this treaty; it had no applicability in the Persian Gulf War. However, US and Coalition actions were consistent with its language. Iraqi actions were consistent with the treaty except as to its provisions on land mines and booby traps.

ROLE OF LEGAL ADVISERS

The Office of General Counsel of the Department of Defense (DOD), as the chief DOD legal office, provided advice to the Secretary of Defense, the Deputy Secretary of Defense, the Under Secretary of Defense for Policy, other senior advisers to the Secretary and to the various components of the Defense legal community on all matters relating to Operations Desert Shield and Desert Storm, including the law of war. For example, the Secretary of Defense tasked the General Counsel to review and opine on such diverse issues as the means of collecting and obligating for defense purposes contributions from third countries; the Wars Powers Resolution; DOD targeting policies; the rules of engagement; the rules pertinent to maritime interception operations; issues relating to the treatment of prisoners of war; sensitive intelligence and special access matters; and similar matters of the highest priority to the Secretary and DOD. In addition, military judge advocates and civilian attorneys with international law expertise provided advice on the law of war and other legal issues at every level of command in all phases of Operations Desert Shield and Desert Storm. Particular attention was given to the review of target lists to ensure the consistency of targets selected for attack with United States law of war obligations.

TAKING OF HOSTAGES

Whatever the purpose, whether for intimidation, concessions, reprisal, or to render areas or legitimate military objects immune from military operations, the taking of hostages is unequivocally and expressly prohibited by Article 34, GC.[1]

Applicability of the GC was triggered by Iraq's invasion of Kuwait on 2 August; thereafter Iraq was an Occupying Power in Kuwait, with express obligations. Under articles 5, 42, and 78, GC, Iraq could intern foreign nationals only if internal security made it "absolutely necessary" (in Iraq) or "imperative" (in Kuwait). Iraq asserted no rights under any of these provisions in defense of its illegal taking of hostages in Iraq and Kuwait.

United Nations Security Council (UNSC) Resolution 664 (18 August) overrode authority inconsistent with its obligations under the GC that Iraq might have claimed to restrict the departure of US citizens and other third-country nationals in Kuwait or Iraq, and clarified the legal status of noncombatants.

Hostage taking by Iraq can be divided into four categories:

- The taking of Kuwaiti nationals as hostages and individual and mass forcible deportations to Iraq, in violation of Articles 34 and 49, GC;
- The taking of third-country nationals in Kuwait as hostages and individual and mass forcible deportations from Kuwait to Iraq, in violation of Articles 34 and 49, GC;
- The taking of foreign nationals within Iraq as hostages, with individual and mass forcible

---

[1] The United States is party to the International Conventional Against Taking of Hostages of 17 December 1979, under which hostage taking is identified as an act of international terrorism.

transfers, in violation of Articles 34 and 35, GC; and

■ Compelling Kuwaiti and other foreign citizens to serve in the armed forces of Iraq, in violation of Article 51, GC.

The taking of hostages, their unlawful deportation, and compelling hostages to serve in the armed forces of Iraq constitute Grave Breaches (that is, major violations of the law of war) under Article 147, GC.

US and other hostages in Iraq, including civilians forcibly deported from Kuwait, were placed in or around military targets as "human shields", in violation of Articles 28 and 38(4), GC. Use of Coalition prisoners of war (POWs) to shield military targets from attack will be considered in the section of this appendix on the treatment of POWs; other abuses of protected civilians will be addressed in the sections on Treatment of Civilians in Occupied Territory and War Crimes.

Iraq released US and other third-party hostages (i.e., other than Kuwaiti citizens) held in either Kuwait or Iraq in December. Because they were permitted to depart well before offensive combat operations began, Iraq's initial taking of hostages from such nations had no effect on US or Coalition force planning or execution of military operations.

Although it was known that some Kuwaiti nationals were being held in Iraq before offensive combat operations began, their presence did not appreciably affect Coalition force planning or execution of military operations. Thus, although the President had declared the United States would not be deterred from attacking legitimate targets because Iraq may have placed protected persons in their vicinity, it does not appear that any Kuwaiti nationals were placed at risk in that fashion after Iraqi release of its third party hostages. Iraq did use its own civilian population for this purpose, however, as will be explained in the section on

targeting, collateral damage and collateral civilian casualties.

Kuwaiti nationals (and other residents of Kuwait) were taken hostage and forcibly deported from Kuwait to Iraq by retreating Iraqi troops as the Coalition forces' liberation of Kuwait reached its final phase. Although the plight of those hostages was a source of great concern to US and other Coalition forces, the fact of their seizure did not have a significant effect on the planning or execution of Coalition military operations.

TREATMENT OF CIVILIANS IN OCCUPIED TERRITORY

The GC governs the treatment of civilians in occupied territories. As previously indicated, all parties to the conflict, including Iraq, are parties to this convention. The treaty's application was triggered by the Iraqi invasion, and was specifically recognized in UNSC resolutions that addressed that crisis.

An earlier law of war treaty that remains relevant is Hague IV, which contains regulations relating to the protection of civilian property (public and private) in occupied territory; in contrast, the GC sets forth the obligations of an occupying power in providing protection for civilians in occupied territory. Cultural property in Kuwait also was protected by the 1954 Hague Cultural Property Convention.

Iraqi actions read like a very long list of violations òf Hague IV, GC, and the 1954 Hague Cultural Property Convention. From the beginning of its invasion of Kuwait, Iraq exhibited an intent not only to refuse to conduct itself as an occupying power, but to deny that it was an occupying power. Its intention was to annex Kuwait as a part of Iraq, and remove any vestige of Kuwait's previous existence as an independent, sovereign nation. (Its transfer of a part of its own civilian population into occupied Kuwait for the purpose of annexation and resettlement constitutes a violation of Article 49, GC.)

A case can be made that Iraqi actions may violate the Genocide Convention, which defines genocide as any of the following acts committed with the intent to destroy, in whole or in part, a national, ethnical, racial or religious group:

- Killing members of the group;
- Causing serious bodily or mental harm to members of the group;
- Deliberately inflicting on the group conditions of life calculated to bring about its physical destruction in whole or in part;
- Imposing measures intended to prevent births within the group; or
- Forcibly transferring children of the group to another group.

Iraq carried out every act of the types condemned by the Genocide Convention, except for forcibly transferring children. Many Kuwaiti citizens were deported forcibly to Iraq; many others were tortured and/or murdered. There were instances of Kuwaiti women of child-bearing age being brutally rendered incapable of having children. Collective executions of innocent Kuwaiti civilians took place routinely. Kuwaiti public records were removed or destroyed, apparently to prevent or impede the reconstitution of Kuwait if Kuwait were liberated. Kuwaiti identification cards and license plates were revoked and replaced with Iraqi credentials, identifying Kuwait as Iraq's 19th province.

In violation of Hague IV and the 1954 Hague Cultural Property Convention, cultural, private and public (municipal and national) property was confiscated; pillage was widespread. (Confiscation of private property is prohibited under any circumstance, as is the confiscation of municipal public property. Confiscation of movable national public property is prohibited without military need and cash compensation,

while immovable national public property may be temporarily confiscated under the concept of usufruct — the right to use another's property so long as it is not damaged.)

Iraqi confiscation appears to have been primarily, if not entirely, part of a program:

- Of erasing any record of the sovereign state of Kuwait;
- Of looting directed by the Iraqi leadership to provide consumer goods for the Iraqi public; and
- Of looting by individual Iraqi soldiers , which was tolerated by Iraqi military commanders and higher civilian and military authorities.

Civilians who remained in Kuwait were denied the necessities for survival, such as food, water, and basic medical care, in violation of Articles 55 and 56, GC. Kuwaiti doctors were forcibly deported to Iraq; Filipino nurses working in the hospitals were raped repeatedly by Iraqi soldiers. Kuwaiti civilians were not permitted any medical care unless they presented Iraqi identification cards; presentation of an Iraqi identification card by a Kuwaiti citizen seldom resulted in any genuine medical care. Medical supplies and equipment in Kuwaiti hospitals necessary for the needs of the civilian population of Kuwait were illegally taken, in violation of Article 57, GC, in brutal disregard for Kuwaiti lives. For example, there are reports that infants died in Kuwaiti hospitals after Iraqis removed them from their incubators, which were shipped to Iraq.

The slightest perceived offense could lead to torture and execution of the purported offender, often in front of family members. Torture and murder of civilians is prohibited by Article 32, GC. Iraqi policy provided for the collective punishment of the family of any individual who served in or was suspected of assisting the Kuwaiti resistance. This punishment routinely took the form of destruction of the family home and execution of all family members. Collective punishment is prohibited expressly by Article 33, GC.

The Iraqi occupation remained brutal until the very end; civilians were murdered in the final days of that occupation to eliminate witnesses to Iraqi repression. The Government of Kuwait estimates that 1,082 civilians were murdered during the occupation. Many more were forcibly deported to Iraq; several thousand remain missing. On their departure, Iraqi forces set off previously placed explosive charges on Kuwait's oil wells, a vengeful act of wanton destruction.

Coalition forces acted briefly as an occupying power. When the Operation Desert Storm ground offensive began, Coalition forces moved into Iraq. Physical seizure and control of Iraqi territory triggered the application of Hague IV and the GC. Both treaties initially had little practical application, since Coalition forces occupied uninhabited desert. As hostilities diminished, the internal conflict that erupted in Iraq caused thousands of civilians to flee the fighting (such as in Al-Basrah, between Iraqi military units and Shi'ite forces) and to enter territory held by Coalition forces. Allied forces provided food, water and medical care to these refugees. As Coaltion forces prepared to withdraw from Iraq, no international relief agency was ready to assume this relief effort. Consequently, refugees were offered the opportunity to move to the refugee camp at Rafha, Saudi Arabia. Approximately 20,000 refugees (including more than 8,000 from the Safwan area) accepted this offer.

In the conflict's latter phases, public and private international relief agency representatives entered the area of conflict, often without sufficient advance notification and coordination with Coalition authorities. While relief agencies undoubtedly were anxious to perform humanitarian missions, their entry onto the battlefield without the advance consent of the parties to the conflict is not consistent with

Article 9, GWS (a provision common to all four 1949 Geneva Conventions), Article 125, GPW, and Article 63, GC. It impeded Coalition efforts to end hostilities as rapidly as possible, and placed these organizations' members at risk from the ongoing hostilities. Coalition aviation units searching for mobile Scud missile launchers in western Iraq were inhibited in their efforts to neutralize that threat by vehicles from those organizations moving through Scud missile operating areas that otherwise were devoid of civilians. The lack of timely, proper coordination by relief agencies with Coalition forces adversely affected air strikes against other Iraqi targets on other occasions. While well-intentioned, these intrusions required increased diligence by Coalition forces, placed Coalition forces at increased risk, and were factors in the failure to resolve the Scud threat.

Whether in territory Coalition forces occupied or in parts of Iraq still under Iraqi control, US and Coalition operations in Iraq were carefully attuned to the fact those operations were being conducted in an area encompassing "the cradle of civilization," near many archaeological sites of great cultural significance. Coalition operations were conducted in a way that balanced maximum possible protection for those cultural sites against protection of Coalition lives and accomplishment of the assigned mission.

While Article 4(1) of the 1954 Hague Convention provides specific protection for cultural property, Article 4(2) permits waiver of that protection where military necessity makes such a waiver imperative; such "imperative military necessity" can occur when an enemy uses cultural property and its immediate surroundings to protect legitimate military targets, in violation of Article 4(1). Coalition forces continued to respect Iraqi cultural property, even where Iraqi forces used such property to shield military targets from attack. However, some indirect damage may have occurred to some Iraqi cultural property due to the concussive effect of munitions directed against Iraqi targets some distance away from the cultural sites.

Since US military doctrine is prepared consistent with US law of war obligations and policies, the provisions of Hague IV, GC, and the 1954 Hague Convention did not have any significant adverse effect on planning or executing military operations.

TARGETING, COLLATERAL DAMAGE AND CIVILIAN CASUALTIES

The law of war with respect to targeting, collateral damage and collateral civilian casualties is derived from the principle of discrimination; that is, the necessity for distinguishing between combatants, who may be attacked, and noncombatants, against whom an intentional attack may not be directed, and between legitimate military targets and civilian objects. Although this is a major part of the foundation on which the law of war is built, it is one of the least codified portions of that law.

As a general principle, the law of war prohibits the intentional destruction of civilian objects not imperatively required by military necessity and the direct, intentional attack of civilians not taking part in hostilities. The United States takes these proscriptions into account in developing and acquiring weapons systems, and in using them in combat. Central Command (CENTCOM) forces adhered to these fundamental law of war proscriptions in conducting military operations during Operation Desert Storm through discriminating target selection and careful matching of available forces and weapons systems to selected targets and Iraqi defenses, without regard to Iraqi violations of its law of war obligations toward the civilian population and civilian objects.

Several treaty provisions specifically address the responsibility to minimize collateral damage to civilian objects and injury to civilians. Article 23(g) of the Annex to Hague IV prohibits destruction not "imperatively demanded by the necessities of war," while Article 27 of that same annex offers protection from intentional attack to "buildings dedicated to religion, art, science, or charitable purposes, historic monuments, hospitals, and places where the sick and wounded are collected, provided they are not being used at the time for military purposes." Similar language is contained in Article 5 of Hague IX, while the conditions for protection of cultural property in the 1954 Hague Cultural Property Convention were set forth in the preceding discussion on the treatment of civilians in occupied territory. In summary, cultural and civilian objects are protected from direct, intentional attack unless they are used for military purposes, such as shielding military objects from attack.

While the prohibition contained in Article 23(g) generally refers to intentional destruction or injury, it also precludes collateral damage of civilian objects or injury to noncombatant civilians that is clearly disproportionate to the military advantage gained in the attack of military objectives, as discussed below. As previously indicated, Hague IV was found to be part of customary international law in the course of war crimes trials following World War II, and continues to be so regarded.

An uncodified but similar provision is the principle of proportionality. It prohibits military action in which the negative effects (such as collateral civilian casualties) clearly outweigh the military gain. This balancing may be done on a target-by-target basis, as frequently was the case during Operation Desert Storm, but also may be weighed in overall terms against campaign objectives. CENTCOM conducted its campaign with a focus on minimizing collateral civilian casualties and damage to civilian objects. Some targets were specifically avoided because the value of destruction of each target was outweighed by the potential risk to nearby civilians or, as in the case of certain archaeological and religious sites, to civilian objects.

Coalition forces took several steps to minimize the risk of injury to noncombatants. To the degree possible and consistent with allowable risk to aircraft and aircrews, aircraft and munitions were selected so that attacks on targets within populated areas would provide the greatest possible accuracy and the least risk to civilian objects and the civilian population. Where required, attacking aircraft were accompanied by support mission aircraft to minimize attacking aircraft aircrew distraction from their assigned mission. Aircrews attacking targets in populated areas were directed not to expend their munitions if they lacked positive identification of their targets. When this occurred, aircrews dropped their bombs on alternate targets or returned to base with their weapons.

One reason for the maneuver plan adopted for the ground campaign was that it avoided populated areas, where Coalition and Iraqi civilian casualties and damage to civilian objects necessarily would have been high. This was a factor in deciding against an amphibious assault into Kuwait City.

The principle of proportionality acknowledges the unfortunate inevitability of collateral civilian casualties and collateral damage to civilian objects when noncombatants and civilian objects are mingled with combatants and targets, even with reasonable efforts by the parties to a conflict to minimize collateral injury and damage.

This proved to be the case in the air campaign. Despite conducting the most discriminate air campaign in history, including extraordinary measures by Coalition aircrews to minimize collateral civilian casualties, the Coalition could not avoid causing some collateral damage and injury.

There are several reasons for this. One is the fact that in any modern society, many objects intended for civilian use also may be used for military purposes. A bridge or highway vital to daily commuter and business traffic can be equally crucial to military traffic, or support for a nation's war effort. Railroads, airports, seaports, and the interstate highway system in the United States have been funded by the Congress in part because because of US national security concerns, for example; each proved invaluable to the movement of US military units to various ports for deployment to Southwest Asia (SWA) for Operations Desert Shield and Desert Storm. Destruction of a bridge, airport, or port facility, or interdiction of a highway can be equally important in impeding an enemy's war effort.

The same is true with regard to major utilities; for example, microwave towers for everyday, peacetime civilian communications can constitute a vital part of a military command and control (C^2) system, while electric power grids can be used simultaneously for military and civilian purposes. Some Iraqi military installations had separate electrical generators; others did not. Industries essential to the manufacturing of CW, BW and conventional weapons depended on the national electric power grid.

Experience in its 1980-1988 war with Iran caused the Government of Iraq to develop a substantial and comprehensive degree of redundancy in its normal, civilian utilities as back-up for its national defense. Much of this redundancy, by necessity, was in urban areas. Attack of these targets necessarily placed the civilian population at risk, unless civilians were evacuated from the surrounding area. Iraqi authorities elected not to move civilians away from objects they knew were legitimate military targets, thereby placing those civilians at risk of injury incidental to Coalition attacks against these targets, notwithstanding efforts by the Coalition to minimize risk to innocent civilians.

When objects are used concurrently for civilian and military purposes, they are liable to attack if there is a military advantage to be gained in their attack. ("Military advantage" is not restricted to tactical gains, but is linked to the full context of a war strategy, in this instance, the execution of the Coalition war plan for liberation of Kuwait.)

Attack of all segments of the Iraqi communications system was essential to destruction of Iraqi military C^2. C^2 was crucial to Iraq's integrated air defense system; it was of equal importance for Iraqi ground forces. Iraqi C^2 was highly centralized. With Saddam Hussein's fear of internal threats to his rule, he has discouraged individual initiative while emphasizing positive control. Iraqi military commanders were authorized to do only that which was directed by highest authority. Destruction of its C^2 capabilities would make Iraqi combat forces unable to respond quickly to Coalition initiatives.

Baghdad bridges crossing the Euphrates River contained the multiple fiber-optic links that provided Saddam Hussein with secure communications to his southern group of forces. Attack of these bridges severed those secure communication links, while restricting movement of Iraqi military forces and deployment of CW and BW warfare capabilities. Civilians using those bridges or near other targets at the time of their attack were at risk of injury incidental to the legitimate attack of those targets.

Another reason for collateral damage to civilian objects and injury to civilians during Operation Desert Storm lay in the policy of the Government of Iraq, which purposely used both Iraqi and Kuwaiti civilian populations and civilian objects as shields for military objects. Contrary to the admonishment against such conduct contained in Article 19, GWS, Articles 18 and 28, GC, Article 4(1), 1954 Hague, and certain principles of customary law codified in Protocol I (discussed below), the Government of Iraq placed military assets (personnel, weapons, and equipment) in civilian populated areas and next to protected objects (mosques, medical facilities, and cultural sites) in an effort to protect them from attack. For this purpose, Iraqi military helicopters were dispersed into residential areas; and military supplies were stored in mosques, schools, and hospitals in Iraq and Kuwait. Similarly, a cache of Iraqi Silkworm surface-to-surface missiles was found inside a school in a populated area in Kuwait City. UN inspectors uncovered chemical bomb production equipment while inspecting a sugar factory in Iraq. The equipment had been moved to the site to escape Coalition air strikes. This intentional mingling of military objects with civilian objects naturally placed the civilian population living nearby, working within, or using those civilian objects at risk from legitimate military attacks on those military objects.

The Coalition targeted specific military objects in populated areas, which the law of war permits; at no time were civilian areas as such attacked. Coalition forces also chose not to attack many military targets in populated areas or in or adjacent to cultural (archaeological) sites, even though attack of those military targets is authorized by the law of war. The attack of legitimate Iraqi military targets, notwithstanding the fact it resulted in collateral injury to civilians and damage to civilian objects, was consistent with the customary practice of nations and the law of war.

The Government of Iraq sought to convey a highly inaccurate image of indiscriminate bombing by the Coalition through a deliberate disinformation campaign. Iraq utilized any collateral damage that occurred — including damage or injury caused by Iraqi surface-to-air missiles and antiaircraft munitions falling to earth in populated areas — in its campaign to convey the misimpression that the Coalition was targeting populated areas and civilian objects. This disinformation campaign was factually incorrect, and did not accurately reflect the high degree of care exercised by the Coalition in attack of Iraqi targets.

For example, on 11 February, a mosque at Al-Basrah was dismantled by Iraqi authorities to feign bomb damage; the dome was removed and the building dismantled. US authorities noted there was no damage to the minaret, courtyard building, or dome foundation which would have been present had the building been struck by Coalition munitions. The nearest bomb crater was outside the facility, the result of an air strike directed against a nearby military target on 30 January. Other examples include use of photographs of damage that occurred during Iraq's war with Iran, as well as of prewar earthquake damage, which were offered by Iraqi officials as proof of bomb damage caused by Coalition air raids.

Minimizing collateral damage and injury is a responsibility shared by attacker and defender. Article 48 of the 1977 Protocol I provides that:

In order to ensure respect for and protection of the civilian population and civilian objects, the Parties to the conflict shall at all times distinguish between the civilian population and combatants and between civilian objects and military objectives and accordingly shall direct their operations only against military objectives.

Paragraph one of Article 49 of Protocol I states that "'Attacks' means acts of violence against the adversary, whether in offense or defense." Use of the word "attacks" in this manner is etymologically inconsistent with its customary use in any of the six official languages of Protocol I. Conversely, the word "attack" or "attacks" historically has referred to and today refers to offensive operations only. Article 49(1) otherwise reflects the applicability of the law of war to actions of both attacker and defender, including the obligation to take appropriate measures to minimize injury to civilians not participating in hostilities.

As previously indicated, the United States in 1987 declined to become a party to Protocol I; nor was Protocol I in effect during the Persian Gulf War, since Iraq is not a party to that treaty. However, the language of Articles 48 and 49(1) (except for the erroneous use of the word "attacks") is generally regarded as a codification of the customary practice of nations, and therefore binding on all.

In the effort to minimize collateral civilian casualties, a substantial responsibility for protection of the civilian population rests with the party controlling the civilian population. Historically, and from a common sense standpoint, the party controlling the civilian population has the opportunity and the responsibility to minimize the risk to the civilian population through the separation of military objects from the civilian population, evacuation of the civilian population from near immovable military objects, and development of air raid precautions. Throughout World War II, for example, both Axis and Allied nations took each of these steps to protect their respective civilian populations from the effects of military operations.

The Government of Iraq elected not to take routine air-raid precautions to protect its civilian population. Civilians were not evacuated in any significant numbers from Baghdad, nor were they removed from proximity to legitimate military targets. There were air raid shelters for less than 1 percent of the civilian population of Baghdad. The Government of Iraq chose instead to use its civilians to shield legitimate military targets from attack, exploiting collateral civilian casualties and damage to civilian objects in its disinformation campaign to erode international and US domestic support for the Coalition effort to liberate Kuwait.

The presence of civilians will not render a target immune from attack; legitimate targets may be attacked wherever located (outside neutral territory and waters). An attacker must exercise reasonable precautions to minimize incidental or collateral injury to the civilian population or damage to civilian objects, consistent with mission accomplishment and allowable risk to the attacking forces. The defending party must exercise reasonable precautions to separate the civilian population and civilian objects from military objectives, and avoid placing military objectives in the midst of the civilian population. As previously indicated, a defender is expressly prohibited from using the civilian population or civilian objects (including cultural property) to shield legitimate targets from attack.

The Government of Iraq was aware of its law of war obligations. In the month preceding the Coalition air campaign, for example, a civil defense exercise was conducted, during which more than one million civilians were evacuated from Baghdad. No government evacuation program was undertaken during the Coalition air campaign. As previously indicated, the Government of Iraq elected instead to mix military objects with the civilian population. Pronouncements that Coalition air forces would not attack populated areas increased Iraqi movement of military objects into populated areas in Iraq and Kuwait to shield them from attack, in callous disregard of its law of war obligations and the safety of its own civilians and Kuwaiti civilians.

Similar actions were taken by the Government of Iraq to use cultural property to protect legitimate targets from attack; a classic example was the positioning of two fighter aircraft adjacent to the ancient temple of Ur (as depicted in the photograph in Volume II, Chapter VI,

"Off Limits Targets" section) on the theory that Coalition respect for the protection of cultural property would preclude the attack of those aircraft. While the law of war permits the attack of the two fighter aircraft, with Iraq bearing responsibility for any damage to the temple, Commander-in-Chief, Central Command (CINCCENT) elected not to attack the aircraft on the basis of respect for cultural property and the belief that positioning of the aircraft adjacent to Ur (without servicing equipment or a runway nearby) effectively had placed each out of action, thereby limiting the value of their destruction by Coalition air forces when weighed against the risk of damage to the temple. Other cultural property similarly remained on the Coalition no-attack list, despite Iraqi placement of valuable military equipment in or near those sites.

Undoubtedly, the most tragic result of this intentional commingling of military objects with the civilian population occurred in the 13 February attack on the Al-Firdus Bunker (also sometimes referred to as the Al-'Amariyah bunker) in Baghdad. Originally constructed during the Iran-Iraq War as an air raid shelter, it had been converted to a military C^2 bunker in the middle of a populated area. While the entrance(s) to a bomb shelter permit easy and rapid entrance and exit, barbed wire had been placed around the Al-Firdus bunker, its entrances had been secured to prevent unauthorized access, and armed guards had been posted. It also had been camouflaged. Knowing Coalition air attacks on targets in Baghdad took advantage of the cover of darkness, Iraqi authorities permitted selected civilians — apparently the families of officer personnel working in the bunker — to enter the Al-'Amariyah Bunker at night to use the former air raid shelter part of the bunker, on a level above the C^2 center. Coalition authorities were unaware of the presence of these civilians in the bunker complex. The 13 February attack of the Al-'Amariyah bunker — a legitimate military target — resulted in the unfortunate deaths of those Iraqi civilians who had taken refuge above the C² center.

An attacker operating in the fog of war may make decisions that will lead to innocent civilians' deaths. The death of civilians always is regrettable, but inevitable when a defender fails to honor his own law of war obligations — or callously disregards them, as was the case with Saddam Hussein. In reviewing an incident such as the attack of the Al-'Amariyah bunker, the law of war recognizes the difficulty of decision making amid the confusion of war. Leaders and commanders necessarily have to make decisions on the basis of their assessment of the information reasonably available to them at the time, rather than what is determined in hindsight.

Protocol I establishes similar legal requirements. Articles 51(7) and 58 of the 1977 Protocol I expressly prohibit a defender from using the civilian population or individual civilians to render certain points or areas immune from military operations, in particular in an attempt to shield military objectives from attack or to shield, favor or impede military operations; obligate a defender to remove the civilian population, individual civilians and civilian objects under the defender's control from near military objectives; avoid locating military objectives within or near densely populated areas; and to take other necessary precautions to protect the civilian population, individual civilians and civilian objects under its control against the dangers resulting from military operations.

It is in this area that deficiencies of the 1977 Protocol I become apparent. As correctly stated in Article 51(8) of Protocol I, a nation confronted with callous actions by its opponent (such as the use of "human shields') is not released from its obligation to exercise reasonable precaution to minimize collateral injury to the civilian population or damage to civilian objects. This obligation was recognized by Coalition forces in the conduct of their operations. In practice, this concept tends to facilitate the disinformation campaign of a callous opponent by focusing international public opinion upon the obligation of the attacking force to minimize collateral civilian casualties and damage to civilian objects — a result fully consistent with Iraq's strategy in this regard. This inherent problem is worsened by the language of Article 52(3) of Protocol I, which states:

> In case of doubt whether an object which is normally dedicated to civilian purposes, such as a place of worship, a house or other dwelling or a school, is being used to make an effective contribution to military action, it shall be presumed not to be so used.

This language, which is not a codification of the customary practice of nations, causes several things to occur that are contrary to the traditional law of war. It shifts the burden for determining the precise use of an object from the party controlling that object (and therefore in possession of the facts as to its use) to the party lacking such control and facts, i.e., from defender to attacker. This imbalance ignores the realities of war in demanding a degree of certainty of an attacker that seldom exists in combat. It also encourages a defender to ignore its obligation to separate the civilian population, individual civilians and civilian objects from military objectives, as the Government of Iraq illustrated during the Persian Gulf War.

In the case of the Al-Firdus bunker, for example — repeatedly and incorrectly referred to by the Government of Iraq and some media representatives as a "civilian bomb shelter" — the Coalition forces had evidence the bunker was being used as an Iraqi command and control center and had no knowledge it was concurrently being used as a bomb shelter for civilians. Under the rule of international law known as military necessity, which permits the attack of structures used to further an enemy's prosecution of a war, this was a legitimate military target. Coalition forces had no obligation to refrain from attacking it. If Coalition forces had known that Iraqi civilians were occupying it as a shelter, they may have withheld an attack until the civilians had removed themselves (although the law of war does not require such restraint). Iraq had an obligation under the law of war to refrain from commingling its civilian population with what was an obviously military target. Alternatively, Iraq could have designated the location as a hospital, safety zone, or a neutral zone, as provided for in Articles 14 and 15, GC.

ENEMY PRISONER OF WAR PROGRAM

This section contains similar information to that contained in Appendix L, but is a more condensed version of that appendix, with emphasis on the legal aspects of the Enemy Prisoner of War (EPW) program. Appendix L used the same base information as Appendix O, but expands to include more operational issues.

Coalition care for EPWs was in strict compliance with the 1949 Geneva convention relative to the treatment of Prisoners of War (hereafter "GPW"). Centralized management of EPW operations began during Operation Desert Shield and continued throughout Operation Desert Storm. The US National Prisoner of War Information Center (NPWIC) became operational before ground operations began and a new automated information program for preserving, cataloging, and accounting for captured personnel (as required by the GPW) was fielded in Operation Desert Shield. Trained Reserve Component (RC) EPW units were activated, and camp advisory teams were sent to Saudi Arabia to account for and to provide technical assistance on custody and treatment of US-transferred EPWs.

EPWs captured by Coalition forces during Operations Desert Shield and Desert Storm were maintained in either a US or Saudi EPW camp. The United States accepted EPWs captured by the United Kingdom (UK) and France, while Saudi Arabia managed a consolidated camp for those EPWs captured by the remaining Coalition forces.

The Army, as the DOD Executive Agent for EPW operations, processed 69,822 Iraqi EPWs captured by British, French, and US forces between 18 January, when the first EPW was captured, and 2 May, when the last EPW in US custody was transferred to Saudi Arabian control. In terms of campaign length vis-a-vis EPWs captured, this was the most extensive US EPW operation since World War II. US forces captured 62,456 EPWs during the conflict. Additionally, 1,492 displaced civilians were evacuated to Saudi Arabia through EPW channels. Some of these initially were believed to be EPWs; others were evacuated for their own safety. French and British forces captured an additional 5,874 EPWs and transferred them to US control. The Arab Command captured 16,921 EPWs. Always of international interest and concern, the humane treatment of and full accountability for EPWs and displaced civilians during this conflict received heightened attention because of religious and cultural sensitivities.

US and other Coalition forces treated EPWs and displaced civilians in accordance with the 1949 Geneva Conventions for the Protection of War Victims. The first three conventions mandate humane treatment and full accountability for all prisoners of war from the moment of capture until their repatriation, release, or death. The fourth convention (GC) requires humane treatment for displaced civilians. The International Committee of the Red Cross (ICRC) was provided access to Coalition EPW facilities and reviewed their findings with Coalition representatives in periodic meetings in Riyadh, Saudi Arabia. While US and Coalition forces worked closely with the ICRC on EPW matters throughout Operation Desert Storm, neither the ICRC nor any other human rights organization played any other role affecting the course of the war. The ICRC was ineffective in providing any protection for US and Coalition POWs in Iraq's custody.

NPWIC was established at the Pentagon during Operation Desert Shield using active duty personnel and became fully operational with Reserve staffing on 21 January. Its mission was to account for EPWs in US custody and to ensure compliance with the 1949 Geneva Conventions. Article 122, GPW requires a captor to establish a National Information Bureau within the shortest time possible after the onset of hostilities. The NPWIC, manned by Army Reserve Individual Mobilization Augmentees, volunteer Reservists and retired personnel, served as a central repository for information relative to EPWs captured by or transferred to US forces, and coordinated information pertaining to EPWs and US POWs in Iraqi hands with the ICRC.

The US and Saudi governments concluded an agreement which allowed the US to transfer captured EPWs to Saudi control after processing by US EPW elements. This agreement was applicable to EPWs captured by the French and British, as those EPWs were processed and maintained in US EPW camps. The US provided camp advisory teams to work with the Government of Saudi Arabia to assist in compliance with the 1949 Geneva Conventions, to facilitate logistic and administrative cooperation, and to maintain accountability for US-transferred EPWs. The size of the host nation EPW camps limited the number of EPWs the United States could transfer, and required that EPWs remain longer in US EPW camps. After active hostilities ended, in order to transfer all EPWs still under US control, the Brooklyn (West) EPW camp, along with its EPWs, was transferred to the Saudi Arabian National Guard.

To help accomplish its multiple missions, the NPWIC and theater EPW units used the Prisoner of War Information System (PWIS-2), an automated system to speed processing and to provide a database of information on captured personnel. The development of PWIS-2 was accelerated during Operation Desert Shield to allow the US to process the massive numbers of EPWs projected from the Kuwaiti Theater of Operations. The system arrived in the field in November with the first EPW unit in SWA. Under the previous manual system, an average of eight EPW could be fully processed per hour per camp. With PWIS-2, EPW units were processing up to 1,500 EPWs per day per camp. Accuracy was at an unprecedented level of 99.9 percent.

Eight EPWs died while in US custody, all as a result of injuries or sickness contracted before capture. One died of malnutrition/dehydration, five as a result of injuries or wounds, and two from unknown causes. Three US-transferred EPWs died in Saudi Arabian camps from wounds received in the Saudi camp, either during an EPW riot or inflicted by another EPW. These deaths were investigated and reported to the ICRC, as required by Articles 120, 122, and 123, GPW.

When Operation Desert Storm began, psychological operations were undertaken to encourage maximum defection or surrender of Iraqi forces. Leaflets to be used as safe conduct passes were widely disseminated over and behind Iraqi lines with great success.

Photographs and videotapes of the first Iraqi EPWs captured were taken and shown by the public media. The capture or detention of EPWs is recognized as newsworthy events and, as such, photography of such events is not prohibited by the GPW. However, Article 13, GPW does prohibit photography that might humiliate or degrade any EPW. Media use of photographs of EPWs raised some apprehension in light of formal US condemnation of the forced videotapes of US and Coalition POWs being made and shown by Iraq. CENTCOM and other DOD officials also expressed concern for the safety of the family of any Iraqi defector who might be identified from media photographs by Iraqi officials. Because of these sensitivities, and consistent with Article 13, GPW, DOD developed guidelines for photographing EPWs. These guidelines limited both the opportunities for photography and the display of EPW photographs taken, while protecting Iraqi EPWs and their families from retribution by the Government of Iraq.

Operation Desert Storm netted a large number of persons thought to be EPWs who were actually displaced civilians. Subsequent interrogations determined that they were innocent civilians who had taken no hostile action against Coalition forces. In some cases, individuals had surrendered to Coalition forces to receive food, water, and lodging, while others were captured because they appeared to be part of hostile forces. Tribunals were conducted to verify the status of detainees. Upon determination of their status as innocent civilians, detainees were transferred from US custody to Safwan, a US-operated refugee camp, or to Rafha, a Saudi Arabian refugee camp.

In March, Coalition forces and Iraqi military representatives signed an agreement for the repatriation of prisoners of war, to be conducted under ICRC auspices. Repatriation of EPWs not in medical channels occurred at Judaydat 'Ar-'ar, near the Jordanian border. Those in medical channels were flown directly to Baghdad on ICRC aircraft.

TREATMENT OF PRISONERS OF WAR

US and Coalition personnel captured by Iraq were POWs protected by the GWS (if wounded, injured, or sick) and GPW. All US POWs captured during the Persian Gulf War were moved to Baghdad by land after their capture.

With some exceptions, depending on their location at the time of capture, their route usually was through Kuwait City to Al-Basrah and then on to Baghdad. Those taken to Kuwait City and Al-Basrah usually were detained there for no more than a few hours or overnight. Limited interrogation of POWs occurred in these cities. Although some were physically abused during their transit to Baghdad, most were treated reasonably well.

On arrival in Baghdad, most Air Force, Navy, and Marine POWs were taken immediately to what the POWs referred to as "The Bunker" (most probably at the Directorate of Military Intelligence) for initial interrogation. They then were taken to what appeared to be the main long-term incarceration site, located in the Iraqi Intelligence Service Regional Headquarters (dubbed "The Biltmore" by the POWs). Since this building was a legitimate military target, the detention of POWs in it was a violation of Article 23, GPW; POWs thus were unnecessarily placed at risk when the facility was bombed on 23 February.

In contravention of Article 26, GPW, all US POWs incarcerated at the "Biltmore" experienced food deprivation. US POWs also were provided inadequate protection from the cold, in violation of Article 25, GPW.

After the 23 February bombing of the "Biltmore" by Coalition aircraft, the POWs were relocated to either Abu Abu Ghurayb Prison (dubbed "Joliet Prison") or Al-Rashid Military Prison ("The Half-Way House"), both near Baghdad. The Army POWs, on the other hand, were believed to have been sent directly to the Al-Rashid Military Prison, where they remained until their repatriation. All US POWs were repatriated from the Al-Rashid Military Prison. The detention of prisoners of war in a prison generally is prohibited by Article 22, GPW.

All US POWs suffered physical abuse at the

hands of their Iraqi captors, in violation of Articles 13, 14, and 17, GPW. Most POWs were tortured, a grave breach, in violation of Article 130, GPW. Some POWs were forced to make public propaganda statements, in violation of Article 13. In addition, none was permitted the rights otherwise afforded them by the GPW, such as the right of correspondence authorized by Article 70. Although the ICRC had access to Iraqi EPWs captured by the Coalition, ICRC members did not see Coalition POWs until the day of their repatriation.

Lack of access to non-US Coalition POW debriefs precludes comment on their treatment. From US POW debriefings, it is known that several Coalition POWs, especially the Saudi and Kuwaiti pilots, were abused physically by their Iraqi captors, in violation of Articles 13 and 17, GPW.

Iraqi POW handling procedures and treatment of Coalition POWs were reasonably predictable, based on a study of Iraqi treatment of Iranians during the eight-year Iran-Iraq war. Iraqi mistreatment of Coalition POWs constituted a Grave Breach of the GPW, as set forth in Article 130 of that treaty.

REPATRIATION OF PRISONERS OF WAR

Article 118, GPW, establishes a POW's right to be repatriated. In conflicts since the GPW's adoption, this principle has become conditional: Each POW must consent to repatriation rather than being forced to return. This proved to be the case after hostilities in this war ended.

No EPW was forcibly repatriated. Coalition forces identified to the ICRC those Iraqi EPWs not desiring repatriation. Once an Iraqi EPW scheduled for repatriation reached the repatriation site, the ICRC reconfirmed his willingness to be repatriated. Those who indicated they no longer desired to return to Iraq were returned to the custody of the detaining power.

On 4 March, Iraq released the first group of 10 Coalition prisoners of war, six of whom were US personnel. The United States simultaneously released 294 Iraqi EPWs for repatriation to Iraq. Of the 294, 10 refused repatriation at the repatriation site and were returned to US custody.

Iraq and the Coalition forces continued repatriation actions through August 1991, at which time 13,318 Iraqi EPWs who refused repatriation remained under Saudi control. On 5 August 1991, Iraqi EPWs still refusing repatriation were reclassified as refugees by the United States (in coordination with Saudi Arabia and the ICRC), concluding application of the GPW.

When US custody of Iraqi EPWs ended, ICRC officials informed the 800th Military Police Brigade (PW) that the treatment of Iraqi EPWs by US forces was the best compliance with the GPW by any nation in any conflict in history. Coalition measures to comply with the GPW had no adverse effect on planning and executing military operations; if anything, by encouraging the surrender of Iraqi military personnel, they improved those operations.

USE OF RUSES AND ACTS OF PERFIDY

Under the law of war, deception includes those measures designed to mislead the enemy by manipulation, distortion, or falsification of evidence to induce him to react in a manner prejudicial to his interests. Ruses are deception of the enemy by legitimate means, and are specifically allowed by Article 24, Annex to Hague IV, and Protocol I. As correctly stated in Article 37(2) of Protocol I:

> Ruses of war are not prohibited. Such ruses are acts which are intended to mislead an adversary or to induce him to act recklessly but which infringe no rule of [the law of war] and which are not perfidious because they do not invite the

confidence of an adversary with respect to protection under that law. The following are examples of ruses: the use of camouflage, decoys, mock operations and misinformation.

Coalition actions that convinced Iraqi military leaders that the ground campaign to liberate Kuwait would be focused in eastern Kuwait, and would include an amphibious assault, are examples of legitimate ruses. These deception measures were crucial to the Coalition's goal of minimizing the number of Coalition casualties and, in all likelihood, resulted in fewer Iraqi casualties as well.

In contrast, perfidy is prohibited by the law of war. Perfidy is defined in Article 37(1) of Protocol I as:

> Acts inviting the confidence of an adversary to lead him to believe that he is entitled to, or is obliged to accord, protection under the [law of war], with intent to betray that confidence . . . .

Perfidious acts include the feigning of an intent to surrender or negotiate under a flag of truce, or the feigning of protected status through improper use of the Red Cross or Red Crescent distinctive emblem.

Perfidious acts are prohibited on the basis that perfidy may damage mutual respect for the law of war, may lead to unnecessary escalation of the conflict, may result in the injury or death of enemy forces legitimately attempting to surrender or discharging their humanitarian duties, or may impede the restoration of peace.

There were few examples of perfidious practices during the Persian Gulf War. The most publicized were those associated with the battle of Ras Al-Khafji, which began on 29 January. As that battle began, Iraqi tanks entered Ras Al-Khafji with their turrets reversed, turning

their guns forward only at the moment action began between Iraqi and Coalition forces. While there was some media speculation that this was an act of perfidy, it was not; a reversed turret is not a recognized indication of surrender per se. Some tactical confusion may have occurred, since Coalition ground forces were operating under a defensive posture at that time, and were to engage Iraqi forces only upon clear indication of hostile intent, or some hostile act.

However, individual acts of perfidy did occur. On one occasion, Iraqi soldiers waved a white flag and laid down their weapons. When a Saudi Arabian patrol advanced to accept their surrender, it was fired upon by Iraqi forces hidden in buildings on either side of the street. During the same battle, an Iraqi officer approached Coalition forces with his hands in the air, indicating his intention to surrender. When near his would-be captors, he drew a concealed pistol from his boot, fired, and was killed during the combat that followed.

Necessarily, these incidents instilled in Coalition forces a greater sense of caution once the ground offensive began. However, there does not appear to have been any centrally directed Iraqi policy to carry out acts of perfidy. The fundamental principles of the law of war applied to Coalition and Iraqi forces throughout the war. The few incidents that did occur did not have a major effect on planning or executing Coalition military operations.

WAR CRIMES

Iraqi war crimes were widespread and premeditated. They included the taking of hostages, forcible deportation, torture and murder of civilians, in violation of the GC; looting of civilian property in violation of Hague IV; looting of cultural property, in violation of the 1954 Hague Cultural Property Convention; indiscriminate attacks in the launching of Scud missiles against cities rather than specific military objectives, in violation of customary international law; violation of Hague VIII in the method of using sea mines; and unnecessary destruction in violation of Article 23(g) of the Annex to Hague IV, as evidenced by the unlawful and wanton release of oil into the Persian Gulf and the unlawful and wanton sabotage of hundreds of Kuwaiti oil wells. The latter acts also constitute a violation of Article 53, GC and a Grave Breach under Article 147, GC.

As indicated earlier, the United States, Iraq, and the members of the Coalition that liberated Kuwait are parties to several law of war treaties. Each assumes good faith in its application and enforcement. Common Article 1 of the four 1949 Geneva Conventions for the Protection of War Victims requires that parties to those treaties "respect and ensure respect" for each of those treaties. The obligation to "respect and ensure respect" was binding upon all parties to the Persian Gulf War. It is an affirmative requirement to take all reasonable and necessary steps to bring individuals responsible for war crimes to justice. In a separate article common to the four 1949 Geneva Conventions, no nation has the authority to absolve itself or any other nation party to those treaties of any liability incurred by the commission of a Grave breach (Article 50, GWS; Article 51, GWS (Sea); Article 130, GPW; and Article 147, GC).

The United States has one of the more comprehensive law of war programs in existence. DOD Directive 5100.77 is the foundation for the US military law of war program. It contains four policies:

- The law of war and obligations of the US Government under that law . . . [will be] observed and enforced by the US Armed Forces.
- A program, designed to prevent violations of the law of war . . . [will be] implemented by the US Armed Forces.
- Alleged violations of the law of war, whether committed by or against US or enemy personnel, . . . [will be] promptly reported, thoroughly investigated, and, where appropriate, remedied by corrective action.
- Violations of the law of war alleged to have been committed by or against allied military or civilian personnel shall be reported through appropriate military command channels for ultimate transmission to appropriate agencies of allied governments.

The Joint Staff, each military department, the unified and specified commands, and subordinate commands have issued implementing directives. It is within this framework that war crimes investigations were conducted in the course of Operations Desert Shield and Desert Storm.

Each service has issued directives to implement DOD Directive 5100.77 with respect to the reporting and investigation of suspected violations of the law of war committed by or against its personnel. DOD Directive 5100.77 appoints the Army as the DOD Executive Agent for administering the DOD Law of War Program with respect to alleged violations of the law of war committed against US personnel. Army Chief of Staff Regulation 11-2 assigns to the Army Judge Advocate General (JAG) responsibility for investigating, collecting, collating, evaluating, and reporting in connection with war crimes alleged to have been committed against US personnel.

Collection of information on Iraqi war crimes began on 3 August, after media reports that US citizens in Kuwait had been taken hostage by Iraqi forces and forcibly deported to Iraq. As previously indicated, these acts constitute a Grave Breach of the GC. Collection of information continued as reports of other Iraqi war crimes were received.

Interagency meetings in late August established a process for informal coordination on war crimes issues, and ensured policy makers were kept informed. On 15 October, the President warned Iraq of its liability for war crimes. The United States was successful in incorporating into UNSC Resolution 674 (29 October) language regarding Iraq's accountability for its war crimes, in particular its potential liability for Grave Breaches of the GC, and inviting States to collect relevant information regarding Iraqi Grave Breaches and provide it to the Security Council.

Initial collection of information on Iraqi war crimes was carried out by the Army JAG's International Affairs Division and CENTCOM's Staff Judge Advocate in Riyadh. Although US hostages in Iraq were released in December, Iraqi abuses in Kuwait continued at such a pace that it became apparent a greater effort would be necessary with regard to collection of evidence and investigation of war crimes. The Army JAG accordingly recommended the mobilization of two Reserve Component Judge Advocate international law detachments. The 199th JAG Detachment was deployed to SWA, while the 208th JAG Detachment served within the Office of the JAG as the War Crimes Documentation Center. The former, in cooperation with the governments of Saudi Arabia and Kuwait, collected information on war crimes committed in Kuwait. The latter collected information from a variety of sources, including other agencies of the US Government, the media, and private sources.

Following Iraq's breach of international peace and security by its invasion of Kuwait, the UNSC, in Resolution 667, decided to take further concrete measures "in response to Iraq's continued violation of the [UN] Charter, of resolutions of the Council and of international law." Specific Iraqi war crimes include:

- The taking of Kuwaiti nationals as hostages, and their individual and mass forcible deportation to Iraq, in violation of Articles 34, 49 and 147, GC.
- The taking of third-country nationals in Kuwait as hostages, and their individual and mass forcible deportation to Iraq, in violation of Articles 34, 49, and 147, GC.
- The taking of third-country nationals in Iraq as hostages, and their individual and mass forcible transfer within Iraq, in violation of Articles 34, 35, and 147, GC.
- Compelling Kuwaiti and other foreign nationals to serve in the armed forces of Iraq, in violations of Articles 51 and 147, GC.
- Use of Kuwaiti and third country nationals as human shields in violation of Articles 28 and 38(4), GC.
- Inhumane treatment of Kuwaiti and third country civilians, to include rape and willful killing, in violation of Articles 27, 32 and 147, GC.
- As noted previously, possible violation of the Genocide Convention, through acts committed with the intent to destroy, in whole or in part, a national group (that is, the Kuwaiti people).
- The transfer of its own civilian population into occupied Kuwait, in violation of Article 49, GC.
- Torture and other inhumane treatment of POWs, in violation of Articles 13, 17, 22, 25, 26, 27, and 130, GPW.
- Using POWs as a shield to render certain points immune from military operations, in violation of Article 23, GPW.
- Unnecessary destruction of Kuwaiti private and public property, in violation of Article 23 (g), Annex to Hague IV.
- Pillage, in violation of Article 47, Annex to Hague IV.
- Illegal confiscation/inadequate safeguarding of Kuwaiti public property, in violation of Article 55, Annex to Hague IV, and Article 147, GC.
- Pillage of Kuwaiti civilian hospitals, in violation of Articles 55, 56, 57, and 147, GC.
- In its indiscriminate Scud missile attacks, unnecessary destruction of Saudi Arabian and Israeli property, in violation of Article 23 (g), Annex to Hague IV.
- In its intentional release of oil into the Persian

Gulf and its sabotage of the Al-Burqan and Ar-Rumaylah oil fields in Kuwait, unnecessary destruction in violation of Articles 23 (g) and 55, Annex to Hague IV, and Articles 53 and 147, GC.

- In its use of drifting naval contact mines and mines lacking devices for their self-neutralization in the event of their breaking loose from their moorings, in violation of Article 1, Hague VIII.

Iraq is a party to the 1925 Geneva Protocol, which prohibits use of CW/BW. Iraq, through its reservation at the time of ratification, pledged no first use of either CW or BW. Although Iraq did not use CW/BW in this war, it violated this treaty in its 1980-88 war against Iran. During the Persian Gulf War, Iraq threatened the use of CW/BW and deployed CW. Although prepared to do so, Iraqi forces did not use either of these weapons of mass destruction during this conflict, perhaps in part due to the success of Coalition efforts to destroy Iraqi CW/BW capabilities, Iraqi C^2, and Iraq's inability to move its weapons to forward sites.

Article 29, GC, states that "The Party to the conflict in whose hands protected persons may be, is responsible for the treatment accorded to them by its agents, irrespective of any individual responsibility which may be incurred." Similarly, Article 12, GPW, declares that "Prisoners of war are in the hands of the enemy Power, but not of the individuals or military units who have captured them. Irrespective of the individual responsibilities that may exist, the Detaining Power is responsible for the treatment given them." Responsibility for the treatment (and mistreatment) of civilian detainees and POW in Iraqi hands, clearly lay with the Government of Iraq and its senior officials.

Criminal responsibility for violations of the law of war rests with a commander, including the national leadership, if he (or she):

- Orders or permits the offense to be

committed, or
- Knew or should have known of the offense (s), had the means to prevent or halt them, and failed to do all which he was capable of doing to prevent the offenses or their recurrence.

In addition, the invasion of Kuwait was ordered by Saddam Hussein and is a crime against peace for which he, as well as the Ba'ath Party leadership and military high command, bear direct responsibility.

The crimes committed against Kuwaiti civilians and property, and against third party nationals, are offenses for which Saddam Hussein, officials of the Ba'ath Party, and his subordinates bear direct responsibility. However, the principal responsibility rests with Saddam Hussein. Saddam Hussein's C^2 of Iraqi military and security forces appeared to be total and unequivocal. There is substantial evidence that each act alleged was taken as a result of his orders, or was taken with his knowledge and approval, or was an act of which he should have known.

It is important to note that, with the possible exception of the Coalition's need to direct considerable effort toward the hunt for Iraqi Scud missiles, no Iraqi action leading to or resulting in a violation of the law of war gained Iraq any military advantages. This "negative gain from negative actions" in essence reinforces the validity of the law of war.

ENVIRONMENTAL TERRORISM

Between seven and nine million barrels of oil were set free in the Gulf by Iraqi action. Five hundred ninety oil well heads were damaged or destroyed. 508 were set on fire, and 82 were damaged so that oil was flowing freely from them.

There has been international examination of these acts. From 9 to 12 July 1991, the

Government of Canada, working with the UN Secretary General, hosted a conference of international experts in Ottawa to consider Iraq's wanton acts of destruction and their law of war implications. There was general agreement the actions constituted violations of the law of war, namely:

■ Article 23g of the Annex to Hague IV, which forbids the destruction of "enemy property, unless . . . imperatively demanded by the necessities of war;" and

■ Article 147 of the GC, which makes a Grave Breach the "extensive destruction . . . of property, not justified by military necessity and carried out unlawfully and wantonly."

The Ottawa Conference of Experts also noted UNSC Resolution 687 (3 April 1991), which reaffirmed that Iraq was liable under international law to compensate any environmental damage and the depletion of natural resources.

Other treaties the Conference of Experts considered were the ENMOD Convention and the 1977 Protocol I, articles 35 and 55 of which contain provisions for the protection of the environment. It was the general conclusion of the experts that the former did not apply to actions of the kinds perpetrated by Iraq, while the latter was not applicable during the Persian Gulf War for reasons previously stated.

Even had Protocol I been in force, there were questions as to whether the Iraqi actions would have violated its environmental provisions. During that treaty's negotiation, there was general agreement that one of its criteria for determining whether a violation had taken place ("long term") was measured in decades. It is not clear the damage Iraq caused, while severe in a layman's sense of the term, would meet the technical-legal use of that term in Protocol I. The prohibitions on damage to the environment contained in Protocol I were not intended to prohibit battlefield damage caused by

conventional operations and, in all likelihood, would not apply to Iraq's actions in the Persian Gulf War.

The Ottawa Conference of Experts did not conclude that new laws or treaties were required; rather, it was the belief of those present that respect for and enforcement of the existing law of war was of greatest importance.

It is not clear why Iraq released oil into the Persian Gulf. Conceivably, Iraq had hoped to interfere with Coalition naval operations in the Gulf, perhaps to impede expected amphibious operations. By threatening desalinization plants, Iraq also may have hoped to disrupt Coalition military operations and Saudi civilian life dependent on a steady flow of fresh water. As it turned out, the cooperative efforts of the Coalition members, the US Coast Guard, and the US National Oceanic and Atmospheric Administration resulted in the oil slick's having a negligible effect on the operations of Coalition naval forces.

Perversely, Iraq's actions did necessitate responsive Coalition operations to protect the environment that inflicted further damage on Kuwaiti property. Specifically, the flow from the Al-Ahmadi terminal was stopped by aerial destruction of vital equipment near the terminal.

As the first Kuwaiti oil wells were ignited by Iraqi forces, there was public speculation the fires and smoke were intended to impair Coalition forces' ability to conduct both air and ground operations, primarily by obscuring visual and electro-optical sensing devices. Review of Iraqi actions makes it clear the oil well destruction had no military purpose, but was simply punitive destruction at its worst. For example, oil well fires to create obscurants could have been accomplished simply through the opening of valves; instead, Iraqi forces set explosive charges on many wells to ensure the greatest possible destruction and maximum difficulty in stopping each fire. Likewise, the Ar-Rumaylah oil field spreads across the Iraq-Kuwait border. Had the purpose of the fires been to create an obscurant, oil wells in that field on each side of the border undoubtedly would have been set ablaze; Iraqi destruction was limited to oil wells on the Kuwaiti side only. As with the release of oil into the Persian Gulf, this aspect of Iraq's wanton destruction of Kuwaiti property had little effect on Coalition offensive combat operations. In fact, the oil well fires had a greater adverse effect on Iraqi military forces.

CONDUCT OF NEUTRAL NATIONS

Neutrality normally is based on a nation's proclamation of neutrality or assumption of a neutral posture with respect to a particular conflict. Iran and Jordan each issued proclamations of neutrality during the Persian Gulf crisis and, as described, refrained from active participation in the war. Other nations, such as Austria and Switzerland, enjoy relative degrees of international guarantees of their neutrality.

Neutrality in the Persian Gulf War was controlled in part by the 1907 Hague V Convention; but traditional concepts of neutral rights and duties are substantially modified when, as in this case, the United Nations authorizes collective action against an aggressor nation.

It was the US position during the Persian Gulf crisis that, regardless of assertions of neutrality, all nations were obligated to avoid hindrance of Coalition operations undertaken pursuant to, or in conjunction with, UNSC decisions, and to provide whatever assistance possible. By virtue of UNSC Resolution 678 (29 November), members were requested "to provide appropriate support for the actions undertaken" by nations pursuant to its authorization of use of all necessary means to uphold and implement prior

resolutions. The language of UNSC Resolution 678 is consistent with Articles 2(5), 2(6), 25, and 49 of the UN Charter. Article 2(5) states:

All Members shall give the United Nations every assistance in any action it takes in accordance with the present Charter, and shall refrain from giving assistance to any state against which the United Nations is taking preventive or enforcement action.

Article 2(6) provides:

The Organization shall ensure that states which are not Members of the United Nations act in accordance with these Principles so far as may be necessary for the maintenance of international peace and security.

Article 25 provides:

The Members of the United Nations agree to accept and carry out the decisions of the Security Council in accordance with the present Charter.

Article 49 declares:

The Members of the United Nations shall join in affording mutual assistance in carrying out the measures decided upon by the Security Council.

This section focuses on the conduct of Jordan, Iran, India and traditionally neutral European nations (primarily Austria and Switzerland) during the course of the hostilities, and the effect of Coalition maritime interceptions on neutral shipping.

UNSC Resolution 661, which called for an economic embargo of Iraq, pursuant to Article 41 of the UN Charter, obligated all member nations to refrain from aiding Iraq. The declarations of "neutrality" by Jordan and Iran were subordinate to their obligation as UN members to comply with UNSC resolutions. Although Jordan's attitude toward Iraq and the

Coalition appeared inconsistent with its UN obligations, mere sympathy for one belligerent does not constitute a violation of traditional neutral duties, nor even a rejection of the obligations imposed by the UNSC resolutions cited. Conduct is the issue.

There were reports that Jordan supplied materials (including munitions) to Iraq during Operations Desert Shield and Desert Storm. Furnishing supplies and munitions to a belligerent traditionally has been regarded as a violation of a neutral's obligations. In this case, it would have been an even more palpable contravention of Jordan's obligations — both because of the request of UNSC Resolution 678 that all States support those seeking to uphold and implement the relevant resolutions, and because the sanctions Resolution 661 established expressly prohibited the supply of war materials to Iraq.

As the US became aware of specific allegations of Jordanian failure to comply with UNSC sanctions, they were raised with the Government of Jordan. Some were without foundation; some were substantiated. Regarding the latter, the Government of Jordan acted to stop the actions and reassured the United States those instances had been the result of individual initiative rather than as a result of government policy. Such logistical assistance as Jordan may have provided Iraq did not substantially improve Iraq's ability to conduct operations, nor did it have an appreciable effect on Coalition forces' operational capabilities.

During actual hostilities, Saudi Arabia stopped pumping oil to Jordan; Jordan obtained petroleum from Iraq, taking delivery by truck. Although not a violation of a neutral's duties under traditional principles of international law, such purchases were inconsistent with UNSC Resolutions 661 and 678.

While the Jordanian importation of oil products from Iraq did not substantially affect Coalition military operations, additional steps were required by Coalition forces to protect Iraqi and Jordanian civilians from the risks of military operations. Jordan imported Iraqi oil by truck across roads in western Iraq during the day and night. These oil trucks were commingled with military and civilian vehicles. At night, some oil trucks were mistaken for mobile Scud launchers or other military vehicles; other trucks and civilian vehicles were struck incidental to attack of legitimate military targets.

This collateral damage and injury, which occurred despite previously described Coalition efforts to minimize damage to civilian objects and injury to noncombatant civilians, is attributable to Jordan's failure to ensure adherence to UNSC sanctions and to warn its nationals of the perils of travel on main supply routes in a combat zone. It also is attributable to mixing of Iraqi military vehicles and convoys with Jordanian civilian traffic traveling in Iraq. Coalition forces continued to take reasonable precautions to minimize collateral damage to civilian vehicles and incidental injury to noncombatant civilians. As a result, the ability to target Iraqi military vehicles and convoys, including mobile Scud missile launchers and support equipment, was impeded.

Iran's conduct during Operations Desert Shield and Desert Storm essentially was consistent with that expected of a neutral under traditional principles of international law, including Hague V. Immediately after the Operation Desert Storm air campaign began, many Iraqi civil and military aircraft began fleeing to Iran, presumably to avoid damage or destruction by Coalition air forces. Under Article 11 of Hague V and traditional law of war principles regarding neutral rights and obligations, when belligerent military aircraft land in a nation not party to a conflict, the neutral must intern the aircraft, aircrew, and accompanying military personnel for the duration of the war. Both Switzerland and Sweden took such actions in the course of World War II, for example, with respect to Allied and German aircraft and aircrews. Some civil (and possibly some military) transport aircraft may have returned to Iraq. With respect to tactical aircraft, however, it appears Iran complied with the traditional obligations of a neutral. US forces nonetheless remained alert to the possibility of a flanking attack by Iraqi aircraft operating from Iran.

Although the situation never arose, the United States advised Iran that, in light of UNSC Resolution 678, Iran would be obligated to return downed Coalition aircraft and aircrew, rather than intern them. This illustrates the modified nature of neutrality in these circumstances. It also was the US position that entry into Iranian (or Jordanian) airspace to rescue downed aviators would be consistent with its international obligations as a belligerent, particularly in light of Resolution 678.

On several occasions, Iran protested alleged entry of its airspace by Coalition aircraft or missiles. The United States expressed regret for any damage that may have occurred within Iranian territory by virtue of inadvertent entry into Iranian airspace. The US replies did not, however, address whether Iranian expectations of airspace inviolability were affected by UNSC Resolution 678.

Although military aircraft must gain permission to enter another State's airspace (except in distress), both Switzerland and Austria routinely granted such clearance for US military transport aircraft prior to the Iraqi invasion of Kuwait. Early in the Persian Gulf crisis, the United States approached the Governments of Austria and Switzerland, seeking permission for overflight of US military transport aircraft carrying equipment and personnel to SWA. Despite initial misgivings, based upon their traditional neutrality, each nation assented. That there was a reluctance to grant permission early in the crisis — that is, when the United States was not involved in the hostilities, and thus not legally a belligerent — demonstrates that the

view by these two States of neutrality may be more expansive than the traditional understanding of the role of neutrality in the law of war. At the same time, while Switzerland is not a UN member, its support for the US effort (through airspace clearances for US military aircraft) preceded UNSC Resolution 678.

Given their reluctance to permit pre-hostilities overflights, it was natural to expect that Switzerland and Austria would weigh very carefully any requests for overflights once offensive actions began, which each did. In light of the UNSC request that all States support the efforts of those acting to uphold and implement UNSC resolutions, each government decided that overflights by US military transport aircraft would not be inconsistent with its neutral obligations. Accordingly, permission for overflights was granted, easing logistical support for combat operations.

In contrast, overflight denial by the Government of India required Marine combat aviation assets in the Western Pacific to fly across the Pacific, the continental US, the Atlantic, and through Europe to reach SWA, substantially increasing the transit route. Air Force transport aircraft delivering ammunition to the theater of operations also were denied overflight permission.

UNSC Resolution 661 directed member states to prevent the import or transshipment of materials originating in Iraq or Kuwait, and further obligated member states to prevent imports to or exports from Iraq and Kuwait. In support of Resolution 661, on 16 August, the United States ordered its warships to intercept all ships believed to be proceeding to or from Iraq or Kuwait, and all vessels bound to or from ports of other nations carrying materials destined for or originating from Iraq or Kuwait. On 25 August, the Security Council adopted Resolution 665, which called upon UN members to enforce sanctions by means of a maritime interception operation. This contemplated intercepting so-called "neutral" shipping as well as that of non-neutral nations. These resolutions modified the obligation of neutral powers to remain impartial with regard to Coalition UN members.

The law of war regarding neutrality traditionally permits neutral nations to engage in non-war-related commerce with belligerent nations. During the Persian Gulf crisis, however, the Coalition Maritime Interception Force (MIF) was directed to prevent all goods (except medical supplies and humanitarian foodstuffs expressly authorized for Iraqi import by the UNSC Sanctions Committee) from leaving or entering Iraqi-controlled ports or Iraq, consistent with the relevant UNSC resolutions. The claim of neutral status by Iran and Jordan, or any of the traditional neutral nations, did not adversely affect the conduct of the Coalition's ability to carry out military operations against Iraq.

THE CONCEPT OF "SURRENDER" IN THE CONDUCT OF COMBAT OPERATIONS

The law of war obligates a party to a conflict to accept the surrender of enemy personnel and thereafter treat them in accordance with the provisions of the 1949 Geneva Conventions for the Protection of War Victims. Article 23(d) of Hague IV prohibits the denial of quarter, that is the refusal to accept an enemy's surrender, while other provisions in that treaty address the use of flags of truce and capitulation.

However, there is a gap in the law of war in defining precisely when surrender takes effect or how it may be accomplished in practical terms. Surrender involves an offer by the surrendering party (a unit or an individual soldier) and an ability to accept on the part of his opponent. The latter may not refuse an offer of surrender when communicated, but that communication must be made at a time when it can be received and properly acted upon — an attempt at surrender in the midst of a hard-fought battle is neither easily communicated nor

received. The issue is one of reasonableness.

A combatant force involved in an armed conflict is not obligated to offer its opponent an opportunity to surrender before carrying out an attack. To minimize Iraqi and Coalition casualties, however, the Coalition engaged in a major psychological operations campaign to encourage Iraqi soldiers to surrender before the Coalition ground offensive. Once that offensive began, the Coalition effort was to defeat Iraqi forces as quickly as possible to minimize the loss of Coalition lives. In the process, Coalition forces continued to accept legitimate Iraqi offers of surrender in a manner consistent with the law of war. The large number of Iraqi prisoners of war is evidence of Coalition compliance with its law of war obligations with regard to surrendering forces.

Situations arose in the course of Operation Desert Storm that have been questioned by some in the post-conflict environment. Two specific cases involve the Coalition's breach of the Iraqi defensive line and attack of Iraqi military forces leaving Kuwait City. Neither situation involved an offer of surrender by Iraqi forces, but it is necessary to discuss each in the context of the law of war concept of surrender.

As explained in Chapter VIII, rapid breach of the Iraqi defense in depth was crucial to the success of the Coalition ground campaign. When the ground campaign began, Iraq had not yet used its air force or extensive helicopter fleet in combat operations, the Iraqi Scud capability had not been eliminated, and most importantly, chemical warfare by Iraq remained a distinct possibility. It was uncertain whether the Coalition deception plan had worked or whether the Coalition effort had lost the element of surprise and there was also no definitive information about the strength and morale of the defending Iraqi soldiers. Because of these uncertainties, and the need to minimize loss of US and other Coalition lives, military necessity required that the assault through the forward

Iraqi defensive line be conducted with maximum speed and violence.

The VII Corps main effort was the initial breaching operation through Iraqi defensive fortifications. This crucial mission was assigned to the 1st Infantry Division (Mechanized). The Division's mission was to conduct a deliberate breach of the Iraqi defensive positions as quickly as possible to expand and secure the breach site, and to pass the 1st UK Armored Division through the lines to continue the attack against the Iraqi forces.

To accomplish the deliberate breaching operation, the 1st Infantry Division (Mechanized) moved forward and plowed through the berms and mine fields erected by the Iraqis. Many Iraqis surrendered during this phase of the attack and were taken prisoner. The division then assaulted the trenches containing other Iraqi soldiers. Once astride the trench lines, the division turned the plow blades of its tanks and combat earthmovers along the Iraqi defense line and, covered by fire from its M-2/-3 armored infantry fighting vehicles, began to fill in the trench line and its heavily bunkered, mutually supporting fighting positions.

In the process, many more Iraqi soldiers surrendered to division personnel; others died in the course of the attack and destruction or bulldozing of their defensive positions.

By nightfall, the division had breached the Iraqi defenses, consolidated its position, and prepared to pass the 1st UK Armoured Division through the lines. Hundreds of Iraqi soldiers had been taken prisoner; US casualties were extremely light.

The tactic used by the 1st Infantry Division (Mechanized) resulted in a number of Iraqi soldiers' dying in their defensive positions as those positions were bulldozed. Marine Corps breaching operations along its axis of attack into Kuwait used different, but also legally acceptable, techniques of assault by fire, bayonet, and the blasting of enemy defensive positions. Both tactics were entirely consistent with the law of war.

Tactics involving the use of armored vehicles against dug-in infantry forces have been common since the first use of armored vehicles in combat. The tactic of using armored vehicles to crush or bury enemy soldiers was briefly discussed in the course of the UN Conference on Certain Conventional Weapons, conducted in Geneva from 1978 to 1980 and attended by the United States and more than 100 other nations. It was left unregulated, however, as it was recognized by the participants to be a common long-standing tactic entirely consistent with the law of war.

In the case in point, military necessity required violent, rapid attack. Had the breaching operation stalled, the VII Corps main effort would have been delayed or, at worst, blunted. This would have had an adverse effect on the entire ground campaign, lengthening the time required to liberate Kuwait, and increasing overall Coalition casualties.

As first stated in US Army General Orders No. 100 (1863), otherwise known as the Lieber Code, military necessity "consists in the necessity of those measures which are indispensable for securing the ends of war, and which are lawful according to the modern law and usages of war...[It] admits of all direct destruction of life or limb of armed enemies." As developed by the practice of nations since that time, the law of war has placed restrictions on the application of force against enemy combatants in very few circumstances (e.g., the first use of chemical or biological weapons). None of these restrictions were at issue during the breaching operations during Operation Desert Storm.

The law of war principle complementary to

military necessity is that of unnecessary suffering (or superfluous injury). That principle does not preclude combat actions that otherwise are lawful, such as that used by the 1st Infantry Division (Mechanized).

In the course of the breaching operations, the Iraqi defenders were given the opportunity to surrender, as indicated by the large number of EPWs taken by the division. However, soldiers must make their intent to surrender clear and unequivocal, and do so rapidly. Fighting from fortified emplacements is not a manifestation of an intent to surrender, and a soldier who fights until the very last possible moment assumes certain risks. His opponent either may not see his surrender, may not recognize his actions as an attempt to surrender in the heat and confusion of battle, or may find it difficult (if not impossible) to halt an onrushing assault to accept a soldier's last-minute effort at surrender.

It was in this context that the breach of the Iraqi defense line occurred. The scenario Coalition forces faced and described herein illustrates the difficulty of defining or effecting "surrender." Nonetheless, the breaching tactics used by US Army and Marine Corps forces assigned this assault mission were entirely consistent with US law of war obligations.

In the early hours of 27 February, CENTCOM received a report that a concentration of vehicles was forming in Kuwait City. It was surmised that Iraqi forces were preparing to depart under the cover of darkness. CINCCENT was concerned about the redeployment of Iraqi forces in Kuwait City, fearing they could join with and provide reinforcements for Republican Guard units west of Kuwait City in an effort to stop the Coalition advance or otherwise endanger Coalition forces.

The concentration of Iraqi military personnel and vehicles, including tanks, invited attack. CINCCENT decided against attack of the Iraqi forces in Kuwait City, since it could lead to

substantial collateral damage to Kuwaiti civilian property and could cause surviving Iraqi units to decide to mount a defense from Kuwait City rather than depart. Iraqi units remaining in Kuwait City would cause the Coalition to engage in military operations in urban terrain, a form of fighting that is costly to attacker, defender, innocent civilians, and civilian objects.

The decision was made to permit Iraqi forces to leave Kuwait City and engage them in the unpopulated area to the north. Once departed, the Iraqi force was stopped by barricades of mines deployed across the highway in front of and behind the column. Air attacks on the trapped vehicles began about 0200. The following morning, CENTCOM leadership viewed the resulting damage. More than two hundred Iraqi tanks had been trapped and destroyed in the ambush, along with hundreds of other military vehicles and various forms of civilian transportation confiscated or seized by Iraqi forces for the redeployment. The vehicles in turn were full of property pillaged from Kuwaiti civilians: appliances, clothing, jewelry, compact disc players, tape recorders, and money, the last step in the Iraqi looting of Kuwait.

Throughout the ground campaign Coalition leaflets had warned Iraqi soldiers that their tanks and other vehicles were subject to attack, but that Iraqi soldiers would not be attacked if they abandoned their vehicles — yet another way in which the Coalition endeavored to minimize Iraqi casualties while encouraging their defection and/or surrender. When the convoy was stopped by the mining operations that blocked the Iraqi axis of advance, most Iraqi soldiers in the vehicles immediately abandoned their vehicles and fled into the desert to avoid attack.

In the aftermath of Operation Desert Storm, some questions were raised regarding this attack, apparently on the supposition that the Iraqi force was retreating. The attack was entirely consistent with military doctrine and the law of war. The law of war permits the attack of enemy combatants and enemy equipment at any time, wherever located, whether advancing, retreating, or standing still. Retreat does not prevent further attack. At the small-unit level, for example, once an objective has been seized and the position consolidated, an attacking force is trained to fire upon the retreating enemy to discourage or prevent a counterattack.

Attacks on retreating enemy forces have been common throughout history. Napoleon suffered some of his worst losses in his retreat from Russia, as did the German Wermacht more than a century later. It is recognized by military professionals that a retreating force remains dangerous. The 1st Marine Division and its 4,000 attached US Army forces and British

Royal Marines, in the famous 1950 march out of the Chosin Reservoir in North Korea, fighting outnumbered by a 4:1 margin, turned its "retreat" into a battle in which it defeated the 20th and 26th Chinese Armies trying to annihilate it, much as Xenophon and his "immortal 10,000" did as they fought their way through hostile Persian forces to the Black Sea in 401 BC.

In the case at hand, neither the composition, degree of unit cohesiveness, nor intent of the Iraqi military forces engaged was known at the time of the attack. At no time did any element within the formation offer to surrender. CENTCOM was under no law of war obligation to offer the Iraqi forces an opportunity to surrender before the attack.

OBSERVATIONS

Accomplishments

- DOD-mandated instruction and training in the law of war were reflected in US operations, which were in keeping with historic US adherence to the precepts of the law of war. Adherence to the law of war impeded neither Coalition planning nor execution; Iraqi violations of the law provided Iraq no advantage.

- CINCCENT conducted a theater campaign directed solely at military targets. As frequently noted during the conduct of the conflict, exceptional care was devoted to minimize collateral damage to civilian population and property.

- The special trust and confidence reposed in the professional capabilities of military commanders by the National Command Authorities permitted commanders at all levels to accomplish their respective missions in an unconstrained manner that simultaneously was consistent with the law of war.

- The willingness of commanders to seek legal advice at every stage of operational planning ensured US respect for the law of war throughout Operations Desert Shield and Desert Storm.

Issue

- A strategy should be developed to respond to Iraqi violations of the law of war, to make clear that a price will be paid for such violations, and to deter future violators.

Appendix P
RESPONSIBILITY SHARING

INTRODUCTION

After the decision to send US forces to Southwest Asia, allied and friendly nations from around the world became involved in confronting Iraqi aggression. Recognizing that confronting aggression is an international responsibility, wealthy and poor nations alike deployed thousands of land, sea and air forces. Particularly in Europe, but also in the Pacific and Indian Ocean areas, countries supported the deployment of US forces by granting transit and overflight rights and access to bases and facilities. Saudi Arabia and the other Gulf states opened their borders to receive these multinational deployments.

These traditional aspects of international cooperation — the contributions of forces, support of the deployment, and basing foreign forces? were among the invaluable and historic contributions of Coalition members around the world. (They are addressed separately in Appendix I.) Without them, it would have been extraordinarily difficult to halt and reverse Iraqi aggression. However, even with these multinational efforts, it was clear from the beginning that large and costly US deployments were essential. Recognizing this requirement and the additional fiscal and economic strains it could place on the nation, the Department of Defense (DOD) developed and shepherded through the interagency process a plan for a new form of international cooperation that became known as "responsibility sharing."

RESPONSIBILITY SHARING TO OFFSET US INCREMENTAL DEFENSE COSTS

The commitment of more than 500,000 US

"[The contributions of our allies] would rank, by a considerable margin, as the world's third largest defense budget.... Few would have imagined this level of foreign participation. There will no doubt be those who will focus attention on whether a particular country paid as much as it might have or as promptly, but these concerns — valid as they are — should not overshadow all that has been accomplished."

Paul Wolfowitz
Under Secretary of Defense (Policy)

troops and associated equipment in Operations Desert Shield and Desert Storm involved large US financial obligations. The United States made its force commitments without regard to whether Coalition and other countries would offset any of these costs. Nevertheless, in recognition of the shared responsibility of confronting Iraqi aggression, Coalition members made financial and other contributions of historic proportions to offset incremental defense costs.

Total US defense costs associated with Operations Desert Shield and Desert Storm consist of three elements:

- Costs associated with the investment in force structure used in Operations Desert Shield and Desert Storm;
- Baseline operating costs for that force structure; and,
- Incremental costs (costs that would not otherwise have been incurred) associated with deploying, operating, and supporting forces used in Operations Desert Shield and Desert Storm.

Through DOD's annual planning, programming,

and budget process, the United States already had determined that national security required undertaking the first two categories of costs. These expenses would have been borne even in the absence of Iraq's invasion of Kuwait. However, Coalition partners in Operations Desert Shield and Desert Storm recognized that one important area of shared responsibility in defeating Iraqi aggression was to help finance US incremental defense costs.

Total US incremental costs for Operations Desert Shield and Desert Storm are estimated at $61 billion. Without responsibility sharing, the US would have had to pay these costs either through a tax increase or through deficit spending, adding to the nations' fiscal difficulties. Instead, in 1990 and 1991, Coalition countries committed almost $54 billion to offset these costs. Roughly two-thirds of these commitments were from the Gulf States directly

confronted by Iraq, with the other one-third coming largely from Japan and Germany. The United States had received, by 11 March 1992, almost $53 billion toward these commitments (more than $47 billion in cash). This amount would rank, by a considerable margin, as the third largest defense budget in the world.

While these historic contributions clearly served a very important role in offsetting the significant financial costs of Operations Desert Shield and Desert Storm, they also served valuable political purposes. First, they enabled Japan and Germany to make major contributions to the Coalition within their domestic political and legal constraints. This has served as an important step in helping these two countries overcome obstacles they face in undertaking international political and security responsibilities commensurate with their economic stature. Second, allied contributions served as additional proof that Iraq was confronting not just the United States, but a worldwide, politically united Coalition, willing to pay the costs of confronting aggression. Finally, financial responsibility sharing gave the contributing countries a vested interest in working to achieve lasting peace among Middle East nations. The discussion below outlines some details involved in responsibility-sharing contributions to the United States in Operations Desert Shield and Desert Storm.

RESPONSIBILITY SHARING FOR CALENDAR YEAR 1990 — DESERT SHIELD COSTS

To encourage other nations to assume their fair share of responsibility for opposing the Iraqi aggression, the President sent two simultaneous missions abroad in early September. The first was headed by the Secretary of the Treasury and included the Deputy Secretary of State and the Under Secretary of Defense for Policy. This mission visited the United Kingdom, France, South Korea, and Japan to discuss Coalition contributions. The second mission was headed

Foreign Contributions Pledged in 1990 and 1991 to Offset US Desert Shield/Storm Costs

($ Millions)

Countries	Commitments	Receipts[1]		
		Cash	In-Kind	Total
Saudi Arabia	16,839	12,002	4,001	16,003
Kuwait [2]	16,057	16,015	43	16,058
UAE	4,088	3,870	218	4,088
Japan	10,012	9,437	571	10,008
Germany [3]	6,572	5,772	683	6,455
Korea	355	150	101	251
Other	29	7	22	29
Total	53,952	47,254	5,639	52,893

[1] Cash receipts are as of 11 March 1992. In-kind receipts are as of 29 February 1992.

[2] While the commitment has been met, Kuwait is continuing to provide assistance-in-kind to US forces remaining in country.

[3] Germany fulfilled its commitment. Germany made available for donations to US over 200 million dollars worth of ammunition, which the US chose not to accept due to the termination of the war.

by the Secretary of State and included the Deputy Secretary of the Treasury and the Deputy Secretary of Defense. This mission visited Saudi Arabia, the Kuwaiti Government in Exile, the United Arab Emirates (UAE), Egypt, Brussels (North Atlantic Treaty Organization and the European Community), Italy, and Germany to discuss contributions to the Coalition effort.

During and shortly after these Presidential missions, various commitments were made to help multinational forces in general and, in particular, to offset US incremental costs for Operation Desert Shield. As a result of these missions and other consultations with foreign nations through diplomatic channels, commitments to the United States came in three principal forms: cash, in-kind airlift and sealift, and in-kind material and equipment. In late September, as part of the Supplemental Appropriations for Operation Desert Shield in the Fiscal Year 1991 Continuing Resolution, Congress expanded the Secretary of Defense's authority to accept contributions of money and property from individuals, foreign governments and international organizations, and established the Defense Cooperation Account (DCA) to receive deposits of monetary contributions (Section 2608, Chapter 155, Title 10 USC). Use of DCA funds was made subject to Congressional authorization and appropriation. Funds deposited in the DCA were authorized to be invested in US securities with interest deposited in the DCA.

Specific commitments by the principal foreign government contributors toward Calendar Year (CY) 1990 US incremental Operation Desert Shield costs, were as follows:

- Saudi Arabia agreed to provide, at no cost to the United States, all fuel, food, water, local transportation, and facilities for all US forces in the Kingdom and surrounding waters. This host nation support (HNS) commitment was implemented through an arrangement

between the US Central Command (CENTCOM) J-4 and the Saudi Military and was titled "Implementation Plan for Logistics Support of the United States Forces in Defense of the Kingdom of Saudi Arabia." Later in CY 1990, Saudi Arabia also committed to reimburse the US for en route transportation costs associated with the second deployment of US forces to the region.

- Japan committed to provide $2 billion to the multinational forces, including about $1.7 billion for US incremental costs. This $1.7 billion was allocated among various forms: cash to cover US transportation expenses, in-kind material and equipment support, and in-kind airlift and sealift.

- Germany agreed to provide about $1 billion worth of support, including some cash for US transportation expenses, lift support, and equipment and other material from its defense stocks (the bulk of the commitment).

- Kuwait agreed to provide $2.5 billion in cash

Foreign Contributions Pledged in 1990 to Offset US Desert Shield/Storm Costs

(\$ Millions)

Countries	Commitments	Receipts[1]		
		Cash	In-Kind	Total
Saudi Arabia	3,339	1,621	882	2,503
Kuwait	2,506	2,500	6	2,506
UAE	1,000	870	130	1,000
Japan	1,680	1,105	571	1,676
Germany[2]	1,072	272	683	955
Korea	80	50	30	80
Other	3	0	3	3
Total	9,680	6,418	2,306	8,724

[1] Cash receipts are as of 11 March 1992. In-kind receipts are as of 29 February 1992. Total may not add due to rounding.

[2] Germany fulfilled its commitment. Germany made available for donations to US over 200 million dollars worth of ammunition, which the US chose not to accept due to the termination of the war.

and some limited in-kind lift.

- The UAE committed to provide $1 billion of support composed of cash and in-kind HNS for US forces in the UAE (e.g., fuel, water, facilities, food, local transportation).
- Korea agreed to provide $80 million for US incremental costs composed of $50 million in cash and $30 million worth of in-kind lift.
- Several other nations provided smaller, but nevertheless important contributions to offset US incremental costs from Operation Desert Shield. This included no-cost HNS by Oman, Bahrain, and Qatar, and in-kind sealift contributions from Denmark.

RESPONSIBILITY SHARING FOR CALENDAR YEAR 1991 DESERT SHIELD AND DESERT STORM INCREMENTAL COSTS

When it became apparent that Operation Desert Shield would extend into 1991, and with the growing likelihood of military conflict, consultations about additional 1991 commitments were conducted with the major foreign contributors to US incremental costs. Subsequently, the following commitments, were made for Operation Desert Shield and what followed as Operation Desert Storm:

- Saudi Arabia agreed to continue providing in-kind HNS and to pay $13.5 billion in cash (less the value of the in-kind HNS).
- The UAE committed to pay $3 billion in addition to in-kind HNS.
- Kuwait agreed to pay $13.5 billion in cash and to provide some in-kind lift.
- Japan committed to provide $9 billion to the multinational forces, of which $8.332 billion in cash was pledged to the United States.
- Germany provided $5.5 billion in cash.
- Korea committed $275 million to the United States, made up of cash, in-kind material, and in-kind airlift and sealift.

Contributions from other countries also increased during Operation Desert Storm. These included no-cost HNS by Oman, Bahrain, and Qatar, and cash and in-kind lift contributions from Italy, Denmark, Luxembourg, Belgium, and Norway.

IN-KIND CONTRIBUTIONS OTHER THAN HOST NATION SUPPORT

Aside from cash and HNS, several countries contributed airlift , sealift, and material and supplies on an in-kind basis. Transportation Command worked with foreign governments in conjunction with elements of the relevant unified commands (e.g., European Command in Europe and Pacific Command in Asia) and US embassies to match US requirements with the contributed lift capabilities. In the case of in-kind equipment, material, and supplies, CENTCOM worked through unified commands and US embassies to match requirements with foreign government offers. Each country's donation had different features in terms of coverage and scope of the in-kind assistance provided.

Foreign Contributions Pledged in 1991 to Offset US Desert Shield/Storm Costs

($ Millions)

Countries	Commitments	Receipts[1]		
		Cash	In-Kind	Total
Saudi Arabia	13,500	10,381	3,119	13,500
Kuwait [2]	13,551	13,515	37	13,552
UAE	3,088	3,000	88	3,088
Japan	8,332	8,332	0	8,332
Germany	5,500	5,500	0	5,500
Korea	275	100	71	171
Other	26	7	19	26
Total	44,272	40,836	3,334	44,169

[1] Cash receipts are as of 11 March 1992. In-kind receipts are as of 29 February 1992. Total may not add due to rounding.

[2] While the commitment has been met, Kuwait is continuing to provide assistance-in-kind to US forces remaining in country.

EQUIPMENT, MATERIAL, AND SUPPLIES

Contributions of in-kind equipment, material, and supplies varied by country. As noted above, these contributions were only accepted against established CENTCOM requirements . The following examples of Germany and Japan demonstrate the differing approaches to in-kind contributions:

- Germany provided almost $550 million worth of equipment and material from existing Defense Ministry stocks. CENTCOM worked with European Command and the US Embassy in Bonn to match these stocks with established requirements. Germany also provided 60 new "Fuchs" nuclear, biological, and chemical (NBC) detection vehicles worth $130 million. This contribution strengthened US abilities to operate in an NBC environment. Germany also provided heavy equipment transporters which helped fill a serious shortfall in US mobility capabilities. Other in-kind contributions included ammunition, chemical protective gear, many types of transport and materials handling equipment (MHE), bulldozers, and miscellaneous supplies (e.g., water cans, tents, medical equipment).
- Japan provided almost $500 million worth of in-kind equipment, material, and supplies. Unlike the German case, however, the Japanese contracted directly with suppliers for delivery of items. Japan worked closely with US forces Japan and CENTCOM to identify requirements. More than 80 percent

of the contracted equipment and supplies were made in the United States or provided by US suppliers. Examples of the types of in-kind support provided included vehicles, construction equipment and materials, and computer and communication equipment.

IN-KIND AIRLIFT AND SEALIFT

In-kind contributions of airlift and sealift gave the US important additional assets to help accomplish the tremendous operation of rapidly transporting US forces and equipment half-way around the world.

In-kind Donations of Airlift and Sealift
(As of 29 February 1992)

Countries	Donated Airlift		Donated Sealift	
	Missions	Value ($000)	Missions	Value ($000)
Korea	89	45,350	1,376	35,700
Japan	119	46,893	420	34,900
Kuwait	1	261	1,334	36,591
Denmark	0	0	*	11,557
Luxembourg	18	6,317	0	0
Italy	23	1,602	0	0
Total	250	100,423	3,130	118,748

*Denmark donated space available on ships.

OBSERVATIONS

Accomplishment

- The sharing of US incremental costs associated with Operations Desert Shield and Desert Storm represents an historic undertaking of unprecedented magnitude in modern times. It not only served to offset almost 90 percent of US incremental costs, but also was an important indicator of the scope and resolve of the multinational Coalition to defeat Iraqi aggression.

Shortcoming

- HNS agreements with Persian Gulf states were not in place initially to provide much needed support items. A concentrated effort was required to produce a November implementation plan for logistics support of the United States in defense of the Kingdom of Saudi Arabia.

Appendix Q

CHEMICAL AND BIOLOGICAL WARFARE DEFENSE

INTRODUCTION

The United States and many other nations have worked actively to eliminate chemical and biological weapons (CW/BW). An array of treaties and other international agreements has been erected to stem the proliferation of such capabilities and to ban their use. Despite these obstacles, Iraq entered the crisis with demonstrated CW and suspected BW capabilities. The inflamed rhetoric of Saddam Hussein implied a possible willingness to use such weapons to inflict mass casualties — perhaps to defeat the Coalition on the battlefield or perhaps to disrupt the will and cohesion of the Coalition. This appendix briefly surveys US defensive measures taken to counter a dangerous threat sustained by Iraq throughout the campaign, albeit one whose specific nature remained largely uncertain to the tactical forces engaged in the theater.

It is not known why Iraq did not use chemical or biological weapons. It is not known what logistic preparations were made to enable such use should it have been ordered by Saddam. Nor is it known what specific actions by the US and other members of the Coalition may have contributed to the Iraqi leader's decision not to use such capabilities. However, we assume US and other Coalition actions had a strong, restraining effect. Saddam already had demonstrated a willingness to inflict mass casualties with CW against enemy troops in the war with Iran, and against his own Kurdish population during and after that war. As evidenced by the Iraqi Scud attacks against civilian populations in Israel, Saudi Arabia, and other Gulf states, Saddam was

> "*O*ne of these days it's going to happen, we're going to have to fight a chemical war. When that happens, we need to be as ready as we can possibly be and we need to be as well trained."
>
> *General H. Norman Schwarzkopf*
> *Commander-in-Chief, Central Command*

willing to exceed the bounds of conventional warfare.

To provide the maximum possible deterrence against such contingencies, the US adopted a range of measures, all resting on the powerful military capabilities arrayed against Iraq. The initial phases of the air campaign opened with a sustained series of attacks on all known CW/BW sites. Stringent measures were taken to minimize the risks to surrounding populations from these strikes, which were intended to disrupt Iraq's capability to use its CW/BW arsenal. These strikes and other measures also were intended to signal Iraqi military leaders in the field that their own interests would not be served obeying orders from Saddam to use CW/BW. Authorization to use CW/BW was assessed to rest solely with the Iraqi leader. The emphasis on speed in planning for the ground offensive was in part driven by the doctrinal view that rapid, sustained maneuver could substantially counter the Iraqi tactic of canalizing attacks into obstacles to create static concentrations of enemy forces vulnerable to CW attack by massed artillery fires.

Repeated statements by senior US officials signaled unmistakably that the US viewed CW/BW use with utmost seriousness. As underscored in the new Regional Defense Strategy, such arsenals of ballistic missiles fitted with nuclear and biological weapons pose a genuinely "strategic" threat to the US and other nations. Countering that threat promises to be an increasingly demanding task in the future and will continue to require the full range of US deterrence and defense capabilities.

While the defensive capabilities of US and other Coalition forces improved rapidly, CW/BW defensive readiness at the outset of the crisis was quite low. Coalition forces embarked on extraordinary measures to correct these weaknesses, largely by building up the preparedness of individuals to protect themselves in the event of CW/BW attack. On balance, these gains did lead to a significant potential for US forces to operate on a contaminated battlefield. While the outcome would have been unaffected, the tempo of the Operation Desert Storm campaign could have been hindered had US troops been forced to remain fully protected by masks and suits. Temperatures during Operation Desert Storm were comparatively cool; data indicate that risks of heat exhaustion would have been sharply higher in the summer, making protracted use of personal protective gear impractical. Studies have also shown that protective equipment dramatically impedes crew performance. The masks hinder communications, and the suits impair the ability to operate equipment. High-speed combat requiring close coordination between crews manning complex systems becomes quite difficult.

THE IRAQI THREAT

Iraq had developed a substantial CW capability including research and development facilities; stockpiles of CW munitions; a variety of delivery systems; and the doctrine and training to employ integrated CW and conventional fires effectively on the battlefield. Iraq was the first nation to use nerve agents on the battlefield — attacking unprepared Iranian troops in 1984. By 1990, Iraq had the largest CW agent production capability in the Third World, annually producing thousands of tons of blister and nerve agents. By the invasion, Iraq had developed BW agents, most likely botulinum toxin and anthrax bacteria. In addition to surface-to-surface ballistic missile warheads, Iraqi delivery means for CW/BW included aerial bombs, artillery shells, rockets, and aircraft-mounted spray tanks.

In contrast to the reasonably comprehensive appreciation of Iraqi CW capabilities and doctrine, intelligence assessments of the BW threat were much more tenuous. (A more detailed discussion of Iraqi military capabilities is in Chapter I.)

COALITION CW/BW DEFENSE MEASURES

CW/BW Defense Force Structure

Deployment of CW/BW defense forces to the theater helped develop a defensive posture. The first units deployed included two Army chemical battalion headquarters; seven heavy decontamination companies; seven dual-purpose (decontamination and smoke generation) companies; four nuclear, biological, and chemical (NBC) reconnaissance platoons; and several CW defense staff augmentation teams. To support units with these limited assets, decontamination areas of responsibility were established. Units deploying in November, following the President's decision to augment Central Command (CENTCOM) forces, included two Army chemical battalion headquarters, five heavy decontamination companies, three smoke generation companies, five dual-purpose companies, and additional staff augmentation teams. The total CW/BW defense force structure included 45 units with 6,028 soldiers, and more than 450 vehicles for reconnaissance, detection, decontamination and smoke generation.

CW/BW Defense Training

During Operation Desert Shield, CW/BW defense training was conducted aggressively at every echelon, from individual survival skills to large scale unit sustainment operations. Individual training began with intensive common task and mask confidence exercises. With the immediacy of the Iraqi threat, proficiency in common individual tasks improved, and the focus shifted to collective unit CW/BW defense survival tasks. The Army Component, Central Command (ARCENT) conducted large scale unit decontamination exercises, mass chemical agent casualty exercises, and command post exercises, which included the warning and reporting system. The Navy Component, Central Command (NAVCENT) conducted chemical casualty handling and equipment decontamination training during shipboard operations and at port facilities. The Air Force Component, Central Command (CENTAF) tested disaster preparedness plans for airfield and equipment decontamination. The Marine Corps Component, Central Command (MARCENT) conducted division-wide decontamination exercises to assess the effects of a large scale CW/BW attack and the ability to defend against it. Special Operations Forces (SOF) conducted intensive training and were the backbone for the conduct of CW/BW defense training for non-US Coalition forces. SOF training teams, CENTCOM mobile training teams, and component staffs improved the Coalition forces' CW/BW defense and support capabilities.

The CW/BW threat prompted immediate and comprehensive medical assistance, technology development, and training. More than 1,500 physicians, nurses, and physician assistants were trained in specialized casualty care by the Army Medical Research Institute of Chemical Defense. The Defense Nuclear Agency's (DNA) Armed Forces Radiobiology Research Institute provided crucial information on biological organisms in desert soil, analyzed the Saudi Arabian water supply for possible contamination, and provided treatment protocols (using new biotechnology agents, for CW/BW agent exposure. The Navy Medical Unit Cairo's laboratory provided analysis and samples of regional organisms and infections.

These CW/BW defense training experiences validated the need for realistic, mission-oriented training, including operating with actual CW/BW defense equipment. Training facilities, such as the Army's Chemical Decontamination Training Facility at Fort McClellan,AL, were vital in giving training personnel confidence in their protective equipment. In turn, these trainers were able to train their own unit personnel better in the use of CW/BW defense protective equipment during preparations for Operation Desert Storm.

CW/BW DEFENSE EQUIPMENT

The systems supporting CW/BW defense are designed to protect against the effects of chemical or biological agents, so forces can survive and continue the mission. These systems perform detection, identification and warning, individual and collective protection, and decontamination of personnel and equipment.

Detection, Identification and Warning Systems

Detectors and alarms are used at the unit level to provide near-real-time detection and warning of the presence of chemical and/or biological agents. Near-real-time detection and warning is important:

- To warn forces adjacent to and downwind of attacks;
- To allow protective measures to be taken to limit dose;
- To initiate therapy early;
- To alert the casualty handling system; and
- To allow units to communicate the "all clear" signal.

Most units deployed to Southwest Asia (SWA) with standard CW detection equipment. Such equipment included the M256 chemical detector kits, and the M8A1 automatic chemical agent alarms. A few newly developed detection systems were fielded for Operations Desert Shield and Desert Storm without benefit of previous field experience. In many cases, this equipment provided unique capabilities never before available in the field, but also presented difficulties since the systems were unfamiliar, were not in final military configurations, or were serviced by special civilian support personnel.

More than 1,300 chemical agent monitors (CAM) were deployed to the theater. Army and

Marine Corps after action reports cited good results with CAMs when the system was used properly to check personnel and equipment for contamination. (The system often was used improperly as a continuous monitor and alarm.) However, it could not detect both nerve and blister agents simultaneously. False alarms reportedly were caused from exposure to certain petroleum products and red fuming nitric acid (a Scud missile fuel oxidizer). Supplies in theater were not adequate to support unit requirements down to the company level.

Ten developmental XM-21 remote sensing chemical agent alarms were fielded by the end of December. The early fielding of five XM-21s with MARCENT, and five with ARCENT, represented the first land-based, stand-off remote chemical detection capability for US forces. Operator surveys indicated the system was easy to operate, and gave few false alarms. Stand-off detection capability provided earlier warning than point detectors.

To improve CW/BW warning and reporting,

THE FOX NBC RECONNAISSANCE VEHICLE

The Fox is a six-wheeled, amphibious, armored vehicle equipped with sensors that detect and identify all known chemical warfare agents. The Fox's four man crew can detect, sample, and analyze surface and air contamination on the move from the safety of the vehicle. The system can conduct NBC reconnaissance missions rapidly across wide expanses of terrain, with high automotive reliability.

DNA rapidly developed the Automated NBC Information System which linked computer support in the United States to forces in the field. This system provided greater identification of potential hazard areas by drawing map overlay contours of different dosage intensity according to specific attack data from the field in order to feed back to the combat commander a more definitive prediction of the probable extent of serious contamination. US forces used this system in more than 600 tests and exercises.

The most effective contamination detection system fielded during Operations Desert Shield and Desert Storm was the German-donated Fuchs (Fox) NBC reconnaissance vehicle. Fielding of the vehicle and training of the crews began in August. Units had just three weeks of training at the German NBC School at Sonthofen or the Army Chemical School at Fort McClellan. Fully trained NBC reconnaissance platoons using Fox vehicles were assigned to ARCENT and MARCENT before the ground offensive started. (British units were also provided with Fuchs systems.) Although repair part shortages existed initially, contractor maintenance kept the vehicles operational. However, more vehicles were needed to meet operational requirements.

Individual Protective Clothing and Equipment

All CW/BW individual defense equipment and clothing was used extensively both in training exercises during the buildup phase and during the offensive part of the conflict. Personnel frequently had to maintain a high level of mission-oriented protective posture (MOPP) as a precaution against Iraqi CW/BW attacks. (MOPP is a doctrinal process where increasing amounts of protective clothing are worn to provide increasing levels of protection, which a commander can change to match the climate, work rate, or threat.)

Individual protective clothing and equipment consists of protective masks, boots, gloves, battle dress overgarments, agent antidote injectors, pyridostigmine bromide tablets (for nerve agent pretreatment), convulsant antidote for nerve agent (CANA), and personal decontamination kits. The CANA provided a capability for preventing or reducing convulsions and resultant brain damage caused by nerve agents. This system was fielded to complement atropine and 2-pam chloride autoinjectors in the nerve agent antidote kits, and pyridostigmine bromide tablets. Protective clothing is worn in various combinations according to the MOPP level. During Operation Desert Shield, extensive training was conducted to acclimatize personnel to the stress the protective gear imposes, so the protective equipment's burden would not unduly slow the pace of offensive operations. Many units donned chemical protective clothing at the start of Operation Desert Storm and continued to wear some items throughout the ground offensive.

Interviews generally indicate soldiers were confident their protective clothing and equipment provided adequate protection. Adding to this confidence was pre-deployment testing of protective masks. The Marine Corps tasked its only US test site to test 450 masks a day, which resulted in a requirement to establish new test sites at Camp Lejeune, NC; Camp Pendleton, CA; and Camp Butler, Okinawa. Similarly, the Army trained deploying chemical specialists in a realistic environment at the Chemical Decontamination Training Facility. The Army also deployed specialized teams equipped with mask leakage detection devices to ensure adequate fits. Individuals with hard-to-fit faces received new M40 protective masks to ensure adequate protection.

Protective mask shortcomings were reported in availability, durability, and suitability. The Marines reported high failure rates during M17 protective mask testing; reasons included poor crimps around the voicemitter, bent drinking tube levers, and outlet valve deterioration. The Marines also reported the shelf lives of many M132A2 replacement filters drawn from Maritime Prepositioning Squadron (MPS) ships had expired and the procedure used to extend the shelf lives was too time consuming. Army surveys cited the mask as uncomfortable for prolonged wear and reported the mask carriers deteriorated because of the abrasive effects of sand. In general, all masks received some criticism for limiting or distorting vision, and the inability to change filters and or eat while in a potentially contaminated environment. Atropine autoinjectors reportedly did not hold up well, breaking or discharging while stored in the mask carrier.

The battle dress overgarment suits, designed primarily for use in a European environment, provide protection against liquid agents, and are more durable than other types of suits. However, this durability and protection is achieved at the expense of greater heat stress imposed on the individual. During Operations Desert Shield and Storm, personnel criticized boots and gloves because of difficulty in performing detailed tasks, and of excessive perspiration. The Marines also reported some overgarments drawn from MPS supplies were damaged by heat or petroleum while in storage.

The Air Force and Marine Corps procured lightweight aircrew and ground personnel CW/BW protective overgarments made of a German-designed material, but these were not fielded before the cessation of hostilities. The Marines also used the British Mark IV protective suit. Initially, operating forces preferred this lightweight suit, but it reportedly lost favor with troops because of its poor durability and protection. The Army is assessing options to field lighter protective clothing for certain missions. The Air Force fielded a multi-man intermittent cooling system for use by ground crews on flight lines. This system included standard flight line air conditioners with an air distribution system hooked up to air cooled vests, to help keep body temperatures down.

Collective Protective Systems (Vehicles and Shelters)

CW/BW collective protection systems were insufficient. Armored vehicles with no collective protection, overpressure, and cooling systems are particularly susceptible in a CW/BW environment in hot climates. The Army took a major step to improve its CW/BW defense readiness posture with its M1A1 swap out program. The newer M1A1s, which have overpressure and cooling systems, can operate in a CW/BW environment with less crew stress. However, during the conflict, significant numbers of combat vehicles had only air-blown mask CW/BW protection with no cooling or overpressure. Troop comments were favorable for systems that provided environmental control for the crew.

Decontamination Equipment

Decontamination equipment is issued at both the personal and unit level, and includes M258A1 individual decontamination kits for removing contamination from clothing and skin; small sprayers, such as the M11 or M13 decontamination apparatus, for decontamination of vehicles and weapons; and the M12A1 power driven decontamination apparatus mounted on a 5-ton truck (available at the chemical defense unit level). The lighter and more transportable M17 lightweight decontamination system also supported ARCENT, MARCENT, and CENTAF. Decontamination equipment was not used during combat operations, but received extensive training use. Adequate supply of water for decontamination operations was a major problem in the desert and there also was a shortage of potable water trailers. Operating forces cited the poor reliability of the older M12A1 system and the newer M17 system. The M12A1 and M17 systems also were criticized for insufficient water pressure and inadequate availability of spare parts. During extended use of the M17 system, high mission failure rates were reported. These water-based decontamination systems, designed for the European theater, were inadequate for desert operations.

LOGISTICS ASPECTS OF CW/BW DEFENSE

Overgarments initially were in short supply, especially in the desert camouflage pattern. Consumption of chemical protective clothing exceeded expectations, causing a drawdown of worldwide theater war reserves stocks. The Army transferred more than 1.1 million overgarments from worldwide theater reserve stocks to augment SWA stock levels. Production of new overgarments was accelerated and almost 300,000 were issued from Defense Logistics Agency stocks by mid-February. In theater, distribution of bulky, high demand items like chemical protective clothing required extensive supply management to satisfy requirements.

High temperatures during the first months of Operation Desert Shield shortened detector battery life considerably. A training battery pack using inexpensive flashlight batteries was fielded on short notice to conserve CAM batteries for combat operations. The harsh desert environment made it necessary to change filters frequently on air intakes of chemical alarms and monitors, as well as on collective protection systems of combat vehicles, vans, and shelters. The industrial base for consumable chemical defense items was pressed to keep pace with the drawdown of war reserve stocks. As a result of experience in SWA, stock levels and resupply procedures are being reconsidered for high demand CW defense items.

The Joint Services Coordination Committee (JSCC) for chemical defense equipment (CDE), a unique joint logistics management initiative, was established, which substantially improved CW/BW defense readiness. The organization effectively managed parts of the industrial base as well as orchestrated the exchange of CDE among the Services and foreign military sales. For example, the Army exchanged protective masks and other CW/BW defense equipment for 1,004 Marine Corps chemical agent alarms to support Army units in SWA. The JSCC was instrumental in ensuring that even non-DOD US civilians living in the region were provided with adequate individual protective equipment. The United States also requested foreign assistance when required. For example, under an American, British, Canadian, Australian Armies Reciprocal Use of Materials Loan, the Canadian government provided 500 CAMs to the United States. More than $250 million of worldwide theater reserve CDE assets were drawn upon.

SUMMARY

An effective CW/BW defense builds confidence in planning and executing operations and is vital to survival in CW and BW environments. US personnel, after intensive preparation in theater, were well trained to conduct sustained combat operations in a CW/BW threat environment, although some defensive equipment deficiencies persisted. Overall, commanders and troops had confidence in the ability to survive CW/BW attacks and continue operations. Iraq had the capability and the experience to use CW, and the capability to use BW, but did not during the Persian Gulf conflict. Although the Coalition's CW/BW defense was not truly tested in combat, many elements of an effective CW/BW defense, including a particularly energetic personal protection readiness program, clearly contributed to the overall deterrent and, importantly, to the ability of the Coalition to press ahead with a bold, offensive strategy.

OBSERVATIONS

Accomplishments

- Coalition forces rapidly raised the state of individual CW/BW defensive readiness.

- Realistic training received emphasis and improved the CW/BW defense readiness posture.

- CW/BW defense equipment fielding initiatives, involving developmental and new items, improved the overall CW/BW defense posture.

- German-donated NBC reconnaissance vehicles were integrated rapidly into Coalition units before the ground offensive started. Users judged this system to be outstanding.

- Establishment of the JSCC for CDE improved CW/BW defense equipment readiness.

Shortcomings

- Chemical protective suits were not optimal for wear in the desert during the summer. Shortcomings were reported in availability, durability, and suitability.

- CW/BW collective protection systems were inadequate. Installation of CW/BW collective protection and cooling systems into combat vehicles was inadequate.

Issues

- Lightweight CW/BW protective clothing and defensive equipment is required, especially for desert climates.

- Integration of CW/BW protection and cooling systems into combat vehicles, and procurement of stand-alone transportable collective protective shelters are required for effective operations in a CW/BW environment.

- BW defense should be emphasized more fully in DOD programs. Inadequacies exist in detectors, vaccines, and protective equipment.

- To ensure effective contamination avoidance on future battlefields, additional NBC reconnaissance vehicles are needed and stand-off chemical and biological detection is required.

- Efforts to replace the water-based decontamination systems should continue.

- Continued force modernization in individual and collective protection, medical support, detection, identification and warning, and decontamination systems are required to ensure force survivability and mission accomplishment under CW/BW battlefield conditions.

Appendix R

ROLE OF WOMEN IN THE THEATER OF OPERATIONS

INTRODUCTION

Department of Defense (DOD) women played a vital role in the theater of operations. By late February, more than 37,000 military women were in the Persian Gulf, making up approximately 6.8 percent of US forces. By Service, there were approximately 26,000 Army, 3,700 Navy, 2,200 Marine, and 5,300 Air Force (USAF) women deployed. Women served in almost all of the hundreds of occupations open to them; as a matter of law and policy, women were excluded from certain specific combat military occupational specialties.

JOB FUNCTIONS OF WOMEN DURING DESERT SHIELD/STORM

Women were administrators, air traffic controllers, logisticians, engineer equipment mechanics, ammunition technicians, ordnance specialists, communicators, radio operators, drivers, law enforcement specialists and guards. Many women truck drivers hauled supplies and equipment into Kuwait. Some brought enemy prisoners of war back to holding facilities. Many flew helicopters and reconnaissance aircraft. Still others served on hospital, supply, oiler and ammunition ships. Others served as public affairs officers and chaplains. Several women commanded brigade, battalion, company, and platoon size units in the combat support and combat service support areas. They endured the same hardships under the same harsh conditions as their male counterparts. The deployment of women was highly successful. Women performed admirably

"They endured the same living conditions, duties, and responsibilities . . . . They performed professionally and without friction or special consideration."

US Marine Officer

and without substantial friction or special considerations.

DEPLOYMENT OF WOMEN TO COMBAT ZONES

Although women did not serve in units whose mission involved direct combat with the enemy, some women were subjected to combat. Five Army women were killed in action and 21 wounded in action. Two women were taken as Prisoners of War (POW). All casualties were the result of indirect causes, i.e., Scud attack, helicopter crash, or mines. One woman Marine driving a truck struck a mine in Kuwait, receiving no injuries. Four Marine women qualified for, and received, the Combat Action Ribbon, having been engaged by, and returned fire against, bypassed Iraqi troops.

Because media attention was afforded to the relatively few cases in which women faced combat conditions, the public perception of the role of women in the Gulf War has tended to be skewed. Army and Marine women served in combat support and service support units ashore. Navy women served on hospital, supply, oiler, and ammunition ships afloat. Ashore, they served in construction battalions, fleet hospitals, and air reconnaissance squadrons, as well as in many support billets. No Navy women saw combat, either directly or indirectly. USAF women served in support billets as well as in tanker, transport, and medical evacuation aircraft. All USAF C-130 squadrons in theater had women maintenance officers. No USAF women saw direct combat.

The National Defense Authorization Act for FY 1992 and 1993 repealed the statutory limitations on the assignment of women to aircraft flying combat missions. The Act also established a Presidential Commission on Assignment of Women in the Armed Forces. The Commission is intended to assess laws and policies restricting the assignment of women service members. The law requires the President to transmit the Commission's report to Congress by 15 December 1992. DOD fully supports the commission. Several other related DOD study efforts also are examining the experience of women service members in the Persian Gulf.

The Army is conducting studies in two categories: "soldier human factors research" during Operations Desert Shield and Desert Storm, and "family factors research" focusing on post Operation Desert Storm family issues. The Navy is studying the issue of women serving in a combat environment. Researchers have surveyed units in the Persian Gulf and are analyzing their data.

DOD is working with the General Accounting Office on a more extensive study to analyze the role of military women in the Persian Gulf. This study will examine issues such as the impact of women on deployment and field operations; women's role in the deployed units; unit operations issues, such as unit cohesion/bonding; and ground deployment issues, such as hygiene. Service historians also have been asked to document contributions made by women in the Persian Gulf.

Data will document the overall number of women who deployed, the skills of those women, the number of single parents and married military couples, and data comparisons with males on the numbers and types of separations from the military. These analyses and assessments will serve as the basis for further evaluation of current policies concerning women in the military. Emerging results of analyses conducted on non-deployable personnel suggest the non-deployability percentages for female personnel were somewhat higher than the percentage for male personnel. Pregnancy accounted for the largest difference in non-deployable percentages. Other differences are not as easily identified and require additional analysis. While non-deployability did not affect the overall conduct of the operation, it is nevertheless an issue that will require further study for future deployment criteria for women.

Several observations have emerged. There were instances of misunderstanding concerning the application of combat restrictions. DOD policies are not designed to shield women from all hostilities, but are designed to limit their exposure to a level which is less than that in direct combat. Direct combat means closing with the enemy by fire, maneuver, or shock effect to destroy or capture, or while repelling assault by fire, close combat, or counterattack. The Risk Rule is used to determine if a non-direct combat position should be closed to women. Noncombat units can be closed to women on grounds of risk of exposure to direct combat, hostile fire, or capture, if the type, degree, and duration of risk is equal to or greater than that experienced by associated combat units (of similar land, sea, or air type) in the same theater of operation.

Finally, the substantial social and cultural differences involving the role of women in Saudi Arabia have received some attention. While there are marked differences, they did not affect the military's role in Operations Desert Shield and Desert Storm. The mission was not one of changing cultural values and beliefs. In fact, the Saudi government ensured US military members, both female and male, were not restricted in the performance of their military duties, even if such duties might counter normal Saudi culture. This was best demonstrated by Saudi acceptance of American women driving military vehicles. However, outside of military duties, Service members were obliged to respect the host country's cultural distinctions of the host country. This courtesy was extended within Saudi Arabia, just as it is within all other countries where US military members serve.

Although US forces had a military, not a civilian mission, this does not mean their presence did not have an effect on Saudi culture. US military men and women deployed to Saudi Arabia were selected based on mission need, with no distinction made for gender, other than application of restrictions contained in US combat exclusion laws and policies. As previously mentioned, this meant US women performed a wide range of critical missions. This fact alone clearly sets a visible example of US principles.

OBSERVATIONS

Accomplishments

- Women were fully integrated into their assigned units.

- Women performed vital roles, under stress, and performed well.

- Current laws and policies were followed.

Issues

- The media and public interest was centered on female casualties and POW.

- In some respects, deployment criteria for women differ among Services. In a few cases, these differences and different interpretations by local commands caused concerns.

Appendix S

MEDIA POLICY

INTRODUCTION

As in all previous American conflicts, the rules for news coverage of Operations Desert Shield and Desert Storm were driven by the need to balance the requirements of operational security against the public's right to know about ongoing military operations. Department of Defense (DOD) policy calls for making available "timely and accurate information so the public, Congress, and the news media may assess and understand the facts about national security and defense strategy," withholding information "only when disclosure would adversely affect national security or threaten the safety or privacy of the men and women of the Armed Forces." The news media feel compelled to report as much information about current newsworthy events as possible.

The challenge to provide full news coverage of Operations Desert Shield and Desert Storm was complicated by several factors:

- The host nation, closed to western media before the operation began, was reluctant to permit reporters to enter the country and was concerned about reporting of cultural sensitivities.
- More than 1,600 news media representatives eventually massed in Saudi Arabia to report about the war.
- The combat actions of Operation Desert Storm used high technology, involved long-range weapons, and occurred on and over a distant, vast, open desert and from ships operating in adjacent bodies of water.
- The combined armor and airmobile attacks

> *"The first essential in military operations is that no information of value shall be given to the enemy. The first essential in newspaper work and broadcasting is wide-open publicity. It is your job and mine to try to reconcile those sometimes diverse considerations."*
>
> *General Dwight D. Eisenhower, 1944*

and drives through Kuwait and Iraq were rapid.
- This was the first major American war to be covered by news media able to broadcast reports instantaneously to the world, including the enemy.

From the beginning of the crisis, DOD worked closely with Central Command (CENTCOM), the Joint Staff (JS), the Services, and news media organizations to balance the media's needs with the military's ability to support them and its responsibility to preserve US combat forces' operational security. The goal was to provide as much information as possible to the American people without endangering the lives or missions of US military personnel.

When the USS Independence (CV 62) battle group arrived in the Gulf of Oman on 7 August and the first Air Force (USAF) F-15s landed on sovereign Saudi territory on 8 August, approximately one week after Iraq invaded Kuwait, there were no western reporters in the Kingdom. The US government urged the Saudi government to begin granting visas to US news organizations, so reporters could cover the US military's arrival. On 10 August, the Secretary of Defense called the Saudi ambassador to inquire about the progress for issuing visas. The ambassador said the Saudis were studying the question but agreed in the meantime to accept a pool of US reporters if the US military would arrange their transportation.

PUBLIC AFFAIRS OPERATIONS

National Media Pool

The DOD National Media Pool, formed in 1985, was alerted the same day. The pool enables reporters to cover the earliest possible US military action in a remote area where there is no other presence of the American news media, while still protecting the element of surprise — an essential part of operational security. Starting with those initial 17 press pool members — representing Associated Press, United Press International, Reuters, Cable News Network, National Public Radio, Time, Scripps-Howard, the Los Angeles Times, and the Milwaukee Journal — the number of reporters, editors, photographers, producers, and technicians grew to nearly 800 by December. Except during the first two weeks of the pool, those reporters all filed their stories independently, directly to their own news organizations.

Joint Information Bureau

To facilitate media coverage of US forces in Saudi Arabia, CENTCOM established a Joint Information Bureau (JIB) in Dhahran and, later, another in Riyadh. Saudi Ministry of Information representatives also were located with the JIB in Dhahran, which let visiting media register with the Saudi government and the JIB at one location. The JIB coordinated with reporters and worked to arrange visits to units the reporters desired to cover. The Saudi government required that a US official escort reporters visiting Saudi bases. The CENTCOM Public Affairs Office (PAO) assumed this responsibility and provided escorts to facilitate coverage on Saudi bases and to US units on the ground and at sea and throughout the theater.

Media Concerns

One of the concerns of news organizations in the Pentagon press corps was that they did not have enough staff in the Persian Gulf to cover hostilities. Since they did not know how the Saudi government would respond to their requests for more visas, and since they couldn't predict what restrictions might be imposed on commercial air traffic in the event of a war, they asked the Pentagon to provide a military plane to take in a group of reporters to act as journalistic reinforcements. A USAF C-141 cargo plane left Andrews Air Force Base, MD, on 17 January, the morning after the bombing began, with 126 news media personnel on board. That plane left as offensive operations began, during the most intensive airlift since the Berlin blockade. The fact that senior military commanders dedicated one cargo airplane to the job of transporting another 126 journalists to Saudi Arabia demonstrated the military's commitment to take reporters to the scene of the action so they could get the story out to the American people.

The Pentagon worked closely with the CENTCOM PAO to determine how best to facilitate coverage of potential hostilities in the Persian Gulf. After several meetings at the Pentagon with military and civilian public affairs officials experienced in previous conflicts, and Pentagon press corps bureau chiefs, the Department published on 14 January a one-page list of ground rules and a one-page list of guidelines for the news media covering operations in the Gulf.

Media On The Battlefield

As early as October, it appeared hostilities in the region could result in a large, fast-moving, and deadly battle. The Pentagon sent a joint public affairs team to Saudi Arabia on 6 October to evaluate the public affairs aspects of hostile action and help CENTCOM prepare for media coverage of any such eventuality. The team was convinced that, given the size and distances involved, the probable speed of advance of US forces, the potential for the enemy to use chemical weapons, and the sheer violence of a large scale armor battle would make open coverage of a ground combat operation impractical, at least during its initial phase.

The team, therefore, recommended that pools of reporters be assigned to units to cover activity within those units. These reporters would stay with units to ensure they would be present with military forces at the beginning of any combat operations. Although the plan was initially rejected, the command ultimately implemented a similar plan calling for ground combat news media pools, all of which would be in place before the ground campaign began.

The second contentious issue was the requirement that in the event of hostilities, all pooled media products undergo a security review. Although most reporting from the theater had been unrestricted, the military was concerned that reporters might not realize the sensitivity of certain information and might inadvertently divulge details of military plans, capabilities, operations, or vulnerabilities that would jeopardize the outcome of an operation or the safety of US or other Coalition forces. The plan called for all pooled media material to be examined by the public affairs escort officer on scene solely for its conformance to the ground rules, not for its potential to express criticism or cause embarrassment. The public affairs escort officer would discuss ground rule problems he found with the reporter, and, if no agreement could be reached about the disputed material, it would be sent immediately to the JIB Dhahran for review by the JIB Director and the appropriate news media representative. If they could not agree, the issue would be elevated to the Assistant Secretary of Defense (Public Affairs) for review with the appropriate bureau chief. The ultimate decision on publication rested with the originating reporter's news organization, not the government or the military.

While the pools were in existence, only five of more than 1,300 print pool stories were appealed through the stages of the review process to Washington for resolution. Four of those were cleared in Washington within a few hours. The fifth story dealt in considerable detail with the methods of intelligence operations in the field. The reporter's editor-in-chief chose to change the story to protect sensitive intelligence procedures.

In addition to 27 reporters on ships and at air bases, when the ground offensive began, CENTCOM had 132 reporters in place with the US ground forces to cover their activity. This let reporters accompany every combat division into battle.

Although plans called for expeditious handling of pool reports, much of it moved far too slowly. The JIB Dhahran reviewed 343 pool reports filed during or immediately after the ground war and found approximately 21 percent arrived at the JIB in less than 12 hours, 69 percent arrived in less than two days, and 10 percent arrived in more than three days. Five reports, hampered either by weather or by poor transportation, arrived at the JIB more than six days after they were filed.

The press arrangements in Southwest Asia were a good faith effort on the part of the military to be as fair as possible to the large number of reporters on the scene, to get as many reporters as possible out with troops during a highly mobile, modern ground war, and to allow as much freedom in reporting as possible, while still preventing the enemy from knowing precisely the nature of Coalition plans.

An unanticipated problem, however, grew out of the security review issue. Reporters were upset with the presence of public affairs escort officers. Although it is a common practice for a public affairs officer to be present during interviews with military personnel, the fact the escort officer had the additional role of reviewing stories for conformance to ground rules led to the public affairs officer being perceived as an impediment. Normally the facilitators of interviews and the media's advocate, public affairs officers now were considered to be inhibiting the flow of information between the troops and the media.

Media Briefings

DOD and CENTCOM conducted extensive briefings on Operation Desert Storm. When the air campaign began, the Secretary of Defense and the Chairman of the Joint Chiefs briefed the news media. Several hours later, during the morning of 17 January, the Commander-in-Chief, CENTCOM, and the CENTCOM Air Forces Commander conducted an extensive briefing in Riyadh. At the Pentagon, during the next 47 days, the JS Directors of Operations and Intelligence — two of the most knowledgeable officials about the operation — along with the Assistant Secretary of Defense for Public Affairs conducted 35 televised news briefings. Likewise, in Saudi Arabia, the command provided the Deputy Director of Operations for daily, televised briefings, and also provided background briefings at the news media's request. The command provided 98 briefings (53 on-the-record and 45 on background). Along with the news reports coming from reporters accompanying our forces in the field, these daily news briefings — conducted by the people responsible for planning and carrying out the operation — provided an unprecedented amount of information about the war to the American people.

OBSERVATIONS

Accomplishments

- DOD acted quickly to move reporters into place to cover the early stages of the American military buildup in Saudi Arabia, providing access for the first western reporters to the early stages of the operation. CENTCOM, in conjunction with DOD, established a pool system, enabling the news media to cover Operation Desert Storm through 159 reporters and photographers who were with combat units. In contrast, 27 reporters were with the D-Day invasion force in 1944 when the first wave of troops went ashore.

- The media pool system placed pool members in positions to witness actual combat or interview troops immediately after combat, as evidenced by the fact approximately 300 reports filed during the ground war were filed from forward deployed units on or near the front lines. Of that number, approximately 60 percent appeared to contain eyewitness accounts of the fighting.

- Pool members were permitted to interview front-line troops. Some 362 stories filed from the front included interviews with front-line troops.

- Frequent public briefings were conducted on details of the operation.

Shortcomings

- Command support for the public affairs effort was uneven. Some component commands were highly cooperative while others did not appear to place a priority on getting the story out. In some cases, this meant lack of communication and transportation assets or priorities to get stories back to the Dhahran JIB in a timely manner.

- Because of the scope and sensitive nature of much of the operational planning, a significant number of PAOs were not able to stay fully abreast of daily developments, nor were they trained to conduct security reviews of pool products. Many were therefore unable to judge operational security violations properly.

- The public affairs escort officers displayed a wide range of expertise in performing their duties. While many received praise from the media and unit commanders for having done excellent jobs, others, overzealously performing their duties, made mistakes which sometimes became news items. Occasional, isolated incidents, such as public affairs officers stepping in front of cameras to stop interviews, telling reporters they could not ask questions about certain subjects, and attempting to have some news media reports altered to eliminate unfavorable information, were reported. Although these incidents were the exception, not the rule, they nonetheless frequently were highlighted in media reports.

Issue

- Media sources have voiced dissatisfaction with some press arrangements, especially with the media pools, the need for military escorts for the news media, and security review of media pool products. DOD is working with news media representatives on ways to improve news coverage of future US military combat operations.

Appendix T
PERFORMANCE OF SELECTED WEAPON SYSTEMS

echnology and sophisticated weapon systems had an enormous effect on the conduct and the outcome of the Persian Gulf conflict. While some equipment, weapons and munitions had been in the inventory for some time, others were new. In fact, some were still in the developmental stages when the war began and were fielded prior to completion of normal test and evaluation schedules. A few systems had been used in combat prior to the Operation Desert Storm, but many were not combat proven. Therefore, an evaluation of the employment and performance of military equipment, weapons and munitions takes on a special significance, and requires a thorough, systematic analysis of all available data.

Weapon systems performance was influenced by a number of factors, including weather conditions, the nature of desert terrain, employment criteria (e.g., rules of engagement, altitude restrictions, attempts to minimize collateral damage), munitions capabilities, and Iraqi capabilities and tactics. These factors should be considered when evaluating the performance of specific systems.

CAVEATS

Scope

This appendix provides a broad overview of the employment and performance of selected weapon systems and is divided into five sections: aircraft systems, ground systems, munitions, naval systems, and space systems. It is not practicable to discuss in this report all the

> *"It is absolutely essential that we review the performance of our people, platforms, weapons, and tactics while our memories are fresh. We want to find out what worked well and what didn't work so well."*
>
> *Admiral F. B. Kelso, II, Chief of Naval Operations*

different systems and forces which contributed to the Coalition's overwhelming victory in Operation Desert Storm. The systems discussed in this appendix were by no means the only systems to play a role in this conflict. Other systems also made contributions to the war effort.

For security reasons, the shortcomings of many weapon systems are classified; therefore, some shortcomings are not listed in the observations sections of this unclassified report.

System Performance and Mission Accomplishment

The accomplishments and shortcomings of individual weapon systems should be considered in the context in which the systems were employed, taking into account the missions assigned to each system. A number of systems were used in more than one mission area, some systems were used in roles other than those for which they originally were designed, and many systems were used together to accomplish specific mission objectives. This appendix should be considered in conjunction with Chapters III through VIII of this report, which discuss the conduct of Operations Desert Shield and Desert Storm, and assess mission area accomplishment.

Data Limitations and Biases

Several limitations and biases in the data on which these assessments were based should be considered when reviewing the following analyses. Much of the data collected remain uncompiled and unanalyzed. The large number of air warfare missions flown, for example, makes data collection a time-consuming task. Data compilation and analysis is likely to require several years. What is presented here is what is currently available, a fraction of what may ultimately be accumulated. Conclusions drawn from the data available now might be changed by data that becomes available in later studies.

Some important data were not collected. Comprehensive battle damage assessment (BDA) data do not exist. It is difficult to assess weapon effectiveness without detailed data on what targets were damaged, to what extent, and by which systems. This assessment is not possible without on-the-ground inspection.

Even where BDA is available, it can be difficult to associate damage with a specific weapon. Many targets were hit with several weapons of the same type or with several different types of weapons or both. In most cases, it is impossible to be sure which weapons did what damage. Effectiveness of the individual weapons cannot always be determined.

The other bias inherent in the data is that data are better for the more advanced systems such as the F-117. Many of the newer, technologically sophisticated systems have on-board recording devices which make the data collection task significantly easier and provide more accurate data. More data are available earlier for these systems than for their less advanced (but perhaps equally effective) counterparts. It may be worthwhile to include mission recording devices on future weapon systems.

AIRCRAFT SYSTEMS

A-6E INTRUDER ATTACK AIRCRAFT

Mission

The A-6 Intruder is a carrier- and land-based, all-weather attack aircraft able to provide accurate weapon delivery day or night. The A-6 contains an all-weather ground mapping radar, a forward looking infrared (FLIR), and a self-contained laser designator for the accurate delivery of laser-guided weapons. The A-6 also can provide close air support (CAS) to ground forces in all weather conditions using a radar beacon to identify friendly forces and obtain targeting information.

System Data

Prime Contractor: Grumman Aerospace Corp.
Crew: One pilot; one bombardier-navigator
Initial Operational Capability: 1965
US Inventory: 350
Length: 55 feet
Wingspan: 53 feet
Weight: 60,400 maximum takeoff
Speed: 560 knots at sea level
Range: 672 miles (combat radius)
Propulsion: Two Pratt and Whitney J-52 P-8B turbojet engines
Armament: Able to carry conventional munitions including gravity and laser-guided

bombs (LGB), Harpoon, High Speed Anti-radiation Missile (HARM), and Standoff Land Attack Missile (SLAM)

Employment

During Operation Desert Storm, the A-6 operated extensively during darkness, inclement weather, and when target areas were obscured by smoke from oil well fires. Although originally designed over 30 years ago, the A-6 has undergone many system improvements. Two squadrons that participated in Operation Desert Storm were equipped with the latest version of the A-6, the A-6E System Weapons Improvement Program (SWIP), an upgrade that includes improved avionics, reliability and maintainability upgrades, and weapon system upgrades that allow use of SLAM, Maverick, HARM, and the Harpoon anti-ship missile to its full capability. These units participated in the first operational SLAM firings. During the war, the A-6 was used in the following mission areas:

- Day-, night-, and all-weather strikes using precision-guided and conventional weapons against point and area targets in support of strategic bombing and battlefield interdiction.
- Close air support (CAS) in direct support of Coalition ground forces.
- Antisurface warfare using missiles and conventional weapons against Iraqi naval units in day- night-, and all-weather conditions.
- Strike support suppression of enemy air defenses (SEAD), including use of HARMs and delivery of Tactical Air-Launched Decoys (TALD).
- Deep strike launch of the new SLAM.

Performance

Overland strike packages were launched from two battle forces; one in the Red Sea, the other in the Persian Gulf. Ninety-five Navy A-6s were used, flying 4,045 sorties. The Red Sea battle force averaged 6.4 strike aircraft per strike while the Arabian Gulf battle force averaged 3.2 strike aircraft per strike. A-6s were used for attacks on high value targets, Iraqi ground forces, Iraqi naval units, artillery, logistics sites, and armor concentrations. With the exception of four strikes early in the war, all Navy ordnance was delivered from medium to high altitude (above 10,000 feet). Typical loads included eight-12 MK-82s, eight-12 MK-20s, six MK 83s, two to four MK 84s, two MK 83 LGBs, or two MK 84 LGBs. Weapons normally were delivered in level flight or in a shallow dive. Target acquisition normally was done using the radar to cue the FLIR. Mission reports indicate about one third of the strike missions required radar deliveries because weather, smoke, or haze prevented FLIR use. Self-protection chaff and flares were used routinely; because of the limited quantity of chaff and flares that can be carried, aircrews tended to husband chaff during the approach to the target to have enough for use in the target area and during departure. A-6s also were used to support strike packages in SEAD by launching TALD or, in the case of the units with the A-6 SWIP, by using HARMs to suppress enemy threat radar systems.

Twenty Marine Corps (USMC) A-6s, flying 854 sorties from land bases, attacked strategic targets (Scud repair/assembly buildings) and interdiction targets (bridges, railroad yards, and ammunition storage areas). At the beginning of the war, A-6s were formed into mixed strike packages (four A-6s and eight F/A-18 bombers with eight F/A-18 fighter suppression escorts, and two EA-6Bs). As the war progressed and air defenses were suppressed, strike packages were reduced to eight bombers and two EA-6Bs. Normal USMC A-6 bomb load was four MK-84 unguided bombs. USMC A-6s also carried LGBs. Delivery tactics were the same as for Navy A-6s. Almost all USMC A-6 missions were flown at night.

Five A-6 aircraft were lost or damaged in combat; two early in the war during low-altitude attacks.

Because of its age, the A-6 required more maintenance manhours per flight hour.

The mission data recorder was unreliable in obtaining necessary battle damage assessment (BDA) information.

OBSERVATIONS

Accomplishments

- Navy and USMC A-6s flew more than 4,700 sorties in support of Operation Desert Storm.

- The A-6 is credited with the first successful combat use of SLAM.

- The A-6 played a key role in the early SEAD effort with HARM and TALD delivery capability.

- A-6s were used extensively at night use because of its all-weather, night-attack capability. The A-6's combination of radar, FLIR, and laser guidance and ranging capability allowed the effective delivery of PGMs and unguided ordnance.

Shortcoming

- The A-6 is an old aircraft and is becoming increasingly more difficult to maintain.

- The A-6's mission data recorder is ineffective for accurate BDA.

Issues

- Improving the on-board navigation system will increase system effectiveness and responsiveness. (The NAVSTAR Global Positioning System currently offers the most promising alternative.)

- Navy plans to operate the A-6 until it is replaced by a new aircraft (designated AX), starting in approximately 2005.

A-10 THUNDERBOLT II ATTACK AIRCRAFT

Mission

The A-10, the Air Force's primary close air support (CAS) aircraft, can strike targets, ranging from armored vehicles to artillery, both near friendly ground forces and in the enemy's second echelon. The OA-10 provides airborne control of tactical air assets that perform CAS missions. The OA-10 locates and identifies targets and then directs aircraft to the targets. The OA-10 and the A-10 are the same airframe.

System Data

Prime Contractor: Fairchild Republic Co.
Crew: One pilot
Initial Operational Capability: 1976
US Inventory: 565
Length: 53.3 ft
Wingspan: 57.5 ft
Weight: 51,000 lbs (maximum takeoff)
Speed: 350 knots
Range: 250 miles (9,500 lbs of ordnance and 1.8 hours of loiter time)
Propulsion: Two General Electric TF34-GE-100 turbofan engines
Armament: Internal 30 mm gatling gun (1,100 rounds high explosive or armor piercing ammunition), 11 external points for carrying most conventional munitions

Employment

A total of 136 A-10s and 12 OA-10s deployed to Saudi Arabia during Operation Desert Shield. All aircraft were based at King Fahd International Airport and used King Kahlid Military City (KKMC) as a forward operating location. This concept let the aircraft return to KKMC between missions, reducing transit time to the Kuwait Theater of Operation and minimized air refuelings.

The aircraft flew 8,077 combat sorties, of which fewer than 1,000 flights supported CAS missions. In addition to traditional missions, A-10s were used for suppression of enemy air defenses and Scud hunting. A-10s sometimes were used during the day to search for and destroy mobile Scud missile systems, and to complete destruction of surface-to-air missile (SAM) sites after those targets had been attacked by other aircraft.

Most sorties were conducted during daylight, but A-10s did perform limited night operations. One of the six squadrons deployed became a dedicated night-attack squadron and trained extensively in night operations during Operation Desert Shield.

Performance

Operating with a reduced threat of radar-guided SAMs, the A-10 was able to engage an average of four to five targets a sortie. A-10s fired 4,801 Maverick missiles, more than 90 percent of those delivered during the war. A-10 air interdiction (AI) operations can be characterized as innovative employment in non-traditional roles. The A-10s long loiter and large payload capability made it ideal for missions such as day Scud hunting and combat search and rescue (CSAR) escort. During the rescue of an F-14 pilot, A-10s escorting a Special Operations Forces (SOF) CSAR helicopter destroyed an Iraqi radio intercept truck that was searching for the pilot. The A-10 also was credited with two air-to-air helicopter kills. The A-10 achieved an outstanding 87.7 percent mission capable (MC) rate.

While its slower speed and long loiter time over the battlefield made it susceptible to enemy fire, the A-10's small vulnerable area allowed many battle-damaged aircraft to return safely to base. Moreover, 10 of the 15 A-10s damaged were returned to action within a day and all but one flew again during the war. Nevertheless, the aircraft suffered six combat losses.

The A-10 is susceptible to threats due to the longer exposure time caused by insufficient engine thrust which limits rate-of-climb, acceleration and maneuver, and cruising speed.

The A-10's night-attack capability is limited to the use of the Maverick seeker or flares. Neither is viable without a mid-to-high altitude sanctuary.

OBSERVATIONS

Accomplishments

- The A-10 performed well in a variety of missions and was particularly effective in AI and CAS roles.

- The A-10 fired 4,801 Maverick missiles with a 94 percent reliability rate.

- The A-10 achieved an 87.7 percent MC rate.

Shortcomings

- The A-10's slow speed and limited maneuverability make it susceptible to antiaircraft artillery and SAMs.

- The A-10 has limited night-attack capability.

Issue

- While the survivability features of the A-10 are good, future aircraft should be designed with higher performance to reduce susceptibility to damage while maintaining low vulnerability.

AH-1 COBRA ATTACK HELICOPTER

Mission

The AH-1's primary mission is to provide close-in fire support and fire support coordination under day, night, and adverse weather conditions. Additional missions include armed escort for assault transport helicopters, point target; and anti-armor operations; anti-helicopter operations; point and limited area defense against threat fixed wing aircraft; and reconnaissance.

System Data

Prime Contractor: Bell Helicopter Textron
Crew: Two
Initial Operational Capability (IOC): AH-1W/1986, AH-1T/1978, AH-1J/1969
US Inventory: 78 AH-1W, 7 AH-1T, 36 AH-1J
Length: 58 ft
Rotor diameter: 48 ft
Maximum Gross Weight: 14,750 lbs (AH-1W)
Speed: 140 knots (cruise)
Range: 140 miles (combat radius)
Endurance: 2.5 hours

Armament: Tow, Hellfire, Sidewinder, and Sidearm missiles, 2.75" and 5" rockets, and 20-mm gun

Employment

The Marine Corps (USMC) deployed four of six active squadrons (50 AH-1Ws) and two reserve squadrons (26 AH-1Js) to support both ashore and afloat operations in Southwest Asia (SWA). In addition, three AH-1Ts were deployed aboard the USS Nassau (LHA 4) with the 26th Marine Expeditionary Unit. These helicopters provided close-in fire support and fire support coordination, conducted point target and anti-armor operations, and reconnaissance. USMC squadrons flew 8,278 hours. The Army deployed 145 AH-1Fs to SWA. Army units flew more than 10,000 hours conducting daylight armed reconnaissance and screening operations.

Performance

During anti-armor and armed reconnaissance

missions, AH-1Ws reportedly destroyed 97 tanks, 104 armored personnel carriers and vehicles, 16 bunkers, and two antiaircraft artillery sites without a loss to enemy fire. Small detachments of two to four AH-1Ws routinely operated from remote forward area rearming points and refueling sites to provide quick reaction, close-in fire support. The AH-1W's weapon flexibility (i.e., dual TOW/Hellfire missile capability) was invaluable.

The AH-1Fs were useful in conducting daylight armed reconnaissance operations and security patrols. For example, two AH-1Fs used TOW missiles and 2.75 inch rockets to destroy light armored personnel carriers. AH-1Fs also used TOW missiles, 20-mm rounds, and 2.75 inch rockets to prevent an Iraqi Republican Guard convoy from crossing a causeway over the Euphrates River. The convoy's lead vehicle was destroyed by a TOW missile, which blocked the causeway.

Small and large scale group surrenders to AH-1Fs and AH-1Ws were common and often occurred after precision guided TOW or Hellfire missiles were fired at enemy armor or fortified positions. For example, a scout weapons team of OH-58s and AH-1Fs, providing security for a refueling operation, flew over Iraqi hardened positions and caused the Iraqi soldiers to surrender, according to after action reports from the 1st Infantry Division.

During Operation Desert Shield, the decision was made to deploy the 24 reserve AH-1Js to SWA. As a result of the continuing requirement to support contingency operations in the

Mediterranean and the Pacific, the Marine Corps activated two Reserve AH-1J squadrons to augment and reinforce AH-1Ws in SWA. The 20-year old AH-1J Cobras were not capable of anti-armor or antiair operations, but provided combat escort and armed reconnaissance for helicopter assault operations. AH-1s lacked a night targeting system, which severely restricted night and adverse weather operations and the use of the Hellfire missile's superior stand-off capability. The lack of an onboard laser designator also was a deficiency. AH-1s did not have a sophisticated navigation system. Because the Global Positioning System (GPS) was essential for accurate navigation in the desert, AH-1Ws were fitted with an interim GPS system before Operation Desert Storm.

The SWA desert environment demanded an unprecedented level of preventive maintenance:

- Canopies required protective covers to minimize degradation from heat and blowing sand.
- Protective blade tape was applied to the leading edge of main rotor blades to prevent sand erosion.
- Despite increased frequency of engine washing, engine life was reduced due to turbine blade sand erosion.
- Because the AH-1W is designed to survive the harsh ocean environment, AH-1Ws successfully withstood the effects of the desert environment. Sealed compartments protected the aircraft's avionics and electronic systems from sand.

OBSERVATIONS

Accomplishment

- The AH-1's weapon flexibility was invaluable. AH-1s destroyed tanks, armored personnel carriers and vehicles, bunkers, and anti-aircraft artillery sites with TOW and Hellfire missiles, rockets and guns.

Shortcomings

- AH-1s lacked a night targeting system, such as a forward-looking infrared (FLIR) and an autonomous laser designator. This severely restricted night and adverse weather operations and the use of Hellfire missiles.

- AH-1s lack a self-contained, precision navigation system like GPS.

- Reserve AH-1Js were not antiarmor capable.

Issues

- The number of AH-1Ws in each of six active and two reserve USMC Cobra squadrons will increase to 18 by FY97.

- Lack of a night targeting system and an on-board laser designator will be alleviated with the introduction of the Cobra Night Targeting System, (IOC FY 93).

- Lack of a navigation FLIR is addressed in a draft operational requirement for a mid-life upgrade to the AH-1W. Lack of a self-contained, precision navigation system will be corrected with the installation of GPS in the AH-1W, scheduled to begin in FY 93.

AH-64 APACHE ATTACK HELICOPTER

Mission

The AH-64 is the Army's primary antiarmor attack helicopter. The AH-64 is able to locate, engage and destroy enemy armored vehicles and other enemy targets in day, night, and other limited visibility conditions.

System Data

Prime Contractor: McDonnell Douglas Helicopter Co.
Crew: Two
Initial Operational Capability: 1986
US Inventory: 616
Length: 49 ft
Rotor Diameter: 48 ft
Maximum Gross Weight: 17,650 lbs
Speed: 145 knots
Range: 162 miles (combat radius)
Endurance: 1.8 hours
Armament: Hellfire missiles, 2.75 inch Hydra rockets, 30 mm cannon
Avionics: Forward-looking infrared (FLIR); Target Acquisition and Designation Sight; Integrated Helmet and Display Sight System; Pilots Night Vision System (PNVS)

Employment

The 274 AH-64s deployed to SWA were used to conduct deep attacks, raids, close battle, and armed reconnaissance missions. These aircraft represented 45 percent of the Army's AH-64 fleet.

AH-64s were used in the first attack of Operation Desert Storm, destroying a critical air defense complex deep inside Iraq. A few days before the start of the Offensive Ground Campaign, AH-64s conducted raids behind fixed Iraqi defensive positions, identified Iraqi border positions and used lasers to designate those positions for artillery-fired Copperhead rounds.

During operations in poor weather, thick smoke, or low visibility, the AH-64 was used as an armed reconnaissance asset, because other aircraft lacked the Apache's survivability, range, mobility and versatility.

Commanders used the AH-64 in a movement to contact role forward of advancing ground forces to assist in keeping our own forces separated from each other while engaging and destroying Iraqi units. The AH-64 destroyed Iraqi equipment and fortifications while providing intelligence to the advance ground elements.

Performance

The AH-64 had the ability to fight from several miles distance, rendering enemy weapon systems less effective. The AH-64s flew more than 18,700 hours with a mission capable rate exceeding 90 percent during the war.

AH-64s conducted armed zone and route reconnaissance deep into enemy territory at night. The aircraft's advanced optical systems helped with navigation and filming terrain and enemy unit dispositions for intelligence analysis. The AH-64 was successful in fast-paced, joint offensive and defensive operations.

The aircraft's auxiliary power unit, environmental control unit, and shaft driven compressor lacked adequate filtration systems to counter the harsh desert environment. Excessive amounts of sand were ingested, damaging these systems. Limited radio transmission ranges hindered the ability to communicate with AH-64s, particularly at low altitudes and during deep interdiction operations.

Though the AH-64 is credited with destroying numerous tanks, trucks and armored vehicles, only one AH-64 was lost to enemy action and its crew was recovered uninjured.

OBSERVATIONS

Accomplishments

- The rapid deployment features of the AH-64 (six in one C-5A) enhanced the antiarmor capability in the theater during the first days of the crisis.

- AH-64s conducted the first attacks in Operation Desert Storm, destroying critical air defenses at night and with total surprise to open an air corridor for Coalition air forces.

- The AH-64 was a valuable maneuver asset during the fast paced, joint ground operations.

- The AH-64 was the only aircraft able to fight in concert with ground forces during certain periods of adverse weather.

Shortcomings

- The harsh desert environment, especially sand, adversely affected aircraft components.

- Limited radio transmission ranges hindered the commanders' ability to communicate with AH-64s.

Issue

- Changes are being considered to improve the aircraft and resolve the shortcomings identified during Southwest Asian operations. These include Global Positioning System for navigation, Single Channel Ground Air Radio System for communications, a flight data recorder, and an improved fire control computer.

AV-8B HARRIER STOVL AIRCRAFT

Mission

The Marine Corps' (USMC's) Short Takeoff and Vertical Landing (STOVL) AV-8B Harrier aircraft conducts deep and close air support (CAS), armed reconnaissance, air defense, and helicopter escort missions. The AV-8B can operate from suitable seagoing platforms, advanced bases, expeditionary airfields, and remote tactical landing sites. Using STOVL technology for basing flexibility, it can respond quickly to the ground commander's need for timely CAS.

System Data

Prime Contractor: McDonnell Douglas
Crew: One Pilot
Initial Operational Capability: 1984

US Inventory: 170
Length: 46.3 ft
Wingspan: 30.3 ft
Weight: 31,000 lbs maximum takeoff
Speed: 0.91 Mach at sea level
Range: 506 miles (combat radius)
Propulsion: One Rolls-Royce Pegasus F402 turbofan engine
Armament: Mk-80 Series Bombs; 25mm Gatling gun; MK-20 Rockeye cluster bomb; AIM-9 Sidewinder; MK-77 Firebombs; 2.75" & 5" rockets; AGM-65E Maverick; mines; CBU-72 fuel air explosive; Laser-guided bombs

Employment

Eighty-six AV-8Bs were deployed in support of Operation Desert Storm. Two AV-8B squadrons (40 aircraft) arrived in the theater on 19 and 20

August to protect against further Iraqi aggression and provide air support for USMC forces. Twenty-six more Harriers were deployed on ships in the Persian Gulf and an additional squadron of 20 aircraft arrived in theater on 22 December. When Operation Desert Storm began, AV-8Bs attacked Iraqi long-range artillery within the Kuwait Theater of Operations (KTO). Other primary targets included armor and troops in the USMC area of responsibility. Immediately before the ground offensive, AV-8Bs conducted intensive operations to prepare the battlefield for ground forces to breach the minefield and obstacle belts in their advance to Kuwait City. AV-8Bs from main bases, amphibious assault ships (LHAs) and unimproved airfields (airfields offering refueling and ammunition with only minor maintenance repair capability) specialized in CAS which required detailed coordination with Coalition ground forces.

Harriers were deployed aboard LHAs to support Marine Expeditionary Brigade operations in the Persian Gulf. A squadron of 20 aircraft had deployed aboard *USS Nassau* (LHA 4) and a detachment of six aircraft was deployed on *USS Tarawa* (LHA 1). The detachment of six aircraft flew to King Abdul Aziz Naval Base on 15 February and operated from this site for the rest of the war. Sea-based combat missions were flown from 20 February through 27 February. AV-8Bs on *USS Nassau* flew 56 combat missions on the third day of the ground offensive for a rate of nearly three sorties per aircraft.

Performance

During multi-aircraft strikes, the Harrier's STOVL capability allowed 24 AV-8Bs to recover at their main base at King Abdul Aziz in less than five minutes. The airfield had an unimproved asphalt surface which needed repair, with minimal taxiways and little ramp space. Twelve aircraft routinely took off in less than two minutes. The aircraft's flexibility

conducting short takeoffs, rolling vertical and vertical landings, allowed compressed launch and recoveries in a dense air traffic control environment. The STOVL capabilities allowed AV-8Bs to continue combat operations when the field was closed to other fixed wing operations because a disabled aircraft blocked the runway. AV-8Bs were able to continue takeoffs and landings from either end of the airfield, in less than 3,000 feet.

Harriers provided a rapid response capability against Iraqi long-range artillery by standing strip alert. Eighteen of these missions were conducted in one hour during the ground war as Marines assaulted north to Kuwait City.

Basing flexibility also allowed the AV-8Bs to be the northern most deployed fixed-wing aircraft in theater. AV-8B operations began at Tanajib forward base only 42 miles south of the Kuwaiti border, on 18 February. Basing closer to the front lines eliminated the requirement for air refueling and provided quick response times. Moreover, aircraft with emergencies were able to recover at forward bases.

Location	To KTO	Load[1]	TOS[2]
Main Base	114 miles	6 X MK-20/MK-82	30 min
Forward Base	42 miles	6 X MK-20/MK-82	45 min
LHA	72 miles	4 X MK-20/MK-82	30 min

[1] Plus 300 rounds 25mm and ALQ-164 DECM pod.
[2] TOS – Time On Station

AV-8B targets included artillery, tanks, armor vehicles, ammunition storage bunkers, convoys, logistics sites, troop locations, airfields, and known antiaircraft artillery /surface-to-air missile (SAM) locations. AV-8Bs expended 7,175 Mk-20 Rockeye cluster bombs, 288 Mk-83 bombs, 4,167 Mk-82 bombs, and 83,373 rounds of 25-mm machine gun ammunition. In the last 10 days of the war, 236 sorties were flown from the forward base, carrying 187 tons of ordnance. From this site, 1,288 MK-20 Rockeye and 1,609 MK-82s were delivered against targets in the KTO. During quick turn-arounds, AV-8Bs routinely were rearmed and refueled in an average of 20 to 25 minutes. One section was turned around in less than 17 minutes.

Harriers based at the front of the battle area provided quick response to air requests with effective combat loads. AV-8B missions were not delayed or complicated by air refueling. Missions were flown from LHAs and forward bases to targets in the KTO. Harriers flew 3,342 sorties in more than 4,317 flight hours while maintaining an 83 percent full mission capable rate and 88 percent mission capable rate. To provide better support for the ground forces, the AV-8Bs frequently operated below the mid-altitude sanctuary.

OBSERVATIONS

Accomplishments

- AV-8Bs were effective and responsive in their primary role of supporting ground forces. The AV-8B was successful in neutralizing the USMC main concern — long-range artillery.

- AV-8Bs maintained an 83 percent full mission capable rate and a 88 percent mission capable rate during combat.

- AV-8Bs aboard the *USS Nassau* proved an LHA can effectively be used as a strike platform.

B-52 STRATOFORTRESS BOMBER

Mission

The B-52 is a multi-mission intercontinental heavy bomber aircraft. It can fly at high subsonic speeds at altitudes up to 50,000 feet and can carry nuclear or conventional ordnance. Numerous modifications have been made to the B-52 including the new Offensive Avionics System, Integrated Conventional Stores Management System, Global Positioning System, and electronic countermeasures improvements making the aircraft more survivable and more accurate. In a conventional scenario, the B-52's large payload and wide variety of munitions allows it to conduct air interdiction, and battlefield air interdiction (BAI) missions. Two types of B-52Gs were used in Operations Desert Shield and Desert Storm.

ALCM B-52G: Primary mission is nuclear deterrence using the Air Launched Cruise Missile, Short Range Attack Missile, and nuclear gravity bombs. Conventionally, the ALCM B-52G has the same internal carriage capability as the conventional B-52G. However, the aircraft is limited to external carriage of up to 1000-lb class munitions.

Conventional B-52G: 41 B-52Gs were modified to improve their conventional capabilities. These aircraft can carry a full range of conventional munitions internally and externally along with standoff munitions such as Have Nap and Harpoon. Other modifications have improved bombing accuracy and ability to conduct conventional operations.

System Data

Prime Contractor: Boeing Aircraft Co.
Crew: Six — aircraft commander, pilot, radar navigator, navigator, electronic warfare officer, and gunner (gunner position recently deleted)
Initial Operational Capability: 1959
US Inventory: 118
Length: 160 ft 11 in
Wingspan: 185 ft
Combat Weight: 488,000 lb
Speed: 440 knots (true air speed at normal cruising altitude of 35,000 feet)

Range: 5,016 miles (unrefueled with typical combat load)
Propulsion: Eight Pratt and Whitney J57-P-43 WB Turbojets
Armament: Approximately 70,000 lbs of mixed ordnance including general purpose bombs, naval mines, standoff munitions, special purpose weapons, and cluster bomb units (CBU). Defensive armament includes four .50-caliber machine guns, chaff, and flares

Employment

Deployment of 20 B-52Gs occurred early in Operation Desert Shield. As the air campaign evolved, the B-52 force grew to 68 B-52Gs, which were used to attack targets in Iraq and Kuwait.

Deployed bomber units developed and flew 335 missions against chemical and nuclear sites, railroad yards, logistics sites, barracks, airfields, weapon sites, Scud missile sites, power production facilities, military industrial sites, and integrated air defense systems. For BAI targets, 442 packages were planned against armor; command, control, and communications (C^3) facilities; infantry and mechanized infantry; minefields; logistics; tactical vehicles; artillery; and ammunition supply points. In addition, B-52 packages were important for psychological operations. A total of 527 BAI sorties were flown during Operation Desert Storm.

Performance

The B-52G bombers which operated in Operation Desert Storm were among the older aircraft in the theater. The aircraft delivered more than 54 million pounds of bombs without a combat loss.

Seven B-52s taking off from Barksdale AFB, LA carrying conventional air-launched cruise missiles (ALCMs) were launched prior to H-Hour as part of Operation Desert Storm.

These round-trip sorties, flying a total distance of over 14,000 miles and remaining aloft for over 35 hours, were the longest combat missions in history and the first combat employment of the conventional ALCM. The B-52s launched 35 conventional ALCMs from outside Iraq's air defense network in Desert Storm's opening hours, with the ALCMs programmed to attack eight targets, including military communications sites and power generation/transmission facilities.

B-52s also struck five targets inside Iraq as part of Operation Desert Storm's initial attack. Four targets were forward operating airfields: As Salman, Glalaysan, Wadi Al Khirr, and Mudaysis. The fifth target was Al Khafi, a forward operating location highway airstrip. It was essential to neutralize these targets in the opening hours of the war. A total of 13 B-52s launched in the opening attack, using mixed loads of weapons (UK-1000, CBU-58, and CBU-89). One B-52 sustained minor damage when it was hit leaving the target area, but there were no casualties.

Night low-level operations against strategic targets continued through the third day of Operation Desert Storm. After striking the Uwayjah petroleum refineries during the air campaign's third night, a B-52G apparently was hit by a missile or antiair artillery, but the aircraft returned to its base safely. After the fourth day, all B-52 missions were conducted at high altitudes.

B-52Gs conducted around-the-clock bombing operations against various targets. B-52s flew 79 offensive counterair sorties against airfields, aircraft on the ground, and airfield supporting infrastructure using general purpose bombs and cluster bomb units. Resulting damage disrupted and prevented air operations.

B-52s flew 954 air interdiction sorties against strategic targets (industrial facilities, C^3 facilities, nuclear/chemical/biological facilities, and short-range ballistic missiles), interdiction targets including Republican Guard units as well as fixed installations such as petroleum, oil and lubricant storage facilities, and railroads. Most raids were conducted at high altitude using radar ground mapping for target acquisition.

B-52Gs flew 527 BAI sorties striking armor, mechanized, and infantry units with a variety of general purpose and cluster bomb munitions. Continual day/night bombing of ground units was devastating to the units' effectiveness.

OBSERVATIONS

Accomplishments

- B-52s carrying conventional ALCMs flew over 14,000 miles and remained aloft for over 35 hours, representing the longest combat sorties in history.

- B-52Gs flew more than 1,600 sorties, dropped more than 72,000 weapons, and delivered more than 27,000 tons of munitions on targets in Iraq and Kuwait without a combat loss.

- The B-52 large payload allowed them to assist breaching operations through enemy ground defenses conducted by Coalition ground forces.

- The B-52G, although comprising only three percent of the total combat aircraft, delivered 30 percent of the total tonnage of air munitions.

Shortcomings

- Lack of available bases in the theater caused three of the four bomber wings to fly 14 to 16 hour missions routinely and thus limited combat sortie rates.

- The B-52's lack of a precision-guided munitions capability limited target selection to large area targets.

- The B-52's lack of stealth attributes required large force protection packages to escort or support their attacks against defended targets.

CH-46 SEA KNIGHT TRANSPORT HELICOPTER

Mission

The CH-46E was designed to move combat troops, support equipment, and supplies rapidly from amphibious assault landing ships and established airfields to advanced bases in undeveloped areas with limited maintenance and logistic support. The Navy also uses the CH-46D model for vertical replenishment, intra-battlegroup logistics, medical evacuation, and search and rescue missions.

System Data

Prime Contractor: Boeing Vertol
Crew: Four
Initial Operational Capability: 1964
US Inventory: 324
Length: 45 ft 8 in
Rotor Diameter: 51 ft
Gross Weight: 24,300 lbs
Max Speed: 145 knots
Range: 110 miles (one way)
Endurance: 2 hours (CH-46D), 1.75 hours (CH-46E)

Armament: Two M2 (.50 caliber) or M60 (7.62 mm) machine guns (CH-46Es only)

Employment

A total of 120 USMC CH-46E aircraft in 10 squadrons (nine active and one reserve) and 42 Navy CH/HH-46D in 21 two aircraft detachments, were deployed to support Operations Desert Shield and Desert Storm. The aircraft were used to transport Marines, Navy personnel, cargo, mail, ordnance, external loads, and to conduct medical evacuation (MEDEVAC) missions and search and rescue missions.

Performance

During Operations Desert Shield and Desert Storm, the Marine CH-46Es supported the scheme of maneuver ashore, and the 21 CH-46D detachments moved approximately 37,000 passengers, 4.6 million pounds of mail, 3.9 million pounds of internal cargo, and 90,000 tons of external cargo, the majority of which was ordnance. Additionally, 313 SAR and MEDEVAC missions were conducted. CH-46Ds and CH-46Es each flew more than 15,000 hours. Mission capable rates during Operation Desert Storm were 87.3 percent for CH-46Ds and 76.2 percent for CH-46Es.

Flight restrictions on rotor head dynamic components reduced the aircraft's gross weight, increased special maintenance inspections, and limited operational capability. The aircraft's limited airspeed and fuel capacity restricted its range to 102 miles with no loiter time. Internal fuel tanks extended the aircraft's range, but limited the aircraft's internal space and cargo-carrying capability.

Inherent limitations of night vision goggles emphasized the requirement for a complementary forward looking infrared (FLIR) system for operations during reduced visibility. The CH-46 lacks an integrated self-contained precision navigation system, which limited its ability to perform missions.

OBSERVATIONS

Accomplishments

- Twenty-one CH-46D detachments moved approximately 37,000 passengers, 4.6 million pounds of mail, 3.9 million pounds of internal cargo, and 90,000 tons of external cargo.

- CH-46Ds flew more than 15,000 hours with MC/FMC rates of 92 and 87 percent respectively.

- CH-46Es flew more than 15,000 hours with a MC rate of 76.5 percent.

- CH-46s conducted 313 SAR and MEDEVAC missions.

Shortcomings

- The CH-46's limited airspeed and fuel capacity restricted its effective range, especially in over-the-horizon operations.

- Turbine blade erosion caused by the desert environment reduced engine life.

- The CH-46s are approaching airframe/dynamic component life limits.

- Lack of spare parts increased aircraft down time.

- Frequent inspection cycles decreased mission availability.

- Lack of self-contained navigational information adversely affected its ability to conduct long range missions. The desert's featureless terrain, coupled with the CH-46's lack of external navigation systems, emphasized the requirement for a self-contained precision navigation capability.

Issues

- NVG limitations emphasized the requirement for a complementary FLIR system for periods of reduced visibility, but there are no plans to install a FLIR system on CH-46 aircraft.

- Dynamic component Upgrade Program will provide newly manufactured dynamic components to increase the useful life of the aircraft, correct safety deficiencies, and reduce maintenance and special inspections.

- The CH-46 upgrade program will increase range and navigational capability.

- A rotor wing head pitch shaft modification will correct a known safety deficiency and reduce the number of required safety inspections.

CH-47D CHINOOK TRANSPORT HELICOPTER

Mission

The CH-47D is a medium lift transport helicopter used primarily to transport personnel, weapons, ammunition, equipment and other cargo in general support of combat units. Most operations consist of transporting supplies and external loads.

System Data

Prime Contractor: Boeing Vertol
Crew: Three
Initial Operational Capability: 1984 ("D" configuration)
US Inventory: 344
Length: 50.75 ft
Rotor Diameter: 60 ft
Maximum Gross Weight: 50,000 pounds
Speed: 140 knots (cruise)
Range: 360 miles

Endurance: 2.2 hours
Armament: Two 7.62 machine guns
Payload: 24,000 pounds

Employment

During Operations Desert Shield and Desert Storm, 163 CH-47s deployed to Southwest Asia (SWA). Ten medium helicopter companies deployed. This represented 47 percent of the CH-47D aircraft fielded.

While in SWA, the CH-47D transported troops and equipment into combat, resupplied the troops in combat, performed medical evacuation, transported bulk supplies, and repositioned reserve forces. It was the only Army helicopter capable of rapidly repositioning extremely heavy equipment in the harsh desert environment.

Performance

The aircraft was used extensively to establish refueling/rearming sites in support of deep operations, to conduct long-range rescue missions, and to move large numbers of enemy prisoners of war. The CH-47D often was the only mode of transportation available to shift large numbers of personnel, equipment, and supplies rapidly across the vast area in which the forces operated. The aircraft was instrumental in maintaining lines of communication and supply to combat units deployed well forward on the battlefield.

The CH-47D normally operates in secure areas; however, during the ground offensive, the CH-47 played an integral part in the air assault. On the first night of the ground campaign, CH-47Ds of the 101st Airborne Division (Air Assault) participated in the largest air assault operation ever conducted. Moving heavy weapons such as the M-198 howitzer, CH-47Ds allowed the 101st Airborne Division (Air Assault) to carry much needed fire support with the initial air assault elements. By the end of the first day of the ground offensive, four teams of CH-47s had lifted 131,000 gallons of fuel and numerous pallets of ammunition. The food and water for the entire air assault force was carried on three CH-47Ds.

The CH-47Ds flew more than 13,700 hours in SWA; the mission capable rate exceeded 75 percent before Operation Storm (the standard is 70 percent) and 85 percent from January through February.

There were reports of infrared and radar-guided missile engagements against CH-47D helicopters; however, no aircraft were lost in these engagements.

OBSERVATIONS

Accomplishments

■ The CH-47D proved to be a reliable asset, flying more than 13,700 hours in support of SWA operations. The aircraft displayed speed and versatility while participating in the largest air assault in history.

■ It provided the ability to move vast amounts of personnel, weapons, supplies, ammunition, fuel and other supplies required to support ground tactical plan.

Shortcomings

■ Heavy divisions reported a need for more CH-47D support.

■ Accurate navigation was difficult in the featureless terrain environment.

■ The aircraft suffered sand erosion problems with the rotor blades, engines, and oil coolers.

Issue

■ Improvements under consideration are, the Global Positioning System for navigation; ANVIS/HUD for NVG operations; Single Channel Ground and Airborne Radio System for communications; and, environmental protection filters and covers.

E-2C HAWKEYE AEW AIRCRAFT

Mission

The E-2C HAWKEYE is an all-weather, carrier-based airborne early warning (AEW) and command and control (C^2) aircraft with a crew of five: pilot, co-pilot, combat information center officer, air control officer, and radar operator. Additional missions include surface surveillance coordination, strike and interceptor control, search and rescue guidance and communications relay.

System Data

Prime Contractor: Grumman Aerospace Co.
Crew: Five
Initial Operational Capability: 1973
US Inventory: 113
Length: 57 ft 8 in.
Wingspan: 80 ft 7 in
Weight: 53,000 lbs maximum takeoff
Cruising Speed: 270 knots
One-way Range: 1,673 miles
Propulsion: Two Allison T56-425A Turboprop engines, 4,910 ESHP each
Armament: None

Employment

The E-2C is both a land-based and carrier-capable aircraft used by the Navy and some foreign countries. Each E-2C is expected to generate about 1.5 sorties a day with a sortie length of approximately 4.5 hours. Normally four or five E-2Cs are embarked on a carrier (CV) and at least one E-2C is kept airborne to provide AEW, C^2, and communications relay functions for a CV task force. Each E-2C carries an APS-138 radar which operates at 400 Mhz; an ALR-73 electronic support measures (ESM) system, identification, friend or foe (IFF) interrogators; one very high frequency, five ultra high frequency, and two high frequency radios; and, several data links including Link-11 (TADIL A) and Link-4A (TADIL C). The E-2C normally cruises at 270 knots at about 25,000 feet.

The E-2C was used in all mission areas including offensive support coordination, intelligence collection, and anti-surface warfare. The first E-2Cs were operational in theater on 7 August. The aircraft operated from three CVs in the Red Sea and three CVs in the Persian Gulf. Three CVs had four E-2Cs embarked while the remainder had five E-2Cs embarked. Beginning on 10 December, four shore-based E-2C aircraft also began operations from Bahrain. Flights were scheduled to support the Persian Gulf Anti-Air Warfare (AAW) Commander by augmenting Airborne Warning and Control System (AWACS) coverage during anticipated periods of peak Iraqi air activity and provide AEW coverage during AWACS refueling. This shore-based coverage remained in operation until USS America (CV-66) and USS Theodore Roosevelt (CV-71) arrived in theater.

Performance

During Operation Desert Storm, 27 E-2C aircraft were in theater. A total of 1,192 sorties were scheduled with 1,183 flown for a total of 4,790 flight hours. Mission capable (MC) rate was 83 percent and full mission capable rate was 69 percent. Total mission completion rate was 99 percent. Overall, the performance of the E-2C over land far exceeded operator expectations. This success was attributable to two major factors: system grooming and operator training.

Overwater radar detection and tracking performance was excellent as expected. Pseudo-Synthetic Video (PSV) and Real-Time Synthetic Video (RTSV) were available consistently for targets at near to medium ranges and only slightly less for targets at longer ranges.

As expected, land/sea interface was the most difficult area for E-2C detection and tracking. Automatic tracking was essentially non-existent. Manual tracking with a dedicated operator who focused on an area of interest was necessary. AMTI video was available on known contacts.

Overland performance consistently exceeded expectations. Radar-only fighter control and continuous tracking of aircraft on the overland low levels were commonplace. The primary threat sector to the north offered the radar's optimum overland environment. While there were only limited opportunities to gather statistical data on detection and tracking of high speed, low altitude targets in the threat sector, tactical aircraft were tracked routinely at medium altitudes. Mission crew debriefs indicated excellent tracking of low-altitude RAF GR-1 aircraft. Both bypass and canceled RTSV proved effective in painting Iraqi tactical aircraft. Only minimal false alarms were encountered. Commercial air targets were routinely detected at long range.

OBSERVATIONS

Accomplishments

- The E-2C coordinated communications shifts, provided situational awareness to Coalition aircraft through all flight phases, and provided backup radar coverage and control for flights in hostile territory.

- Integration of E-2C and AWACS radar pictures provided superior situational awareness to both platforms and exceptional E-2C target area control of strike aircraft.

Shortcomings

- Lack of an over-the-horizon communications suite was a distinct disadvantage. The addition of a satellite communications capability in the E-2C would have added tactical flexibility when operating at extended distances from the CV battle group.

- The lack of in-flight refueling capability limited the E-2C's range and endurance.

Issue

- The next upgrade of the E-2C — the Group-II-APS-145 equipped aircraft ?will resolve many of the identified shortcomings.

E-3 AWACS AIRCRAFT

Mission

The E-3 Airborne Warning and Control System (AWACS) provides highly mobile, survivable airborne surveillance and command and control (C^2) functions for tactical and air defense forces. It provides all-altitude surveillance of airborne targets over land and water. The AWACS missions are to detect enemy aircraft, control defensive friendly fighters, control strike aircraft and provide a long-range air picture to theater commanders and other command forces.

System Data

Prime Contractor: Boeing Aerospace Co, airborne radar built by Westinghouse
Crew: Flight crew of four plus 19 to 29 mission specialists
Initial Operational Capability: 1977
US Inventory: 33
Length: 145 ft, 6in
Wingspan: 130 ft, 10in
Weight: 325,000 lbs
Cruise Speed: 460 knots
Range: 24 hours flight time refueled (limited by crew rest requirements), more than 11 hours flight time unrefueled
Propulsion: Four Pratt and Whitney TF-33-PW-100A turbofan engines
Armament: None

Employment

The E-3 is a land-based airborne early warning and control aircraft used by the Air Force (USAF), the Royal Saudi Air Force, North Atlantic Treaty Organization (NATO), and other countries. E-3s normally are operated as individual aircraft, often maintaining a surveillance station around the clock using multiple aircraft in sequence. Only E-3B/C aircraft were deployed to Operations Desert Shield and Desert Storm.

Five E-3s initially were deployed to Riyadh, Saudi Arabia, arriving on 8 August and an E-3 orbit was established the next day about 110 to 125 miles from the Kuwaiti and Iraqi borders. During Operation Desert Shield, there was a gradual buildup of E-3s in Riyadh until 11 were available by 16 January. On 15 January, three E-3s deployed to Incirlik, Turkey, to begin operations in Southeast Turkey, about 120 miles from the Iraqi border. (In addition, NATO-owned E-3s were used in the Mediterranean to monitor the flow of aircraft towards Southwest Asia and for maritime interception surveillance. They also flew over Turkish territory to maintain Turkish air sovereignty.)

Performance

At the start of Operation Desert Storm, four US E-3s were airborne over Saudi Arabia (three forward, one to the rear) and one US E-3 over southeast Turkey. In addition, there was a Saudi E-3 in southern Saudi Arabia used primarily for communications relay. The rearmost US E-3 in Saudi Arabia was primarily used to manage air refueling operations. This configuration of airborne E-3s was maintained 24 hours a day throughout most of Operation Desert Storm. E-3s, at times, overflew Iraq to provide additional radar coverage against deep target areas. E-3s did benefit from airborne combat air patrol established near the E-3 orbit to protect all high value airborne assets (HVAA) to include AWACS, Joint Surveillance Target Attack Radar System, and Rivet Joint.

E-3s supported all daily air tasking order activity, controlling an average of 2,240 sorties a day and a total of more than 90,000 sorties during the war. AWACS provided direct support of offensive counter air and defensive counter air combat patrols. During Desert Storm, AWACS flew 448 sorties for 5,546 flying hours. In addition to controlling combat aircraft, AWACS helped to ensure there were no Coalition mid-air collisions. No AWACS were damaged and no AWACS personnel were injured as a result of enemy action.

Throughout Operations Desert Shield and Desert Storm, AWACS provided the primary air picture to the appropriate theater C^2 centers through voice and electronic data links for 100 percent of tasked station time. The E-3, operating in conjunction with Marine Corps (USMC), Navy, Army, USAF, and Saudi Arabian units, provided an air picture that spanned from the Persian Gulf to the Red Sea, providing real time information to most Coalition command centers. The E-3 established a data sharing network with the RC-135 Rivet Joint, Airborne Battle Command and Control Center, Tactical Air Control Center (TACC) and Navy E-2s. The complete theater air picture was passed through this network. The TACC relayed information data link to USMC and Army units, and the Saudi Arabian-led Coalition C^2 centers. AWACS also provided primary support to all aircraft requiring pre- and post-strike air refueling in northern Saudi Arabia

---

OBSERVATIONS

Accomplishments

- AWACS demonstrated excellent deployability, arriving in theater on 8 August.

- During Operation Desert Storm, E-3s provided medium altitude radar coverage of Iraqi airspace while operating from Saudi and Turkish airspace.

- AWACS provided threat warning to all assigned strike packages inside hostile territory and provided threat warning and deconfliction of all HVAA in theater.

Issue

- The usefulness of long-distance, communications between widely separated E-3s covering related areas should be investigated.

EA-6B PROWLER ECM AIRCRAFT

Mission

The EA-6B is a four-seat carrier- and land-based aircraft incorporating comprehensive electronic countermeasures (ECM) equipment to jam enemy radars and communications. The tactical jammers are carried in external pods. The radar intercept receivers, mission computers and aircrew displays are carried internally.

System Data

Prime Contractor: Grumman Aerospace Co.
Crew: One pilot; three electronic countermeasures officers
Initial Operational Capability: 1971
US Inventory: 133
Length: 59 ft.
Wingspan: 53 ft.
Weight: 61,500 lbs maximum takeoff
Speed: Maximum 0.99 Mach; Cruise 0.72 Mach
Range: 852 miles
Propulsion: Two Pratt and Whitney J-52 P-408 turbojet engines
Armament: High Speed Anti-radiation Missile (HARM)
Onboard Weapons System: ALQ-99 Tactical Jamming System; ASQ-191 Communications Jamming System
External Stores (five stations available): ALQ-99 Jamming Pod (five max); AGM-88 high-speed anti-radiation missile (four maximum), external fuel tanks (five maximum), ALE-41 Chaff Pod (five maximum), and ALQ-167 Jamming Pod (four maximum)

Employment

The Navy and Marine Corps (USMC) used the EA-6B Prowler to provide ECM during Operations Desert Shield and Desert Storm. The Prowler's mission was to deny the enemy the use of the electromagnetic spectrum. This ECM support contributed substantially to Coalition effectiveness by denying early warning and tracking data to enemy integrated air defense system (IADS) operators and by disrupting the firing solution of enemy anti-aircraft weapons. EA-6B support was considered essential for every Navy and USMC strike. The aircraft also supported coalition strikes involving aircraft of all types. It was the Navy's platform of choice for High Speed Anti-Radiation Missile (HARM) use.

The first Navy EA-6Bs arrived in the north Arabian Sea on 7 August. The first USMC EA-6Bs were operationally ready on 28 August. At the start of Operation Desert Storm, Navy EA-6Bs operated from aircraft carriers (CVs) in the Red Sea and the Persian Gulf; three CVs in the Red Sea had five EA-6Bs each while three CVs in the Persian Gulf had four EA-6Bs each. The 12 USMC EA-6Bs operated from Shaikh Isa, Bahrain. Navy Prowlers in the Red Sea generated 1.2 sorties a day per aircraft, with an average length of five hours per sortie. Persian Gulf Prowlers generated 1.3 sorties a day per aircraft with an average length of three hours per sortie. USMC Prowlers generated 1.3 sorties a day per aircraft with an average length of 2.7 hours a sortie.

On the first day of Operation Desert Storm, three Navy EA-6s with jammer pods, but no HARMs, supported a strike on Al Taqaddum west of Baghdad; three EA-6s with jammer pods and one HARM each supported an attack on H-3 in western Iraq; four EA-6s with jammer pods and one HARM each supported an attack on H-2/H-3 in western Iraq; and, two EA-6s with two HARMs and one EA-6 with only jamming pods supported attacks on H-2/H-3 and Al Asad. On the first raid of the war, two USMC EA-6s jammed Iraqi EW/GCI radars to screen Coalition inflight refueling operations, while five other EA-6s supported a large F/A-18 strike on Tallil airfield.

Performance

ECM aircraft performance is difficult to quantify. The mission is to support strike aircraft by suppressing the enemy Integrated Air Defense Systems (IADS). This can be accomplished in several different ways; effectiveness is measured by the success of the supported strike.

Prowlers flew 1,623 combat sorties, totaling 4,600 flying hours, with no combat losses; Prowlers launched over 150 HARMs. EA-6B systems jammed Iraqi radar systems, and the perceived threat of destruction from EA-6B HARMs forced Iraqi radars off the air and surface-to-air systems into highly ineffective operating modes.

OBSERVATIONS

Accomplishments

- EA-6Bs flew 1,623 combat sorties totaling 4,600 flight hours with no combat losses.

- EA-6Bs successfully provided ECM jamming and launched over 150 HARMs in support of Coalition forces.

Issue

- The next version of the EA-6B is known as the Advanced Capability (ADVCAP) Prowler. ADVCAP production begins as a remanufacture program in FY-93. New production of EA-6Bs was completed in FY-89. The EA-6B is projected to be the Navy and USMC tactical ECM aircraft well into the next century.

F-4G WILD WEASEL ECM AIRCRAFT

Mission

The F-4G Wild Weasel's mission is to destroy, neutralize, or degrade enemy radar-directed surface-to-air threats (i.e., Suppression of Enemy Air Defenses (SEAD)). The F-4G aircraft is essentially a F-4E/ARN-101 aircraft specially modified to carry the AN/APR-47 Radar Attack and Warning System which detects, identifies, and locates pulsed and continuous wave radar emitters. Although the F-4G can carry virtually every type of air-to-air and air-to-surface munition, the preferred SEAD ordnance is the AGM-88 High Speed Anti-radiation Missile (HARM).

System Data

Prime Contractor: McDonnell Douglas Aircraft Co
Crew: Two, One pilot and One Electronic Warfare Officer
Initial Operational Capability: 1978

US Inventory: 99
Length: 63 ft
Wingspan: 39 feet
Weight: 58,000 lbs maximum takeoff
Speed: Mach 2+ at 40,000 feet
Range: 600 miles
Propulsion: Two General Electric J79-GE-15 turbojet engines
Armament: Rockeye cluster bombs, air-to-surface missiles such as Shrike, HARM and Maverick and air-to-air missiles.

Employment

The Air Force (USAF) committed 63 percent (62 aircraft) of its F-4Gs to support Operation Desert Storm. Most aircraft operated from Bahrain, but 12 F-4Gs deployed to Incirlik, Turkey. The F-4Gs were used to conduct autonomous operations, direct support, and area SEAD missions. During autonomous operations, F-4Gs attacked targets in a particular geographic area to reduce the enemy air defense threat or roll back the air defenses for upcoming Coalition air operations. During direct support missions, F-4Gs joined other aircraft during a particular airstrike and provided SEAD to support that specific mission. On area suppression missions, F-4Gs were not tied to a particular strike force, but provided SEAD support for numerous strikes against various targets. The majority of F-4G missions were in the direct support role. Virtually all F-4G missions required inflight refueling.

Performance

Potential measures of performance for the F-4G force include availability, use, and mission completion rates, sorties launched, total flying time, on-station time, numbers of missiles launched and numbers of radars and other emitters damaged, destroyed, or kept off the air, the number of Coalition raids and aircraft which were saved from potential engagement, and other measures. Only limited data are now available to show how well the F-4G and associated weapons performed.

There is considerable imprecision in intelligence estimating and battle damage assessment in electronic combat, however, the general perceived threat of destruction reduced Iraqi propensity to operate their equipment. Indeed, the potential threat of physical destruction by Anti-Radiation Missiles in general (launched from any platform: F-4G, EA-6, F/A-18) perhaps was the biggest single factor in Operation Desert Storm SEAD, as evidenced by the dramatic decrease in emissions after day one of Operation Desert Storm.

OBSERVATIONS

Accomplishments

- More than 2,700 F-4G combat sorties were flown during Operation Desert Storm, with only one combat loss.

- The perceived threat of destruction appears to have forced Iraqi radars off the air and SAM systems into highly ineffective operating modes.

F-14 TOMCAT FIGHTER

Mission

The Navy F-14 Tomcat is a variable-sweep wing, supersonic air superiority fighter capable of engaging multiple targets simultaneously from sea level to above 80,000 feet. The F-14 uses the AIM-54 long-range air-to-air missile (AAM), the AIM-7 medium-range AAM, the AIM-9 short-range AAM and the 20mm M-61A1 cannon.

There are three variants of the F-14:

F-14A — Most F-14s, equipped with the AWG-9 radar and TF-30 engines.

F-14B — New production aircraft and remanufactured F-14As equipped with F110 engines that improve thrust by 30 percent. ALR-67 compatibility and some minor structural improvements also separate the F-14B from the F-14A.

F-14D — New production aircraft and remanufactured F-14As equipped with the F110 engines, new digital APG-71 radar, digital avionics and Infrared Search and Track System. The same ALR-67 compatibility and structural improvements as the F-14B. Although listed here as a F-14 variant, the D model has not reached IOC and did not participate in Desert Storm.

System Data

Prime Contractor: Grumman Aerospace
Crew: One Pilot and One Radar Intercept Officer (RIO)
Initial Operational Capability: 1972, F-14A; 1988, F-14B; 1993, F-14D
US Inventory: 479
Length: 62 ft 8 in
Wingspan: 64 ft 1.5 in
Weight: 72,935 lbs
Speed: 780 knots / Mach 1.88
Range: 704 miles unrefueled (fighter escort

mission); 495 miles unrefueled (Combat Air Patrol) with one hour loiter
Propulsion: F-14A: Two PW TF30-P-414As rated at 17,077 lbs in AB each; F-14B/D: Two GE F110-GE-400s rated at 23,600 lbs. in AB each
Armament: Maximum of eight AAMs; AIM-54 Phoenix, AIM-7 Sparrow, AIM-9 Sidewinder, 20mm M-61A1 Cannon
Imagery System: Tactical Air Reconnaissance Pod System (TARPS)

Employment

The F-14A and F-14B variants were used during Operation Desert Storm for fighter sweep, CAP and escort missions. Operations were conducted day and night, at all altitudes, depending on the threat and specific mission objectives. The additional capability of the TARPS provided daytime imagery for battle damage assessment, pre-strike planning, maritime interception operations and detection of Scud missile launch site locations.

Barrier CAP missions also were flown to protect Coalition naval forces and Gulf Cooperation Council coastlines throughout the war. Later in the conflict, F-14s were used to establish and maintain CAPs to intercept Iraqi aircraft attempting to flee to Iran.

During Operation Desert Storm, 99 F-14s flew 4,182 sorties for a total of 14,248 flight hours, more than any other Navy fixed wing aircraft. The 16 F-14s configured to carry TARPS flew 751 sorties for a total of 2,552 flight hours. The F-14s were deployed aboard five of the six carriers in theater and operated from the Red Sea and the Persian Gulf.

Performance

The F-14 never was fully challenged in its primary air superiority mission. Iraqi fighters never directly threatened Navy strike groups escorted by F-14s nor attempted forward quarter engagements against F-14 CAP or sweep missions.

The F-14 had the most flight hours of any Navy fixed wing aircraft and maintained a mission capable (MC) rate of 77 percent.

TARPS aircraft were distributed among five carriers to provide theater and strike planning support and maintained an 88 percent MC rate.

One F-14 was lost to a possible surface-to-air missile during an overland high value unit CAP mission. This loss was the only F-14 lost during Operations Desert Shield and Desert Storm.

OBSERVATIONS

Accomplishments

- F-14s conducted six intercepts against hostile aircraft, and achieved one air-to-air kill (helicopter).

- The Iraqis did not attempt a direct confrontation with F-14s.

- The F-14's range and endurance capability was an asset, since most missions required extensive flight time.

- The F-14 maintained a 77 percent MC rate.

- F-14s maintained three 24-hour CAP stations in the Persian Gulf and one in the Red Sea throughout the war, two more stations were added before the ground offensive began.

- TARPS systems had an 88 percent reliability rate.

F-15C EAGLE FIGHTER

Mission

The F-15C's mission is air superiority through offensive and defensive counter air (OCA/DCA). The F-15C provides close-in visual and medium-range, all-weather capability against any threat aircraft.

System Data

Prime Contractor: McDonnell-Douglas
Crew: One pilot
Initial Operational Capability: 1979
US Inventory: 417
Length: 63 ft
Wingspan: 42 ft
Weight: 68,000 lbs (maximum takeoff)
Speed: Mach 2.3
Range: 330 to 720 mile combat radius (configuration dependent)
Propulsion: Two Pratt and Whitney F100-PW-100 turbofan engines

Armament: One M-61A1 20 mm cannon, four AIM-9L/M Sidewinder and four AIM-7 Sparrow missiles

Employment

F-15Cs are used generally in two-aircraft formations with multiples of two comprising actual flights. Specific numbers and methods of use are tailored to individual mission objectives.

F-15C OCA/DCA missions generally are categorized as sweep, combat air patrol (CAP), or force protection. Sweep missions establish air superiority in designated areas for a specified time period by seeking out and destroying enemy aircraft within the designated area. CAP missions are used within the air defense concept to protect ground or airborne assets from attack by enemy aircraft, while the force protection mission protects friendly airborne forces from attack by enemy air. During Operation Desert

Storm F-15Cs were used to intercept and destroy Iraqi aircraft, including those attempting to flee into Iran.

Twenty-four F-15Cs were among the first US-based aircraft to deploy on 7 August, a total of 118 F-15Cs eventually deployed. This force represented about 28 percent of the Air Force inventory. F-15Cs flew 5,906 OCA/DCA missions during Operation Desert Storm.

Performance

The F-15C helped attain air superiority within the first few days of the air campaign and air supremacy within 10 days. F-15Cs achieved 33 of the 38 air-to-air kills in Operation Desert Storm. This was accomplished with no F-15C losses and no incidents of air-to-air fratricide.

While F-15C pilots were well prepared to fly OCA/DCA missions and the weapon system (aircraft and weapons) proved ready and reliable, there were some system problems. Because of the distances involved and the short range radios on the F-15C, pilots had some difficulty maintaining voice contact with AWACS aircraft while maintaining CAPs over Iraq. This difficulty may have prevented timely interception of some Iraqi aircraft attempting to flee to Iran. Also, F-15Cs experienced problems with video tape recorders used to record weapons delivery. This hampered documentation of air-to-air engagements and verification of air-to-air kills.

OBSERVATIONS

Accomplishments

- The F-15C was a significant contributor to attaining air superiority in the first 10 days of hostilities.

- The F-15C achieved 33 of 38 air-to-air kills and there were no F-15C combat losses.

- There were no incidents of air-to-air fratricide.

- F-15Cs flew 5,906 OCA/DCA missions.

Shortcomings

- A low power (5 watts) radio made long-range communication difficult.

- A poor quality video recording system degraded weapons delivery documentation.

F-15E EAGLE FIGHTER

Mission

The F-15E is a high performance, supersonic, all-weather, dual role fighter. In the air superiority role, its primary weapons are radar guided and infrared homing air-to-air missiles and a 20-mm gun. In the air-to-surface role, the aircraft carries Low-Altitude Navigation and Targeting Infrared for Night (LANTIRN) targeting and navigation pods and can carry guided and unguided air-to-ground weapons. During Operation Desert Storm, the F-15E was used in offensive counter air (OCA), strategic bombing, air interdiction (AI), close air support, and suppression of enemy air defenses roles.

System Data

Prime Contractor: McDonnell Douglas Corp.
Crew: Two, pilot and weapon systems officer
Initial Operational Capability: 1989
US Inventory: 125
Length: 63.75 ft
Wingspan: 42 feet, 10 inches
Weight: 73,000 lbs maximum takeoff
Speed: Supersonic

Range: 960 mile radius
Propulsion: Two Pratt and Whitney F100-PW-220 or -229 turbofan engines
Armament: Typical weapons used during Operation Desert Storm were:
12 MK-82 (500lb general purpose bomb) or,
five MK-84 (2000lb general purpose bomb) or,
eight GBU-12 (500lb laser-guided bomb) or,
four GBU-10 (2000lb laser-guided bomb) or,
six CBU-87 (Combined effects munitions) or,
six CBU-89 (Gator mine, anti-armor/personnel) or,
six CBU-52 (Anti-personnel cluster munitions) or,
12 MK-20 (Anti-armor cluster munitions) or,
500 rounds 20 mm
four Aim-9Ms

Employment

The two F-15E squadrons that participated in Operations Desert Shield and Desert Storm had just reached operational readiness when they deployed. Operational test and evaluation on the LANTIRN pods was conducted in the area of responsibility (AOR), including the targeting pods, which were shipped to the theater after deployment. At the beginning of hostilities, 48 F-15Es were in-place and conducting operations out of Al-Kharj, Saudi Arabia.

Performance

F-15E missions were conducted almost entirely at night. The aircraft's highly flexible avionics package and the solid foundations of training and tactics provided a good baseline for the successful execution of all F-15E mission profiles.

The first night low-altitude mission and the preplanned AI packages were profiles that had been practiced extensively before the air campaign and presented very few unanticipated problems.

Two aircraft were lost during combat. The first loss occurred on 17 January during an OCA mission and the second on 19 January during an AI mission.

The F-15E's mission capable rate was 85.9 percent.

OBSERVATIONS

Accomplishments

- The LANTIRN targeting pod proved invaluable not only in destroying targets with LGBs, but also in locating the target and providing real time bomb damage assessment.

- The F-15E accomplished successfully LANTIRN operational test and evaluation in the AOR, including pods shipped after deployment.

- Forty-eight F-15Es flew 2,210 sorties and dropped 1,700 GBU 10/12s using LANTIRN, along with other ordnance.

- F-15E flexibility was demonstrated in anti-armor missions. On several occasions, 16 armored vehicles were destroyed on a single sortie by two F-15s carrying eight GBU-12s each.

Issue

- Improving the on-board navigation system will improve system effectiveness and responsiveness. (The NAVSTAR Global Positioning System currently offers the most promising alternative.)

F-16 FIGHTING FALCON MULTI-ROLE AIRCRAFT

Mission

The F-16 Fighting Falcon is the Air Force's primary multi-role aircraft, able to deliver a wide range of air-to-surface and air-to-air weapons. The F-16 was used during Operation Desert Storm for strategic attack, offensive counter air, suppression of enemy air defenses, air interdiction, and close air support.

System Data (F-16C)

Prime Contractor: General Dynamics Corp.
Crew: One Pilot
Initial Operational Capability: 1984
US Inventory: 1759
Length: 49.3 ft
Wingspan: 32.8 ft
Weight: 42,300 lb maximum takeoff
Cruise Speed: High subsonic
Range: 510 to 600 miles (High Profile)
Propulsion: One F110-GE-100 turbofan engine
Armament: Most air-to-air missiles and air-to-surface missiles and bombs

Employment

The F-16's involvement in Operations Desert Shield and Desert Storm began on 10 August with the deployment of 24 F-16Cs to Al-Dhafra, United Arab Emirates (UAE). A second squadron of F-16Cs arrived there the next day. Upon arrival, 12 F-16Cs were reconfigured for air-to-air combat and placed on alert. On 13 August, F-16s from Al-Dhafra, UAE, began flying training and orientation flights as aircraft and weapons continued to arrive in theater. As munition stockpiles built up, additional aircraft were placed on CAS alert to respond to any Iraqi incursion into Saudi Arabia.

From September through January, F-16s continued to arrive in theater. As the units arrived, they trained alongside other Coalition air forces in the Gulf region. F-16s refined established tactics and techniques and developed new procedures tailored to the desert environment. Specific training included medium altitude weapon deliveries and large force operations. Training also included extensive use of air refueling and airspace control procedures. During this time, Low Altitude Navigation Targeting Infrared for Night (LANTIRN) units received a full complement of navigation pods and accomplished Operational Test and Evaluation of this portion of the weapons system while preparing for and executing Operation Desert Storm. The complete LANTIRN system consists of a navigation pod and a targeting pod containing a laser designator, all integrated and mounted externally beneath the aircraft; however, because of the limited number available, no F-16s were equipped with LANTIRN targeting pods.

A total of 251 F-16s participated in Operation Desert Storm, attacking oil refineries, communications facilities, surface-to-air missile sites, Scud facilities, Republican Guard headquarters, airfield facilities, runways, aircraft bunkers, and chemical weapons bunkers. On 19 January, 56 F-16s attacked the Baghdad Nuclear Research Center in the largest single raid of the war. During Operation Desert Storm, F-16s continued to strike targets supporting all facets of the air campaign from strategic attack to CAS.

During the air campaign, F-16s used a two-aircraft formation as the basic fighting element. This basic two-aircraft element combined with other elements to form flights of four aircraft. These flights of four were then joined with other flights to form strike packages as large as 56 aircraft. In the early stages of the campaign, large packages were routine. However, as air supremacy was gained and targeting priorities changed, F-16s were used more as two-aircraft elements or as flights of four rather than in large packages.

Typical weapons loads used during Operation Desert Storm were:

- six MK-82s (500lb general purpose bomb) or,
- two MK-84s (2000Lb general purpose bomb) or,
- four CBU-52/58/71 (cluster bomb unit, anti-personnel) or,
- four CBU-87 (Combined effects munition) or,
- four CBU-89 (Gator mine, anti-personnel) or,
- four AGM-65 Maverick (electro-optical/IR guided missile) or,
- two AGM-69/88 (Shrike/high-speed anti-radiation missile)
- 510 rounds 20 mm Armor Piercing Incendiary/High Explosive Incendiary
- two AIM-9Ms

There was a requirement during the conflict for current and accurate target information in the interdiction mission area. This role was filled by F-16s in the Killer Scout mission, which essentially was armed reconnaissance that coordinated air strikes. Airspace was divided in 36x36 mile kill boxes. The Air Tasking Order assigned kill boxes. In the assigned boxes, scouts provided continuous daylight coverage for a two-aircraft formation and located targets in their area. Scouts provided target type and location updates as well as threat status and position information of other friendly aircraft. The intent was to strike assigned targets as soon as possible and keep traffic flowing through the Kuwait Theater of Operations.

Performance

F-16s proved effective when using GPS in conjunction with off-board sensors and LANTIRN.

Infrared Mavericks (AGM-65D/Gs) provided F-16s with a precision weapon that allowed standoff at medium altitude. When used in conjunction with the radar it provided beyond visual range targeting.

Five F-16s were lost in combat.

OBSERVATIONS

Accomplishments

■ More than 13,480 combat sorties were flown against targets including airfields, Republican Guard positions and strategic targets near Baghdad.

■ F-16s had a mission capable rate of 88.8 percent, and the highest use rate of all USAF aircraft in theater (1.35 sorties per aircraft per day).

■ F-16s using GPS, on board radar, and LANTIRN Forward-looking infrared proved successful.

Issue

■ The F-16 LANTIRN units are now receiving and qualifying with their targeting pods.

F-111 AARDVARK STRIKE AIRCRAFT

Mission

The F-111 is a land-based supersonic tactical
strike aircraft. It has variable sweep wings, a
terrain-following radar, a self-contained inertial
navigation system and a radar bombing system
— a combination that enables low-level attacks
in all weather conditions.

Two F-111 models participated in Operations
Desert Shield and Desert Storm; the F-111E and
the F-111F. The major difference between the
F-111E and the F-111F is the F-model's Pave
Tack pod which provides an infrared
target-acquisition and laser-designation
capability to attack point targets in clear weather
at night with laser-guided weapons.

System Data

Prime Contractor: General Dynamics
Crew Size: Two; one Pilot, one Weapon
System Officer

Initial Operational Capability: 1967 (F-111A)
US Inventory: 79 F-111Es and 83 F-111Fs
Length: 73.5 ft
Wingspan: 32 to 63 feet
Weight: 100,000 lbs maximum takeoff
Speed: 1.2 Mach at sea level
Range: 828 miles (combat radius)
Propulsion: Two Pratt and Whitney TF-30
turbofan engines
Armament: General purpose bombs (MK-82,
MK-84), Guided weapons (GBU-10, GBU-12,
GBU-15, GBU-24, GBU-28), and cluster
munitions (CBU-87, CBU-89)

Employment

The United States used 66 F-111Fs from bases
inside Saudi Arabia and 18 F-111Es as part of
the EUCOM supported Operation Proven Force
based at Incirlik Air Base, Turkey. The first
F-111 unit to deploy to the Gulf region was the
492nd Tactical Fighter Squadron (TFS) from
Lakenheath Air Base, United Kingdom (UK).

The 492nd TFS sent 18 of its F-111Fs to At-Taif, Saudi Arabia, on 25 August 1990. On 2 September, the 493rd TFS deployed 14 of its F-111Fs to At-Taif and on 29 November, the 494th TFS sent 20 F-111Fs to At-Taif. The 495th TFS sent the last F-111Fs from Lakenheath to Saudi Arabia on 11 December.

The 20th Tactical Fighter Wing from Upper Heyford, UK, was participating in routine training exercises at Incirlik Air Base, when tensions were rising between Iraq and Kuwait. The 77 TFS's 14 F-111Es remained in Turkey and represented the only US land-based offensive air capability in the Southern region until F-16Cs arrived in the region on 10 August. The 55th TFS replaced the 77th TFS on 31 August but eventually was replaced by the 79th TFS before Operation Desert Storm began. The 79 TFS remained on station in Turkey and operated as part of the Operation Proven Force composite wing until the war ended.

During Operation Desert Shield, the F-111Fs participated in composite force training missions aimed at increasing interoperability with the other night-capable air assets.

F-111s were tasked to attack airfield aircraft and facilities; hardened aircraft shelters; command, control, communications and intelligence facilities; bunkers, nuclear, biological, and chemical warfare facilities; bridges; air defense assets; and armor. Many of these missions were conducted in adverse weather conditions with an average sortie length of more than three hours. The Pave Tack forward-looking infrared (FLIR) system proved to be an invaluable asset at night, providing pinpoint accurate deliveries of laser-guided weapons.

Performance

The F-111's long range reduced aerial refueling requirements, freeing these resources to support other missions. The F-111 was used in a non-traditional anti-tank role. The Iraqi decision to deploy armor in fixed target positions allowed these positions to be determined. This enabled the F-111s to detect and attack the dug-in armor using the Pave Tack FLIR in conjunction with laser-guided bombs. The F-111 also demonstrated a capability to attack high-contrast targets with extreme precision when it used the TV-guided GBU-15s to destroy the oil facilities that Iraq used to pump oil into the Gulf.

The F-111 posted an 85 percent mission capable rate. No F-111s were lost during the war and only one sustained battle damage in more than 4,000 sorties.

OBSERVATIONS

Accomplishments

- The F-111's Pave Tack FLIR provided precision weapon capability at night allowing the aircraft to continue bombing round-the-clock. The ability to work at night allowed the F-111 to operate in a reduced threat environment, since electro-optical and infrared guided surface-to-air weapons require visual acquisition.

- The F-111F was credited with hitting the oil pumping manifold off the Kuwaiti coast, thwarting the Iraqi attempt to further spread Kuwaiti crude oil over the Gulf.

- The Pave Tack system's capability to provide video of the target from acquisition to impact provided immediate feedback for battle damage assessment.

- The F-111F successfully used the GBU-28 laser-guided bomb against a deeply buried command and control facility in Iraq.

Issue

- A planned avionics upgrade will provide a more accurate and reliable INS, especially if integrated with the NAVSTAR Global Positioning System.

F-117A NIGHTHAWK STEALTH FIGHTER

Mission

The F-117A Stealth fighter's mission is to penetrate dense threat environments and attack high-value/high-leverage targets with pinpoint accuracy using conventional laser-guided bombs.

System Data

Prime Contractor: Lockheed Aircraft
Crew: One pilot
Initial Operational Capability: Mid-1980s
US Inventory: 56
Length: 66 feet
Wingspan: 43.3 feet
Weight: 52,500 lbs maximum takeoff
Speed: High Subsonic
Range: 540 to 720 mile combat radius
Propulsion: Two General Electric F404-GE-F102 turbojet engines
Armament: Two laser-guided bombs (LGBs)

Employment

From September through December, the F-117s refined established tactics and techniques and developed new procedures tailored to the desert environment. Training included extensive use of air refueling. In addition to air refueling, training involved mock attacks at night on buildings and structures similar to the potential targets in Iraq.

During the first Operation Desert Storm attack, the F-117s were targeted against the Iraqi Integrated Air Defense System (IADS), specifically the integrated operations centers in the south and west. The F-117's second attack targeted key command and communications (C^2) centers in downtown Baghdad. These attacks were designed to quickly isolate field commanders from the decision makers in Baghdad.

On subsequent nights, the F-117s focused their attacks on other target categories to include hardened aircraft shelters at Iraqi airfields; nuclear, biological and chemical warfare research, production, and storage areas; bridges; Scud missile production and storage facilities; as well as the command, control, and communications targets. Before the ground offensive began, the F-117s were tasked to strike the oil pumping stations used by the Iraqis to feed the fire trenches along the Saudi/Kuwait border. The F-117 was effective in this role, removing both a physical and a potential psychological weapon from the Iraqi arsenal.

Performance

The F-117 achieved tactical surprise on the first night of the war, when it attacked about 35 percent of that night's strategic targets. It flew into the highest threat areas and was exposed to these threats for a relatively long time. The F-117 attacks helped disrupt the Iraqi IADS, and destroyed C^2 centers in Baghdad.

The F-117 was used by planners to strike the most heavily defended targets in the most populated areas. By virtue of its stealth characteristics, the F-117 allowed operations without the full range of support assets required by non-stealthy aircraft. Typically, F-117 sorties used little or no direct electronic combat or fighter support. These factors allowed planners to attack a far wider array of targets than would have been possible without them.

Over the course of the war, the deployed F-117s flew approximately two percent of the total attack sorties, yet struck about 40 percent of the strategic targets attacked. It was the only aircraft to attack targets in downtown Baghdad and to hit targets in all 12 target categories. The F-117's high accuracy limited collateral damage, particularly in Baghdad. No F-117s were lost or damaged due to air defenses, an outcome which strongly suggests stealth technology was effective.

The mission planning system designed specifically for the F-117 is time consuming and labor intensive.

OBSERVATIONS

Accomplishments

- The F-117 flew 1,296 sorties, mostly against targets in the heavily defended areas of downtown Baghdad, without the loss of a single aircraft.

- The F-117 was a weapons system of choice by planners to attack targets in downtown Baghdad. It struck targets in all 12 air target categories.

Shortcoming

- The F-117 has a slow, tedious mission-planning system.

Issues

- The mission planning system is undergoing a complete revision to make it more user friendly and adaptable to changing conditions. The USAF also is incorporating the F-117A's mission requirements into an upgraded Air Force Mission Support System.

- Improving the on-board navigation system will improve system effectiveness and responsiveness. The NAVSTAR Global Positioning System currently offers the most promising alternative.

F/A-18A/C HORNET STRIKE FIGHTER

Mission

The F/A-18 Hornet strike fighter is a twin-engine, twin-tail, high performance, multi-mission tactical aircraft operated by the Navy and Marine Corps (USMC). The Hornet uses selected external equipment to accomplish specific fighter or attack missions. When used as a fighter, the F/A-18 provides cover for tactical air projection over land and sea and complements Fleet air defense. The primary attack missions are interdiction, close air support, defense suppression, and strikes against land/seaborne targets.

System Data

Prime Contractor: McDonnell Douglas
Crew: One pilot
Initial Operational Capability: 1983 (F/A-18A)
US Inventory: 526
Length: 56 feet

Wingspan: 37.5 feet
Maximum Gross Weight: 51,900 lbs
Speed: 725 kts , 1.8+ Mach
Combat Radius: 440 miles (fighter mission); 500 miles (attack mission)
Propulsion: Two General Electric F404-GE-400 afterburning, low-/ bypass turbofan engines each capable of producing 16,000 pounds thrust
Armament: Nine external stations, including two wingtip stations for AIM-9 Sidewinder air-to-air missiles; two outboard wing stations for an assortment of air-to-air and air-to-ground weapons, including AIM-7 Sparrows, AIM-9 Sidewinders, AGM-84 Harpoons, AGM-88 high-speed anti-radiation missiles (HARM) and AGM-65 Maverick missiles; two inboard wing stations for external fuel tanks or air-to-ground weapons; two nacelle fuselage stations for Sparrows, AN/ASQ-173 Laser Detector Tracker Strike Camera, AN/AAS-38 targeting forward-looking infrared (FLIR) or AN/AAR-50 navigation FLIR; and a center

station for fuel tank or air-to-ground weapons. Air-to-ground weapons include GBU-10 and 12 laser-guided bombs (LGBs), MK-80 series general purpose bombs, and CBU-59 cluster bombs. A M61 20-mm six-barrel gun is mounted in the nose and has a director gunsight.

Employment

Ninety Navy F/A-18 A/Cs, operating from four aircraft carriers, participated in Operation Desert Storm combat operations. The multi-mission Hornet was used in all areas of the offensive counter air (OCA) and defensive counter air (DCA) mission. The OCA sweeps were flown in the early days of the war to engage Iraqi aircraft that may have been in the target area. Typical F/A-18 load for this mission was two AIM-9, two AIM-7, and full 20-mm ammunition (FAMMO).

Thirty-six USMC F/A-18A and 36 F/A-18C aircraft deployed to SWA. USMC F/A-18s were used in strategic air strikes, suppression of enemy air defense (SEAD), Republican Guard attacks, battlefield preparation, and air support during the ground offensive. Strikes were launched from Skaikh Isa, Bahrain, with a typical load of two fuel tanks, two Sparrow AAMs, two Sidewinder AAMs, and five MK-83 Rockeye, or MK-84 bombs, or Walleye, or Maverick missiles. F/A-18 also used FLIR and HARM.

Dedicated combat air patrol (CAP) missions were flown around the clock by units in the Persian Gulf to maintain a fighter presence on the three assigned CAP stations. Typical load for this mission was two AIM-9, two AIM-7, FAMMO, and a forward-looking infrared (FLIR) pod.

The F/A-18 Hornet was heavily tasked to conduct SEAD missions during the first part of the war. Normal mission load consisted of two AIM-9, two AIM-7, FAMMO, and two AGM-88 High-Speed Anti-Radiation Missiles (HARM).

OCA airfield attack was conducted by units operating both in the Red Sea and the Persian Gulf. Typical load for this mission was two AIM-9, five or more MK-83s, or two or more MK-84s, one AIM-7, FAMMO and a FLIR pod.

In the airfield attack mission, bunkers and aircraft revetments were attacked with MK-84 bombs with electrically delayed fuzes. Hangers and buildings were attacked with MK-80 series bombs with instantaneous and variable time fuzes. Primary target acquisition systems used were visual, radar, inertial navigation, and FLIR. To remain clear of the Iraqi air defense systems typical attacks were from a 30 degree or greater dive beginning at 30,000 to 35,000 feet with release between 20,000 and 10,000 feet, at an airspeed of 480 to 540 knots.

DCA escort was flown on occasion by units in the Persian Gulf. Typical load for this mission was two AIM-9, one AIM-7, FAMMO and occasionally a HARM.

All aircraft flew with operable electronic countermeasures equipment. This equipment included the ALR-67 Radar Warning Receiver, an ALE-39 chaff/flare dispensing unit, and an ALQ-126B DECM set.

Performance

The F/A-18 Hornet proved highly reliable and survivable. More than 17,500 tons of ordnance were delivered against a variety of targets. Self-escort capability reduced support assets that would otherwise have been required.

The F/A-18 demonstrated exceptional flexibility and rapid turn around times. Its availability was near continuous (99 percent) and its survivability was impressive. Three USMC F/A-18s damaged by surface to air missiles and one by anti-air artillery all returned to base and flew again within 36 hours. Only one Navy F/A-18 was lost in combat.

The successful performance of the multi-mission F/A-18 Hornet was highlighted on 17 January when a division of F/A-18s encountered two Iraqi Mig-21s about 35 miles from the intended target. The F/A-18s acquired, identified, and destroyed the two MIGs, rapidly shifted to the air-to-ground role, rolled in on the assigned target, and dropped MK-84s with pinpoint accuracy.

OBSERVATIONS

Accomplishments

- F/A-18s were reliable and experienced good survivability in combat.

- Multi-mission philosophy created flexibility for the Operation Desert Storm commander. F/A-18s participated in virtually every conceivable mission during Operation Desert Storm.

- F/A-18s conducted 10 intercepts (established radar contact) against hostile aircraft, with two air-to-air shoot downs.

- F/A-18s demonstrated the capability to acquire strike targets with visual, radar, inertial navigation coordinates and FLIR.

Issue

- Improving the on-board navigation system will improve system effectiveness and responsiveness. The NAVSTAR Global Positioning System currently offers the most promising alternative.

F/A-18D HORNET STRIKE FIGHTER

Mission

This two-seat all-weather, day/night Marine Corps (USMC) aircraft's mission is to attack and destroy surface targets, conduct multi-sensor imagery reconnaissance, supporting arms coordination, and intercept and engage enemy aircraft.

System Data

Prime Contractor: McDonnell Douglas
Crew: One pilot, one weapon system officer
Initial Operational Capability: 1989
US Inventory: 29
Length: 56 feet
Wingspan: 37.5 feet
Maximum Gross Weight: 51,900 lbs
Cruise Speed: high subsonic to supersonic
Combat Radius: 410 miles (fighter mission), 465 miles (attack mission)
Propulsion: Two General Electric F404-GE-400 turbofan engines
Armament: Nine external stations, including two wingtip stations for AIM-9 Sidewinder air-to-air missiles; two outboard wing stations for an assortment of air-to-air and air-to-ground weapons, including AIM-7 Sparrows, AIM-9 Sidewinders, AGM-84 Harpoons, AGM-88 high-speed anti-radiation missiles (HARM) and AGM-65 Maverick missiles; two inboard wing stations for external fuel tanks or air-to-ground weapons; two nacelle fuselage stations for Sparrows, AN/ASQ-173 laser detector tracker strike camera, AN/AAS-38 targeting forward-looking infrared (FLIR) or AN/AAR-50 navigation FLIR; and a center station for fuel tank or air-to-ground weapons. Air-to-ground weapons include GBU-10 and 12 laser-guided bombs, MK-80 series general purpose bombs, and CBU-59 cluster bombs. A M61 20-mm six-barrel gun is mounted in the nose and has a director gunsight

Employment

The USMC deployed 12 F/A-18D aircraft to Southwest Asia. The F/A-18s were used in tactical air coordinator and airborne forward air control roles. These aircraft flew into target areas ahead of Coalition strike aircraft to locate and identify high value targets during tactical air missions. F/A-18s provided almost 24-hour battlefield coverage for close air support (CAS) missions.

Performance

The F/A-18Ds flew 557 sorties and achieved a 14 sorties a day sustained sortie rate. The aircraft's mission capable rate was 85.9 percent. Ordnance expended included 2,325 rockets and 27,000 rounds of 20-mm cannon ammunition.

F/A-18Ds located and identified high value targets not only for USMC tactical air strikes but also for Air Force, Navy and Kuwaiti Air Force strikes.

The F/A-18 demonstrated good survivability during Operation Desert Storm. Throughout the air campaign and ground offensive, no F/A-18Ds were lost to enemy fire and only two sustained battle damage (one from a surface-to-air missile and one from anti-air artillery; both returned to service within less than 36 hours) even though the aircraft spent more time in threat areas because of its air control mission.

OBSERVATIONS

Accomplishments

- F/A-18Ds located and identified high value targets for Coalition CAS sorties.

- F/A-18Ds were effective in controlling as many as 20 aircraft in a 30-minute period, providing not only target identification and location, but also threat and overall battlefield updates.

JOINT SURVEILLANCE AND TARGET ATTACK RADAR SYSTEM (JSTARS)

Mission

The Joint Surveillance and Target Attack Radar System (JSTARS) is a joint Army/Air Force (USAF) development program designed to provide near real time (NRT) wide-area surveillance and deep targeting capability to ground and air commanders for indications and warning, situation development, and target development. The USAF is responsible for developing the E-8 aircraft, a military version of the Boeing 707, the airborne radar, the aircraft self-defense suite and air-to-ground communications. The JSTARS radar provides information on both moving and fixed targets.

A frequency hopping, Ku Band surveillance control data link (SCDL) is the primary communications means between the E-8 and ground station modules (GSM). The SCDL provides Ground Station Module (GSM) operators the same radar data available to

on-board operators for processing, analyzing, and disseminating to operational and tactical ground commanders. The Army is responsible for developing the GSM.

Interim GSM (IGSM) is a full scale development model. The system will receive, process, and analyze data from several sensors in addition to JSTARS (e.g., Small Aerostat Surveillance System and OV-1D side-looking airborne radar). However, it can operate only with one sensor at a time. Six IGSMs, mounted on five-ton trucks, were deployed.

System Data

Prime Contractor: Grumman Aerospace Corp
Crew: Flight crew of four plus 17 to 25 mission specialists
Initial Operational Capability: Projected FY 97
US Inventory: Two research and development aircraft

Length: 145 ft
Wingspan: 146 ft
Combat Weight: 325,000 lb
Cruise Speed: 480 mph
Range: 3,000 miles
Propulsion: Four TF-33 turbofan engines
Armament: None

Employment

Two E-8s deployed to Riyadh, Saudi Arabia on 12 January and the first operational mission was flown two days later. Six IGSMs were sent to Saudi Arabia, arriving on 12 January. An IGSM was allocated to both Air Force Component, Central Command (AFCENT) and Army Component, Central Command (ARCENT) in Riyadh; one was deployed with Marine Component, Central Command (MARCENT) at various locations; one was sent to ARCENT forward at King Khalid Military City; and one, was assigned to both VII Corps and XVIII Airborne Corps. Only two E-8 missions were flown before Operation Desert Storm began, one

primarily for testing. Iraqi ground equipment was detected on both flights.

Performance

hroughout Operation Desert Storm, JSTARS (with external sensor cueing) was able to detect, locate, and track high value targets, such as Scud missile launchers, convoys, river crossing sites, logistics sites, assembly areas, and retreat routes.

On 29 January, JSTARS detected a convoy moving south from the suburbs of Kuwait City. JSTARS tracked the convoy and passed the target to the Airborne Battlefield Command and Control Center, which called in Coalition aircraft. These aircraft reportedly destroyed 58 of 61 vehicles in the convoy. Later that day, during the battle for Al-Khafji, JSTARS confirmed no Iraqi reinforcements were being sent, permitting a rapid and accurate assessment of the tactical situation which helped in plan the JFC-E for the counterattack.

OBSERVATIONS

Accomplishments

- JSTARS proved it could deploy to an area and operate with existing command, control, communications, and intelligence (C^3I) assets.

- JSTARS provided NRT monitoring of major enemy ground movements.

- JSTARS real-time monitoring of Coalition force movement helped coalition force command and control and reduced fratricide.

- Deployment of E-8/IGSM systems still in full scale development (i.e., Initial Operational Capability planned for FY97) worked well and provided significant C^3I contributions.

- JSTARS performed well in combat conditions. Operation Desert Storm re-validated the need for a system to locate and track moving ground targets across a wide area and quickly relay this information to commanders.

Shortcoming

- The two available JSTARS aircraft could not meet Central Command's requirements. Because JSTARS is a development system, spare parts were at a premium and often had to come from the non-flying platform to meet mission requirements.

Issues

- JSTARS program managers are working with the acquisition community to improve JSTARS support for future contingencies.

- The USAF and Army are reviewing JSTARS concepts of operation with respect to tactical integration of JSTARS and air/ground users.

- Incorporating the NAVSTAR Global Positioning System with on-board navigation will improve system effectiveness and make JSTARS more compatible with intelligence collection systems.

KC-135 STRATOTANKER REFUELING AIRCRAFT

Mission

Purchased to refuel strategic long-range bombers, the KC-135 also provides aerial refueling support to all Air Force (USAF), Navy, and Marine Corps (USMC) aircraft as well as allied aircraft. KC-135s have the additional ability to transport passengers and cargo. There are four variants of the KC-135; the KC-135A, KC-135E, KC-135Q and KC-135R.

System Data

Prime Contractor: Boeing
Crew: Four
Initial Operational Capability: 1957 (KC-135A)
US Inventory: 629; 182 KC-135As, 158 KC-135Es; 235 KC-135Rs; 54 KC-135Qs
Length: 136 ft 3 in
Wingspan: 130 ft 10 in

Maximum takeoff weight: 203,288 lbs (KC-135R), 189,000 lbs (KC-135A/Q), 193,000 lbs (KC-135E)
Cruise Speed: 460 knots
Range: 11,270 miles
Propulsion: Four F108-CF 100 jet engines (KC-135R)
Armament: None

Employment

Tankers established air refueling bridges across the Atlantic and Pacific oceans to move fighter aircraft to the Gulf region. These aircraft also supported airlift aircraft deploying ground units to the region. During the conflict, KC-135 tankers were assigned to specific strike formations.

More tankers were involved in the Gulf War operations than the 230 aircraft identified in Joint Staff plans for regional contingency operations. During Operations Desert Shield and Desert Storm, 262 KC-135s supported the theater along with 46 KC-10s. In addition to refueling sorties, KC-135s flew 913 airlift sorties, transporting passengers and cargo to the theater and within the theater. US tankers refueled aircraft from the armed forces of Italy, Oman, Bahrain, Saudi Arabia, and the United Arab Emirates. The crucial limiting factor affecting air refueling was airspace. A combination of air refueling tracks and anchors were used to maximize tanker availability. Tankers performed some refuelings over enemy territory. The Air Reserve Component (ARC) of the tanker force participated in all phases of operations, comprising 37 percent of the tanker fleet in the theater. Twelve of 13 Air National Guard units and all three Air Force Reserve tanker units were activated.

Performance

KC-135s flew almost 23,000 refueling sorties, delivering more than 136 million gallons of fuel to more than 69,000 receivers. No air refuelings were missed for reasons other than weather. Mission capable (MC) rates exceeded 90 percent which is greater than the peacetime rate.

Aircrew performance, both active duty and ARC, was excellent due to both normal training (including worldwide operations and joint and combined exercises) and the intensive training

and flying time expended to hone skills before Operation Desert Storm.

KC-135A and Q model performance was marginal in the hot weather conditions, even with thrust augmentation. This augmentation is provided by 5,500 lbs of water injected into the engines during takeoff. This requirement makes these models dependent on demineralization plants and water trucks and reduces the fuel capacity. The performance of the KC-135A and Q limited their use in Operations Desert Shield and Desert Storm. Missions supported by one KC-135R required two KC-135A or Q aircraft for the same level of support. In addition to performance factors, some beddown locations were unavailable to A and Q models because of noise and/or pollution considerations.

The KC-135 requires installation of a single-point boom drogue adapter before refueling probe-equipped aircraft (Navy, USMC, and certain allied aircraft). Probe/drogue receivers found this fixed attachment on the KC-135 less desirable than the separate hose systems on other tankers because it leaves less margin for error during engagement, refueling, and disengagement. Some refueling incidents resulted in damage to the refueling probe itself, or to the drogue, requiring the mission to abort. The designed hose length, response, and basket configuration mandate proficiency and training in addition to that required for KC-10, KC-130 and KA-6D hose/basket systems.

OBSERVATIONS

Accomplishments

- KC-135s flew almost 23,000 refueling sorties, providing more than 136 million gallons of fuel to more than 69,000 receivers.

- Mission capable rate exceeded 90 percent, greater than the peacetime rate.

Shortcomings

- KC-135A and Q model performance was marginal, limiting their use.

- The KC-135 requires installation of a drogue adapter on its boom before refueling probe-equipped receivers, which limits its flexibility to refuel all types of aircraft.

Issues

- Performance problems associated with the KC-135A and Q models will be corrected by upgrading them to the R model configuration by 1995.

- A program to equip KC-135s with two wing mounted air refueling pods for probe and drogue operations is in research and development with production planned for 1994. This modification would correct the problems associated with refueling aircraft equipped with probes.

- The Navy uses JP-5 jet fuel for carrier operations because it is less volatile than other grades. However, JP-5 was not as readily available throughout the theater. Refueling carrier-based aircraft with grades other than JP-5 caused safety concerns once the aircraft were back on the carriers. This problem could be a constraining factor in future operations and is under review by a joint USAF/Navy review board.

LIGHT AIRBORNE MULTIPURPOSE SYSTEM (LAMPS) HELICOPTER

Mission

Light Airborne Multipurpose System (LAMPS) is an integrated ship/helicopter system. The helicopter uses avionics and electronics to extend the range of shipboard sensors and weapons. Primary missions are anti-submarine warfare and anti-surface warfare (ASUW). Secondary missions include logistics support, search and rescue, and medical evacuation. LAMPS MK I aircraft support FF 1052, CG 27, and NRF FFG 7 class ships as well as DD 963, DDG 993, CG 47, and FFG 7 class ships awaiting LAMPS MK III modifications. LAMPS MK III aircraft support DD 963, CG 47, and FFG 7 class ships. LAMPS MK III ships have mechanical launch and recovery provisions to permit helicopter operations in severe weather.

System Data

	SH-2F (MARK I)	SH-60B (MARK III)
Prime Contractor:	Kaman Aerospace	Sikorsky/IBM
Crew:	Two pilots, one crew	Two pilots, one crew

	SH-2F (MARK I)	SH-60B (MARK III)
Initial Operational Capability:	1973	1984
US Inventory:	111	126
Length:	52 ft 7 in	64 ft 10 in
Rotor Diameter:	44 feet	53 ft 8 in
Gross weight:	13,500 lbs	21,700 lbs
Maximum speed:	150 knots	180 knots
Range:	360 miles	500 miles
Endurance:	three hrs	four hrs
Propulsion:	T-58 turboshaft (2)	T-700 turboshaft (2)
Armament:	2 ASW torpedoes M-60 machine gun	3 ASW torpedoes M-60 machine gun

Employment

The Navy deployed 46 LAMPS aircraft (34 LAMPS MK III SH-60Bs and 12 LAMPS MK 1 SH-2Fs). One SH-2F was equipped with a prototype Magic Lantern laser mine-detection system. LAMPS helicopters operated throughout the Persian Gulf, Red Sea, Gulf of Oman, Gulf of Aden, and Eastern Mediterranean Sea performing maritime interception operations (MIO), detection and targeting missions, mine hunting and destruction, explosive ordnance disposal (EOD) team support, special warfare operations, battle damage assessment, combat search and rescue, and coastal surveillance. Joint operations were conducted with Army and British helicopters and Kuwaiti surface combatants. United Nations Security Council sanctions were enforced through hundreds of merchant shipping queries. LAMPS helicopters provided close-in protective machine gun coverage for boarding parties, detected floating and moored mines and worked in direct support of EOD teams conducting mine destruction. SH-60B crews rescued an Air Force F-16 pilot and a Navy F-18 pilot.

LAMPS helicopters were tasked to find Iraqi patrol boats and minelayers, search oil platforms for Iraqi military activity, and monitor the spread of oil caused by Iraq's environmental terrorism.

Performance

During Operation Desert Storm, LAMPS helicopters flew 10,123 hours in 4,102 sorties. The mission capable (MC) rate was 87 percent and the full mission capable (FMC) rate was 80 percent.

OBSERVATIONS

Accomplishments

- Detected and targeted enemy surface threats which resulted in successful coordinated attacks with armed British Lynx and Army OH-58D helicopters.

- Participated in 11 MIO take downs as gunships in coordinated efforts with SEALs aboard SH-3s.

- Visually located many mines.

- Conducted two successful over-water pilot rescues in the northern Persian Gulf.

- Participated in coordinated attacks with SEALs and OH-58D against Iraqi forces on Qurah Island. Two minelayers were destroyed, 67 enemy prisoners of war (EPWs) were taken, and many documents were captured.

- Along with OH-58Ds from USS Nicholas (FFG 47), engaged nine oil platforms in the Ad-Dawrah oil fields, taking 23 EPWs.

Shortcomings

- The LAMPS helicopters lack a stand off air-to-surface weapon like the British Lynx's Sea Skua missile.

- The LAMPS helicopters lack adequate visual identification equipment for surveillance and targeting (particularly night vision) and a Global Positioning System for more accurate navigation.

Issue

- The Penguin air-to-surface missile for the SH-60B (Initial Operational Capability FY-93) will provide an air-to-surface standoff weapon capability.

MH-53E SEA STALLION MINE COUNTERMEASURE HELICOPTER

Mission

The primary missions of MH-53E aviation mine countermeasure (AMCM) helicopters are to detect and sweep mines, and to conduct precursor sweeps for surface mine countermeasure forces. AMCM helicopters tow a cable with a mechanical cutting device which cuts mine mooring cables releasing the mines to the surface. The helicopters also use acoustic and magnetic mine countermeasure (MCM) sleds, which simulate a ship's propellers and magnetic signature, detonating influence mines. Additionally, they tow a side scanning sonar device to locate moored and bottom mines.

System Data

Prime Contractor: United Technologies Sikorsky Aircraft
Crew: Two pilots, and two to five crewmen
Initial Operational Capability: 1988
US Inventory: 30
Length: 99 ft
Rotor Diameter: 79 ft
Weight: 73,500 lbs (maximum gross weight)
Speed: 150 knots
Range: 750 nm
Propulsion: Three T-64-416 engines
Armament: Two 50-caliber machine guns
MCM systems:
Mk 103 moored sweep

Mk 104 acoustic sweep
Mk 105 magnetic sweep
Mk 106 magnetic/acoustic sweep
RAYDIST/GPS navigation
AN/AQS-14 minehunting sonar

Employment

On 7 October, six MH-53 AMCM Super Stallion helicopters arrived in the Persian Gulf on Air Force C-5As. After Operation Desert Storm began, Coalition MCM platform's principal mission was to clear a path to the Kuwaiti coast for naval gun fire support and a possible amphibious landing. After the cease-fire, these platforms platforms cleared port approaches and harbors, including Kuwait City's port.

Performance

The air-transportable AMCM helicopters provided rapid response for MCM operations. Their high speed provided great flexibility during Coalition MCM operations. AMCM helicopters were the preferred platform for shallow water MCM operations. Using the Mk 106 magnetic/acoustic sweep, the helicopters cleared hundreds of square miles of the northern Persian Gulf. AMCM assets swept over thirty mines and coordinated explosive ordnance disposal (EOD) team mine destruction. The AMCM helicopters averaged four missions per day and sustained an average aircraft availability rate of 83 percent.

OBSERVATIONS

Accomplishment

■ This was the first operational deployment of the MH-53E helicopter; the AMCM successfully completed their missions.

Shortcomings

■ AMCM helicopters did not have a dedicated surface platform to serve as a flight deck and support ship.

■ The MH-53E was not certified to conduct night MCM operations.

Issue

■ Programs are being considered to provide AMCM with improved Global Positioning System navigation, night certification, airborne neutralization and sweep systems, and electro-optical minehunting capability.

■ The AMCM helicopters lacked a dedicated support ship which could provide a flight deck, command and control, logistics, maintenance, and EOD team support.

OH-58D SCOUT HELICOPTER

Mission

The OH-58D is the Army's first true scout helicopter. Its primary missions are reconnaissance, intelligence gathering, surveillance, and target acquisition and/or designation during day or night operations, and in adverse weather.

The OH-58D's mast-mounted sight (MMS) provides day and night target acquisition sensors and a laser rangefinder/designator. The laser designator lets the OH-58D use laser-guided weapons including Hellfire and other precision munitions. The MMS is above the rotor to increase aircraft survivability by allowing the aircraft to hover closer to the ground or behind hills or berms. The OH-58D's highly accurate inertial navigation system permits precise target location information, which can be passed to other aircraft or artillery elements with an automatic target handover system.

In 1987 and 1988, 15 OH-58Ds were modified with air-to-air and air-to-ground weapons. The modifications include Air-to-Air Stinger (ATAS) and Air-to-Ground Hellfire, Hydra 70 rockets, and a .50-caliber machine gun. These aircraft were designated Prime Chance aircraft.

System Data (Prime Chance aircraft)

Prime Contractor: Bell Helicopter
Crew: Two
Initial Operational Capability: 1987
US Inventory: 168
Length: 33.8 ft
Rotor Diameter: 35 ft
Maximum Gross Weight: 5,400 pounds
Speed: 112 knots (cruise)
Range: 324 miles
Endurance: 2.4 hours
Propulsion: 650hp T-703-AD-700
Armament: Prime Chance only; combination of two of the following: ATAS, Hellfire missiles, .50 Caliber Machine Gun, Hydra 70 rockets

Employment

The Army deployed 132 of 168 (79 percent) of the OH-58D combat fleet to Southwest Asia (SWA). The OH-58D was used as a scout and armed reconnaissance helicopter. As an unarmed scout helicopter, it was used primarily to conduct reconnaissance at night and provided intelligence directly to the ground maneuver commander. The OH-58D designated targets for attack aircraft such as the AH-64 with Hellfire. Operating from naval vessels, seven OH-58Ds were used as reconnaissance and attack assets in the maritime campaign.

OH-58Ds also operated with Marine Corps attack helicopters, coordinated fire support, and led Joint Air Attack Team missions with fixed wing attack aircraft. OH-58Ds also designated targets for F-111s, and other fixed-wing aircraft.

In combat engagements, OH-58Ds contributed to field artillery effectiveness by providing aerial observation for standard artillery munitions and terminal guidance for laser-guided Copperhead rounds.

Performance

The Prime Chance OH-58Ds supporting the maritime campaign in the Persian Gulf used Hellfire anti-armor missiles, 2.75" aerial rockets, and .50-cal machine gun, to attack targets, such as fortified oil platforms and Iraqi forces on islands, from stand-off ranges.

Prime Chance OH-58Ds participated in liberating the first Kuwaiti territory in the conflict. Around noon on 24 January, OH-58Ds operating from *USS Curts* (FFG 38) attempted to rescue 22 Iraqis from a sinking minelayer near Qaruh Island. As the helicopters assisted the survivors, Iraqi forces on the Island fired on the helicopters. As the helicopters engaged the island defenses with rocket and machine gun fire, *USS Curts* maneuvered closer to the island and attacked the positions with its 76-mm guns. Navy SEALs from Naval Special Warfare Group 1 landed on Qaruh aboard helicopters from *USS Leftwich* (DD 984). With the OH-58Ds, *USS Nicholas* (FFG 47), and *USS Curts* covering the island, the SEALs reclaimed the island and raised the Kuwaiti flag on Qaruh Island. The Coalition forces captured 67 enemy prisoners of war (EPWs) during the battle and obtained intelligence about Iraqi minefields in the area.

OH-58Ds operated with AH-64s on raids to destroy radar sites and antiaircraft positions. These missions included seeking out and designating targets for AH-64s. Acting as a covering force to provide early warning, OH-58Ds led the 2nd Armored Cavalry Regiment's main effort into Iraq and Kuwait during Operation Desert Storm. While providing aerial observation for field artillery missions, OH-58Ds successfully designated 12 targets which were destroyed by Copperhead artillery rounds. While operating near friendly ground units, the OH-58D guided close air support sorties onto targets with laser designation.

The OH-58D mission capable rate was more than 85 percent. While flying more than 8,700 hours in SWA, the operating tempo exceeded 23 hours an aircraft per month. The normal peacetime operating tempo is 14 hours an aircraft.

OBSERVATIONS

Accomplishments

- Eighty-one percent of the Army's entire OH-58D combat fleet supported operations in SWA. During operations in SWA the OH-58D flew more than 8,700 hours.

- The Prime Chance OH-58Ds were dedicated to joint missions and provided the Navy its only night forward-firing helicopter platform.

- Operating with Naval forces, OH-58Ds participated in liberating the first Kuwaiti territory in the conflict.

PIONEER UNMANNED AERIAL VEHICLE (UAV)

Mission

The Pioneer unmanned aerial vehicle (UAV) system provides near-real time (NRT) day or night reconnaissance, surveillance, target acquisition (RSTA), battle damage assessment (BDA) and battlefield management within line-of-sight of the ground control station. Pioneer systems are used by the Army, Navy, and Marine Corps (USMC).

System Data

Prime Contractor: AAI Corp
Crew: Ground crew, three; flight controllers, three
Initial Operational Capability: 1986 (Interim System)
US Inventory: 50
Length: 14 ft
Wingspan: 17 ft
Max gross weight: 448 lbs
Range: Greater than 120 miles
Mission altitude: 1000 to 12,000 ft

Max altitude: 15,000 ft
Propulsion: 26 horsepower, aviation gas engine
Armament: None
Guidance: UHF/C band telemetry
Sensors: Electro-optical; Infrared, or Television

Employment

The Navy used Pioneer from the battleships USS Missouri (BB63) and USS Wisconsin (BB64). Pioneer flew 151 sorties for a total of 520 flight hours. Sorties conducted included RSTA, Naval Gunfire Support, BDA, Maritime Interception Operations (MIO) and battlefield management. Information collected was provided to theater and component commanders. For example, as a result of Pioneer, Iraqi patrol boats were detected and a strike on two high-speed boats was directed. In the surveillance role: two Silkworm antiship missile sites were located; 320 ships identified; antiaircraft artillery positions were determined; pre- and post-assault reconnaissance of Faylaka Island was conducted, including the surrender of Iraqi troops; and, major Iraqi armor movements and the retreat from Kuwait were detected.

The Army's Pioneer UAV system is assigned within the UAV Platoon, Fort Huachuca, AZ. This supports the Army's training base and provides a UAV contingency capability for activities such as Operations Desert Shield and Desert Storm.

During Operations Desert Shield and Desert Storm, the Army's UAV platoon was assigned to VII Corps and provided support throughout the Corps area. VII Corps was quick to recognize its value and began requesting more missions than the unit could fly. Targets of interest included tanks, bunkers, command posts, artillery batteries, free rocket over ground (FROG) sites, and convoys. In many instances, the number of targets discovered were so great they could not be engaged quickly. In addition, the Pioneer was used to observe Iraqi retrograde operations.

The USMC used the Pioneer UAV with three Remotely Piloted Vehicle (RPV) Companies operating from Al-Jubai airport, Abu Hadriyah, Al-Mish'ab, and Al-Qarrah.

The USMC Pioneer UAV was used primarily for RSTA. This is because of the current lack of payloads other than electro-optical (day television) and forward looking infrared. One Pioneer vehicle was configured for radio (Very High Frequency/Ultra High Frequency)) relay; however it was not used during the operation. RSTA objectives are to collect information via pre-planned reconnaissance and surveillance, detect, recognize, and identify targets. This information was used to engage targets by gunfire spot adjustment techniques (including naval gunfire) or directing close air support assets toward the target. Targets included troops, tanks, artillery pieces, surface-to-air missile sites (including dummy sites), FROG sites, aircraft

hangars, and ground emplacements (trenches, bunkers, supply depots).

Pioneer was an outstanding asset for determining BDA. Its high survivability, long endurance, and NRT video allowed for varying aspect angles and repetitive views during extended periods. The video quality allowed immediate decisions on whether additional attacks were required. For example, a "dummy" SAM site was not engaged because the video allowed the determination that the site was not operational. BDA was performed on the targets previously mentioned.

Performance

The Navy Pioneer UAV system's availability exceeded expectations. Established sortie rates indicated a deployed unit could sustain 60 flight hours a month. During combat operations, units flew more than 125 hours a month. This tempo stretched the current logistic support structure's limits.

Direct control of Pioneer by the Naval tactical commander provided a high degree of responsiveness and flexibility. Airspace deconfliction worked well in the theater of operations. System survivability was well demonstrated. Low signature resulted in only one air vehicle shot down. Three other UAV were hit but were recovered and subsequently repaired and returned to service. During Desert Storm Navy UAVs flew 64 sorties for 213 hours while providing NGFS for 83 missions.

The Army Pioneer UAV provided a quick-fire link that allowed targets to be engaged quickly. The Pioneer helped the tactical commander conduct situation development, targeting, route reconnaissance, and BDA. The UAV platoon also moved during combat to support the forward movement of battle. This was managed by completing a hastily constructed runway near the front line of troops. Army

UAVs flew 46 sorties and 155 flight hours during the war.

USMC Pioneer operations were conducted at various altitudes depending on the mission assigned. Marine UAV companies flew 138 missions and 318 hours during Operation Desert Shield and 185 missions and 662 hours during Operation Desert Storm.

OBSERVATIONS

Accomplishments

- Pioneer successfully conducted RSTA, Command and Control (C^2), and BDA missions throughout the campaign. Much USMC success in enemy location and validation resulted from hours of UAV video depicting details of exact Iraqi positions.

- Pioneer demonstrated the flexibility to operate from runways and roads.

- Pioneer provided a quick-fire link between real-time video and the shooters.

- Pioneer validated the use of UAVs in the same airspace with manned aircraft.

- Operators provided the first successful integration of ship-based UAVs into combat operations.

Shortcomings

- Shipboard launch and recovery systems were cumbersome and required increased logistic support.

- The Pioneer UAV uses aviation gasoline which is difficult to obtain and raises safety issues with shipboard storage of the fuel.

- The Army Pioneer's launch and recovery system required a runway. This made use difficult in remote combat areas near the forward line of troops.

- The proliferation of different video formats between Services complicates the sharing of products.

Issue

- The shortcomings are being addressed by the Services in requirements documents in support of future UAVs under development by the UAV Joint Project Office.

S-3B VIKING MULTI-MISSION AIRCRAFT

Mission

The S-3B aircraft is a carrier-based, fixed wing, multi-mission aircraft designed to provide the carrier battle force with a quick reaction outer zone anti-submarine warfare, and anti-surface warfare, surveillance, localization and attack capability. During Operation Desert Storm, the S-3B was used in many additional roles including command and control (C-2) and in-flight refueling.

System Data

Prime Contractor: Lockheed Aircraft
Crew: Four, one pilot and three crewman
Initial Operational Capability: 1974 (S-3A); 1988 (S-3B)
US Inventory: 78
Length: 53.4 feet,
Wingspan: 68.7 feet
Weight: 52,540 lbs maximum takeoff
Maximum speed: 457 knots
Range: 3,168 miles (unrefueled)

Propulsion: Two G.E.TF-34 Turbofan engines
Armament: Harpoon, Mk-80 series bombs, MK-46 Torpedo, all naval mines

Employment

Forty-one S-3 aircraft in theater operated from five aircraft carriers; they flew 1,674 sorties and 4,948 hours supporting Operation Desert Storm. The S-3 multi-mission capability was demonstrated throughout the conflict in a variety of missions:

S-3Bs participated in armed scout missions in the Red Sea and Persian Gulf augmenting armed surface reconnaissance aircraft assigned to strike missions.

S-3 aircraft provided inflight refueling to Combat Air Patrol (CAP) aircraft in the Red Sea and Persian Gulf. Combat tanking was provided to returning strike aircraft. The S-3 provided recovery and emergency fuel for long-range strike aircraft returning to ship. The S-3's extended range and endurance was ideally suited for this mission.

S-3B aircraft smoothed transition and established communication connectivity for strike leaders going to targets in western and central Iraq and the Kuwait Theater of Operations (KTO). S-3B aircraft provided C^2 backup when E-2C aircraft were unavailable.

S-3B aircrews also flew SEAD missions in the KTO during the early days of the war.

S-3 aircraft were tasked with transfer of crucial personnel to and from the Fleet and Central Command (CENTCOM) headquarters. Additionally, the S-3 was used to deliver the air tasking order (ATO) from CENTCOM headquarters to the carrier battle group commanders at sea.

Performance

S-3B aircraft provided command, control and communications links among controlling agencies, strike leaders and the battle group commander during strikes. Targets in western and central Iraq and the KTO required crossing most of Saudi Arabia for Red Sea based aircraft. Coordination was required through three USAF AWACS sectors. S-3Bs improved transition and established communications to and from the areas for the strike leaders.

S-3Bs participated extensively in Maritime Interception Operations (MIO) in both the Red Sea and Persian Gulf. A total of 530 sorties was devoted to reconnaissance and interception operations.

As an adjunct to MIO, S-3Bs flew armed scout missions.

S-3Bs flew 68 sorties in support of Persian Gulf MCM.

S-3B aircraft flew 80 sorties dedicated to Counter-Counter targeting/antisurface missile defense.

S-3Bs provided aerial refueling to battle group organic assets in both the Red Sea and Persian Gulf. A total of 562 dedicated tanker missions was flown and an additional 482 sorties provided fuel to fighter and attack aircraft. Missions included tanking for CAP aircraft in the Red Sea and Persian Gulf, overhead recovery tanking, and emergency tanker support. The S-3B provided a tanker hose multiplier to the battle group commander.

The S-3B provided crucial logistic support to the battle group commander. The S-3B was the only reliable platform for delivering the daily air tasking order from Saudi Arabia to the battle group commanders. Additionally, the S-3B provided fast reliable transportation of crucial staff personnel between CENTCOM headquarters and the battle groups.

OBSERVATIONS

Accomplishments

- The S-3B provided effective C^2 to strike leaders in SEAD and overland strike missions.

- The S-3B located and identified many surface contacts in a maritime interception role.

- The S-3B provided vital organic tanking capability to battle group aircraft.

SH-3H SEA KING MULTI-MISSION HELICOPTER

Mission

The SH-3H aircraft is a carrier-based, multi-mission antisubmarine warfare (ASW)/fleet support helicopter designed for inner zone ASW protection to the carrier battle group. The SH-3H also can conduct missions involving combat search and rescue (CSAR), naval special warfare (NSW), visual mine search and destruction, anti-ship missile defense (ASMD), surface surveillance and logistics support.

System Data

Prime Contractor: Sikorsky Aircraft
Crew: Two pilots, two door gunners/rescue swimmers
Initial Operational Capability: 1961 (SH-3A)
US Inventory: 113 SH-3Hs
Length: 73 ft
Rotor Diameter: 62 ft

Weight : 21,000 lbs
Maximum speed: 120 knots
Range: 650 miles
Endurance: 5.5 hours
Propulsion: Two T58-GE-10/T58-GE-402 engines
Armament: Two M-60D machine guns
Avionics Systems: Night vision goggle (NVG) compatible cockpit kits; AQS-13E active dipping sonar; AN/ASQ-81 magnetic anomaly detection system (MAD); sonar data computer, AKT-22 Acoustic Data, Link, ARS-6 downed aircrew locating system (DALS)

Employment

Thirty-nine SH-3H helicopters were deployed from one reserve and six active squadrons; 34 aircraft were embarked on six aircraft carriers, two were forward deployed aboard a Spruance class destroyer at a CSAR station in the North Persian Gulf and three reserve helicopters were stationed outside the Gulf. Since Iraq was not considered an ASW threat, the ASW equipment was stripped from SH-3H aircraft to provide more logistics capability.

The SH-3H was reconfigured with additional troop seats and armed with M-60D machine guns to support the following operations:

- **Maritime Interception Operations (MIO)** — SH-3H aircraft provided transport for boarding teams and insertion of SEAL teams for takedowns of non-cooperative merchant vessels in support of the United Nations embargo. Eleven non-cooperative take downs were conducted.
- **Surface Surveillance** — Day and night surveillance of surface shipping using stabilized binoculars and NVGs to visually identify contacts of interest. Additionally, visual surveillance of oil slick boundaries was conducted.
- **Combat Search and Rescue** — A two-aircraft detachment was maintained aboard a destroyer forward deployed to the

northern Persian Gulf. Aircraft were airborne or on deck in an alert status and were tasked to support returning strike aircraft.

- **Logistics Support** — Around-the-clock logistics support consisted of cargo and personnel transport throughout battle force and ashore.
- **Mine Detection** — Visual searches were conducted for floating mines and Explosive Ordnance Detachment (EOD) or SEAL team members were inserted to destroy them. Twenty-three mines were destroyed in this fashion.

Performance

Aircraft use was 94.9 hours a month. The six embarked squadrons logged 5,781 hours maintaining 81 percent full mission capable (FMC) and 84 percent MC rates. The lack of an ASW threat allowed significant diversification of the missions that the SH-3H could perform for the battle force.

OBSERVATIONS

Accomplishments

- SH-3 helicopter insertions of SEAL teams onto non-cooperative merchant shipping proved to be a crucial element of the MIO. SH-3s also inserted SEAL teams, who captured two islands and a fortified oil platform.

- Although SH-3s normally operate from aircraft carriers, an SH-3 SAR detachment was successfully deployed aboard a destroyer in the northern Persian Gulf.

- Eighty-five EPWs were transported to custody.

- Twenty-three mines were sighted by SH-3s and destroyed by EOD teams.

Issue

- Replacement of the SH-3H by SH-60F ASW helicopters plus HH-60H CSAR/NSW helicopters began in 1990. The first airwing outfitted with this configuration arrived in the Persian Gulf three weeks after the end of the conflict. This combination should correct the deficiencies cited above with the exception of sensors and forward firing weapons.

UH-60 BLACK HAWK UTILITY HELICOPTER

Mission

The UH-60 Black Hawk is the Army's primary assault helicopter, able to transport a combat-equipped infantry squad of 11 soldiers, or an external cargo load of up to 8,000 pounds. It transports troops and equipment into combat, resupplies the troops while in combat, performs aerial medical evacuation (MEDEVAC), search and rescue, and command and control (C^2). Special Black Hawk variants perform electronic warfare (EH-60) and support special operations missions (MH-60A and MH-60K).

The Black Hawk is replacing the UH-1 Iroquois in assault helicopter companies, cavalry squadrons, attack helicopter battalions, MEDEVAC units, special operations units, and aviation maintenance companies.

System Data

Prime Contractor: Sikorsky Helicopter Company

Crew: Two pilots and one crew chief/gunner
Initial Operational Capability: 1976
US Inventory: 1061
Length: 57.4 ft
Rotor Diameter: 53.7 ft
Maximum Gross Weight: 20,500 pounds; useful payload: 3,500 pounds
Maximum External Load: 8,000 pounds
Maximum Speed: 145 knots (cruise)
Range: 396 miles (803 miles with External Stores Support System (ESSS) and Extended Range Fuel System (ERFS)
Mission Endurance: 2.3 hours (5.4 hours with ESSS and ERFS)
Propulsion: Two T700-GE-700C engines,
Armament: Two M60 machine guns (7.62mm)

Employment

The Army deployed 489 Black Hawks to Southwest Asia (SWA), which is 46 percent of the total inventory. Eighteen UH-60 assault companies were deployed. Additional UH-60s deployed with MEDEVAC units, cavalry squadrons, maintenance companies, AH-64

Apache battalions, and special operations units.

These helicopters performed combat, combat support, and combat service support missions, logging more than 44,000 hours. UH-60s were used for artillery deployment and emplacement, evacuation of enemy prisoners of war, and support of OH-58D's conducting Persian Gulf operations. UH-60s also performed many MEDEVAC missions, including the transportation of patients to and from hospital ships.

The extended range fuel system (ERFS) was particularly beneficial in providing additional range required to operate within the area of operations. UH-60s routinely transported soldiers, equipment, repair parts, supplies, food, and water between unit locations.

Seventeen UH-60s had the new AN/ASC-15B C^2 console installed. The airborne C^2 consoles provided secure very high frequency, ultra high frequency, frequency modulation, high frequency, and tactical satellite (TACSAT) communications, allowing commanders to maintain control of fast paced operations over extended ranges.

The 101st Airborne Division (Air Assault) conducted the largest air assault in history using 60 UH-60s and 30 CH-47s simultaneously to air assault soldiers and combat equipment to the Euphrates River Valley. This operation established blocking positions preventing the withdrawal of the Iraqi ground forces.

Performance

The UH-60 is a vast improvement from the UH-1. Its highly survivable airframe provides the ground commander the capability of transporting a useful load (internal and external) in a high altitude or hot environment. There were only two UH-60 combat losses.

The UH-60 mission capable rate was 82 percent. It was, however, affected by the sand. The UH-60 made multiple landings and takeoffs in the desert while conducting sling-load operations that required hovering for prolonged periods of time. These operations caused the aircraft to be exposed to excessive sand blasting and sand ingestion. Engines, auxiliary power units, rotor blades, and pitch change rod end bearings were the primary components susceptible to damage.

From a systems capabilities standpoint, the aircraft had insufficient navigational equipment. Due to a lack of identifiable terrain, the crew was unable to update the doppler navigational system. Global Positioning System (GPS) will solve this shortcoming.

In addition to aircraft and systems capabilities shortfalls, additional training was required using night-vision goggles (NVG). Acclimation to the desert environment took time and training. Lack of terrain definition caused the crews to fly higher and slower. Limited definition with night-vision goggles restricted sling-load operations at night.

OBSERVATIONS

Accomplishments

■ UH-60s flew more than 44,000 hours supporting operations in SWA and were used in the largest air assault in history.

■ UH-60 demonstrated extreme flexibility and versatility by supporting air assaults, MEDEVAC, C2, special operations, electronic warfare, and EPW evacuation.

Shortcomings

■ Precision navigation was difficult in the featureless terrain environment.

■ Communications during low-level operations was extremely difficult across extended ranges.

■ Complete aircraft survivability equipment are not installed fleet wide.

■ The aircraft suffered from sand and harsh environmental factors present in a desert environment. Rotor blades, engines and oil coolers were affected by sand erosion.

■ Flight in low-light conditions was extremely difficult.

GROUND SYSTEMS

ASSAULT AMPHIBIAN VEHICLE (AAV)

Mission

The Marine Corps (USMC) AAV7A1 family of vehicles carry the surface assault infantry elements of the landing force and their equipment from amphibious ships to inland objectives. Once ashore, the AAV7A1 family of vehicles supports maneuver warfare and performs combat support (CS) and combat service support (CSS) missions as appropriate. There are three AAV variants:

The **AAVP7A1** is the baseline variant and the primary means of providing armored protected mobility to the Marine Air/Ground Task Force Ground Combat Element. Following closely behind tank units, the AAVP7A1 provides suppressive fires against enemy infantry and lightly armored vehicles. The AAVP7A1 carries infantry forward to maintain an attack's momentum; they dismount and remount as the

tactical situation requires. Although optimally used as a troop carrier in tactical situations, the AAVP7A1 can be called upon to support CSS efforts as a logistics carrier. It also can be configured with special countermine systems to conduct hasty and deliberate minefield breaching operations.

The **AAVC7A1** is used as a mobile command post for infantry regiment and battalion commanders during ship-to-shore movement and operations ashore. It provides the commander with the ability to communicate with combat, CS and CSS units.

The **AAVR7A1** provides recovery and field maintenance support for the AAV7A1 family of vehicles during operations ashore. The AAVR7A1 can recover other AAVs or smaller vehicles. It provides an overhead crane capability to remove AAV power packs and provides equipment and tools for organizational maintenance in the field.

System Data

Prime Contractor: FMC Corporation
Crew: Three
Initial Operational Capability: FY 1985
US Inventory: 1,153
Weight: 57,000 pounds
Load Capacity (maximum): 21 combat equipped Marines or 10,000 pounds of cargo
Cruising Range: Land at 25 mph: 300 miles, Water at 2,600 rpm: 7 hours
Cruising Speed: Land: 20-30 mph, water: 6 mph
Surfability (combat loaded): Able to negotiate 6-foot plunging surf combat loaded and survive 10-ft plunging surf
Armor: 1.4 to 1.75 inches of aluminum armor plate
Armament: M85 .50 caliber machine gun in the electric drive turret, or the Mk 19, MOD 3 40-mm machine gun and M2HB .50 caliber machine gun

Employment

AAVP7A1s were used to provide high-speed, armor-protected mobility to the maneuver elements of the ground forces, along with providing fire support for embarked infantry. The AAVP7A1s also were used extensively as host vehicles for the special mission kits used during minefield breaching, carrying line charges and combat engineer teams.

AAVC7A1s were used as the principal command and control (C^2) vehicle by the maneuver element commanders to communicate with subordinate units and higher headquarters. These commanders also used the AAVC7A1 to coordinate fire support and logistics support.

AAVR7A1s were used to provide battlefield maintenance repairs in support of the AAV family of vehicles and for battlefield recovery of AAVs.

During Operation Desert Storm, 473 AAVP7A1s, 40 AAVC7A1s, and 19 AAVR7A1s were used. Aboard amphibious task force shipping, an additional 93 AAVP7A1s, six AAVC7A1s, and four AAVR7A1s were deployed.

Performance

Despite suspension and power shortfalls, the AAVP7A1 proved very reliable in the desert environment. The vehicle met all standards and specifications. AAVP7A1 availability exceeded 93 percent.

The AAVC7A1 proved effective in the desert environment, although some overheating of the vehicle's communication systems was experienced. The vehicles were used extensively for C^2. The vehicle met all minimum standards and specifications. AAVC7A1 availability exceeded 95 percent.

The AAVR7A1 proved very reliable in the desert environment. The vehicle exceeded standards and specifications. AAVR7A1 availability was 100 percent.

The firing sights for the M85, Mk 19 and M2HB machine guns were visual only, with no night or low visibility capability beyond what the gunner could see. During low visibility and darkness, the AAV7A1 vehicles were unable to engage targets effectively beyond visual range, and often engaged targets well below the machine gun's maximum effective range.

The AAV7A1's suspension system was over stressed, limiting its cross-country mobility and speed because of the added weight of several production improvements and special engineer mission kits, coupled with life cycle fatigue. Similarly, stress was placed on the propulsion system. This was an important factor in the

AAVs' inability to keep pace with the main battle tank.

The AAV7A1 family of vehicles' amphibious capabilities were not tested under combat conditions. However, amphibious planning identified the AAV7A1 family's short range and lack of open ocean capability as limitations in planning over-the-horizon assaults.

OBSERVATIONS

Accomplishments

- All variants performed to mission standards.

- Performance in the desert environment was satisfactory.

- The overall AAV availability rate was 96 percent.

Shortcomings

- AAVs lacked an adequate sight capability and precision onboard navigation equipment.

- AAVs were unable to keep up with the main battle tank while traveling cross-country in the desert terrain.

Issues

- The most widely proclaimed deficiency was the lack of an adequate sighting device for night fighting. The vehicle could not sight to its weapons systems' maximum effective ranges. Potential solutions are being reviewed.

- The suspension system problem was identified before Operation Desert Storm and is being corrected under a funded product improvement program. An advanced propulsion system initiative is being reviewed.

- The flat, featureless terrain made precision land navigation and position locating difficult. During reduced visibility, navigation capability was further degraded. This deficiency is being corrected through the planned procurement and fielding throughout the USMC of a Global Positioning System and the Position Location Reference System. Provisions for installation of this equipment in the AAV were funded in FY 92. These product improvements will correct the most significant deficiencies in its ground support role.

BRADLEY FIGHTING VEHICLE

Mission

The Bradley Fighting Vehicle provides mechanized infantry, armored cavalry, and scout units with a full-tracked, lightly armored fighting vehicle with the mobility, lethality, and survivability to operate with the M-1 tank as a member of the combined arms team.

There are two Bradley variants:

M2 Series Infantry Fighting Vehicle (IFV) — The M2 Bradley provides tactical mobility, limited armor protection, and antiarmor capability to the infantry squad, whose mission is to close with and destroy the enemy. The addition of improvements to the vehicle have resulted in four models: the basic model (A0), A1(-), A1, and A2.

M3 Series Cavalry Fighting Vehicle (CFV) — The M3 Bradley provides tactical mobility, limited armor protection, and antiarmor capability to the scout squad, whose mission is to conduct screening, reconnaissance, and security missions. As with the M2 Bradley, there are four M3 models: the basic model (A0), A1(-), A1, and A2.

System Data

Prime Contractor: FMC Corporation
Crew: Nine-man Infantry squad (three are vehicle crew) (IFV); five-man Scout Section (three are vehicle crew) (CFV)
Initial Operational Capability: 1984
US Inventory: 5,774
Weight (Combat Loaded): 50,000 lbs (A0/A1(-)/A1 models); 60.000 lbs (A2 model) 66,000 lbs (A2 with add-on armor tiles)
Length: 21.5 ft
Height: 9.75 ft
Width: 10.5 ft
Engine: Cummins VTA 903-500 HP Diesel (A0/A1(-)/A1); Cummins VTA 903-600 HP Turbo Diesel (A2)
Maximum Speed: 41 mph (A0/A1(-)/A1); 38 mph (A2)
Cross Country Speed: 30-35 mph
Fuel Capacity: 175 gallons diesel or JP-8
Cruising Range: 300 miles (A0/A1(-)/A1), 275 miles (A2)
Main Armament: M242 25-mm cannon
Secondary Armament: M240C 7.62-mm coaxial machine gun, two-tube (Basic) TOW missile launcher (A0/A1(-)), two-tube TOW2 (T2SS) missile launcher (A1/A2), Six M231

5.56-mm firing port weapons
(M2A0/M2A1(-)/M2A1only), Two M231
5.56mm firing port weapons (M2A2 only)

Employment

Units initially deployed to the Persian Gulf were largely equipped with the basic model Bradley. Recognizing the threat posed by Iraqi weapon systems, the Army opted to modernize the fleet in theater. Six hundred ninety-two A2 models were shipped from new production and POMCUS stocks to support this effort. The A2 version's survivability is improved with add-on armor, an interior spall liner, larger engine, and improved ammunition storage. Of the 2,200 Bradleys in theater during the ground campaign, the A1 and A2 models comprised 33 percent and 48 percent, respectively.

Fighting Vehicles complemented tanks in providing anti-armor lethality and high speed maneuver in the offensive. In the heavy force, these systems were generally in the spearhead of the high speed maneuver that took Coalition forces deep into the enemy's rear areas to defeat the Republican Guard and cut off avenues of supply and avenues of withdrawal.

Performance

Division-level after action reports indicate the Bradley fleet maintained an availability rate of more than 90 percent through the 100 hours of high-speed ground war. Units completed long-distance, cross-country movements (100 to 300 miles) with no major breakdowns. While some success may be attributed to the fact that many vehicles were new, consistent performance of operator level Preventive Maintenance Checks and Services was crucial to desert operations. Soldier interviews provide favorable comments on ease of maintenance, reliability of transmissions, and engine power.

Thermal imaging systems (TIS) allowed crews to acquire and engage targets at long ranges through smoke and sand, both day and night. TOW engagement ranges of 2,500 to 3,500 meters were common. The Bradley's 25-mm cannon also was rated by crews as accurate, effective, and lethal. High explosive and armor piercing rounds were effective against light armor, trucks, and bunkers at maximum ranges. However, the lack of a laser range finder was identified as a deficiency. TOW gunners had difficulty determining if targets were within range. When firing the 25-mm gun, lead and elevation became a matter of guesswork, since exact ranges were unknown. Higher resolution thermal sights also are needed to provide better target identification capability at long range.

The Bradley A2 model's survivability improvements proved effective as evidenced by several examples of vehicles which took significant hits without flash fires or catastrophic loss. Most damage was found to be penetrator related with little damage from spall. Unless combustibles or ammunition were in the penetrator path, there was very little collateral damage. Fire-suppression systems worked extremely well. The Bradley's mobility and ability to detect and kill enemy targets before they could respond also contributed to the Bradley's survivability. However, the fact that fire from friendly forces caused more Bradley losses than enemy fire confirms the need for a combat vehicle identification system to prevent fratricide.

Other deficiencies were identified during interviews with vehicle crews and commanders. Without positional navigation devices, land navigation in the desert would have been extremely difficult. Because of the Bradley's current configuration, vehicle exhaust tended to blow into the vehicle commander's face. Stowage capacity for individual equipment aboard the Bradley was inadequate. Support and command and control (C^2) vehicles had difficulty maintaining pace with maneuver forces.

OBSERVATIONS

Accomplishments

- Used successfully with the M-1 tank in fast paced, complex offensive and defensive operations.

- Operational readiness rate exceeded 90 percent throughout the campaign.

- Thermal sights provided day and night, all weather target acquisition.

- The TOW II missile and 25-mm cannon were accurate and lethal.

- Survivability validated modernization efforts.

Shortcomings

- Gunnery accuracy was hindered by lack of a laser range finder.

- Detection, recognition, and identification of targets were hindered by lack of high resolution thermal sights.

- The M-2/3 lacks a combat vehicle identification capability and an onboard vehicle navigation device.

- Vehicle exhaust should be redirected away from the commander's hatch.

- Equipment storage capacity is inadequate.

Issue

- Action is under way to resolve identified shortcomings. The crisis occurred midway through the Army's modernization program. As the A2 model is fielded to deployable units, it will be less likely the basic model will deploy. Requirements are being developed to resolve other deficiencies. Efforts are under way to develop a solution for all combat vehicles to improve combat identification and avoid fire from friendly forces. The Army also is considering the second generation forward looking infrared to enhance TIS resolution. Finally, the Army is considering an upgrade program for its fleet of C^2 and support vehicles which would improve their ability to maintain pace with the maneuver forces.

LAND MINE COUNTERMEASURE AND OBSTACLE BREACHING SYSTEMS

Mission

Land mine countermeasure (MCM) and obstacle breaching systems are used by combat engineers to breach both man-made (e.g., minefields and tank ditches) and natural obstacles so ground forces can maneuver. Of critical importance during Operation Desert Storm were MCM systems. Selected MCM systems used by the US Marine Corps and the US Army were:

Anti-Personnel Obstacle Breaching System (APOBS): This portable system is an explosive item and is used to breach a continuous footpath (0.6 x 45 meters) through anti-personnel minefields and associated wire obstacles during an assault. It can neutralize single impulse type anti-personnel mines.

M58 Single Shot Line Charge/Mine Clearing Line Charge (MICLIC): This explosive line charge is mounted on a trailer towed by an armored or wheeled vehicle, and is rocket-propelled across a suspected minefield. It is used to breach a continuous path (8m by 100 m) through minefields containing single impulse, non-blast-hardened pressure mines and associated wire obstacles.

Mk 154 Triple Shot Line Charge: This system consists of three individual explosive line charges mounted on an Assault Amphibian Vehicle (AAV). It can clear an 8 by 300 meter area of single impulse, pressure-actuated mines and is capable of waterborne or land use.

Track-Width Mine Roller (TWMR): The TWMR consists of two reinforced, weighted roller devices which are extended in front of the tracks of the tank on which it is mounted. The system activates single impulse, pressure fuzed mines in its path. Its primary purpose is to detect the limits of a suspected minefield or expediently verify a mine cleared lane.

Full-Width Mine Rake (FWMR): The FWMR is mounted on the dozer blade of the M-60 tank or M728 Combat Engineer Vehicle (CEV). It can clear surface and buried mines (12 inches deep) in sandy soils across the full-width of the armored vehicle's path. It physically moves mines to the side and has the advantage of clearing the full-width of the lane.

Other systems used by the US Marine Corps and the US Army to breach obstacles other than minefields were:

M-9 Armored Combat Earthmover (ACE): This system is a highly mobile, survivable, tracked and armored earthmover. It provides a capability to perform offensive and defensive excavation missions without requiring a heavy transporter to move between sites.

M728 Combat Engineer Vehicle (CEV): The CEV consists of a basic M60A1 tank with a hydraulically operated debris blade, 165mm turret mounted demolition gun, retractable boom and winch. It provides engineers in the forward combat area with a versatile, armor-protected means of clearing rubble, filling tank ditches, and a reduction of defended strongpoints. During Operation Desert Storm it mounted the FWMR for the US Army forces.

Armored Vehicle Launched Bridge (AVLB): The AVLB is a standard M48 or M60 tank chassis modified (turret and weapons removed) to transport, launch and retrieve a 60 foot span Military Load Class 60 bridge. It is used to span short gaps (e.g., tank ditches) during an assault, without exposing personnel to direct small arms fire.

Pipe Fascines: This system is an expedient, inexpensive method to cross anti-tank ditches or other gaps up to 10 meters wide. Pipe bundles are dumped into the gap and then used by the assaulting force to cross the obstacle. The fascine bundles include varying numbers of pipes, depending on the depth of the obstacle.

D-7 Tractor Protective Kit (TPK): The TPK is an easily installed, bolt-on, armor kit that provides the D-7 tractor and its operator with protection from small arms fire and from explosion fragments.

System Data

Anti-Personnel Obstacle Breaching System (APOBS)
  Manufacturer: US Navy Laboratories (Panama City and Indian Head Island)
  Weight: 120 pounds
  Number deployed to SWA: 36

M58 Single Shot Line Charge/Mine Clearing Line Charge (MICLIC)
  Prime Contractor: Morton Thiokol
  Number deployed to SWA: More than 300

Mk 154 Triple Shot Line Charge
  Prime Contractor: General Motors of Canada
  Number deployed to SWA: 62

Track-Width Mine Roller (TWMR)
  Prime Contractor: Urdan and Minowitz
  Number deployed to SWA: At least 58 units

Full-Width Mine Rake (FWMR)
  Manufacturer: US Army Belvoir Research, Development and Engineering Center (BRDEC) and Letterkenny Army Depot
  Weight: Approximately 3500 lbs
  Dimensions: 180.5" wide, 92.3" long, and 42" high
  Number deployed to SWA: 59

Armored Combat Earthmover (M-9 ACE)
  Prime Contractor: Boeing McGlaughlin York (BMY)
  Crew: One
  Gross weight: 54,000 lbs
  Engine: Cummins Diesel (295 hp at 2,600 rpm)
  Bridge Classification: 17 tons
  Maximum speed: 30 mph

Ascending grade: 60 percent
Gradability: 20 percent
Trench width: 62 inches
Number deployed to SWA: 151

M728 Combat Engineer Vehicle (CEV)
Prime Contractor: General Dynamics
Military Load Classification: 60
Number deployed to SWA: Exceeding 55

Armored Vehicle Launched Bridge (AVLB)
Prime Contractor: Chrysler Corp. and
Allison Steel
Military Load Classification: 60
Number deployed to SWA: Exceeding 110

Pipe Fascine
Prime Contractor: TD Molding
Military Load Class: 70 tons
Dimensions: 181 inches long, 186.6 inches
wide
Weight: 5,513 pounds
Number deployed to SWA: 78 bundles

D-7 Tractor Protective Kit (TPK)
Manufacturer: Marine Corps Logistics
Base, Albany, GA
Weight: 9,000 lbs
Level of protection: 14.4-mm all purpose
rounds at 200 meters
Number deployed to SWA: 26

Employment

Many different systems were used in SWA to
breach minefields and obstacles. During
Operation Desert Storm, the Marine Corps fired
49 single shot and 55 triple shot line charges.
The US Army used their MICLICs in a limited
manner, and depended on the FWMR mounted
on a CEV when breaching suspected minefields.
Due to the difficulty of transporting the TWMR
using heavy semitrailers, the US Army did not
use TWMRs.

The ACE proved very effective for breaching
earthen berms, filling tank ditches, and cutting
through wire fences. It also was used to make
protective defilade positions for vehicles and
weapon systems. The M9 ACE was used by the
Marine Corps to breach fences, small berms,
and potential minefields when other MCM
equipment was unavailable.

To cross ditches and other gaps, facines were
used by the US Marine Corps and AVLBs by
the US Army. On occasion, bunkers and other
strong points were eliminated using the
demolition gun on the CEV.

After minefields were cleared, non-standard
marking systems had to be fabricated since no
effective method was available. Individual units
used flags, colored barrels, panels, and other
methods.

Performance

APOBS achieved minimal success. Some
charges only partially detonated and combat
engineers used others improperly. This
performance can be attributed partly to operator
unfamiliarity with the ordnance.

Some explosive charge detonation problems
were encountered with the M58/MICLIC single
shot line charge. Operators experienced
difficulty in correctly orienting the trailer on
which the line charge was mounted. The vehicle
towing the line charge could not back out of a
plowed lane with the trailer in tow. It was
difficult to tow the line charge from the staging
area to the obstacle area and keep the system
operational. The Mk 154 triple shot line charge
performed better than the M58/MICLIC, but
only 49 percent were successfully deployed and
command detonated as designed.

Because of the soft soil conditions in the desert,
the FWMR was an effective tool, creating easily
visible lanes for follow-on forces. The FWMR
was one of only two systems available for
assaulting forces when encountering
blast-hardened mines.

Generally, the TWMR was unsuccessful in breaching operations. Specifically, it failed to breach several minefields consisting of continuous pressure mines. It was slow, cumbersome, and bogged down in soft sand. The US Army did not use the TWMR for breaching.

The M9 ACE was a versatile system. The soft desert soil caused some traction problems, which limited its speed to about 20 mph. Overall, the ACE quickly and effectively performed its missions.

TPKs performed as intended and at least one D-7 operator was protected from the explosion of a land mine.

Each use of pipe fascine required four bundles from two AAVs to breach adequately ditches that were usually three to four meters wide and two to three meters deep. The AAVs laying the pipes often were exposed to flanking anti-tank and /or anti-armor fire during employment. An excavation vehicle was required to reduce the escarpment after the breach was completed using the pipe fascines.

The CEV and AVLB performed their roles effectively when they were able to keep pace with maneuver forces. Mounting the FWMR on the CEV provided the only full-width breaching capability for the US Army.

OBSERVATIONS

Accomplishments

- The Mk 154 successfully cleared breach points for vehicle passage.

- The FWMR was developed and fielded in under four months, and was very effective in clearing lanes, leaving a visible path through minefields after line charges cleared wire obstacles and marked a path.

- The M9 ACE was successful in myriad tasks, including obstacle reduction.

Shortcomings

- The M58/MICLIC single shot line charge and associated trailer were not as rugged as required. There also was no means of ensuring correct orientation of the charge from inside an enclosed vehicle.

- Line charges, both the single shot and triple shot were ineffective against the modern, blast-hardened land mines encountered in SWA.

- Minefield breaching forces did not have adequate standard systems to mark lanes through minefields once they were breached and verified cleared.

- The TWMR bogged down too easily in softer soils, was cumbersome to transport to the obstacle area, and generally did not provide high confidence that a lane was actually clear of mines.

- No system was available for rapid self-breaching of scatterable mines, if they had been encountered away from a deliberate breach site.

- No real-time standoff minefield detection capability existed.

- The pipe fascine was successfully used in obstacle and ditch crossings; however, the vehicle carrying the bundles was extremely vulnerable to enemy fire when deploying the bundles. This breaching method is recommended as an expedient only.

Issues

- There is a need for dedicated counterobstacle vehicles, as mobile and survivable as the maneuver forces, designed specifically to counter the land mine threat.

- There is a need for a self-breaching capability for all units in the forward combat areas, designed to counter scatterable mines.

- There is a need for a strong RDT&E program to advance standoff mine detection, neutralization and marking capability.

LIGHT ARMORED VEHICLE (LAV)

Mission

The Light Armored Vehicle (LAV) is operated by a Marine Corps (USMC) Light Armored Infantry (LAI) battalion, which conducts reconnaissance; security and economy of force operations; and, within its capabilities, limited offensive and defensive operations. The LAV consists of six variants. The nucleus of the battalion is the LAV-25 Scout/Reconnaissance vehicle. The remaining variants exist in smaller numbers to complement and support the LAV-25.

System Data

Prime Contractor: Diesel Division, General Motors of Canada
Initial Operational Capability: 1985
US Inventory: 724
Propulsion: 275 hp diesel engine
Maximum speed: 62 mph (land), 6 mph (water)

Maximum range: 410 miles
Maximum trench: 81 inches
Maximum grade: 60 percent head on
Maximum side slope: 30 percent angle

LAV-25

Crew: Seven (commander, driver, gunner, and four scouts)
Combat weight: 28,200 lbs.
Armament: M242 25-mm chain gun (fires high explosive and armor-piercing ammunition), M240 7.62-mm machine gun (coaxially mounted with chain gun), M240 7.62-mm machine gun (pintle mount).

LAV ANTITANK (LAV-AT)

Crew: Four (commander, gunner, loader, and driver)
Combat weight: 27,650 lbs.
Armament: TOW missile system, M240 7.62-mm machine gun (ring mount)

LAV MORTAR (LAV-M)

Crew: Five (commander, driver, and three mortar men)
Combat weight: 26,700 lbs.
Armament: M252 81-mm mortar, M240 7.62-mm machine gun (ring mount)

LAV LOGISTICS (LAV-L)

Crew: Three (commander, driver, cargo handler)
Combat weight: 28,200 lbs.
Payload: 5,240 lbs.
Armament: M250 7.62-mm machine gun (ring mount)

LAV COMMAND AND CONTROL (LAV-C2)

Crew: Seven (commander, driver plus five radio operator/staff members)
Combat weight: 27,060 lbs
Radios: Four VHF, one UHF, one HF
Armament: M240 7.62-mm machine gun (ring mount)

LAV RECOVERY (LAV-R)

Crew: Three (commander, driver, and boom operator)
Combat weight: 28,320 lbs.
Armament: M240 7.62-mm machine gun (ring mount)

Employment

More than 350 LAVs of all types were used in SWA, (193 LAV-25, 54 LAV-AT, 26 LAV-M, 30 LAV-C2, 47 LAV-L, 22 LAV-R). LAI units were in frequent and sometimes sustained contact with Iraqi forces before and during the ground campaign. LAI units provided a protective screen for the Marine divisions. LAI units scouted Iraqi minefields and the breach points which eventually were used on G-Day. Additionally, they performed economy of force missions and feints, which successfully deceived the enemy as to friendly intentions.

Performance

Land-based LAVs proved flexible, responsive and adaptable. They experienced no special maintenance reliability problems as a result of the desert environment. Operational readiness (OR) throughout Operation Desert Shield ranged from 88 to 98.5 percent, with 95 percent being typical. Highest readiness rates were achieved just before G-Day. During the Offensive Ground Campaign, readiness exceeded 94 percent. This readiness was achieved through an intense maintenance effort and extensive use of parts obtained through selective interchange with other LAVs in theater.

Afloat LAVs experienced a lower OR rate (as low as 76 percent at one point, with 93 percent the average). Although vehicles operated ashore were at higher risk for breakage, component failures can happen when the vehicle sits idle aboard a ship. Crewmen performing preventive maintenance aboard ship will discover systems and parts that fail. The lower OR rate for vehicles afloat reflects the inability to use parts sources available to units ashore.

The LAV-25 does not have a thermal imaging capability. Its passive night sight is marginally effective, requires significant ambient illumination, and provides no capability on an obscured battlefield (night or day). Without thermal imaging, the LAI battalion experienced severe operational restrictions low visibility conditions.

The Global Positioning System (GPS) received praise from all users. It was provided on a temporary basis and in insufficient numbers to equip each vehicle. Because of the extended dispersion and frontages at which LAI companies and platoons operate, users felt strongly that each LAV-25 and LAV-AT should have GPS.

OBSERVATIONS

Accomplishments

- Deployed rapidly in operationally significant numbers.

- Demonstrated high maintenance reliability.

- Proved to be flexible, adaptable, and responsive.

- Provided protective screen for USMC forces.

- Provided effective reconnaissance.

Shortcomings

- Because of a lack of thermal sights, LAVs had reduced effectiveness at night and on the obscured battlefield.

Issue

- A thermal imaging system for the LAV-25 is an initiative for FY 94.

M1A1 ABRAMS TANK

Mission

The M1A1 Abrams tank is a full-tracked, armored combat vehicle capable of sustained offensive and defensive combat in a nuclear, biological, and chemical (NBC) environment. It used by both the US Army and the US Marine Corps (USMC), and is designed to close with and destroy enemy forces using shock action, firepower, and mobility in coordination with supporting ground and air forces in all battlefield conditions.

There are three variants:

M1 — The M1 tank is the initial model, which was introduced in 1981. It has a 105-mm gun along with enhanced survivability and improved fire control.

M1A1 — The M1A1 is the basic A1 model. The major improvements from the basic M1 model include a 120-mm main gun, NBC overpressure system, and armor packages.

M1A1 Heavy Armor (HA) — The M1A1

Heavy Armor model is the same as the A1 model except that some specific armor packages (made from depleted uranium) are added.

System Data

Prime Contractor: General Dynamics
Crew: Four
Initial Operational Capability: FY 1985 (M1A1); FY 1987 (M1A1HA)
US inventory: 2,445 (M1A1); 1,753 (M1A1HA)
Combat weight: 67.5 tons (loaded with enhanced armor and T158 track)
Engine: 1,500 hp, air-cooled turbine
Cross country speed: 30 miles per hour
Weapons:
Main armament: M256 120-mm smooth bore cannon
Coaxial weapon: M240 7.62-mm machine gun
Loader's weapon: M240 7.62-mm machine gun
Commander's weapon: M2 .50 caliber machine gun
Main gun basic load: 40 rounds
Fuel capacity: 498 gallons of DF-2, DF-1, DFA, or JP-8
Operational range: 127 miles (NBC protection

on), 130 miles (NBC protection off)
Cruising range: 279 miles (NBC protection
on), 289 miles (NBC protection off) at 29 mph
on dry, level roads

Employment

During Operation Desert Storm, the Army
used 1,178 M1A1 and 594 M1A1(HA) tanks
(approximately 2,300 M1A1 series tanks
were deployed, but 528 tanks were placed in
operationally ready float status and theater
war reserve stock). These tanks were used in
Operation Desert Storm to provide anti-armor
lethality and high-speed maneuver in the
Coalition's heavy forces. The M1A1 tank was
the spearhead during the ground campaign.
The USMC deployed 16 M1A1 and 60
M1A1(HA) tanks in Operation Desert Storm.
These tanks were fielded quickly to counter the
Iraqi armored threat and then used to exploit
obstacle belt penetrations during the ground
offensive.

Because of the threat posed by Iraqi T72M-1
tanks and chemical weapons, efforts were
made to place the latest M1A1 and M1A1
(HA) tanks into Army units. M1A1s from
stocks in Europe and M1A1(HA)s from
production facilities were shipped to Saudi
Arabia and an all-out effort was conducted
between November and 15 January to
modernize the armor fleet. These tanks provided
crews with better survivability because of the
special armor packages and NBC overpressure
system.

Performance

After-action reports from divisions and brigades
indicate readiness rates greater than 90 percent,
based on vehicles able to "shoot, move, and
communicate." These statistics were achieved
by units moving between 200 and 370
kilometers in 100 hours of high-speed offensive
maneuver (e.g., the 3d Armored Division moved
more than 300 tanks at night across 200

kilometers without any breakdowns). Several
factors contributed to this success. First, many
new, low-mileage systems were used. Second,
parts from reserve tanks in the United States and
Europe and excess tanks in the theater of
operations were used to bring some tanks to full
operational status. Third, Heavy Equipment
Transporters (HET) were used to move tanks
forward in theater as much as possible.
Although the HET shortage was a problem,
movement of tanks by HETs greatly reduced
wear. Finally, extensive preventive maintenance
kept tanks in running order. Reductions in
thrown tracks by ensuring proper track tension
was applied and the reduction of engine wear
and replacement by seal inspections and proper,
frequent cleaning of filters were major
contributors to the high operational readiness
rate.

The capability of the M1A1 tank's equipment,
coupled with crew skill and training, enabled
M1A1 crews to "see first, shoot first," resulting
in many one-round kills on armored vehicles.
Thermal Imaging Systems allowed detection of
Iraqi targets day and night in smoke and haze at
great distance. Iraqi systems lacked this
capability. Targets were routinely identified out
to 1,500 meters and detected at much greater
ranges with the median detection range of 2,600
meters. M1A1 crews were able to engage Iraqi
tanks well beyond the range of Iraqi T-72s and
reports from enemy prisoners of war indicate
they could only return fire at muzzle flashes. An
Armor School report stated, "120-mm
ammunition consistently achieved catastrophic
kills against T-72 tanks, even when [the T-72s
were] behind thick berms." An example of the
agility, mobility, and lethality of the M1A1 tank
was demonstrated by the 2nd Brigade, 1st
Armored Division at the Battle of Medina
Ridge. In a 45-minute battle, the unit achieved
tactical surprise by moving quickly and silently
and destroyed 100 Iraqi tanks and more than 30
BMPs. Finally, interviews with crews indicate
many engagements occurred "on the move" (15
to 25 km/hr), and involved engagements at all

angles. The M1A1 frequently outran other US systems on the battlefield.

The low loss rate points to the survivability of the M1A1 tank. Vehicle speed and agility, identification and early engagement of the enemy at long range, thermal capabilities, armor protection, training, and crew survivability measures all contributed to M1A1 survivability

Several sources reported impacts of 125-mm armor-piercing ammunition on M1A1s without a single penetration, but these reports have not been corroborated. Of the 18 combat damage incidents reported, nine were permanent losses caused by fire from friendly forces. The damage inflicted on the other nine M1A1s were mostly from mines and are considered repairable.

OBSERVATIONS

Accomplishments

- The M1A1 series tanks were used successfully in fast-paced, complex offensive and defensive operations in all environments; they demonstrated all weather and night capability through sandstorms, rain, and haze from oil field fires with little degradation.

- M1A1 systems overmatched Iraqi systems in acquisition, fire control, lethality, mobility, and survivability.

- Operational readiness rates were more than 90 percent throughout the campaign.

- Many first round hits occurred while the vehicle was on the move.

- M1A1 ammunition produced catastrophic kills against Iraqi armor.

Shortcomings

- The M1A1 lacked a positive combat vehicle identification system, such as higher resolution thermal sights which would improve detection, recognition, and identification.

- The M1A1 did not have an onboard vehicle navigation device.

- M1A1 fuel consumption was high.

- Other combat support and combat service support systems are not as mobile as the M1A1 and this restrains the overall maneuver speed.

Issues

- Shortcomings identified during Operation Desert Storm are being corrected. A commanders' independent thermal viewer and an onboard position/navigation device will be organic equipment on the new M1A2 tank.

- Programs have begun to improve combat vehicle identification and prevent fratricide incidents. The Army is looking at second generation forward looking infrared to improve recognition and identification for TIS.

MULTIPLE LAUNCH ROCKET SYSTEM (MLRS) AND ARMY TACTICAL MISSILE SYSTEM (ATACMS)

Mission

The multiple launch rocket system (MLRS) is a long-range free-flight rocket system that provides general support artillery fires to division and corps level tactical units. At the division level, MLRS is organized into a nine-launcher battery. At the corps level, MLRS units consist of one or more battalions of 27 launchers.

In addition to the command and control, fire direction and logistic support elements common to all field artillery units, the MLRS consists of self-propelled loader launcher (SPLL) and a family of MLRS munitions. During Operations Desert Shield and Desert Storm, two different types of MLRS munitions were used: the Army Tactical Missile System (ATACMS) and the M77 rocket. The M77 rocket is packaged in six-round pods. When fully loaded with two pods, the SPLL can fire 12 rockets in less than one minute. The rocket consists of a solid rocket motor and a warhead containing 644 dual purpose grenades for use against personnel and lightly armored targets. An area coverage weapon system, one MLRS M77 rocket can dispense its grenades across four to five acres. If a launcher were to fire its full load of 12 rockets, the target area coverage would exceed 30 acres.

ATACMS, a multi-purpose system, is a ballistic missile fired from the M270 MLRS launcher. ATACMS replaced the conventional Lance missile system and is used to attack soft, stationary, semi-fixed targets (e.g., surface-to-surface missile sites, air defense sites, logistics sites, and command, control, communications, and intelligence facilities). ATACMS is the operational commanders' deep strike weapon system.

System Data

MLRS

Prime Contractor: LTV Aerospace and Defense Co.
Crew: Three (driver, gunner and section chief)
Initial Operational Capability: 1983 (MLRS); 1990 (ATACMS)

M270 Launcher (lightly armored, self-propelled, tracked vehicle, variant of Bradley armored fighting vehicle chassis)
  Weight: 25 tons
  Propulsion: 500 hp diesel engine
  Maximum. speed: 40 mph
  Cruising range: 298 miles

M77 Rocket
  Length: 155 inches
  Weight: 675 lbs
  Range: 32 km
  Guidance: unguided
  Warhead: 644 M77 antipersonnel and antimaterial grenades

ATACMS

  Length: 13 feet
  Propulsion: Solid propellant rocket motor
  Guidance System: Inertial navigation

Employment

During Operation Desert Shield, 189 MLRS SPLLs were deployed to the theater. MLRS fired 9,660 rockets in combat at targets such as artillery, convoys, logistics sites, and troop positions. First operational in August 1990, ATACMS production was accelerated soon after the crisis began. Two deep attack capable MLRS batteries (18 SPLLs), specially configured with deep battle kits to fire ATACMS, were deployed to Saudi Arabia. A conversion team with nine deep battle kits also deployed to Saudi Arabia to convert standard MLRS to ATACMS capable batteries. ATACMS was used against a variety of targets including surface-to-air missile sites, rocket and artillery batteries, logistics and refueling sites, and convoys.

Performance

In combat for the first time, MLRS performed well. MLRS rocket fires had a tremendous psychological impact on Iraqi soldiers. Enemy soldiers were terrified of its destructive force, which they sometimes referred to as "steel rain." The MLRS rockets proved to be extremely effective against personnel and unarmored vehicles. In addition to its lethality, two other attributes exemplified this system's performance: long range capability and the ability to keep pace with the fast moving M1A1 tank and M2/3 armored fighting vehicles. However, US rocket systems were out-ranged by the Iraqi Astros II multiple rocket launcher (60 km). Accurate targeting of Iraqi positions by ground and air units overcame this disadvantage.

ATACMS apparently silenced targeted air defense sites; electronic emissions ceased soon after sites were attacked by ATACMS. Coalition aircraft flying through flight corridors cleared by ATACMS strikes reported no enemy air defense radar activities. Based on demonstrated performance during suppression of enemy air defense missions, Army Component, Central Command requested all available ATACMS assets for use in the ground offensive.

ATACMS was a highly responsive system. A-10 pilots requested a short notice ATACMS strike on an air defense site and ATACMS responded within minutes, completely destroying the target. During one ATACMS strike, more than 200 unarmored vehicles were destroyed as they attempted to cross a bridge.

OBSERVATIONS

Accomplishments

- MLRS was lethal and extremely effective at long ranges against a variety of targets.

- MLRS was responsive and delivered large volumes of accurate fires in day or night and during all types of weather, especially intense rain and dust storms.

- MLRS was very maneuverable and was the only field artillery system that kept up with fast-paced maneuver advances.

- ATACMS accuracy met or exceeded operational requirements, and ATACMS destroyed or silenced most targets attacked.

Shortcomings

- Ground commanders desired an ATACMS and rocket system with even greater range.

- The M77 rocket was not effective against moving armored targets like tanks.

PATRIOT AIR DEFENSE SYSTEM

Mission

The Patriot Air Defense System provides medium-to-high altitude air defense of ground forces and crucial assets against air breathing threats (ABTs) and tactical ballistic missiles (TBM).

System Data

Prime Contractor: Raytheon
Patriot battery (fire unit): One radar, one engagement control station, one to eight launchers with four missiles on each launcher, and one electrical power plant
Crew: Launcher crew — three; van crew — three (up to eight launchers per van in a fire unit)
Initial Operational Capability: 1982
Guidance: Command guidance and semi-active homing

A Patriot battery includes up to eight launchers, each with four MIM-104 missiles, and support equipment, including a multi-function phased-array radar, weapons control computer, electric power plant, and equipment to interface with other parts of the air defense system and higher headquarters. Missiles with Patriot anti-tactical missile capability (PAC-2) enhancements (warhead and fuze improvements in addition to PAC-1 software improvements) are capable of anti-tactical ballistic missile (ATBM) defense as well as defense against ABTs. PAC-1 missiles are used only for defense against ABTs.

Employment

Patriot units normally are deployed as directed by the battalion commander based on the area to be defended and the expected axis of attack. The configuration provides coverage against both air-breathing and TBM threats. Patriot units are positioned in overlapping or independent configurations, depending upon weapons available and the number and location of assets to be protected. Overlapping coverage is preferred because of the redundancy it offers during attacks as well as the fact it offers more continuous coverage while individual fire units stand down for periodic maintenance, and movement.

Twenty-one US batteries (132 launchers) deployed to Saudi Arabia. Four batteries (two US and two Dutch batteries for a total of 26 launchers) deployed to Turkey. None of the four batteries in Turkey was involved in any engagements. Seven Patriot batteries (four US, one Dutch, and two Israel Defense Force (IDF) batteries for a total of of 48 launchers) were used in Israel. The two IDF batteries received abbreviated training in the United States, and the crews were supplemented by US maintenance personnel. The Dutch battery did not deploy to Israel until several days before the end of the war and was not involved in any Scud engagements. Patriot batteries in Saudi Arabia were used primarily to protect crucial assets (e.g., airfields, ports,oil production and refinery facilities, logistics bases, command and control centers, and Corps maneuver elements). In Israel, Patriot provided limited area defense for selected population centers. In Turkey, Patriot batteries were positioned to defend Turkish air bases.

Performance

The Patriot system does not have embedded digital data collection, which prevented a detailed and quantitative analysis of each firing. Therefore, a complete quantitative analysis of Patriot effectiveness is not available. The Army developed preliminary quantitative results based upon the best operational data then available. Action continues to obtain and analyze additional data from diverse sources and agencies. Even with the results of this continuing analysis, a finite, quantitative scoring of Patriot effectiveness may not be possible.

The system's operational success during the Gulf War can, however, be measured qualitatively. Patriot batteries provided valuable protection of Saudi ports and airfields, and served as a confidence-building asset to Coalition forces and civilians. The system played an important role in keeping Israel out of the war and strengthening Coalition resolve. The Patriot system was designed to defend small areas, like Saudi Arabian airfields. During the war, however, Patriot was also used to protect large cities, such as those in Israel. Consequently, Scud damage generally was greater in Israel, where the areas surrounding defended assets were more densely developed, than in Saudi Arabia, where defended assets often were more isolated.

Patriot had a mission capable rate of 95 percent in SWA.

OBSERVATIONS

Accomplishments

- A system designed to shoot down aircraft was modified to provide a successful ATBM system.

- Patriot was successful politically — it helped keep Israel out of the war and strengthened Coalition resolve.

Issue

- Shortcomings have been identified and continue to be addressed through software changes and funding for improvements. Two major software changes were made during Operation Desert Storm that greatly improved Patriot's capability to identify and destroy the Scud warhead. Funding has been appropriated for near- and mid-term upgrades, which will let Patriot engage TBMs at a higher altitude and greater range.

TACTICAL WHEELED VEHICLES (HEAVY FLEET)

US Army Heavy Equipment Transporter (HET).

USMC Logistic Vehicle System (LVS).

Mission

The Army's heavy fleet of tactical wheeled vehicles consists of old and new vehicles, as well as a mix of both commercial and tactical models. The missions performed were contingent on the type of vehicle, tactical or commercial. The heavy expanded mobility tactical truck (HEMTT) provides fuel and ammunition to combat units. The tractor version pulls heavy systems such as the Patriot missile system. The wrecker version performs recovery roles. The HEMTT is an 8X8 diesel powered 10-ton truck. The heavy equipment transporter (HET) mission is to transport tanks and other heavy equipment. The tractor is an M911 with an 8X6 diesel engine with pusher axle. The companion trailer is the M747 rated at 60 tons. The line haul tractor (LHT) (M915 and M915A1) pull M872 series 34-ton semitrailers. The M915 series is a 6X4 diesel powered vehicle. It is a commercial-type vehicle designed for highway use. The engineer tractors are M916 light equipment transporters and the M920 medium equipment transporter. The mission of these vehicles is to transport engineer equipment such as bulldozers. The M916 is a diesel-powered 6X6. The M920 is a diesel-powered 8X6.

The Marine Corps's (USMC) Logistic Vehicle System (LVS) is composed of two separate chassis units coupled together through an articulation joint to form an 8X8, diesel-powered vehicle. The front power unit, Mk 48, when coupled with the five rear body units, (Mk 14 container hauler; Mk 15 wrecker recovery vehicle; Mk 16 fifth wheel; Mk 17 dropside cargo hauler with crane; and the Mk 18 ribbon bridge transporter/self loading container hauler) transports bulk and containerized liquid and dry cargo. Four primary combinations, (Mk 48/Mk 14, Mk 48/Mk 15, Mk 48/Mk 16, and Mk 48/Mk 17) were used during Operations Desert Shield and Desert Storm. The Mk 18 was undergoing its initial production test and was not deployed.

System Data (US Army Heavy Fleet)

Heavy Expanded Mobility Tactical Truck (M977)

Prime Contractor: Oshkosh Truck Corporation
Crew: Two
Initial Operational Capability: 1985
US Inventory: 11,177
Curb weight: 35,500 pounds
Payload: 24,500 pounds
Length: 401 inches
Width: 96 inches
Height: 112 inches
Propulsion: 445 hp diesel engine
Trailer towing capacity: 40,000 pounds
Range: 300 miles

Heavy Equipment Transporter (M911/M747)

Prime Contractor: Oshkosh Truck Corporation
Crew: Two
Initial Operational Capability: 1978
US Inventory: 750
Curb weight: 39,952 pounds
Payload: 106,000 pounds
Length: 369 inches
Width: 114 inches
Height: 144 inches
Propulsion: 435 hp diesel engine
Trailer towing capacity: N/A
Range: 420 miles

Line Haul Tractor (M915)

Prime Contractor: Freightliner
Crew: Two
Initial Operational Capability: 1979
US Inventory: 4,667
Curb weight: 19,720 pounds
Payload: 54,000 pounds
Length: 262 inches
Width: 96 inches
Height: 142 inches
Propulsion: 400 hp diesel engine
Trailer towing capacity: N/A
Range: 357 miles

Light Equipment Transporter (M916)
Prime Contractor: Freightliner
Crew: Two
Initial Operational Capability: 1980
US Inventory: 1,759
Curb weight: 24,971 pounds
Payload: 50,000 pounds
Length: 294 inches
Width: 96 inches
Height: 142 inches
Trailer towing capacity: N/A
Range: 357 miles

Medium Equipment Transporter (M920)
Prime Contractor: AM General (Not in production)
Crew: Two
Initial Operational Capability: 1980
US Inventory: 992
Curb weight: 30,270 pounds
Payload: 55,000 pounds
Length: 319 inches
Width: 96 inches
Height: 142 inches
Trailer towing capacity: N/A
Range: 357 miles

System Data (USMC Logistic Vehicle System)

US Inventory: 1,655
Initial Operational Capability: 1985
Propulsion: 445 hp diesel engine

Mk 48/Mk 14 Container Hauler
Prime Contractor: Oshkosh Truck Corp
Crew: Two
Curb Weight: 40,200 pounds
Payload: 25,000 pounds cross-country, 45,000 pounds highway
Length: 456 inches
Width: 96 inches
Towed Load: 60,000 pounds
Range: 300 miles

Mk 48/Mk 15 Wrecker Recovery Vehicle
Prime Contractor: Oshkosh Truck Corporation

Crew: Two
Curb Weight: 52,300 pounds
Payload: 20,000 pounds cross-country; 45,000 pounds highway
Length: 444 inches
Width: 96 inches
Towed Load: 60,000 pounds
Range: 300 miles

MK48/Mk16 Fifth Wheel Semitrailer Adapter
Prime Contractor: Oshkosh Truck Corporation
Crew: Two
Curb Weight: 40,500 pounds
Payload: 188,000 pounds (gross combination weight rating)
Length: 397 inches
Width: 96 inches
Towed Load: M870 and M-1000 Semitrailers
Range: 300 miles

MK48/Mk 17 Dropside Cargo With Crane
Prime Contractor: Oshkosh Truck Corporation
Crew: Two
Curb Weight: 47,800 pounds
Payload: 20,000 pounds cross-country; 40,000 pounds highway
Length: 456 inches
Width: 96 inches
Towed Load: 60,000 pounds
Range: 300 miles

Employment

The HEMTT provided fuel and ammunition to armor, artillery, and infantry units. To support the theater campaign plan, 1,343 HEMTTs were sent in excess of normal unit allowances. The purpose of these vehicles was to augment or replace 5,000 gallon tankers and 22-ton semi-trailers in divisions and Armored Cavalry Regiments. The HEMTT tanker has a capacity of 2,500 gallons. Therefore, 5,000 gallon tankers were replaced on a two-for-one basis. The cargo HEMTTs augmented the semi-trailers in the forward areas or replaced them on a one-for-one basis. Of the 11,177 HEMTTs in the Army's inventory, 4,410 were deployed.

The LHT was used in the line haul mode as in any commercial tractor or trailer operation. Its primary limitation was little or no off-road capability. Of the 4,667 M915 in the Army's inventory, 2,337 were deployed. The HETs were used to move tanks and other equipment to the forward areas. This was a change in doctrine for the Army. Previously, the HET mission had been to remove damaged equipment from collection points to repair facilities and to bring new equipment to units. A secondary mission was unit transportation. Executing the theater campaign plan required moving many tracked vehicles across great distances by truck. Using HETs for this purpose saved wear and tear on the equipment, so the tracked vehicles were ready for battle when needed. Initially, the Army did not have enough assets to meet this requirement. A worldwide search was conducted and 1,404 HETs were found to meet the 1,295 requirement. The HETs were provided from Egypt, Italy, Germany, Saudi Arabia, US leased and US off-the-shelf procurements. The employment doctrine developed for Operation Desert Storm has become the Army's new doctrine for heavy HET employment. Of the 750 HETs in the inventory, 497 were deployed. The engineer tractors transported engineer equipment. Of the 1,759 M916, 468 were deployed. Of the 992 M920, 152 were deployed.

The USMC's LVS was developed to provide a common, multipurpose, heavy-lift vehicle sized for both expeditionary and division level transportation requirements. The bulk of I Marine Expeditionary Force supplies and equipment were moved from port to the forward operating areas by the LVS. Of the 1,655 LVSs in the USMC inventory, 615 were deployed.

Performance

The HEMTT's operational readiness rate of greater than 90 percent exceeded Army standards. It operated superbly in terrain that had become a quagmire because of rain. The HEMTT kept up with the tracked vehicles. One commander substituted HEMTTs for tracked ammunition carriers because of their greater reliability and mobility. LHT (M915) performed their line haul mission well and were able to move large quantities of supplies. Their lack of mobility limited their use mainly to improved roads. If it went off-road, the surface had to be hard or the vehicle had to be assisted by a HEMTT. The military HET was overloaded when carrying the M1A1 tank. The new HET, capable of transporting the M1A1 tank with the tank crew in its cab, was not available. The HET maintained an operational readiness rate approaching 90 percent.

One vehicle the Army did not deploy was the Palletized Load System (PLS). The British and French Armies deployed this system. PLS vehicles were used to transport fuel, water, ammunition, containers and Multiple Launch Rocket System rocket pods. Both the UK and France were pleased with the performance of the PLS system. US commanders indicated during interviews that the US PLS would have enabled the logistics system to operate more effectively.

The LVS was a highly mobile, extremely flexible, heavy-wheeled vehicle. The tandem-tow (two Mk 14 trailers or Mk 17/Mk 14 combination) doubled each LVS' carrying capacity without an increase of crew. This combination could be operated well on both highway or rough terrain. The Mk 48/Mk 16 facilitated the movement of Material Handling Equipments (MHE) using M870 trailers. The Mk 48/Mk 17 rear body unit was able to offload itself and other vehicles thus providing relief for MHE. The Mk 48/Mk 15 was an excellent recovery asset for all vehicles. The LVS also was able to keep pace with forward mechanized units during offensive operations. The LVS readiness rating ranged from 92 percent to 95 percent throughout Operations Desert Shield and Desert Storm.

OBSERVATIONS

Accomplishments

- The HEMTT was praised for its performance by both commanders and soldiers.
- A new doctrine developed for HET employment.
- The reliability and mobility of the LVS was a significant factor in the accomplishment of the USMC's mission.

Shortcomings

- The M1A1 tank overloaded the HET.
- The HET lacks cross-country mobility.
- The LHT was not mobile off roadways.
- LHTs created problems for forward units because trailers could not be off-loaded and 40-ft containers were difficult to handle.

Issues

- PLS would have made logistics operations more efficient in Operations Desert Shield and Desert Storm. The British and French proved the system was effective, delivering all types of cargo and reducing truck requirements. The French were able to load flatracks for their system while the truck was in transit. The driver could drop his load at the destination without waiting for the cargo to be off-loaded.
- A new HET version will replace the current HET. It has a 70-ton capacity, super single radial tires, central tire inflation system and can transport the tank crew. HET unit structure has been increased from 36 to 96 trucks per company to meet the new doctrine requirement.

TACTICAL WHEELED VEHICLES (MEDIUM FLEET)

Mission

The medium fleet consists of both 2- and 5-ton vehicles; the fleet deployed for Operations Desert Shield and Desert Storm consisted of both old and new vehicles. The 2-ton truck performs unit missions such as unit supply vehicle, mess truck, communications systems carrier, maintenance van, water truck, fuel truck and troop transport. The 2-ton truck fleet consisted of a mix of gas powered and multi-fueled vehicles. The 5-ton truck missions include general cargo and troop transport; tractor prime mover for 22-ton cargo semitrailers and 5,000 gallon fuel tankers in Corps and Divisional units; fuel and ammunition transport; prime mover for the 155-mm towed howitzer, wrecker operations and repair van. In Operations Desert Shield and Desert Storm there were gas powered, diesels and multi-fuels.

System Data

2-Ton Truck (M44 Series)

Prime Contractor: AM General Corporation
Crew: One driver
Initial Operational Capability: 1953
US Inventory: 68,700
Curb weight: 13,200 pounds
Payload: 5000 pounds
Length: 278 inches
Width: 93 inches
Height: 112 inches
Propulsion: Gasoline and multi-fuel 140 to 160 hp engines
Trailer towing capacity: 6,000 pounds
Range: 300 miles

5-Ton Truck (M39 Series, M809 Series, M939 Series, M939A1 Series, M939A2 Series)

Prime Contractor: BMY Wheeled Vehicles Division of Harsco Corporation
Crew: One driver (assistant with tractor)
Initial Operational Capability: 1989
US Inventory: 15,195
Curb weight: 22,175 pounds
Payload: 10,000 pounds
Length: 310 inches

Width: 98 inches
Height: 120 inches
Propulsion: 240 hp diesel engine.
Trailer towing capacity: 15,000 pounds
Range: 300 miles

Employment

The 2-ton truck was used in its standard mission roles. Of the 67,700 2-ton trucks in the Army's inventory, 14,000 were used Operations Desert Shield and Desert Storm. The 5-ton truck performed all of its missions. Particularly important was the movement of 5,000 gallon fuel semitrailers to the forward areas. It was also a key vehicle for transporting mine clearing battalion equipment. The Army was issuing the M939A2 series 5-ton truck at the start of Operations Desert Shield and Desert Storm. The 1st Infantry Division was changed before its deployment. All other divisions deployed with a mix of vehicles. Only 1,185 of the 9,700 new M939A2 5-ton trucks were used in Operations Desert Shield and Desert Storm. There were 2,000 of the 3,800 M939A1 and 12,136 of the 45,800 older series trucks used.

Performance

The 2-ton truck was the poorest performing vehicle in Operations Desert Shield and Desert Storm, because of its age and mobility problems. The 5-ton truck had mixed performance. The older vehicles did not perform as well as the newer vehicles, yet the operational readiness rates exceeded the Army's standard. The vehicles had varying degrees of mobility. The older M39, M809 and early M939 models with dual rear wheels did not perform as well as the M939A1, which has super single radial tires or the M939A2 which has central tire inflation system in addition to super single radial tires.

OBSERVATIONS

Accomplishment

■ Newer M939A1 and M939A2 5-ton truck models performed better than older models and readiness rates exceeded Army standards.

Shortcoming

■ The 2-ton truck was underpowered and experienced poor mobility.

Issues

■ A family of medical tactical vehicles (FMTV) which is a 4X4 that contains a more powerful engine, super single radial tires, and central tire inflation system is being procured. Older 5-ton trucks will be replaced by the 5-ton FMTV version. Between the two versions of FMTV, the Army has developed a concept that will provide major component commonality and reduce parts stock problems.

■ A Service Life Extension Program (SLEP) is required because new vehicles cannot be procured fast enough to replace older trucks. SLEP will provide a more powerful engine and super single radial tires resulting in greater reliability and increased mobility, while reducing operation and support costs.

TACTICAL WHEELED VEHICLES (LIGHT FLEET)

Mission

The light fleet TWVs deployed to Operations Desert Shield and Desert Storm consisted of the high mobility multi-purpose wheeled vehicle (HMMWV), combat unit cargo vehicle (CUCV) (a modified Chevrolet Blazer), the M-151 Jeep, the M561 Gama Goat and the M880 Dodge pickup truck. The HMMWV is a light, highly mobile, diesel powered, tactical vehicle that uses a common 1-1/4 ton payload chassis. The HMMWV versions are: cargo/troop carrier, armament carrier, communications system carrier, ambulance, TOW missile carrier, and light artillery prime mover. The CUCV is a light commercial-type 4-wheel drive vehicle powered by the same engine as the HMMWV with 1-1/4 ton capacity and less mobility than the HMMWV. The CUCV was designed for use in units that operate in rear areas. The versions are: cargo, ambulance, communications shelter, and command vehicle. The Jeep, Gama Goat and M880 are being retired. These vehicles were deployed with units to Southwest Asia (SWA) because the program to replace them had not been completed. All these type vehicles are expected to be out of the inventory by the end of FY 93.

System Data

HMMWV

Prime Contractor: AM General
Crew: Two to four
Initial Operational Capability: 1984
US Inventory: 59,883
Curb weight: 5,200 to 7,180 pounds (depending on model)
Payload: 2149 to 3177 pounds (depending on model)
Length: 180 to 203 inches
Width: 85 inches
Height: 72 to 105 inches
Propulsion: 6.2 liter diesel engine
Trailer towing capacity: 3,400 pounds
Range: 300 miles

CUCV

Prime Contractor: General Motors Corp, Chevrolet Division
Crew: Two
Initial Operational Capability: 1983
US Inventory: 58,604
Curb weight: 5,900 pounds
Payload: 2,900 pounds
Length: 185 to 222 inches (depending on model)
Width: 80 inches
Height: 76 to 101 inches (depending on model)
Trailer towing capacity: 3,000 pounds
Range: 250 miles

Employment

The Army used 20,000 of its 59,883 HMMWVs in Operations Desert Shield and Desert Storm. When the crisis began, the Army was replacing older vehicles with the HMMWV in its divisions and Armored Cavalry Regiments. The 82 Airborne Division and the 1st Infantry Division changes were completed before deployment. More than 5,000 HMMWVs were shipped to the theater to replace older vehicles in various units.

The Army also deployed 13,291 of its 58,604 CUCVs. In Operations Desert Shield and Desert Storm, operation of the CUCV was limited because of SWA's harsh terrain.

Performance

The HMMWV was the light vehicle of choice for soldiers in Operations Desert Shield and Desert Storm because of its superb performance. The HMMWV met or exceeded all expectations. It demonstrated excellent cross-country capability and its 90 percent operational readiness rate exceeded Army standards. The large payload capacity also was a tremendous asset for units. It proved to be a rugged cross-country vehicle. (The only complaint from soldiers was that the seat was too hard.) The CUCV had limited off-road capability and was not able to meet all the forward forces' requirements. However, it performed well when used within its limitations. The outdated M-151, M880 and Gama Goat did not perform well.

OBSERVATIONS

Accomplishments

- Versatile and reliable, the HMMWV maintained an operational readiness rate that exceeded Army standards. Its cross-country mobility and large payload capacity made it the light vehicle of choice among soldiers.

Shortcomings

- HMMWV's hard seat made rides uncomfortable for soldiers. HMMWVs in current production have a new seat that improves comfort. The Army also is installing new seats in the older vehicles.

- The CUCV had limited off-road mobility.

Issues

- A heavy HMMWV version intended to provide better artillery towing and transport heavy shelters will be fielded in FY 93.

- The Army is studying the possibility of installing tires that improve traction and, thus mobility, on the CUCV.

- Future procurements will favor HMMWV-like vehicles. However, there still is a role for a CUCV-type vehicle for units that operate in rear areas with improved roads.

TRAILBLAZER RADIO INTERCEPT AND DIRECTION FINDING SYSTEM

Mission

Trailblazer is a semi-automatic high frequency/very high frequency (HF/VHF) communications intercept and VHF radio intercept and direction finding (DF) system. It can locate a VHF transmitter within five seconds to a distance of approximately 30 km. It is targeted against Division and below command posts, maneuver, artillery and air defense units.

System Data

Frequency: 0.5-500 MHz (Intercept), 20-80 MHz (DF)
Targets: Single channel tactical HF and VHF tactical radios and jammers

Range: 30 KM (VHF); 70+ KM (HF)

Employment

Five Trailblazers deployed to Southwest Asia. In accordance with the deception plan and operational security policy, all systems were used initially in local force protection missions, rather than for collection operations against Iraqi forces.

Performance

When the Operation Desert Storm operations order required friendly forces to move to the west of the Iraqi forces, Trailblazer was used to confirm that selected breach routes were unopposed to a distance of 20 km. Targeting the few active enemy communications emitters, Trailblazer's DF system located Iraqi transmitters. However, the enemy's radio silence and the speed of the Coalition advance combined to limit Trailblazer's contribution after the ground offensive started. The Trailblazer, mounted on a Vietnam-era M1015A1 tracked carrier, could not keep up with the M1 tanks and M2 fighting vehicles.

OBSERVATIONS

Accomplishment

■ Trailblazer provided accurate VHF emitter locations to 150 km.

Shortcomings

■ The M1015A1 tracked carrier, common to Trailblazer, the Teampack Electronic Intelligence System, and the Tacjam Electronic Countermeasures System, is mechanically unreliable and lacks the mobility and speed to keep pace with the supported combat force.

Issue

■ Corrective action is under way to mount Trailblazer on 5-ton trucks for speed and mobility. New systems are being designed for the Electronic Fighting Vehicle System, which will be mounted on a Multiple Launch Rocket System chassis.

TROJAN SPIRIT SATELLITE COMMUNICATIONS SYSTEM

Mission

Trojan Spirit is a mobile satellite communications system mounted on a High Mobility Multi-purpose Wheeled Vehicle (HMMWV) providing Sensitive Compartmented Information-level communications and automation for all-source intelligence purposes. Trojan Spirit's mission is to provide voice, data, and facsimile communications at Army component, corps, division, separate brigade, armored cavalry command posts (CP) and maneuver brigades, and organic or assigned intelligence units, linking them with supporting or supported intelligence units both in the continental US and overseas.

System Data

Prime Contractor: Electrospace Systems
Initial Operational Capability: 1991
Configuration: One HMMWV with two trailers (satellite terminal and power generation) or in two HMMWVs
Communications: C and Ku-Band capable.

Uses leased and government-owned satellite channels for worldwide connectivity

Employment

Army Component, Central Command (ARCENT) used the total production run of 13 Trojan Spirit systems in Operations Desert Shield and Desert Storm in Southwest Asia. ARCENT used three Trojan Spirits at the component Main and Mobile CPs. One provided all-source collection management and intelligence dissemination support from the echelon above corps intelligence center at the ARCENT Main CP (Riyadh) to the VII Corps and XVIII Airborne Corps and the theater reserve division (1st Cavalry Division).

XVIII Airborne Corps used one Trojan Spirit at its Main CP, using it for all-source intelligence and for communicating to the system used at the 101st Airborne Division (Air Assault) subordinate to the corps.

VII Corps used two Trojan Spirits, one at its Main CP and one at its Military Intelligence

Brigade Operations Center at another location. These systems provided all-source intelligence and imagery intelligence support to the Commander, VII Corps, and communicated with systems at VII Corps divisions.

ARCENT also provided one Trojan Spirit to Marine Corps Component Comander (MARCENT) for all source connectivity to ARCENT, since ARCENT was responsible for ground order of battle in the theater.

Performance

Overall readiness rates for Trojan Spirits, first fielded in mid-January before the air campaign began, was more than 90 percent. Key intelligence support was provided by Trojan Spirit:

- Allowed ARCENT to inform both US corps the Iraqi Republican Guards divisions were moving to block ARCENT's attack; influenced the disposition of the attacking forces in both US corps;
- Provided the only means to communicate intelligence on the enemy situation from the ARCENT to 1st Cavalry Division once the division began its rapid, cross-desert attack as theater reserve against the Republican Guards;
- Provided a means to communicate imagery

from VII Corps' supporting MI Brigade to the 1st Armored Division, allowing the division to attack some 20 targets with artillery and attack helicopters;
- Linked the 101st Airborne Division (Air Assault) with the XVIII Airborne Corps after the division assault into Iraq, with its Trojan Spirit deployed and operating in position near the Euphrates River. In this manner, XVIII Airborne Corps could warn 101st Airborne Division (Air Assault) of any threat approaching the division's position from Baghdad;
- Provided a rapid, reliable, secure means of intelligence dissemination and collection management from division through component level, at times the only means of communicating intelligence information to mobile forces. This occurred when immediate precedence record traffic via AUTODIN took eight to 12 hours to reach addressees. During the air campaign, this connectivity was particularly important to 1st Cavalry Division, in blocking position and performing raids across the Iraq-Kuwait border, as other US forces moved to attack positions;
- During the air campaign, provided a means to communicate intelligence on Iraqi movements and battle damage between ARCENT and the two corps, and MARCENT.

OBSERVATIONS

Accomplishment

- Provided a rapid, reliable, secure means of intelligence dissemination and collection management from division through component level, at times the only means of communicating intelligence information to mobile forces.

Shortcomings

- Not every division had a system, and units typically received only one of three required.

- Lacked tactical mobility of the satellite terminal trailer, and time to integrate the system into unit operations.

Issue

- A proposal to field and integrate a modified version, adapted for mobility, and with new satellite channels to Army Force Package One units in sufficient quantities is being considered.

MUNITIONS

AIR-LAUNCHED CRUISE MISSILE

Mission

The AGM-86C air-launched cruise missile (ALCM) was designed to attack soft ground targets using a high explosive blast/fragmentation warhead. It is a conventional variant of the AGM-86B nuclear ALCM. A global positioning system (GPS) aided by an inertial navigation system (INS) provides all-weather capability.

System Data

Prime Contractor: Boeing Aerospace
Initial Operational Capability: 1988
Length: 20 ft, 9 in
Wingspan: 12 ft
Cruise Speed: 500 mph
Propulsion: Williams F107-WR-101 turbofan
Guidance: GPS/INS
Armament: Blast/fragmentation

Employment

During the first night of Operation Desert Storm, 35 conventional ALCMs were launched from seven B-52G aircraft which took off from Barksdale AFB, LA. The bombers launched the missiles on the one-time mission approximately two hours after the strategic air campaign began. These ALCMs were launched against 8 targets in Iraq, including power generation and transmission facilities and military communications sites.

Performance

A complete assessment of the AGM-86C's effectiveness is difficult to determine because of incomplete battle damage assessment (BDA) and the inability to distinguish damage caused by other munitions that struck some of the same targets. All missiles launched successfully transitioned to cruise flight. Demonstrated accuracy appears consistent with the results obtained from testing.

OBSERVATIONS

Accomplishments

- The AGM-86C ALCM played an important role in Operation Desert Storm.

- All missiles that were launched successfully transitioned to cruise flight.

LASER GUIDED BOMBS (LGB)

Mission

Laser-guided bombs (LGBs) are close-in weapons capable of striking point targets. There are three weight classes of LGBs: 500 lb, 1000 lb, and 2,000 lb. The weapon consists of a bomb body with a guidance kit which detects a target illuminated by a laser beam.

System Data

Prime Contractor: Texas Instruments
Initial Operational Capability: Early-1970
Range: Up to 7 miles
Guidance: Passive laser tri-Service seeker.
Armament: Blast fragmentation high explosive warhead (500, 1,000, and 2,000 lb), or penetrator (BLU-109 Improved 2000 lb)

Employment

LGBs delivered by the F-111, F-15E, F-117, F/A-18, and the A-6E were used primarily against hardened airfield facilities, such as aircraft shelters and bunkers, and also against bridges, artillery and armor. The GBU-12 (500 lb) was used extensively against vehicles and armor. All LGBs were used against point targets because of their high accuracy.

Performance

Approximately 9,300 LGBs were dropped. More than 4,500 of these were GBU-12 (500 lb); over 2,500 were GBU-10 (2,000 lb); over 200 were GBU-16 (1,000 lb), and almost 2,000 were GBU-24/27 (1,600 of which were 2,000-lb penetrators).

Although there is a lack of comprehensive bomb damage assessment data, LGBs appear to have performed well. After action reports indicate the LGBs were effective. Because of their precision, LGBs were the weapon of choice when accuracy was required, such as against military targets in downtown Baghdad and bridges.

While there were some instances of weapons failing to guide; overall, LGBs were responsible for minimizing collateral damage.

LGBs used against tanks and armored vehicles, hardened command and control bunkers, and aircraft shelters were also effective. However, while post war examination and analysis of Iraqi targets confirms the success of LGBs, battle damage assessment (BDA) by reconnaissance assets during the conflict was difficult to determine. LGBs would often penetrate into the facility leaving only a small penetration hole although interiors were determined to have been destroyed or severely damaged. Further data on precision-guided ordnance effectiveness is unavailable unless an extensive bomb damage assessment study is completed.

OBSERVATIONS

Accomplishment

- Demonstrated LGB accuracy was consistent with results from pre-war testing.

Shortcoming

- There were some shortages of LGB guidance kits in theater.

Issue

- Additional LGB kits are being procured to build up the operational inventory.

MAVERICK AIR-TO-GROUND MISSILE

Mission

Maverick is a stand-off weapon capable of striking point targets. There are six variants. Maverick A and B versions have an electro-optical (EO) television guidance system. The D and F variants have an imaging infrared (IR) guidance system operated much like that of the A or B, except that infrared video overcomes the daylight only limitation. The E variant uses a laser seeker to guide against designated targets such as protected command bunkers and armored vehicles. Laser designation can be performed by ground Modular Universal Laser Emitter (MULE) or airborne systems. The F and G variants have essentially the same guidance system as the D with a heavier weight penetrator warhead in the F and G variants.

System Data

Prime Contractor: Hughes/Raytheon
Initial Operational Capability: AGM-65D in 1983; AGM-65F/G in 1989
Length: 8.8 ft
Cruise Speed: Supersonic
Range: Up to 15 miles
Propulsion: Single stage solid propellant rocket motor with dual thrust
Guidance: Television (AGM-65A/B); Laser Maverick (AGM-65E) - Passive laser tri-Service seeker; IIR Maverick (AGM-65D/F/G) - Passive imaging infrared seeker with digital centroid tracking
Armament: Shape-Charge Jet and Blast 125 pound warhead (A/B/D); blast fragmentation 300 lb high explosive warhead (E/F/G)

Employment

The Maverick can be used from the A-6, A-10, AV-8B, F-16, F-4G, and F/A-18. The missile has a launch and leave capability that lets a pilot fire the weapon and immediately take evasive action or attack another target. The shape-charge jet and blast warhead is designed to work against armor and other moderately hard targets but can also be effectively used against targets such as radar control facilities and other above-ground facilities.

Maverick attacks were conducted typically in close air support (CAS) or air interdiction (AI) missions. Both IR and TV Mavericks were used. Most were fired at ranges averaging 3.5 miles or less, which is considerably less than the weapon's maximum range. The predominant target set for IR Maverick was armor. Attack aircraft in many cases would be assigned to a "kill box" in which an airborne Forward Air Controller (FAC) would also be assigned. The FAC would enter the Kill Box to find the targets. Attack aircraft would then be directed to the target by the FAC.

Performance

Maverick success rate (successful launch and guidance to the target) was approximately 80 to 90 percent for the more than 5,100 AGM-65s fired. These results are consistent with Air Force performance before Operation Desert Storm. Laser Maverick performance was reported as three hits for five missiles fired. The misses were attributed to weak MULE batteries.

OBSERVATIONS

Accomplishments

- A-10s delivered more than 4,800 of the more than 5,100 Mavericks used in the war.

- Maverick demonstrated accuracy consistent with results from pre-war testing.

Shortcoming

- Maverick use requires comprehensive training because of the cockpit workload in the battlefield environment. This can cause aircrews to become unduly preoccupied and predictable targets for enemy anti-aircraft fire while attempting delivery.

SIDEWINDER AIR-TO-AIR MISSILE

Mission

The AIM-9 Sidewinder is an advanced, short-range, supersonic, air-to-air missile. The AIM-9 Sidewinder's primary role is air superiority, but the missile also is used extensively to provide aircraft self defense capability. The Sidewinder uses a passive infrared (IR) target acquisition system.

System Data

Prime Contractor: Ford Aerospace
Initial Operational Capability: 1982 (AIM-9M)
Length: 9 feet, 5 inches
Diameter: 5 inches
Wingspan: 2 feet, 0.75 inches
Weight: 195 lbs

Warhead: AIM 9L, 20.8 lbs; AIM-9M, 7.4 lbs blast fragmentation
Propulsion: Solid propellant rocket motor
Guidance: Passive IR homing

Employment

The AIM-9 Sidewinder missile was used within visual range, day and night, in clear weather.

Performance

A small number of Sidewinders (less than 20) were fired during Desert Storm. Success rate of the AIM-9 was consistent with the results of previous testing. More realistic pilot training and improved missile technology played major roles in the missile's success.

OBSERVATIONS

Accomplishment

- The Sidewinders fired during Desert Storm performed well and the success rate was consistent with previous operational testing.

SPARROW AIR-TO-AIR MISSILE

Mission

The AIM-7 Sparrow is a semi-active radar-guided, air-to-air missile with a high-explosive warhead. It has all-weather, all-altitude operational capability and can attack high performance aircraft from all angles, including head-on. With its quick reaction time and high maneuverability, the Sparrow can attack targets traveling at supersonic speeds and at all altitudes. The missile also can operate in an electronic countermeasures environment. It can be carried on the F-14, F/A-18, F-15, Air Defense F-16, and F-4G.

System Data

Prime Contractor: Raytheon
Initial Operational Capability: 1983 (AIM-7M)
Weight: 500 lbs
Length: 12 ft
Diameter: 8 in
Wingspan: 40 in
Warhead: High explosive, 85 lbs

Guidance: Radar, semi-active continuous wave or pulsed doppler

Employment

The Sparrow was used by F-14, F-15, and F/A-18 aircraft during Operation Desert Storm. The missile was used both day and night, in clear or adverse weather, in visual and beyond visual range (BVR) tactical situations. Improved performance can be attributed to realistic pilot training programs such as Red Flag and Top Gun, as well as cockpit display technology.

Performance

There were 71 AIM-7 Sparrow firing attempts. The Air Force (USAF) accounted for 67 of the 71 attempts. USAF hit rate was nearly triple the success rate in Southeast Asia (SEA). The Navy's experience was similar.

Results most likely were due to several factors. The AIM-7M is much improved over earlier versions. The success rate of Sparrows launched within the missile's envelope was double the success rate in SEA. A larger percentage of the launch attempts were in the envelope and a much greater percentage were successful against targets at low altitude. Some firings were successful against helicopters.

OBSERVATIONS

Accomplishments

■ Technological improvements to the Sparrow resulted in improved performance.

■ Realistic advanced fighter weapons training at Service training schools resulted in improved pilot performance.

■ Combat results show previous Weapons System Evaluation Program test firings conducted by the Services in peacetime to have been fairly accurate at depicting pilot, aircraft, and air-to-air missile capabilities and limitations.

STANDOFF LAND ATTACK MISSILE (SLAM)

Mission

The Standoff Land Attack Missile (SLAM) is a tactical weapon designed for deployment aboard aircraft carriers. Launched from A-6E and F/A-18 aircraft, it provides a standoff air-to-surface day/night/marginal weather capability. It satisfies intermediate tactical needs between long-range cruise missiles and short-range freefall munitions in land attacks against fixed, above-ground, high-value targets.

System Data

Prime Contractor: McDonnell Douglas Missile Co.
Initial Operational Capability: Pre-Initial Operational Capability Deployment
Length: 14.75 ft
Weight: 1385 pounds
Cruise Speed: MACH 0.8
Range: More than 50 miles
Propulsion: Turbojet engine
Guidance: Target location and mission data are loaded into the missile before takeoff. While the missile is in-flight, a satellite Global Positioning System (GPS) receiver/processor updates the missile's inertial navigation system. This points the missile's imaging infrared (IR) seeker directly at the target. The IR seeker sends a video image to the cockpit via a Walleye data link pod. The pilot selects a specific aimpoint on the target and gives the commands for seeker lock on. After seeker lock on, the missile makes an autonomous precision strike.
Armament: 500 lb high explosive
Fuze: Provides instantaneous and delayed detonation options

Employment

SLAM was used to attack heavily defended targets from standoff ranges outside of surface-to-air missile and antiaircraft artillery envelopes.

Performance

Seven SLAMs were launched from either A-6E or F/A-18 aircraft at standoff ranges outside Iraqi target defenses. Missiles were controlled from A-7E or F/A-18 aircraft through AWW-9 data link pods.

The new AWW-13 data link pod was unavailable for use, requiring the use of the older, less reliable AWW-9 pod. Initial AWW-9 pod reliability was low, requiring dedicated maintenance efforts by a team of civilian technicians and Navy maintenance personnel to improve performance.

OBSERVATIONS

Accomplishments

- SLAM provides a standoff capability and was used successfully for the first time in combat without the loss of aircraft or crew.

- Recorded infrared video of the missile as it struck the target provided verification of aimpoint accuracy (BIA — bomb impact assessment).

Shortcoming

- The AWW-9 data link pod was unreliable.

Issue

- The new AWW-13 advanced data link pod currently entering the Fleet should resolve data link pod reliability problems.

TACTICAL AIR-LAUNCHED DECOY

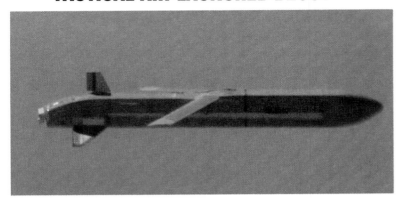

Mission

The ADM-141 Tactical Air-Launched Decoy (TALD) is an expendable aerial decoy used to improve strike aircraft survivability by deceiving and saturating hostile radar-controlled air defenses.

System Data

Prime Contractor: Brunswick Defense Corp.
Initial Operational Capability: 1987
Weight: 400 lbs
Length: 7.67 ft
Maximum Range: 86 miles at maximum launch altitude/minimum decoy speed
Launch Platforms: F/A-18, A-6, A-7, S-3
Launch Altitude: 100 to 40,000 ft
Speed: 250 to 500 knots
Radar Return Enhancement: Active and passive

Employment

TALDs are small, unpowered decoys carried by tactical aircraft on standard bomb racks. TALD's size, weight and carriage approximate that of a 500-lb bomb. Up to eight TALDs can be carried by a single Navy or Marine (USMC) aircraft.

Significant numbers of TALD were used in the early stages of Operation Desert Storm supporting suppression of enemy air defenses (SEAD) operations. TALD was launched by both Navy and USMC tactical aircraft and were used in varying quantities in both dedicated TALD missions and combined TALD/Strike payloads.

Performance

TALD proved to be a key element in the suppression arsenal. Pilots reported SAMs were launched in response to TALD launches. Furthermore, it is likely that TALD contributed to Iraqi claims of massive Coalition aircraft losses early in the theater campaign.

OBSERVATIONS

Accomplishments

■ Southwest Asia (SWA) provided the first combat use of TALD. Despite a lack of experience with the weapon system, it was easily loaded by loading crews and deployed by aircrew.

■ TALD was an integral part of SEAD strike planning. Aircrew confidence in the weapon system increased as a result of battlefield observation of its effectiveness.

■ TALD probably was responsible for the early Iraqi claims of extensive allied aircraft losses.

■ TALD exposed enemy SAM site radars and made them more susceptible to HARM.

Shortcomings

■ TALD launch and carriage restrictions placed some aircraft within the range of long-range SAMs.

■ While TALD was extremely effective against the Iraqi integrated air defense systems, the glide path might be more easily discriminated by more sophisticated radars or operators.

TOMAHAWK MISSILE

Mission

Tomahawk is a stand-off, deep strike weapon capable of striking ships and targets ashore from surface combatants or submarines. Tomahawk's objective is to deliver pinpoint attacks against targets in heavily defended areas where the probability of the loss of manned aircraft is too high.

There are three conventionally-armed Tomahawk variants:

Tomahawk Antiship Missile (TASM) (BGM-109B) contains a guidance system similar to the Harpoon anti-ship missile. TASM uses an active radar seeker and passive identification and direction-finding equipment to seek out, lock on, and strike targets ranging from frigates to high value carriers. Its sea-skimming altitude and evasive flight path help the missile conceal the direction of its launch and elude enemy defenses as it approaches the surface target.

TLAM-C (BGM-109C) can neutralize important targets ashore, such as command and control (C^2) systems, airfields, and air defense systems with its 1,000-lb warhead.

Submunition TLAM-D (BGM-109D) is a variant of the TLAM-C, can strike area targets and can render aircraft and air defense sites inactive. It can attack multiple targets by dispensing 166 combined effects bomblets (CEB) submunitions in partial loads which provide armor-piercing, fragmentation, and incendiary effects.

System Data (TLAM-C/D)

Prime Contractor: McDonnell/Douglas; General Dynamics
Initial Operational Capability: 1986 (TLAM-C)
Length: 20.5 feet
Cruise Speed: High subsonic (Mach 0.5 to .75)
Range: Greater than 500 miles
Propulsion: Solid propellant rocket motor for

boost mode; turbofan engine for cruise mode

Guidance: Terrain-Contour Matching (TERCOM) uses a radar altimeter to produce terrain profiles at preselected points along the route. These profiles are compared with reference maps in the guidance computer to determine if flight corrections are needed. Each TERCOM update increases the precision of TLAM's flight; Digital Scene-Matching Area Correlation (DSMAC); more precise than TERCOM, produces digital scenes of natural and man-made terrain features and compares them with scenes stored in a computer. Used during terminal homing phase to guide TLAM-C/D to a direct hit.

Armament: TLAM-C — 1000-lb high explosive, TLAM-D — 166 BLU-97/B combined effects bomblets in 24 packages

Employment

Only the TLAM-C and D variants were used during Operation Desert Storm. TLAM's employment emphasized its primary attributes — precision strike capability and survivability. It was one of only two systems used to strike targets in downtown Baghdad — the most heavily defended target complex — during the initial phase of the air campaign. Tomahawk was the only weapon used for daylight attacks against Baghdad during the entire campaign.

TLAM missions were an integral part of the air campaign. They were fully integrated into the daily Air Tasking Order with other air assets. Unlike tactical air strikes, however, TLAM missions did not require Airborne Warning and Control System (AWACS), tanker, fighter or electronic warfare coordination. As a result, TLAM sometimes was the only asset that could conduct short notice strikes (provided that a TLAM mission package already had been prepared). For example, when suspected Scud missile loading activity was detected at a missile storage facility, 13 TLAM were fired at

previously attacked aimpoints to disrupt the activity until tactical air strikes could be conducted.

Overall, 282 of 288 Tomahawks were successfully launched by 16 surface ships and two submarines. Of these, 64 percent were launched during the first 48 hours of the war. These strikes were almost exclusively against chemical weapons facilities, electrical power and distribution facilities, and high level leadership C^2 facilities. The attacks on leadership and C^2 facilities paved the way for Coalition aircraft to strike Baghdad and other heavily defended areas.

Performance

Mission planners at the Cruise Missile Support Activities, located at Atlantic and Pacific commands, began planning targets soon after the invasion of Kuwait. Throughout Operation Desert Shield, planners continued to develop TLAM strike missions and plans. By H-Hour, with the assistance of national sensors to supplement existing information, several hundred TLAM missions were available to support the air campaign.

The key to timely mission planning was the availability of TERCOM maps from the Defense Mapping Agency and DSMAC scenes based on recent imagery. Once missions are transmitted to Tomahawk platforms, missiles can be ready to fire very quickly. Tomahawk targeting capability against relocatable targets was demonstrated in one instance by a short notice attack against an Iraqi communications facility. Although Tomahawk is affected by some types of adverse weather, weather conditions during Operation Desert Storm never precluded a TLAM mission.

Of 288 missiles launched, 282 successfully achieved cruise flight for a 98 percent launch success rate. An assessment of TLAM effectiveness — its success in reaching and damaging the intended target — is much more difficult to determine because of incomplete battle damage assessment (BDA) and the inability to distinguish missile damage from damage caused by other assets, including other Tomahawks. During Operation Desert Storm, Tomahawk was sometimes used to disrupt functions in a target facility, rather than to destroy the facility. TLAM also was used only to damage a facility to a level that would require a moderate period of time to repair instead of complete destruction.

All assigned TLAM missions were executed either by the first-assigned platform using the intended missile or its backup, or by reassigning the mission to another launch platform. On several occasions, Navy Component Central Command (NAVCENT) elected not to use backup missiles, or another platform, because the missile was one of several targeted at the designated aim point and sufficient redundancy existed.

TLAM's demonstrated accuracy was consistent with results from pre-combat testing. The observed accuracy of TLAM, for which unambiguous target imagery is available, met or exceeded the accuracy mission planners predicted.

OBSERVATIONS

Accomplishments

- The Tomahawk cruise missile played an important role as the only weapon system to attack central Baghdad in daylight. The cruise missile concept, incorporating an unmanned, low-observable platform able to strike accurately over long distances, was validated as a significant weapon for future conflicts.

- The demonstrated launching system success rate was 98 percent.

- TLAMs demonstrated accuracy that was consistent with results from pre-combat testing.

Issue

- Block III missile improvements, planned well before the invasion of Kuwait, are funded in the FY92 budget. Significant improvements in Tomahawk C^2 systems included with the Block III improvements will be fielded in 1993. These improvements will increase flexibility and reduce communication requirements associated with targeting conventional Tomahawk missions.

- Additional improvements in the Tomahawk weapons system based upon experience gained during Operation Desert Storm are under review for inclusion in Tomahawk Block III missile development.

Naval Systems

AIRCRAFT CARRIER (CV/CVN)

Mission

The aircraft carrier's mission, as the center piece of the Navy's battle group, is to conduct prompt and sustained combat operations at sea, through sea control and power projection. In the exercise of sea control, the carrier and its embarked aircraft can, under all conditions of weather and visibility, detect and destroy enemy aircraft, submarines, and surface ships; strike base areas; and conduct reconnaissance, patrol, and offensive mining operations. In the exercise of power projection, the carrier strikes enemy air and naval bases and port facilities; conducts interdiction strikes and close air support in conjunction with amphibious operations and land campaigns; and conducts deep strikes against the enemy's infrastructure and strategic targets.

There are two aircraft carrier variants, the conventionally powered aircraft carrier (CV) and the nuclear powered aircraft carrier (CVN).

The newer, more capable CVNs are replacing older conventional CVs in the fleet.

System Data (Nimitz Class)

Length overall: 1,092 ft
Beam, maximum: 257 ft
Full Load displacement: 96,300 tons
Aircraft embarked: 85 to 90
Aircraft Catapults: Four
Complement: 6,300
Propulsion Plant: Nuclear power
Speed: 30+ knots

Employment

At the time of the Iraqi invasion of Kuwait, the Navy already was on station in the region. Battle Groups led by *USS Independence* (CV 62) and *USS Dwight D.Eisenhower* (CVN 69) moved from the Indian Ocean and Eastern Mediterranean Sea to take up positions in the Gulf of Oman and Red Sea respectively — ready to begin sustained combat operations.

When Operation Desert Storm began, there were six aircraft carriers on station in the Red Sea and Persian Gulf. USS America (CV 66) and *USS Theodore Roosevelt* (CVN 71) left Norfolk on 28 December, and arrived on station just before Operation Desert Storm. They joined *USS Midway* (CV41), *USS Saratoga* (CV 60), *USS John F.Kennedy* (CV 67), and *USS Ranger* (CV 61), which already were on station.

Performance

Navy carrier-based aircraft contributed to the destruction of Iraq's air and naval forces, antiair defenses, ballistic missile launchers, communications networks, electrical power systems, and more.

E-2C Hawkeyes (discussed separately in this appendix) operated around the clock in conjunction with Coalition Airborne Warning and Control Systems to track Iraq's air force and provide air traffic control. Navy carrier-based aircraft flew continuous combat air patrols to protect Coalition naval forces, sealift shipping and airfields, and provided reconnaissance.

Carrier-based aviation made a major contribution to the destruction of the Iraqi Navy. Within the first three weeks of the air campaign, A-6s, F/A-18 and S-3s sank and disabled many of Iraq's missile gunboats, minesweepers, patrol craft and other small ships. Silkworm antiship missile sites and armed hovercraft also were attacked.

Operation Desert Storm marked the first combat use of some of the Navy's newest carrier-based aircraft including the F-14A+, the F/A-18C, and the F/A-18D night-attack aircraft. S-3B aircraft also used their inverse synthetic aperture radar to locate mobile Scud launchers.

As the war progressed, the Navy's strike mission changed from strategic air attacks and battlefield preparation to tactical targets and battlefield air interdiction. On the last full day of war, the six carrier battle groups flew 600 combat missions. Nearly 20,000 carrier-based sorties were flown delivering more than 21 million pounds of ordnance.

OBSERVATIONS

Accomplishments

- Within one hour of the start of the 2 August attack, the *USS Independence* (CV 62) battle group (forward-deployed to the Indian Ocean) and the *USS Dwight D. Eisenhower* (CVN 69) battle group (forward-deployed to the eastern Mediterranean Sea) were ordered to the Gulf of Oman and the Red Sea, respectively.

- The flexibility of the aircraft carrier allowed for the concentration of air power where it was most needed. For example, USS America redeployed from the Red Sea, where it had been used to attack Baghdad and western Iraq, to the Persian Gulf where it could be used to support the ground campaign.

- The centralized location of all required strike assets (i.e., fighters, bombers, electronic warfare support aircraft, etc) on an aircraft carrier allowed an entire strike package to plan and prepare for complex strikes. This capability also provided an effective, rapid reaction strike capability if a short-notice contingency strike was required.

- Carrier-based aircraft flew approximately 20,000 sorties from 17 January to 28 February.

Shortcomings

- Because of the extended ranges involved during attacks on Iraq, naval air assets required refueling from land-based tankers. However, the Persian Gulf Battle Force was able to move closer to Kuwait as the war progressed, which reduced the need for non-organic tanking support.

- For safety reasons, naval aircraft use JP-5 fuel for carrier-based operations. Refueling from land-based aircraft with other than JP-5 allowed mission completion, but presented an increased fire hazard when the aircraft returned to its aircraft carrier.

Issue

- The Navy and Air Force have established a flag-level board to address many issues involved with joint operations, such as in-flight refueling and fuel compatibility.

MINE COUNTERMEASURES SHIP

Mission

The surface mine countermeasures ship (SMCM) provides the capability to conduct a mine survey of harbors, port approaches, large ocean areas, including potential amphibious objective areas and sea lines of communication. These platforms can detect, locate and neutralize all existing types of bottom and moored mines.

System Data (MCM 1 Avenger Class Mine Countermeasure Ship)

Prime Contractor: Peterson Builders/Marinette Marine
Initial Operational Capability: 1987
Inventory: 14 (Planned)
Length: 224
Displacement: 1,312 tons
Beam: 39 ft
Draft: 11.5 ft
Speed: 14 knots
Complement: Six officers, 75 enlisted
Propulsion: Four diesel engines
MCM Systems: AN/SLQ-48 Mine Neutralization System, AN/SSN-2 Precision Inertial Navigation System (PINS) AN/SQQ-32 advanced minehunting sonar AN/SLQ-37 influence minesweeping system AN/WQN-1 channel finder
Armament: None

Employment

The US mine warfare concept was designed around a European war scenario, which relied on North Atlantic Treaty Organization (NATO) allies to participate substantially in mine warfare operations, especially in MCM. The Navy's MCM capabilities in the Persian Gulf consisted of surface mine countermeasures (SMCM), aviation mine countermeasures (AMCM), and explosive ordnance disposal (EOD) teams. One newly commissioned Avenger class (MCM 1) MCM ship and three older MSO 422/508 class minesweepers deployed to the Persian Gulf on 30 September. After Operation Desert Storm began, the Coalition mine countermeasures (MCM) forces cleared paths to the Kuwaiti coast for naval gunfire support and amphibious operations. After the cease fire, these platforms cleared port approaches and harbors, including Kuwait City's port.

USS Avenger (MCM 1) used the AN/SQQ-32 MCM sonar to detect moored and bottom mines in shallow or deep waters. *USS Avenger* also used the AN/SLQ-48 mine neutralization system (MNS) to locate, examine, and destroy mines. The MNS consists of a remotely piloted submersible vehicle equipped with sonar and two television cameras for locating mines, explosives for neutralizing mines, and cable cutters for cutting a mine's mooring so it floats to the surface for destruction. The other US minesweepers used the AN/SQQ-14 MCM sonar to detect bottom and moored mines and mechanical minesweeping gear to cut mine cables.

Performance

USS Avenger developed engineering problems while deployed; all four diesels engines had to be replaced during her deployment. However, *USS Avenger's* MCM suite was effective. For example, on 27 February, *USS Avenger,* using the AN/SQQ-32 MCM sonar, detected, classified and marked a bottom influence mine (similar to the type that struck *USS Princeton*) at a distance of 900 yards. Because of the mine's unique shape and construction (glass reinforced plastic), it had been assessed to be undetectable by sonar. The AN/SLQ-48 was the most sophisticated mine neutralization system used in MCM operations and PINS proved to be the most precise and reliable navigation system of all Coalition MCM assets.

OBSERVATIONS

Accomplishments

- *USS Avenger,* using the AN/SQQ-32 MCM sonar, detected, classified, and marked a bottom influence mine similar to the type that struck *USS Princeton.*

- The AN/SLQ-48 was the most sophisticated MNS used in MCM operations and PINS proved to be the most precise and reliable navigation system of all Coalition MCM assets.

Shortcomings

- The SMCM ships lacked a dedicated support ship for C^3, logistic, maintenance, and explosive ordnance disposal team support.

- USS Avenger's as-received material condition was poor. This shortcoming initially prevented her from contributing the most sophisticated and effective MCM systems to the Coalition's MCM operations.

NAVAL GUNFIRE SUPPORT (NGFS)

Mission

Iowa Class battleship 16-inch/50 caliber guns provide intermediate-range naval gunfire support (NGFS) for battlefield area interdiction (BAI) and direct support for forces ashore. Each 16-inch gun can fire a 2,700-lb armor-piercing shell more than 23 miles every 30 seconds. A battleship can deliver more than 20 tons of ordnance on target in one minute and 1,458 tons in one hour.

System Data

Calibre: 16 inch
Projectile weight: 2,240 lbs; 2,700 lbs armor piercing
Rate of Fire: Two rounds per minute/one per minute sustained
Maximum range: 26 miles
Maximum effective range: 20 miles
Rounds per ship: 1220
Guns per battleship: Nine

Employment

During Operation Desert Storm, the Navy's two commissioned battleships, *USS Missouri* (BB 63) and *USS Wisconsin* (BB 64), fired 1,102 16-inch rounds in 83 NGFS missions against targets such as artillery batteries, small boats in port, anti-aircraft sites, bunkers, infantry in trenches, ammunition storage sites, command posts, and tanks. Total ordnance delivered was the equivalent of 542 A-6 missions. Unmanned aerial vehicles (UAVs) were used during most missions for surveillance, targeting, spotting, and battle damage assessment (BDA), and greatly increased the 16-inch gun's effectiveness.

Performance

The 16-inch gun missions can be divided into three categories of targets: BAI into the Kuwaiti Theater of Operations from 4 to 12 February, support of the amphibious raid on the island of Faylakah, and support of ground operations from 20 to 26 February.

Spotting and BDA were provided almost exclusively by UAVs. Two-thirds of the missions received spotting, as well as almost 90 percent of the shells fired, which is a high percentage historically. The battleship fired an average of 19 rounds per mission when spotting was provided. For missions where spotting was not used, three or four shells per mission were fired, mostly for harassment fire against troop and artillery positions.

According to US Navy sources, BDA was obtained in 70 percent (37 of 52) of the missions where spotting was used. Included in the targets reportedly destroyed, neutralized or heavily damaged were three area targets (an artillery/mortar battery and two ammunition/logistic sites) and seven point targets (two surface-to-air missiles or antiaircraft artillery sites, three command/observation posts, a building and a radar/electronic warfare/communication site).

OBSERVATIONS

Accomplishments

- Battleship 16-inch guns and UAVs provided an effective delivery of ordnance against various targets.

- NGFS missions were unaffected by cloud cover or oil field smoke over the targets because the UAVs were able to operate below these conditions.

- The 16-inch guns were reliable and fired all assigned missions without placing aircraft or air crews at risk.

Shortcoming

- The threat of mines kept the battleships from following Coalition ground forces as they advanced rapidly north.

Issue

- USS Wisconsin was decommissioned on 30 September, 1991. With the decommissioning of USS Missouri in March, 1992, the Navy's existing 5-inch and 76-mm guns provide the only NGFS capability.

SPACE SYSTEMS

DEFENSE METEOROLOGICAL SATELLITE PROGRAM (DMSP)

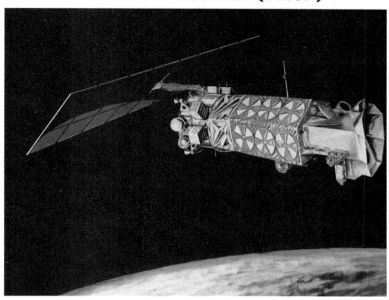

Mission

Defense Meteorological Satellite Program (DMSP) satellites provide direct readout of theater cloud conditions to fixed and mobile terminals. The satellite program is designed to collect and disseminate global visible and infrared cloud cover, and other specialized meteorological, oceanographic, and solar geophysical data to support Department of Defense operations and other high priority programs, and tactical field units worldwide.

System Data

Prime Contractor: General Electric
Initial Operational Capability: 1966
Length: 12 ft
Diameter: 4 ft
Weight: 1830 lbs
Orbit: Circular Sun Synchronous Polar
Altitude: 540 miles
Prime Sensor: Optical linescan system

Bands: Visible and IR
Resolution: 0.36 — 1.8 miles

Employment

Three DMSP satellites were available during Operations Desert Shield and Desert Storm. DMSP flights 8 and 9 were available throughout the entire conflict and flight 10 was launched 1 December. Six Mark IV vans (deployable DMSP receiving stations) were deployed. One Air Force (USAF) van was deployed to Riyadh and provided imagery to Central Command (CENTCOM) staff and a Tactical Forecast Unit (TFU). Five Marine (USMC) Mark IV vans were deployed in support of USMC aviation and amphibious operations. Some Navy ships with embarked meteorological personnel (aircraft carriers and aviation-capable amphibious ships) were equipped to receive direct DMSP broadcasts of weather information. Other ships with meteorological personnel relied on civilian weather satellites.

TFU managed Mark IV operations at Riyadh and produced a standard weather report transmitted by high frequency (HF) radio to Army and Air Force (USAF) users in theater. Weather images were faxed from the USAF Mark IV van to USAF units by land lines. Army units received weather images from non-military weather satellites through a commercial receiver which could only receive a civil weather broadcast. The Army chose to use these receivers because the Mark IV van required considerable airlift space (75 percent of a C-141 load) and, therefore, could not meet Army mobility requirements.

Performance

Coalition forces used DMSP and civil weather satellite data to predict rapidly changing weather patterns and to monitor the burning oil wells. Weather information was used extensively to plan and execute attack missions, infer wind direction and potential chemical agent spread, and to alert US forces of sandstorms or other weather phenomena. This access to current weather data allowed US forces to capitalize on night vision and IR targeting capabilities.

Weather satellites provided key support to US forces in Saudi Arabia and surrounding areas in planning missions, preparing weapons systems, readying defenses, and moving troops. Weather data became especially crucial in the desert where heavy coastal fogs and sandstorms reduced visibility to zero and rains turned desert sands into bogs. Weather data also was used in target selection and in determining the best type of aircraft and munitions to use.

Information on rapidly changing weather patterns was crucial to tactical planners. SWA weather patterns changed within minutes. For example, on 24 January, one DMSP readout showed Baghdad in central Iraq covered by clouds and Basra near the Gulf coast clear. Approximately an hour and a half later, a second DMSP image showed Baghdad clear and Basra overcast.

OBSERVATIONS

Accomplishment

■ Weather data was vital to military operations and was widely available to US forces. Both DMSP and non-military satellites played key roles in providing meteorological data on a timely basis. Each provided unique and time crucial data not accessible from another source.

Shortcomings

■ Rapidly changing weather patterns in Southwest Asia resulted in tactical units not always having timely and accurate information on target area weather conditions.

■ Field units did not have total access to DMSP data. Small tactical DMSP receive terminals will be available for all field units in the next few years.

■ Some Navy ships with embarked meteorological personnel did not have access to DMSP data. The required antenna/receiver system has been procured and will be installed as funding permits.

DEFENSE SATELLITE COMMUNICATIONS SYSTEM (DSCS)

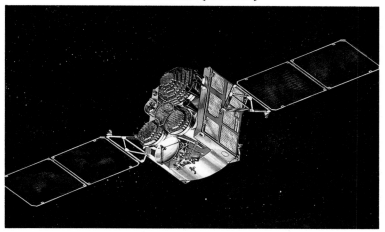

Mission

As part of the Defense Communications System, the Defense Satellite Communications System (DSCS) provides communications connectivity for: tactical warning and assessment information transfer; intelligence data transfer to processing segments from remote locations as well as overhead intelligence platforms; missile warning conference; and command and control between the National Command Authorities and deployed military commanders.

System Data

Prime Contractor: TRW/GE (DSCS II and III satellites)
Initial Operational Capability: DSCS II (Nov 71); DSCS III (Oct 82)
Inventory: DSCS II — 4; DSCS III — 4
Satellites: DSCS IIIs
Three axis, stabilized in geosynchronous orbit
10-year design life/seven-year mean-mission life
Electro-magnetic pulse hardened

Employment

The operational DSCS consists of space, control, and terminal segments. The DSCS Space Segment consists of five operational satellites and three reserves in orbit. These are a mix of DSCS IIs and IIIs over the East Atlantic, West Atlantic, East Pacific, West Pacific, and Indian Ocean. Two additional DSCS IIs have severely limited capability and a DSCS III, launched in 1982, which is severely degraded, provide the reserve satellite support in orbit.

The DSCS II satellites, developed in the late 1960s, have no unique military features to sustain operations in hostile environments, such as jamming and nuclear scintillation. The DSCS III satellites were developed in the late 1970s and incorporated unique military features to make them jam resistant and nuclear hardened.

The DSCS strategic terminal segment has a range of antennae from large fixed terminals with 60-foot parabolic antennas to 30-inch antennae supporting users such as the National Emergency Airborne Command Post. Ground Mobile Forces (GMF) terminals equipped with eight and 20-foot antennas and the Navy shipboard terminals equipped with four-foot antennae support the DSCS tactical user requirements.

The DSCS requires users to share power and bandwidth of an individual transponder channel. As a result, discipline is imposed on all user terminals to assure they conform to their specific frequency and power assignment. Should a user terminal vary from its assigned parameters, it will adversely affect other users and possibly could disrupt the entire satellite channel and eliminate space segment access for hundreds of users. Network control is performed through the DSCS Operations Centers (DSCSOCs), located with large fixed DSCS ground terminals. These DSCSOCs have direct connectivity to all user terminals in their area of control to assure continuous operation and support resolution of terminal problems when the terminal operators can not resolve them. The tactical users, such as GMF and the Navy, are sub-networks operated within assigned allocation.

Performance

DSCS played a major role in providing command, control and intelligence information during Operations Desert Shield and Desert Storm. Before the invasion of Kuwait, there were only four tactical DSCS terminals in the area of responsibility (AOR). By 5 January, more than 120 tactical DSCS terminals had been deployed to serve in major support roles, providing communications for combat, combat support and service support operations. The Joint Forces Air Component Commander used DSCS daily to transmit the air tasking order to air bases. DSCS supported a 75 percent increase in intelligence relay to the continental United States for processing and return to the theater. Tactical GMF terminals moved with offensive forces as they deployed to the West for a flank attack. Antennae were loaded on flatbed vehicles to avoid disassembly. As forces made intermediary stops, connectivity to higher command headquarters was established immediately using the DSCS satellite. By the end of the war, 33 GMF tactical terminals were supporting combat forces in Kuwait and Iraq, providing command, control, and intelligence communications.

OBSERVATIONS

Accomplishments

■ The DSCS was the principal multi-channel transmission system for intra- and inter-theater communications during the early phase of Operation Desert Shield. DSCS initially provided 75 percent of all inter-theater connectivity and was used extensively to support intra-theater requirements covering deployment of forces across long distances not supportable by terrestrial systems.

■ Commercial augmentation of satellite communications also proved helpful.

Shortcomings

■ Satellite communications were vulnerable to jamming and spoofing.

■ The overall satellite constellation lacks redundancy and there is no capability to launch replacement satellites quickly.

■ Some older ground segment terminal equipment requires extensive maintenance.

Issue

■ Current DSCS fixed ground terminal equipment is 1970s technology and has exceeded its life-cycle. Components and repair parts no longer are manufactured. The heavy terminal/medium terminal (HT/MT) part of the DSCS program provides for modernizing the terminal with state-of-the-art technology, extending the life cycle another 15 years and reducing operating and support costs. Funds are programmed with contract award scheduled for early FY 92 and modernization to start in FY 94.

GLOBAL POSITIONING SYSTEM (GPS) NAVSTAR-GPS

Mission

Global Positioning System (GPS) is a satellite based, radio-navigation system that provides precise, world wide, three-dimensional position, velocity, and timing data. NAVSTAR-GPS satellites operate in inclined, semi-synchronous, 12- hour orbits. When GPS is fully operational in 1993, it will consist of a constellation of satellites that will provide continuous three-dimensional, worldwide coverage. During the Persian Gulf War, 16 GPS satellites provided navigation and positioning data. When the constellation is fully deployed, there will be 24 satellites (21 primary systems and three spares).

System Data

Prime Contractor: Rockwell International
Projected Full Operational Capability: 1993
Size: 5 feet x 17 ft 6 in
Weight: 2,000 pounds (on orbit)
Launcher: DELTA II ELV with PAM-D upper stage
Orbit: Circular, 55 degree inclination
Altitude: 13,000 miles; Orbital Period: 11.996 solar hours
Design Life: 7.5 years
Constellation: Six planes, four satellites per plane
Control segment: Master Control Station (MCS), Falcon Air Force Base, CO
Monitor Stations: Hawaii, Colorado Springs, Ascension Island, Diego Garcia, Kwajalein Island
Ground (control) Antennas: Ascension, Diego Garcia, Kwajalein

Employment

Navigation in a featureless desert posed significant challenges. There were almost no man-made or natural features to confirm positions. A precise navigation means was required to aid combat forces. GPS met this need.

GPS receivers were used throughout the theater to assist forces at sea, on land, and in the air. For example, GPS fixed navigational positions during mine clearing operations and provided launch coordinates for ships firing TLAM. Among other uses, GPS guided maneuver units, helped minimize fratricide, registered artillery and precisely located land mines. The Air Force used GPS to guide aircraft to targets.

Because of the immediate need for GPS receivers, Coalition forces relied on commercial GPS receivers. Almost 85 percent of the receivers US forces used were commercial, non-crypto capable models. The lack of secure GPS receivers meant that, had the enemy the capability to do so, he might have benefited from the system also. By March, 4,490 commercial and 842 military GPS receivers had been deployed.

Performance

The GPS constellation was improved to support US forces in the operating area by changing the launch plane of a GPS satellite launched in October. There was adequate two-dimensional coverage (latitude and longitude) for almost the entire day and three dimensional (latitude, longitude, and altitude) coverage for about 19 hours a day. (By comparison, troops at Fort Bragg, NC, could receive good 3-D coverage for about 15 hours a day.)

The heavy reliance on commercial receivers forced the US to keep Selective Availability (SA) off. SA is the intentional corruption/degradation of positioning and timing data so that non-military users do not receive military data. Throughout the war, commercial and military versions of the GPS receivers displayed comparable accuracies. The military receiver provided about 16 meters spherical error probable accuracy, while the commercial small, lightweight receiver (SLGR) provided about 25 meters accuracy. This variation in accuracy often is caused by satellite geometry and user dynamics. If SA is employed, the commercial SLGR gives a much less accurate position.

OBSERVATIONS

Accomplishments

- GPS was used more extensively than planned and met navigation and positioning requirements.

- The GPS satellite constellation was optimized for use in the AOR.

Shortcomings

- There were not enough military versions of the GPS receiver available, which led to the off-the-self purchase of thousands of commercial, non-SA receivers. The reliance on commercial receivers required keeping SA off.

- The United States shipped as many receivers as possible for more than six months, but was still unable to satisfy unit demand.

Issues

- The GPS Joint Program Office is procuring a military version of the small lightweight receiver which will be available in 1994.

- GPS should be considered for incorporation into all weapon systems and platforms.

MULTI-SPECTRAL IMAGERY: LANDSAT

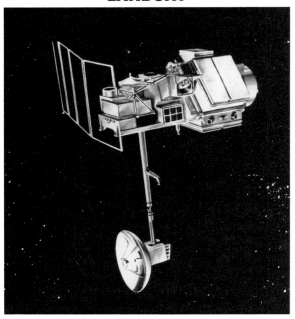

Mission

LANDSAT provides multi-spectral surface imaging for geological and ecological mapping and surface-change detection. LANDSAT is designed and used for civil and commercial peacetime uses. However, military applications inherent in the remote sensing capabilities of multi-spectral imagery (MSI) have been developed and are being expanded. In addition to LANDSAT, the French SPOT — Satellite Probatoire d'Observation de la Terre (Exploratory Satellite for Earth Observation) also provides MSI data. The former Soviet Union's (Meteor Prioida) and Japanese (MOS-1) also have MSI systems.

LANDSAT is managed by the Department of Commerce, National Oceanographic and Atmospheric Administration. It is operated by Earth Observation Satellite Corp., a contractor.

System Data

Orbital parameters: 98.2 Inclination, 438-mile altitude.
Weight: 4,270 lbs
Initial Operational Capability: LANDSAT-5 launched in 1984, originally had been expected to operate only until early 1989
Thematic mapper: Seven-band scanning radiometer. Operates from 0.45 to 2.35 microns.
Resolution: 98 ft
Four band scanning radiometer: Operates from 0.5 to 1.1 microns, resolution , 262 ft
Thermal infrared band: Single band. Operates from 10.4 to 12.5 microns, resolution, 394 ft
Scene size: 185 km by 170 km

Employment

MSI provided direct war-fighting support during Operation Desert Storm. Because of MSI's unique nature, military planners were able to obtain information normally not available. Furthermore, MSI showed features of the earth beyond human visual detection capability.

Performance

When US forces deployed to Southwest Asia, many maps of Kuwait, Iraq, and Saudi Arabia available to US forces were 10 to 30 years old. To correct this deficiency, MSI satellite systems were used to image the theater; the Defense Mapping Agency (DMA) prepared new maps based on these images. Since MSI maps are images of the earth, they show existing roads, trails, airfields, etc. Clear, open areas, which may be suitable for military purposes, also stand out and are easily factored into planning. For example, after the 82nd Airborne Division obtained a LANDSAT map of Kuwait City, it asked for national imagery to determine if there were traps or obstructions that would prevent an airborne landing. MSI images may be able to show subsurface features down to 30 meters, depending on water clarity. The Navy used MSI data in planning amphibious operations during Operations Desert Shield and Desert Storm.

OBSERVATIONS

Accomplishments

■ GPS was used more extensively than planned and met navigation and positioning requirements.

■ The GPS satellite constellation was optimized for use in the AOR.

Shortcomings

■ There were not enough military versions of the GPS receiver available, which led to the off-the-self purchase of thousands of commercial, non-SA receivers. The reliance on commercial receivers required keeping SA off.

■ The United States shipped as many receivers as possible for more than six months, but was still unable to satisfy unit demand.

Issues

■ The GPS Joint Program Office is procuring a military version of the small lightweight receiver which will be available in 1994.

■ GPS should be considered for incorporation into all weapon systems and platforms.

GLOSSARY

A

A-box	fire support box; subdivision of a kill box [USMC]
AAA	antiaircraft artillery
AADC	Area Air Defense Commander
AAR	after-action review
AAV	assault amphibian vehicle; fully tracked vehicle able to carry Marines and equipment from assault ship to inland objectives and during subsequent operations ashore [USMC]
AAW	antiair warfare; action to destroy or reduce to an acceptable level the enemy air and missile threat [Navy; USMC]
ABCCC	Airborne Battlefield Command and Control Center; aircraft equipped with communications, data link, and display equipment; airborne command post or communications and intelligence relay facility
ABDR	Aircraft Battle Damage Repair [USAF]
ABFDS	Aerial Bulk Fuel Delivery System [USAF]
AC	Active Component
ACA	Airspace Control Authority
ACAA	automatic chemical agent alarm
ACC	1) Arab Cooperation Council; 2) Airspace Coordination Center [CENTCOM]
ACINT	acoustic intelligence
ACE	1) Airborne Command Element [USAF]; 2) armored combat excavator [Army]; 3) Air Combat Element [NATO]; 4) Aviation Combat Element; the task-organized Marine Air-Ground Task Force element that contains aviation and aviation support forces. It includes aviation command (including air control), combat, combat support, and combat service support units needed to accomplish a mission [USMC]
ACR	Armored Cavalry Regiment [Army]
ACV	1) armored combat vehicle; 2) air cushion vehicle
ADA	air defense artillery
A/DACG	Arrival/Departure Airfield Control Group
ADOC	Air Defense Operations Center; an area and airspace above it within which established procedures minimize interference between air defense and other operations
ADR	Aircraft Damage Repair [Navy]
ADSS	ANVIS Display Symbology System
ADVCAP	advanced capability
AE	assault echelon; the element of a force scheduled for initial assault on the objective area
AEW	airborne early warning; detection of enemy air or surface units by radar or other equipment in an airborne vehicle and transmission of a warning to friendly units
AFB	Air Force Base
AF/SA	Headquarters USAF Studies and Analysis Agency
AF/XO	Headquarters USAF Plans and Operations

AFCS	Automatic Flight Control System; a system that includes all equipment to control automatically the flight of an aircraft or missile to a path or attitude described by internal or external references
AFID	anti-fratricide identification device
AFLC	Air Force Logistics Command
AFMSS	Air Force Mission Support System
AFOE	assault follow-on echelon; the additional forces, supplies and equipment needed for a landing force to continue operations ashore after an amphibious landing. Normally embarked aboard amphibious shipping or Military Sealift Command ships able to unload without port facilities [Navy; USMC]
AFR	Air Force Reserve
AFRC	Armed Forces Recreation Center
AFRRI	Armed Forces Radiobiology Research Institute
AFRTS	Armed Forces Radio and Television Service
AFSAC	Air Force Special Activities Center
AFSOC	Air Force Special Operations Command
AFSOCCENT	Air Force Special Operations Command, CENTCOM
AFSOUTH	Allied Forces, South [NATO]
AG	Adjutant General [Army]
AGMC	Aerospace Guidance and Meteorology Center [USAF]
AI	air interdiction; air operations to destroy, neutralize or delay the enemy's military potential before it can be brought to bear effectively against friendly forces, at such distance from friendly forces that detailed integration of each air mission with the fire and movement of friendly forces is not required
AIMD	Aircraft Intermediate Maintenance Detachment [Navy, USMC]
air superiority	that degree of dominance in the air battle of one force over another which permits operations by the former and its related land, sea, and air forces at a given time and place without prohibitive interference by the opposing force
air supremacy	that degree of air superiority wherein the opposing air force is incapable of effective interference
AIRBOC	air rapid-bloom off-board chaff countermeasures cartridge
AJCM	anti-jam control modem
ALC	Air Logistics Center [USAF]
ALCE	Airlift Control Element [USAF]
ALCM	air-launched cruise missile
ALFS	airborne low-frequency sonar
ALO	air liaison officer; an officer (aviator/pilot), attached to a ground unit, who functions as the primary advisor to the ground commander on air operations
AMC	Army Materiel Command
AMCM	aviation mine countermeasures [Navy]
AMRAAM	advanced medium-range air-to-air missile
AMTI	airborne moving-target indicator
ANG	Air National Guard
ANGLICO	Air-Naval Gunfire Liaison Company; a company with liaison and communications teams designed to coordinate naval gunfire and air support for ground forces [USMC]

ANZUS	Australia-New Zealand-United States Treaty
AO	area of operations
AOA	amphibious objective area; a geographic area, delineated in the initial directive, for command and control, within which is located the objective(s) to be secured by an amphibious task force
AOR	area of responsibility; a defined land area in which responsibility is specifically assigned to the the area commander for development and maintenance of installations, movement control and tactical operations involving troops under his control, along with parallel authority to exercise these functions
APC	armored personnel carrier; a lightly armored, highly mobile, full-tracked vehicle, amphibious and air-droppable, used primarily for transporting personnel and their individual equipment during tactical operations
APF	Afloat Prepositioning Force
APOD	aerial port of debarkation
APOE	aerial port of embarkation
APS	afloat pre-positioned ship
APU	auxiliary power unit
ARC	1) Air Reserve Components; 2) American Red Cross
ARCENT	Army Component, Central Command
ARG	Amphibious Ready Group
ARNG	Army National Guard
ARSOC	Army Special Operations Command
ARSOFTF	Army Special Operations Forces Task Force
ASARS	Advanced Synthetic Aperture Radar System [USAF]
ASBPO	Armed Services Blood Program Office
ASE	aircraft survivability equipment
ASL	1) allowable supply list; 2) authorized stockage list [Army]
ASM	armed scout mission
ASMD	antiship missile defense
ASR	armed surface reconnaissance [Navy]
assault shipping	shipping assigned to an amphibious task force used to transport the assault echelon to the objective area [Navy]
ASUW	antisurface warfare
ASW	antisubmarine warfare
ATACMS	Army Tactical Missile System
ATAF	Allied Tactical Air Force [NATO]
ATAS	air-to-air Stinger
ATBM	antitactical ballistic missile
ATC	1) Air Transportable Clinic [USAF]; 2) air traffic control
ATCC	Antiterrorism Coordinating Committee
ATF	Amphibious Task Force ; naval force and landing force, with supporting forces, organized and equipped for amphibious operations[Navy; USMC]
ATGM	anti-tank guided munition
ATH	Air Transportable Hospital [USAF]
ATHS	Airborne Target Handover System
ATO	air tasking order

AUTODIN	Automatic Digital Network
AUTOVON	Automatic Voice Network; formerly the principal long-haul, unsecure voice communications network within the Defense Communications System; replaced by Defense Switched Network
AVGAS	aviation gasoline
AVIM	Aviation Intermediate-level Maintenance
AVLB	armored vehicle-launched bridge
AVSCOM	Aviation Systems Command [Army]
AVUM	Aviation Unit-level Maintenance [Army]
AWACS	Airborne Warning and Control System; air surveillance and control provided by airborne early warning vehicles equipped with search and height-finding radar and communications equipment for controlling weapons

B

BAAF	Bahrain Amiri Air Force
BAI	battlefield air interdiction
BASE-LITE	base imagery transmission equipment
BCTP	Battalion Command Training Program
BDA	battle damage assessment
BEEF	Base Emergency Engineering Force [USAF]
BFV	Bradley fighting vehicle
BGTT	Battle Group Tactical Training Continuum [Navy]
Black Hole	CENTCOM air campaign planning staff offices
BLSSS	Base-Level Self-sufficiency Spares [USAF]
BLT	Battalion Landing Team; in an amphibious operation, an infantry battalion normally reinforced by necessary combat and service elements [USMC]
BMW	Bombardment Wing [USAF]
BUU	basic user unit [USMC]
BVR	beyond visual range
BW	biological warfare; use of biological agents to produce casualties in man or animal and damage to plants or materiel; or defense against such use; also biological weapon

C

C-Day	the unnamed day on which a deployment operation begins or is to begin (in the case of Operation Desert Shield, 7 August 1990)
CA	Civil Affairs; those phases of the activities of a commander which embrace the relationship between the military forces and civil authorities and people in a friendly or occupied country or area when military forces are present
CAB	Combat Aviation Brigade
CAF	Canadian Air Force
CAFMS	Computer-assisted Force Management System
CAG	Civil Affairs Group
CALS	Committee on Ammunition Logistics Support
CAM	chemical agent monitor
CANA	convalescent antidote for nerve agent

CAP	combat air patrol; an aircraft patrol provided over an objective area, over the force protected, over the crucial area of a combat zone, or over an air defense area, to intercept and destroy hostile aircraft before they reach their target
Capstone	Army program that aligns units, regardless of component, into a wartime command structure
CAS	close air support; air action against hostile targets near friendly forces, which require detailed integration of each air mission with the fire and movement of those forces
CATF	Commander, Amphibious Task Force [Navy]
CATM	captive airborne training missile
CAX	combined arms exercise [USMC]
CBPS	chemical biological protective shelter
CBS	Columbia Broadcasting System
CCJ5-SPG	Central Command J5-Special Planning Group
CDC	Combat Development Command [USMC]
CDE	chemical defense equipment
CDTF	Chemical Decontamination Training Facility
CEM	combined effects munition
CENTAF	Air Force Component, Central Command
CENTCOM	US Central Command
CEP	circular error probable; an indicator of the accuracy of a weapon system, used as a factor in determining probable damage to a target; the radius of a circle in which half of a missile's projectiles are expected to fall
CFV	cavalry fighting vehicle
CHAMPUS	Civilian Health and Medical Program for the Uniformed Services
Checkmate	Headquarters USAF Air Staff planning group
CI	1) counterintelligence; activities concerned with identifying and counteracting the security threat posed by hostile intelligence services or organizations, or by individuals engaged in espionage, sabotage, subversion or terrorism; 2) civilian internee; a civilian interned during armed conflict or occupation for security reasons or for protection or because he has committed an offense against the detaining power
CIA	Central Intelligence Agency
CIC	1) Combat Information Center [Navy]; 2) Combined Intelligence Center [CENTCOM]
CILMC	Contingency Intermediate-level Maintenance Center
CINC	Commander-in-Chief
CINCCENT	Commander-in-Chief, Central Command
CINCEUR	Commander-in-Chief, European Command
CINCFOR	Commander-in-Chief, Forces Command
CINCLANT	Commander-in-Chief, Atlantic Command
CINCPAC	Commander-in-Chief, Pacific Command
CINCSPACE	Commander-in-Chief, Space Command
CINCSAC	Commander-in-Chief, Strategic Air Command
CINCSO	Commander-in-Chief, Southern Command
CINCSOC	Commander-in-Chief, Special Operations Command
CINCTRANS	Commander-in-Chief, Transportation Command
CITV	commanders' independent thermal viewer

CJCS	Chairman, Joint Chiefs of Staff
CLF	1) Combat Logistics Force; 2) Commander, Landing Force [Navy, USMC]
CLSF	Combined Logistics Stores Facility
CLSS	Combat Logistics Support System
CLSU	Communications Security Logistics Support Unit
CMEF	Commander, Middle East Force
CMTC	Combat Maneuver Training Center
CNN	Cable News Network
CNO	Chief of Naval Operations; the Navy's senior uniformed leader
COCOM	combatant command (command authority)
COE	Corps of Engineers [Army]
COMCARGRU	Commander, Carrier Group
COMCRUDESGRU	Commander, Cruiser Destroyer Group
COMDESRON	Commander, Destroyer Squadron
COMINT	communications intelligence; technical and intelligence information derived from foreign communications by other than the intended recipients
COMSAT	communications satellite
COMSEC	communications security; protection against unauthorized receipt of telecommunications
COMTAC	Commander, Tactical Air Command
CONOPS	1) concept of operations; 2) contingency operations
CONUS	Continental United States
COP	Concept Outline Plan
COSCOM	Corps Support Command
CP	command post; a unit or subunit headquarters where the commander and staff perform their activities
CPX	command post exercise
CRAF	Civil Reserve Air Fleet
CRC	CONUS Replacement Center
cross level	shifting of people and/or equipment from one unit to another to make the receiving unit ready for deployment
CS	combat support
CSAR	combat search and rescue
CSG	Cryptologic Support Group [NSA]
CSH	Combat Support Hospital
CSOA	combined special operations area
CSS	combat service support; assistance provided operating forces primarily in administrative services, chaplain services, civil affairs, finance, legal services, health services, military police, supply, maintenance, transportation, construction, troop construction, acquisition and disposal of real property, facilities engineering, topographic and geodetic engineering functions, food service, graves registration, laundry, dry cleaning, bath, property disposal and other logistics services
CSSA	1) CENTAF Supply Support Activity [USAF]; 2) combat service support area; area from which logistics support is provided to forward units and where logistics operations are conducted. [USMC]

CSSD	Combat Service Support Detachment; task-organized service support unit assigned to support directly specific forward units, sites, or airfields [USMC]
CSSE	Combat Service Support Element; those elements whose primary missions are to provide service support to combat forces and which are a part, or prepared to become a part of a theater, command or task force formed for combat operations
CT	counterterrorism; offensive measures to prevent, deter and respond to terrorism
CTC	Combat Training Center [Army]
CTT	Coordination and Training Team [SOF]
CUCV	commercial utility cargo vehicle
CVBG	Aircraft Carrier Battle Group
CW	chemical warfare; all aspects of military operations involving the use of lethal and incapacitating munitions/agents and the warning and protective measures associated with such offensive operations; also chemical weapon
CWC	Composite Warfare Commander [Navy]
CY	calendar year
C^2	command and control
C^3	command, control, and communications
C^3I	command, control, communications, and intelligence
C^3IC	Coalition Coordination, Communication, and Integration Center
C^4	command, control, communications, and computers

D

D-Day	the unnamed day on which a particular operation begins or will begin; (in the case of Operation Desert Storm, 17 January 1991)
DA	direct action [SOF]
DAMA	demand assigned multiple access; multiplexing system which permits one satellite channel to be shared by multiple users simultaneously
DARPA	Defense Advanced Research Projects Agency
DARS	daily aerial reconnaissance and surveillance [CENTCOM]
DAS	direct air support
DASC	Direct Air Support Center; a subordinate operational component of a tactical air control system designed for control and direction of close air support and other tactical air support operations, normally collocated with fire support coordination elements
DASC-A	Direct Air Support Center Airborne
DCA	1) Defense Communications Agency; 2) Defense Cooperation Account; 3) defensive counter-air
DCI	Director of Central Intelligence
DCP	director of air campaign plans [CENTCOM]
DCS	1) Defense Communications System; 2) Digital Computer System
DDI	Deputy Director for Intelligence [CIA]
DDN	Defense Data Network

DDO	Directorate of Operations [CIA]
DDS	1) Defense Dissemination System; 2) dry deck shelter [Navy]
DEFSMAC	Defense Special Missile and Astronautics Center
DESCOM	Depot System Command [Army]
DEPMEDS	Deployable Medical Systems
DF	direction finding; a procedure for obtaining bearings of radio frequency emitters by using a highly directional antenna and a display unit on an intercept receiver or ancillary equipment
DFR/E	Defense Fuel Region/Europe
DFR/ME	Defense Fuel Region/Middle East
DFSC	Defense Fuel Supply Center
DFSP	Defense Fuel Support Point
DIA	Defense Intelligence Agency
DIAC	Defense Intelligence Analysis Center
DIPEC	Defense Industrial Plant Equipment Center
DISA	Defense Information Systems Agency
DISCOM	Division Support Command
DLA	Defense Logistics Agency
DLR	depot-level repairable
DMA	Defense Mapping Agency
DMI	Directorate of Military Intelligence [Iraq; Israel; Egypt]
DMPI	designated mean point of impact
DMRIS	Defense Medical Regulating Information System
DMSP	Defense Meteorological Satellite Program
DNA	Defense Nuclear Agency
DNBI	disease, non-battle injury
DOD	Department of Defense
DOD-JIC	DOD Joint Intelligence Center
DODEX	DOD Intelligence Information System Extension
DOS	day of supply; a unit or quantity of supplies adopted as a standard of measurement, used in estimating the average daily expenditure under stated conditions
DPG	Defense Planning Guidance
DPSC	Defense Personnel Support Center
DSA	defense special assessment [DIA]
DSCS	Defense Satellite Communications System
DSCSOC	Defense Satellite Communications System Operations Center
DSMAC	digital scene-matching area correlation
DSN	Defense Switched Network
DSNET	Defense Secure Network
DSP	Defense Support Program
DTED	digital terrain elevation data
DVITS	Digital Video Imagery Transmission System

E

E&E	evasion and escape; procedures to emerge from a hostile area
EAC	1) echelons above corps; 2) Eastern Area Command

EBC	echelons below corps	FARP	forward arming and refueling point; a temporary facility, organized, equipped, and deployed by an aviation commander, and normally located in the main battle area closer to the area of operation than to the aviation unit's combat service area, to provide fuel and ammunition necessary for use by the aviation maneuver units in combat
EC	European Community		
ECCM	electronic counter-countermeasures; that division of electronic warfare involving actions to ensure friendly use of the electromagnetic spectrum despite the enemy's use of electronic warfare		
ECM	electronic countermeasures; that division of electronic warfare involving actions to prevent or reduce an enemy's effective use of the electromagnetic spectrum	FAST	1) forward area ID and TRAP broadcast; 2) Fleet Antiterrorist Security Team [USMC]
		FASTCAL	Field Assistance Support Team for Calibration
EFVS	Electronic Fighting Vehicle System	FBI	Federal Bureau of Investigation
EHF	extremely high frequency	FCTC	Fleet Combat Training Center [Navy]
ELANT	East Atlantic Satellite	FDA	Food and Drug Administration
ELINT	electronics intelligence; information derived from foreign non-communications electromagnetic radiations emanating from other than nuclear detonations or radioactive sources	FDL	Fast Deployment Logistics
		FDR/FA	flight data recorder/fault analyzer
		FEBA	forward edge of the battle area; the foremost limits of a series of areas in which ground combat units are deployed, excluding the areas where the covering or screening forces are operating, designated to coordinate fire support, and the positioning or maneuver of units
ELT	English language training		
ELV	expendable launch vehicle		
EMIS	electromagnetic isotope separation		
EMP	electromagnetic pulse; the electromagnetic radiation from a nuclear explosion caused by Compton-recoil electrons and photoelectrons from photons scattered in the materials of the nuclear device or in a surrounding medium	FEWS	Follow-on Early Warning System
		FFC-A	Forward Forces Command
		FHE	Forward Headquarters Element
		FID	Foreign Internal Defense; participation by civilian and military agencies of a government in any action taken by another government to free and protect its society from subversion, lawlessness, and insurgency
ENWGS	Enhanced Naval Warfare Gaming System		
EOB	electronic order of battle		
EOD	explosive ordnance disposal; the detection, identification, field evaluation, rendering-safe, recovery and final disposal of unexploded ordnance	FIE	fly-in echelon; Marines, supplies and equipment deployed by strategic airlift during an operation [USMC]
		FIST	Fleet imagery support terminal
EOSAT	Earth Observable Satellite Corp.	FLIR	forward-looking infrared
EPDS	Electronic Processing and Dissemination System	FLOT	forward line of own troops; indicates the most forward positions of friendly forces in any kind of military operation at a specific time
EPW	enemy prisoner of war		
ESM	1) electronic surveillance methods; 2) electronic warfare support measures		
		FLTCORGRU	Fleet Coordinating Group
EUCOM	US European Command	FLTSAT	Fleet Satellite
EUCOMM-Z	US European Command Communications Zone	FLTSATCOM	Fleet Satellite Communications
EVAC	evacuation hospital	FMF	Fleet Marine Force
EW	electronic warfare; military action involving the use of electromagnetic energy to determine, exploit, reduce or prevent hostile use of the electromagnetic spectrum through damage, destruction, and disruption while retaining friendly use of the electromagnetic spectrum	FMO	Frequency Management Office
		FMS	Foreign Military Sales; that part of US security assistance authorized by the Foreign Assistance Act of 1961, as amended, and the Arms Export Control Act of 1976, as amended; the recipient reimburses for defense articles and services transferred
		FMTV	family of medium tactical vehicles

F

FA	field artillery	FOB	forward operating base
FAC	forward air controller; an officer (aviator/pilot) member of the tactical air control party who, from a forward ground or airborne position, controls aircraft in close air support of ground troops	FOL	forward operating location
		FORSCOM	Forces Command
		FROG	free rocket over ground
		FSA	fire support area; a maneuver area assigned to fire support ships from which to deliver gunfire support of an amphibious operation
FAE	fuel air explosive		
FAF	French Air Force		
FAISS-E	FORSCOM Automated Intelligence Support System		
FAMMO	full ammo [Navy]		

FSCL	Fire support coordination line; a line established by the ground commander to ensure coordination of fire not under his control, but which may affect current tactical operations
FSS	fast sealift ship
FSSG	Force Service Support Group; combat service support element of a Marine Expeditionary Force [USMC]
FTD	Foreign Technology Division [USAF]
FY	fiscal year

G

G-Day	the first day of the ground campaign (in the case of Operation Desert Storm, 24 February 1991)
GA	Tabun, a nerve agent
GB	Sarin, a nerve agent
GC	Geneva Convention Relative to the Protection of Civilian Persons in Time of War
GCC	Gulf Cooperation Council
GCE	ground combat element; ground maneuver element of a Marine Air-Ground Task Force; task organized around an infantry or armor unit with combat, combat support, and combat service support attachments [USMC].
GCI	ground controlled interception; a technique that permits control of friendly aircraft or guided missiles to effect interception
GD	Soman, a nerve agent
GF	a nerve agent
GHQ	General Headquarters
GMF	Ground Mobile Force
GNA	Goldwater-Nichols Department of Defense Reorganization Act of 1986
GPS	Global Positioning System
GPW	Geneva Convention Relative to the Treatment of Prisoners of War
GRCA	ground reference coverage area
GSM	ground station module
GWS	Geneva Convention Relative to the Treatment of Wounded or Sick Prisoners of War

H

H-Hour	the specific time at which an operation or exercise begins or is scheduled to begin; (in the case of Operation Desert Storm, 0300 local time, 17 January 1991); initial time of arrival of first aircraft over target
HARM	high-speed anti-radiation missile
HEMTT	heavy expanded mobility tactical truck
HET	heavy equipment transporter
HF	high frequency
HFDF	high frequency direction finding

HIDACZ	High Density Airspace Control Zone; doctrinal innovation used during Gulf crisis to delineate airspace under the control of I Marine Expeditionary Force; it enabled I MEF to control airspace over and forward of its units in response to the changing tactical situation
HIRSS	Hover Infrared Suppressor Subsystem
HLPS	heavy-lift preposition ship
HMMWV	high-mobility multi-purpose wheeled vehicle
HNS	host nation support; civil and military assistance given in peace and war by a host nation to allied forces on or in transit through the host nation's territory
HQDA	Headquarters, Department of the Army
HSB	high speed boat
HSC	Health Services Command
HSEP	Hospital Surgical Expansion Package [USAF]
HSS	health service support
HU	Hospital Unit; a team split from a Field Hospital
HUD	heads-up display; a display of flight, navigation, attack or other information superimposed on a pilot's forward field of view
HUMINT	human resources intelligence; intelligence derived from human beings as both sources and collectors, where the human being is the primary collection instrument
HVAA	high-value airborne assets

I

I&W	indications and warning; those intelligence activities intended to detect and report time-sensitive intelligence information on foreign developments that could involve a threat to the United States or allied military, political, or economic interests or to US citizens abroad
IADS	Integrated Air Defense System [Iraq]
IAF	Italian Air Force
IATACS	Improved Army Tactical Communications System
IBAHRS	Inflatable Body and Head Restraint System
ICBM	intercontinental ballistic missile; a ballistic missile with a range from about 3,,000 to 8,,000 nautical miles
ICMMP	Integrated CONUS Medical Mobilization Plan
ICON	imagery communications and operations Node
ICRC	International Committee of the Red Cross/Crescent
IDF	Israel Defense Force
IES	Imagery Exploitation System
IFF	identification, friend or foe; a system using electromagnetic transmissions to which equipment carried by friendly forces automatically responds, for example, by emitting pulses, thereby distinguishing themselves from enemy forces
IGSM	interim ground station module [JSTARS]
IHADSS	Integrated Helmet and Display Sight System [Army]

IIR	1) imaging infrared; 2) Intelligence Information Report	JCS	Joint Chiefs of Staff
IIS	Iraqi Intelligence Service	JCSE	Joint Communications Support Element
IMA	individual mobilization augmentee; a Reservist not assigned to a troop program unit, but with a specific mobilization mission and assignment, normally at a major headquarters	JFACC	Joint Force Air Component Commander; assigned by joint force commander; duties normally include planning, coordination, allocation and tasking based on the joint force commander's apportionment decision; recommends apportionment of air sorties to various missions or geographic areas
IMET	international military education and training; formal or informal instruction provided to foreign military students, units, and forces on a non-reimbursable basis by offices or employees of the United States, contract technicians and contractors	JFC	Joint Forces Command
		JFC-E	Joint Forces Command-East
		JFC-N	Joint Forces Command-North
		JFLC	Joint Forces Land Component
IMINT	imagery intelligence; intelligence derived from visual photography, infrared sensors, lasers, electro-optics and radar sensors such as synthetic aperture radar	JFLCC	Joint Forces Land Component Commander
		JIC	Joint Intelligence Center
		JIF	Joint Interrogation Facility
INMARSAT	International Maritime Satellite	JILE	Joint Intelligence Liaison Element; provided by the Central Intelligence Agency to support a unified command or joint task force
INS	Inertial Navigation System; a self-contained navigation system using inertial detectors, which automatically provides vehicle position, heading and velocity	JIPC	Joint Imagery Production Complex
		JITC	Joint Interoperability Test Center
IO	Indian Ocean satellite	JMRO	Joint Medical Regulating Office
IOC	1) Intercept Operations Center [Iraq]; 2) initial operational capability; the first capability to use effectively a weapon, item of equipment, or system by a military unit	JOC	Joint Operations Center; a jointly manned facility of a joint force commander's headquarters established for planning, monitoring, and guiding execution of the commander's decisions
IPDS	Imagery Processing and Dissemination System	JOPES	Joint Operation Planning and Execution System
IPSA	Iraqi Pipeline Saudi Arabia	JOTS	Joint Operational Tactical System [Navy]
IR	infrared	JPO	Joint Petroleum Office
IRDS	infrared detection set	JPTS	jet petroleum, thermally stable
IRR	Individual Ready Reserve; members of the Ready Reserve not assigned to the Selected Reserve and not on active duty	JRC	Joint Reconnaissance Center
		JRCC	Joint Rescue Coordination Center; an installation staffed by supervisory personnel from all participating services, with facilities to direct and coordinate all available search and rescue facilities within a specified area
ISA	Intermediate Supply Activity [USMC]		
ISAR	inverse synthetic aperture radar [Navy]		
ISE	Intelligence Support Element	JROC	Joint Requirements Oversight Council
ITAC	Intelligence and Threat Analysis Center [Army]	JRTC	Joint Readiness Training Center
ITALD	improved tactical air-launched decoy	JS	Joint Staff
ITF	Intelligence Task Force [DIA]	JSCAT	Joint Staff Crisis Action Team
		JSCC	Joint Services Coordination Committee
		JSCP	Joint Strategic Capabilities Plan

J

J-1	director of personnel	JSOTF	Joint Special Operations Task Force
J-2	director of Intelligence	JSPS	Joint Strategic Planning System
J-3	director of operations	JSTARS	Joint Surveillance Target Attack Radar System
J-4/7	director of logistics and security assistance	JTC3A	Joint Tactical Command, Control and Communications Agency
J-5	director of plans and policy		
J-6	director of command and control, communications and computer systems	JTF	Joint Task Force; a force composed of assigned or attached elements of the Army, Navy, Marine Corps, and the Air Force, or two or more services, which is constituted and so designated by the Secretary of Defense or by the commander of a unified command, a specified command, or an existing joint task force
JAAT	Joint Air Attack Team		
JAG	Judge Advocate General		
JAIC	Joint Air Intelligence Center		
JBPO	Joint Blood Program Office		
JCEOI	joint communications electronics operations instructions	JTFME	Joint Task Force Middle East
		JTIDS	Joint Tactical Information Distribution System

K

KAF	Kuwaiti Air Force
kill box	geographic area designated for air strikes
KKMC	King Khalid Military City
KTF	Kuwait Civil Affairs Task Force
KTO	Kuwait Theater of Operations

L

LABCOM	Laboratory Command [Army]
LAI	light armored infantry; a mechanized infantry unit mounted in light armored vehicles with the mission of reconnaissance, screening, and conducting raids [USMC]
LAMPS	Light Airborne Multipurpose System [Navy]
LAN	local area network
landing force	a task organization of troop units, aviation and ground, assigned to an amphibious assault; highest troop echelon in the amphibious operation
LANTCOM	Atlantic Command
LANTIRN	low-altitude navigation and targeting infrared for night
LAR	logistics assistance representative
LAV	light armored vehicle ; eight-wheeled lightly armored family of vehicles used by Marine Light Armored Infantry battalions.[USMC]
LCAC	landing craft, air cushion; capable of carrying 60 tons from ship to shore at overwater speeds of more than 40 knots and ranges exceeding 50 miles
LCC	Land Component Commander
LCU	landing craft, utility
LEDET	Law Enforcement Detachment [Coast Guard]
LET	light equipment transporter
LGB	laser-guided bomb (see LGW)
LGW	laser guided weapon; a weapon which uses a seeker to detect laser energy reflected from a target and through signal processing guides itself to the point from which the laser energy is being reflected
LHA	amphibious assault ship, general purpose
LHT	line-haul tractor
littoral	the shore area between low and high tides
LNO	liaison officer
LOC	line of communication; land, water or air route which connects an operating military force with a base of operations and along which supplies and military forces move
LOROP	long range oblique photography
LOTS	logistics over the shore; the loading or unloading of ships without the benefit of fixed port facilities, in friendly or non-defended territory and, in time of war, during phases of theater development in which there is no enemy opposition
LPV	laser-protective visor
LRC	Logistics Readiness Center [USAF]

LRI	long-range international
LRU	line-replaceable unit [USAF]
LVS	Logistics Vehicle System; heavy transporter truck system capable of cross country movement [USMC]

M

M-box	maneuver box; subdivision of a kill box [USMC]
MAC	Military Airlift Command
MACCS	Marine Air Command and Control System; tactical air command and control system which gives the tactical air commander the means to command, control, and coordinate all air operations within an assigned sector and to coordinate air operations with other services; it includes command and control agencies with communications-electronic equipment that incorporates a capability from manual through semiautomatic control. [USMC]
MACG	Marine Air Control Group; command within the Marine Aircraft Wing that contains the units and systems necessary to provide task-organized air command and control detachments to a Marine Air-Ground Task Force [USMC]
MACSAT	multiple access commercial satellite
MAG	Marine Aircraft Group; task organized aviation unit roughly equivalent in size to an Air Force wing. A composite MAG normally is the Aviation Combat Element for a Marine Expeditionary Brigade [USMC]
MAGTF	Marine Air-Ground Task Force; task organization of Marine air, ground, and combat service support forces under a single command and structured to accomplish a specific mission [USMC]
MAP	master attack plan
MARCENT	Marine Forces, Central Command; Marine component command ; it coordinated all administrative, logistical, and interservice issues for Marine forces ashore in Southwest Asia.
MARDIV	Marine Division
MARS	Military Affiliate Radio Station
MASH	Mobile Army Surgical Hospital
MASS	MICAP (mission critical parts) Asset Sourcing System
Maverick	air-to-surface missile with launch and leave capability; stand-off, outside point defense weapon able to strike point targets
MAW	Marine Aircraft Wing
MC	mission capable
MCAGCC	Marine Corps Air-Ground Combat Center, 29 Palms, CA
MCIC	Marine Corps Intelligence Center
MCLB	Marine Corps Logistics Base
MCM	mine countermeasures; all methods for preventing or reducing damage or danger from mines
MCSF	Mobile Cryptologic Support Facility
MCSSD	Mobile Combat Service Support Detachment [USMC]
MEA	munitions effectiveness assessment

MEB	Marine Expeditionary Brigade; Marine Air-Ground Task Force normally built around a command element, a regimental landing team, a composite aircraft group, and a service support group [USMC]	MORE-CT	meals, ordered ready-to-eat, contingency test
		MP	Military Police
		MPA	maritime patrol aircraft
MEDEVAC	medical evacuation	MPES	Medical Planning and Execution System
MEDSOM	Medical Supply Optical and Maintenance [Army]	MPF	Maritime Prepositioning Force; combination of a Maritime Prepositioning Squadron and its associated Marine Expeditionary Brigade [USMC]
MEF	1) Middle East Force; 2) Marine Expeditionary Force; Marine Air-Ground Task Force normally consisting of a command element, one or more Marine divisions, one or more aircraft wings, and a force service support group [USMC]		
		MPLH	multipurpose light helicopter
		MPM	medical planning module
		MPS	Maritime Prepositioning Squadron
MEL	mobile erector launcher [Iraq]	MRE	meal, ready-to-eat
MEPES	Medical Planning and Execution System	MRS	Mobility Requirements Study
MET	medium equipment transporter	MRSA	Materiel Readiness Support Agency
METL	mission-essential task list	MSC	Military Sealift Command
METSAT	meterological satellite	MSE	mobile subscriber equipment
METT-T	mission, enemy, terrain, troops and time available	MSI	multi-spectral imagery
MEU	Marine Expeditionary Unit	MSR	main supply route; the route or routes designated within an area of operations upon which the bulk of traffic flows in support of military operations
MEU (SOC)	Marine Expeditionary Unit (Special Operations Capable); forward deployed amphibious Marine Air-Ground Task Force composed of a command element, a battalion landing team, a composite helicopter/AV-8B squadron, and service support element; capable of limited combat operations, especially rapidly planned amphibious raids and maritime special operations [USMC]		
		MTBF	mean time between failures
		MTF	medical treatment facility
		MTI	moving-target indicator; a radar presentation which shows only targets in motion
		MTMC	Military Traffic Management Command
		MTO	mission type order; order issued to a lower unit that includes the accomplishment of the total mission assigned to the higher headquarters, or to a unit to perform a mission without specifying how it is to be accomplished
MEWSS	Mobile Electronic Warfare Support System; light armored vehicle specially equipped with electronic warfare equipment used to conduct tactical electronic warfare and signals intelligence operations [USMC]		
MEZ	Missile Engagement Zone; in air defense, airspace of defined dimensions within which the responsibility for engagement normally rests with a particular weapon system	MTT	Mobile Training Team; one or more US personnel drawn from Service resources and sent on temporary duty to a foreign nation to give instruction
		MULE	modular universal laser equipment
		MUST	Medical Unit, Self-contained, Transportable
MHE	materiel-handling equipment	MWR	Morale, Welfare and Recreation
MI	Military Intelligence; intelligence on any foreign military or military-related situation or activity which is significant to military policy making or the planning and conduct of military operations and activities		

N

NAC	Northern Area Command
MIB	Military Intelligence Board
MICAP	mission critical parts [USAF]
MIF	Maritime Interception Force
MILSATCOM	military satellite communications
MIMI	Ministry of Industry and Military Industrialization [Iraq]
MIPE	Mobile Intelligence Processing Element
MIO	Maritime Interception Operations
MITT	mobile integrated tactical terminal
MLRS	Multiple Launch Rocket System
MMS	mast-mounted sight [Army]
MNS	1) Mine Neutralization System [Navy]; 2) mission need statement
MOC	Mobile Operations Center [USAF]
MOD	Minister (Ministry) of Defense
MODA	Minister (Ministry) of Defense and Aviation [Saudi Arabia]
MOPP	mission-oriented protective posture

NAC	Northern Area Command
NADEP	Naval Aircraft Depot
NAEW	NATO airborne early warning
NAF	Naval Air Facility
NAS	Naval Air Station
NATO	North Atlantic Treaty Organization
NAVCENT	Naval Component, Central Command
NAVEUR	Naval Forces, Europe
NAVOCFORMED	Naval On-call Force, Mediterranean
NAVSPACECOM	Naval Space Command
NAVSPECWARGRU	Navy Special Warfare Group
NBC	Nuclear/biological/chemical
NCA	National Command Authorities; the President and Secretary of Defense or their duly deputized alternates or successors
NCP	Non-US Coalition Partner
NCS	National Communications System

NCTR	Non-cooperative target resolution	OPCOM	operational command; authority granted to a commander to assign missions or tasks to subordinate commander, to deploy units, reassign forces and to retain or delegate operational and/or tactical control as deemed necessary; does not necessarily include administration or logistics [NATO]
NDI	non-developmental item		
NDMS	National Disaster Medical System		
NEO	Non-combatant evacuation operations		
NETT	New Equipment Training Team [USA]		
NGFS	Naval gunfire support		
NIC	National Intelligence Council	OPCON	operational control; authority delegated to a commander to direct forces assigned so the commander can accomplish specific missions or tasks, usually limited by function, time or location; to deploy units concerned, and to retain or assign tactical control of those units; does not necessarily include administration or logistics
NITF	national imagery transmission format		
NLSF	Navy Logistics Support Force		
NMIC	National Military Intelligence Center [DIA]		
NMIST	National Military Intelligence Support Team [DIA]		
NOAA	National Oceanographic and Atmospheric Administration		
NOIC	Naval Operational Intelligence Center	OPLAN	Operation Plan; a plan for a single or series of connected operations to be carried out simultaneously or in succession
NORAD	North American Aerospace Defense Command		
NPIC	National Photographic Interpretation Center	OPORD	Operation Order; a directive, usually formal, issued by a commander to subordinate commanders to effect the coordinated execution of an operation
NPWIC	National Prisoner of War Information Center		
NRT	near-real time; delay caused by automated processing and display between the occurrence of an event and reception of the data at some other locations	OPSEC	operations security; the process of denying adversaries information about friendly capabilities and intentions by identifying, controlling and protecting indicators associated with military operations
NSA	National Security Agency		
NSC	National Security Council	OPTEMPO	operating tempo; the pace of operations, such as the number of sorties flown, miles steamed, etc., in a given period
NSOC	1) National Signals Intelligence Operations Center [NSA]; 2) Navy Satellite Operations Center		
NSW	Naval Special Warfare	OP^3	Overt Peacetime Psychological Operations Program
NSWC	Navy Surface Warfare Center	OR	operational readiness
NSWTG	Naval Special Warfare Task Group	OSD	Office of the Secretary of Defense
NSWTG-CENT	Naval Special Warfare Task Group, Central Command	OTH	over the horizon
		OUTS	Operational Unit Transportable System
NTC	National Training Center, Fort Irwin, CA	Over-the-horizon assault	amphibious assault conducted from ships located beyond visual and coastal surveillance radar ranges of shore defenders, normally 30 to 60 miles [USMC]
NTIC	Navy Tactical Intelligence Center		
NTPF	Near-term Prepositioning Force		
NTPS	Near-term Prepositioned Ships		
NTU	new threat upgrade [Navy]		
NVG	night-vision goggles		

O

O&M	operations and maintenance
OASD, SO/LIC	Office of the Assistant Secretary of Defense for Special Operations and Low Intensity Conflict
OCA	offensive counterair; actions to destroy, disrupt or limit enemy air power as close to its source as possible
OCAC	Operations, Control and Analysis Center
OFP	Operational Flight Program
OICC	Operational Intelligence Crisis Center [DIA]
OIP	Optical Improvement Program
OMB	Office of Management and Budget

P

PACOM	Pacific Command
PASSEX	passing exercises
PBW	Bombardment Wing (Provisional)
PC-LITE	processor, laptop-imagery transmission equipment
PD	Probability of detection; the probability that the search object will be detected under given conditions if it is in the area searched
PGM	Precision-guided munition
PLGR	precise lightweight Global Positioning System receiver
PLO	Palestine Liberation Organization
PLRS	Position Location Reporting System
PLS	Palletized Load System
PNVS	Pilot Night-vision System
POG	Psychological Operations Group
POL	petroleum, oil and lubricants; a broad term which includes all petroleum and associated products used by the armed forces

POMCUS	prepositioned overseas materiel configured to unit sets		RGFC	Republican Guard Forces Command [Iraq]
PORTS	Portable Remote Telecommunications System		RHIB	rigid-hull inflatable boat
POW	prisoner of war; a detained person as defined in Articles 4 and 5 of the Geneva Convention Relative to the Treatment of Prisoners of War of August 12, 1949; in particular, one who, while engaged in combat under orders of his government, is captured by the armed forces of the enemy		RIB	rubberized inflatable boat
			RIBS	Readiness in Base Services [USAF]
			RIT	remote imagery transceiver
			R/L	receive location
			RLG	ring laser gyro
			RLT	Regimental Landing Team; task organization for landing, composed of an infantry regiment reinforced by those elements required for beginning its combat mission ashore [USMC]
PREPO	Prepositioned force, equipment, or supplies			
PRM	Presidential Review Memorandum			
PSHD	Port Security Harbor Defense		ROE	rules of engagement; directives issued by competent military authority which delineate the circumstances and limitations under which US forces will initiate and/or continue combat engagement with other forces encountered
PSV	pseudo-synthetic video			
PSYOP	psychological operations; planned operations to convey selected information and indicators to foreign audiences to influence their emotions, motives, objective reasoning, and ultimately, the behavior of foreign governments, organizations, groups and individuals			
			ROEX	rules of engagement exercise
			RO/RO	roll-on/roll-off ship ; a Military Sealift Command ship built so vehicles and equipment can be loaded by driving them up stern or bow ramps into the holds; a RO/RO greatly simplifies rapid deployment of ground forces and enables ships to be unloaded without extensive port facilities [Navy].
PWIC	Prisoner of War Information Center			
PWIS	Prisoner of War Information System			
			ROWPU	reverse osmosis water purification unit
			RPV	remotely piloted vehicle; an unmanned vehicle able to be controlled from a distant location through a communications link; normally designed to be recoverable

Q

QEAF	Qatari Emiri Air Force

			RRF	Ready Reserve Fleet
			RRFWG	Ready Reserve Force Working Group
			RSADF	Royal Saudi Air Defense Force

R

R&D	research and development		RSAF	Royal Saudi Air Force
R&M	reliability and maintainability [USAF]		RSCG	Royal Saudi Coast Guard
R&R	rest and recuperation; withdrawal of individuals from combat or duty in a combat area for short periods		RSLF	Royal Saudi Land Force
			RSNF	Royal Saudi Naval Force
			RSSC	Regional Signals Intelligence Support Center [NSA]
RAF	Royal Air Force [UK]		RSTA	reconnaissance, surveillance and target acquisition
RC	Reserve Component		RTSV	real-time synthetic video
RCCM	regional contingency construction management		RWR	radar warning receiver
RCHB	Reserve Cargo-handling Battalion [Navy]			
RDF	Rapid Deployment Force			
RDF	radio direction finding; radio locations in which only the direction of a station is determined by means of its emissions			

S

RDJTF	Rapid Deployment Joint Task Force		SA	selective availability [GPS]
RECCE	reconnaissance; action undertaken to obtain, by visual observation or other detection methods, information about the activities and resources of an enemy or potential enemy; or to secure data concerning the meteorological, hydrographic or geographic characteristics of a particular area		SAAF	Saudi Arabian Armed Forces
			SAAM	special assignment airlift mission
			sabkas	marshy salt flats, fed by underground water table
			SAC	Strategic Air Command
			SAFE	safe areas for evasion
			SAM	surface-to-air missile; a surface-launched missile designed to operate against a target above the surface
RED HORSE	Rapid Engineer Deployable, Heavy Operational Repair Squadron, Engineer [USAF]			
REDCOM	Readiness Command (1971)			
REFORGER	Return of Forces to Germany		SAMS	School of Advanced Military Studies [Army]
Regiment	Marine infantry unit equivalent in size to an Army brigade. A regiment fights as a task-organized force with other combat arms units attached; reinforced regiment normally numbers more than 4,,000 Marines [USMC]		SANG	Saudi Arabian National Guard
			SAS	Special Air Service [UK]
			SATCOM	satellite communications
RFI	request for information		SBU	Small Boat Unit

SBSS	Standard Base Supply System	SOAF	Sultanate of Oman Air Force
SCDL	surveillance control data link	SOAR	Special Operations Aviation Regiment
SCI	sensitive compartmented information; all information and materials bearing special community controls indicating restricted handling within present and future community intelligence collection programs and their end products for which community systems of compartmentation have been or will be formally established	SOC	Sector Operations Center [Iraq]
		SOCCENT	Special Operations Command, CENTCOM
		SOCCT	Special Operations Combat Control Team
		SOCEUR	Special Operations Command, Europe
		SOCOM	Special Operations Command
		SOCRATES	Special Operations Command Research Analysis and Threat Evaluation System; a program for assessing the level of foreign technology
SDC	shaft-driven compressor		
SDV	swimmer delivery vehicle [Navy]		
SEA	sea echelon area [Navy]	SOF	Special Operations Forces
Seabee	construction engineer [Navy]	SOFA	Status of Forces Agreement
SEAD	supression of enemy air defenses; activity which neutralizes, destroys or temporarily degrades enemy air defenses in a specific area by physical attack and/or electronic warfare	SOG	Special Operations Group [USAF]
		SOP	Standard (Standing) Operating Procedure; set of instructions covering those features of operations which lend themselves to a definite or standardized procedure without loss of effectiveness; applicable unless ordered otherwise
SEAL	sea, air and land; Navy officers and enlisted members specially trained and equipped for unconventional and paramilitary operations including surveillance and reconnaissance in and from restricted waters, rivers and coastal areas. Seals also are able to train allies in special operations [Navy]		
		SOS	Special Operations Squadron [USAF]
		SOSB	1) Special Operations Signal Battalion; 2) Special Operations Support Battalion
		SOTA	Signals intelligence operational tasking authority
SEP	spherical error probable	SOW	Special Operations Wing [USAF]
SERE	survival, evasion, resistance and escape	SPACC	Space Control Center
SEVENTHFLT	7th Fleet, the Navy command whose area of operations includes the Western Pacific and Indian Oceans	SPACECOM	Space Command
		SPEAR	Special Project Evaluation and Antiairwarfare Research [Navy]
SF	Special Forces	SPG	Special Planning Group [SOF]
SFG	Special Forces Group	SPINS	special instructions
SFOD	Special Forces Operational Detachment	SPOD	sea port of debarkation
SH	Station Hospital	SPOE	sea port of embarkation
shamal	sand/wind storm; literally means "north"	SR	special reconnaissance [SOF]
SHAPE	Supreme Headquarters, Allied Powers, Europe	SRA	Specialized Repair Activity
SHF	super-high frequency	SRAM	short-range air-to-surface attack missile
short ton	2,,000 pounds or 0.907 metric tons	SRBM	short-range ballistic missile; ballistic missile with a range of about 600 nautical miles
SI	special intelligence		
SIA	station of initial assignment [USMC]	SRIG	Surveillance, Reconnaissance and Intelligence Group; intelligence command of roughly regimental size that contains reconnaissance, interrogator, counterintelligence, unmanned aerial vehicles, intelligence analysis, signals intelligence, and special communications units.; detachments task organized for assignment to Marine Air-Ground Task Force command elements [USMC]
SIDS	Secondary Imagery Dissemination System		
SIGINT	signals intelligence; a category of intelligence including all communications intelligence, electronic intelligence and telemetry intelligence		
SINCGARS	Single-channel Ground and Airborne Radio System		
SITREP	situation report; a report giving the situation in the area of a reporting unit or formation	SRP	Sealift Readiness Program
		SSA	Special Support Activity [NSA]
SLAM	standoff land-attack missile	SSCRA	Soldiers and Sailors Civil Relief Act
SLAR	side-looking airborne radar; an airborne radar, viewing at right angles to the axis of the vehicle, which produces a presentation of terrain or moving targets	SSM	surface-to-surface missile; a surface-launched missile designed to operate against a target on the surface
		SSN	nuclear-powered attack submarine
SLAT	strike leader attack training [Navy]	SSO	Special Security Office
SLEP	Service Life Extension Program	STANAVFORCHAN	Standing Naval Force, Channel
SLGR	small, lightweight ground receiver [GPS]	STAR	scheduled theater airlift route
SMCM	surface mine countermeasures [Navy]	Stop loss	program designed to retain on active duty service members with skills crucial to an operation
SME	Squadron Medical Element [USAF]		
SMESA	Special Middle East Sealift Arrangement [MSC]		
SNEP	Saudi Naval Expansion Program	STOVL	short takeoff and vertical landing

STRICOM	Strike Command (1960s)
STU	secure telephone unit
SUCAP	surface combat air patrol
SUPCOM	Support Command
SWA	Southwest Asia
SWAPDOP	Southwest Asia Petroleum Distribution Operational Project
SWIP	Systems Weapon Improvement Program
SYERS	Senior Year Electro-optical Reconnaissance System [USAF]

T

T&E	Test and evaluation
TAA	tactical assembly area
TAC	Tactical Air Command; Air Force organization designed to conduct offensive and defensive air operations in conjunction with land or sea forces
TACAIR	tactical air
TACC	Tactical Air Command Center; principal Marine Corps air operation installation from which aircraft and air warning functions of tactical air operations are directed; it is the senior agency of the Marine Corps Air Command and Control System [USMC]
TACINTEL	tactical intelligence; intelligence required for planning and conduct of tactical operations
TACON	tactical control; detailed and usually local direction and control of movements or maneuvers needed to accomplish missions or tasks assigned
TACP	tactical air control party; subordinate operational component of a tactical air control system designed to provide air liaison to land forces and for the control of aircraft operating in close proximity to ground forces
TACSAT	tactical satellite
TACTRAGRU	Tactical Training Group [Navy]
TADMs	TR-1 ASARS Data Manipulation System [UK]
TADS	target acquisition and designation Sight [Army]
TADSIXS-B	Tactical Data Information Exchange System-B
TAF	Tactical Air Force
TAH	hospital ship
TAI	target of interest
takedown	forcible boarding of a ship by helicopter-borne forces, to compel the ship to stop and comply with maritime interception operations
TALD	tactical air-launched decoy
TAMMIS	Theater Army Medical Management and Information System
TAMP	Theater Aviation Maintenance Program
TAOC	Tactical Air Operations Center; subordinate operational component of the Marine Air Command and Control System designed for direction and control of all en route air traffic and air defense operations, to include manned interceptors and surface-to-air weapons, in an assigned sector; under the operational control of the Tactical Air Command Center [USMC]
TAR	training and administration into the Reserve [Navy]

TARPS	Tactical Aerial Reconnaissance Pod System [Navy]
TAACOM	Theater Area Army Command
TASM	Tomahawk antiship missile
TASOSC	Theater Army Special Operations Support Command
TAVB	aviation logistics ship; a Military Sealift Command ship, normally roll-on/roll-off, on which aviation intermediate maintenance facilities and supplies are embarked during Marine amphibious or Maritime Prepositioning Force operations. [Navy, USMC]
TAW	Tactical Airlift Wing [Air Force]
TBM	tactical ballistic missile
TBTC	Transportable Blood Transshipment Center
TCAE	Technical Control and Analysis Element
TDF	tactical digital facsimile
TDRSS	Tracking and Data Relay Satellite System
TDY	temporary duty
TEAM	Tactical EA-6B Mission Support Element
TEL	transporter erector launcher
TENCAP	tactical exploitation of national capabilities
TERCOM	terrain contour matching
TERPES	Tactical Electronic Reconnaissance Processing and Evaluation System
TERS	Tactical Event Reporting System
TF	Task Force; a temporary grouping of units, under one commander, formed to carry out a specific mission or operation
TFS	Tactical Fighter Squadron [USAF]
TFU	Tactical Forecast Unit [USAF]
TFW	Tactical Fighter Wing [USAF]
throughput capacity	rate at which personnel and equipment are received and processed
THMT	tactical high-mobility terminal
TI	total inventory
TIBS	Tactical Information Broadcast System [USAF]
TIS	Thermal Imaging System
TLAM	Tomahawk land-attack missile
TMIS	Theater Medical Information System
TNMCS	total not-mission capable, supply [USAF]
TO&E	Table of Organization and Equipment
TOSS	Tactical Operations Support System
TOT	time on target; time at which aircraft are scheduled to attack/photograph the target
TPFDD	time-phased force and deployment data
TPFDL	time-phased force and deployment list
TPU	Troop Program Unit
TPW	target planning worksheet
TRAC	tactical radar correlator [Army]
TRADOC	Training and Doctrine Command [Army]
TRAM	tractor, rubber-tired, articulated, multipurpose
TRANSCOM	Transportation Command
TRAP	tactical receive equipment and related applications
TRI-TAC	Joint Tactical Communications Program
TSS	Tactical Shelter System

TTAD	temporary tour of active duty
TTU	Transportation Terminal Unit; designed to conduct port operations [Army]
TWV	tactical wheeled vehicle

U

UAE	United Arab Emirates
UAEAF	United Arab Emirates Air Force
UAV	unmanned aerial vehicle
UHF	ultra-high frequency
UIC	unit indentification code; a six-character, alphanumeric code that uniquely identifies each Active, Reserve and National Guard unit of the Armed Forces
UK	United Kingdom
ULCS	unit-level circuit switch
UMMIPS	Uniform Material Movement and Issue Priority System
UN	United Nations
UNAAF	Unified Action Armed Forces; publication setting forth the principle, doctrines, and functions governing the activities and performance of the Armed Forces of the United States when two or more Services or elements thereof are acting together
UNSC	United Nations Security Council
USAF	United States Air Force
USAFE	US Air Forces, Europe
USAMMCE	US Army Medical Materiel Center
USAMMCSA	US Army Medical Materiel Center
USAR	US Army Reserve
USAREUR	US Army, Europe
USASG	US Army Support Group
USCG	United States Coast Guard

USDAO	US Defense Attache Office
USIA	US Information Agency
USMC	United States Marine Corps
USMCMG	US Mine Counter Measures Group
USMCR	United States Marine Corps Reserve
USMTM	United States Military Training Mission
USNR	United States Naval Reserve
USO	United Service Organizations
USSR	Union of Soviet Socialist Republics
UW	unconventional warfare; broad spectrum of military and paramilitary operations conducted in enemy-held, enemy-controlled or politically sensitive territory

V

VA	Department of Veterans Affairs
VCJCS	Vice Chairman, Joint Chiefs of Staff
VHF	very-high frequency
VLS	Vertical Launch System
VS-17	fluorescent orange panel

W

WATCHCON	watch condition
WEU	West European Union
WMP	War and Mobilization Plan [USAF]
WRM	war reserve materiel
WRSK	War Readiness Spares Kit [USAF]
WSEP	Weapons System Evaluation Program
WSIP II	Weapons System Improvement Program
WWIMS	Worldwide Indicators and Monitoring System
WWMCCS	Worldwide Military Command and Control System